Learning in U.S. and
Soviet Foreign Policy

Learning in U.S. and Soviet Foreign Policy

EDITED BY

George W. Breslauer and Philip E. Tetlock

Committee on International Conflict and Cooperation
Commission on Behavioral and Social Sciences and Education
National Research Council

Westview Press
BOULDER • SAN FRANCISCO • OXFORD

This work was supported by a grant from the University of California, Berkeley, through funds provided by the John D. and Catherine T. MacArthur Foundation. The contents hereof do not necessarily represent the views of the University of California or the John D. and Catherine T. MacArthur Foundation.

NOTICE: The project that is the subject of this report was approved by the Governing Board of the National Research Council, whose members are drawn from the councils of the National Academy of Sciences, the National Academy of Engineering, and the Institute of Medicine. The members of the committee responsible for the report were chosen for their special competences and with regard for appropriate balance.

This report has been reviewed by a group other than the authors according to procedures approved by a Report Review Committee consisting of members of the National Academy of Sciences, the National Academy of Engineering, and the Institute of Medicine.

The National Research Council was organized by the National Academy of Sciences in 1916 to associate the broad community of science and technology with the Academy's purposes of furthering knowledge and advising the federal government. Functioning in accordance with general policies determined by the Academy, the Council has become the principal operating agency of both the National Academy of Sciences and the National Academy of Engineering in providing services to the government, the public, and the scientific and engineering communities. The Council is administered jointly by both Academies and the Institute of Medicine. Dr. Frank Press and Dr. Robert M. White are chairman and vice chairman, respectively, of the National Research Council.

Published in 1991 in the United States of America by Westview Press, Inc., 5500 Central Avenue, Boulder, Colorado 80301, and in the United Kingdom by Westview Press, 36 Lonsdale Road, Summertown, Oxford OX2 7EW

Library of Congress Cataloging-in-Publication Data
Learning in U.S. and Soviet foreign policy / [edited by] George W. Breslauer and Philip E. Tetlock.
     p.   cm.
Includes index.
ISBN 0-8133-8264-5. — ISBN 0-8133-8265-3
   1. United States—Foreign relations—1945-   —Case studies.
2. Soviet Union—Foreign relations—1945-   —Case studies.
I. Breslauer, George W.   II. Tetlock, Philip.   III. Title: Learning in US and Soviet foreign policy.
E840.L39   1991
327.73047—dc20   91-8909
                                                                                   CIP

Printed and bound in the United States of America

The paper used in this publication meets the requirements of the American National Standard for Permanence of Paper for Printed Library Materials Z39.48-1984.

10   9   8   7   6   5   4   3   2   1

Contents

Tables and Figures

TABLES

FIGURES

CHAPTER 9

Foreword

This book addresses an aspect of the theory and practice of foreign policy that has assumed increasing emphasis in the study of international relations in the past decade. It became increasingly obvious to specialists in this field that existing theories of international relations did not lend much help in understanding the role of learning in the conduct of foreign policy. A number of political scientists—among them Lloyd Etheredge and Hugh Heclo—had already called attention to the need for developing a more systematic way of understanding *government learning*, or the lack thereof, and *political learning* more generally. And Ernest May and Richard Neustadt, among others, called attention to the risks entailed when, as is often the case, policy makers resort to a very simple type of learning—the use of a particular historical analogy—to diagnose and deal with a current foreign policy problem.

The volume is a distinctive, pioneering study in several respects. It is comparative across both issue areas and countries and hence should be of interest to a variety of scholars. Not only does it provide a comprehensive analytical assessment of the role of learning (and nonlearning) in the development of U.S.–Soviet relations, but it also makes a unique contribution to the development of theoretical and methodological tools for the study of foreign policy change. The volume throws considerable light on the complexity of the relationship between policy-relevant beliefs held by political leaders and the content of their foreign policy. For example, the authors find that a change in beliefs does not necessarily result in a change of policy and that, indeed, policy change often takes place in the absence of a prior change in beliefs. The volume provides an extremely interesting and valuable exploration of the possible relevance of a variety of different concepts of learning. It reveals disagreements among the authors as to which approach to learning is most relevant to particular policy changes and as to why on other occasions policy change did not occur. In the introductory and summary chapters, volume editors Philip Tetlock and George Breslauer provide invaluable discussions of the study's experience with the elusive concept of learning and of what can be learned about learning.

I believe this volume is a valuable and timely contribution to scholarship in the area of international relations.

Alexander George

Professor Emeritus of International Relations, Stanford University

Distinguished Fellow 1990–1991, United States Institute of Peace

Preface

The project that produced this volume began under the sponsorship of the National Research Council's Committee on International Conflict and Cooperation (formerly called the Committee on the Contributions of the Social and Behavioral Sciences to the Prevention of Nuclear War). Our purpose was to explore the conditions under which foreign policy makers change their beliefs and, as a result, change policy as well. We decided to use as our base of evidence the record of U.S. and Soviet foreign policy evolution in selected issue areas from World War II to the present.

A planning conference of prospective contributors was held at the National Academy of Sciences in Washington, D.C., in April 1987. Draft chapters were discussed at a workshop in Berkeley, California, in November 1988. At each meeting, specialists on U.S. and Soviet foreign policy discussed with international relations theorists and learning theorists the ways in which case studies of foreign policy evolution could illuminate the conditions under which foreign policy makers learn from experience.

One result of those discussions was a paper by Philip Tetlock that presented to the authors a menu of conceptions and types of learning, asking them to specify when, if at all, any or all of these types of belief change take place and result in (or from) changes in policy. In Chapter 1, we discuss the diverse definitions of learning employed in everyday and scholarly discourse. In Chapter 2, Tetlock summarizes some of the findings of the case studies, grouped around diverse types of learning, and focuses on conditions under which each takes place. In Chapter 3, Ernst Haas, one of the leading theorists of learning in international relations, presents an alternative conceptualization that informed the frameworks adopted by several of the contributors (see Chapters 4, 15, 19, and 20).

By giving equal time to studies of both U.S. and Soviet foreign policy and to diverse theories of learning in international relations, we have produced a large volume that will be of interest to several audiences. Students and specialists interested in the concept of learning, its diverse usages, and the distinctive forms it takes in international relations will be especially interested in the theoretical and synthesizing essays grouped together in Parts I and IV. Students looking for a series of interpretive histories of the foreign policies of the superpowers will be drawn to several of the essays in Parts II and III. Students and specialists interested in analyses that explore correlates of cognitive and policy changes without presenting a narrative history will be drawn to other chapters in Parts II and III. Indeed, a number of these case studies make rich contributions to our thinking about the nature of learning in foreign policy in the course of interpreting the history of a policy realm.

We are grateful to the National Research Council for undertaking this project. For invaluable assistance during all phases of this project, we are immensely grateful to committee staff members Jo Husbands and, especially, Mary Thomas. Our thanks go as well to Christine McShane for copy editing the volume, and to Estelle Miller and Linda Humphrey for composition services. We would also like to thank the Committee on International Conflict and Cooperation for its oversight of the project and for its strong support of our role as editors. We are also grateful to the MacArthur Interdisciplinary Group on International Security Studies of the University of California at Berkeley and to the Institute on Global Conflict and Cooperation for supplementary financial support during the writing and publication processes. Finally, we are indebted to the many scholars who communicated suggestions for the improvement of the individual chapters, but especially to Alexander George for his characteristically detailed, trenchant, and persistent criticisms.

George W. Breslauer
Philip E. Tetlock

Contributors

RICHARD D. ANDERSON, JR., Department of Political Science, University of California, Los Angeles

COIT D. BLACKER, School of International Relations, University of Southern California

GEORGE W. BRESLAUER, Department of Political Science, University of California, Berkeley

ALEXANDER DALLIN, Department of History, Stanford University

BANNING N. GARRETT, Center for Strategic and International Studies, Washington, D.C.

FRANKLYN GRIFFITHS, Department of Political Science, University of Toronto

ERNST B. HAAS, Department of Political Science, University of California, Berkeley

JONATHAN HASLAM, King's College, Cambridge, England

TED HOPF, Department of Political Science, University of Michigan

YUEN FOONG KHONG, Center for International Affairs, Harvard University

DEBORAH WELCH LARSON, Department of Political Science, University of California, Los Angeles

PETER R. LAVOY, Department of Political Science, University of California, Berkeley

ROBERT LEGVOLD, W. Averell Harriman Institute for Advanced Study of the Soviet Union, Columbia University

ROBERT A. LEVINE, The RAND Corporation, Santa Monica, Calif.

STEVEN L. SPIEGEL, Department of Political Science, University of California, Los Angeles

PHILIP E. TETLOCK, Department of Psychology, University of California, Berkeley

WALLACE J. THIES, Department of Politics, Catholic University of America

STEVEN WEBER, Department of Political Science, University of California, Berkeley

ALLEN S. WHITING, Department of Political Science, University of Arizona

Committee on International Conflict and Cooperation

CHARLES TILLY (Chair), Center for Studies of Social Change, New School for Social Research
ROBERT M. AXELROD, Institute of Public Policy Studies, University of Michigan
BARRY M. BLECHMAN, Defense Forecasts, Inc., Washington, D.C.
GEORGE W. BRESLAUER, Department of Political Science, University of California, Berkeley
JOHN L. COMAROFF, Department of Anthropology, University of Chicago
LYNN R. EDEN, Center for International Security and Arms Control, Stanford University
BARRY EICHENGREEN, Department of Economics, University of California, Berkeley
RICHARD E. ERICSON, Department of Economics, Columbia University
ROBERT W. FOGEL, Center for Population Economics, University of Chicago
WILLIAM A. GAMSON, Department of Sociology, Boston College
ALBERT O. HIRSCHMAN, School of Social Science, Institute for Advanced Study, Princeton, N.J.
ROBERT JERVIS, Institute for War and Peace Studies, Columbia University
ROBERT KEOHANE, Department of Government, Harvard University
GAIL LAPIDUS, Center for Slavic and East European Studies, University of California, Berkeley
R. DUNCAN LUCE, Irvine Research Unit in Mathematical Behavioral Science, School of Social Science, University of California, Irvine
HERBERT A. SIMON, Department of Psychology, Carnegie Mellon University
JACK SNYDER, Department of Political Science, Columbia University
PHILIP E. TETLOCK, Department of Psychology, University of California, Berkeley
SIDNEY VERBA, Department of Government, Harvard University

PAUL C. STERN, Study Director
JO L. HUSBANDS, Senior Research Associate
DANIEL DRUCKMAN, Senior Staff Officer
LEE WALKER, Research Associate
MARY E. THOMAS, Senior Program Assistant

PART I

Perspectives on Learning

1

Introduction

George W. Breslauer and Philip E. Tetlock

Are makers of foreign policy capable of learning? This by no means rhetorical question inspired the research project that produced the present volume. On one hand, it is tempting to conclude that learning must occur. National leaders who fail to adjust policies to changing circumstances will eventually be faced with ineffective policies and, perhaps, loss of personal authority and power. On the other hand, the obstacles to learning look formidable indeed. We would underscore four such obstacles.

First, the international environment is extraordinarily complex. Many causal factors are at work, interacting with each other in ways that make it difficult for anyone to fathom the real causes of events or trends. Even when we sense that one factor or another contributed to outcomes, it is daunting to assign relative weights and to distinguish decisive from contributory-but-not-decisive causes, or to distinguish between necessary and sufficient conditions.

Second, the international environment is highly uncertain. It is difficult to know what would have happened if a policy maker had adopted a different policy. Moreover, leaders of other states often have incentives to misrepresent their intentions and capabilities. And on the home front, accurate perception of international affairs is impeded by the highly partisan nature of controversies over the degree to which values are under threat or need to be promoted.

Third, the international environment is highly labile or changeable. Consider the many sharp and sudden qualitative discontinuities that have emerged in the international scene since World War II: weapons of unprecedented destructive power; delivery systems of unprecedented speed; dramatic shifts in leadership; startling reversals of international alignments (such as the sudden emergence of the Sino-Soviet-American strategic triangle); and the emergence of an increasingly multipolar economic-technological system. Frequently, by the time observers had finally decided how to characterize the situation, that characterization had become obsolete. Imagine the difficulties facing policy makers under these conditions!

Fourth, policy makers are ultimately human beings—limited-capacity information processors who can cope with only so much information per unit of time. It should not be surprising that they reach out for simplifying rules of thumb or heuristics. This need for simplicity and order is exacerbated by the political context of policy making, the need to appease multiple constituencies, and the time pressures that bear down on policy makers. It is little wonder that Henry Kissinger observed: "It is an illusion to believe that leaders gain in profundity while they gain experience. . . . The convictions that leaders have formed before reaching high office are the intellectual capital they will consume as long as they continue in office."[1]

In order to determine whether, when, and how often policy makers reevaluate their "intellectual capital," we asked a number of specialists on U.S. and Soviet foreign policy to examine regional and functional realms of policy since World War II. We posed five key questions to these specialists:

(1) Under what conditions do policy makers' beliefs change?

(2) What forms do such changes take? Reevaluation of tactics, strategies, or basic assumptions and goals? Movement toward simplicity or complexity? Reduced or expanded capacity for self-criticism and coping with trade-offs?

(3) When are these cognitive changes translated into policy, overcoming institutional and domestic political impediments?

(4) When do these cognitive and political changes move policy in the direction of a more realistic or efficient matching of means and ends?

(5) When are we more or less justified in making judgments about performance improvement?

As the table of contents indicates, these questions have been addressed in parallel chapters or integrated studies on U.S. and Soviet foreign policy toward arms control, détente, Western Europe, China, the Middle East, Third World intervention, and nuclear nonproliferation. In addition to the case studies, we have included several chapters on approaches to the conceptualization and study of learning in international relations (Chapters

2 and 3) and a theoretical statement about the possible impact of politics on learning in Soviet foreign policy (Chapter 4).

The case studies are a rich source of information about the first three of our questions in particular. They focus principally on how and why prevailing beliefs change, and on how and why this is translated into a collective process of changing policy. The case material also provides some insight into questions four and five, which we draw out further in Parts I and IV of the volume. However, further empirical and philosophical work driven exclusively by the last two questions remains an important agenda for the future.

Efforts to address questions four and five highlight the difficulties involved in applying the concept of *learning* to the study of international relations. There is a wide range of ways in which the term is used in both everyday language and in various professional subcultures that international relations researchers have occasion to draw on. What's more, there is a tension between the everyday and the professional usages. Everyday usages usually require us to make implicit judgments about the nature of reality that, in the complex, uncertain, and changing context of international relations, would strike many academic observers as highly speculative or tendentious. By contrast, professional usage often avoids this dilemma, but at the price of violating the seemingly commonsense meaning of the term.

THE ORDINARY LANGUAGE CONCEPTION OF LEARNING

In its everyday usage, *learning* is a deceptively straightforward concept. When a child burns his finger on the stove, and his parent says, "I hope you learned your lesson," the implication is that there was only one clear lesson to be learned: don't touch hot stoves or you will injure yourself. In its simplest usage, then, *to learn* has a tight connection with the verb, *to know*. Indeed, learning might simply be thought of as *coming to know*. The child who "learns his lesson" has come to know that hot stoves burn fingers.

In most of its usages, the meaning of the verb, *to know*, is distinguishable from the meaning of the verb, *to believe*. When using the verb, *to know*, the speaker of the sentence is vouching that the sentence is true. The person who categorizes something as an instance of knowing assumes the validity of the belief in question. Thus, it makes sense to say: "He believes that the stove is hot, but he is wrong." It does not make sense to say: "He knows that the stove is hot, but he is wrong." Similarly with the verb, *to learn*. If we say, in ordinary usage, that "He learned the stove was hot," we are vouching for the validity of his knowledge that the stove was indeed hot. It would not make sense to say, "He learned the stove was hot, but he was wrong." To convey that thought, we would use different terminology. We might say, "He drew the conclusion that the stove was hot, but he was wrong." From the point of view of the learner, learning that something is so might be merely a matter of acquiring a belief, but from the point of view of the person who *describes* the change *as an instance of learning*, the new belief has to be valid, or true, or justified, or realistic.

At issue in these cases is the observer's judgment about the correspondence between the learner's perception of reality and reality itself. In other cases, we might be dealing with more complex mental operations. That is, we might be faced, not with a situation of *learning that*, but rather with a situation of *learning how*. Learning how to do something entails acquiring behavior that succeeds in accomplishing what the actor tries to do. In the simplest, everyday usage, we would then say that the boy learned to avoid burning his finger by improving his understanding of when the stove was hot *or* by developing ways of avoiding the stove altogether *or* by wearing special protective garments when using the stove, etc. In these cases, the learner acquires a small or large repertoire of beliefs that he translates into a small or large repertoire of behaviors that adequately services the goal of avoiding getting his finger burned.

Thus, when we, as observers, say that the boy learned to avoid burning his finger, we are vouching for two things: (1) that the boy has not been burned again (or his incidence of being burned has declined) and (2) that such an outcome was a product of his having acquired a set of beliefs and behaviors that improved his performance on this score. It would not make sense to say that the boy learned how to avoid getting burned if the outcome was a product of luck, coincidence, or nonexposure to a hot stove during the period of observation.

Learning how, in this conceptualization, entails a claim on the part of the observer that the actor has improved his performance in relation to the attainment of certain goals, and that this has happened as a result of behavioral change that is preceded and driven by improvement in the actor's understanding of his environment. Presumably, this also means that the actor held the goals that the observer imputes to him.

The hot stove is a useful introduction to the idea of learning because it is so simple and straightforward. There is no ambiguity or dissensus about goals: almost everybody except suicidals and extreme masochists wants to avoid being burned. The causal linkage between the heat of the stove and the impact on the finger is simple and direct. Ways to avoid getting burned are not terribly complicated. It is tempting therefore to assume that everyday usage of the term *learning* is equally straightforward.

But such is not the case when we think of more complicated cases.

When everyday usage, as reflected in journalism and public discourse, turns to larger issues of social, political, and economic life, the ease of our exercise is undermined by the complexity of those issues, the ambiguities of what constitutes reality, the controversies surrounding how the world really works, and the ease with which normative and theoretical issues become confused. When Bob Dylan asks, "When Will They Ever Learn?" he is really asking: "When will they come to agree with my claim that war is not worth the lives lost in the process?" This is a very complex claim, however simple and appealing it might appear to be. It entails a *value* judgment about the relative worth of lives lost versus the goals attained by warfare. It further entails an implicitly counterfactual claim about the state of the world that would have obtained in the absence of warfare (or of a given war). That counterfactual claim, in turn, will invariably rest on implicit or explicit theoretical assumptions about cause and effect in international politics.

The point can be clarified by reference to the difference between the Vietnam War and World War II. In the eyes of those alienated by the Vietnam War, Bob Dylan's claims were compelling: the massive loss of life (both Vietnamese and American) was a disproportionate price to pay for containing the spread of communism, even if the war had been won by the United States. Presumably, this conclusion is based on both a value judgment (the worth of human lives) and a theory of cause-effect relations in international politics (the impact on the rest of the world, and on American national security, of an uncontested incorporation of Vietnam into the communist world).

Dylan's claims might be less compelling had they been made in 1945, with reference to World War II. In the eyes of many people, the loss of life was not disproportionate to the goal of defeating German and Japanese fascism. This claim may or may not be based on a lower valuation of human life, or on a higher valuation of communism relative to fascism. It is usually, however, justified on the basis of counterfactual claims about what the world would have looked like had the United States not entered the war, had Hitler defeated England and Russia, and had Japan not been defeated in the Far East. Those claims, in turn, will typically be informed by theories of warfare, political control, even human nature that have greater or lesser plausibility in the eyes of different social scientists.

Thus, when we begin to apply the ordinary usage of *learning* to the complex world of public affairs, we run up against the limits of our knowledge (we consciously use this last term). If, as observers, we may only use the term *learning* to describe changes in beliefs that we can vouch to be "more true" than earlier beliefs; or if we can only use the term to describe changes in behavior that we can vouch to be more efficient or effective in achieving certain ends (be they ours or the actor's), then we will rarely be allowed to use the term. The result would be that a word that is commonly used in day-to-day life falls victim to the limits of social science and is therefore largely purged from use by social scientists.

BEHAVIORAL AND SOCIAL SCIENCE
CONCEPTIONS OF LEARNING

Such has not been the fate of the term. *Learning* has been employed extensively in the literature of cognitive psychology, organization theory, political science, and international relations. However, this disciplinary diffusion of the term has resulted in great variation in definitions.

Learning theorists in experimental psychology have long relied on a behavioral definition that corresponds in logic to the *learning how* variant of the hot stove example: a change in the probability of a category of response as a result of experience. For example, did the pigeon learn that a pellet of food would appear with every three pecks of the key when the green light was on? This example is based on clear specification of what reality is, and on whether the pigeon's behavioral repertoire changed in ways likely to increase the probability that it would attain the goals we impute to it (wanting food). And since the experimenter controls the reward contingency, he is in a good position to make strong inferences about the relative efficacy of the behavioral strategies of the pigeon.

Such trial-and-error learning corresponds to one definition of the term that Tetlock discusses in Chapter 2. Even when we exit the experimental situation and deal with the real world of interpersonal or international relations, this approach is not as divorced from everyday usage as it might appear. For it corresponds to a form of *learning that* previous behaviors (or policies) were not "working" in the given time frame in advancing the goals that drove them. When a policy maker learns in this minimalist sense, he has not necessarily learned anything deeper about how the world works or about how to advance his goals. He has only learned that the previous policy was not "working." Learning, for these purposes, refers to a change in the probability of a response in the face of changing reward contingencies.

Cognitive theorists, in contrast, use a different definition of learning. To them, learning entails increased differentiation and integration of mental structures (schemata). People working in this tradition pay little attention to the underlying external reality, much less to determining whether increased complexity of thought necessarily makes an individual more knowledgeable about the environment. It follows that such a definition also means that the observer is not focusing on whether increased complexity results in behavioral patterns that improve performance in pursuit of goals held by either the actor or the observer. By the everyday definition suggested at the beginning of this chapter, which related to both *learning that* and *learning how*, cognitive theorists are not focusing on learning, but rather on changes in the content and structure of beliefs. This has yielded a huge literature on factors that facilitate, and factors that impede, changes in beliefs.[2] But it has not tackled the more complex issues that arise in judging whether and when changes in beliefs are more or less justified in light of the "true" nature of reality.

When political scientists focus on learning among policy makers at the level of the nation-state, they face analogous problems. They may choose to ask simple descriptive questions: "When do policy makers' beliefs change?" and the subsidiary query, "What forms do these changes take?" They may relate their findings to the literature on cognitive psychology to build inductive theory about what it takes for policy makers to change their minds, challenge their own assumptions, and overcome the cognitive conservatism of the human mind.[3] They may seek to test Henry Kissinger's suggestion, quoted earlier, that policy makers do not have the time or incentive to reevaluate their beliefs on the job; that they must live off the intellectual capital they brought with them into office. When they state the research problem in this way, political scientists follow cognitive psychologists in avoiding judgments about the realism of the beliefs in question.

This approach to learning is divorced from the everyday usage of the term as "coming to know," but it is not at all divorced from a commonsense usage as "coming to believe." Even in everyday language, it is not odd to say, "he learned the wrong lesson" or "he thought he had learned, but he was wrong." When political scientists make broad claims about the mental operations, or behavioral tendencies, of that class of human beings that especially interests them—politicians—they often advance empirical generalizations that do not require the observer to vouch for the correspondence between beliefs and reality, or between behavior and performance. Thus, they may ask: "How do policy makers typically learn?" In this case, the connection is with the verb, *to believe*. How and why do policy makers typically come to believe what they do? How do they draw lessons? And why do they typically draw the lessons they do? Jervis, for example, explores the impact of many factors (formative experiences, early political socialization, analogical reasoning, and the like) on the ways in which policy makers "learn from history."[4] In these cases, it makes sense, even on the basis of linguistic intuition, to speak of learning propensities or learning tendencies, which are calculated from the observation of how categories of people come to believe what they do. The observer need not vouch for the validity of the beliefs.

Defining the research problem as one of belief system change narrows the focus to a very specific subset of change. That subset is restricted in three senses: to the level of *the individual*; to changes in *cognition* (beliefs and preferences), not changes in behavior; and to changes that do not require a judgment about correspondence with reality or improvements of performance (i.e., to *believing that*, not *knowing that* or *knowing how*). These restrictions could be viewed as prudent or imprudent, depending on one's view of the capacity of social science and philosophy to supply grounded theories that we could use to judge whether policy makers have become more or less realistic in their perceptions, and more or less effective in pursuing their (or our) goals.

Yet even this does not exhaust the variety of usages of the term *learning*. A number of our contributors (Haas, Anderson, Lavoy, and Weber) insist on a distinction between *adaptation* and *learning*. They treat the distinction as essentially one of degree: a function of the extent to which core beliefs or goals have changed. Many of the types of learning that Tetlock (Chapter 2) treats as trial-and-error learning or as changes in cognitive content, these contributors refer to as types of adaptation, with the term *learning* reserved for fundamental changes in understanding of cause-effect relations in international politics or revaluations of goals. In these cases, however, there is not very much at stake in the choice of definition. The differences between these particular contributors are more matters of definitional taste.

A more consequential distinction arises over cases in which there is a disjunction or clash between behavioral and cognitive definitions of learning. Although it is often the case that people *learn how* as a result of a better understanding of their environment (*learning that*), these two types of knowledge can be dissociated, both in everyday usage and in the complex, political world of international relations. One can have a good understanding of the physics of riding a bicycle but not know how to do it or, more commonly, one can know how to ride a bike but know nothing about the underlying laws of physics. In security policy, one can improve one's performance as a result of mindlessly or intuitively adapting to an unprecedented rush of events that one understands poorly. More generally, as Larson (Chapter 10) argues, one can change one's behaviors and only later bring one's beliefs into line with the new behavioral patterns. Or, as Anderson argues (Chapter 4), one can change one's behavior as a result of political pressures that constitute one's immediate frame of reference, with little immediate or later change in beliefs. Some of our contributors prefer to define such cases of behavioral change that precedes (or proceeds independently of) understanding as adaptation rather than learning. As long as the reader is clear as to the usage being employed, this strikes us as a defensible approach to differentiating among related phenomena.

The real challenge is to discern empirically when behavioral change is in fact not accompanied or preceded by cognitive restructuring or improved understanding.

A still more substantial epistemological issue is one that preoccupies organization theorists and students of political organization: the problem of aggregating individual cognition and behavior to the level of the policy-making *unit* as a whole. In analyzing circumstances in which a leader has autocratic authority within an organization or state, and in which implementation of his wishes is not problematic, it might not be necessary to worry about aggregation. We can focus on the cognitive and behavioral dynamics of the individual alone. But when the individual's cognitive dynamics, policy preferences, and political behavior are constrained or shaped by norms, preferences, and powers of other individuals distributed throughout the structure of governance, we must factor these elements into our study of changes in the prevailing beliefs that inform organizational or national policies.

Organization theorists and political scientists seeking to build theories of change will more often be interested in these kinds of redirection of prevailing assumptions and policies. Moreover, they are especially sensitive to the political and social, not just individual-psychological, costs of, and pressures for, redirection. Hence, they will focus their attention on the aggregation of individual learning to the level of the larger unit, anthropomorphizing the institution. Organization theorists will inquire into the conditions for "organizational learning."[5] Political scientists may ask, "Can governments learn?"[6] or may inquire into the conditions for "social learning."[7]

Even though the aggregation of change to the level of organizations, governments, and communities may be justified for the purposes of sociological, economic, and political analysis, it does not at all ease the definitional differences between those who adopt broad versus narrow definitions of learning. Haas (Chapter 3) and Anderson (Chapter 4), for example, focus on collective learning, and distinguish sharply between many types of *adaptation* and a very narrow phenomenon called *learning*. Tetlock (Chapter 2), by contrast, distinguishes among many types of learning, at both the individual and the collective level, and absorbs the concept of adaptation into his typology of learning. Nor does the process of aggregation ease the epistemological dilemma of distinguishing between changes in belief, on one hand, and improved understanding or performance, on the other. Collective learning, as with individual learning, may be associated with a collectivity's coming to *know that*, coming to *know how*, or coming to *believe that*.

On this score, however, economists and organization theorists are advantaged in tackling the task of evaluating levels of understanding and performance by the greater scientific maturity of their disciplines. Much of organization theory is built on observation of the behavior of firms in competitive marketplaces. The imputation of goals to those firms is not problematic: we know that their boards of directors seek to have the firm survive, maintain or expand its market shares, and become increasingly profitable. These objectives are easily quantified. Moreover, we have very large samples of firms to examine to determine which types of strategies did or did not meet these goals. And we can observe whether executives in fact learned from experience and improved their strategies.

What's more, the environment of firms is more learner-friendly than is the environment of international politics. Firms receive more frequent and more unambiguous feedback about their performance levels than do leaders of states. Countries get fewer observations and more ambiguous feedback that does not tell them why things are going wrong. This allows vested interests greater latitude to reinterpret the data in ways consistent with their biases. Leaders of firms see themselves and their competitors as essentially similar in nature or analogous in the tasks they perform and the environments in which they compete. Leaders of states, in contrast, tend to adopt or be constrained by ideologies that emphasize how different they are from their competitors. Hence, leaders of states are less likely than are leaders of firms to learn from the mistakes of their competitors. (Might this explain why the Soviet Union intervened in Afghanistan despite the U.S. loss in Vietnam?) To be sure, neither organization theory nor economics qualifies as a highly advanced science with high predictive capability. But the development of both inductive and deductive theory in those disciplines that is relevant to the tasks of matching beliefs to reality, and of evaluating performance, is fairly advanced, especially relative to political science and international relations.

Thus, when dealing with governments in the international system, we find that many of the goals pursued by states are not easily quantified as performance indicators. Is the United States more or less secure today than it was 10 years ago? Are the United States and the Soviet Union farther from nuclear war today than they were 10 years ago? Is the United States materially more secure than it was before Reaganomics? Is the Middle East more stable today than it was 10 years ago? Moreover, when seeking to define the nature of reality, we are forced to factor into our counterfactuals a far greater number and array of imponderables than do organization theorists and economists. Our understanding of cause-effect relationships in the international system is underdeveloped relative to the more quantifiable and paradigmatic social science disciplines.

These attributes of international politics compound the dilemmas of scholars seeking to identify learning in U.S. and Soviet foreign policy making that corresponds to learning as knowledge acquisition (*learning that*). The task would be simpler (though still difficult, given problems of access to information) were we simply to treat learning as *coming to believe*: When do policy makers change their minds? In what ways? However, if we choose to use *learning* in its everyday usage, we are forced to vouch for the greater realism of belief changes we judge to constitute learning. In like manner, when addressing not *learning that* but *learning how* (i.e., knowledge-informed performance improvement), we must vouch for our ability to impute the goals being pursued by the policy makers so as to judge whether performance toward the realization of those goals has improved.

Vouching for the greater realism of beliefs or goals is not a hopeless exercise. We are certainly not radical subjectivists who believe that there is no reality beyond that constructed by the human mind. Throughout the case studies in this volume, authors identify changes in belief in Washington and Moscow that they are confident in calling more realistic. Perhaps the best test of this judgment is that these empirical beliefs are no longer highly controversial among a wide range of both liberals and conservatives in this country. Take a most poignant and entertaining example noted in the chapter by Stephen Spiegel: "Americans have come a long way since Truman's ambassador to the United Nations implored Arabs and Jews to 'settle this problem in a true Christian spirit.'" Beyond this trivial example, it is safe to say that the top 300 or so leaders of both superpowers, over the past 30 years: (1) have come to a more complex appreciation of the nature of the nuclear revolution in weaponry; (2) have developed a more sophisticated and less stereotyped understanding of the complexity of the adversary's political processes (even though they may remain befuddled by that complexity); (3) have learned that many indigenous processes in the Third World are out of the direct control of either superpower; and (4) have come to understand that the multiplicity of foreign policy goals they hold are often in conflict with one another, that they are often irreconcilable, or that the costs of pursuing them simultaneously may ultimately prove to be prohibitive. Other examples could be cited.

Taken individually or together, these cases of learning correspond to *learning that*. In and of themselves they do not tell us whether such belief changes have altered policies enacted, or whether policy has become more effective as a result. That is, greater realism along certain dimensions of belief may often[8] be a necessary condition, but is certainly not a sufficient condition, for improved performance (*learning how*). To see whether leaders have learned how, we must specify the goals by which performance is to be evaluated, determine that changes in belief drove the enactment of new policies, and evaluate the greater or lesser effectiveness of those policies. This analytical step forces us to rely on cause-effect calculations that are more complex, and judgments that are more far-reaching, about the reciprocal and continuing interaction of policy and the international environments toward which policy is directed. It also forces us to go beyond empirical judgments about the power of weaponry, the intentions of the adversary, and the nature of indigenous forces at work in regional conflicts. We must now draw on theoretical arguments about the long-term and short-term consequences of continuing interaction among multiple states and among economic, political, and social forces at home and abroad.

Our existing bodies of knowledge, both empirical and theoretical, may help us deal with selected questions about short-term causation. We can conduct counterfactual analysis to inquire: What would it have taken to avoid the Korean War, or the October 1973 Middle East war, or the invasion of Afghanistan? We may remain uncertain about many of the facts, but that is more a matter of archival access than logical impossibility. The persuasiveness of short-term counterfactual arguments hinges on three things: (1) the richness of the empirical evidence available; (2) the degree to which one can draw on well-validated theoretical and empirical generalizations in filling in the missing hypothetical data points; and (3) the degree to which one can achieve consensus concerning the nature of the situation to which one is applying the theoretical and empirical generalizations.

On this last point, a great deal depends on the closeness of the "causal calls." It is easy, for example, to imagine Kennedy's losing the 1960 election to Nixon if evidence had become public concerning Kennedy's philandering. It is harder, however, to imagine Johnson's 1964 election being overturned. When the causal competition is intense, the addition of only a weak theoretical cause may make a critical difference; when the outcome appears already highly overdetermined, the addition of even a moderately strong theoretical causal candidate may not make much of an impression on analysts.

Our existing bodies of knowledge, both empirical and theoretical, may help us deal with selected questions about short-term causation, but the medium-range consequences often become unfathomable and a matter of theoretical or normative faith. The evolution of historical scenarios is often highly contingent on later branchings and decision points. For similar reasons, we usually evaluate leaders in terms of the relatively short-term consequences of their initiatives: did Roosevelt extricate America from the Depression? Did he mobilize the country to prosecute World War II? We do not frequently ask: Did Roosevelt create the preconditions for the imperial presidency that Nixon later abused?

Thus, when asking whether policy makers have *learned how*, we face a major intellectual challenge. Even if we knew the goals being pursued by policy makers, the changes in beliefs, and the resultant changes in policy, we would still be faced with the task of defining a time span over which performance will be judged. Firms regularly go out of business; states rarely fail to survive. So mere long-term survival is not a very demanding criterion for performance evaluation. Below that threshold, performance may appear to be effective in the short term, only to be judged ineffective after a few more years have passed. In 1979, Soviet policy in the Third World during the previous five years appeared to be a resounding success. Five years later, in 1984, the opposite verdict was being reached, both by most Soviets leaders and by most outside observers.

Herein lies the irony and the dilemma. We are often better equipped empirically to judge performance over short time periods, yet it may require longer time periods to make meaningful generalizations about the effectiveness of policies driven by certain assumptions. To take another striking case, Pike and Ward have recently argued that the U.S. willingness to fight the Vietnam War for as long as it did, even though it lost the military war, was responsible for the growing prosperity, stability, and unity of Southeast Asia today.[9] What, then, are the appropriate lessons of Angola and Vietnam for Soviet and U.S. policy makers? If we, as observers, deign to define what those lessons should be, we must have a criterion by which to judge whether U.S. and Soviet leaders have drawn the right lessons (i.e., learned, defined as *coming to know that*). But the utility and persuasiveness of that criterion will hinge on the validity of the lessons we, as observers, have drawn. Would a Palestinian state in the Middle East increase or decrease the long-term stability of the region? That happens to have been the issue dividing the superpowers and regional leaders for decades. Which side failed to learn, in this sense of the term? It may be that both U.S. and Soviet policy planners have learned a great deal about the Middle East in recent decades (*learning that*), but that neither of them has learned how to solve the Arab-Israeli conflict.

Some theorists of international politics might argue an opposite case: that we are better able to project the long-term consequences than the short-term results of events and policies. The counterproductivity of Soviet policy in Africa in the 1970s, they might argue, was not evident immediately, but was predictable as a longer-term consequence of the inherent balancing tendencies within world politics. Or another example: reentry of China into a period of relative openness to the outside world will eventually be a matter of economic and strategic necessity. In the coming 30–50 years, it is surely inevitable. But how confident can we be in predicting its eventuation in the next 3–5 years?

Were there substantial consensus within the social science community about the range of applicability of different theories of international relations, this would be a generalizable and powerful argument. However, most of our theories do not allow us such confidence regarding the prediction of trends; and most of the questions we would like to address, given the threat of nuclear war or ecological disaster, pertain to the coming 10 years or so. Hence, the defensibility of many inferences about learning (defined as *knowing that*) will be a function of the defensibility of the theoretical framework that has been deployed to generate counterfactual claims.

If we have a well-validated theory that has been carefully applied to widely agreed-on antecedent conditions in the real world, the counterfactual will be persuasive. For example, if the earth were as hot as Venus, life as we know it would never have arisen on our planet. This counterfactual is particularly persuasive, because there is so little controversy over the validity of the underlying theoretical laws and generalizations that are drawn on to fill in the missing data points in the counterfactual world. In short, we have a lot of confidence in the basic laws of biochemistry.

If we have controversy over both the merits of the theory and the antecedent conditions to which it is applied, the counterfactual will probably persuade only its authors and a few close friends. Unfortunately, much theory of international relations that is relevant to Soviet and U.S. security policy (the subject matter of this volume) is inadequately developed and validated to make persuasive the major counterfactuals we would like to deploy. Consider, for example, the following counterfactual claim. Even if the United States had invaded Cuba in 1962 in order to destroy the intermediate-range ballistic missiles there, the conflict would not have escalated into a nuclear war. This counterfactual is quite persuasive to neorealists who believe that Khrushchev would have been constrained by the balance of power prevailing at the time. It is less persuasive to conflict-spiral theorists who believe that there is potential for crises to escalate out of control as a result of the irrationality of human actors, organizational factors, and random accidents. For both policy makers and analysts, then, international relations is a learner-unfriendly environment!

This accounts in part for the differential uses of the concept *learning* in literature on foreign policy and international relations. This is not the place for a thorough review of that literature, but a few examples will be useful. Nye distinguishes between simple and complex learning, but each is descriptive of a given level of change in beliefs and/or goals, without evaluating whether those changes entailed greater realism or not. Alternatively, Haas (Chapter 3) proposes that application of the term *learning* be restricted to complex learning that is driven by consensual knowledge developed by an epistemic community, which results in institutionalized changes in both goals and cause-effect relationships, and in a closer matching of ends and means. Haas avoids judging the longer-term realism or effectiveness of the change, instead suggesting that only centuries of retrospective distance will allow us to make such judgments. Yet he avoids equating learning only with change in fundamental beliefs by demanding that it be driven by a scientific consensus among those who subscribe to a common epistemology. This definition eases the observer's task of reality testing. It also makes it far easier to apply Haas's framework to issues, such as economics, ecology, and other scientific-technical domains, in which a substantial measure of scientific consensus is more easily attained than in the political and security realms of international relations.

Etheredge, in contrast, believes that performance evaluation and reality depiction by the observer are essential to using the term *learning* in security policy analysis. He compares U.S. policy in Latin America in the early 1950s with that in the late 1950s, early 1960s, and 1980s to see whether policy makers drew the lessons from previous experience that he feels they ought to have drawn.[10] This scholar, in other words, is more confident in his ability to generate and defend counterfactually grounded claims concerning long-term international trends.

This volume is a product of our effort to employ the learning concept in ways that would allow us to explore changes in beliefs and performance levels in superpower relations, without falling into the trap of radical subjectivism, on one hand, or theoretical and normative overconfidence, on the other.[11] These are two opposing categories of errors: the Scylla and Charybdis of learning analysis.

The core problem, as we see it, is this. It is impossible to purge *learning* from our vocabulary; no history of any era could be written without using the term in one or the other of its everyday usages. But which usage should we employ for purposes of advancing our understanding of governmental decision making? If we work with a highly restrictive conception of learning, we run the risk of having nothing to explain. If we work with an expansive conception of learning, virtually anything qualifies. If we restrict learning to knowledge acquisition, rather than belief change, there emerge as many conceptions of learning as there are distinct political/theoretical viewpoints on the U.S.–Soviet relationship. Any thoughtful observer with a reasonably well-articulated theory of cause and effect in the international realm can then make attributions of learning or nonlearning.

Nor is this simply a matter of political preference or theoretical bias. There may sometimes be a number of equally plausible ways to interpret the evidence, movement toward any of which might constitute learning. If we abandon epistemological monism in favor of pluralism, we can talk (in principle) about learning within different conceptual frameworks. For example, there would then be different types of learning from the perspective of different variants of deterrence and conflict-spiral interpretations of the U.S.–Soviet relationship. Given the deep dissensus in the political science community over what constitutes knowledge of the U.S.–Soviet relationship, this pluralistic conception of learning strikes us as reasonable. It mirrors our image of the level of scientific maturity of the field, and allows us to focus initially on learning as *coming to believe*, rather than *coming to know*.

Beyond the epistemological challenge lie empirical challenges as well. The empirical materials were often deficient for specifying policy makers' goals (especially on the Soviet side). Both we and our contributors found it easier to treat belief change as a dependent variable than as an independent variable. That is, it was normally easier to specify when and why beliefs changed than it was to determine the relationship between changes in beliefs, on one hand, and policy change or performance improvement, on the other. For policies and performance may change or improve for reasons other than, or in interaction with, belief change (for example: political coalition building; see Anderson, Chapter 4).

Beyond this empirical question of what caused behavioral change, there was always the danger that individual contributors' different theoretical assumptions drove their conclusions about performance evaluation and realism. This factor almost certainly accounts for some differences in tone, focus, and conclusions among the case studies. Nonetheless, we found the case studies to be sufficiently comparable to permit us to mine them for purposes of documenting instances of certain types of belief change and their circumstantial correlates (see Chapter 2) and for pushing beyond the material in the case studies to expand our thinking about the relationship between learning and cooperation in U.S.–Soviet interaction (see Chapters 20 and 21).

Thus, as it has developed, the volume has expanded to perform several functions: (1) to expose the reader to a wide range of perspectives on the usages of a learning construct for thinking about foreign policy; (2) to present new empirical case studies on parallel aspects of Soviet and U.S. foreign policy that bear on the conditions under which leaders in each capital change their beliefs and policies; and (3) to push beyond the case studies' priority focus on learning as *coming to believe that* to examine instances of learning as *coming to know that* and *coming to know how*: in the latter case, exploring the role of belief-change in Soviet–U.S. learning how to cooperate (see Chapters 20 and 21).

NOTES

1. Henry Kissinger, *White House Years* (New York: Little, Brown, 1979), 54.
2. See W.J. McGuire, "The Nature of Attitudes and Attitude Change," in *Handbook of Social Psychology*, eds. G. Lindzey and E. Aronson (Reading, Mass.:

Addison-Wesley, 1980); and R.E. Nisbett and L. Ross, *Human Inference: Strategies and Shortcomings of Social Judgment* (Englewood Cliffs, N.J.: Prentice-Hall, 1980).

3. Robert Jervis, *Perception and Misperception in International Politics* (Princeton, N.J.: Princeton University Press, 1976), Chapter 3.

4. Ibid.

5. James G. March, *Decisions and Organizations* (Oxford: Basil Blackwell, 1988); M.L. Tushman and E. Romanelli, "Organizational Evolution: A Metamorphosis Model of Convergence and Reorientation," in *Research in Organizational Behavior*, eds. B. Staw and L.L. Cummings (Greenwich, Conn.: JAI Press, 1985); Chris Argyris and Donald A. Schon, *Organizational Learning: A Theory of Action Perspective* (Menlo Park, Calif.: Addison-Wesley, 1978).

6. Lloyd Etheredge, *Can Governments Learn?* (New York: Pergamon, 1985).

7. Karl Deutsch, *The Nerves of Government* (New York: Free Press, 1966).

8. Not always, though, because people sometimes do the right thing for the wrong reasons.

9. Douglas Pike and Benjamin Ward, "Losing and Winning: Korea and Vietnam as Success Stories," *Washington Quarterly* (Summer 1987).

10. Etheredge, *Can Governments Learn?*

11. Radical subjectivism: "given that nobody really knows what would have happened if _____ , one person's opinion must be as good as another's!" Theoretical and normative overconfidence: "from our special epistemic vantage point, we know what would have happened if _____ , or we know what goals policy makers should have pursued in this situation."

2

Learning in U.S. and Soviet Foreign Policy: In Search of an Elusive Concept

Philip E. Tetlock

This book appears at a key transitional point in international relations. The bitter cold war between the United States and the Soviet Union is, if not permanently over, at least in deep remission. The old bipolar world has given way to a new, increasingly multipolar order. It is timely, therefore, to look back over the 45 years since World War II— to look back not only at what American and Soviet leaders thought they were doing at particular junctures in history, but also at the sometimes gradual and sometimes dramatic transformations that occurred in the thinking of these leaders. These transformations raise a complex mixture of empirical and normative questions: Under what conditions are policy makers likely to change their minds? How do psychological, institutional, and domestic political processes interact to impede or facilitate changes in point of view? When are changes in point of view actually translated into policy? And when are we justified in saying that policy makers were either too slow or too quick to change their minds?

A retrospective assessment of this sort immediately runs into an enormous obstacle: the difficulty of saying anything about the past half century of U.S.–Soviet interaction that is simultaneously not platitudinous and not controversial. Observations that evoke general agreement across the political spectrum sound pretty obvious. There is broad consensus, for example, that the two superpowers created weapon systems of enormous destructive power, competed for influence in virtually every region of the globe, and eventually reached numerous agreements to limit both their military and geopolitical competition. Beyond these least-common-denominator observations, however, the consensus quickly fades. We find sharp controversy over the nature of U.S. and Soviet goals and over the appropriateness of the policies each superpower has pursued to achieve its goals. Different observers offer starkly different conclusions concerning the lessons that the superpowers should draw from the last 45 years of intense interaction. Hawks point to one set of lessons: the importance of communicating one's determination to deter aggression and the grave consequences of even perceived weakness.[1] Doves point to another set: the importance of avoiding self-defeating arms races and the tragic consequences of exaggerating the hostility of the other side.[2] Self-styled owls point to a third set of lessons: the importance of striking the right balance between deterrence and reassurance and of appreciating the complexities of nuclear command and control systems.[3] Finally, there are the theorists of imperial overstretch who remind us of the inevitable decline of all great powers and the need never to lose sight of the economic and technological underpinnings of military power.[4] In short, the lessons one extracts from experience depend very much on one's prior point of view.[5]

It is important to acknowledge the multitude of lessons we can draw from the historical record. The danger of overconfidence is real.[6] We often hear political pundits forcefully argue that, if only their prescriptions had prevailed, the world would be a better place today. Given the shaky epistemological status of historical counterfactuals, such arguments should be viewed with measured skepticism. It is hard to say for sure what would have happened when multiple causes were at work, the causes interacted in largely unknown ways, and the links between causes and effects were highly probabilistic.[7] The honest response is to admit that we frequently do not know how history would have unfolded had someone done something differently. Was the Cuban missile crisis triggered by the perceived weakness or the perceived strength of the Kennedy administration?[8] Or was it the product of just another "hare-brained scheme" of General Secretary Khrushchev? Did the new Gorbachevian thinking about foreign policy arise because of or despite the Reagan defense build-up?[9] Or was Reagan irrelevant? These questions intrigue us—in part because they are so important and in part because they lie tantalizingly outside our analytical grasp. History provides no control groups that allow us to assess the impact of the presence versus absence of hypothesized causes. The control groups exist (if that is the right word) only in the imaginations of political analysts.[10]

The U.S.–Soviet relationship is a far-from-perfect laboratory for testing abstract hypotheses about learning. In an epistemologically pristine world, analysts could calibrate the precise rates at which U.S. and Soviet policy makers came to realize the truth about each other, the strategic implications of the nuclear revolution, and the dynamics of regional conflicts.

In this, less-than-ideal world, we must scale back our objectives. To be sure, we can still pose questions about learning in the more limited, descriptive meaning of the term. Investigators can ask: "Who drew what lessons from which experiences and with what political consequences?" without any implication that they themselves know what policy makers should have done. We need to be exceptionally careful, however, in using the term *learning* in its more expansive, normative sense. We cannot replay history the way we can a game of chess. There is inevitably controversy over whether policy makers drew the right or wrong lessons from particular experiences.

This chapter is intended to serve an integrative function for the volume as a whole. As such, it has multiple objectives. First and most important, I attempt to clear away the definitional underbrush that threatens to obscure common themes running through the case studies of U.S. and Soviet learning in a wide range of policy arenas. Different investigators use the term *learning* in different—sometimes downright incompatible—ways. I distinguish five usages here: (1) the neorealist approach to learning (learning involves the rational adjustment of policy in response to the reward and punishment contingencies of the international environment); (2) the belief system approach (learning involves change in the cognitive content of one's image of the international environment and the best ways to cope with that environment); (3) the cognitive structural approach (learning involves change in the cognitive structure of one's image of the international environment: change in the direction of greater complexity and greater capacity for self-criticism); (4) the organizational and political cultural approach (learning involves change in the institutional procedures or cultural norms that shape how governments respond to international events); and (5) the efficiency conception of learning (learning involves acquiring the ability to match means and ends more effectively than one could in the past: either by employing more appropriate means or by pursuing more realistic goals). This latter conception of learning raises vexing problems of counterfactual assessment (what would have happened if . . .), problems that neorealists can escape (because they make strong assumptions about the rationality of security policies in the first place—there is not much room for improvement), that cognitivists can escape (because they make no assumptions about the relative efficacy of different policies—their focus is purely intrapsychic), and that organization theorists can escape (one can document patterns of institutional change without making any assumptions about the adaptiveness of these changes).

In addition to mapping out different conceptions of learning, this chapter has a number of other objectives. Assessing whether learning—in any of the previous senses—has occurred turns out to be a hazardous undertaking. Methodological and theoretical traps abound. One theoretical trap is to use the term *learning* so loosely that it becomes synonymous with any new policy initiative by a government. Learning—at a psychological or institutional level of analysis—is by no means the only possible explanation for policy change.[11] The alternatives are, however, the subject of some controversy. Different writers emphasize different alternatives to learning and draw the line between learning and other processes at different places. Haas (Chapter 3), for instance, argues that governments often change course in a mechanistic or cybernetic fashion, with little or no reassessment of basic beliefs and goals. He calls this process adaptation, not learning. Anderson (Chapter 4) notes that governments often change course as the result of shifting coalitional patterns that reflect who is now "in" and "out"—coalitional dynamics that have little or nothing to do with the international situation (see also Thies, Chapter 6). And March notes that governments often patch policies together in "garbage-can" fashion.[12] The ultimate product will depend much more on chance conjunctions of persons, ideas, and issues than it does on rational planning responsive to external events. Another type of trap—more methodological than theoretical—is to take foreign policy rhetoric too seriously as evidence of how policy makers actually think. Policy makers sometimes know more than they let be known. If we underestimate what policy makers understood in the past, we run a serious risk of overestimating what they have learned in the present. A final trap raises both methodological and theoretical issues: the danger of social scientists' using the term *learning* in so self-serving a manner that it becomes synonymous with the adoption of policies that the investigator deems correct. Judgments of learning become, in this case, thinly veiled partisan pronouncements.

There is a lot of room for disagreement rooted in divergent political and theoretical perspectives on U.S.–Soviet relations, disagreements that occasionally surface in this volume. There is also, however, enormous potential for advancing our understanding of U.S.–Soviet relations in particular and of foreign policy theory in general. Insofar as we can identify cognitive psychological, institutional, and domestic political processes that facilitate or impede different types of learning, and we can separate our factual from our value judgments of what has been learned, we will be in a much stronger position to fashion policy-relevant theory in a complex and rapidly changing international environment.

CONCEPTIONS OF LEARNING

How one thinks about learning in international relations is profoundly shaped by theoretical first principles. If one believes that it is useful to black-box the foreign policy-making process and simply look for lawful regularities between international events and governmental responses (as some neorealists believe), then one will be reasonably content working with a minimalist or reward/punishment conception of learning. If not, one will need to take into account the psychological, institutional, and domestic political processes that shape which international events governments heed and which ones they ignore. Among scholars in the latter camp, however, disagreements emerge over the relative importance of mediating variables, with some scholars assigning primacy to the beliefs and preferences of individual decision makers (advocates of the belief system and cognitive structural approaches to learning) and others assigning primacy to political institutions and processes (scholars who prefer to think about learning in organizational or cultural terms). Finally, there is the normative question. It is one thing to describe shifts in beliefs, goals, institutional procedures, and cultural norms; it is quite another to draw strong conclusions about the appropriateness of these shifts. Here again, we see large differences among the contributors to this volume. Some authors explicitly distance themselves from normatively loaded definitions of learning. Such questions are, in their view, unanswerable (Levine, Chapter 5)—or, if answerable, only so in the distant future (Haas, Chapter 4). Others are willing—albeit with some trepidation—to make judgments about whether policy makers became more or less realistic in the time period under study (Blacker, Chapter 12; Garrett, Chapter 7; Legvold, Chapter 18; Weber, Chapter 20). Still others (like myself) are decidedly ambivalent about the role social scientists can play in this regard (Breslauer, Chapter 15; Spiegel, Chapter 8).

THE NEOREALIST CONCEPTION OF LEARNING

Learning takes on a simple, perhaps deceptively simple, meaning here. One does not need to make elaborate, highly speculative inferences concerning what was going on inside the minds of particular policy makers at particular times. One simply posits that governments respond in a rational (or, at least, reasonable) manner to the reward and punishment contingencies of the international environment.[13] From this standpoint, the problem of learning is largely a pseudo-problem. Neorealists assume that there is little leeway for slow learners in a rapidly changing international environment. National leaders either respond in a prudent and timely manner to shifts in the balance of power or they are replaced by more realistic leaders. The choice is between learning and being selected out of the game in ruthless Darwinian fashion. Waltz, for example, explicitly compares international systems to unregulated economic markets.[14] Both, he notes, are self-help systems in which the component units (firms or nations) must either fend for themselves or enter into alliances with powerful protectors. National governments that display little capacity to learn have little chance to survive.

This neorealist approach to learning is a useful starting point. It calls our attention to the structural incentives in the international environment for particular types of policies. Neorealists and game theorists lead us to expect policy makers to be highly attuned to these incentive structures.[15] In general, the expectation is for a high baseline of military, political, and economic competition within the international environment, an expectation that follows from the security dilemma and the anarchic nature of the international system.[16] These theorists also, however, allow for the possibility of cooperation. The rational actor premises underlying neorealist and game theoretic approaches lead us to expect cooperation when cooperation is indeed prudent—when, for example, the penalties for noncooperation are steep (e.g., violating arms control agreements motivates the other side to develop destabilizing first-strike weapons systems), the rewards for cooperation are high (e.g., the economic and security benefits of reduced military competition), and the shadow of the future looms large (it does not pay to cross an adversary with whom one expects to deal over a protracted period of time).[17] Some observers argue that these conditions were clearly satisfied in the case of the Soviet Union in the late 1980s.[18] The massive Reagan defense build-up made clear to the Soviets that the penalties for noncooperation were steep (sharp Western responses to the build-up of intercontinental ballistic missiles, SS-20s in eastern Europe, and Third World activism); the prospect of revitalizing the stagnant Soviet economy by redirecting scarce resources from defense to economic modernization greatly enhanced the rewards of cooperation; and the shadow of the future loomed ominously indeed (it doesn't pay to cross adversaries who may have decisive technological and economic advantages in long-term competition). Gorbachev, in short, need not have been a nice guy.[19] Why invoke altruism when enlightened self-interest is up to the explanatory task?

Although useful up to a point, the neorealist conception of learning is profoundly unsatisfying. One reason is that the neorealist approach is so epistemologically restrictive; it rules out most of the questions our contributors to this volume find most interesting. Our contributors are not content with merely describing shifts in superpower response thresholds in response to external events. They want to explore the psychological, institutional, and political processes that lead governments to define their interests in certain ways and to adopt certain policies in pursuit of those interests—policies with which governments occasionally persist even in the face of repeated punishment. Just as pigeons sometimes fail to respond to changing reinforcement contingencies,[20] and just as economic actors sometimes fail to respond in a timely fashion to changing market signals,[21] so foreign policy actors are sometimes slow to respond to changes in the distribution or even the nature of geopolitical power. There is a hollow tautological ring to purely structuralist explanations of foreign policy that presume a frictionless capacity of unitary rational actors to adjust strategies in response to new events. It is possible to generate post hoc geopolitical rationalizations for a wide range of policy decisions. If it is easy to argue that the conciliatory Gorbachevian initiatives of the late 1980s were dictated by systemic necessity, it is equally easy to argue that, had the Soviet Union moved in a militant, neo-Stalinist direction in the late 1980s, that response too would have been dictated by systemic necessity: What better way to hold on to superpower status than by reasserting discipline on the domestic front and by devoting massive resources to defense programs?[22]

Our objections to the neorealist approach are not, however, just methodological; they are also substantive. It sounds uncontroversial, even platitudinous, to claim that, ceteris paribus, governments persist with policies that yield desired consequences and modify and eventually abandon policies that yield undesired ones (a political restatement of the earliest behaviorist law of learning, Thorndike's Law of Effect). What counts, though, as a good or bad outcome? The answer is sometimes obvious, sometimes not. The Bay of Pigs can be uncontroversially classified as the sort of outcome the Kennedy administration strove thereafter to avoid; it is not clear, however, whether the Strategic Arms Limitation Treaties— SALT I and SALT II—should be placed in the good or bad outcome category. The lessons one draws from the early arms control treaties largely reflect one's overall political outlook. Many liberals and moderates saw the consequences of the early treaties with the Soviets as, on balance, positive; many conservatives concluded the opposite. There is so much room for disagreement here because there is so much uncertainty concerning the causal connections between policies and outcomes. We do not know which outcomes were the result of the policies adopted and which would have occurred anyway.

A straightforward reward-punishment model of learning in international politics fails because it fails to address how decision makers cope with the causal ambiguity inherent in complex historical flows of events.[23] The feedback that decision makers receive from their policies is often equivocal and subject to widely varying political interpretations. Moreover, feedback to a policy may be delayed. What appears to be a prudent policy at one time may appear to be extraordinarily foolish at another. In the 1950s and 1960s, supporters of covert action cited the coup sponsored by the Central Intelligence Agency (CIA) against Iranian Prime Minister Mossadegh as a good example of how to advance U.S. strategic interests in the Middle East and elsewhere; after the fundamentalist Islamic revolution of 1979, opponents of covert action argued that a reappraisal was in order. To invoke another example, Soviet policy in the Third World seemed to bear fruit in the 1970s, with pro-Soviet governments sprouting up in such diverse locations as Indochina, Afghanistan, Ethiopia, and Nicaragua. By the late 1980s, a reappraisal was in order. Geostrategic assets increasingly looked like liabilities. In an international environment that is complex to the point of indeterminate, even rational actors may be unable to anticipate the long-range consequences of their actions.[24]

THE COGNITIVE PSYCHOLOGICAL APPROACH TO LEARNING

If what counts as a rewarding or punishing consequence in the international environment critically depends on the ideological assumptions of the beholder, it is no longer adequate to black-box the policy-making process and limit the study of learning to documenting action-outcome covariations. It becomes necessary to study how policy makers think about events within the international system. The belief system approach to learning rests on a pair of simple functionalist premises:

(a) The international environment is extraordinarily complex;
(b) People—limited capacity information processors that we are— frequently resort to simplifying assumptions to deal with the complexity, uncertainty, and painful trade-offs inherent in foreign policy problems.[25]

Policy makers, like ordinary mortals, see the world through a glass darkly— through the simplified images they create of the international scene. Policy makers may act rationally, but only within the context of their subjective representations of reality (Simon's principle of bounded rationality).[26] To understand foreign policy, we must understand the simplified images of reality that decision makers rely on in interpreting events and choosing among courses of action.[27] Policies that make eminent sense within one assumptive framework look foolish, even treasonous, within other frameworks. Neo-Stalinists—who subscribed to the two-camp thesis that conflict between the imperialist and socialist states was inevitable—looked with horror on the policy initiatives of Gorbachev and the rhetoric of interdependence that accompanied those initiatives. Conversely, many liberal advocates of arms control were equally horrified as the Reagan administration attempted to dismantle the arms control understandings of the 1970s and escape mutually assured destruction (MAD) via the strategic defense initiative (SDI).

Foreign policy belief systems have enormous cognitive and political utility. They provide policy makers with ready answers to basic questions about the world with which they must deal. What are the fundamental objectives of the leaders of other states? What risks are my adversaries prepared to take to achieve those objectives? Is conflict inevitable? What form is the conflict likely to take? Foreign policy belief systems also facilitate decision making by providing guidelines for choosing among options. They provide frameworks for estimating the consequences of different options (If we fail to do x, the Soviets are likely to do y . . .) and for assessing the significance of those consequences (How will vital national interests be affected?).

There is, however, a price to be paid for these benefits. In their efforts to maintain stable, internally consistent belief systems, policy makers may fashion images of the world that are more orderly and regular than reality itself. Belief systems may facilitate the learning of lessons consistent with the underlying assumptions but impede the learning of anything else.

Empirical and theoretical work on belief systems leads to a variety of predictions concerning the conditions under which learning is likely to take place and the forms that learning is likely to take.[28] I summarize here four hypotheses that have been advanced in the literature and that receive support in many of the case studies commissioned for this volume.

Hypothesis 1: Several lines of work suggest that foreign policy belief systems are organized hierarchically with fundamental assumptions and policy objectives at the apex of the system, strategic policy beliefs and preferences at an intermediate level, and tactical beliefs and preferences at the base of the system.[29] If so, it is reasonable to ask at what juncture in belief systems learning occurs. Given the powerful cognitive psychological and political accountability pressures to demonstrate consistency in policies over time, a plausible hypothesis is that most learning takes place at the level of tinkering with tactics. Policy makers rarely have the time or the inclination to start questioning the fundamental premises of policy; they are, however, willing to make frequent tactical adjustments to cope with unforeseen events.

Three examples of such tactical learning (or adaptation, in Haas's terms) should suffice:

(1) Spiegel (Chapter 8) argues that fundamental U.S. objectives in the Middle East have been remarkably constant over the last 40 years: protecting Israel, maintaining access to oil, blocking Soviet influence, and promoting peace. Most debate within administrations has focused on the relative weight of particular objectives—weights that hinge largely on the threats or opportunities most salient at the moment. Events such as wars, oil embargoes, coups, and uprisings prime or activate different objectives, and administrations respond by making mostly tactical adjustments.

(2) Haslam (Chapter 13) argues that the Soviet policy toward Germany between 1945 and 1985 was anchored in a unilateralist approach to

national security that emphasized reliance on both territorial expansion and the Soviet army as an instrument for oppressing local populations. Although the Soviets made numerous tactical adjustments to mollify the West (especially after 1953 when they became more interested in détente), Soviet leaders adamantly refused to give up the territorial control they had won at such a cost in blood in World War II. Reconsideration of the German question—and of the possibility that Stalin's method of preventing a repetition of the last war might be eroding long-term Soviet national security—were simply too emotionally and politically explosive issues to take on in the 1945–1985 period.

(3) Thies (Chapter 6) notes that the Eisenhower administration was convinced of the need to reduce defense spending "to a level the economy could support without undue strain over the long haul." Eisenhower turned to the doctrine of massive retaliation to reconcile what he saw as the contradictory needs to deter Soviet expansionism and to maintain economic growth and political stability. This escape from the guns-versus-butter trade-off ("more bang for the buck" in nuclear weapons) had a significant price tag of its own. It placed the political onus on NATO of threatening to begin a nuclear war in response (in principle) to even minor Soviet acts of aggression. The Eisenhower administration did not, however, question the premises of its policy. Instead, it adopted what Thies terms a "schizophrenic" public stance: simultaneously threatening to employ "big weapons" to protect "free people" and attempting to control the resultant political damage in Europe by suggesting that it really would not be necessary to follow through on those threats. This tactical bandaid may have sufficed as long as the American homeland was reasonably safe from Soviet nuclear retaliation and the deterrent threat retained credibility. As it became increasingly apparent that we lived in a MAD world, it also became clear that Eisenhower's escape from the guns-versus-butter dilemma was a temporary one.

Hypothesis 2: A logically related hypothesis is that policy makers reconsider their basic strategic approach to a problem only after repeated failures to come up with a tactical solution. One can make a strong case, for example, that the U.S. decision to withdraw from Vietnam and the Soviet decision to withdraw from Afghanistan were made only after it became clear that, given the political constraints on the use of force, a military solution was not attainable. Similarly, one can make a strong case that the Soviet decision to accept the Reagan "zero option" for intermediate-range nuclear weapons in Europe was made only after the failure of repeated diplomatic and political efforts to halt the deployment of Pershing and cruise missiles (Haslam, Chapter 13).

Hypothesis 3: A third, closely linked hypothesis is that policy makers reconsider basic goals or objectives only after repeated failures to come up with a strategic solution. This type of "fundamental learning"[30] may occur only when current policies appear to lead to either undeniable logical contradictions or unpalatable empirical consequences. Weber (Chapter 20) argues that, in the domain of nuclear arms control, there are only two reasonably clear-cut examples of fundamental learning: McNamara's acceptance of the radical strategic implications of mutually assured destruction in the 1960s (motivated in part by the growing incredibility of the doctrine of massive retaliation—Thies, Chapter 6) and Gorbachev's embrace of both MAD and the doctrine of sufficiency in the 1980s (motivated in part by the counterproductive effects of adopting a war-fighting nuclear posture in the 1970s—Blacker, Chapter 12). To this list, Garrett (Chapter 7) would add the Nixon-Kissinger initiatives to Beijing, which required restructuring the dominant American image of the People's Republic of China: from that of a revolutionary pariah state to that of a rational national actor in a balance-of-power system. The old cold war policies toward China were yielding little and, given the domestic constraints and international trends Nixon and Kissinger confronted, there were compelling realpolitik reasons to use China as a counterweight to growing Soviet power.[31] Finally, the most recent example of fundamental learning is the wholesale abandonment of the Brezhnev Doctrine by the Gorbachev leadership— the acid test being the willingness to accept German reunification within NATO (Haslam, Chapter 13). Here one sees a sharp, qualitative shift in the Soviet conception of security. The buffer state or *cordon sanitaire* model, rooted in a fear of invasion from the West, gave way to an understanding of security grounded in the economic and political interdependence of states.

Hypothesis 4: The previous three hypotheses are consistent with McGuire's principle of least resistance in attitude change.[32] All other things being equal, people try to accommodate new evidence and arguments by minimizing the number of related cognitions that must be changed in the process of incorporating the new evidence into the belief system. For instance, it was cognitively easier for John Foster Dulles to dismiss Soviet troop cuts in eastern Europe in the mid-1950s as a propagandistic gesture necessitated by economic weakness than it was to consider seriously the possibility that the expansionist model of Soviet intentions underlying the containment policy was fundamentally flawed.[33] Only in the face of repeated disconfirming instances are policy makers willing to reappraise basic premises.

Repeated disappointment may be a necessary but almost certainly not a sufficient condition for fundamental reappraisal to occur. Philosophers of science have noted the tenacity with which old-generation scientists hold on to basic assumptions underlying their research programs.[34] When unexpected results emerge, the first intellectual instinct of scientists loyal to the research program is to challenge the appropriateness of the re-search methods that produced the results (analogous to challenging tactics). If a number of theoretically credible methods lead to the same conclusion, the second reaction is to challenge the middle-range theories that generated the disconfirmed hypothesis (analogous to challenging strategy after repeated failures). Only if it proves impossible to improvise a middle-range theory consistent with the observed facts are some scientists willing to reconsider their commitment to the hard-core objectives of the research program (analogous to challenging fundamental policy objectives after repeated strategic failures). The fourth hypothesis maintains that this latter type of learning is often so cognitively difficult, that it typically occurs only in the presence of massive personnel shifts. Two examples of fundamental learning discussed in this book—the Nixon-Kissinger reconceptualization of the role of China in the international system (Garrett, Chapter 7) and Gorbachev's reconceptualization of the entire system (Blacker, Chapter 12; Breslauer, Chapters 15 and 21; Legvold, Chapter 18)—depended very much on massive personnel shifts. What Max Planck observed of physicists may also be true of national leaders: one must wait for the old generation to retire or die before new ideas can be thoroughly explored.

How does one know, however, whether learning of the fundamental type has occurred? The debate over Gorbachev illustrates the inferential problems involved. Even into the late 1980s, some conservatives continued to argue that the Gorbachevian policies did not reflect a fundamental reevaluation of Soviet goals, but rather a strategic shift, an effort to achieve a *peredyshka* or breathing spell in which to revitalize the Soviet system and then resume competition with the West on more advantageous terms. In one sense, debates over levels of learning are unresolvable. For any given Gorbachevian act, it was possible to come up with rival tactical and fundamental explanations. The scales of plausibility began to tip dramatically, however, when one broadened the range of evidence considered and took into account a wide array of foreign policy acts. If fundamental goals have indeed been reevaluated, we should expect policy in many arenas to change (as it did). Moreover, we should expect major institutional and domestic political re-structuring in response to this reevaluation (restructuring that clearly has occurred under Gorbachev; see Legvold, Chapter 18 and Blacker, Chapter 12). Even so, there is ultimately no well-defined evidential standard for distinguishing among levels of learning. As late as 1974, James Jesus Angleton, the director of U.S. counterintelligence, resisted revising his monolithic image of international communism by dismissing the Sino-Soviet split as a strategic feint.[35] And as late as 1989, some diehard essentialists still harbored dark suspicions about Gorbachev's true motives.[36]

THE COGNITIVE STRUCTURALIST APPROACH TO LEARNING

Some contributors use the terms *learning* and *changing one's mind* interchangeably. Within the belief system approach to learning, for example, one might say that, as a result of an event, decision makers adjusted their views on the likely effectiveness of a particular policy or their views on the feasibility or desirability of achieving a given goal. Learning, in this view, involves adjustments in the content of a belief system—shifts in subjective probability estimates that could, in principle, be modeled as a Bayesian process of "updating priors."[37] Dallin (Chapter 11), for instance, notes that many conservatives lowered their estimates of the likelihood of expansionist Soviet acts in response to the Gorbachevian initiatives of 1985–1989. Changes in belief systems also involve shifts in goals and even values. Blacker (Chapter 12), for example, suggests that Brezhnev gradually became more accepting of mutual nuclear vulnerability in the 1970s. There need not, of course, be any implication of approval on the analyst's part of the lessons that policy makers have learned. The term *learning* is used in a purely descriptive fashion to characterize the direction and magnitude of the shifts that have occurred on certain issues within the belief systems of certain individuals.

Belief systems, however, vary not only in content, but also in structure. In his pioneering study of government learning, Etheredge[38] attaches special significance to this cognitive structural dimension of belief systems, defining learning in terms of increased cognitive differentiation and integration of thought and increased capacity for self-reflection.[39] I focus here on four structural dimensions of belief systems of special relevance to learning in foreign policy: (1) the cognitive complexity of the idea elements within a belief system, (2) the evaluative complexity of the idea elements, (3) the degree of interrelatedness or integration among idea elements, and (4) the capacity for self-reflection or metacognition. Learning can take the form of change on each of these structural dimensions:

(1) *Cognitive complexity* refers to the number of logically distinct arguments or considerations that a policy maker takes into account in judging an event or arriving at a decision. Two individuals, for example, may hold identical policy positions, each favoring or opposing ballistic missile defense with equal intensity—but differ greatly in the cognitive complexity of the reasons underlying their stands. One individual may have a complex rationale for opposing missile defense, a rationale that takes into account the vicissitudes of U.S.–Soviet strategic nuclear competition, the transience of technological advantages, the destabilizing effects of undermining mutually assured destruction, and the enormous expense

of the proposed projects. The other individual may have a simple rationale that is anchored in only one set of objections to ballistic missile
defense. These differences in cognitive structure may, moreover, be consequential. There are strong logical and psychological grounds for expecting policy preferences buttressed by a cognitively complex array of
beliefs to be much more resistant to change than a preference buttressed
by only a single argument.

(2) *Evaluative complexity* refers to the degree of inconsistency or tension that exists among the considerations that a policy maker uses to
judge events or make choices. A degree of cognitive complexity is obviously
necessary for evaluative complexity. If there is only one idea element in
one's belief system, and that element is not self-contradictory (e.g., "This
statement is false"), then one's belief system must be evaluatively consistent.
Cognitive complexity is not, however, a sufficient condition for evaluative
complexity. One can have an extremely cognitively complex belief system,
with many arguments converging on the same conclusion, that still may
be evaluatively simple because there is little or no tension among these
mutually reinforcing arguments. Or one can have a belief system characterized by both cognitive and evaluative complexity, in which some
arguments point the decision maker in one policy direction and other
arguments point in the opposite direction. Evaluative complexity implies
conflict, dissonance, and dialectical tension among cognitions.

(3) *Cognitive integration* refers to the development of complex rules,
schemata, and trade-off principles for coping with evaluative tensions
among the values within a belief system. Policy makers often want contradictory things: to promote economic efficiency but not at the expense
of producing domestic instability, to deter the other side but to avoid
triggering an uncontrollable arms race spiral, or to pursue a sound foreign
policy but not to antagonize key political constituencies. Cognitive integration
is critical for establishing priority rules or boundary conditions among
such competing objectives. One must decide how much of one value one
is prepared to sacrifice to achieve gains on other values. Moreover, at the
highest levels of cognitive integration, one must confront the need to
make flexible or contingent trade-off judgments in which the relative
weight one places on competing values changes with the domestic or
international situation.

(4) *Self-reflection* or *metacognition* can be viewed as a special form of
cognitive integration. It refers to the capacity to view one's own mental
processes with a degree of detachment and to comment on those processes
from a logical or even epistemological standpoint. Policy makers don't
just think; they (perhaps rarely) think about thinking. Examples of
metacognition include self-conscious attempts to design a decision-making
system that avoids the problems of earlier systems (e.g., how to achieve

high-quality, multidimensional policy analysis without diffusing too much authority, taking too much time, or exacerbating bureaucratic in-fighting?) and self-conscious efforts to articulate standards of evidence and proof (e.g., at what point do we decide that we need to begin revising basic assumptions about an adversary's intentions or capabilities?).

From the standpoint of cognitive consistency theory, we should expect most learning in foreign policy to take the form of increases in cognitive but not evaluative complexity.[40] This prediction also follows from Jervis's characterization of "belief system overkill."[41] Policy makers, he notes, are often not satisfied to argue that, on balance, the policy they prefer is better than the alternatives. They feel a psychological and political need—two needs that are difficult to disentangle—to argue that their policy is, in decision theory terms, dominant or better on all possible criteria. In this way, policy makers can avoid confronting cognitively difficult, emotionally wrenching, and politically embarrassing trade-offs.[42]

A cognitive consistency analysis suggests that most learning in foreign policy involves the acquisition of progressively more elaborate justifications that support what one has done or plans to do. All learning, however, certainly does not fit this restrictive template. Several chapters make reference to learning that involves increases in evaluative complexity. Spiegel, for example, notes a long-term trend for U.S. policy toward the Middle East to be informed by an increasingly more evaluatively complex image of regional dynamics than U.S. policy in the 1940s: a greater appreciation for cross-cutting inter-Arab rivalries and for ways of balancing U.S. interests vis-à-vis the Israelis and Arabs (Chapter 8). Griffiths notes a long-term trend from Stalin to Gorbachev for Soviet views of the United States to make greater allowance for evaluative inconsistency.[43] The simple Stalinist image of a society dominated by a cohesive group of monopoly capitalists has been superseded by a much more multidimensional image of a pluralistic society in which policy is the product of competing interest groups, institutions, and factions. Breslauer (Chapter 15) notes growing recognition among Soviet elites—through the 1970s and 1980s—of the tension between supporting "progressive" Third World regimes and enjoying the benefits of détente. Finally, Legvold (Chapter 18) notes that the overall Gorbachevian conception of international security is more evaluatively complex than the Brezhnevite conception. The Gorbachevian concept explicitly acknowledges the reality of what U.S. academics call the security dilemma—one can undermine one's own security by building up one's conventional or nuclear forces to the point at which they breed fear, anxiety, and hostility in other powers, setting up the potential for a conflict spiral (see also Blacker, Chapter 12; Haslam, Chapter 13; Whiting, Chapter 14).

Increasing evaluative complexity might be applauded as a sign of greater realism; it can also, however, be dangerous. In part, this is so because reality is sometimes simple. Chamberlain would probably enjoy higher historical esteem today if he had held a less evaluatively complex view of Hitler's intentions in 1938. And, in part, this is so because increased evaluative complexity—in the absence of cognitive integration—can induce confusion, even paralysis, within a decision-making system (the Hamlet syndrome). Recognizing that conflicting points of view compete for dominance within the government of one's adversary is not useful if the knowledge merely adds to one's uncertainty and causes one to temporize and vacillate. Recognizing a tension between objectives is not useful if one merely randomly shifts from one objective to another as a function of whichever one is more salient or politically expedient at the moment (a common criticism of the Carter administration—Garrett, Chapter 7). Learning at the level of cognitive integration—establishing flexible but reasonably well-defined guidelines for resolving conflicts among goals— would seem a critical precondition for successful coping in a complex international environment—an observation that leads naturally to the efficiency conception of learning.

THE EFFICIENCY DEFINITION OF LEARNING

It is possible to assess learning at the level of individual belief systems or political structures without taking any stand on whether governments are becoming more adroit or adept at achieving the goals they value. It is not possible to avoid this extraordinarily important—but also extraordinarily difficult—issue when we try to assess learning in the efficiency sense of the term. According to this definition, learning has occurred whenever policy makers have learned to match means and ends in more efficient or effective ways. Learning in this sense *can take two very distinct forms*—one can discover more effective strategies for pursuing one's original goals, or one can redefine one's goals in more realistic ways. A chess player, for example, might learn to play the game more effectively or learn to keep his morale and self-esteem intact by giving up trying to defeat much stronger players.

Assessing whether learning in the efficiency sense has occurred is quite straightforward in highly controlled environments with well-defined functional properties (call them learner-friendly environments). We can be reasonably confident that we have learned a great deal about how to conduct recombinant DNA research, to construct more powerful supercomputers, and, of course, to design and deliver nuclear weapons. These environments are learner-friendly in four key respects: (a) There are well-defined evidential standards for determining success and failure; (b) it is possible to conduct controlled experiments to eliminate alternative causal hypotheses; (c) it is possible to draw on well-replicated and precise laws of physical and biological science in designing the relevant technologies; and (d) investigators tend to get quick and unambiguous feedback concerning the correctness of their predictions.

Assessing whether learning in the efficiency sense has occurred in post-World War II superpower relations is much more complex—for we don't have any of the just-mentioned methodological and theoretical advantages. Elegant controlled experiments are impossible. There is no sophisticated research literature that political analysts can draw upon for well-documented scientific laws and principles. Indeed, even the most tentative generalizations about deterrence or decision making evoke spirited debate within the professional community.[44] We also lack a large, carefully quantified, and uncontroversial data base that we can rely on for assessing the accuracy of past expectations or predictions. Policy makers rarely receive quick or unequivocal feedback concerning the accuracy of their predictions. In fact, the issue of who should take credit or blame for particular outcomes is typically hotly contested. In the United States, for example, many conservatives are eager to assign credit to the Reagan administration's defense build-up for the more conciliatory Soviet foreign policy of the late 1980s. According to this view, the Soviets recognized that they could not compete on a prolonged basis in the kind of intense military-technological arms race to which the Reagan administration had committed the United States. Gorbachev was merely following the old Bolshevik operational code dictum: in probing your opponent with a bayonet, when you strike mush, keep pushing, and when you strike steel, draw back.[45] We should not be surprised, from this perspective, that the Soviets have pulled back in response to the recent political and military assertiveness of the West.

By contrast, many liberals and moderates argue that the new Gorbachevian approach to foreign policy would have emerged on the scene pretty much regardless of who occupied the White House (indeed, if anything, Gorbachev's approach emerged *despite*, not because of, Reagan's policies). In this view, the Gorbachev leadership is a natural stage in the internal evolution of the Soviet political-economic system and an inevitable consequence of the generational transfer of power to a new, better educated, and more politically sophisticated leadership cohort.[46] Whereas physical and biological scientists can turn to well-designed experiments with control groups to address causal questions that intrigue them, here the control groups exist only in the imaginations of political analysts. We must rely on highly speculative forms of counterfactual analysis: what would have happened if X had or had not occurred? It is easy to slip into tautological patterns of reasoning in the face of such ambiguity and complexity. It is tempting to allow one's preconceptions to fill in the missing data points for the no-Reagan control condition. Counterfactual history is in this respect rather like the Rorschach inkblot test. People often see what they want or expect to see. And what one sees may tell us as much about the inner mental workings of the observer as it does about the external political workings of the world.

Some contributors to this volume have voiced skepticism concerning the very possibility of learning in the efficiency sense in U.S. and Soviet foreign policy. In his study of U.S. arms control policy, Levine (Chapter 5) forcefully argues that little changed from 1960 to 1985 in our thinking about arms control, despite massive changes in the technological, strategic, and political environments. Arms control debates, he maintains, have ultimately been theological in nature. We have no concrete or generally accepted evidence that allows us to determine which policies increased or decreased the likelihood of nuclear war. He notes that we learn from experience and, fortunately, we have had no experience of nuclear warfare since 1945.

Levine's point is well taken. We simply do not know whether nuclear war would have occurred if we had travelled down a different—more conciliatory or more hawkish—policy path. As Joseph Nye notes, much of what passes for nuclear knowledge "rests upon elaborate counterfactual arguments, abstractions based on assumptions about rational actors, assumptions about the other nation's unknown intentions and simple intuitions."[47] It is easy for the nuclear theologians to construct a dizzying variety of theories to account for *the nonoccurrence of a unique event.*

Where does all this leave us? Should we give up on assessing whether learning in the efficiency sense has occurred? Some analysts may conclude that the task is hopeless. We suspect, however, that this response would be too extreme. It is difficult, but not inherently impossible, to draw inferences about whether learning in the efficiency sense has occurred in particular foreign policy contexts. To be sure, making the inference does require a lot of confidence in the analyst's grasp of the underlying geopolitical reality and of what would have happened if other policies had been pursued. Nonetheless, such confidence may sometimes be justified. Most scholarly observers agree that it was prudent for U.S. policy makers to recognize the strategic significance of the Sino-Soviet split (Garrett, Chapter 7), that the Camp David accord advanced U.S. influence in the Middle East (Spiegel, Chapter 8), that it was inappropriate to rely on the Korean analogy as a detailed guide to policy in Vietnam (Khong, Chapter 9), and that supplying certain types of nuclear technologies substantially increases the risk of a country "going nuclear" (Lavoy, Chapter 19). Most observers also agree that Soviet policy makers—under Gorbachev—have begun to pursue both more adaptive tactics and realistic goals in their dealings with China (Whiting, Chapter 14), in arms control negotiations with the

United States (Blacker, Chapter 12), and in their relations with Western Europe (Haslam, Chapter 13) and the Third World (Breslauer, Chapter 15; Hopf, Chapter 16). Indeed, not only are many observers willing to make inferences of this sort, many are also inclined to wonder why it took policy makers so long to recognize the need to modify tactics or redefine goals—at which point they invoke combinations of cognitive psychological, institutional, and domestic political explanations. What Victor Hugo said of God might equally aptly be said of policy makers: they see the truth, but slowly. Perceptions may systematically lag behind reality.[48]

INTERRELATIONSHIPS AMONG TYPES OF LEARNING

Assuming that we are justified in making at least tentative inferences about learning in the efficiency sense, an interesting theoretical question arises: How is learning in the efficiency sense related to learning in the "cognitive content" and "structural" senses? Here we discover a plethora of possible answers. Much depends on the hypothesized degree of correspondence between the thought patterns of decision makers and the geopolitical environment that they confront. Learning in the cognitive content sense (adjusting tactics, strategies, and goals) may be quite adaptive in an environment that is undergoing dramatic change but quite maladaptive in an environment that superficially is in flux but in reality is highly stable and requires constancy of purpose (an argument that conservative advocates of containment advanced in the late 1980s with respect to U.S. policy toward the Soviet Union). And even in highly labile environments, learning in the cognitive content sense is at most a necessary, not a sufficient, condition for learning in the efficiency sense. The mere fact that one adjusts one's tactics, strategies, or goals does not imply that one is doing so wisely. Policy adjustments may confuse the bureaucracy, erode one's domestic base of support (which, in turn, reduces one's long-term flexibility), antagonize allies, and trigger undesired responses from adversaries.

Learning in the cognitive structural sense is also related in subtle and context-dependent ways to learning in the efficiency sense. In many cases, one can make a strong case that cognitive structural learning is close to being a necessary—although certainly not a sufficient—condition for learning in the efficiency sense. That conclusion seems to follow from how many contributors have characterized the policy problems confronting U.S. and Soviet decision makers. Spiegel (Chapter 8), for example, describes the often sharp tensions among the objectives that have driven U.S. policy toward the Arab-Israeli conflict, including the protection of Israel, the containment of Soviet influence, continued access to Middle Eastern oil, and the promotion of conservative Arab regimes. Thies (Chapter 6) notes the multiple policy objectives that U.S. administrations struggled to juggle in the early post-World War II period, including the need to keep defense spending and taxes within domestically tolerable limits, to keep the European allies solvent and secure, and to maintain a deterrent threat that was both potent and credible. Breslauer (Chapter 15) has noted the conflicts among Soviet goals in the Middle East, especially the tension between expanding influence in hardline Arab states and promoting détente with the United States. And Griffiths (Chapter 17) has noted a similar tension at a more abstract level in the formulation of Soviet foreign policy goals: on one hand, the desire to reap the benefits of improved relations with the successful "state monopoly capitalist states" of the West (trade, technology transfer) and, on the other hand, the desire to accelerate the "general crisis of capitalism" by assisting socialist victories in the Third World. It is logically impossible to cope with trade-offs of this sort without thinking about foreign policy problems in evaluatively complex and cognitively integrated ways.

Appreciating the trade-off structure of one's environment is certainly not, however, a sufficient condition for effective matching of means to ends. It is possible to display impressive cognitive structural learning and still fail. Spiegel (Chapter 8), for example, portrays the Middle Eastern policies of Eisenhower and Dulles as complex, innovative, well-organized, and profoundly unsuccessful. The effort to forge an Arab NATO (the Baghdad Pact) fizzled; the Soviets made significant inroads in the Middle East, and the efforts to promote peace in the region met with total failure. Khong (Chapter 9) portrays Johnson administration policy in the Vietnam war as a moderately complex, balanced attempt to avoid the mistakes in Korea (namely, provoking massive Chinese entry into the conflict) and simultaneously contain communist influence in Indochina—an attempt that also obviously failed.

The sources of these failures are, of course, endlessly debatable. Perhaps failure was inevitable given the structure of the situation: the realities of power within the region and domestic political constraints. Perhaps a more thoughtful and creative leadership could have crafted policies that would have worked out better. Perhaps there is an inherent element of unpredictability in foreign policy outcomes, and mistakes are inevitable no matter how well-informed or sophisticated the leadership. Whatever the correct combination of interpretations, the key point is that the relatively complex lessons policy makers drew from experience were not sufficient for guiding events in the desired historical direction.

Indeed, even the necessary-but-not-sufficient-condition interpretation of the relationship between cognitive structural and efficiency learning may be too strong. Not only is it possible to be complex and wrong, it may also be possible to be simple and right.[49] Cognitive structural learning is probably not even necessary for effective matching of means to ends. The simple-minded and determined pursuit of a single, well-defined objective may sometimes yield better results than complex attempts to achieve many, poorly defined objectives. For example, after reading Khong's study of decision making within the Johnson administration, one cannot help but wonder whether a simple dovish *or* hawkish policy would not have worked out better from an American standpoint than the complex, sometimes downright confusing, mixed policy that was actually pursued. The Johnson administration may have simultaneously overestimated both the winnability of the ground war in the south (encouraging excessive optimism that the projected troop commitments would be sufficient to do the job) and the danger of provoking Chinese entry into the war (failing to take into sufficient account the rising Sino-Soviet hostility, historical enmity between the Vietnamese and Chinese, and the chaos of Mao's Cultural Revolution). And after reading Dallin's description of the simplistic, stereotype-driven policies of the early Reagan administration toward the Soviet Union, one cannot help but wonder whether, indeed, the Reagan administration did the right thing for the wrong reasons. We may never know for sure (it would require a remarkable Soviet willingness to declassify records of their internal deliberations), but the unprecedented, peacetime expansion of American military strength—combined with what many Soviets regarded as the technological trump card of SDI—all may have combined to persuade a Soviet leadership beset with internal problems to adopt a much more conciliatory foreign policy posture than they otherwise would have.

If these speculative arguments are valid, the relationships between learning in the cognitive structural sense and learning in the efficiency sense are extraordinarily complex. Perhaps the strongest claim that can be made is that learning in the cognitive structural sense—developing a more nuanced, differentiated, and integrated view of one's environment—increases the *likelihood* both of pursuing policies that lead to achieving important goals and of setting realistic goals, especially when the environment is highly complex and rapidly changing.[50] Cognitive structural learning is clearly no guarantee, however, of success.

LEARNING AT THE LEVEL OF INSTITUTIONS AND POLITICAL CULTURES

So far, all the conceptions of learning considered here have been intrapsychic in focus: that is, learning occurs within the minds of particular policy makers. National security decisions are not, however, the product of isolated individuals. Such decisions are the product of political actors (a) who work within complex normative systems regulated by rules of accountability and constrained by standard operating procedures[51] and (b) who are often in intense competition with each other for influence and power and spend easily as much time negotiating with each other as they do with foreign governments.[52]

A number of writers argue that learning can take place not only at an individual level of analysis but also at the level of organizations and political cultures.[53] Just as individuals are capable of change in response to events, so too are institutions and political systems. This volume offers numerous examples of such collective learning—examples that fall into three broad categories, described below.

(1) Policy makers may create or dismantle institutions with the objective of avoiding the mistakes or repeating the successes of the past. To reduce the danger of a Soviet blitzkrieg invasion of Western Europe, Western leaders created a unified NATO command structure that was modeled on SHAEF (Supreme Headquarters, Allied Expeditionary Force), which directed the Normandy invasion and follow-up campaign in World War II (Thies, Chapter 6). To reduce the likelihood of a return to a Brezhnevite foreign policy, Gorbachev has instituted a system of public accountability of key decision makers—a system that bears some resemblance to the U.S. system of congressional accountability (Legvold, Chapter 18). To reduce the demonstrated ability of the foreign policy bureaucracy to subvert policy initiatives, Nixon and Kissinger centralized a great deal of authority in themselves and worked under a veil of secrecy (Garrett, Chapter 7).

(2) Policy makers may draw systematically on the knowledge base of an epistemic community and attempt to institutionalize the access of that community to the decision-making process (Breslauer, Chapter 15; Haas, Chapter 3; Lavoy, Chapter 19; Weber, Chapter 20; Whiting, Chapter 14). Weber notes, for instance, the willingness of defense secretary Robert McNamara to draw on the insights of academic strategists such as Thomas Schelling in rethinking the premises of nuclear deterrence. Lavoy notes the receptivity of the Carter administration to the highly complex nonproliferation problems that arise in transferring and monitoring commercial nuclear technologies. Whiting and Breslauer note the growing willingness of the Gorbachev leadership to draw on special area expertise (on China and the Middle East, respectively) in crafting policy toward those regions of the globe. Of course, epistemic communities can fall in and out of favor—as many social scientists discovered when the Reagan administration came to power and MAD theorizing was no longer in vogue (although—because it had been successfully institutionalized in the 1970s—the MAD doctrine significantly constrained the counterforce and ballistic missile defense initiatives of the Reagan period; Weber, Chapter 20). Other reminders of the reversibility of influence include the "red scare" purges of American Sinologists in the late 1940s (a purge that may have inhibited pre-Korean-War overtures to the People's Republic of China

to distance itself from the Soviet Union); the "yellow peril" scare that, for all practical purposes, destroyed the Soviet Sinological community in the late 1960s and cut the top leadership off from the advice of people with in-depth knowledge of Chinese politics and culture (Whiting, Chapter 14); and the dramatic deemphasis on nuclear nonproliferation from the Carter to the Reagan administration (Lavoy, Chapter 19).

(3) Policy makers may set cultural, political, and intellectual forces in motion that they lose the ability to control. Legvold (Chapter 18) describes the synergistic effects that relatively open debate has had on the quality of "foreign policy dialogue" within the Soviet Union. The top leadership sketches an idea—in vague or inchoate form, such as reasonable sufficiency or interdependence—and scholars (who may have been waiting decades for the opportunity to elaborate on these ideas) draw out a rich web of implications: the nature of the nuclear security dilemma, the danger of conflict spirals, and the need to consider explicitly the nonmilitary dimensions of security issues. The leadership, in turn, draws on many of these more specific and easier-to-operationalize-in-policy notions. Legvold describes the process well: "Ideas are inspired by ideas. People are sparked to thoughts they never had by others' equally novel thoughts." These changing norms of intellectual debate have important effects (see also Griffiths, Chapter 17).

The normative environment is not, of course, always quite so hospitable to creative questioning of the underlying premises of policy. A groupthink-like atmosphere sometimes falls on intellectual debate over policy issues. George Ball's objections to the Korean analogy in guiding the early decisions to enter the Vietnam War were apparently given short shrift.[54]   The McCarthyite atmosphere of the late 1940s and 1950s inhibited U.S. politicians and intellectuals from advocating a conciliatory policy toward Mao—a leader some thought of as a prospective "Asian Tito" (Garrett, Chapter 7). When people feel that their political careers are on the line, they are understandably reluctant to express doubts about popular policies or support for deviant ideas. According to Janis, President Kennedy felt that such a normative atmosphere stifled critical questioning that could have prevented the Bay of Pigs disaster and bent over backward in organizing the executive committee deliberations during the Cuban missile crisis to avoid a repeat performance.[55]

In summary, there is nothing immutable about the normative, institutional, and political mechanisms that regulate the policy-making process. There is also nothing inevitable about the value judgments that we attach to particular institutional or political changes. Changes that one observer lauds, another may ridicule. One source of normative disagreement is quite straightforward and, in principle, empirically resolvable. An institutional procedure that is adaptive for some purposes may be maladaptive for others. We just need to specify the normative boundary conditions. External accountability demands are a good example. Policy makers sometimes respond to such demands by engaging in preemptive self-criticism: anticipating valid objections that skeptics could raise to what they are doing and modifying policy to take those objections into consideration. The result is sometimes a better decision-making process.[56] For instance, Thies (Chapter 6) notes that Dean Acheson's self-described conversion on German rearmament was speeded by his discomfort at having to acknowledge a logical inconsistency in Truman administration policy before a Senate committee: on one hand, he agreed that no viable defense of Europe was possible without a German contribution and, on the other hand, he had to admit that there were no current plans for rearming Germany and including it in NATO defense plans. External accountability demands can also, however, be impediments to good policy making; too many cooks can spoil the broth. A policy that must gain the acceptance of a broad spectrum of political actors may be so diluted that it accomplishes none of its intended objectives. Sometimes the need to act quickly and secretly may be great enough to justify circumventing external accountability checks—as some might conclude from Garrett's study of the Nixon-Kissinger policy toward China.

Another source of normative disagreement is much less easily resolved—disagreements rooted in competing political assumptions and values. Weber, for example, views the gradual elite acceptance of the MAD doctrine as a positive development of the late 1960s and 1970s. He notes that in this period the "SALT solution" to nuclear deterrence in a MAD world was "firmly institutionalized" within the U.S. government. The Defense Department and National Security Council became accustomed to using SALT assumptions as starting points in formulating security policy and negotiation proposals. This embedding of SALT assumptions into the standard operating procedures of the national security bureaucracy was not viewed, however, in such a favorable light by conservatives such as Richard Perle and Caspar Weinberger. Nuclear use theorists saw this residual SALT influence not as a manifestation of institutional learning, but rather as an obstacle to crafting and mobilizing support for policies that would effectively close the "window of vulnerability" and deter new acts of Soviet expansionism.

Blacker (Chapter 12) observes an interesting mirror-image example of obstacles to institutional learning on the Soviet side—an observation that underscores Weber's claim that U.S. and Soviet nuclear policies have been badly out of synchrony. Although the Soviet political leadership grudgingly came to accept the strategic implications of MAD between 1972 and 1985, the Soviet military leadership was more resistant. They apparently saw their institutional mission as one of minimizing damage to the Soviet Union (in the event that war occurs) by maximizing damage to U.S. nuclear forces and by undertaking as extensive protective measures as SALT permitted. Thus, in the Soviet case, the military functioned as a brake on the fundamental learning about nuclear deterrence that occurred under McNamara in the United States and under Gorbachev in the Soviet Union. Although most Western observers saw Soviet military resistance to accepting MAD as backward, rigid, and parochial (rooted in short-sighted self-interest), the situation probably looked very different to those hard liners who remained in positions of influence in Moscow. From their point of view, the press organs of the military may have been one of the last bastions of lucidity in an age filled with naive talk about the end of the international class struggle and reasonable sufficiency in deterrence. Our judgments about what constitutes institutional learning versus an institutional obstacle to learning depend in no small degree on our political perspective.[57]

CONCEPTUAL AND EMPIRICAL PROBLEMS IN ASSESSING LEARNING

If we define the concept of learning sufficiently broadly—for instance, by subsuming all of the previously discussed definitions and making it synonymous with any attempt by a government to cope with changing circumstances—the concept loses all explanatory force; it becomes an empty tautology. If everything governments do is a manifestation of learning, nothing has been explained.

What are the theoretical alternatives to a learning framework? Under what conditions do investigators run the risk of concluding that the superpowers have learned (in one or another sense) when learning has not actually occurred? There are many possible pitfalls, five of which I identify here: (1) observers may confuse learning with adaptation; they may conclude that a government has learned when it has merely adapted in automaton fashion to changing stimulus conditions; (2) observers may confuse learning with political competition; they may attribute policy shifts to learning when those shifts are best explained by internecine bargaining among political rivals who have staked out distinctive foreign policy platforms for themselves in an effort to woo the support of key constituencies; (3) observers may confuse learning with the random ebb and flow of event streams within organized policy-making anarchies: much hinges on what problems are salient at the moment, who attends which meetings and controls the agenda, and who decides what counts as a solution; (4) observers may falsely conclude that learning occurred because they underestimated what policy makers knew in the first place; (5) observers may allow their own political biases and preferences to color their judgments of when learning has occurred.

ADAPTATION VERSUS LEARNING

Haas (Chapter 3) draws a sharp distinction between adaptation and learning—a distinction that a number of our contributors find useful (Lavoy, Chapter 19; Weber, Chapter 20). Adaptation has a mechanistic or cybernetic ring to it: one adapts or changes one's behavior in response to new events but without questioning one's beliefs about basic causation or underlying values. It hardly makes sense, for instance, to say that a thermostat—which activates or cuts off the operation of a furnace at a specified temperature—has learned each time the antecedent conditions for switching the furnace on or off have been satisfied. Equally so, it makes little sense to say that policy makers have learned if they are mindlessly relying on standard operating procedures to keep a few feedback variables within a politically tolerable range (e.g., make sure that the negotiations on conventional forces in Europe don't advance too quickly but avoid provoking the other side into a walk-out).[58] As long as policy makers are reasonably successful in performing this sort of cybernetic balancing act, there is little incentive for them to learn in Haas's sense of the term—to undertake the psychologically and politically stressful task of reformulating basic assumptions and goals.[59]

By contrast, learning involves a transformation in mode of thinking—a reassessment of fundamental beliefs and values that draws on the consensual knowledge of an epistemic community. There is nothing piecemeal or ad hoc about learning in this view. It entails a systematic restructuring of how policy makers approach a major problem such as strategic arms control, ozone depletion, or international debt. Policy makers have learned when they adopt a new, typically more complex, theory of the causal processes at work in a domain—a theory that guides the selection of objectives and options and that, in the eyes of the relevant scientific community, is more realistic than the conceptual framework that previously guided policy.[60]

The distinction between adaptation and learning is an intriguing one. There is a big difference between claiming: (a) the Soviet government has initiated a new policy because it has carefully reassessed the assumptions underlying the old policy, found those assumptions wanting, and drawn on the consensual knowledge of epistemic communities inside and outside the country to formulate an alternate set of premises and goals for guiding their actions (an interpretation endorsed to varying degrees by all our Sovietological contributors, but most forcefully by Legvold, Chapter 18) and (b) the Soviet government has changed its policy course in the last few years but has not altered its basic view of the world or its basic objectives. According to this (less and less influential) interpretation, the policy changes observed are merely the result of activating different components of a complex knowledge structure (a master plan for global hegemony). This knowledge structure specifies the relative importance that policy makers should place on competitive versus conciliatory strategies under different economic and geopolitical circumstances. In principle, the knowledge structure could be operationalized in the form of production rules:[61] under conditions A, B, and C, do x_1 and x_2; under conditions D, E, and F, do x_3 and x_4 . . . . Nothing has been learned in this view—the perceptual preconditions for activating one or another policy recipe have simply changed.

The Haasian distinction would subsume the reward-punishment and trial-and-error approaches to learning under the rubric of adaptation. One could easily imagine a cybernetic mechanism—wired up to assess the positive or negative value of the outcomes of its actions—adjusting its conduct to the reward and punishment contingencies of the environment. Indeed, such cybernetic mechanisms already exist. Commercially available computer chess programs can now play at a master level of sophistication (better than 95 percent of human players). The Haasian conception would also call into serious question what we called earlier the belief system approach to learning. Merely changing one's judgment about the probability or desirability of an event (adjusting beliefs and goals) is a necessary but not a sufficient condition for learning in the Haasian sense. To qualify as learning in this latter sense, policy makers must draw on the consensual knowledge of an epistemic community—be they economists, arms control specialists, physicists, or psychologists. This constraint on the term *learning* will also probably strike many scholarly observers as useful. It would sound odd to say that a policy maker who displayed growing symptoms of paranoid schizophrenia—like Secretary of Defense Forrestal in 1948—was learning something about his environment, although he quite demonstrably changed both his beliefs and his goals.

Although theoretically provocative, the distinctions Haas raises are difficult to operationalize. There is no neat nonarbitrary line dividing adaptation from learning. It will often be ambiguous whether policy makers are responding in a more cybernetic or in a more thoughtful fashion to events. Indeed, it may well be possible to mimic—via production rule systems—virtually any hypothesized example of learning in international politics.[62] That would leave us in an ironic situation. The danger at the beginning of this section was that the concept of learning was so diffuse that it could be invoked to explain any government policy. The danger now is that the empirical threshold for identifying learning has been raised so high that nothing will qualify.

Difficult empirical problems also arise in deciding whether policy shifts have truly been informed or guided by the consensual knowledge of an epistemic community. As Haas (Chapter 3) and Anderson (Chapter 4) are well aware, politicians may not internalize the ideas promoted by epistemic communities; they may merely use these ideas to appeal to influential constituencies, to outflank rivals, and to gain tactical advantages in ongoing struggles for power. The consensual knowledge of epistemic communities may be employed to justify rather than guide policy. An equally tricky issue concerns exactly what counts as an epistemic community. Must it be a group of scholars or scientists who subscribe to a common set of rigorous procedures for evaluating evidence and claims? Or would Nancy Reagan's calls for advice from her astrologer count as attempts to draw on the consensual knowledge of an epistemic community? Although this question can be easily answered in my opinion (and I suspect in Haas's opinion), the underlying issue raised by the question cannot be so readily resolved. Different groups resemble to varying degrees the ideal type of an epistemic community united around a consensual core of knowledge. We may decide to disqualify a group because it fails to live up to Popperian standards of scientific argumentation, because it lacks scholarly credibility, because there is too much internal dissension, or perhaps for a host of other reasons.

In short, the boundaries between adaptation and learning are fuzzy. This fuzziness does not, of course, mean that the distinction is useless; it does mean that those who choose to employ it should do so circumspectly.

POLITICAL COMPETITION VERSUS LEARNING

Anderson (Chapter 4) has advanced a political competition model of change in Soviet foreign policy—one that, mutatis mutandis, could be readily applied to U.S. foreign policy (see Thies, Chapter 6). In Anderson's model, "foreign policy changes in response to variation in the distribution of authority among contenders for leadership, who compete for authority by proposing distinctive foreign policy strategies." International events may influence policy, but only *indirectly* by altering the relative credibility of competing foreign policy views in the eyes of key constituencies. Moreover, it is probably quite common for foreign policy to change completely independently of international events. Policy makers' influence may wax and wane as a result of purely domestic events: poor agricultural or economic performance, a scandal such as Watergate, or the like.

According to the political competition model, Politburo members consider three sets of information in deciding what foreign policy stands to advocate: (a) the international environment; (b) the policy preferences of domestic constituencies; and (c) the policy stands of rival Politburo members. Each competitor confronts tough trade-offs in formulating a political strategy. On one hand, each wants to maximize his share of domestic support by advancing a position close to the median of elite constituency preferences. On the other hand, each also needs to carve out a distinctive policy position (to give constituencies a reason to support oneself as opposed to one's rivals), a plausible policy position (a position that does not lead to demonstrably false predictions or undesirable consequences), and a viable policy position (one that stands a good chance of actually being implemented—why support someone who is consistently on the losing side of Politburo arguments?). Politburo members respond to these trade-offs by developing moderately contrasting positions on foreign policy and resolving their differences via bargaining (trading support on one issue for support on another). Foreign policy may oscillate a great deal, from this point of view, for reasons that have little or nothing to do with learning about the international scene. The key question is: Which combination of Politburo members can put together a minimal winning coalition, and what compromises did they have to make in order to do so?

Taken to its logical extreme, the political competition model paints a portrait of Soviet decision making as autistic. Policy makers—who know little about the outside world—compete for influence by inventing policy platforms calculated to appeal to elite constituencies who know even less about the outside world. International reality does, however, have ways of insinuating itself into the process. As Anderson notes, the effects on domestic bargaining can mimic those of learning about the international situation. Working with a cognitive structural conception of learning (increased "integrative complexity of images of the world and of policy"), Anderson notes how the bargaining-for-influence process can prompt pseudo-learning in leaders' statements on foreign policy. He writes: "Rival leaders use their public statements not only to appeal to their own followers but to offer bargaining concessions to rivals and to signal acceptance of compromises." Just as if genuine cognitive structural learning had occurred, leaders advance increasingly multidimensional arguments that take into account objections and qualifications that their rivals deem important.

Although the political competition model initially looks very different from a learning theory approach, on closer inspection the two perspectives blur into each other—in much the same way that adaptation and learning blur into each other. One obvious question to pose is why call the evolution of public images stimulated by bargaining *pseudo-learning*. It could be, of course, that, as soon as it becomes politically feasible to do so, many Politburo members drop all the complex qualifications they attached to their earlier rhetorical positions. But it could also be the case that, as a result of internal debate, Politburo members with different perspectives on the international scene influence each other and gradually form genuinely more complex views of reality (a process that researchers in group dynamics call informational influence). In addition, the ground rules for political competition may themselves evolve as the constituencies to be wooed slowly but surely develop a more sophisticated grasp of the international system and the Soviet Union's place in it. It appears—over time—to have become increasingly difficult to sell a hard-line Stalinist interpretation of U.S. foreign policy as dominated by monopoly-capitalists and bent on encircling and destroying the Soviet Union.[63] This evolution of elite views may occur at least partly in response to events—an evolution that might aptly be characterized as a rolling consensus in which views once considered mainstream become peripheral and peripheral views either disappear (literally fall off the spectrum) or themselves become mainstream (Griffiths, Chapter 17). As elite constituencies become "smarter," Politburo members campaigning for the support of those constituencies must come up with increasingly sophisticated appeals—or drop out of the political game. Processes of learning and political competition may sometimes mutually reinforce each other.[64]

THE GARBAGE CAN MODEL OF ORGANIZATIONAL CHOICE VERSUS LEARNING

Thus far, the alternatives we have considered to learning—cybernetic adaptation and political competition—have been deterministic. March's pioneering work on the "garbage can model of organizational choice" suggests another possibility.[65] The foreign policies of the superpowers may be the product of "organized anarchies" in which the "outputs" (final decisions) depend more on a temporal than a causal logic. Much hinges on chance conjunctions of persons, issues, and events. The interrelations among four event streams are especially crucial: (1) problems (what do people inside and outside the foreign policy-making system care about—demonstrating strength to the Soviets, shifting scarce capital from defense to domestic programs, hostages in Lebanon, . . .); (2) solutions (a political solution is always someone's product—the nuclear freeze or SDI—a product that person is eager to promote); (3) participants (policy makers come and go for a variety of personal, administrative, and political reasons), and (4) choice opportunities (there are numerous occasions when governments are under great pressure to do something—the situation calls for a response, and even a nonresponse will qualify by default).

Not surprisingly, given its emphasis on randomness, the garbage can process does not solve problems terribly well. In a series of carefully designed computer simulations, March has shown, however, that garbage can models do enable reasonable choices to be made even when the organization is beset with internecine conflicts, ambiguity about its goals, a rapidly changing environment that is continually throwing up new challenges, and decision makers with little time and limited cognitive capacity. In short, garbage can models muddle through under difficult circumstances.

Observers of foreign policy may be struck by the resemblance between the day-to-day chaos of high-level governmental functioning and the garbage can model. A pessimistic interpretation of this resemblance is that long-term learning in foreign policy is impossible. Different lessons from experience will be activated depending on what problems events make salient, which decision makers are on hand to advance their preferred solutions, and what choice opportunities have arisen. A more balanced interpretation would acknowledge a large stochastic element in superpower foreign policies, but allow for the possibility that learning at an institutional or cultural level can prevent people with oddball ideas from getting into the central event streams of the policy-making system or, at a minimum, prevent those ideas from being taken seriously when they do get into the event stream. As with Anderson's political competition model, it is not difficult to build learning parameters into the garbage can model.[66] Governments may learn how to make decisions: how much time and energy to allocate to certain categories of problem (e.g., governments may learn that some problems are just intractable and there are greater payoffs to devoting effort elsewhere), how to prevent certain problems from arising (e.g., through skillful managing of political opponents or use of the press or diplomacy), whom to include and whom to exclude from particular decisions (e.g., through control of the agenda and timing of meetings), and which types of ideas to take seriously and which ones to disregard. Indeed, it is highly unlikely that a government that failed to learn how to exercise some control over the event streams that constitute it could survive for any protracted period of time.

THE DANGER OF UNDERESTIMATING POLICY MAKERS

Many claims about the occurrence or nonoccurrence of learning ultimately rest on inferences about what policy makers thought from what policy makers have said. As our contributors are well aware (see especially Dallin, Chapter 11; Whiting, Chapter 14), one is on tenuous grounds drawing confident cognitive conclusions from public political pronouncements. Policy makers may say things in public that they would privately acknowledge to be simplistic, naive, and even demagogic. Shifts in public statements over time more often reflect shifts in impression management goals and tactics than they do shifts in ways of thinking.[67]

Sometimes this distinction between true private beliefs and public posturing is an easy one to make. We have access to both private and public statements. Drawing on declassified documents, Thies (Chapter 6) argues that U.S. officials in the early postwar period deliberately exaggerated the risk of a Soviet invasion of Western Europe in order to rally domestic support (and mute criticism of) the Marshall Plan and the NATO alliance. It was not so much that they expected a Soviet blitzkrieg as they felt it politically useful to raise the specter of such an event. Garrett (Chapter 7) argues—again based on declassified documents—that Eisenhower and Dulles were well aware that Mao was not merely a Soviet puppet and that the communist monolith was more myth than reality. They were pursuing a "wedge-through-pressure" strategy toward China: by isolating China and increasing its dependence on the Soviet Union, they thought they could increase friction between the two major communist powers (an hypothesis that Garrett claims was borne out by subsequent events). And there is, of course, the famous quote from an exasperated Dean Rusk during the Vietnam War: "I'm not the village idiot. I know that Ho is not Hitler."[68] We know from Khong's (Chapter 9) careful analysis of the internal deliberations of the Johnson administration that the reasoning behind the decision to commit ground troops to South Vietnam was considerably more complex than the ritualistic "no more Munichs" rhetoric addressed to the American public.

Analysts of Soviet learning have a much more difficult time drawing sharp distinctions between private beliefs and public posturing. They have to work, virtually exclusively, with public records. As a result, much is left to one's imagination. We do not know, as Whiting (Chapter 14) notes, what the Soviets thought they could achieve through a massive conventional and nuclear buildup of forces along the Chinese border. Did they hope to pressure the Chinese Communist Party into overthrowing Mao and replacing him with a more pro-Soviet leader? Or did they merely hope to deter an irrational Mao from attacking Soviet Siberia? Without knowing what the original Soviet expectations were, it is hard to say what, if anything, they learned from the experience. There is also, of course, much ambiguity about Gorbachev. Did he envision in March 1985 the dramatic transformations that have occurred in Soviet security policy in the last five years? Or has he been engaged in a synergistic learning process of the sort sketched by Legvold (Chapter 18)—one in which the top leadership signals that it is acceptable to elaborate on certain ideas (e.g., nuclear sufficiency), the policy community does so in rich detail, the leadership picks up on many of the new ideas and identifies further directions for elaboration, and so on? Lacking any solid baseline for comparison, one must rely on educated guesses about learning from the available data: the evolution of actual policy over time, public statements from various sources, and the conditions under which shifts in statements precede versus follow shifts in policy.

THE DANGER OF PROJECTING ONE'S
NORMATIVE PREFERENCES

It is difficult—indeed unnatural—to use the term *learning* in a completely value-neutral way. When a political observer says that learning has occurred, more often than not the observer approves of the policy shifts being described. The study of learning, from this perspective, is under the implicit or explicit control of political agenda. We should expect cognitive accolades to be showered on policy makers who act in approved ways and cognitive insults to be showered on policy makers who stray from the "correct" path. It is thus not surprising that Western analysts laud the conciliatory initiatives of the Gorbachev leadership—a leadership that is intellectually sophisticated enough to appreciate the interactive logic of the security dilemma and the subtle trade-offs among its domestic and foreign policy goals. Nor is it surprising that observers of liberal inclination laud McNamara's recognition of the strategic implications of MAD as insightful and perceptive and criticize the Reagan administration for "unlearning" these important lessons (an administration that allowed its worst-case ideological assumptions about Soviet intentions to exert too much influence on policy).

We need to be vigilant that the term *learning* is not just used as a synonym for policy shifts with which the analyst sympathizes. As discussed earlier, the connections between cognitive and institutional conceptions of learning and learning in the efficiency sense can be tenuous indeed. Policy makers may fashion policies on the basis of assumptions that experts would deem simplistic, and those policies may actually work out quite well. Or policy makers may make Herculean efforts to be responsive to new evidence and to confront complex trade-offs only in the end to be identified with a policy failure. Learning is a multidimensional concept whose parts do not always cohere as one might expect. Historical analysts need to be on guard against what psychologists call halo effects (the mistaken assumption that all good things go together). As also discussed earlier, we need to maintain a certain humility about our ability to make conclusive judgments about learning in the efficiency sense. There are many normatively loaded questions that lie outside the scope of current knowledge. Do we see in Gorbachev the fulfillment of George Kennan's 1947 prophecy that containment would eventually cause the Soviet state to mellow? Or would such a leadership have emerged in response to a wide range of Western policy postures? Or are we relying on too short a time perspective? Might Gorbachev's successors pursue a quite different set of foreign policy priorities? Often the most that analysts can honestly claim is that "at this point in history, a particular policy has not led to Armageddon and may even have played some role in producing consequences that, given my values, I welcome."

Just as it is possible to pretend to know more than one does, it is also possible to pretend to know less. One can take the pursuit of value-neutrality to ludicrous extremes. Few would argue that social scientists should keep their silence, no matter how preposterous the premises or malignant the values underlying government policy. Who, for instance, would propose that social scientists should act as though they are totally agnostic on whether the monolithic neo-Stalinist image or the pluralistic Gorbachevian image of U.S. foreign policy is more correct? Or on whether the winnability of all-out nuclear war is an open issue? These questions raise substantive issues on which social and physical sciences directly bear. In Haas's terminology, there are relevant epistemic communities.

Aspiring to total value neutrality in an intellectual enterprise of this nature is not only unrealistic, it is also undesirable. In part, this is so because it requires us to understate our substantive knowledge. We know a good deal about the technical feasibility of various types of ballistic missile defense, about the rapidity with which technical innovations diffuse, about the complex trade-offs one confronts in making economic and security policy, and about the indigenous dynamics of particular regional conflicts. There is little to be gained and much to be lost from assuming that one person's opinion is as good as another's.

The quest for total value neutrality is misguided for another, equally important reason: it requires us to understate the procedural knowledge of relevant epistemic communities. Not only do we possess knowledge, we know how to go about generating new knowledge. Most scientists subscribe to a common set of epistemic norms. They believe, for example, that claims to knowledge should be stated in a format that allows empirical testing of either the claims or the logical implications of those claims. They also believe that these empirical tests need to be conducted in a fashion that minimizes the potential influence of the personal or institutional interests of the investigator. Investigators who fail to play by these basic rules of the scientific game (the most efficient method of generating knowledge human beings have yet devised) rightly lose their credibility in the eyes of colleagues. To be sure, adapting these epistemic rules to the domain of foreign policy is a complex undertaking—not least of all because of the equivocal and delayed nature of the feedback one receives concerning the correctness of one's policies. Nonetheless, one can make a strong case that policy makers who resist treating foreign policy beliefs as testable propositions and who assimilate virtually any evidence into those beliefs have failed to learn how to learn. These policy makers will be slow to update their beliefs in response to new events, slow to revise their expectations about future events, and slow to acknowledge the need to adjust policy as circumstances change. In short, failure to live up to the epistemic ideals of science may be the best evidence of limited, long-term potential for learning in the efficiency sense.

CONCLUDING REMARKS

The chapters in this volume are a heterogeneous lot. This diversity reflects the state of the art. There is no single way of looking at learning

in U.S.–Soviet relations. Much depends on one's disciplinary orientation. Different schools of thought sensitize us to different issues. Neorealists
remind us not to forget the incentive structures intrinsic to the international
system at any given moment: the balance and distribution of power and
the relative rates of change in the economic and technological underpinnings of that power. Cognitive psychologists remind us that policy makers react not to the international environment as such, but rather to their
mental representations of that environment. To understand the evolution
of policy, we need to understand our cognitive biases and limitations:
our tendencies to oversimplify complex problems, to be oblivious to trade-
offs, and to assimilate new evidence into our preconceptions. Organization theorists remind us of the powerful inertial forces at work in institutions: the rigidity of standard operating procedures, the parochialism of
bureaucratic fiefdoms, and the paralyzing effects of internecine rivalries.
Students of domestic political affairs remind us of the need to place
foreign policy in the context of ongoing struggles for influence among
powerful constituencies in the country at large. Politicians are less interested
in understanding the outside world than they are in putting together
combinations of foreign policy ideas that will enable them to assemble
winning coalitions.

These different approaches—or levels of analysis in Allison's terms[69]—are
not mutually exclusive. They serve as beacons that selectively illuminate
some facets of the evolving U.S.–Soviet relationship and leave other facets very much in the dark. Each level of analysis highlights distinctive
determinants of learning or of failures to learn at particular junctures in
post–World War II history. From a neorealist perspective, learning can
be viewed as the rational adjustment of policy in response to the shifting
reward and punishment contingencies of the international environment.
From a cognitive psychological perspective, learning can be viewed as
the not-so-rational adjustment of the content and structure of foreign
policy belief systems in response to the often equivocal feedback of the
international environment. The superpowers may respond to reality,
but not always in a timely or appropriate manner. From an organization
theory perspective, learning can be viewed as the adjustment of institutional
norms and procedures in ways designed to minimize the likelihood of
past mistakes (or what have come to be thought of as mistakes) and
maximize the likelihood of past successes (or what most people currently
think of as successes). The reality that the superpowers respond to is
largely filtered through elaborate institutional screening mechanisms that
no single individual fully understands. From a domestic political perspective,
learning appears to be very much a hit-or-miss affair. Competing politicians
use foreign policy ideas as weapons in their struggles for influence. There
is no guarantee whatsoever that policy ideas which capture the imaginations

of key domestic constituencies will capture important aspects of international reality. If anything, there are reasons for expecting the opposite (Anderson, Chapter 4).

There is, of course, no elegant theoretical formula for integrating these different levels of analysis. If one were simply to sum up—in impressionistic fashion—the grounds for optimism and pessimism, one would have good cause for deep depression. There are far more theoretical impediments to, than facilitators of, learning: the ambiguous nature of the policy feedback that national leaders receive; the cognitive, institutional, and domestic political limits on rationality; and the confusion and time pressure that often surround the policy-making process. Such a summation exercise would lead, however, not only to an artificially precise conclusion, but quite possibly to a prematurely pessimistic one. There are countervailing arguments for guarded optimism. Policy makers may not be as obtuse as they are sometimes depicted in the research literature. When learning becomes especially critical (Haas's trilogy of urgency, desirability, and feasibility), our leaders may often rise to the occasion. Moreover, the world may be more forgiving of slow learners than the harsher variants of neorealism lead one to suppose. If the world is populated largely by other slow learners, our leaders may often be protected from the consequences of their folly. A chess metaphor provides an appropriate closing note: errors of judgment that grand masters would mercilessly exploit frequently go unnoticed by less perceptive players. Slow learners can survive, sometimes even prosper, as long as they play mostly with each other.

NOTES

I am grateful for the detailed and thoughtful comments of George Breslauer, Alexander George, Ernst Haas, Robert Jervis, and Charles McGuire on earlier versions of this chapter. Comments concerning the chapter should be sent to Philip E. Tetlock, Institute of Personality Assessment and Research, Room 2C, 2150 Kittredge Street, University of California, Berkeley, CA 94720.

1. Z. Brzezinski, *Game Plan: A Geostrategic Framework for the Conduct of the US–Soviet Contest* (Boston: Atlantic Monthly Press, 1986); R. Pipes, *Survival Is Not Enough: Soviet Realities and America's Future* (New York: Simon and Schuster, 1984).

2. M. Deutsch, "The Prevention of World War III: A Psychological Perspective," *Political Psychology*, 4 (1983); R. White, *Fearful Warriors: A Psychological Study of US–Soviet Relations* (New York: Free Press, 1984).

3. G.T. Allison, A. Carnesale, and J.S. Nye, *Hawks, Doves and Owls: An Agenda for Avoiding Nuclear War* (New York: Norton, 1985); J.D. Steinbruner, "Choices and Trade-offs," in A. Carter et al. (eds.), *Managing Nuclear Operations* (Washington, D.C.: The Brookings Institution, 1987).

4. P. Kennedy, *The Rise and Fall of the Great Powers: Economic Change and Military Conflict from 1500–2000* (New York: Random House, 1987); D. Calleo, *Be-*

yond American Hegemony (New York: Basic Books, 1987); M. Olson, *The Rise and Decline of Nations* (New Haven: Yale University Press, 1982).

5. For discussions of the theory-driven (as opposed to data-driven) nature of social thought, see R.E. Nisbett and L. Ross, *Human Inference: Strategies and Short-comings of Social Judgment* (Englewood Cliffs, N.J.: Prentice Hall, 1980); O.R. Holsti and J.N. Rosenau, *American Leadership in World Affairs: Vietnam and the Breakdown of Consensus* (London: Allen & Unwin, 1984); R.E. Neustadt and E.R. May, *Thinking in Time: The Uses of History for Decision Makers* (New York: Free Press, 1984).

6. B. Fischhoff, "Nuclear Decisions: Cognitive Limits to the Thinkable," in P.E. Tetlock, J.L. Husbands, R. Jervis, P.C. Stern, and C. Tilly (eds.), *Behavior, Society, and Nuclear War* (Vol. 2) (New York: Oxford University Press, 1990).

7. P.E. Tetlock, "Methodological Themes and Variations," in P.E. Tetlock et al. (eds.), *Behavior, Society, and Nuclear War* (Vol. 1) (New York: Oxford University Press, 1989).

8. Within the Kennedy administration, many of the ExComm members at the time believed that Khrushchev's gamble was based on his perception of President Kennedy as a young, inexperienced, and weak leader (a perception derived from the summit meeting at Vienna and Kennedy's handling of the Bay of Pigs affair in 1961). Many scholars now believe, however, that Khrushchev's decision to deploy missiles in Cuba was motivated by U.S. strength, not weakness (specifically, the massive advantage in intercontinental ballistic missiles the United States had achieved by 1962). Of course, these hypotheses need not to be mutually exclusive explanations for Khrushchev's behavior. Perceptions of U.S. strength might have generated the perceived need to redress the nuclear balance, while the belief that Kennedy was weak could have led Khrushchev to conclude that the gamble was a safe one, as Kennedy would ultimately accept the Soviet fait accompli. U.S. and Soviet officials and scholars discuss Khrushchev's perceptions and motives in J. Blight and D. Welch, *On the Brink: Americans and Soviets Reexamine the Cuban Missile Crisis* (New York: Noonday Press, 1989).

9. Many conservative analysts claimed that the events of the late 1980s vindicated the policies of the Reagan administration. For instance, Burton Yale Pines, vice president of the Heritage Foundation, argued in 1989 that "the emerging situation is notably a victory for Ronald Reagan's policies. By rebuilding the U.S. arsenal and launching such advanced programs as the Strategic Defense Initiative, Reagan signaled strongly that America no longer would tolerate the shift of global correlation of forces in Moscow's favor. . . . Under Reagan, the U.S. raised the price of Soviet expansionism and adventurism to levels that the Kremlin's leaders apparently concluded are unacceptable." Burton Yale Pines, "Waiting for Mr. X," *Policy Review*, 49 (Summer 1989):2–3. See also Richard Pipes, "Paper Perestroika: Gorbachev and American Strategy," *Policy Review*, 47 (Winter 1989); Richard Pipes, "Gorbachev's Russia: Breakdown or Crackdown?" *Commentary* (March 1990); Paul Nitze, "America: An Honest Broker," *Foreign Affairs*, 69, no. 4 (Fall 1990). Other analysts have taken the opposing view and argued that the Reagan administration can take little or no credit for the massive changes in Soviet politics under Gorbachev: see S. Talbott, "Rethinking the Red Menace," *Time* (January 1, 1990); J. Snyder, "The Gorbachev Revolution: A Waning of Soviet Expansionism?" *International Security*, 12 (Winter 1987/88); S. Bialer, "Gorbachev's Program of Change: Sources, Significance, and Prospects," *Political Science Quarterly*, 103 (1988).

10. For a recent review of the central role that counterfactual arguments play in comparative politics and international relations, see J. Fearon, "Counterfactuals and Hypothesis Testing in Political Science," *World Politics*, in press.

11. For a useful overview of sources of policy change, see C. Hermann, "Changing Course: When Governments Choose to Redirect Foreign Policy," *International Studies Quarterly*, 34 (1990):3–21.

12. J.G. March, *Decisions and Organizations* (Oxford: Basil Blackwell, 1988).

13. R. Keohane, *Neorealism and Its Critics* (New York: Columbia University Press, 1988).

14. K.N. Waltz, *Theory of International Politics* (Reading, Mass.: Addison-Wesley, 1979).

15. K.A. Oye (ed.), *Cooperation Under Anarchy* (Princeton, N.J.: Princeton University Press, 1986).

16. K.N. Waltz, *Theory of International Politics*.

17. R. Axelrod and R.O. Keohane, "Achieving Cooperation Under Anarchy: Strategies and Institutions," *World Politics*, 38 (1985):226–54.

18. B. Pines, "Waiting for Mr. X"; R. Pipes, "Paper Perestroika."

19. G.T. Allison, "Testing Gorbachev," *Foreign Affairs*, 67 (1988).

20. R. Herrnstein, "Superstition: A Corollary of the Principles of Operant Conditioning," in W.K. Honig (ed.), *Operant Behavior* (New York: Appleton-Century-Crofts, 1966).

21. J. March, *Decisions and Organizations*.

22. Many Sovietologists expected such a retrenchment. For example, Philip Stewart argued in 1986 that: "Gorbachev, perceiving the Soviet Union as threatened abroad by resurgent 'imperialism' and at home by a stagnant economy, has articulated a defensive, strongly nationalist foreign policy designed to protect the Soviet Union during a lengthy period of domestic rebuilding." He concluded that the reshuffling of the Politburo in 1985 and 1986 had created a fundamental shift in its prevailing outlook. Stewart was not optimistic about the future, however, as he believed that "this shift may be characterized as movement from the moderate, outward, and western orientation of the Brezhnev era to a tough, uncompromising, predominantly inward, nationalist or self-reliant perspective that is reminiscent of the late-Stalin era." P. Stewart, "Gorbachev and Obstacles Toward Détente," *Political Science Quarterly*, 101 (1986):2.

23. J. March, *Decisions and Organizations*.

24. Perhaps the most we can realistically hope for is to move from one type of policy mistake to another before the consequences of any given mistake become unbearable. For instance, in his historical analysis of U.S. policy toward Europe, Thies (Chapter 6) argues that "in their zeal to avoid the mistakes of their predecessors, U.S. officials have often been blind or at least insensitive to the shortcomings of their own approach." Eisenhower and Dulles shunned the Truman policy of endowing the North Atlantic Treaty Organization (NATO) with sufficient conventional forces to deter a Soviet invasion on the ground that such a policy would prove prohibitively expensive and politically unsustainable. As a result, they turned to a policy of massive retaliation, which raised alarm among the Europeans (who happened to live at ground zero) and became increasingly incredible as the Soviets acquired the capability to strike the American homeland (why should the United States give up New York to save Paris?). The Kennedy and Johnson

administrations were so determined to boost U.S. military capabilities and to acquire a wider range of conventional and nuclear options (between doing nothing and all-out nuclear war) that they provided the Europeans with a ready excuse for not increasing their own forces (sowing the seeds for much future discord). The Reagan administration was so motivated to overturn the image of weakness and vacillation from the Carter years that it may have seriously endangered the political unity of NATO through blustery rhetoric about nuclear shots across the bow. Learning, in this view, is a trial-and-error process.

25. A.L. George, *Presidential Decision-Making in Foreign Policy: The Effective Use of Information and Advice* (Boulder, Colo.: Westview Press, 1980); R. Jervis, *Perception and Misperception in International Politics* (Princeton, N.J.: Princeton University Press, 1976); P.E. Tetlock and C. McGuire, "Cognitive Perspectives on Foreign Policy," in S. Long (ed.), *Political Behavior Annual* (Vol. 1) (Boulder, Colo.: Westview Press, 1986). (Reprinted in R. White [ed.], *Psychology and the Prevention of Nuclear War*, New York: New York University Press); R.E. Nisbett and L. Ross, *Human Inference*.

26. H.A. Simon, *Models of Man* (New York: Wiley, 1957).

27. A. George, "The 'Operational Code': A Neglected Approach to the Study of Political Leaders and Decision-Making," *International Studies Quarterly*, 13 (1969); P.E. Tetlock, "Policymakers' Images of International Conflict," *Journal of Social Issues*, 39 (1983).

28. R.P. Abelson and A. Levi, "Decision-Making and Decision Theory," in E. Aronson and G. Lindzey (eds.), *Handbook of Social Psychology* (Vol. 2) (Hillsdale, N.J.: Erlbaum, 1985); R. Axelrod, *Structure of Decision* (Princeton, N.J.: Princeton University Press, 1976); O.R. Holsti, "Foreign Policy Formation Viewed Cognitively," in R. Axelrod (ed.), *Structure of Decision*; P. Tetlock and C. McGuire, "Cognitive Perspectives on Foreign Policy."

29. O.R. Holsti, "The 'Operational Code' as an Approach to Analysis of Belief Systems" (Final report to the National Science Foundation, Grant SOC 75-15368, Duke University, 1977); A. George, "The Operational Code."

30. J. Nye, "Nuclear Learning and U.S.–Soviet Security Regimes," *International Organizations*, 41 (1988).

31. The different conclusions that Larson (Chapter 10) and Garrett (Chapter 7) draw concerning the occurrence of learning in the Nixon-Kissinger period are traceable to two distinct analytical sources. Larsen, on one hand, argues that Nixon and Kissinger were cognitively predisposed all along to exploit the Sino-Soviet rivalry. Both individuals were guided by realpolitik assumptions (or in the cognitive psychological terminology employed by Larson, *schemata*). Garrett, on the other hand, is more impressed by the capacity of Nixon and Kissinger to transcend the prevailing wisdom about China in 1969 (a nation "gone mad" during the Cultural Revolution) and to pursue a policy anchored in very different premises. If one limits one's conception of learning to a strictly individual level of analysis, the key question is "What did Nixon and Kissinger know about U.S.–Sino–Soviet relations and when did they know it?" If one broadens one's conception of learning to a governmental level of analysis, the question of what Nixon or Kissinger believed at particular times is of only secondary or biographical interest. The key point is that the individuals who assumed key posts of authority in 1969 had a more complex and perhaps realistic view of the international environment than did their predecessors.

32. W.J. McGuire, "The Nature of Attitudes and Attitude Change," in G. Lindzey and E. Aronson (eds.), *Handbook of Social Psychology* (3rd. ed.) (Reading, Mass.: Addison-Wesley, 1985).

33. O.R. Holsti, "Cognitive Dynamics and Images of the Enemy," in R. Fagen (ed.), *Enemies in Politics* (Chicago: Rand McNally, 1967). Recent historical work does, however, cast some doubt on the depiction of Dulles as a hopelessly closed-minded ideologue (Thies, Chapter 6).

34. T. Kuhn, *The Structure of Scientific Revolutions* (Chicago: University of Chicago Press, 1970); I. Lakatos, "Falsification and the Methodology of Scientific Research Programs," in I. Lakatos and A. Musgrave (eds.), *Criticism and Growth of Knowledge* (London: Cambridge University Press, 1970), 91–196.

35. D.C. Martin, *Wilderness of Mirrors* (New York: Ballantine Books, 1981).

36. R. Pipes, "Paper Perestroika."

37. The pros and cons of the Bayesian approach to revising foreign policy beliefs are thoroughly discussed in N. Schweitzer, "Bayesian Analysis of Intelligence: A Focus on the Middle East," *International Interactions*, 4 (1977); Z. Maoz, "Scientific Logic and Intuition in Intelligence Forecasts," in J.D. Singer and R.J. Stoll (eds.), *Quantitative Indicators in World Politics* (New York: Praeger, 1984). For a review of the psychological research literature on whether people actually are good or bad Bayesians, see P. Slovic, B. Fischhoff, and S. Lichtenstein, "Behavioral Decision Theory," *Annual Review of Psychology*, 28 (1977).

38. L. Etheredge, *Can Governments Learn?* (New York: Pergamon Press, 1985).

39. P.E. Tetlock, "A Value Pluralism Model of Ideological Reasoning," *Journal of Personality and Social Psychology*, 50 (1986):819–27; P.E. Tetlock, "Monitoring the Integrative Complexity of American and Soviet Policy Rhetoric: What Can Be Learned?" *Journal of Social Issues*, 44 (1988). This work demonstrates that it is possible to develop reasonably rigorous content analytic measures of the structural complexity of political arguments and thought.

40. R.P. Abelson et al. (eds.), *Theories of Cognitive Consistency: A Sourcebook* (Chicago: Rand McNally, 1969).

41. R. Jervis, *Perception and Misperception in International Politics.*

42. D. Kahneman, P. Slovic, and A. Tversky (eds.), *Judgment Under Uncertainty* (Cambridge: Cambridge University Press, 1982); J.D. Steinbruner, *A Cybernetic Theory of Decision* (Princeton, N.J.: Princeton University Press, 1974); R. Abelson and A. Levi, "Decision-Making and Decision Theory"; P. Tetlock, "A Value Pluralism Model."

43. F. Griffiths, "Sources of American Conduct: Soviet Perspectives and Their Implications," *International Security*, 9 (1984); Chapter 17 in this volume.

44. R.N. Lebow and J. Stein, "Beyond Deterrence," *Journal of Social Issues*, 43 (1987); C. Achen and D. Snidal, "Rational Deterrence Theory and Comparative Case Studies," *World Politics*, 41 (1989); G. Downs, "Arms Races and War," in P.E. Tetlock et al. (eds.), *Behavior, Society, and Nuclear War* (Vol. 2); R. Jervis, "Rational Deterrence: Theory and Evidence," *World Politics*, 41 (1989); A. George and R. Smoke, "Deterrence and Foreign Policy," *World Politics*, 41 (1989).

45. N. Leites, *A Study of Bolshevism* (New York: Free Press, 1953); A. George, "The Operational Code."

46. J. Hough, *Russia and the West: Gorbachev and the Politics of Reform* (New York: Simon and Schuster, 1988).

47. J. Nye, "Nuclear Learning," 382.

48. R. Jervis, *Perception and Misperception*.

49. P. Suedfeld, "Are Simple Decisions Always Worse?" *Society*, 25, no. 5 (1988); P.E. Tetlock and R. Boettger, "Accountability: A Social Magnifier of the Dilution Effect," *Journal of Personality and Social Psychology*, 52 (1989).

50. I.L. Janis, *Crucial Decisions: Leadership in Policymaking and Crisis Management* (New York: Free Press, 1988).

51. M. Halperin, *Bureaucratic Politics and Foreign Policy* (Washington, D.C.: The Brookings Institution, 1974); J.D. Steinbruner, *A Cybernetic Theory*.

52. R. Putnam, "Diplomacy and Domestic Politics: The Logic of Two-Level Games," *International Organizations*, 42 (1988):427–60; Anderson, Chapter 4 in this volume.

53. J. March, *Decisions and Organizations*.

54. I.L. Janis, *Victims of Groupthink* (2nd ed.) (Boston: Houghton-Mifflin, 1982); D.M. Barret, "The Mythology Surrounding Lyndon Johnson, His Advisers, and the 1965 Decision to Escalate the Vietnam War," *Political Science Quarterly*, 103 (1988); Khong, Chapter 9 in this volume.

55. I.L. Janis, *Victims of Groupthink*.

56. P.E. Tetlock, "Accountability: The Neglected Social Context of Judgment and Choice," in B.M. Staw and L. Cummings (eds.), *Research in Organizational Behavior* (Vol. 1) (Greenwich, Conn.: JAI Press, 1985), 297–332. See, however, P.E. Tetlock and R. Boettger, "Accountability," for an example of how preemptive self-criticism can erode rather than enhance judgmental effectiveness.

57. There are numerous other examples—both in this book and elsewhere—of the difficulty of determining what counts as an institutional impediment to learning. Haas (Chapter 3) provides a good general definition: "Institutional missions become encapsulated in routines that aid the career patterns of officials rather than solve problems." Operationalizing that definition is, however, more troublesome. Is the nuclear triad—the underpinning of U.S. strategic deterrence—an example of prudent redundancy or merely a rationalization that ensures that each of the three major services gets its slice of the budgetary pie? Does the NATO military bureaucracy inflate estimates of Soviet strength because it has a vested interest in doing so (Thies, Chapter 6) or because overestimation is a prudent precaution in the politically fickle democracies of the West? As C. Wright Mills noted, one person's reason is another's rationalization.

58. S. Talbott, *Deadly Gambits* (New York: Alfred Knopf, 1985).

59. J.D. Steinbruner, *A Cybernetic Theory*.

60. Haas's conception of learning overlaps in significant ways with both the cognitive structural and efficiency conceptions sketched here. His conception is, however, identical to neither. For Haas, policy makers learn when they draw on the "consensual knowledge of an epistemic community" to reconceptualize the problems confronting them. Often this consensual knowledge requires thinking about problems in more differentiated and integrated ways—what Haas calls "nested problem sets," which involve placing a problem in a broader systemic frame of reference (e.g., thinking about the nuclear arms race not only in a strategic but also in an economic or ecological framework). Often this consensual knowledge will guide policy in more realistic or adaptive directions (in large part

because most epistemic communities rely on the self-correcting norms of science to weed out deviant or crackpot ideas). Learning in the Haasian sense need not, however, entail movement toward greater complexity of thought (consensual knowledge may consist of simple but powerful generalizations) or movement toward greater efficiency (policy makers may be persuaded to adopt a body of consensual knowledge that turns out in hindsight to have been seriously flawed).

61. M.K. Singley and J.R. Anderson, *The Transfer of Cognitive Skills* (Cambridge, Mass.: Harvard University Press, 1989); H.A. Simon, *Models of Thought* (New Haven: Yale University Press, 1987).

62. M.K. Singley and J.R. Anderson, *Transfer of Cognitive Skills*; H.A. Simon, *Models of Thought*.

63. F. Griffiths, "Sources of American Conduct"; Chapter 17 in this volume.

64. Thies (Chapter 6) independently advances a political competition model of his own to explain the twists and turns of U.S. policy toward Europe since 1945. He notes that "competition for control of the executive branch encourages ambitious individuals to formulate alternative policies intended to improve on those of the incumbent administration." The new ideas of aspiring U.S. politicians—like those of aspiring Politburo members—need to be distinctive (otherwise why should others support them?), to appeal to important constituencies (otherwise why bother to campaign at all?), and to be plausible (who wants a platform that leads to demonstrably incorrect predictions?). The political stimulus to creativity does not, however, as Thies notes, guarantee learning. Indeed it can inspire demagoguery and, once the challengers gain power, overreactions to the shortcomings of earlier policies.

65. M.D. Cohen, J.G. March, and J.P. Olson, "A Garbage Can Model of Organizational Choice," *Administrative Quarterly*, 17 (1972); J. March, *Decisions and Organizations*.

66. J. March, *Decisions and Organizations*.

67. P. Tetlock, "Monitoring Integrative Complexity."

68. R. Jervis, *Perception and Misperception*, 22.

69. G.T. Allison, *Essence of Decision* (Boston: Little Brown, 1971).

3

Collective Learning: Some Theoretical Speculations

Ernst B. Haas

Between 1948 and 1952, the leaders of several Western European countries decided that the conditions that had pitted their states against each other in two world wars could not be permitted to continue; these leaders concluded that a new European order was needed in which the sovereign power of the nation-state was to be weakened in the interest of peace and welfare. Their capacity to reason enabled them to arrive at a more or less agreed notion of why the past was unacceptable. Their concern for finding a formula making an alternative political order legitimate compelled them to search for a compromise among the diverse and clashing reasons favoring change. The result was a new constitution for integrating Western Europe—the institutions that eventually became the European Economic Community. Knowledge, or what passed for knowledge, about the causes of the two world wars, the Great Depression, the violation of human rights, the stagnation of industrial development, and the dynamics of virulent nationalism conditioned the rationality, the compromises, the rationalization formula. European governments "learned," through the marshaling of knowledge, to redefine their old interests into a new formula of regional governance.

This essay is about the ability of governments to learn new routines when they recognize that the established practices are inadequate for solving whatever is considered a problem. Altering established practices that prove to be unacceptable may lead either to more international collaboration or to more national self-sufficiency and isolation, to more complex international interdependencies, or to simpler patterns. In either case we want to know how whose knowledge is being used to define the reasons for changing one's ways while also retaining the integrity of the bureaucratic entity in question and protecting the cohesion of the society of which the bureaucracy is a part. In this essay the ability to mount and institutionalize a revolution is not considered learning.

Provisionally, I define learning as any change in behavior due to a change in perception about how to solve a problem. The prospective learners are not individuals but entities in government: departments, working groups, ministries, conferences, services—segments of a bureaucracy or a legislature.

These speculations ought to be read as an effort to devise a coding scheme for giving us a way to judge whether bureaucracies and organizations learn. I begin with a discussion of bounded rationality as the condition limiting what and how learning occurs, then introduce the concepts of consensual knowledge as a constituent of learning and of epistemic communities as agents of learning. I then posit the notion of nested problem sets as the things to be learned. That done, I show why most familiar notions of adaptation and learning are not appropriate guides to the discussion of foreign policy learning by government bureaucracies. Two codes are then offered. One gives us the tools for making judgments about adaptive and learning routines in decision making that cannot be fully analytical; the other allows us to judge whether cognitive changes that result in novel definitions of problems to be solved give us nearly nondecomposable problem sets. I end with a discussion of why learning is not necessarily preferable to mere adaptation and why it is impossible to design routines that will institutionalize learning by bureaucracies.

I. CONSENSUAL KNOWLEDGE AND POLITICAL INNOVATION

BOUNDED RATIONALITY DOMINATES DECISION MAKING

If kings were philosophers and philosophers practiced the kind of rational choice postulated in microeconomic models, then new consensual knowledge would painlessly bring about policy innovations suggested as uniquely rational by that very knowledge. Suppose that no inexpensive cure for acid rain were available and politicians and bureaucrats resist the costly remedies suggested by scientists; the result is a policy of inaction. Suppose further that suddenly it is discovered that the pollutants are not transported by air currents but by some other agent, thereby making the installation of expensive antipollution equipment unnecessary. Instead a different regulatory mechanism is employed. New knowledge will have led directly to policy innovation. Technical rationality would have driven the decision; means alone were at stake as ends remained constant.

The questioning of prior cause-effect beliefs, however, is hardly ever a rational process if judged by strict standards of technically rational choice. Matters proceed in a much sloppier way. Thought about environmental protection and resource conservation again exemplifies the sloppiness. Here a change in the urgency for choice made politicians seek out bodies of knowledge thought likely to advance their instrumental cause. The creators of that knowledge may also seek out friendly politicians in the search for allies. Before the claims to knowledge become truly consensual, the interplay will take the form of an ideological debate, as happened in the early days of the international environmental movement, when the interests of the developed and the developing worlds were at loggerheads.

Knowledge and interest, instead of being in harmony, may well suggest opposing lines of action. We are unable to predict when the interplay between interest and knowledge becomes stable, and we can only claim that learning has an elective affinity with the more fundamental changes in scientific and technical understanding. The form of rational choice Max Weber termed *technical* and Herbert Simon calls *substantive* does not describe the process.

"If we accept values as given and consistent," says Simon, "if we postulate an objective description of the world as it really is, and if we assume that the decision maker's computational powers are unlimited, then two important consequences follow. First, we do not need to distinguish between the real world and the decision maker's perception of it; he or she perceives the world as it really is. Second, we can predict the choices that will be made by a rational decision maker entirely from our knowledge of the real world and without a knowledge of the decision maker's perceptions or modes of calculation. (We do, of course, have to know his or her utility function.)"[1]

Bureaucrats choose "under ambiguity," not in the way just sketched. Decision making "under ambiguity" differs fundamentally from what is normally considered to be rational behavior by individuals seeking to optimize or maximize. Problems of ambiguity include the following. There is often no determined or even probable outcome to be associated with a decision-making routine. Choice is often constrained by a condition of strategic interdependence in which the opposing choosers find themselves, a condition of which they are fully aware. Preferences are often not clear, or not clearly ordered, because the decision is not being made by a single individual but by a bureaucratic entity. There may also be a mismatch between the assumed causal links constituting the problem the organization is called on to resolve, and the causal theory underlying the internal arrangements of units, plans, and programs designed to solve the problem. Decision-making models that are supposed to draw on the lessons of history, that are predicated on the actors' deliberately learning from prior mistakes, are badly flawed because the lessons of history are rarely unambiguous: different actors certainly offer varying and equally plausible interpretations of past events that often mar decision making in the present. Learning, under such circumstances, consists of recognizing the desirability of a different process of decision making, a process that copes a little better with ambiguity. Simon explicitly avoids specifying what, substantively speaking, ought to be learned. Under procedural rationality, learning means designing and mastering an alternative process.[2] Decisions made under ambiguity remain rational because the choosers do the best they can under the circumstances. They do not act randomly. They attempt to think about trade-offs even though they are unable to rank-order their preferences. In short, they "satisfice."

CONSENSUAL KNOWLEDGE

Our concern is this: How does knowledge about nature and society make the trip from lecture halls, think tanks, libraries, and documents to the minds of political actors? How does knowledge, by its nature debatable and debated, become sufficiently accepted to enter the decision-making process? No doubt the political interests experienced by actors are one determinant of which kind of knowledge will be preferred as a basis for decision. Consensual knowledge is not absolutely different from political ideology; on the contrary, the line between the two is often barely visible. Some will say that consensual knowledge is merely science-derived transideological and transcultural ideology. I would contest such a claim with only a mild amendment, not challenge it fundamentally, yet make a case that political choice infused with consensual knowledge is more pervasive than choice informed exclusively by immediate calculations of material interest or by the unmodified dominance of substantive value.

By consensual knowledge I mean generally accepted understandings about cause-and-effect linkages about any set of phenomena considered important by society, provided only that the finality of the accepted chain of causation is subject to continuous testing and examination through adversary procedures. Cause-effect chains are derived from information, scientific and nonscientific, available about a given subject and considered authoritative by the interested parties—although the authoritativeness is always temporary. Consensual knowledge is socially constructed and therefore inseparable from the vagaries of human communication. It is not true or perfect or complete knowledge.

We lack a totally consensual criterion for determining truth, perfection and completeness. It may even be true that what is claimed as consensual knowledge by a bureaucracy is known to be flawed. Yet even this guilty knowledge may be presented to the public as valid merely to protect the mission and the integrity of the organization. In so doing, the nonknowledge interests of the parties concerned are also being protected. Knowledge is not in principle opposed to interest; it is, in the extreme case, the handmaiden of interest.

Consensual knowledge may originate as an ideology. It differs from ideologies only in that it is constantly challenged from within and without and must justify itself by submitting its claims to truth tests considered generally acceptable. Unless such testing takes place, it is impossible to speak of any kind of error correction because the criteria for determining acceptable and undesired outcomes would differ with the actor concerned. Consensual knowledge differs from ideology-derived interests because it constantly has to prove itself against rival formulas claiming to solve problems better. The acceptability, the very quality of consensus, that makes the kind of knowledge of concern to us different from other claims "to know" is the fact that it must survive in the process of social selection, in the demonstrated ability to excel in solving problems.

I hold that such a process describes generally how governments and public organizations have learned to deal with most of the problems their constituents have imposed on them in the twentieth century, with the exception of changed behavior due entirely to the success of a political revolution that simply gets rid of competing notions of cause and effect. Our conceptions of what constitutes a problem to be solved by way of public policy have been irretrievably infected by the knowledge of nature and society that has gained widespread acceptance.

EPISTEMIC COMMUNITIES AS PURVEYORS
OF CONSENSUAL KNOWLEDGE

All public organizations are staffed by professional civil servants who participate in the making of decisions and who implement most of the operational measures. Bureaucracies are made up of people who usually carry the professional qualifications relating to their organizations' tasks: law, agriculture, medicine, and the like. They are a conduit for introducing into public policy the knowledge produced by their disciplines. Moreover, these professionals often act in concert with like-minded professionals not in the employ of the organizations but linked to them through service on advisory panels of experts. Public organizations are exposed to knowledge through the medium of *epistemic communities*, defined by Holzner and Marx as "those knowledge-oriented work communities in which cultural standards and social arrangements interpenetrate around a primary commitment to epistemic criteria in knowledge production and application."[3]

I accept this definition as far as it goes. However, it must be augmented to suit the specific circumstances of learning in public organizations constrained by institutional habit. For me, an epistemic community is a group of professionals (usually recruited from several disciplines) who share a commitment to a common causal model and a common set of political values. They are united by a belief in the truth of their model and by a commitment to translate this truth into public policy, in the conviction that human welfare will be enhanced as a result.

Epistemic communities profess belief in extracommunity reality tests. They are, in principle, open to the constant reexamination of prevailing beliefs about cause and effect, ends and means. They are ready to see more complex cause-effect chains, or to simplify these in line with new knowledge. Yet, being human, they also resist reality tests likely to disturb their claims to novelty and relevance; epistemic communities exhibit both the Mertonian norms of science and its counter-norms. Rival epistemic groups thus exhibit the same behaviors as do rival schools of scientists. The ultimate test of truth is the collective decision by the users of knowledge as to which claim is more successful in solving a problem agreed by all as requiring solution. It is a common property of epistemic communities that they accept this judgment as legitimate.

I have put emphasis on the procedural aspects of epistemic behavior, on how the members of an epistemic community defend what they think is true. This involves the procedures of science, scientific methodology, and the sociological canons for judging its generality. The substantive aspect of belief requires even more emphasis. Members of an epistemic community profess belief not merely in scientific procedures of verification, beliefs that may be almost instinctive and hardly require explicit articulation; these people are primarily and overtly concerned with substantive knowledge claims about whatever issue or problem attracts them to public organizations and political decision makers. Their knowledge about communicable diseases, deep-sea mineral deposits, nuclear fusion, or exchange rate stability gives them their claim to be heard.

If the epistemic community involved in the decision has no opposition, its claim to knowledge is consensual for all. In the absence of this condition, the decision is going to be characterized by conflict among rival claimants to knowledge. Decisions, in short, have to be studied in terms of the knowledge brought to bear. That knowledge is either consensual or it is not.

The lack of consensual knowledge does not mean that no knowledge is involved in the decision. A decision about environmental protection may be informed by the separate bodies of information of toxicologists, meteorologists, soil chemists, and agricultural economists even if these professionals cannot yet agree among themselves on an integrated, consensual view of how their separate disciplinary lores cohere. Separate issues will not be combined on the basis of knowledge. Hence, more accurately, a decision is based on knowledge that is or is not *becoming* more consensual.

Political goals are determined by the ideologies to which decision makers subscribe. Ideologies vary considerably in terms of their determinateness; they suggest the concrete interests a politician chooses to advocate and defend. Political goals are derived from interests.

Goals can be either "specific" or "interconnected," "static" or "expanding." A specific goal seeks the attainment of a single outcome—a higher per capita income, cleaner air, or cheaper fuel prices. An interconnected goal envisages causal connections between these separate desired outcomes. Actors espousing such goals define the superordinate problem to be solved in more complex ways than actors who remain committed to the attainment of specific goals. Static goals remain constant over long periods of time. Expanding goals refer to situations in which politicians feel compelled to enlarge their targets to include new goals in order to be able to satisfy the demands associated with the original ones. Interconnected and expanding goals tend to go together because they are justified by the same cause-effect chain. A commitment to them creates a dependence on knowledge producers whose advice becomes a crucial input. No such commitment follows from the tendency of politicians to entertain static and specific goals because the fragmented knowledge offered to them by separate professional and disciplinary groups (not organized as epistemic communities) is deemed by the decision makers to be adequate.[4]

When we combine the codings for the kind of knowledge involved in decision making with the types of goals politicians are able to entertain, we obtain the four situations captured in Figure 1. Each cell represents a decision-making style that might be associated, empirically, with a subunit within a public organization that combines experts with politicians as a team.

		Goals considered by politicians are:	
		Specific, static	Interconnected, expanding
Beliefs of experts about knowledge become:	More consensual	Pragmatic	Analytic
	Not more consensual	Eclectic	Skeptic

FIGURE 1 Decision-making styles.

This way of relating knowledge to political goals allows us to state a number of additional propositions about bureaucratic learning. Public policy can feature several ways of combining interests with scientific information, running from decisions dominated by scientific metaphor to the subordination of science to immediate political interest. These alternatives imply several different ways in which issues on a policy agenda can be combined and subsumed in terms of imputed cause-effect chains. The analytic decision-making style implies a nexus of issues in which consensual knowledge defines what can be meaningfully combined with what: opportunistic combinations are excluded. The eclectic style suggests the opposite: issues are combined exclusively on the basis of tactical-instrumental concerns. The skeptic and pragmatic styles, however, feature a combination of the two. Fully substantively defined linkages are not possible, but totally opportunistic combinations are not rational either. I suggest that the pragmatic style lends itself most readily to learning under conditions of bounded rationality.

It follows that knowledge-infused learning is most likely associated with discussions and negotiations dominated by analytically and pragmatically minded decision makers, and that skeptics and eclectics are far less likely to learn as a result of their efforts at problem-solving. Analytically and pragmatically minded decision makers will most likely succeed in creating abstractly nested hierarchies of causal relations that respect what is known about affinities among phenomena; skeptics and eclectics will not succeed in establishing such nests and will persist in reordering their priorities and causal understanding in such a way as to ignore and neglect systemic connections grasped by others.

NESTED PROBLEM SETS APPLIED TO POLITICAL DECISIONS

How does it happen that public policies designed to improve our material life, our health, and our ability to live in peace politically acquire a serious debt to the work of physicists, chemists, biologists, economists, and sociologists? How does it happen that this debt can take the form of new ways of thinking, of defining problems, of anticipating new problems and possibilities? In short, how is it that science can be linked to charting and planning the future of societies? The answer requires the idea of nested problem sets. Nested problem sets are bundles of public policies arranged so as to define and solve human problems in such a way as to be consistent with the knowledge claimed by prior intellectual aggregation associated with scientific investigation. If there is consensus on the intellectual aggregation, the nested problem set is also likely to become consensual; if there is continuing disagreement among rival ways of aggregating, the rivalry will be reflected in competing nests.

The rearrangement of nests of concepts relating to public policy oc-curs in political organizations, not in scientific endeavors: bureaucracies, legislatures, parties, pressure groups, courts. It is there that ideas of how things could be different are argued out, compared, voted on, fought about, and funded. We can think of the components of these nests as hierarchies of information undergoing rearrangement into ever more complex flow charts. Items are moved about, subsumed under different headings designed to serve more complex purposes. We change arrows of causa-tion between boxes as our understandings of causes and effects undergo change, and as the purpose to which the information is to be put be-comes more comprehensive. Nesting involves the combination, elimina-tion, substitution, and subsuming of concepts intended to lead to more comprehensive political action, thus giving us the political counterpart to intellectual aggregation.

I now develop one example of the evolution of a larger flow chart: the notion of international security. Compared with beliefs and practices before 1945, it is a distinct innovation. The intellectual disciplines that partake of this nesting enterprise include political science, physics and engineering, international economics, development economics, psychology, and ecology, among many others. Their concerns are marked by the tension between ensuring the military security of individual countries *while also* seeking to protect the world against the more extreme possible consequences of that security. The problem set seeks to balance the need for national security with the survival of the entire globe. The tension is best illustrated with the scenario about nuclear winter: a nuclear exchange of a certain magnitude can endanger the biological survival of enough species (because of its interruption of generalized biochemical processes) so as to endanger entire ecosystems and the economies and human life support systems that derive from them.[5] A similar tension is implicit in the need for national security on one hand, and on the other the prevention of the military capabilities involved from having consequences the mili-tary planners themselves wish to avoid, thereby linking thought about arms control, crisis prevention, the mental stability of leaders, and even the pace of economic and social change to the need for national military security. The greater one's awareness of the possible implications of nuclear and other technologically advanced weapons, the more compelling the intellectual need to fashion policies that ensure *both* national security and international survival. The manifestation of this (incompletely ag-gregated) problem set is the arena of international negotiations on arms control and environmental protection, which of course cross-cut with other emerging problem sets.

We know that one major difference between the intellectual pyramids of scientific information and the politician's problem sets is the time horizon that dominates the thinking of each. Political actors are forced to focus on the short run, on effects sufficiently visible to inspire or frighten their followers. Epistemic communities typically use longer time scales in their projections. Many of the debates between rival nests are over the time span involved. Many of the unresolved tensions within single sets suffer from the same debility.

John Ruggie's discussion of social time as an explanatory concept helps to elucidate the issue, without being able to resolve it. The example of nuclear winter illustrates the distinctions. Changes in the basic conditions that trigger demands eventually reflected in problem sets can be incremental, conjunctural, and secular in character, on a scale from shorter to longer. The difference between the three involves an awareness of the breadth of issues affected. Incremental changes are at first discernible only with respect to the things that are visibly changing—pollution is rising or falling, wars are larger or fewer in number. Most observations about social and economic trends are of this kind; the number of people and activities influenced by them remains cognitively narrow. When we talk about conjunctural changes, we are interested in identifying more than the immediate visible consequences. We are concerned with the relationship between the incremental rates of change and their not-so-visible effects on economic welfare and peace. When we seek to identify secular changes, we are in search of still more remote consequences, such as the carrying capacity of the globe. Nuclear winter, in an incremental perspective, is just a matter of the numbers of the immediate damage and suffering engendered by a massive nuclear exchange. In the conjunctural perspective, it forces us to focus on demographic consequences for the surviving generations of life forms. In the secular perspective it focuses our attention on the more abstract notion of global carrying capacity, both in terms of physical and cultural resources. The problems identified in an incremental time scale do not disappear if they are subjected to the secular scale, but they are redefined and reconceptualized, therefore suggesting a different cognitive and political flow chart.[6]

Nesting and intellectual aggregation are most complex and comprehensive the closer we approach the secular form of social time. The more complex the nesting and the time frame, the less acceptable the simple continuation of present policies and practices. Even the adequacy of the sovereign territorial state as the source of most public policy is thrown into doubt in a secular time perspective because it cannot develop policies able to stave off the more remote but very unpalatable effects identified. Aggregated knowledge explains this implication by pointing to the larger number of tightly coupled systems; the larger the number and the tighter the coupling, the more massive becomes the pattern of uncontrollable positive feedbacks poisoning the future. The political actors come to the same conclusion by simply growing aware of the unprecedented scale of human suffering made visible by secular time—as long as basic values remain the same. If humankind were to turn Buddhist the material values that make social time so relevant would lose their salience, and the consequences to be averted might seem more tolerable.

At each higher level of aggregation, alleged and experienced interdependencies become more complexly linked. At each higher level, earlier ideological cleavages become less salient. And at each higher level the terms of political conflict are more easily redefined in such a way as to make unilateral insistence, the desire for absolute victory by one side, less attractive. The more complexly we nest our problem sets, the more we enmesh ourselves in the fate of others.

II. COLLECTIVE ACTION, ADAPTATION, AND LEARNING

DEFINITIONS: LEARNING VERSUS ADAPTATION

I argue that problems are redefined through one of two complicated processes that I call *adaptation* and *learning*. These processes differ in their dependence on new knowledge that may be introduced into decision making (Table 1).

By learning I mean the process by which consensual knowledge is used to specify causal relationships in new ways, so that the result has

TABLE 1 The Processes of Adaptation and Learning

Adaptation	*Learning*
Behavior changes as actors add new activities (or drop old ones) without examining the implicit theories underlying their programs. Underlying values are not questioned.	Behavior changes as actors question original implicit theories underlying programs and examine their original values.
Ultimate purpose of the organization is not questioned. Emphasis is on altering means of action, not ends. Technical rationality triumphs.	Ultimate purpose is redefined, as means as well as ends are questioned. Substantive rationality triumphs.
New ends (purposes) are added without worrying about their coherence with existing ends. Change is incremental without any attempt at nesting purposes logically.	New nested problem sets are constructed because new ends are devised on the basis of consensual knowledge that has become available, as provided by epistemic communities.

implications for the content of public policy. Learning in and by bureaucracies implies that the organization's members are induced to question earlier beliefs about the appropriateness of ends of action, and to think about the selection of new ones, to revalue themselves. And as the members of the organization go through this process, it is likely that they will arrive at a common understanding of what causes the particular problems of concern. A common understanding of causes is likely to trigger a shared understanding of solutions, and the new chain implies a set of larger meanings about life and nature not previously held in common by the participants.

Learning may involve the elaboration of new cause-effect chains more (or less) elaborate than the ones being questioned and replaced. The resulting conceptualization of the world may be more (or less) holistic than the earlier one. It may imply progress or regress, depending on the normative commitment of the observer, or the preferred reading of history.

Questioning an established cause-effect schema involves the disaggregation of a problem as it had been initially conceived. The problem first has to be taken apart; its parts have to be identified and sorted into patterns different from the ones that had been featured in an earlier round. That done, the problem has to be reaggregated into a differently nested set, either more complex and comprehensive than the original one, or less so.

Changes in patterns of collective action due to adaptation are far less searing for the participants because it demands less self-reflection. By adaptation I mean two slightly different processes of changing one's problem-solving behavior that avoid a thorough revaluation of one's beliefs about basic causation. Adaptive behavior, in the first instance, is any determination that a tried and true set of means is no longer appropriate or effective in attaining a stipulated end. A recognition of the failure of technical rationality, when it leads to the selection of a new set of means (or policy instruments), is an adaptive act on the part of a bureaucracy. Such a step may be difficult because of entrenched bureaucratic interests and time-hallowed conceptions of bureaucratic missions. It may be costly in terms of positions and budget items lost. It may hurt individual careers. I call it adaptive precisely because the changes are made in recognition of real costs.

A more ambitious version of adaptive behavior also occurs. Sometimes the choice of new means still proves ineffective, given original ends. If the decision makers then conclude that an alternative set of ends ought to be considered, *without at the same time questioning the underlying cognitive schemata that establish a belief in cause-and-effect relations*, we are still encountering adaptation. The choice of new ends is like trial-and-error selection, not choice informed by new knowledge. Because it is organizationally and emotionally a less painful process than full-scale learning, adaptive behavior is encountered far more often in international relations than is true learning.

WHAT ADAPTATION AND LEARNING ARE NOT

My definitions differ from others often used in the international relations literature. Functionalists claim that learning consists of changing one's attitude and behavior as a result of association with *successful* functional international arrangements (i.e., nonpolitical arrangements dedicated to economic, technological, or humanitarian purposes). Evidence of such learning is the demand that additional functional organizations, designed on the model of the first one, be set up, and that those who participated in the work of these organizations developed positive attitudes toward them.[7] These formulations are less than fully helpful because they do not tell us *what* has to be learned, *how* cognitive processes have to be reorganized. Most important, they fail to spell out the institutional and political blocks to the development of positive attitudes; nor do they even ask which forms of design are likely to overcome such blockages. To argue that form follows function, and that function follows participation and positive experience, flies in the face of experience with disappointment and with unintended consequences.

Nor do bureaucracies learn as do individuals, even though they are made up of individuals. Institutional routines interfere. Lessons learned by one bureaucrat do not necessarily become the collective wisdom of that unit. Lessons learned are informed by the interests professed by the learner. We do not assume that the interests will change only because a given routine used in their implementation has failed. Such approaches equate learning with error correction by individuals. But the observer then has to specify what the "correct" perception ought to be, and the "correct" perception inevitably turns out to be the one preferred by the observer.[8]

Learning and Adaptation in Error Correction

Adaptation and learning, in the literature on biological and cultural evolution, are synonyms. Both are tied up with survival and stability. Neither is a serviceable concept for me, as derived from neodarwinian thinking, because they depend on the idea of homeostasis. Since few organizations possess this property, we must first show how the notions of adaptation and learning differ in this context from the more familiar usage in biology and anthropology. In cybernetic-biological discourse, the organism learns in order to adapt. What does it learn? It develops behaviors (which are often not based on genetic endowment) that enable it to survive under changing environmental conditions. It does so by keeping its main bodily functions within a physiologically favorable range: the organism's functions are stable if changes remain within a range that permits it to survive. Survival and stability are linked concepts; stability makes survival possible. What is learned is to compensate behaviorally for some challenge to stability. This involves short-term and longer-term feedback mechanisms of varying complexities. Conceptually, then, stability and survival are brought about through adaptive behavior, which is always behavior that leads to an improvement of the organism's life chances. Adaptation—learned behavior in the biologist's language—is always for the better.[9]

Whether adaptation is always for the better depends on who assesses the outcome. Adaptation, in our context, is the ability to change one's behavior so as to meet challenges in the form of new demands without having to revaluate one's entire program and the reasoning on which that program depends for its legitimacy. This, of course, assumes that the challenges come slowly and can be dealt with in a piecemeal fashion. Adaptation is incremental adjustment, muddling-through. It relies largely on technical rationality. Since ultimate ends are not questioned, the change in behavior takes the form of a search for more adequate means to meet the new demands.

This is no mean feat. Organizations are usually bombarded with divergent demands from a variety of coalitions, and their survival is by no means a certainty. Being able to adapt without basic revaluation is a considerable achievement for the organization's leaders and members. It is a very worthwhile enterprise to try to understand how mere survival is made possible given the global setting. To be able to adapt is to be very skillful in living with one another in a conflict-ridden world.

If error correction is not a useful guidepost for understanding learning, neither is effectiveness. The judgment of whether one's performance is effective pertains to technical rationality, not value rationality. It is useful in explaining how adaptation occurs, not learning as I define it. Technical criteria for evaluating the performance of organizations do not speak to the satisfaction or dissatisfaction of the clients, who may value such abstract aims as equity, quality of life, or the enjoyment of individual rights even if the organization falls short of mundane technically effective performance. Notions of affect, imitation, intelligence, effectiveness, and therapy must be banished from our discussion of learning.

Organizational Survival-seeking Behavior Is Not Adaptation

Standard organization theory assumes that the entity under study seeks a maximum of control over its environment. Organizations are envisaged as systems seeking to get the better over external elements and actors who might reduce the autonomy of the entity. Boundary maintenance is therefore crucial, whether the environment is envisaged as being made up of customers, suppliers, competitors, political clients, or other bureaucracies. While it is understood that the organization must satisfy those environmental forces on whom the organization depends, maximum attainable control over them is seen as the best way to achieve autonomy. Autonomy, in turn, is valued because it guarantees the survival of the organization in a setting of competition; and survival calls for adaptation.

Therefore, the organization must consistently review its operations in order to make sure that boundaries are maintained in such a fashion as to favor survival. Review implies the identification of past errors in decision making and their correction. To adapt, for theorists of organizations, then, means to change operations in the face of a changing environment so as to be more certain of surviving and prospering. If the prevalence of competition among organizations is the challenge to survival, then principles of wise management are the techniques to ensure that natural selection favors you rather than your competitor. Successful adaptation implies using the techniques of management and design found to be theoretically and practically appropriate: to make a profit in producing refrigerators, providing software services, or growing soybeans. In the case of public organizations the mission may be helping the handicapped, improving agricultural productivity in Mali, or perfecting a defense against missile attack. The purpose is not questioned; the means for achieving it are constantly reviewed in order to remove possible error. It bears repeating that the exercise of technical rationality presumes an agreed, known, and stable preference ordering among the decision makers.

None of these assumptions is consistently met by bureaucracies in the foreign policy area. These bureaucracies normally do not compete for market shares, profits, or potential clienteles. While their survival is not ensured at all, failure to survive is not due to being a poor competitor. They do strive to survive, of course, but they do so by seeking to please their clients with more appropriate programs. The point is that these programs do not result from the exclusive exercise of technical rationality. Conflict among coalitions precludes the existence of agreed and stable preference orderings. Survival for public bureaucracies implies more than simple adaptation because it may involve the questioning of underlying goals of action; then criteria of efficiency no longer suffice.

Learning and Adaptation Differ From Avoidance of Misperception

It is common to equate adaptation (and learning) with trial-and-error processes of changing one's behavior, with relatively unself-conscious experimentation, again suggesting a misleading parallel to natural selection. I argue that the identification of both adaptation and learning with simple error correction is inappropriate in the study of international politics.

Error occurs when decision makers take the kinds of shortcuts described by cognitive psychologists: errors of bias, judgment, and attribution. Such errors certainly violate the canons of technically rational choice. A different kind of error arises in prisoners' dilemma situations. The less than fully rational result of a rational choice is due to the situational constraint in which the choosers find themselves. In both cases the decision makers could, in principle, avoid their mistakes if the institutional constraints and incentives in which they chose had been different, or if the source of their errors had been pointed out to them.

Why are these flaws in decision making relevant for us? The prevalence of cognitive shortcomings is undeniable, but they refer to individual decision makers, not bureaucratic entities. If entire units were often characterized by such traits, it is doubtful that they would survive for long. If they do show these attributes and survive anyway, the cognitive shortcomings cannot be very debilitating. Adaptation can still occur. In short, this type of error is relevant only if the error-prone chooser is really crazy and if the psychological mechanism underlying it is "hard-wired."

Errors associated with a situation of strategic interdependence are the stuff of microeconomic decision theory. Again, some mechanism for adapting to such constraints must be available because the casualty rate among public bureaucracies is very low. No learning or adaptation at all would be in evidence if such errors were normal operating procedure. However formidable they look in logic, their practical impact cannot be very great.

But what are we to make of such errors as an unwanted war, or of an unintended arms race, or of the continuation of an ineffective policy (like area bombing after the shortcomings of that tactic had been documented at the end of World War II)? Why do these "motivated" errors recur? They recur, we are told, because actors use unsystematic methods of analysis resulting in the nonuse of available knowledge. They recur also because of bureaucratic rivalries. Institutional missions become encapsulated in routines that aid the career patterns of officials rather than solve problems. Operational codes are enshrined even though they militate against the calculation of trade-offs.

Such behaviors are rooted in the routines of collective decision making. Institutionalized conduct and expectations, triggered by such things as civil service rules and bureaucratically sanctioned codes of interpersonal ties and loyalties, are the culprits. These, to be sure, may possibly be aggravated by cognitive errors committed by individual decision makers.

Motivated errors are due to ailments common in all types of organizations. But they are *not* necessarily irrational. Since these organizational ailments are part of a larger culture that *has* adapted, and since they occur

in organizations that *have* survived, they cannot be obviously self-de-
structive. In short, there must be good organizational reasons why these
practices persist even though they do lead to unwanted consequences.
Motivated errors are part of normal organizational life. We therefore
should not treat them as a simple mismatch of ends and means that can
be corrected by appealing to the canons of technical rationality. But can
the persistence of motivated error be considered allowable in an organization that is expected to adapt or to learn?

If the notion of error means anything it must mean that actors recognize
as wrong the persistence of decision-making routines that produce undesired
outcomes. Successful adaptation implies the willingness to reconsider
the tie between means and ends and to reformulate the organization's
program accordingly. Successful adaptation may also call for adding
new purposes or dropping old ones, without necessarily involving a searching
examination of assumptions about cause-effect links. Both activities also
imply error correction.

But I argued that the persistence of motivated errors is not only natural
but may actually contribute to the continued functioning of the organizations;
how then can I argue that adaptation includes the correction of some
motivated errors? The answer is that small incremental institutional
change is required by adaptive behavior even though sudden and drastic
reform is not to be expected. Civil service rules may be relaxed. New
interdepartmental committees may weaken the force of tenacious bureaucratic
politics. Information gathering and monitoring may be expanded by
means of new routines. All these constitute marginal changes in practices
that may have led to motivated errors in the past; they do not add up to
a complete self-examination. But they are adaptive in the sense that
recognized flaws in decision making are removed. Adaptation is change
that seeks to perfect the matching of ends and means without questioning
the theory of causation defining the organization's task. *Adaptation does
not require new consensual knowledge.*

I reserve the term *learning* for the situations in which an organization
is induced to question the basic beliefs underlying the selection of ends.
True revaluation is attempted when beliefs of cause and effect are examined.
Revaluation involves the recognition of connections among factors thought
to constitute causes of whatever problem is to be solved, connections
that had previously gone unrecognized. Revaluation implies shifting
one's cognitive horizon toward beliefs about causes different from previous
beliefs. Revaluation is made possible by the existence of bodies of knowledge
not previously available. Learning involves the penetration of political
objectives and programs by new knowledge-mediated understandings of
connections.

Once a bureaucracy questions older beliefs and struggles to institutionalize new ways of linking knowledge to the task it is supposed to carry out, it must necessarily also question behaviors identified with past failures. These behaviors may well have been rooted in practices we identify as motivated errors. While some of these practices undoubtedly contributed to the past survival and adaptation of the organization that is now questioning itself, some other practices (such as mode of recruiting personnel and the kind of professional training personnel is expected to have) will now appear to be wholly indefensible. Overcoming motivated errors is a core aspect of learning.

Have the Soviet Union and the United States learned anything in their relations with each other, in a specific region of the world like the Middle East or on an issue like arms control? The case studies contained in this volume shed little light on the question. This ought not to surprise us. Few of the case studies were written with my mode of analysis as their guide. My scheme was not designed to explore learning and adaptation with respect to security and military issues. If it nevertheless has something to offer here, as the essays of Peter Lavoy and Steven Weber suggest, the results ought to be seen as serendipitous. None of the case studies permits a coding of events in terms of the categories offered in this or the next section.

It is therefore reassuring that almost all of the essays confirm my argument that adaptation is much more common than learning. Governments, like the rest of us, prefer not to question themselves too profoundly; they will tinker in less searching ways for as long as they can, once they sense that past policies do not produce the expected results. To be sure, many of the contributors find no adaptation worthy of note; Richard Anderson offers a compelling scheme that enables him to claim that cognitively based adaptation on the part of the Soviet leadership is impossible. Wallace Thies, Steven Spiegel, and Jonathan Haslam see evidence of adaptation, but explain it in terms of personnel changes, not cognitive revaluation. Robert Levine, Deborah Larson, and Allen Whiting explain whatever little adaptation they perceive as being due to slight alterations in means to attain one's unchanging goals more effectively.

I take courage from the fact that occasional learning and considerable adaptive changes attributable to the kinds of cognitive processes I stress were discovered by Alexander Dallin for the United States, and by George Breslauer, Coit Blacker and Robert Legvold for the Soviet Union. While Weber and Lavoy document much adaptation and a bit of learning for both governments, they also note that the process remains asymmetrical, systematically reciprocal, and altogether a weak reed. We must conclude that nothing irreversible has occurred to totally alter the cognitive universe of Soviet and U.S. foreign policy makers.

III. LEARNING AND ADAPTATION
UNDER BOUNDED RATIONALITY

Adaptive behavior is common whereas true learning is very rare. The very nature of bureaucratic institutions is such that the dice are loaded in favor of the less demanding behavior associated with adaptation. This is true even if we restrict the type of rationality required for learning to the bounded variety, not the fully analytic procedures that are inapplicable to governmental decision making. The case for the difficulty of learning under conditions of bounded rationality is starkly made by John Steinbruner, who reminds us that the recurrence and imperfect mastery of misperceptions by the actors must be taken for granted. That leaves us with the boundedly rational patterns of choice Steinbruner calls *cybernetic* and *cognitive*. They will provide our initial framework for summarizing whether, when, and where adaptation and/or learning has taken place in the diplomatic encounters we call the cold war and U.S.–Soviet détente.

For Steinbruner, decision makers are motivated by wishing to survive rather than serve some overriding organizational mission. Choice routines seek to limit the complexity of the real world and to reduce uncertainty by imposing limits on incoming information and by seeking to segment the problem to be solved. Outcomes are not systematically assessed and the choice of response is limited by these constraints. Both modes result in outputs that are suboptimal though they generally suffice to ensure the survival of the unit. Both decision-making modes may ignore new knowledge or use it very selectively; neither is able to make full use of consensual knowledge. The cognitive and cybernetic decision-making paradigms lead to actor choices that Janice Stein (whose treatment I follow here) labels *satisficing, single-value calculus* and *lexicographic calculus*.[10] They are choices that represent adaptive behavior among like-minded actors, not among antagonists.

If the common decisional routines lead merely to adaptive behavior, what can be said about learning under conditions of bounded rationality? Steinbruner's cybernetic and cognitive paradigms of behavior are juxtaposed by him to an analytic paradigm, a routine that adheres strictly to the canons of technical rationality. At the extreme, such a routine is inconsistent with some of the conditions that define bounded rationality: when outcomes of choice cannot be predicted with confidence, when the values of the actors are not ranked and trade-offs cannot be calculated, when cost-benefit criteria of analysis cannot be systematically used and comprehensive searches are not possible. But real-life decision makers do not necessarily operate at the extreme; it is quite possible (and Stein documents such instances) that some of the limitations on analytic behavior are operative and some are not, or that some are operative most of the time and some only intermittently. In short, approximations to analytic decision making are conceivable; the pure case, the beloved straw man of the critic, is not to be taken seriously. An imperfect analytic mode is the vehicle under which learning can be imagined to occur. Says Stein:

> The cybernetic explanation suggests that decision makers rely on selective feedback and programmed operations to make their choices. In an analytic process, decision makers approach their problem with a blueprint or a causal model of the environment; they concentrate on understanding and explanation. A cybernetic decision maker follows routine procedures without necessarily understanding the effects of individual ingredients or their interaction together to produce the final product. If the stew is too thick, the cook adds water, if it is too thin a little more flour. The chef substitutes trial-and-error experimentation and learning for causal knowledge. Cybernetic decision makers follow programmed procedures without understanding the reasons for them. Moreover, they do not care that they do not fully understand; it is not the reasons but the result that counts. They concentrate on the immediate effect rather than the precedent cause. Even then cybernetic decision makers generally emphasize the consequence rather than the range of outcomes which their actions may produce.[11]

The behavior I call learning takes place under the decision-making conditions Stein labels *constrained optimizing*. It may not only characterize the like-minded members of the same government or coalition, but it may also include antagonists seeking an accommodation, such as the encounters of Soviet and U.S. bureaucracies of concern to us. How can that process be conceptualized?

The changes in actor behavior associated with cybernetic and cognitive modes of decision making avoid self-reflection. Under cybernetic conditions change in behavior comes about by following a programmed formula responding to selective feedback from the results of earlier decisions. Under cognitive conditions, change occurs because of reinforcement, inconsistency management and pressures generated within small groups. Under the analytic paradigm, however, the change in behavior is associated with a redefinition of cause-effect schemata, with "lateral and upward expansion."[12] Robert Cutler summarizes the difference between the adaptive and the learning modes as shown in Table 2.

The constrained optimizers are able to reflect on their past failings as they benefit from multiple iterations of action-response-action sequences that led to less-than-desired outcomes. The logic of iterated prisoners' dilemma gaming as well as the logic of the reciprocity formula derived from exchange theory explain how and why antagonists may learn to cooperate.[13] The perception of the inadequacy of past noncooperative policies leads to the reflection about alternatives, not a sudden spurt of altruism or the meek desire to turn the other cheek.

TABLE 2 Basic Postulates of the Decisional Paradigms

	Analytic Paradigm	Cybernetic and Cognitive Paradigm(s)
Decision maker's basic motivating value	Achievement of an optimal, or at least acceptable, result in the external world (64)	Survival, as directly reflected in the internal state of the decision-making mechanism (65)
Decision maker's central attitudinal focus	Finding an optimal [or acceptable] solution under given constraints (56)	Elimination of the variety [complexity] inherent in any significant decision problems (56)
Decision maker's behavioral pattern	Direct calculation of alternative outcomes (56)	Control of uncertainty (62) Segmentation of problems (78)
Decision maker's modus operandi	Assumption of alternative outcomes (34) Assumption of sensitivity to pertinent information (35)	Focus on only a few of the incoming variables (46) Elimination of serious calculation of probable outcomes (66)

NOTE: All entries in the table are either direct citations or paraphrases of Steinbruner (see text note 10), which is referenced by the page numbers in parentheses. Material in brackets has been added by Robert Cutler (see text note 10: Table 1, p. 58).

Our job is to identify episodes in U.S.–Soviet relations in order to see whether changes in behavior can be spotted that conform to either the adaptive or the learning modes. We postulate that the three decision-making paradigms are not mutually exclusive in real life, that any single bureaucracy can combine elements of all three. Steinbruner invented three types of actors—grooved, uncommitted, and theoretical thinkers—to correspond, respectively, to bureaucrats, politicians, and experts active in a *single* bureaucracy.[14] (Table 3). Stein and Tanter discovered seven separate decision-making paths that capture the three paradigms and actors in intermingled action. I shall use four of these paths to sketch the code to be used in judging U.S.–Soviet behavior.

A decision-making unit, informed by its beliefs and norms and triggered into action by some stimulus, typically engages in diagnosis, search, revision, and evaluation before finally choosing. Each of these five steps is handled differently, depending on which mixture of analytic, cybernetic, and cognitive elements prevails and whether theoretical or grooved or uncommitted thinkers have their way.[15] Figure 2 shows the sequence

TABLE 3 Styles of Thinking Within Organizations

	Grooved Thinking	Uncommitted Thinking	Theoretical Thinking
Organizational conditions	In organizations that have been conceded competence over a certain range of tasks, at levels where problems nearly always fall readily into a small number of basic types.	High levels in an organizational hierarchy, where intersecting information channels carry relatively abstracted, aggregated information.	Usually within a particular information channel in an organizational unit, formal or informal, which has a restricted scope of concern.
Chief cognitive characteristic	Stability has been well established by long exercise over an extended sequence of decisions. Experience offers powerful analogs for new decisions.	Consistency and stability principles prevent overall integration of divergent patterns of thought, each urged on the decision maker by a different "sponsor."	When highly generalized conceptions become established, they provide the mind with a basis for handling the uncertainty of the immediate decision problem.
Other characteristics	Operates in a very short-range time frame and with a quite low level of abstraction.	Due to the organizational setting, the reality principle forces a more abstract intellectual framework than for the grooved thinker. But abstraction is made difficult by uncertainty.	Beliefs are generally organized around a single transcendent value, inferentially related to specific objectives.
	Attention given only to that small number of variables which are pertinent to a decision problem.	Uncommitted thinker deals in a more extended time frame than grooved thinker, with a greater range of problems and greater scope of individual problems.	Since thought processes are less dependent on incoming information to establish coherent beliefs, inconsistency mechanisms are widely employed to cope with it.
	Simplicity principle tends to organize problem conceptions around a single value. Reality principle operates to provide a ready-made, well-anchored structure to which new problems can be fitted.	Decision maker will oscillate among competing belief patterns, compromising stability somewhat, in favor of simplicity.	Likely to be found in small, closely knit groups which interact regularly over issues of common concern. This pattern of interaction provides social reinforcement.

NOTE: All entries in the table are either direct citations or close paraphrases of Steinbruner, taken from pages 125-135 (see text note 10). Reprinted by permission.

and lists the four types of choice of interest to us. Figure 3 shows the mixture of paradigms leading to choice.

Constrained optimizing, clearly, resembles true optimizing, although the search for solutions is dominated by the actors' ideologies rather than by the use of analytic techniques, permitting enough theoretical thinking to be considered learning behavior. The other three relevant modes of choosing do not allow sufficient independence from grooved and uncommitted thinking to leave much of a door for knowledge to enter the picture. To satisfice means that one picks the first solution that apparently meets most of the obviously more salient values, without formal search and without attempting a ranking of values, indeed without any formal decision rules. Decision makers relying on a single-value calculus find it too painful to choose among competing values and pick their solutions by seeking to maximize one value on which they can agree because of their acceptance of prior beliefs. Lexicographers, however, "choose the option which best discriminates among rank-ordered dimensions of value."[16]

IV. WHY ADAPTATION IS EASIER THAN LEARNING

The stimuli that lead to learning come mostly from the external environment in which a bureaucracy is placed. Such endogenous concerns as the coordination of units, sources of revenue, staff-line relations, or internal monitoring reflect adaptation or learning; they do not trigger it. Can we say something about the environmental conditions most likely to lead to learning? Are there plausible predictors of learning? None is obvious; several are possible. I review them without settling the issue. The predictors are the *desirability* of finding new cause-effect chains, the *possibility* of finding them, and the *urgency* for finding them.

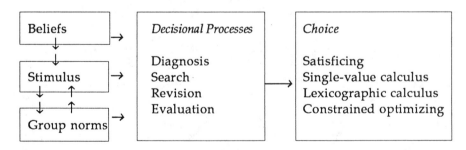

FIGURE 2   National security decision making.

Search	Revision	Evaluation	Choice
Cognitive/ $\longrightarrow$ cybernetic	Cognitive/ $\longrightarrow$ cybernetic	Cybernetic $\longrightarrow$	Satisficing
Cybernetic $\longrightarrow$	Cybernetic/ $\longrightarrow$ cognitive	Cognitive $\longrightarrow$	Single-value calculus
Analytic $\longrightarrow$	Cognitive $\longrightarrow$	Cognitive $\longrightarrow$	Lexicographic calculus
Cognitive $\longrightarrow$	Cognitive/ $\longrightarrow$ analytic	Modified $\longrightarrow$ analytic	Constrained optimizing

FIGURE 3 Multiple paths to choice.

Desirability refers to the incentives motivating the bureaucratic units to engage in some soul-searching. We hypothesize that actors' career goals and political opportunities to prosper are heavily identified with pleasing a certain constituency, with helping that constituency to solve its problems. Issues that can be approached in terms of the proper conjunction of incentives on the part of decision makers are more likely to be dealt with than issues that do not offer the same opportunities. From the vantage point of desirability, it makes more sense to reexamine one's ends and values with respect to fighting epidemics than mounting campaigns in favor of human rights.

The existence of political incentives may not be enough to trigger learning. The possibility of redefining ends along new causal chains must also exist. This possibility, of course, is a function of the state of scientific knowledge, the degree of consensus it enjoys, and the availability of epistemic communities for spreading the word. The possibility of learning refers to the availability of new means that entitle actors to consider new ends not previously accessible to them.

One would think that the urgency of the problem involved has something to do with the rate of learning. Is there a crisis that calls out for immediate action, such as a famine, the imminent bankruptcy of a large country and its creditors, or an AIDS epidemic? If the requisite knowledge exists (or can rapidly be found) and if political incentives are aligned with crisis management, we would expect rapid learning to occur. We would also expect that a crisis combined with the special salience of certain issues would increase the sense of urgency. Is health the most salient, or is malnutrition? Is either more salient than economic development or debt relief? Are programs and problems involving money for economic development the most salient? At this point I speculate that learning is triggered in situations showing high desirability, reasonable possibility, and the conjunction of high issue salience and a crisis.

ATTRIBUTES OF BUREAUCRATIC DECISION MAKING

These intuitive predictions of the conditions under which learning is likely to prevail over adaptive behavior are based on a particular conceptualization of the bargaining process among bureaucratic units, on the way knowledge is used to define and redefine problem sets (and solutions), and on the extent to which these practices are successfully institutionalized by actors. We now turn to the discussion of each of these attributes of bureaucratic decision making.

Bureaucratic Bargaining

Reconsider the argument illustrated by Figure 1. My argument was based on the assumption that *all* participants in decision making are located in a single cell, that the negotiation in question can be described in terms of the characteristics of a single cell. This assumption is unrealistic. It is truer to life to imagine a bargaining situation in which the participants are located in different cells. Analysis would then have to focus on the interaction between, say, a set of negotiators characterized by eclectic style favoring tactical linkages and another made up of skeptics committed to the fragmented linkage of issues, as they confront each other in a bargaining situation.

How, then, shall we code the bargaining styles that pit differently minded coalitions against each other in single negotiating encounters? The first point to be noted is that decisions can either be based on similar decision-making styles and modes of linkage or on dissimilar ones. I predict that negotiations in which the bargaining coalitions live in the same cell, when they profess similar modes of linking issues and merging knowledge with political goals, are more likely to produce lasting agreements than when dissimilar modes encounter each other.

Agreements based on similar decision-making styles and modes of issue linkage sometimes emerge after first suffering through encounters that were dissimilar. The progression illustrates the important differences between the pragmatic/fragmented mode that is merely adaptive and the analytic/substantive mode that favors learning. Pragmatists, unlike analytic thinkers, experiment with combining two or three issues. Once they are convinced that the combination is conceptually faulty or politically unacceptable, they are willing to decompose the issue package.

Pragmatists prefer to link issues substantively at all times, but they will accept tactical linkages when they must. Moreover, they will bargain with opponents not willing to make substantive linkages, thus permitting the fragmented pattern to operate. Therefore, this mode permits only tentative movement toward the growth of consensual concepts, because for the pragmatist nothing is ever final and complete. The social and economic goals to which politicians subscribe may not be expanding as the expert wishes. Therefore, the varying concepts that permit nesting of goals and policies continue to coexist and to compete. Improved knowledge cannot be used to order goals in any final way. As single goals change and coalitions among bargainers shift, so does the order of priorities acceptable to the pragmatist. Improved knowledge may help in the ordering. But since it too is rarely final and complete, pragmatists must work on the border of relative and temporary certainty, of social goals that are only occasionally ordered consensually. Hence they are willing to settle for stop-and-go tactics, attempts to construct more encompassing concepts followed by periods of retrenchment and disaggregation.

These conclusions, to become credible, must be justified in terms of a more refined typology of bargaining situations than has been offered so far, a three-level typology. The following situations must be covered. (1) Intragovernmental negotiations are important because they (a) determine the outcomes the international negotiator ought to seek and (b) ratify the accord he or she brings home. (2) Intracoalitional negotiations seek to unify a single bloc or alliance of governments behind a preferred position (or range of positions) before the full international talks begin. Both types are essentially encounters among the like-minded, a feature that ought to caution us about the generalizability of studies of national-level decision making. (3) Finally, the international negotiations themselves must be studied, and we must remind ourselves that these are negotiations among antagonists, parties that cannot be expected to share many meanings or that dispose, between them, of a large "win-set."[17]

Therefore, arriving at an agreement at the international level is more difficult than at the other two levels, especially if we recall that the size of the win-set at levels 1 and 2 determines the range of possible outcomes at level 3. The possibility of agreement at level 2 is also constrained (at least in the case of pluralistic and/or democratic polities) by the number of actors and the complexity of their demands at level 1: the larger the number and the more intricate their nested demands, the smaller the win-set. Moreover, bargaining styles at level 1 will tend toward dissimilarity if there are very numerous participating constituencies. Styles will tend to be quite similar at level 2 because the knowledge that the coalition will eventually have to face an opposing coalition is a powerful incentive to hold the members together. We know that dissimilarity has an elective affinity for adaptive behavior; therefore, bargaining at level 3, which probably pits opposing styles against each other, is not likely to lead to learning.

Problem Definition

Assume now that the bargaining has resulted in an agreement that will take the form of a new program of action. Such a decision seeks to define a commonly experienced problem that is to be solved by way of collaborative measures. Assume also the decision is just the latest effort to tackle the problem. Each time the problem is defined slightly differently from the previous attempt. Each time the components of the problem are nested more (or less) complexly than before. As we know, a nested problem set contains a theory about what causes the dissatisfaction that constitutes the problem, how various institutions, processes, and physical parameters are thought to bring about the unhappiness, and what can be done about it. Differently arranged nests correspond to different sets of Chinese boxes (or Russian dolls), each governed by the shape of its largest box (or doll). What matters in a discussion of learning is the determination that the more recently constructed box (the most recent compromise derived from the conjunction of consensual knowledge and shared goals) is more (or less) decomposable than its predecessors, that problems have been redefined by respecting new knowledge.

How then shall we describe problem definition? My discussion now elaborates on the distinctions introduced in Figure 4. The dominance of the analytic/substantive mode results in the elaboration of a *nondecomposable* set of tightly interrelated issues and concerns.[18] To the extent that the set is derived from a single overarching principle or norm, such as the predominance of a higher quality of life or improved international equity, the set is hierarchically arranged (cell 4). The prevalence of the pragmatic/fragmented bargaining style tends to yield a *nearly nondecomposable* nested set (cell 3). Less hierarchy is evident in the nesting because the bargainers have to do some compromising among the basic principles in putting the set together. Not all parts of the set are equally tightly and equally permanently linked to the other parts, so that some decomposition is always possible. A *fully decomposable* set is the result of bargaining in the eclectic/tactical style (cell 1). Whatever arrangement is reached remains subject to relatively easy dismemberment as bits and pieces of the problem can be tackled. Bargaining that features the skeptic/fragmented style is more difficult to code and classify (cell 2). It depends on the style of the opposing coalitions. If they are eclectically minded, the result will also be a fully decomposable set. But if they are analytically or pragmatically minded, then the outcome is likely to be a nearly nondecomposable set.

Politicians' response to more elaborately integrated
theoretical knowledge:

		Little use	Much use
Epistemic communities achieve:	More consensual knowledge	3. Selective use of knowledge to suit ideological need; some systematic nesting across ideologies	4. General use of knowledge bridges ideologies: extensive nesting
	Not more consensual knowledge	1. Knowledge used very selectively and opportunistically; no nesting	2. Opposing alliances between sets of epistemic communities and sets of politicians; each alliance attempts systematic nesting

FIGURE 4 Political choice and scientific discovery.

Institutionalization

We now need some evaluative variables for assessing whether adaptation or learning leads to permanent changes in the bureaucratic unit being studied. I shall use the notions of institutionalization and governmental legitimacy/authority for that purpose. The judgment in each case is a simple bivariate one: the features to be elaborated either do or do not develop.

I define institutionalization as the development of new organs, principles of action, and administrative practices that are designed to improve the performance of the polity or organization in the wake of some major disappointment with earlier performance.

Institutionalization, so defined, assumes that decision-making routines that actively search for consensual knowledge were used; evidence that this was done would include any and all of the following: the organization may establish a think tank to work up consensual knowledge; it may decide to use modeling techniques found to be useful in other decision-making contexts in order to reduce uncertainty; program budgeting may be adopted in order to monitor performance more systematically and to gain insight about failures in performance; recruitment practices may be changed to reflect the need for personnel adept in these activities and skills; rules of deliberation may be changed so as to give incentives for serious nonconfrontational discussion rather than relying on posturing and voting. If most of these practices develop, I conclude that learning is taking place. Adaptation, as opposed to learning, features attempts to use one or two of these innovations in an ad hoc manner. It must be stressed that the episodic use of these innovations does not amount to successful institutionalization. Successful institutionalization takes place only when these innovations are consistently used and fully integrated into the regular decision-making process.

Crisis management can be used as a shorthand indicator for successful institutionalization. A crisis is a sudden concatenation of circumstances that threatens the major values of the bulk of the actors—a major war, a famine, a depression. A crisis presents the actors with an unfamiliar set of problems in the sense that the causes of the disturbance are seen as complex and not amenable to single-shot solutions. It is not that they never experienced war, famine or depression previously. A crisis consists not in the recurrence of these events, but in the actors' recognition that the recurrence is due to the fact that previous institutional routines have been insufficient to avert it. Successful crisis management incorporates in a single institutional response the qualities and routines described above.

Attributes as Predictors

We are discussing elective affinities among traits and attributes, not tight causal schemes. The core attributes of adaptive as opposed to learning behavior are summarized in Table 4. On the basis of this summary we can claim that, on balance, certain international efforts at collaboration display learning, such as the program of the World Bank, the World Health Organization, and the International Atomic Energy Agency.[19] Others, such as the United Nations and the International Labor Organization, have displayed adaptive behavior. Similar judgments can be made of nation-states. For instance, late Manchu China, the Ottoman government after 1879, modern Pakistan, and Russia after 1861 sought to practice adaptation in the face of external and internal challenges; all failed in the attempt. Britain since 1945 and India since independence have successfully practiced adaptation, though not learning. The United States, during the New Deal and World War II years, was a successful learner; so was Japan between 1867 and 1981; so were France and Germany after 1950. The United States, the Soviet Union, and Japan certainly practiced successful adaptation in recent decades, internally as well as in their foreign relations. Some might actually consider the changes in policy as evidence of learning, though the lack of institutionalization and long-term near nondecomposability under a strategic variable make me hesitate to advance this claim.

Two major conditions then underlie successful learning in and by governments. There must be a relatively stable coalition of like-minded

TABLE 4   Attributes of Adaptation and Learning Behavior

Attribute	Adaptation	Learning
Consensuality of scientific knowledge	Not becoming more consensual, except among some coalitions of the like-minded; epistemic communities remain weak	Becomes more consensual in general because of strong epistemic communities
Character of political goals	Specific and static; specific with some demand for movement toward expanding goals	Interconnected and expanding
Issue linkage	Skeptic or eclectic	Fragmented, some substantive
Bargaining		
intragovernmental	Similar	Dissimilar
intrabloc	Dissimilar	Similar
intergovernmental	Dissimilar	Almost similar
Problem definition	Nesting results in decomposable sets not rationally coordinated with core strategic variable	Nesting results in apparently nondecomposable sets that become nearly nondecomposable, though remaining coordinated by means of a core strategic variable
Institutionalization of innovations	Gradual and unsystematic; undesired events not perceived as a general crisis	Sudden and systematic, triggered by crisis

actors. These actors must profess goals that do not differ fundamentally from government to government, agency to agency. And there must be sufficient consensual knowledge available to provide the rationale for the novel nesting of problems and solutions. Both conditions must be met. The existence of either, by itself, does not permit learning.

It seems clear that the shock of war and of disappointment with economic development are major occasions for learning to think anew about the adequacy of international institutions in the second half of the twentieth century. Threats to the environment and to the global commons can also be powerful stimuli. The most consistent and the most impressive sequences of attempted problem solving, resulting in the elaboration of more complex problem sets, all hinged on the demands for programs, services, and rules that conform to Western political principles and responded to secular knowledge purveyed by epistemic communities. The logical and epistemological properties featured in modern Western thought were important facilitators of learning because they helped focus research and program making around the substantive strategic variables that determine degrees of decomposability.

All institutional actors are habit-driven, but not to the same degree and not at a constant rate through time. To be able to learn demands that the bonds of habit be light. Adaptation, however, is quite possible in all but the most taboo-ridden organizations. Few modern public organizations are so encrusted with habit and routine as to be unable to shift from ineffective to more efficacious means, or to add new purposes to old ones, though neither the new nor the old need be attained with speed and efficiency. While most habit-driven organizations can adapt, only a few seem to be able to learn.

How rapidly and how readily organizations are willing to reexamine and revaluate themselves is a wholly empirical question. No formalized script can capture the process. As argued above, we can only claim that epistemic communities, as triggers for learning, are likely to be listened to when political decision makers find it congruent with their career interests to listen; and this is more likely to happen when knowledge promises better solutions to old problems in a setting of crisis. Rosenau makes the same point, though he does not qualify it sufficiently to limit it to learning as opposed to any change in organizational behavior:

> In short, be they individuals or collectivities, officials or citizens, educated or illiterate, Western or Eastern, actors are conceived as learners and not as constants on the world scene. And as learning entities, they can never succeed in cutting off *all* feedback that runs counter to their orientations. Thus being open to learning, they are capable of changing. This can occur in one or both of two ways: (a) when the external stimuli are so persistently and startlingly different as to jolt habitual modes and foster new patterns more appropriate to the evolving circumstances; or (b) when new skills, capabilities, and/or responsibilities develop within the actor, forcing the old, habitual ways to yield to new ones. Externally induced habit change is exemplified by the political adjustments that follow the waging and termination of an international war or the socioeconomic adjustments that accompany, say, a fundamentalist revolution or a sharp and enduring shift in the cost of energy. Internally induced habit change is illustrated by the consequences of the microelectronic revolution for people's analytic capabilities. When basic change does occur, of course, its external and internal stimuli are interactive and reinforcing. Together they eventually produce new characteristic modes of coping with change, which, through time, evolve as new habit functions.[20]

For these reasons, then, the game should not be seen as heroic epistemic communities facing off against silent, undifferentiated, but malign habit. Rather we should see the game as a slow historical movement in which *some* epistemic communities successfully shake up *some* aspects of habitual behavior. Organizations, because they adapt and sometimes even learn, permit change to occur even if they do not actively favor it. Habit is neither totally banished nor is it an inevitable block to new ways. But, given the culturally very heterogeneous world in which we live, how can we expect meanings and symbols to be shared sufficiently widely among nations so as to allow learning based on consensual knowledge to occur?

IS LEARNING BETTER THAN ADAPTATION?

We now know which aspects of collective behavior have an elective affinity with learning to manage interdependence, to cope with crises so that they are less likely to recur. Can we flatly assert that to learn is always better than to practice the more modest behavior we call adaptation?

It all depends on what *best* is taken to mean in this context. Suppose there is no stable coalition of the like-minded and there is not enough consensual knowledge to give us nested problem sets, the two major conditions underlying the possibility of learning. Would that force us to conclude that adaptive change should not be attempted? How can we tell that the lessons learned by the organizations are the right lessons? How can we be sure until all the outcomes are known and until we can gauge the degree of satisfaction they engender?

To argue that the learning model is the best compels us to assert that the substance of the problem definition it attempts is normatively preferable to the other two models. We would have to be confident that the particular nesting of problems attempted by an organization is the right nesting, the one most likely to deliver the desired outcome. I reiterate that all knowledge experienced by actors is socially constructed. Since there is no such thing as final and true consensual knowledge, it is impossible to make a credible claim that one way of nesting problems is superior to another—except in the case of incontrovertible physical evidence. We have no warrant for confidence *unless the routines and skills associated with the learning model consistently produce the outcomes desired more reliably than is the case in the adaptive mode.*

Let us now suppose that these routines do perform better than the practices associated with adaptation. Let us suppose further that the beneficiaries, the clients of the organizations' programs, agree among themselves that better health, more peace, higher living standards, and a wholesome physical environment constitute the utopia toward which our organizations should labor. Given all of these suppositions, we would be entitled to say that the learning model is practically and morally superior to the other ways of defining problems and their solutions. We would have the right to state this conclusion not only because the learning model performs better but also because it alone contains the concepts and techniques necessary for reflecting on failure and thinking about doing better with a different definition of the problem.

These suppositions are not realistic. Most states endorse peace in general but feel that it can be attained only if their archrivals are eliminated or chastened. Few governments profess a desire for peace at any price, and neither do their citizens. In principle everyone prefers good health to bad, but does this preference predict that governments are willing to budget for better health when there are competing claims for military funds? Few quarrel with the desirability of higher living standards, but most decision makers disagree as to whether the improvement should take the form of industrialization under state or private auspices, favor urban or rural dwellers, sacrifice agriculture to industry, or the reverse. Everybody wants to be free of toxic chemicals, but not everyone is equally willing to put this goal ahead of defense, industrialization, or urban amenities. In short, the existence of universal, mass-based values does not ensure agreement on how to order them. The disagreement is the stuff of national and international politics.

But we do know that the learning model provides a mechanism for the blunting of the differences among these preferences. That is its great virtue. It offers routines and institutions for working out fragments of value consensus. In the successful learning organizations, this blunting takes the form of a rapprochement among competing ideologies when their adherents realize that uncompromising persistence in one's preferred ideology involves undesirable costs *and* when a compromise would not fatally undermine one's preferred ideology. If we agree that the particular values likely to be enhanced by the learning model are indeed to be preferred to others, then the model is indeed the best. Even if we agree merely that self-correcting procedures for making decisions are superior to fixed routines, then the learning model is still to be preferred.

Unfortunately, we cannot be sure of any of this. We do not know whether appropriate routines for self-correction will be followed when outcomes prove disappointing. We dare not assume that the consensual knowledge of one epoch will remain consensual, that political goals agreed to at one point will continue to be preferred by those who matter most. We are not yet in a position to judge whether the compromises among ideologies that have occurred will be institutionalized. Therefore, since international interdependence will not soon come to an end, models of behavior that merely enable the organizations to adapt should be valued. They provide a hedge against time, an opportunity to preserve what is still desired, even in the absence of learning.

BETWEEN ADAPTATION AND LEARNING: WHY LEARNING CANNOT BE DESIGNED

My discussion of the moral superiority of learning is inconclusive. Any notion of superiority is hedged about by doubts, by counterpoint that can be summed up as the tyranny of the *fortuna* of habit over the *virtù* of learning.

Machiavelli, some of us suspect, often exaggerated. It seems a distinct overstatement to juxtapose habit to learning with the starkness he used to contrast *virtù* with the sluggishness of routinized fate. There is certainly an elective affinity between habit and adaptation; the persistence of established patterns and routines is responsible for some of the behaviors we associate with adaptation. The affinity of the imaginative and creative forces the author of *The Prince* identified as *virtù* with the behavior pattern I have called learning is equally clear. I argue that usually neither adaptation nor learning wins any final and full victories, that the two coexist and interact. I also urge that no acceptable social scientific account of events is possible without bearing in mind the interaction of the two modes. Hence, the case for the superiority of learning cannot be made on value-neutral social science grounds.

One reason for this state of affairs is the ingrained tendency of political actors not to be readily persuaded by scientific knowledge. Historically, scientific knowledge that eventually becomes consensual rarely provides a breathtaking new paradigm for politics. On the contrary, political advocacy and political routine seek to adapt new discoveries to previously held convictions. Discoveries in astronomy and biology in the sixteenth and seventeenth centuries were by no means used immediately as the basis for a fresh view of humankind and nature. That came much later. These discoveries were instead pressed into service to reaffirm prior beliefs about humankind and nature, some of which had been accepted since the time of Plato. They served as affirmations of the great chain of being, the principle that God's perfect reason foreordains and preprograms everything, that everything that can be logically, is or will be.

Nothing much has changed since. New discoveries in the sciences and new technological inventions are immediately incorporated into prior beliefs, religious and secular. Few of us consider them as possible radical breakpoints with the past, as the occasion for formulating metaphors for politics that had not been thought of before. In the area of environmental politics, for instance, liberals, socialists, and conservatives selectively incorporate and reject scientific findings into their programs; many actors reject the arguments of ecologists as romantic or reactionary, but some embrace ecology as a new view of politics, a metaphor symbolizing and representing humankind's place in, and unity with, nature.

Sensitivity to the notion of habit-driven behavior should teach us to expect nothing else. Once set up, the organization will be animated by various bureaucratic networks. The components of these networks exist at the national as well as the intergovernmental levels, among governmental units and among nongovernmental organizations with a stake in the agenda. Actual discussion, negotiation, study and—eventually—action are the result of activities within and among these bureaucratic networks. Private interests and parties are involved in most instances, though the intensity of the involvement differs with each issue area. Involvement is most intense in organizations with a mission involving scientific, engineering, and medical personnel.

Whenever the leadership of an organization heavily dependent on scientific and technical personnel fears that knowledge has changed so as to put into question the mission of their organization, the scientific component risks being corrupted because scientific questioning is choked off. The original knowledge then becomes dogma. Systematic evaluation of organizational performance is avoided because it might threaten the dogma. The corruption of science and scientific objectivity will lead the organization away from learning.

The emphasis on habit-driven behavior leads us to another sobering conclusion: if solutions to conflicting welfare claims are being offered that imply obvious redistributive or regulatory interventions, which are certain to make very visible short-term losses to important constituencies, then the acceptance of the relevant knowledge by governments is very much in doubt. Hence, the amount of analytic decision making to be expected is limited by the immediacy and clarity of the welfare trade-offs, and substantive linkages will be few. Epistemic communities can realistically aim at the elaboration of more intelligently nested problem sets only if they are in control over all levels of bureaucratic activity, national and intergovernmental. That control, however, is likely to differ sharply with the degree of consensus about the applicable knowledge, and agreement about the publicness of the good being provided. Science as such can be expected to generate policy-relevant knowledge only if governments perceive the need for it to solve problems they cannot avoid solving, and if they cannot think of a way of doing this without making use of knowledge offered by epistemic communities.

But somehow the game goes on. Scientific knowledge does find its way into policy making that leads to substantive linkages, cognitively similar bargaining styles, and newly nested problem sets that aim at more effective problem solving. If *virtù* wins no final victory, neither does Dame Fortuna. The limitations of habit, real though they are, are often transcended by appropriate behaviors because no political routine is totally frozen. Almost certainly, the social democrat will never walk away with a complete victory; but neither will the classical conservative. They are condemned to interact with each other for a very long time. Therefore, they can be expected to experience interdependence in such a way as to arrive at programs and rules that make them both see their enmeshment as a nearly nondecomposable system.

In that case they are acting out an evolutionary logic. Past events, past mistakes of policy, and past discoveries of science create a dynamic in which all actors, despite the ideological commitments that define their perceived interests, will be forced to consider the other's interests as if they were their own. Not only interests, but the fates of actors become intertwined, not only in the observer's judgment but also in the minds of the actors. The reality of the cognitively evolutionary pattern, in turn, limits and suggests the kinds of theories of organization on which we can draw in considering the deliberate design of organizations that can learn.

The learning mode can never be expected to win a final victory over the adaptive mode. The two will continue to coexist within the same organization and among organizations. Total learning is not within the grasp of the political being because of the drag of habit and the limits of social learning. The creative passion for designing better bureaucracies encounters the inertia of embedded perceptions and interests. Both forces will determine the eventual outcome. Probably this result will fully satisfy nobody, but it will set the pattern for the next round of change just the same.

NOTES

Portions of this essay are taken or adapted from the author's *When Knowledge Is Power* (Berkeley: University of California Press, 1990). I gratefully acknowledge the publisher's permission to use the material.

1. Herbert A. Simon, "Rationality in Psychology and Economics," in Robin M. Hogarth and Melvin W. Reder, eds., *Rational Choice* (Chicago: University of Chicago Press, 1986), 26–27.

2. James G. March, *Decisions and Organizations* (London: Basil Blackwell, 1988), 12–14.

3. Burkhart Holzner and John H. Marx, *Knowledge Application* (Boston: Allyn and Bacon, 1979), 108. My use of the notion of reality testing relies on their discussion; see pp.103–10, 139–40.

4. There is of course a logical possibility governing decision making that differs from the four we envisage here. Interests need not be informed by knowl-

edge (as here defined) at all. Ideology may be the source of interest, unaided by any notion of technical information, structured or not, consensual or disputed. In such a situation a politician's sense of interest retains its immunity from the truth tests to which epistemic communities are subject. These possibilities do not concern us here. I am elaborating a notion of organizational decision making in which knowledge, consensual or not, shapes and deflects raw interest. I am not here interested in goals based on interests uninformed by knowledge.

I feel justified in taking this position because it is hard to imagine any political issue in modern international relations that is not informed to some extent by experts' claims that command some respect, mixed with a fair amount of ridicule and even contempt. The point is that, even though the knowledge claimed by experts may be partisan knowledge, it still enters the decision-making process. This is the situation covered by the southwest cell on Figure 1.

5. Carl Sagan, "Nuclear War and Climatic Catastrophe: Some Policy Implications," *Foreign Affairs* 62 (1983–84); 257–92, among many studies on this topic. Burns H. Weston, ed., *Toward Nuclear Disarmament and Global Security* (Boulder, Colo.: Westview Press, 1984).

6. John Gerard Ruggie, "Social Time and International Policy," in Margaret P. Karns, ed., *Persistent Patterns and Emergent Structures in a Waning Century* (New York: Praeger, 1986).

7. See Robert E. Riggs and I. Jostein Mykletun, *Beyond Functionalism* (Minneapolis and Oslo: University of Minnesota Press and Universitetsforlaget, 1979), 166–76, for a full statement of the relationship between functionalist thought and learning.

8. One author defines individual learning as "changes in *intelligence* and *effectiveness*" and to operationalize the growth of intelligence as "(1) growth of *realism*, recognizing the different elements and processes actually operating in the world; (2) growth of *intellectual integration* in which these different elements and processes are integrated with one another in thought; (3) growth of reflective *perspective* about the conduct of the first two processes, the conception of the problem, and the results which the decision maker desires to achieve." Lloyd S. Etheredge, *Can Governments Learn?* (New York: Pergamon, 1985), 66, emphasis in original.

Etheredge's book and his "Government Learning" (in Samuel Long, ed., *Handbook of Political Behavior* [New York: Plenum, 1981]) are among the first systematic efforts to conceptualize learning by public organizations, even if the lessons learned turn out to be the things the author preferred. The therapeutic component of the theory lies in the emphasis on internal communication, openness, participation, heterodoxy, competition among ideas, and personal creativeness and its rewards. Etheredge explicitly equates government learning with lessons learned by single policy makers. The character of the routines suggested is thought to generalize learning to other decision makers. Abraham Maslow rides high in this approach as in C. Argyris and D.A. Schön, *Organizational Learning* (Reading, Mass.: Addison-Wesley, 1978).

9. I am indebted for this conceptualization to W. Ross Ashby, *Design for a Brain* (New York: John Wiley, 1960, 2nd ed.), especially chs. 1, 5, 9. My treatment of adaptation eschews an argument using evolutionary theory either as metaphor or analogy.

10. John D. Steinbruner, *The Cybernetic Theory of Decision* (Princeton, N.J.: Princeton University Press, 1974). For an excellent summary of this theory, which also goes a long way toward explaining the separate status of the cognitive paradigm, see Robert Cutler, "The Cybernetic Theory Reconsidered," *Michigan Journal of Political Science* 1, 2 (Fall 1981). I have relied on this piece very heavily. Finally, this section draws heavily and gratefully on Janice Gross Stein and Raymond Tanter, *Rational Decision-Making* (Columbus: Ohio State University Press, 1980).

11. Stein and Tanter, *Rational Decision-Making*, 33–34.

12. Cutler, "The Cybernetic Theory Reconsidered," 60 (Table 2, last line).

13. Robert Axelrod, *The Evolution of Cooperation* (New York: Basic Books, 1984) and the GRIT process documented by Deborah Welch Larson in "Crisis Prevention and the Austrian State Treaty," *International Organization* (Winter 1987), 27–60. Robert O. Keohane, "Reciprocity in International Relations," *International Organization* (Winter 1986), 1–27.

14. Cutler, "The Cybernetic Theory Reconsidered," 62 (Table 3 in the original).

15. Figure 2 is adapted from Stein and Tanter, *Rational Decision-Making*, 64 (Fig. 3.1 in the original). The characteristics of the three paradigms with respect to each decisional step are listed on their Table 3.1, p. 65. Figure 3 is adapted from their Fig 3.2, p. 65. I disregard three "paths to choice" as unlikely to be relevant.

16. Stein and Tanter, *Rational Decision-Making*, 46. *Satisficing* is defined on p. 35 and *single-value calculation* on p. 45.

17. The logic of this discussion is derived from Robert D. Putnam, "Diplomacy and Domestic Politics: The Logic of Two-Level Games," *International Organization* 42, 3 (Summer 1988); 427–60. A win-set for any one constituency is "the set of all possible [level 2 and 3] agreements that would 'win'—that is, gain the necessary majority among the constituents—when simply voted up or down " (ibid., 437). Putnam uses the notion of a set as meaning the *number* of possibly acceptable agreements, without worrying about the content of the agreements in terms of the complexity or type of linked issues in the set. Nor is Putnam responsible for my connecting his logic with my concern with bargaining styles.

18. The source of the vocabulary of decomposability is, of course, Herbert Simon's work. For a recent discussion of these distinctions see Simon, *Reason in Human Affairs* (Stanford, Calif.: Stanford University Press, 1983).

19. For evidence of these judgments see Ernst B. Haas, *When Knowledge Is Power* (Berkeley: University of California Press, 1989).

20. James N. Rosenau, "Before Cooperation: Hegemons, Regimes and Habit-Driven Actors," *International Organization* 40, 4 (Autumn 1986), 864–5.

4

Why Competitive Politics Inhibits Learning in Soviet Foreign Policy

Richard D. Anderson, Jr.

Recollect: To recall with additions something not previously known.

— Ambrose Bierce
The Devil's Dictionary[1]

Political competition among Politburo members to shape Soviet foreign policy should inhibit their learning from events or trends in the international situation. Success in political competition depends on the relative persuasiveness to constituents of rival leaders' foreign policy postures, which include both policy recommendations and images of the world situation. When devising foreign policy recommendations, each competitor must simultaneously (a) contemplate world developments, (b) assess the relative persuasiveness of various policy recommendations and associated images of the world situation, and (c) evaluate possible compromises with rivals. According to at least one school of cognitive psychologists, when any person simultaneously considers a variety of information, the probability that the person will learn from any given piece of information is strongly related to the person's previous development of mental organization attuned to that particular information. Mental organization in turn depends on (a) past exposure to information previously comprehended as similar and (b) past motivation to have organized that information into memory. During their rise to the national leadership, Politburo members receive much practice in persuading constituents and in evaluating compromises, and the theory of political competition implies that they have developed strong motivation to learn how to make these assessments. However, most receive much less information about the behavior of foreign governments, and this kind of information has made less difference to most of their careers. Therefore, the probable organization of most Soviet leaders' minds for sensitivity to information about competitive politics should interfere with their prospects for learning from world developments.

Scholarly attention to learning in foreign policy is motivated by concern about how foreign policy changes. Political competition theory, which derives from the work of Schumpeter and Dahl, offers an alternative to the prevalent explanation of change in Soviet foreign policy. Prevalent theories attribute observed change in Soviet foreign policy exclusively to the Politburo's reevaluation of its international situation. According to this explanation, Soviet foreign policy changes when the Politburo recognizes that its existing strategy is not working or that its existing goals have become less urgent or feasible. By contrast, political competition theory says that foreign policy changes in response to variation in the distribution of authority among contenders for leadership, who compete for authority by proposing distinctive foreign policy strategies. The distribution of authority among the leaders may vary because domestic or international developments alter the relative credibility of their foreign policy stands in the eyes of constituents—but policy may also change independently of domestic or international events if leaders change their bargaining strategies or the postures that they use to build authority.

Accordingly, political competition differs from the prevalent theories in expecting foreign policy change normally to occur by "adaptation" rather than by "learning." *Adaptation* refers to a switch from one behavioral routine in the repertoire of an individual or organization to another routine; the second routine may either have previously appeared in the repertoire or be innovated. *Learning* is notorious for the variety of meanings attached to it. In my view, the most general meaning of learning, subsuming all the others, is change in "integrative complexity," i.e., in how a person discriminates among phenomena and therefore in what information the person can recall.

When analysts of Soviet foreign policy argue that the Politburo's reevaluation of the effectiveness of a strategy or of the feasibility or urgency of a goal has produced policy change, they characteristically imply that Soviet decision makers' assessment of the international situation manifests a high degree of integrative complexity. Consider the standard explanations of why the Soviet Union turned to détente in the early 1970s. Analysts' lists of the Politburo's reasons for this policy change characteristically include: West Germany's shift to Ostpolitik, growing hostility from China, U.S. eagerness to withdraw from Vietnam, the attainment of strategic parity, and the promise of international trade to remedy deteriorating Soviet economic performance. Often other factors are added to this list, such as the reinvigoration of the North Atlantic Treaty Organization (NATO) and the Soviet leaders' growing confidence, after the intervention in Czechoslovakia, in their ability to restrain change in Eastern Europe.[2] The Soviet leaders could not have chosen their détente policy by reason of these factors unless they were able to discriminate each development, evaluate it in comparison to considerations weighing against détente, and recall all the positive and negative factors during decision making. Consequently, explanations attributing policy change to reevaluation of the situation customarily impute to the Soviet leaders relatively developed learning about the international situation.

By contrast, normally expecting policy change to occur by adaptation, political competition theory imputes to the Politburo no great degree of learning about the international situation. Rather than depending on a complex evaluation of many factors, the credibility of a contender's whole policy posture may hinge on some single dramatic event. When one contender's credibility declines, policy shifts from the existing compromise toward the alternatives favored by rivals. Although this process places little demand on learning about the international situation, political competition theory does require that Politburo members have developed high integrative complexity enabling them to evaluate the changing persuasiveness of various policy recommendations and the foreign policy postures of rivals.

Whether political competition theory or the reevaluation theories offer a more convincing explanation of change in Soviet foreign policy is a matter for extended empirical investigation. Elsewhere I have offered evidence that political competition theory supplies a more convincing explanation for the shift to détente during the early Brezhnev years.[3] Here my purpose is solely theoretical. On the assumption that political competition theory would survive additional empirical investigation, I will explore this theory's expectations concerning the ability of Soviet foreign policy makers to learn from events or trends in the outside world.

The exploration will proceed in four stages. First, an explanation of how competitive politics shapes and changes foreign policy indicates that in making foreign policy, Politburo members must consider three different categories of information: (1) selected aspects of the international situation, (2) persuasiveness of policy recommendations and images of the outside world in the eyes of domestic constituencies, and (3) policy recommendations of other Politburo members. Second, the intraleadership bargaining caused by political competition produces effects on policy that in some respects mimic the changes in integrative complexity associated with learning. Third, a psychological theory of expert decision making explains why the likelihood that Soviet leaders are particularly familiar with information on the persuasiveness of recommendations and on the acceptability of policy compromises to rivals is likely to interfere with actual, as opposed to mimetic, learning about the international situation. Fourth, a hypothesis to test this expectation against evidence of the verbal and nonverbal behavior of Soviet leaders is presented, and the consequences of this hypothesis for failure to learn from errors in Soviet foreign policy are identified.

The conclusion relates my theory to Haas's long-standing view that learning by public organizations must originate outside politics. Of course, a definition of learning as change in integrative complexity restricts the concept of learning to organisms with brains in which complex integration can develop. Thus my topic is personal learning rather than Haas's organizational learning—yet they come to the same thing. Group learning can be said to occur when individuals in the group develop complementary integrative complexity—e.g., when the students in a political science class learn enough concepts that they can enter the scholarly community defined by the practice of a certain discourse on politics. (Without assuming the possibility of learning by at least some groups, presumably none of us would teach.) Haas's variable "consensus knowledge" is group learning in this sense. In discounting the likelihood that consensus learning among competitive politicians can extend to an elaborated understanding of the world situations that they cite when justifying their policies, political competition theory offers an explanation why Haas has found that politicians must rely on scientists—working in institutional settings quite different from competitive politics—to produce improvements in understanding these situations.

COMPETITIVE POLITICS AND INFORMATION IN SOVIET FOREIGN POLICY

Political competition theory takes two variables—the distribution of different foreign policy postures among competing Politburo members and the selection of compromises among the different policy recommendations implicit in the postures—to be the determinants of Soviet foreign policy. These variables shape policy because foreign policy postures contribute to contending Politburo members' ability to solve their problem of building authority, while bargaining solves their problem of sharing it over time. Central to my purpose here is this point: if these variables explain Soviet foreign policy, they also indicate what information Politburo members consider when they decide about foreign policy.

As Hodnett observes, the crucial problem confronting any Politburo member is how to maintain his or her seat on the Politburo and, if pos-

104

sible, to improve it.[4] To the extent that this problem has even figured in the analysis of Soviet foreign policy, analysts have usually deemed it sufficient to explore the consequences of the dependence of any individual's membership in the Politburo on the continuing approval of the other members, and particularly of the general secretary.[5]

If, however, retention in the Politburo depended solely on peer approval, no member would have any incentive to disagree in public with other members over policy. If a member did dissociate himself publicly from the agreed-on policy, that member would risk giving the others an incentive to remove him from the Politburo. Hence the notion that all Politburo members depend solely on peer approval for their retention in the leadership leads to the prediction that Politburo members will not advocate different policies in public, and many observers claim to find the expected uniformity in Politburo members' public statements. Alternatively this reasoning leads to the prediction that Politburo members who do violate the norm of adherence to the consensus in public statements will pay for this violation by loss of influence within the leadership. Observation of public differences over policy among Politburo members who retain or improve their positions in the leadership would refute both expectations.

By contrast, political competition theory explains observations of public differences among Politburo members with the argument that each member's retention in the Politburo must depend on maintaining approval beyond the member's peers. To achieve retention, any member must first ensure that the Politburo as an institution remains authoritative, i.e., the Politburo must be able to obtain voluntary compliance with its dictates from enough persons beyond its membership to enforce its will on all others. These persons will presumably offer voluntary compliance only if they expect the Politburo's decrees to advance some purposes of their own. Any Politburo member who secured identification with the purposes of these outsiders would be in a position to contribute to maintenance of the authority of the Politburo as a whole; as a result, however, that Politburo member would also be in a position to exact approval for his or her own retention from the rest of the members. In turn, if they did not seek identification with outside supporters, they would find their retention dependent on that member's approval and lack any means of exacting reciprocity. Consequently, for the Politburo to persist as an authoritative institution, at least some Politburo members should seek approval for themselves as individuals from persons outside the Politburo; if these outsiders are too numerous for face-to-face communication, the Politburo members should do so publicly. If several Politburo members act in this manner, the supporters become "constituents," i.e., persons whose continuing approval affects the prospects for a leader's retention of office.

If Soviet leaders seek identification with supporters outside the Politburo, they should offer political "postures" consisting of sets of goals, images describing the situation and justifying those goals as urgent and feasible, and strategies to achieve the goals given the described situation. These postures offer potential supporters *reasons for allegiance* to the leader. Therefore the leader will be more likely to gain allegiance from the supporters if the leader designs the posture with consideration of its persuasiveness to existing audiences of supporters. Successful leaders are likely to be those who have learned to assess the relative persuasiveness to constituents of alternative postures. The distribution of persuasiveness must be one component of the information considered by Soviet leaders in making foreign policy.

The postures of competing leaders must moreover be *different*. Beginning with Downs, many analysts argued on formal grounds that the electoral programs of rival candidates should converge on the point favored by the median constituent. Within a few years of Downs's argument, however, empirical studies of actual leaders in the United States belied this expectation.[6] Downs and subsequent arguments for convergence omitted the consideration that, if competitors for leadership converge on a common program, constituents will lack any reason to prefer one competitor to another. Consequently, each competitor must trade off between: (a) obtaining support from the largest possible share of the available constituents by offering a posture converging on the median point and (b) maintaining constituents' reason to offer support by advocating a posture distinguishable from those of rivals.

If leaders' foreign policy postures differ, then the leaders must decide foreign policy by *bargaining*. Constituents presumably care not only whether a leader has an appealing posture but also whether the leadership as a whole acts on that leader's posture. Consequently, in this bargaining each leader must seek to ensure that the overall policy of the state, both foreign and domestic, conforms no more closely to any rival's posture than to the leader's own. Otherwise constituents, to whom the posture may still appeal, are likely to regard it as futile and may shift their allegiance to a politically more effective rival.

The expectations that the postures must differ and that the policy must be chosen by bargaining indicate two more components of the information that Soviet leaders must consider in deciding foreign policy: (a) they must consider their rivals' postures and (b) they must consider a variety of possible compromises, which they must evaluate according to the compromises' relative persuasiveness to constituencies.

Political competition also encourages Soviet leaders to learn about the international situation, because competition produces incentives for leaders to display *effectiveness* in foreign policy. If a leader's foreign policy recommendations are adopted by the Politburo but fail to achieve progress toward promised effects, the leader should lose credibility in the eyes of constituents. If information that contradicts the leader's image of the international situation reaches constituents, this too should reduce the leader's credibility.

According to political competition theory, leaders' concern for their credibility is the avenue by which international events and trends influence the course of foreign policy. If international developments weaken constituents' credence in the leader's image of the world or block progress toward the achievement of the leader's goals, then the leader is giving the constituents less convincing reasons for voluntary compliance with Politburo instructions. In this case the leader's contribution to the authority of the Politburo diminishes, and rivals' reason to defer to the leader in bargaining over policy also diminishes. Therefore foreign policy will change in response to some international events and trends: specifically, those regarded by the leadership as likely to alter the distribution of constituent credibility among the leaders' postures. Thus, according to political competition theory, a selected subset of information about the international environment must be a final category of information considered by Soviet leaders deciding foreign policy.

In sum, the problem of retaining membership in the Politburo induces Soviet leaders to build authority by developing contrasting substantive postures on foreign policy and to decide policy by bargaining. Consequently, when the Politburo decides on foreign policy, Politburo members have incentives to consider three categories of information: (1) persuasiveness to constituencies, (2) the postures of rivals and possible compromises among their policy recommendations and images of the international situation, and (3) selected information about the international situation expected to bear on the credibility of their policies in constituents' eyes. These categories are, moreover, enumerated in order of strategic priority for the Politburo member. No leader can expect to control bargaining over policy unless the leader's policy recommendations first persuade some constituents; policy effectiveness cannot maintain a leader's credibility in the eyes of constituents unless the policy recommendation first moves through the bargaining to the point of enactment.

MIMICRY OF LEARNING BY COMPETITIVE POLITICS

In certain respects, the effects of both bargaining and authority building on foreign policy may mimic learning about the international situation. Learning is associated with change in integrative complexity and accompanying variation in both the content and flexibility of policy. Bargaining and authority building can separately cause both the state's foreign policy and individual leaders' images of the international situation to display change in integrative complexity, independent of learning about the international situation, in response to variation in competitive circumstances within the leadership. Alternatively, of course, changes in competitive circumstances may simply cause policy to oscillate within the contract zone formed by the expressed preferences of the contending leaders, without any change in integrative complexity.

Bargaining introduces increased complexity both into foreign policy and into leaders' images of the international situation. When each rival for leadership advocates a different strategy justified by a different image of the international situation, trade offs among these images and strategies during bargaining are likely to produce a foreign policy marked by a balance of conflicting purposes and information.

George Breslauer's chapter in this volume (Chapter 15) offers a useful example of how bargaining introduces complexity into policy. He notes that over time Soviet policy toward the Middle East displayed a shifting mix of four orientations. Although Breslauer examines attitudes of officials below the supreme leadership, within the Politburo one leader was the principal representative of each of these orientations in global policy. Shelepin advocated an extreme form of sectarian extremism and Brezhnev (until 1969) a moderate form, Kosygin (and Brezhnev after 1969) advocated a collaborative international strategy that encompassed occasional efforts for U.S.–Soviet crisis management in the Middle East, and Podgorny advocated what Breslauer calls "ecumenical activism," a strategy of promoting anti–U.S. coalitions with foreign governments regardless of their ideological orientation. Given bargaining among adherents of these contrasting postures and variation over time in their relative credibility, one should not be surprised to find that Soviet policy combined the different orientations in varying mixes at different stages or that the enacted policy was more complex than the policy preferred by any individual leader.

Bargaining can also change the complexity of individual leaders' statements on foreign policy. In competitive politics, rival leaders use their public statements not only to appeal to their own followers but to offer bargaining concessions to rivals and to signal acceptance of compromises. Because the process of policy bargaining is ongoing, whenever the observer cuts into the process, he or she should expect to find each contender for leadership offering a mix of images and policy recommendations, including some favored by the contender and some conceded to rivals. Thus Soviet leaders' statements on foreign policy frequently manifest a complex design in which a variety of arguments for a certain policy are followed by a *however* or a *but* introducing the advocacy of a contrasting policy.

Complexity of policy and leaders' commentary may also vary over time as bargaining produces a rearrangement of issue linkages and a change in the uniformity of images used to justify foreign policy. Variation in issue linkages arises because leaders find that issue separation eases the search for acceptable compromises. By defining issues as separable, rival leaders increase the number of possible issue trades and consequently enlarge the bargaining space.

Policies chosen by issue trading can be rationalized by a single uniform image of the international situation or by multiple, contrasting images. Policies subordinated to multiple images typically feature self-contradictory rationales. For example, the rationale for the post-Khrushchev bid for rapprochement with Maoist China combined Brezhnev's image of Chinese willingness to negotiate a reconciliation with his rivals' image of a reconciliation achieved by obtaining Chinese concessions on all the issues of ideology and domestic and foreign policy in dispute between the two national leaderships. Not surprisingly, this Soviet policy failed to produce any progress in Sino-Soviet talks.

Issue trading can produce variation in the complexity of policy because leaders can engage either in separate one-for-one swaps or in some more complex combination. For example, an issue trade during early 1965 resulted in a policy that U.S. escalation in Vietnam prohibited further diplomatic initiatives toward the United States and any of its main European allies. Further bargaining produced a more complex compromise in which the prohibition on diplomatic initiatives was confined to bilateral U.S.–Soviet issues and the Vietnam issue was cited to justify new initiatives toward a variety of West European states.

Authority building can produce variation in complexity separately from bargaining. Leaders may find they can build authority in a given constituency by identifying themselves with some single value of greatest importance to those constituents. But they may also want to assemble a constituency that represents a coalition of persons who are most attracted by different, competing values. In the latter case a leader will offer a more complex posture.

For example, in the immediate post-Khrushchev leadership, Podgorny, whose place in the leadership was vulnerable, designed a posture that in retrospect looks remarkably shrewd. In both foreign and domestic policy Podgorny positioned himself as a moderate relative to the two principal rivals Brezhnev and Kosygin. Podgorny justified his posture, which promoted a global coalition combining radical states and cooperative capitalist governments against the United States, as avoiding the extremes both of Brezhnev's proposals to wall off the socialist from the capitalist countries and of Kosygin's excessive confidence in U.S. restraint from global interventionism. In order to appear as a moderate, however, Podgorny necessarily defined a more complex image of the outside world than either Brezhnev or Kosygin.

Change in the complexity of a leader's posture is particularly likely to accompany shifts in the composition of the constituency. Although political competition theory basically expects a given leader's global posture to remain stable over time, this basic expectation does not apply when a leader decides to attempt expansion of the constituency—to enter the phase of "inclusion."

The leader engaged in inclusion attempts to expand the constituency by a developing a new posture that combines (a) previous appeals intended to retain original constituents with (b) selective incorporation of variants of rivals' proposals intended to lure some of their constituents.[7] Consequently an inclusion posture will display more complex design than the original posture. Inclusion postures typically contain arguments that the success of the leader's original policy proposals justifies a shift to new policies. An example is Brezhnev's 1971 argument for arms control (a variant of Kosygin's earlier proposal, which Brezhnev incorporated into his own inclusion posture). Brezhnev argued that his own earlier doubts about U.S. readiness to negotiate had been justified but that the successes of his military program and Soviet economic progress would now compel U.S. concessions in the Strategic Arms Limitation Treaty (SALT) talks.[8]

In addition to producing increased complexity in the leader's public posture, inclusion behavior by an ascendant leader will also produce policy change that imitates learning. An ascendant leader is one whose authority markedly exceeds that of any rival. Increasing a leader's control over policy, ascendancy allows the leader to impose increasing integration across issues and more uniformity on the image that rationalizes a policy, as well as enabling the policy to become more flexible. All these changes look like learning.

An ascendant leader should design the inclusion posture with an eye to the ensuing bargaining over policy. If rivals' postures differ, their differences will produce at least some issue cleavages dividing them. The ascendant leader can incorporate into the inclusion posture intermediate proposals on those issues. In the bargaining these proposals will occupy a pivot, which enables the leader's proposals to define policy on those issues, since movement of the ascendant leader's proposals with respect to any rival's preferences gains in support from one rival what is lost in support from others. Occupancy of the pivot will be stable, as rivals cannot eliminate the pivot by altering their postures except at the expense of accelerating the erosion of their appeal to constituents. The ascendant leader's prospect of controlling policy also improves because this leader is now backed by a larger constituency, which has expanded to include any of the rivals' formerly marginal constituents who prefer the ascendant leader's intermediate proposal to the postures of rivals.

In the presence of a pivot, bargaining shows a greater tendency to integrate policies across issues and to subordinate policy to some unified image of the situation. As the leader's recommendation will be the compromise outcome on every issue for which the leader occupies a pivot, the separation of these issues is no longer required in order to increase the availability of possible compromises. Since these issues are no longer involved in issue trading, the policy rationale need no longer combine multiple images; instead the rationale in the leader's inclusion posture becomes the uniform image justifying policy on those issues. Of course, on issues for which the leader does not occupy the pivot, bargaining may continue to display the previous pattern of issue separation and subordination to multiple images of the situation.

Because the removal of contradictions in images of the situation and the recognition of interrelationships among issues formerly thought to be separate are hallmarks of learning, the foreign policies of an inclusion stage sometimes appear to outsiders as if learning has taken place. Less separation of issues can also increase flexibility in international negotiations, when ability to integrate issues in the domestic bargaining enables the ascendant leader to make more issue trades in the international bargaining. For example, integration of formerly separate Soviet policies toward Western Europe and toward the United States promoted détente by enabling Brezhnev to make a concession to the United States when the Soviets stopped trying to negotiate European security at a forum excluding the United States and instead accepted U.S. participation in what became the Helsinki Conference. Increasing integration of issues and greater policy flexibility led Marshall Shulman to speculate that the détente policies of Brezhnev's inclusion stage (1970 to early 1973) showed a "learning trend," a greater recognition that the dangers of strategic confrontation outweighed the importance of regional disputes like Nixon's mining of the Haiphong harbor.[9] But if the change represented learning by the Politburo, dramatic change should have been observed in the global postures of all the senior Soviet leaders, instead of its having been confined to Brezhnev, as would be expected from the hypothesis of inclusion. Moreover, if the Politburo had learned to refrain from strategic confrontation, the Soviet Union should never have delivered the arms for either Egypt's attack on Israel in October 1973 or the final North Vietnamese offensive in 1975.

In sum, when observers study learning in a foreign policy produced by political competition, their observations must control for the effects of variation in bargaining and in the composition of leaders' constituencies. Over time these processes can change the complexity of policy, the degree of integration across issues, and the degree of uniformity of images contained in rationales for policy.

One might of course argue that such changes count as learning—and perhaps they should, in some minimal sense. Rather than learning from the international situation directly, leaders may learn new information or new conceptions of the international situation from the mutual exchange of viewpoints during political bargaining. As I shall demonstrate below, however, neither bargaining and nor shifts in authority building raise the integrative complexity displayed by Soviet leaders above a very low ceiling. Furthermore, exposure to rivals' images of the world situation does not correct the errors that Soviet leaders make as the result of their own oversimplified images. For these reasons the changes in leaders' rhetoric seem more likely to represent their choice to vary the integrative complexity within a space below that ceiling and already available to the leaders, rather than to mark the raising of that ceiling that would constitute real learning. If so, the appearance of learning created by bargaining and shifts in authority building would be mimetic.

PSYCHOLOGICAL THEORIES OF EXPERT DECISION MAKING

In attributing change in the complexity of both foreign policy and leaders' commentary on the international situation to variations in competitive circumstances within the leadership and its constituencies, political competition theory portrays leaders as experts in responding to and manipulating these circumstances. Psychologists who study expert performance conclude that experts differ from novices mainly in their ability to remember more information about the situations in which their expertise enables superior performance. Their ability to consider more information during decision making depends on having previously developed a "content-specific" mental organization tailored to that information. Requiring extended experience with the information in question and the learning of appropriate motivation, this mental organization also affects the prospects that an expert will learn from novel information. In the presence of familiar cues, the mental organization that makes expertise possible will interfere with learning from, or even noticing, novel cues. This line of argument suggests that if Soviet leaders are experts at domestic political competition, learning from the international situation may be very hard for them.

Emphasizing that retention of authority will vary with the effectiveness of a leader's policy recommendations, political competition theory implies that Soviet leaders have an *interest* in learning about the international situation, albeit less interest than in learning constituency attitudes and rivals' postures. As Robert Jervis observes, however, "Knowing what a person's interests are does not tell us how he will see his environment or go about selecting the best route to reach his goals."[10]

To address these problems of perception and choice, Jervis and others have turned to theories borrowed from cognitive and social psychologists.[11] These fields of psychology feature a great multitude of theories. The

overlaps and mutual contradictions among all these psychological theories raise the question of how political scientists should decide which
theory to borrow. Jervis adopted an eclectic approach of drawing suggestive
propositions from psychological theories regardless of whether the source
theories were mutually consistent.[12] Deborah Welch Larson has used
political documents to test which psychological theory best accounts for
the behavior of national leaders in a particular case.[13] An alternative approach
is to decide by psychological criteria which theory is most convincing
and to use that theory to generate hypotheses about the expected behavior
of political leaders across cases.

The particular theories borrowed by Jervis—cognitive dissonance, cognitive
consistency seeking, attribution theory, and prospect theory—have been
seriously challenged by other psychologists who raise issues of the ecological
validity of the experiments through which the theories developed. In
particular, these critics have amassed evidence questioning whether any
laboratory experiment, and especially ones presenting inexperienced subjects
with unfamiliar, insignificant tasks and at most very brief training, can
reproduce the conditions that trigger competent performance.[14] Assuming that national political leaders making foreign policy are experienced
subjects competently performing tasks familiar to them, I have therefore
preferred to draw on psychological theories developed through study of
experts in the performance of their special skills.

As the main issue for understanding both performance and learning,
these theories identify the determination of how a decision maker represents
the task.[15] The answer depends on what the decision maker remembers
about the task, and that depends in turn on what the decision maker
already knows.

Experimental observation indicates that the degree of expertness in
performance is related to the ability to recall information, but that this
ability is content-specific, i.e., experts can remember much more information
than novices about the specific content of their expertise, but experts
perform no better at remembering information in general. The original
experiments by Herbert Simon with chess players showed that improvements in competitive performance in chess correlated with more ability
to replace chess pieces in the correct locations on a empty board after a
brief glimpse of the original board. However, more expert chess players
manifest this superior ability only when the original positioning of the
pieces is taken from an actual game and not when the pieces have been
placed randomly on the board. Similar results have been obtained in
observations of competitors in bridge, the Asian board game *go*, distance
running, marksmanship, long jumping, basketball and volleyball, table
tennis, skiing, and baseball; of noncompetitive experts, particularly pianists
and other musicians, typists, and Morse code operators; and of cognitive

development in young children.[16] The range of these observations indicates that physical and intellective skills are identical in this respect. Content specificity is evidently a general feature of human thought. Judith Reitman summarizes the findings of this research:

> Experts differ from nonexperts more in perceptual-memorial abilities than in logical, problem solving abilities normally thought characteristic of thinking. There is something about the expert's accrued past experience and the similarity of the current situation to that experience that allows him to reduce masses of specialized information, without concomitant loss of detail, into units his limited capacity can handle.[17]

The dependence of all performance on "accrued past experience" is the fundamental critique of the experiments through which psychologists developed the theories that have previously been applied to foreign policy research. As the child development specialist Ann Brown comments, "Experimental psychologists often operate as if they wished to control for . . . developmental variations in knowledge as a source of extraneous variability"[18] even though variations in prior learning are the main source of variability in performance.

Placement of variations in expertise at the center of theoretical attention has developed a new conception of learning—an approach that I call *cognitive constructivism*. This new approach is still far from understanding mind, but I would join its advocates in arguing that constructivism progresses beyond alternative conceptions and would additionally suggest that their findings are rich in implications for politics. Constructivism is an alternative to all four conceptions of individual learning distinguished by Philip Tetlock: (1) change in cognitive *content* or the transition from one belief system to another, (2) change in cognitive *structure* from less to more elaborate or vice versa, (3) change in *efficiency* of action to greater "adeptness or adroitness," and (4) rational adjustment to change in the incentives presented by the international situation. (Tetlock's fifth category, institutional learning, is seen as an epiphenomenon of learning at the individual level.)

While cognitive constructivism shares with Tetlock's cognitive structuralism the emphasis on change in integrative complexity as the crux of learning (and indeed many students of expertise, including Simon and Reitman, should be classified as structuralists), constructivism differs from structuralism in regarding content, efficiency, and recognition of shifts in incentives not as distinctive approaches to learning, but instead as *aspects* of change in integrative complexity.

The fundamental difference between cognitive constructivism and cognitive structuralism concerns how the mind is organized. Structuralists see the mind as a *hierarchy* consisting of few abstractions or goals at the top, cause-and-effect linkages at the middle level, and many concrete experiences at the bottom.[19] Constructivists view mental organization as *heterarchy.*[20] In a heterarchy, the lowest level consists of abstract units of information, with the precise unit depending on the particular information to be organized. Intermediate levels consist of many increasingly complex combinations of the lowest-level units, with each unit incorporated into many different combinations. The top level integrates the intermediate combinations into a potentially unlimited variety of possible intentions to act.[21] Hierarchies narrow toward the top; heterarchies widen. In structuralists' hierarchy, the goals are abstract and the experiences concrete; in constructivists' heterarchies, the experiences are abstract and the intentions are concrete.

A cognitive constructivist's classic example of a heterarchy is a natural language.[22] In English, about 50 phonemes occupy the lowest level; each is an abstraction of a range of sounds produced by English speakers. Thousands of syllables, hundreds of thousands of words, many millions of possible sentences and even more narratives occupy ascending intermediate levels. A capacity to intend an infinity of meanings is at the top. Another example of a heterarchy is knowledge of how to play chess. The abstract units are the 32 chessmen and 64 squares; the intermediate levels are many possible arrangements of a few chessmen into strong or weak formations on the board, and many more possible board positions consisting of various combinations of those formations; and the top level is a very large inventory of strategies for winning the game by transitioning from less to more favorable board positions.

As these examples suggest, cognitive constructivism emphasizes that any person's mind must consist of many distinct special-purpose heterarchies, not of any single multipurpose hierarchy.[23] Constructivists understand these special-purpose heterarchies not as *holding the content* of a person's knowledge but as *being* the knowledge.[24] Their viewpoint cannot be understood without a radical break from the family of metaphors that English has accustomed us to use in thinking about mind, for the very term *content* implies that the mind "holds" (contains) information, "comprehends" (prehensilely takes hold of) ideas.[25] Structuralists often distinguish "procedural" or "knowing how" knowledge from "declarative" or "knowing that" knowledge. A structuralist might regard a political leader's belief system as the declarative content of the leader's procedural mental organization. To Guy Claxton, by contrast, this distinction characterizes not mind but the structuralist's assumptions: "declarative and procedural knowledge are not basically different types of knowledge; they are . . . different questions we can ask about what we know . . . ."[26] To a constructivist, a political leader's belief system would be an observed feature, inferred from the leader's communicative and other behavior,[27] produced by a mental heterarchy observable only in the organization of the leader's expression of beliefs.

Similarly, to constructivists, adeptness or adroitness is also an observable feature of behavior produced by the presence of a heterarchy. To qualify as adept or adroit, a person must match any change in circumstances with appropriate change in behavior. This characterization is just as apt when the circumstances that change are conceived to be "incentives" as it is when the circumstances are conceived to be changes in the positioning of chess pieces on a board. The expert's increasingly numerous discriminations at ascending intermediate levels enable him or her to make fine distinctions between one situation and another, and the very large number of possible intended actions enables the expert to generate a behavior tailored specifically for that situation.

When constructivists take developmental variation in knowledge as crucial to understanding performance, information about developmental processes becomes necessary to predict what a person will learn.[28] Development of elaborate heterarchies appears to depend minimally on two prerequisites: practice over very numerous trials with consistent feedback leading to simplification and abstraction of the representation of the experience; and a motivation that impels the learner to abandon memorial strategies until finding one appropriate for abstracting and integrating simplified cues from the repeated experience. Novices attempt to represent situations by considering as many aspects of the situation as they can, including many irrelevant ones.[29] But because they have not yet developed appropriate strategies for integrating only the relevant cues, they shift from one aspect of a situation to another, losing consistency in the process. Expertise develops by contrast when the learner begins to isolate from the situation certain cues, suitable for higher-order integration, from the total stimulus presented by the situation.[30]

In effect, to become expert in recalling some information, a person must learn to ignore other information that may be present. The need to ignore information is a consequence of the multiplicity of heterarchies existing in any person's mind. Constructivists deny the existence of any central executive that regulates which heterarchy becomes active at a given time. The possibility that information will maintain activation of any particular heterarchy therefore depends on mechanisms that resist conscious or unconscious noticing of information likely to activate other heterarchies.[31]

While enabling the remarkable performances of memory and flexibility that we admire as expert, the expert's learned tunnel vision has a cost: "interference." This phenomenon is familiar to anyone who has begun learning a second language. When speech in the native language is audible, the learner cannot comprehend even minimally complex speech or text presented in the second language. During the 1970s constructivists studying a variety of cognitive activities converged on "the working hypothesis that the same cognitive principles are operating in both comprehension and learning."[32] If comprehension and learning are two ways of referring to the same process, then the presence of information that someone comprehends should interfere with learning, and the interference with novel information will be greater, the more expertise the person displays. In short, if a person's expertise interferes with remembering novel information, and if a person cannot learn from information that the person cannot remember, then expertise with familiar information will impair learning of unfamiliar information.

In application to Soviet political leaders, the constructivists' hypothesis about the improbability of learning from novel information in the presence of familiar cues implies that Politburo members are unlikely to learn about international situations. From a very early stage in their careers, Communist Party procedures have obligated future Politburo members to demonstrate knowledge of arguments persuasive to officials. The system of adult political education compels party members to participate in lecturing the general population on party policy. This experience probably offers the lecturer little information on the persuasiveness of policy arguments to the popular audience, which is reported to react mainly with passivity, but preparation of draft lectures and obtaining party superiors' approval for the drafts affords consistent feedback on persuasiveness to officials.[33] As the Politburo member rises through an official career, continuing participation in committee decision making, "premised on the existence of conflicting organizational interests,"[34] affords the future Politburo member extended practice in evaluating the acceptability to other officials of compromise proposals.

While Politburo members therefore have extended experience with the persuasiveness of policy arguments to the members of future constituencies and with evaluation of compromises, very few of them obtain much experience in dealing with foreign officials (except, perhaps, from Eastern Europe). Among Politburo members one might cite Gromyko, the long-time foreign minister, and Andropov, former head of the KGB, as exceptions to this generalization. But even in their case, diplomats and intelligence officials in any government (and especially in the Soviet government) spend far more time talking to other officials of their own government than to foreigners.

Consequently, when Politburo members decide foreign policy, they must make some very practiced evaluations (the relative persuasiveness to constituents of information about the international situation and the relative acceptability of possible policy compromises) and some relatively unpracticed evaluations (effects of Soviet policies on foreign states' behavior, reasons for foreign states' actions). Their probable expertise in evaluating persuasiveness to constituents and policy compromises is likely to interfere with their evaluation of the international situation. That is, they are likely to form perceptions of the international situation by the criterion of persuasiveness to their various constituencies and usefulness in justifying policy compromises and to use images chosen on these grounds to represent the international situation, instead of forming their perceptions of the international situation by monitoring the situation itself. Literally, they will lack the prior learning necessary to remember information about the international situation that would enable them to correct and improve their perceptions. Consequently over time they are unlikely to learn from the international situation by forming a heterarchy appropriate to the international context. Their beliefs about the international situation are unlikely to change as the situation changes or to become more discriminating over time; they are unlikely to become more adept or adroit at manipulation of the situation; and incentives present in the international situation will fail to affect their policy choices.

This hypothesis should be understood as qualified by recognition that expertise in any specialty is somewhat helpful in organizing information about problems in general. Most people can see the obvious. Therefore one should assume that Soviet leaders will make some limited discriminations about international situations. In fact, political competition theory requires some such assumption. If Soviet leaders and their constituencies were entirely oblivious to events and trends in the international situation, these events and trends could not affect the distribution of credibility among the leaders, and this mechanism of policy change could not occur.

The question is, what events will be "obvious"? This question can be addressed (although scarcely answered) by considering how people solve problems at which they are novices. In a series of subtle experiments Amos Tversky and Daniel Kahneman have shown that novices display a strong propensity to misestimate probabilities.[35] Constructivists would accept Tversky and Kahneman's experimental findings but reject their interpretation.[36] In contrast to Tversky and Kahneman's interpretation ascribing the misestimates of probability to three "heuristics" supposedly fundamental to all human reasoning, Whiting comments that any model identifying a "general-purpose acquisition strategy" (e.g., their three heuristics) should be regarded as "inapplicable to any skilled performance."[37] Instead of heuristics, the reason for the misestimates observed by Tversky and Kahneman could be novices' usual propensities to incorporate irrelevant information and not to incorporate enough information into problem solving.

A constructivist reinterpretation would attribute Tversky and Kahneman's findings to their subjects' lack of knowledge relevant to evaluating the probability distributions presented in the experiments. This reinterpretation would begin with the experimental observation that novices' probability assessments vary with the number of probability terms discriminated by the assessor.[38] The simplest discrimination is between sure things and uncertain prospects. Consequently, as the probability of an event increases to closely approximate certainty, novices' performance in judging relative probability should improve markedly, as a step function. Some experiments confirm this expectation. The errors found by Tversky and Kahneman in novices' responses to one problem asking them to distinguish close relative probabilities became less frequent as the gap between the relative probabilities widened and much less frequent when the difference approached one.[39] Similar results have been found on other problems.[40]

This finding—that even novices' errors markedly diminish as probabilities approach certainty—can be applied to foreign policy by considering how much discrimination would be required for a constituent or a rival to decide whether an international event or trend had discredited an image offered by a Politburo member. Some events directly contradict images: for example, U.S. bombing of North Vietnam in 1965 directly contradicted Kosygin's expressed hope that the United States would refrain from escalation. At the same time, the bombing did not contradict Brezhnev's expressed concern that the United States might escalate. Consequently, Kosygin's credibility should have decreased relative to Brezhnev's, and policy accordingly moved toward Brezhnev's preference for increased Soviet aid to North Vietnam. In contrast, events or trends that require even slightly complicated analysis to determine their relation to a leader's image are unlikely to affect credibility. Competing leaders are therefore often able to offer opposite analyses of the international situation without apparent influence on the credibility of each rival in the eyes of their respective supporters. Instead of changing people's opinions, advocacy of contending arguments stabilizes the distribution of constituency attitudes.[41] Opinion research has found that some dramatic events dilute constituents' credence in a particular argument without converting them to an opposing viewpoint.

RESTRICTIONS ON LEARNING AND ERRORS IN SOVIET FOREIGN POLICY

Consideration of Politburo members' developmental experience suggests that they should know much more about constituency attitudes and the acceptability of compromises than about the international situation. Consequently, when making foreign policy, they should be expected to form their perceptions of the international situation, not by monitoring complex information about the situation, but by evaluating the relative persuasiveness of various images of the international situation to their own and rivals' constituents. Given the absence of direct information about the Soviet leaders' perceptions—as opposed to their expressed images—of the international situation, how can observers ever confirm or disconfirm this expectation? Here I offer a hypothesis and an account of my own and others' observations to show that the integrative complexity of Soviet leaders' images of the international situation appears substantially lower than the integrative complexity of their images of their own competitive politics. The disparity between the two contexts in Soviet leaders' integrative complexity, and especially the failure of the integrative complexity of Soviet leaders' images of the international situation to vary outside a quite restricted range, argue strongly in favor of the hypothesis. The impact of interference from competitive politics on learning about international situations is evident in the record of errors, characteristically featuring neglect of relevant information, in Soviet leaders' foreign policy decisions.

I have argued that Soviet leaders have learned much more about domestic political competition than about international situations. Learning is marked by change in integrative complexity allowing for a degree of discrimination among features of a situation appropriate for analysis of that situation. If situations are simple, learning will produce simplicity of representation as the learner discards irrelevancies; if situations are complex, learning will manifest more complex representations. (Consider for example the difference in learned representations of tic-tac-toe and chess.) If political competition theory offers a valid explanation of state foreign policies, international situations must generally be more complex than political competition at home. The international situation, comprising the foreign policies of many states, will be determined by the interaction of the political competitions in many states, while the domestic political competition takes place only among the leaders within the particular state. Therefore, if Soviet leaders displayed equally apt learning about both situations, their image of the international situation would display more integrative complexity than their image of the domestic political situation. Observations show the reverse of this expectation.

Integrative complexity can be observed by the number of discriminations in a person's image of a situation. Analyses of Soviet leaders' public statements about the international situation consistently find remarkably low degrees of discrimination. Most attention has been devoted to arguments that the propensity of states to issue initiatives for collaboration is associated with increases in the integrative complexity of their images of the international scene. Thus Snyder and Diesing's review of international crises finds that, across governments, "soft-liners" favoring cooperative

crisis resolution are "much more sensitive to divisions within the opposing government." The "hard-liners" see "no point in paying much attention
to the opponents' internal divisions . . . ."[42]   The most careful measurement of covariation between initiatives for collaboration or competition
and change in the integrative complexity of rhetoric has been undertaken
by Tetlock.   He concludes: "For both the United States and the Soviet
Union, low integrative complexity was associated with undertaking major military-political interventions in other countries . . . ; high integrative
complexity was associated with the successful culmination of negotiations
on issues that had been major sources of tension in the superpower relationship . . . ."[43]

While valid and unquestionably important, the focus of these studies
on variations in integrative complexity diverts attention from the point
that, even when the integrative complexity of Soviet and American leaders'
images of the international situation peaks, it remains remarkably low.
While corroborating Snyder and Diesing's finding that advocates of cooperative diplomacy comment more about divisions in other governments, my own review of all Politburo speeches and writings during
1964–1967 and 1970–1972 found no instances in which a Politburo member distinguished more than two points of view within an opposing government (e.g., "imperialist" versus "sober-thinking" factions) or classified
the states in any global region into more than two categories (e.g., "progressive" and "reactionary" states in the Third World). In many instances
Politburo members described a foreign government or group of governments as monolithic.[44]   Tetlock's findings reinforce the point.   Although
Tetlock devised a seven-point scale, his review of "official policy statements"
by the U.S and Soviet governments, encompassing every three-month
interval from 1945 through 1986, never found a quarter in which the
statements' "mean integrative complexity" exceeded the midpoint on the
scale—and there were only six quarters during which either government's
score exceeded 3 on his scale.[45] This finding emerged even when Tetlock
discarded the five lowest scores in each quarter (half his data).

Moreover, Tetlock found that national leaders failed to integrate different aspects of their assessments of world situations. Tetlock's integrative
complexity measure combines a measure of "differentiation" with a measure
of "integration." Rather than assessing differentiation in images of foreign
governments, Tetlock measured differentiation by the "number of evaluatively
independent dimensions of judgment" used in interpreting events. He
then separately measured "integration" by whether the leader isolated
the evaluative dimensions ("low"), recognized trade-offs between pairs
of dimensions ("medium"), or recognized contingent relationships among
multiple dimensions ("high"). The score of 3—the maximum mean for
any quarter—was assigned to statements displaying medium to high

differentiation but low integration.[46] In other words, although the leaders observed by Tetlock offered a variety of justifications in recommending their policies, they generally failed even to recognize the presence of trade-offs among the various justifications by which they sought to gain approval for their proposals.

Accordingly, despite variation depending on a leader's policy preferences, the integrative complexity of national leaders' commentary on the international situation is consistently low. Soviet leaders' responses to domestic competitive circumstances, by contrast, display a higher degree of integrative complexity than their commentary on the international situation.

Political competitors should manifest a high degree of discrimination with regard to the persuasiveness of their postures to constituencies and with regard to the possible compromises defined by rivals' policy recommendations. Observers cannot easily see Politburo members' discrimination of the relative persuasiveness of their postures to constituencies. Indeed, the only reason for an observer to infer that Politburo members monitor their persuasiveness to constituencies is the evidence that some Soviet leaders carefully individuate their public postures. However, the core hypotheses of political competition theory include an expectation that observable policies will always represent compromises among the observable policy recommendations of rival leaders. A finding that a large number of observed policies consistently conformed to the expectations of a bargaining model applied to the observed policy recommendations would be hard to understand without the assumption that the Soviet policy makers were taking into account each others' expressed preferences. Hence the number of different recommendations can be taken as an index of the degree of discrimination in each rival Politburo member's perception of his competitive circumstances.

Analysis of bargaining indicates that Politburo members' discrimination of rivals' policy recommendations varied by issue. A few of the compromises found in my analysis of issue trading during the first half of the Brezhnev period would have demanded no higher level of discrimination than the dichotomous classifications often manifest in Politburo members' descriptions of foreign governments. For example, the policy adopted during 1965 of reducing the implicit subsidy to most Eastern European governments represented a compromise between Politburo opponents and advocates of economic reform. But most of the compromises demanded substantially more elaborate discrimination. Four to six distinct recommendations affected Soviet policy toward Vietnam. Five to nine distinct stances can be observed in the making of Soviet policy toward China in 1965. Five separate stances influenced policy toward Western Europe during 1966–1967.

Brezhnev's détente strategy shows the complexity of Politburo members' representations of their domestic competition. Brezhnev's strategy discriminated between Kosygin's advocacy of, and Podgorny and Suslov's resistance to, U.S.–Soviet cooperation. He defined a pivot intermediate between these two poles. In order to cross-pressure the opposition, he discerned issues dividing Podgorny from Suslov and also separating both of them from other opponents of détente such as Petr Shelest. He also perceived inducements useful for converting less powerful figures, including the defense minister Grechko, the Central Committee officials Kirilenko and Pel'she, and Kosygin's deputy Mazurov, into supporters of his policy. To carry out his strategy, Brezhnev must have kept track of policy preferences on several issues for at least seven different leaders. Since the success of a pivot strategy of the kind used by Brezhnev depends on each other bargainer's awareness of the relationship among the pivot, their own recommendations, and the alternatives, all the other leaders must also have been using the same complex perception of the bargaining.

In sum, in bargaining within the Politburo Soviet leaders manifest a range of discrimination substantially exceeding (although overlapping at the low end) the discrimination evident in their images of foreign governments. This finding is the reverse of what one should expect if Soviet leaders were equally likely to learn about their own competitive politics and about more complex international politics.

Two objections might be raised to this tentative conclusion. First, it is sometimes supposed that the images of the international situation in public statements by political leaders are merely instrumental and that they use some more sophisticated perception in private formulation of policy. Second, I have of course compared two different manifestations of integrative complexity: Soviet leaders' statements about the international situation with the process of policy compromise within the Politburo. One behavior is verbal, the other nonverbal.

The former objection cannot be directly refuted by observations of the Soviet case, as no records are available of private deliberations over foreign policy by the Politburo. One may note that the level of integrative complexity observed by Tetlock in Politburo statements approximates the level found in U.S. government statements. Some records of private deliberations by U.S. leaders are available. In the recently published minutes and transcripts of tape recordings of White House deliberations during the Cuban missile crisis, President Kennedy and his advisers never distinguish more than two policy preferences (soft and hard lines) in their discussions of Soviet purposes, and Kennedy strongly prefers a monolithic image of Soviet motives. Their statements also do not contain any more complex images of any other foreign governments.[47] This limited degree of discrimination replicates that observed in both Soviet public statements and (by Snyder and Diesing) in the public statements of a variety of other governments.

The latter objection raises the issue of whether the oversimplifications in Soviet leaders' verbal commentary on the international situation correspond with errors in policy making. If the integrative complexity of Soviet leaders' perceptions of the international situation were as low as the observed range of discrimination in their images, then observers should expect that their conduct of policy would manifest the errors expected from novice decision making: i.e., incorporation of irrelevant information and neglect of relevant information.

My survey of Soviet foreign policy during the first half of the Brezhnev era discovered many errors featuring these novice traits. At the outset I should note that not all misrepresentations of the international situations in Soviet leaders' public statements bear the unintentional character necessary to qualify as errors. Consider for example the disagreement in late 1970 between Suslov and Brezhnev over whether the Bundestag was likely to ratify the Moscow Treaty on Renunciation of Force signed in August. Even when the Bundestag ultimately did ratify the treaty in 1972, ratification never gained a majority: the vote was 248 for, 10 against, and 238 abstentions. In the interim the treaty had survived a vote of no confidence in the Brandt government by two votes and passage through a Bundestag committee by one vote. Twenty months in advance, an accurate estimate of the treaty's chances for ratification should have given its prospects as slightly better than even. Had both Brezhnev (who sponsored the treaty) and Suslov (whose global posture oriented him against it) converged on an accurate representation of the treaty's prospects, their images of this crucial feature of the international situation would not have satisfied their joint need to maintain differentiation. According to political competition theory, in political competitors' priorities, maintenance of differentiation should outrank the credibility of their images. Consequently each of them deviated slightly from the accurate estimate. Suslov rated the treaty's prospects as no better than even, while Brezhnev expressed confidence that the treaty's German backers would overcome its opponents. Looking very much as if each man intentionally shaded his estimate, this instance seems to be a case in which the limitation on the complexity of leaders' images of foreign governments to no more than a dichotomous representation still allowed both Brezhnev and Suslov to consider their competitive requirements together with enough information about the West German situation for an accurate image. Thus their misrepresentations of this situation do not appear to have been errors.

In contrast, many examples display what appear to be unintentional biases in Soviet leaders' assessments of their international situation. A bias can be inferred to be unintentional when the leader suffers competitive disadvantage from the discrediting of the misestimate. An example is Brezhnev's selection of the NATO proposal for a multilateral force (MLF) as his proof of the aggressiveness of capitalist governments. Brezhnev incorporated irrelevant information in the form of his insistence on the severity of the MLF's nuclear threat to Soviet security. Adding only 200 missiles on vulnerable surface ships to the 1,000 invulnerable Minuteman, 600 bombers, and hundreds of Polaris missiles already in the U.S. strategic arsenal, the MLF added marginally to the threat. The constraint on the complexity of leaders' images of the international situation caused Brezhnev to neglect relevant information. He depicted an uncertain prospect as a sure thing by his denial of any significance to complex negotiations within NATO over whether to deploy MLF. Two days after Brezhnev launched his campaign against MLF, President Johnson decided to end U.S. support of the proposal. Instead of revising his image of the NATO threat when news of Johnson's decision arrived, Brezhnev instead intensified his insistence on the urgency of blocking MLF. When internal disagreements caused NATO to abandon the project six months later, Brezhnev found himself bereft of an issue to give credence to his image of an urgent nuclear threat to European security. The resulting loss of credibility left him unable to resist rivals' pressures for a new round of diplomatic initiatives to Western European countries in the fall of 1965.

During the first half of Brezhnev's tenure, neglect of relevant information caused every senior Politburo member to advance an image of the international situation built around fundamental misjudgments that soon disadvantaged him in the competition when discredited by international events. Brezhnev exaggerated Western European willingness to grant the Federal Republic of Germany access to nuclear weapons and Chinese willingness to forgo the ideological dispute. Kosygin underestimated American commitment to the defense of South Vietnam and overestimated Western European willingness to relax the Common Market trade preferences. Suslov exaggerated the potential for Western European communists to lead leftist electoral coalitions. Podgorny overestimated Western European readiness to reach a security settlement without the United States and exaggerated the attractiveness of economic partnership with the Soviet Union. Mikoyan expected Third World leaders to comply with escalated political demands at the same time as they accepted cuts in Soviet economic aid. Shelepin bet on the growing influence of American Nazis or on American resort to nuclear weapons in Vietnam. In 1971 Podgorny misjudged Egyptian President Sadat's willingness to delay recovery of Sinai. In 1972 Brezhnev and Kosygin overestimated their ability to restrain Egypt's desire for war against Israel and underestimated the severity of the American public reaction to the ensuing Arab attack on Israel. In each of these cases, errors in the leader's image enhanced the initial credibility of his policy recommendations at the expense of exposing them to later discrediting by events unanticipated in the leader's image. It was as if the leader chose his image of the international situation by considering its contribution to his persuasiveness to constituents and only the most obvious features of the situation itself.

The prevalence of errors attributable to Politburo members' neglect of relevant information about the international situation is understandable if the limits on integrative complexity manifest in Soviet leaders' statements result from the real limitations on their ability to recall this information during foreign policy decision making in a competitive context. Such cognitive limitations, attributable to the cueing of their expertise tailored to persuading constituents and evaluating the acceptability of compromises to rivals, would impair their chances of learning from international events or trends. If decision making in a competitive context blocks Politburo members' recall of information about the outside world more complex than the monolithic or dichotomous images found in their public statements, then they cannot gradually develop the heterarchy capable of organizing more complex information by abstracting and by discarding irrelevancies. Soviet leaders' misperceptions are well described by Baruch Fischhoff's observation that "Upon careful examination, many apparent errors prove to represent deft resolution of the wrong problem."[48] When Politburo members err in evaluating their international situation, they do so as a cost of their adroitness in evaluating their competitive circumstances.

CONCLUSION

Observations of a discrepancy in integrative complexity between Politburo members' perceptions of their competitive circumstances and their images of the international situation disconfirm the hypothesis that they will learn equally from both situations. This evidence challenges any theory which says that change in Soviet foreign policy results from complex reevaluations of the international situation.

The finding that Soviet leaders are unlikely to learn from international events or trends supports Haas's longstanding contention that social learning must take place outside politics. Political organizations can learn because politicians are sensitive to change in constituency attitudes. Constituencies include scientists, who work in institutional settings that allow them to develop mental organization attuned to monitoring information from the situation, and not just from the attitudes prevalent among any social group, including other scientists. When other constituents develop deference to scientific knowledge and scientists develop a con-

sensus in favor of a given form of action, politicians' sensitivity to constituency attitudes will cause them to adopt the scientific consensus as
the basis for policy. This expectation has an odd corollary: the differentiation
of policy recommendations necessary to political competition can only
occur when either scientists fail to achieve consensus or important social
constituencies fail to develop deference to scientific opinion. In a world
in which constituencies always deferred to experts and experts always
agreed on optimal solutions, politics would indeed become "the administration
of things."

At the same time the findings presented here revise Haas's view of
organizational learning in two respects. First, Haas has tended to see
political competitors' interest as the obstacle to learning by organizational
leaderships. Interest can cause organizational leaders to misrepresent
the outside world, as Brezhnev's disagreement with Suslov over the chances
for Bundestag ratification of the German treaty exemplifies. But when
retention of authority depends on designing images of the situation and
policy recommendations that external events do not promptly discredit,
political competitors have an interest in understanding aspects of their
situation beyond the competitive considerations of persuasiveness to
constituencies and compromise with rivals. "Interest" cannot explain
observations that political competitors often are remarkably oblivious to
these noncompetitive features of their situation. How can interest explain
disastrous misperceptions like Stalin's withholding of ammunition from
the military units guarding the western frontier in June 1941? The problem
appears instead to be the character of political learning. Misperceptions
are a cost of expertise.

Second, reevaluation of images of the environment, reassessment of
the ideas of cause and effect underlying strategies, or even reconsideration
of goals do not necessarily establish that organizational learning, rather
than adaptation, has occurred. When people compete for leadership of
an organization by offering contending postures comprising goals, images
of the situation, and strategies, all of these components of the organization's
routines for responding to the outside world become outcomes of bargaining.
Stability in organization routines develops not because organizations are
"habit-driven actors" (in James Rosenau's phrase). Habits drive persons;
in application to organizations, habit is a misleading metaphor because
it distracts attention from the role of leadership and bargaining in cumulating
an organization's repertoire of routines from the habits of the organization's
individual members. Organizational routines are stable to the extent
that the composition and relative power of underlying constituencies
seldom change very much. When membership in constituencies does
change radically—e.g., when the leader of the Soviet Communist Party
compels his colleagues to let votes by noncommunists affect the compo-

sition of the government—organizations can adapt their goals, their images of the world, and their strategies very dramatically, without necessarily learning at all.

NOTES

1. Quoted from Guy Claxton, "Remembering and Understanding" in Claxton, ed., *Cognitive Psychology: New Directions*, (London: Rutledge and Kegan Paul, 1980), 197.

2. Some of the many sources advancing similar lists of factors include: Harry Gelman, *The Brezhnev Politburo and the Decline of Détente* (Ithaca, N.Y.: Cornell University Press, 1984), 116–35; Bruce Parrott, *Politics and Technology in the Soviet Union* (Cambridge, Mass.: MIT Press, 1983), 231; Erik P. Hoffman and Robbin F. Laird, *The Politics of Economic Modernization in the Soviet Union* (Ithaca, N.Y.: Cornell University Press, 1982), 139; A. James McAdams, *East Germany and Détente: Building Authority After the Wall* (Cambridge, Mass.: Cambridge University Press, 1985), 95–96; W.E. Griffith, "The Soviets and Western Europe: An Overview," in Herbert Ellison, ed., *Soviet Policy Toward Western Europe: Implications for the Atlantic Alliance* (Seattle: University of Washington Press, 1983), 1321; Robert Legvold, "France and Soviet Policy," in Ellison, ed., *Soviet Policy Toward Western Europe*, 66–68; Gerhard Wettig, *Europaeische Sicherheit: Das Europaeische Staatensystem in der Sowjetischen Aussenpolitik 1966–1972* (Cologne: Bertelsmann Universitaetsverlag, 1972), 154–63; Coit D. Blacker, "The Kremlin and Détente: Soviet Conceptions, Hopes and Expectations," in Alexander George, ed., *Managing U.S.–Soviet Rivalry: Problems of Crisis Prevention* (Boulder, Colo.: Westview Press, 1983), 121–29; George W. Breslauer, "Why Détente Failed," in George, ed., *Managing U.S.–Soviet Rivalry*, 331–32; Samuel B. Payne, *The Soviet Union and SALT* (Cambridge, Mass.: MIT Press, 1980), 20; Lawrence T. Caldwell, "Soviet Attitudes To SALT," Adelphi Papers no. 75 (London: The Institute for Strategic Studies, 1971), 5–6; Raymond L. Garthoff, *Détente and Confrontation: American-Soviet Relations from Nixon to Reagan* (Washington, D.C.: Brookings, 1985), 101–102; Marshall D. Shulman, "SALT and the Soviet Union," in Mason Willrich and John B. Rhinelander, eds., *SALT: The Moscow Agreements and Beyond* (New York: The Free Press, 1974), 101–102.

3. Richard D. Anderson, Jr., "Competitive Politics and Soviet Foreign Policy: Authority Building and Bargaining in the Brezhnev Politburo," (Ph.D. Diss., University of California, Berkeley, 1989).

4. Grey Hodnett, "The Pattern of Leadership Politics," in Seweryn Bialer, ed., *The Domestic Context of Soviet Foreign Policy* (Boulder, Colo.: Westview, 1981), 108.

5. Hodnett, in "The Pattern of Leadership Politics," 108, says that his formulation of the Politburo member's "personal political problem" is "oversimplif[ied]." Cf. Gelman, *The Brezhnev Politburo*, particularly Chapter II, "The Political Mechanics of the Brezhnev Regime," and Chapter III, "The Politburo as Battleground"; Dennis Ross, "Coalition Maintenance in the Soviet Union" *World Politics*, 32, 2 (Jan. 1980): 258–80; and Ross, "Risk-Aversion in Soviet Decisionmaking," in Jiri Valenta and William Potter, eds., *Soviet Decisionmaking for National Security* (London: George Allen and Unwin, 1984).

6. George Rabinowitz and Stuart Elaine MacDonald, "A Directional Theory of Issue Voting," *American Political Science Review*, 83, 2 (March 1989): 93–121.

7. *Inclusion* is Kenneth Jowitt's term. See his "An Organizational Approach to the Study of Political Culture in Marxist-Leninist Systems," *American Political Science Review*, 68, 3 (September 1974): 1171–91, and "Inclusion and Mobilization in European Leninist Regimes," *World Politics* 28, 1 (October 1975) 69–96. On constituency expansion and change in leaders' postures, cf. Richard Fenno, *Home Style: House Members in Their Districts* (Boston: Little, Brown and Co., 1978), 172–73. The term *selective incorporation* is taken in slightly modified form from George W. Breslauer, *Khrushchev and Brezhnev as Leaders: Building Authority in Soviet Politics* (London: George Allen and Unwin, 1982). Breslauer observes inclusion authority building more thoroughly than any predecessor.

8. *Pravda*, June 12, 1971.

9. Shulman, "SALT and the Soviet Union," 105.

10. Robert Jervis, *Perception and Misperception in International Politics* (Princeton, N.J.: Princeton University Press, 1976), 8.

11. R. Jervis, Janice Gross Stein, and R.N. Lebow, eds., *Psychology and Deterrence* (Baltimore: Johns Hopkins University Press, 1985); Deborah Welch Larson, *Origins of Containment: A Psychological Explanation* (Princeton, N.J.: Princeton University Press, 1985); John D. Steinbruner, *The Cybernetic Theory of Decision: New Dimensions of Political Analysis* (Princeton, N.J.: Princeton University Press, 1974); Irving L. Janis and Leon Mann, *Decision Making: A Psychological Analysis of Conflict, Choice and Commitment* (New York: The Free Press, 1977), 129–32.

12. Jervis, *Perception and Misperception*, passim.

13. Larson, *Origins of Containment*, 57–58.

14. The most powerful criticism of experimental psychology's ecological validity is Ebbe B. Ebbesen and Vladimir J. Konecni, "On the External Validity of Decision Making Research: What Do We Know About Decisions in the Real World?" in Thomas S. Wallsten, ed., *Cognitive Processes in Choice and Decision Behavior* (Hillsdale, N.J.: Lawrence Erlbaum Associates, 1980). Cf. Philip E. Tetlock, "Accountability: The Neglected Social Context of Judgment and Choice," *Research in Organizational Behavior* VII (JAI Press, 1985): 297–332; Claxton, "Cognitive Psychology: A Suitable Case for What Sort of Treatment?" in Claxton, ed., *Cognitive Psychology*, 12–13; K.J. Gergen, "Experimentation in Social Psychology: A Reappraisal," *European Journal of Social Psychology* 8 (1978): 507–27; H.T.A. Whiting, "Dimensions of Control in Motor Learning," in G.E. Stelmach and J. Requin, eds., *Tutorials in Motor Behavior* (Amsterdam: North Holland Publishing Company, 1980), 538; L.H. Shaffer, "Analyzing Piano Performance: A Study of Concert Pianists," in Stelmach and Requin, eds., *Tutorials in Motor Behavior*, 444; K.M. Newell, "Coordination, Control and Skill," in David Goodman, Robert B. Wilberg, and Ian M. Franks, eds., *Differing Perspectives in Motor Learning, Memory and Control* (Amsterdam: Elsevier Science Publishers, 1985), 306. For admissions of the importance of this problem from the other side, see: Richard A. Schmidt, "On the Underlying Structure of Well-Learned Motor Responses: A Discussion of Namikas and Schneider and Fisk," in Richard A. Magill, ed., *Memory and Control of Action* (Amsterdam: North-Holland Publishing Company, 1983), 146; Robert S. Lockhart, "Remembering Events: Discussion of Papers by Jacoby and Craik, Battig, and Nelson," in L.S. Cermak

and F.I. Craik, eds., *Levels of Processing in Human Memory* (Hillsdale, N.J.: Erlbaum, 1979), 78.

15. John S. Carroll, "Analyzing Decision Behavior: The Magician's Audience," in Wallsten, ed., *Cognitive Processes*, 70.

16. Herbert A. Simon, *Models of Thought* (New Haven: Yale University Press, 1979), p. 369–421; Fran Allard, Sheree Graham, and M.E. Paarsalu, "Perception in Sport: Basketball," *Journal of Sport Psychology* 2 (1980): 14–21; Allard and Janet L. Starkes, "Perception in Sport: Volleyball," *Journal of Sport Psychology* 2 (1980): 22–33; Neil Charness, "Components of Skill in Bridge," *Canadian Journal of Psychology* 33 (1979): 1–16; Charness, "Memory for Chess Positions," *Journal of Experimental Psychology: Human Learning and Memory* 2 (1976): 641–53; Judith S. Reitman, "Skilled Perception in Go: Deducing Memory Structures from Inter-Response Times," *Cognitive Psychology* 8 (1976): 336–56; G.A. Arutyunyan, V.S. Gurfinkel, and M.L. Mirskii, "Investigation of Aiming at a Target," *Biophysics* 13 (1968): 642–45; Arutyunyan et. al., "Organization of Movements on Execution by Man of an Exact Postural Task," *Biophysics* 14 (1969): 1162–67; D.N. Lee, "Visuo-Motor Coordination in Space-Time," in Stelmach and Requin, eds., *Tutorials in Motor Behavior*, 285–86; David J. Ostry, "Execution-Time Movement Control," in Stelmach and Requin, eds., *Tutorials in Motor Behavior*, 462–67; Thomas J. and Karl U. Smith, "Cybernetic Factors in Motor Performance and Development," in Goodman et al., eds., *Differing Perspectives in Motor Learning*, 248–52; Whiting, "Dimensions of Control in Motor Learning," 547; B.P.L.M. den Brinker, J.R.L.W. Stabler, H.T.A. Whiting, and P.C.W. van Wieringen, "A Multidimensional Analysis of Some Persistent Problems in Motor Learning," in Goodman et. al., eds., "Differing Perspectives in Motor Learning," G. Namikas, "Vertical Processes and Motor Performance," in Magill, ed., *Memory and Control of Action*, 105; Shaffer, "Analyzing Piano Performance," 444–54; Carroll, "Analyzing Decision Behavior," 73; Ann L. Brown, "Theories of Memory and the Problems of Development: Activity, Growth and Knowledge," in Cermak and Craik, eds., *Levels of Processing in Human Memory*, 228–42.

17. Reitman, "Skilled Perception in Go," 336.

18. Brown, "Theories of Memory," 250–51.

19. E.g., Denis J. Glencross, "Levels and Strategies of Response Organization," in Stelmach and Requin, eds., *Tutorials in Motor Behavior*, 553.

20. The application of "heterarchy" to skilled performance evidently originates with Walter Schneider and Arthur D. Fisk, "Attention Theory and Mechanisms for Skilled Performance," in Magill, ed., *Memory and Control of Action*, 120–22.

21. Alfred Gell, "On Dance Structures: A Reply to Williams," *Journal of Human Movement Studies* 5, 1 (March 1979): 28.

22. Whiting, "Dimensions of Control in Motor Learning," 544; Janet L. Lachman and Roy Lachman, "Comprehension and Cognition: A State of the Art Inquiry," in Cermak and Craik, eds., *Levels of Processing in Human Memory*, 190–202.

23. This viewpoint is most fully developed in Howard Gardner, *Frames of Mind: The Theory of Multiple Intelligences* (New York: Basic Books, 1983).

24. Paul A. Kolers and William E. Smythe, "Symbol Manipulation: Alternatives to the Computational View of Mind," *Journal of Verbal Learning and Verbal Behavior* 23 (1984): 289–314.

25. Cf. D. Alan Allport, "Patterns and Actions: Cognitive Mechanisms are Content-Specific," in Claxton, ed., *Cognitive Psychology*, 48.

26. Claxton, "Remembering and Understanding," in Claxton, ed., *Cognitive Psychology*, 229–30.

27. An exhaustive discussion of techniques for inferring belief systems is found in Robert Axelrod, ed., *Structure of Decision: The Cognitive Maps of Political Elites* (Princeton, N.J.: Princeton University Press, 1976). Axelrod and his coauthors do not offer any solution to the problem of how to test the inference that observed behaviors correspond to mental structures. For discussions of the futility of their method in the face of this problem, see Axelrod, "Limitations," 252–53; Ole Holsti, "Foreign Policy Formulation Viewed Cognitively," 44.

28. J.D. Bransford, J.J. Franks, C.D. Morris, and B.S. Stein, "Some General Constraints on Learning and Memory Research," in Cermak and Craik, eds., *Levels of Processing in Human Memory*, 332.

29. L.L. Jacoby and F.I. Craik, "Effects of Elaboration of Processing at Encoding and Retrieval: Trace Distinctiveness and Recovery of Initial Context," in Cermak and Craik, eds., *Levels of Processing in Human Memory*, 10; Charness, "Components of Skill in Bridge," 11; Nigel Harvey and Kerry Greer, "Action: The Mechanisms of Motor Control," in Claxton, ed., *Cognitive Psychology*, 103; Hillel J. Einhorn, "Learning From Experience and Suboptimal Rules in Decision Making," in Wallsten, ed., *Cognitive Processes*, 5.

30. Whiting, "Dimensions of Control in Motor Learning," 547.

31. Beth Kerr, "Memory, Action and Motor Control," in Magill, ed., *Memory and Control of Action*, 49–52; Allport, "Patterns and Actions," 38–39, 55–58; Allport, "Attention and Performance," in Claxton, ed., *Cognitive Psychology*, 122–23.

32. James G. Greeno, "Processes of Learning and Comprehension," in Lee W. Gregg, ed., *Knowledge and Cognition* (Potomac, Md.: Lawrence Erlbaum Associates, 1974), 27; Jacoby and Craik, "Effects of Elaboration of Processing," 8; Claxton, "Remembering and Understanding," 230.

33. Thomas F. Remington, *The Truth of Authority: Ideology and Communication in the Soviet Union* (Pittsburgh, Pa.: University of Pittsburgh Press, 1988), 83–96.

34. Ellen Jones, "Committee Decision Making in the Soviet Union," *World Politics*, 36, 2 (January 1984): 167, 181–87.

35. Their own and others' findings are collected in Daniel Kahneman, Paul Slovic, and Amos Tversky, eds., *Judgment Under Uncertainty: Heuristics and Biases* (Cambridge, Mass.: Cambridge University Press, 1982).

36. See particularly Ebbesen and Konecni, "On the External Validity of Decision Making Research," 24.

37. Whiting, "Dimensions of Control in Motor Learning," 538.

38. George N. Wright, Lawrence D. Phillips, Peter C. Whaley, Gerry T. Choo, Kee-Ong Ng, Irene Tan, and Aylene Wisudha, "Cultural Differences in Probabilistic Thinking," *Journal of Cross-Cultural Psychology*, 9, 3 (September 1978): 285–99.

39. Maya Bar-Hillel, "Studies of Representativeness," in Kahneman, Slovic, and Tversky, eds., *Judgement Under Uncertainty*, 81.

40. Gordon F. Pitz, "Subjective Probability Distributions for Imperfectly Known Quantities," in Gregg, ed., *Knowledge and Cognition*, 37–38; Dennis L. Jennings, Teresa M. Amabile, and Lee Ross, "Informal Covariation Assessment: Data-based Ver-

sus Theory-based Judgments," in Kahneman, Slovic, and Tversky, eds., *Judgment Under Uncertainty*, 221.

41. Murray Edelman, *Constructing the Political Spectacle* (Chicago: University of Chicago, 1988), 18–19.

42. Glenn H. Snyder and Paul Diesing, *Conflict Among Nations: Bargaining, Decision Making, and System Structure in International Crises* (Princeton, N.J.: Princeton University Press, 1977), 303–304.

43. Tetlock, "Monitoring the Integrative Complexity of American and Soviet Policy Rhetoric: What Can be Learned," *Journal of Social Issues*, 44, 2 (1988): 113.

44. Anderson, *Competitive Politics*.

45. Tetlock, "Monitoring the Integrative Complexity," 109–111.

46. Tetlock, "Integrative Complexity of American and Soviet Foreign Policy Statements: A Time Series Analysis," *Journal of Personality and Social Psychology*, 69 (1985), 1570–71.

47. "White House Tapes and Minutes of the Cuban Missile Crisis," *International Security*, 10, 1 (Summer 1985): 164–203.

48. Baruch Fischhoff, "For Those Condemned to Study the Past: Heuristics and Biases in Hindsight," in Kahneman, Slovic and Tversky, eds., *Judgment Under Uncertainty*, 340.

PART II

Case Studies of U.S. Foreign Policy

5

The Evolution of U.S. Policy Toward Arms Control

Robert A. Levine

We wrote this book twenty-five years ago and are reprinting it now without any changes. . . . This study presents basic ideas that are as valid as they were twenty-five years ago.

— Thomas C. Schelling and Morton H. Halperin
Preface to 1985 edition of *Strategy and Arms Control*[1]

ISSUES

Like conceptions of God, which vary from Michelangelo's awesome patriarch creating man in His own image to the Unitarians' abstract universal principle of order, arms control is what one defines it to be. This essay uses a standard broad definition, encompassing all measures intended to decrease the likelihood of war or mitigate its destructive effects if it does occur. The definition covers unilateral as well as multilateral measures, tacit agreements as well as explicit ones, and structural steps (possibly involving increases in numbers of weapons) as well as arms reductions. It is the definition used by Schelling and Halperin in 1960 and in 1985.

The essay focuses on *strategic nuclear* arms control—control over the intercontinental weapons that might be exchanged by the United States and the Soviet Union. Even though the subject of arms control presents endless horizons extending to all aspects of international relations, this focus makes it possible to examine the new issues that have risen in the first (nearly) half-century of the nuclear age. Too frequently, however, discussions of strategic arms control ignore the connections to other aspects of military and international political policy; the intention here is to examine the relationship of arms control to its context.

The opening reference to the Deity is intended also to illustrate another point: the ongoing discussion of nuclear arms control is quite theological. No concrete or generally accepted evidence exists of the effects of divine or nuclear intervention; the resulting discussions are precise, detailed, and deductive—and frequently highly emotional—but never empirical. No final proof of any point, compelling enough to convince all parties, has been adduced, and in both the religious and the nuclear cases the possibility of proof through Armageddon is distinct enough that nobody wants to push for it.

The new theology directs policy today much as the old did in the Middle Ages. And theology changes only slowly. Twenty-five years is an instant, and Schelling and Halperin are quite correct: their ideas are as valid now as then, and if we obtain evidence that they were wrong in some particular, it will be too late.

Whether this relatively immutable theology can still encompass learning depends, of course, on the definition of the term. The definition of learning implicit in this paper when it was first written was the simple one later made explicit in the guidelines for the project as: "the capacity (or incapacity) of governments to adjust or adapt their policies in response to changing circumstances." Subsequently, however, it was suggested that the project would be more fruitful if other, more intricate, concepts were considered: "minimalist"; "cognitive content"; "cognitive structuralist"; "efficiency." They have been considered, and for several reasons the paper sticks to the original definition of governments adapting to changing circumstances. First and foremost, I consider myself competent only to treat this form of governmental learning.[2] Second, if one is interested in the *making* of policy, then learning as it is manifested in the making of policy is the most important topic—which is not to denigrate those who are interested in and expert on learning as such; but I am not. Third, individuals have learned in all directions in this area—some learned from the nuclear developments of the 1960s and from Vietnam that it is difficult for policy to manipulate the world, some learned from Prague and Afghanistan that it is oversimple to concentrate on weapons disembodied from politics. Tracking individual learning would be a very different exercise. And fourth, I must admit to some unease at one more definition of learning that sometimes seems implicit in the use to which the more esoteric definitions can be put: "Learning is other people agreeing to what I already believe."

In any case, this paper sticks to the simple definition, of governmental adaptation to changing circumstances. Applying this definition to the topic assigned, one can say that U.S. policy toward arms control *has* evolved since the 1960s but largely because the weapons to be controlled have changed, and to a lesser extent because the political imperatives have shifted. Learning in U.S. foreign policy, however, has had little to do with it. Circumstantial learning depends on experience, and fortunately we have had no nuclear experience since 1945.

One of the most convenient simple structures for examining nuclear theory and policy remains Herman Kahn's 1960 division of nuclear deterrence into "Type I Deterrence [which] is the deterrence of a direct attack," and "Type II Deterrence [which] is defined as using strategic threats to deter an enemy from engaging in very provocative attacks, other than a direct attack on the United States itself."[3] For those who accept the legitimacy of nuclear deterrence at all (compared with those few who want to move directly to a nonnuclear world—and think we can), Type I deterrence is a clear and agreed objective. Type II is more controversial.

The *unilateral* objective of Type I deterrence is to avoid nuclear war by the threat of second-strike retaliation so terrible that the enemy will never mount a first strike. *Multilateral* Type I deterrence aims at mutual stability—each side deterring the other so that neither side will start a war, and both sides having confidence that this is the case. In the early 1960s, this looked relatively simple. It took more than one warhead to dig out a hardened retaliatory weapon, so that there seemed a disadvantage to going first. Deterrence thus seemed safe, so many of the Type I issues revolved around the avoidance of undeterrable accidental nuclear war. But later in the decade, the advent of the multiple independently targetable reentry vehicle (MIRV) reversed the equation—one multiple-warhead missile could kill more than one retaliatory weapon—and the worst theoretical fears of several years earlier seemed to be coming to pass. In particular, MIRV raised questions of preemption, the attempt to mount a nuclear strike against an enemy because of the belief that he is about to strike you, so that the issue is not war versus no-war, but powerful first strike versus feeble second strike. Preemption still governs much of the discussion of Type I deterrence.

For the United States, Type II deterrence means using the threat of nuclear attack to deter anything other than nuclear attack on the United States—which in practice has come to mean deterrence of a Soviet attack against Western Europe. In the years after 1960, it became clear from Vietnam and other wars that nuclear deterrence was too big a stick to use on such Third World conflicts. It may have been relevant to the Cuban missile crisis—that remains a subject of disagreement—but in any case, that crisis was between the United States and the Soviet Union, Cuba being merely the locale.

In the future, oil or other issues in the Middle East may become so crucial to the well-being of the West that Type II deterrence based on American nuclear weapons may become relevant. Currently, and for the last quarter-century, however, Type II deterrence has been effectively limited to Europe. As such, it raises different issues from Type I. Ultimately the issues are political and psychological, revolving around the two questions: *Do the Soviets believe that the United States will use nuclear weapons against an attack on our European allies? Do the allies believe the Soviets believe?*

The questions become particularly sharp because the almost-universal belief in the West (and, indications are, in the East as well) is that the Soviets have strong conventional dominance on the European continent and would thus have no reason to use nuclear weapons initially in any aggression. As a result, the central military issue of Type II deterrence becomes one of American willingness to mount what in the context of Type I deterrence is a *first strike*, a nuclear attack against Soviet forces and perhaps Soviet territory, without the other side having used nuclear weapons at all yet.

Since Type I deterrence is deterrence of a first strike—in the context of multilateral stability, a first strike by either side—some obvious tension exists between the objective of maintaining such stability and the U.S. objective of deterring Soviet conventional aggression in Europe by threatening such a strike. This tension provides much of the material for ongoing disagreements over nuclear arms policy. The disagreements center on two issues: the use of sophisticated strategies for the controlled use of nuclear weapons—what one significant publication has called "discriminate deterrence"[4]—and the emphasis that should be put on arms control agreements, the explicit multilateral portion of the wider set of arms controls defined here.

Three schools of thought on these issues exist in the United States. Using titles I have applied to them elsewhere,[5] they are:

1. *The Extenders* (for extended deterrence, another term for Type II), the advocates of discriminate deterrence, who believe that, since nuclear weapons may be used in the future, we should plan to use them in a controlled manner that may limit damage to us and to the world, compared with an uncontrolled holocaust. The Extenders argue that such demonstrated planning to use the weapons in a relatively "rational" manner will make their use credible, and this credibility of response will increase U.S. Type I deterrence. But they also argue that because we may *want* to use nuclear weapons first to defend Western Europe, the same credibility of use increases Type II deterrence. The Europeans who are the primary beneficiaries of Type II, however, worry that the increased credibility of discriminate deterrence stems from our willingness to use nuclear weapons

in Europe in a way that will avoid subjecting the United States to attack, and they object to that particular form of discrimination. The Extenders treat the United States and the Soviet Union asymmetrically, believing that, if we are strong enough to deter them (Types I and II), then that is all the stability necessary. Their test for arms control agreements depends on the same sort of stability. Albert Wohlstetter is the prototypical Extender.

2. *The Disarmers*, who agree that we may want to use nuclear weapons first, and therefore reject all deterrence. For better or for worse, the Disarmers have had little to do with ongoing U.S. policy toward arms control, which has been based on deterrence, and this essay focuses therefore on the other two schools.

3. *The Limiters* (for limited deterrence), who, in contrast to the other two schools, aim at downgrading the presumption that we may want to use nuclear weapons. Their focus is on Type I mutual stability, and their emphasis is on explicit nuclear arms control agreements to increase that stability. They do not believe that discriminate deterrence can work, and, while they favor discriminating nuclear planning over nondiscriminating, they prefer weapons, strategies, and rhetoric that stress Type I deterrence. Their belief is that deterrence is "existential," in the term applied by McGeorge Bundy, i.e., that the very existence of nuclear weapons, with the open-ended and unknown Pandora possibilities were they to be used, suffices to deter that use. This does not mean that we should do anything stupid, such as simplifying our retaliatory forces to the point at which the enemy can wipe them out and avoid retaliation. It does mean that planning should stress defensive complexities designed to make the enemy's task more difficult, rather than the offensive complexities for nuclear use supported by the Extenders. The concept of existential deterrence extends to Type II as well as Type I: the possibility that any war in Europe might turn nuclear suffices to deter the events, Soviet aggression in particular, that might start such a war. Some Limiters, Robert McNamara for example, believe that the North Atlantic Treaty Organization (NATO) should build up its conventional forces enough to throw into doubt Soviet victory even in a purely conventional conflict, and then should explicitly eschew first use of nuclear weapons in Europe; they feel that even such a "no first use" declaration would preserve existential Type II deterrence, while it would improve the stability of mutual Type I deterrence. Others, however, fear that such a declaration would not only increase the danger of Soviet aggression in Europe, but also destroy NATO.

In fact, the Limiters' explicit dependence on existential deterrence—the stabilizing of Type I to the possible detriment of Type II—scares the West Europeans as much as the Extenders' discriminating deterrence. The Europeans' real preference is for Western Europe to be covered by the umbrella of American Type I deterrence—for an attack on Stuttgart to be treated by the U.S. president as the precise equivalent of an attack on San Francisco. The fact that this is impossible has led to the independent nuclear deterrents of France and Great Britain. And the additional fact that Germany is by definition Type II to all three NATO nuclear powers has led to most of the political complications in NATO over the last 20 years or more.

This is the context in which U.S. policy toward arms control has evolved. It has evolved slowly; each of the issues discussed above was raised in the late 1950s and the early 1960s, and today's debate over each would be quite recognizable to those who discussed the issues then. Indeed, they are mostly the same people.

HISTORY

Until the late 1950s, the discussion of strategic nuclear policy was embryonic at best, and many strategic developments went largely unrecognized, at least compared with the intense scrutiny with which such developments were examined in the 1960s and subsequently. Certainly the advent of the nuclear age in 1945 impelled a deluge of writings, but these ranged from the scientific to the high philosophical; few bore on the strategic issues of procuring, deploying, and planning to use (or not use) nuclear weapons. Writings about arms control were largely confined to disarmament as such—reducing the numbers of nuclear weapons or getting rid of them completely—rather than the intricate discussions of the later years that emphasized prevention or control.

The postwar era began with a U.S. monopoly of nuclear weapons. Although the Soviets broke this before long and both sides developed hydrogen weapons in the early 1950s, the unexamined U.S. assumptions behind John Foster Dulles's "massive retaliation" policy were that nuclear weapons provided a very cost-effective way of containing inherent Soviet aggressiveness throughout the world; we had a lot more weapons than they did; and nuclear war would consist of U.S. attacks on Soviet cities, as on Hiroshima and Nagasaki, with our air defenses hindering their retaliation (or first strike). Although massive retaliation was highly controversial, most of those who challenged it publicly did so on moral and philosophical grounds rather than strategic ones, which questioned feasibility or examined potential Soviet response or initiation. One major exception among early analysts was Bernard Brodie.[6]

By the late 1950s, however, the advent of the modern missile, based on German V-2 technology at the end of World War II and dramatized by the launching of the Soviet sputnik in 1957, forced public questioning of the earlier, unexamined premises. It was believed in the United States, far too pessimistically as it later turned out, that the Soviets were about to overtake us in means of intercontinental delivery of nuclear warheads (the "missile gap").

In fact, private reexamination of strategic premises had already been under way for several years; it began to enter the public debate by the late 1950s. Threaded throughout the discussion from then until now are the names of five analysts whose writings and actions have been seminal in the debate over the entire period: Albert Wohlstetter, Thomas Schelling, Robert McNamara, McGeorge Bundy, and Henry Kissinger.[7] The earliest major contributions came from Wohlstetter and Schelling. Through the 1950s, Wohlstetter headed a RAND Corporation team that started out to optimize the U.S. strategic basing system and ended by questioning the premises on which the system was based.[8] In 1959 he went public with an article the crucial point of which was that nuclear deterrence, far from being automatic, required care to make sure that the enemy did not wipe out our entire retaliatory capability in a first strike, thus leaving us naked.[9]

The problems raised by Wohlstetter's "The Delicate Balance" were considered crucial by a group of analysts that could be considered then and through the early 1960s as a single school of thought. This school has since divided over the central issue of the extension of the use of nuclear weapons beyond simple deterrence or defeat of a Soviet nuclear attack. Wohlstetter has become a leading Extender, stressing the importance of careful planning for a variety of deterrent uses and, if necessary, actual uses for nuclear weapons—what has now become *discriminate deterrence*. (The commission that coined the term was cochaired by Wohlstetter.)

Schelling, then and still a Harvard professor of economics, can now be counted among the Limiters; but his most important initial and continuing contribution has been to set the terms of reference that have been used for much of the discussion of strategic nuclear policy and arms control over the past quarter-century. His 1960 book, *The Strategy of Conflict*, laid out in a fairly abstract manner a set of propositions derived from economics and game theory concerning the ways opponents do and can deal with each other, and the conditions for stability in such conflicts.[10] In 1961, his and Halperin's *Strategy and Arms Control* applied the propositions, still somewhat abstractly, to possible rules for nuclear stabilization. They stressed the then-novel idea that many arms control steps could be unilateral (e.g., protection of Side A's retaliatory forces so that A is not tempted to a first strike, particularly a preemptive first strike), as well as multilateral in the classic treaty form.

The use of nuclear weapons to strike at enemy forces rather than populations, to deter and to signal, to control and to stabilize, and to work politically without being used militarily has, in fact, been the basis for U.S. nuclear arms policy over the entire period since the expiration of massive retaliation. (One question frequently raised is whether such considerations also form the basis of Soviet policy and, if not, what the implications of the asymmetry may be.)

Although Wohlstetter and Schelling were not in substantial disagreement with one another in the late 1950s and early 1960s, they did represent a geographic division. Through 1960, the centers of American thinking on nuclear arms policy and arms control were Santa Monica, California, where RAND is located, and Cambridge, Massachusetts, where Schelling and others had organized the Joint Harvard-MIT Faculty Seminar on Arms Control. With the election of John Kennedy as president, many of those who had been involved in the early discussions joined the Defense Department in the new administration. From RAND came Henry Rowen, Charles Hitch, Alain Enthoven (a junior analyst on the basing study), and later Daniel Ellsberg; from the Cambridge seminar, McGeorge Bundy moved in as Kennedy's national security adviser, Harvard Law School professor John McNaughton took a key assistant secretaryship, and Halperin later joined in a junior role. Those who remained in Santa Monica and Cambridge, including Wohlstetter and Schelling, consulted with their colleagues and others, and many of the ideas that had been incubated in academe and the think tanks entered directly into national policy.

It is a commonplace among sophisticated observers of academic/policy interaction that ideas generated on the campus enter actual policy only through the strong distorting filter of politics, if at all. Although the general rule applied to this case as to all others, the never-never abstract and theological nature of nuclear strategy, combined with the Kennedy administration's suspicions of the uniformed military establishment, meant that more of the raw unrefined product than usual seeped through and entered national strategy. The movie *Dr. Strangelove* satirized the strategic consultants, among others; the material was gathered largely at cocktail parties thrown for director Stanley Kubrick and author Peter George by the consultants in Cambridge and Santa Monica. The strategic views of the consultants were substantially distorted by the caricature, but the extent of their influence was not.

Robert McNamara, the third seminal contributor, was appointed secretary of defense as a manager, not a strategist. He learned quickly from his new staff, notably from William Kaufmann, a consultant with deep roots in both Cambridge and Santa Monica. One thing they all soon learned was that the missile gap existed in reverse; the United States was still far ahead of the Soviet Union in delivery systems as well as warheads. This, plus the fact that the United States was taking steps to protect its nuclear forces—through emphasis on the sea-based portion, hardening of land-missile sites, and airborne alert for bombers—meant that it would take many first-strike missiles to kill a single retaliatory missile. Since the Soviets had many fewer, they could not strike first; and in most foreseeable circumstances, we would not. Putting a discount rather than a premium on a first strike meant the preemption fears that had preoccupied many of the academic arms controllers were ill-founded, and stability based on unilateral measures was at hand.

Another lesson was that the plans set forth in the early 1950s for a massive conventional defense of Western Europe to be mounted by the member nations of the North Atlantic Treaty Organization (NATO) were seen by the nations at risk as far too costly to put into place; Type II U.S. nuclear deterrence of Soviet invasion of Western Europe, nuclear or nonnuclear, was still considered basic. The political road to nuclear war remained dangerously open, and the Berlin crises of the first year of the Kennedy administration led Kennedy, McNamara, and the Defense Department to think seriously about the use of nuclear weapons. In October 1962, the Cuban missile crisis again stimulated serious consideration of "what if" we had to use the weapons. Some analysts believed that our ability to do so and "win" made an important contribution to the successful resolution of the crisis, although Bundy argues strongly that the nuclear balance had very little to do with it.[11] In any case, the two years of crises in 1961 and 1962 confirmed the belief in the need for containing the aggressive hostility of the Soviet Union. By 1963, however, the resolution of the missile crisis made possible the first significant arms control agreement between the United States and the Soviet Union, the Atmospheric Test Ban Treaty. The treaty had little to do with stability as such, however, and few analysts thought that it implied more than a tactical change in the relations between the two superpowers.

All these events led to very concrete planning as well as thinking about the uses of nuclear weapons. McNamara was the swing man. Initially, he adopted the ideas of the nuclear strategists with whom he surrounded himself. In a still-famous 1962 speech made in Ann Arbor, Michigan, he contended that our "principal military objectives, in the event of a nuclear war stemming from a major attack on the [NATO] Alliance, should be the destruction of the enemy's military forces, not of his civilian population."[12] In other speeches and statements made earlier in the year he espoused the "city-avoidance" counterforce theory of nuclear targeting, both as a commonsense humanitarian philosophy and as a strategy for using the threat of nuclear attack (or additional echelons of attack after the first exchange) as a bargaining device, particularly in a NATO (Type II) context.[13]

The Ann Arbor speech was the high-water mark of "declaratory" counterforce policy in the 1960s. Five years later, toward the end of his tenure as secretary of defense, McNamara stressed not the details of bargaining, but the pure Type I functions of nuclear weapons used as a threat of near-total devastation to the enemy: "Now it is imperative to understand that assured destruction is the very essence of the whole deterrence concept. . . . It means the certainty of suicide to the aggressor—not merely to his military forces but to his society as a whole."[14] This was not the *"mutual* assured destruction" (MAD) that the Extenders contend deliberately puts our population at risk to Soviet attack, but it is a major move away from the details of counterforce and nuclear bargaining. It moved McNamara toward the Limiters' school, signaling the development of the Limiters as more than a tolerated loyal opposition considered to be lightweights within the policy establishment. And it earned the strong and continuing opposition of Wohlstetter and others who remained steadfast Extenders.

The change was, in fact, primarily in *declaratory* policy—what was *said* about nuclear weapons and plans. The actual nuclear strategy of the United States, once McNamara achieved control of it early in his tenure, emphasized the targeting of enemy military forces, not populations. This shifted only marginally back and forth as McNamara revised his views and, indeed, has remained relatively constant through various changes in declaratory emphasis from then until now. McNamara has not written of the events that led him to shift his emphasis; others have speculated. Perhaps the demonstration in Vietnam that detailed calculations do not always work out precisely as planned had something to do with it. Within the strategic nuclear realm itself, events had moved away from the comfortable stability of "it takes more than one to kill one" of the theorists of a few years earlier. The Soviets had begun to build very large warheads, and many of them, which put even well-protected hard sites at additional risk. Perhaps more important, however, the advent of MIRV, the multiple independently targetable reentry vehicle, meant that one missile with a lot of warheads could kill more than one enemy missile in a silo, and the equation was reversed toward a new premium on a first strike.

It is not clear to what extent MIRV was a reaction to the then-developing anti-ballistic missile (ABM) capability, to what extent ABM was a reaction to MIRV, or whether perhaps both were results of the inexorable advance of military technology. McNamara was dubious about ABM, going along with the concept of its development on the questionable rationale of the need for a defense against Chinese missiles. What is clearer from his 1967 speech, however, is that the action-reaction arms race typified by MIRV and ABM had been one factor leading him to shift away from the stress on detailed counterforce. He had begun to believe that such details could lead to no conclusion.

The ABM itself became a major—perhaps *the* major—factor in the debate in the late 1960s. The Soviets had been working on the system throughout most of the 1960s. Some Americans believed this to be a part of the general Soviet attempt to achieve a strategic advantage, but others suggested a strong Soviet bias toward defense because of the traumas of World War II, as illustrated by the massive Soviet investment in air defense. In any case, knowledge of the Soviet efforts led to pressure for similar U.S. systems.

In a debate with many similarities to the more recent one over the Strategic Defense Initiative (SDI) (but lacking any discussion of the possibility of an absolute hard-shell protection of the United States set forth in President Reagan's more recent dream), the Extenders favored ABM as one more tool to sophisticate the U.S. nuclear arsenal and strategy. Most of the Limiters opposed it, primarily on the basis that an effective ABM would be destabilizing because it could be taken as an effort to allow a U.S. first strike by protecting targets in this country from ragged Soviet retaliation against such a strike.

For a variety of reasons, rather than becoming another stride in the arms race, ABM development in the late 1960s and early 1970s provided an opportunity for the first U.S.–Soviet arms control agreement. Unlike the Atmospheric Test Ban Treaty, it potentially affected the stability of the nuclear arms balance for better or for worse. The arguments of the Limiters undoubtedly had some effect in encouraging U.S. acceptance of the ABM treaty signed in 1972. Perhaps more important, however, were President Nixon's political imperatives (and perhaps similar pressures on Brezhnev). And a major permissive factor was that useful deployment of the ABM proved difficult enough that, even after the treaty was signed permitting one ABM complex each to the United States and the Soviet Union, we soon abandoned our efforts as being insufficiently cost-effective, given the technology of the times, and strategically meaningless.

Together with the ABM limitations, the Strategic Arms Limitation Treaty (SALT) of 1972 put the first limitations on offensive missiles.[15] Lawrence Freedman characterizes the basic bargain of SALT: "Implicit in the agreement was a trade of Soviet numerical superiority in missiles for U.S. superiority in technology and bombers."[16] The Extenders detested this trade-off, the more so because it allowed the Soviets to multiply their advantage by putting more MIRVed warheads on their heavier missiles. In any case, SALT, signed in 1972, became SALT I, as an interim SALT II imposing further limits on bomber delivery systems in addition to missiles was negotiated, again over the strong opposition of the Extenders.

Deterioration of U.S.–Soviet relations, largely because of Soviet aggression in Afghanistan, meant that President Carter never presented SALT II to the Senate for ratification. It was then disowned but its limitations observed through Thanksgiving 1986 by President Reagan. Although such atmospherics of U.S.–Soviet relations had an important positive effect on making the ABM treaty and SALT I possible in 1972, and a major negative effect in making ratification of SALT II impossible in 1979, they bore little relationship to longer-run and more fundamental U.S. views of the Soviet Union. Most Americans' views remained in the range bounded at one end by the belief that the Soviets would remain highly aggressive and attempt to increase their military power no matter what we did (the Extenders' view) and at the other end by the belief that Soviet aggressiveness was tempered by prudence and a desire to shift resources away from the arms race, with their military posture designed in substantial measure in reaction to our own (the Limiters).

To a great extent, the détente of the early 1970s had been the handiwork of Henry Kissinger, the fifth of the major voices in the arms debate. Kissinger differed from the others less in viewpoint than in frame of reference. In the late 1950s and early 1960s, his policy recommendations as a member of the Cambridge branch of the consulting debaters put him well within the establishment consensus that included Schelling, Wohlstetter, McNamara, and everyone else who aspired to have a real effect on real policy. When McNamara and others veered off toward the Limiter school, Kissinger remained an Extender.

Unlike the other three, Kissinger took a primarily *political* view of the issues. From the 1950s, he concentrated more on the effects of potential or actual use of nuclear weapons on world power structures than on the logic and arithmetic of nuclear exchange. In 1957, he espoused a "limited" nuclear war strategy in Europe, contrasting it to Dulles's massive retaliation as a better instrument to protect real U.S. interests in Western Europe.[17] A few years later, he changed this view toward conventional defense, not massive retaliation, but he continued to promote the concept that nuclear and other weapons were instruments in an essentially political conflict between the superpowers.[18] Political conflict might lead to nuclear war, and it was to the political sphere that we must look to prevent such war as well as to promote our own interests. Kissinger's Ph.D. dissertation had been about the post-Napoleonic balance-of-power stability created in Europe by Metternich and Castlereagh, and his objective, as writer and later as public official, was to reproduce that kind of stability in the world, without sacrificing U.S. interests. His early writings, his activities in office, and his current columns and comments have added an important real-world political dimension to the strategic debate.

Because of his different way of thinking, Kissinger had become something of an outsider in Washington and among the academic debaters after the first year or two of the Kennedy administration. When Nixon made him national security adviser and then secretary of state, he directed much of his early effort toward such nonnuclear issues as Vietnam, the Middle East, and China, but he was central in creating the atmosphere of détente with the Soviet Union that made the ABM treaty and SALT I possible. He was a key negotiator on the treaties, but preparation of U.S. positions on the precise numbers and definitions was more within the realm of the Department of Defense.

SALT I and the ABM treaty were consistent with the stress on assured destruction as the central deterrent to strategic nuclear war between the United States and the Soviet Union that McNamara had begun in the previous administration. In 1974, however, James Schlesinger, a RAND alumnus and Extender analyst in good standing (and a Harvard College classmate of Kissinger), became secretary of defense. Schlesinger moved declaratory policy back toward the emphasis on selectivity, counterforce, and potential bargaining and away from the sole objective of deterrence of attack on ourselves; and he made appropriate adjustments in actual strategic options. His aim, he told the House Armed Services Committee, was "that the President of the United States, under conditions in which there is a major assault against the interests of the United States or its allies, will have strategic options other than the destruction of the society and the urban industrial base of the society attacking us."[19]

At the same time, however, SALT II, which the Extenders believed put additional limits on U.S. capabilities to actually implement such a selective strategy, was agreed to in principle by President Ford and Chairman Brezhnev; it took several more years to negotiate the details, and by the time it was ready to present to the Senate for ratification, President Carter decided not to do so because of Afghanistan. The Extenders believed that SALT I and the ABM treaty, abetted by the defense budget cutbacks of the first Carter years, had allowed the Soviets to take a giant step toward catching up to us in strategic capabilities and laying the groundwork to surpass us dangerously. The Limiters too agree that effective "parity" was the condition coming out of the 1970s, but the Extenders' attribution of causation to U.S. carelessness and political error is far more controversial. To the Limiters, the U.S. strategic dominance that lasted at least through the early 1960s was inherently transitory and convergence between the superpowers inevitable. Their belief all along has been that strategic superiority is militarily meaningless in the nuclear age and is therefore politically useless.

Nobody interested in nuclear arms control and stability was very happy in the years after 1972. The two major schools attributed the slowing of progress and the decline of hopes to rather different causes, however. Two thoughtful analysts, one from each school, have summed up their own discontent. Paul Nitze, an Extender who has been in the thick of arms control negotiations and debates since the Kennedy administration, lays the blame on continuing Soviet efforts to squeeze out the last drop of advantage:

From 1972, when the Soviets passed the United States in number, size, and throwweight of offensive missile systems, they proceeded to develop and deploy one generation after another of more modern systems . . . . Once the Soviets judged the military correlation of forces had become favorable, they were adamant in refusing to consider any agreement which would result in rough equality or which would improve crisis stability.[20]

Schelling presents a Limiters' view of the same years and events. In addition to criticizing U.S. and Soviet arms control positions that he believes substituted mindless numerical limitations on weapons for consideration of their stabilizing or destabilizing characteristics, Schelling attacks the counterforce doctrine that he sees as the central U.S. strategic concept of those years:

Since 1972, the control of strategic weapons has made little or no progress, and the effort on our side has not seemed to be informed by any coherent theory of what arms control is supposed to accomplish. . . . Ten years ago, late in the Nixon administration, secretaries of defense began to pronounce a new doctrine for the selection of nuclear weapons. This doctrine entailed a more comprehensive target system than anything compatible with the McNamara doctrine. . . . What has happened is that a capacity to maintain control over the course of war has come to be identified with a vigorous and extended counterforce campaign, while retaliatory targeting has been identified with what Herman Kahn used to call "spasm."[21]

WHERE WE ARE

President Reagan and his advisers came into office on a national security platform that stressed the rebuilding of U.S. defenses that they contended had been allowed to deteriorate drastically by both President Carter and the Republican administrations preceding him. This applied very specifically to the strategic nuclear area, in which the administration initiated a variety of weapons systems intended to implement the Extenders' nuclear control precepts. These programs dominated the strategic nuclear policy of the first three quarters of the Reagan era. Then quite suddenly, without voluntarily abandoning the plans or the weapons of nuclear control (the refusal of the Congress to appropriate the full funding requested for the programs forced some abandonment), the administration shifted the emphasis to the arms controls favored by the Limiters.

One measure of the nuclear emphasis is that in addition to benefiting from a defense budget that more than doubled from fiscal 1982 (President Carter's last budget request) to fiscal 1989 (President Reagan's latest request as of this writing), strategic forces went up as a percentage of the whole from 7.7 percent to 8.0 percent. More specifically applicable to nuclear control doctrines as such, however, are two controversies of the period, one having to do with the choice between two intercontinental ballistic missiles (ICBMs), the other concerning President Reagan's Strategic Defense Initiative.

1. *ICBMs.* The large MIRVed MX missile has been the subject of much controversy since the Carter administration. The many warheads made it an excellent counterforce weapon, but as accelerating technology threw into doubt the capability of even super-hard shelters to protect second-strike retaliatory capabilities, and thus made missile mobility appear relatively more attractive, the MX's size presented problems. Both the Carter and the Reagan administrations presented exotic schemes for keeping the elephants on the move, but the implementable plans remained shelter-centered, and as a result MX appeared an attractive MIRVed Type II weapon with dubious second-strike Type I capabilities. This did not appeal to the Limiters, or even all of the Extenders.

In 1963, President Reagan appointed retired Air Force General Brent Scowcroft, who had directed President Ford's National Security Council, to head a bipartisan Commission on Strategic Forces. The commission presented a report that endorsed the mobile MX, but stressed even more the additional need for a much smaller, much more mobile weapon:

> The Commission believes that a single-warhead missile weighing about fifteen tons (rather than the nearly 100 tons of MX) may offer greater flexibility in the long run effort to obtain an ICBM force that is highly survivable, even when viewed in isolation, and that can consequently serve as a hedge against potential threats to the submarine force.[22]

The proposed small ICBM, called Midgetman, was embraced by many Democrats in Congress, and the conceptual controversy became a political one as well. The uneasy compromise was to go ahead with both MX and Midgetman, but the Reagan administration was never enthusiastic about Midgetman, nor would the Congress vote anywhere near the administration's desires on MX. The administration saw MX as a large, accurate, counterforce weapon, essential for either a Type I retaliatory mission (which the Extenders contended should be strictly counterforce) or for a Type II "first" strike. In addition, by the end of the decade, because Midgetman's small size and mobility would make it hard for inspectors to find, it seemed paradoxically to interfere with the administration's new enthusiasm for arms agreements. The Air Force backed MX largely because it provided more bang (i.e., warheads) for a buck. The Democrats favoring Midgetman did so on the Limiter grounds that the mobility would make it an ideal untargetable Type I weapon, while the single warhead pretty well disqualified it for a first strike. By 1988, budgetary pressures were forcing hard decisions, and President Reagan's budget for fiscal 1989 proposed continued heavy programming for MX with a few hundreds of millions of dollars to keep Midgetman alive in case the next president wanted to revive it. This was the situation going into the Bush administration.

2. *SDI.* When President Reagan proposed his Strategic Defense Initiative in 1983, his clear objective, from which he never retreated in subsequent years, was to provide an ICBM shield that would physically prevent nuclear attack on the U.S. population as well as weapons, thus rendering Type I deterrence unnecessary. His thoughts about Type II deterrence were less clear: at various times he implied that the shield would cover our allies also; but West Europeans doubted that and tended to see SDI as a device that would allow the United States to retreat from the nuclear world, including the Type II commitment to use nuclear weapons against conventional aggression.

In any case, however, nobody except the president himself, Defense Secretary Weinberger, and a few zealots ever took the population-protecting hard-shell version seriously. For the Extenders in and around the administration, the stated objective for SDI was sufficient protection of U.S. missiles that they could be used in a strong counterattack even after an enemy first strike. As such, this is a respectable Type I objective, if confused somewhat by the president's grander design. The difficulty is, however, that an ABM system strong enough to defend against a coordinated enemy first strike, is a fortiori likely to be capable of fully defeating a ragged enemy retaliatory second strike, mounted after our own first strike had hit its ICBM force. SDI is thus necessarily a Type II weapon system as well as a Type I, and this disturbed the Limiters. In addition, the seeming necessity to break the existing ABM treaty in order to deploy SDI, and probably even to test it, was antithetical to the arms agreement stress of the Limiters. As the Reagan administration ended, however, the combination of budgetary pressures and increasing doubts about how well the thing would work at all, together with the subtraction of President Reagan's strong political influence, seemed to be relegating SDI to a hedge against accidental or third-party-caused war. This much smaller version, proposed by Senator Sam Nunn, would be limited enough to have little deterrent effect—Type I or Type II—vis-à-vis the Soviet Union.

If the first Reagan years stressed the controlled use of nuclear weapons, however, and the concept continued to dominate the unilateral weapons and strategic choices of the administration, suddenly and surprisingly the emphasis in the last several years shifted to arms agreements with the Soviets. Although the dynamic of what happened is not yet clear, most of the impetus seemed to come from Gorbachev. President Reagan's first term in office was characterized by the "evil empire" speech, which indicated a mind-set toward the Soviet Union rather more extreme than those of presidents Ford and Carter, even though his general treatment of the opponent, as a power so antithetical and cynical as to preclude other than a public relations treatment of arms negotiations, was consistent with the policies of his predecessors. But when Gorbachev, both by report and by face-to-face meeting at Geneva, appeared to be quite different, Reagan was, in a real sense, radicalized. Historians—or the president in his memoirs—may suggest how much additional motivation stemmed from Reagan's desire to improve his place in history; in any case, after Geneva came Reykjavik, then the Intermediate-Range Nuclear Forces (INF) treaty at the Washington summit, and at this writing a serious possibility of a Strategic Arms Reduction Talks (START) treaty cutting the number of missiles of both superpowers in half. Much of what has happened had come as a result of Soviet acceptance of previous Western positions (e.g., the swap of *all* the Soviet SS-20 missiles for NATO's INF, on-site verification), some of which had been put forth only because of the certain belief that they were unacceptable to the Soviets.

Nonetheless, even if the Soviets were the prime movers, Reagan's acceptance of Gorbachev's acceptance is in itself a remarkable turnabout. It is a turn toward arms agreements as a means of achieving stable mutual Type I deterrence. Both the substance of the turn and the way it was initiated, at the unprepared and uncoordinated (with our NATO allies) Reykjavik meeting, have shaken the confidence of European NATO members in the umbrella of Type II deterrence that is supposed to protect them. That, however, falls outside the scope of this essay.

LEARNING

What does all this imply about learning in U.S. foreign policy? Not much. In the 25 years from 1960 to 1985, U.S. policy toward arms control—arms control in the broad or narrow sense—evolved only slowly. The Type I/Type II issues of deterrence were much the same at the end of the period as at the beginning. Table 1 below is reproduced from the relevant portions of two tables in my 1963 book, *The Arms Debate*.[23] Translating the Anti-War Marginalists of the earlier period to the current Limiters, and consolidating the other two schools, the Middle Marginalists and the Anti-Communists, to become the Extenders, the differences in viewpoint at the beginning of the 1960s changed only marginally to become those recognizable in the mid-1980s. And this was true in spite of truly major technological, political, and strategic changes over the same period:

TABLE 1 1963 Values, Analyses, and Recommendations

	Anti-War Marginalists	*Middle Marginalists*	*Anti-Communist Marginalists*
Values	Prevention of war	Prevention of war Melioration of war	Defense of freedom against communism Forcing communist retreat
Analyses: War	War will be thermonuclear	War tends to become thermonuclear	War is a spectrum
	Weapons can only be used to prevent war if anything	Weapons are primarily to deter war but we may have to strike (first or second)	Weapons are political instruments
	War starts by accident, irrationality, miscalculation	Rationality can exert substantial control over irrationality; accidental war requires both an accident and a wrong response; the "Paradox of Deterrence"; war can be self-generating	War starts primarily for political reasons
	"Limited wars" escalate		Nuclear weapons dominate war and conventional forces are important mainly for "psychology"
	Arms races cause wars	Escalation can be controlled through proper attention to tactical nuclear weapons, conventional forces, etc.	The arms race can be exploited
	Once war starts, control and melioration are impossible	The arms race can perhaps be controlled	Control is possible and is necessary for the political exploitation of war
		Control and melioration of war may be possible, particularly in those cases where we strike first	

Opponent	U.S.S.R. is becoming consolidationist in order to conserve its successes; clashes of interest are psychological U.S.S.R. is moving away from military means to achieve its objectives	U.S.S.R. is still carefully aggressive in the short run but perhaps it may change in the long; clashes of interest are real U.S.S.R. uses military means for political ends, but is willing to take little nuclear risk	U.S.S.R. is implacably aggressive and out to bury us, with no sign of change U.S.S.R. is carrying on a "protracted conflict" with all means, although it now shies away from high nuclear risk
Recommendations Strategic; Arms control	Short run: stable deterrence Long run: world peace through universal disarmament to be gained by negotiations that may start with unilateral initiatives	Short run: make war less likely and/or terrible by controls over numbers and/or uses of armaments to be gained by unilateral steps and/or tacit or explicit multilateral agreements Long run: a series of short runs	Short run: unilateral control over warfare to make war thinkable as a political tool Long run: agreement with communists delineating areas of conflict and common interest
Deterrence	Only as a part of short-run stable deterrence	Various mixes of arms control and political deterrence; of controlled counterforce and/or countercity targets; of second and first strike	Controlled deterrence as a political weapon; "win second strike" as a shield against enemy escalation

• Technologically, although ABM had been thought of by the early 1960s, it hardly came up in the debate. Even more important, however, MIRV, which has turned on end the basic strategic balance, changing it from the stable it-takes-more-than-one-to-kill-one to the unstable one-shot-kills-many, is not mentioned at all in the literature of the early 1960s.

• Politically, the Soviet-Chinese rift was beginning to be recognized in the West in the early 1960s, but it had not yet affected strategic discussions. Most Sovietologists did not expect the diffusion of multicentric communism, and only a few saw the loosening of Soviet bonds on the East European satellites.

• Internally, the Soviet Union was thought to be strong and vigorous, in contrast to the current Western perception that it is in severe internal economic and perhaps even political trouble. True, Krushchev then was thought of by some Westerners as Gorbachev is now, but Krushchev did not last.

• Strategically, after the missile-gap scare of the late 1950s, which had wound down by the end of 1961, it was recognized that the United States was still far ahead of the Soviet Union in nuclear delivery capabilities. Today, parity is recognized by all; Soviet superiority is feared by a few.

It seems quite clear that, lacking specific experience in the strategic nuclear era to learn from, little was learned by the policy-making institutions of the United States or the schools of thought in the debate. It was the Middle Ages of arms control and other strategic thinking; theology dominated. The issues changed slowly; the attitudes remained the same.

What about the rapid Reagan changes after 1985? These certainly mark a change of policy; they do not mark new learning. Whatever may have moved President Reagan from within (e.g., his place in history), the external change he reacted to was not a new understanding of old facts, but a very new set of facts, those surrounding General Secretary Gorbachev.

In adopting the goal of arms agreement long espoused by the Limiters, the president had not learned from that school. Indeed, his one attempted move toward the truly new—his attempt at Reykjavik to abolish all nuclear weapons or all missiles or all of something that was never quite clear—was well outside the teachings of the Limiters as well as the Extenders; fortunately, the president quickly forgot about it. Aside from the abolition, however, Reagan did move toward the arms agreement prescriptions of the Limiters. But he did so without abandoning the controlled-nuclear-use policies of the Extenders; his continued insistence on the MX missile indicated constancy in that regard, as did the swan-song report of some of his defense advisers, the *Discriminate Deterrence* document whose central recommendation in regard to nuclear weapons was to retain our "capabilities for discriminate nuclear strikes."[24]

Nor is such learning likely to characterize the Bush administration, as it starts into business by pursuing a set of policies that proceed for the most part from those of the last Reagan years and continue well within the Extender/Limiter bounds. The likely changes in U.S. policy will not stem from U.S. learning, nor should they, given the dearth of nuclear evidence from which to learn. In a very real sense, our general policies have been right all along: unilateral pursuit of nuclear control while seeking arms agreements consistent with that control. True, until 1985 the latter was never really tested by Soviet acceptance of the basic principles. That is why the impetus to current changes has come not from Western learning, but from the East.

In 1986, a French analyst wrote: "In the bundle of factors that have, since 1954, determined the evolution of the Franco-German dialogue on matters of security, the Soviet Union has appeared, without doubt, as the only constant."[25] What was true of the Franco-German security dialogue was even more true of the U.S.–Soviet security dialogue on nuclear weapons and stability; it did not change between 1954 (really, since 1948) and 1985, because of the constancy of the Soviet Union. Immediately after that writing, however, Gorbachev changed the Soviet Union's foreign as well as domestic policies. The changes have been radical and visible; whether they are permanent and fundamental remains to be seen. The Reagan adaptations—negotiate seriously but keep your powder dry— were appropriate. They were not based on new learning, however, because the old lessons covered the possibilities.

Gorbachev's own radical changes were undoubtedly based on Soviet interests as he saw them. Their apparent direction was toward stability and away from attempts to achieve a "correlation of forces," in the Soviet phrase, that would gain political advantages vis-à-vis the West. Now, to the extent that this new direction is real as well as apparent, the intriguing question arises of the extent to which the substance of the Soviet moves has been itself based on real learning—from Schelling, Halperin, Kahn, Wohlstetter, and the other U.S. instructors on the subject of the principles of nuclear stability.

But that is the subject of another essay in this volume.

NOTES

1. Thomas C. Schelling and Morton H. Halperin, *Strategy and Arms Control* (Elmsford, N.Y.: Pergamon Press, 1985) xi.

2. I was trained as an economist. For the first half of the 1980s, however, I was charged with supervising a group of psychologists who specialized in learning. I learned that I was not going to learn much about learning.

3. Herman Kahn, *On Thermonuclear War* (Princeton, N.J.: Princeton University Press, 1960), 126. Kahn also delineates "Type III . . . 'tit-for-tat,' graduated or

controlled deterrence," but this is a less useful concept, obscuring the essential difference between the single objective of using nuclear weapons to avoid the use of nuclear weapons, and all other objectives. Type III terminology (although not the concept of graduation) has fallen into disuse.

4. *Discriminate Deterrence: Report of the Commission on Integrated Long-Term Strategy* (Washington, D.C.: U.S. Government Printing Office, January 1988).

5. Robert A. Levine, *The Strategic Nuclear Debate*, RAND Corporation Report R-3565 (Santa Monica, Calif., November 1987).

6. The first several chapters of Fred Kaplan's *Wizards of Armageddon* (New York: Simon and Schuster, 1983), present an excellent picture of Brodie's early thinking and writing.

7. Evaluation of individual contributions is not a purpose of this essay. Not only are the five people listed seminal contributors, but they also represent different aspects of strategic policy making at crucial times throughout the period. A fuller list of still-active major participants over a long period of time would have to include, at a minimum, Morton Halperin, William Kaufmann, George Kennan, Paul Nitze, and Henry Rowen.

8. The two other major members of the team, Henry Rowen and Fred Hoffman, have also continued to be active in the debate throughout the entire period, Hoffman being one of the developers of the strategic implications of President Reagan's Strategic Defense Initiative (SDI).

9. Albert Wohlstetter, "The Delicate Balance of Terror," *Foreign Affairs* (January 1959).

10. Thomas C. Schelling, *The Strategy of Conflict* (Cambridge, Mass.: Harvard University Press, 1960).

11. McGeorge Bundy, *Danger and Survival: Choices About the Bomb in the First Fifty Years* (New York: Random House, 1988), Chapter IX.

12. Robert S. McNamara, "Defense Arrangements of the North Atlantic Community," Department of State *Bulletin*, July 9, 1962, 67.

13. See the many quotes from McNamara in 1962, in William W. Kaufmann, *The McNamara Strategy* (New York: Harper and Row, 1964), Ch. 2, "The Search for Options." Kaufmann had drafted the Ann Arbor speech and many of the others.

14. Robert S. McNamara, "The Dynamics of Nuclear Strategy," Department of State *Bulletin*, October 9, 1967, 443–44. The speech was drafted by Morton Halperin, then in the Defense Department. Halperin, by then on his way to becoming a strong Limiter, shifted to the National Security Council staff in the first year of the Nixon administration, where he was so strange an anomaly that his phone was tapped by his superiors before he quit.

15. The ABM treaty is sometimes considered part of SALT, sometimes a separate entity.

16. Lawrence Freedman, *The Evolution of Nuclear Strategy* (New York: St. Martin's Press, 1981), 357.

17. Henry A. Kissinger, *Nuclear Weapons and Foreign Policy* (New York: Harper and Row, 1957).

18. Henry A. Kissinger, *The Necessity for Choice* (New York: Harper and Row, 1960).

19. James Schlesinger, testimony before U.S. House of Representatives, Committee on Armed Services, *Military Posture and Procurement of Aircraft, Missiles, Tracked Combat Vehicles, Torpedoes and Other Weapons*, Title I, H.R. 12564, Part 1 of Hearings on Military Posture, Department of Defense Authorization for Appropriations for Fiscal Year 1975, 1974, 46.

20. Paul Nitze, "The Objectives of Arms Control," *Current Policy* 677 (Department of State Bureau of Public Affairs, Washington, D.C., March 28, 1985), 5.

21. Thomas C. Schelling, "What Went Wrong with Arms Control," *Foreign Affairs* (Winter 1985/86), 224–30.

22. *Report of the President's Commission on Strategic Forces* (Washington, D.C.: U.S. Government Printing Office, April 1983), 15.

23. Robert A. Levine, *The Arms Debate* (Cambridge, Mass.: Harvard University Press, 1963), Table 1, 212–13, and Table 2, 278.

24. *Discriminate Deterrence*, 2.

25. Nicole Gnessoto, "Le dialogue franco-allemand depuis 1954: patience et longueur de temps," in Karl Kaiser and Pierre Lellouche, eds., *Le couple franco-allemand et la défense de l'Europe* (Paris: IFRI, 1986), 11.

6

Learning in U.S. Policy
Toward Europe

Wallace J. Thies

U.S. policy toward Europe during the cold war can be viewed as either a radical departure from isolationism or a continuation of initiatives taken in response to World War II. On February 3, 1939, President Roosevelt told a news conference that his foreign policy had "not changed and it is not going to change. . . . We are against any entangling alliances, obviously." Ten years later his successor, Harry Truman, signed the North Atlantic Treaty, telling the audience at the signing ceremony that had there been such a pact in 1914 and 1939 the two world wars would not have occurred.[1] After World War I, U.S. forces were quickly withdrawn from Europe and suggestions that the United States should attempt to influence events there were met for the most part during the interwar years with apathy and even scorn.[2] After World War II, most U.S. forces were again withdrawn but some were left behind, and since 1951 the United States has routinely stationed hundreds of thousands of servicemen in Europe on a more or less permanent basis. During the 1930s, the Western democracies effectively demoralized each other through their inability to collaborate in the face of the dynamism exhibited by Germany, Italy, and Japan.[3] After World War II, the formation of the North Atlantic Treaty Organization (NATO) and its assorted councils, committees, and military commands signified acceptance by the United States and its European allies of a degree of peacetime collaboration unprecedented in the history of alliances.[4]

And yet, the policies followed by the United States since World War II can also be seen as the product of a world view that came to be widely held among elite groups concerned about foreign policy as a result of the events that preceded the war and the experience of close collaboration with other countries, especially Great Britain, during the war itself. The failure of the United States to play a constructive role during the 1930s convinced many Americans of the need for policies that would ensure that the events that had precipitated the second world war were not repeated during the postwar period.[5] Military and economic aid to the countries of Western Europe was facilitated by precedents established during the war, especially the Lend-Lease Act and U.S. leadership in the creation of the United Nations Relief and Rehabilitation Administration.[6] The idea of an integrated coalition force, which was adopted by NATO members as a means of strengthening deterrence and ensuring effective resistance in the event of war, was largely the product of the favorable experiences of American and British officers with SHAEF (Supreme Headquarters, Allied Expeditionary Forces), the unified command that planned the cross-Channel invasion and directed the campaign that culminated in the German surrender.[7] The various combined boards and committees established by the United States and Great Britain to oversee the war effort served as precedents that influenced both the design of NATO and the activities assigned to its military commands and supporting agencies.[8]

Since the formation of NATO the goals pursued by the United States in its policies toward Europe have remained essentially the same: to prevent all or even part of Western Europe from falling under Soviet control, and to do so in a way that economized on U.S. resources and left the United States free to defend its interests elsewhere in the world. The strategies devised to attain these ends have varied in response to innovations in weaponry and changing perceptions of Soviet intentions; declaratory policy has also changed as successive administrations have sought to set themselves apart from their predecessors. This blend of continuity and change makes U.S. policy toward Europe a useful case study of the extent to which U.S. leaders have learned from the experiences of their predecessors. If every incident were a unique occurrence, learning would not be possible, for the past would offer no guide to the future. If ends and means never varied at all, learning would also be impossible, because policy makers would have no grounds for concluding that one combination was superior to another. It is precisely because U.S. policy toward Europe has incorporated elements of both stability and change that a review of its development since 1945 should yield insights into four aspects of learning in U.S. policy:

1. To what extent have U.S. officials been influenced to adopt new policies in response to exposure to certain experiences (the reward-punishment definition of learning)?

2. To what extent have U.S. officials changed their views concerning tactics, strategy, and general policy objectives (the cognitive content definition of learning)?

3. To what extent have U.S. officials acquired a more sophisticated understanding of the political/strategic environment (the cognitive structural definition of learning)?

4. To what extent have U.S. officials learned to pursue their goals more effectively as a result of their own experiences and those of their predecessors (the efficiency definition of learning)?

THE TRUMAN ADMINISTRATION AND THE FORMATION OF NATO

The Truman administration's acceptance of a peacetime alliance with the countries of Western Europe has often been described as a revolutionary departure from traditional U.S. isolationism, but this view overlooks important changes in the outlook of U.S. officials that preceded by several years the signing of the North Atlantic Treaty in 1949.[9] The imposition of communist governments on Poland, Hungary, Romania, and Bulgaria; Soviet pressures on Turkey and Iran; and the efforts of communist parties in Greece, Italy, France, and elsewhere to gain power by means both violent and nonviolent suggested to many in the United States a repetition of the tactics used by Germany in the 1930s to isolate and gobble up vulnerable territories on its southern and eastern borders.[10] By the time the British informed the State Department of their intention to withdraw from Greece and Turkey, the Truman administration was for the most part agreed that if the United States should stand aside and do nothing, as it had during the 1930s, the balance of power would grow progressively less favorable to the democratic states, Soviet ambitions would expand, and the likelihood of war would increase.[11] From this conviction flowed the decisions to extend military and economic aid to Greece and Turkey, to sponsor the European Recovery Program, and to undertake the rehabilitation of West Germany and its reintegration into the economic and political life of Western Europe.

The frequency with which analogies between Nazi Germany and Soviet Russia were bandied about in the media and in the speeches and writings of members of the articulate public during the postwar years did not mean, however, that U.S. officials were unaware of the differences between Germany and the Soviet Union.[12] Within the Truman administration, analogies between Hitlerism and Stalinism were viewed as misleading and dangerous because they diverted attention away from the real threat posed by the Soviets.[13] Unlike Nazi Germany, the Soviet Union had no timetable for conquest and preferred to make gains by political rather than military means.[14] Soviet activities constituted an assault against the West, but it was an assault that was limited to "territory thought most favorable to the interior lines of the Soviets, where their military power was superior, and [to] political issues in international discussions, where stubborn and skillful opposition to American proposals could be successful at little cost."[15] The Soviets could be counted on to make a grab for anything that came within their reach, but they were not expected to press their demands to the point of war.[16] The possibility of war could never be completely discounted, but in view of the enormous devastation suffered by the Soviet Union during World War II and the leadership's fear of mutinies and large-scale defections in the event of a major international conflict, "Russia cannot possibly be regarded as a power that has solved all its internal problems, is armed to the teeth and ready to plunge the world into war."[17]

More serious than the danger of a Soviet invasion was the possibility that the peoples of Western Europe would become so demoralized by the rigors of war and reconstruction that they would turn in desperation to the Communists in their search for rulers who could ensure adequate supplies of food and fuel; alternatively, they might become vulnerable to Communist-led coups carried out under the shadow of Soviet military power.[18] "The Russians don't want to invade anyone," George Kennan wrote to Walter Lippmann in April 1948, but the possibility that they might do so was eroding the nerves of governments and publics in Western Europe and diverting their attention from the more pressing problems of economic reconstruction and domestic political stability.[19] "[A]s things stand today," Kennan told an audience at the National War College in October 1947, "it is not Russian military power which is threatening us, it is Russian political power. . . . If it is not entirely a military threat, I doubt that it can be met effectively by military means."[20]

On the basis of their assessment of the similarities and differences between the political/military environment that produced the second world war and the one that prevailed during the years immediately following the war, officials in the Truman administration drew several conclusions concerning the policies required of the United States. First, even though the danger of a Soviet invasion was low, the United States could not withdraw to the sidelines as it had after the first world war and leave the European democracies to fend for themselves. The Soviets "did not separate their military, political and economic policies but had rather a single integrated policy and used the threat of armed force to enhance fear."[21] The war, in other words, was already in progress.[22] Without a sense of confidence in the future, consumers in Western Europe would not save, business leaders would not invest, and economic recovery would grind to a halt. Despair would grow, governments would be unable to halt the spread of chaos, and Western Europe would fall to the Communists as a result of internal decay. "Which is better," President Truman asked in a memorandum on the budgetary choices facing the country, "to spend twenty or thirty billion dollars to keep the peace or to do as we did in 1920 and then have to spend 100 billion dollars for four years to fight a war?"[23]

Second, however, since the danger of war was low, the United States and its European partners could afford to move slowly and deliberately in responding to the Soviet threat. What was needed was not a crash program but rather a carefully tailored collective effort that put a premium on European initiative and self-help in order to make the most of the limited resources available to the United States. Even before the end of 1947 a consensus had begun to form in the Truman administration that the advance of Soviet power in Europe had been halted, at least for the moment, and that this outcome was largely although not exclusively due to the refusal of the United States to withdraw the remaining U.S. military forces in Europe prior to the conclusion of satisfactory peace settlements and to the prospect of U.S. aid in the form of the Marshall Plan.[24] The burden that this effort had entailed weighed heavily on U.S. officials—in the words of an influential paper prepared within the State Department:

> We have borne almost single handedly the burden of the international effort to stop the Kremlin's political advance. But this has stretched our resources dangerously far in several respects. . . . In these circumstances it is clearly unwise for us to continue the attempt to carry alone, or largely single handed, the opposition to Soviet expansion. It is urgently necessary for us to restore something of the balance of power in Europe and Asia by strengthening local forces of independence and by getting them to assume part of our burden.[25]

The best way to do this was by prodding the Europeans to take a more realistic view of the challenges that they faced and the solutions available to them. Soviet efforts to intimidate and subvert the democratic states of Western Europe were likely to continue for a very long time, but the most appropriate response was not to prepare for war but rather to redouble efforts to secure prompt passage of the European Recovery Program (ERP) combined with efforts to bring West Germany into a more normal relationship with its neighbors, preferably by means of greater political and economic integration in Western Europe.[26] ERP was the key to economic recovery, which would make possible an increase in the military strength of the European democracies, thereby contributing to the goal of restoring "something of the balance of power." Soviet attempts to subvert the recovery process were to be met by a determined effort to move West Germany to self-government, without which it would be impossible to persuade German workers to make the exertions needed to revive the productive power of German factories and mines. Economic revival in Germany would make an important contribution to economic recovery in Western Europe; more important, by insisting on a coordinated program based on self-help and mutual aid as the price of U.S. aid, the combination of ERP and political rehabilitation in Germany would open the door to a Europe that was integrated both politically and economically. Implicit in the Truman administration's view was the belief that a politically united Western Europe that could draw on the resources of western Germany would comprise a unit of sufficient size and strength to withstand Soviet efforts at intimidation and subversion largely on its own.[27]

The Communist coup in Czechoslovakia and later the blockade of West Berlin demonstrated the limits of this line of reasoning and compelled the administration to consider stronger measures—most prominently a formal security arrangement for the North Atlantic area—to achieve the goal of reviving the confidence of the European democracies. Military power "cast shadows and influenced policy," and as of 1948 it was the Soviets who were casting the longer shadow.[28] Yet even as the Truman administration was conducting the negotiations that culminated in the North Atlantic Treaty, it strove mightily to keep the talks focused more on what the Europeans could do for themselves than on what the United States might do for them. European security, in the words of Undersecretary of State Robert Lovett, would have to be "rebuilt on a much sounder basis than in the past"—the United States could not afford to "rebuild a fire-trap." Rival nationalisms would have to be subordinated to the goal of defending a common Western civilization against the threat from the east. The price of an alliance with the United States was thus an end to the Franco-German quarrel and the reintegration of West Germany into the political and economic life of Western Europe.[29]

In sum, the goal of the Truman administration during the years following World War II was the creation of a favorable political/military posture from which to thwart Soviet political ploys backed by the threat of an invasion while gradually assembling the forces and contingency plans needed to hedge against the unlikely but still real possibility that war might occur.[30] U.S. officials absorbed the "lessons of the 1930s," but they also recognized that there were important differences between the challenges posed by Nazi Germany and the Soviet Union. They sought to walk a fine line between the political and the military dangers facing the West in the hope that it would be possible to evolve a posture adequate to deal with both. The policy that was the product of these perspectives was one that recognized that spending too much on defense could be as dangerous as spending too little, since excessive military spending could stifle economic recovery and frighten the peoples of Western Europe into believing that war was imminent and that neutralism offered the only chance for survival.[31] It was a policy that subordinated the creation of larger forces-in-being to the goal of economic recovery, that assigned a higher priority to deterring Soviet adventurism than to preparing a robust defense, and that pursued deterrence more through the assembling of a unified Western coalition than through specific threats of retaliation. It was recognized by U.S. officials that such a policy entailed distinct military risks, but these were judged tolerable in view of the widely shared belief that the Soviets did not want war.[32] U.S. officials were aware that giving too much weight to either the political or the military dimension of the Soviet challenge could be disastrous, yet they were on the whole confident that the West in general and the United States in particular were capable of surmounting the dangers that they faced. In Kennan's words, "The West could win this cold war."[33]

THE IMPACT OF THE KOREAN WAR

The North Korean invasion of South Korea raised the subjective probability of war in Europe and resulted in an abrupt change in both the assumptions and the time perspective on which U.S. policy was based. The war in Korea suggested that prudent planning could no longer be based on the assumption that the Soviet challenge was essentially political in nature.[34] The heightened concern about the possibility of a Soviet military adventure provided the impetus needed to persuade Americans and Europeans alike of the need for immediate increases in the size of their armed forces, which henceforth would be organized as an integrated force under a unified command.

The sense of urgency generated by the attack on South Korea can be seen most clearly in the quickened pace of the buildup conducted by the NATO members during 1951 and 1952. Between December 1949 and May 1950, the number of divisions available to NATO members in Western Europe increased by only 2, from 12 to 14, most of which were understrength, short on equipment, and ill prepared for war.[35] The December 1950 meeting of the NATO council in Brussels agreed on General Eisenhower as commander of the integrated force that was to be created during 1951; Eisenhower's headquarters was established in Paris in January and activated as an operational command in April. Overall, NATO forces in Western Europe increased from 15 divisions and fewer than 1,000 aircraft in April 1951 to approximately 35 divisions, in varying degrees of readiness, and slightly fewer than 3,000 aircraft by December 1951.[36] By the end of 1953, the ground forces commanded by Eisenhower's successor, General Matthew Ridgway, had increased to about 100 divisions (about 25 active-duty divisions and 40 to 50 reserve divisions in Western Europe, plus 14 Turkish and 8 Greek divisions), backed by an extensive infrastructure of airfields, communication facilities, and pipelines.[37]

These were impressive achievements, but of greater long-term significance was a set of attitudes that came to be widely held in both the United States and Western Europe as a result of the experience of responding to the challenge posed by the Korean War. Fears that the attack on South Korea was but a precursor of an attack on Western Europe dissipated quickly during the winter of 1950–1951, and the subsequent stalemate on the Korean peninsula, the start of truce talks in the summer of 1951, and the increasing unpopularity of the war and the sacrifices that it entailed combined to reduce the urgency of the rearmament effort. The NATO buildup was sustained throughout 1951 and 1952, but only by means of extraordinary measures such as the creation in October 1951 of the Temporary Council Committee (TCC) and its executive board of W. Averill Harriman, Sir Edwin Plowden, and Jean Monnet. These were charged with examining the financial and economic resources and the military programs and plans of NATO members in order to devise a three-year program that would provide the forces needed for a robust conventional defense of Western Europe.[38] The force goals proposed by the TCC for 1952 called for approximately 50 active and reserve divisions and 4,000 aircraft in Western Europe by the end of the year, to be followed by additional increases during 1953 and 1954.[39] This program was endorsed by the NATO council during its meeting in Lisbon in February 1952 and the goals set for 1952 were for the most part achieved on schedule, but at the cost of a defense burden that loomed so large as to be politically unsustainable for the remaining two years of the Lisbon program.[40] By the end of 1952, retrenchment was very much on the minds of Western leaders on both sides of the Atlantic.[41]

In the United States, Congress cut $4.3 billion from President Truman's $50.9 billion defense budget for fiscal 1953, "absolutely and proportionately the largest congressional cut in the military budget between 1946 and 1961."[42] Cuts in the U.S. effort encouraged a slackening in Western Europe. British officials took the lead in proposing what Churchill called a "reshaping of defense concepts," which would entail less reliance on ground forces and more on the deterrent effect of nuclear weapons. Efforts to scale down the ambitious force goals approved at Lisbon received official sanction at the December 1952 meeting of the NATO council in Paris. The council agreed that "while there was a continuing need for progressively increasing the number of NATO forces, the emphasis during 1953 should be on improving combat efficiency."[43]

The slackening of the rearmament effort coincided with a change of administration and of strategic doctrine in the United States. Eisenhower's administration took office committed to reducing defense expenditures to a level the economy could support without undue strain over the long haul. The alternatives, it was believed, were either excessive inflation as a result of continued deficit financing or a stifling of economic activity by the increased taxes needed to close the budget gap. Either way, the result was expected to be what administration officials referred to as "national bankruptcy."[44] The budget cuts necessary to eliminate the deficit inherited from the Truman administration could be achieved only by significant reductions in defense spending, which in turn would require substantial cuts in conventional forces, especially the Army and the Marine Corps. The manpower reductions that the Eisenhower administration planned to make would be offset by increased reliance on firepower in the form of nuclear weapons, both tactical and strategic. The doctrinal basis for these changes was provided by NSC 162/2, approved by Eisenhower in October 1953, which rejected the assumption that a general war or even a large-scale limited war could be fought without nuclear weapons. NSC 162/2 authorized the services to plan to employ nuclear weapons in any future conflict in which their use would be militarily advantageous.[45]

Concurrent with its efforts to reshape U.S. strategic doctrine, the Eisenhower administration pressed for a shift in NATO strategy in the direction of greater reliance on nuclear weapons, both strategic and tactical, as instruments of both deterrence and defense. Tactical nuclear weapons had not figured prominently in NATO planning prior to 1952 because they were not expected to be available in quantity prior to the completion of the three-year program accepted at Lisbon; the Lisbon goals were thus the product of a belief that there was no alternative to a largely conventional defense of Europe. The rising volume of complaints emanating from European capitals during 1952 concerning the burdens imposed by the rearmament effort were interpreted by U.S. officials to mean that the Lisbon program could be completed only if the United States paid a larger share of the cost in the form of increased military and economic aid. This option not only conflicted with Eisenhower's determination to reduce government spending; more important, a strategy based on large conventional forces was one that, in his view, played to Soviet strength.[46] Unexpectedly rapid progress in the development and production of tactical nuclear weapons during 1951 and 1952 suggested the possibility of substituting greater firepower for the additional divisions that were to be formed by NATO members during 1953 and 1954. U.S. officials pushed for adoption of a nuclear strategy by NATO, and in December 1954 the NATO council "brought NATO strategy into line with American strategy and authorized SHAPE to base its military planning on the assumption that nuclear weapons would be used in future conflicts." A goal of 30 nuclear-armed active-duty divisions was later set for the European central region, but as of 1960 only 22 had been deployed.[47]

The failure to complete the three-year program agreed on at Lisbon and the subsequent scaling back of force goals in the face of pleas of financial hardship had the effect of saddling NATO with a lingering sense of the inadequacy of Western armies and a belief that democratic states could never match the ability of the Soviet Union and its satellites to mobilize manpower for military purposes.[48] The letdown was all the greater because even the proponents of the Lisbon program had conceded that the goal was not to build a force that could triumph in a prolonged conventional war. While numerically inferior to the forces of the Soviet Union and its allies, the force envisaged at Lisbon was to be large enough to create doubts in Moscow about the wisdom of an attack (thereby reinforcing the deterrent effect of the U.S. Strategic Air Command) and if need be to hold a defensive line long enough to permit mobilization of additional Western manpower and the destruction of much of the Soviet Union's war-making capacity by means of a strategic air offensive.[49]

Soviet conventional superiority was thus accepted as a fact of life during the Eisenhower years, both in the United States and in Western Europe. Official NATO estimates credited the Soviets alone with an army of 175 divisions, of which 140 were believed to be operational standing divisions, backed by a capability to mobilize as many as 400 divisions in 30 days.[50] Faced with a force of this size, the 20 or so divisions available to NATO members along the central front in Germany appeared so vastly outnumbered that the West had no choice but to rely on early and massive use of nuclear weapons in the event of a Soviet attack.

There was, however, considerable evidence available that the military balance was nowhere near as unfavorable to the West as the conventional wisdom suggested; what was lacking in NATO capitals was the will to seek it out and put it to use. The Soviets did not respond to the NATO buildup during 1950–1952 by attempting to maintain the numerical superiority that they possessed prior to the Korean War; instead, they continued to maintain the same 22 divisions in East Germany that had been there in 1948.[51] More important, it was known as early as 1951 that the figure of 175 divisions that was accepted in the West as an accurate description of Soviet ground forces was essentially a chimera that concealed an army very different in structure from those in the West:

> Much hysterical nonsense is printed about Russian strength, the most widely published figure being 175 divisions. These "divisions" include artillery divisions, engineer divisions, and low grade infantry divisions, along with crack guards and armored divisions; and all are smaller than western divisions. By our measure, the Russians may have between 70 and 80 divisions in their standing army, with perhaps twenty-five close to the line that divides Europe.[52]

It was also known in the early 1950s that, while the Soviet army was organized into a larger number of divisions than those fielded by Western armies, only those along the frontier in Germany and in the Far East were kept at full strength; the rest were maintained at substantially less than full strength.[53]

As a result, far from leaving the West hopelessly outnumbered, the NATO-wide rearmament effort of the early 1950s gained for the West rough parity on the ground, despite the failure of the NATO countries to complete the three-year program agreed on at Lisbon. The combined armed forces of the NATO countries increased from about 4.2 million in 1950 to 5.8 million in 1951, 6.6 million in 1952, and 6.7 million in 1953. By comparison, the combined armed forces of the Soviet Union and its Eastern European allies were estimated to be about 6.0 million in 1954.[54] No single measure adequately captures the complexities involved in assessing the relative military capabilities of NATO and the Warsaw Pact, but a focus on total regular armed forces is revealing of the overall level of effort by each side and of the forces that could be brought to bear relatively quickly in the event of another war.

Along the central front in Germany, the military balance during the first year of Eisenhower's presidency was actually quite favorable to the West:

> Stripped of words and propaganda, the Atlantic effort in Europe has reached the point where, in Germany, . . . we can mass a heavier weight of armor and men than can the Russians. At the critical German front, we can mass 500,000 men against the Russians' 300,000.[55]

The NATO buildup during the early 1950s was of such a magnitude that Ridgway's successor as supreme allied commander, Europe (SACEUR), General Alfred Gruenther, asserted in June 1954 that the Soviets would be severely defeated if they were foolish enough to attack, although he warned that the relatively favorable military balance then prevailing might not endure.[56]

The armed forces of the NATO countries declined in size after 1953, but this was the result of policy decisions rather than an iron law of political economy. The assumptions that future wars would inevitably be nuclear and that nuclear weapons could substitute for manpower were used by the Eisenhower administration to justify sharp reductions in U.S. forces. Total U.S. active-duty forces fell from roughly 3.5 million in 1953 to 2.5 million by 1960. Most of the cuts were absorbed by the ground forces: the Army declined from 1.5 million in 1953 to 870,000 in 1960; the Marines from 243,000 in 1954 to 175,000 in 1960.[57] The Europeans were only too willing to emulate the example set by the United

States. British forces peaked at about 900,000 in 1953, declining to about 520,000 in 1960. A West German army of 12 divisions by 1957 had been envisioned at the time of West Germany's entrance into NATO in 1955, but by 1950 only 7 divisions had been created.[58]

Despite these reductions, the conventional balance in Europe did not tilt sharply in favor of the Warsaw Pact. Soviet forces were also cut back after the death of Stalin, from a peak of about 5.0 million in 1955 to about 3.6 million by 1960. Polish forces declined from about 500,000 in 1950 to about 200,000 in 1960, while the Hungarian army was virtually disbanded after the uprising there in 1956.[59] As of Eisenhower's last year in office, the combined armed forces of the NATO countries were roughly one-third again as large as those of the Warsaw Pact.[60] Figures published by Hanson Baldwin in 1959 indicated that NATO members had earmarked 2.2 million soldiers to hold a defensive line in Western Europe; facing them were 1.77 million Soviet troops backed by 1.2 million soldiers from the satellite countries. Even if one assumed that the satellite forces were 100 percent reliable and that the Soviets would commit all of their available forces to an attack on Western Europe (leaving none behind for rear-area security, ensuring the reliability of the satellites, and so on), the ratio of attacking to defending forces would have been only 1.3:1, hardly an overwhelming margin of superiority.[61]

But while the private assessments of NATO military commanders and intelligence officers, as reflected in their off-the-record comments to sympathetic journalists, presented a picture of rough parity on the ground, official NATO estimates continued to credit the Soviets with overwhelming conventional superiority.[62] The basis for the disparity can be traced to the prevailing mood of skepticism concerning the ability of democratic states to act responsibly in the realm of military affairs:

> [NATO military commanders] know that if they pause for praise, parliaments and peoples will relax instantly, slash budgets, strip down taxes—before the necessary planes and pilots are supplied, before the war reserves are in the warehouses, before the almost finished creation of their devotion receives its capping, final increment of strength. Their duty then, as they see it, is to moan rather than boast, to exhort rather than comfort and to flog reluctant civilians along the path of duty, however great the strain and unwilling the flesh.[63]

Eisenhower's administration was for the most part content to accept without challenge the simple division counts provided by NATO that suggested that the West was hopelessly outnumbered because of its belief that the United States should not attempt to build larger conventional forces, not even for an area as important as Western Europe. The purpose of NSC 162/2 was to support the president's efforts to reduce military spending by closing off the possibility that any of the services might generate "requirements" for manpower and equipment larger than what the administration was prepared to provide by claiming that conventional resistance was feasible.[64] In Eisenhower's view, the United States should serve as a center of production and inspiration but not as a supplier of troops:

> Our view in the central position must be directed to many sectors. We cannot concentrate all our forces in any one sector, even one as important as Western Europe. We must largely sit here with great, mobile, powerful reserves ready to support our policies, our rights, our interests wherever they may be in danger in the world.[65]

Any attempt to field larger conventional forces would also have stirred up trouble with the Taft wing of the Republican party, which had made its belief in the inadequacy of Western armies the cornerstone for its claims that the United States should withdraw to the Western Hemisphere and use air and naval power to prevent any increase in the area under Communist control.[66]

In retrospect, there is a certain irony in the way in which the attitudes of U.S. officials evolved during the 1950s. In 1948 and 1949, when the armies of the NATO countries really were outnumbered and outgunned, officials in the Truman administration took a coolly calculating view of the situation in Europe, resolved not to be panicked into emergency measures, and opted for a program intended to result in a slow but steady rebuilding of Western strength. Yet by 1953, the sense of futility resulting from the failure to complete the full three-year program agreed on at Lisbon pushed U.S. officials to consider the substitution of nuclear weapons for manpower even though the force increases achieved during 1951 and 1952 were of such a magnitude that rough parity in conventional forces had already been achieved.[67]

Eisenhower told a press conference on December 15, 1954, that, to preserve the free enterprise system at a level of taxation that the American people would support, he preferred to base his military policies on preparations to meet the great threat (all-out war) and to rely on improvisation to handle smaller ones.[68] His views in this regard are indicative of his determination to avoid a repetition of the unpleasantness associated with the Korean War rearmament effort. For the NATO countries as a whole, per capita consumption in 1951 was approximately equal to that of 1950, but some countries—notably the United States, Great Britain, Canada, the Netherlands, and Norway—experienced a decline in living standards.[69] Over the period 1950–1954, however, both the Western European and North American members of NATO achieved such a substantial rise in production that living standards rose even as defense expenditures were climbing rapidly. By 1954 the real increase in production was such that government expenditures, including defense, were absorbing only about one-half of the increase in total output achieved since 1950. Per capita consumption within the NATO countries increased by 7 percent over the period 1950–1954.[70] By 1956, all of the European members of NATO had achieved new peaks of economic strength and prosperity.[71] In effect, the Eisenhower administration turned to a nuclear strategy to justify reductions in defense spending and the number of men under arms at a time when the economic strength of the United States and its allies was increasing, not declining.[72]

THE STRATEGY OF "RETALIATION"

A second legacy of the Korean War, closely related to the belief that the West was hopelessly outclassed in conventional forces, is perhaps best described as the militarization of U.S. perspectives on the struggle for Europe. Prior to the invasion of South Korea, the policies of the Truman administration had been based on the belief that the Soviet Union sought the fruits of war but without the risks and exertions and thus that the struggle for Europe was essentially a political/psychological contest in which alliances and armed forces served as instruments of intimidation and reassurance rather than conquest and destruction. Officials in the Truman administration were able to take a relatively relaxed view of the military threat posed by the presence of Soviet forces in Central Europe because it was generally accepted within the U.S. military establishment that, in the unlikely event of war, a strategic air offensive from bases in Britain and North Africa could degrade Soviet war-making potential to the point at which another cross-Channel invasion and liberation of Western Europe would be possible.[73]

The opening weeks of the Korean War effectively dispelled the combination of prideful memories of World War II and naive optimism concerning the military value of strategic airpower that the Truman administration had used to rationalize the low and inflexible ceilings on military spending that had been imposed in 1948, 1949, and 1950.[74] Even with sizable U.S. forces nearby in Japan, the first two months of the war were essentially one defeat after another for the United Nations side. "If they had gone into Greece," Acheson told the Senate Foreign Relations Committee on July 24, 1950, "we don't have any troops within a thousand miles of Greece. We couldn't have done anything about Iran; we would have a terrible time doing anything about Berlin."[75]

In the pre-Korea period, merely agreeing on a plan for assembling the forces needed to defend Western Europe was regarded as a great achievement.[76] The ease with which the North Koreans had overrun most of South Korea in a matter of weeks made the elaborate NATO structure, with its layers of committees and working groups, appear to be little more than an empty shell incapable of repelling an attack.[77] The perilous condition of MacArthur's forces after the Chinese counterattack at the end of November 1950 contributed to the climate of military pessimism that accompanied Eisenhower's appointment as SACEUR in December. Eisenhower's appointment had been intended to alleviate the anxieties that had developed in Europe as a result of events in Korea, but the very act of recalling the commander who had supervised the cross-Channel invasion in 1944 contributed to a growing awareness in Europe and the United States that the availability of nuclear weapons could make it impossible even to assemble the forces needed to seize and hold a beachhead on the continent, much less carry out another OVERLORD-style landing.[78] Korea dramatized Europe's vulnerability, while the increased range and destructiveness of modern weapons placed a premium on finding ways to stop an invasion as far to the east as possible. From the second half of 1950 onward, U.S. officials were to grow increasingly preoccupied with invasion scenarios, to the neglect of the pre-Korea focus on the political/ psychological dimension of the contest for Europe.

This preoccupation with invasion scenarios is apparent in several aspects of U.S. policy as it developed during the 1950s. The war in Korea and the rearmament effort that it inspired transformed the Atlantic Alliance from a loosely organized coalition based on a U.S. pledge to come to Europe's aid in the event of a confrontation with the Soviet Union to an integrated multinational organization charged with assembling and directing the forces needed to meet and contain a Soviet attack. In Western Europe, fear that an invasion was imminent had begun to decline as early as the winter of 1950–1951. The death of Stalin in March 1953, the armistice in Korea in July, and the increased emphasis on "peaceful coexistence" in Soviet foreign policy in the mid-1950s combined to lower even further the subjective probability of war. In response to these changes in the political climate, the Europeans were more than willing to jettison a rearmament effort that they had never been enthusiastic about anyway in favor of a return to the pre-Korea conception of the alliance, namely as a means to commit the United States to come to their defense. U.S. officials, at whose insistence the transformation of the alliance had been undertaken, continued to see it as a tool to redress what was believed to be a serious military imbalance in Europe.[79]

The Eisenhower administration thus inherited from its predecessor the leading role in the effort to find a way to defend the territories of the European allies against a Soviet attack, but this imperative collided head on with the belief that the West was hopelessly outnumbered on the ground and with the desire, felt in both the United States and Western Europe, to reduce military spending in order to free resources for other uses.[80] The Truman administration had confronted an analogous situation in the pre-Korea period: it too believed the West was outnumbered and outgunned, and it too was committed to restricting military spending in order to speed economic recovery in Western Europe. The Truman administration had judged the resulting imbalance in conventional forces tolerable in part because of its belief that the past was not a reliable guide to the future: Stalin was not Hitler, the Soviet Union did not have a timetable for conquest, war was not imminent, and the West accordingly had time to rebuild its military strength. The Eisenhower administration was more a prisoner of the recent past, and it thus evolved a strategy designed to prevent a repetition of the last war—in this case, the Korean War.

Indicative of the Eisenhower administration's concern with preventing additional Korea-style invasions was an article published by John Foster Dulles in the summer of 1952.[81] Dulles accepted without challenge the view that the West was greatly outnumbered by the Soviets and their allies: "We cannot build a 20,000 mile Maginot line or match the Red armies, man for man, gun for gun, and tank for tank at any particular time or place their general staff selects. To attempt that would mean real strength nowhere and bankruptcy everywhere." To compensate for the Soviets' advantages in manpower and interior lines of communication, "the free world [must] develop the will and organize the means to retaliate instantly against open aggression by Red armies, so that if it occurred anywhere, we could and would strike back where it hurts, by means of our own choosing." "In the hands of statesmen," Dulles argued, nuclear weapons and the air and naval forces needed to deliver them could serve as "effective political weapons in defense of the peace." Was there, however, much danger of "open aggression by Red armies" in Europe?

At the time the NATO rearmament effort had been launched in 1950, U.S. and European officials were generally agreed that a Korea-style invasion would be a serious danger only if the Soviets were allowed to gain parity in strategic nuclear forces to go along with their pre-Korea superiority in conventional forces.[82] As of 1952, the U.S. lead in strategic nuclear forces was growing rather than shrinking, and the Soviet advantage in conventional forces was being narrowed as a result of the NATO-wide buildup begun in 1950.[83] In a prescient comment, Theodore H. White predicted that the Soviets would be led to change their tactics as a result of the shifting military balance in Europe: "Since they cannot shake Europe and the Alliance apart by force or the threat of force, they must now attempt to seduce it into disunion or magnetize it apart by political and economic war."[84]

The possibility that the Soviets might rely more on political rather than military means to erode the position of the NATO allies was precisely the aspect of Dulles's strategy that Eisenhower himself professed to be most concerned with. In a comment on a preliminary draft of Dulles's *Life* article, Eisenhower wrote:

> There is only one point that bothered me. . . . It is this: What should we do if Soviet *political* aggression, as in Czechoslovakia, successively chips away exposed positions of the free world? So far as our resulting economic situation is concerned, such an eventuality would be just as bad for us as if the area had been captured by force. To my mind, this is the case where the theory of "retaliation" falls down.[85]

Dulles promised to remedy the deficiency in the final draft, but the published version failed to deal with the issue Eisenhower had raised. Eisenhower warned Dulles again in July 1952 that "exclusive reliance on a mere power of retaliation is not a complete answer to the broad Soviet threat," but the policies that he allowed his administration to embark on during his first year in office suggest that he neglected to take his own warning seriously.[86]

As explained by Dulles in a speech before the Council on Foreign Relations on January 12, 1954, the Eisenhower administration had made a "basic decision" to depend primarily on a "great capacity to retaliate, instantly, by means and at places of our choosing."[87] "Massive retaliation" was in essence a strategy for reducing military spending but without appearing to back away from the commitment to defend Europe against Korea-style attacks. In effect, the administration proposed to squeeze the maximum mileage out of U.S. strategic nuclear forces, which it had to maintain anyway to deter a Soviet attack on the United States, by threatening to employ those forces in response to attacks on U.S. allies overseas. Concurrently, tactical nuclear weapons would be integrated into NATO's force structure and war plans, thereby adding to the credibility of the administration's threats not to be drawn into another limited war and improving the ability of NATO's forces to retard a Soviet advance. Implicit in the administration's approach was the assumption that if the United States was prepared to cope with the challenge of all-out war, it would also be prepared to cope with lesser challenges that might come its way.[88]

In the late 1940s, the Truman administration had been prepared to accept certain military risks in pursuit of a favorable political-military posture from which to engage in a long-term contest for influence with the Soviets. In the early 1950s, the Eisenhower administration saw no alternative to accepting certain political risks for the sake of a military strategy that would justify reductions in defense spending, without which the West would be too exhausted to make it through the long term. Eisenhower himself warned in his State of the Union address in 1955 that "Undue reliance on one weapon or preparation for only one kind of warfare simply invites an enemy to resort to another," but he nonetheless countenanced policies intended to foreclose the option of preparing for more than one kind of warfare in Europe.[89] The result was to heighten the vulnerability of the West to two kinds of Soviet challenges: on one hand, Soviet peace offensives intended to convince the publics of Western Europe that it was the Americans who were the principal threat to peace; on the other hand, limited challenges to the political arrangements that had evolved in Europe after the second world war, in order to place on NATO the onus of threatening a nuclear war in order to uphold the status quo. By emphasizing its determination to respond to all but the most minor contingencies with nuclear weapons, the Eisenhower administration in effect opened the door to a renewal of the kind of political warfare that the Atlantic alliance had been created to counter.[90]

A good example of the box into which the administration maneuvered itself can be found in Eisenhower's comments to a press conference on March 11, 1959, at a time of heightened tension as a result of the Soviet ultimatum on Berlin delivered in November 1958. Eisenhower reiterated the West's determination to defend West Berlin, but he also stated that NATO would not fight a ground war in Western Europe because it was outnumbered. In Eisenhower's view, the disparity in conventional forces was so great that he could see no use for a few thousand more soldiers in West Berlin or a few more divisions in Western Europe. While he was confident that the Soviets would not start a war over Berlin, he implied that if they did the United States would defend its interests with nuclear weapons if necessary, although he conceded that a nuclear war could not "free anything" and would be "self-defeating."[91]

Eisenhower's comments suggest that he and his advisers were not unaware of the drawbacks associated with threats to cross the nuclear threshold. This gave U.S. policy a schizophrenic quality during the Eisenhower years. Determination to cling to the nuclear-oriented strategy formulated during 1952 and 1953 (so as not to forgo the savings achieved by cutting conventional forces) was combined with a search for expedients that would make it unnecessary to confront explicitly the full implications of what the administration proposed to do in the event it was called on to make good its threats. A favorite theme of Eisenhower's second secretary of defense, Neil McElroy, was that "We better never let anyone get the mistaken idea that we are not going to use our big weapons if needed. The free peoples are a minority group in the world, and unless we have serious resolution to use, if need be, the big stuff in order to deter aggression or protect the free world, you are going to get into a limited war."[92] But since it was the fear that the United States would use the "big stuff" to defend Western Europe that heightened the vulnerability of NATO to Soviet peace offensives and limited challenges to the status quo, others in the administration tried to minimize the significance of its threats of massive retaliation by suggesting that it would not be necessary to go through with them.

One way in which this was done was through suggestions that the growing availability of short-range, low-yield nuclear weapons offered the prospect of victory in an East-West conflict but without harming civilians and without precipitating World War III.[93] At other times, administration spokesmen suggested that deterrence of a Soviet attack might rest on the threat of limited, graduated reprisals intended to impose unacceptable costs by means of selective strikes rather than wholesale destruction of an invader's forces.[94] This was a way of suggesting that it would be possible to fight a relatively painless nuclear war because the bombs would explode far away from the territory being defended. Sometimes both arguments were combined in an attempt to put the best possible gloss on the administration's policy. In an October 1957 article in *Foreign Affairs*, Dulles wrote that U.S. allies had until then been dependent on a strategy of deterrence based on the United States' capacity for massive retaliation against an aggressor, a strategy that had been chosen only because there was no viable alternative to it. With the development of smaller and cleaner nuclear weapons, however, "their use need not involve vast destruction and widespread harm to humanity." "In the future," Dulles continued, "it may thus be feasible to place less reliance upon deterrence of vast retaliatory power. It may be possible to defend countries by nuclear weapons so mobile, or so placed, as to make military involvement with conventional forces a hazardous attempt." Nations near the Soviet Union could possess "an effective defense against full scale conventional attack" but without endangering themselves or friendly peoples in the area.[95]

A strong case can be made that U.S. policy toward Europe during the Eisenhower years resulted in the worst of both worlds: threats of "massive retaliation" made the United States appear irresponsible and generated fears in Europe of the consequences of resisting Soviet pressures, while the disclaimers and clarifications issued by administration spokesmen undercut the credibility of its threats and encouraged the Soviets to raise the level of tensions in order to sow discord in the West. U.S. declaratory policy was hardly a model of consistency during the Eisenhower years. Eisenhower himself repeatedly proclaimed U.S. unwillingness and inability to fight a war of local resistance and emphasized his conviction that any war in Europe would inevitably involve a thermonuclear exchange. Yet he also conceded that such a war would be "self-defeating" and would bring about the "destruction of civilization as we know it."[96] Dulles told the Council on Foreign Relations in January 1954 that the West should rely on the deterrent value of "massive retaliatory power," but he also told a Senate committee in April 1957 that "With modern weapons, any general war could not be won by anybody. It would be a disaster of worldwide proportions, which would threaten indeed the very existence of the human race. . . ."[97] Dulles and McElroy may not have believed that the United States would fight a limited war in Europe, but their successors conveyed a different message. In April 1959, Secretary of State designate Christian Herter told the Senate Foreign Relations Committee that the West would not be justified in launching a nuclear war in the initial stage of a Soviet attack, and that the president would not involve the United States in an all-out war "unless the facts showed that we were in danger of devastation ourselves." Thomas Gates, Eisenhower's third secretary of defense, told the Associated Press in April 1960 that "We must be prepared for military actions of varying degrees and sizes anywhere in the world and be able to contain quickly such action. We must put out the fire of limited war in situations that range from another Korea sized conflict to one involving a small number of infantry or marines."[98]

The inconsistencies in declaratory policy, however, may have seemed a small cost compared to the administration's successes in reducing the burden of defense expenditures on the nation's economy:

> Expenditures for national defense remained remarkably stable [during the Eisenhower years], ranging from a low of $40.2 billion in fiscal 1955 to a high of $47.7 billion in fiscal 1961. More revealing are military expenditures as a percentage of the total budget—these figures actually declined, from 65.7% in fiscal 1954 to 48.5% in fiscal 1961. Defense spending as a percentage of gross national product also went down, from 12.8% in fiscal 1954 to 9.1% in fiscal 1961.[99]

The administration's critics were often scornful of what they saw as empty threats of massive retaliation, yet Eisenhower himself appears to have been convinced that such threats were more than enough to deter a Soviet Union that was plainly inferior to the United States in nuclear weapons' stockpiles and the means for their delivery.[100] "They're not ready for war and they know it," he commented in 1955. "They also know that if they go to war, they're going to end up losing everything they have. That . . . tends to make people conservative."[101]

FROM "RETALIATION" TO "FLEXIBLE RESPONSE"

Eisenhower's policies were based on the belief that the United States could safely threaten the Soviet Union with a nuclear riposte because the latter not only lacked the means for extensive retaliation but was not expected to acquire such a capability until the early 1960s.[102] The Kennedy administration was strongly influenced by evidence that had begun to accumulate as early as 1955 of a growing Soviet capability for intercontinental nuclear strikes.[103] During the Eisenhower years, the U.S. contribution to NATO planning was based largely on the assumption that there was only one contingency worthy of serious consideration, namely an all-out attack across the north German plain.[104] Kennedy and his advisers rejected the fixation on a single contingency and the deliberate narrowing of options that had been the product of the nuclear-oriented approach of their predecessors. Their concern for the vulnerability of the United States to Soviet retaliation led them to search for ways to limit and control the use of violence in order to prevent escalation to all-out war. Eisenhower's policies assumed that there was a ceiling on defense spending that, if breached, would involve an unacceptable risk of economic catastrophe. Kennedy and his advisers rejected what they saw as "the mistaken notion that the economy is unable to bear any extra burdens"; hence they saw no reason to hold defense spending below the level needed to acquire additional forces to permit nonnuclear responses to nonnuclear attacks.[105]

Kennedy and his advisers had been impressed by the difficulties their predecessors encountered in formulating responses that were both effective and in proportion to the challenges offered by the Soviets to exposed Western positions such as Berlin. As explained by Walt Rostow:

> It should be noted that we have generally been at a disadvantage in crises, since the Communists command a more flexible set of tools for imposing strain on the Free World—and a greater freedom to use them—than we normally command. We are often caught in circumstances where our only available riposte is so disproportionate to the immediate circumstances that its use risks unwanted escalation or serious political costs to the free community. This asymmetry makes it attractive for the Communists to apply limited debilitating pressure upon us in situations where we find it difficult to impose on them an equivalent price for their intrusions.[106]

Although the Kennedy administration's goals in Europe were essentially the same as those pursued by Eisenhower and Dulles, the latter had placed a higher value on the subsidiary goal of economizing on U.S. resources. "[A]s a consequence, they had been prepared to run the risks either of not acting at all, or of responding at levels beyond the original provocation. Kennedy, possessed of an economic rationale for disregarding costs, placed his emphasis on minimizing risks by giving the United States sufficient flexibility to respond without either escalation or humiliation."[107] The importance attached by Kennedy and his advisers to the availability of nonnuclear options was seemingly validated by the outcome of the Cuban missile crisis, which Kennedy himself attributed to the presence of usable conventional forces, which left the Soviets with no choice but to yield or risk nuclear war.[108]

In line with this view, the Kennedy administration placed special emphasis on strengthening NATO's capabilities for conventional resistance.[109] To provide the range of options called for by the strategy of flexible response, the number of active Army divisions was increased from 11 to 16 and the divisions themselves were restructured to improve readiness and reduce reliance on nuclear weapons. The strength of the U.S. Seventh Army in West Germany was increased from about 200,000 in 1961 to 240,000 in 1963, while the Army as a whole increased from about 870,000 in 1960 to 975,000 in 1963.[110]

The Kennedy administration also pressed for larger conventional forces from the European allies, but its arguments were received coolly by the Europeans, who were skeptical of both the practicality and the wisdom of Kennedy's approach.[111] On one hand, if the 25 or so divisions available to the alliance in Central Europe were facing 175 or more Soviet divisions, as the traditional method of assessing the military balance there suggested, what was the point of adding a few more to the NATO side? On the other hand, the Europeans argued, greater reliance on conventional forces could only imply lack of confidence in the nuclear deterrent.[112] As a result, the prerequisite to securing a larger conventional contribution from the European allies was a reexamination of the balance of forces in Central Europe, to determine whether a conventional option was feasible or not.

During the 1950s, it had been standard practice to base assessments of the military balance in Europe on simple division counts, a methodology that led inexorably to the conclusion that NATO had no choice but to rely on threats of escalation across the nuclear threshold since there did not appear to be any way that the 25 or so active-duty divisions along the NATO side of the central front could hope to withstand for long an assault by the 175 divisions that were traditionally credited to the Soviet Union alone. The misleading nature of comparisons of this kind was demonstrated anew by the systems analysts brought into the Defense Department by the Kennedy administration, who in effect rediscovered what had been known to well-connected journalists since the start of the 1950s:

> As early as 1962 it became apparent that there was something badly wrong with merely counting divisions. . . . [T]he United States had nearly a million men on active duty in the Army, organized into 16 combat divisions plus support. The Soviet Army numbered roughly two million men, only enough by our standards to support an army of about 40 divisions. Yet the Soviets were supposed to be supporting an army of 175 divisions. . . .

A more detailed review of the 175 divisions indicated that at least one-half of them were cadre divisions (that is, essentially paper units) with perhaps 10% of their manpower on board and far from 100% of their equipment. If these divisions were to be counted for the Soviets in the total comparison of military strength, our low priority National Guard and reserve divisions, numbering somewhere between 40 and 50, ought also to be counted, together with similar units for our NATO allies. Part of the problem, it appeared, was that the grand total of the Soviet force structure, including many paper units that had little real military power, was being compared with the total of combat-ready units for the NATO allies.[113]

The reaction to this reassessment of the balance in Europe was testimony to the durability of images formed a decade earlier, when the failure of NATO members to complete the rearmament program agreed on at Lisbon in 1952 had saddled the alliance with the conviction that democracies were incapable of competing with dictatorial regimes when it came to mobilizing manpower for military purposes:

The initial reaction of the Services and the NATO commanders to these studies was not to reexamine their estimates, but to explain away the differences on other grounds. A whole new set of arguments was raised to account for the overwhelming Soviet conventional superiority. The arguments came in various forms, but they all made essentially the same point: these differences could be accounted for by the higher standard of living and better treatment of the individual soldier in a Western army. Many of our soldiers, it seemed, had to man typewriters and post exchanges and medical facilities, while most Russian soldiers were out in the field with their rifles. At one briefing it was explained at great length that the Army had to have a fancy mobile field kitchen to give each of our soldiers a hot meal every day, while the Russian soldiers were accustomed to eating soup out of one huge kettle. Apparently, we were going to lose a war in Europe because U.S. soldiers didn't eat soup. . . .
   In each case, [we] tried to check out the details of the arguments. One of the striking things about this operation was the extent to which the experts fell back on hearsay and how little factual information was available to prove or disapprove their contentions. . . . The arguments that 'we have more medical personnel who don't fight,' 'half our people are behind type-writers,' 'the Russians all eat soup but we have to have a lot of cooks,' and so on appeared to be nothing more than myth—myth that says the Soviets are poor, tough, and accustomed to hardship while we are wealthy, soft, and pampered.[114]

The Kennedy administration's conclusions on the state of the military balance in Europe were never fully accepted by the Europeans, who viewed reassessments of this kind as either a device to extract from them pledges to increase defense spending and/or as a pretext to withdraw a portion of the U.S. forces stationed in Europe. "Flexible response" was not officially endorsed by the NATO allies until 1967, and even then it was not accompanied by significant changes in the alliance's conventional force posture.[115] Foot dragging by the Europeans accounted in part for the failure of the alliance to develop its capabilities for conventional resistance to the extent desired by the Kennedy administration, but a portion of the blame must be assigned to the manner in which the Kennedy and Johnson administrations implemented their own strategy.

U.S. officials during the 1960s attempted to revise the conventional wisdom of the 1950s by arguing that the alliance had had a conventional option all along. By 1965, civilian analysts in the Defense Department had come to the conclusion that NATO and the Warsaw Pact had approximate equality on the ground; by 1968 their studies suggested that NATO was *superior* to the Warsaw Pact both in immediately available forces and in reinforcement capability.[116] Officials in the Kennedy and Johnson administrations were not content merely to discredit the conventional wisdom of the Eisenhower years, pressing instead for additional increases in the alliance's conventional forces so as to raise even higher the threshold beyond which nuclear weapons might have to be employed. But neither were they prepared to dispense entirely with the deterrent effect of nuclear weapons; indeed, both wished to retain that aspect of the Eisenhower-Dulles strategy that sought to keep the Soviets uncertain of how the United States might respond to an attack.[117]

The result once again was a set of policies that were something less than a model of consistency. Kennedy and his advisers had reservations about the usefulness of tactical nuclear weapons in an area as densely populated as Western Europe, yet they increased the number of U.S. tactical nuclear weapons deployed there by 60 percent.[118] The Kennedy and Johnson administrations encouraged the European allies to increase their conventional forces, but by increasing the number of U.S. tactical nuclear weapons in Europe they in effect provided the Europeans with an excuse not to do so. Both administrations placed a premium on the controlled use of force so as to minimize pressures for escalation in the event of war, but they also wanted to keep the Soviets uncertain of the circumstances under which a conventional attack might be met by a nuclear response, which could have appeared to the latter as heightening rather than diminishing the attractiveness of a preemptive nuclear strike in a future crisis.

A more important problem centered on the purposes that flexibility was intended to serve. The Truman and Eisenhower administrations had accepted and even encouraged a constriction of available military means because they saw this as crucial to the realization of important intermediate goals, such as freeing resources to fund economic recovery in Western Europe and later removing the drag of high taxation and deficit spending from the U.S. economy. The Kennedy and Johnson administrations encouraged a multiplication of military means but without linking the greater flexibility that they sought to some broader purpose other than the ability to respond to challenges in kind. For both of them flexibility was essentially an end in itself.

U.S. efforts during the 1960s to strengthen the West's capabilities for conventional war put NATO in a stronger military position vis-à-vis the Soviet Union, but since the resulting increase in military strength was not linked to any broader political goal, the rationale for maintaining the larger conventional forces sought by the Kennedy and Johnson administrations proved difficult to sustain. The strengthened NATO military posture may have encouraged the greater restraint exhibited by the Soviets after the Cuban missile crisis had exposed as fraudulent Khrushchev's claims of Soviet strategic superiority, but as the situation in Europe became more stable, the need for large conventional forces seemed to diminish. As a result, formal acceptance by NATO in 1967 of the strategy of "flexible response" coincided with the start of a period of relative decline in NATO's conventional strength that would continue unabated throughout the Nixon and Ford years.

CARTER'S EFFORTS TO REVITALIZE THE ALLIANCE

Between 1964 and 1968, the combined armed forces of the NATO countries increased from 5.84 million to 6.2 million, but this was almost entirely the result of the expansion of U.S. forces as a result of the Vietnam War. U.S. military manpower rose from 2.69 million in 1964 to 3.5 million in 1968 while the combined forces of all other NATO members declined from 3.15 million to 3.02 million. Between 1964 and 1968, Belgium, Britain, Canada, France, and the United States all reduced their ground forces along the central front in Europe; these reductions were only partially offset by increases in West German and Dutch forces. The United States also drew down substantially U.S. tactical air units deployed in Europe in order to meet the needs of those fighting in Southeast Asia. Overall, U.S. military personnel in Europe declined from 436,000 in 1964 to 314,000 in 1968.[119]

These reductions appear not to have adversely affected the military balance in Europe, at least in the short run. The combined armed forces of the Warsaw Pact countries also declined slightly between 1964 and 1968, largely as a result of reductions in Soviet and Romanian forces. In 1968, the combined armed forces of the NATO countries were more than 50 percent larger than those of the Warsaw Pact, the most favorable ratio achieved by the NATO countries between 1960 and 1982.[120] Even if the

U.S. increases for the Vietnam War are excluded, the NATO countries still maintained roughly 30 percent more men under arms than the countries of the Warsaw Pact. In the center region, NATO in 1968 had more men under arms than did the Warsaw Pact, and the latter's advantage in tanks was offset by NATO advantages in armored personnel carriers, artillery, and vehicles and by a significant NATO qualitative advantage in tactical airpower.[121]

Between 1968 and 1977, however, the combined armed forces of the Warsaw Pact countries increased from 4.27 million to 4.75 million, with the largest increases achieved by those members facing NATO forces along the central front: the Soviet Union, East Germany, and Poland. These increases were not matched by the NATO countries. Instead, the combined armed forces of the NATO countries declined for nine consecutive years between 1968 and 1977. Most of the decline was accounted for by reductions in U.S. forces due to the disengagement from Vietnam, but most of the European members reduced their forces as well. Overall, total NATO forces decreased by 26 percent between 1968 and 1977. By 1977, the combined armed forces of the NATO countries were only 1.5 percent larger than those of the Warsaw Pact, the least favorable ratio for the period 1960–1982.[122]

These shifts in the military balance went largely unnoticed during the first half of the 1970s in part because of the preoccupation of governments and publics with the ambitious effort by Nixon and Kissinger to wrap the Soviets in a web of understandings and agreements that would give them an incentive to practice self-restraint and in part because of hopes that the military balance in Europe could be stabilized through the negotiations on Mutual and Balanced Force Reductions (MBFR).[123] The benefits of détente never materialized to the degree expected in the United States and the MBFR negotiations proceeded inconclusively even as the shifts in the military balance mentioned earlier continued: between 1973 and 1977, the combined armed forces of the NATO countries declined by about 400,000 while those of the Warsaw Pact rose by about 300,000.[124] As a result, both the Carter and the Reagan administrations moved to redress what by the end of the 1970s was widely perceived as a worsening military situation in Europe.

At President Carter's order, officials in the Defense Department made NATO their "first order of business," and within three months of the inauguration a series of memoranda detailing an action program for the alliance had been drafted and approved by Secretary of Defense Harold Brown.[125] Underlying this burst of activity was a concern that the shifts in the military balance that had occurred earlier during the 1970s could, if left unchecked, render useless the strategy of flexible response. NATO planning during the Nixon and Ford years had been based on an assumption that the Warsaw Pact countries would require at least 30 days to mobilize prior to an attack. Thus, even if NATO's decision to move to a war footing lagged a week behind that of the pact, it would still have roughly three weeks to mobilize reserves and bring up reinforcements. Soviet improvements during the 1970s in the offensive striking power of their forces and in their reinforcement capability led officials in the Carter administration to question whether that much warning time would be available in a crisis. They proposed instead that NATO be prepared to respond effectively to a Warsaw Pact attack launched after only 5–7 days of preparation.[126]

Carter administration officials also questioned whether NATO forces were still capable of implementing a "forward defense" with conventional forces, whereby a Soviet attack along the central front would be met with nonnuclear resistance as far to the east as possible in order to minimize destruction in the NATO countries and ensure West Germany's support for the alliance. An interagency review of the global military balance, sent to the president in June 1977, concluded that the Warsaw Pact countries had achieved a 2:1 advantage in forces along the central front as a result of improvements during the 1970s. While this advantage was deemed "too small in itself for the attacker to have any expectation of quick or substantial victory," the report concluded that "the chance of NATO stopping an attack with minimal loss of territory and then achieving its full objective of recovering that land which had been lost appears remote at the present time."[127]

These considerations led officials in the Carter administration to conclude that first priority for NATO should be to strengthen the alliance's conventional forces, and especially their ability to respond to an attack launched with little or no warning. The centerpiece of the administration's efforts in this regard was the proposals presented personally by President Carter to the NATO council in London in May 1977. Because the military balance in Europe had been shifting against the West for nearly a decade, the president proposed that the alliance undertake a series of "quick fixes" intended to remedy its most pressing needs immediately plus a long-term defense program backed by a commitment to real increases in defense spending of at least 3 percent per year.[128]

Taken as a whole, the Carter proposals for redressing the conventional balance in Europe constituted the most ambitious plan for strengthening the alliance's forces since the program agreed on at Lisbon in 1952. The precedent set at Lisbon did not augur well for the Carter proposals. The three-year buildup proposed by the TCC had been accepted in large part because of fears of Soviet adventurism if they were allowed to gain parity in strategic nuclear forces to go along with their perceived advantage in conventional forces. As U.S. superiority in strategic nuclear forces became more apparent and as international tensions declined following the death of Stalin, the willingness of all of the NATO allies to complete the full three-year program agreed on at Lisbon declined markedly, and the program itself was for all practical purposes dropped at the end of the first year.

By 1977, the subjective probability of war in Europe was already very low and there was little on the horizon that the Carter administration could point to as justification for a prolonged and costly effort to strengthen the alliance's conventional forces other than a vaguely defined goal of making it through the 1980s. As a result, while the program of "quick fixes" was agreed to by the NATO allies during 1977 and a long-term defense program incorporating about 100 recommendations was drafted during 1977 and 1978, only modest improvements to the Alliance's conventional forces were actually achieved during 1977–1979.[129] The progress in this regard was so modest that in the aftermath of the Soviet invasion of Afghanistan the Carter administration proposed yet another package of quick fixes and longer-term improvements to the alliance's conventional forces—one that bore a striking resemblance to the program presented by President Carter in London just three years before.[130] Despite efforts to make this latest package more palatable to the Europeans by giving them substantial advance warning of what the administration would be proposing, the former consented only grudgingly and complained about the propensity of the Americans to come in with a new program every year.[131] As 1980 came to an end, the alliance was widely said to be in its worst state ever, despite (or perhaps because of) Carter's reliance on carefully crafted packages and elaborate consultative procedures, which seemed to result only in endless nitpicking over who would pay for what.[132] This was an outcome that Carter's successor was determined to avoid, although he too would have difficulty articulating the goals that a revitalized alliance was supposed to achieve.

THE REAGAN YEARS: FROM UNILATERALISM TO U-TURN

The Reagan administration took office convinced of the need for much stronger measures to redress what it saw as a very unfavorable military balance in Europe and inspired by the belief that a reassertion of U.S. leadership would be welcomed by the European allies.[133] The objective of strengthening NATO's capabilities for both conventional and nuclear warfare, however, was pursued in such an abrasive fashion during Reagan's first term that the results achieved often seemed to be the opposite of those intended.

At the start of its tenure, the Reagan administration attempted to distance itself from its predecessor's practice of confronting the Europeans with numerical or percentage goals to be achieved within a certain time frame. As explained by Deputy Secretary of Defense Carlucci, what the alliance needed was "more emphasis on specific force increases and defense improvements" rather than "more rhetoric or disputes about percentages."[134] The promise of a new approach was for the most part welcomed by the Europeans, but by the summer of 1981 the Reagan administration had managed to irritate many of the governments it had pledged to reassure by reacting sharply and critically in public to announcements by the Europeans that they might not meet the goal of 3 percent real annual increases in defense spending—the same goal that Reagan's spokesmen had derided as indicative of the failings of their predecessors.[135]

The apparent eagerness of the Europeans to escape from their earlier pledges of modest annual increases in defense spending was met in Washington first with dismay and exasperation and then threats of reprisals if the Europeans did not do more to emulate the administration's plans for double-digit percentage increases in defense spending. "The American people," Secretary of Defense Weinberger explained, "may not wish to bear the burden of necessary defense expenditures if they think some are doing less as we do more."[136] The threat to draw down U.S. forces in Europe embodied in the various amendments proposed by Senator Mansfield between 1967 and 1971 had not persuaded the Europeans to become more self-reliant. Between 1970 and 1974, all of the European allies except West Germany, Greece, Italy, and Portugal had reduced rather than increased the size of their armed forces. During the same period, five of the European allies reduced the share of national income devoted to defense (France, Greece, the Netherlands, Norway, and Turkey); three stayed the same (Denmark, Luxembourg, and Great Britain); only West Germany, Italy, and Portugal raised their shares; and Portuguese resources were being frittered away in Africa rather than spent constructively in Europe.[137] If the Europeans had been unresponsive to threats of troop withdrawals at a time when the United States was already redeploying units from Europe to Asia, they were even less likely to respond to threats from an administration that was publicly committed to rebuilding U.S. military strength, but this did not dissuade the Reagan administration from making them anyway. Threats that the Europeans should shape up or the Americans would ship out were no more successful in the 1980s than they had been in the 1970s: between 1980 and 1984, six of the European allies reduced the size of their armed forces (Belgium, Denmark, France, West Germany, the Netherlands, and Norway); one stayed the same (Luxembourg); only five managed an increase, including the three that could least afford to do so (Greece, Turkey, Portugal, Italy, and Great Britain). Seven of the European allies reduced the share of national income devoted to defense; only five increased it (France, Greece, Italy, the Netherlands, and Great Britain).[138]

An apparent inability to learn from the past also characterized the Reagan administration's approach to strategic questions. During the 1950s, uncritical acceptance by the Eisenhower administration of the "fact" of overwhelming Soviet conventional superiority had resulted in serious problems within the alliance, most notably concern in Europe about the judgment of U.S. officials and the wisdom of too close an alignment with the United States. During the 1980s, easy acceptance by the Reagan administration of the need to offset what was presumed to be massive Soviet conventional superiority likewise led to serious problems for the alliance, most notably the popular revolt against U.S. policies within large segments of the publics of Western Europe.[139]

During the Eisenhower years, greater reliance on nuclear weapons for deterrence and defense against a Soviet attack had spawned important albeit unsuccessful protest movements in Western Europe, most notably the *Kampf dem Atomtod* ("Struggle Against Atomic Death") in West Germany and the Campaign for Nuclear Disarmament in Great Britain.[140] Pressures from the Reagan administration to modernize the alliance's theater-based nuclear arsenal contributed to a resurgence of antinuclear and anti-American demonstrations in Western Europe, but rather than treat the peace movement as a symptom of societies troubled by their dependence on the United States and thus in need of reassurance, the Reagan administration responded to it as a failure of nerve in the face of Soviet military superiority. Lectures by U.S. officials on the proper way to counter Soviet military might appear to have deepened rather than alleviated the anxieties felt by European publics.[141] The more that officials in Washington spoke of the need to engage the Soviets and their proxies in a variety of theaters and to prevail against them in either conventional or nuclear wars, the more they contributed to fears in Europe of becoming pawns in a U.S.–Soviet struggle that would be fought on and over the homelands of the European allies.[142] The more that U.S. officials focused on ways to make nuclear weapons more "usable" (enhanced radiation weapons, nuclear "demonstration shots"[143]), the more they contributed to fears in Europe of an America prepare to fight to the last European for the sake of destroying the Soviet Union.[144] The more that U.S. officials insisted on the need to retain the option of escalation across the nuclear threshold, the more they contributed to an impression that the Soviets had long sought to foster—namely, that of the Americans as outsiders who cannot be trusted and who are themselves the principal danger to peace in Europe.[145]

During President Reagan's second term, both the tone and the substance of U.S. policy toward Europe changed considerably, a development that appears to have been due in part to the intensification of the U.S.–

Soviet dialogue as symbolized by the five summit conferences held between 1985 and 1988. Shortly after the conclusion of the Geneva summit in November 1985, Reagan was quoted as telling the other members of his delegation that "I have to believe that . . . [the Soviets] share with us the desire to get something done, and to get things straightened out." Gorbachev, the president told reporters, "is just as sincere as we are in wanting an answer."[146]

The "fresh start" in U.S.–Soviet relations that the Geneva summit was intended to bring about thus opened the door to both a more purposeful search for areas of agreement with the Soviet Union and a more solicitous attitude toward the European allies. During Reagan's first term, administration officials had been prone to lecture the Europeans on their lack of understanding of the Soviet threat. By the time of the Geneva summit, however, the Soviet Union was no longer the "focus of evil" but rather a partner in the search for negotiated arms reductions. During Reagan's first term, arms control initiatives had been viewed as either public relations exercises intended to placate European publics and/or as delaying tactics that could buy time for the administration's rearmament effort to establish a margin of superiority over the Soviets.[147] During the second term, arms control initiatives were pursued more seriously, culminating in the 1987 Intermediate Nuclear Forces (INF) Treaty, which banned the deployment by the United States and the Soviet Union of all but very short-range nuclear missiles in Europe. During Reagan's first term, U.S. defense spending rose at an average annual rate of 8.3 percent, measured in real terms, and U.S. officials had frequently criticized the Europeans for their failure to follow the example set by the United States.[148] Beginning in fiscal 1986, however, U.S. defense spending declined in real terms, a trend that continued throughout Reagan's second term, which made it difficult for U.S. officials to argue that the Europeans were the ones not pulling their weight within the alliance.[149] The hectoring tendencies of the administration's first term were thus replaced by a determination to pay more attention to the views of the European allies, as symbolized by Reagan's stopover in Brussels on the way home from the Geneva summit to report personally to the heads of other NATO governments on his talks with Gorbachev.

The Carter and Reagan presidencies have often been viewed as strikingly different in substance and style, but in terms of their policies toward Europe what stands out in retrospect are the similarities rather than the differences. Both were characterized by a determination to reassert U.S. influence within the councils of the alliance, yet neither appears to have had a vision of Europe's future analogous to that of the Truman administration at the time NATO was formed. Instead, both pursued a reassertion of U.S. leadership as an end in itself. Because neither possessed a coherent vision of what Europe was to become, neither was a paragon of consistency in the policies that they offered. Carter ran for office in 1976 on a pledge to reduce U.S. defense spending but then proposed in 1977 that NATO members commit themselves to 3 percent real annual increases in their defense budgets. Reagan condemned the Europeans for offering subsidized credits to facilitate Soviet purchases of the equipment needed to build the Siberian natural gas pipeline, but he also offered to sell the Soviets grain at prices subsidized by the U.S. Treasury. Carter encouraged the Europeans to request the deployment of enhanced radiation weapons with U.S. forces in Europe but then cancelled production after the request had become public knowledge. Reagan insisted that Pershing 2s and ground-launched cruise missiles were necessary to recouple U.S. strategic nuclear forces to the defense of Western Europe but then proposed as his contribution to arms control the complete elimination of the weapons by which "recoupling" was to be achieved.

The abrupt end of Carter's presidency after one term meant that he and his subordinates had less chance to learn from their mistakes (e.g., the reversal over the neutron bomb) than did their successors. Reagan and his associates became more solicitous of the opinions of the European allies, but relations between the United States and its NATO partners continued to be plagued during his second term by the president's propensity for rhetorical excess, delivered in such a casual manner as to leave his audience wondering if he had thought through the implications of his pronouncements.[150] The Reykjavik summit, in the words of one European commentator, "succeeded in alienating virtually every sector of European public opinion":

> The forces of the right were everywhere horrified by the president's declared objective of "eliminating all ballistic missiles from the face of the earth" by 1996 and his aspiration to create a "a world without nuclear weapons." The left blamed him for making this aspiration unacceptable to the Soviets by his insistence on retaining his Strategic Defense Initiative (SDI). Moderates in all countries were deeply disturbed by what James Schlesinger has so rightly called the "casual utopianism and indifferent preparation" of the whole exercise.[151]

CONCLUSIONS: LEARNING IN U.S. POLICY

Under what conditions, to what extent, and in what ways have U.S. officials learned from the past? Viewed from the perspective of the reward-punishment definition of learning, changes in policy in response to the experiences of one's predecessors stand out clearly. Truman's policies were strongly influenced by the failure of the democratic states to resist German and Japanese expansionism during the 1930s. Dulles's strategy of retaliation was a reaction to the higher taxes and larger deficits that were the result of the Truman administration's efforts to fight a limited war in Korea while simultaneously assembling the forces needed to provide a robust conventional defense of Western Europe. Kennedy's strategy of flexible response was a reaction to the difficulties that Eisenhower and Dulles encountered in responding to limited challenges to the status quo. Carter's NATO-first orientation was a reaction to the alleged neglect of Europe by Nixon and Ford. Reagan's military buildup was a reaction to his predecessor's belief that modest improvements over a period of years would suffice to restore rough parity between NATO and the Warsaw Pact.

Whether these changes in policy constitute learning in the cognitive content or cognitive structural senses is more difficult to judge. The review in the preceding sections suggests that the most important changes in U.S. policy have occurred as a result of turnover among elites owing to the electoral cycle.[152] These changes are consistent with the hypothesis that individuals rethink and revise their beliefs as they assimilate the experiences of their predecessors, but they are also consistent with the simple displacement of one set of beliefs (those of the incumbents) by those of their successors. This suggests that any discussion of learning in U.S. policy be conducted in terms of an attempt to differentiate between factors that encourage individuals to put forward proposals for policy change and those that encourage individuals to change their views about what is necessary and/or desirable.

Concerning the first of these, the competition for control of the executive branch encourages ambitious individuals to formulate alternative policies intended to improve on those of the incumbent administration, but this is not necessarily indicative of learning in either the cognitive content or cognitive structural senses. Learning in the cognitive content sense implies a willingness to change tactics, strategy, or overall goals in response to new information. Learning in the cognitive structural sense suggests the emergence of a more sophisticated understanding of the political/strategic environment by individuals who (1) recognize the need for adjustments in means and/or ends as a result of exposure to an experience, (2) take note of similarities and differences between situations separated in time in order to identify past mistakes and the changes needed to avoid their recurrence, and (3) revise their beliefs on what is necessary or desirable in response to their analysis of the changing political/strategic environment. Both of these kinds of learning require intellectual effort and a willingness to alter values and beliefs that presumably have served well the needs of those who hold them. The review in the preceding sections suggests that these forms of learning are unlikely in the absence of stimuli powerful enough to overcome the intellectual inertia associated with familiar ideas and long-held beliefs.

The policies of the Truman administration were in a sense the most forward looking of those reviewed earlier because of their concern to bring about a Europe that was economically vibrant, politically integrated, and militarily strong enough to look after itself. The experience of World War II served as a powerful stimulus to reject isolationism in favor of a design intended to prevent the recurrence of such a catastrophe, while the belief that U.S. resources were limited provided an incentive to examine carefully the analogy between Nazi Germany and the Soviet Union and to formulate reasons why the Soviets would not behave like the Germans.

From the early 1950s until the end of the 1980s, however, the situation in Europe was for the most part so stable and so tolerable that incumbent administrations and their would-be successors discussed policy alternatives less in terms of overall goals than of alleged strategic or tactical mistakes by their predecessors. A stable political situation and a low subjective probability of war are not conducive to a thorough reexamination of ends and means. The defensive orientation of U.S. policy and the desire of every administration since Truman's to economize on the application of U.S. resources in order to preserve freedom of action elsewhere has encouraged seekers of elective and appointive office to search for ways to pursue more efficiently or at less risk the same goals sought by those they hope to replace. Electoral competition in a milieu in which there is general agreement about overall goals encourages would-be office holders to refine and repackage their beliefs in an attempt to make them more appealing to others, but it does not necessarily impel them to rethink and revise those beliefs in light of lessons from the past.

It could be argued that a concern to avoid the mistakes of one's predecessors would require those preparing to mount a challenge for control of the executive branch to elaborate a set of cause-and-effect relationships capable of explaining how the promised improvements in performance would be achieved, thereby bringing about the kind of deepened understanding of the political/strategic environment associated with learning in the cognitive structural sense. In practice, however, the relatively stable situation that prevailed in Europe during the cold war and the corresponding absence of any compelling reasons to rethink what the United States should be trying to accomplish there meant that the arguments advanced by those seeking control of the executive branch were often strongly influenced by impressionistic judgments that were not empirically grounded. Dulles assumed that there was no alternative to threats of massive retaliation because the West was hopelessly outnumbered in conventional forces, even though by 1954 the combined armed forces of the NATO countries were larger than those of the Soviet Union and its allies. Eisenhower believed that national bankruptcy would result if defense spending was not curtailed, even though production and private consumption in the NATO countries rose during the Korean War, at the same time that defense spending was also rising. The Reagan administration was sharply critical of the Europeans for failing to match increases in defense spending by the United States during the 1980s, even though during the 1970s most of the European allies had steadily increased defense spending at a time when the United States was cutting back.[153]

Once the former challengers have gained power, moreover, a different kind of inertial tendency works to retard the formation of new ideas and approaches. In the U.S. system, responsibility for defense and foreign affairs is divided between the executive and legislative branches, neither of which is a unified entity but rather a coalition of "quasi-sovereign powers" that contest for primacy in the making of policy.[154] Within the executive branch, responsibility is divided among the Departments of State, Defense, Treasury, Commerce, the intelligence community, and the Executive Office of the President, each of which is further divided into semiautonomous agencies or bureaus. Simply to get all of the actors involved to operate within the framework of a unified policy consensus can sorely tax the energy and patience of presidents and their inner circle of advisers. Once the policy machine has been set in motion, senior officials are often reluctant to go through the exertions required to formulate a new consensus by suggesting that strategy and/or supporting policies be changed. Logically, the Soviet explosion of an atomic bomb in 1949 should have been followed by a reevaluation of NATO's strategy of relying on U.S. nuclear striking power to counterbalance Soviet conventional superiority.[155] But since estimates of the likelihood of war remained low even after the Soviet atomic explosion, there was little incentive for the Truman administration to consider a change in strategy, especially one that might imply costly changes in defense policy, which could soak up funds intended to speed economic recovery in Europe. Dulles's strategy of retaliation was based in part on the assumption that the greater firepower of nuclear weapons could provide an effective substitute for the manpower reductions that Eisenhower's administration was determined to make. Studies and war games conducted during the 1950s suggested that the opposite was true and that "[m]ore manpower would probably be needed to fight a tactical nuclear war than a non-nuclear war," yet the administration clung to its nuclear-oriented strategy rather than forgo the goal of reducing defense spending.[156]

If inertia is a powerful force militating against attitudinal and policy change, under what conditions might it be overcome? The review in the preceding sections suggests three ways in which the inertial tendencies discussed above can be overcome: through the shock of a sudden and unexpected event, through the gradual accumulation of such a mass of evidence that the issue of policy change can no longer be put off, or through the prospect of substantial budgetary savings if policy is changed.

Concerning the first of these, prior to the Korean War both the Truman administration and the Congress had been satisfied with a military aid program that allotted roughly $1 billion to the NATO allies during fiscal 1950—a figure that had been selected more on the basis of judgments of what the American public would tolerate than of the military situation in Europe. For fiscal 1951, the administration again requested approximately $1 billion for the European allies on the grounds that Congress might reject the whole program if asked to provide more than the previous year's figure. The shock caused by the invasion of South Korea made these figures appear totally inadequate. The $1 billion request for fiscal 1951 had required two months of detailed examination prior to congressional approval, but an emergency supplemental appropriation allocating more than $4 billion to the NATO allies was rushed through after the outbreak of war with very little study.[157]

Once the path of policy has been altered, pressures for logical consistency can become an important stimulus for additional policy change. Congress readily accepted the Truman administration's conclusion that war in Korea required an across-the-board rearmament effort to shore up vulnerable areas such as Western Europe, but many in Congress felt it illogical and unfair that U.S. manpower and equipment should be expended to defend German territory unless the Germans themselves shared in the effort. Acheson's self-described "conversion" on German rearmament was apparently speeded by his discomfort in having to admit to the Senate Appropriations Committee that no defense of Europe was possible without a German contribution and that there were no plans as of August 1950 for rearming Germany so that it too could contribute to NATO's defensive shield.[158]

Attitudinal change can also occur as a result of a gradual accumulation of evidence suggesting the need for policy change, especially if accompanied by a recent unpleasant experience that influences the interpretation of new information.[159] J.M. Jones has described the Truman administration's decision to become actively involved in European affairs as a response to "accumulating facts that had been shouting for recognition for a long time":

> For decades, massive historical caravans had been observed moving slowly toward predictable destinations: Great Britain toward loss of Empire and inability to maintain the balance of power in Europe and order in Asia; Western continental Europe toward instability and weakness; the United States toward economic and military preeminence in political isolation; and the Soviet Union toward a fundamental challenge of Western civilization.

Suddenly during the Fifteen Weeks of 1947 it was discovered that all four caravans were on the point of arrival. According to a logical projection of historical trends, these destinations would shortly be reached and the world stage set for an inevitable war between two titans, the Soviet Union, astride Europe and Asia, and America standing alone.[160]

Acheson used a similar argument during a February 27, 1947, meeting with the congressional leadership to discuss military and economic aid to Greece and Turkey. The persuasiveness of his appeal was very likely heightened because it was cast in such a way as to suggest parallels between the consequences of U.S. inaction during the 1930s and the likely consequences of U.S. inaction against the Soviet Union:

The Russians had any number of bets, Acheson went on. If they won any one of them, they won all. If they could seize control over Turkey, they would almost inevitably extend their control over Greece and Iran. If they controlled Greece, Turkey would sooner or later succumb, with or without a war, and then Iran. If they dominated Italy, where Communist pressures were increasing, they could probably take Greece, Turkey, and the Middle East. Their aim, Acheson emphasized, was control of the eastern Mediterranean and the Middle East. From there the possibilities for penetration of South Asia and Africa were limitless.

As for Europe, Acheson continued, it was clear that the Soviet Union, employing the instruments of Communist infiltration and subversion, was trying to complete the encirclement of Germany. In France, with four Communists in the Cabinet, one of them Minister of Defense, with Communists controlling the largest trade union and infiltrating government offices, factories, and the armed services, with nearly a third of the electorate voting Communist, and with economic conditions worsening, the Russians could pull the plug any time they chose. In Italy a similar if less immediately dangerous situation existed, but it was growing worse. In Hungary and Austria the Communists were tightening the noose on democratic governments. If Greece and the eastern Mediterranean should fall to Soviet control, the material and psychological effects in the countries that were so precariously maintaining their freedoms and democratic institutions would be devastating, and probably conclusive.[161]

Reasonable people can disagree over the accuracy of Acheson's assessment, but at the time it would have been difficult for his listeners to accuse him of exaggerating because only a decade earlier the United States had stood by while the Nazis had intimidated, subverted, and attacked neighboring states, and the result had been the second world war.

Finally, attitudinal change can also be the product of the prospect of substantial budgetary savings. The evidence available suggests that the inertial tendencies discussed above constitute less of an obstacle to attitudinal change when the policy changes in question promise budgetary savings rather than additional expenditures. The Eisenhower administration was unwilling to abandon its strategy of massive retaliation because the alternative seemed to be a costly expansion of general-purpose forces suitable for employment in limited wars. It was, however, willing to embrace the concept of limited nuclear war because it was cheaper to equip existing Army and Air Force units with tactical nuclear weapons than to spend enough on strategic nuclear forces to maintain, in the face of fears of a "bomber gap" and later a "missile gap," the degree of strategic superiority on which massive retaliation had initially been based.[162] Policy initiatives that require spending money, like the collectively funded purchase by NATO members of a fleet of AWACS early warning aircraft, often require months if not years of intricate negotiations over who will pay what share of the cost before agreement can be reached among all the parties involved.[163] In the aftermath of the collapse of Communist rule in Eastern Europe, in contrast, NATO members have moved with alacrity to claim for themselves a share of the troop reductions expected to be agreed on by NATO and the Warsaw Pact, with the Bush administration in the forefront of the scramble.[164]

Concerning learning in the efficiency sense, the record of U.S. policy since World War II suggests that for the most part U.S. officials have not become progressively more skillful at reconciling policy goals with available means. The desire of incoming administrations to distance themselves from the alleged mistakes of their predecessors has often meant that old lessons must be learned anew, as if there had been no relevant experience.[165] Benjamin Cohen notes that in the realm of international economic policy, the Carter administration went through a difficult learning process, first reasserting its determination to take the lead in fostering global economic recovery and then discovering the advantages of collaboration with the other advanced democratic states for the sake of joint management of what the United States could no longer control alone. With the accession of the Reagan administration, the pendulum swung back to unilateral initiatives, as if the Carter learning process had never occurred. President Reagan and his associates apparently felt it inconceivable that the United States could not reclaim its accustomed autonomy and influence. All that was needed was renewed vigor and incisive action in support of U.S. interests.[166]

This tendency of incoming administrations to distance themselves from their predecessors suggests that for U.S. officials, there is a difference between the learned past and the remembered past. They may have learned while in school or during their apprenticeship that there is a historical record of policy toward Europe stretching back many years, if not decades, but what they remember and respond to are the mistakes of their immediate predecessors. In their zeal to avoid them, officials have often been blind or at least insensitive to the shortcomings of their own approach. Eisenhower and Dulles were so convinced of the folly of the Truman administration's efforts to endow NATO with the conventional forces needed to defend against a Soviet invasion that they appear not to have understood the fears that their own emphasis on massive retaliation caused in Europe, especially among the publics of the European allies. The Kennedy and Johnson administrations were so intent on acquiring a wider range of conventional options that they dismissed the concern of the European allies for the effect of flexible response on the credibility of the alliance's nuclear threats as a thinly disguised effort by nations in decline to avoid sharing the burdens being borne by the United States. The Reagan administration was so concerned to avoid the impression of weakness conveyed by the Carter administration that it appears not to have understood how its own blustery rhetoric was at least partly responsible for the apparent surge in neutralist and pacifist sentiment that it sought to blame on the policies of the Carterites.

Some aspects of the learned past are so salient that senior officials cannot help but bear them in mind as they go about their business. Hungary was invaded by the Soviets in 1956 after announcing that it would leave the Warsaw Pact, which helps explain why the Bush administration was so circumspect about the future of that organization even as communist governments were being toppled throughout eastern Europe. But for the most part the historical record is too distant, too complicated, too cluttered with small details to be of much use to individuals who are used to receiving information in the form of "executive summaries" and "talking points" that they can use in their next meeting. What James Fallows has written of President Carter could usefully be applied to many of the "in-and-outers" who have populated the upper reaches of the executive branch since the second world war: they see their task less in terms of understanding problems than in terms of fixing them.[167] The heavy workload and short tenure in office characteristic of the senior levels of the Departments of State and Defense are not conducive to a thorough reexamination of the historical record in search of clues to a better understanding of current problems. Hence problems are relentlessly recast in technical terms: How many division equivalents are necessary to stop a Soviet invasion comprised of "x" divisions? What percentage increase in defense spending is needed to support the latest package of conventional force improvements? How many NATO missiles and aircraft are needed to offset Soviet theater nuclear forces?

The resulting militarization of U.S. perspectives has itself been an impediment to learning in the efficiency sense. In the late 1940s, the Truman administration was willing to accept certain military risks for the sake of a favorable political-military posture from which to engage in a long-term contest for influence with the Soviet Union. The military strategy underlying Truman's policies offered only the bleakest of prospects in the event of war—retreat, occupation of most or all of Western Europe by Soviet forces, and a prolonged war of attrition to liberate countries abandoned at the start of the fighting—but military strategy was subordinate to broader political considerations, which dictated holding down defense spending in order to free resources to speed economic recovery in Western Europe. The situation may have looked bleak in the short run, but over the long run the administration was confident of the West's ability to meet whatever challenges the Soviets might offer provided it stuck to the main task of reviving and renewing the societies of Western Europe and did not allow itself to be distracted by Soviet efforts to play on the fears of countries that were weak at present but were expected to recover both their self-confidence and their military strength.

The transformation of NATO in the early 1950s into an organization charged with assembling the forces needed to meet and defeat a Soviet invasion resulted in the displacement of the pre-Korea focus on the political-psychological dimension of the struggle for Europe by a preoccupation with invasion scenarios, which subsequently proved strongly resistant to change. Resistance to change was in part the product of vested interests within the armed forces, which attempted to maintain the impression that they were overmatched and thus in need of additional resources to ensure the safety of the West, but organizational interests are only part of the explanation. The record of U.S. policy toward Europe since the early 1950s suggests that U.S. officials have gradually lost sight of the larger goals that military power was originally intended to serve and have instead pursued military power as an end in itself.[168] The militarization of U.S. perspectives in the aftermath of the Korean War and the concern to amass the forces and firepower needed to stop a Soviet invasion in its tracks inclined many U.S. officials toward strategies that depended heavily on early and massive use of nuclear weapons and which in effect threatened to destroy Western Europe in order to save it. This preoccupation with strategies that threatened escalation across the nuclear threshold in the event of war has caused the Europeans to worry not only that the United States might not defend them in their hour of need but also that it might defend them so well that their countries would not survive. The preoccupation with invasion scenarios in effect heightened the vulnerability of the alliance to the very political warfare it was created to defeat.

With the collapse of communist rule in eastern Europe, the credibility of invasion scenarios has dropped precipitously, thereby necessitating a return to the kind of broad political/strategic issues with which American officials were preoccupied at the time the Alliance was created. German reunification, the status of the formerly German territories transferred to

Poland and the Soviet Union after World War II, the further development of the European Community (EC), the future of the newly democratic governments of Eastern Europe caught between the EC in the West and the Soviet Union to the East—the list of problems on Europe's horizon practically cries out for a renewed attempt to articulate a vision of what Europe should be and its relationship to the United States.

For nearly 40 years NATO in general and U.S. policy in particular have been sustained by the mission of organizing the West's resources to meet and defeat a Warsaw Pact invasion. With the latter in a shambles, Soviet forces withdrawing from Eastern Europe, and a reunited Germany moving toward economic hegemony over the continent, U.S. officials can scarcely avoid any longer the challenge of rethinking what the United States should be attempting to accomplish through its policies toward Europe. Whether the challenge will be met in time remains to be seen, but on balance the record of U.S. policy since the Korean War does not provide much basis for optimism in this regard.

NOTES

1. Herbert Feis, *From Trust to Terror* (New York: W.W. Norton, 1970), 381, 379.

2. Selig Adler, *The Isolationist Impulse* (New York: Free Press, 1957); Adler, *The Uncertain Giant: American Foreign Policy Between the Wars* (New York: MacMillan, 1965), Chapter 7. See also H. Feis, *From Trust to Terror*, 307.

3. H. Bradford Westerfield, *The Instruments of America's Foreign Policy* (New York: Thomas Y. Crowell, 1962), 43.

4. Robert Osgood, *NATO: The Entangling Alliance* (Chicago: University of Chicago Press, 1962), 18–19; Wallace J. Thies, *An Alliance in Crisis: The Politics of Integration in the Atlantic Alliance* (forthcoming), Chapters 1, 3, 4.

5. See, for example, Secretary of State George C. Marshall's remarks at Princeton University, February 22, 1947, quoted in Joseph M. Jones, *The Fifteen Weeks* (New York: Harcourt Brace, 1955), 108–109; and President Eisenhower's comments in a 1955 letter to Winston Churchill, quoted in John Lewis Gaddis, *Strategies of Containment* (New York: Oxford University Press, 1982), 131. See also Robert Divine, *Eisenhower and the Cold War* (New York: Oxford University Press, 1981), 10.

6. Lawrence Kaplan, *A Community of Interests: NATO and the Military Assistance Program, 1948–1952* (Washington, D.C.: U.S. Government Printing Office, 1980), 4.

7. Alan Bullock, *Ernest Bevin, Foreign Secretary* (New York: W.W. Norton,1983), 804–805; Forrest C. Pogue, "SHAEF—A Retrospect on Coalition Command," *Journal of Modern History*, 23 (December 1951): 329–35.

8. Robert Jordan, *The NATO International Staff/Secretariat, 1952–1957* (London: Oxford University Press, 1967), 229.

9. L. Kaplan, *A Community of Interests*, 1; Lawrence Kaplan, *NATO and the United States* (Boston: Twayne Publishers, 1988), 1; Armin Rappaport, "The American Revolution of 1949," *NATO Letter*, 12 (February 1964): 3–8.

10. See, for example, the comments by Secretary of State George C. Marshall,

quoted in Les Adler and Thomas Paterson, "Red Fascism: The Merger of Nazi Germany and Soviet Russia in the American Image of Totalitarianism, 1930s–1950s," *American Historical Review*, 75 (April 1970): 1057.

11. The British embassy in Washington conveyed two notes to this effect to Undersecretary of State Dean Acheson on February 21, 1947. The views of U.S. officials at the time these notes were passed are described in J. Jones, *The Fifteen Weeks*, 129–70.

12. L. Adler and T. Paterson, "Red Fascism."

13. See, for example, the remarks by George Kennan to the ambassadors of Great Britain, France, Canada, and the Benelux states, July 7, 1948, in U.S. Department of State, *Foreign Relations of the United States* (hereafter *FRUS*), vol. 3 (Washington, D.C.: U.S. Government Printing Office, 1948), 157.

14. J.L. Gaddis, *Strategies of Containment*, 34–35.

15. Dean Acheson, *Present at the Creation* (New York: New American Library, 1970), 262.

16. See, for example, the October 7, 1946, memorandum by George Kennan, quoted in David Mayers, "Containment and the Primacy of Diplomacy: George Kennan's Views, 1947–1948," *International Security*, 11 (Summer 1986): 130–31; Forrestal's diary entry for March 16, 1948, in Walter Millis (ed.), *The Forrestal Diaries* (New York: Viking Press, 1951), 395; and the September 1949 remarks by John Foster Dulles, quoted in R. Osgood, *The Entangling Alliance*, 50.

17. Remarks by George Kennan, "Organization Meeting on Russia," June 12, 1946, quoted in D. Mayers, "Containment," 145–46. Kennan reiterated this judgment in a September 1948 lecture at the National War College, quoted in J.L. Gaddis, *Strategies of Containment*, 35.

18. J. Jones, *The Fifteen Weeks*, 82–84; D. Acheson, *Present at the Creation*, 302; J.L. Gaddis, *Strategies of Containment*, 35.

19. George Kennan to Walter Lippmann, April 6, 1948, quoted in D. Mayers, "Containment," 141. See also J.L. Gaddis, *Strategies of Containment*, 35.

20. Quoted in J.L. Gaddis, *Strategies of Containment*, 40. See also, D. Mayers, "Containment," 141.

21. Remarks by Charles E. Bohlen, July 7, 1949, *FRUS*, vol. 3, 1948, 157.

22. Remarks by George Kennan, ibid.

23. Undated memorandum, quoted in J.L. Gaddis, *Strategies of Containment*, 62.

24. This view was argued most cogently in a paper prepared under Kennan's supervision by the State Department's Policy Planning Staff, PPS-13, November 6, 1947, a summary of which was presented to the Cabinet by Marshall on November 7, 1947; *FRUS*, vol. 1, 1947, 770–77.

25. Ibid., 772–73. See also J.L. Gaddis, *Strategies of Containment*, 57.

26. The administration's policy, as explained by Marshall and affirmed by Truman at a meeting on the defense budget on May 7, 1948, "was based on the assumption that there would not be war and that we should not plunge into war preparations which would bring about the very thing we were taking steps to prevent" (W. Millis, *The Forrestal Diaries*, 432). See also PPS-13, *FRUS*, vol. 1, 1947, 774; *FRUS*, vol. 2, 1948, 70–72; J.L. Gaddis, *Strategies of Containment*, 38–39; D. Acheson, *Present at the Creation*, 442; and David McLellan, *Dean Acheson, The State Department Years* (New York: Dodd Mead, 1976), 146–47.

27. The importance of greater political and economic integration in Western Europe in the thinking of U.S. officials is discussed in W. Thies, *An Alliance in Crisis,* Chapter 3.

28. Remarks by George Kennan, July 7, 1948, FRUS, vol. 3, 1948, 157.

29. Remarks by Robert Lovett, ibid., 151 (see also 156, 166). For a detailed account of the negotiations that culminated in the signing of the North Atlantic Treaty, see W. Thies, *An Alliance in Crisis,* Chapter 3. An account that emphasizes heavily the determination of U.S. officials to use the creation of a new security arrangement for Europe to resolve the German question is that of Timothy Ireland, *Creating the Entangling Alliance* (Westport, Conn.: Greenwood Press, 1981).

30. See, for example, Kennan's comments during the July 7, 1948, meeting with the ambassadors of Great Britain, France, Canada, and the Benelux states, *FRUS,* vol. 3, 1948, 157.

31. See, for example, comments by Charles Bohlen during the meeting on July 7, 1948, ibid.

32. See, for example, James Forrestal's characterization of U.S. policy as a "calculated risk," quoted in J.L. Gaddis, *Strategies of Containment,* 61–62.

33. *FRUS,* vol. 3, 1948, 157. See also George Kennan to Walter Lippmann, April 6, 1948, quoted in D. Mayers, "Containment," 142. Truman's confidence in the ability of the West to meet the Soviet challenge is discussed by H. Feis, *From Trust to Terror,* 86.

34. See, for example, Truman's message to Congress of August 1, 1950, quoted in L. Kaplan, *A Community of Interests,* 105; the account of the September 1950 meetings of the NATO council in D. Acheson, *Present at the Creation,* 574–75; and the statements by Truman, Acheson, and Secretary of Defense Louis Johnson, quoted in R. Osgood, *The Entangling Alliance,* 69–70.

35. Lord Ismay, *NATO: The First Five Years* (Paris: 1954), 29; Roger Hilsman, "NATO: The Developing Strategic Context," in Klaus Knorr (ed.), *NATO and American Security* (Princeton, N.J.: Princeton University Press, 1959), 17.

36. L. Ismay, *The First Five Years,* 40, 102. These totals do not include Greek and Turkish forces, which did not come under NATO command until 1952.

37. Ibid., 107, 114–24; R. Hilsman, "The Developing Strategic Context," 22–23; Coral Bell, *Negotiation From Strength* (London: Chatto & Windus, 1962), 51.

38. The work of the TCC and its executive board is described in more detail in W. Thies, *An Alliance in Crisis,* Chapter 5; R. Jordan, *The NATO International Staff/Secretariat,* 203–11; and L. Ismay, *The First Five Years,* 44–48.

39. Walter S. Poole, *The History of the Joint Chiefs of Staff: The JCS and National Policy, vol. 4, 1950–1952* (Wilmington, Del.: Michael Glazier, 1980), 276.

40. L. Ismay, *The First Five Years,* 103.

41. These pressures are discussed more fully in Ronald Ritchie, *NATO: The Economics of an Alliance* (Toronto, Ont.: The Ryerson Press, 1956), 52–61. See also D. Acheson, *Present at the Creation,* 902–904.

42. Samuel Huntington, *The Common Defense* (New York: Columbia University Press, 1961), 63.

43. Charles J.V. Murphy, "A New Strategy for NATO," *Fortune* (January 1953): 80–81; L. Ismay, *The First Five Years,* 104; S. Huntington, *The Common Defense,* 63–64; C. Bell, *Negotiation From Strength,* 138, 143; R. Hilsman, "The Developing Strategic Context," 26.

44. The views of the Eisenhower administration are discussed in more detail in S. Huntington, *The Common Defense*, 64–88; Glenn Snyder, "The New Look," in Warner Schilling, Paul Hammond, and Glenn Snyder, *Strategy, Politics, and Defense Budgets* (New York: Columbia University Press, 1962). See also J.L. Gaddis, *Strategies of Containment*, 134.

45. J.L. Gaddis, *Strategies of Containment*, 148; S. Huntington, *The Common Defense*, 74; C. Bell, *Negotiation From Strength*, 130; R. Hilsman, "The Developing Strategic Context," 26.

46. R. Hilsman, "The Developing Strategic Context," 15–16; C. Murphy, "A New Strategy," 80, 83; S. Huntington, *The Common Defense*, 78–79; J.L. Gaddis, *Strategies of Containment*, 139–40.

47. S. Huntington, *The Common Defense*, 80–81; R. Hilsman, "The Developing Strategic Context," 27–34; C. Bell, *Negotiation From Strength*, 49; Alain Enthoven and K. Wayne Smith, *How Much Is Enough?* (New York: Harper & Row, 1971), 120–21; International Institute for Strategic Studies, *The Communist Bloc and the Free World: The Military Balance, 1960* (London: 1961), 8 (hereafter, IISS, *Military Balance*).

48. A. Enthoven and K. Smith, *How Much Is Enough?*, 118–21, 138–41; Robert Osgood, *The Entangling Alliance*, 20, 39–40, 64.

49. See, for example, D. McLellan, *Dean Acheson*, 344–45. See also Acheson's comment to Churchill in January 1952, quoted in J.L. Gaddis, *Strategies of Containment*, 123–24.

50. R. Osgood, *The Entangling Alliance*, 118. See also Col. Andrew Goodpaster, "The Development of SHAPE," *International Organization*, 9 (1955): 259; Ben T. Moore, *NATO and the Future of Europe* (New York: Harper, 1958), 70; A. Enthoven and K. Smith, *How Much Is Enough?*, 120–21, 133.

51. Theodore H. White, *Fire in the Ashes* (New York: William Sloane Associates, 1953), 303–304.

52. Theodore H. White, "The Job Eisenhower Faces: The Tangled Skein of NATO," *The Reporter*, 4 (February 6, 1951):12. White's conclusions in this regard were later confirmed by the systems analysis office within the Defense Department (A. Enthoven and K. Smith, *How Much is Enough?*, 132–42).

53. T. White, *Fire in the Ashes*, 293.

54. L. Ismay, *The First Five Years*, 110–12.

55. T. White, *Fire in the Ashes*, 296. See also R. Hilsman, "The Developing Strategic Context," 23–24; and Alastair Buchan, *NATO in the 1960s*, rev. ed. (New York: Praeger, 1963), 43.

56. Quoted in L. Ismay, *The First Five Years*, 108–109. See also Edmund Taylor, "The Atlantic Alliance: After Gruenther, What?," *The Reporter*, 12 (June 2, 1955): 18; and Norman Padelford, "Political Cooperation in the North Atlantic Community," *International Organization*, 9 (August 1955): 353.

57. S. Huntington, *The Common Defense*, 79, 95; J.L. Gaddis, *Strategies of Containment*, 166; C. Bell, *Negotiation From Strength*, 138; IISS, *Military Balance, 1960*, 13–14.

58. IISS, *Military Balance, 1971–1972*, 63; C. Bell, *Negotiation From Strength*, 148.

59. Reliable data on the armed forces of the Eastern European states during the 1950s are difficult to compile. The figures cited here are from *The Statesman's Yearbook* for 1951, 1957, 1960–1961, 1961–1962; IISS, *Military Balance, 1960*, 6; IISS, *Military Balance, 1971–1972*, 63.

60. Wallace J. Thies, *The Atlantic Alliance, Nuclear Weapons and European Attitudes: Re-examining the Conventional Wisdom* (University of California, Berkeley: Institute of International Studies, 1983), 48–51; A. Enthoven and K. Smith, *How Much Is Enough?*, 134.

61. Baldwin's figures are reproduced in R. Osgood, *The Entangling Alliance*, 375, fn. 22. See also R. Hilsman, "The Developing Strategic Context," 33; and General Maxwell Taylor, *The Uncertain Trumpet* (New York: Harper, 1959), 136–39.

62. Most prominently Theodore H. White, Hanson Baldwin, and Edmund Taylor. White's writings in particular suggest very good connections at SHAPE and elsewhere.

63. T. White, *Fire in the Ashes*, 302–303. See also William T.R. Fox and Annette Baker Fox, *NATO and the Range of American Choice* (New York: Columbia University Press, 1966), 37; R. Ritchie, *The Economics of an Alliance*, 56; R. Osgood, *The Entangling Alliance*, 39–40.

64. G. Snyder, "The New Look," 437; S. Huntington, *The Common Defense*, 74.

65. Quoted in R. Osgood, *The Entangling Alliance* , 78.

66. The views of Senator Robert Taft and former President Herbert Hoover are summarized in *FRUS*, vol. 3, 1951, 14; D. Acheson, *Present at the Creation*, 630–37; D. McLellan, *Dean Acheson*, 340–45; and L. Kaplan, *A Community of Interests*, 149–53.

67. White goes further in this regard, arguing that by 1953, the power balance in Central Europe had "shifted from the Russians to the Atlantic forces" (*Fire in the Ashes*, 296).

68. R. Osgood, *The Entangling Alliance*, 391, fn. 98.

69. R. Ritchie, *The Economics of an Alliance*, 56.

70. Ibid., 54; Lincoln Gordon, "Economic Aspects of Coalition Diplomacy— The NATO Experience," *International Organization*, 10 (November 1956): 533.

71. R. Ritchie, *The Economics of an Alliance*, 14; see also 52–53.

72. Ibid., 14.

73. For U.S. military planning during the late 1940s, see Gregg Herken, *The Winning Weapon* (New York: Random House, 1982); Kenneth Condit, *The History of the Joint Chiefs of Staff: The JCS and National Policy, vol. 2, 1947–1949* (Wilmington, Del.: Michael Glazier, n.d.), Chapters 9–10; and David Alan Rosenberg, "American Atomic Strategy and the Hydrogen Bomb Decision," *Journal of American History*, 66 (June 1979): 62–87.

74. See, for example, K. Condit, Chapters 1, 6, 7, 8; S. Huntington, *The Common Defense*, 33–47; Walter Millis et al., *Arms and the State* (New York: Twentieth Century Fund, 1958), 197–258; Warner Schilling, "The Politics of National Defense: Fiscal 1950," in W. Schilling, P. Hammond and G. Snyder, eds., *Strategy, Politics, and Defense Budgets*, 5ff.

75. Quoted in J.L. Gaddis, *Strategies of Containment*, 110.

76. See, for example, the remarks by Secretary of Defense Louis Johnson to the House Foreign Affairs Committee on June 5, 1950, quoted in L. Kaplan, *A Community of Interests*, 86.

77. Ibid., 105.

78. R. Osgood, *The Entangling Alliance*, 35; J.L. Gaddis, *Strategies of Containment*, 166; R. Hilsman, "The Developing Strategic Context, " 19.

79. R. Osgood, *The Entangling Alliance*, 114–15; W. Fox and A. Fox, *NATO and the Range of American Choice*, 38.

80. See, for example, the statements by Eisenhower and Ridgway, quoted in R. Osgood, *The Entangling Alliance*, 383–84, fn. 67.

81. "A Policy of Boldness," *Life*, May 19, 1952, 146–160, summarized in J.L. Gaddis, *Strategies of Containment*, 121–22. See also R. Divine, *Eisenhower and the Cold War*, 12–14.

82. J.L. Gaddis, *Strategies of Containment*, 96–101.

83. S. Huntington, *The Common Defense*, 61–62, 298–312.

84. T. White, *Fire in the Ashes*, 304.

85. Quoted in J.L. Gaddis, *Strategies of Containment*, 128 (emphasis in original); see also R. Divine, *Eisenhower and the Cold War*, 14.

86. This exchange between Dulles and Eisenhower is described in J.L. Gaddis, *Strategies of Containment*, 128.

87. John Foster Dulles, "The Evolution of Foreign Policy," Department of State *Bulletin*, (January 25, 1954): 108.

88. See, for example, the statements by Secretary of Defense Neil McElroy, Air Force Chief of Staff Thomas White, and Air Force Vice Chief of Staff Curtis Lemay, quoted in R. Osgood, *The Entangling Alliance*, 391, fn. 98. See also George Rathjens, "NATO Strategy: Total War," in K. Knorr, *NATO and American Security*, 66–67.

89. Quoted in J.L. Gaddis, *Strategies of Containment*, 166.

90. R. Osgood, *The Entangling Alliance*, 142.

91. Ibid., 160.

92. Secretary of Defense Neil McElroy, quoted in ibid., 141–42.

93. See, for example, the remarks by Dulles, quoted in ibid., 158.

94. S. Huntington, *The Common Defense*, 105–106.

95. Quoted in R. Osgood, *The Entangling Alliance*, 158–59.

96. Ibid., 197.

97. J.F. Dulles, "The Evolution of Foreign Policy;" R. Osgood, *The Entangling Alliance*, 158.

98. Quoted in R. Osgood, *The Entangling Alliance*, 143–44.

99. J.L. Gaddis, *Strategies of Containment*, 164.

100. See, for example, William Kaufmann, "The Requirements of Deterrence," and "Limited Warfare," both in Kaufmann (ed.), *Military Policy and National Security* (Princeton, N.J.: Princeton University Press, 1956). See also Bernard Brodie, "Unlimited Weapons and Limited War," *The Reporter* (November 18, 1954); Robert Osgood, *Limited War: The Challenge to American Strategy* (Chicago: University of Chicago Press, 1957); and Henry Kissinger, *Nuclear Weapons and Foreign Policy* (Garden City, N.Y.: Doubleday, 1958).

101. Quoted in J.L. Gaddis, *Strategies of Containment*, 175.

102. S. Huntington, *The Common Defense*, 65, 69.

103. In particular, the bomber fly-by that accompanied the 1955 May Day parade in Moscow, the successful test of an intercontinental ballistic missile during the summer of 1957, and the launching of the first artificial earth satellite (Sputnik) in October 1957.

104. W. Fox and A. Fox, *NATO and the Range of American Choice*, 38; B. Moore, *NATO and the Future of Europe*, 71.

105. Paul Samuelson, quoted in J.L. Gaddis, *Strategies of Containment*, 204, suggested the contrast between the economic assumptions of the Eisenhower and Kennedy administrations.

106. Quoted in ibid., 214.

107. Ibid.

108. Ibid., 216.

109. Ibid., 216–217.

110. Ibid., 216; Jerome Kahan, *Security in the Nuclear Age* (Washington, D.C.: Brookings, 1975), 75; IISS, *Military Balance, 1960*, 13; IISS, *Military Balance, 1961*, 10; IISS, *Military Balance, 1963–1964*, 22.

111. Henry Kissinger, *The Troubled Partnership* (New York: Doubleday Anchor Books, 1966), 106; C. Bell, *Negotiation From Strength*, 150–51; J. Kahan, *Security in the Nuclear Age*, 78.

112. J.L. Gaddis, *Strategies of Containment*, 217.

113. A. Enthoven and K. Smith, *How Much Is Enough?*, 134–36; also 140–41, 147–48. See also J.L. Gaddis, *Strategies of Containment*, 207.

114. A. Enthoven and K. Smith, *How Much Is Enough?*, 138–40.

115. The number of active-duty divisions along the NATO side of the central front increased from 22 in 1960 to 27 in 1963, but this was entirely the result of a long-planned expansion of the West German army from 7 to 12 divisions.

116. A. Enthoven and K. Smith, *How Much Is Enough?*, 140–41, 147–51.

117. J.L. Gaddis, *Strategies of Containment*, 220.

118. Ibid., 220–21.

119. IISS, *Military Balance, 1964–1965*, 15–25; IISS, *Military Balance, 1966–1967*, 27; IISS, *Military Balance, 1968–1969*, 18–32; IISS, *Military Balance, 1969–1970*, 5. See also U.S. Department of Defense, *Annual Report for Fiscal Year 1982* (Washington, D.C.: U.S. Government Printing Office, 1981), B–5.

120. W. Thies, *The Atlantic Alliance*, 48–51.

121. A. Enthoven and K. Smith, *How Much Is Enough?*, 147–49, 151, 154–56.

122. W. Thies, *The Atlantic Alliance*, 48–51.

123. U.S. policies toward Europe during the Nixon–Ford years are discussed in more detail in Lawrence Kaplan, "NATO: The Second Generation," in Lawrence Kaplan and Kenneth Clawson (eds.), *NATO After Thirty Years* (Wilmington, Del.: Scholarly Resources, Inc., 1981), 4–21.

124. W. Thies, *The Atlantic Alliance*, 48–51.

125. "Mondale Discusses SALT at NATO," *Aviation Week and Space Technology* (hereafter *AW&ST*) (January 31, 1977): 14; "Defense Department Sustains Effort to Aid NATO Standardization," *AW&ST* (April 25, 1977): 32.

126. Clarence A. Robinson, Jr., "U.S. Shapes Goals for NATO Summit," *AW&ST* (May 8, 1978): 18; Bernard Weinraub, "Army to Shift More Men and Equipment to Europe," *New York Times* (hereafter *NYT*) (October 19, 1977): A5.

127. Quoted in Richard Burt, "U.S. Analysis Doubts There Can Be Victor in Major Atomic War," *NYT* (January 6, 1978): A4.

128. *Weekly Compilation of Presidential Documents* (May 16, 1977): 696–700. See also the press briefing by Ambassador Henry Owen, ibid., 701–704.

129. Clarence A. Robinson, Jr., "Strength Sought at Least Cost," *AW&ST* (August 8, 1977): 36; "Short–Term Initiatives Readied by NATO," *AW&ST* (August 15, 1977):

54–55; "NATO Defense Principles Approved," *AW&ST* (May 22, 1978): 27; Eugene Kozicharow, "NATO Defense Spending to Increase," *AW&ST* (May 29, 1978): 17; "That's Better," *The Economist* (June 3, 1978): 56; Charles Corddry, "U.S. Demands an End to 'Lag' by NATO Allies," *Baltimore Sun* (April 24, 1980): A5; John Fialka, "U.S. Asks European Allies to Boost Defense Posture," *Washington Star* (April 24, 1980): A6; Norman Kempster, "NATO Allies Have Only Enough Bullets, Bombs to Fight 3 or 4 Weeks, U.S. Says," *Los Angeles Times* (April 24, 1980): 26.

130. Bradley Graham, "U.S. Freed to Boost Forces in Mideast," *Washington Post* (May 14, 1980): A21; Michael Burns, "NATO Backs U.S. Bid to Speed Up Alliance's Long-Range Defense Plans," *Baltimore Sun* (May 14, 1980): A2; "More for Asia, Less for Europe," *The Economist* (May 17, 1980): 42; Eugene Kozicharow, "NATO to Boost European Defense Program," *AW&ST* (May 19, 1980): 19.

131. "Get Moving," *The Economist* (April 19, 1980): 47; "NATO Calls on Iran to Free U.S. Hostages," *Washington Star* (May 14, 1980): 8.

132. Wallace J. Thies, "Crises and the Study of Alliance Politics," *Armed Forces and Society*, 15 (Spring 1989): 349ff; see also Wallace J. Thies, "The 'Demise' of NATO—A Postmortem," *Parameters*, 20 (June 1990): 17–30.

133. The administration's perceptions of the military balance in Europe are discussed in Robert Reinhold, "U.S. Warns Its Allies They Must Increase Military Spending," *NYT* (February 22, 1981): 1, 8, 9; Bradley Graham, "U.S. Calls on Allies to Boost Defense Outlay," *Los Angeles Times* (February 22, 1981): 1, 22; "NATO Urged to Stress Strength Over Arms Control," *AW&ST* (April 13, 1981): 18–19; "NATO Modernization, Arms Control Stressed," *AW&ST* (April 27, 1981): 69, 72, 77. The administration's belief in the importance of U.S. leadership is discussed in Ronald Steel, "Will Europe Behave?," *New Republic* (December 6, 1980): 13; Miles Kahler, "The United States and Western Europe: The Diplomatic Consequences of Mr. Reagan," in Kenneth Oye et al. (eds.), *Eagle Defiant* (Boston: Little Brown, 1983), 280; Roger Hansen, "The Reagan Doctrine and Global Containment: Revival or Recessional," *SAIS Review*, 7 (Winter–Spring 1987): 53.

134. R. Reinhold, "U.S. Warns Its Allies," *NYT* (February 22, 1981); B. Graham, "U.S. Calls on Allies," *Los Angeles Times* (February 22, 1981). See also Richard Halloran, "Allies Found Lagging on Arms Outlay," *NYT* (July 29, 1981): 5.

135. "Holding Steady?," *The Economist* (April 18, 1981): 54–55; John Tagliabue, "Bonn Budget Plan for the Military Cut in Real Terms," *NYT* (July 13, 1981): 1, 5; Steven Weisman, "U.S. Critical of Bonn's Plan to Curb Military Spending," *NYT* (August 1, 1981): 2; Halloran, "Allies Found Lagging," *NYT* (July 29, 1981).

136. Quoted in Richard Barnet, *The Alliance* (New York: Simon and Schuster, 1983), 428.

137. W. Thies, *The Atlantic Alliance*, 49; *NATO Review*, 24 (1, February 1976): 27.

138. The data cited here are drawn from U.S. Arms Control and Disarmament Agency, *World Military Expenditures and Arms Transfers, 1988* (Washington, D.C.: U.S. Government Printing Office, 1989), 34ff. Spain is not included because it did not join the alliance until 1982.

139. See, for example, former Secretary of State Haig's comment that the United States would have to triple the size of its armed forces and put its economy on a war footing in order to provide a nonnuclear defense of Western Europe; Bernard Gwertzman, "U.S. Refuses to Bar Possible First Use of Nuclear Arms," *NYT* (April 7, 1982): 1, 6.

140. See, for example, Jeffrey Boutwell, "Politics and the Peace Movement in West Germany," *International Security*, 7 (Spring 1983): 72–92; Frank Myers, "The Failure of Protest Against Postwar British Defense Policy," in Solomon Wenk (ed.), *Doves and Diplomats* (Westport, Conn.: Greenwood Press, 1978), 240–64.

141. See, for example, Secretary Haig's comments on the need to retain the option of nuclear first use, in B. Gwertzman, "U.S. Refuses to Bar Possible First–Use," *NYT* (April 7, 1982).

142. These fears are described in more detail in David Capitanchik and Richard Eichenberg, *Defense and Public Opinion* (Royal Institute of International Affairs: Chatham House Papers #20, 1983), 22–25, 53–56, 61–66.

143. See, for example, the comments by Secretary of State Haig, Secretary of Defense Weinberger, and President Reagan, cited in Seyom Brown, *The Faces of Power*, rev. ed. (New York: Columbia University Press, 1983), 587–88. See also the essay by M. Kahler in K. Oye et al. (eds.), *Eagle Defiant*, 283–86.

144. Harald Mueller and Thomas Risse–Kappen, "Origins of Estrangement: The Peace Movement and the Changed Image of America in West Germany," *International Security*, 12 (Summer 1987) 82–83.

145. Ibid. In an October 1983 survey, 73 percent of British respondents said they believed the U.S. promise that Great Britain would have veto power over the firing of the ground-launched cruise missiles based there could not be trusted; Barnaby Feder, "Britons Shying Away From Missiles," *NYT* (October 31, 1983): 9.

146. Lou Cannon, "Reagan Tells Aides of Geneva's Promise," *Washington Post* (November 23, 1985): A1, A12. See also Michael Mandelbaum and Strobe Talbott, *Reagan and Gorbachev* (New York: Vintage Books, 1987).

147. The Reagan administration's lack of interest during its first term in serious arms control negotiations is described in Strobe Talbott, *Deadly Gambits* (New York: Vintage, 1984).

148. The figure cited here is average annual real growth in Department of Defense budget authority for the period fiscal 1982 to fiscal 1985. During the same period, average annual real growth in outlays was 6.75 percent. For a more detailed treatment of changes in the defense budget during the 1980s, see Stephen Alexis Cain, "The FY 1980/1991 Defense Budget: Preliminary Analysis," (Washington, D.C.: Center on Budget and Policy Priorities, 1989), especially Table 1. See also House Armed Services Committee, *HASC Tasks* (April 1988): 1.

149. Between fiscal 1986 and fiscal 1989, Defense Department budget authority in real terms declined at an average annual rate of 2.8 percent; outlays increased by 5.8 percent and 0.4 percent in fiscal 1986 and fiscal 1987, but declined by 0.3 percent and 0.7 percent in fiscal 1988 and fiscal 1989 (S. Cain, Table 1). The figures for fiscal 1989 included in this table represent estimates by the Office of Management and Budget.

150. See, for example, the president's pronouncement during an interview with Soviet journalists published in November 1985 that deployment of his proposed space-based missile defense system would come only after an agreement to eliminate offensive nuclear missiles (David Hoffman, "Reagan Says SDI Deployment Depends on Nuclear–Missile Ban," *Washington Post* (November 5, 1985): A1, A24.

151. Michael Howard, "A European Perspective on the Reagan Years," *Foreign Affairs: America and the World, 1987–1988*, (Council on Foreign Relations), 479. For

Schlesinger's article, see "Reykjavik and Revelations: A Turn of the Tide?," *Foreign Affairs: America and the World, 1986*, (Council on Foreign Relations), 430.

152. J.L. Gaddis, *Strategies of Containment*, 354.

153. W. Thies, *The Atlantic Alliance*, 22–23.

154. W. Schilling, "The Politics of National Defense," 22.

155. R. Osgood, *The Entangling Alliance*, 52.

156. A. Enthoven and K. Smith, *How Much Is Enough?*, 125; R. Osgood, *The Entangling Alliance*, 106–107, 125, 388.

157. L. Kaplan, *A Community of Interests*, 104, 76, 105.

158. Ibid., 110; D. Acheson, *Present at the Creation*, 565, 567.

159. Robert Jervis, *Perception and Misperception in International Politics* (Princeton, N.J.: Princeton University Press, 1976), 217.

160. J. Jones, *The Fifteen Weeks*, 130, 9; see also D. Acheson, *Present at the Creation*, 294.

161. J. Jones, *The Fifteen Weeks*, , 140–141.

162. S. Huntington, *The Common Defense*, 88–106.

163. The story of the AWACS purchase is told in Arnold Lee Tessmer, *The Politics of Compromise: NATO and AWACS* (Washington, D.C.: National Defense University Press, 1988).

164. This judgment is based on interviews conducted at NATO headquarters in Brussels during the summer of 1989.

165. This point was suggested by R. Jervis, *Perception and Misperception*, 222.

166. "An Explosion in the Kitchen? Relations With the Advanced Industrial States," in Oye et al. (eds.), *Eagle Defiant*, 111–13.

167. James Fallows, "The Passionless Presidency," *Atlantic Monthly* (May 1979): 44. This point was suggested by Richard Neustadt and Ernest May, *Thinking in Time* (New York: Free Press, 1986), xiv.

168. This point was suggested by R. Jervis, *Perception and Misperception*, 234–35. See also Wallace J. Thies, "On NATO Strategy: Escalation and the Nuclear Allergy," *Parameters*, 18 (September 1988): 18–33.

7

The Strategic Basis of Learning in U.S. Policy Toward China, 1949–1988

Banning N. Garrett

INTRODUCTION

This chapter focuses on the strategic basis of learning in the formulation and implementation of U.S. policy toward China.[1] For more than four decades, U.S. policy makers have shaped China policy based largely on their perceptions of the strategic environment and considerations of U.S. strategy rather than solely on issues in bilateral relations with China. These factors have included: the East-West struggle, the global strategic environment, and U.S. strategy toward the Soviet Union; and the strategic environment in Asia and the requirements for containing communism and a favorable balance of power in the Asia-Pacific region. In formulating policy, U.S. officials have also considered developments in China's domestic economic and political situation; Chinese military deployments and capabilities, especially nuclear weapons; and Beijing's changing foreign policies. Although U.S. policy toward China has not been shaped by domestic politics in the United States, the president's policy-making flexibility has frequently been constrained by calculations of unacceptable political costs of a change in policy.

Strategic considerations and assessments have often provided the key to China policy. They have facilitated learning by policy makers at critical points leading to policy breakthroughs. The remarkable change in U.S. policy that made possible the Sino-American rapprochement in the 1969–1972 period, for example, was based on a reassessment of the strategic environment and U.S. strategy by the Nixon administration. Strategic concerns have also led to policy paralysis. Calls for change in China policy based on bilateral considerations have been rejected or ignored by senior officials on the basis of failure to perceive changes in the strategic environment that required a reassessment of policy toward China or an unshakable commitment to a current strategy and strategic objectives.

In the late 1940s, as the Nationalist regime was collapsing on the Chinese mainland and was retreating to Taiwan, many U.S. policy makers advocated a subtle strategy aimed at encouraging the Chinese Communists to pursue a course independent of Moscow and to reach an accommodation with the United States. The United States was implementing such a policy toward Yugoslavia in response to Marshal Tito's break with Stalin in 1948, and there were probes from Chinese Communist leaders indicating that encouraging "Titoism" in China was a viable option.

This cognitive complexity of U.S. policy makers' understanding of processes in China and of their policy discussions during the late 1940s contrasts with two decades following the outbreak of the Korean War in June 1950. The Titoist option was abandoned, U.S. policy making toward China became frozen in ideological rigidity, and Sino-American relations became stalemated in hostile confrontation. Throughout the 1950s, however, senior policy makers continued to base U.S. policy on perceptions of nationalist tendencies in China and growing differences between Beijing and Moscow, despite their public portrayal of Beijing and Moscow as immutable allies in a monolithic Sino-Soviet bloc. They believed that in the long run those differences—exacerbated by a U.S. strategy of putting pressure on China aimed at driving a wedge between the two communist powers—would lead to an irreconcilable rift between China and the Soviet Union. That rift, they maintained privately, would make possible realization of the balance-of-power strategy toward China and the Soviet Union in Asia that had been advocated in the late 1940s.

As the U.S. sought to isolate China and increase the Chinese burden on Moscow, however, deep mistrust and hostility developed between Washington and Beijing that proved to be a major obstacle to exploitation of the success of the wedge strategy when the Sino-Soviet dispute finally emerged publicly in 1960. U.S. policy makers' own anticommunist rhetoric as well as pressure from domestic critics, especially "China lobby" supporters of the Nationalists on Taiwan, posed nearly insurmountable obstacles to changing China policy even if it had been perceived that strategic benefits might accrue to the United States from such a policy shift. And during the periods of nascent U.S.–Soviet détente in the late 1950s and again after the October 1962 Cuban missile crisis, China was perceived in Washington to be a more aggressive and militant foe than was the Soviet Union. In the early 1960s, Washington even considered active pursuit of joint action with the Soviet Union to contain China.

China as well as the United States was locked into a confrontational policy in this period. During most of the 1950s and 1960s, China was committed to militant "anti-imperialism" and unwilling to pursue new initiatives toward the United States that could break the deadlock in Sino-American relations.[2]

In perhaps one of the most dramatic examples of learning in the history of U.S. foreign policy, this impasse in relations was overcome by the carefully orchestrated transformation of the U.S.–Chinese relationship in the period between 1969 and 1972. The key factor making possible the U.S. policy shift leading to the rapprochement with China was a change in strategic perspective and global strategy under a new administration in response to changing international circumstances. The administration's new strategy and its policy initiatives toward China profoundly affected the global balance of power, strengthened U.S. leverage over the Soviet Union and North Vietnam, and substantially improved the U.S. strategic position globally and in Asia.

There are other turning points in Sino-American relations since the 1969–1972 rapprochement that illustrate the strategic basis of learning and change in U.S. policy toward China. In 1978 there was a major shift in policy toward China under the Carter administration that resulted not from changing views of the president's senior advisers but rather from the impact of external events on the outcome of policy struggles among senior officials seeking presidential support for competing strategies. That shift was preceded by an extended period of debate within the U.S. government over its strategy for containment of the Soviet Union and China's role in that strategy. Senior officials' views of these issues were influenced by new ideas from outside the government as well as by changes in the international environment. Altered circumstances internationally provided the opportunity for some officials to successfully press for implementation of a preexisting policy option. In this case, the U.S. government can be said to have learned even though individual policy makers did not change their views, and it is still uncertain whether the president was aware that his policy choices vis-à-vis China implied a shift in strategy toward the Soviet Union.

In the first two years of the Reagan administration, perceived U.S. strategic interests vis-à-vis the Soviet Union forced Washington to retreat from efforts to roll back the clock on U.S. policy toward Taiwan while simultaneously enhancing anti-Soviet cooperation with Beijing. The Reagan administration came to realize that its initial objectives toward China were incompatible and therefore impractical. The administration had to relearn the lessons of the past about the limits of China's flexibility on the Taiwan issue that had been established by the experience of the three previous administrations. In the mid-1980s, the Reagan administration successfully adjusted China policy in response to perceived changes in the U.S.–Soviet balance of power and the Soviet threat and to China's adoption of an independent foreign policy.

APPROACH

This study does not recount the history of Sino-American relations but rather examines American officials' thinking about China policy and U.S. geopolitical strategy. Consequently, the study does not provide a detailed account of developments in U.S. policy toward China but rather analyzes the considerations in formulating U.S. policy. The primary sources for the study are memoirs of key policy makers, secondary accounts, government documents, and interviews with participants in the policy-making process. Documents on U.S. policy in the late 1940s and early 1950s that have recently been declassified have led to reassessments of that period by several historians. This study's account of learning in U.S. policy toward China in the 1940s and 1950s has drawn heavily on the works of these scholars.

Although policy makers' memoirs are critical sources for understanding the thinking of presidents and senior officials, they can also be incomplete and self-serving. To some extent, this can be compensated for by reference to other accounts of the period and by interviews with former officials and others involved in the policy-making process. It will be possible to draw a more complete picture of their views as government documents of the last three decades are declassified.

1949–1960: DRIVING A WEDGE

Strategic considerations were predominant in U.S. policy making toward China even in the 1940s and 1950s, despite the ideological rhetoric and the domestic political pressures that often appeared to most observers as the driving forces behind U.S. policy. Although anticommunism and domestic politics were factors that constrained the flexibility of the Truman and Eisenhower administrations, they were not the key factors shaping U.S. policy.

U.S. policy toward the Chinese Communist Party (CCP) in the late 1940s and the People's Republic of China (PRC) after October 1949 was predicated on the notion that the CCP and Communist China would eventually split with the Soviet Union and counterbalance Soviet power in Asia. This underlying perspective formed the basis of a strategy aimed at driving a wedge between the Soviet Union and its communist allies. This strategy was revealed only recently in declassified documents and contrasts sharply with the simplistic public descriptions by Truman and Eisenhower administration officials of a monolithic Sino-Soviet bloc and of the Chinese communists as mere puppets of the Soviet Union.

A key objective of U.S. policy at the end of World War II was to separate communist movements and governments from the perceived source of their inspiration and control—the Soviet Union. "What is remarkable about American policy toward international communism in the early days of the Cold War," historian John Lewis Gaddis writes, "is how quickly the possibility of encouraging heretical growths came to be seen, and acted upon."[3] The central assumption of U.S. strategy from the beginning, according to Gaddis, "was that the interests of communists outside the Soviet Union—and of left-wing non-communist movements as well—would not always coincide with those of the Kremlin."

Events in the late 1940s—especially the defection of Yugoslavia from the Soviet camp in mid-1948—vindicated the view that there were potential clashes of interest within the communist world and that these differences could be encouraged and exploited by the United States. President Truman endorsed a National Security Council paper in November 1948 that called for efforts to bring about "the gradual retraction of undue Russian power and influence from the present perimeter areas around traditional Russian boundaries and the emergence of satellite countries as entities independent of the USSR."[4]

By that time, U.S. officials were convinced that defections from Moscow's control were more likely in Asia than in Eastern Europe. George Kennan, then director of the Policy Planning Staff, told students at the Naval War College in October 1948: "I can't say to you today whether Titoism is going to spread in Europe," but "I am almost certain that it is going to spread in Asia."[5]

Many State Department officials foresaw a near-term Communist Chinese split with the Soviet Union. "We anticipate the possibility that great strains will develop between Peiping [Beijing] and Moscow," a department memorandum stated in November 1949. "These strains would not only work to our advantage but would contribute to the desired end of permitting China to develop its own life independently rather than as a Russian satellite."[6] Some officials advocated actively seeking to entice the CCP into pursuing a course independent of the Soviet Union that would make possible some form of Sino-American cooperation.[7] Secretary of State Acheson and his Foreign Service advisers, especially George Kennan, favored a realpolitik containment strategy that would rely on a nationalist and independent Communist China to counterbalance Soviet power in Asia.[8]

State Department officials' hopes for a fissure in the emerging ties between the CCP and the Soviet Union and establishment of a cooperative relationship with a Chinese Communist government were encouraged by CCP probes to the United States in the 1940s.[9] CCP leaders first approached the United States toward the end of World War II. Mao Zedong even sent a secret message offering to visit Washington to meet with President Roosevelt.[10] CCP leaders continued to probe the United States in the last days of the Chinese civil war, despite U.S. support for the faltering Nationalists who eventually retreated to Taiwan.[11]

As early as August 1948, some U.S. officials had suggested that Mao Zedong could be another Marshal Tito.[12] The potential for Chinese Titoism was hotly debated within the Truman administration during this period.[13] Many State Department officials foresaw the possibility that the Chinese Communists would conclude that the Soviet Union—not the United States— was China's main enemy.[14] Secretary of State Acheson, stressing the importance of nationalism as a historical force, told an executive session of the Senate Foreign Relations Committee in March 1950 that it was inevitable that the Chinese Communists would come into conflict with the Soviet Union "because the very basic objectives of Moscow are hostile to the very basic objectives of China."[15] Acheson also suggested in January 1950 that Soviet pressures on China would make the CCP realize the advantages of dealing with the United States.[16]

President Truman had authorized a policy in March 1949 based on the assumption of basic conflicts of interest between China and the Soviet Union. The objective of this policy was to seek "to exploit through political and economic means any rifts between the Chinese Communists and the USSR and between the Stalinist and other elements in China both within and outside of the communist structure."[17] Truman had remarked to Senator Arthur Vandenberg during the year "that the Russians will turn out to be the 'foreign devils' in China and that the situation will establish a Chinese government that we can recognize and support."[18] Truman also indicated in November 1949 that he found merit in the suggestion that Washington attempt to exploit differences between Moscow and Beijing by having economic and political relations with China as it did with Yugoslavia.[19] Despite this recommendation and Acheson's desire to reach accommodation with China, however, there was little support in the Truman administration for active steps to encourage Chinese Titoism.[20] In addition, other policies toward China adopted at the same time were hostile to the CCP and appear to have been based on assumptions contradictory to the Titoist hypothesis.[21]

Washington also received conflicting signals from the Chinese Communists during this period, which may have reflected the splits within the CCP leadership. Despite the probes from some CCP leaders for establishing ties with the United States, party propaganda was increasingly hostile to the United States. More significantly, the Chinese Communists deeply antagonized the United States by placing the U.S. consul general in Mukden, Angus Ward, and his staff under virtual house arrest for a year beginning in November 1948. In June 1949, Mao Zedong announced a policy of "leaning to the side of socialism" that seemed to place the CCP firmly in the Soviet camp and rule out near-term prospects for a rapprochement with the United States.[22] And in mid-February 1950, the Sino-Soviet Treaty was announced in Moscow, thus seeming to solidify an alliance between the Soviet Union and the newly established People's Republic of China.

These events led to the virtual abandonment of hopes in Washington—especially in the State Department—for near-term accommodation with the CCP, although many officials continued to predict that a fissure might soon develop between the CCP and the Communist Party of the Soviet Union (CPSU). Active steps to entice the CCP into a more accommodating and independent stance had been rejected earlier as likely to open the administration to charges of appeasement of communism. Now the strategy of passively waiting for the Chinese Communists to split with the Soviet Union in the near term was perceived as increasingly unviable, especially following Chinese intervention in the Korean War in November 1951.[23]

While privately U.S. policy makers did not reject the prospect of a Sino-Soviet split, they increasingly viewed such a development as only a long-term possibility.[24] In a December 1950 response to British Prime Minister Clement Attlee's plea for a differentiated U.S. policy toward China and the Soviet Union on the grounds that there was still "a chance of Titoism," Secretary of State Acheson said that, although few of President Truman's advisers would disagree with Attlee's appraisal, the question was whether it was "possible to act on it." "Perhaps in ten or fifteen years," Acheson prophetically noted in the private conversation, "we might see a change in the Chinese attitude, but we do not have that time available."[25] The secretary of state also noted that the American public would not accept a policy of accommodation with China in Asia while standing up to the Soviet Union in Europe.[26]

Following Chinese intervention in Korea, American policy makers publicly insisted that the CCP was a puppet of Moscow—a "Soviet Manchukuo"—and implied that the United States would support the Nationalists' goal of overthrowing the communist regime.[27] Washington placed Taiwan inside the U.S. defense perimeter and eventually concluded a mutual defense treaty with the Republic of China, thus solidifying U.S. support for the Nationalist Chinese and endorsing their claim to being the rightful government of all of China.[28] U.S. policy makers definitively dismissed the possibility of actively exploiting differences between China and the Soviet Union in the short term, thus ruling out a balance of power strategy in Asia that encouraged China to pursue a course independent of the Soviet

Union and more amenable to U.S. interests in Asia.[29] The United States was set on a path of including Communist China as an object of its strategy of containment of the Soviet Union and international communism.[30]

Nevertheless, the secret long-term U.S. strategic objective remained to drive a wedge between China and the Soviet Union.[31] According to NSC 48/5, approved by President Truman in May 1951, the U.S. goal was to "detach China as an effective ally of the USSR and support the development of an independent China which has renounced aggression."[32] Rusk's condemnation the following day of the Chinese government as a Slavic Manchukuo was aimed at encouraging Chinese Titoism by discrediting Moscow in the eyes of Beijing—rather than at indicating a U.S. government belief that China was an inalienable puppet of the Soviet Union.[33]

President Eisenhower and his secretary of state John Foster Dulles also supported a policy of trying to split Beijing from Moscow in the long run, despite their public statements insisting that the Soviet Union and China formed an inseparable, monolithic communist threat to the United States and its allies. Throughout the 1950s, Eisenhower and Dulles pursued a wedge-through-pressure strategy aimed at straining China's relationship with the Soviet Union by creating excessive Chinese demands on Moscow for political, military, and economic support.[34] Historian John Lewis Gaddis has recently revealed that Secretary of State Dulles—"the very symbol of the American tendency to see communism as monolithic"—privately acknowledged the existence of differences between China and the Soviet Union and advocated a sophisticated strategy for exploiting those differences.[35]

Dulles's wedge strategy was articulated in a briefing by the secretary of state for President Eisenhower, British Prime Minister Winston Churchill, and French Foreign Minister Georges Bidault at a December 1953 meeting in Bermuda. Dulles maintained that the Chinese would not willingly submit to dictation from Moscow and that this situation "may eventually give us an opportunity for promoting division between the Soviet Union and Communist China in our own common interest." Dulles went on to recommend that the best means of exacerbating differences between Beijing and Moscow "would be to keep the Chinese under maximum pressure rather than by relieving such pressure." This pressure, Dulles explained, would compel the Chinese to make more demands on the Soviet Union that the Soviets would be unable to meet, thus increasing the strain in the relationship. Such a strategy was a better course, Dulles concluded, than seeking "to divide the Chinese and the Soviets by a sort of competition with Russia as to who would treat China best."[36] Although Dulles and Eisenhower continued to perceive signs of differences between China and the Soviet Union and agreed to open ambassadorial-level talks with

the Chinese in 1955, they consistently rejected pursuit of a more conciliatory policy aimed at weaning the Chinese away from the Soviet Union,
not only to avoid a competition with Russia, but also in fear of alienating
domestic constituencies and unsettling allies.[37] They did, however, seek
to strain relations between China and the Soviet Union at key points in
the 1950s—especially during the crises over the offshore islands of Quemoy
and Matsu in 1954–1955 and again in 1958—by taking steps aimed at
heightening the perceived burden in Moscow of the Sino-Soviet alliance
and Chinese distrust of Moscow.[38]

While Dulles and Eisenhower secretly sought to undermine the Sino-
Soviet bloc by driving a wedge between Beijing and Moscow, the secretary
of state publicly based U.S. policy on the assumption that the U.S. government
regarded the Communist Chinese regime as "a passing phase and not a
perpetual phase." In a major policy speech in San Francisco, June 28,
1957, Dulles said: "We owe it to ourselves, our allies, and the Chinese
people to do all that we can to contribute to that passing."[39] The policy
consequences of this declared objective were the same as that of the
wedge strategy—with one important exception. While the wedge strategy
sought to isolate and pressure mainland China to force a rupture in ties
with the Soviet Union, its goal was only to foster an independent communist
regime. The passing phase objective, however, suggested that the United
States sought not only to force a fissure in the communist world but also
to replace the communist regime in Beijing with an anticommunist government under Chiang Kai-shek and the Nationalists. In practice, however, U.S. policy was guided by the more limited objectives of the wedge
strategy. Dulles and Eisenhower were committed to keeping a leash on
Chiang Kai-shek rather than supporting a Nationalist invasion of the
mainland. Despite Dulles's rhetoric, the administration's more realistic
hope was that the Soviet-Chinese alliance was a passing phase, not that
the communist regime in Beijing would collapse.

By encouraging a Sino-Soviet split, the wedge strategy was aimed at
making possible a U.S. balance of power strategy in Asia as well as at
weakening the global strategic position of the Soviet Union. Gaddis
reveals, for example, that Dulles commented privately to the British ambassador in February 1955 that the long-term objective of U.S. policy in
East Asia was to bring about "sufficient independence between Peiping
[Beijing] and Moscow as to create the beginning of a balance of power
relationship."[40]

The U.S. wedge strategy was effective, although it was not necessarily
the primary factor leading to the Sino-Soviet split.[41] U.S. pressure on China
in the 1950s exacerbated differences between the two communist powers
by increasing the Chinese burden on the Soviet Union and by demonstrating
to China the limits of Soviet support. In addition, U.S. efforts in the late

1950s to improve relations with Moscow while maintaining a hard line toward Beijing intensified China's concern that the Soviet Union's commitment to Chinese security was rapidly diminishing. By 1959, the Chinese were also suspicious that the "spirit of Camp David" would lead to super-power cooperation and even possible collusion against China.[42]

Although the wedge strategy presumed the possibility—indeed, the long-run likelihood—of a Sino-Soviet split, the Eisenhower administration did not perceive the growing differences between Beijing and Moscow as presenting a potential strategic opportunity to achieve a new modus vivendi with China and to reshape the global and regional configurations of power based on an emerging tripolarity.[43] Rather, they viewed signs of differences between Beijing and Moscow as disputes over the best means of defeating the United States. Dulles commented in early 1959 that, although there might be a struggle between Chinese leader Mao Zedong and Soviet leader Nikita Khrushchev over ideological leadership of international communism, there was "no early prospect of a division there which would be helpful to the West."[44]

By the time the open Sino-Soviet rift occurred in 1960, the chasm dividing Washington and Beijing was far wider than it had been when the possibility of Chinese Titoism was first discussed within the Truman administration in the late 1940s. Not only had the United States and China engaged in military conflict in Korea, but also the hostility had continued after the war, especially in the confrontations over Quemoy and Matsu. The United States objected to Chinese support for revolutionary movements in Indochina and elsewhere in Asia, and Beijing's threats against Formosa were viewed as signs of aggressive Chinese intentions. The United States had maintained a trade embargo against China and continued seeking to isolate China internationally while covertly and overtly supporting the Nationalists' irredentist ambitions short of unleashing Chiang Kai-shek for an attack on the mainland. In addition, U.S. policy makers' flexibility in changing U.S. policy toward China was constrained by the growing anticommunist hysteria in the United States, the extensive political clout of the pro-Nationalist China lobby, the administration's own rhetoric about international communism and the Communist regime in Beijing as a passing phase, and Western perceptions of China as a hostile totalitarian state threatening U.S. interests throughout Asia.[45]

Thus, at the very time in the late 1950s and early 1960s that the wedge strategy was succeeding, U.S. policy makers did not perceive the Sino-Soviet split as presenting exploitable strategic opportunities such as they had envisioned in formulation of the wedge strategy a decade earlier. Rather than seeking a new modus vivendi with China—much less a reconciliation—in pursuit of a new balance of power in Asia, the United States at the beginning of the 1960s perceived China as an even more aggressive and unpredictably dangerous enemy than the Soviet Union. Not only did containment of China remain the primary U.S. strategic objective in Asia, but also both the Kennedy and Johnson administrations seriously considered joint action with the Soviet Union against China in the early 1960s. Not until the end of the decade, under President Nixon, did the United States adopt a policy aimed at capitalizing strategically on the deep fissure in the communist world.

The decade-long hiatus between the open Sino-Soviet split and the Sino-American rapprochement was not just a question of strategic vision in the White House, however. During the 1960s, the mutual antagonism between the United States and China was further strained by Chinese hostility toward the United States and its allies, the Cultural Revolution, the growing U.S. involvement in the Vietnam War—including the U.S. assumption that China was the beneficiary if not the instigator of the conflict—and Beijing's successful development of nuclear weapons.

1961–1968: A MORE DANGEROUS ENEMY

Although neither President Kennedy nor President Johnson viewed the Sino-Soviet rift as creating exploitable strategic opportunities for the United States, they did perceive China as increasingly independent of the Soviet Union and often more troublesome than the Soviet Union in a nascent tripolar configuration of power.[46] In addition, the Soviets' growing conflict with the Chinese was viewed as preoccupying Moscow to the strategic benefit of the United States.[47] Kennedy and Johnson were also unwilling to pay the domestic political cost of adopting a more conciliatory U.S. policy toward China as was being advocated both inside and outside the U.S. government.

Although President Kennedy publicly acknowledged the existence of the Sino-Soviet split, he insisted that the differences between the Soviet Union and China were over means, not goals. "A dispute over how to bury the West," Kennedy insisted, "is no grounds for Western rejoicing."[48] Secretary of State Rusk warned that it was too soon to conclude that the basic unity of the socialist camp could not be easily reestablished in the event of a conflict with the West.[49]

President Kennedy viewed the Chinese as more hostile—and unpredictably adventurous—than the Soviets. He insisted in late 1962 that the world would be "far worse off" if China rather than the Soviet Union "dominated the Communist movement" because Chinese leaders "believe in war as a means of bringing about the Communist world" and that if there is a "nuclear third world war, they can survive it anyway with seven hundred and fifty million people."[50] In August 1963, following the signing of the

U.S.–Soviet Nuclear Test Ban Treaty and 14 months before China exploded its first nuclear bomb, Kennedy publicly warned that a nuclear-armed China could present a "potentially more dangerous situation than any we've found since the end of the Second war."[51] President Kennedy—and later President Johnson—secretly considered preventive military action against China's nascent nuclear capability, either unilaterally or jointly with the Soviet Union.[52] In addition, the Kennedy administration reportedly gave serious consideration in 1962 to supporting a Nationalist invasion of the mainland to instigate an uprising against the Communist regime.[53]

Besides perceiving the Chinese as irrational and dangerous, President Kennedy also had concluded at the beginning of his administration that domestic politics posed an insurmountable obstacle to change on the key issues in U.S. policy toward China, admission of the People's Republic into the United Nations and adoption of a "two Chinas policy," recognizing both Beijing and Taipei and thus ending U.S. support for continuation of the Chinese civil war.[54] According to Theodore Sorensen, Kennedy said privately that even if China had not become an emotional and political issue in the United States, any U.S. initiative at that time toward negotiations with China, diplomatic recognition of Beijing, or admission of China to the U.N. would be regarded as rewarding aggression.[55] Kennedy administration officials, according to Roger Hilsman, former assistant secretary of state for Far Eastern affairs, concluded in 1962 that the Chinese would view U.S. initiatives toward accommodation as "proof of the efficacy of their hardline," and thus that before "increased flexibility" in U.S. policy would work, "there probably had to be more firmness."[56]

Despite Kennedy's hostility toward China, he did not rule out eventual adoption of a more flexible China policy. He confided to a close adviser early in his administration that he favored a shift in policy but that any change would have to be deferred until his second administration because of the likely political opposition at home.[57] Dean Rusk, who was publicly viewed at the time as extraordinarily rigid on U.S. policy toward China in both the Kennedy and Johnson administrations,[58] insisted more than two decades later that he had favored a change in policy in 1961 but that Kennedy was adamant in postponing a consideration of a policy change. According to Rusk, Kennedy directed his secretary of state to ensure that there were no leaks to the press about any administration discussions of a new policy.[59]

In December 1963, Roger Hilsman made a public speech in San Francisco suggesting a new China policy of flexibility as well as firmness.[60] The speech was prepared before—but delivered three weeks after—President Kennedy was assassinated. It was not the harbinger of a dramatic shift in policy under the Johnson administration, however.

The escalation of the Vietnam War precluded a major change in China policy. Rusk and Johnson publicly defended the escalation of U.S. involvement in the Vietnam War as necessary to halt "Chinese expansion" in Asia. "Over this war—and all Asia—is another reality," Johnson asserted in April 1965, "the deepening shadow of Communist China. The rulers in Hanoi are urged on by Peking. . . . The contest in Vietnam is part of a wider pattern of aggressive purposes."[61] The Johnson administration's apprehension about aggressive Chinese intentions increased further with the publication of Lin Piao's *Long Live the Victory of People's War* in the fall of 1965—which the administration viewed as a Chinese *Mein Kampf*—and the advent of the Cultural Revolution a few months later.[62]

Johnson, like Kennedy, feared China's emerging nuclear capability and considered preventive military strikes against Chinese nuclear weapons facilities, either unilaterally or jointly with the Soviet Union.[63] Johnson's concern about Chinese nuclear weapons was publicly indicated by Secretary of State Dean Rusk, who raised the specter of 1 billion hostile Chinese armed with nuclear weapons at a news conference in October 1967.[64]

Despite the unmitigated hostility toward China expressed by U.S. leaders, administration officials privately recognized that America's favorable global strategic position had become dependent on the split between China and the Soviet Union. Insight into the Johnson administration's strategic view of China is provided by a top secret briefing by strategist Paul Nitze, then secretary of the navy, in January 1967.[65] A basic objective of U.S. foreign policy, Nitze said, was to maintain a favorable global balance of power vis-à-vis the Soviet Union, and within that bipolar balance, a favorable balance in Asia. The critical factor in Asia, Nitze asserted, was the status of the Sino-Soviet relationship. "A renewed coalition between the two and against the U.S. would affect the global balance of power, would set an Asian balance of power against the U.S., and could bring Soviet nuclear power into confrontation with the United States on the shifting ground of Asia." While Nitze emphasized that a second objective of U.S. policy was to prevent the Chinese from achieving hegemony in Asia, he also warned against taking action "to protect the rimland states" of Asia that "could force the Chinese regime toward a closer accommodation with the U.S.S.R."[66]

This strategic view did not imply need for any near-term change in China policy, which remained virtually frozen during the Johnson administration. U.S. fears of hostile and aggressive Chinese intentions had increased during the decade with the Sino-Indian war, China's acquisition of nuclear weapons, China's alleged responsibility for the Vietnam War, and the advent of the Cultural Revolution.[67]

Nevertheless, the hostility in the United States toward China born of the Korean War and the McCarthy era was fading.[68] There were increasing calls from congressional leaders, scholars, and other public figures for opening doors to Beijing. The pro-Taiwan China lobby had weakened substantially, and there was a more open debate about China in the press. Public opinion on China was also changing slowly, with increasing support for admission of China to the U.N., negotiations with Beijing on Vietnam, and easing of the U.S. trade embargo against the People's Republic.[69] There was also pressure in the State Department for a new China policy and a reassessment of China's alleged aggressiveness.[70]

By 1968, the presidential candidates of both parties were urging adoption of a more flexible China policy. Vice President Hubert Humphrey called for the "building of peaceful bridges to the people of Mainland China." Governor Nelson Rockefeller, campaigning for the Republican nomination, called for more "contact and communication" with China. The other leading Republican candidate, former Vice President Richard Nixon, had urged in *Foreign Affairs* magazine the previous year that the United States should "come urgently to grips with the reality of China."[71] Nixon added that "we simply cannot afford to leave China forever outside the family of nations, there to nurture its fantasies, cherish its hates and threaten its neighbors. There is no place on this small planet for a billion of its potentially most able people to live in angry isolation." Although Nixon had been a leading member of the China lobby, he had privately argued as far back as 1954 that it was important to end the isolation of China.[72] And in a comment foreshadowing his triangular strategy, Nixon had privately told Romanian President Nicholae Ceausescu in 1967 that he "doubted that any true détente with the Soviets could be achieved until some kind of *rapprochement* could be reached with Communist China."[73]

Despite shifts in public opinion and support for change in policy toward China in both political parties, there was no movement toward a change in U.S. policy toward China as Lyndon Johnson's presidency became consumed by the Vietnam War. The Johnson administration did not change its public portrayal of China or privately engage in a process of reassessing U.S. global strategy to find a new path to make possible a breakthrough in Sino-American relations or in the Vietnam War.

Containment of China continued to be the primary objective of U.S. strategy in Asia. In addition, the U.S. flirtation with the possibility of joint action with the Soviet Union against Chinese nuclear facilities, the 1963 Nuclear Test Ban Treaty, and the 1968 Non-Proliferation Treaty suggested a growing U.S. tendency to view containment of China as a shared concern with the Soviet Union. The Chinese, for their part, perceived the United States as colluding with the Soviet Union against China. Changing strategic assessments in Beijing, Washington, and Moscow were, however, about to provide the basis for a breakthrough in Sino-American relations.

1969–1972: BREAKING THE STRATEGIC IMPASSE

Changing international circumstances and a shift in U.S. global strategy provided the keys to change in U.S. policy toward China under the Nixon administration. President Richard Nixon and his national security adviser, Henry Kissinger, viewed China policy as an element of U.S. strategy toward the Soviet Union—not as only a regional issue in Asia or a bilateral issue between Beijing and Washington. Nixon and Kissinger finally capitalized on the Sino-Soviet split that had been produced, in part, by the wedge-through-pressure strategy of the Eisenhower administration in the 1950s but was left unexploited by the United States in the 1960s. They changed the U.S. perspective on China from anticommunist containment to balance-of-power pragmatism. On this basis they seized opportunities to transform the Sino-American relationship in a profound and enduring manner that realized the balance-of-power objectives of Dean Acheson and George Kennan in the Truman administration in the 1949–1950 period. In the process, they shaped a new context for succeeding administrations' perceptions of China and the requirements of America's China policy.[74]

The limits of U.S. power and the need for a reassessment of U.S. strategy had become readily apparent to U.S. policy makers by January 1969 when Richard Nixon took office. The 1968 Tet offensive in Vietnam had demonstrated Washington's inability to effectively apply its overwhelming military power to achieve political objectives in Southeast Asia. The Soviet Union was continuing to narrow the economic and technological gap with the United States and approaching parity in strategic nuclear forces.[75] This deteriorating U.S. strategic position was in part the result of a massive Soviet military buildup, spurred by the humiliation of the 1962 Cuban missile crisis, that was occurring at a time when the United States was pouring immense human and material resources into a black hole in Southeast Asia rather than into maintaining U.S. military superiority over the Soviet Union.[76] The intractable war in Vietnam and the civil rights movement at home had sparked a domestic crisis of unprecedented scope in the postwar era.[77] American economic hegemony was also in decline. The U.S. share of the gross world product and of world trade had fallen substantially since 1950 as Western Europe and Japan—with U.S. assistance—had rebounded from the devastation of World War II to become economic competitors. Economic recovery in the Soviet Union had also led to a narrowing of the Soviet–U.S. economic gap.[78]

The ability of the United States to manage global strategic realities appeared to be rapidly diminishing in the late 1960s. Throughout the 1950s and most of the 1960s, the United States had strategic nuclear superiority over the Soviet Union. Washington had maintained a "2 1/2 war" strategy based on the premise that the United States must be prepared to simultaneously fight major conventional wars against the Soviet Union in Europe and against China in Asia as well as a minor brushfire war such as in Vietnam. By 1969, however, the Soviets had nearly achieved strategic parity and the 2 1/2 war strategy had lost its credibility.[79]

While the challenge from the Soviet Union was growing and the credibility of America's strategic posture was in jeopardy, the ability of China to threaten U.S. interests in Asia was diminishing. The Cultural Revolution had turned China inward in a devastating domestic political struggle that severely disrupted China's economy and further weakened its position in the Asian balance of power as well as vis-à-vis its emerging primary enemy, the Soviet Union. The Sino-Soviet conflict, which had broken into the open in 1960, had created a second military front for Beijing, which was already concerned with managing perceived military threats from the U.S.–backed Nationalists on Taiwan and from the United States. The U.S. threat to China had appeared to be growing in the mid-1960s as the United States expanded its military role in Indochina, despite private U.S. assurances to Beijing that China would not be attacked if it did not enter the war.[80]

The Sino-Soviet split complicated the strategic situation for the Soviet Union as well as for China. Beijing's hostility to Moscow had created a second front for Soviet military planners—a development that was little appreciated by U.S. policy makers prior to the Nixon administration.[81]

Development of a new strategy had been beyond the capability of the Johnson administration, which had become hamstrung by its own ideological preconceptions and mired in an unwinnable and increasingly unpopular war that it justified as necessary to contain Chinese communism. A new U.S. strategy had to be found that (1) acknowledged the limits of U.S. power in Asia and the growing global power of the Soviet Union by capitalizing on U.S. strengths and exploiting the weaknesses of U.S. adversaries; (2) came to grips with the need for a new policy toward Beijing; and (3) differentiated between North Vietnam, China, and the Soviet Union in practice as well as in theory.

It was left to a new administration to reassess the strategic environment in nonideological, realpolitik terms and recognize opportunities as well as dangers in the global situation facing the United States at the end of the 1960s. Based on such an analysis of changing strategic realities and policy requirements, Nixon and Kissinger sought to develop a global strategy that would (1) ease domestic opposition to U.S. involvement in Vietnam while offering the prospect of a favorable outcome of the war; (2) manage the threat to U.S. interests posed by the seemingly relentless growth of Soviet military capabilities and a shift in the trend in the balance of power favoring the Soviet Union; and (3) move away from an unviable 2 1/2 war military strategy to a 1 1/2 war strategy that no longer presumed a simultaneous conflict with the Soviet Union and China.[82]

Both Nixon and Kissinger believed that this new strategy should include activating the triangular relationship among the United States, the Soviet Union, and China to create a new global configuration of power. Careful manipulation of the strategic triangle, they believed, would provide greater incentives for the Soviet Union to be more conciliatory and restrained in its international behavior—especially its support of North Vietnam—and to take other steps aimed at improving relations with the United States and slowing the development of Sino-American relations.[83]

At the beginning of the first administration, however, Nixon and Kissinger had yet to understand the thinking of Chinese leaders and saw little prospect for a breakthrough in Sino-American relations. Although they viewed rapprochement with Beijing as a strategic requirement for the United States, they also shared many of the perceptions of China that had paralyzed U.S. policy toward China for two decades, including the view that China was responsible for the Vietnam War, that the Chinese were dangerously aggressive, and that Beijing was the culpable party in the Sino-Soviet split. "Originally we had not thought reconciliation possible," Kissinger writes in his memoirs. "We were convinced that the Chinese were fanatic and hostile. But even though we could not initially see a way to achieve it, both Nixon and I believed in the importance of an opening to the People's Republic of China."[84] In the next few months, Nixon and Kissinger began reassessing their preconceptions about China and realizing that their theoretical ideas about establishing a triangular framework could be implemented in practice through a patient and highly secretive diplomacy that capitalized on fortuitous unfolding events as well as on long-term trends.

Less than two months after Nixon was inaugurated, the conflict between the Soviet Union and China exploded into open military clashes along the Sino-Soviet border.[85] Sporadic border clashes, Soviet hints of a possible large-scale attack on China,[86] and increasing signs of Chinese interest in rapprochement with the United States to counterbalance the growing Soviet threat[87] presented both dangers and opportunities to Nixon and Kissinger. The danger was that the border clashes could escalate into a major, possibly nuclear, war between the two communist powers.[88] At worst, the United States would be dragged into a global conflict. Even if that did not occur, a successful Soviet military move to provoke leadership or policy changes in Beijing that led to a renewal of the Sino-Soviet alliance would shift the global balance of power against the United States.

The U.S. president and his national security adviser perceived an opportunity to begin implementing their strategy aimed at creating a new, more favorable configuration of global power. They concluded that U.S.

policy steps to begin actively exploiting the potential U.S. leverage in the Soviet-American-Chinese strategic triangle could prevent both Sino-Soviet war and Sino-Soviet rapprochement while also providing the United States with a new source of pressure on both Moscow and Hanoi.

In the first few months of the administration, Nixon and Kissinger gained insight into not only Chinese views and national interests but also Soviet leaders' concern about the possibility of steps by Washington to thaw Sino-American relations. Former Kissinger aide William Hyland recounts that Soviet Ambassador to Washington Anatoly Dobrynin told Kissinger in early 1969 that China was the Soviet Union's "main security problem."[89] Hyland comments that "after years of soaking up the bitter anti-Chinese atmospherics in Washington during the Johnson administration, and especially from Dean Rusk, Dobrynin assumed that complaints about Chinese behavior would continue to be sympathetically received." Dobrynin "outsmarted himself," however, Hyland notes. The Soviet ambassador's remarks and other private Soviet warnings to the United States against seeking to use China against the Soviet Union indicated to Nixon and Kissinger that the Soviets' extreme sensitivity to the prospect of any improvement in Washington-Beijing ties provided a potential new source of U.S. leverage over Moscow.[90]

Nixon and Kissinger took small, unilateral steps toward improving relations with Beijing beginning in July 1969, thus initiating a process of signaling that led to a dialogue and greater mutual understanding between the United States and China in the following two years. They also signaled the Soviet Union that the United States would neither side with Moscow against Beijing nor tolerate unilateral Soviet military pressure on China. The administration rejected Soviet overtures for joint U.S.–Soviet military measures or U.S. acquiescence to Soviet military action to destroy China's nuclear capabilities[91]—a dramatic reversal from the 1963–1964 period when Washington apparently approached the Soviet Union with a similar proposal. The United States also indicated publicly that it was opposed to a Soviet attack on China, thus signaling Beijing of its concern for Chinese security and rejection of U.S.–Soviet collusion.[92] At a National Security Council meeting August 14, 1969, Nixon, according to Kissinger, "startled his Cabinet colleagues by his revolutionary thesis (which I strongly shared) that the Soviet Union was the more aggressive party and that it was against our interests to let China be 'smashed' in a Sino-Soviet war."[93]

The Nixon-Kissinger strategic logic was new and confusing not only for the Soviets, but also for other officials in the administration. Kissinger recounts that he and Nixon were alone among senior policy makers in being convinced "that the United States could not accept a Soviet military assault on China. We had held this view before there was contact [with

China] of any sort; we imposed contingency planning on a reluctant bureaucracy as early as the summer of 1969."[94] Kissinger further explained that "this reflected no agreement between Peking and Washington. . . . It was based on a sober geopolitical assessment. If Moscow succeeded in humiliating Peking and reducing it to impotence, the whole weight of the Soviet military effort could be thrown against the West. Such a demonstration of Soviet ruthlessness and American impotence . . . would encourage accommodation to other Soviet demands from Japan to Western Europe, not to speak of the many smaller countries on the Soviet periphery."

Although the Sino-Soviet schism had been a reality for a decade, the Nixon administration was the first to develop a strategy to exploit the Beijing-Moscow rift to enhance the U.S. position in the global balance of power, create a new context for resolving the Vietnam issue, and transform the Sino-American relationship.[95] In the process, Nixon and Kissinger based their strategy toward China not on the assessments and recommendations of most China experts inside and outside the U.S. government— although these experts played an important role in developing the tactics of rapprochement—but rather on its own balance of power, national interest perspective, and realpolitik strategy toward the Soviet Union. The thinking of the president and his national security adviser more closely correlated with leadership perspectives and concerns in Beijing and Moscow than did the relatively parochial views of most area specialists.

Many, if not most, U.S. experts on China had supported adoption of a new China policy since the early 1960s, including U.S. recognition of the People's Republic and its admission to the United Nations.[96] For the most part, however, they based their views on bilateral considerations and failed to appreciate the strategic perspective of Chinese leaders and thus the basis for new policies toward Sino-American relations in Beijing as well as in Washington. Kissinger claims that this failure was demonstrated on the eve of his secret July 1971 visit to Beijing. "The academic China experts were convinced that the issues of primary concern to China were Vietnam and Taiwan," Kissinger writes. "This turned out to be quite wrong. Arms control was another priority issue urged on me; the Chinese never raised this matter and rebuffed us when we did; they consistently took the Gaullist view that the whole subject was just another form of U.S.–Soviet collusion. Another nearly universal expert opinion was that *before* U.S.–Chinese relations could improve, we had to recognize Peking as the sole government of China or at least allow Peking into the United Nations. This too was wrong: the breakthrough occurred months before the latter event took place, and seven years before President Carter did the former. Bilateral trade and exchanges were another professional priority . . . these turned out to be of marginal interest to the Chinese, doled out when necessary for symbolic purposes. It was widely held, again, that China would insist on reassurance that we were withdrawing from Asia. The opposite was true. The Chinese desperately wanted us *in* Asia as a counterweight to the Soviet Union."[97]

Kissinger is partly to blame for the limited vision of some China specialists. He intentionally kept the China-watching community in the dark about the administration's secret contacts with Beijing and its evolving strategy toward China, thus complicating the analytical tasks of the government as well as academic Sinologists advising him. Some government and academic Sinologists, however, although they were not privy to the administration's policy initiatives and secret contacts, did provide crucial assistance to Kissinger as he developed his understanding of China during the 1969–1971 period leading up to his secret visit to Beijing. They correctly perceived the strategic situation faced by Beijing and helped shape Kissinger's thinking about China in the crucial period of mid-1969.[98]

Nevertheless, the presidential vantage point and Nixon and Kissinger's strategic view provided a unique and prescient guide to Chinese thinking in assessing the possibilities for implementing their triangular, balance-of-power strategy. Nixon and Kissinger came to understand Chinese leaders' primary concerns about the Soviet Union and the need for the United States to remain a power in Asia as a counterbalance to the Soviet Union. Shared U.S. and Chinese concern about the Soviet Union thus provided the basis for the efforts by both U.S. and Chinese leaders to dramatically transform the Sino-American relationship in the 1969–1972 period.

Based on this perspective, Nixon and Kissinger had developed a China policy that was based primarily on the Soviet-American-Chinese triangular relationship and rejected policies that focused solely on U.S.–Soviet or Sino-American relations. Kissinger explains this by recounting an analysis he provided Nixon in August 1969 of the schools of thought in the U.S. government about China's role in U.S. strategy toward the Soviet Union. The "Slavophiles," Kissinger told Nixon, "argued that the Soviets were so suspicious of U.S.–Chinese collusion that any effort to improve relations with China would make Soviet-American cooperation impossible. Those who held this view believed that we should give top priority to improving relations with the Soviet Union and, for this reason, should avoid efforts to increase contact with Peking."[99] The "Sinophiles," Kissinger writes, "argued that our relations with the Soviet Union should not be a major factor in shaping our China policy. Marginal actions to increase Soviet nervousness might be useful but fundamental changes in the U.S.–China relationship should be guided by other considerations." The third group, which advocated what Kissinger terms "a kind of 'Realpolitik' approach," argued that expanded contacts with China would provide the United States with leverage over the Soviet Union. "Not surprisingly," Kissinger writes, "I was on the side of the Realpolitikers."

During the 1971–1972 period, Nixon and Kissinger were successful at achieving both a rapprochement with China and détente with the Soviet Union, including the first Strategic Arms Limitation Treaty (SALT I). China ended its enmity toward the United States and tacitly supported maintaining a strong U.S. position in Asia as Beijing as well as Washington sought to create a new global and regional balance of power to contain the Soviet Union. In addition, "playing the China card"—as U.S. steps to improve ties with China to gain leverage over the Soviet Union came to be called—had been successful in prompting Moscow to take steps to improve relations with Washington during this critical period.[100]

The "Sinophile" and "Slavophile" positions had little influence not only in the Nixon administration's formulation of policy toward China and the strategic triangle but also in the Ford administration.[101] Even as the circle of officials involved in the policy-making process widened under President Ford, the debates over China policy nevertheless involved primarily a struggle between officials advocating rival realpolitik strategies for managing Soviet power rather than Sinophile or Slavophile alternatives.

1973–1976: CHINA THE KEY ISSUE
IN THE SOVIET POLICY DISPUTE

Nixon and Kissinger had reassessed the strategic environment and developed a new global strategy to exploit U.S. strengths and Soviet weaknesses, including Moscow's fear of China. They succeeded in identifying and seizing opportunities to transform the global strategic alignment of power capitalizing on the Sino-Soviet split and creating a new strategic reality and a new balance of power, thus realizing objectives of the Truman and Eisenhower administrations. The high point of their success was in 1972 when China and the Soviet Union competed to have better relations with the United States. By late 1973, however, the Nixon administration's détente policy toward the Soviet Union was being attacked by domestic critics for having failed to slow the buildup of Soviet military power and the expansion of Soviet global influence.[102] As Kissinger's détente strategy came unraveled in the next two years, some officials maintained that managing a new strategic reality required adoption of a new realpolitik strategy. A key element of the debate became the role of China in U.S. strategy toward the Soviet Union.

Détente came under increasing attack from within the administration—especially from Defense Secretary James Schlesinger—and from congressional critics. Kissinger's efforts to finalize the SALT II agreement based on the

1974 Ford-Brezhnev Vladivostok formula were stalled and his strategy of "strategic enmeshment" of the Soviet Union was undermined by Senate amendments in 1974 that tied improved U.S.–Soviet trade relations to Soviet emigration policies and severely limited Export-Import Bank credit commitments to the Soviet Union, thus leading Moscow to abrogate the 1972 U.S.–Soviet trade agreement.[103] Soviet actions in the Middle East and Angola in the 1973–1975 period eroded the credibility of détente and further strained superpower relations. Kissinger was also under attack for the July 1975 Helsinki agreement and for his failure to criticize the Soviets directly for human rights violations. Although he tried to defend and repair his faltering détente policy, Kissinger was also becoming increasingly disenchanted with Soviet behavior and Moscow's view of détente.

The U.S. détente policy was under attack from the Chinese as well. They had begun accusing Kissinger of "appeasement" of the Soviet Union and indicating that U.S. weakness vis-à-vis Moscow raised serious doubts about the reliability and usefulness of the United States as a strategic counter to the Soviets.[104] Chinese leaders' disillusionment with the United States was compounded by the failure of the Nixon and Ford administrations to follow through on the Shanghai communiqué and normalize relations with Beijing.

Nixon and Kissinger had sought to use the "new relationship" with China to gain leverage over the Soviet Union. They had not envisioned a quasi-alliance with Beijing against Moscow. The United States would not take sides in the Sino-Soviet dispute, Kissinger insisted, but rather would be "evenhanded" in dealing with the Soviet Union and China. Such an evenhanded policy was necessary, Kissinger had maintained, to exploit Moscow's fears of Sino-American ties without provoking a counterproductive Soviet reaction. Developing military and strategic ties with China implied abandonment of evenhandedness and movement toward alignment with China against the Soviet Union to further strengthen the U.S. position in the balance of power. Thus, the idea of U.S.–Chinese military ties seemed to pose a direct challenge to Kissinger's policy of détente. Kissinger may also have felt constrained by secret promises to Soviet leaders that the United States would not develop military ties with China.[105]

As Sino-American relations deteriorated in the mid-1970s, however, Soviet fear that Sino-American relations would strengthen and lead to growing U.S.–Chinese anti-Soviet cooperation greatly diminished, thus sharply reducing U.S. leverage over Moscow. Administration officials asserted in November 1975 that, although the Soviets' concern over Sino-American ties had moderated their behavior in the early 1970s, it was no longer a factor restraining Soviet "adventurism" in Portugal and Angola.[106]

The United States needed to establish a new momentum in relations with China to regain leverage over the Soviet Union. The White House viewed concessions to China on Taiwan to improve U.S.–Chinese ties, however, as precluded by the conservative challenge to President Ford's ambitions for the Republican nomination for president in 1976.

In this strategic and political context Kissinger apparently became more receptive to the notion of steps toward China in the security realm to bolster relations with Beijing and regain leverage over Moscow. Such steps would relate more directly to China's primary security concern, the Soviet threat, than would concessions on Taiwan to normalize Sino-American relations. Thus, Kissinger's concern that a U.S. "tilt" toward Beijing would provoke an unacceptable response from Moscow apparently diminished or was set aside in the fall of 1975.[107]

The events and debates of the 1974–1975 period revealed an apparent contradiction in the Nixon-Kissinger triangular strategy. The United States was trying to strengthen détente by using Soviet fears of Sino-American collusion to pressure Moscow to compromise in bilateral negotiations and to cooperate in resolution of regional conflicts. The Chinese, however, were seeking to undermine détente and to pull the United States into an anti-Soviet coalition. Thus, if U.S. policy toward China were successful in furthering détente, China would perceive its security as diminished, the usefulness of the Washington connection for Beijing would be put in doubt, Sino-American relations would probably deteriorate, and U.S. leverage over Moscow would again be reduced. The Nixon-Kissinger strategy also implied that if the Soviet Union were accommodating to the United States, Washington would slow development of U.S.–Chinese relations, thus giving the Soviet Union a "veto" over U.S. policy toward China.

U.S. triangular policy was thus at an impasse by 1975. The U.S. position in the balance of power was deteriorating despite the initial rapprochement with China. The Soviet Union continued to build up not only its strategic forces in an apparent bid for nuclear superiority, but also its naval forces in a drive to challenge the U.S. navy globally and its land and air forces in the Far East to intimidate China. In addition, détente had failed to deter Moscow from using military force to seize opportunities in the Third World to expand Soviet influence. At the same time, the United States was reducing its military spending and its military and political involvement in the Third World while turning attention to mounting economic problems at home.

American policy makers were forced to reassess U.S. strategy in an effort to regain momentum in Sino-American relations and counter the adverse trend in the U.S.–Soviet balance of power to regain leverage over Moscow. The appropriate U.S. response to the deterioration of détente thus became the focus of an intense and prolonged dispute within the U.S. government.

In this case, U.S. policy makers turned to a highly controversial new idea that did not originate with senior policy makers. That idea was to abandon evenhandedness and develop a military-strategic relationship with China in a coalition strategy to contain expanding Soviet power. U.S.–Chinese military ties became a serious policy option favored by some top officials in the Ford and then Carter administrations that was pushed forward by external events as well as by internal policy struggles.

When the idea of developing an anti-Soviet defense relationship with China was first proposed in 1973–1974, it was criticized as unrealistic and even irresponsible by many U.S. officials.[108] Soviet experts insisted that abandonment of a policy of evenhandedness in favor of a tilt toward China in the triangular relationship through development of a security relationship with Beijing would undermine efforts to improve U.S.–Soviet relations and to negotiate a SALT II agreement with Moscow. And although the idea of Sino-American military ties was stimulated in part by quiet Chinese probes to the United States as early as 1973, many China specialists inside and outside the government contended that Beijing would not abandon self-reliance and seek a defense relationship with the United States. A minority of China experts maintained that Beijing's probes to the United States were an indication of serious interest in military ties with the United States to counter Soviet power and that Chinese leaders would not be restrained by their avowed commitment to independence and self-reliance.

While most Soviet and China specialists opposed the idea of U.S.–Chinese military ties, some defense planners were attracted to the strategic logic and purported benefits for both the United States and China of a U.S.–Chinese defense relationship. Secretary of Defense James Schlesinger, who was briefed on the pros and cons of military ties with China in late 1974, became the leading supporter of the idea within the administration.

By the fall of 1975, the outlines of a sharp debate over China's role in U.S. strategy toward the Soviet Union had emerged with military ties as the key issue. This debate was an inextricable part of the larger struggle over détente in which Schlesinger was pitted against Secretary of State Kissinger.

According to its advocates, the benefits of U.S.–Chinese defense ties— ranging from exchange of defense attachés to sales of advanced weapons and intelligence sharing—included:[109]

(1) Gaining leverage over Moscow to restrain Soviet behavior internationally and to pressure the Soviets to be more forthcoming in the SALT II talks and in other bilateral negotiations—leverage that had seemingly been lost since the initial opening to China had successfully nudged the Soviets forward in the SALT I negotiations;

(2) Preventing a Sino-Soviet rapprochement by maintaining suspicion and tension between Beijing and Moscow while tying Chinese leaders, including senior military officers, to the policy of tilting toward the United States;

(3) Giving Moscow reason to plan for possible U.S. wartime aid to China in the event of a new Sino-Soviet military conflict or possible Chinese involvement in a U.S.–Soviet conflict, thus complicating Soviet wartime planning; and

(4) Strengthening China's military capability through the transfer of certain advanced weapons and military technology, thus helping China deter the Soviet Union and possibly leading Moscow to redeploy some of its conventional forces to the Far East, thereby reducing pressure on the North Atlantic Treaty Organization (NATO) in the West.

As realpolitik strategists, both Kissinger and Schlesinger were attracted to the idea of military ties with China—but for different and conflicting reasons. Although both officials viewed China in a triangular context, they saw China's role in the strategic triangle differently primarily on the basis of their opposing views of U.S.–Soviet relations and on their diverging institutional concerns.

For Kissinger, détente was fundamentally a diplomatic approach to the problem of managing the threat posed by growing Soviet power, although he viewed strong U.S. military power—including maintenance of "essential equivalence" of strategic forces in the face of a major Soviet nuclear arms buildup—as a prerequisite for carrying out this strategy. The problem for Kissinger was strengthening the American position in the peacetime balance of power through political means at a time of Vietnam War–induced cuts in defense spending. Since Kissinger sought to pressure Moscow by manipulating Soviet anxiety about possible Sino-American collusion against the Soviet Union, any gestures toward military ties with China would be aimed at maintaining and increasing Washington's diplomatic leverage over the Soviets. At the same time, such attempts to gain leverage would be judged as counterproductive if moves toward China compelled Moscow to adopt a harder line in negotiations with the United States or engage in more aggressive international behavior.

For Schlesinger, coping with Soviet power was more a military than a diplomatic problem for U.S. global strategy. In his view, détente had not slowed the buildup of Soviet strategic and conventional military power, nor had it altered the long-term hegemonistic goals of Soviet leaders. The benefits accruing to the United States in the global military balance resulting from the Sino-Soviet split and then China's tilt toward the United States had become increasingly important in the effort to maintain or improve the American military position vis-à-vis the Soviet Union, especially in the Far East, at a time of declining U.S. defense spending. As a strategic ally bolstered by U.S. military assistance, China offered greater potential to tie down a substantial portion of Soviet military capabilities and resources and to greatly complicate Soviet defense planning for both conventional and nuclear war with the West. From Schlesinger's primarily military point of view—including his concern about the wartime balance of forces—the preservation of détente and success in the SALT II negotiations had a lower priority than did the maintenance of a favorable balance of military power.

Thus, Kissinger viewed steps toward military ties with China as aimed not only at directly strengthening the faltering Sino-American relationship but also at salvaging détente by pressuring Moscow to restrain its international behavior and become more accommodating to the United States. Schlesinger, who opposed détente, was less concerned about provoking a negative political reaction from Moscow than with containing expansion of Soviet power by strengthening the Western global strategic position through a military buildup and establishment of an anti-Soviet strategic relationship with Beijing.

Although Schlesinger was ousted by President Ford in November 1975 as a result of his policy disputes with Kissinger—including disputes over China—the issue of whether to seek a strategic, anti-Soviet military relationship with Beijing was not settled in the Ford administration. The secretary of state even took several cautious steps toward military ties with China over the next 12 months as he sought to reassure Beijing of U.S. concern about Chinese security and to signal the Soviet Union that a strategic tilt toward China by the United States was possible if Moscow were not more accommodating.[110]

1977–1980: NORMALIZATION ON A STRATEGIC BASIS

The unresolved strategic debates between Kissinger and Schlesinger over China and Soviet policy carried over into the Carter administration. Senior officials holding opposing strategic and policy ideas did not change their views, however. Neither Secretary of State Cyrus Vance nor National Security Adviser Zbigniew Brzezinski succeeded in persuading the other of his opposing view, but rather one or the other official won presidential support on specific policy issues: external events and domestic pressure led the president to decide in favor of policy options representing the strategic views of one faction over the other.

From the beginning of the Carter administration, Secretary of State Vance was concerned with strengthening U.S.–Soviet détente and finalizing a SALT II agreement. Improving relations with China was a low priority for the new secretary of state. Even more cautious than Kissinger in 1974, Vance viewed the development of strategic/military ties with China—"playing the China card"—as unnecessarily provocative toward Moscow and likely to undermine U.S.–Soviet relations. Vance notes in his memoirs that "to me, the suggestion of a U.S.–PRC security relationship was an unwise notion that posed substantial risks for our relations with Moscow and for our relations with Tokyo and other Asian allies."[111] National Security Adviser Brzezinski, however, viewed military ties with China as a means of strengthening the U.S. position in the balance of power and pressuring Moscow to be more cautious in its international behavior.[112]

There were no significant differences among senior policy makers on the desirability or terms of normalization of relations with China.[113] Vance notes, however, that "although everyone in the administration agreed that normalization would serve U.S. interests, we had different reasons for reaching this conclusion. Brzezinski looked at normalization largely in light of the impact it would have on the U.S.–Soviet geopolitical competition. [Secretary of Defense Harold] Brown emphasized the contribution that improved relations with Peking, including a modest security relationship, could make to our ability to counter Soviet military power. . . . I believed that China constituted a political, economic, and cultural weight in the world that the United States could not ignore. Better relations would help our foreign policy across the board—by producing increased regional stability and, in the long run, a more stable global order."[114] These differences reflected differing bureaucratic interests as well as conflicting strategic outlooks.

Brzezinski notes that although he supported normalization of relations with China, he thought the United States might be able "to promote a strategic connection even without normalization."[115] From the beginning of the administration, Brzezinski pressed for playing the China card in the triangular relationship by developing a strategic, anti-Soviet relationship with the People's Republic.

President Carter's predisposition toward détente and arms control favored Vance's strategy of seeking accommodation with Moscow and avoiding actions that might antagonize the Soviet Union. Nevertheless, Carter soon came into conflict with Moscow for his statements criticizing human rights in the Soviet Union and his new arms reductions proposal presented to Soviet leaders by Vance in March 1977. In response, at Brzezinski's urging Carter considered playing the China card for the first time.

In contrast with the sharply restricted discussions of this issue in the Nixon and Ford administrations, the option of military ties with China was the subject of an extensive interagency review, Presidential Review Memorandum (PRM) 24, in the Carter administration. The review pitted officials from the Pentagon, the National Security Council (NSC), and the Central Intelligence Agency (CIA) in favor of military ties against State Department officials, who argued that such moves might be too provocative toward the Soviet Union. Although the idea of developing military ties with China—such as transfer of military-related technology or allowing Western European arms sales to Beijing—was rejected by President Carter in June 1977, the issue continued to be the subject of intense debate within the administration for the rest of the year.[116]

The conclusions of PRM-24 were leaked to the press June 24. Five days later, Vance, in part reacting to the leak, emphasized in a speech to the Asia Society in New York that Sino-American relations would be dealt with primarily in a bilateral context and that they would "threaten no one," i.e., the Soviet Union.[117] Besides reassuring Moscow that the United States was not moving toward an anti-Soviet strategic relationship with China, Vance also successfully urged President Carter to tone down his human rights criticisms of the Soviet Union and back away from his tough SALT reductions proposals. At the same time, Carter decided to forge ahead with efforts to normalize Sino-American relations and directed Vance to present a proposal for normalization during a visit to Beijing in August.

In this period, the NSC concluded a major interagency study of the global balance of power—PRM-10—which concluded that the growth in Soviet military and economic power was slowing down and that long-term trends favored the United States.[118] The conclusions of PRM-10 offered a more relaxed view of the Soviet Union than Ford administration studies, which had warned of a continuing Soviet military buildup outstripping the United States and a Soviet reach for nuclear superiority.[119] PRM-10, which was conducted by government officials under the leadership of a consultant to Brzezinski at the NSC, Harvard Professor Samuel P. Huntington, not only concluded that the U.S.–Soviet military balance was roughly equal at present, but it also looked beyond strictly military factors to contrast the strength and scope of the U.S. economy and capacity for technological innovation with forecasts of impending Soviet capital and labor shortages. In addition, PRM-10 noted Moscow's problems with political succession, agricultural failures, and the continuing Sino-Soviet split as factors exacerbating Soviet long-term weakness and shifting the balance of power toward the United States.

PRM-10 seemed to suggest that the United States could be less alarmed by the "Soviet threat" and proceed with SALT and other efforts to enhance U.S.–Soviet cooperation. Vance and other pro-détente, pro-arms control officials in the administration argued on the basis of the PRM-10 assessments that Soviet weaknesses and American strengths provided a basis for Soviet interest in accommodation with Washington. Brzezinski and others, however, viewed the conclusions of PRM-10 as arguing for exploitation of Moscow's vulnerabilities to obtain concessions in bilateral negotiations and restrain the expansion of Soviet power—a view that did not prevail within the administration until the following spring.

The administration's foreign policy, especially toward the Soviet Union, and the implications of the PRM-10 assessment as communicated to the Chinese by Vance during his August visit to Beijing, created immediate problems for Sino-American relations. Publicly, the two sides reached an impasse over the terms of normalization, with the Chinese charging that the Carter administration had retreated from its predecessor's position on normalization. Privately, however, administration officials acknowledged that fundamental differences in strategic views between the two sides were also a crucial element in the impasse during Vance's visit.[120]

The secretary of state's views of the policy implications of PRM-10 posed a direct challenge to China's view of the United States as a declining superpower and the Soviet Union as the superpower on the ascendancy. The Chinese position provided the strategic rationale underlying Beijing's drive to establish an informal working alliance with the United States against the Soviet Union. To the Chinese, Vance's interpretation of PRM-10 also raised questions about the usefulness of the United States as a quasi-ally if Washington failed to see the need to take a strong stand against Moscow's global expansion.[121] "Normalization to Beijing would signify a further Chinese tilt toward the United States, and the Chinese were seeking the sense of strategic orientation which the Nixon administration had earlier provided," according to then-NSC China specialist Michel Oksenberg.[122] But Vance's statements and the administration's foreign policy in August 1977 indicated to the Chinese that the "signs were more in the other direction—of an administration oblivious to the Soviet global design."

In early 1978, the China card once again rose to the top of the deck in response to Soviet and Cuban military intervention in Ethiopia and Moscow's recalcitrance in bilateral negotiations with the United States, especially the SALT talks.[123] This time President Carter, under intense domestic political pressure to respond to the Soviet "challenge," took a much harder line publicly in his statements on relations with Moscow, including in his March 17 Wake Forest speech written by Brzezinski and his NSC staff. Carter also sided with Brzezinski on the issue of strategic ties with China, and—against the advice of Vance—sent the anti-Soviet national security adviser to Beijing in late May, signifying to both China and the Soviet Union that the United States had made an important shift in its global strategy.

Brzezinski's visit was intended to play the China card, and it was perceived that way in Moscow as well as in Beijing. In his private conversations with Chinese leaders, Brzezinski indicated that the United

States had changed its global strategy and now sought to cooperate with Beijing against Moscow. The national security adviser said that he and President Carter "believe the United States and China share certain common fundamental interests and have similar long-term strategic concerns. The most important of these is our position on global and regional hegemony. . . . We have been allies before. We should cooperate again in the face of a common threat. For one of the central features of our era—a feature which causes us to draw together—is the emergence of the Soviet Union as a global power."[124] In his public statements during the visit, Brzezinski asserted that Washington views its relations with China "from a long-term strategic view." He departed sharply from Vance's statement the previous June that the U.S.–Chinese relationship would "threaten no one" by asserting that "only those aspiring to dominate others have any reason to fear the further development of American-Chinese relations."

Brzezinski's aides provided the Chinese with detailed briefings on PRM-10. They communicated the national security adviser's view that chronic Soviet weaknesses and long-term U.S. advantages should be exploited to extract greater concessions from the Soviet Union and to contain its global expansion, even at the expense of possible deterioration in U.S.–Soviet relations—a view that was far more acceptable to the Chinese and suggested greater American willingness to pursue a potentially provocative informal alliance with Beijing against Moscow. Brzezinski writes that he was instructed by President Carter to "stress to the Chinese how determined we were to respond assertively to the Soviet military buildup and to Soviet proxy expansionism around the world."[125] In addition, Brzezinski discussed with the Chinese the sale to China of U.S. dual-purpose, military-related technology and Western European arms.

Brzezinski's visit provided the breakthrough that set the two countries on the path to normalization of relations seven months later. Both U.S. and Chinese officials indicated that common strategic views and concerns provided the context for rapid movement toward full diplomatic ties. The national security adviser's aides told the New York Times shortly after Brzezinski's return from Beijing that the two sides had agreed normalization was not only a bilateral matter but also strategically important to offset the Soviet Union.[126] Brzezinski told the Times that "the basic significance of the trip was to underline the long-term strategic nature of the United States relationship to China." Three years later, Brzezinski said that he had taken to Beijing "a secret Presidential instruction in my briefcase empowering me to start a new phase in the American-Chinese relationship."[127] He said that he had taken "as my point of departure our common strategic interests" vis-à-vis the Soviet Union, which were used as "a vehicle for moving forward toward normalization, and then for heavily enlarging the scope of the whole relationship."

Chinese officials, who had expressed dissatisfaction with Vance's Beijing visit, termed the talks with Brzezinski "beneficial" and were clearly pleased. They later told visiting Americans that normalization of relations with the United States was a strategic issue for China based on common concern about the Soviet threat.[128]

Brzezinski's China trip demonstrated to the administration that general agreement between the United States and China on strategic views and concerns created the political will to compromise to achieve normalization of Sino-American relations and forward movement in the overall relationship. The national security adviser's visit to Beijing did not indicate, however, that a new consensus had been reached within the administration on U.S. strategy toward the Soviet Union and China's role in that strategy. On the contrary, Vance and other senior administration officials sought to limit the damage of the tilt toward Beijing by maintaining at least a public image of evenhandedness in Washington's dealings with the Soviet Union and China.[129] They also sought to slow if not reverse the momentum of the new phase in Sino-American relations. The direction of the Sino-American relationship in the Carter administration had been set, however, resulting first in the normalization of relations on a strategic basis January 1, 1979, and finally, in the wake of the Soviet invasion of Afghanistan, a presidential decision in January 1980 later to allow sales to China of nonlethal military equipment.

1981–1982: INCOMPATIBLE OBJECTIVES

President Reagan, a longtime supporter of Taiwan who also had supported the idea of arming Communist China against the Soviet Union since the mid-1970s, would learn that his objectives with China were incompatible. Reagan wanted to roll back the clock on U.S. relations with Taiwan by upgrading ties with Taipei to an official status after they had been severed under the terms of the normalization agreement with Beijing. At the same time, he wanted to strengthen U.S. strategic cooperation with China to counter Soviet power.

Some officials in the Reagan administration believed that, strategically, China needed the United States more than the United States needed China and that therefore Beijing would have no choice but to accept an upgrading of U.S. relations with Taiwan.[130] The Chinese, however, threatened to downgrade Sino-American relations in an effort to demonstrate to the Reagan administration that China was not weak and would therefore not accept a retrogression in U.S. commitments to China on the Taiwan issue. Even after Reagan backed down on reestablishing official ties with Taipei, U.S.–Chinese contention over Taiwan continued on the issue of U.S. arms sales to Taiwan.

Some administration officials, including Secretary of State Alexander

Haig, argued for a bureaucratic compromise between those advocating upgrading arms sales to Taiwan and those supporting strategic ties with China. His solution was a policy of U.S. sales of arms to both China and Taiwan, which he contended the Chinese would accept. During his visit to Beijing in June 1981, Haig announced that the United States had lifted the ban on arms sales to China and asserted that "U.S. and Chinese perceptions of the international situation have never been closer. Our common resolve to coordinate our independent policies in order to limit the Soviet Union's opportunities for exploiting its military power has likewise grown stronger."[131]

Haig miscalculated, however. The Chinese reacted strongly to the U.S. effort to buy Beijing's acquiescence to upgraded arms sales to Taiwan, warning that continued U.S. arms sales to Taiwan were a "key stumbling block" in the development of Sino-American relations and putting the strategic relationship with the United States on hold. Pro-Taiwan White House officials nevertheless sought to gain presidential approval for sale to Taipei of a new jet fighter, the FX, which would increase the level of sophistication of arms sales to Taipei. This time Haig warned Reagan in an internal memorandum that Sino-American relations were at a "critical juncture" and maintained that "careful management" of relations with Beijing was essential "if we are to avoid a setback which could gravely damage our global strategic policy."[132] In the memorandum, Haig noted that the administration had given the impression to the Chinese that "we wanted to reverse normalization and pursue a 'two China's policy,'" and that this had "transformed the aircraft replacement question, which might have been manageable, into a symbolic challenge to China's sovereignty and territorial integrity."

After compromises by both sides, the United States and China released a joint communiqué August 17, 1982, on U.S. arms sales to Taiwan that not only reaffirmed but went farther toward recognizing Chinese sovereignty over Taiwan than previous U.S. commitments to China in the 1972 Shanghai and the 1978 normalization communiqués.[133] Thus, the Reagan administration achieved a modus vivendi with Beijing on Taiwan that eventually led to stabilization and steady improvement in Sino-American bilateral relations.

1983–1988: CHANGING STRATEGIC REALITIES

While the administration had to relearn lessons on Taiwan, it was able under Haig's successor George Shultz to recognize a new strategic situation in the mid-1980s and to adjust U.S. triangular policy accordingly. Haig had sought to develop strategic ties with China as part of an anti-Soviet coalition strategy similar to that pursued by Zbigniew Brzezinski.[134]

Like Brzezinski, Haig viewed strategic and military ties with Beijing as a deterrent to aggressive actions by the Soviet Union, punishment for the Soviets' global expansionist activity, and a source of leverage over Moscow in Soviet-American relations. Officials traveling in Haig's party to China in June 1981 told the press that the administration's announced decision to sell arms to China was viewed as a way to "get Moscow's attention." They emphasized the triangular context of the arms sales decision, noting that it signaled Moscow that a Sino-American alliance, although not yet politically feasible, had moved a step closer to realization.

Haig's view was increasingly out of step with Chinese thinking, however, and the administration's efforts to use common strategic concerns about the Soviet Union to win Beijing's acceptance of arms sales to Taiwan may have provided impetus to China's movement toward an "independent foreign policy." The Chinese viewed increasing Soviet economic difficulties and global overextension, combined with the U.S.-led effort to check Soviet expansion in the aftermath of the Afghanistan invasion, as diminishing the Soviet threat to China and increasing Beijing's room for maneuver in international relations.[135] They may have also been wary of being dragged into a U.S.–Soviet confrontation as superpower tensions increased during the first two years of the Reagan presidency. In October 1982, China officially adopted an "independent foreign policy" to facilitate easing of tensions with the Soviet Union and to maximize China's diplomatic maneuverability as the Soviet threat to China began to diminish and the U.S. global position strengthened. The Chinese—who in 1979 had called for a "united front" with the United States against the Soviet Union—publicly rejected a strategic relationship with the United States. Privately, however, the Chinese continued to insist that U.S.–Chinese relations were based on common strategic interests.

Shultz, who took office in mid-1982, saw less need for the tactical use of relations with China to influence Soviet behavior than had his predecessor. Like Haig, he supported a coalition strategy to contain Soviet power. But the new secretary of state emphasized the economic rather than the strategic-military underpinnings of the global coalition. Whereas Haig had viewed China through a Eurocentric lens, in which Beijing's primary role was to buttress NATO deterrence of Soviet expansion in Europe and the Middle East, Shultz stressed China's regional role in Asia and the increasing economic and political significance of the region to the United States.[136]

American officials scaled down their expectations of the role that China could play—and would be willing to play—as an active strategic partner in a global coalition. The administration also rejected the tactical use of China as a card to influence Soviet behavior. China's importance to the United States was viewed as stemming primarily from its passive role as a strategic counterweight to Soviet power and from its pursuit of parallel strategic interests with the United States in Afghanistan, Cambodia, and other areas involving Soviet expansionist activities in the Third World and Asia. It was considered essential to long-term U.S. objectives to maintain Beijing's pro-Western strategic posture and to assist China in strengthening its military capability for deterrence of the Soviet Union. The most effective means of achieving U.S. goals, in the administration view, was to support China's economic modernization effort through development of bilateral economic ties and the transfer of technology—including defense-related advanced technology.[137]

The administration's decision to deemphasize China's global strategic role was not only the result of its increasing focus on regional concerns in Asia and perceived changes in Chinese views of the international situation. There was also an assessment in Washington that the trend in the balance of power was beginning to shift in favor of the United States. The Soviets were perceived as facing mounting internal economic and political difficulties and international isolation on one hand, and the resurgence of U.S. power on the other, as the Reagan administration engaged in an unprecedented military buildup, the U.S. economy strengthened, and the United States began reasserting its global power. This administration view of the shift in the balance of power, held by 1983, was summarized by Shultz in the Spring 1985 issue of *Foreign Affairs*: "Today, our key alliances are more united than ever before. The United States is restoring its military strength and economic vigor and has regained its self-assurance; we have a President with a fresh mandate from the people for an active role of leadership. The Soviets, in contrast, face profound structural economic difficulties and restless allies; their diplomacy and their clients are on the defensive in many parts of the world. We have reason to be confident that the 'correlation of forces' is shifting back in our favor."[138]

In this new situation, Shultz and other U.S. officials saw less need for an overt strategic relationship with China to compensate for Soviet advantages in the global balance of power than Brzezinski had judged necessary in the late 1970s or Haig had advocated in 1981–1982. The changing international situation had also decreased Beijing's perceived requirement for overt strategic cooperation with the United States to counter the Soviet threat to Chinese security.

Following the misperceptions and miscalculations in the first two years of the Reagan administration, Chinese and American leaders increasingly shared perceptions of the strategic environment and the strategic requirements for further development of Sino-American relations and for effective management of the evolving Soviet threat. They had also reached an enduring modus vivendi on Taiwan.

CONCLUSION: LEARNING IN POLICY MAKING TOWARD CHINA

This study suggests that learning by senior policy makers in formulating and implementing U.S. China policy—even at the level of tactics—has often been closely related to and facilitated by policy makers' reassessment of the strategic situation and their perception that a change in strategy and/or strategic objectives was required to meet changing conditions or to overcome the failure of past policies. In circumstances viewed as requiring changes in policy on the level of strategy or strategic objectives, policy makers have been especially committed to enhancing their understanding of the international situation and considering new policy options. Their interest has then increased in ideas for changes in tactical policy—ideas that may have been on the shelf or even vigorously advocated by lower-level officials for a considerable period of time. Conversely, policy makers' relative comfort with the strategic situation and/or current strategy has reduced their interest in cognitive-structural learning and in considering new tactical initiatives.

This conclusion is contrary to the hypotheses that policy makers learn mostly at the level of tactics and that only after repeated failures to arrive at a tactical solution to a problem do they consider the possibility of a shift in strategy or a change in objectives. In U.S. policy making toward China, learning has not been primarily the result of repeated failures at the tactical level leading to a search for a new strategy or reconsideration of basic goals. On the contrary, a perceived need or opportunity for a change in goals and strategies has led to a willingness to engage in cognitive-structural learning—developing a more nuanced, differentiated, and integrated view of one's environment—and then to consideration of tactical policy shifts as a means of implementing a new strategy or achieving new strategic objectives.

This study has not addressed the issue of learning by U.S. policy makers in tactical interaction with China. Such learning by policy makers at the level of tactics has also taken place in the process of implementing U.S. strategy, such as the signaling process between China and the United States that began in 1969 and led to Kissinger's secret trip to Beijing in July 1971. Tactical learning has probably been greater for lower-level officials responsible for day-to-day bilateral relations, however, than for senior policy makers for whom learning has been first and foremost at the level of strategy and strategic objectives.

COGNITIVE-STRUCTURAL LEARNING

U.S. strategy and the strategic perspectives of senior officials have been primary factors determining the extent of cognitive-structural learning by policy makers. The Dulles-Eisenhower wedge-through-pressure strategy, for example, reinforced the isolation of China and curtailed the interaction through which leaders of the two countries might have improved their understanding of each other's viewpoints. The Eisenhower administration's virulent anticommunism and the McCarthy purges of the State Department also dampened any pressure from below for a reconsideration of tactics, strategy, or objectives that might have led to cognitive-structural learning at the top. More importantly, the hard-line strategy of seeking to increase pressure on China while minimizing both official and unofficial contacts between the two countries precluded the interactive learning that characterized the periods before 1950 and after 1969.

Although Dulles and Eisenhower apparently had a more complex understanding of Sino-Soviet relations than most government officials and the public believed they had, their strategic perspective and strategy toward China stifled the learning process both within the government and between the United States and China. Even the success of the wedge-through-pressure strategy by the end of the 1950s failed to advance the learning process. Relations with Beijing had become even more strained during the Eisenhower administration than they had been a decade earlier, and U.S. policy makers had come to perceive China as an even more hostile, aggressive, and unpredictable nation than the Soviet Union.

Changing strategic realities in the early 1960s, including the Sino-Soviet split, led to reassessments of the "China threat" by the Kennedy and Johnson administrations, although not to revision of the strategic goal of containing and isolating Chinese communism. Both Kennedy and Johnson considered a departure from past U.S. strategy in response to China's development of a nuclear weapons capability in the 1963–1964 period, however, when they seriously weighed the possibility of joint action with the Soviet Union to eliminate Chinese nuclear facilities. Such a cooperative action with Moscow against Beijing would have implied a containment strategy against China in which the Soviet Union was a U.S. ally.[139] However, the strategic view of China held by senior policy makers in the Kennedy and Johnson administrations did not lead to reassessment of basic assumptions about Chinese intentions and U.S. objectives toward China.

By contrast, President Nixon's response to the strategic impasse inherited from the Johnson administration provided the most important impetus to learning in China policy since the creative period at the end of the 1940s. The shifting U.S.–Soviet balance of power and the Vietnam quagmire had created new, overriding strategic realities in the late 1960s that made a sharp disjuncture in U.S. thinking about China and China policy both possible and necessary. Although changing views of China in the United States helped pave the way for acceptance of a new China policy, bilateral considerations for improving relations with Beijing were unpersuasive to policy makers, including the view espoused by Richard Nixon himself in *Foreign Affairs* in 1967 that one quarter of the world's population should not be left in "angry isolation." Writing about Sino-American relations in 1982, Richard Nixon commented that "the key factor that brought us together ten years ago was our common concern with the Soviet threat."[140]

The Nixon administration's dramatic shift in U.S. policy toward China necessitated cognizance by Nixon and Kissinger of the opportunities as well as dangers presented to the United States at the end of the 1960s by the extraordinary convergence of changing global, regional, and domestic circumstances and Chinese policies. The reevaluation by Nixon and Kissinger involved reassessment of past policies and of changing global strategic realities and options. This included reexamining assumptions about Chinese intentions and foreign policies, especially toward the United States, the conflict in Vietnam, and the Soviet Union. The reassessment also questioned U.S. strategy toward the Soviet Union and Vietnam and U.S. objectives as well as strategy toward China.

By the mid-1970s, the U.S. connection with China was no longer producing the leverage over the Soviet Union that it had yielded at the beginning of the decade. U.S. policy makers searched for a new means to enhance the leverage value of the Sino-American relationship in the strategic triangle as well as to move forward in bilateral relations with Beijing. In the Ford and Carter administrations, proposed steps toward military ties with China as means of regaining momentum in Sino-American relations and the triangle became a focal point of debate over strategy toward the Soviet Union.

The Carter administration's adoption of a new strategy toward China and the Soviet Union in the spring of 1978 created a new context to manage old as well as emerging problems, including the expansion of Soviet power. The convergence of American and Chinese strategic views proved to be the key to breaking the deadlock that had developed in the Sino-American relationship and moving forward rapidly toward normalization of relations. The buildup of Soviet military power and Soviet expansionist activities in the Third World had intensified the struggle over Soviet policy and U.S.–Chinese military ties within the Carter administration. New Soviet actions in Ethiopia and Zaire had been seized upon by Zbigniew Brzezinski to push for implementation of policies based on his hard-line strategy toward the Soviet Union. This strategy included developing a strategic, military relationship with China to counter Soviet power. The national security adviser finally won President Carter's support for such a tilt toward China in the U.S.–Soviet–Chinese triangular relationship in late winter 1978 when Carter agreed to send Brzezinski to Beijing to forge a strategic relationship with China as a means of strengthening

U.S. containment of the Soviet Union. Sino-American agreement on strategy toward the Soviet Union proved critical to moving forward in bilateral ties, especially normalization of Sino-American relations. Chinese leaders agreed to begin normalization negotiations, which were completed six months later.

By changing its policies in response to perceived strategic dangers and opportunities, the U.S. government "learned" even though senior advisers to the president did not change their views on U.S. strategy and the international situation. Senior policy makers—especially Vance and Brzezinski—saw no prospect of persuading each other to change their strategic views. Rather, they fought over specific options that all the participants understood as embodying strategic choices.

Although President Carter's decision to send Brzezinski to Beijing represented a landmark victory within the administration for the national security adviser's strategic view, Carter may not have perceived this or other key decisions as backing for the general strategic policy view of one adviser or the other—even if his advisers and Soviet and Chinese leaders reached that conclusion.

The Reagan administration learned that its ideological commitment to Taiwan was incompatible with its strategic objectives and strategy for achieving those goals. The administration miscalculated in its assessment that Chinese leaders would acquiesce to a reversal of previous U.S. policies on Taiwan because of China's perceived strategic weakness and reliance on the United States to counter Soviet power. U.S. policy makers' interactions with China since 1969 had led three previous administrations to understand the limits of Chinese flexibility on Taiwan, which the Reagan administration had sought to exceed.

In the mid-1980s, China's role in U.S. strategy and Washington's policy options in relations with Beijing had to be adjusted in response to changes in U.S. and Chinese assessments of the balance of power and the international situation. The Reagan administration had sought in the early 1980s to dramatically increase U.S. military power and to strengthen the U.S.-led global coalition against the Soviet Union in response to a perceived continuation of the Soviet expansionism and military buildup of the 1970s. Secretary of State Haig viewed China as a key link in the coalition and a major source of pressure on the Soviet Union that could be best exploited by an overt strategic-military relationship between Washington and Beijing. The shift in the U.S.–Soviet balance of power in favor of the United States, mounting Soviet internal economic difficulties, and Moscow's subsequent restraint in its international behavior, however, reduced the perceived necessity in Beijing and later in Washington for an overt Sino-American strategic alignment to contain Soviet power.[141]

President Reagan and other administration officials adjusted U.S. policy toward China to compensate for developments in the global strategic environment and changes in Chinese policy, including Beijing's proclamation of an "independent foreign policy" and a reduced need and desire for overt strategic relations with the United States and China's efforts to improve relations with the Soviet Union. This adjustment in U.S. policy was the result not of failure of the previous policy of an open quasi-alliance with China against the Soviet Union, but rather of that strategy's success in containing Soviet expansion and encouraging the Soviet Union to revise its global strategy.

INTERACTIVE LEARNING

In the process of developing the new relationship between the United States and China, both Chinese and U.S. leaders greatly improved their understanding of each other's perspective and intentions. This interactive learning process between the United States and China was especially intense and ultimately successful in the 1969–1971 period as Washington and Beijing overcame a nearly total lack of contact and probed each other to determine the possibilities for transforming the relationship. As the two sides began to interact through secret channels in 1969, it became evident to U.S. leaders—and presumably to Chinese leaders as well—that they were viewing the world in a similar, balance-of-power, national interest framework rather than from an anticommunist—or an anti-imperialist—ideological perspective. Common strategic concerns about the Soviet Union provided the basis for establishing a dialogue and setting aside past differences to build the foundation for a new relationship.

Interactive learning on the strategic level also occurred between the United States and China during the Carter administration. U.S. strategy toward the Soviet Union as explained by Secretary Vance to Chinese leaders in August 1977 was at odds with Beijing's assessment of the strategic environment, the appropriate response to the expansion of Soviet power, and the desirable basis for development of Sino-American relations. Chinese leaders expressed their disagreement with Vance's strategic assessment and global strategy and indicated that their strategic difference with the United States was a major impediment to improvement in relations between Beijing and Washington. Brzezinski's articulation nine months later of a new U.S. strategy toward the Soviet Union that paralleled Chinese thinking and called for development of a strategic relationship between China and the United States paved the way for normalization of bilateral relations and ended Chinese criticism of U.S. policy toward the Soviet Union.

In response to the potential crisis in relations that developed over the sale of U.S. arms to Taiwan in the 1981–1982 period, both the United States and China sought to "limit damage" and find a mutually acceptable resolution of the issue rather than allow the volatile dispute to lead to a regression in Sino-American relations. A crisis was averted not only by an intense learning process at the tactical level but also by a belief on both sides that a retrogression in Sino-American relations would undermine the common strategic concerns of both countries.

Following the 1969–1972 Sino-American rapprochement, the interactive learning process broadened beyond exchanges between top leaders. An increasing number of lower-level officials and nongovernmental individuals as well as government and private organizations became involved in the relationship as China and the United States interacted in a growing number of economic, political, cultural, and military arenas. Learning gradually became institutionalized in the U.S. government bureaucracy. A new conventional wisdom emerged in which China was a friendly country rather than an enemy.

THE IMPACT OF PERSONNEL SHIFTS

Although senior policy makers may have difficulty redefining fundamental premises or objectives of policies to which they feel committed, fundamental learning does not always depend on wholesale personnel shifts. Change in administrations preceded the profound shift in U.S. objectives and strategy in the 1969–1971 period, but not prior to the strategic shifts in the Carter administration in 1978 and to the policy adjustments in the Reagan administration in 1982–1983. In those cases, the president, at the urging of certain advisers and in reaction to events, changed policies substantially. In 1978, this was true at the level of strategy toward the Soviet Union, and in 1982–1983 it constituted more of a strategic adjustment to accommodate changes in Chinese and U.S. perceptions of changes in the U.S.–Soviet balance of power.[142]

Strategic assessments may thus be even more important in stimulating learning by policy makers than changes in administration or in key personnel—unless new administrations or personnel are responsible for new strategic assessments. The dramatic changes in U.S. Soviet policy in the last years of the Reagan administration and the beginning of the Bush administration may provide further evidence of this thesis. In both administrations, new strategic assessments of Soviet policies and intentions and changes in the strategic environment led to substantive changes in U.S. policy toward the Soviet Union, culminating in President Bush's call in the spring of 1989 for a new long-term strategy of moving "beyond containment" to integrate the Soviet Union into the world community on the basis of a more cooperative East-West relationship.

Strategic considerations were also responsible for President Bush's unwillingness to take harsher steps to punish and isolate China in the aftermath of the Tiananmen massacre in June 1989. These concerns were evident in Bush's decision to violate his stated policy of suspending high-level contacts with China by sending his national security adviser to Beijing secretly in July and openly again in December to seek to restore Sino-American relations. The rapidly changing international environment, including the decommunization of Eastern Europe, the political and economic transformation of the Soviet Union toward a multiparty democracy and a free-market economy, and the evolution of U.S. strategy toward the Soviet Union as the post–World War II Cold War era came to an end, however, created the basis—and the need—for another reassessment of China's role in U.S. strategy. By the beginning of the 1990s, the Bush administration had already concluded that China's strategic importance to the United States as a counter to Soviet power had diminished significantly, thus requiring development of a broader foundation for U.S. policy toward China while also freeing the hand of the president in managing Sino-American relations.

NOTES

1. The author wishes to thank Robert Ross and George Breslauer for their insightful comments on an earlier draft of this chapter.

2. The United States and China did learn tacit crisis management, however, to limit the scope of the Korean War and to avoid direct military conflict in confrontations over Quemoy and Matsu in the 1950s and Indochina in the 1960s.

3. John Lewis Gaddis, *The Long Peace: Inquiries Into the History of the Cold War* (New York: Oxford University Press, 1987), 149–50. In this pathbreaking study, Gaddis writes that on the basis of new evidence he had provisionally concluded that "despite what they said in public, American policy-makers at no point during the postwar era actually believed in the existence of an international communist monolith." Ibid., 148.

4. Cited by Gaddis, *The Long Peace*, 159. Gaddis notes that Titoism in Yugoslavia had developed "quite independently of anything the United States had done," and that "it is not at all clear that it was ever within Washington's power to affect, in any substantial way, the relationship between Moscow and its East European satellites in the first place." Ibid., 160.

5. Ibid., 161.

6. Ibid., 76–77. Nancy Tucker notes that President Truman had concluded that the Soviet Union preferred a divided and weak neighbor to a unified China under a dynamic Communist leadership. Nancy Bernkopf Tucker, *Patterns in the Dust: Chinese-American Relations and the Recognition Controversy, 1949–1950* (New York: Columbia University Press, 1983), 16.

7. The debates and responses to CCP probes during this period are detailed by Robert M. Blum, *Drawing the Line: The Origin of the American Containment Policy in East Asia* (New York: W.W. Norton, 1982), 50–79. See also Tucker, *Patterns in the Dust*, 16–18.

8. Waldo Heinrichs, "American China Policy and the Cold War in Asia: A

New Look," in *Uncertain Years: Chinese-American Relations, 1947-1950*, eds. Dorothy Borg and Waldo Heinrichs (New York: Columbia University Press, 1980), 285.

9. See Michael Hunt, "Mao Tse-tung and the Issue of Accommodation with the United States, 1948–1950," in *Uncertain Years*, eds. Dorothy Borg and Waldo Heinrichs.

10. See Barbara Tuchman, "If Mao Had Come to Washington: An Essay in Alternatives," *Foreign Affairs* 51, no. 1 (October 1972).

11. In the spring of 1949, as the communist armies were rolling toward complete victory on the mainland, China's future premier Zhou Enlai sent a secret message to senior American officials asking for U.S. economic aid and indicating that Zhou's liberal wing of the Communist Party wanted China to steer an independent course with good working relations between China and the United States. Zhou added, according to the report of the consul general, Edmund O. Clubb, that the radicals wanted an alliance with the Soviet Union while liberals, including Zhou, viewed Soviet foreign policy as crazy and a risk of war with the United States. Zhou reportedly said China under the Communists would serve in the international sphere as a mediator between the Western powers and the Soviet Union. Cited by Robert M. Blum, *Drawing the Line*, 56. Blum also details other Chinese Communist probes to the United States in Chapter 4. See Michael Hunt, "Mao Tse-tung and the Issue of Accommodation with the United States, 1948–1950," and Warren I. Cohen, "Acheson, His Advisers, and China, 1949–1950," in *Uncertain Years*, eds. Dorothy Borg and Waldo Heinrichs.

12. Robert M. Blum, *Drawing the Line*, 10. The United States successfully followed a balance of power policy toward the regime of Marshal Tito in Yugoslavia in this same 1948–1951 period in response to the opportunity presented by Tito's split with Stalin in mid-1948, thus demonstrating that Washington was capable of pursuing a nonideological strategy to counterbalance Soviet power by developing economic, political, and military ties with a communist country threatened by Soviet coercion. There was no domestic "Yugoslavia lobby" to oppose this policy of aiding a "communist" power, although the administration was cautious about publicly embracing the communist regime in fear of both domestic criticism and discrediting Tito. See Gaddis, *The Long Peace*, 158–59, and Philip Windsor, "Yugoslavia, 1951, and Czechoslovakia, 1968," in *Force Without War: U.S. Armed Forces as a Political Instrument*, eds. Barry M. Blechman and Stephen S. Kaplan (Washington, D.C.: Brookings, 1978), especially 455–56; and David Allan Mayers, *Cracking the Monolith: U.S. Policy Against the Sino-Soviet Alliance, 1949–1955* (Baton Rouge: Louisiana State University Press, 1986) , 25–26.

13. See Robert M. Blum, *Drawing the Line*, Chapter 4.

14. In September 1950, for example, Secretary of State Dean Acheson insisted publicly that China would be "crazy" to enter the Korean War because it faced the danger of the "great cloud from the north, Russian penetration" aimed at those areas in northern China under Soviet control. Acheson added that "I give the people in Peiping credit for being intelligent enough to see what is happening to them." Cited by Robert Blum, *The United States and China in World Affairs* (New York: McGraw Hill, 1966), 113. See also Gaddis, *The Long Peace*, 169, fn.

15. Ibid., 165.

16. Tucker, *Patterns in the Dust*, 188. See also Cohen, "Acheson, His Advisers, and China."

17. Cited by Robert M. Blum, *Drawing the Line*, 32, and Gaddis, *The Long Peace*, 163.

18. Cited by Tucker, *Patterns in the Dust*, 175.

19. Ibid.

20. Robert M. Blum notes that "the policy of encouraging the eventual emergence of a Communist China free of Soviet domination still lacked the appeal to either American military leaders or members of Congress who wanted the United States to do something more active to stop communism in Asia. The State Department also had to take account of the political reality that President Truman, much less Congress, would not allow the proffering of any American aid to the Mao Tsetung regime unless it drastically and publicly changed its attitude toward the United States." Blum, *Drawing the Line*, 59–60. Whether the United States and the CCP missed a historic opportunity for an accommodation in the late 1940s is still a subject of debate in both the United States and China that is beyond the scope of this paper. See, for example, the papers and discussions in Dorothy Borg and Waldo Heinrichs, eds., *Uncertain Years*; Mayers, *Cracking the Monolith*, 163–64; and Michael Schaller, *The U.S. Crusade in China, 1938–1945* (New York: Columbia University Press, 1979), 303–304.

21. Robert M. Blum notes that there was little inducement in the policies approved in March 1949 toward the CCP, the Nationalists, and Formosa for the Chinese Communists to lean to the side of the West. Other than "controlled trade" with the West and Japan, the policies adopted in the "March 3 package" were "disagreeable" from the CCP perspective, including "continued recognition of the Nationalists; a program of covert aid to pro-Western groups on the mainland; possible future overt support for some anti-Communist force that might rise up against the Communists; and the policy of severing Formosa from the mainland." Many of these policies, Blum contends, "were designed in opposition to the Titoist hypothesis and appeared to rest on the counter-hypothesis that all Communists were in the same camp and should be staunchly opposed by the use of all practical devices." Blum, *Drawing the Line*, 35.

22. See Hunt, "Mao Tse-tung and the Issue of Accommodation," 209–16, and Blum, *Drawing the Line*, 63. Hunt suggests that the failure of the United States to respond positively to CCP probes—rather than unquestioning affinity with the Soviet Union—led Mao to enunciate this policy. Ibid., 216.

23. See Tucker, *Patterns in the Dust*, 195–207, on the decisive and negative impact of the outbreak of the Korean War on U.S. policy toward China and the prospects for normalization of Sino-American relations.

24. Gaddis, *The Long Peace*, 169–71. See also Mayers, *Cracking the Monolith*, 81–83.

25. See Mayers, *Cracking the Monolith*, 93, and Gaddis, *The Long Peace*, 170. Gaddis notes that Acheson told Winston Churchill in early 1952 that a Sino-Soviet split had seemed a real possibility before the outbreak of the Korean War, but that Chinese intervention "had made this hope seem very distant and impossible of attainment at present. I did not think that over any period of time with which we could now be concerned it was possible to create a divergence between the two communists [sic] groups" (173).

26. Tucker notes that prior to the outbreak of the Korean War in June 1950, pressure from the China lobby in support of the Nationalist Chinese was not a major factor in U.S. policy toward China. Tucker, *Patterns in the Dust*, 99.

27. Dean Rusk, chief of the Far Eastern Branch of the State Department, told the China Institute in New York on May 18, 1951, that "the Peiping regime may be a colonial Russian government—a Slavic Manchukuo on a larger scale. It is not the government of China. It does not pass the first test. It is not Chinese." Rusk's speech also included a statement implying support for Nationalist Chinese leader Chiang Kai-shek's effort to retake control of the mainland: "As the Chinese people move to assert their freedom and to work out their destiny in accordance with their own historical purposes, they can count upon tremendous support from free peoples in other parts of the world." Rusk had not cleared the speech and was taken to task by Acheson, who finally agreed that it did not represent a departure from U.S. policy. Thomas J. Schoenbaum, *Waging Peace and War: Dean Rusk in the Truman, Kennedy and Johnson Years* (New York: Simon and Schuster, 1988), 223–24.

28. Robert Blum contends that this policy was set de facto as a result of President Truman's decision June 27, 1950—before China's entry into the Korean War—to send the Seventh Fleet to the Taiwan Straits despite Truman's declaration in the order that the future status of Taiwan would be determined later. Blum, *The United States and China*, 112. Another (different) scholar, Robert M. Blum, however, uncovered documents demonstrating that in March 1949, before the CCP's consolidation of power on the mainland or the Nationalists' final retreat to Formosa [Taiwan], President Truman agreed to a secret policy aimed at maintaining a pro-U.S. regime on Formosa that was separate from the mainland. Blum, *Drawing the Line*, 37. According to Blum, the United States wanted to gain control of Formosa for strategic and military reasons, whether through the Nationalist occupation or Taiwan independence. Washington wanted especially to prevent Soviet military presence on the island as a result of Communist Chinese occupation. See also Gaddis, *The Long Peace*, 74–75, 80–81; and Tucker, *Patterns in the Dust*, 199–200.

29. See Mayers, *Cracking the Monolith*, 94. Robert Sutter suggests that "American policy refused to recognize that the vital interests of the United States and the Chinese Communists in East Asia could be compatible. . . ." Robert Sutter, *China Watch: Sino-American Reconciliation* (Baltimore: Johns Hopkins University Press, 1978), 4.

30. For an analysis of U.S. perceptions of Sino-Soviet differences and covert efforts to exploit those differences during the Korean War, see Mayers, *Cracking the Monolith*, 95–107 and 115–25.

31. Gaddis notes that even after Chinese intervention in Korea, the administration continued to believe strongly enough in the possibility of exploiting eventual differences between the Soviet Union and China that in early 1951 the State Department authorized secret contacts with the Chinese, possibly to seek a cease-fire in return for U.S. recognition of the People's Republic of China. The contacts produced no results, however. Gaddis, *The Long Peace*, 170.

32. Ibid., 172. See also Mayers, *Cracking the Monolith*, 102.

33. Gaddis, *The Long Peace*, 172–73. According to Rusk's sympathetic biographer, Thomas J. Schoenbaum, "many years later, Rusk seemed to be genuinely uneasy about this speech, dismissing it either as campaign-style oratory or as an attempt to shame the Chinese into splitting with the Soviets." Schoenbaum,

Waging Peace and War, 223. Tucker notes that speeches by U.S. officials in 1950 repeatedly referred to the CCP as Soviet puppets, hoping to shame Beijing into a demonstration of anti-Russian nationalism. Tucker, *Patterns in the Dust*, 193.

34. The Truman administration also viewed China as placing an excessive burden on the Soviet Union that could be exacerbated by an economic boycott of China by the West. See Tucker, *Patterns in the Dust*, 178.

35. Gaddis, *The Long Peace*, 148. See also Mayers, *Cracking the Monolith*, 119–120.

36. The existence of this briefing was discovered by Gaddis in 1979 and led to a reconsideration of his previous views not only of Dulles but also of U.S. statements about "monolithic communism" throughout the cold war. See Gaddis, *The Long Peace*, 147–48. A National Security Council study, NSC 166/1, dated November 3, 1953, outlined the differences between the Soviet Union and China and how they could be exacerbated by U.S. pressure on Beijing. See Mayers, *Cracking the Monolith*, 121–23 and 149–50.

37. Gaddis, *The Long Peace*, 186. See also Mayers, *Cracking the Monolith*, 145–48.

38. After the Chinese backed down in the Quemoy-Matsu crisis in 1958, Eisenhower privately wondered whether the Soviets did not foresee a future threat from China. Nevertheless, he discussed with Dulles, according to the secretary of state's notes, the U.S. policy of "holding firm until changes would occur within the Sino-Soviet bloc. He felt these were inevitable but realized that the policy we were following might not be popular. There were some who wanted to give in; others who wanted to attack. The policy that required patience was rarely popular." Cited by Gaddis, *The Long Peace*, 187. Interestingly, in his memoirs Eisenhower does not express his views about differences between China and the Soviet Union while reporting without comment private statements to him by both Khrushchev in September 1959 and Nationalist Chinese leader Chiang Kai-shek in June 1960 denying the existence of a rift between Moscow and Beijing. Dwight D. Eisenhower, *The White House Years—Waging Peace, 1956–1961* (New York: Doubleday, 1965), 445, 564. See also Mayers, *Cracking the Monolith*, 127–50 and 154 on implementation of the wedge-through-pressure strategy during the 1950s.

39. Roger Hilsman notes that, on the basis of this assumption, U.S. policy was "to act and speak as to encourage Chinese overseas and on the mainland to look to the Nationalists on Taiwan as the government of all of China. The policy, moreover, was to abstain 'from any act to encourage the Communist regime, morally, politically, or materially,' and this included refusing to extend diplomatic recognition, opposing the seating of Communist China in the UN, putting an embargo on any trade or cultural exchanges, and encouraging our friends and allies to follow suit." Roger Hilsman, *To Move a Nation: The Politics of Foreign Policy in the Administration of John F. Kennedy* (New York: Doubleday, 1967), 301.

40. Gaddis, *The Long Peace*, 184.

41. "Though American policy was not ultimately responsible for the shattering of Sino-Soviet cooperation, by early 1956 the Dulles-Eisenhower version of containment, of applied pressure, seems to have contributed, as its authors hoped, to the weakening of Russian and Chinese pledges to each other." Mayers, *Cracking the Monolith*, 151–57.

42. Ibid., 156.

43. Although the Eisenhower administration did not wholly exclude the possibility of a more conciliatory approach to China, according to Gaddis, it was not prepared to resume the Truman administration's attempt to split the Chinese from the Soviets through accommodation. See Gaddis, *The Long Peace*, 185–86. In 1955, the Eisenhower administration agreed reluctantly, however, to a Chinese offer to open a channel for direct Sino-American discussions—the Ambassadorial Talks—that continued sporadically for the next 15 years. Although the talks did not lead to a Sino–U.S. reconciliation, they did provide a forum for crisis management and for the initial Sino-American contacts under the Nixon administration. For an account of the Warsaw talks, see Kenneth Young, *Negotiating With the Chinese Communists: The United States Experience, 1953–1967* (New York: McGraw Hill, 1978).

44. Cited by Gaddis, *The Long Peace*, 187.

45. Mayers, *Cracking the Monolith*, 157.

46. President Kennedy did not differentiate in policy toward China and the Soviet Union, however, in the first two years of his administration, according to Gerald Segal. Although some U.S. officials viewed China as acting as a "semi-independent seat of power" pursuing its own interest in the Laos crisis of 1961–1962, Segal maintains, Kennedy did not accept this differentiated view of China and the Soviet Union until 1963. Gerald Segal, *The Great Power Triangle* (New York: St. Martin's Press, 1982), 12–15.

47. "The taunts and threats" to Khrushchev's leadership from the Chinese, Theodore Sorensen wrote of the Kennedy administration's perception of the Sino-Soviet rift, caused the Soviet premier "to reshuffle his priorities, removing conflict with the West from the top of his agenda. They also required him to prove concretely the value of coexistence and to isolate the more reckless Chinese." Nevertheless, Sorensen noted, President Kennedy "derived little comfort from the Soviet-Chinese dispute, and thought, on the contrary, that it might increase the dangers of desperation in Moscow or irresponsibility in Peking." Sorensen, *Kennedy* (New York: Harper and Row, 1965), 724–26.

48. Sorensen, *Kennedy*, 206.

49. Foster Rhea Dulles, *American Foreign Policy Toward Communist China* (New York: Thomas Y. Crowell, 1972), 206. Roger Hilsman reports that in early 1962 U.S. government officials for the first time entertained the notion of a permanent Sino-Soviet split. As director of intelligence at the State Department he gave a public speech in November 1962 that asserted: "we cannot foresee any genuine reconciliation of the dispute," but nevertheless argued against the notion of a complete and final break. "Communist ideology," Hilsman's speech concluded, "with its goal of world revolution, still provides an overall basis for unity between Peiping and Moscow. So long as both partners see the United States as the greatest obstacle to the attainment of this goal, they will try to patch over their differences and unite against a common enemy." Hilsman, *To Move a Nation*, 344–345.

50. Cited by Young, *Negotiating With the Chinese Communists*, 253–54.

51. Cited by Robert Blum, *The United States and China*, 128.

52. Raymond Garthoff notes that he was involved in these internal delibera-

tions in the mid-1960s. See his *Détente and Confrontation: American-Soviet Relations from Nixon to Reagan* (Washington, D.C.: The Brookings Institution, 1985), 984n. For a discussion of Kennedy administration debates over China's nuclear potential, see Franz Schurmann, *The Logic of World Power* (New York: Pantheon, 1974), 388–98. See also Murray Marder, "The Secret War We Fought with China," *Washington Post* 5 July, 1981. Joseph Alsop, in "Go Versus No-Go," *New York Times Magazine* 11 March, 1973, reported that President Kennedy considered approaching the Soviets about joint action against China's nuclear weapons facilities: "President Kennedy, who took an exceedingly dark view of the Chinese nuclear program, had ordered exploration of the idea of destroying that program in some sort of collaboration with the Soviets."

53. See Hilsman, *To Move a Nation*, 310–20. The Kennedy adminstration assured the Chinese in the Warsaw talks, however, that Washington would not provide assistance to the Nationalist Chinese for an assault on the mainland.

54. Ibid., 302–303.

55. Sorensen, *Kennedy*, 665.

56. Hilsman, *To Move a Nation*, 346.

57. See Arthur M. Schlesinger, Jr., *A Thousand Days: John F. Kennedy in the White House* (Boston: Houghton Mifflin, 1965), 479–480. President Kennedy faced opposition to changing China policy not only from the China lobby but also from the outgoing president. Eisenhower privately warned Kennedy that he would return to public life if the new administration supported U.N. admission for Communist China. See also Dulles, *American Foreign Policy Toward Communist China*, 193–95. For a discussion of a new China policy in a second Kennedy administration, see Hilsman, *To Move a Nation*, 340–57; 580–81.

58. See Dulles, *American Foreign Policy Toward Communist China*, 192, 231, and James C. Thomson, "On the Making of U.S. China Policy, 1961–9: A Study in Bureaucratic Politics," *China Quarterly*, 50 (April–June 1972).

59. Schoenbaum writes that Secretary of State Rusk raised the issue of changing China policy privately with Kennedy in May 1961. "He found Kennedy unreceptive to his arguments. The politics of the matter, Kennedy explained, made it impossible to contemplate any change for the time being. . . . It was a question to be deferred to his second term if he received a greater mandate in the 1964 election. Rusk got up to leave, and Kennedy called him back. 'What's more, Mr. Secretary,' he said, 'I don't want to read in the *Washington Post* and *The New York Times* that the State Department is thinking about a change in China policy.'" Schoenbaum, *Waging Peace and War*, 388.

60. The December 13 speech also rejected the public position of Dulles that the Communist regime was a passing phase: "We have no reason to believe that there is a present likelihood that the Communist regime will be overthrown." Hilsman, *To Move a Nation*, 351.

61. Dulles, *American Foreign Policy Toward Communist China*, 213.

62. Ibid., 224–26.

63. It is not generally known that the Johnson administration apparently approached the Soviet Union about joint action against the Chinese nuclear weapons program shortly before China exploded its first nuclear bomb on October 16, 1964. A declassified memorandum for the record by President Johnson's national

security adviser McGeorge Bundy, September 15, 1964, said that the president had approved decisions to closely consider "appropriate military actions against Chinese nuclear facilities" if "we should find ourselves in military hostilities at any level with the Chinese Communists." Bundy also said the president had approved exploring with the Soviets the possibility of joint action against Chinese nuclear facilities, including "even a possible agreement to cooperate in preventive military action." Bundy noted that the secretary of state (Dean Rusk) "now intends to consult promptly with the Soviet Ambassador." Memo from the Lyndon Baines Johnson Library, declassified September 14, 1977, and provided to the author by Ronald J. Bee. In his memoirs, Johnson writes only that he was concerned about the long-run implications of the Chinese nuclear test but that he did not mention it in his discussion with Soviet ambassador Anatoly Dobrynin later that same day. Lyndon Baines Johnson, *The Vantage Point: Perspectives of the Presidency* (New York: Holt, Rinehart and Winston, 1971), 469.

64. Dulles, *American Foreign Policy Toward Communist China*, 213–14.

65. Paul Nitze, Secretary of the Navy, "Remarks to National War College and Industrial College of the Armed Forces," Ft. Lesley J. McNair, Washington, D.C., 18 January 1967 (Top Secret, declassified 13 June 1972).

66. Nitze also asserted that "we want eventually . . . a China with which the U.S. can live in some degree of mutual accommodation—not one which views much of the rest of the world as a fertile field for revolution and the United States as its implacable enemy." Nitze, "Remarks to National War College."

67. By 1967, 71 percent of the respondents in a Gallup poll agreed with the proposition that China would be a greater threat to world peace by 1970, while only 20 percent were more concerned about the Soviet Union. Cited by Warren Cohen, "American Perceptions of China," in *Dragon and Eagle*, eds. Michel Oksenberg and Robert B. Oxnam (New York: Basic Books, 1973), 80.

68. Ibid., 81–83.

69. Dulles, *American Foreign Policy Toward Communist China*, 226–27.

70. See Thomson, "On the Making of U.S. China Policy."

71. Richard M. Nixon, "Asia After Vietnam," *Foreign Affairs* 46, no.1 (October 1967): 121.

72. Henry Brandon, *The Retreat of American Power* (New York: Doubleday, 1973), 181–82. In an August 1954 National Security Council meeting, Vice President Nixon ruled out accommodation with Communist China "over the period of the next 25 or 50 years," suggesting that a U.S. policy of accommodation toward Beijing would allow "Communist Chinese power to sweep over Asia." This did not mean that the United States must go to war with China, Nixon said, but rather that "a tough coexistence policy may be in the long run the best method of driving a wedge between China and Russia." Gaddis, *The Long Peace*, 181–82. According to Seymour Hersh, however, Nixon had at least since 1960 sought the political benefits of initiating a U.S. opening to China. Seymour M. Hersh, *The Price of Power: Kissinger in the Nixon White House* (New York: Summit Books, 1983), 350.

73. Richard M. Nixon, *RN: The Memoirs of Richard Nixon* (New York: Warner, 1978), 347–48.

74. Franz Schurmann rejects a commonly held view that Henry Kissinger was the primary architect of U.S. foreign policy during the Nixon presidency and

ascribes the key role as "the creator of the grand design and its chief operative" to Richard Nixon. Franz Schurmann, *The Foreign Politics of Richard Nixon: The Grand Design* (Berkeley: Institute of International Studies, University of California, 1987), 2–3, 22–26. In this paper, I have not sought to establish which man was the primary innovator but rather to discuss the strategic thinking behind the shift in U.S. policy, which was uniquely shared and implemented by the two men.

75. In his discussion of the situation facing the Nixon administration in 1969, Kissinger notes that Americans "never fully understood that while our absolute power was growing, our *relative* position was bound to decline as the USSR recovered from World War II. Our military and diplomatic position was never more favorable than at the very beginning of the containment policy in the late 1940s." Henry A. Kissinger, *White House Years* (Boston: Little, Brown, 1979), 62 (emphasis in original).

76. Paul Kennedy notes that "while the United States was pouring money into Vietnam, the USSR was devoting steadily larger sums to its nuclear forces—so that it achieved a rough strategic parity—and to its navy, which in these years emerged as a major force in global gunboat diplomacy; and this increasing imbalance was worsened by the American electorate's turn against military expenditures for most of the 1970s." Paul Kennedy, *The Rise and Fall of the Great Powers* (New York: Random House, 1987), 406–407.

77. See Schurmann's discussion of the domestic political and economic crises facing Richard Nixon when he took office in 1969. Schurmann, *The Foreign Politics of Richard Nixon*, 7–13, 68–76.

78. See Kennedy, *The Rise and Fall of the Great Powers*, 432–37; and Kenneth A. Oye, "Constrained Confidence and the Evolution of Reagan Foreign Policy," in *Eagle Resurgent? The Reagan Era in American Foreign Policy*, eds. Kenneth Oye, Robert J. Lieber, and Donald Rothchild (Boston: Little, Brown and Company, 1987), 10.

79. Kissinger writes that the United States never had the military capability to implement such a demanding strategy, despite Washington's declaratory policy, and that if a war broke out simultaneously with the Soviet Union and China it would therefore likely lead to use of nuclear weapons. Kissinger, *White House Years*, 222.

80. These assurances were relayed to Chinese leaders in the Sino-American Ambassadorial Talks. See Young, *Negotiating With the Chinese Communists*, 268–75, and Franz Schurmann, *The Logic of World Power* (New York: Pantheon, 1974), 515. Chinese scholar Wang Jisi writes that "the insistence that American forces were sent to Viet Nam because of the 'Chinese Communist expansion' . . . made it impossible to break the deadlock in Sino-American relations. In 1965–1967, the principal issue argued between Beijing and Washington in the Warsaw ambassadorial talks was Viet Nam. Although the Johnson Administration tried to convey a message in Warsaw to Beijing that it had no intention of invading China or crushing North Viet Nam, Beijing found it hard to trust such a promise." Wang Jisi, "From Kennedy to Nixon: America's East Asia and China Policy," *Beijing Review* (May 16–22, 1988).

81. A few policy makers may have vaguely perceived the benefits of two-front deterrence of the Soviet Union in the 1950s. Chester Bowles, U.S. representative

to India, wrote to Dulles in February 1953: "With an uncertain China on its Pacific flank the Soviet Union would surely be forced to abandon its present policies of naked threats . . . in Europe and the Middle East and adopt some less explosive tactics." Cited by Mayers, *Cracking the Monolith*, 125.

82. Kissinger comments on this shift in strategy that "what started out as a highly esoteric discussion of military strategy turned into one of our most important signals to the People's Republic of China that we meant to improve our relations with it." The announcement of the shift in U.S. strategy in the president's first *Foreign Policy Report to the Congress* on February 18, 1970, indicated to Beijing that "We would no longer treat a conflict with the USSR as automatically involving the People's Republic. We would treat our two adversaries on the basis of their actions toward us, not their ideology; we publicly acknowledged their differences and the unlikelihood of their cooperation." Kissinger, *White House Years*, 220, 222.

83. Ibid., 164.

84. Ibid., 163.

85. Nixon and Kissinger may have missed an opportunity to begin their own dialogue with China shortly after the new administration took power in January 1969, according to Seymour Hersh (*The Price of Power*, 354–55), who argues that the rapprochement with China could have been achieved much earlier.

86. Soviet defector Arkady Shevchenko reports that the Soviet leadership seriously considered nuclear strikes against China in the summer of 1969. Moscow was dissuaded from an attack in part by indications that the United States would react strongly against the Soviet Union, according to Shevchenko. Arkady Shevchenko, *Breaking with Moscow* (New York: Alfred A. Knopf, 1985), 164–66.

87. Sutter maintains that Chinese leaders had perceived a growing threat of Soviet attack on China since Moscow's invasion of Czechoslovakia in August 1968 and that they realized "they could move closer to the United States in order to readjust Sino-Soviet relations and form a new balance of power in East Asia favorable to Chinese interests." Sutter, *China Watch*, 2.

88. For Kissinger, the Sino-Soviet conflict provided a learning experience after he was in office. He initially tended to take the Soviet point of view on the conflict and see the Chinese as more irrational and likely to attack the Soviet Union, according to Marvin and Bernard Kalb in *Kissinger* (Boston: Little, Brown, 1974). But by August 1969, after a briefing by University of Michigan China expert Allen Whiting, Kalb and Kalb say, Kissinger had changed his views (see pp. 226–27). For a catalogue of Soviet threats to China, see Sutter, *China Watch*, 86–89.

89. William G. Hyland, *Mortal Rivals: Superpower Relations From Nixon to Reagan* (New York: Random House, 1987), 24.

90. Moscow's "paranoia" about Sino-American cooperation was impressed on Kissinger from the first days of the Nixon administration. The Soviets expressed their concern to him about the possibility of a Sino-American rapprochement beginning in early 1969, according to his *White House Years* (167–70, 179). Soviet Ambassador Anatoly Dobrynin warned in October 1969, while discussing the opening of the U.S.–Soviet Strategic Arms Limitation Talks (SALT) , that any attempt to manipulate the Sino-Soviet conflict would undermine efforts to improve relations between Washington and Moscow. Ibid., 187.

91. See Kissinger, *White House Years*, 177 and 182–91. Kissinger reports that a Soviet embassy official in Washington asked a State Department official August 18, 1969, how the United States would react to a Soviet attack on Chinese nuclear facilities. Kissinger writes that he and Nixon saw support for China as a "strategic necessity" in the event of a Sino-Soviet war, although he does not spell out what kind of support might be forthcoming. Kissinger also notes that U.S. negotiator Gerard Smith was approached at the SALT I talks in Vienna in July 1970 by the Soviet negotiator Vladimir Semenov, who suggested U.S.–Soviet joint action against China. John Newhouse, in *Cold Dawn: The Story of SALT* (New York: Holt Rinehart and Winston, 1973), 188–89, reports on Soviet probes to the United States during the SALT negotiations. See also H.R. Haldeman, *The Ends of Power* (New York: New York Times Books, 1978), 984n; and A. Doak Barnett, *China and the Major Powers in East Asia* (Washington, D.C.: Brookings Institution, 1977), 78–79. Columnist Joseph Alsop reported in the *New York Times Magazine*, 11 March 1973, that the Soviets had approached Nixon in March 1969 to gain U.S. support for a "surgical strike" against China's nuclear installations in Xinjiang and that Nixon refused and later informed the Chinese of the request. Cited by Schurmann, *The Foreign Politics of Richard Nixon*, 101. See also Garthoff, *Détente and Confrontation*, 209–10.

92. CIA Director Richard Helms, in an unprecedented background briefing, told a select group of reporters in late August 1969 that the Soviets had approached European Communist leaders about the possibility of a Soviet preemptive strike against Chinese nuclear facilities. Helms indicated that the United States opposed such action. Kissinger, *White House Years*, 184. See also Hyland, *Mortal Rivals*, 25–28. A Chinese official, who was working closely with Premier Zhou Enlai at the time, told me in 1982 that he had been very surprised to discover that the Soviets were considering a preemptive strike against China. The official said Helms's press conference, by showing that the United States opposed such a strike, "was very important and unexpected. It helped pave the way for the rapprochement."

93. Kissinger adds that "it was a major event in American foreign policy when a President declared that we had a strategic interest in the survival of a major Communist country, long an enemy, and with which we had no contact." Kissinger, *White House Years*, 182. Kissinger had initially viewed the Chinese as the more irrational party in the Sino-Soviet dispute and more likely to attack the Soviet Union, according to Marvin and Bernard Kalb. Kalb and Kalb report that Kissinger was dissuaded of this view by Allen Whiting, who in August 1969 convinced the national security adviser of the seriousness of the Soviet military threat to China and urged that the administration seize the opportunity of Chinese leaders' fear of Soviet attack and need for a U.S. counterweight to Soviet power to orchestrate a historic breakthrough in Sino-American relations. See Kalb and Kalb, *Kissinger*, 226-27.

94. Kissinger, *White House Years*, 764. Tad Szulc reports that in mid-February 1970 Kissinger set up a special projects staff to develop contingency planning for the United States in the event of a Sino-Soviet war. Tad Szulc, *The Illusion of Peace* (New York: Viking Press, 1978), 206.

95. See Kennedy, *The Rise and Fall of the Great Powers*, 407–8.

96. They insisted that these steps were both desirable and necessary prerequisites to any improvement in Sino-American relations. Kissinger writes that during the

transition period to the new administration, several distinguished China experts wrote a memorandum urging the United States to make unilateral concessions to Beijing, including severing of U.S. ties to Taiwan and support for China's admission to the United Nations. At the same time, these experts failed to note either China's concern about the Soviet threat to Chinese security and the geopolitical opportunities this presented the United States or the "possibility that the Chinese might have an incentive to move toward us without American concessions because of their need for an American counterweight to the Soviet Union." Kissinger, *White House Years*, 165. Seymour Hersh also reports on this memorandum from eight prominent China scholars from Harvard, Columbia, and the Massachusetts Institute of Technology in the *The Price of Power*, 357n.

97. Kissinger, *White House Years*, 705. Alexander Haig writes of his visit to China in January 1972 in preparation for Nixon's visit the following month: "Though he never stated the case in so many words, I reported to President Nixon that the import of what [Chinese Premier] Zhou [Enlai] said to me was: don't lose in Vietnam; don't withdraw from Southeast Asia." Alexander Haig, *Caveat: Realism, Reagan, and Foreign Policy* (New York: Macmillan, 1984), 202.

98. At a critical point in August 1969 when the Soviet Union was threatening to attack China, critical analysis and advice was provided to Kissinger by University of Michigan China expert Allen Whiting, who had served from 1962 to 1966 as director of the State Department's Office of Research and Analysis for the Far East. Whiting, on the basis of discussions with his former colleagues whose assessments apparently were not reaching the White House, warned Kissinger that the Soviets had been making extraordinary preparations for an attack on China's nuclear facilities with conventional weapons. Whiting reportedly noted his colleagues' concern that the Chinese would believe the United States had tacitly approved such a Soviet attack. He suggested that a private U.S. assurance to Chinese leaders that the United States would not condone a Soviet strike on China's nuclear facilities might improve prospects for Chinese concessions on the major obstacle to a breakthrough in Sino-American relations—Taiwan. Whiting maintained that Taiwan was a secondary concern to Chinese leaders compared with the perceived threat to China from the Soviet Union. Hersh, *The Price of Power*, 357–59. Hersh also reports that Whiting frequently visited Washington in the summer of 1969, where he met with his former intelligence colleagues and learned, he says, that they felt "cut off from the White House. They felt useless and unwanted. Henry wasn't asking any questions, because if he asked, the bureaucracy might know what he was planning." Although Whiting is not credited in Kissinger's memoirs, Kissinger did mention to the Kalb brothers that he had been influenced by Whiting's analysis. Kalb and Kalb, *Kissinger*, 226–27.

99. Kissinger, *White House Years*, 182. Kissinger writes that many Soviet experts "rejected as either absurd or reckless" the argument that better ties with China could actually foster improvement in U.S.–Soviet relations." Kissinger cites a September 1969 State Department paper asserting that U.S. overtures to China would "introduce irritants" into the U.S.–Soviet relationship and that "if a significant improvement in the Sino-American relationship should come about, the Soviets might well adopt a harder line both at home and in international affairs." Kissinger, *White House Years*, 189.

100. Former Kissinger aide William Hyland, not a disinterested commentator, remarks that Kissinger's secret visit to China in July 1971 was especially successful in gaining leverage over Moscow. "Playing the China card was clearly a success. Within a few weeks, there was a breakthrough in the Berlin talks, the SALT negotiations began to move again and the Soviets agreed to a Nixon summit in Moscow for the following spring." Hyland, *Mortal Rivals*, 35. See Garthoff, *Détente and Confrontation*, 240–42. See also Newhouse, *Cold Dawn*, 100 and 109–12, on the China factor in detente and the SALT negotiations.

101. Government Soviet experts' concern that any U.S. efforts to improve ties with China might undermine efforts to ease relations with the Soviet Union predate the Nixon administration. James C. Thomson, former assistant secretary of state for Far Eastern affairs, reveals similar concerns expressed in the Kennedy administration. He argues that the "China purges of the '50s had produced an unintended result: priority status for Soviet specialists and Soviet-American relations." The senior China specialists had been banished, he writes, and in their absence "U.S. policy was inevitably skewed towards Moscow to an unhealthy degree; indeed, vivid Soviet descriptions of Chinese 'irrationality' began to be accepted and repeated among American policy-makers." Thomson notes that in the 1962–1963 period, from the Cuban missile crisis to the Atmospheric Nuclear Test Ban Treaty, "efforts to undertake small unilateral initiatives towards China—most notably with regard to the travel ban—were regularly rejected on the ground that they might jeopardize the process of Soviet-American rapprochement." Thomson, "On the Making of U.S. China Policy," 228–29.

102. The key event stimulating opposition to détente in the United States was the U.S.–Soviet confrontation during the October 1973 war in the Middle East. See Garthoff, *Détente and Confrontation*, 405–8.

103. See Hyland, *Mortal Rivals*, 98–109, and Garthoff, *Détente and Confrontation*, 454–56, on the battles over the Jackson-Vanik and the Stevenson amendments.

104. See Banning Garrett and Bonnie Glaser, "From Nixon to Reagan: China's Changing Role in American Strategy," in *Eagle Resurgent: The Reagan Era in American Foreign Policy*, eds. Kenneth Oye, Robert Lieber, and Donald Rothchild, 262.

105. "Between 1972 and 1974, Kissinger had repeatedly tried to mollify Brezhnev by promising that we would not enter into any military arrangements with China directed against Russia," according to Kissinger aide Hyland, *Mortal Rivals*, 64.

106. Leslie Gelb, "Washington Senses Loss of Leverage Against Soviets," *New York Times*, 30 November 1975. The administration official interviewed by Gelb was probably either Kissinger or his deputy Winston Lord. Peter Osnos, writing from Moscow for the *Washington Post*, 7 December 1975, concluded that the Soviets "apparently believe that relations between China and the United States are essentially stalled," and consequently seem relatively unconcerned about possible Sino-American collusion against them.

107. Kissinger's memoirs for the period of the Ford administration have not been written and there is no other public record of Kissinger's thinking on the issue of U.S.–Chinese military ties in this period. My assessment of Kissinger's views is based on interviews with officials and consultants in Washington as well as on my own judgment of the reasons for his actions on the issue.

108. For a detailed analysis and history of the struggle over U.S. military ties

with China, see Banning Garrett, *The 'China Card' and Its Origins: U.S. Bureaucratic Politics and the Strategic Triangle*, Ph.D. Dissertation, Brandeis University, 1983, University Microfilms, 1984.

109. These ideas were proposed by Michael Pillsbury, then a RAND consultant, who wrote the first study exploring the subject in early 1974. Pillsbury went public with his ideas in September 1975 in "U.S.–Chinese Military Ties?" *Foreign Policy* no. 20 (Fall 1975). Publication of his article was encouraged by high-level administration officials. Ironically, these ideas were initially sparked by Soviet claims that the United States was already providing China with arms, thus indicating Soviet sensitivity to such a policy.

110. See Garrett, *The 'China Card' and Its Origins*, 262–63 for a summary of these steps.

111. Vance records his consistent opposition to steps toward developing military and strategic ties with China advocated by Brzezinski for fear of provoking Moscow and damaging United States–Soviet relations. See Cyrus Vance, *Hard Choices: Critical Years in American Foreign Policy* (New York: Simon and Schuster, 1983), 101–102, 110–19, and 390–91. Like Kissinger, however, Vance viewed U.S.–Chinese relations as contributing to a more favorable balance of power. Vance notes his view at the beginning of the administration that "[a]s long as we maintained a realistic appreciation of the limits of Sino-American cooperation, especially in security matters, and carefully managed the complex interrelationships between China, the Soviet Union, and ourselves, better U.S. relations with China would contribute to strengthening the balance of power both in Asia and globally." Ibid., 45–46.

112. Brzezinski writes in his memoirs that from the beginning of the administration, he believed that improving relations with China was of strategic importance to the United States. Zbigniew Brzezinski, *Power and Principle: Memoirs of the National Security Adviser, 1977–1981* (New York: Farrar, Straus and Giroux, 1983), 3, 196.

113. Part I of Presidential Review Memorandum (PRM) 24, completed in May 1977, reportedly recommended that the United States meet China's basic conditions for normalization and warned that U.S.–Chinese relations would stagnate or erode unless forward progress were made toward normalizing relations. The study also warned that failure to make progress in relations with China could lead to improved Sino-Soviet relations while U.S. success in moving forward with Beijing could prompt improvements in U.S.–Soviet relations, as had happened in the 1971–1973 period. According to Brzezinski's aide Michel Oksenberg, this position was supported by both Vance and Brzezinski. See Michel Oksenberg, "A Decade of Sino-American Relations," *Foreign Affairs*, 61, no. 1 (Fall 1982): 181–82.

114. Vance, *Hard Choices*, 78–79.

115. Brzezinski, *Power and Principle*, 198.

116. Vance notes that "although my views on this issue largely prevailed throughout 1977, we were to debate this issue again during the remainder of my term as secretary of state." Vance, *Hard Choices*, 78.

117. For Vance's account of the PRM-24 debate, see *Hard Choices*, 78; for Brzezinski's account, see *Power and Principle*, 200.

118. See the *New York Times* 8 July 1977 and 6 January 1978 on the contents of

PRM-10. Brzezinski writes that PRM-10 "reinforced my previous predisposition to push on behalf of American-Chinese accommodation. I saw in such accommodation, together with our own enhanced defense efforts, the best way for creating greater geopolitical and strategic stability." Brzezinski, *Power and Principle*, 178.

119. The document presenting the hard-line point of view on Soviet intentions and the strategic balance under the Ford administration was the so-called Team B report done for the CIA by a group of conservative outsiders. See the *New York Times* 26 December 1976 and the *Washington Post* 2 January 1977.

120. See Garrett and Glaser, "From Nixon to Reagan," 265.

121. In published articles and private statements over the next several months, the Chinese criticized the United States for underestimating the Soviet threat and pursuing a policy of appeasement. See Garrett, *The 'China Card' and Its Origins*, 111–13.

122. Michel Oksenberg, "A Decade of Sino-American Relations," 193.

123. For details on this period, see Garrett, *The 'China Card' and Its Origins*, Chapter 4.

124. Brzezinski, *Power and Principle*, 211.

125. Ibid., 207.

126. *New York Times*, 28 May 1978.

127. George Urban, "A Long Conversation with Dr. Zbigniew Brzezinski," *Encounter* (May 1981).

128. Chinese officials, including Deng Xiaoping, made this point to Rep. Lester L. Wolff (Democrat–N.Y.) in July 1978. See "A New Realism: Factfinding Mission to the People's Republic of China, July 3–13, 1978," House Subcommittee on Asian and Pacific Affairs, (Washington: GPO, December 1978), 24–26.

129. Vance notes that he sent President Carter a letter outside bureaucratic channels in late May 1978 that asserted, among other recommendations on U.S.–Soviet relations, that "we should be careful how we managed the U.S.–PRC–USSR triangular relationship and should avoid trying to play China off against the Soviets." Vance, *Hard Choices*, 102.

130. See Secretary of State Alexander Haig's memoirs for an insider's account of differences within the Reagan administration in the 1981–1982 period over Taiwan and China's strategic importance to the United States. Haig, *Caveat*, 195–200.

131. See Garrett and Glaser, "From Nixon to Reagan," 269–79, for a detailed account of this period.

132. The 26 November 1981 memorandum was leaked to Tad Szulc and quoted in "The Reagan Administration's Push Toward China Came from Warsaw," *Los Angeles Times* 17 January 1982.

133. For Secretary of State Alexander Haig's account of the negotiations with the Chinese and within the administration that led to the 17 August 1982 joint communiqué on U.S. arms sales to Taiwan, see *Caveat*, 204–17.

134. In his memoirs, Haig writes: "In terms of the strategic interests of the United States and the West in the last quarter of the twentieth century, China may be the most important country in the world." Haig, *Caveat*, 194.

135. See Banning Garrett and Bonnie Glaser, "Chinese Estimates of the U.S.–

Soviet Balance of Power," *Occasional Paper* no. 33, Asia Program, Wilson Center, July 1988, 27–30, 53.

136. In "New Realities and New Ways of Thinking," *Foreign Affairs* 63, no. 4 (Spring 1985), George Shultz stressed the growing economic importance of the region to the United States. In a major Asia policy speech, March 5, 1983, to the World Affairs Council of North California in San Francisco, Shultz intentionally deemphasized China's global role when he noted that the Sino-American relationship "can be a potent force for stability in the future of the region."

137. By early 1983, Shultz and the administration were ascribing the leading role in U.S. strategy for Asia to Japan, not China. See Richard Nations, "A Tilt Towards Tokyo: The Reagan Administration Charts a New Course for Asian Policy," *Far Eastern Economic Review* (April 21, 1983).

138. George Shultz, "New Realities and New Ways of Thinking," *Foreign Affairs* 63, no. 4 (Spring 1985).

139. From a balance-of-power perspective, cooperation with the Soviet Union against China was unthinkable—success of such a strategy would further weaken and isolate China or even lead China to rejoin forces with the Soviet Union. Such a strategy would thus strengthen the Soviet Union's position in the global balance of power while weakening that of the United States and its allies.

140. The former president added that this "overriding strategic concern dominated our dialogue." Richard Nixon, "America and China: The Next 10 Years," *New York Times* 11 October 1982.

141. For an analysis of China's evolving assessments of the Soviet-American balance of power and its implications for Chinese policy, see Garrett and Glaser, "Chinese Estimates of the U.S.–Soviet Balance of Power."

142. The Reagan administration's shift in emphasis from strategic-military to economic underpinnings of U.S. global containment strategy toward the Soviet Union and subsequent changing view of China's role in U.S. global strategy represented in large part the views of the new secretary of state George Shultz, who replaced Alexander Haig in mid-1982.

8

Learning in U.S. Foreign Policy: The Case of the Middle East

Steven L. Spiegel

The major theme of this chapter is that government learning, as suggested by policy toward the Arab-Israeli dispute, is rare and occurs primarily via personnel shifts. When learning does occur at the individual level it tends to be prompted by pain (disillusionment, embarrassment), and it takes the form of a slow, incremental process, accompanied by shifts in the relative weighting of consistent, long-term objectives and the adjustment of tactics. In general, policy makers are more willing and able to change tactics rather than strategy, and strategies rather than goals.

I believe that dramatic, qualitative transformations in beliefs and preferences are rare. Sudden, sharp shifts into new ways of looking at the world by elites in power almost never occur, even in response to crises. Generally, individuals in power may adjust their priorities and tactics, but sudden policy changes are caused by the arrival of new personnel. Otherwise, change may involve a gradual revision of policy beliefs and preferences (a slow, cumulative process). Most often, "outs" develop ideas which are then assimilated by top-level policy makers coming to power or advisers are selected from within the bureaucracy or the policy elite outside the government who expose the top levels to alternative positions.

Such changes occur in the context of the definition of American interests in the Middle East, which has been consistent for 40 years and has been the source of a remarkable consensus:

- the need to protect oil supplies and the pipelines and waterways through which oil is delivered to the rest of the world;

264

- the importance of preventing the expansion of Soviet control in the area;
- the significance of protecting Israel's security;
- the requirement that as many as possible pro-American Arab regimes retain power over time;
- the advisability of pursuing an Arab-Israeli settlement as an end in itself and as a means of promoting America's other interests in the area.

The relative weight of these issues changes over time as perceived threats to U.S. interests and perceived opportunities for enhancing these interests are altered. Thus, there was particular concern with the Soviet threat in the 1950s and early 1980s; with the oil crisis in the 1970s; with the security of pro-Western regimes in the 1960s; with the potential for possible breakthroughs in the peace process in the 1970s and from 1988 onward.

In the short term, the changes in American policy revolve around the relative weight of particular objectives (e.g., the pursuit of containment, oil, peace, the protection of pro-American regimes), enhancing the impact of strategies and tactics. Because there is a consensus on long-term interests, differences over strategy and tactics become central to policy debate. Changes assume a variety of forms: the priority of the Middle East; the conception of how the peace process should be pursued; the approach to possible alternatives (e.g., step by step, comprehensive, international conference, autonomy); the relative importance of individual Arab states or Israel to the United States; the use of arms sales and aid; the use of carrots or sticks toward local parties; and the willingness to challenge or cooperate with the Soviet Union.

THREE PARADIGMS

Often, government policies are seen as in conflict (especially efforts to protect pro-American Arab states and Israel or to sell arms to both sides). Therefore, coalitions advocating alternative paradigms have evolved over the years. They have made it easier for key policy makers to resolve inherent contradictions and to handle domestic and external pressures. Three paradigms represent a combination of preferred objectives, which lead in turn to particular strategies and even tactics for implementing them. The consensus on fundamental U.S. interests underlies the discussion of the three paradigms that follows, but the paradigms reflect differing assessments of the perceived threats and opportunities that confront U.S. policy makers and differences over the optimal means available to the United States for fulfilling objectives.

1. *Soviet-centered*. Under this view, the Soviet threat is the critical issue facing American policy in the area and the United States must adapt to continuing challenges as local developments evolve. There are two strategies for dealing with this concern: (1) attempt to organize the Arabs for thwarting Soviet advances in the Persian Gulf and distance U.S. policy from Israel or (2) use Israel as a strategic asset and try to develop strong relations with as many pro-American Arab states as possible.

The first approach dominated the American national security bureaucracy prior to the Nixon administration and was pursued with particular vigor during the Eisenhower years. Yet even among those who advocated this alternative, there were differences over tactics: whether to organize the states of the area in an anti-Soviet coalition (the Baghdad Pact); to align with Nasser's Egypt as the likely premier power of the area; or to use economic aid or arms sales as the prime means of influence. The notion of an anti-Soviet, Arab-oriented strategy was resurrected at the Pentagon under Caspar Weinberger. He received considerable support from Joint Chiefs nervous about the new American responsibilities in the Persian Gulf necessitated by the fall of the Iranian shah, the Soviet invasion of Afghanistan, and the enunciation of the Carter Doctrine.

The second group, which sees Israel as a key asset of American interests, was advocated by supporters of Israel as early as the 1940s. It can be seen in embryonic form in the argument of Truman's special counsel, Clark Clifford, that a democratic Jewish state in Palestine would thwart Soviet aims in the region.[1] Both Nixon and Kissinger flirted with the idea during the administration's first term, especially during the September 1970 Jordan crisis. Yet until the Reagan administration, the powerful Senator Henry Jackson was the prime exponent of the view (backed by many in the American Jewish community and among conservative policy analysts). In the Reagan era, the view was enhanced by a variety of powerful figures, including Alexander Haig, Jeane Kirkpatrick, Richard Perle, John Lehman, and Jack Kemp.

2. *Palestinian-centered*. According to this group, the way to solve American Middle East dilemmas in the security, political-diplomatic, and economic arenas is to solve the Arab-Israeli dispute. The way to solve this conflict is to address the Palestinian question squarely. Most members of this group favor more intricate dealings between the United States and the Palestine Liberation Organization (PLO) and believe that U.S. interests would best be served should Israel accept a Palestinian state on the West Bank and the Gaza Strip.

In the 1950s, there was early support for this perspective, especially among those either linked to the oil industry or concerned about the oil question. There was also an overlap with the anti-Soviet position, as suggested in a later period by the strongly pro-Palestinian position of

John Connally in the 1980 campaign. As early as the 1950s, however, the power of the conception for American liberals can be seen in the concern of Senator John F. Kennedy for the Palestinian refugee issue. This stance was later revitalized in the 1970s and 1980s by such figures as Jimmy Carter, Jesse Jackson, Donald McHenry, George McGovern, Cyrus Vance, Warren Christopher, Harold Saunders, George Ball, William Quandt, and Zbigniew Brzezinski.

3. *Regional Pragmatists.* This paradigm is a broadly pragmatic, regional orientation. Its adherents reject any one-dimensional interpretation of Mideast events and solutions. Rather, they see Mideast policy as multi-layered, involving a host of competing objectives and solutions. They favor close American involvement in the peace process but are open to a variety of avenues and directions. Pragmatism rather than ideology or rigid support for a particular solution is one of their distinguishing characteristics. Members of this group generally favor strategic cooperation with Israel, are cautious about dealings with the PLO, favor improved ties with Arab states but not at the expense of Israel, and are carefully prepared to test whether the Soviet Union under Gorbachev has genuinely altered its policies toward the Arab-Israeli dispute. The disparate nature of this approach is mirrored by the diversity of its adherents: George Shultz and Walter Mondale; Henry Kissinger and Sol Linowitz; Lawrence Eagleburger and Samuel Lewis.

Truman, beset by competing forces, sought somehow to evolve such an approach, but could not. Johnson, in his support for Israel and the conservative Arab states, similarly groped toward it. Neither president, nor their respective aides, was able to produce a fully developed policy, even though their approaches moved in the direction of regional pragmatism. This integrated approach, long sought by Congress, became popular within the executive branch only in the Reagan administration under a president and a secretary of state committed to supporting strongly both pro-American Arab regimes and the Israelis.

In practice, there is much common ground between "strategic consensus" policy makers and the regional pragmatists, but only the pragmatists are prepared to entertain the possibility of Soviet involvement in the peace process. The anti-Soviet Arab-oriented group and the Palestinian-centered group also share much in common. The major difference between the two is that the former group is preoccupied with establishing close relations with Arab countries to build a bulwark of facilities and relationships that will serve as a block to Soviet advances. The Palestinian-centered group focuses on the Palestinian question and does not concentrate on the thrust of Soviet expansionism. Even conservatives in this camp focus primarily on threats to oil supplies rather than Soviet policies per se. In essence, then, there are two floating coalitions that influence U.S. Mideast policy, and many individual policy makers identify with some of the ideas advocated by both camps within their coalition.

These paradigms provide guides both to policy makers struggling with decisions and to analysts seeking an understanding of ongoing events. Over the 40-odd years of heavy U.S. involvement in the area, both the fundamental problems policy makers encounter and the perspectives with which they face them have grown increasingly complex. Arguments in favor of support for Israel now include a strategic-military dimension as well as moral, ethnic, religious, romantic, and humanitarian concerns. Americans are also more likely to distinguish among Arabs: between Egypt and Saudi Arabia; between Jordan and the Palestinians; between the PLO and the residents of the occupied territories; and even between Shiites and Sunnis, fundamentalists, radicals, and moderates. Americans have come a long way since Truman's ambassador to the United Nations implored Arabs and Jews to "settle this problem in a true Christian spirit."[2]

An increased sensitivity for the complexity of the area has been accompanied by unpredictability. For example, three secretaries of state with long tenure, Acheson, Dulles, and Rusk, shared an Arab-oriented anti-Soviet tilt, which helped give the State Department a reputation as inevitably weighing in against the Israelis. However, since the 1970s, a series of secretaries with widely differing views have made the State Department's role and positions on the Middle East more difficult to anticipate. Even most officials in the Near East Bureau, long the hotbed of Arabism in the American government, now accept that the United States will have a strong relationship with Israel. The precise role of the bureau will depend on the assistant secretary and his or her relationship to the secretary. However, the bureau can be expected to advocate the applicability of U.N. Resolution 242 to all fronts; to accept a workable autonomy as long as its time frame is circumscribed; to reflect the positions of embassies in the Arab world; and to be the source of proposals, from time to time, advocating concessions to the PLO and/or a more sympathetic approach to the Palestinians.

Similarly, the American Jewish community, long a source of nearly unquestioned support for official Israeli views, is today in ferment. In the 1980s, criticism of Israel by American Jews has increased substantially. There are a variety of reasons for these changes: (1) a sympathetic administration in Washington made criticism less risky to Israel's interests; (2) this environment was reinforced by widespread American resentment of Arabs over the energy crisis, terrorism, and the failure of the peace process early in the Reagan era; (3) the preoccupation of the Arab world with the Iran-Iraq War seemed to enhance Israeli security; (4) a series of scandals and mishaps from the war in Lebanon, to the Pollard affair, to the *intifada* raised serious questions about Israeli judgment and policies; and (5) the emergence of a government of two voices (Likud and Labor) meant that Israelis were no longer speaking with one message but were exporting their own internal differences and practically inviting American Jews to voice their own opinions. By the transition to the Bush administration, these discussions were accelerated by the apparent newfound moderation of the PLO hierarchy under Yasser Arafat.

Many within the leadership and even more the followership of American Jewry still support Israeli positions in an unquestioned fashion, and the media tend to give undue coverage to critics, thereby presenting a distorted view. Yet a line has been broken that has at least partially legitimized critiques of Israeli national security positions from both the left and the right (despite greater public attention to the left).

As suggested by increased diversity within both the State Department and the American Jewish community, the competition in Washington over Arab-Israeli policy is still keen, but individuals select from reigning paradigms to pursue their own policy preferences, whatever their institutional base. The discussion in elite journals and think tanks frames the debate and deepens fundamental concepts, but individual policy makers find one or another prism most convincing. Once in power, they adapt to changing conditions in terms of these preferences.

As the following review of the record demonstrates, officials rarely make fundamental changes while in office. Rather the principal adjustments and innovations are made by analysts and academics out of power. The paradigm adopted by key policy makers who assume power determines which interpretations of events emerge victorious and are applied as policy.

COGNITIVE CHANGE THROUGH NEW ADMINISTRATIONS

Given this discussion as background, it is not surprising to find that a new administration comes to power with a new set of ideas designed to apply to a situation that developed before it took office. Instead of policy makers changing their minds, policies are altered because the decision makers themselves are different. This is the single most frequent example of change, and it occurs in every administration transition.

ROOSEVELT TO TRUMAN

Franklin D. Roosevelt had pursued an almost duplicitous policy in which the Jews were made public promises of support for Zionist aims followed by secret letters to Arab leaders confirming that no changes would be allowed without "prior consultation." The Arabs were thus routinely granted in secret a veto over what the president regularly offered in public. Roosevelt apparently assumed he would be able to overcome this contradiction by means of his personal impact. He particularly hoped to bribe the Saudis into backing Zionist aims in Palestine. However, at his meeting with King Ibn Saud on his way home from Yalta shortly before his death, this president failed completely. The king suggested that in the Arab tradition the Jews as victors be given defeated Germany. Roosevelt had no time left to apply the lessons of his experience, but he did shock Jewish leaders with his negative report to Congress upon returning to the United States.[3]

Harry S. Truman, less geopolitically sophisticated, less concerned with oil, more honest and forthright, had to address the tragic repercussions of the Holocaust. He was also saddled with the American army's responsibility for Jewish displaced persons who sought entry into a Palestine closed by British obeisance to Arab sensitivities. He inadvertently set the United States on a new course by resort to three principles: (1) Humanitarian concerns demanded that at least some of the Jews in Europe be admitted to Palestine but did not necessarily demand a Jewish state; (2) This issue was the type of problem to be handled by the fledgling United Nations, superseding even the necessity of continued British rule; and (3) The United States would contribute neither arms nor men to resolve a conflict seen as peripheral to immediate U.S. security needs but would try to help by diplomatic and perhaps even economic means.[4]

The contrast between Truman and his predecessor can be seen most dramatically in 1948 when, after initial waffling, the president chose to recognize the establishment of the state of Israel 11 minutes after its birth, thereby finally rejecting one of Roosevelt's favorite fantasies, a U.N. trusteeship. It is not accidental that David Niles, who served both presidents as Jewish adviser in the White House, later commented, "There are serious doubts in my mind that Israel would have come into being if Roosevelt had lived."[5]

TRUMAN TO EISENHOWER

As Truman once told Secretary of Defense James Forrestal, a Zionist opponent, he was only trying to do "what's right."[6] But Dwight Eisenhower, judging from his position as army chief of staff in 1947 and later as Columbia University's president, concluded that Truman had allowed domestic politics to control his policy.[7] By the time he had served as the first commander of the North Atlantic Treaty Organization (NATO) and was running for president, he had determined that the Middle East needed a "mini-NATO." Early in his presidency, he told B'nai B'rith president Phillip Klutznick that he was not sure, had he occupied the Oval Office in 1948, that he would have extended Israel recognition as Truman had.[8]

Instead, Eisenhower and his top foreign policy lieutenant, John Foster

Dulles, set about according the Arab-Israeli arena an attention it had lacked under Truman. The result was a priority and a coherence then unprecedented in American policy toward the region.

Eisenhower and Dulles were convinced the area would soon be the victim of international communism and they set about anticipating the threat. Believing the Arabs would be central to withstanding the anticipated Soviet onslaught, they correctly identified revolutionary Egypt as the most important country in the new Arab Middle East. Therefore, they sought to distance American policy from Britain, France, and Israel; to organize key states in a mini-NATO that the United States would not join; to offer arms to the two Arab leaders, Egypt and Iraq; to improve their chances of success by promoting secretly an Arab-Israeli peace (Project Alpha; the Anderson mission) and publicly novel technical arrangements (the Johnson Plan). Rarely has American policy been so innovative, integrated, organized, and unsuccessful. Yet we can only marvel in retrospect at the manner in which the commanders of the "New Look" took various paltry efforts by the departing Truman administration and transformed American policy into a dynamic movement for substantive change. Despite their gerontological image, in the Middle East Eisenhower and Dulles bordered on the radical.

EISENHOWER TO KENNEDY

By the time he reached office, John F. Kennedy found a Middle East policy hanging on to the threads of a weakened Arab conservatism. Reversing course, he accorded the very countries Eisenhower had shunned, Egypt and Israel, a new position in American calculations. Nasser received attention as the type of "progressive nationalist" Kennedy was trying to court worldwide. For the first time, Israel was sold defensive arms (Hawk antiaircraft missiles) in an explicit rejection of Eisenhower's past behavior. Policy toward the U.S. approach to the peace process was altered as well. Instead of fantasized master strokes and technical initiatives, Kennedy focused on the refugee question and operated through the United Nations rather than unilaterally. Perhaps most important, the overall priority of the area was reduced by comparison with the Eisenhower era.[9]

KENNEDY TO JOHNSON

Transitions in which vice presidents suddenly assume office involve less change because a smaller number of personnel are affected. Yet even here we can see the impact of a more conservative captain of the ship of state. Reacting to Kennedy's experiences with Nasser during the Yemen War, Johnson took steps that led to a deterioration in U.S.–Egyptian relations. He was also the first president to embark on a generalized arms sales policy to conservative, pro-American Arab states. This approach, in turn, led him to broaden arms sales to Israel to include offensive weapons, even jet fighters. Unlike Eisenhower and Kennedy, he expressed a sentimental, romantic attachment to Israel embodied in comparisons to the people studied in Sunday school, the prophets of the Bible, and a private analogy to Texas (leaving the Arabs as Mexicans). Well before the Six Day War, U.S. policy toward the region had been altered, reflecting Johnson's preference for Israel and conservative Arab countries like Saudi Arabia, Libya, and Jordan, instead of a flirtation with pro-Vietcong "radicals" like Egypt, Iraq, and Algeria.[10]

JOHNSON TO NIXON

Richard Nixon believed that his predecessor had been too passive in response to the 1967 war and the Mideast powder keg that it had created.[11] Assuming that the Soviet Union had won a major victory, he sought to use the peace process as a means of reducing Moscow's influence and resurrecting relations with the Arab world that had been severely damaged by Israel's victory. Yet he was unprepared to distance the United States from Israel the way Eisenhower had. For the first time, a U.S. president and national security adviser saw the Israelis as potentially useful to American interests. Nixon and Kissinger, however, were preoccupied with other issues, and prime authority for developing a Mideast policy that would meet Nixon's objectives was left to the State Department. With the war of attrition raging along the Suez Canal, Big Four (Britain, France, the United States, and the Soviet Union) talks were conducted at the United Nations; Big Two (the United States and the Soviet Union) talks were held in Washington; and U.S.–Israeli relations were strained amidst Jerusalem's arguments that the new administration had veered away from its predecessor's opposition to an imposed peace and willingness to sell Israel arms. The outcome of this maneuvering was the secretary of state's enunciation of the Rogers Plan in December 1969. The proposal epitomized the new administration's distinctiveness and represented the first U.S. attempt after 1967 to propose a comprehensive framework for a Mideast settlement.[12]

NIXON TO FORD

The hypothesis that policies are altered when personalities change is ironically confirmed in the Nixon to Ford transition, because throughout the four years of this presidential term Henry Kissinger was the chief functionary of Mideast policy. During Watergate, Nixon's preoccupation with the scandal necessitated Kissinger's immediate control over policy making. When Ford assumed the presidency, his own lack of expertise and experience led him to defer to his secretary of state, who had already been established as the central foreign policy player in the administration. Thus Kissinger continued on his shuttle diplomacy course without any visible alterations in the fundamental approach that he had been pursuing before Nixon resigned.[13]

FORD TO CARTER

This transition is a classic example of the impact of a new presidential elite. The Middle East had been a top priority issue during the Ford era, and it was a matter of major concern to the new president and his advisers. Yet the differences in philosophy, tactics, and approach are striking. Assuming office at a time when Soviet policy, alliance policy, and energy policy encouraged attention to the Arab-Israeli dispute, the new Carter team rejected Kissinger's emphasis on small steps leading eventually to a breakthrough. Instead, the president elaborated a north-south orientation rooted in improving relations with the Third World, promoting economic interdependence, and overcoming the energy crisis. This focus led to advocacy of a comprehensive Arab-Israeli settlement, which would begin with a Geneva conference and lead to a resolution of the dispute "in all its parts." If possible, the Soviets would be treated as potential partners in peacekeeping rather than as dangerous adversaries.

Carter broke new ground by replacing Kissinger's limited definition of peace as *nonbelligerency* with an all-encompassing concept then called *normalization*, by focusing attention on the Palestinians as a central issue in the conflict and by stressing the need for major territorial compromises by Israel. Thus, Kissinger's policy had been reversed: a cautious focus on process had been turned into a risky preoccupation with the outcome of negotiations; a carrot-and-stick manipulation of the parties had been transformed into a "holy mission" designed to sweep the regional players along in its wake; an effort to stop the Soviets in the area through diplomacy had been turned into a strategy that necessarily engaged them. Reacting to the October 1973 war, intellectuals and specialists out of power, working under the auspices of such institutions as the Trilateral Commission and the Brookings Institution, had produced a new set of concepts that incoming Washington officials set out to apply.[14] In a process that constantly repeats itself, different individuals had drawn different lessons from the same history.

CARTER TO REAGAN

Philosophy and tactics were again reversed with the arrival of a new team in 1981. In the wake of the fall of the shah and the Soviet invasion of Afghanistan, the new president was impressed with the idea that the Arab-Israeli dispute had been overemphasized by his predecessor by comparison with other regional issues and thrusts. Reagan and his new secretary of state sought to refocus U.S. policy on the Soviet threat, to rally local parties to the anti-Soviet cause, to use Israel as an asset to U.S. interests while simultaneously reinforcing U.S. support for friendly Arab countries. Gone were Carter's deemphasis on the use of force, his fascination with the Palestinians, his sympathy for the Third World, and his preoccupation with energy and economic concerns.

In a host of subtle ways the new focus can be seen in the emphasis on terrorism and the diminished concern with human rights; in the more relaxed attitude toward Israeli settlements on the West Bank; and in the increased involvement with Lebanon and the Persian Gulf. The old administration had been dominated by liberal Palestinian-centered activists. The new team was split between strategic consensus advocates (Reagan, Haig) and Arab-oriented anti-Soviet proponents led by Caspar Weinberger. The defense secretary pressed for arms sales to Arab friends, especially AWACS jets to Saudi Arabia, and sought to distance the administration from Israel. The mixed message of the new Reagan era was in direct contrast to Carter's single-minded focus on settling the Arab-Israeli dispute.[15]

TWO TYPES OF POLICY ALTERATION

In all of these transitions we see U.S. policy altered in one of two ways. First, when a newly elected president assumes office there is a wholesale changing of the guard. The new team has developed a novel framework in response to a recent crisis and the perceived errors of its predecessor. There may be serious tactical and even philosophical differences within the new entourage as it gropes toward dealing with these inherited challenges, but no one is satisfied with the previous administration's answer or methods.

Second, when a president assumes office suddenly and a team is already in place, the degree of change depends on his policy differences with his predecessor (realized or not) and the personnel changes he makes. Conveniently, three archetypical cases appear in our sample. Though he did not know it, Truman had major differences with his predecessor on Palestine. His inability to balance competing forces at home served to accentuate the volatility and inconsistency that were to become the trademark of his Mideast policy. Johnson differed only subtly from Kennedy on the Middle East, but his overpowering personality pressed his predecessor's aides in a new, more conservative direction. Ford was content to let his secretary of state/national security adviser continue the Nixon-Kissinger policy framework he accepted.

COGNITIVE CHANGE THROUGH NEW PERSONNEL WITHIN AN ADMINISTRATION

The second type of change occurs when new personnel arrive within an administration. The higher the level of replacement (depending on the precise organization of the administration), the more likely policy changes will result. Several examples will serve to illustrate this point.

1. The first case is the transition from John Foster Dulles to Christian A. Herter in 1959. As has often been noted, Eisenhower appeared far more interested in accommodative policies, especially toward the U.S.S.R., after Dulles's death. Goodwill trips, meetings, and gestures distinguish his last two years in office. Similarly, the Middle East policy was also quieter under the less ideological Herter, with no dramatic programs or strong anticommunist initiatives.

The last major act toward the region under Dulles was an intervention into Lebanon in July 1958. During the Herter era, there was a tentative willingness to consider new approaches to Israel and Egypt for the first time since Suez. Given the administration's past record and the persistent suspicion of Nasser, it is likely that had Dulles lived there would have been continuing efforts to thwart the advance of what were perceived as communist-supported radicals in the area.[16] Recent research has demonstrated that Eisenhower was more intricately engaged in policy making than was generally realized at the time.[17] Yet he interacted differently with Dulles than with Herter; the former seems to have brought out his activist anticommunist inclinations, whereas under Herter he had a greater tendency to show his more optimistic, conciliatory side.

2. From the outset of the Nixon administration, Secretary of State William P. Rogers had promoted an activist policy toward the Middle East peace process, but by 1973 he had been able to achieve only one controversial Egyptian-Israeli cease-fire (along the Suez Canal in August 1970). His image was one of failure: the Rogers Plan I—1969; the Egyptian violations of the August 1970 cease-fire; the failure to begin Egyptian-Israeli proximity talks; the flap over the mid-1971 Bergus "Phantom" memorandum; the inability to gain the president's backing for pressure on Israel; the aborted limited settlement approach in 1971. By 1973 few regional participants abroad or bureaucratic participants at home took the secretary of state seriously.

By contrast, Rogers's archrival, Henry Kissinger, had attained an almost mythical international reputation for diplomatic achievement. When he assumed the post of secretary of state in September 1973, all involved players anticipated that if he turned his attention to the Middle East he would be treated with respect and his efforts would be more innovative and skillful than Rogers's. We now know that after the Vietnam settlement in early 1973, Nixon sought to shift a reluctant Kissinger toward the Middle East.[18] Instead, the Middle East issue was the first problem the new secretary of state addressed seriously after taking office, shortly before the October 1973 war, as he shuttled between the Arab and Israeli delegations at the U.N. General Assembly, seeking a point of diplomatic breakthrough. It can be reasonably concluded that if Rogers had still been secretary of state after October 1973 and had still been in charge of Mideast diplomacy, the American reaction would have been less manipulative, skillful, consistent, unified; in short, less effective and successful.

3. On a lower bureaucratic level, it is useful to contrast the impact of the transition between Daniel Patrick Moynihan and William Scranton as ambassador to the United Nations in 1975–1976. Moynihan (with the occasional rearguard assistance of Secretary of Defense James Schlesinger) represented an alternative foreign policy direction in a Ford administration largely ruled by Henry Kissinger. Skeptical of détente and more ready to confront the Third World and defend Israel vociferously, Moynihan delivered stirring speeches that thrilled the hearts of supporters of Israel and conservatives alike. When he left to run for the Senate, he was replaced by William Scranton. The former Pennsylvania governor and presidential candidate had already infuriated Israel and her supporters in late 1968 by declaring while on a mission for President-elect Nixon that the United States should pursue a more "evenhanded" policy in the Middle East. In his first speech to the Security Council, he criticized Israeli policies in Jerusalem and the West Bank, calling them an "obstacle" to Mideast peace. Although the speech was written in the State Department, Moynihan would certainly have at least protested and demonstrated his displeasure publicly.[19]

There have been similar transitions at the U.N. (the diplomatic Adlai Stevenson to an Arthur Goldberg closely associated with the pro-Israel cause; Charles Yost, former ambassador to Syria, to the politically ambitious George Bush; vocal supporter of Israel Jeane Kirkpatrick to diplomatic troubleshooter Vernon Walters). Sometimes the president seeks to signal a change of emphasis for diplomatic or political reasons (Yost to Bush). Sometimes the impact on the Middle East is accidental (Stevenson to Goldberg). But the U.N. ambassadorship is a peculiarly apt way of illustrating how changing lower-level officials does shift the emphasis of Mideast policy, at least in particular contexts.

4. The best example of an immediate change precipitated by a personnel shift within an administration is the transition from Alexander Haig to George Shultz, regarding the Palestinians. Haig had concentrated on the Lebanon and Persian Gulf problems during his tenure at the State Department and had been inhibited from addressing the Palestinian question fully by the controversy over a Sinai multinational force he confronted when he assumed office, by the Sadat assassination in October 1981, and by the tensions surrounding the final Israeli withdrawal from the Sinai in April 1982. His concerns were also different from those of the Carter team: strategic consensus against the U.S.S.R., strategic cooperation with

Israel, and a regional rather than a strictly Arab-Israeli approach to the area.

Shultz, however, took a very different stand in 1982. During the election campaign, he had told a reporter that Ronald Reagan's fascination with Israel was the only issue on which the two disagreed.[20] In his confirmation hearings he reiterated that the time had come to pay more attention directly to the Palestinian issue. "The crisis in Lebanon makes painfully and totally clear a central reality in the Middle East: the legitimate needs and problems of the Palestinian people must be addressed and resolved—urgently and in all their dimensions."[21] The result of his early weeks at Foggy Bottom was the Reagan Plan, enunciated on September 1, in which he convinced the president to outline an American plan for "self-government by the Palestinians of the West Bank and Gaza in association with Jordan." Both Israeli annexation and an independent Palestinian state were ruled out. In case anyone might have doubts, Haig declared that he did not agree that a peace plan should have been made public.[22] Haig has also claimed he opposed the president's announcement of U.S. participation in a multinational force for Lebanon shortly before he left office.[23] He was clearly less critical of the Israeli invasion than Shultz. Given a passive president, it is clear that had he remained in office the United States' Mideast policy would have been different in 1982.

There are a host of other personnel changes that have led to subtle and even dramatic alterations in the positions of a particular bureaucratic agency or even of the presidential elite as a whole. One especially significant change was the replacement of Philip Habib as Mideast negotiator by Robert McFarlane in 1983. McFarlane was far more inclined to use the U.S. military presence in Lebanon in an activist role, and the acceptance of his advice in Washington led to a fundamental shift in the Marines' function, which would shortly have disastrous consequences.[24] McFarlane's gung-ho philosophy was expanded when he became national security adviser a few weeks later, replacing William Clark. In this new role, he aligned with Shultz against Weinberger to promote closer strategic ties with Israel and an expanded role in Lebanon—winning the first, losing the second.[25] When Frank Carlucci replaced John Poindexter at the National Security Council, it was clear to all that the gung-ho philosophy that had led to the Iran-Contra affair was dead.

The policy implications of personnel shifts are rarely as clear as those cited above. More typical are the subtle alterations of Mideast policy created by such transitions as Carlucci for Weinberger in 1988 and James Schlesinger for Melvin Laird in 1973 (even though Elliott Richardson was in office for three months in between the two). In both cases, Pentagon chiefs less opposed to ties with Israel replaced imposing figures who sought to avoid entanglements with Jerusalem.

This review of personnel shifts reinforces the first hypothesis that policy changes are primarily achieved by bringing new players to power. At times, this is a conscious effort on the part of the president and his closest advisers, especially when the Mideast is a high priority or the outgoing official is considered too vociferous (e.g., Yost to Bush) or too adventurous (e.g., Poindexter to Carlucci). Most often, the policy maker is selected for reasons that are at most marginally related to Mideast policy. The impact is achieved by the different approach the official brings to office (e.g., Stevenson to Goldberg; Carlucci to Weinberger).

In these first two hypotheses we have tried to show that rather than cognitive change's occurring as a consequence of learning, it most often evolves because new officials arrive with new approaches and assumptions. Either the newcomers have long perceived alternate paradigms, or they learned from the previous administration's failures. On occasion, the appointment of officials within a term reflects the learning of the presidential entourage who are seeking to change policies by changing personnel, but this is rare. Policy makers are usually selected, especially during a presidential term, because they are seen as providing continuity with the overall global philosophy of the administration and/or because they appear to exhibit particular required talents. The changes in Mideast policy that they provide are then incidental to their anticipated impact.

COGNITIVE CHANGE EARLY IN AN ADMINISTRATION

We turn now to policy changes that are effected by officials in power. When policies do not work, they must be adapted, which is usually accomplished by changing tactics, on occasion by changing strategies or even objectives, and almost never by changing paradigms. This section deals with cognitive change that occurs when a new administration discovers that its new policy is impractical. New administrations frequently arrive with a flourish, filled with the confidence born of electoral success. The ideas new officials have developed on the outside may seem effective, but instead quickly misfire, usually within the first year. Three varied cases exemplify this process in America's experience with the Middle East.

1. The Nixon administration was committed to an activist diplomacy that it believed could lead America to sponsor a comprehensive peace accord in the area. When it could not gain Soviet acquiescence in its program, the president authorized the secretary of state to declare, in what became known as the Rogers Plan, that Israel should withdraw from "all but unsubstantial" areas captured in 1967 in return for an Arab

commitment to nonbelligerence. Varied details applying to both Egypt and Jordan were revealed both publicly and privately.[26]

The administration thus made a bid to deal with all of the factors that had created the Arab-Israeli crisis after 1967. The plan did not work. It was roundly denounced by the Israeli government and its supporters at home. The Arabs greeted it with confused and diffident skepticism. A frustrated Israel began a series of deep penetration raids into Egypt, which led to an escalation of their conflict, including a new dangerous level of Soviet involvement.

The administration never acknowledged that it had acted in error. Nixon later claimed that he never anticipated the Rogers Plan would work, but he thought its presentation would demonstrate to the Arabs that the United States was capable of acting in an evenhanded fashion.[27] Yet at the time he was careful in public to separate himself implicitly from the Rogers initiative without renouncing it explicitly.

The plan was soon superseded by a series of Middle East efforts, all of which rested on the opposite concept from comprehensiveness: a step-by-step approach. Though this strategy was pursued initially by Rogers, it was closer to Kissinger's preferred methods. Hence, a new strategy was being pursued in the service of a consistent objective. In 1975 and 1976, when pressures rose for a return to a comprehensive approach, Kissinger would remind associates of the dangers as epitomized by the failure of the Rogers Plan.[28] The lesson of the early fiasco had become engrained in the modus operandi of the administration.

2. The incoming Carter team was unimpressed by Kissinger's lessons. It embraced comprehensiveness with a flurry of activity as it aimed to reconvene a Geneva conference. By early fall the strategy was in deep trouble over bitter differences about how to organize a conference, over unexpected divisions in the Arab camp, over confusion about the impact of newly elected Israeli Prime Minister Menachem Begin, over the failure to gain PLO acceptance of critical U.N. Resolutions 242 and 338 after secret diplomacy, over a Carter agreement with the Soviets on October 1 on a set of principles to govern the conduct of the conference by the superpower cochairmen. The Carter team nevertheless continued to work assiduously to break the logjam, but its efforts were halted when Anwar Sadat changed the rules of Mideast diplomacy by his shocking trip to Jerusalem in 1977.

The Carter administration reacted very differently from the Nixon team to its initial failure. Instead of changing policies, it attempted slowly to adapt the new development to its strategy. In other words, it changed tactics in the service of the same strategy. Initially confused in its response, Secretary of State Vance demonstrated the administration's preference for comprehensiveness when he stated on his first visit to the area after

Sadat's visit, "In my talks with President Sadat and Prime Minister Begin, I stressed the United States' firm commitment to a comprehensive peace. . . . In each of the countries that I visited, I affirmed the continued commitment of the United States to the search for peace."[29] National Security Adviser Brzezinski placed the continuity of policy in a philosophical context when he explained that the Carter team's policies were like three concentric circles: Egypt and Israel as the innermost circle; the Palestinian question as the second ring; the Golan Heights as the peripheral arena.[30] In other words, the administration would pursue comprehensiveness without a conference and in stages—the minimal adjustment necessitated by Sadat's trip. Camp David fit this grand design, as the President explained in a breakfast meeting with reporters shortly afterward and at the Egyptian-Israeli peace treaty signing ceremony.[31] The conflicts with Israel that ensued over the Palestinian question throughout the remainder of the term reflected this strategy, and the president fully expected to devote more attention to it after the election when he would no longer be encumbered by the same type of political constraints.[32]

3. The third case involves the first year of a secretary of state's tenure rather than the initial period of a particular administration. Attempting to redirect Mideast policy toward the Palestinian question, George Shultz developed the Reagan Plan and attempted to implement it while pursuing an Israeli-Lebanese accord. By mid-1983 his policy was in a shambles. After the failure of the Arab states to support his Reagan Plan and Syria's sabotaging of his Lebanese-Israeli agreement, Shultz became disillusioned with Arab unwillingness or inability to support U.S. initiatives. There is evidence that in pursuing his new policy toward Israel, he was returning to previous attitudes espoused at the University of Chicago and in the Nixon administration.[33] The transformation is nevertheless the most dramatic in the history of American policy toward the area. It is the only clear example we have of a paradigm shift in office, from Palestinian-centered to regional pragmatist.

No leading American official has ever made such a fundamental change in policy toward the Arab-Israeli dispute. The reasons for Shultz's shift are still a matter of speculation, but there appear to be several factors that help to explain it. (1) His policy did not work. (2) Between February and August 1983 the two Israeli officials most unpopular in Washington, Defense Minister Sharon and Prime Minister Begin, left office. (3) The president was more comfortable with the new policy. (4) The influential undersecretary of state for political affairs, Lawrence Eagleburger, strongly urged the shift. (5) Shultz was personally offended by Arab behavior in this period. (6) Key White House staff figures, looking toward the 1984 elections, favored the change. (7) The new national security adviser, Robert McFarlane, also backed the new route.

These three cases represent varied responses to early failures. In the first, a new strategy is adopted; in the second, only tactics are altered; in the third, a paradigm shift occurs. The Nixon administration shifted from comprehensiveness to step by step, even while continuing to seek to reverse the decline in U.S.-Arab relations. The Carter team adjusted to a new form of comprehensiveness after Anwar Sadat's trip to Jerusalem sealed the fate of a Geneva conference. Only George Shultz made a fundamental shift to a new paradigm after his initial failures. As particularly suggested by the Rogers Plan, it may be possible to shift tactics early in an administration without undue discomfort. Later, change is ever more difficult. An administration that is actively involved in the area is most likely to make major changes early because its commitment to a particular strategy has not yet hardened; its inexperience encourages adjustment and it has more time than an older presidency to recoup politically at home and diplomatically abroad.

COGNITIVE CHANGE IN MIDCOURSE

Once policies have been formed and committed, changes are difficult and a consequence of disillusionment often accompanied by personal embarrassment. Yet in the course of an administration, changes are often necessary either because developments abroad create new situations or because strategies have failed. Changes are easier to make if external developments can be used as an excuse than if failure must be admitted. In either case, these changes are not the quick responses to the first experience discussed above, but the gradual accumulation of lessons and the combination of adjustments distinctive of the typical policy team. These are isolated cases of limited learning by policy makers in power. They again indicate persistent efforts to fit developments into preexisting assumptions and to react accordingly.

1. Having slowly constructed a complex policy, Eisenhower and Dulles watched with growing agitation as it gradually disintegrated. They had expected to see Nasser join a Middle East defense organization backed by the United States and to sell him arms. Instead, he would accept neither U.S. conditions nor plans and turned to the Soviets for weapons. Perplexed, Eisenhower and Dulles tried again by organizing the Aswan Dam offer and moving forward in a secret peace process. When Nasser again refused U.S. conditions and would not engage in a peace process with Israel, they reluctantly concluded that he could not be trusted after all. Newly released documents demonstrate the pain and agonizing reappraisal that greeted this realization. Perhaps, thought Eisenhower in March 1956, King Ibn Saud could replace Nasser as the leading Arab

figure, but a meeting with the weak Saudi monarch the following year ended that alternative.[34]

As they groped for a new policy after Suez, the two U.S. leaders produced a multilateral form of their initial conception. Any observer must be struck by the striking similarity between the Baghdad Pact and the Eisenhower Doctrine. Although the form and content had changed, the substance of aiding the local parties to resist international communism and its local lackeys remained the same. The intervention into Lebanon was precipitated by the fall of the linchpin of U.S. policy throughout the era: the pro-Western government of Iraq. Thus, the Eisenhower record shows little evidence of learning in the sense of recognizing failure and adjusting accordingly. Instead, an ideological lens made policy learning and adjustment more difficult. The preoccupation with international communism masked a misunderstanding of regional dynamics.

2. In his thousand days John F. Kennedy suffered two setbacks in his Mideast policy, but the degree of his disillusionment was minimal. Although he had secretly backed an effort to ameliorate the condition of the Palestinian refugees, he had not expected it to succeed and therefore had given it a "U.N. cover." By the fall of 1962 he was under a variety of both Arab and Jewish pressures to bury it, which he did without great remorse because of limited political and psychological capital expended. Many frustrated State Department officials, of course, were furious. Rather than learning a lesson, Kennedy merely confirmed his original suspicions and assumptions.[35]

This president had invested heavily in efforts to promote new relations with Nasser. By 1963, Egypt's engagement in the Yemen War had made the establishment of a new relationship with Nasser far more costly in political terms. It had already resulted in an improvement of U.S. relations with a Saudi Arabia threatened by Nasser's activity. But given Kennedy's extensive political and economic investment in Nasser, any change in policy was gradual and confused. When he died, the president was learning the difficulties of a new policy toward Nasser, but he was resisting any major alteration of his course.

3. During the crisis preceding the Six Day War, several members of Congress argued that the Middle East was a more crucial arena than Southeast Asia for U.S. interests; the implication for many doves was that U.S. policy should therefore be redirected.[36] In his last 18 months in office, Johnson did increase the priority of the Middle East, but he would not abandon a Vietnam policy that had become the preoccupation of his administration.

4. Ford and Kissinger conducted a highly publicized reassessment of U.S. Mideast policy after the failure of Egyptian-Israeli talks in March 1975 as a means of pressuring Israel to become more conciliatory. Ap-

parently an agonizing reappraisal, it was actually a favorite Kissinger tactic gone awry. Throughout the Nixon period, Israel had been treated to a subtle carrot-and-stick manipulation typical of a godfather approach, the crux of which even Nixon himself later admitted.[37]

In March 1975 Kissinger produced a Ford letter warning the Israelis that the United States would reassess its Mideast policy if they did not become more conciliatory. In response, they reminded him that "coincidentally" Nixon had sent a similar message when the talks Kissinger was mediating between Israel and Syria had almost broken down the previous year. Ford was not amused and ordered the reassessment.[38] Kissinger appeared to be willing to consider a new comprehensive approach, but quickly acquiesced when Egypt and Israel signaled their desire to resume negotiations. There is therefore little sign of learning here, except for reinforcement of the step-by-step approach.

5. By his own admission Jimmy Carter was appalled by the Soviet invasion of Afghanistan, which he considered a personal affront. Combined with the fall of the shah and the hostage crisis, it epitomized American weakness, shattered his already battered image, and undoubtedly led to his electoral defeat. The invasion also led to his disillusionment with Soviet policies and to his declaration of the Carter Doctrine, in which the United States committed itself to the protection of the Persian Gulf. The rhetorical and substantive changes caused by these events were certainly a consequence of disillusionment accompanied by painful personal embarrassment, as in his admission of lack of knowledge of Soviet objectives.

Despite the supposed widespread impact of these events, policies toward the Arabs and the Israelis remained totally unchanged, except that Carter had less time to deal with the issue. Brzezinski's second circle—the Palestinians—remained intact and would certainly have been more vigorously pursued in 1981. Those critics of the administration who argued that the Persian Gulf events had made the Palestinian question less pressing and Israel more valuable to the United States were simply ignored. Brzezinski rose in influence at the expense of Vance, who eventually resigned. Yet these two key advisers were in substantial agreement on the Arab-Israeli dispute. As in other administrations, there is little sign of learning here in the sense of producing a new approach to the Arab-Israeli conflict in response to major events. The broad administration consensus and the success at Camp David restricted any incentive to reexamine prior assumptions.

6. The Reagan Plan having failed in 1983, George Shultz pursued a more cautious policy in the Middle East until 1988. Faced with a Palestinian uprising and a waning administration, Shultz promulgated a new peace approach for imminent negotiations now appropriately labeled the *Shultz Initiative*. In deference to the preferences of Mikhail Gorbachev, King

Hussein, and Shimon Peres, he included a ceremonial international conference—an adjustment from previous stands. But the fundamental error of the Reagan Plan was repeated: the assumption that the very act of presenting a proposal dramatically would cause its acceptance. The events of 1982–1983 were repeated: Israel's prime minister rejected it; King Hussein moved grandly in a new direction; the United States suffered an ignominious defeat. It is hard to see what Shultz had learned from his painful experiences five years earlier.

Thus, except for the quick early shock of reality, policy makers learn lessons very slowly, if at all. Ironically, successes and failures may both dampen incentives for learning. For example, the establishment of the Baghdad Pact and the Camp David meetings convinced Eisenhower and Carter respectively that they were on the right track. As in the case of the Reagan Plan, incentives for learning and policy change may dwindle, if from an early policy failure the inference is drawn that the Middle East problem does not admit of a solution—no policy change can bring about success.

However, incentives for learning and policy change may increase after policy failure if it is coupled with the expectation that conditions will worsen if a fresh approach is not pursued. This kind of situation usually leads to learning at the level of tactics, when it occurs. For example, there are occasional bitter pills, particularly triggered by arms sales issues that require frequent reactions. Nixon learned that habitual arms sales disputes with Israel were politically costly at home and abroad; by the end of his first term, he sought to arrange longer-term programs to avoid constant battles. Ronald Reagan's administration learned early that frequent suspensions of arms to Israel were not effective in changing Israeli policy. It also learned that battles with Congress over Arab arms sales were difficult, and a major victory could not often be repeated successfully. Carter learned that he could not restrict arms sales to the area the way he had intended. But learning is exceptional. This is the level of tactics, and these cases do not form the centerpiece of Mideast policy in these administrations.

Instead of learning, repeated errors are a more striking pattern. An example of strategy error and nonlearning can be found in early 1955, when Eisenhower and Dulles were certain that Nasser had no choice but to accept U.S. conditions for arms sales; they would not be blackmailed. Having been proven wrong once, they were certain a year later that he would accept their terms on the Aswan Dam; they would not be blackmailed. By the time he finally did propose a deal in June 1956, they had concluded he could not afford both the dam and his increased arms commitments. Besides, wiretaps of the Egyptian embassy convinced them he was not serious.[39] Twice in two years they had mishandled the Egyptian leader.

An example of nonlearning on the tactical level can be seen when Kissinger rudely and almost gleefully watched Rogers's failure to arrange supervision of the cease-fire along the Suez Canal in August 1970. When his turn came in October 1973, he made the same mistake.

Another example of tactical nonlearning occurred when Jimmy Carter thought he learned after the uproar over his October 1, 1977, U.S.–Soviet communiqué that Mideast decisions must be carefully considered by high-ranking domestic and foreign policy advisers. He then committed the same error at the end of February 1980 over a controversial U.N. Security Council resolution. As in 1977, he did not fully understand the implications of his approval on relations with Israel and on his own domestic political standing. In both cases he does not seem to have fully understood the document under consideration.

Carter was unusually able in his ability to assimilate details and to translate this newly learned material into concrete action. But the details he gained regarding the niceties of Arab-Israeli diplomacy fit into a constant overall philosophy. Thus, at the outset of the administration he repeatedly misspoke concerning diplomatic details, but he was clearly committed to some kind of Palestinian homeland. By the end of the administration, his theme concerning Palestinian rights remained substantially unchanged.[40] Carter's learning ability seems to have been confined to assimilating factual data within a narrow and rigid framework.

These isolated cases of learning suggest the limited ability of policy makers for cognitive change. Instead, we typically see new developments reinterpreted to fit into the prepackaged framework (the paradigm and its accompanying objectives and strategies) with which policy makers enter office. Only unusually flexible and often inexperienced individuals are able to change in midcourse, and only critical situations can force most officials to alter their preconceptions.

COGNITIVE CHANGE DURING CRISES

Even crises are not necessarily the occasions of major changes they are usually supposed. As a result of crises the priorities of issues may be increased, but altered circumstances, especially crises, do not necessarily change minds but often afford the opportunity for the playing out of preexisting assumptions.

1. Thus, three years before Suez, Eisenhower and Dulles had decided to separate U.S. policy from that of Britain, France, and Israel. The two leaders then spent the next period assuming that Britain and France's

colonial heritage meant that the United States, as a noncolonial power, would have to distinguish itself from its allies.[41] Therefore, they acted as mediator in pressing for a successful treaty mandating Britain's departure from the Suez Canal zone. They also assumed Israel was a heavy burden for U.S. diplomacy and sought to make their differences with Jerusalem clear as Arab-Israeli tensions continued. The documents now show that they took evenhandedness so seriously that they even placed a ship in the Mediterranean whose mission was to come to the aid of any victim of aggression—Arab or Israeli. In the fall of 1956 the ship was removed at the insistence of the Pentagon, but their mind-set before Suez prepared them for an olympian neutrality.[42] The aggressors as determined by the United States would be punished. When war actually arrived, their prior disillusionment with Nasser inhibited aid to the victim, but their sanctions against Britain, France, and Israel are well known.

At the time of the intervention in Lebanon, Dulles entered Eisenhower's office to find the president already committed to action. The coup that had just occurred in Iraq could not be allowed to spread. But how to justify U.S. intervention? Eisenhower commented that he was ". . . giving deep thought to finding a moral ground on which to stand if we have to go further."[43] Both Eisenhower and Dulles operated on a series of premises that permitted them to see their actions as the playing out of an international code of justice and legal norms. Suez and Lebanon were fit into their conceptual framework. They made adjustments in response to events, as in the enunciation of the Eisenhower Doctrine after Suez or the Lebanese intervention itself. But their assumptions about the direction, purpose, and course of U.S. Mideast policy remained unaltered.

2. Lyndon Johnson's administration suggested after the Six Day War that it would not repeat Eisenhower's pressure on Israel to withdraw in 1957 without explicit Arab commitments to nonbelligerence. In a sense, this stance meant a change of U.S. policy, but not for Lyndon Johnson. As senate majority leader, Johnson had been one of Eisenhower's major critics in 1957. Instead of teaching him a lesson, the Six Day War and the crisis that led up to it confirmed this president's preconceptions and reinforced his determination not to insist on Israeli withdrawals without Arab acceptance of nonbelligerence.

3. The Nixon administration is usually seen as having markedly changed directions after October 1973, but the issue was only accorded increased priority with an accompanying tactical adjustment to the new conditions and the addition of another policy objective—ending the oil embargo. Certainly there was no change in strategy. We have already noted that the administration had moved to a limited settlement approach by mid-1970, and Henry Kissinger had already begun dealing actively on the Arab-Israeli peace front prior to the war. His efforts had been delayed

because Rogers tarried in departing, not because Nixon and Kissinger failed to comprehend the Middle East's significance. Throughout the administration Nixon had seen the Arab-Israeli peace process as a prime means of eroding Soviet influence in the region. By mid-1973 it was a simple conceptual step to include the growing energy crunch as another issue that peace efforts would alleviate. Indeed, Nixon delineated a policy a month beforehand that is conventionally seen as having been initiated after the war.[44]

The Arabs succeeded in grabbing the administration's attention and the war destroyed a myth of Israeli invincibility that had been generated by the events of June 1967 and September 1970. In this sense the lessons learned previously had been wrong, and the stark realization reinforced a sense of urgency; hence, the increase in priority and the tactical adjustments. Nixon had been correct in believing the Middle East was of prime importance, but he, and especially Kissinger, had believed that more time was available before an explosion might occur.[45] But the impact of this newfound priority was a reaffirmation of a strategy developed years earlier both in the Middle East and in experiences with other diplomatic problems.

In one sense the nuclear alert that ended the war represented a major challenge to détente. Indeed, the origins of the public's disillusionment with this approach to the U.S.S.R. can be found in this crisis, especially because the two U.S. leaders had oversold détente for domestic purposes. Nixon used the alert as an excuse for reaffirming the importance of his leadership, but it actually fit his preconception of the U.S.–Soviet relationship: negotiation cum confrontation. The president and the secretary of state might have anticipated that they would not confront this kind of tension after agreements to control superpower participation in Third World conflict had been reached at the superpower summits in 1972 and 1973 and after the agreement they reached in Moscow on a cease-fire to end the war. But Nixon and Kissinger's basic modus operandi included challenges to negotiating partners, and even at the height of the crisis they acted as if this "misunderstanding" with the Soviets was normal.[46] Thus, the nuclear alert did not represent a major challenge to their prior assumptions.

However, the war and the nuclear alert reinforced the fear that the Arab-Israeli conflict could lead to a superpower confrontation. The Six Day War had raised these concerns for the Johnson administration and the Nixon team had entered office fully aware of the threat, which had encouraged its early talks with the Soviets on the Arab-Israeli problem. For the decision makers who experienced the eerie uncertainty of possible confrontation with the U.S.S.R. on the night of October 24, 1973, the danger of escalation added increased urgency to the need to reach a settlement, a concern that would also influence the Carter administration as well.

Finally, Nixon believed that the Six Day War had been a defeat for the United States to Moscow's benefit, because Israel's victory had led several key Arab states to be isolated from Washington.[47] The lesson he drew from 1967 was that the United States could not afford another massive Israeli victory. But as he had demonstrated in the September 1970 Jordan crisis, his conception of the U.S.–Soviet relationship demanded that no client state associated with the United States (e.g., Jordan, Israel) could be defeated by a client of the U.S.S.R. (e.g., Syria, Egypt).[48] Thus, Nixon entered office committed to the notion that neither Israel nor an Arab state could be allowed to win a war. For this reason, much U.S.–Israeli discussion in this period was focused on convincing Israel not to preempt again as it had in 1967. Secretary of Defense Melvin Laird was one of the leaders of this point of view. Kissinger acquiesced.[49]

The key to understanding U.S. diplomacy during the war is this preference for a stalemate, which is why American efforts were carefully and successfully balanced to produce a particular result. Neither side would be allowed to win or lose. As in the other cases we have discussed here, this policy was not an improvised reaction to crisis but the victory of a conception learned years earlier.

LEARNING IN PERSPECTIVE

We see, then, that learning primarily occurs by "outs" who bring a set of assumptions to power, which they apply as events unfold. Rarely are developments so shocking that they cause a redefinition of the basic premises on which the policy makers in power are acting. A brief review of the administrations since Truman will serve to consolidate my major points.

TRUMAN

Truman's initial reaction to the Palestinian question was humanitarian and cautiously diffident: the Jewish refugees should be aided; the U.N. should deal with the issue; however fascinating the Zionist objective or a Jewish state might be, it was not necessary so long as the refugees could be assisted by other means or the U.N. could find a better way of settling the Palestinian question. Truman was confronted by vehement Jews and their supporters, in and out of the administration and in Congress, who wanted American support for the Zionists. The national security bureaucracy and its allies among Arabists, missionaries, and oilmen pulled him in the opposite direction. Subsequently, the president wavered back and forth. In late 1947, for example, he endorsed partition favoring the Zionists but accepted an arms embargo that discriminated primarily against them. In 1948 he accepted trusteeship, which reversed partition, and then recognized the state of Israel as soon as it was established.

By 1949, the infant state had won a full-fledged victory against the unanimous predictions of the entire national security bureaucracy. Yet there is no evidence that these events led to a reassessment. In the State Department in particular U.S. policy, when it differed with officials' recommendations, was seen as a mistake. Truman grumbled to aides sympathetic with the Arabs that underdogs, when suddenly thrust into positions of authority, act just as reprehensibly as those who opposed them. "If the Jews hold me to my contract, they will have to keep theirs."[50] If the Israelis wanted to keep part of the Galilee, which they had conquered in the war, they would have to relinquish the Negev Desert granted them in the 1947 partition (a favorite State Department scheme). In a recently released State Department document, a similar position was still being touted in early 1951.[51]

The diaries of Eddie Jacobson, Truman's Jewish former haberdashery partner, likewise reveal that as in 1948 the president regularly made promises that were totally opposite to State Department strategy. In 1950 he told Jacobson that Israel would receive arms when it needed them; he then approved the Tripartite Declaration. At one point, Truman promised Jacobson he would aid in gaining a congressional committee's approval of assistance to Israel, then he did nothing and refused to allow the disclosure of his personal support. In early 1952 a paper preparing Truman for a meeting with Prime Minister Winston Churchill included Israel as a member of the then-contemplated Middle East Defense Organization. The State Department, however, had no intention of allowing Israeli participation.[52]

The Truman era is distinctive for the minor impact Israel's establishment and victory over the Arabs had on prevailing attitudes. The anti-Soviet Arab-oriented paradigm prevailing in the bureaucracy was so powerful that even the White House could only raise occasional questions. After making the minimal adjustment to Israel's existence, all engaged parties continued on without changing their basic assumptions about U.S. policy toward the area. Only the priority of the issue was lowered with the end of the Arab-Israeli War.

EISENHOWER

Eisenhower and Dulles entered office with a new set of premises built on perceived Truman errors, especially his presumed genuflection to the pressures of domestic politics. Eisenhower, however, had actually been one of Truman's critics within the national security bureaucracy in 1947. Learning here, therefore, was practically nonexistent. As the administration unfolded and one failure succeeded another, the president and his secretary of state tried to impose their preconceptions on an ever-narrowing environment. By 1958 Baghdad and Cairo, the two pillars of their contemplated anti-Soviet strategy, were in the Kremlin's orbit. Iraq's Kassem and Egypt's Nasser competed with each other for Moscow's favors.

Yet the successful intervention into Lebanon gave the policy a temporary appearance of effectiveness. The absence of learning can best be depicted by Eisenhower's comment in his memoirs that "[i]f he [Nasser] was not a Communist, he certainly succeeded in making us very suspicious of him."[53] One of the major changes from the Truman era was the inclination to see the Middle East as an example of the international communist conspiracy at work, hardly an advance in sophistication.

KENNEDY

Kennedy's team came to power convinced that the Arab-Israeli dispute would gradually wither away. With the Soviets now saddled with balancing the Iraqi-Egyptian rivalry and Nasser preoccupied with consolidating his union with Syria, the issue seemed to be on ice. Although the problems of ameliorating the conflict and initiating a new relationship with Nasser proved to be more intractable than anticipated, little time was expended on assimilating the consequences of unanticipated developments, especially the Yemen War.

JOHNSON

The more conservative Johnson was comfortable dealing with the pro-American Arab regimes. He similarly adjusted to the Six Day War in terms of his 1957 experience: pressuring Israel to withdraw from occupied territory without reciprocal Arab concessions was a mistake. But if the war raised the possibility that the Vietnam involvement might be occurring at the expense of other strategically important regions like the Middle East, Johnson's administration ignored it. Arthur Goldberg was delegated to help negotiate U.N. Resolution 242, and then the issue was left to a U.N. mediator (Gunnar Jarring). Johnson did learn that the Middle East was a critical region, yet he remained preoccupied with Vietnam.[54]

NIXON

The Nixon presidency was the first in which an important degree of learning occurred during an administration's tenure in office. In the first year it concluded that a comprehensive strategy would not work and that coordination with the U.S.S.R., Britain, and France was not viable. Kissinger himself, who opposed these efforts from the beginning, had much to learn about the details of Mideast diplomacy. When first informed of the content of U.N. Resolution 242 at a dinner party, he thought the contents were a joke.[55] On the tactical level, the administration also learned gradually how to combine the carrot and the stick toward Israel, with an emerging understanding that the carrot was more effective.

Having combined initial premises with early experiences, the Nixon administration was eventually set in a specific pattern. The emergence of Kissinger added coherence; the October 1973 war added urgency to a brew that had been mixed at the outset. Nixon's aides learned to ignore his occasional temperamental outbursts in which he would hearken back to the original notions of comprehensiveness and pressure on Israel.[56] The Watergate scandal was obviously causing him to hope he could salvage his office by Mideast diplomatic miracles.

FORD

Ford and Kissinger had to relearn the lesson that undue pressure on Israel was an ineffective tactic during the 1975 reassessment of Mideast policy. By 1976 diplomacy had stalled. Whatever initiatives might have been taken by Ford and Kissinger in 1977, had they remained in office, they would likely have pursued policy according to the premises that had been followed since 1969. The learning of lessons had declined as the policy was implemented. Although there were signs of a possible initiative toward the Palestinians in late 1974 and early 1975 that would have represented a major change in strategy, Kissinger signed a memorandum of agreement with Israel in 1975 prohibiting a U.S.-PLO dialogue until the organization recognized U.N. Resolutions 242 and 338 and recognized Israel's right to exist. Limited steps achieved dramatically had become his strategy, not spectacular and risky achievement by plodding, behind-the-scenes effort.

CARTER

The onset of the Carter administration suggested that the major learning in the development of America's more complex Middle East policy was still occurring among those out of power. Yet the list of initial miscalculations by the Carter group is impressive: that Labor's continued dominance in Israel could be taken for granted; that Syria and the PLO could be coaxed into the peace process or delivered by the Saudis; that the Arabs were united; that comprehensiveness could work; that the American domestic scene would find a U.S. invitation to bring the U.S.S.R. back into the peace process acceptable; that the energy crisis could be ameliorated by settling the Arab-Israeli dispute. To their credit, Carter and his aides did gradually and begrudgingly adjust their flawed strategy as events confronted them with insurmountable obstacles to continuing in their chosen path. Thus, they brokered an Egyptian-Israeli peace treaty—a separate peace they vehemently opposed, while insisting that it was part of a new comprehensive strategy.

They then confronted several new challenges: the 1979 energy crisis (over the fall of the shah, not over the Arabs and Israel as they had predicted), the hostage crisis, and the Soviet invasion of Afghanistan. In response, the Carter Doctrine was declared, acknowledging the threat to the Persian Gulf separate from the Arab-Israeli dispute. Yet the summer 1979 crisis over amending U.N. Resolution 242 (which led to Andrew Young's resignation) and the March 1980 domestic crisis over a U.N. resolution critical of Israel demonstrated that the main objective of the administration remained unchanged: to achieve a breakthrough with Arab radicals, including the Palestinians, which would set the stage for the achievement of a comprehensive Arab-Israeli settlement. In this sense, the Carter team's learning was limited to narrow adjustments necessitated by major events.

REAGAN

The Reagan administration came to power assuming an even more simplistic view of the area: the disputing parties must be organized into a strategic consensus that would withstand Soviet expansion more effectively than in the past. A minority view, led by Caspar Weinberger and centered at the Pentagon, favored appealing to the Arabs, so that the Persian Gulf could be defended more effectively through bases and other military arrangements. When both groups failed, the new secretary of state, George Shultz, undertook a major initiative toward resolving the Palestinian question and later he pressed negotiations for an Israeli agreement to withdrawals from Lebanon.

When these efforts failed too, the rarest of developments occurred: a diametrically altered strategy in midterm rooted in a shift of guiding paradigms. Shultz now moved toward closer ties with Israel in the hopes that frustrated Arabs would finally have to sue for peace, creating an arena for a renewed U.S. initiative. In 1988, the Palestinian *intifada* finally did create a basis for a new Shultz peace campaign.

In moves backed by Weinberger and Chief of Staff James Baker, the administration also suddenly walked out of Lebanon in early 1984.[57] Jordan's King Hussein in turn tried to respond to Shultz's diplomatic moves between 1985 and 1988, but the U.S. response was tentative, and the Israelis were hobbled by internal division. Meanwhile, the National Security Council became embroiled in secret dealings with Iran, which exploded in the major scandal of the administration and led to an increased U.S. role in the Persian Gulf in order to assuage incensed Arab leaders.

There was no learning process in any of these manipulations, except that officials clearly never again wanted to appear to be trading arms for hostages. The confusion in administration policy evolved as a consequence of a passive president, poorly versed in foreign affairs and uninterested in details; an unusually high turnover in major officials, especially at the National Security Council; a decline in the quality of personnel; a series of strategies lacking in coherence and derisive of lessons previously learned.

The irony of the Reagan era's Mideast policy is that one of the objectives in the revised Shultz strategy was fulfilled, even while the overall strategy failed to bring about a breakthrough in the peace process. Having challenged the Arab parties to make a move toward Israel as a consequence of the United States' growing intimacy with Jerusalem and his own passivity toward the peace process, Shultz could not react effectively when the Arab upheaval emerged in 1988. Impaired by a lame duck status and caught unprepared, the secretary of state repeated his tactic of issuing a position and then trying to gain support with the same negative results as the Reagan Plan.

Thus, the Reagan administration paradoxically exhibited the greatest amount of learning (one of its major figures shifted paradigms and it changed strategies in midcourse on such issues as Israel and Lebanon, Iran and Iraq). Yet, with the exception of the Truman administration, it manifested the weakest ability to adjust when challenges arose. Unlike the Nixon and Carter administrations, the Reagan team was not able to benefit from early mistakes to develop a workable strategy. Rather, its initial flexibility masked an inability to devise effective amendments to strategic concepts when troubles emerged.

THE IMPACT OF INTERNAL ADMINISTRATION UNITY

This discussion of the Reagan administration brings us to the last subject of this essay: the problem of process as opposed to substance. First, does the relative unity of an administration contribute to learning? This study suggests the precise opposite, but only in restricted conditions. We find both that unity inhibits learning and that disunity and low priority may inhibit effective learning even more.

The two most unified administrations in Arab-Israeli policy were led by Eisenhower and Carter. On one hand, as we have seen, they both made adjustments when challenges to their assumptions arose, but their fundamental premises remained constant throughout their period in office. Thus, ideas developed out of power on an issue regarded as having high priority had a direct and immediate impact. On the other hand, the administration's unity inhibited its ability to move in another direction when it might have been merited. Under unusual circumstances, the Ford administration was also united, despite occasional dissent from peripheral figures like Schlesinger and Moynihan. It also exhibited a pattern of rigid adherence to a particular program.

The combination of disunity and low priority may inhibit effective learning even further. In the Truman and Johnson administrations, presidential attention was focused elsewhere, except for short periods of crisis. While the national security bureaucracy moved in one direction (especially under Truman), significant elements of the White House staff and isolated pockets in the bureaucracy moved in another (especially under Johnson). The president, seeking to balance conflicting advice, acted cautiously, with the result that U.S. policy was inconsistent, passive, reactive, and confused. Only when particular tasks were assigned to individual officials were major negotiations achieved (e.g., the Tripartite Declaration, U.N. Resolution 242), but these are isolated accomplishments removed from these administrations' general records.

The Kennedy administration was also seriously divided on the Middle East (especially between national security and White House officials), with the issue regarded as a low priority. We can only postulate what might have happened had Kennedy lived. Either the divisions would have continued and been unresolved, as under Truman and Johnson, or a policy czar would have emerged and settled the matter, as under Nixon. As indicated by his decisiveness regarding the demise of the Johnson Plan, perhaps the president himself would have brought unity to policy— an unusual pattern rarely achieved since Roosevelt.

The greatest degree of learning seems to have occurred in the two cases in which policy was high priority and the administration was divided: the Nixon and Reagan first terms. The bitter disputes between Rogers and Kissinger and between both secretaries of state and Weinberger increased the penalty of committing errors or of failing to learn from them. As a consequence, in both cases strategies were fundamentally revamped after initial miscalculations. However, both periods are distinctive for their ineffectiveness. Learning did not translate into successful achievement of diplomatic objectives, and the internal divisions helped to impede success by confusing foreign governments as to U.S. intentions and even the precise nature of U.S. policy.

We can never, of course, be certain that if policy makers had all been following the same paradigm the outcome would have been more successful. We do know, however, that during these periods policy makers were working at cross purposes. It is reasonable to postulate that external conditions were sufficiently fluid that a differently organized administration could well have (indeed probably would have) led to more effective U.S. policies and more efficient use of whatever lessons may have been learned from particular experiences.

THE IMPACT OF DOMESTIC POLITICS

The final issue to be considered in this study is the question of the domestic impact on learning. The Arab-Israeli dispute is a problem that is famous for its entanglement with domestic politics and the interest of nongovernmental groups. Many analysts of U.S. policy in the Middle East assume that political leaders are constrained by domestic politics, a situation that would inhibit learning.[58] The record is far more complex, suggesting that domestic constraints actually contribute to learning under particular conditions.

The paradigms discussed at the outset have largely been developed by analysts out of power. Without the vibrancy of domestic discussion, they would doubtless not have been articulated as clearly and the differences between competing positions would not have emerged as sharply. Only the Arab-oriented anti-Soviet perspective was developed in the State Department. The strategic consensus anti-Soviet paradigm and the Palestinian-centered position have their origins in popular discourse, although both have supporters within government. The regional pragmatist paradigm was strongly developed in a nongovernmental setting, but many of those who have supported and refined it are either members of Congress or "in-and-outers."

Policy makers also operate under domestic constraints, and therefore political and organizational processes can block cognitive change from leading to policy changes after new ideas have developed. Thus, Truman was prevented from developing a consistent approach to the Arab-Israeli issue by his unwillingness to challenge or reject permanently one of two vocal and dramatically opposed camps (one centered in the State Department, the other in the Jewish community and among White House aides). Eisenhower and Dulles were prepared to ignore domestic pressures, but their policy was undermined by their inability to overcome the bitter rivalry between Iraq and Egypt and their respective competing supporters in the national security bureaucracy. Kennedy was cautious in his opening to Egypt and in his pursuit of the Johnson Plan because of his fear of domestic repercussions. Ford and Carter flirted with options favoring a dialogue with the PLO. Yet when they faced opposition from Israel and Sadat and they could not gain PLO acceptance of their conditions, they concluded that a confrontation with domestic groups constituted a serious burden not worth the heavy cost. Reagan at first accepted the cost of confronting Israel's supporters over arms sales to the Arabs. As the administration continued and the Arab states failed to back the peace process as anticipated, his team became more willing to accede to the preferences of the pro-Israeli forces in Congress opposed to most arms sales to Arab states. Thus, domestic constraints are especially strong when reinforced by outside pressures.

Yet, while domestic politics inhibits decision makers, it also expands their horizons. During the Truman and Eisenhower administrations, Zionist supporters kept an alternative Mideast strategy in the public discussion when policy practitioners were slow to adjust to changing regional conditions. Kennedy actually instructed one of his chief aides (Myer Feldman, deputy special counsel) to make arguments favorable to Israel. This president's political dependence on American Jews encouraged an innovative strategy balancing closer ties with radical Arab regimes and Israel. To the surprise of many analysts, the latter did not interfere with the former. Relations with Israel were improved and refined. The problems with Nasser occurred because of intra-Arab rivalries (especially over Yemen) and not because of Kennedy's approach to Israel.

Congress and the domestic political arena pressed for the sale of Phantom jets to Israel in 1968, which would never have been undertaken if left to the bureaucracy. Again, the dire consequences of a further deterioration in relations with the Arabs predicted by opponents did not occur—yielding a gradual recognition in Washington that arms sales to Israel were not as dangerous to contacts with the Arabs as predicted. Indeed, Kissinger soon argued, in a position that was eventually widely accepted, that it was the very close relationship to Israel advocated by the pro-Israeli forces that made the United States attractive to Arabs seeking to use diplomacy to regain their territory.

Similarly, pressure from pro-Israeli forces contributed strongly to the major adjustments of the Nixon period from comprehensiveness as a negotiating tactic to step by step and from carrot-and-stick tensions to quieter, longer-term arms deals with Israel. One of the supreme ironies of the Carter era is that he achieved his greatest success at Camp David by making the kinds of adjustments in reaction to Sadat's diplomacy that his critics had been begging him to consider. Domestic pressures had encouraged him in this direction and, as he was fully aware, increased the price of failure. Different domestic groups, sympathetic to the Palestinians, kept their cause alive during the Reagan era at a time of diminished official concern. They have promoted the conclusion, which is likely to be accepted, that a major lesson of the 1980s was that Washington cannot afford to ignore this issue.

LEARNING AND OUTCOMES

The question is often asked about the relationship between learning and successful policies. The most dramatic two cases of success for the United States in the post-1945 period are the Kissinger shuttle diplomacy and the Carter achievement at Camp David. In each case, successes followed adjustments in response to early failures. The Nixon administration changed strategies when comprehensiveness did not succeed and after October 1973 raised the priority of the Middle East, broadened its objectives, and made tactical adjustments within the context of a consistent strategy. The Carter administration retained its fundamental strategy but made tactical adjustments in response to Sadat's trip to Jerusalem. Clearly, without these midcourse correctives, neither policy would have succeeded. Yet we do not know whether the Nixon administration would have been able to avert the October 1973 war if its divisions had not prevented more effective learning in its first term, and whether the Carter administration would have been able to achieve quicker progress on the Sinai and further progress on the Palestinian question if it had not been wedded to a rigid Middle East consensus. We do know that other issues (China, the U.S.S.R., and Vietnam for Nixon; Iran and Afghanistan for Carter) impeded the time available for the Arab-Israeli issue during periods of less success in both administrations.

We can see from the Nixon and Carter examples that, whether caused by error or insufficient attention, inhibited or nonexistent learning contributed to policy failures. In the Eisenhower era, a willingness to alter strategies (perhaps by embracing Israel or Egypt—two very different approaches) might have averted the Suez crisis and earlier might have moved Nasser in a more moderate direction before his policy became solidified. Perhaps if the Johnson administration had learned from the June 1967 crisis that it had overvalued Vietnam and paid more attention to the Middle East, an early Israeli withdrawal from occupied territories might have been achieved. The administration's success in reaching agreement on U.N. Resolution 242 in November 1967 suggests that diplomatic openings may have been wider than appeared to be the case at the time. While it is impossible to prove a case from counterfactual speculation, we can at least raise inferences about the possible relationship between the absence of learning and policy failures.

However, we can with confidence identify one dramatic case in which learning did not result in success. Secretary of State Shultz's paradigm shift and strategy change in 1983 did not improve the outcome of his policies. An alternative strategy had also failed and, as suggested earlier, part of the problem was that he employed similarly unsuccessful tactics when opportunities arose in both 1982 and 1988 (the Reagan Plan, the Shultz Initiative). Moreover, it is likely that his second strategy, like his first, was insufficiently subtle and complex, reflecting inexperience and a tendency to favor too exclusively one side (the Arabs) and then the other (the Israelis).

This essay has concentrated on learning by individuals and therefore, as we have shown, the examples of learning are rare, with the exception of occasional adjustments in tactics and priorities. However, over time Americans have collectively learned a host of lessons from exposure to and experience in the Middle East. We have only to compare the U.S. approach to the area at the end of the 1980s with assumptions, paradigms, and strategies four decades earlier. By comparison, U.S. policy in the 1940s appears crude. There was little understanding of inter-Arab rivalries, of the conflicting objectives of individual Arab states, of the potential for balancing U.S. interests vis-à-vis both the Arabs and the Israelis, of the means by which the United States might usefully facilitate an Arab-Israeli settlement. As the Soviet Union became more active in the area, the reaction was alarmist—even apocalyptic.

As the years have progressed, Americans have learned how to maneuver among the parties, and they have frequently discovered wider levels of flexibility than they had previously supposed. Over the years, Americans have tried various types of pressures and incentives, gradually learning that the latter are more effective. They have learned about the limits of their influence and the inhibitions on Soviet influence as well. Meanwhile, they have learned more about the peoples of the area themselves—the dynamics and content of Jewish and Islamic religious life and of Israeli and Arab mores, beliefs, and cultures. The State Department, for example, has learned that American Jews can serve in Arab countries and that foreign service officers can serve in both Israel and the Arab states.

Critics might argue that lessons have been inadequately or wrongly learned (e.g., the possibilities of successfully pressuring individual Arab states or Israel) or that a lack of understanding of indigenous bargaining strategies remains in Washington's dealings with the area. Yet, when compared with the minimal level of individual learning, collective and institutional progress appears more impressive. Americans have a better sense of the Middle East today than in the 1940s because they are more involved, there is more media attention to the area, and there is more collective experience. But that is different from individual learning, and each new individual starts from a different place. Thus, while in the long term collective and institutional learning may occur, in the short run individuals are paramount and in general they are not learners.

CONCLUSION

This examination of U.S. policy toward the Middle East suggests that in the United States outside groups and individuals out of government are a major factor in the learning process. Once in power, officials bring a policy framework that has usually been developed in reaction to a recent crisis. Elites in power adjust priorities and tactics cautiously— even in response to major events. Elites out of power develop new strategies. Once implemented, policies are changed only with great reluctance and only after dramatic developments have mandated adjustments. Even then, alterations are usually minimal and consistent with original premises. For those in and out of government who seek change, the easiest way to accomplish the goal is to change players. Otherwise, change will in most cases be a painful process.

NOTES

The author would like to thank Alexander George and the editors for their comments on an earlier draft of this manuscript.

1. Peter Grose, *Israel in the Mind of America* (New York: Alfred A. Knopf, 1983), 269–70.

2. George T. Mazuzan, *Warren R. Austin at the U.N., 1946–1953* (Kent, Ohio: Kent State University Press, 1977), 99; *Time*, 5 February 1951, 16.

3. Grose, *Israel in the Mind of America*, 154.

4. *Foreign Relations of the United States 1947*, vol. V (Washington, D.C.: U.S. Government Printing Office), 1177–78. In the confusion between 1947 and 1948, the president at times suggested he would accept the participation of Americans in a U.N. "police force or constabulary," but this was not to include "organized troop units." He did not have a "military" presence in mind.

5. Howard M. Sachar, *Europe Leaves the Middle East, 1936–1954* (New York: Alfred A. Knopf, 1972), 454.

6. John M. Blum, ed., *The Price of Vision: The Diary of Henry A. Wallace, 1942–46* (Boston: Houghton Mifflin, 1973), 607.

7. Robert J. Donovan, *Eisenhower: The Inside Story* (New York: Harper & Row, 1956), 67; Donald Neff, *Warriors at Suez* (New York: Linden Press, 1981), 107.

8. Author's interview with Philip Klutznick.

9. Steven L. Spiegel, *The Other Arab-Israeli Conflict: Making America's Middle East Policy, From Truman to Reagan* (Chicago: University of Chicago Press, 1985), 110–16; Mordechai Gazit, *President Kennedy's Policy Toward the Arab States and Israel* (Tel Aviv: Shiloah Center for Middle Eastern and African Studies, 1983), 39.

10. Spiegel, *The Other Arab-Israeli Conflict*, 121–25.

11. Richard M. Nixon, 27 January 1969, *Public Papers of the Presidents of the United States: Richard M. Nixon* (1969) (Washington, D.C.: U.S. Government Printing Office, 1971): 18.

12. Spiegel, *The Other Arab-Israeli Conflict*, 188.

13. Ibid., 312–14.

14. Ibid., 323, 327.

15. Ibid., 395–400.

16. Dwight D. Eisenhower, *The White House Years—Waging Peace, 1956–1961* (New York: Doubleday, 1965), 265; Documents from the Bipartisan Leadership Meeting of 12 August 1956, 5; Cablegram to Secretary of State Dulles, 12 December 1956, 1–2; Memorandum for the Secretary of State from the Under Secretary, 16 March 1956, 1–2.

17. Fred I. Greenstein, *The Hidden Hand Presidency: Eisenhower as Leader* (New York: Basic Books, Inc., 1982), 5–6.

18. Richard M. Nixon, *The Memoirs of Richard Nixon* (New York: Grosset & Dunlap, 1978), 787.

19. Bernard Reich, *Quest for Peace* (New Jersey: Transaction Books, 1977), 94;

New York Times, 14 December 1968, 1; *Near East Report*, 20 (1976): 31 March, 51; 21 April, 69; 28 April, 72; 16 June, 104; 6 October, 170.

20. Laurence T. Barrett, *Gambling With History: Reagan in the White House* (New York: Doubleday, 1983), 248; *New York Times*, 20 November 1980, B12.

21. *New York Times*, 14 July 1982, A12.

22. *New York Times*, 15 September 1982, 1, A12; Alexander M. Haig, Jr., *Caveat—Realism, Reagan and Foreign Policy* (New York: Macmillan, 1984), 346.

23. Haig, *Caveat*, 351.

24. Martin Indyk, "Reagan and the Middle East: Learning the Art of the Possible," *SAIS Review*, Winter-Spring 1987, 7(1), 124–25 (The John Hopkins University).

25. Ibid.

26. William Rogers, "A Lasting Peace in the Middle East: An American View," an address by Secretary of State William P. Rogers before the 1969 Galaxy Conference on Adult Education (Washington, D.C.: U.S. Government Printing Office, 1970); Mahmoud Riad, *The Struggle for Peace in the Middle East* (New York: Quartet Books, 1981), 111.

27. Nixon, *Memoirs*, 479.

28. Edward R.F. Sheehan, *The Arabs, Israelis, and Kissinger* (New York: Readers Digest Press, 1976), 164–74.

29. "Statement from Andrews Air Force Base," 15 December 1977, Department of State *Bulletin*, Jan.–June 1978, 78(2010), 46.

30. Interview with Zbigniew Brzezinski, "Issues and Answers," American Broadcasting Company, 10 December 1977; Zbigniew Brzezinski, *Power and Principle* (New York: Farrar, Straus & Giroux, 1983), 113–14.

31. Jimmy Carter, *Public Papers of the President*, 13 October 1978, 1780; Moshe Dayan, *Breakthrough* (New York: Alfred A. Knopf, 1981), 187.

32. "Middle East Policy Survey," 24 October 1980, 18, 2–3.

33. Bernard Gwertzman, "Reagan Turns to Israel," *New York Times Magazine*, 27 November 1983, 63; author's confidential interviews.

34. Dwight D. Eisenhower Diaries, Conversation with Acting Secretary of State Herbert Hoover, Jr., and Robert B. Anderson, Afternoon of March 12, 1956 (Document 110), 1–2; Memorandum from the Secretary of State, 28 March 1956 (Document 1), 1–2.

35. Memorandum, conversation with Israeli Foreign Minister Meir, 27 December 1962, 7.

36. I.L. Kenen, *Israel's Defense Line* (New York: Prometheus Books, 1981), 196–97; *Near East Report*, 21 (1967), 40–44.

37. David Frost interview with Richard Nixon, *New York Times*, 13 May 1977, A8.

38. Sheehan, *The Arabs, Israelis, and Kissinger*, 159–65, 174.

39. Eisenhower, *Waging Peace*, 33.

40. Jimmy Carter, *Public Papers of the President*, 12 May 1977, 861; 13 April 1980, 682.

41. Memorandum of Conference with the President, 30 October 1956; Transcript of phone call from John Foster Dulles to the President, 30 October 1956, 4:54 pm, 5; Memorandum of Conference with the President, 29 October 1956.

42. Memorandum for Mr. MacArthur from J.W. Hanes, Jr., 1 May 1956; Memorandum of Conversation with the President, 13 July 1956, 2–3; Memorandum for the President from Secretary Dulles, 28 September 1956.

43. Memorandum of Conference with the President, 15 July 1958, 11:25 am, 1.

44. Richard Nixon, *Public Papers of the President*, 5 September 1973, 736.

45. Author's interview with James Schlesinger; *New York Times*, 13 May 1977, A11; Marvin Kalb and Bernard Kalb, *Kissinger* (Boston: Little, Brown, 1974), 455; Henry Kissinger, *Years of Upheaval* (Boston: Little, Brown, 1982), 465.

46. Richard Nixon, *Public Papers of the President*, 26 October 1973, 896–97, 901–902, 904.

47. Nixon, *Memoirs*, 283.

48. Henry Kissinger, *White House Years* (Boston: Little, Brown, 1979), 617–19; Nixon, *Memoirs*, 483.

49. Author's confidential interviews.

50. *Foreign Relations of the United States 1948*, vol. V, Part II (Washington, D.C.: U.S. Government Printing Office, 1976), 1565–67.

51. *Foreign Relations of the United States 1951*, vol. V (Washington, D.C.: U.S. Government Printing Office, 1976), 560.

52. Diary Papers of Edward Jacobson, 5 May 1950, 12; Kenen, *Israel's Defense Line*, 75; "Steering Group on Preparations for Talks Between the President and Prime Minister Churchill," 4 January 1952, 2.

53. Eisenhower, *Waging Peace*, 265.

54. Compare statements of President Johnson between November 1966 and May 1968, *Public Papers of the President*, 13 November 1966, 1378; 4 June 1968, 680.

55. Kissinger, *White House Years*, 341.

56. Kissinger, *Years of Upheaval*, 546–51; author's confidential interviews.

57. Indyk, *Reagan and the Middle East*, 124–25.

58. Sheehan, *The Arabs, Israelis, and Kissinger*; William Quandt, *Camp David: Peacemaking and Politics* (Washington, D.C.: Brookings Institution, 1986); Paul Findley, *They Dare to Speak Out* (Westport, Conn.: Lawrence Hill and Co., 1985); Edward Tivnan, *The Lobby: Jewish Political Power and American Foreign Policy* (New York: Simon & Schuster, 1987).

9

The Lessons of Korea and the
Vietnam Decisions of 1965

Yuen Foong Khong

I would suggest to you that if we had not gone into Korea, I think it would
have been very unlikely that we would have gotten into Vietnam.

— George Ball
July 1986[1]

In thinking about the nature of the challenge posed by the Vietnam
conflict and in assessing the options available to the United States, U.S.
policy makers consistently looked to the lessons of history for guidance.
President Dwight Eisenhower was very much impressed by the lesson of
the 1930s—Munich, Manchuria, and Ethiopia—as were Lyndon Johnson
and his secretary of state, Dean Rusk. In the early 1960s John F. Kennedy
and his advisers seemed to find the experiences of Malaya, the Philippines,
and Greece more pertinent. The most drastic version of the domino
theory, wherein the collapse of South Vietnam was to lead to the inexorable
communization of the rest of Southeast Asia, was also popular from the
mid-1950s to the early 1960s. In addition, the lessons of Berlin, Cuba,
Turkey, and the two world wars were often cited in public by officials.
But the lesson or historical analogy most frequently evoked throughout
the period was Korea.

This essay focuses on the impact of the Korean analogy on the U.S.
decision to intervene with military force in Vietnam in 1965. I argue that
the Korean analogy—or rather what U.S. decision makers considered to
be major lessons of the U.S. experience in the Korean War—played a

major role in the U.S. decision to intervene. More specifically, the Korean analogy or the "lessons of Korea" performed five diagnostic tasks central to political decision making: (1) it helped condition the U.S. definition of the situation or problem in Vietnam; (2) it shaped the assessment of the political and (3) moral stakes; (4) it provided a prediction about the likelihood of success; and (5) it warned about the dangers of certain options. When the contents of these diagnoses are teased out from the empirical record, they can explain why the Johnson administration decided to intervene in Vietnam and why the intervention took the form that it did. Toward the end of my analysis, I will compare my analogical explanation with the containment explanation of Vietnam and suggest that the analogical explanation provides insights not found in the containment explanation.

Figure 1 shows the total number of historical analogies used (in public) per quarter for the years 1961–1966. The source used for this count is the Department of State *Bulletin*. Note the precipitous climb in the use of analogies in the first half of 1965, the period in which the Johnson administration was planning the escalation of the Vietnam War. Table 1 identifies the most important analogies and their frequency of use per year. The two most obvious points are also the most important. Like the

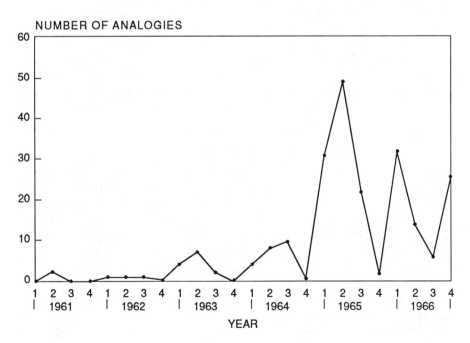

FIGURE 1   Total number of historical analogies used per quarter, 1961–1966. Source: Department of State *Bulletin*.

TABLE 1   The 10 Most Frequently Used Public Analogies

ANALOGY	1950–60	1961	1962	1963	1964	1965	1966	TOTAL
1. KOREA	8	1	2	1	7	23	21	63
2. 1930s	1	-	-	-	-	30	11	42
3. GREECE	-	-	-	3	2	13	14	32
4. MALAYA	-	-	1	5	2	9	5	22
5. BERLIN	1	-	-	-	4	6	8	19
6. PHILIPPINES	-	-	-	2	2	8	3	15
7. CUBA	-	1	-	-	5	5	3	14
8. TURKEY	-	-	-	1	1	3	5	10
9. WORLD WAR II	-	-	-	-	-	4	5	9
10. GERMANY	1	-	-	1	-	3	3	8

Source: Department of State *Bulletin*.

pattern revealed in Figure 1, the use of analogies in public increased dramatically in 1965. Whether the analogies were used for analysis, explanation, or justification—and they need not be mutually exclusive—will be dealt with later; the point now is that, as the decision makers contemplated intervening militarily in Vietnam, they referred to historical analogies more frequently. Second, the Korean analogy was by far the most frequently invoked "lesson of the past." This suggests that it may have played a special role in the analysis or justification of the U.S. role in the Vietnam War; it also supports the notion that the last successful war exercises a major impact on the way a nation looks at the next war.[2]

THE PUBLIC LESSONS OF KOREA

In January 1965, Assistant Secretary of State for Far Eastern Affairs William Bundy shared his thoughts on "American Policy in South Vietnam and Southeast Asia" with the members of the Washington (Missouri) Chamber of Commerce. Like most of his other speeches, this one was long, detailed, but never condescending. Like many of his other speeches, this one referred to the Korean analogy. This speech, however, was distinguished by the systematic manner in which Bundy drew on the lessons of Korea to illuminate the problem in South Vietnam.

Bundy began by surveying the postwar history of the Far East. He described the inability of the United States to prevent China from turning communist in 1949 and lamented its consequences: "[T]here came to power . . . a Communist regime . . . imbued above all with a primitive Communist ideology in its most virulent and expansionist form." Bundy then turned to the case of Korea. In Korea, the United States succeeded in foiling the expansionist plans of North Korea and its backers, China and the Soviet Union, at the cost of 150,000 American casualties and $18 billion. But South Korea remained independent. This historical sketch was necessary to understand U.S. policy toward South Vietnam, for the policy was not the result of "some abstract design from a drawing board," but rather "the fruit of history and experience." As Bundy put it:

In essence, our policy derives from (1) the fact of the Communist nations of Asia and their policies; (2) the lessons of the thirties and of Korea; (3) the logical extension of that fact and these lessons to what has happened in Southeast Asia.[3]

By the "fact of the Communist nations of Asia and their policies," Bundy meant primarily China and North Vietnam and their expansionist tendencies. The lessons of the 1930s were nested in the lessons of Korea:

In retrospect, our action in Korea reflected three elements:
  • a recognition that aggression of any sort must be met early and head-on or it will have to be met later and in tougher circumstances. We had relearned the lessons of the 1930s—Manchuria, Ethiopia, the Rhineland, Czechoslovakia.
  • a recognition that a defense line in Asia, stated in terms of an island perimeter, did not adequately define our vital interest, that those vital interests could be affected by action on the mainland of Asia.
  • an understanding that, for the future, a power vacuum was an invitation to aggression, that there must be local political, economic, and military strength in making aggression unprofitable, but also that there must be a demonstrated willingness of a major external power both to assist and to intervene if required.[4]

Applied to the problem of South Vietnam, these lessons suggested that external aggression—by North Vietnam, with the backing of China and the Soviet Union, against South Vietnam— was the issue. The stakes were vital for, if such aggression was not stopped now, it would have to be stopped later under more difficult conditions. Somewhat more implicit, there was also the suggestion that action by the United States was likely to succeed.

The aggression from the North thesis was most forcefully articulated in a white paper issued by the State Department in February 1965. The report downplayed the parallels between Vietnam and the experiences of Greece, Malaya, and the Philippines. In Greece, the report argued, the guerrillas used a friendly neighbor as a sanctuary; in Malaya, the guerrillas were physically distinguishable from the peasants; in the Philippines, the guerrillas were separated physically from their source of moral and physical support, i.e., China. None of these conditions obtained in the case of Vietnam. Korea was a better analog: "North Vietnam's commitment to seize control of the South is no less total than was the commitment of the regime in North Korea in 1950. . . . Above all, the war in Vietnam is not a spontaneous and local rebellion against the established government."[5]

William Bundy's deputy, Leonard Unger, sardonically brushed aside the suggestion that an indigenous revolt was occurring in South Vietnam: "Certainly, they [the Vietcong] are Vietnamese, and the North Koreans who swept across their boundary in 1950 to attack South Korea were also Koreans."[6] Years after he made the fateful decisions of 1965, Johnson would lecture Doris Kearns on the same point, with the same analogy:

> How . . . can you . . . say that South Vietnam is not a separate country with a traditionally recognized boundary? . . . . Oh sure, there were some Koreans in both North and South Korea who believed their country was one country, yet was there any doubt that North Korean aggression took place?[7]

A fundamental lesson of Korea was, therefore, that international communism was at work. In 1950, North Korea, with the backing of the Soviet Union (and by implication China), attempted to invade South Korea. In 1965, North Vietnam, backed by the two communist giants, was trying to take over South Vietnam. This argument fits the standard definition of analogical reasoning, which can be expressed in the form, AX:BX::AY:BY. North Korea (A) and North Vietnam (B) were similar in that both were communist states (X). North Korea (A), supported by the Soviet Union and China, tried to invade the South (action Y); therefore North Vietnam's (B) role in South Vietnam was probably backed by the same communist giants and was also just as aggressive (action Y).

The Korean analogy did not just describe the nature of the conflict in Vietnam. If aggression (on the part of the North Vietnamese) was the definition of the situation suggested by the Korean analogy, then military action (on the part of the United States) was the prescription. In 1950, the United States met North Korea "early" and "head-on." In the 1930s no one met Mussolini and Hitler early and head-on; that only postponed the reckoning until "later" and under "tougher circumstances." Applied to Vietnam, this contrast between the path of 1950 and that of the 1930s offered an unambiguous lesson: meet the North Vietnamese now lest one has to meet them later in tougher circumstances.

Implicit in the prescription of military intervention now was the prognostication of success without excessive costs. That was why the path of 1950 (Korea) was preferable to the path of the 1930s. The prediction of eventual success was one of the most attractive characteristics of the

Korean analogy. Applied to Vietnam, it implied that timely intervention by the United States was likely to succeed in preventing South Vietnam from going communist, much like U.S. intervention in Korea succeeded in foiling North Korea's attempt to conquer the South.

Moreover, if Vietnam was analogous to Korea in that Northern aggression was to blame, if the stakes were as vital, and if U.S. intervention was likely to work, then it could be argued that the United States was obligated to help South Vietnam.[8] In other words, underlying the picture given by the Korean analogy also stood a strong normative invocation: it was morally right for the United States to come to the help of South Vietnam.[9] The policy implication of these public lessons of Korea is not hard to deduce: if necessary, the United States would intervene to keep South Vietnam independent.

THE USES OF THE ANALOGIES: DIAGNOSIS, JUSTIFICATION, AND ADVOCACY

Relying on the public statements of policy makers to document what they learned from the U.S. experience in the Korean War and how they applied those lessons to Vietnam is an appropriate point of departure. However, we must do more than that if we want to claim that the Korean analogy influenced the decision outcome. For focusing only on the public analogies makes us susceptible to the following objections: What if the policy makers did not take the Korean and other analogies they used seriously? What if the analogies were used primarily for justifying and advocating policy instead of analyzing it? These are legitimate objections. If officials used analogies only to convince the public and to justify the wisdom and moral rightness of their policies, then examining their analogies amounts to a study of political rhetoric. To make this analysis more than a study of political rhetoric, it is necessary to make a distinction between analogies used in public and those used in private. If analogies were used to persuade the public, then they ought not to show up frequently in the documents and the private deliberations of the policy makers. The opposite, however, was true. As will be seen later, references to historical analogies abound in the documents and the deliberations of the period. This should allow us to be more confident about the claim that analogies were not simply used for justification but that they played important diagnostic roles.

Still, it might be argued that even those historical analogies used in private were used for advocacy, not diagnosis. An experienced bureaucrat might latch onto a salient analogy to advocate a particular policy even though he might not believe in that analogy. Analogies, in this view, are used to prop up decisions that the policy maker has already made. That is possible. The three uses of analogies—justification, policy advocacy, and diagnosis—need not be mutually exclusive. Indeed, in practice, these uses are probably difficult to separate. The policy maker who, say, used the Korean analogy to inform his diagnosis of the stakes in Vietnam would have no problems using the same analogy to justify or advocate his preferred policy. For the purposes of our analysis, it can be readily granted that some policy advocacy and justification might be at work when a policy maker uses an analogy. What is important to my case is that we also allow for the possibility that the analogy may also be used for diagnosis. Once this is allowed, an analysis of a policy maker's analogies is simultaneously an analysis of his decision making.

It is the policy maker who used analogies he personally did not believe in to justify or advocate a particular policy that poses a problem for my analysis. In such cases, analyzing their analogies is tantamount to analyzing epiphenomena. One might learn something about the properties of analogies that make them such attractive tools of persuasion—not an unimportant task—but one is unlikely to unveil the reasoning behind their decisions. If, however, policy makers believed in the analogies they used, their using the same analogies for advocacy and public justification need not detract from the diagnostic role that the analogies may have played in their decision making. A study of those analogies can be one way to probe the reasoning behind their decisions.

Three arguments are offered in defense of the assumption that the United States' Vietnam decision makers believed in the analogies they used. First, it is the simpler and more parsimonious assumption. One need not document deceitful or manipulative practices on the part of the policy makers, as the public persuasion and private advocacy theses must. At the least, the latter must document inconsistencies between the analogies used by policy makers and their true beliefs. This is difficult to do. Moreover, since both the justification and advocacy theses focus on how a policy maker sells his favored option, they beg the question of how he came to favor that option. It is consequently simpler to assume that the policy maker took his analogies seriously: it gives an indication of how he arrived at his decision and it also explains why he might use the analogies to sell his policy.

Second, there is overwhelming evidence that those who formulated U.S. Vietnam policy were serious about the analogies they used. The memoirs and private papers of many of the principals indicate that they used basically the same analogies in public and in private to make sense of the situation in Vietnam. For example, Robert McNamara has written that one reason why he pressured President Johnson to call up the reserves in 1965 was because he believed that the reserves played a critical role in resolving the Berlin crisis of 1961.[10] Also, when asked whether they believed in the analogies they used, the former policy makers, virtually to a man, asserted that they did.[11] Dean Rusk, for example, spoke of "advocacy with integrity" and challenged his critics to find "any instance where I thought one thing and said another."[12]

It would be unusual, it could be claimed, for former policy makers to say anything other than that they were serious about the analogies they used 25 years ago. Yet it is possible to perform a check. A policy maker who used an analogy for advocacy without believing in it would grab the most effective analogy to bolster his preferred option. There need be no correlation between the most effective analogy and his personal experience. Yet the most avid users of historical analogies almost always invoked parallels with which they were most familiar. Lyndon Johnson and Dean Rusk, for example, were both deeply affected by the Korean War. As a senator, Johnson was extremely moved by Truman's decisiveness in responding to the attack by North Korea against the South; Rusk, after all, was the person who designated the 38th parallel as the dividing line between North and South Korea. Johnson would always remember how Truman protected U.S. vital interests in Asia; Rusk would subsequently be uncompromising toward those bent on crossing designated "boundaries."[13] Finally, George Ball, who had worked closely with the French, was much more attuned than his colleagues to the similarities between the U.S. and the French experiences in Vietnam. Ball was so convinced of the relevance of the French parallel—and its implications—that he continued to use the analogy even when it was obvious that the analogy was not the most effective tool for advocating his preferred policy.[14]

Perhaps the strongest argument in favor of the "they believed in the analogies they used" assumption is to be found in cognitive psychology. Recent findings in cognitive psychology—schema theory to be precise—suggest that a major way human beings make sense of new situations is through analogical reasoning.[15] Comprehension, in other words, is to a significant extent an analogical enterprise. Human beings make sense of new experience through schemas, "the building blocks of cognition" or "a generic concept stored in memory, referring to objects, situations, events or people."[16] For example, policy makers may abstract from the events of the 1930s—aggressive fascism, appeasement, general war—and other similar incidents to form a schema: "aggression unchallenged is aggression unleashed."[17] Policy makers with this Munich schema stored in their memory will match new incidents (e.g., Ho Chi Minh's attempts to "reunify" North and South Vietnam) against the schema; they are likely to process incoming information, especially if it is ambiguous, in terms of the Munich schema.[18] In other words, the notion of the schema provides independent corroboration for the assumptions that policy makers take their analogies seriously and that they also often rely on them to make sense of their external environment. In the next section, I examine how some of the principal decision makers relied on analogies in private to make sense of the challenge in Vietnam.

THE PRIVATE LESSONS OF KOREA

On the fourth day after Congress passed the Tonkin Gulf resolution, William Bundy began contemplating the "Next Courses of Action in Southeast Asia." A few days later, the chairman of the Joint Chiefs of Staff sent a memorandum with the same title to the secretary of defense. Armed with the resolution, administration officials were ready to do more to "convince Hanoi that they were facing a determined foe and that they should get out of South Vietnam and Laos."[19] In the months of August to October 1964, a consensus was developing among Johnson's advisers that "doing more" meant going beyond reprisals against specific acts by Hanoi; the idea of launching a systematic air war against North Vietnam became increasingly popular.[20] It was in this context that George Ball wrote a long memorandum on October 5, 1964, in which he expressed his "skeptical thoughts on the assumptions of our Viet-nam policy" to Dean Rusk, Robert McNamara, and McGeorge Bundy.[21]

Titled "How valid are the assumptions underlying our Vietnam policies," this document has been hailed by later analysts as "remarkable" and "prescient."[22] Two successive Saturday afternoons were reserved to debate the issues raised by Ball. When it became obvious after the first meeting that Ball's arguments had not made the slightest dent on his superiors' convictions, the second meeting was cancelled.[23] Five months later, the memorandum reached the president's desk. Johnson demanded to know why he had not seen it earlier. A meeting was called to discuss Ball's arguments and Johnson "showed that he had read the document, for he challenged specific points [Ball] . . . made and even remembered the page numbers where those arguments occurred."[24]

Ball's memorandum began with the observation that the political situation in Saigon was going from bad to worse. It was obvious that "[w]ithin the next few weeks, we must face a major decision of national policy." As Ball saw it, the United States had four options. The first option was to continue to support the South Vietnamese effort, in full realization that it might not be enough. The second option was to take over the war in South Vietnam by introducing U.S. troops. Third, the United States could bomb the North in hope of forcing them to stop supporting the Southern insurgency. Bombing might also improve the U.S. bargaining position, making possible a political solution through negotiation. The fourth option was a political settlement through negotiation but without direct U.S. military involvement.

Through a comprehensive analysis that considered the effectiveness and the likely costs of each of the options, Ball dismissed the first three and came out in favor of the fourth. The first two options were not serious possibilities. Option one, it was widely acknowledged, would not be enough to prevent the collapse of South Vietnam. Option two, introducing ground troops, was something everyone was keen to postpone for the moment. The main purpose of Ball's memorandum, therefore, was to question the assumptions of those who favored option three. The most important of these assumptions, if Ball's memo is any indication, was the belief that the Korean and Vietnam conflicts were analogous.

In the foreword of the memorandum and under the subheading "South Viet-nam is Not Korea," Ball warned: "In approaching this problem, I want to emphasize one key point at the outset: The problem of South Viet-nam is *sui generis*. South Viet-nam is not Korea, and in making fundamental decisions it would be a mistake for us to rely too heavily on the Korean analogy."[25] He then went on to list five principal differences between the U.S. position in South Vietnam in 1964 and the U.S. position in Korea in 1951:

a. We were in South Korea under a clear United Nations mandate. Our presence in South Viet-nam depends upon the continuing request of the GVN plus the SEATO protocol.
b. At their peak, United Nations forces in South Korea (other than ours and those of the ROK) included 53,000 infantrymen and 1000 other troops provided by fifty-three nations. In Vietnam, we are doing it alone with no substantial help from any other country.
c. In 1950, the Korean government under Syngman Rhee was stable. It had the general support of the principal elements in the country. There was little factional fighting and jockeying for power. In South Viet-nam, we face governmental chaos.
d. The Korean War started only two years after Korean independence. The Korean people were still excited by their newfound freedom; they were fresh for the war. In contrast, the people of Indochina have been fighting for almost twenty years—first against the French, then for the last ten against the NVN. All evidence points to the fact that they are tired of conflict.
e. Finally, the Korean War started with a massive land invasion by 100,000 troops. This was a classical type of invasion across an established border. It was so reported within twelve hours by the United Nations Commission on the spot. It gave us an unassailable political and legal base for counteraction.

In South Viet-nam, there has been no invasion—only slow infiltration. Insurgency is by its nature ambiguous. The Viet Cong insurgency does have substantial indigenous support. Americans know that the insurgency is actively directed and supported by Hanoi, but the rest of the world is not so sure. The testimony of the ICC has been fuzzy on this point—and we have been unable to disclose our most solid evidence for fear of compromising intelligence sources.

As a result, many nations remain unpersuaded that Hanoi is the principal source of the revolt. And, as the weakness of the Saigon Government becomes more and more evident, an increasing number of governments will be inclined to believe that the Viet Cong insurgency is, in fact, an internal rebellion.[26]

Ball's analysis questioned the diagnoses and moral sanction provided by the Korean analogy. There had been no invasion in South Vietnam, Ball claimed. The Vietcong enjoyed substantial indigenous support. Ball came close to saying that the Vietnam conflict was an internal rebellion.[27] Adherents to the Korean analogy were inclined to discount the indigenous support enjoyed by the Vietcong. From the president down to William Bundy, the problem in South Vietnam was diagnosed as Northern communist aggression; the Vietcong's tactics might be different from those of the North Koreans, but they were basically similar in their aggressive designs on the South.

For Ball, a United Nations mandate and non-U.S. troops accorded an international legitimacy to the U.S. role in Korea. The absence of a similar mandate and support for the United States in Vietnam raised questions about the moral legitimacy of a U.S. counteraction against North Vietnam. A less direct but very prescient attack against a third lesson of Korea was Ball's point about the absence of a Syngman Rhee in South Vietnam. That the United States succeeded in Korea was partially attributable to Rhee and the stability his government enjoyed; the governmental chaos in South Vietnam throughout 1964 implied that success was probably most difficult in Vietnam.

If the differences outlined above between Korea and Vietnam were political, dissimilarities that Ball identified later in his memorandum focused on military strategy. Bombing North Vietnam, Ball argued, was unlikely to reduce Hanoi's support for the Southern insurgency. In fact, the North Vietnamese were likely to retaliate by sending substantially more ground forces into South Vietnam. Since the United States could not "counter [North Vietnamese] ground forces by air power alone, as we quickly learned in Korea," it was important that "we should remember that in South Vietnam the nature of the terrain reduces the premium on modern firepower and logistic equipment even more than it did in Korea." In short, an air offensive by the United States against the North was likely to lead to a series of escalatory measures terminating in the introduction of U.S. land forces.

Ball then went on to worry about protracted fighting on the ground.

China might intervene and U.S. forces would begin to take substantial casualties:

> At this point, we should certainly expect mounting pressure for the use of at least tactical nuclear weapons. The American people would not again accept the frustrations and anxieties that resulted from our abstention from nuclear combat in Korea.
>
> The rationalization of a departure from the self-denying ordinance of Korea would be that we did not have battlefield nuclear weapons in 1950— yet we do have them today.[28]

Unlike in 1951, the United States in 1964 would be less willing to tolerate heavy casualties; also unlike in 1951, it would be more difficult for the United States to resist using tactical nuclear weapons. Ball was not speculating in the abstract. It was known that a segment of the military was uninterested in fighting the North Vietnamese Korea-style. As a working group of the Joint Chiefs of Staff put it in November 1964, "Certainly no responsible person proposes to go about such a war [against the North Vietnamese and Chinese], if it should occur, on a basis remotely resembling Korea. 'Possibly even the use of nuclear weapons at some point' is of course why we spend billions to have them."[29] It was precisely this kind of reasoning that worried Ball. The use of tactical nuclear weapons in Asia was unacceptable to him because he believed it would damage the U.S. world position. The United States would be accused of using nuclear weapons only against Asians.

Toward the end of Part One of the memorandum, Ball came back to his theme that South Vietnam was not another Korea: "As has been repeatedly pointed out in this memorandum, the issues in Indochina are not clearly defined, as they were in Korea." Again, in arguing against those who wanted to bomb the North to the negotiating table, Ball sought to slight the Korean analogy:

> Let me reiterate once more that Indochina is not Korea. In bombing North Viet-nam, we would *not* be seeking to stop massive and overt aggression south of the Yalu River on behalf of the UN. We would appear instead to be a great power raining destruction on a small power because we accused that small power of instigating what much of the world would quite wrongly regard as an indigenous rebellion.[30]

But who really thought that Vietnam was another Korea? "Practically everybody," was Ball's answer in an interview conducted in 1986. Ball elaborated on the theme:

> After all in 1961, when we got involved in this thing, it hadn't been many years since we were in Korea. Naturally the Korea business over-

hung everything and it was easy for people to say, well, look we fought the Korean war at some cost, we prevailed, nowadays there is a similar challenge in the same part of the world, how could we not pick this challenge up?[31]

In his memoirs, Johnson intimated that "[w]hen a President faces a decision involving war or peace, he draws back and thinks of the past and of the future in the widest possible terms."[32] To be sure, Johnson was informed by many lessons of many pasts, but Korea preoccupied him.[33] Perhaps he was inspired by Truman's decisiveness in June 1950, perhaps their geographical proximity made it easy to link Vietnam and Korea together, or perhaps Korea was the last major war fought—and won, according to elite opinion in the mid-1950s—by the United States.[34] Whatever it was that attracted Johnson to the Korean precedent, a major lesson he drew was that the United States made a mistake in withdrawing from Korea in June 1949; it emboldened the communists, forcing the United States to return to Korea one year later to save the South. He was not disposed toward repeating the same mistake in Vietnam.[35]

Dean Rusk was the other firm believer in the Korean analogy. According to his former deputy, Rusk "was enormously impressed by the analogy of Korea because he had been deeply engaged himself in the Korean War." Rusk was "convinced that what he had done in Korea was a good thing to do and we had finally won in Korea and therefore by applying enough effort and enough time we should be able to prevail in Vietnam as we had in Korea. . . ."[36] Yet, according to Ball:

> I don't want to suggest that he was over-simplified in any sense but he was very much impressed. As he used to say to me why do you take such a gloomy view of the prospects? We had very bad patches in Korea and we finally came through and I think this was a sustaining thought on his part. He saw this fundamentally as an extension of—an attempt on the part of the major communist powers to extend their influence in Southeast Asia. He never recognized that this was fundamentally a Tonkinese initiative and that it was a local conflict and that the great power involvement was peripheral rather than fundamental. . . . [H]e saw the role of North Vietnam fundamentally as an extension of the role of the Chinese and Soviets. This was something which I continually challenged but nevertheless, he has never gotten over the view that this was like the Korean War and that as he has said, the only qualification that he has ever publicly said since then is that he underestimated the staying power of . . . the North Vietnamese.[37]

Based on Ball's account, the Korean analogy was instructive to Rusk because it suggested that the challenge in South Vietnam was similar to the challenge in South Korea. Just as communist expansionism—backed by China and the Soviet Union—threatened South Korea's political independence in 1950, it was threatening South Vietnam's political independence in the 1960s. Both were cases of unlawful communist aggression against viable political regimes. Rusk's public statements reinforced the seriousness with which he took the comparison:

> The fact that the demarcation line between North and South Viet-nam was intended to be temporary does not make the assault on South Viet-nam any less of an aggression. The demarcation lines between North and South Korea and between East and West Germany are temporary. But that did not make the North Korean invasion of South Korea a permissible use of force.[38]

As noted earlier, Ball's memorandum challenged Rusk's reliance on the Korean analogy to diagnose the nature of the conflict in Vietnam. Ball pointed out that, in South Vietnam, there was no invasion, only slow infiltration; moreover, the insurgency had substantial indigenous support. This and other differences that Ball tried to point out were regarded by Rusk, McNamara, and McGeorge Bundy as "nuances" that did not negate the basic similarities between communist aggression in Korea and Vietnam.[39] Similarly, Rusk's assistant secretary for Far Eastern affairs, William Bundy, once asked a subordinate to draft a speech that would, among other things, "dispose of the canard that the Vietnam conflict was a civil war." When the aide replied, "But in some ways, of course, it is a civil war," Bundy reportedly snapped, "Don't play word games with me!"[40]

Rusk's suggestion-by-analogy that North Vietnam's "assault" against South Vietnam was as impermissible a use of force as North Korea's attack against South Korea illustrates the normative power of the diagnosis provided by the Korean analogy. McGeorge Bundy found this normative lesson of the Korean analogy particularly instructive. For Bundy, it was just for the United States to help South Korea repel the North Korean invasion in 1950. North Vietnam's infiltration of South Vietnam was also an act of aggression; as such, it was also just for the United States to help the South Vietnamese against the North.[41]

Even more important than serving as a diagnostic or evaluative aid, the Korean analogy suggested to Dean Rusk and to those around him that, despite bad spells, the United States could still succeed in Vietnam. As the above passages show, Ball believed that this had a strong impact on Dean Rusk. Rusk does not deny this. According to Rusk, things looked very dark for the South Koreans and the United States when they were driven to Pusan by the North Koreans. "We did not quickly come to the conclusion that it was hopeless. This influenced our thinking about Vietnam to a degree."[42] This is hardly surprising. Given his experience with the Korean War—the most recent conflict in his memory, in the same part of the world—it was reasonable to compare Vietnam with Korea. It would have been unusual for him or anyone for that matter to have refrained from consulting his previous experiences to assess the situation in Vietnam.

Despite Ball's systematic isolation of the key differences between Vietnam and Korea, despite his worry that his superiors might rely too heavily on the Korean analogy in making decisions about Vietnam, there was one lesson that he shared with them. And that was not to provoke China, lest it intervene on behalf of North Vietnam as it intervened on behalf of North Korea in 1950. Ball dealt at length with this possibility. Although the most recent Special National Intelligence Estimate (SNIE) concluded that China was "unlikely" to intervene—by ground or by air—even in face of sustained U.S. air attacks against North Vietnam, Ball argued that "we would be imprudent to undertake escalation without assuming that there was a *fair chance* that China would intervene. We made a contrary assumption in Korea in October 1950 with highly unfortunate consequences." He then cited liberally from a book detailing the conversation between President Truman and General MacArthur regarding the possibility of Chinese intervention in Korea. The point of the passage was that, despite MacArthur's assurances, China did cross the Yalu.[43]

Johnson's memoirs indicate that he was mindful of this lesson each time he contemplated using force against the North Vietnamese.[44] Ball's passage about the Truman-MacArthur exchange had an impact on Johnson; as will be seen shortly, Johnson would replay the Truman-MacArthur conversation "with a difference" in two crucial meetings with his advisers. The "China crosses the Yalu" syndrome also had a profound impact on Dean Rusk. Rusk was contrite about his failure to forecast China's intervention in the Korean War; he was determined to avoid repeating the mistake in Vietnam.[45] William Sullivan, chairman of the Vietnam Working Group charged with planning the possible escalation of the Vietnam War in early 1964, believed that the Korean analogy played a crucial role in constraining United States military strategy:

> In several instances the precedent of the Korean conflict was evoked to suggest that China would become directly involved in ground combat if United States forces were to strike north of the [17th] parallel. I believed that the prevalence of such a conviction played a major role in determining how the war was actually fought.[46]

The private lessons that Johnson and his advisers drew from Korea and applied to Vietnam may be summarized as follows: South Vietnam and South Korea were analogous in terms of the threat they faced— Northern aggression; the stakes (for the United States) in both countries were high, and in both cases it was morally and legally right to assist in their resistance against aggression. In other words, the Korean analogy was used in private to help define the nature of the problem in Vietnam and to assess the stakes of the conflict. It also affirmed the morality of the U.S. position.

Thus the policy makers seemed to affirm in private what they said in public. Two other lessons that were implicit in the public use of the Korean analogy became explicit in private. One was the prediction that, as in Korea, the United States would eventually convince the communists that victory was not possible. The second was the lesson of MacArthur: if the United States pushed the North Vietnamese too hard, the Chinese might intervene as they did when MacArthur carried the war to North Korea. That the public lessons of Korea echoed the private reasoning of the Johnson administration suggests that the Korean analogy was not merely used for public justification; the analogy did inform the thinking of the principal policy makers.

THE FEBRUARY AND JULY DECISIONS

The two most important decisions of the Vietnam war were made in 1965. In February, in the face of the deteriorating situation in South Vietnam, Lyndon Johnson was asked to decide whether to launch a major air war against North Vietnam. Five months later, in face of the imminent collapse of South Vietnam, Johnson was asked to decide whether to launch a ground war in South Vietnam with 100,000 U.S. troops. Assuming that Johnson and his advisers took the Korea-Vietnam analogy seriously, it does not take much to deduce that they were likely to decide in favor of intervention. In what follows, I shall attempt something more interesting and demanding: I shall demonstrate the relevance of the Korean analogy in Vietnam decision making by using it to explain the actual options selected. This requires the Korean analogy to explain decision outcomes at a very specific or concrete level—it must not only be able to distinguish between prointervention and anti-intervention options, it should also be able to suggest, between prointervention options, the one more likely to be chosen. If the Korean analogy passes this demanding test, it acquires added explanatory power; it also adds to the stock of evidence that the analogy played a critical role in the decision-making process. The context of the 1965 decisions needs to be clarified before this test is performed.

Neither Ball's October 5, 1964, nor his subsequent memoranda had much effect on the proponents of escalation. Secretary of Defense McNamara thought that Ball was acting with "reckless disloyalty in . . . putting these kinds of thoughts in print in raising the questions."[47] When the president called his principal advisers in to discuss Ball's memorandum on February 24, 1965, McNamara again "responded with a pyrotechnic display of facts and statistics to prove that [Ball] . . . overstated the difficulties . . . and suggesting at least by nuance, that [Ball] . . . was not only prejudiced but ill-informed."[48]

As the situation in South Vietnam grew progressively worse through the fall of 1964, the (William) Bundy Working Group on Vietnam went through successive drafts of "New Courses of Action in Southeast Asia." By late November, the group had settled on three options. Option A was "to continue present policies indefinitely." This meant providing "maximum assistance within South Vietnam"—strengthening the pacification program, improving the police program, the economic program, etc.—but excluding the introduction of U.S. combat troops or a "United States taking over of command." Limited actions in Laos (Ho Chi Minh Trail) and covert actions by the South Vietnamese against the North would also be included, as would specific reprisals by the United States against "VC 'spectaculars' such as Bien Hoa."

Option B "would add to present actions a systematic program of military pressures [i.e., air attacks] against the North, with increasing pressure for actions to be continued at a fairly rapid pace and without interruption" until U.S. objectives were obtained. Option C differed from B in terms of the pace and scale of the air attacks: "The military scenario should give the impression of a steady deliberate approach," beginning with "graduated military moves against infiltration targets, first in Laos and then in the DRV, and then against other targets in North Vietnam." Under option C, the air war against North Vietnam would be slow-paced and more cautious.[49]

Negotiations would play no role under option A or B and a minor role under option C. As the authors of the paper put it, "[b]asic to this option [A] is the continued rejection of negotiations." Option B would approach negotiations "with absolutely inflexible insistence on our present objectives." Option C, which would include an "orchestration of . . . communications with Hanoi and/or Peiping," and "indicating from the outset a willingness to negotiate" seemed to take negotiations more seriously until the "early negotiating actions" were specified. The United States would insist on three fundamentals: "(a) that the DRV cease its assistance to and direction of the VC; (b) that an independent and secure GVN be re-established; and (c) that there be adequate international supervising and verification machinery."[50] These were precisely the same "present objectives" about which option B was to be "absolutely inflexible." If these "objectives" or "fundamentals" were to be "insisted on" by option C as well, then negotiations would seem improbable. The United States gave up nothing; the DRV was expected to give up the very things they were fighting for.

After a long National Security Council meeting on December 1, option B was dropped. Options A and C were renamed Phase I and Phase II, respectively, suggesting that they were to be conceived of as stages in a two-part plan.[51] A February 7, 1965, memorandum written by McGeorge Bundy after he witnessed the results of a Vietcong attack on the Pleiku barracks in South Vietnam started a reluctant Johnson on the path of approving option C (now known as Phase II and later code-named "Operation Rolling Thunder"). McGeorge Bundy painted a grim picture: the situation in Vietnam was deteriorating and, without new United States action, defeat seemed inevitable within a year. There was not much time to turn things around. "The [U.S.] stakes in Vietnam," according to Bundy, were "extremely high." The chances of success, defined as "changing the course of the contest in Vietnam," were estimated to be between 25 percent and 75 percent.[52]

On February 10, the Vietcong attacked the U.S. barracks in Qui Nhon, killing 23 U.S. servicemen. Three days later, President Johnson formally approved option C. Turmoil within the South Vietnamese government made it impossible for the United States to obtain the pro forma approval from the Vietnamese authorities until nearly two weeks later. On March 2, option C, now code-named "Operation Rolling Thunder," was launched.

Sustained bombing of North Vietnam failed to change the course of the contest in Vietnam. Morale in South Vietnam did improve but it was temporary. Most observers agree that with the decision to bomb North Vietnam, the United States had crossed the Rubicon. George Kahin also argues, plausibly I believe, that another Rubicon had been crossed, this time in Hanoi. Hitherto, Hanoi had sent military, technical, and supply cadres—mostly former Southerners—into South Vietnam. Hanoi had refrained from sending regular combat units into South Vietnam for fear of instigating the United States into escalating the conflict. The launching of Operation Rolling Thunder, according to Kahin, "removed the constraints that had previously kept Hanoi from sending its own ground combat units into the South."[53]

It was the Vietcong, however, who dealt a series of catastrophic defeats to the ARVN (South Vietnamese Army) during the summer of 1965. In May, a regiment-sized Vietcong unit decimated two ARVN battalions. U.S. officers who witnessed the battle "went away with the distinct impression that the RVNAF were close to collapse." In June, another battalion of ARVN's finest reserves were decimated at Dong Xoai.[54] "The Viet Cong," according to General Westmoreland, were "destroying battalions faster than they can be reconstituted and faster than they were planned to be organized under the buildup program."[55] Moreover, Westmoreland continued, North Vietnam's 325th and 304th Divisions were either already in South Vietnam or close enough to reinforce the Vietcong. In light of this situation, he saw "no course of action open to us except to reinforce our efforts in SVN with additional United States or Third Country forces as rapidly as is practicable during the critical weeks ahead." Westmoreland asked for 32,000 additional U.S. ground troops, with the caveat that more might be required later. By late June 1965, the request was increased to 100,000 or 44 battalions.[56]

Confronted with Westmoreland's request, President Johnson sent Robert McNamara once again to Vietnam to assess the situation and to obtain some answers that he, the president, wanted. Should the United States intervene to "prevent the loss of Southeast Asia" to "aggressive forces moving illegally across international frontiers?" Would United States forces be effective fighting the Vietcong in unfamiliar terrain? Would "non-Vietnamese fighting men revive memories of the French colonial years and arouse anti-foreign sentiments?"[57] On his return from South Vietnam, Secretary McNamara answered the first two questions in the affirmative in a July 20 memorandum to the president. The third question was not answered. More important, McNamara painted an even bleaker picture of the situation in South Vietnam than McGeorge Bundy did six months earlier. "The situation in South Vietnam is worse than a year ago (when it was worse than a year before that)." Despite the bombing campaign, the South Vietnamese government "is liable to provide security to fewer and fewer people in less and less territory." As such, the "DRV/VC seem to believe that SVN is on the run and near collapse; they show no signs of settling for less than complete takeover."

The United States could do one of three things. The first option, "cut our losses and withdraw under the best conditions that can be arranged," was certain to humiliate the United States and damage its future effectiveness on the world scene. The second option, "continue at about the present level," suffered from the disadvantage that as the U.S. position weakened, it would "almost certainly confront us later with a choice between withdrawal and an emergency expansion of forces, perhaps too late to do any good." It should not come as a surprise, then, that McNamara recommended the third option: "Expand promptly and substantially the United States military pressure against the VC in the South. . . . This . . . would stave off defeat in the short run and offer a good chance of producing a favorable settlement in the longer run." Thus the memorandum's answers to Johnson's first two questions were, yes, substantial U.S. forces—100,000 by October, perhaps another 100,000 in early 1966—were necessary to prevent a takeover and, yes, with these soldiers the United States has, in the concluding sentence of the memorandum, "a good chance of achieving an acceptable outcome within a reasonable time in Vietnam."[58]

The next day, July 21, President Johnson met with his advisers to consider McNamara's recommendations. The most complete account of these meetings, drawing on three largely similar accounts, has been assembled by George Kahin. As he explains: "There are three records of this [meeting]: an unsigned account from the NSC files rendered in abbreviated, semiverbatim style; the slightly less comprehensive but apparently verbatim record of the president's aide Jack Valenti; and the extensive and more inclusive summary by Cooper . . . . The three accounts are here woven together, relying as much as possible on Valenti's generally more detailed version, but closing its gaps with appropriate passages from the other two." The account provided below is Kahin's, with some extraneous passages deleted and cross-checked with original sources.[59]

Present at this meeting were: McGeorge Bundy, Chester Cooper, Jack Valenti, and Horace Busby from the White House; Rusk, Ball, William Bundy, ambassador to South Vietnam Henry Cabot Lodge; ambassador to Thailand Leonard Unger from the State Department; McNamara, Vance, McNaughton from the Defense Department; General Wheeler, chairman of the Joint Chiefs of Staff; Admiral Raborn and Richard Helms of the Central Intelligence Agency; and Leonard Marks and Carl Rowan of the U.S. Information Agency. The president began with some substantive questions:

PRESIDENT: What I would like to know is what has happened in recent months that requires this kind of decision on my part. What are the alternatives? I want this discussed in full detail, from everyone around this table. Have we wrung every single soldier out of every country that we can? Who else can help us here? Are we the sole defenders in the world? Have we done all we can in this direction? What are the compelling reasons for this call-up? What results can we expect? Again, I ask you what are the alternatives? I don't want us to make snap judgments. I want us to consider all our options. We know we can tell the South Vietnamese we are coming home. Is that the option we should take? What would flow from that? The negotiations, the pause, all the other approaches we have explored, are these enough? Should we try others?

[Cooper account]

McNamara discussed the situation: the VC has greatly expanded its control of the country, populous areas are now isolated, both the VC and ARVN have been suffering heavy casualties. Unless the United States steps in with additional forces, the VC will push the GVN into small enclaves and become increasingly ineffective. The VC now controls about 25 percent of the population. (CIA Director Raborn estimated that the VC controlled about 25 percent of the population during the day and about 50 percent at night.) A year ago, the VC controlled less than 20 percent.

The President felt that our mission should be as limited as we dare make it. General Wheeler agreed, but felt that we should engage in offensive operations to seek out and fight the VC main force units. Although this is difficult because of lack of tactical intelligence we know where these base areas are.

Director Raborn reported the CIA's estimate that the VC will avoid major confrontations with United States forces and concentrate on destroying our LOCs (lines of communication) and on guerrilla war generally. General Wheeler felt that the VC will have to "come out and fight" and that this will probably take place in the highlands where they will probably attempt to establish a government seat.

[Valenti account]

BALL: Isn't it possible that the VC will do what they did against the French—stay away from confrontation and not accommodate us?

WHEELER: Yes, that is possible, but by constantly harassing them, they will have to fight somewhere.

McNAMARA: If the VC doesn't fight in large units, it will give the ARVN a chance to resecure hostile areas. We don't know what VC tactics will be when the VC is confronted by 175,000 Americans.

RABORN: We agree. By 1965's end, we expect NVN (North Vietnam) to increase its forces. It will attempt to gain a substantial victory before our buildup is complete.

PRESIDENT: Is anyone here of the opinion we should not do what the memorandum says? If so, I want to hear from them now, in detail.

BALL: Mr. President, I can foresee a perilous voyage, very dangerous. I have great and grave apprehensions that we can win under these conditions. But let me be clear. If the decision is to go ahead, I am committed.

PRESIDENT: But, George, is there another course in the national interest that is better than the one McNamara proposes? We know it is dangerous and perilous, but the big question is, can it be avoided?

BALL: There is no course that will allow us to cut our losses. If we get bogged down, our cost might be substantially greater. The pressures to create a larger war would be irresistible. The qualifications I have are not due to the fact that I think we are in a bad moral position.

PRESIDENT: Tell me then, what other road can I go?

BALL: Take what precautions we can, Mr. President. Take our losses, let their government fall apart, negotiate, discuss, knowing full well there will be a probable takeover by the Communists. This is disagreeable, I know.

PRESIDENT: I can take disagreeable decisions. But I want to know can we make a case for your thoughts? Can we discuss it fully?

BALL: We have discussed it. I have had my day in court.

PRESIDENT: I don't think we have made any full commitment, George. You have pointed out the danger, but you haven't really proposed an alternative course. We haven't always been right. We have no mortgage on victory. Right now, I am concerned that we have very little alternative to what we are doing. I want another meeting, more meetings, before we take any definitive action. We must look at all other courses of possibility carefully. Right now I feel it would be more dangerous to lose this now, than endanger a greater number of troops. I want this fully discussed.

RUSK: What we have done since 1954 to 1961 has not been good enough. We should have probably committed ourselves heavier in 1961.

ROWAN: What bothers me most is the weakness of the Ky government. Unless we put the screws on the Ky government, 175,000 men will do us no good.

LODGE: There is not a tradition of a national government in Saigon. There are no roots in the country. Not until there is tranquillity can you have any stability. I don't think we ought to take this government seriously. There is simply no one who can do anything. We have to do what we think we ought to do regardless of what the Saigon government does. As we move ahead on a new phase, we have the right and the duty to do certain things with or without the government's approval.

PRESIDENT: George, do you think we have another course?

BALL: I would not recommend that you follow McNamara's course.

PRESIDENT: Are you able to outline your doubts? Can you offer another course of action? I think it's desirable to hear you out, truly hear you out, then I can determine if your suggestions are sound and ready to be followed, which I am prepared to do if I am convinced.

BALL: Yes, Mr. President. I think I can present to you the least bad of two courses. What I would present is a course that is costly, but can be limited to short-term costs.

PRESIDENT: Alright, let's meet again at 2:30 this afternoon to discuss George's proposals. Meanwhile, let Bob tell us why we need to risk all these Americans' lives. I don't choose to do that casually.

McNamara and Wheeler proceeded to outline the reasons for more troops. Essentially, they said, 75,000 men [the number of U.S. troops already in South Vietnam at the time of the NSC meeting] are just enough to protect the bases. The extra men, they insisted, would stabilize the situation, and then improve it. It also would give the ARVN a breathing space, they said. We would limit the incursion of more troops to 100,000 because it might not be possible to absorb more in South Vietnam at this time. . . .

PRESIDENT: It seems to me that you will lose a greater number of men. I don't like that.

WHEELER: Not precisely true, Mr. President. The more men we have there, the greater the likelihood of smaller losses.

PRESIDENT: Tell me this. What will happen if we put 100,000 more men and then two, three years later you tell me you need 500,000 more? How would you expect me to respond to that? And what makes you think if we put in 100,000 men, Ho Chi Minh won't put in another 100,000, and match us every bit of the way?

WHEELER: This means greater bodies of men from North Vietnam, which will allow us to cream them.

PRESIDENT: But what are the chances of more North Vietnamese soldiers coming in?

WHEELER: About a fifty-fifty chance. The North would be foolhardy to put one-quarter of their forces in SVN. It would expose them too greatly in the North.

. . .

[Valenti account—2:30 p.m., July 21]

PRESIDENT: Alright, George.

BALL: We cannot win, Mr. President. This war will be long and protracted. The most we can hope for is a messy conclusion. There remains a great danger of intrusion by the Chinese. But the biggest problem is the problem of the long war. The Korean experience was a galling one. The correlation between Korean casualties and public opinion showed support stabilized at 50 percent. As casualties increase, the pressure to strike at the very jugular of North Vietnam will become very great. I am concerned about world opinion. If we could win in a year's time, and win decisively, world opinion would be alright. However, if the war is long and protracted, as I believe it will be, then we will suffer because the world's greatest power cannot defeat guerrillas. Then there is the problem of national politics. Every great captain in history was not afraid to make a tactical withdrawal if conditions were unfavorable to him. The enemy cannot even be seen in Vietnam. He is indigenous to the country. I truly have serious doubt that an army of westerners can successfully fight orientals in an Asian jungle.

PRESIDENT: This is important. Can westerners, in the absence of accurate intelligence, successfully fight Asians in jungle rice paddies? I want McNamara and General Wheeler to seriously ponder this question.

BALL: I think we all have underestimated the seriousness of this situation. It is like giving cobalt treatment to a terminal cancer case. I think a long, protracted war will disclose our weakness, not our strength. The least harmful way to cut losses in SVN is to let the government decide it doesn't want us to stay there. Therefore, we should put such proposals to the GVN that they can't accept. Then, it would move to a neutralist position. I have no illusions that after we were asked to leave South Vietnam, that country would soon come under Hanoi control. What about Thailand? It would be our main problem. Thailand has proven a good ally so far, though history shows it has never been a staunch ally. If we wanted to make a stand in Thailand, we might be able to make it. Another problem would be South Korea. We have two divisions there now. There would be a problem with Taiwan, but as long as the Generalissimo is there, they have no place to go. Indonesia is a problem, as is Malaysia. Japan thinks we are propping up a lifeless government and are on a sticky wicket. Between a long war and cutting our losses, the Japanese would go for the latter. My information on Japan comes from Reischauer.

PRESIDENT: But George, wouldn't all these countries say that Uncle Sam was a paper tiger, wouldn't we lose credibility breaking the word of three presidents, if we did as you have proposed? It would seem to be an irreparable blow. But I gather you don't think so.

BALL: No, sir. The worse blow would be that the mightiest power on earth is unable to defeat a handful of guerrillas.

PRESIDENT: Then you are not basically troubled by what the world would say about our pulling out?

BALL: If we were actively helping a country with a stable viable government, it would be a vastly different story. Western Europeans look upon us as if we got ourselves into an imprudent situation.

PRESIDENT: But I believe that these Vietnamese are trying to fight. They're like Republicans who try to stay in power, but don't stay there long. Excuse me, Cabot.

BALL: Thieu spoke the other day and said the Communists would win the election.

PRESIDENT: I don't believe that. Does anyone believe that? (His hand circled the table. McNamara, Lodge, Bill Bundy, Leonard Unger all expressed views contrary to Ball's.)

McNAMARA: Ky will fall soon. He is weak. We can't have elections there until there is physical security, and even then there will be no elections because as Cabot said, there is no democratic tradition. (Wheeler suggested that McNamara was right about Ky, but said, "I am very impressed with Thieu.")

PRESIDENT: There are two basic troublings within me. First, that westerners can even win a war in Asia. Second, I don't see how you can fight a war under direction of other people whose government changes every month. Now, go ahead, George and make your other points.

BALL: The costs, as well as our western European allies, are not relevant to their (European) situation. What they are concerned about is their own security, that is, troops in Berlin have real meaning, troops in Vietnam have none.

PRESIDENT: Are you saying that pulling out of Korea would be akin to pulling out of Vietnam?

McGEORGE BUNDY: It is not analogous. We had a status quo in Korea. It would not be that way in Vietnam.

BALL: We will pay a higher cost in Vietnam. This is a decision one makes against an alternative. On one hand, a long, protracted war, costly, very costly, with North Vietnam digging in for the long term. This is their life and driving force. The Chinese are taking the long-term view by ordering blood plasma from Japan. On the other hand, there are short-term losses if we pull out. On balance, we come out ahead of the McNamara plan. Of course, it is distasteful either way.

[Cooper account]

Mr. Bundy [McGeorge] agreed with the McNamara proposals. He felt that no government which could hold power is likely to be one that is likely to invite us out. The basic lesson of Mr. Ball's view is that: 1) The post-monsoon season will not see us in the clear. 2) No single speech will be sufficient to reassure the American people. We will have to face up to the serious ominous implications of our new policy. This is not a continuation of our present approach. . . . There are no early victories in store, although casualties are likely to be heavy.

Mr. Bundy did not believe that Mr. Ball's "cancer analogy" was a good one. Immaturity and weakness, yes. A non-Communist society is struggling to be born. Before we take our decision to the American people, Ambassador Taylor should go back to the GVN and get greater, more positive assurances. There will be time to decide our policy won't work after we have given it a good try. (Mr. Ball disagreed here, feeling that the larger our commitment, the more difficult would be the decision to get out. "We won't get out; we'll double our bet and get lost in the rice paddies.")

Mr. Bundy felt that the kind of shift in US policy suggested by Mr. Ball would be "disastrous." He would rather maintain our present commitment and "waffle through" than withdraw. The country is in the mood to accept grim news.

[Valenti account]

RUSK: If the Communist world finds out we will not pursue our commitments to the end, I don't know where they will stay their hand. I have to say I am more optimistic than some of my colleagues. I don't believe the VC have made large advances among the Vietnamese people. It is difficult to worry about massive casualties when we say we can't find the enemy. I feel strongly that one dead man is a massive casualty, but in the sense that we are talking, I don't see large casualties unless the Chinese come in.

[Cooper account]

McNamara felt that Mr. Ball understated the cost of cutting our losses. He agreed with Mr. Rusk on the international effect of such an action at this time. Mr. Ball also overstates the cost of his (McNamara's) proposal. He agreed that it would take at least two years to pacify the country and we must be prepared to increase our forces by another 100,000.

General Wheeler said that it was unreasonable to expect to "win" in a year regardless of the number of US troops involved. We might start to reverse the unfavorable trend in a year and make definite progress in three years. The President wondered whether we could win without using nuclear weapons if China entered the war.

General Wheeler felt that we could in "Southeast Asia." He believes US forces can operate in the terrains of Southeast Asia. This is the first "war of National Liberation"; if we walk out of this one, we will just have to face others.

The President asked why, when we've been undertaking military efforts for 20 months, this new effort will be successful.

General Wheeler felt that our additional forces will stave off a deteriorating situation.

[Valenti account]

LODGE : I feel there is a greater threat to start World War III if we don't go in. Can't we see the similarity to our own indolence at Munich? I simply can't be as pessimistic as Ball. We have great seaports in Vietnam. We don't need to fight on roads. We have the sea. Let us visualize meeting the VC on our own terms. We don't have to spend all our time in the jungles. . . . The Vietnamese have been dealt more casualties than, per capita, we suffered in the Civil War. The Vietnamese soldier is an uncomplaining soldier. He has ideas he will die for.

UNGER: I agree this is what we have to do. We have spotted some things we want to pay attention to.

[Cooper account]

The President stressed his desire to get more third country troops into South Vietnam. He also raised the possibility of a Vietnam Task Force which will meet daily.

The meeting adjourned at 5:30.

Johnson consulted the military the next day (July 22). Present were: General Wheeler, Chairman, JCS; General Harold Johnson, Army Chief of Staff; General McConnell; Admiral David McDonald, Chief of Naval Operations; General Wallace Greene, Jr., Commandant of the Marine Corps; Harold Brown, Secretary of the Air Force; Paul Nitze, Secretary of the Navy; Stanley Resor, Secretary of the Army; and Eugene Zuckert, Assistant Secretary of the Air Force. The civilian advisers present were McGeorge Bundy, McNamara, Clifford, Vance, and Valenti.[60]

PRESIDENT: I asked Secretary McNamara to invite you here to counsel with you on these problems and the ways to meet them. Hear from the chiefs the alternatives open to you and then recommendations on those alternatives from a military point (of view). Options open to us: one, leave the country— the "bugging out" approach; two, maintain present force and lose slowly; three, add 100,000 men—recognizing that may not be enough—and adding more next year. Disadvantages of number three—risk of escalation, casualties will be high, and may be a long war without victory. I would like you to start by stating our present position and where we can go.

McDONALD: Sending Marines has improved situation. I agree with McNamara that we are committed to the extent that we can't move out. If we continue the way we are, it will be a slow, sure victory for the other side. By putting more men in it will turn the tide and let us know what further we need to do. I wish we had done this long before.

. . .

PRESIDENT: Paul, what is your view?

NITZE: In that area not occupied by US forces, it is worse, as I observed on my trip out there. We have two alternatives— support Vietnam all over the country or stick to the secure position we do have. Make it clear to populace that we are on their side. Gradually turn the tide of losses by aiding Vietnam at certain points. If we just maintained what we have— more the Pres. problem than ours—to acknowledge that we couldn't beat the VC, the shape of the world will change.

PRESIDENT: What are our chances of success?

NITZE: If we want to turn the tide, by putting in more men, it would be about sixty-forty.

PRESIDENT: If we gave Westmoreland all he asked for, what are our chances? I don't agree that North Vietnam and China won't come in.

NITZE: Expand the area we could maintain. In the Philippines and Greece it was shown that guerrillas (can lose).

PRESIDENT: Would you send in more forces than Westmoreland requests?

NITZE: Yes. Depends on how quickly they. . . .

PRESIDENT: How many? Two hundred thousand instead of 100,000?

NITZE: We would need another 100,000 in January.

PRESIDENT: Can you do that?

NITZE: Yes.

McNAMARA: The current plan is to introduce 100,000—with the possibility of a second 100,000 by first of the year.

PRESIDENT: What reaction is this going to produce?

WHEELER: Since we are not proposing an invasion of North Vietnam, the Soviets will step up material and propaganda—same with the Chicoms [Chinese Communists]. North Vietnam (might) introduce more regular troops.

PRESIDENT: Why wouldn't North Vietnam pour in more men? Also, call on volunteers from China and Russia?

WHEELER: First, they may decide they can't win by putting in the forces they can't afford. At most they would put in two more divisions. Beyond that, they strip their country and invite a counter move on our part. Second, on volunteers—the one thing all North Vietnam fears is the Chinese. For them to invite Chinese volunteers is to invite China taking over North Vietnam. Weight of judgment is that North Vietnam may reinforce their forces, but they can't match us on a buildup. From military view, we can handle, if we are determined to do so, China and North Vietnam.

PRESIDENT: (Don't you) anticipate retaliation by the Soviets in the Berlin area?

WHEELER: You may have some flare-up but lines are so tightly drawn in Berlin, that it raises the risk of escalation too quickly. Lemnitzer thinks there will be no flare-up in Berlin. In Korea, if Soviets undertook operations it would be dangerous.

PRESIDENT: Admiral, would you summarize what you think we ought to do?

McDONALD: First, supply the forces Westmoreland has asked for. Second, prepare to furnish more men—100,000—in 1966. Third, commensurate building in air and naval forces, step up attacks on North Vietnam. Fourth, bring in needed reserves and draft calls.

PRESIDENT: Any ideas on what cost of this would be?

McNAMARA: Yes. $12 billion dollars in 1966.

PRESIDENT: Any idea what effect this will have on our economy?

McNAMARA: It would not require wage and price controls in my judgment. The price index ought not go up more than one point or two.

GENERAL McCONNELL: If you put in these requested forces and increase air and sea effort, we can at least turn the tide to where we are not losing anymore. We need to be sure we get the best we can out of South Vietnam. We need to bomb all military targets available to us in North Vietnam. As to whether we can come to a satisfactory solution with these forces, I don't know. With these forces properly employed, and cutting of their (VC) supplies, we can do better than we are doing.

. . .

PRESIDENT: Doesn't it really mean if we follow Westmoreland's request we are in a new war? (Isn't) this going off the diving board?

McNAMARA: This is a major change in US policy. We have relied on South Vietnam to carry the brunt. Now we would be responsible for satisfactory military outcome.

PRESIDENT: Are we in agreement we would rather be out of there and make our stand somewhere else?

GENERAL JOHNSON: The least desirable alternative is getting out. The second least is doing what we are doing. Best is to get in and get the job done.

PRESIDENT: But I don't know how we are going to get that job done. There are millions of Chinese. I think they are going to put their stack in. Is this the best place to do this? We don't have the allies we had in Korea. Can we get our allies to cut off supplying North Vietnamese?

McNAMARA: No, we can't prevent Japan, Britain (and the others) to charter ships to Haiphong.

. . .

PRESIDENT: Are we starting something that in two or three years we simply can't finish?

BROWN: It is costly to us to strangle slowly, but chances of losing are less if we move in.

PRESIDENT: Suppose we told Ky of requirements we need—he turns them down—and we have to get out and make our stand in Thailand.

BROWN: The Thais will go with the winner.

PRESIDENT: If we didn't stop in Thailand, where would we stop?

McNAMARA: Laos, Cambodia, Thailand, Burma surely affect Malaysia. In 2–3 years communist domination would stop there, but ripple effect would be great (in) Japan, India. We would have to give up some bases. Ayub [Khan, head of Pakistan government] would move closer to China. Greece, Turkey would move to neutralist positions. Communist agitation would increase in Africa.

GREENE: Situation is as tough as when it started. But not as bad as it could be. Marines in the First Corps area is example of benefits. (Here are the stakes as I see them.) One, national security stake; (it is a) matter of time before we (would have to) go in some place else. Two, pledge we made. Three, prestige before the rest of the world. If you accept these stakes, there are two courses of action. One, get out. Two, stay in and win. How to win? The enclave concept will work. I would like to introduce enough Marines to do this. Two Marine divisions and one air wing. Extend. 28,000 there—(we need an) additional 72,000.

McNAMARA: Greene suggests these men over and above Westmoreland's request.

PRESIDENT: Then you will need 80,000 more Marines to carry this out?

GREENE: Yes. I am convinced we are making progress with the South Vietnamese, in food and construction. We are getting evidence of intelligence from the South Vietnamese. In the North, we haven't been hitting the right targets. We should hit pol (petroleum) storage—essential to their transportation. Also, airfields, MGs and IL28s. As soon as SAM installations are operable.

PRESIDENT: What would they do?

GREENE: Nothing. We can test it by attacking pol storage. Then we should attack industrial complex in North Vietnam. Then we ought to blockade Cambodia—and stop supplies from coming down. How long will it take? Five years, plus 500,000 troops. I think the (American) people will back you.

PRESIDENT: How would you tell the American people what these stakes are?

GREENE: The place where they will stick by you is the national security stake.

GENERAL JOHNSON: We are in a face-down. The solution, unfortunately, is long-term. Once the military (problem) is solved, the problem of political solution will be more difficult.

PRESIDENT: If we come in with hundreds of thousands of men and billions of dollars, won't this cause China and Russia to come in?

GENERAL JOHNSON: No. I don't think they will.

PRESIDENT: MacArthur didn't think they would come in either.

GENERAL JOHNSON: Yes, but this is not comparable to Korea. . . .

PRESIDENT: But China has plenty of divisions to move in, don't they?

GENERAL JOHNSON: Yes, they do.

PRESIDENT: Then what would we do?

GENERAL JOHNSON: If so, we have another ball game.

PRESIDENT: But I have to take into account they will.

GENERAL JOHNSON: I would increase the build-up near North Vietnam and increase action in Korea.

PRESIDENT: If they move in thirty-one divisions, what does it take on our part?

McNAMARA: Under favorable conditions they could sustain thirty-one divisions and assuming the Thais contributed forces, it would take 300,000 plus what we need to combat the VC.

PRESIDENT: But remember they're going to write stories about this—the Bay of Pigs—and about my advisors. That's why I want you to think very carefully about alternatives and plans. Looking back on the Dominican Republic would you have done any differently, General?

GENERAL JOHNSON: I would have cleaned out part of the city and gone in—with same numbers.

PRESIDENT: Are you concerned about Chinese forces moving into North Vietnam?
GENERAL JOHNSON: There is no evidence of forces—only teams involved in logistics. (They) could be investigating areas which they could control later.

The historical precedents invoked in debate during the July 21 and 22 meetings included the following: France in the 1950s (Ball), Philippines and Greece (Nitze), Munich (Lodge), and, most prominently, Korea (President Johnson, Ball). That the Vietcong would use the same guerrilla tactics that they used against the French to fight the United States seemed likely to Ball. More important was the implication that if the Vietcong used the same tactics, they were likely to defeat the United States in the same way that they defeated the French. Ball's one sentence reference to Vietcong strategy against the French must be understood in light of his June 18 memorandum, "Keeping the Power of Decision in the South Viet-nam Crisis," in which he drew repeatedly on the French experience in Vietnam to warn Lyndon Johnson of the slim prospects of victory.[61]

Those, like Paul Nitze, who were less pessimistic than Ball, would find the Philippines and Greece analogy more instructive. Nitze invoked the Philippines and Greece analogy to show that guerrillas could lose when Johnson worried aloud about "our chances of success" even with the extra 100,000 troops. Nitze's use of the Philippines and Greece analogy is important because it exemplified a central tendency of the policy makers: the willingness to be guided by analogies predicting desired outcomes. With the exception of the president and George Ball, virtually all the historical analogies used by administration officials in the 1960s, in private and especially in public, were analogies suggesting the probability of victory. Analogies with the slightest hint of defeat were scrupulously avoided.

The most dramatic use of a historical analogy in the meetings was Ambassador Henry Cabot Lodge's remark about Munich and World War III. It is also probably the strongest evidence we have of the influence of the Munich analogy on the decision makers. The question of Munich is a question of stakes and consequences. "Our [Western?] indolence at Munich" resulted in World War II; our indolence in South Vietnam might bring about an equally disastrous consequence: "I feel there is greater threat to start World War III if we don't go in." With consequences so drastic, stakes so high, it would be difficult to deny Westmoreland's request for the 100,000 troops.

It might be worth noting that Lodge's remark was the last in a series of blows (following McGeorge Bundy, Rusk, and McNamara) dealt to George Ball's anti-intervention arguments. Of greater significance was what failed to occur after Lodge's reference to Munich. No one questioned his analogy. McGeorge Bundy, resident critic of specious analogies, fell silent. In June, Bundy had signed an incisive nine-page memorandum disputing Ball's United States 1965–French 1954 analogy.[62] In the July 21 meeting, he had also rejected Ball's cancer analogy and the President's Korea-Vietnam analogy. Bundy's silence in the wake of Lodge's Munich remark is interesting but not surprising. Like most of the senior decision makers present, he was convinced of the appropriateness of the Munich analogy. In their public speeches, their memoirs, or their writings, they often made the point that Neville Chamberlain's appeasement of Hitler at Munich helped start World War II; for that reason, the United States could not allow Ho Chi Minh to take over South Vietnam, lest that lead to another world war.[63]

Yet the analogy most frequently and explicitly invoked in these meetings was Korea. The president seemed preoccupied with the lessons of Korea. This is in accord with Johnson's memoirs, in which he repeatedly referred to the Korean precedent. Johnson believed that the United States did one crucial thing right in 1950 and that was the decision to use U.S. troops to resist aggression in Korea. Johnson was so proud of Truman's decision that he wrote an admiring letter to the president, praising the latter for his courage in responding to the challenge in Korea and reaffirming America's capacity for world leadership. Johnson would later look to Truman's decisiveness for inspiration.[64]

But the United States made three mistakes in Korea, according to Johnson. The first mistake in Korea was the withdrawal of U.S. occupation forces in June 1949. One year later, the United States was back in Korea, resisting aggression. When Johnson asked Ball in the July 21 meeting, "Are you saying that pulling out of Korea would be akin to pulling out of Vietnam?," he was trying to draw out the consequences of Ball's position. Ball had earlier maintained that "troops in Berlin have real meaning, troops in Vietnam have none." Johnson believed that a U.S. withdrawal from South Vietnam would allow the North Vietnamese to invade South Vietnam, just as the withdrawal of U.S. occupation forces from South Korea in 1949 encouraged the North Koreans to invade the South in 1950. Ball did not contest the implications of his position as sketched by Johnson; he merely saw it as the lesser of two evils. Johnson, however, saw withdrawal as the greater of the two evils:

> . . . I could see us repeating the same sharp reversal once again in Asia . . .
> but this time in a nuclear world with all the dangers and possible horrors
> that go with it. Above all else, I did not want to lead this nation and the
> world into nuclear war or even the risk of such a war.[65]

The second mistake was Truman's failure to ask Congress for an expression of its backing of the U.S. effort in Korea. With respect to South Vietnam, this problem was solved in 1964 during the Tonkin Gulf incident—Johnson sought, and received, an overwhelming expression of support from Congress in the form of the Tonkin Gulf resolution. As noted earlier, the Johnson administration began planning the escalation of the Vietnam War less than a week after they were armed with the resolution.

The third mistake made by the United States in Korea was getting into a protracted war with China. This was a mistake that Johnson was determined to avert in Vietnam. Secretary of State Rusk was even more determined to do the same. George Ball (as most others) was aware of this and opened the June 21 afternoon session—his last chance to argue against intervention—by explicitly linking the possibility of Chinese intervention in Vietnam to the Korean experience. Ball's opening argument (quoted earlier) was a point blank statement: "We cannot win, Mr. President. This war will be long and protracted. . . . There remains a great danger of intrusion by the Chinese." The biggest problem, however, was the problem of a protracted war:

> The Korean experience was a galling one. The correlation between Korean casualties and public opinion showed support stabilized at 50 percent. As casualties increase, the pressure to strike at the very jugular of North Vietnam will become very great.

Ball did not need to explain why it was taboo to hit at the jugular of North Vietnam. Everyone around the table knew. China would intervene. It did so in 1950 when the United States crossed the 38th parallel and moved in on the jugular of North Korea.

Johnson's concern about Chinese intervention in Vietnam did not surface in his July 21 meeting with his civilian advisers; it occupied center stage in his meeting with his military advisers the next day. A major theme, at least on the part of the president, was concern about Chinese and Soviet intervention. Wouldn't Hanoi ask for volunteers from China and Russia in response to the 100,000 U.S. troops? "There are millions of Chinese. I think they are going to put their stack in. . . . We don't have the allies we had in Korea." By the time General Wallace Greene, commandant of the marine corps, spoke about the United States winning in Vietnam by hitting North Vietnam's petroleum storage, air fields, and "industrial complex" and blockading Cambodia, Lyndon Johnson had had enough. He asked, "If we come in with hundreds of thousands of men and billions of dollars, won't this cause China and Russia to come in?" To General Harold Johnson's (army chief of staff) "No," Lyndon Johnson replied, "MacArthur didn't think they would come in either."

That Lyndon Johnson and his civilian advisers were mindful of not provoking China into another war because of the lessons learned in the Korean War is not controversial. In fact, one of the few things about which there is a strong consensus among Johnson's former military and civilian advisers is that the Korean analogy—more specifically, the specter of Chinese intervention—constrained U.S. strategy in Vietnam decisively. For many that was lamentable because it doomed the United States to failure; others were relieved that that happened. What is most interesting, however, is the extent to which this particular lesson of Korea—apparitions of MacArthur, of hordes of Chinese Communists crossing the border—were invoked in both the December 1964 and the July 1965 meetings. Nor would this be the only time when the ghost of MacArthur would haunt the president. Slightly more than a year after these decisions, when the Vietnam War was still going badly and the United States was taking heavy casualties, as George Ball predicted, Johnson wanted General Westmoreland to address the American public. Mindful of General MacArthur's open attack on Truman before Congress in 1951, Johnson warned Westmoreland as the latter was about to face the media, "I hope you don't pull a MacArthur on me."[66]

LINKING BELIEFS AND DECISIONS

How can it be shown that the above beliefs about Vietnam— based on reasoning by analogy—influenced the policy makers' decisions? Alexander George has developed two procedures, "the congruence method" and "process tracing," to assess the impact of cognitive beliefs on decisional choices. I will use George's construction of these procedures to demonstrate how the Korean analogy affected the Vietnam decisions of 1965. George developed the procedures to test how well the Operational Code explained policy choice. Since I believe that the historical analogy is a more manageable unit of analysis than the Operational Code, I shall, in using George's procedures, replace the Operational Code with the appropriate historical analogy.[67]

The idea behind the congruence procedure is simple. The aim is to check for congruence or consistency between a policy maker's beliefs and his policy choice. According to George:

> The determination of consistency is made deductively. From the actor's . . . beliefs, the investigator deduces what implications they have for decision. If the characteristics of the decision are consistent with the actor's beliefs, there is at least a presumption that the beliefs may have played a causal role in this particular instance of decision-making.[68]

Although success at establishing consistency between beliefs and policy choice allows one to "presume" that beliefs may have played a causal role, that is insufficient for George. George worries about spurious consistency and overly causal imputation of cause and effect. Moreover, since experimental designs are not possible for single case analysis, George searches for "the functional equivalent of experimental design." To this end, George designs a series of ingenious thought experiments that "causal interpretations in single-case analysis" could undergo; he proposes that we subject such interpretations to this "series of hurdles . . . before granting them plausibility."[69]

The gist of George's "functional equivalent of experimental design" is shown in Figure 2. Say belief X (Operational Code for George, the lessons of Korea for us) has been shown to be consistent with option C, the option chosen. One must then ask, can X explain and predict only option C? Or would option B—not chosen by the decision maker—also have been consistent with X? If so, then X "may be part of the explanation, but its ability to discriminate among alternative outcomes and its predictive power are weakened." Next, it is necessary to ask: are there any options tabled that would not be consistent with X? Option A, for example, may have been proposed by some advisers but, because the option was not consistent with X (the decision maker's beliefs), it was not given a sympathetic hearing. When this happens, "important explanatory and predictive power" can be attributed to X "on the grounds that its presence tended

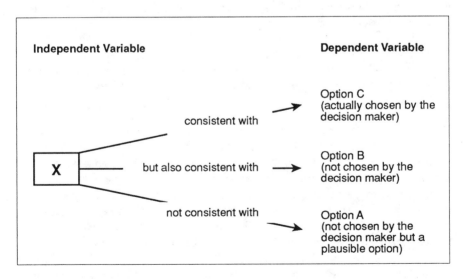

FIGURE 2   The congruence procedure fitted with experimental design.
Source: Adapted from Alexander George.

to exclude adoption of other policy options" (e.g., A) that might have been chosen by other decision makers having belief Y rather than X.[70]

George's methodological thoroughness is further illustrated by his unwillingness to let the relationship between options A, B, and C go unexamined. He toys with the following ideas: suppose C differs in some ways from B, yet both options share something in common—both are "hard, refractory" responses to an adversary's actions while option A, by contrast, is a "conciliatory" response. When such is the relationship between options A, B, and C, the belief X:

> acquires added explanatory and predictive power of a quite useful kind, for it does discriminate between conciliatory and refractory responses (though not by itself between variants of a conciliatory response). In this sense . . . beliefs introduce choice propensities into an actor's decision-making. In other words, the actor's adherence to belief [X] . . . does not determine in a linear, specific way his decision choice, but it does bound and delimit the general range or type of response he is likely to make in a given situation.[71]

In the attempt below to demonstrate how certain beliefs about the lessons of Korea "bound and delimit" the U.S. response to the deteriorating situation in South Vietnam in 1965, I rely on the congruence procedure as outlined above. I also use process tracing, which George defines as "a more direct and potentially more satisfactory approach [than the congruence procedure] to causal interpretation in single case analysis" because it "attempt[s] to trace the process—the intervening steps—by which beliefs influence behavior." More specifically:

> Process-tracing seeks to establish the ways in which the actor's beliefs influenced his receptivity to and assessment of incoming information about the situation, his definition of the situation, his identification and evaluation of options, as well as, finally, his choice of a course of action.[72]

There is no doubt that the congruence procedure, because it works by correlation, is not as convincing as the process-tracing procedure, which works by attempting to reconstruct the decision-making process. Yet the two procedures complement one another in important ways and, for the purposes of this analysis, cannot be strictly separated. In using the congruence procedure to explain why the Johnson administration chose the escalatory options that it did in 1965, for example, I found it impossible to keep process tracing away for long. To go back to the earlier example of options A, B, and C, it should be apparent that any description of these options beyond the abstract "conciliatory" and "refractory" requires some process tracing. This, I think, explains the difference between George's approach and the approach taken here. Both his independent variable

(Operational Code) and his dependent variable (refractory or conciliatory actions) are at a higher level of abstraction than mine. Accordingly, for George, the information requirements for establishing congruence are not that demanding. With a more specific independent variable like the lessons of Korea, and an equally specific dependent variable like the actual option selected, more information is required to establish congruence and to distinguish between options. The source of this information has to be the policy process—the content of the option chosen and the options not chosen, the policy maker's estimate of their respective probabilities of success, the respective dangers they pose, etc.

The precise label adopted for my adaptation of George's methods is unimportant. It may be called *congruence plus*, acknowledging the congruence procedure template supplemented by significant process tracing; or it may be labeled *process tracing minus*, to reflect both its connection to the congruence procedure and the omission of one important aspect of process tracing. That aspect is information processing—how "the actor's beliefs influenced his receptivity to and assessment of incoming information"—an aspect that is dealt with at greater length elsewhere.[73]

THE LESSONS OF KOREA AND OPTION C (AIR WAR)

Figure 3 shows the relationship between the lessons of Korea and the actual options considered by the policy makers in February and July 1965. The February options, it will be recalled, were defined by William Bundy's Working Group on Vietnam; the July options were those listed by President Johnson in the final National Security Council Meeting on July 27. Johnson's listing of options differed from McNamara's listing in that it included options D and E, which he considered but rejected. Including these two options imposes a more demanding test on the Korean analogy, but, if the analogy survives the test, its explanatory power will be significantly increased.

These were the two most important decisions of the Vietnam War. The February decision launched the air war against North Vietnam; the July decision launched the U.S. ground war in South Vietnam. The timing of the decision was influenced primarily by the precarious state of South Vietnam—each time it was perceived that South Vietnam was on the verge of collapse, U.S. policy makers agonized over what the United States should do. The Korean analogy is unable to say why the decision to begin Operation Rolling Thunder was not made a few months earlier or later; what it can do is to give some clues to (a) the basic query why the United States decided in favor of military intervention, and (b) the specific query why escalation took the form that it did, i.e., why certain options were chosen over others.

338

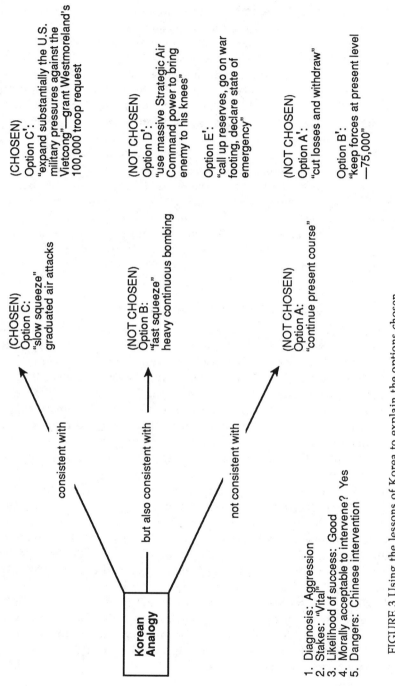

Dec. 1964–Feb. 1965 (Air War)

July 1965 (Ground War)

(CHOSEN)
Option C:
"slow squeeze"
graduated air attacks

(CHOSEN)
Option C':
"expand substantially the U.S. military pressures against the Vietcong"—grant Westmoreland's 100,000 troop request

consistent with

(NOT CHOSEN)
Option B:
"fast squeeze"
heavy continuous bombing

(NOT CHOSEN)
Option D':
"use massive Strategic Air Command power to bring enemy to his knees"

but also consistent with

Option E':
"call up reserves, go on war footing, declare state of emergency"

(NOT CHOSEN)
Option A:
"continue present course"

(NOT CHOSEN)
Option A':
"cut losses and withdraw"

not consistent with

Option B':
"keep forces at present level —75,000"

Korean Analogy

1. Diagnosis: Aggression
2. Stakes: "Vital"
3. Likelihood of success: Good
4. Morally acceptable to intervene? Yes
5. Dangers: Chinese intervention

FIGURE 3 Using the lessons of Korea to explain the options chosen.

The first four lessons of Korea enumerated in Figure 3 are lessons obtained from our earlier discussion of the public lessons of Korea. A careful reading of presidential speeches and the Department of State *Bulletin* in the year preceding the two decisions would have allowed an analyst to derive the same lessons. Memoirs and internal documents would have sharpened the analysis, but they are not essential. This is in accord with Alexander George's observation that the congruence procedure is not extremely demanding in terms of data requirements.[74]

With knowledge of the public lessons of Korea, it is easy to see why option A was rejected in February.[75] "Continue the present course" would not have arrested the deteriorating situation in South Vietnam. In a January memorandum to Dean Rusk titled "Notes on the South Vietnamese Situation and Alternatives," William Bundy offered the "prognosis that the situation in Vietnam is now likely to come apart more rapidly than we had anticipated in November [1964]."[76] Later in the month, Bundy's brother, McGeorge, told Johnson that he and McNamara were convinced that "our current policy can only lead to disastrous defeat."[77] The implications of option A were unacceptable. Option A was fundamentally at odds with the first four lessons of Korea: (a) aggression must not be rewarded, (b) the stakes in Vietnam were extremely high, (c) "whenever the US stood firm, the challenge was successfully met," and (d) like Korea, the United States was morally right.

A believer in the lessons of Korea would find options B and C (air war column, Figure 3) to be consistent with his beliefs. Both options entailed starting a sustained air war against North Vietnam; B involved heavy, continuous bombing; C's pace would be slower and more cautious. It seems that knowing that someone subscribed to the Korean analogy is not enough to predict which of the two options he would choose. In fact, if the Korean analogy was correct about the diagnosis, the high stakes, the good chance of the United States' succeeding, option B should be the favored choice. However, the option selected was C. Was something else at work? Could the Korean analogy explain what it was?

It would have been possible to infer from the public record that an administration highly attuned to the first four lessons of Korea would also have been alerted to a fifth lesson: excessive military pressure against the North might provoke Chinese intervention as in Korea. Dean Rusk's public statements in 1964–1965, for example, showed an interesting pattern. Rusk would refer to a string of historical analogies—Korea would always be among them—to characterize the nature of the conflict and stakes in Vietnam. He insisted that the United States would have to respond to this kind of communist expansionism. Rusk would then point out that the U.S. response was restrained and that U.S. objectives were limited.[78] In the context of the total amount of military power available to the United States, the U.S. response in Vietnam was restrained. If this is interpreted as an attempt not to appear too provocative to Hanoi and China, one may say this about the Korean analogy: while the first four lessons goaded the United States toward a strong response, the fifth lesson—the specter of Chinese intervention—restrained Johnson and his advisers from doing the "full squeeze."

It is the private record, however, that brings out the restraining function of the Korean analogy most fully. Up to this point, the congruence procedure has relied on the public record to sketch the lessons of Korea. The only reason for not turning to the private record is to see if a coherent statement of the lessons of Korea with some explanatory power can be constructed by relying on public statements. There is no reason not to use the private record to tease out the fifth lesson of Korea.

The private record shows—and this has been repeatedly confirmed by those involved in policy making in the 1960s—that the fear of Chinese military intervention in North Vietnam played a decisive role in constraining U.S. military strategy in 1965. With the exception of the joint chiefs of staff, who accepted the first four but not the fifth lesson of Korea, all of Johnson's advisers were determined to avoid MacArthur's mistake in Korea.[79] The political scientist Allen Whiting, head of the Far East division of the State Department's Office of Intelligence and Research and author of the respected *China Crosses the Yalu*, continually warned his two bosses, Dean Rusk and George Ball, about the dangers of Chinese intervention.[80] Rusk himself was said to have been contrite for failing to foresee the Chinese reaction in 1950; he was determined not to let it happen again in Vietnam.[81]

Lyndon Johnson shared this determination to avoid MacArthur's mistake. Recently declassified material about the December 1, 1964, meeting, which touched on the possibility of initiating an air war and in which options A, B, and C were discussed, portrays Johnson as being preoccupied with Saigon's weakness. "No point in hitting North if South not together," said Johnson. When Maxwell Taylor, U.S. ambassador to South Vietnam, doubted that Hanoi would "slap back" if the United States "slapped" Hanoi, the president retorted : "Didn't MacArthur say the same?"[82] This December discussion about the bombing options provides a telling prelude about Johnson's state of mind; it shows how attuned he was to the possibility of Chinese intervention. Eight months later (in the July meetings discussed above), when it became clear that bombing was not working and he had to decide whether to start a ground war with U.S. troops as well, Johnson would use exactly the same MacArthur analogy to challenge his military advisers who wanted to strike Hanoi harder.

The private record thus shows that there was a fifth lesson—the need to avoid MacArthur's mistake of provoking China into a war with the

United States—that was very much on the minds of the major policy makers. With all five lessons counted, the Korean analogy is able to discriminate between options B and C in the February decision to launch an air war. Although both options B and C were in the main consistent with the lessons of Korea, option C was more fully consistent than option B. Option C took the fifth lesson of Korea seriously; option B was more cavalier about it.[83]

THE LESSONS OF KOREA AND OPTION C' (GROUND WAR)

The same logic is applicable to the July decision to grant General Westmoreland's request for 100,000 troops. Options A' and B' were inconsistent with the five lessons of Korea. Despite or perhaps because of the bombing of North Vietnam, the situation in South Vietnam was "worse than a year ago (when it was worse than a year before that)." The odds were "less than even" that the South Vietnamese government would last out the year. "The DRV/VC seem to believe that South Vietnam is on the run and near collapse; they show no signs of settling for less than a complete takeover."[84] Given the situation, option B', "continue the present course," would not be enough to stave off a South Vietnam and U.S. defeat. Option A', withdrawal, would guarantee such a defeat. Again, if the stakes in Vietnam were so high, the moral issue so clear, and success so possible (if only the United States tried harder), options A' and B' and their consequences were unacceptable.

Options C', D', and E' were all consistent with the lessons of Korea. Again, the first four lessons, on first glance, would have predisposed their believer toward options D' and E'. These were the options in which U.S. military strength and determination would be most unambiguously brought to bear in the Vietnam conflict and, as such, have the greatest likelihood of convincing the North Vietnamese and the National Liberation Front to stop and desist. As the record of the June 22 meeting showed, the joint chiefs were very much interested in D'; they and their boss, McNamara, also saw calling up the reserves—the major part of E'—as important in "turning the tide." But once the fifth lesson of Korea is factored into the analysis, it becomes obvious why option D' was rejected. Crippling Hanoi—bombing its petroleum storage, airfields, MGs, and IL28s, as the joint chiefs urged—would have been too provocative to China. As the minutes of the July 22 meeting showed, Johnson referred to MacArthur again when his military advisers wanted to bring Hanoi to its knees.

The rejection of Option E' can also be explained with the fifth lesson of Korea factored in. Despite strong pressure from his secretary of defense to call up the reserves because of their "essential role" in "resolving the

1961 Berlin crisis," and despite pressures from the military to "go on a war footing," the president hesitated.[85] Johnson agonized over this issue and the final decision, in my reading of the documents, was a close call. Johnson's sensitivity to the need to avoid the excesses of the Korean War made him reluctant to call up the reserves and to set the United States in a war posture: these steps were considered to be too provocative to China and the Soviet Union. As I have tried to show above, this concern about not provoking the communists was based on Johnson's interpretation of the U.S. mistake in the Korean War. Johnson himself cited this in his memoirs as the reason why he did not call up the reserves.[86]

The one option left that was fully consistent with all the lessons of Korea was C': that was the option selected. By testing for congruence between the lessons of Korea and the actual policy options forwarded in February and July 1965, it was possible to discover which options were likely to be rejected. Options inconsistent with the tenets of the Korean analogy were rejected. By combining the various lessons of Korea, it was further possible to discover which, among the remaining options, were not fully compatible with the tenets of the Korean analogy. Through this process of elimination, it was possible to arrive at the actual option selected for the two most important decisions of the Vietnam War. The Korean analogy seems able to shed light on why the Johnson administration decided to intervene in Vietnam and, perhaps even more interesting, it seems able to explain why the interventions took the form that they did, namely options C and C'.

THE KOREAN ANALOGY AND CONTAINMENT

While the Korean analogy provides a good explanation of the war decisions of 1965, the analyst impressed by the basic continuity of the United States' containment policy might wonder what explanatory mileage has been gained through the preceding analysis. Wouldn't knowing that the United States acted to contain communism in the postwar period be sufficient to explain the decision to intervene in Vietnam? Vietnam, in this view, is another episode in the continuing saga of containment. Thus Leslie Gelb and Richard Betts explain the decision in terms of the pursuit of "the core consensual goal of postwar [U.S.] foreign policy," the containment of communism.[87] Applied to Vietnam, this meant that it was considered vital to America's security that South Vietnam remained noncommunist.[88] Agreeing with the containment thesis, George Herring has argued that "[t]he United States involvement in Vietnam was not primarily a result of errors of judgment or of the personality quirks of the policy makers, although these things existed in abundance. It was a logical, if not inevitable, outgrowth of a world view and policy, the policy of containment, which Americans in and out of government accepted without serious question for more than two decades."[89]

The point I wish to make is simple: the Korean analogy can do what the containment thesis does, and more. That is, the Korean analogy can explain not only why it was important for the United States to intervene in Vietnam, but it can also explain why the intervention took the forms that it did, i.e., options C and C'. The idea behind containment is that, left on its own, communism is likely to spread in a way that will threaten world peace or the vital interests of the United States (the two are almost always considered synonymous). As the only power with the military and economic might to counter this spread of communism, the United States had to demonstrate that it possessed the will to stop communism. Thus Vietnam. These notions are implicit or explicit in the Korean analogy. As William Bundy put it in 1965, U.S. policy toward South Vietnam "derives from . . . the fact of the Communist nations of Asia and their [expansionist] policies and . . . the lessons of the thirties and of Korea"; more specifically, "our action in Korea" suggested that "aggression of any sort must be met early and head-on or it will have to be met later and under tougher circumstances."[90] Applied to the conflict in Vietnam, the message of Korea is clear: it is necessary to prevent South Vietnam from falling under communism. In this sense, there is substantial overlap between the containment and lessons of Korea explanations. This overlap should not be surprising because, after all, Korea was an instance of containment and a successful one at that.

To say that Korea was an instance of containment raises an interesting issue: why not adopt the containment explanation then, since it appears to be the more parsimonious explanation? One need know only that in the postwar period, the United States acted to prevent the spread of communism: hence Vietnam. Using the Korean analogy explanation requires one to identify the relevant analogy and then to specify its content in order to explain Vietnam. Although more parsimonious, the containment explanation is so broad that it runs into empirical difficulties. If containment is the leitmotif of U.S. foreign policy, then how does one account for the absence of decisive U.S. actions in China (1949), Vietnam (1954), Laos (1961), Indonesia (1965), Czechoslovakia (1968), Angola (1975), and Nicaragua (1979)? Why didn't the United States decide in favor of military intervention when each of these countries was in danger of turning communist? The inability of containment to explain U.S. inaction in 1954 with respect to Vietnam is particularly troublesome. The 1950s, after all, were the height of the containment period. It makes one wonder whether the containment thesis gets the 1965 decision right by chance. One possible argument that containment theorists may advance to explain the above "anomalies" is to point out that U.S. policy makers made assessments that indicated that the stakes were not as vital or that the dangers were too great or that the United States was unlikely to succeed. This, of course, begs the question of how they arrived at these assessments. As we have seen in the case of Vietnam, the Korean analogy played a major role in determining such assessments.[91]

The major advantage, however, of focusing on the Korean analogy is that it is capable of greater accuracy. What it loses in parsimony and sweep, it gains in accuracy. By accuracy I mean its ability to say something about the "choice propensities" of the policy makers. Thus if one returns to the policy options presented to the decision makers in July 1965, one can compare the explanatory power of the two approaches. The containment thesis will have little trouble dismissing options A' and B': given that "withdrawal" or "keep forces at present level" will lead to the communization of South Vietnam, the United States cannot choose this option. As I have argued earlier, the Korean analogy will also predispose its adherents toward dismissing options A' and B'.

The containment explanation is unable to discriminate between the prointervention options. If the "core consensual goal" of combating communism was decisive, it stands to reason that one would prefer the harsher options (D' and E') instead of C' since they were more likely to be effective. Yet Johnson chose C'. It will not do to argue that Johnson chose C' first with full knowledge that he could escalate to D' and E' if C' did not work—that is not supported by the empirical record. Moreover, a politician as astute as Johnson knows that choosing C' in July 1965 might lead to domestic and international repercussions that might make it much more difficult for him to exercise D' or E' if C' does not work.

The Korean analogy does a better job of explaining the choice of C'. Knowing that Johnson wanted to avoid MacArthur's mistake at all costs helps explain why he chose C' over D' and E' in 1965. It is instructive to note that while Johnson did more of C' by increasing the number of U.S. troops in South Vietnam to over 500,000 by 1967, he did not escalate to D' or E', the import of containment notwithstanding.

It might be argued that it is unfair to expect a high level explanation like containment to explain low-level tendencies like the selection of policy options. That may be the case. The tougher question, perhaps, is the following: is it necessary for students of U.S. foreign policy to explain the choice of policy options? In my view, it is one of the more interesting and important things to be explained. The success or failure of a given policy, more often than not, depends on the choice of options tabled to further it. If none of the options tabled are palatable or capable of achieving the stated objectives, decision makers might want to consider revising or abandoning the policy. Almost two decades after America's withdrawal from Vietnam, former officials, military men, and civilians continue to believe that if Johnson had chosen the harsher options, the United States could have brought North Vietnam to the negotiating table sooner or perhaps even won the war. We will never know if that could have been. What we do know is that the debate is premised on the assumption that which option gets chosen—and let us include George Ball's option of withdrawal here to widen the range of choices—may mean the difference between victory and wisdom and defeat and humiliation. Anything that might be responsible for such variation in policy outcomes deserves to be explained.

NOTES

Unless otherwise noted, all documents cited are located in the Lyndon Baines Johnson Library, Austin, Texas.

1. Personal interview with George Ball, July 23, 1986.
2. See Robert Jervis, *Perception and Misperception in International Politics* (Princeton, N.J.: Princeton University Press, 1976), 266–70.
3. Department of State *Bulletin*, February 8, 1965, 171.
4. Ibid., 168.
5. Ibid., March 22, 1965, 404.
6. Ibid., May 10, 1965, 712. Leonard Unger also affirmed this view in a personal interview, August 13, 1985.
7. Doris Kearns, *Lyndon Johnson and the American Dream* (New York: Harper and Row, 1976), 328.
8. For a more involved discussion of the normative component of the Korean analogy, see Yuen Foong Khong, "Seduction by Analogy in Vietnam: The Malaya and Korea Analogies," in Kenneth Thompson ed., *Institutions and Leadership: Prospects for the Future* (Lanham, Md.: University Press of America, 1987), 65–77.
9. McGeorge Bundy, a less avid user of analogies than most of his colleagues, nevertheless found this lesson of Korea very pertinent. Personal interview with McGeorge Bundy, April 11, 1986.
10. Letter from Robert McNamara to Larry Berman, cited in Berman, *Planning a Tragedy: The Americanization of the War in Vietnam* (New York: W.W. Norton, 1982), 104.
11. Personal interviews with Dean Rusk, William Bundy, Leonard Unger, George Ball, and James Thomson, 1985–1986.
12. Personal interview with Dean Rusk, August 21, 1986.
13. See Lyndon Johnson, *The Vantage Point* (New York: Holt, Rinehart and Winston, 1971), 31, 47–48, 115. For Dean Rusk's views, see Department of State *Bulletin*, May 10, 1965, 697.
14. See for example, Ball's memorandum to the president, "Keeping the Power of Decision in the South Viet-Nam Crisis," June 18, 1965, National Security File.

William Bundy believed that Ball's reliance on the analogy of France in the 1950s made him "much less effective" in policy debates. Personal interview with William Bundy, April 11, 1986.

15. Terry Winograd, "A Framework for Understanding Discourse," in Marcel A. Just and Patricia A. Carpenter, eds., *Cognitive Processes in Comprehension* (Hillsdale, N.J.: Lawrence Erlbaum Associates, 1977); David Rummelhart and Andrew Ortony, "The Representation of Knowledge in Memory," in Richard Anders, Rand Spiro, and William Montague, eds., *Schooling and the Acquisition of Knowledge* (Hillsdale, N.J.: Lawrence Erlbaum Associates, 1977).

16. David Rumelhart, "Schemata: The Building Blocks of Cognition," in Rand Spiro, Bertram Bruce, and William Brewer, eds., *Theoretical Issues in Reading Comprehension* (Hillsdale, N.J.: Lawrence Erlbaum Associates, 1980), 34; Deborah Welch Larson, *Origins of Containment: A Psychological Explanation* (Princeton, N.J.: Princeton University Press, 1985), 51.

17. This is adapted from Deborah Larson's excellent discussion of cognitive scripts in *Origins of Containment*, esp. p. 54. See also Robert Abelson, "Script Processing in Attitude Formation and Decision-Making," in John Carroll and John Payne, eds., *Cognition and Social Behavior* (Hillsdale, N.J.: Lawrence Erlbaum Associates, 1976), pp. 33–45, and Robert Jervis, *Perception and Misperception*, 217–24.

18. See Alexander George's important discussion of information processing in "The Causal Nexus Between Cognitive Beliefs and Decision-Making Behavior: The 'Operational Code' Belief System," in Lawrence Falkowski, ed., *Psychological Models in International Politics* (Boulder, Colo.: Westview Press, 1979), 96–101. See also Ole Holsti, "Foreign Policy Decision Makers Viewed Psychologically: Cognitive Processes Approaches," in G. Matthew Bonham and Michael Shapiro, eds., *Thought and Action in Foreign Policy* (Basel, Stuttgart: Birkhauser, 1977), esp. 25–27.

19. *The Pentagon Papers: The Defense Department History of United States Decisionmaking on Vietnam*, 4 vols. (The Senator Gravel edition; Boston: Beacon Press, 1971), III, 130–31.

20. Ibid., 206, 524–29, 550–64.

21. Memo to Dean Rusk, Robert McNamara, and McGeorge Bundy from George Ball, "How Valid Are the Assumptions Underlying Our Viet-Nam Policies?" reproduced in *The Atlantic Monthly*, 320 (July 1972): 35–49.

22. Leslie Gelb and Richard Betts, *The Irony of Vietnam: The System Worked* (Washington, D.C.: Brookings, 1979), 111; Richard Neustadt and Ernest May, *Thinking in Time: The Uses of History for Decision Makers* (New York: Free Press, 1986), 170.

23. Personal interview with George Ball, July 23, 1986.

24. George Ball, *The Past Has Another Pattern* (New York: W.W. Norton, 1982), 392.

25. George Ball, "How Valid Are the Assumptions," 36.

26. Ibid., 37.

27. Ball called the Vietnam conflict a "civil war" in a July 1, 1965, memorandum to Lyndon Johnson. See *Pentagon Papers*, IV, 615.

28. Ball, "How Valid Are the Assumptions," 41–42.

29. *Pentagon Papers*, III, 623.

30. Ball, "How Valid Are the Assumptions," 46. Original emphasis.

31. Ball interview, July 23, 1986.

32. Lyndon Johnson, *The Vantage Point*, 151.

33. Ibid., 115, 117, 131, 152–53.

34. See the following for elite opinion surmising that the Korean War was a victory for the United States: Adlai Stevenson, "Korea in Perspective," *Foreign Affairs* 30 (April 1952): 352; Averell Harriman, "Leadership in World Affairs," *Foreign Affairs* 32 (July 1954): 526; Dean Rusk, "The President," *Foreign Affairs* 38 (April 1960): 363–64. See also Richard Rovere's early assessment that "History will cite Korea . . . as the turning point of the world struggle against Communism and as the scene of a great victory for American arms, one the future will celebrate even though the present does not . . . ," in *The Eisenhower Years: Affairs of State* (New York: Farrar, Strauss and Cudahy, 1956), 145.

35. Johnson, *The Vantage Point*, 152–53.

36. Ball interview, July 23, 1986.

37. Ibid.

38. Department of State *Bulletin*, May 10, 1965, 697. The same point was made by Rusk in a personal interview, August 21, 1986.

39. Ball interview, July 23, 1986.

40. Personal interview with James Thomson, October 31, 1986. The incident is also recounted, without identifying the assistant secretary of state, in James Thomson, "How Could Vietnam Happen," *The Atlantic Monthly* (April 1986): 50.

41. Personal interview with McGeorge Bundy, April 11, 1986.

42. Personal interview with Dean Rusk, August 31, 1986.

43. Ball, "How Valid Are the Assumptions," 40–41. Original emphasis.

44. Lyndon Johnson, *The Vantage Point*, 125, 140, 149.

45. David Halberstam, *The Best and the Brightest* (New York: Random House, 1972), 326.

46. Personal letter to the author, May 5, 1986. The basic theme was reiterated by William Sullivan in a personal interview, July 23, 1986.

47. Ball interview, July 23, 1986.

48. Ball, *The Past Has Another Pattern*, 392. Although Johnson formally approved Operation Rolling Thunder on February 13, sustained bombing was not initiated until March 2, 1965. The meeting to discuss Ball's memorandum should be understood in this context. See George T. Kahin's, *Intervention: How America Became Involved in Vietnam* (New York: Alfred Knopf, 1986), 286–305, for a meticulous analysis of Johnson's reluctance to escalate the Vietnam War.

49. *Pentagon Papers*, III, 659–60.

50. Ibid., 664. My account differs slightly from Kahin's. My reading of the document suggests that option C left a little room for the possibility of negotiations; Kahin believes otherwise. See *Intervention*, 247.

51. Kahin, *Intervention*, 252.

52. *Pentagon Papers*, III, 687–91.

53. Kahin, *Intervention*, 306.

54. *Pentagon Papers*, III, 392.

55. Ibid., IV, 609.

56. Ibid., III, 462–73.

57. Johnson, *The Vantage Point*, 144. These three were not the only questions Johnson asked, but McNamara's memorandum seemed to address two of them intently.

58. *Pentagon Papers*, IV, 620–22.

59. See George T. Kahin, *Intervention* (Copyright © by George T. Kahin. Reprinted by permission of Alfred A. Knopf, Inc.), 370–78. The documents he uses are Meeting on Vietnam, July 21, 1965, Notes (by Jack Valenti), Papers of Lyndon Baines Johnson, Meeting Notes File and Meeting with Foreign Policy Advisors, July 21, 1965, Memorandum for the Record (by Chester Cooper), Papers of Lyndon Baines Johnson, Meeting Notes File.

60. What follows is from George T. Kahin, *Intervention* (Copyright © by George T. Kahin. Reprinted by permission of Alfred A. Knopf, Inc.), 379–85. The document he uses is Meeting on Vietnam, July 22, 1965, Papers of Lyndon Baines Johnson, Meeting Notes File. Larry Berman was probably the first to publish the record of this meeting. See his *Planning a Tragedy*, 112–19.

61. Memo, George Ball to the president, "Keeping the Power of Decision in the South Viet-Nam Crisis," June 18, 1965, National Security Council History, Deployment of Major U.S. Forces to Vietnam, National Security File.

62. Memo, McGeorge Bundy to the president, "France in Vietnam, 1954, and the U.S. in Vietnam, 1965—A Useful Analogy?" June 30, 1965, National Security Council History, Deployment of Major U.S. Forces to Vietnam, National Security File.

63. David Halberstam has observed that McGeorge Bundy's "Munich lecture was legendary at Harvard. . . . It was done with great verve, Bundy imitating the various participants, his voice cracking with emotion as little Czechoslovakia fell, the German tanks rolling in just as the bells from Memorial Hall sounded. The lesson was of course interventionism, and the wise use of force." Halberstam, *The Best and the Brightest*, 56.

64. Johnson, *The Vantage Point*, 47–48.

65. Ibid., 152–53.

66. William Westmoreland, *A Soldier Reports* (New York: Doubleday, 1976), 159.

67. Alexander George, "The Causal Nexus," 95–124. For the reasons why I have focused on analogies instead of the Operational Code, see Yuen Foong Khong, "From Rotten Apples to Falling Dominoes to Munich: The Problem of Reasoning by Analogy About Vietnam" (Ph.D. diss., Harvard University, 1987), 13–22.

68. Ibid., 106.

69. Ibid., 105.

70. Ibid., 111.

71. Ibid., 112.

72. Ibid., 113.

73. See Yuen Foong Khong, *Analogies at War: Korea, Munich, Dien Bien Phu and the Vietnam Decisions of 1965* (Princeton, N.J.: Princeton University Press, forthcoming).

74. George, "The Causal Nexus," 105, 113.

75. Option A or Phase I might have been actually tried for a very brief period, but the point is that by February, Johnson had to decide whether to go beyond this option.

76. *Pentagon Papers*, III, 685.

77. Cited in Johnson, *The Vantage Point*, 122.

78. See for example, Dean Rusk's "Total Victory for Freedom," wherein Rusk reassures the audience that the "United States intends to avoid the extremes. . . .

we do not intend to strike out rashly into a major war in that area." Department of State *Bulletin*, October 5, 1964, 466. A few days later, Rusk's assistant secretary of state for Far Eastern affairs went so far as to say that "[w]e do not aim at overthrowing the Communist regime of North Viet-Nam but rather at inducing it to call off the war it directs and supports in South Viet-Nam." Department of State *Bulletin*, October 19, 1964, 537.

79. Personal interviews with William Sullivan, George Ball, and John Roche, July 5, 1986.

80. Ball interview, July 23, 1986; see also Allen Whiting, *The Chinese Calculus of Deterrence* (Ann Arbor: University of Michigan Press, 1975), 184–88.

81. Halberstam, *The Best and the Brightest*, 326.

82. Cited in Kahin, *Intervention*, 252.

83. The relative weights of the five lessons of Korea are determined empirically. The first four lessons predisposed policy makers toward military intervention, but the fifth lesson played a major role in preventing the United States from going all out.

84. *Pentagon Papers*, IV, 620.

85. Personal letter from Robert McNamara to Larry Berman, cited in Berman, *Planning a Tragedy*, 104.

86. Lyndon Johnson, *The Vantage Point*, 149. Larry Berman has suggested that another reason why Johnson was reluctant to call up the reserves was that the economic costs would have been so great that it would have undermined Johnson's Great Society. See Berman, *Planning a Tragedy*, 145–53.

87. Leslie Gelb and Richard Betts, *The Irony of Vietnam*, 2.

88. Ibid., esp. 181–200.

89. George Herring, *America's Longest War: The United States and Vietnam, 1950–75* (New York: John Wiley & Sons, 1979), x.

90. Department of State *Bulletin*, February 8, 1965, 168–71.

91. No claims are being made here about the ability of the Korean analogy or an analogical approach to explain the above "anomalies" that containment is unable to explain; the scope of my approach is narrower and less ambitious than that of the containment thesis.

10

Learning in U.S.–Soviet Relations: The Nixon-Kissinger Structure of Peace

Deborah Welch Larson

It is an illusion to believe that leaders gain in profundity while they gain experience. . . . The convictions that leaders have formed before reaching high office are the intellectual capital they will consume as long as they continue in office.

—Henry A. Kissinger, *White House Years*[1]

INTRODUCTION

Can policy makers learn? Or is international politics a dreary recurrence of similar events, a mechanical action-reaction to an anarchic environment? Learning refers to change in the *cognitive content* of policy makers' beliefs that enables them to match ends to means more *efficiently*. Examples of learning might include abstraction of a new concept,[2] or change in the image of the opponent.[3] If learning does occur, what factors prompt leaders to alter their convictions?

Major theoretical perspectives in international relations either focus on obstacles to learning or omit the important causal factors. Structural realist theory explains why states learn to adapt to the conventions of the balance-of-power system, but is too general and abstract to deal with creative statecraft. Liberal theory suggests that better information about ends-means relationships should cause leaders to reevaluate their presuppositions, but it neglects the psychological obstacles to receiving information incongruent with one's beliefs. In this essay, I present a cognitive framework that not only explains why leaders change their beliefs but also accounts for individual variations in using new information. In order to investigate the possibility and causes of learning, I examine the Nixon-Kissinger détente policy from 1969–1973. Most foreign policy analysts regard the Nixon-Kissinger détente period as perhaps the most creative and innovative in U.S. foreign policy. Clearly, if effective learning is possible in international politics, the Nixon-Kissinger era should be an exemplar.

What were the intellectual origins of the Nixon-Kissinger paradigm for U.S.–Soviet relations? Did Nixon and Kissinger change their beliefs about the world? What factors account for the major change in the U.S. approach to dealing with the Soviet Union? In general, which theory best explains learning or its absence in the U.S. relations with the Soviet Union?

I have focused on Richard Nixon and Henry Kissinger because they maintained a tight grip on the threads of foreign policy. All important agreements of the Nixon-Kissinger détente era were negotiated in the "backchannel" between Kissinger and Soviet Ambassador Anatoly Dobrynin. Furthermore, using individuals as the unit of analysis avoids the ecological fallacy of inferring that aggregate-level changes in state policy reflect individual attitude change.

To avoid problems of hindsight and distorted memory, I have relied for the most part on contemporary statements by Nixon and Kissinger as sources of evidence for their beliefs and preferences. Of course, politicians and other public officials make statements to serve goals other than representing their private beliefs. Consequently, I have used an *indirect* method of inference: before judging whether a particular statement represented the subject's true beliefs, I tried to ascertain his communication goal and strategy and its likely effect on content. By looking at *who* said *what to whom* under *what circumstances*, the analyst can often determine *what purpose* the communicator was trying to achieve.[4]

I shall argue that learning depends on the complexity and content of decision makers' belief systems. Policy makers who know more learn less. Moreover, change takes place first at the more peripheral-level beliefs, rather than touching core assumptions. Thus, Kissinger and Nixon did not change their fundamental beliefs about the Soviet Union or the best means of maintaining world order. Precedents for the Nixon-Kissinger foreign policy can be found in Kissinger's earlier writings and some of Nixon's speeches.

THEORETICAL EXPLANATIONS OF LEARNING

Structural realists have a very limited conception of learning; states are "socialized" to the rules of the balance-of-power system or fail to survive.[5] Applied to the Nixon-Kissinger era, structural realism suggests that the United States and China would seek a rapprochement to balance against the Soviet threat. The theory does not explain, however, why Nixon and Kissinger should adopt more benign views about the Soviet Union nor why they should seek a détente with both states at the same time.

In contrast, liberals argue that new technological information and better knowledge of cause-effect relationships may alter policy makers' beliefs about the world. Diffusion of consensual knowledge may lead states to reevaluate their interests.[6] Thus, liberal realism suggests that consensual knowledge about the arms race, technological developments in weaponry, or the Soviet Union led Nixon and Kissinger to adopt new, more effective ways of reaching their goals. What liberals often fail to consider, however, is that decisions on state cooperation are *political*; different scientists have different opinions on technological questions based on their ideology and beliefs. Policy makers can usually find a scientist who supports their beliefs.

The "new institutionalism" suggests that states do not adapt well to changes in the environment. Elites resist changes that might upset their prerogatives and privileges. Bureaucratic agencies follow standard operating procedures to coordinate their operations, but routinization inhibits responsiveness to new conditions that cannot be handled by existing routines. Thus, when it occurs, learning is a seismic realignment in response to crises, not a smooth incremental process of structural adaptation.[7] An institutionalist perspective suggests that the Nixon administration would learn in response to major crises—for example, in Vietnam or the Middle East—that could not be handled by their cold war beliefs and institutions.

COGNITIVE THEORY OF LEARNING

Cognitive psychology illuminates why learning is so difficult in the international environment. Effective learning requires accurate, reliable feedback about the relationship between situational conditions and the most appropriate response. But the consequences of foreign policy decisions often do not become apparent for years, and cannot easily be traced to a particular action. Moreover, exogenous, unpredictable changes in the international environment such as the 1973 oil price hike may affect the success or failure of foreign policy initiatives. It then becomes difficult for the analyst as well as the policy maker to determine whether a policy might have worked if the situation had been different.[8]

In addition to the problems created by lack of feedback, policy makers assimilate new information to preexisting beliefs. Availability of more accurate information on the benefits of cooperation does not guarantee that it will be applied. Whether decision makers actually absorb new information requires attention and the ability to fit this data into their cognitive structures.[9] People who have a complex, integrated set of schemas can better accommodate contradictory information *without* changing their beliefs, because they can formulate conditional generalizations or qualifications. By contrast, the nonexpert with a simple set of schemas is apt to change his mind readily, but these changes may not endure because there is little structure on which to fasten new concepts and data. This suggests that individuals with moderate knowledge of a policy domain are more susceptible to belief change.

People are more likely to learn a new concept through repeated, successive exposures to a phenomenon. When they encounter behavior that is unexpected and cannot be fit into preexisting schemas, decision makers try to formulate an explanation for it. The act of explaining a surprising event may lead to the formation of a new attitude. But the degree of change is apt to be quite limited; individuals can store exceptional instances without inferring that they are representative. Thus, people respond to discrepant data by adopting a more complex, shaded view of the world without changing their fundamental assumptions.[10]

Dramatic change such as a religious conversion may require a prior change in behavior. Decision makers are rationalizing rather than rational animals. They use their behavior as a guide to what they believe. Thus, policy change may precede and *cause* a change in policy makers' attitudes or beliefs.[11]

PREEXISTING BELIEFS OF KISSINGER AND NIXON

KISSINGER'S EARLIER WRITINGS

To determine whether Kissinger's views of the Soviet Union did, in fact, change, we should start by examining his voluminous policy pieces as well as more scholarly works. Judging by his writings in the 1950s and 1960s, Kissinger's views about how to deal with the Soviet Union and world order show substantial continuity. Indeed, he repeats the same ideas over and over. Recurring themes include emphasis on concrete interests instead of atmospherics, the problem of establishing a legitimate world order, and the role of diplomacy.

Kissinger claimed that past U.S. policy had aimed at reducing tensions as an end in itself. But tensions were caused by differences over concrete issues. Past détentes with the Soviet Union failed to endure because many in the West were content with changes in Soviet tone, confusing atmosphere with substance. A lasting détente would require resolution of political disputes. Therefore, U.S. policy should aim at settling differences with the Soviets.[12]

For similar reasons, Kissinger had contempt for summits and "personal diplomacy." He cited the "spirit of Geneva" as proof that good personal relations, "atmospherics," had no lasting effect on Soviet policies. A year after Geneva, in 1956, the Soviets had invaded Hungary. To believe that meetings between personalities could magically solve difficulties was not only an illusion. It also gave the Soviets a lever by which to demoralize the West and press extreme demands under the guise of "relaxation of tensions" or "peaceful coexistence." If the Soviets convinced the West that all tensions were due to misunderstanding or the absence of personal rapport among leading statesmen, they would remove any justification for U.S. policy makers to insist on concrete settlements.[13]

Since tensions were caused by conflicts of interest, Kissinger also believed that arms control had no intrinsic value. Arms did not cause tensions; political differences did. In *The Necessity for Choice*, Kissinger grudgingly accepted the ideas of thinning out of forces in Central Europe and establishing a nuclear-free zone. But he rationalized that these objectives were negotiable because they were trivial. The cold war in Europe was caused by the power vacuum in Central Europe and the problem of German reunification, not Soviet armed forces. As long as Germany remained divided, the danger of an explosion existed.[14] In sum, Kissinger favored limited cooperation with the Soviets on arms control, but he subordinated the issue to solving the political issues of a divided Europe.

In the late 1950s, some in the West argued that acceptance of the status quo in Central Europe would lead to greater stability. Once its position in Eastern Europe was recognized, the Soviets would become a status quo power. Kissinger disagreed. Moreover, for the United States to recognize the division of Germany would leave a hostile, dissatisfied power in Central Europe. In 1962, he wrote that "the West may have to acquiesce in the division of Germany but it cannot agree to it." Allied cohesion and stability in Europe required that the blame for the division of Germany be placed on the Soviet Union.[15]

Although skeptical about the likelihood of reaching any substantive agreement with the Soviets, Kissinger argued that domestic public opinion and alliance cohesion required that the United States be receptive to negotiations with the Soviets. In the late 1950s, Kissinger criticized Secretary of State John Foster Dulles for refusing to meet with Soviet representatives until they had "proved" their good intentions by deeds rather than words. Dulles believed that negotiations with the Soviets were a necessary evil until Soviet society had been transformed. At the same time, Dulles feared that summit meetings and other forms of negotiation would undermine the Western democracies' will to resist.[16]

Kissinger noted that Dulles's policies had consequences precisely opposite to those intended. The secretary of state's rigidity hastened the demoralization of the West that he was trying to prevent. According to Kissinger, the tension that Dulles thought was essential could be supported only if the peoples of the West understood that their leaders were making every effort to end it. "The free world requires an attitude of conciliation for its very cohesion," Kissinger wrote. "It cannot be asked to wait rigidly in the face of mounting tensions without making an effort to break the deadlock."[17]

The idea that a Soviet change of heart had to precede negotiations led various foreign policy analysts in the West to engage in verbal gymnastics to prove that the Soviets had indeed changed. "More attention was paid to whether we should negotiate than to what we should negotiate about," Kissinger wrote. "It caused us to make an issue of what should have been taken for granted: our willingness to negotiate."[18] Furthermore, it distracted the United States from developing a concrete program for settlement. In sum, "negotiations with the Soviet Union must be justified by our purposes, not theirs."[19] In 1968, Kissinger argued that focusing on Soviet motives confused the debate and deflected the United States from elaborating its purposes. "Soviet trends are too ambiguous to offer a reliable guide—it is possible that not even Soviet leaders fully understand the dynamics of their system."[20]

To be sure, diplomacy was difficult in a bipolar world because "any relative weakening of one side is tantamount to an absolute strengthening of the other."[21] A multipolar period offered greater scope for creative diplomacy and statecraft. From his study of eighteenth- and nineteenth-century diplomacy, Kissinger observed that subtlety of maneuver could substitute for physical strength. Assembling a coalition could exert pressure against a more powerful state or mobilize defensive support. A country's bargaining position depended on its availability as an alliance partner for as many other countries as possible. Where Kissinger changed was in his judgment that the world had become politically multipolar. In 1968, Kissinger wrote that "the most profound challenge to American policy will be philosophical: to develop some concept of order in a world which is bipolar militarily but multipolar politically."[22]

Establishing a stable world order would require formulating a concept of legitimacy. A recurring theme in both Kissinger's policy and scholarly writings was the distinction between a legitimate and a revolutionary world order. When the major powers regarded the rules of the game as legitimate, diplomacy was feasible. For negotiators had a common understanding of what was fair and reasonable. "It is the legitimizing principle which establishes the relative 'justice' of competing claims and the mode of their adjustment," Kissinger wrote in *A World Restored*.[23] In a revolutionary period, however, major states did not accept the existing distribution of power or a common code of behavior. As a result, negotiating proposals were made more for propaganda than to harmonize interests. Applying this reasoning to U.S.–Soviet relations, Kissinger reasoned that successful negotiations with the Soviets would require prior agreement on a code of conduct.[24]

NIXON'S PREPRESIDENTIAL VIEWS

It is difficult to characterize change in Nixon's cognitions as "learning," for his statements on foreign policy and U.S.–Soviet relations have little structure or consistency. Nixon was a chameleon whose views shifted with each audience. As Garry Wills commented, "there is one Nixon only, though there seem to be new ones all the time—he will try to be what people want."[25]

For example, in a speech made on the eve of Khrushchev's 1959 visit to the United States, Nixon cautioned his audience against confusing "protestations of good will, personal charm and affability" with a "change of attitude." He even quoted Henry Kissinger: "We must guard against succumbing to the illusion of relaxation while the causes of the cold war remain unsolved and new crises build up in an atmosphere of blandness and normalcy." Yet, Nixon also identified "great forces" working for peace that would, in the end, ensure a settlement of U.S.–Soviet differences. One was the "awesome destructive power of nuclear weapons," which meant that "the time when one nation could gain an advantage over another which would assure victory in war in any real sense is gone."[26] Thus, Nixon had accepted mutual assured destruction even before the Soviets had acquired nuclear parity with the United States.

Vice President Nixon also suggested that disarmament and political conflict resolution were in Khrushchev's self-interest. The communist world also had its problems and weaknesses. There was the desire of the Soviet people for an increasing share of their limited productivity, so much of which now went into armaments. "And while it is too early to conclude that he may be troubled by his Chinese ally," Nixon said, "[Khrushchev] may well be deeply concerned by the nightmare which is taking form on his long common border with China." Nixon had recognized the Sino-Soviet split and its implications for U.S.–Soviet détente before it was openly acknowledged. Finally, Khrushchev was bound to be influenced by the "diabolical enormity of nuclear weapons."[27] The implication of Nixon's remarks was that, if Soviet internal weakness and external threats gave them an incentive to cooperate, then the United States should reciprocate.

By 1963, Nixon was out of power and his political views had therefore changed. Whereas he had earlier argued that the Soviets had internal difficulties and that communism was not monolithic, now he claimed that it was "dangerous nonsense" to point out that there were troubles in

the Soviet camp. While Red China and Russia were having their differences, "we cannot take too much comfort in the fact that what they are
debating about is not how to beat each other but how to beat us." They
were simply arguing over "what kind of a shovel they should use to dig
the grave of the United States." To be sure, communism had its troubles.
"But we must face up to the fact that in 40 years it has extended its
power to over a billion people and a third of the world and it has yet to
give up an inch of territory any place in the world."[28] (Apparently Nixon
forgot about the 1955 Soviet withdrawal from Austria, when he was vice
president.)

"Peaceful coexistence" was another word for "creeping surrender."
Nor did Nixon agree that the Soviets would become more accommodating if the United States recognized their position in Eastern Europe. "For
the Communist the status quo is just a launching pad for their next
conquest."[29] As for détente, Nixon declared that "I believe that with
regard to the Soviet Union the test ban marks the beginning of the most
dangerous period of the cold war since it began 18 years ago." Since the
Communist bloc aimed at destroying the free world, cooperation with
the Soviets was not in the U.S. interest.[30]

PROBING THE SOVIET UNION, 1969

INITIAL ATTITUDES

It is ironic that Nixon and Kissinger became identified with détente.
At first, they intended only a limited accommodation. Their image of the
Soviet Union differed greatly from that of proponents of détente. They
did not believe that the desire for trade and economic growth would
lead the Soviets to become more conservative. Nixon and Kissinger rejected the idea that face-to-face meetings between the president and the
Soviet leader—so-called personal diplomacy—could lessen tensions. Nixon
believed that a summit meeting that did not produce concrete agreements
would raise expectations too high and then backfire against him politically.
In language reminiscent of Dulles in 1958, Nixon insisted that there could
be no summit meeting without "adequate preparation" and the prospect
for concrete agreements.

In a memorandum to the State Department setting down his policy,
Nixon wrote: "In the past, we have often attempted to settle things in a
fit of enthusiasm, relying on personal diplomacy. But the 'spirit' that
permeated various meetings lacked a solid basis of mutual interest, and
therefore, every summit meeting was followed by a crisis in less than a
year."[31]

Nixon and Kissinger based their policy toward the Soviet Union on the principles of negotiation, nuclear sufficiency, and linkage. But they were responsive to domestic political constraints and strategic opportunities, and swiftly changed tactics whenever existing policies were not working. Nixon was the political tactician; Kissinger the diplomatic strategist. Together, they were able to shift course to meet changed world and domestic conditions.

Negotiation

The major source of change in Nixon's beliefs was assuming the role of the presidency. In his inaugural address, President Nixon declared that "after a period of confrontation, we are entering an era of conciliation. Let all nations know that during this administration our lines of communication will be open."[32] The hawkish, political, combative, anticommunist, anti-Democratic Nixon of the past seemed to be gone. Columnist James Reston speculated that Nixon was able to express his personal views now that he was president rather than official spokesman for the Republican party.[33]

Sufficiency

Nixon also returned to his earlier views on the disutility of nuclear superiority. At his first press conference a week after inauguration, Nixon surprised news reporters with his offhand acceptance of "sufficiency" as a goal for U.S. policy instead of superiority. "Our objective," he said, "is to be sure that the United States has sufficient military power to defend our interests and to maintain the commitments which this Administration determines are in the interest of the United States around the world." Nixon said, "I think 'sufficiency' is a better term, actually, than either 'superiority' or 'parity.'" He explained that wars occurred when each side believed it had a chance to win. Therefore, parity did not "necessarily assure that a war may not occur." For the United States to talk about superiority had a detrimental effect on the Soviet Union and gave impetus to the arms race.[34] This was a new Nixon. In an October 24 speech made during the 1968 campaign, Nixon had warned of a "security gap" with the Soviets and called for returning to the objective of "clear-cut military superiority."[35] Not to be outdone, then Secretary of Defense Clark Clifford had claimed that he was not giving up the idea of superiority either. At hearings before the Senate Preparedness Subcommittee in spring 1968, representatives from the Pentagon gave assurances that they would not allow the Soviets to match U.S. strategic capability.[36]

Eisenhower originally used the term sufficiency in reaction to Democratic charges of a "bomber gap." The policy meant maintaining adequate or sufficient nuclear forces, instead of trying to maintain U.S. superiority in long-range bombers as the Air Force advocated. In 1956, Secretary of the Air Force Donald A. Quarles called for a policy of "sufficiency." Neither the United States nor the Soviet Union could prevent the other side from inflicting catastrophic damage on its homeland. Moreover, this situation of mutual deterrence could exist even if there was a wide numerical disparity between the opposing forces. Consequently, beyond a certain point what mattered was not the relative strength of nuclear forces, but the "absolute power in the hands of each and . . . the substantial invulnerability of this power to interdiction."[37]

Although the Eisenhower administration had laid the groundwork by introducing the concept of sufficiency, many Americans found it difficult to accept the loss of their military superiority. In a *Foreign Affairs* article, McGeorge Bundy observed that while "Presidents and Politburos know in their hearts that the only thing they want from strategic weapons is never to have to use them . . . the public in both countries has been allowed by its leaders to believe that somewhere in ever-growing strength there is safety, and that it still means something to be 'ahead.'"[38]

Nixon had not thought through what sufficiency would mean for U.S. force structure and doctrine.[39] Institutional constraints interfered with Nixon's ability to implement sufficiency in nuclear forces. Powerful groups within the Pentagon and Congress objected to legitimizing the U.S. loss of military superiority. Several days after President Nixon's avowal of sufficiency, Secretary of Defense Melvin Laird declared, "I am not giving up the idea of maintaining a superior force in the United States." He said he would be willing to describe missile superiority for the United States as "sufficiency."[40] In December 1969, the House Appropriations Committee cut $5.3 billion from the Defense budget, the largest cut since 1954, yet stated that "this country must maintain its military superiority" over the Soviet Union.[41]

Why did Nixon change his mind about seeking military superiority? In his memoirs, Nixon recalls that he had realized that the concept of superiority was meaningless, because the United States and the Soviet Union had reached the point at which "each nation had the capacity to destroy the other."[42]

The president had also realized that retaining superiority was no longer achievable in view of congressional pressure to reorder priorities toward solving the problems of the cities and poverty. In December 1968, before the Nixon administration took office, the president-elect had ordered a study on the U.S. strategic posture. The study, carried out by Morton Halperin and Laurence E. Lynn, Jr., was completed in January and showed that the United States could not regain the superiority that it had in the 1950s. The Soviets were building Polaris-type submarines and intercontinental ballistic missiles (ICBMs) larger than any in the U.S. arsenal. The Pentagon did not want to increase the number of existing weapons that were designed in the 1950s but to wait for a new generation of technology. New missile systems, however, required about eight years from testing to deployment. Consequently, Kissinger recommended to the president that the goal of U.S. military policy should be sufficiency rather than superiority. Nixon immediately accepted the idea.[43] Congress would not support the defense programs necessary to maintain numerical equality in all weapons categories, much less to attain superiority. Influential senators and the establishment press argued that unmet domestic needs and internal political divisions were a greater threat to U.S. security than the Soviet Union. As McGeorge Bundy observed,

> Strategic parity is a simple and inescapable reality, not an American negotiating position. The retaliatory capacity of the Russians has long since reached a level such that the United States *cannot* achieve any superiority worth having.[44]

In sum, convinced that nuclear superiority was no longer militarily meaningful nor politically feasible, Nixon now preferred U.S.–Soviet parity.

LINKAGE: RHETORIC AND REALITY

On January 20, 1969, Nixon's inauguration day, the Soviets announced that they were ready to "start a serious exchange of views" on the control of nuclear missiles. At the same time, they emphasized that they were "not more interested than the United States" in beginning the talks.[45] Strategic Arms Limitation Treaty (SALT) negotiations had been scheduled to begin in 1968 by the Johnson administration, but were cancelled because of the Soviet invasion of Czechoslovakia.

On one hand, Nixon's acceptance of parity logically implied that he should favor arms control as a more efficient means of ensuring a nuclear balance. On the other hand, he believed that the arms race was merely a symptom of political conflict, not the cause. As a result, Nixon linked arms control to progress toward a settlement in Vietnam or the Middle East. At the same January 27 press conference at which he introduced the concept of sufficiency, Nixon declared that "I want to have strategic arms talks in a way and at a time that will promote, if possible, progress on outstanding political problems at the same time." He specifically mentioned the Middle East, although he was more concerned about Vietnam.[46]

In his memoirs, Kissinger recalled that they attached two meanings to linkage. First, what might be called *tactical* linkage referred to a diplomat's use of an issue in negotiation as leverage on another issue. Second, in *inherent* linkage, a great power's actions in one part of the world had consequences beyond the issue or region directly involved. In his memoirs Kissinger recalled that "linkage was a reality, not a decision. Displays of American impotence in one part of the world, such as Asia or Africa, would inevitably erode our credibility in other parts of the world, such as the Middle East." For example, the United States could not withdraw from the war in Vietnam without losing credibility in the Middle East.[47]

Nixon's interpretation of linkage was fuzzy and inconsistent. He was criticized for using tactical linkage, in other words, making arms control negotiations with the Soviets contingent on political settlements on unrelated issues. In practice, however, the Nixon administration defined linkage more loosely as consistent behavior across issue areas. In other words, instead of asking for a quid pro quo on issue B in return for a U.S. concession on issue A, Nixon expected the Soviets to show a cooperative attitude on the major issues at stake in the U.S.–Soviet relationship. The Nixon administration could not trust Soviet good intentions if they cooperated in areas of interest to them, while trying to achieve unilateral advantage at the expense of the United States in other parts of the world. For example, in December 1968, Henry Kissinger told KGB operative Boris Sedov that the president-elect was serious about negotiation but would "judge the Soviet Union's purposes by its willingness to move forward on a broad front, especially by its attitude on the Middle East and Vietnam."[48] On his March 1969 European trip, Nixon denied that he was setting conditions for negotiations, or even that he had any desire for a package deal. Instead, he called for "signs of good faith" across the board, so that progress in one area would not be undermined by crises in another.[49] According to columnist Max Frankel, Nixon emphasized that he was not making political deals a "condition" for arms control talks, but pointed out that he could not "be expected to develop trust for the Russians in one area if he is given cause for suspicion and hostility in another."[50] In this sense, Nixon's approach to linkage was reminiscent of President Eisenhower's insistence that the Soviets should prove their good faith by "deeds" rather than words before he would agree to a summit meeting.[51]

Kissinger justified linkage on the grounds of fairness and reciprocity. He argued that separating "issues into distinct compartments would encourage the Soviet leaders to believe that they could use cooperation in one area as a safety valve while striving for unilateral advantages elsewhere. This was unacceptable."[52] At a reception at the Soviet embassy on February 14, 1969, Kissinger told Dobrynin that the "Nixon Administration was prepared to relax tensions on the basis of reciprocity."[53]

At the time, columnists speculated that the president's national security adviser, Henry Kissinger, had conceived of linkage.[54] In fact, it was Nixon's idea. In a 1963 interview with *U.S. News and World Report*, Nixon argued that the United States should make trade agreements with the Soviets only when they served our political objectives. "If the Soviet

Union needs wheat—as it does—then we should make that particular trade agreement only if we get the Soviet Union to make some political agreement, for example, like the withdrawal of troops from an area that is to receive wheat—Hungary, Cuba." Nixon argued that "trade is the biggest lever the United States has in negotiating with the Soviet Union."[55] In the 1950s, Kissinger had argued against making willingness to negotiate with the Soviets contingent on proof of Soviet good intentions.

SOVIET PEACE OFFENSIVE, 1969

The Soviets made the first moves toward a détente, reinforcing Nixon and Kissinger's belief that the Soviets needed arms control and would be prepared to make sacrifices to achieve it. At his meeting with Nixon on February 17, 1969, Dobrynin hinted at a summit and asked when the United States would be ready to engage in talks on limiting strategic arms. Nixon was noncommittal; he said that summits had to have careful preparation. Furthermore, freezing arms would not ensure peace unless there was also political restraint.[56]

Nixon also made it clear that any important issues should be taken up with Henry Kissinger, his national security adviser. Secretary of State William Rogers was not to be informed. The Kissinger-Dobrynin connection was the backchannel. All major agreements achieved during the Nixon-Ford administrations—SALT I, Berlin, the Basic Principles Agreement, and Agreement on Prevention of Nuclear War—were first negotiated in the backchannel. The backchannel was therefore an example of institutional learning.

In a memo to the president summarizing his first meeting with Dobrynin, Kissinger argued that the conciliatory Soviet line and interest in negotiations were motivated by fear that Nixon might undertake new costly weapons programs that Moscow would have to match. Kissinger recommended that "we should seek to utilize this Soviet interest, stemming as I think it does from anxiety, to induce them to come to grips with the real sources of tension, notably in the Middle East, but also in Vietnam."[57] Thinking that the Soviets needed SALT more than the United States did, the Nixon administration tried to use the prospect of arms control negotiations to persuade the Soviets to cooperate in solving conflicts of interest, reflecting their belief that arms races were a symptom, not the cause, of tensions.

The Soviets followed up Dobrynin's meeting with other conciliatory gestures to improve relations with the United States. In March 1969, the Soviet government agreed to a new rapid communications link between the U.S. embassy in Moscow and the State Department, which they had previously held up for months. The Soviets also proposed reviving the U.S. consul office in Leningrad and establishing a new Soviet consulate in San Francisco. In conversations with foreigners, Soviet officials stressed that they wanted to end the arms race in order to shift resources into the civilian sector of the economy. For the first time since World War II, the Soviet celebration of May Day was not accompanied by a parade of the latest tanks and military equipment rumbling across Red Square. Secretary General of the Communist Party Leonid I. Brezhnev made a speech calling for peaceful coexistence while omitting the ritual denunciations of the United States, West Germany, and Israel. In a July speech to the Supreme Soviet, Foreign Minister Andrei Gromyko called for a new era of friendly relations with the United States and suggested Soviet interest in a summit conference with President Nixon. Diplomats in Moscow interpreted Gromyko's conciliatory words as evidence that the Soviets had made a high-level decision to seek an improved atmosphere with the West. The Soviets clearly wanted a détente with the United States in 1969.[58]

Soviet peace initiatives reinforced Nixon's and Kissinger's initial mistaken impression that the Soviets were desperate for SALT. In mid-April, Kissinger linked SALT talks to a settlement of the Vietnam War. He informed Dobrynin that U.S.–Soviet relations were "at a crossroads,"[59] and "a settlement in Vietnam was the key to everything."[60] Kissinger proposed sending Cyrus R. Vance to Moscow to negotiate principles of strategic arms limitation. While there, Vance would be empowered to meet with a North Vietnamese representative to discuss a political and military settlement in Vietnam. Dobrynin asked if the United States was making a Vietnam settlement a condition for progress on the Middle East, economic relations, and strategic arms. Kissinger replied that we were prepared to continue talking, but talks would move more rapidly if Vietnam were out of the way. Dobrynin pointed out that the United States should understand the limits of Soviet influence on Hanoi; the Soviet Union would never threaten to cut off supplies to their North Vietnamese allies. The Soviets did not formally reply to Nixon's offer to send a special emissary to Moscow, because they were afraid of the U.S. reaction.[61]

SOVIET REACTION TO LINKAGE

In fact, the Soviets deeply resented linkage, because it implied that they needed a SALT agreement more than the United States. The Soviets let it be known that they were annoyed by the Nixon administration's delay in starting arms control talks. The Soviet press interpreted Nixon's call for simultaneous negotiations as "missile talks last."[62] In a May letter to Nixon, Soviet Premier Aleksei Kosygin complained that "taking into account the complexity of each of these problems by itself, it is hardly worthwhile to attempt somehow to link one with another."[63]

Aside from the damaging effects of linkage on their reputation, the Soviets were concerned about the implications for the strategic balance of delaying the SALT talks while the Nixon administration completed accelerated tests of the multiple independently targetable reentry vehicle (MIRV) missiles and took steps to deploy an antiballistic missile (ABM) system. After Nixon's ABM decision was announced, the Soviet press lifted its ban on criticism, accusing the president of stepping up the arms race and reviving the cold war. Soviet officials stressed to foreigners that they wanted to end the arms race in order to transfer resources into the civilian sector of the economy. In June, the communist Party newspaper *Pravda* carried an article complaining about the U.S. policy of proceeding with new defensive and offensive missile systems while failing to set a date for the start of arms control talks. According to Western diplomats, the Soviets had decided to go ahead with SALT talks in 1968 on the assumption that the two nations had reached rough parity. The Soviets were worried that U.S. deployment of these large new weapons systems could upset the balance of forces. To the Soviets, Nixon's policy amounted to a return to the old U.S. policy of "negotiation from strength" and was a repudiation of parity.[64]

Linking the strategic arms talks to a Vietnam settlement was ineffective, because the Soviets had limited leverage over Hanoi, particularly in view of their rivalry with China. Cutting off military aid to the North Vietnamese would have cast doubt on the credibility of Soviet alliances. Nor would a Soviet aid cutoff have had much effect, considering that China was available as an alternative supplier. Indeed, that the Soviet Union conducted negotiations with the United States while it escalated the war in 1972 damaged Soviet relations with Hanoi.[65]

DOMESTIC OPPOSITION TO LINKAGE

Soviet pressure for SALT made it politically impossible for Nixon to delay arms talks.[66] Domestic opposition pressured Kissinger and Nixon to abandon the policy of linking SALT to unrelated issues. The *New York Times*, the *Washington Post*, and other publications claimed that since the United States had an interest in arms control, no additional Soviet concessions on unrelated issues should be demanded as a precondition for negotiations. For example, in the *New York Times*, Robert Kleiman pointed out that neither Eisenhower nor Kennedy allowed the Berlin crisis to obstruct negotiations for a test ban; nor did the Soviet Union allow U.S. bombing of North Vietnam to block completion of the nuclear nonproliferation treaty; the SALT talks "serve mutual interests of far greater importance."[67]

For the most part, however, critics objected not so much to linking issues per se, but to making negotiations contingent on solving difficult political issues while the United States deployed new destabilizing defensive and offensive systems. For example, Senator Albert Gore complained that "ABMs will be all over the place" if "we wait until peace and love prevail in the Middle East and there is a settlement in Southeast Asia."[68] Democratic leader Senator Mike Mansfield urged Nixon to postpone talks aimed at solving long-term political issues and concentrate instead on negotiating a nuclear arms moratorium before the deployment of new weapons systems gained "irreversible momentum" in both the United States and the Soviet Union.[69] The *New York Times* warned that "unless the United States and the Soviet Union can reach an arms control agreement before both sides proceed much further on these multiple warheads, the strategic arms race will enter a new, more costly and more terrifying round."[70]

THE ABM DEBATE

Congressional opposition to the ABM system had been building. On March 7, 1969, the Senate Foreign Relations Committee urged the Nixon administration to delay deployment of an ABM system while it sought a strategic arms control agreement with the Soviet Union. Three prominent Republican senators—John Sherman of Kentucky, Jacob K. Javits of New York, and Charles H. Percy of Illinois—met personally with Kissinger to persuade the administration to wait. Meanwhile, Senator Mike Mansfield, his voice shrill with emotion, spoke from the floor of the Senate: "Having spoken so long and so loudly of a distant danger, we are not able to hear the rising voice of need at hand." "The multibillion-dollar Sentinel system does not meet these difficulties anymore than Vietnam has met them. On the contrary, it may well act to intensify them."[71]

Nixon did not want to give up the ABM system unilaterally. Kissinger agreed, recalling that he "considered it highly dangerous to stop programs in the area of our traditional superiority—advanced technology—without any Soviet reciprocity."[72] On one hand, the Soviets were building ICBMs; we were not. On the other hand, the United States planned to construct a nationwide ABM system, while the Soviets had left the Moscow system in abeyance. Thus, a reciprocal deal would involve a trade of ICBMs for ABMs.

On March 14, 1969, Nixon announced his program for a modified ABM system consisting of 2 sites designed to protect missiles, but eventually to include 12 sites nationwide by 1973. Although Nixon emphasized that the system would protect the U.S. nuclear deterrent rather than cities, some of the proposed future sites were not near missile bases. Kissinger claimed that the system differed from Johnson's planned deployment "primarily in covering all of the United States with radars, providing a better base for rapid expansion against the Soviet Union, and concentrating somewhat more on defending ICBM bases."[73] Nixon claimed that the U.S. decision to deploy an ABM would not discourage the Soviets from entering arms control negotiations; indeed, four days after Johnson announced the Sentinel system the Soviet Union agreed to talks. By ostensibly moving the system away from cities and giving it an anti-Soviet justification, Nixon cleverly defused most domestic opposition. The most vigorous opponents were citizens of protected cities, who objected to having missile sites next door. Congressional opponents admitted that they had been outwitted by Nixon but vowed to continue the struggle for the next two months before the system came to a vote. According to the *New York Times*, "it would have taken bold executive leadership to reverse the policy on the Sentinel antiballistic missile system which Mr. Nixon inherited from the Johnson administration; to overrule Secretary of Defense Laird and the Pentagon planners; and to confront the military-minded Congressmen on Capitol Hill who automatically equate more weapons with more security."[74] James Reston judged that Nixon dealt with the issue of arms control "politically and nationally, and within this frame, he was not only effective but brilliant." "For students of domestic politics, public relations, and bedside manners, President Nixon's press conference on the ABM was a fascinating performance, but it was a tactic and not a policy, and it reduced the great issue of world arms control down to a national political controversy over the President's techniques."[75]

Despite Nixon's political ploy, the Senate Foreign Relations subcommittee on disarmament chaired by J.W. Fulbright of Arkansas conducted televised hearings on the ABM issue throughout the summer. Secretary Laird and representatives of the Pentagon justified the ABM on the grounds that Soviet deployment of the SS-9 suggested that they were going for a "first-strike capability." "The Soviets are going for a first-strike capability, and there is no question about it," Laird declared. The size of the SS-9 warhead and its accuracy suggested to the secretary that "this weapon can only be aimed at destroying our retaliatory force."[76] Consequently, the United States needed an ABM system to protect its nuclear deterrent. On June 19, Nixon as well asserted that recent intelligence data had convinced him that the Safeguard ABM system was "even more important" than ever. He said that the data showed that the Soviet Union had made rapid progress in developing multiple warhead missiles and that these missiles were targeted "to fall in somewhat the precise area" in which the U.S. Minuteman silos were located.[77]

The Nixon administration's charges about Soviet motives, however, backfired because skeptical members of Congress had other sources of information. During the hearings, Senator Stuart Symington of Missouri pointed out that "only a few months ago we were told by Dr. [Alain] Enthoven [former secretary of defense for systems analysis] that the SS-9 was built for a second-strike purpose."[78] The intelligence community sent out reports suggesting that the Soviets were moving rapidly to strengthen their nuclear forces as a deterrent, but were not striving for a first-strike capability. Senator Fulbright pointed out that, even if the Soviet buildup endangered U.S. land-based forces, the ABM was not the only counterresponse; the United States could deploy additional Minuteman missiles at less cost than an antimissile system. Moreover, the Soviets could overwhelm a U.S. ABM system by deploying additional SS-9s or other smaller missiles. Dr. George W. Rathjens of the Massachusetts Institute of Technology argued that other conclusions could be drawn from the Soviet SS-9 program—that the Soviets wanted warheads large enough to destroy American cities or that they wanted warheads large enough to penetrate a possible large-scale U.S. ABM deployment.[79] Even after Nixon agreed to arms control talks, in August a congressional amendment to halt deployment of a Safeguard system was defeated by the narrowest possible margin of 50-51, with Vice President Agnew casting a tie-breaking vote.[80]

THE MIRV ISSUE

Congress also pressured President Nixon to propose to the Soviets an immediate mutual moratorium on testing MIRVs. Members of Congress argued that, if neither side had MIRVs, then the United States and the Soviet Union would not have to deploy expensive ABM systems. The Nixon administration had justified the Safeguard ABM system on the grounds that it was needed to protect the U.S. Minuteman force against a disabling first strike from SS-9 missiles fitted with multiple warheads. Once the United States had obtained an operational MIRV capability, the Minuteman III would have three reentry vehicles. Poseidon launchers could carry up to 14 reentry vehicles.[81]

But the timing of a MIRV ban was critical. On one hand, strategic analysts believed that a treaty limiting MIRVs could not be verified once either side had acquired an operational deployment capability without on-site inspection to see how many warheads a launcher carried, a procedure unacceptable to both the Soviets and the United States. On the other hand, satellites or radar tracking could monitor Soviet testing of MIRVs. Consequently, beginning SALT negotiations before the United States finished its test series was urgent if there was to be any hope at all of an agreement banning MIRVs. Navy and Air Force testing of MIRVs was scheduled to resume late in May and continue through July.[82]

Reflecting this sense of urgency, Republican Senator Edward Brooke sponsored a sense-of-the-Senate resolution calling on the president to propose to the Soviet Union an immediate and mutual moratorium on flight testing of MIRVs accompanied by SALT negotiations.[83] "Unless there is an immediate suspension of such tests before the program is completed,"

Senator Brooke said, "neither side is likely to believe that the other has actually refrained from deploying MIRV's."[84]   The *New York Times* supported the test moratorium, arguing that the United States was more likely to persuade the Soviet Union not to build these systems by "offering to forgo them for the United States, not by forcing a race that is more likely to become irreversible than to strengthen the American bargaining position in negotiating a standdown."[85]   On June 5, Senators William B. Saxbe and J.W. Fulbright joined with 43 other members of Congress in a statement warning that:

> Once testing has passed the point where deployment is possible, we can no longer have a self-policing arms agreement with the Russians.
> Once large-scale ABM deployment begins and MIRV testing has been completed, the nuclear genie will be out of the bottle, and it is unlikely that the stability we now enjoy will ever return again.[86]

The Nixon administration was deeply divided on the question of a MIRV test ban. Secretary of State William Rogers and Gerard C. Smith, the head of the Arms Control and Disarmament Agency (ACDA), favored negotiating a MIRV ban and an immediate moratorium on testing before the "point of no return."[87]

The Pentagon argued against a test moratorium by claiming that the Soviets would cheat and that MIRVs were necessary to penetrate a Soviet "thick" ABM system. Deputy director of the ACDA Philip J. Farley testified to Congress that a moratorium on MIRV testing could not be verified by national technical means. Moreover, Farley said, the Soviets might *already* have sufficient knowledge and experience to deploy MIRVs without further testing. A Defense Department advisory panel headed by Daniel Fink, a former Defense Department official employed by a major MIRV contractor, agreed that the Soviets could acquire an operational MIRV capability through secret testing. The Pentagon's top scientist, John S. Foster, testified before the House of Representatives Foreign Affairs Subcommittee that the Soviets could get around a test moratorium, either with clandestine space shots or with tests on the ground that could not be detected.[88]   As the *New York Times* pointed out, this argument was reminiscent of the opposition to the ratification of the 1963 nuclear test ban treaty, when "it was said that the Soviet Union would evade the ban by testing behind the moon or in far outer space."[89]   Analysts at the Central Intelligence Agency (CIA) angrily challenged this contention, insisting that the Soviet Union could not develop, test to operational confidence, deploy, and continue confidence testing of a MIRV system without being detected repeatedly by U.S. radar, satellites, communications monitoring, and other intelligence means. The United States, the CIA argued, would never buy and deploy a system it had not tested extensively. Why should it be assumed that the Soviet Union would not only do so, but risk its survival by employing such a weapons system in a "first strike?"[90]

The Air Force and the Navy continued their tests of multiple warheads for Minuteman III and Poseidon missiles throughout the summer. In June, the Air Force quietly awarded an $88 million contract for MIRVs to General Electric, which suggests that the Nixon administration stalled on the SALT talks until MIRV testing had been completed.[91]

LINKAGE ABANDONED

The State Department simply ignored Nixon's instructions that there were to be no SALT talks until the Soviets showed willingness to negotiate on a broad range of issues. On March 27, Secretary of State Rogers testified before the Senate Foreign Relations Committee that the administration had "already agreed with the Soviet Union that we will have these talks very soon." "We hope that such talks can begin within the next few months," he said.[92] In June, Rogers told Soviet ambassador Dobrynin that the Nixon administration hoped to begin talks on strategic arms limitations that summer. State Department officials then reported the conversation to the press.[93]

Nixon himself was inconsistent. On his European tour, Nixon told a group of 20 leading French politicians, labor leaders, industrialists, academics, and journalists that it would be a "crime" not to take advantage of the Soviet Union's willingness to take part in arms talks with the United States. He also said that, although the causes of world tension were political, a negotiation on limitation of armaments would reduce the magnitude of these tensions.[94] It would not be at all surprising if the Soviets were confused about the U.S. position on linkage.

Nixon lashed out at his critics in a June 4 speech to the Air Force Academy, calling those who favored arms control negotiations and a mutual moratorium on MIRV testing "unilateral disarmers" or "isolationists." Senator Gore commented that "it sounded like the old Nixon I used to know."[95] Nixon returned to the cold war theme that a worldwide American presence was necessary for global stability, attacking those who too quickly "grow weary of the weight of free world leadership." Contrary to his earlier statements to a French audience, Nixon argued that "the adversaries in the world are not in conflict because they are armed." "They are armed because they are in conflict."[96]

Less than a week later, however, on June 11, Nixon authorized Secretary of State Rogers to propose to Dobrynin that they begin talks with the Soviets at the end of July, implicitly abandoning linkage. Nixon even claimed that "[w]e are considering the possibility of a moratorium on tests as part of an arms control agreement."[97] For the remainder of the

Nixon administration, the United States and the Soviet Union decoupled strategic arms negotiations from other issues in their relationship. Nixon had learned that domestic political opposition to the arms race deprived him of the bargaining leverage needed to link arms negotiations to other issues. To paraphrase Kissinger, the American people would finance an arms race only if reasonable effort was made to end it.

TRADE LINKAGE

Nixon believed that the Soviets needed trade and credits more than the United States needed expanded trade with the Soviets. Therefore, he could use trade as leverage on Soviet policies in other areas.

The administration had to take a position on various bills in Congress liberalizing exports to the Soviet Union, because the 1949 Export Control Law was scheduled to expire on June 30, 1969. Angry at the Soviet refusal to provide any help in settling the Vietnam War, Nixon tried to retaliate by refusing to expand trade. On May 28, the Nixon administration announced that it had decided not to encourage further trade with Communist countries "in present circumstances" as part of its policy of linkage. Democratic senators Edmund Muskie and Walter F. Mondale were bitterly critical of the administration's decision, charging that the United States was losing business to Western Europe.[98]

Nixon and Kissinger exaggerated the Soviet need for American trade and the extent to which the Soviets would make concessions on unrelated issues in return for liberalized export controls. It is true that Brezhnev enthusiastically advocated increased trade with the West, reversing the Stalinist policy of autarchy. Several Politburo members, however, were markedly reserved about expanded trade with the West, and many Central Committee members actively opposed the idea. Some Soviet leaders argued that the West would exploit Soviet economic dependence. Increased economic interdependence could also contaminate the Soviet people with capitalist notions. Brezhnev did not gain control of the Politburo, thereby ensuring support for his economic policies, until 1973, when he abandoned the Soviet policy of autarchy.[99] In May 1971, as will be discussed below, Nixon and Kissinger made trade concessions to the Soviets, without a political quid pro quo, to persuade them to agree to a face-saving, cosmetic agreement on SALT.

In part, the failure of linkage may be attributed to Kissinger and Nixon's miscalculation of Soviet interests in détente and arms control. But more important, because Nixon and Kissinger articulated the strategy publicly, the Soviets viewed linkage not as a term referring to mutually profitable exchange, but as attempted blackmail.

SALT NEGOTIATIONS, NOVEMBER 1969

When the State Department proposed SALT talks with the Soviets in June 1969, they delayed answering until October. Soviet leaders were wary about U.S. intentions as a result of the Nixon administration's decisions to proceed with both an ABM deployment program and testing of MIRVs. Some Soviet military leaders, including Marshal Nikolai I. Krylov, commander of the strategic missile forces, claimed that the United States was preparing for a surprise attack against the Soviet Union and that the best defense was overwhelming strategic superiority. In addition, only a few weeks after Nixon's invitation to begin arms talks, U.S. officials announced that the president would visit Romania in August, which could have been interpreted as a U.S. policy of encouraging Eastern European independence from Soviet tutelage. Finally, Soviet officials probably did not want to start SALT talks when conflict with China placed them on the "psychological defensive." In other words, Soviet officials feared that their border dispute with China might cause U.S. officials to believe that the Soviets were rushing into arms talks to seek agreement at any cost to avoid trouble both in the East and the West. Thus, it was no coincidence that Dobrynin delivered the Soviet proposal on starting the talks on the same day that Sino-Soviet negotiations began in Beijing. Kissinger claimed, however, that the Soviets wanted to wait until the end of the Senate's ABM debate (in August) so that they would not undermine critics' arguments that the ABM was incompatible with arms control negotiations.[100]

President Nixon was ambivalent about SALT and arms control. He probably would not have agreed to negotiations, if Johnson had not already scheduled talks and initiated the process. Nixon was wary, but willing to be shown that arms control talks could bear fruit.[101] Exploratory negotiations began in November 1969 at Helsinki.

FROM NEGOTIATION TO CONFRONTATION, 1970

A FAILURE TO LEARN: THE MIRV BAN ISSUE

The second round of SALT talks was scheduled to begin on April 16, 1970. This was the last chance to obtain a negotiated ban on MIRVs. In June, the first Minuteman IIIs were deployed.[102]

From the perspective of liberal realism, the Nixon administration should have favored a ban on testing, production, and deployment of MIRVs. Scientists, members of Congress, and analysts agreed that deployment of MIRVs would endanger the stability of the nuclear balance. If the accuracy and yield of the warheads were increased, MIRVs could provide a first-strike capability, endangering mutual deterrence and strategic stability. Moreover, in the long run, the risk posed by MIRVs affected the United States more than the Soviet Union. The United States had a temporary advantage in MIRV technology, because the Soviets had only tested multiple reentry vehicles (MRVs), which could not be independently targeted. Once they had acquired MIRVs, however, the Soviets would be able to put more warheads on a missile than the United States because the SS-9 had greater throw-weight. In July 1969, a *New York Times* editorial warned that Soviet MIRVs would make the U.S. Minuteman and other land-based forces obsolete. While the joint chiefs of staff wanted MIRVs to restore the U.S. lead in the offensive missile race, "the search for superiority in the nuclear missile era is illusory." "The question that must be faced is whether American security will be better maintained with MIRV's on both sides—or on neither."[103]

Nixon did not oppose a MIRV ban out of domestic political consider-ations. Congress would certainly have ratified a MIRV ban if concluded *before* either side had acquired an operational deployment capability, particularly if the negotiations had been accompanied by a ban on testing to prevent the Soviets from catching up with the United States. On April 9, by a margin of 72 to 6, the Senate passed the Brooke resolution, which called on President Nixon to propose that both sides immediately suspend deployment of offensive and defensive nuclear strategic weapons. An arms control panel made up of former Kennedy and Johnson administration officials recommended to the American Assembly, a nonpartisan discus-sion group at Columbia University, that the Nixon administration support the Brooke resolution and accompany it with a six-month unilateral postponement of MIRV deployments.[104] In 1971, even conservative Senator Henry Jackson advocated a one-year freeze on MIRVs to reverse the decline in U.S. security.[105]

But all the public debate on MIRVs—including congressional hearings, resolutions, editorials, meetings between the president and key congres-sional leaders—was, as Nixon put it, "irrelevant."[106] Nixon's task was to devise a proposal for a MIRV ban that would satisfy public pressure yet be unacceptable to the Soviets. Thus, at the meeting of the National Security Council (NSC) to discuss a MIRV ban, Nixon added a requirement for on-site inspection. Since the Soviets had insisted since the beginning of the negotiations that SALT would have to be verified through national technical means, the Soviet delegation rejected the proposal immediately. Another reason why the Soviets found the proposal objectionable was that it banned testing and deployment of MIRVs, but not production, which would allow the United States to maintain a stockpile of MIRVs, but merely not deploy them. In November 1970, the Soviets told Smith that they had never considered the U.S. MIRV proposal as genuine; instead, it was a "cheap sop" to appease congressional opinion.[107]

The Soviet government might have accepted a MIRV ban on testing as well as production if monitored by national surveillance methods. The Soviets had sent signals that they were interested in a ban on test-ing, production, and deployment of MIRVs. Soviet embassy officials, in informal contacts with legislators or their aides, indicated Soviet interest in a MIRV ban. The Soviet Defense Ministry's newspaper *Krasnaia zvezda* hinted at such a position. The *New York Times* reported that the Soviet leadership was divided over the wisdom of halting MIRVs, but would be receptive to an *American* proposal. At a private meeting of the Council of Foreign Relations in March, Dobryin suggested that the Soviets would be responsive to a U.S. offer of a moratorium or limitation on testing multiple warheads.[108]

Contrary to his later statement that he wished he had thought through more carefully the implications of a MIRVed world, Kissinger was not ignorant or uninformed about the destabilizing potential of MIRVs. In addition to being exposed to congressional hearings and editorials on MIRVs, he met weekly with a group of academics and scientists who briefed him on the technology and strategic implications of multiple warhead missiles.[109]

If Kissinger and Nixon were primarily concerned about verifying a MIRV ban, it seems odd that they added the on-site inspection requirement only *after* the critical NSC meeting at which various SALT proposals were discussed. Unlike other components of the U.S. SALT proposals, the NSC and the verification panel did not discuss the details of on-site inspection or if it would be effective in monitoring a ban. Officials who advocated on-site inspection had not made a technical study of verification requirements; they either wanted it to ensure that the Soviets would reject a MIRV ban (Defense representatives) or because they thought that the United States should be "tough" with the Soviets to teach them a lesson. An interagency study of the verification requirements of a MIRV ban was not completed until two months *after* the United States had decided to demand on-site inspection.[110]

The Nixon administration's failure to make use of technological information in MIRVs can best be explained from institutional and cognitive perspectives. The Pentagon and the joint chiefs adamantly opposed restraints on the development of MIRVs. MIRVs were cost-effective, cheap, and technologically sound. Moreover, MIRVs provided the means of covering nuclear targets in the Soviet Union given budgetary constraints. The military believed that the U.S. technological advantage could and should be maintained. Even if the Soviets did acquire MIRVs, who could tell when that would be? So much bureaucratic momentum had developed behind MIRVs, so many other weapons programs had been sacrificed for them, and their envisioned use was so entrenched in projected U.S. force structure, that the military would have vigorously and loudly objected to their cancellation. Early in 1969, Nixon and Kissinger had concluded that they could not obtain the Pentagon's support for a treaty limiting both ABMs and MIRVs. For *political* reasons, Nixon decided to concentrate on ABMs. MIRVs were the price paid for the joint chiefs' acceptance of an ABM treaty.[111]

But a cognitive perspective is needed to explain why Kissinger and Nixon were ready to abandon a MIRV ban. Politicians choose the issues on which to fight; their preferences determine the costs they are willing to incur. Beliefs about the opponent and the world, in turn, determine preferences. Nixon and Kissinger attached no intrinsic value to arms control. As both repeated numerous times, they believed that arms races were a symptom of conflict rather than its cause; statecraft should aim at solving political issues. Instead of using SALT to restrain arms expenditures or stabilize the strategic balance, they viewed arms control as a means of pressuring the Soviets to make concessions on peripheral areas or as distraction for an antiwar public opposed to Nixon's escalation of the war in Vietnam. For example, in April 1970, Kissinger remarked to Dobrynin that on SALT the "main problem was to get concrete about *something*," implying that the substance of the agreement was of little concern. Kissinger also suggested to Dobrynin that the United States would be satisfied with a *limited* SALT agreement restricted to ABMs, rather than a comprehensive proposal linking offensive and defensive limitations.[112]

DELINKING THE CAMBODIAN INVASION

Although the Nixon administration tried to link SALT to Soviet willingness to settle the Vietnam War, the president decoupled his own escalation of the war from relations with the Soviet Union. On April 30, Nixon announced that U.S. troops had invaded Cambodia to clean out suspected North Vietnamese sanctuaries.

Soviet leaders accused Nixon of "bad faith" and insincerity. In the first press conference held by a Soviet government leader since Khrushchev, Kosygin said that the Cambodian intervention raised doubts about Nixon's sincerity in seeking an "era of negotiation."[113] Western diplomats were surprised that Kosygin had delivered the Soviet denunciation of the Cambodian action himself and by the Soviet premier's personal attack on Nixon. In an implicit reference to linkage, Kosygin said that "the United States must not think that Moscow is more interested in better relations than Washington."[114] In a June speech to the Supreme Soviet, Brezhnev angrily complained that the Nixon administration's declarations of love for peace went counter to its "aggressive actions."[115] Soviet President Podgorny characterized U.S.–Soviet relations as "in a kind of frozen state."[116]

The Soviets did not, however, link Cambodia to the SALT negotiations. Smith expected the Soviets to suspend SALT talks for 90 days, while U.S. troops were in Cambodia. The head of ACDA advised Nixon that the "minimal" Soviet response proved that the Soviets were serious about reaching a SALT agreement.[117]

In support of decoupling SALT from Vietnam, Nixon used the same arguments that had been used against him by critics of linkage: while the United States and the Soviet Union were far apart on policy toward Southeast Asia and the Middle East, they had mutual interests in the problem of arms control. "The Soviet Union," he said, "has just as great an interest as we have in seeing that there is some limitation on nuclear arms."[118] In fact, Nixon's professed interest in arms control was for domestic political consumption. He was bored by the details of various arms control negotiating proposals and left it up to Kissinger to develop a negotiating position.

BRANDT'S OSTPOLITIK

The détente that developed in Europe grew out of a disjuncture between cold war institutions and East-West interactions. The rigid political separation between Eastern and Western Europe was incongruent with expanding economic contacts and political interdependence. East-West détente developed first in Europe, based on increasing trade and contacts. Economic interdependence led to improved political relations. By 1973, West Germany was the Soviet Union's largest Western trading partner. But this structural opportunity for change required a diplomatic strategy for its exploitation. West German Chancellor Willy Brandt played a leading role both in promoting European détente and in prodding the U.S.–Soviet tension reduction process into motion.

During the cold war, the West German government had refused to recognize governments that had any dealings with East Germany—the Hallstein Doctrine. Gradually, this policy became unrealistic as more and more governments recognized East Germany. The West German government risked isolation.

In September 1969, the Social Democratic Party (SPD) came to power for the first time under Willy Brandt. Brandt cautiously began a policy of détente with the Soviet Union and East Germany. His strategy was to negotiate first with the Soviet Union, offering them a nonuse of force agreement and recognition of existing boundaries in Europe, while relying on the Soviets to pressure East Germany for a Berlin agreement and regularized relations between East and West Germany.

The Soviets were receptive to West German overtures. Previously, the Soviets had insisted that West Germany recognize East Germany as a precondition for negotiations. But the Soviets regarded it more likely that they could reach an agreement with SPD than the Christian Democrats. They also wanted advanced West German technology and recognition of East Germany.

On August 12, 1970, Brandt and Prime Minister Kosygin signed a nonaggression pact providing for West German recognition of existing boundaries in Europe as "inviolable but not unchangeable." Both sides agreed to work toward détente and increase economic, technological, and cultural cooperation. Bonn agreed to de facto (but not de jure) recognition of East Germany, abandonment of the Hallstein doctrine, and entry of both German states into the United Nations.

Bonn declared that the Bundestag would ratify the treaty only if a Berlin agreement ensuring Western access were reached. This was not tactical linkage of one issue to another for bargaining purposes; Brandt had a two-vote coalition majority and would have difficulty persuading the German parliament to ratify the nonaggression treaty unless the Soviets made reciprocal concessions on Berlin. After the Soviet-FRG nonaggression pact was signed in August 1970, the Soviets had an interest in concluding an agreement on Berlin that would enable Brandt to get his Ostpolitik treaties through the German Parliament.

Kissinger was suspicious of Brandt's Ostpolitik, fearing that the German leader might succumb to the lure of German reunification and make unilateral concessions to the Soviet Union. Kissinger feared another Rapallo, in which German nationalism made common cause with Soviet diplomatic isolation. Kissinger was also concerned that the Soviets would establish a selective détente with West Europe without U.S. participation and drive a wedge into the North Atlantic Treaty Organization (NATO). While there was nothing that the United States could do to stop Brandt, Kissinger advised Nixon to refrain from approving the West German leader's negotiating strategy so that the United States would not assume blame in the eyes of the German public for hardening the division of Germany.[119]

Kissinger recognized that he had leverage over the pace of West German rapprochement, however, because Brandt needed U.S. help in negotiating access guarantees to West Berlin. West Germany did not have legal authority to negotiate on the status of West Berlin because theoretically it was still under occupation. Only the four occupying powers had authority to negotiate on Berlin—the United States, France, Britain, and the Soviet Union.[120]

COLD WAR IN U.S.–SOVIET RELATIONS

The budding U.S.–Soviet détente was nipped by a series of crises in the Middle East, Cuba, and Berlin. Protestations of desire for peace were drowned out by charges of cheating and bad faith. The superpowers were prisoners of their small clients. Although nuclear parity made it impossible for the superpowers to resort to war, it provided no compelling imperative for them to resolve their conflicts. Neither the United States nor the Soviet Union was willing to restrain itself outside the main confrontational arena in Europe.

Nixon and Kissinger overreacted to Soviet behavior, largely because they still assumed that the Soviets controlled their clients and acted according to plan.

In early September, the State Department charged that the Soviets had violated a recently negotiated cease-fire by helping the Egyptians move antiaircraft missiles along the Suez Canal. A State Department official said that the implications of Soviet actions were disturbing, not only because of their effect on the continuing Arab-Israeli crisis, but also in terms of how much credence could be placed on Soviet promises in SALT.[121]

Stung by the charges, the Soviet government said that it had not violated the terms of the Middle East cease-fire, because it had never been a party to the agreement. No Soviet personnel were manning antiaircraft missiles in the Suez Canal zone, the Soviet government said. The Soviets claimed that the "old Nixon" was showing his colors, stirring up an anticommunist campaign in time for the elections.[122]

On September 20, Syrian tanks invaded Jordan—with Soviet connivance, in Nixon's view. Nixon put on a show of force with the U.S. Sixth Fleet in the eastern Mediterranean. In a September 25 background briefing, Kissinger accused the Soviets of establishing a submarine base at Cienfuegos in violation of the Khrushchev-Kennedy agreement that ended the Cuban missile crisis.

On October 9, the Soviets retaliated by announcing that they had decided not to send Soviet Premier Kosygin to address the United Nations at its twenty-fifth anniversary session because of the "officially inspired" anti-Soviet campaign. Soviet officials said they were particularly offended by the charges made by high U.S. officials and leading newspapers that the Soviet Union could not be trusted.[123]

Nixon administration officials expressed deep concern about Soviet intentions. In an October 11 television appearance, Laird and Rogers catalogued examples of Soviet bad faith in areas ranging from the Soviet missile buildup to the Middle East and Vietnam.[124] American officials claimed that they had been trying to move toward a "generation of peace" by not trying to squeeze the greatest advantage out of every bargaining situation, since nuclear parity between the United States and the Soviet Union imposed the need for restraint. The administration wondered whether the Soviet Union was willing to exercise similar restraint.[125]

For their part, the Soviets claimed that Nixon was "not a reliable man"; he talked about wanting an "era of negotiation" but his actions in North Vietnam, Cambodia, the Middle East, and Cuba made serious negotiations impossible. The Soviets complained that the president did not want to deal with the subject at hand, but was always asking them to prove their good faith by making concessions on some other problem. This "Kissinger doctrine of linkage," they said, was unacceptable.[126] In a private meeting with Secretary of State Rogers, Gromyko did clear up U.S. misperceptions of Soviet policy in Berlin. During the Berlin talks, the Western powers became irritated by interruptions in air travel, which they interpreted as an attempt by the Soviets to block the negotiations. Gromyko blamed a wayward Soviet air controller for interference in the corridor, and he assured Rogers that Moscow was not demanding the removal of all West German federal officers from Berlin as the price for continuing the Berlin negotiations.[127]

In his October 23 speech to the United Nations, Nixon tried to signal his desire for accommodation while reminding the Soviets that the benefits they would gain from cooperating with the United States were contingent on Soviet restraint in Third World areas. He contrasted détente with "power politics in which nations sought to exploit every volatile situation for their own advantage, or to squeeze the maximum advantage for themselves out of every negotiation."[128] Today, especially where the nuclear powers were concerned, he warned the Soviets, such policies invited the risk of confrontation that could spell disaster.[129] Nixon's conciliatory gesture, however, was not credible against the background of U.S.–Soviet conflict.

Some Soviet analysts recommended that the administration set up a high-level strategy group to screen out U.S. actions that could adversely affect the debate in the Politburo over whether to pursue a détente with the United States. The Kremlin was making plans for the twenty-fourth communist party congress in March, the first since 1956. The State Department, the CIA, and Soviet experts put pressure on the White House to send a signal to the Soviets to influence forthcoming decisions on the trade-off between guns and butter, SALT and other issues. Two steps recommended were that the United States adopt a more reasonable proposal in the SALT talks to meet Soviet concerns that it was trying to freeze the Soviet Union into a position of inferiority, and that the Nixon administration expand trade with the Soviet Union beyond a case-by-case basis. Premier Kosygin had remarked to Senator Muskie, "We are *not* sure that Washington is not serious about the SALT talks, but we are not sure that it is."[130] While the White House had tried to keep the Soviets guessing about whether they were facing the "new Nixon" or the "old Nixon," that strategy could boomerang now.[131]

BREAKTHROUGH IN U.S.–SOVIET RELATIONS, 1971

In his annual foreign policy report in February 1971, Nixon asserted that "the postwar order of international relations—the configuration of power that emerged from the Second World War—is gone."[132] Western Europe and Japan had regained their economic vitality and political self-assurance. The Stalinist bloc had fragmented. New nations were acting with self-assurance on the world stage. The rigidity of the bipolar world had given way to the fluidity of a new age of multipolar diplomacy.

Nixon continued to affirm the doctrine of linkage while abandoning it in practice: "It is a fact of international politics . . . that major issues are related."[133] "Aggressive action in one area is bound to exert a disturbing influence in other areas," he warned. Nuclear weapons required that both the United States and the Soviet Union practice self-restraint in pursuit of their national interests. The United States had shown restraint in the SALT negotiations, in diplomatic initiatives in the Middle East, and in talks on Berlin. "Such a policy of restraint," he said, "requires reciprocity—concretely expressed in actions."[134]

THE SOVIET SIGNAL?

Nixon also noted that the Soviets had given no reason for their recent halt in ICBM construction nor any guarantee that the slowdown would continue. The president expressed concern that the "halt" might be a delay intended to permit the Soviet Union to install new technical advances, such as multiple warheads on its missiles. If so, he warned, the United States would react appropriately. Unless the United States had a firmer indication of Soviet intentions, Nixon would have to continue work on the ABM system. Several times in the foreign policy report, Nixon stated that the significance of the Soviet delay was "unclear" or "ambiguous," appealing to the Soviets to show that their action was an intentional signal.[135]

On December 16, 1970, Secretary of Defense Melvin Laird had announced that the Soviets had halted work on the SS-9. Actually, the pause in the Soviet buildup had been detected earlier in the spring, but Laird was reluctant to publicize the information while the defense budget was under congressional consideration. After the SALT negotiations began, the Soviets stopped constructing ICBM silos, other than completing existing groups, 10 silos for SS-11s and SS-13s. In October 1970, the Soviets abandoned construction of 18 SS-9s.[136]

The Soviet signal created public pressure for the Nixon administration to reciprocate. Nixon publicly applauded the halt, saying that he sensed an overwhelming common interest by the two powers to avoid a nuclear competition and "the escalating burden of arms."[137] Smith wrote the president a letter urging that the United States match Soviet restraint by deferring expansion of the ABM program beyond the requested two sites.[138] Pentagon officials objected that the Soviets' major objective was to halt the U.S. ABM program. To slow down or stop the missile defense program unilaterally, they said, would remove U.S. leverage in pressing for the Soviets to stop their ICBM program.[139] Many members of Congress called for the United States to accept the Soviet SALT proposal for an immediate agreement confined to ABMs only.

Irritated by news leaks about the negotiations, the Soviets broke their year-long silence with an article in *Pravda,* accusing Washington of trying to gain a unilateral military advantage by its refusal to discuss limits on U.S. fighter-bombers stationed near the Soviet Union. *Pravda* warned that if U.S. strategists hoped to obtain Soviet consent "to any agreement violating the principle of reciprocal security and insuring unilateral military advantages for the United States they are mistaken."[140] A few days later, *Izvestiia* criticized Smith for testifying against an ABM-only agreement in a secret briefing of the Senate Foreign Relations Committee.[141]

Almost immediately after his February plea that the Soviets reveal their intentions, Nixon got his answer in the form of alarming new intelligence showing the construction of new Soviet silos in Kazakhstan, near existing SS-9 and SS-11 fields. Laird passed on the intelligence to Senator Henry Jackson, who appeared on the television program "Face the Nation" on March 7 to announce the discovery of monster holes, much larger than those dug for the SS-9, which suggested that the Soviets were deploying "huge new missiles." Jackson believed that the new missile was MIRVed and superior to the SS-9. He predicted that the Soviets would use this huge buildup not to make a first strike on the United States, but to assume greater and greater international political risks in the 1970s.[142] In late April, at least 40 silos were spotted at half a dozen sites in the Soviet Union. A month later 60 silos were found. "If this pace continues much longer, we'll have to call it a crash program," one official said.[143] The final total reached in October was 91 new silos. Not all the new silos were for SS-9s; 66 appeared to be for SS-11s, a much smaller and less accurate missile that would not threaten the U.S. Minuteman force.[144]

Unlike their earlier charges of Soviet cheating and bad faith, this time the Nixon administration took a cautious, low-key attitude toward the new intelligence findings. President Nixon commented that "I do not believe our expressing, as a government, trepidation about this would be helpful."[145] A Pentagon spokesman commented that "We are not sure exactly what it is or what the Soviets' intentions are."[146] Defense Department officials pointed out that there were several possible interpretations—the Soviet Union was installing multiple warheads on SS-9s, it was introducing other refinements, or that it was introducing an entirely new missile, as Jackson had suggested.[147]

Evidence of the new Soviet ICBM construction made Nixon and Kissinger *more,* not less, eager to negotiate on arms limitations. Through their ICBM buildup, the Soviets had finally proved what they had stated many times, that they did not need SALT more than the United States. Nixon realized that while the SALT talks continued, the nuclear balance was changing in the Soviets' favor. In addition to their ICBM construction program, the Soviets were increasing their submarine fleet rapidly and would reach parity with the United States in three years. The Soviets already had more ICBMs than the United States. The ABM program was under attack again in Congress and had barely survived the most recent vote. The longer the negotiations lasted, the worse the U.S. position became. Nixon did not think that he could persuade Congress to agree to a major buildup of strategic weapons at a time when the Soviets were professing their desire for an arms limitation treaty. Since December 1970, the Soviets had been suggesting that they favored an ABM treaty combined with a less formal agreement on offensive arms, such as a freeze. President Nixon instructed Kissinger to follow up these Soviet hints and obtain a more limited agreement that would freeze the Soviet construction of dangerous new ICBMs. A freeze, of course, would recognize Soviet superiority in numbers of missile launchers.[148] Conservative Senator Jackson had reached the same conclusion. He proposed a one-year agreement with the Soviet Union freezing land-based missiles to "arrest the decline in the security" of the U.S. nuclear deterrent. A freeze was necessary, because if the Soviets deployed these 25-megaton missiles, within a year they could add more megatonnage than the United States had in its entire Minuteman system.[149]

While allowing Kissinger to negotiate secretly with Dobrynin in the backchannel, Nixon wrote Smith that he agreed that the new intelligence about Soviet ICBM construction lent urgency to the SALT negotiations. While avoiding any impression that the United States was under pressure of any deadline or was eager to rush in with concessions, Nixon wanted Smith to convey to Semenov his concern and the adverse impact that the momentum of the Soviet buildup was having on domestic opinion in the United States. Nixon also told Smith to point out that the administration had deliberately refrained from public speculation about the significance of the ICBM construction, and had chosen not to make an issue of it in the 1971 defense budget. When confronted with Smith's protests, Semenov replied that the United States had been modernizing its strategic armaments, and naturally the Soviet Union was doing the same. The Soviet negotiator replied that it was completely natural and understandable that the U.S. government had shown restraint in its comments. Indeed, Semenov said, in the physical sciences this sort of phenomenon was known as an aberration. But he conceded that each side read what the other side was saying with greater attention than it gave to statements made by its own people, and we could help each other by pointing out such comments.[150]

When Smith asked Dobrynin about the meaning of the Soviet resumption of ICBM construction, he claimed that Soviet embassies were not informed about such developments. But the Soviets found a way to reassure the United States about the military significance of the new missiles, through multiple channels of information. Soviet diplomats reassured the U.S. delegation at Vienna that the silos were part of a "modernization" program similar to the U.S. improvement of its Minuteman and Polaris missiles. Then the Soviets backed up their words with deeds. Satellite reconnaissance data from March 4 to April 12, 1971, showed silo liners next to the new holes. The Soviets had placed a full set of liners next to the silos, in rank order and face upward so that they could be photographed properly, along with missile cannisters so that the diameter of the missiles could be calculated. The CIA concluded that, instead of deploying a new "monster missile," the Soviets had dug larger holes so that they could place a concrete shell around the missiles, part of an effort to "harden" the silos so that they would be less vulnerable to U.S. MIRVs.[151] Still, although they were not yet deploying MIRVs, the Soviets *were* constructing new ICBMs while the United States was not.

BREZHNEV LAUNCHES DÉTENTE

In spring 1971, U.S–Soviet relations achieved a breakthrough on Europe and SALT simultaneously. At the twenty-fourth party congress in March 1971, Leonid I. Brezhnev consolidated his authority and proclaimed a policy of peaceful coexistence with the West. In his speech, Brezhnev stressed that his country wanted improved relations with the capitalist world since that might contribute to a further rise in Soviet consumers' standard of living. The Soviet leader complained about the "frequent zig zags in United States foreign policy, which are apparently connected with some kind of domestic political moves from short-term consider-ations."[152]

While urging the United States to take Brezhnev's call for improved relations seriously, however, Foreign Minister Gromyko said that Nixon's desire to move from confrontation to an era of negotiations "should be supported by practical deeds." As areas in which agreements were pos-sible, Gromyko mentioned the Berlin talks, a general European security conference, the Middle East, and the strategic arms talks.[153]

Soviet experts at the Institute of the U.S.A. and Canada used the word *flexibility* to describe inconsistency in the Nixon administration's policy. The Soviets complained that if Nixon were sincerely interested in peace and the well-being of the American people, he would have ended the Vietnam War, cut back on U.S. overseas commitments, and sought closer ties with the Soviets. Instead, Nixon reduced U.S. troop strength in Vietnam while supporting forays into Laos and Cambodia. While speaking of an "era of negotiation," the president created a mood of confrontation. The Soviets still complained about Nixon's trip to Romania in 1969, which they regarded as an effort to split Communist ranks.[154]

American experts, for their part, did not immediately perceive the significance of the change in Soviet policy. For example, James Reston commented that Brezhnev's speech was "long, vague, and hopeful . . . but essentially it is an exercise in public relations rather than a practical basis for serious negotiation." The tone was conciliatory, but the substance was familiar and one-sided. Brezhnev wanted recognition of World War II territorial changes, dissolution of the Warsaw Pact and NATO, the "dismantling of foreign bases," and the "abolition of the remaining colonial regimes"—Western, that is. Reston concluded that for all Brezhnev's conciliatory proposals, "his strategic and political aims remain the same."[155]

The Soviets backed up their conciliatory rhetoric with a series of concessions.[156] After the party congress, Soviet officials told U.S. diplomats that they had been instructed to negotiate seriously with the United States.[157] At the United Nations disarmament conference at Geneva, the Soviet Union agreed to the West's position that a separate ban on bacteriological weapons should be negotiated first, leaving aside the more difficult problem of limiting chemical weapons.[158]

On May 14, 1971, Brezhnev proposed mutual balanced force reductions in Central Europe, declaring that the United States should try "tasting the wine." Brezhnev's unexpected offer undercut Senator Mike Mansfield's resolution to cut U.S. troops in Europe by 150,000, predicted to pass the Senate on May 19.[159]

On May 20, 1971, President Nixon announced that the United States and the Soviet Union had agreed to concentrate that year on negotiating an ABM agreement. "Together with concluding an agreement to limit ABMs, they will agree on certain measures with respect to the limitation of offensive strategic weapons."[160] In other words, the United States gave up its demand for a comprehensive agreement limiting both offensive and defensive weapons, and the Soviet Union softened its demand for an initial agreement limited to defensive weapons only.[161]

The United States had conceded more than the Soviets, because the central issue of the sequence of negotiations for offensive and defensive limitations was still unsettled. Kissinger had tried to persuade the Soviets to agree to simultaneous negotiations for an ABM treaty and offensive limitations, because after an agreement on defensive systems was reached, the United States would have given up its bargaining leverage. The Soviets wanted an ABM treaty completed before considering possible limitations on offensive weapons.[162] But the drafting of the May 20 agreement was imprecise and could permit either interpretation. The language referring to offensive weapons limitations merely said that the two sides agreed to try to agree on "certain measures."[163]

In return for this Soviet "concession," Nixon privately promised the Soviets a grain agreement and the rescission of an executive order requiring that 50 percent of grain sold to the Soviets be carried on U.S. ships. To implement this promise, Nixon had Charles Colson make political concessions to the maritime unions so that they would agree to unload grain from Soviet ships, a task that was not accomplished until autumn.[164] In other words, instead of linking liberalized trade to Soviet concessions on other issues, the Nixon administration made secret trade concessions to the Soviets in return for a cosmetic, face-saving SALT agreement that did not solve the real issue.

Although Nixon was troubled by the evidence of an intensive Soviet missile buildup, he decided that the risks of abandoning SALT talks and retaliating with a new U.S. crash missile program were greater.[165] The Soviets reciprocated by unilaterally halting their construction of ICBMs after the May 20 agreement was reached, a year before the interim agreement on offensive forces formalized this obligation.[166]

The Soviets and the United States reached cooperative agreements in a variety of issue areas. The first major advance in 15 months of Berlin talks came on June 7, 1971, when the Soviets compromised with the West on vehicular access to West Berlin.[167] The final Berlin agreement was signed on August 23, 1971, providing access guarantees for Western powers and West Germans to West Berlin. In September, the United States and the Soviet Union agreed to upgrade the "hot line" with satellite transmission and to reduce the risk of an accidental war by agreeing to measures for mutual notification and consultation in case of nuclear accidents.[168]

Since the various agreements on Berlin, SALT, accidental war, and the hot line satisfied Nixon's criteria for concrete agreements, in October 1971 he announced that he would visit Moscow.

WHY DID THE SOVIETS SHIFT?

It should be noted that the thaw in U.S.–Soviet relations *preceded* President Nixon's July announcement of his visit to China. While U.S.–Chinese relations had been improving as symbolized by "Ping-Pong" diplomacy, no one, including the Soviets, expected such a dramatic departure.[169] Thus, while the Sino-American rapprochement contributed to the developing U.S.–Soviet détente, it was not the most important causal factor.

Several possible explanations for the new initiatives in Soviet policy can be advanced. The Soviets had an interest in reaching an agreement on Berlin so that Brandt could get the Ostpolitik treaties ratified. But the United States had a veto over the Berlin agreement. Thus, the Soviets were led to abandon their 1966–1970 policy of seeking a "selective détente" with Western Europe to drive a wedge between the United States and its allies.[170] Brezhnev had domestic political motives for détente with the United States; he had based his campaign for leadership on the argument that the Soviets should obtain Western technology and trade to raise the Soviet standard of living.[171] In addition, the Soviets recognized that they had overestimated the effect of domestic demonstrations on Nixon's ability to engage in competitive policies in the Third World. In 1970, even Brezhnev was talking about the breakup of the capitalist system in America. Soviet experts on the United States warned that Nixon might overreact to the demonstrations by intervening abroad to prove that the United States had full freedom of action and was prepared for worsening of tensions.[172]

THE MAY 1972 SUMMIT

Nevertheless, Nixon was still suspicious of Soviet motives and ambivalent about détente. In his February 1972 foreign policy report, Nixon announced that there were "serious grounds" for believing that a "fundamental shift" in U.S.–Soviet relations might occur. He said it was unclear, however, whether the Soviets had permanently changed their policy or had made a tactical shift for their own advantage.[173] President Nixon also said that the Soviets regarded international tension as "normal," hostility as "inevitable," détente as a transitory opportunity to seek tactical advantage, and negotiation as harsh competition for unilateral gain.[174]

Despite Nixon's rhetoric about a new multipolar system, he continued to believe that the Soviets were responsible for North Vietnamese behavior.[175] When the North Vietnamese launched a major offensive on March 30, Nixon was convinced that the Soviets were in collusion with Hanoi to tie his hands behind his back so that he could not escalate the war. President Nixon ordered Kissinger to threaten to cancel the summit during the security adviser's April 1972 visit to Moscow if the Soviets did not bring the Vietnam War to an end. Through his negotiations with the North Vietnamese, however, Kissinger had learned that the Soviets had very little influence on the highly motivated, independent North Vietnamese.[176] Kissinger believed that it was dangerous to threaten the Soviets, and simply ignored the president's instructions.[177]

Nixon was willing to risk losing the main achievements of his policy toward the Soviet Union—the concrete agreements reached with the Soviet Union on economic and political issues, the summit, and the emerging détente—so that he could achieve a settlement of the Vietnam War. On the eve of the summit in Moscow, Nixon ordered the mining of North Vietnamese ports and the bombing of Haiphong.

Influenced by the "lessons of history," Nixon considered cancelling the summit himself to avoid the humiliation of having the Soviets do so in an election year when he stepped up the pressure on North Vietnam. Nixon blamed his 1960 defeat in part on Khrushchev's cancellation of President Eisenhower's visit to Moscow over the U-2 incident.[178] In fact, the Soviets believed that Khrushchev had made a major blunder by impulsively walking out of the Paris summit, and Soviet editors and journalists contrasted favorably Brezhnev's decision to go ahead with the summit despite the mining of North Vietnamese harbors.[179]

In addition, the Soviets may have been worried about West German ratification of the Soviet-German nonaggression treaty and therefore unwilling to risk raising the level of international tension. On April 27, 1972, Chancellor Willy Brandt survived an unprecedented no-confidence motion by one vote. Since the Christian Democrats had based their campaign against Brandt on opposition to the treaties recognizing the division of Germany and loss of prewar territories, many political observers wondered whether the nonaggression treaties with Poland and the Soviet Union would pass the Bundestag. Moscow refused to implement the Berlin agreement until the treaties were ratified.[180]

At the summit in Moscow, Nixon and Brezhnev signed a dazzling array of agreements, including the Basic Principles of Mutual Relations, the SALT accords, and establishment of a joint commission of economic relations as well as cooperation in science and technology, medicine, public health, environmental protection, collaboration in space exploration, and avoidance of incidents at sea. The Basic Principles agreement was consistent with Kissinger's long-standing belief that a stable international order required agreement on the legitimate ends and means of international politics.

For Nixon and Kissinger, learning took place at the level of tactical beliefs rather than the fundamental image of the opponent or strategy. By 1972 Nixon had learned that he could not expect simultaneous progress on the major issues at stake in U.S.–Soviet relations. In order to move toward negotiations with the Soviets, Nixon learned to decouple difficult issues from more manageable problems, to insulate competition in the Third World from the overall U.S.–Soviet security interdependence. The conflict of interest with the Soviets over the Middle East was too intractable. He eventually realized as well that the Soviets had limited leverage over Hanoi, and that they would not end the Vietnam War in return for trade concessions. The Soviets refused to be restrained and cooperative in all geographic locations and issue areas. Threatening to hold the U.S.–Soviet cooperation hostage whenever the Soviets behaved competitively in other areas had generated crisis and confrontation, not negotiation. In short, he abandoned linkage.

Instead of linkage, Nixon adopted a policy of step-by-step agreements, hoping to give the Soviet officials a stake in international order and to institutionalize more cooperative Soviet behavior.[181] Arms control could contribute to that objective; it need not follow the resolution of political issues. By 1972, Nixon regarded arms control as the "crown jewel" of the summit.[182]

DÉTENTE UNDONE, 1973

Brezhnev's June visit to the United States marked the halcyon days of U.S.–Soviet détente. But Nixon's failure to articulate an alternative strategy to linkage ultimately led to the unraveling of détente. Nixon's Democratic opponents used linkage against him, by tieing increased Jewish emigration to congressional approval of the Soviet trade agreement. In August 1972, the Soviet government had imposed an exit tax on emigrants. Two months later, Senator Henry Jackson proposed an amendment that denied most-favored-nation status to any Communist state that restricted emigration. Nixon and Kissinger believed that it was unrealistic to link issues to concessions within a state's domestic jurisdiction.[183]

In April 1973, Nixon submitted to Congress the U.S.–Soviet trade agreement that provided for credits and most-favored-nation status in return for settlement of the Soviet lend-lease debt.

During Brezhnev's visit, Senator Jackson and other Democratic senators threatened not to ratify the agreement giving the Soviets most-favored-nation status unless the Soviet government modified their policies on Jewish emigration. Brezhnev had come prepared with facts and figures showing that Jewish emigration had increased, and that only applicants whose presence was vital to national security were denied permission to leave. In interviews with the press and congressional leaders, the Soviet party secretary spent more time emphasizing the mutual benefits that both states would derive from large-scale, long-term trade agreements involving exchange of Soviet natural resources for U.S. technology and credits.[184]

Brezhnev and other Soviet officials regarded congressional attempts at linkage as an intrusion in their domestic affairs and a violation of sovereignty. Moreover, Brezhnev had based his détente policy on the expectation that massive infusions of Western capital and technological know-how would revitalize the sagging Soviet economy. The dispute over Soviet most-favored-nation status and credits and the Jackson amendment destroyed détente, as the Soviets had no incentive for restraint once anticipated economic benefits had been denied.

CONCLUSIONS

Nixon and Kissinger assumed power with an unusually well-developed strategy for moving the Soviet Union from confrontation to negotiation. As a result of their experience in office, they changed their initial preconceptions about the best tactics to use in dealing with the Soviet Union. When their initial approach failed to provide the Soviets with an incentive to restrain themselves either in the Third World or the arms race, Nixon and Kissinger decoupled SALT from U.S.–Soviet competition in the Third World, accepted nuclear parity with the Soviets, and agreed to make small agreements on arms control as a first step toward more substantive resolution of political differences.

Kissinger and Nixon did not change their fundamental beliefs about the Soviet Union or world order. This is not surprising, for policy makers must make quick decisions without having time to think. As Kissinger recalled, "there is little time for leaders to reflect. They are locked in an endless battle in which the urgent constantly gains on the important."[185] Policy makers assimilate what is new to what they already know. They act first, and rationalize later.

This case suggests that learning cannot be explained without focusing on individuals. People differ—in their receptivity to new information and ability to incorporate new data into their belief systems. Individuals such as Kissinger who have a complex belief system are able to integrate discrepant information without changing their presuppositions because they can add qualifications or subtypes.[186] While in office, Kissinger adopted a more modulated, subtle notion of linkage than his original idea of requiring that the Soviets cooperate on different issues. In his authoritative statement to the Senate Foreign Relations Committee on détente, Kissinger did not use the term linkage except to criticize those who tried to influence Soviet domestic policy. Instead, Kissinger said that the administration's approach was based on the belief that "in moving forward across a wide spectrum of negotiations, progress in one area adds momentum to progress in other areas."[187] "If we succeed," he said, "then no agreement stands alone as an isolated accomplishment vulnerable to the next crisis." This was a very different notion from the original conception of linkage. It implied a step-by-step approach to conflict, taking issues apart and solving the easiest first to create negotiating momentum. This notion of linkage also implied that "by acquiring a stake in this network of relationships with the West the Soviet Union may become more conscious of what it would lose by a return to confrontation."[188]

Kissinger adopted a more differentiated concept of linkage because the negotiations on Berlin and SALT proceeded on parallel but separate tracks. Although Kissinger and the Soviets delayed the talks on separate occasions to ensure that they ended simultaneously, no one tried to trade a concession for an equivalent return within the other negotiation. Although the China initiative gave the Soviets an incentive to speed up summit preparations, the process of U.S.–Soviet tension reduction had already gathered momentum before Nixon's visit to China was announced. Indeed, Brandt deserves much of the credit for establishing the groundwork for the Nixon-Kissinger "structure of peace" by giving the Soviets an incentive to cooperate with the West. The Soviets did not make concessions on the Middle East or Vietnam as the price for SALT.

As for Nixon, he was an other-directed politician, who had few enduring beliefs. Thus, Nixon's beliefs changed readily, but the changes did not last.

To explain learning, one must also focus on *types* of beliefs—from tactical, to strategic, to more central beliefs. Beliefs determine the *content* and *sequence* of lessons learned. People change less central beliefs first. Moreover, intellectuals and experts can more readily accommodate discrepant information without altering fundamental assumptions. Thus, one cannot explain why one lesson was learned rather than another without considering preexisting beliefs.

It is difficult otherwise to explain why Nixon and Kissinger were unreceptive to the domestic debate on MIRVs. Prominent arms control theorists, scientists, and members of Congress agreed that MIRVs would destabilize the strategic balance, increase the risk of preemption, and ultimately make the U.S. Minuteman force obsolete. If liberal theory were correct, the United States should have proposed a ban on MIRVs in 1969–1970, and détente with the Soviets might have occurred two years earlier. But Nixon and Kissinger believed that "nations are not in conflict because they are armed; they are armed because they are in conflict."

One might argue that an institutional framework better explains Nixon and Kissinger's inattention to the MIRV problem. The Pentagon thought only of its institutional interests in targeting and preferred a world in which both sides had MIRV to neither. Yet the content and intensity of beliefs determine the cost that politicians are willing to incur in support of policy positions. Nixon was not afraid to take unpopular positions that went against the grain of bureaucratic prejudices—as demonstrated by his dramatic coup in visiting China, pursuing SALT, and the bombing of Hanoi and mining of Haiphong. Indeed, he welcomed the opportunity to prove himself.

An institutionalist perspective better explains failure to learn than the reverse. Bureaucratic and domestic constraints interfered with Nixon and Kissinger's attempts to implement such strategic innovations as "sufficiency" and "linkage." For example, while Nixon repeatedly said that he recognized that the quest for nuclear superiority was futile once both sides had assured destructive capabilities, his administration accelerated deployment of MIRVs before the SALT negotiations were under way and sought counterforce capabilities, largely to satisfy the Pentagon.[189] Crises do not lead to learning because, in the stress and uncertainty of the moment, policy makers cannot obtain accurate information about whether their mistaken policies were responsible. Even if they do have such information, the need to appear in charge and confident before the bureaucracy and the electorate would inhibit them from making use of these lessons.

Nixon was more responsive to the domestic context of learning than the international one. He abandoned the policy of linking SALT to progress on Vietnam and the Middle East because Congress objected to financing nuclear weapons programs before an effort was made to negotiate limitations. Similarly, Nixon accepted "sufficiency" and mutual assured destruction in the SALT agreements because the post-Vietnam congressional emphasis on solving internal problems deprived him of the options of trying to maintain U.S. strategic superiority or of deploying an antiballistic missile system.

The Nixon-Kissinger case suggests that leaders respond more to domestic political changes than to environmental rewards and punishments. But it would also be simplistic to attribute change entirely to domestic politics. The relationship between leadership and domestic politics is more complex and interactive; Nixon, for example, conformed to domestic preferences on ABMs but not on MIRVs. His personal beliefs combined with an acute sensitivity to political costs and benefits determined his receptivity to public preferences.

Nixon was able to defuse much domestic opposition by claiming that he needed certain weapons systems as bargaining chips or for national security. President Nixon was also adept at packaging problems to cut the ground out from under his critics, as he did by supposedly moving the ABM system away from cities and by proposing a MIRV ban with on-site inspection.

The Nixon-Kissinger case has implications for the "levels of analysis" problem in international relations. Should the unit of analysis be the individual, state, or system? What is the relative explanatory weight of each?

Domestic political constraints, the technological imperatives of the arms race, and geopolitical pressures created by strategic overextension ensured that U.S. policy toward the Soviet Union would not be confrontational. Nixon and Kissinger's beliefs about the importance of concrete agreement rather than atmospherics, the futility of seeking nuclear superiority, and the importance of developing a legitimate, consensual framework for world order determined that U.S.–Soviet relations would go beyond coexistence to substantive cooperation.

This raises the more general question whether cognitive change is essential for creativity and innovation in foreign policy. Perhaps a change in leadership combined with a transitional period in the international system would be sufficient. Thus, more research needs to be done into the causes of creative statecraft.

Even if cognitive change is not essential for policy innovation, it may be that such changes will not endure without a cognitive basis of legitimation. In other words, because Nixon and Kissinger did not explain to the American public that their success resulted from decoupling rather than linkage, the policy of détente ultimately became unraveled as domestic opponents used linkage to influence Soviet domestic politics, contrary to Kissinger's original intentions.

Thus far, available research suggests that leaders change fundamental beliefs about the enemy only when forced by the pressure of circumstances to realign. For example, Harry S Truman did not change his beliefs that the Soviet Union would cooperate with the United States until several months *after* congressional budget cutting forced him to exaggerate the Soviet threat in the Truman Doctrine speech.[190] But clearly more empirical research needs to be done to determine whether it is possible for leaders to change their assumptions about the adversary incrementally by testing the evidence.

NOTES

1. Henry A. Kissinger, *White House Years* (Boston: Little, Brown, 1979), 54.

2. John R. Anderson, *Cognitive Psychology and Its Implications* (San Francisco: W.H. Freeman, 1980), 137–48, 331–43.

3. Jennifer Crocker, Susan T. Fiske, and Shelley E. Taylor, "Schematic Bases of Belief Change," in *Attitudinal Judgment*, ed. J. Richard Eiser (New York: Springer-Verlag), 197–226.

4. For further discussion, see Deborah Welch Larson, "Research Note: Problems of Content Analysis in Foreign-Policy Research: Notes From the Study of the Origins of Cold War Belief Systems," *International Studies Quarterly* 32 (1988): 241–55.

5. Kenneth N. Waltz, *Theory of International Politics* (Reading, Mass.: Addison-Wesley, 1979), 76-77.

6. Joseph S. Nye, Jr., "Nuclear Learning and U.S.–Soviet Security Regimes," *International Organization* 42 (Summer 1987): 378, 380; Joseph S. Nye, Jr., "Neorealism and Neoliberalism," *World Politics* 40 (January 1988): 235–51; Robert O. Keohane and Joseph S. Nye, Jr., "Power and Interdependence Revisited," *International Organization* 41 (Autumn 1987): 725–53.

7. Stephen Krasner, "Sovereignty: An Institutional Perspective," *Comparative Political Studies* 21 (Spring 1988): 66–94.

8. Amos Tversky and Daniel Kahneman, "Rational Choice and the Framing of Decisions," in *Rational Choice: The Contrast Between Economics and Psychology*, eds. Robin M. Hogarth and Melvin W. Reder (Chicago: University of Chicago Press, 1986): 90–91.

9. Robert Jervis, *Perception and Misperception in International Politics* (Princeton, N.J.: Princeton University Press, 1976), 217–82.

10. Susan T. Fiske and Shelley E. Taylor, *Social Cognition* (Reading, Mass.: Addison-Wesley, 1984), 163–64.

11. Deborah Welch Larson, *Origins of Containment: A Psychological Explanation* (Princeton, N.J.: Princeton University Press, 1985), 42–50.

12. Henry A. Kissinger, "Central Issues of American Foreign Policy," 1968 report to the Brookings Institution, reprinted in *American Foreign Policy*, 3rd ed. (New York: W.W. Norton, 1977), 88.

13. Henry A. Kissinger, *The Necessity for Choice* (Garden City, N.Y.: Doubleday, 1962), 194–95, 196–97.

14. Ibid., 161–63.

15. Ibid., 132–33.

16. Ibid., 199–200.

17. Ibid., 200–201.

18. Ibid., 203.

19. Ibid., 210.

20. Kissinger, "Central Issues of American Foreign Policy," in *American Foreign Policy*, 89.

21. Kissinger, *Necessity for Choice*, 177–78.

22. Kissinger, "Central Issues," 79.

23. Henry A. Kissinger, *A World Restored* (Boston: Houghton Mifflin, Sentry edition, 1973), 145.

24. Kissinger, "Central Issues," 57.

25. James Chace, "The Five-Power World of Richard Nixon," *New York Times Magazine*, 20 February 1972, 15.

26. "Nikita S. Khrushchev: The Man and His Mission," speech by Richard M. Nixon, American Dental Association, 14 September 1959, *Vital Speeches*, 15 October 1959, 16–18.

27. "Appraisal of Summit Conference," speech by Richard M. Nixon, 23 April 1960, American Society of Newspaper Editors, *Vital Speeches*, 1 June 1960, 486.

28. "American Policy Abroad," speech by Richard M. Nixon, American Society of Newspaper Editors, *Vital Speeches*, 1 June 1963, 487.

29. Ibid., 487–88.

30. "Where Nixon Stands," *U.S. News and World Report*, 14 October 1963, 89.

31. Kissinger, *White House Years*, 135–36.

32. Robert B. Semple, Jr., "A Role for Disaffected and the Young Pledged," *New York Times*, 21 January 1969, 22.

33. James Reston, "From Partisan to President of All," *New York Times*, 21 January 1969, 21.

34. Hedrick Smith, "President Links Political Issues to Missile Talks," *New York Times*, 28 January 1969, 1; I.F. Stone, "Nixon and the Arms Race: How Much is 'Sufficiency'?," *New York Review of Books*, 27 March 1969, 6.

35. Smith, "President Links Political Issues," 1.

36. John Newhouse, *Cold Dawn: The Story of SALT* (New York: Holt, Rinehart and Winston), 106–107.

37. Jerome H. Kahan, *Security in the Nuclear Age* (Washington, D.C.: Brookings Institution, 1975), 31–34; Gerard Smith, *Doubletalk: The Story of SALT I* (New York: Doubleday, 1980; Lanham, Md.: University Press of America, 1985), 23.

38. McGeorge Bundy, "To Cap the Volcano," *Foreign Affairs* (October 1969): 13.

39. Raymond L. Garthoff, *Détente and Confrontation: American–Soviet Relations From Nixon to Reagan* (Washington, D.C.: Brookings Institution, 1985), 56–57.

40. William Beecher, "Laird Supports Antimissile Net," *New York Times*, 31 January 1969, 1.

41. John W. Finney, "Pentagon Budget Cut $5.3 Billion by House Panel," *New York Times*, 4 December 1969, 1.

42. Richard Nixon, *RN* (New York: Grosset & Dunlap, 1978), 415.

43. Marvin Kalb and Bernard Kalb, *Kissinger* (Boston: Little, Brown, 1974), 106–107; Smith, *Doubletalk*, 23.

44. McGeorge Bundy, "How to Wind Down the Nuclear Arms Race," *New York Times*, 16 November 1969, IV-156.

45. Theodore Shabad, "Soviet Tells U.S. That It is Ready for Missile Talks," *New York Times*, 21 January 1969, 1.

46. Text of President Nixon's news conference on January 27, 1969, *New York Times*, 28 January 1969, 12.

47. Kissinger, *White House Years*, 129.

48. Kissinger, *White House Years*, 127.

49. Max Frankel, "Nixon Is Hopeful Moscow Will Help in Peacemaking," *New York Times*, 5 March 1969, 9.

50. Max Frankel, "Nixon Foreign-Affairs Gambles," *New York Times*, 16 March 1969, 15.

51. On the comparison between Eisenhower and Nixon, see Robert Kleiman, "Nixon's Choice: Stability or Upward Spiral in Missiles?," *New York Times*, 17 February 1969, 34.

52. Kissinger, *White House Years*, 113, 127, 129, 136.

53. Ibid., 113.

54. See, for example, James Reston, "The Kissinger Approach to the Soviets," *New York Times*, 29 January 1969, 40.

55. "Where Nixon Stands," *U.S. News and World Report*, 14 October 1963, 89.

56. Kissinger, *White House Years*, 143.

57. Ibid.

58. James Reston, "Washington: President Nixon and the New Soviet Line," *New York Times*, 19 March 1969, 46; Bernard Gwertzman, "Nixon's ABM Plans Arouse Soviet Press Critics," *New York Times*, 28 March 1969, 15; Henry Kamm, "Soviet May Day, Stressing Peace, Omits Arms Show," *New York Times*, 2 May 1969, 1; Bernard Gwertzman, "Gromyko Calls for New Era of Closer U.S.–Soviet Relations," *New York Times*, 11 July 1969, 1; Garthoff, *Détente and Confrontation*, 71–73.

59. Nixon, *RN*, 391.

60. Kissinger, *White House Years*, 266–68.

61. Garthoff, *Détente and Confrontation*, 250–51.

62. Juan d'Onis, "Malik Rejects Position of U.S. on Linkage of East-West Issues," *New York Times*, 19 February 1969, 6; Gwertzman, "Nixon's ABM Plans Arouse Soviet Press Critics," *New York Times*, 28 March 1969, 15; Garthoff, *Détente and Confrontation*, 184–85; Robert Kleiman, "Nixon's Great Gamble in Soviet-American Relations," *New York Times*, 7 April 1969, 42.

63. Kissinger, *White House Years*, 144.

64. Gwertzman, "Nixon's ABM Plans Arouse Soviet Press Critics," *New York Times,* 28 March 1965, 15; Bernard Gwertzman, "*Pravda* Voices Soviet Displeasure with U.S. Over Missile Policies and Delay on Arms-Control Talks," *New York Times,* 11 June 1969, 11.

65. Harry Gelman, *The Brezhnev Politburo and the Decline of Détente* (Ithaca: Cornell University Press, 1984), 109.

66. In an interview with Seymour M. Hersh, Morton Halperin, then a leading adviser to Kissinger on SALT, recalled that the White House permitted the formal SALT talks to begin in November 1969 only because of Soviet pressure. "We were confronted with it, and it would have been politically disastrous to Nixon and personally harmful to Henry not to go ahead with it." See Seymour M. Hersh, *The Price of Power: Kissinger in the Nixon White House* (New York: Summit Books, 1983), 147–48.

67. Kleiman, "Nixon's Choice: Stability or Upward Spiral in Missiles?," *New York Times,* 17 February 1969, 34.

68. John W. Finney, "Laird Sees 'Rapid' Soviet Missile Gains," *New York Times,* 21 February 1969, 1.

69. "Pact to Curb Arms Urged by Mansfield," *New York Times,* 13 April 1969, 61.

70. "The First Three Months," *New York Times* editorial, 20 April 1969, IV-12.

71. John W. Finney, "Sentinel Delay Urged in Senate," *New York Times,* 8 March 1969, 1.

72. Kissinger, *White House Years,* 205.

73. Kissinger, *White House Years,* 209; Robert B. Semple, Jr., "Nixon's Decision," *New York Times,* 16 March 1969, IV-1; Robert B. Semple, Jr., "Nixon Proposes ABM Revisions," *New York Times,* 15 March 1969, 1; John W. Finney, "Nixon Chances of Getting Senate Approval in Doubt," *New York Times,* 15 March 1969, 1; Max Frankel, "Nixon Takes Middle Ground in First Difficult Decision," *New York Times,* 15 March 1969, 18.

74. "The Useless 'Safeguard,'" *New York Times* editorial, 15 March 1969, 21.

75. James Reston, "Washington: President Nixon's Priorities," *New York Times,* 16 March 1969, IV-14.

76. *Intelligence and the ABM,* Hearings Before the Committee on Foreign Relations, U.S. Senate, 91st Cong., 1st sess., 23 June 1969, 6, 49; John W. Finney, "Fulbright Says Laird Uses Fear to Promote ABM," *New York Times,* 22 March 1969, 1.

77. Robert B. Semple, Jr., "Nixon Considers MIRV Tests Move," *New York Times,* 20 June 1969, 1.

78. Finney, "Fulbright Says Laird Uses Fear to Promote ABM," *New York Times,* 22 March 1969, 1.

79. *Strategic and Foreign Policy Implications of ABM Systems,* Hearings Before the Committee on Foreign Relations, 28 March 1969, 358; Semple, Jr., "Nixon Considers MIRV Tests Move," *New York Times,* 20 June 1969, 1; *Intelligence and the ABM,* Hearings Before the Committee on Foreign Relations, 8 July 1969, vi.

80. Warren Weaver, "ABM Foes Beaten," *New York Times,* 7 August 1969, 1.

81. John W. Finney, "Moratorium on Strategic Arms Suggested by Senate ABM Foes," *New York Times,* 25 April 1969, 27.

82. John W. Finney, "Missile Testing Divides U.S. Aides," *New York Times,* 22 May 1969, 1.

83. John W. Finney, "Critic Says Pentagon Chart Shows ABM to be 'Poor Defense,'" *New York Times,* 4 June 1969, 4; John W. Finney, "Case is Critical of Missile Policy," *New York Times,* 6 June 1969, 1.

84. Peter Grose, "U.S. Intends to Continue Missile Tests," *New York Times,* 6 June 1969, 1.

85. "ABM: The Central Issue," *New York Times* editorial, 22 May 1969, 46.

86. Grose, "U.S. Intends to Continue," 1.

87. John W. Finney, "Missile Testing Divides U.S. Aides," *New York Times,* 22 May 1969, 1.

88. John W. Finney, "U.S. Aide Cautions on MIRV Test Ban," *New York Times,* 2 July 1969, 13.

89. Robert Kleiman, "Nixon Confronts a Momentous Decision on the Hydra-Headed MIRV," *New York Times,* 17 August 1969, IV-2; "MIRV Responsibility," *New York Times* editorial, 29 July 1969, 36.

90. Kleiman, "Hydra-Headed MIRV," IV-2.

91. Peter Grose, "U.S. Intends to Continue Missile Tests," *New York Times,* 6 June 1969, 11; "MIRV Madness," *New York Times* editorial, 29 June 1969, IV-10.

92. James F. Clarity, "Rogers Says U.S. Can End ABM Work If Soviet Does," *New York Times,* 28 March 1969, 1.

93. "U.S. Assures Soviet on Arms-Curb Talks," *New York Times,* 16 June 1969, 11.

94. Henry Tanner, "Nixon Terms Arms Talks With Soviet Urgent Duty," *New York Times,* 2 March 1969, 1.

95. John W. Finney, "President's Speech Stirs Resentment in Congress," *New York Times,* 5 June 1969, 1.

96. Robert B. Semple, Jr., "He Chides Critics," *New York Times,* 5 June 1969, 1.

97. Robert B. Semple, Jr., "Nixon Considers MIRV Tests Move," *New York Times,* 20 June 1969, 1.

98. Edwin L. Dale, "Nixon Against Easing Curb on Trading with Red Bloc," *New York Times,* 29 May 1969, 1; Kissinger, *White House Years,* 152–54; Garthoff, *Détente and Confrontation,* 90–91.

99. Garthoff, *Détente and Confrontation,* 88–89.

100. Bernard Gwertzman, "Soviet Leaders Held Split Over Strategic Arms Talks," *New York Times,* 27 October 1969, 1; Garthoff, *Détente and Confrontation,* 131–32; Kissinger, *White House Years,* 145.

101. Max Frankel, "New Arms Talks: Risk and Opportunity," *New York Times,* 27 October, 1969, 1.

102. Greenwood, *Making the MIRV,* 134–35.

103. "MIRV Nightmare," *New York Times* editorial, 18 July 1969, 32.

104. John W. Finney, "Arms Panel Urges Halt in Weapons Deployment," *New York Times,* 5 April 1970, 3.

105. Tad Szulc, "A Missile Freeze Urged by Jackson," *New York Times,* 29 March 1971, 9.

106. Greenwood, *Making the MIRV,* 134–35.

107. Garthoff, *Détente and Confrontation,* 139–40; Smith, *Doubletalk,* 176.

108. Garthoff, *Détente and Confrontation*, 140; Greenwood, *Making the MIRV*, 134; Robert Kleiman, "New Roadblock to Arms Control Progress," *New York Times*, 11 January 1970, IV-14; William Beecher, "Soviet Diplomats Said to Hint Interest in MIRV Curbs," *New York Times*, 12 March 1970, 14.

109. See Hersh, *Price of Power*, 150–56.

110. Garthoff, *Détente and Confrontation*, 138–39; Smith, *Doubletalk*, 171.

111. Greenwood, *Making the MIRV*, 138–39; Hersh, *Price of Power*, 155; Garthoff, *Détente and Confrontation*, 135; Smith, *Doubletalk*, 119, 161; John Newhouse, *Cold Dawn*, 180–81.

112. Garthoff, *Détente and Confrontation*, 148–49.

113. Bernard Gwertzman, "Kosygin Attacks Nixon for Moving G.I.'s to Cambodia," *New York Times*, 5 May 1970, 1

114. "Kosygin Reports Impasse on China," *New York Times*, 11 June 1970, 7.

115. Bernard Gwertzman, "Brezhnev Says U.S. Spurs Aggression as It Talks Peace," *New York Times*, 13 June 1970, 1.

116. "Chilly Breeze from Moscow," *New York Times* editorial, 13 June 1970, 30.

117. Smith, *Doubletalk*, 137, 152.

118. "Cambodia Sweep Termed Success," *New York Times*, 10 May 1970, 23.

119. Kissinger, *White House Years*, 408–12, 423–24, 529–34; Hersh, *Price of Power*, 416.

120. What linkage meant in this instance was not trading concessions on SALT, for example, for reciprocal concessions on Berlin. Instead, Kissinger tried to see that negotiations on Berlin and SALT concluded simultaneously. As Kissinger recalled, "the linkage was never made explicit, but it was clearly reflected in the pace of our negotiations" (*White House Years*, 821–22). Kissinger did not trust the Soviets to cooperate on SALT once they had achieved stabilization of the status quo in Europe. Thus, Kissinger resorted to the device of having Ambassador Rush take a vacation for extended periods.

121. *New York Times*, 26 September 1970, 2; Kissinger, *White House Years*, 585–91.

122. Bernard Gwertzman, "Kosygin Forgoes Visit to the U.N.," *New York Times*, 10 October, 1970, 1.

123. Ibid.

124. Tad Szulc, "U.S. Sees Big Rise in Defense Costs If Arms Talks Fail," *New York Times*, 12 October 1970, 1.

125. "U.S. Sees a Peril in Asia Cease-Fire," *New York Times*, 14 October 1970, 1; Max Frankel, "U.S.-Soviet Ties: An Uncertain Crisis," *New York Times*, 15 October 1970, 12; James F. Clarity, "U.S. and Russia: Chill in the Air Again," *New York Times*, 18 October 1970, IV-1; "The Rogers-Gromyko Talks," *New York Times*, 20 October 1970, 46.

126. James Reston, "Nixon and Brezhnev," *New York Times*, 20 December 1970, IV-11.

127. Hedrick Smith, "U.S. and Russia: The Mood is a Bit Warmer," *New York Times*, 25 October 1970, IV-4.

128. Text of Nixon's speech to the United Nations, October 23 1970, *New York Times*, 24 October 1970, 10; Robert Kleiman, "U.S. Strategy on the Kremlin Debate," *New York Times*, 8 February 1971, 33.

129. Ibid.

130. Robert Kleiman, "U.S. Strategy on the Kremlin Debate," *New York Times*, 8 February 1971, 33.

131. Ibid.

132. Richard Nixon, "U.S. Foreign Policy for the 1970s: Building for Peace," 25 February 1971, 3–4.

133. Ibid., 161–62.

134. Ibid., 158.

135. Ibid., 177; Hedrick Smith, "President Says Arms Pact Should Limit All Missiles," *New York Times*, 26 February 1971, 1.

136. Newhouse, *Cold Dawn*, 198; Smith, *Doubletalk*, 206–207; Lawrence Freedman, *U.S. Intelligence and the Soviet Strategic Threat*, 2nd ed. (Princeton, N.J.: Princeton University Press, 1986), 156-57; Raymond L. Garthoff, "SALT and the Soviet Military," 24 (January-February 1975): 30.

137. "President Terms Cuba Off Limits for Soviet Subs," *New York Times*, 5 January 1971, 21.

138. Smith, *Doubletalk*, 202, 204–205; Kissinger, *White House Years*, 811–12.

139. William Beecher, "Pentagon Seeks Missile Defense Around Capital," *New York Times*, 27 January 1971, 1.

140. Bernard Gwertzman, "Moscow Assails U.S. Arms Stand," *New York Times*, 4 February 1971, 6.

141. Bernard Gwertzman, "Soviet Assails U.S. for Opposing a Limited ABM Pact," *New York Times*, 7 February 1971, 3.

142. Newhouse, *Cold Dawn*, 201.

143. William Beecher, "U.S. Expects Soviet to Test Large New Missiles Soon," *New York Times* 19 May 1971, 1.

144. Newhouse, *Cold Dawn*, 202.

145. Freedman, *U.S. Intelligence and the Soviet Strategic Threat*, 164–65.

146. Hedrick Smith, "Missile Activity in Soviet Found," *New York Times*, 8 March 1971, 1.

147. Ibid.

148. Smith, *Doubletalk*, 208–209, 226; Freedman, *U.S. Intelligence and the Soviet Strategic Threat*, 166; Newhouse, *Cold Dawn*, 204–205.

149. Tad Szulc, "A Missile Freeze Urged by Jackson," *New York Times*, 29 March 1971, 9.

150. Smith, *Doubletalk*, 212–13.

151. William Beecher, "U.S. Expects Soviet to Test Large New Missiles Soon," *New York Times*, 19 May 1971, 1; John W. Finney, "C.I.A. Said to Doubt Pentagon's View on Missile Threat," *New York Times*, 16 May 1971, 4; Freedman, *U.S. Intelligence and the Soviet Strategic Threat*, 165.

152. Bernard Gwertzman, "Peace and Consumer Gain Stressed at Soviet Parley," *New York Times*, 31 March 1971, 15; Garthoff, *Détente and Confrontation*, 42. Brezhnev had not yet completely removed his opponents from the Politburo. Consequently, there were limits to how far he could go in signing trade agreements with the West.

153. Bernard Gwertzman, "Gromyko Urges Serious Effort to Ease Tensions," *New York Times*, 4 April 1971, 1.

154. Bernard Gwertzman, "Nixon 'Flexibility' Impresses Russians," *New York Times,* 22 March 1971, 10.

155. James Reston, "Brezhnev's World View," *New York Times,* 31 March 1971, 45.

156. Bernard Gwertzman, "Soviet Cautious," *New York Times,* 21 May 1971, 2.

157. Bernard Gwertzman, "Soviet Defends Its Policy of Improving U.S. Relations," *New York Times,* 25 June 1971, 4.

158. Victor Lusinchi, "Russian Move Opens Way for Biological Arms Ban," *New York Times,* 31 March 1971, 1.

159. Kissinger, *White House Years,* 938–39, 946–47; Garthoff, *Détente and Confrontation,* 115–16.

160. Harrison E. Salisbury, "Signs of 'Détente' Are Popping Up All Over," *New York Times,* 23 May 1971, IV-1.

161. Max Frankel, "Compromise Set," *New York Times,* 21 May 1971, 1; Garthoff, *Détente and Confrontation,* 417; Kissinger, *White House Years,* 820–21.

162. Kissinger, *White House Years,* 803, 814–16, 818–19; Smith, *Doubletalk,* 222–23, 226–27, 230–33.

163. Frankel, "Compromise Set," *New York Times* 21 May 1971, 2; Smith, *Doubletalk,* 223, 244.

164. Garthoff, *Détente and Confrontation,* 92; Hersh, *Price of Power,* 345–48.

165. James Reston, "Cautious Nixon Strategy," *New York Times,* 21 May 1971, 39.

166. Garthoff, *Détente and Confrontation,* 183.

167. Max Frankel, "Diplomatic Thaws Spur New Questions in Washington," *New York Times,* 25 May 1971, 12; "Doing Business With Brezhnev," *New York Times,* 17 October 1971, IV-10; Tad Szulc, "Would You Believe a Genuine Détente?" *New York Times,* 20 June 1971, IV-4.

168. Tad Szulc, "Accord Reported to Prevent War by Atomic Error," *New York Times,* 13 September 1971, 1.

169. For example, on April 19, *New York Times* columnist and editorial board member Harry Schwartz commented that President Nixon could score a major political coup if he toured the People's Republic of China in summer 1972, during the Democratic Party convention. "At the moment," he wrote, "any such ambitious agenda of near-term Chinese-American cooperation is sheer fantasy. There is still too much suspicion and fear between the two powers to expect so rapid an evolution of relations." "Triangular Politics and China," *New York Times,* 19 April 1971, 37.

170. Frankel, "Diplomatic Thaws Spur New Questions in Washington," *New York Times,* 25 May 1971,12; Bernard Gwertzman, "Brezhnev's Future Priorities," *New York Times,* 12 April 1971, 18; Robert Kleiman, "Mr. Nixon and Berlin," *New York Times,* 4 September 1971, 21; Garthoff, *Détente and Confrontation,* 14.

171. Gelman, *The Brezhnev Politburo and the Decline of Détente,* 126–30.

172. Gwertzman, "Nixon 'Flexibility' Impresses Russians," *New York Times,* 22 March 1971, 10.

173. Richard Nixon, "U.S. Foreign Policy for the 1970s: The Emerging Structure of Peace," 9 February 1972, 5–6.

174. Ibid., 17–18.

175. Stanley Hoffmann, "Statecraft Demands Imagination," *New York Times*, 7 March 1972, 39.

176. Kissinger, *White House Years*, 268–69, 1135.

177. Ibid., 1134, 1156.

178. Ibid., 1159–60.

179. Harry Schwartz, "Moscow's Smile," *New York Times*, 7 August 1972, 27; Garthoff, *Détente and Confrontation*, 102.

180. *New York Times*, 28 April 1972, 11; "Survival at Bonn," *New York Times* editorial, 28 April 1972, 40.

181. Henry Brandon, "Nixon's Way With the Russians," *New York Times Magazine*, 21 January 1973, 36.

182. Garthoff, *Détente and Confrontation*, 184–85.

183. Henry Kissinger, *Years of Upheaval* (Boston: Little, Brown, 1982), 254.

184. Hedrick Smith, "Brezhnev Praises Nixon for 'Realistic' Approach," *New York Times*, 15 June 1973, 2.

185. Kissinger, *White House Years*, 54.

186. Fiske and Taylor, *Social Cognition*, 174; Crocker, Fiske, and Taylor, "Schematic Bases of Belief Change," 204.

187. U.S. Senate, *Détente*, Hearings Before the Committee on Foreign Relations, 93d Congress, 2nd sess. (Washington: U.S. Government Printing Office, 1975), 249.

188. Ibid.

189. Alton Frye, *A Responsible Congress: The Politics of National Security* (New York: McGraw-Hill, 1975), 69.

190. Larson, *Origins of Containment*.

11

Learning in U.S. Policy Toward the Soviet Union in the 1980s

Alexander Dallin

THE PROBLEM AND THE SOURCES

U.S. policy toward the Soviet Union during the Reagan years exhibited a sharp shift—from sweeping, systematic hostility at the start, to a sequence of hopeful summits and accords at the end. What accounted for this change of rhetoric and behavior? And to what extent can these and other developments in the same period be explained in terms of individual or organizational learning?

The body of material surveyed for this chapter consists primarily of the public pronouncements of the president, the national security adviser, and the secretary of state—their prepared speeches and formal remarks as well as press conferences and impromptu comments—and of some of their subordinates in the executive branch. Memoirs of contemporaries—mostly of a disappointing kiss-and-tell variety—as well as secondary studies have been consulted, and a small number of interviews have been conducted. However, a serious problem of sources remains.

It is whether the published record available to us adequately reflects the thinking, the beliefs, and the values of the office holders concerned. Alas, within the confines of this undertaking there is no way to go significantly beyond the public record, although at a future point this may be possible, both through more extensive interviews with former officials and through perusal of still unavailable government files. Even then, of course, legitimate questions would remain regarding the congruence of articulations and beliefs. Not only did the president's deputy press secretary, Larry Speakes, later reveal that he himself had made up quotations he had given the media as verbatim statements by the president,[1] but more generally in the age of media hype and "spin control" there are increasing grounds to question whether the written (or oral) record bears any verisimilitude to the author's perceptions or convictions. While it may be assumed that there is a reasonably close fit in regard to the secretary of state or the national security adviser, this cannot be assumed about the president except in unedited, spontaneous, off-the-cuff remarks.

COLD WAR FUNDAMENTALISM: THE BACKGROUND

Given the available record of earlier comments by incoming President Reagan and some of his entourage, the dominant mind set in the new administration with regard to the Soviet Union can be sketched rather more clearly than would have been possible for a number of his predecessors. There are repeated and articulate expressions by Ronald Reagan and those around him of a consistent ideological and political outlook on communism—of what has been called American *cold war fundamentalism*. (To the Reagan team the fact that the Soviet Union was communist mattered a good deal more than did the fact that, in its dominant culture, it was Russian. A generation earlier, it is true, Ronald Reagan had argued that communism was a myth concealing traditional Russian objectives. For many White House staffers this was, in any event, a distinction without a difference.) Communism—or socialism, or Marxism-Leninism, as Ronald Reagan almost interchangeably referred to it—was something he had learned about both from personal experience and from capsule distillations, largely from bitter enemies of it. So was totalitarianism:

> . . . [O]nly one so-called revolution puts itself above God, insists on total control over the peoples' lives, and is driven by the desire to seize more and more lands. . . . Two visions of the world remain locked in dispute.[2]

Some observers would see Reagan's anti-Soviet evangelism as an extension of his domestic views: "The struggle to defend freedom and morality abroad is a more intense version of the battle to preserve these virtues at home. In the eyes of Reagan and other conservatives the communism of the Soviet Union represents the end point, the logical culmination of dangerous currents—big government, atheism, and relaxed moral standards."[3]

Reagan's personal history had indeed included some experience with what he later remembered as communism during his days in Hollywood. As he volunteered in an interview toward the end of his first year in office:

[QUESTION:]. . . Your stand against communism—and it's well known—is tough and has always been tough. But I gather that since you've become President, you've sort of run into the new realism of "We're in this world together."

THE PRESIDENT: No, not at all. I had my earliest experience with communism, and it is pretty much the same. I know that it sounds kind of foolish maybe to link Hollywood, an experience there, to the world situation, and yet, the tactics seemed to be pretty much the same. But that much rewritten history of Hollywood and distorted history has hidden from many people what actually took place back there in the late forties after World War II. It was a Communist attempt to gain control of the motion picture industry, because at that time the Hollywood motion picture industry provided the film for 75 percent of the playing time in all the theaters of the world. It was the greatest propaganda device, if someone wanted to use it for that, that's ever been known. . . . I was right in the middle of it as president of the Screen Actors Guild. . . .

This is how I knew it from the inside, and I think I learned a lot there. And the funny thing is, I didn't start with a bias. As a matter of fact, I started the other way.[4]

The *Los Angeles Times* had quoted Reagan at the time as saying about the allegation of a "red" takeover of Hollywood, "The Russians sent their first team, their ace string, here to take us over"—a story that can only be described as fantasy.[5]

His view of communism, as the interviewer mentioned, was indeed tough, and there is nothing to suggest that he was prepared to make any significant distinction between American and Soviet communists, between those in and out of power, or between those in 1917 and those in the 1980s. "They" had been, and presumably remained, all of them, wedded to world revolution or Soviet world domination (which, in the Reagan world view, amounted to very much the same thing). Marxism-Leninism required it, and if he had any questions whether that belief system was bound to have operational consequences for all communists and for all communist regimes, no such doubts were apparent:

They are the ones that seek, whether it's out of paranoia on their part—and believe me, everyone's an enemy, and so they have to be aggressive—or whether it is the Marxist-Leninist theory, more than a theory—commitment—that was handed them, and that was that they must support uprisings wherever they take place in the world to bring about a one-world communist state.[6]

It was a given that—as President Reagan made certain to state at his very first news conference after his inauguration in January 1981, in reply to a question about Soviet intentions, "their goal must be the promotion of world communism and a one-world socialist or communist state. . . . The only morality they recognize is what will further their cause: meaning they reserve unto themselves the right to commit any crime, to lie, to cheat, to obtain that. . . ."[7] It seemed as if the new president, a seasoned actor, had rehearsed the answer in advance.

But ideology and conviction were one thing; policy and conduct were another.[8] Inevitably perhaps, many inconsistencies and contradictions developed that suggested to some observers, not for the first time, that the presidential bark was worse than the bite. Practical considerations—bluntly, domestic politics—led Reagan to terminate the ban on wheat shipments to the Soviet Union that Jimmy Carter had imposed after the Soviet invasion of Afghanistan. After some slight hesitation, not all communist regimes were treated alike. U.S. policy toward Red China and Yugoslavia did differ from that toward Moscow; a policy of differentiation sought to make qualitative distinctions in dealing with East European communist regimes. Later, as the second term went on, references to the Soviet commitment to a single worldwide communist state and to revolution abroad became rare (except in regard to Central America). It is not clear what impact the perception of China's departure from anything resembling orthodox communism had on the judgment of American policy makers; the president would typically dismiss the problem of reconciling his view of China with his ideological perspective by finding that China had not really been communist. Perhaps this provided an unstated precedent for later divorcing his practical, operational approach to the Soviet Union from his theoretical view of Marxism-Leninism. In any event, he was prepared to remark, when questioned on Red Square during his visit to Moscow in 1988, that his identification of the Soviet system as the "evil empire" belonged to an earlier era that had passed. But then, what else could he have said, with Mikhail Gorbachev as genial host at his side? In any event, the implication was that it was the Soviet Union that had changed, not Ronald Reagan.

Whether the salient changes that characterized American conduct and rhetoric regarding the Soviet Union were tactical or fundamental remained an open question. The most general trend characterizing the evolution of American policy toward the Soviet Union in the 1980s was an increasing departure from the rigidity of ideological stereotypes and their replacement by a more open-ended (if not totally open-minded) pragmatism in dealing with the Soviet Union.

It is likely that this shift was facilitated by a certain divorce of rhetoric

from policy even in the first term. Entirely apart from the inconsistencies and contradictions noted above, on a practical level there was a
sense that the United States had nothing to negotiate with the Soviet
Union about. This made it easy to adopt a posture of ostracism and
global alarm; it similarly made it easier, later, once an agenda of negotiations
appeared, to adjust policies and modify the rhetoric that backed them.

LEARNING FROM HISTORY:
IN SEARCH OF A USABLE PAST

In the course of the 1980s administration paradigms regarding the
Soviet Union underwent significant changes; they fit at least a minimalist
definition of learning as reflected in verbal or behavioral change. Whether
or not the key actors of the Reagan administration learned from experience is explored below. While historical imagery seems to have gone
along with these changes in paradigms and policies, there is no indication
that anything significant was ever learned from history, either before or
after the paradigm change.

In fact, it is apparently the case that (with some exceptions) U.S. political elites tend to be relatively impervious to historical information
(accurate or otherwise). As the authors of an important recent study put
it, "We sensed around us—in our classes, in the media, in Washington—
a host of people who did not know any history to speak of and were
unaware of suffering any lack . . . ."[9] It was as if intellectuals, like court
jesters and purveyors of staples and spices to Her Majesty, were at times
used to supply historical data as examples, precedents, or moral lessons.
And if the knowledge of history and its application to political values
and strategies, particularly to foreign policy-relevant perspectives, have
typically been scanty for U.S. decision-making circles, this lack was particularly glaring and pervasive for most of the personnel brought into
the executive branch in 1981.

The available information provides no reason to think that historical
evidence was viewed or accepted as a significant input capable of challenging or reversing accepted views of the president and those around
him; it did figure among the anecdotes, stereotypes, one-liners, and 3×5
cards used to illustrate comfortable notions dearly held. In other words,
history might selectively be part of the script, and the script might indeed be modified over time. At times, history was *used,* but it did not *inform.*
When the task was to explain why progress on arms control was slow
and difficult, reference was often made to the "historical record" of repeated Soviet violations of earlier treaties and agreements. When an
arms control agreement (such as the Intermediate-range Nuclear Forces—
INF—agreement) was concluded, this litany was tacitly dropped (only to

be picked up by critics of the treaty in Congress or on the political far right).

Moreover, the available information argues strongly that for public pronouncements from the White House the key variable determining the use of historical images and references was who the president's speechwriters and closest advisers were (and what their assumptions amounted to) at any given time. Insiders knew or could guess which of several possible writers had left his or her footprint on particular presidential speeches or remarks. Not only Patrick Buchanan was thus tasked, in effect, to put words in the president's mouth. To give but one example, this was apparently the case with the president's references to the "evil empire" in speaking of the Soviet system to a gathering of evangelical fundamentalists in 1983.[10]

No doubt key figures in the Reagan administration assumed that the historical record strongly bore out their assumptions about communism, about the superpowers, about war and peace, and about the way the world was spinning. History, in this light, was a device for validation, one of many. It served much as did another anecdote on the teleprompter or underscoring on the computer screen.

A more complete picture requires adding several elements. First, even in the first Reagan years in the White House, there were some people around the administration who had a distinctly less ideological approach and tended to adopt a more moderate and agnostic view of the Soviet Union and U.S.–Soviet relations. Professional bureaucrats or conservative business leaders with an efficiency orientation or an agenda of decontrol, they were either not interested in the more abstract and sweeping judgments concerning communism and its putative mission, even if they accepted the Reagan thesis in general terms and made sure not to question it in public; or else they found the hard-line pronouncements concerning the Russians counterproductive. This was true, for instance, of some professional foreign service officers, some journalists recruited into the government, and some business leaders in the Department of Commerce.

More generally, throughout the Reagan years, different subelites in Washington functioned with different paradigms and unreconciled images of the Soviet Union. But all those involved in, or on the fringes of, the security field may be assumed to have substantially shared the dominant attitude of "peace through strength," discussed below, which referred to appeasement in the 1930s and to détente in the 1970s as the prime exhibits of the folly of those failing to heed that dictum.

Second, there were a few intellectuals in, or close to, the administration who had a better knowledge of history and at times used it to support their views. In most instances, their arguments placed them rather far on the right end of the ideological spectrum. Richard Pipes, a prominent

Harvard professor of Russian history, served for some two years as senior specialist on Soviet affairs in the National Security Council. In his case, the views he held were, and are, well known thanks to his many publications and public appearances. In the early 1980s he maintained, as he had for a generation, that short of a major catastrophe—a Hiroshima or a Holocaust—the dominant political culture of a country, developed cumulatively over centuries, could not be altered, and that the Russian past in substance predetermined the Soviet present and future. By implication, there were no grounds to expect any significant change in the Soviet system or in communism. Pipes contributed memoranda and arguments, parts of which showed up in presidential speeches and documents and, more generally, provided intellectual backbone and footnotes to the more sweeping anti-Soviet orientation. He left the administration with some frustration over its perceived need to make political compromises.[11]

Others who made contributions of an intellectual sort included Jeane Kirkpatrick, a political scientist; Eugene Rostow, a lawyer; and (by laxer criteria) perhaps Richard V. Allen and Edward Rowney. Though hardly experts on Soviet history or politics, they had strong views that placed them too at the intransigent end of the Washington rainbow. So did a few analysts with close ties to key administration figures, such as senior staffers of the Heritage Foundation and Irving Kristol, of *The Wall Street Journal*, who would declare as late as 1987 that:

> The Soviet Union believes it has the right to intervene anywhere, any time it's convenient. That is part of its Marxist-Leninist doctrine. It doesn't believe in the principle of nonintervention, and since it does not, neither can we.[12]

The most frequent and most consistently invoked historical references were simple and straightforward. They tended to appear in regard to verities that invited reinforcement by reference to historical stereotypes. Two historical images dominated the rhetoric dealing with the Soviet Union.

One was the Hitler analogy. This consisted of two parts. The more generally accepted element was the argument stressing the failure of appeasement in the 1930s. The practical payoff of the argument was to defend larger spending on defense. You cannot satiate an aggressor by giving him some of what he asks for: he will only ask for more. As the president told a group of foreign television journalists, "the civilized world [cannot] ignore the conduct of a country that today is bombing helpless women and children, is using chemical warfare, places like Cambodia and Afghanistan. I don't think that we can remain silent, as too many of us in the world did when Hitler was coming to power, in the face of this kind of conduct."[13] What he had in mind was put more systematically in a prepared text:

> It's always very easy and very tempting politically to come up with arguments for neglecting defense spending in time of peace. One of the great tragedies of the century was that it was only after the balance of power was allowed to erode and a ruthless adversary, Adolf Hitler, deliberately weighed the risks and decided to strike that the importance of a strong defense was realized too late. That was what happened in the years leading up to World War II. And especially for those of us who lived through that nightmare, it's a mistake that America and the free world must never make again.[14]

France and Britain facing the Nazis, and Munich 1938 in particular, were the references used. There was not a single effort, on the record, to ask whether the assumptions regarding Nazi Germany were equally applicable to the Soviet Union: by implication, they must be.

That indeed was the second part of the argument, advanced by only some in the administration. It was perhaps most revealingly put by Assistant Secretary of Defense Richard Perle in a talk at the Kennan Institute in Washington. When he was uncertain about the next Soviet move, he confessed, he would ask himself, "What would Hitler have done?" Here the assumed similarity in behavior among all totalitarian regimes went quite far, and it cannot be said that all high officials of the Reagan administration (if they asked themselves this question) would have accepted the imputed identity. Jeane Kirkpatrick had a special role in having the "totalitarian" category more widely used. On the record, there was no discussion of the possible changes in the Soviet system since Stalin's days that might have made the label inappropriate; nor any question whether there might not be fundamental differences between the Nazi and the Soviet models, whatever the similarities.

The second, and closely related, formula invoking historical precedents was "peace through strength." In simplest terms, the argument was that the record of the past invariably showed that weakness not only led to the adversary's victory in war but also tempted the adversary into aggression. It argued that recent history was replete with compelling examples: the failure of the Western democracies to arm and stand up to Hitler in the 1930s; the failure of the Western allies to show strength and resolve in dealing with Stalin at Yalta and after the end of the war; and— within the experience of the actors in the Reagan administration—the years of détente (if truth be told, under Richard Nixon and Gerald Ford, as well as Jimmy Carter) that witnessed a precipitous decline in American prestige, with the surrender of Southeast Asia to the communists as its symbol; the emergence of Soviet client regimes in Nicaragua, Angola, South Yemen, and Ethiopia; and the hostage crisis in Teheran as the aftermath. All these were cited as examples of the failure to heed the dictum that strength, and only strength, could guard the peace.

In retrospect, "détente, as it existed, was only a cover under which the Soviet Union built up the greatest military power in the world."[15] What then?

> This stretch of 37 years since World War II [Ronald Reagan declared in 1982] has been the result of our maintaining a balance of power between the United States and the Soviet Union and between the strategic nuclear capabilities of either side. As long as this balance has been maintained, both sides have been given an overwhelming incentive for peace. In the 1970s the United States altered this balance by, in effect, unilaterally restraining our own military defenses while the Soviet Union engaged in an unprecedented build-up of both its conventional and nuclear forces. . . . If steps are not taken to modernize our defense, the United States will progressively lose the ability to deter the Soviet Union from employing force or threats of force against us and against our allies.[16]

The obvious implication for the Reagan policy makers was the priority objective of regaining a position of strength to deal with the Soviet Union, whether to intimidate, deter, or negotiate. There was relatively little elaboration of this simplistic formula. What kind of strength was needed: Was it only military, or also economic and moral? How was it measured—in dollars appropriated for defense, in weapons acquired or deployed, or in some other way? Was it material power that mattered, or perceptions? The notion of military sufficiency did not enter the argument, nor any sense that different defense strategies called for different configurations of men and weapons, that qualitative differences could matter greatly, or that arms control had to be integrated into the desired defense agenda even if it meant making nonsense of the formula "more is better," in defense. Nor, finally, was the question raised in this context what constraints were imposed by the magnitude of revenues and by alternative demands on scarce federal resources. The argument and the historical references were apparently considered powerful and effective, although—or perhaps because—they were so simple.

THE PARADIGM CHANGE

From the start the Reagan administration, like any other, faced the problem of reconciling its new experiences with preexisting assumptions and expectations. Throughout the Reagan years, there was an unresolved tension between ideological and pragmatic (essentialist versus mechanistic) approaches. In essence, over time, the pragmatic elements got stronger. By 1984 one could speak of an unadvertised (and as yet incomplete) paradigm change. At the outset, the dominant assumption in the highest administration circles had been that ultimately the Soviet system must go—either because totalitarian systems, inherently expansionist, did not change; or because Soviet conduct showed a troubling continuity of behavior that had been characteristic throughout Russian history. In his address to the British Parliament on June 8, 1982, Reagan came close to calling for a crusade to rid the world of the Soviet scourge and pledging all the help needed to internal forces working to subvert it (much as he would later seek to do to the Contras fighting the Sandinista regime or to the Mujahaddin in Afghanistan). There were, he said, "totalitarian forces in the world who seek subversion and conflict around the globe to further their barbarous assault on the human spirit. What then is our course? Must civilization perish in a hail of fiery atoms? Must freedom wither in a quiet, deadening accommodation with totalitarian evil?"

The Soviet system, he declared, was "inherently unstable," and "the very repressiveness of the state ultimately drives people to resist it, if necessary by force." The president's speechwriters had incorporated suggestions received from the National Security Council staff, which included references to historians' writings "since the exodus from Egypt" about those who "sacrificed and struggled for freedom—the stand at Thermopylae, the revolt of Spartacus, the storming of the Bastille, the Warsaw uprising in World War II." The West "must not hesitate to declare our ultimate objectives and to take concrete actions to move toward them." Part of those objectives was the mission "to foster the infrastructure of democracy," "to help others to gain their freedom as well." Destabilizing the Soviet Union, bankrupting it, and fighting it by proxies were three of the strategies being explored.[17]

Meanwhile a well-connected official in the U.S. Information Agency (USIA), Scott Thompson, was giving lectures explaining that it was time to "take the struggle directly to the enemy, on his own ground."[18] Officials at the Voice of America urged a more militant policy aimed at "destabilizing" the Soviet system by promoting disaffection "by peoples against rulers." Consultants spoke of using an "Islamic card" against Moscow. Serious papers were produced by senior academic consultants to the administration discussing the ways in which the United States might be able to intervene in Eastern Europe if civil strife erupted there.

For the time being, in any event, while it was impolitic to say so in public, it was taken for granted (and this was Secretary Haig's understanding) that "there was nothing substantial . . . to negotiate until the USSR began to demonstrate its willingness to behave like a responsible power."[19]

At the end of 1983 the superpowers appeared to be once more on a collision course. The bitterness over the shooting down of the KAL-007 airliner, the struggle over the deployment of Pershing-2s and cruise missiles in Europe, the Soviet walkout from the INF, Strategic Arms Reduction Talks (START), and conventional arms control negotiations were only some of the dramatic highlights of the new confrontation. The U.S. landing in Grenada in October 1983 was also calculated to impress third parties (and the American public) with U.S. determination and readiness to act.

But then the signals began to change. At first, these changes were almost universally dismissed as verbal ploys. In a speech on January 16, 1984, which high government officials later pointed to as the first public indication that the earlier intransigence was being jettisoned, the president declared in a carefully prepared text that "we should always remember that we do have common interests." There was, in essence, no alternative to coexistence:

> . . . [O]ur two peoples [the president said] share common bonds and interests. . . . Avoiding war and reducing arms is a starting point in our relationship with the Soviet Union, but we seek to accomplish more. With a good-faith effort on both sides, I believe the United States and the Soviet Union could begin rising above the mistrust and ill will that cloud our relations. We could establish a basis for greater mutual understanding and constructive cooperation, and there's no better time to make that good-faith effort than now.[20]

Even so, the overall problem of accepting the reality of Soviet power, rather than trying to change the Soviet system, presented serious political and conceptual problems for the administration. They were illustrated, for instance, in this exchange between Congressman Lee Hamilton and Assistant Secretary of State Richard Burt, in June 1984:

> MR. HAMILTON: The President said the other day that if the Soviets want to keep their Mickey Mouse system, that is ok. Now, if you look at that statement, it would seem to suggest that we are giving up the idea of trying to influence their internal situation, their politics, or their economic system. Is that a fair statement?
> MR. BURT: No, I don't think it is. I think that we recognize that we have the responsibility to steer the Soviet Union toward a course of more humane treatment of its people; human rights remains, as I said, one of the key aspects of our policy toward the Soviet Union.
> I think what the President was saying there was that we do not have, as a short-term goal, changing the whole system of Soviet Government. But that is not to say that we cannot influence the Soviet Government . . . .
> MR. HAMILTON: Do you believe that the security interests of the United States require major changes in the internal structure of the Soviet Union?

MR. BURT: Well, that is really a philosophical statement. . . .

MR. HAMILTON: It is not out of order, because it is philosophical.

MR. BURT: I know. . . . We would like a Soviet Union that shared in our values. But I think we also have to work with the Soviet Union as it is, and we have to be able to protect our security interests with the current regime in power . . . .[21]

Without turning on the president's belief system, Burt was essentially shifting to a new argument for dealing with the Soviet Union. Whether or not significant change in the Soviet system was possible, there was a strong case to be made for the need to deal with the Soviet Union as it was. The following year Robert C. McFarlane, the national security adviser, would go even further, and more optimistically, in a public address:

No one has ever convinced me that there is some law of nature requiring two populous and powerful nations halfway around the world from each other to be locked in permanent hostility. . . . I think the real sources of conflict are things that can—and do—change. If there is a military rivalry between two great countries, it's caused less by the arms themselves than by the way the two sides think about military security. If there is a geopolitical rivalry, it's not caused by the facts of geography but by the way the two sides define their political security and their other interests. If there is a clash of ideas—well, not even ideologies are permanent. . . . They are subject to what is sometimes called "reality therapy"—the test of time and experience. Sometimes, with any luck, they can be cast off. Mental prison walls do come down.[22]

This approach, also reflected in a variety of ways in the cautious but open-ended statements of Secretary of State George Shultz, set the stage both for more serious arms control negotiations and before long for the sequence of summits between Ronald Reagan and Mikhail Gorbachev.

EXPLANATIONS OF CHANGE

How to explain the change in American policy? A number of alternative explanations may be proposed, and it should be said from the start that the case for none is totally persuasive.

One important explanation of change was the awareness of the White House and other policy makers of American public opinion, as reflected in polls, and of congressional pronouncements on foreign affairs and arms control in particular. An influential part of the media provided support and articulation to these sentiments. There was evidence of a widespread desire to continue, or resume, arms control negotiations and to explore the possibilities of improved U.S.–Soviet relations, and the administration hated to be on the defensive. In the words of a conservative observer:

> If our experience in recent years conveys one clear lesson, it is that the public will not support a policy that does not hold out the hope of improvement in our relationship with the Soviet Union, and that does not actively seek improvement. In this respect, as in so many others, there has been a marked change since the period of the Cold War.[23]

It is true, some astute analysts of American foreign policy have suggested, that over the past generation considerations of American domestic politics have come to play an increasing role in the formulation, and especially the rhetoric, of U.S. foreign policy. Governing, it has been said, has increasingly been seen by sitting presidents as a campaign for reelection, and generally "foreign policy and domestic politics have become inseparable, especially during election 'years,' which now stretch into eighteen months or more."[24] The importance of broad trends in public opinion was bound to become particularly salient in 1984 as the presidential and congressional elections approached. While no one suggested that the president was in trouble, it was manifestly prudent to take the wind out of the sails of political critics.

As there is no way of measuring the relative importance of this factor, it might be suggested that its specific weight was increased by the perceived utility of the polling data for some political actors, who used it to underline a point they wished to make in any case. This circumstance leads us back to the role of personnel changes, discussed below. In any case, as one analyst writes:

> It would be easy to dismiss Reagan's recast image as a conciliator in 1984 as simply the product of election year politics. . . . But it would be a mistake to view Reagan's approach in 1984 as simply a departure from previous positions which was dictated by electoral politics.[25]

For one thing, the shift marked the beginning of a policy that grew in scope and importance regardless of the electoral campaign and continued for years beyond it. For another, what evidence we have suggests that the initial impetus for the shift came from State Department officials—typically, those least concerned with domestic opinion and politics. Moreover, Ronald Reagan's opponent in the election, Walter Mondale, can scarcely be said to have articulated an alternative strategy for dealing with the Soviet Union. Yet the fact that the White House was prepared to pick up the idea at that time—it presumably had not approved analogous proposals on earlier occasions—may indeed be related to the political scene and the looming electoral contest (as well as to other factors mentioned below).

Reinforcing this trend is a second explanation, pressure from allies in the North Atlantic Treaty Organization (NATO) to negotiate with the Soviet Union, along the lines of the two-track policy adopted in 1979. Peace movements in Europe were growing in strength; Reagan's policies had antagonized many Western Europeans; and European leaders such as West German chancellor Kohl had been urging Reagan for some time to seek a personal meeting with the Soviet leader, precisely to stem the deterioration of superpower relations. But the European allies had no effective means of pressuring Washington (short of threatening a major crisis); the Reagan administration had been prepared to ignore earlier importuning from abroad; and in fact on several occasions (notably the Siberian pipeline controversy) American nationalists seemed to enjoy underlining American power and manliness by slighting or ignoring the junior partners of the Atlantic alliance.

Third, if there was a rational basis for the change of policies and its timing within the mind set of the Reaganauts, it was the perception of growing U.S. military strength—precisely the position of strength from which, history ostensibly taught, it would be necessary to deal with the Soviet Union. Accurately or not, it was now argued that the "window of vulnerability" that the Reagan administration had encountered when it came to office had been closed. Washington could take credit for creating the new and altered situation in which it could successfully embark on a new round of talks with the Russians.

At the very least the assertion of new U.S. strength provided a plausible rationale for the new approach; "SDI would bring the Russians back to the bargaining table"; and no doubt some personnel in the executive branch subscribed to this view. True, an alternative view held that precisely because of its newly won strength the United States did not need to negotiate—a perspective somewhat akin to Karl Deutsch's remark that power is the ability not to have to learn—but George Shultz and those in his camp firmly and explicitly rejected this approach.

Fourth, at a later date the momentum was reinforced by the Geneva, Washington, and Moscow summits, the INF treaty, and reactions to them both at home and abroad. But these were the self-fulfilling expectations of benefits from success in negotiating, not the causes of its initial approval. Similarly, a major argument in favor of the new policy from about 1986 on was the perception of Soviet weakness, receptivity, and flexibility and the conclusions reached in the United States about the nature and significance of changes taking place in the Soviet Union under Gorbachev (including their implications for foreign policy). But these findings could not have a bearing on the initial policy option in January

1984: it came more than a year before Gorbachev's elevation to general secretary in Moscow.

A fifth argument focuses on the pattern of personnel replacement in Washington that preceded and accompanied a significant change of outlook and policy. Of the various factors we can trace, the change of personalities in key positions was probably the single most important development that correlates positively with the policy change. The transition years (1982–1984) saw the departure of Alexander Haig, Richard V. Allen, William Clark, Jeane Kirkpatrick, Richard Pipes, Eugene Rostow, and others—all among the more ideological cold warriors; and the arrival of George P. Shultz, Robert J. McFarlane, Jack Matlock, and others of their general orientation. (Later, if we are to believe White House correspondents as well as Donald Regan and her own account, Nancy Reagan emerged as an important influence on her husband and, thereby, on public policy.)[26]

What is important here is the appearance of new actors, presumably with somewhat different values and approaches from those of their predecessors, rather than learning by those who continued on the job. Yet it is difficult to believe that the change in orientation that accompanied this personnel shift was itself an accident. There is nothing to indicate a concerted effort to install moderates in place of the departing hard liners. More plausible is the hypothesis that the first team had tended to consist of true believers and men (and an occasional woman) ideologically or personally close to Ronald Reagan. As they left—some of them as failures—their replacements had to be sought elsewhere in the Republican fold or in government service, which meant typically people of a less ideological mold. Once George Shultz was appointed, he was likely to select as his subordinates people with an outlook closer to his own. And the removal of William Clark and Edward Meese from the White House made it possible to seek successors with conservative professionalism rather than cronies or ideologues.

One further explanatory hypothesis centers on the assumed concern of President Reagan, first, for his self-image and legacy and, second, for his ability, in effect, to deliver peace. Those who know Reagan personally—including members of the opposite party—have no hesitation in asserting that he genuinely cared about both policy and image when it came to peace, including the ambitious vision of denuclearization; in all likelihood, Nancy Reagan reinforced this quest for a legacy of the president as the architect of world peace; and the president does not appear to have sensed any tension between these objectives and his earlier strategy toward the Soviet Union. But even if we accept this picture as probably accurate, it does not in itself explain why, in the final year of his first term in office, Reagan chose to follow a course that seemed to reverse what he had earlier embarked on.

Finally, it may be suggested that the new approach served to produce a better match between means and ends. If the globalism and military buildup of the Reagan years were open to charges of overstretch insofar as U.S. resources were concerned, the new policy might appear to contain a grain of awareness of the limits of power that even the mightiest nation must recognize. In this light the new policy meant reducing excessive goals and recognizing the formidable costs involved in any effort to bankrupt the Soviet economy, let alone to threaten credibly to destroy the Soviet regime. Such a realization would invite the application of the "efficiency" definition of learning. Alas, it seems entirely inappropriate for 1983–1984: there is no basis for thinking that the change of U.S. policy was the product of such a sweeping, detached, rational insight.

Perhaps it should also be underlined that, according to the way the Reagan administration functioned, there was relatively little concern about the disjunction—tactical or inadvertent, no matter—between an essentialist ideological stance and a pragmatic exploration of negotiations with Moscow. Such seeming inconsistencies had happened before and did not seem overly troubling. This too, however, fails to explain why and how the decisions were reached to embark on the new course.

We are thus left with the sense that a number of things came together that made it possible for some of the professionals to convince the secretary of state and for him, in turn, to prevail once crucial personnel changes had occurred, at a time when political considerations grew in salience around the White House. This, rather than a rational, principled reconsideration, nor an explicit acknowledgment of lessons learned, is what appears to have taken place.

If the above serves to explain the start of an overt (though still cautious) movement in a new direction from early 1984 on, in 1985–1986 and thereafter the Gorbachev regime began to give evidence of significant innovations in both Soviet foreign policy and domestic policies, the recognition of which served to reinforce the new American approach.

But what was particularly important beginning with the Geneva summit was Ronald Reagan's personal meeting with and impression of the Soviet leader. It was characteristic that firsthand experience mattered so greatly to this president: the personal relationship was not inhibited by, nor did it reshape, the ideological edifice that might have been expected to block the interpersonal rapprochement. Time and again he would later say that this Soviet leader was quite different from earlier ones (whom, if truth be told, he had never met—a fact that sometimes seemed to escape him when he kept saying that this man was so unlike all the others he had known; the closest he came to acknowledging it was to remark about Gorbachev's predecessors, "They kept dying on me").

The Reagans' brief but triumphal trip to Moscow in 1988 only cemented his new attitudes. To him as to the first lady it seemed important to have direct evidence that churches were being reopened and services were permitted; this, as well as improvements in Soviet human rights practices, and the fact that he was able to meet with dissidents and address university students, removed some of the most blatant charges that had earlier been leveled against the Soviet regime.

Strongest perhaps, psychologically, was the president's ability to take credit for the changes taking place in the Soviet Union and in Soviet foreign policy. Related to it as a significant element in the Reagan personality was his pervasive optimism. Unlike some of his associates who were prone to project their prophecies of gloom onto the future march of totalitarianism, Reagan had tended to foresee its early demise. And while some of his hard-line advisers and subordinates greeted the Gorbachev revolution with ill-concealed skepticism, the president soon affirmatively tended to see what he wished to see (and what he perceived to be politically smart), namely, progress in the U.S.–Soviet relationship.

Actually, Ronald Reagan's knowledge of Soviet affairs had scarcely undergone any substantial improvement. An interview with visiting Soviet journalists, late in the second term, showed Reagan as awkward and as ignorant as ever when it came to Soviet history, Marxism-Leninism, and Kremlin policy.[27] And perhaps most important, there is no evidence that his new and positive experience with Gorbachev, including the conclusion of the INF treaty and progress on other agreements, led him to rethink any of the underlying assumptions of the older policy—the catechism of the Committee on the Present Danger. Several former officials who claim to know Reagan well privately agree that, after all his experience with Gorbachev and the "new Russia," his basic view of communism had scarcely changed. There is nothing to suggest that, as far as Ronald Reagan was concerned, the altered U.S.–Soviet relationship prompted, or required, any systematic, ideological reconceptualization. It was as if the Soviet Union was not truly communist any longer but that its experience had confirmed that communism was bound to be a failure.

As the second term went on, the Pentagon, whose civilian appointees—from Caspar Weinberger to Richard Perle and Fred Iklé—had often obstructed the State Department's endeavors, lost much of its clout with the resignation of its key actors. The National Security Council was in the throes of the Iran-Contra affair and the scandal it led to. Both by his efforts and by default, George Shultz appeared to be in the driver's seat when it came to U.S.–Soviet relations. He had gained a keen understanding of, and fine personal rapport with, his opposite number, Edvard Shevardnadze. All this eased the change of policies.

It was apparently not so unusual for Reagan to go along like a good trooper, as he had on the movie set in earlier days. It was not his habit to worry whether he believed in the script he acted out. John P. Sears, his former campaign manager, asserts that as governor of California Reagan "seldom came up with an original idea and often, like a performer waiting for a writer to feed him his lines and for a director to show him how to say them, he waited for others to advise him what to do."[28] It may not be too far-fetched to refer to a more general thesis regarding the role of film in the shaping of Reagan:

> The presidential character . . . was produced from the convergence of two substitutions that generated cold war countersubversion in the 1940s and undid its 1980s revival—the political replacement of Nazism by Communism . . . and the psychological shift from an embodied self to a simulacrum on film. Reagan . . . found out who he was through the roles he played on film. . . . The confusion between life and film produced *Ronald Reagan*, the image that has fixed our gaze.

"Reagan's easy slippage between movies and reality," Michael Rogin suggests, "is synecdochic for a political culture increasingly impervious to distinctions between fiction and history."[29]

In this light it may not be inappropriate to suggest that Ronald Reagan unwittingly sought to act out two different self-images, both larger than life. One was the Western in which he was the happy cold warrior fighting the good fight for good against evil. In the other he would end up riding off into the sunset, having brought peace on earth. The foreign policy of his two terms reflected and nourished both fantasies.

WITH THE BENEFIT OF HINDSIGHT

While the changes that U.S. policy toward the Soviet Union underwent in the course of the 1980s naturally found reflection in the rhetoric used by the White House and other government agencies, they involved the introduction of no new lessons from history or experience. They did involve a muting of earlier themes of the Soviet threat, including the recitation of Soviet takeovers, aggressions, and abuses of human rights. The Hitler analogy had all but disappeared by 1986–1987. At a time when Moscow was virtually advertising its economic weakness, and when in the United States the unprecedented national debt was becoming a major political issue, pressures for greater (but costly) U.S. strength abated to a considerable extent. Even the manifest failures of communism, as exemplified by the Soviet Union, no longer appeared to invite the gloating predictions of 1981–1982 from the president that that system was bound to be relegated to the trashcan of history.

While academics and journalists sparred over the propriety or adequacy of comparing Gorbachev with Peter the Great or with Nikita Khrushchev, the White House and the secretary of state had apparently no interest in such analogies and whatever they implied. Accurately perhaps, there was a suspicion that in some respects the Soviet scene had become unprecedented. Historical precision did not seem to matter to the "spin meisters" who knew how to hype every photo opportunity and managed to turn events such as the Reykjavik summit into purported showcases of American diplomatic skill. In fact, historical accuracy seemed almost irrelevant; time and again the president referred to nonexistent documents (such as the Ten Commandments of "Nikolai" Lenin) or offered ostensible quotes from the Soviet classics that no one else was able to find, just as he asserted that there was no word in Russian for *freedom*.[30] If history was merely a means, then it did not really matter.

One could also note a (perhaps understandable) reluctance to advertise the errors implicit in the administration's earlier historical and political science references. While the term *totalitarian* was less frequently used in official Washington parlance to describe Gorbachev's Soviet Union than it had been before his accession, there was certainly no explicit statement that its use had been wrong. If now changes in the Soviet system were acknowledged and welcomed, there was no recognition of the fact that earlier dogmatic insistence on the unchangeability of the Soviet regime had itself been a product of rigid American ideology. As Soviet troops withdrew from Afghanistan, there was considerable relief and self-congratulation in Washington, but (perhaps understandably again) nobody seemed to dwell on the fact that this was an occurrence unprecedented for those who had posited (slightly inaccurately if we consider Austria, Manchuria, Northern Iran, and Bornholm) that the Soviet Union had never withdrawn from any territory it had occupied.

Nobody cared to point out the logical fallacies. If the changes occurring in the Soviet Union were both significant and autonomous, then some of the assumptions about the dynamics of Russian history had been wrong. And if these changes were the result of American containment, then those who—40 years earlier, in the case of George Kennan's "X" article—had argued that it could indeed bring about a mellowing of the Soviet system, were being proven to have been more correct than those, in the Reagan entourage or elsewhere, who had insisted that the Soviet system could not and would not change.

Who indeed likes to advertise erroneous assumptions later proven wrong? After all, some doubt remained among skeptics in the administration about Soviet use of chemical warfare even when the protracted yellow rain campaign had been dismissed as spurious. Earlier on, administration officials had indignantly cited an ostensible Brezhnev speech in Prague in the early 1970s in which he had allegedly told his audience that détente was a temporary device to lull the West to sleep—a speech widely understood to have been the invention of American or British "black propaganda."

Other issues remained unsettled even if the weight of professional judgment went against the arguments earlier voiced by high administration spokespersons. Thus, in the early and mid-1980s, a number of U.S. officials had spoken of the Soviet intervention in Afghanistan as part of the century-old Russian drive to the Indian Ocean (or the Persian Gulf) or the even older Russian quest for a warm-water port. As Jeane Kirkpatrick told the United Nations General Assembly in 1984:

> Why did the Soviet Union invade Afghanistan in the first place? Perhaps history best explains it. Those who believe the Soviet Union is, at base, a contemporary embodiment of historic Russian goals, see the Afghan policy in that light.Since the time of the czars, it is said by those who argue along that line, Russian leaders have pursued the dream of a warm-water port on the Indian Ocean. Domination of Afghanistan is thus essential to the fulfillment of historic territorial aspirations.[31]

To many observers familiar with the geography of the area (there were no ports, warm or cold, within sight or smell of Afghanistan, and the topography made it most unsuitable as a passageway), with czarist motivations (primarily anti-British), with Soviet priorities, and with at least some of the circumstances of the Soviet invasion in 1979 (repeated importuning by Kabul and alarm at the prospect of having clients and comrades go down the drain), these historical references seemed woefully wide of the mark; as events in Afghanistan unfolded, they became even more obviously inept. But at best they were tacitly jettisoned rather than acknowledged to have been wrong *expressio verbis*.

Toward the end of the Reagan era, there was virtually an exhaustion of historical references with regard to Soviet affairs. The situation must have appeared strikingly unprecedented, or else its shapers found no good historical examples for analogical argument or even dramatic illustration. At high-level meetings of Soviet and American officials, it was typically the Moscow representatives who made reference to the days of George Washington or Abraham Lincoln (or Franklin D. Roosevelt) when Russo-American relations were reportedly good—admittedly, at a time when they had little to do with each other, and long before either country became a superpower. But while there seemed to be no learning from history, there is some reason to conclude that another kind of learning was going on.

A MATTER OF LEARNING

U.S. policy makers in the 1980s moved from an incomplete in-group consensus around an essentialist, ideological view of the U.S.–Soviet competition, to a markedly more pragmatic and agnostic approach to U.S.–Soviet relations and Soviet objectives. While there is a strong case to be made for evidence of learning, the modal response in Washington appeared to reduce the scope of what was being learned to a minimum. Rather than isolating and dismissing the Soviets as hopeless and hostile, administration officials and their envoys discovered that, for whatever combination of reasons, negotiating with them worked. As for long-term Soviet objectives, the easiest way to handle them was to adopt an agnostic perspective: it was not clear whether Moscow had in effect abandoned any of its global aspirations or its traditional Marxist-Leninist world view. Where early on in the Reagan years the key spokespersons had professed certainty, remarks such as "We do not know" or "We are not sure" recur frequently in the second term in official commentary on Soviet affairs. As Mr. Reagan told a group of high school students, "It is virtually impossible for us to understand their system . . . ."[32]

What made it easier to downgrade the alarm about the Soviet threat was the simultaneous sense of greater U.S. strength, for which the administration took credit, and of newly evident and self-advertised Soviet weakness and difficulties—in its economy, in advanced technology, in its society, even in its ability to carry through meaningful reforms. The good news was that Moscow itself now confirmed the president's long-standing insistence that socialism and statism were bound to make any country that became their victim a basket case. Moreover, the fact that the Soviet leadership was prepared to make unilateral and asymmetrical concessions to the United States was taken to be reassuring.

Although a variety of authoritative figures were to claim that the U.S. reorientation concerning the Soviet Union that occurred toward the middle of the Reagan years—never so advertised at the time—had been part of the original design, intended to take place once the United States had regained its position of strength, the weight of evidence overwhelmingly points in the opposite direction: the paradigm change ultimately involved the muting of beliefs and attitudes that administration ideologues had held dear, and was resisted by some and misunderstood by others.

True, both within the administration and even more among the corps of American experts on world affairs, arms control, and Soviet politics, there were serious cleavages over the nature and implications of changes in the Soviet Union and in U.S.–Soviet relations.[33] But, as the end of the Reagan years approached, such arguments appeared to have remarkably little to do with the conduct of U.S.–Soviet relations, even when strategic arms control negotiations stalled and concern remained about Soviet espionage, technology transfer, and Soviet activities in the Third World. In 1988, far more significant than precedents or analogs, once again, were internal and unresolved differences in the executive branch over U.S. defense policy (for instance, a coherent plan for conventional arms reduction negotiations with the Soviet Union) and over the extent to which foreign policy events ought to be tailored to the electoral campaign.

The primitive verities of 1980–1981 had all but vanished, and (it must be assumed) a greater sense of complexity of the real world had indeed impressed itself on U.S. policy makers. Yet there was not a corresponding shift in historical examples and precedents to accompany the new posture of minimum assured self-satisfaction. Perhaps after all, *not* reaching for historical clichés also constituted a form of learning.

But what about those other forms of learning? How much had the president and those around him learned by the time they left the White House? The honest answer must be that we do not know what learning did take place. This is particularly true if we recognize that some insights learned may not have been translated into behavior, nor publicly revealed in any other way.

It is clear that the minimalist definition of learning is satisfied by the evidence of U.S. policy change. But this is hardly an interesting conclusion. At the other end of the spectrum, the efficiency definition of learning—a better match of means and ends—not only presents some conceptual problems but, even if accepted, defies ready application and testing. A case can be made for the proposition that, as it moved toward the end of its incumbency, the Reagan administration, just as others have, revealed a growing urge to show tangible results. One way to do this is to adjust objectives, that is, scale them down to make them more attainable. This did indeed provide a better fit of means and ends. But by all odds what prompted this adjustment was a matter of self-image and domestic policy: it had nothing to do with a changed perception of the Soviet Union or of U.S.–Soviet relations. Moreover, President Reagan's behavior at Reykjavik— well into his second term in office—showed how he was personally prepared to buy into a much more ambitious—not to say utopian—agenda. On balance, then, it is difficult to assert that by the efficiency criterion that learning did demonstrably take place.

This leaves us with the cognitive-structuralist definition of learning. Did Ronald Reagan and those around him, during his years in the White House, acquire a more accurate and complex understanding of the Soviet Union and Soviet conduct? Here the answer has to be a qualified "yes," even if the conclusions they overtly drew from this were constrained in various ways, for reasons rooted primarily in domestic politics, personality, and ideological constructs.

No less important, unlike his secretary of state, who was relatively open to learning and assimilated the lessons into his subsequent behavior, the president in particular resisted significant learning beyond his discovery that Mikhail Gorbachev was a leader he could deal with (who was pleasant, who was prepared to make unilateral concessions and whom, incidentally, Margaret Thatcher also thought well of). Gorbachev surely did not fit Reagan's image of the head of the evil empire—clearly a case of cognitive dissonance for the president. The way he handled it was to redefine Gorbachev as someone who had departed from the Bolshevik mold. In brief, the learning concerned policy toward Gorbachev and Gorbachev's Soviet Union; it did not extend to the president's beliefs about communism.

Even U.S. policy escaped searching scrutiny because in the course of the 1980s the Soviet Union itself underwent major change, and it was hard to tell what part the United States had played in bringing about *perestroika, glasnost,* and the new political thinking. Administration figures later sought to take credit for their role, but—to take one concrete case—in regard to the Strategic Defense Initiative (SDI), subsequent claims that it was meant to pressure the Soviets into a more conciliatory posture on arms control are totally without merit: SDI was announced before the Soviet walkout from the arms talks; the purpose of the program was far more sweeping and comprehensive than a contrived effort to influence the behavior of the opposite numbers in Moscow. It may well be that there were unintended (and ultimately beneficial) consequences of SDI research and funding for U.S.–Soviet relations, but if so, they were outcomes not anticipated by those who launched the whole thing. That the policy that the Reagan administration pursued in the second term led to an improvement in U.S.–Soviet relations is manifest; whether it was the product of cognitive learning remains in doubt.

Outside the White House, American attitudes and perceptions regarding the Soviet Union changed a good deal—largely, one may surmise, as a consequence of the changed Soviet behavior and rhetoric. Certainly the experience of even Ronald Reagan made it easier to negotiate this transformation of the American mood. How serious was the failure of learning to extend to underlying assumptions about communism and the Soviet Union (at least as far as the president and those who thought like him were concerned)? One might think of the ideological tenets as a body of beliefs insulated from reality testing—in effect, ritual pronouncements of negligible operational value. This view is reinforced by the evidence that each time a concrete need was perceived to deal or negotiate with the Soviet Union, China, or another communist state, a convenient rationale was found to justify doing so without imperiling the ideological edifice. In this sense, ideology and learning may be thought of as reciprocals: the stronger the former, the harder it is for the latter.

The balance looks rather different, however, if we posit that true learning requires intellectual integration of new insights or information into a broader construct of beliefs. Thus, for instance, Lloyd Etheridge has proposed three criteria to assess the growth of intelligence:

> (1) growth of realism, recognizing the different elements and processes actually operating in the world; (2) growth of intellectual integration in which these different elements and processes are integrated with one another in thought; (3) growth of reflective perspective about the conduct of the first two processes, the conception of the problem, and the results which the decision maker desires to achieve.[34]

In these terms, a growth of realism is clearly apparent. But it is precisely the disjunction of policy and belief, resisting intellectual integration, and the absence of any growth of reflective perspective about these processes that remain strikingly characteristic of the White House in the 1980s. Indeed, one might speculate that one of the consequences of this—what might be called the absence of organizational learning—was the failure to transmit the operational insights, as a systematic body of thought, to the successor administration.

NOTES

The author would like to thank Jeanne Tayler for help with research for this chapter; and George W. Breslauer, Gail W. Lapidus, Philip Tetlock, and Stephen Weber for very helpful comments on an earlier version of this chapter.

1. *The New York Times*, 14 April 1988; Larry Speakes, *Speaking Out* (New York: Scribner's, 1988), 36. We must dismiss as deliberately manipulative, rather than revealing, the remarks and speeches delivered by the president on public occasions during his brief visit to the Soviet Union in 1988. Carefully massaged with the assistance of professionals such as Librarian of Congress James Billington, writer-historian Susan Massie—a friend of the Reagans—and, it was reported, émigré comedian Yakov Smirnov, these were aimed first and foremost at Soviet audiences.

2. Remarks at the annual observance of Captive Nations Week, 19 July 1983, in *Public Papers of the Presidents of the United States: Ronald Reagan (1983)* (Washington, D.C.: U.S. Government Printing Office, 1985), 2:1053.

3. Robert Dallek, *Ronald Reagan: The Politics of Symbolism* (Cambridge, Mass.: Harvard University Press, 1984), 129–30.

4. "Interview with the President," 28 December 1981, in *Public Papers of the Presidents of the United States: Ronald Reagan (1981)* (Washington, D.C.: U.S. Government Printing Office, 1982), 1:1197.

5. Cited in Michael Paul Rogin, *Ronald Reagan, The Movie* (Berkeley: University of California Press, 1987), 27.

6. Interview with *People* Magazine, 12 June 1983, in *Public Papers of the Presidens (1983)*, 2:1714.

7. *The New York Times*, 30 January 1981. For a more detailed account of the author's views and some further evidence, see Alexander Dallin and Gail W. Lapidus, "Reagan and the Russians: American Policy Toward the Soviet Union," in Kenneth Oye et al., eds., *Eagle Resurgent?* rev. ed. (Boston: Little, Brown, 1987), 193–254.

The same theme came up several times in the president's on-the-record conversations. In an interview with Walter Cronkite, on March 3, 1981, Reagan remarked, "They have told us that their goal is the Marxian philosophy of world revolution and a single, one-world communist state and that they're dedicated to that." And in an interview with three correspondents of the *Los Angeles Times*, on January 20, 1982, he reiterated, "That religion of theirs, which is Marxism-Leninism, requires them to support world revolution and bring about the one-world communist state. And they've never denied that." *Public Papers of the Presidents (1981)*, 1:193; *Public Papers of the Presidents of the United States: Ronald Reagan (1982)* (U.S. Government Printing Office, 1983), 64.

8. On the role of domestic politics, cf. I.M. Destler, Leslie Gelb, and Anthony Lake, *Our Own Worst Enemy* (New York: Simon & Schuster, 1984).

9. Richard E. Neustadt and Ernest R. May, *Thinking in Time* (Glencoe, Ill.: Free Press, 1986), xi.

10. According to Bob Woodward, the speech was crafted by Anthony R. Dolan, a protégé of CIA chief William J. Casey and William F. Buckley, Jr., and "a true believer in the conservative cause" (Bob Woodward, *Veil* [New York: Simon & Schuster, 1987], 235–36.) This is not to suggest that the president disagreed with it but merely to attribute the initiative for the images used to the particular speechwriter involved.

11. For the author's more extensive critique of the views identified with the hard-line continuity school among historians of Russia, see Alexander Dallin, "The Uses and Abuses of Russian History," in Terry L. Thompson and Richard Shelton, eds., *Soviet Society and Culture: Essays in Honor of Vera S. Dunham* (Boulder, Colo.: Westview Press, 1988), 181–94.

12. *The Reagan Doctrine and Beyond* (Washington, D.C.: American Enterprise Institute, 1987), 27.

13. Interview, 26 May 1983, in *Public Papers of the Presidents (1983)*, 1:774.

14. Radio address, 19 February 1983, in *Public Papers of the Presidents (1983)*, 1:258.

15. Interview at the Williamsburg Economic Summit, 31 May 1983, in *Public Papers of the Presidents (1983)*, 1:802.

16. Ronald Reagan, radio address to the nation, 17 April 1982, in *Public Papers of the Presidents (1982)*, 503–504.

Western unity was another, subordinate theme introduced in this argument. In the president's commencement address at Eureka College, his alma mater, in

May 1982, his speechwriters introduced this passage: ". . . Soviet aggressiveness has grown as Soviet military power has increased. To compensate, we must learn from the lessons of the past. When the West has stood united and firm, the Soviet Union has taken heed. . . . Through unity, you'll remember from your modern history courses, the West secured the withdrawal of occupation forces from Austria and the recognition of its rights in Berlin" *Public Papers of the Presidents (1982)*, 600. Others would seriously dispute that there was Western unity in negotiating over Austria.

It is curious that the Cuban missile crisis of 1962 rarely figured among the historical examples of superior strength and political will that worked to deter hostile action—perhaps because that crisis was handled by a Democratic administration with which none of the Reagan team's actors was identified.

17. See *U.S. Foreign Policy and World Realities: Addresses by President Ronald W. Reagan 1982* (Stanford, Calif.: The Hoover Institution, 1982), 16–24.

18. Cited in Michael Mandelbaum and Strobe Talbott, *Reagan and Gorbachev* (New York: Vintage, 1987), 48.

19. Alexander M. Haig, Jr., *Caveat—Realism, Reagan and Foreign Policy* (New York: Macmillan, 1984); also cited in Mandelbaum and Talbott, *Reagan and Gorbachev*, 28.

20. Radio address to the nation, 11 February 1984, in *Public Papers of the Presidents of the United States: Ronald Reagan (1984)*, (Washington, D.C.: U.S. Government Printing Office, 1986), 192.

21. U.S. House of Representatives, Committee on Foreign Affairs, *Developments in Europe*, Hearings, 24 June 1984, 7–8. It might be said that the same theme was launched by Secretary Shultz in his major statement before the Senate Foreign Relations Committee the previous summer, when he declared (in a text carefully honed by his staff) that while this country had a vision "that inspires America's role in the world," "it does not, however, lead us to regard mutual hostility with the U.S.S.R. as an immutable fact of international life" (Shultz, "U.S.–Soviet Relations," Department of State *Bulletin*, July 1983, 100).

22. Robert C. McFarlane, "U.S.–Soviet Relations in the Late 20th Century," Department of State *Bulletin*, October 1985, 34ff.

23. Robert W. Tucker, "Toward a New Détente," *The New York Times Magazine*, 9 December 1984.

24. Destler et al., *Our Own Worst Enemy*. See also Miroslav Nincic, "U.S. Soviet Policy and the Electoral Connection," *World Politics*, 42 (April 1990): 370–96.

25. John D. Lees and Michael Turner, eds., *Reagan's First Four Years* (Manchester: Manchester University Press, 1988), 130–31.

26. On crediting Shultz, McFarlane (and Nancy Reagan) with key roles in bringing about the Geneva summit, see, e.g., Jane Mayer and Doyle McManus, *Landslide* (New York: Houghton Mifflin, 1988), 158ff. The importance of Shultz's appointment is confirmed from the opposite perspective by those members of the Reagan White House who felt betrayed by the changes of policy. See an otherwise highly loaded account, Constantine Menges, *Inside the Security Council* (New York: Simon & Schuster, 1988), 371–78. See also Nancy Reagan, *My Turn* (New York: Random House, 1989).

27. Reagan interview with Valentin Zorin and Boris Kalyagin, 20 May 1988, in *Public Papers of the Presidents of the United States: Ronald Reagan (1988)*, (Washington, D.C.: U.S. Government Printing Office, 1990), 686–91.

28. Cited in Dallek, *Ronald Reagan*, 12.

29. Rogin, *Ronald Reagan, The Movie*, 3, 9, 31.

30. In all probability Reagan had confused it with the statement that there was no noun for *privacy* in Russian, although there was an adjectival form for *private* (as in fact is true in several other European languages as well).

31. Jeane J. Kirkpatrick, "Afghanistan: Five Years of Tragedy," November 14, 1984, Department of State *Bulletin*, January 1985, 47.

32. Remarks to students and faculty of Fallston High School, 4 December 1985, in *Public Papers of the Presidents of the United States: Ronald Reagan (1985)*, (Washington, D.C.: U.S. Goverment Printing Office, 1988), 1452.

33. Balancing those who argue for a greater American effort to "help" Gorbachev, Richard Nixon and Henry Kissinger are examples of critical skeptics in regard to the "new" Reagan policy. In Kissinger's words, "Even were Gorbachev committed to peace in the Western sense, there is little in the history of either czars or commissars to supply comfort to the Soviet Union's neighbors. . . . [The objectives] that Stalin pursued after the war and that Brezhnev carried out in Afghanistan date back to imperial Russia:Soviet domination of the Balkans and the Dardanelles; a major voice in Poland; and Soviet hegemony over Iran. . . . Twice before the West deluded itself by basing its policies on favorable assessments of Soviet leaders: with Stalin in 1944 and Khrushchev in 1956" (Henry Kissinger, "A Memo to the Next President," *Newsweek*, 19 September 1988, 34ff.) Similarly, Lt. Gen. William E. Odom, formerly head of the National Security Agency and Army intelligence, found that "little fundamental change has occurred" in Gorbachev's Russia, which remains a one-party state that monopolizes the media and fails to place law above politics ("Has the Soviet Union Really Changed?" *U.S. News and World Report*, 3 April 1989.)

34. Lloyd S. Etheridge, *Can Governments Learn? American Foreign Policy and Central American Revolutions* (London: Pergamon Press, 1985), 66.

PART III

Case Studies of Soviet Foreign Policy

12

Learning in the Nuclear Age: Soviet Strategic Arms Control Policy, 1969–1989

Coit D. Blacker

For 20 years U.S. and Soviet policy makers have sought, with varying degrees of success, to negotiate meaningful limitations on important components of their strategic nuclear arsenals. That Soviet leaders have learned *something* from and about this complex and consuming process as a consequence of their participation would appear self-evident, even to the casual observer. A comparison of the proposals put forward by Soviet negotiators in the early 1970s, during the first phase of the Strategic Arms Limitation Treaty (SALT), with those advanced since the coming to power of Mikhail Gorbachev, for example, reveals striking differences in substance, emphasis, and tone.

The central question, then, is not whether the Soviets have learned as a result of their arms control negotiating experience with the United States; on that point the evidence seems unambiguous, whatever the particular definition of learning being applied. The more interesting issues are what has been learned (and who has been learning), why and how has learning occurred, and what kinds of learning appear to have taken place. There is, as well, a fourth issue of rather more immediate relevance: How and to what extent has this learning process materially affected both the content and the conduct of Soviet arms control policies in the period since March 1985?

In addition to the well-known problems that attend any analysis of Soviet policy—from the relative paucity and questionable reliability of the data to the subjective character of the interpretative exercise—there is a special difficulty that arises in assessing the evolution of Soviet attitudes toward nuclear arms control. This difficulty is not the exclusive preserve of the Sovietological community, however; any analyst attempting a comparable effort regarding U.S. arms control policy will confront a very similar problem. Beliefs, convictions, perceptions, and policy prescriptions regarding nuclear arms control derive in large measure from a prior or preexisting set of beliefs, convictions, perceptions, and policy prescriptions regarding the military utility of nuclear weapons. In other words, one's views about nuclear arms control are heavily influenced, if not determined, by one's views about nuclear weapons and the likely implications of their use in war. Although nonmilitary factors can and do influence the substance of arms control proposals in important ways, steps to limit or otherwise constrain military forces through international negotiation are first and foremost a subset of national security policy.

The implications for this analysis are clear. If, on one hand, senior Soviet leaders believe that a nuclear war can be fought and won and if they also believe that they have both the material resources and the political will to develop and maintain a "war-winning" posture, then their interest in negotiations to limit central strategic systems is likely to be either cosmetic—Soviet participation is expected to produce some political advantage or at least prevent an erosion of the country's international political stature—or narrowly self-serving in military terms. At a minimum, Soviet leaders would not, given this set of values, warmly embrace an agreement to *stabilize* (to employ the term favored by the U.S. arms control community) the military relationship with Washington, based on the logic of assured destruction. By the same token, in the actual process of negotiation the Kremlin could be expected to advance proposals designed to contribute in some measurable way to the Soviet Union's ability to prevail in the event of war. Any agreement that the two sides might reach as a consequence of the negotiations would have to meet, we can assume, the same rigorous standard.

If, on the other hand, senior Soviet leaders are convinced that a strategic nuclear exchange between the superpowers will produce no victors, then their calculus concerning the potential utility of arms control agreements is likely to be very different. They will have a much stronger interest, for example, in measures to constrain the military competition, and to render it more stable, than they will in the pursuit of illusory military advantages. Assuming that U.S. policy makers were to share this perspective, the bilateral incentive to conclude far-reaching agreements to limit both the quantitative and the qualitative dimensions of the strategic arms race would be great. Under such conditions, a strong mutuality of interest would inform the U.S.–Soviet search for progress in arms control, opening up the possibility of genuine and sustained accommodation, at least in this one area of superpower relations.

The history of Soviet arms control policy since the late 1960s is perhaps best understood as a prolonged struggle between these two competing tendencies regarding the nature and predictable consequences of war in the nuclear age. It is the story of the slow erosion of confidence in the first set of beliefs, once held by virtually all important Soviet decision makers, followed by an effort to preserve as much of the original vision as possible, even when confronted by a mounting body of disconfirming evidence, which is in turn abandoned by a new collection of Soviet leaders, deeply if unevenly impressed by the logic of the second set of images. The process by which key elements of the Soviet leadership moved from essential confidence in the first set of core beliefs to explicit advocacy of the second is the subject of this analysis.[1]

THE LOGIC OF IMAGES:
SOVIET BELIEF SYSTEMS IN THE NUCLEAR AGE

The strategic arms control policies of the Soviet Union can be divided into two analytically distinct phases: from the initiation of the SALT talks in 1969 to the collapse of the Strategic Arms Reduction Talks (START) negotiations in late 1983, and from 1985 to the present. The two periods are linked by an extended transition (which actually begins several years before the Soviet walkout in 1983) in which elements of the old line coexist uneasily with elements of the new.

Such a temporal division of the period under review is controversial. While useful for purposes of discussion, it is, of course, subjectively derived, reflecting the peculiar judgments and biases of the analyst. Some observers date the beginnings of the transition in Soviet thinking regarding nuclear weapons and arms control to the early 1970s, when Soviet leaders chose to endorse the antiballistic missile treaty; that decision rendered impossible, at least for the life of the agreement, any realistic effort to limit damage to the Soviet Union in the event of a strategic nuclear exchange with the United States—certainly a fundamental requirement of any military strategy that has victory as its overarching objective. Others cite the January 1977 speech of Leonid Brezhnev in which the late Soviet leader renounced strategic superiority as a goal of Soviet policy (the beginnings of the so-called Tula line, named for the city in which Brezhnev made these remarks). Still others reject outright the notion of any fundamental shift in Soviet military strategy and arms control policies during these years, pointing, among other factors, to the Kremlin's continuing deployment of highly capable offensive and defensive strategic weapon systems far in excess of those required for deterrence, but absolutely essential to the maintenance of a damage-limiting posture.

It is unlikely that the present effort will resolve this issue, nor is this its central purpose. What follows is an interpretation of the evidence that is advanced less for what it might contribute to the ongoing debate over the content and evolution of Soviet military strategy, as important as that issue surely is, than for what it might suggest about the issue of learning in Soviet arms control policy.

PHASE I: 1969–1983

What distinguishes this notional first phase in Soviet thinking from the second? As suggested, the key issue would appear to be differing assessments regarding the wagability and winability of nuclear war. From the late 1950s to the late 1970s, the overwhelming impression, gleaned largely from Soviet military writings, is of a policy-making community committed to the proposition that from the predictable chaos and devastation of nuclear war one side must surely prevail.[2] This is not to suggest that Soviet leaders regarded the prospect of such a conflict with equanimity or complacency during this or any other time. On the contrary, senior Soviet officials, military as well as political, were emphatic that the first and overriding purpose of the country's military power was to *deter* the outbreak of war with the West. Should deterrence fail, however, and a strategic nuclear war erupt between the two superpowers, the goal of Soviet military policy during these years would have been to terminate hostilities on terms favorable to Moscow.

Not all ranking Soviet leaders were of a single mind on these issues. As early as 1954, Soviet premier Georgi Malenkov cast doubt on the thesis that one side must prevail in a nuclear war when he cautioned that such an explosion could spell the end of world civilization.[3] It is interesting to note, however, that in their successful campaign to oust him from his leadership position, Malenkov's opponents used the premier's pronouncements on the nature of war in the nuclear age as a weapon against him, portraying the beleaguered leader as unreliable on defense- and security-related issues.[4] Nikita Krushchev, for one, took the message to heart; he never repeated the Malenkov formula, at least not in public, although he did warn explicitly about the devastation certain to attend any strategic nuclear exchange between the superpowers.[5] Unlike Malenkov, however, Krushchev remained faithful to the notion of a Soviet victory in the unlikely event of a nuclear war, relying for such an outcome on the material and moral superiority of the socialist way of life.

Throughout this first phase in Soviet policy, voices critical of the thesis that a nuclear war could be fought and won continued to be heard. Overwhelmingly, however, those in leadership positions echoed the views of the professional military who with few exceptions argued that, with proper preparation and the requisite forces, the Soviet Union could expect to emerge battered but victorious in any nuclear war with the United States.[6]

Interestingly, at no time during these years nor, for that matter, during the years that followed, did Soviet leaders believe themselves to be in a position actually to *achieve* this ambitious military objective. From the beginning of the nuclear age to the late 1960s, the leadership was only too aware of the decisive strategic advantage enjoyed by the United States—an advantage so pronounced, according to one senior Soviet military official writing in the early 1980s, that it was the Americans, and not the Soviets, who could expect to prevail should the cold war ever turn hot.[7] Determining which side might win was essentially beside the point, anyway, a derivative issue. The larger issue at stake was victory itself: Could the concept of military victory continue to have operational meaning in a world of nuclear-armed superpowers? Could it be achieved under contemporary conditions? If so, how and at what cost? For the better part of 20 years, from the unveiling of the Soviet Union's revised military doctrine in 1960 to the turbulence manifest in Soviet strategic thinking at the end of the 1970s, the answer to those questions was yes.

Given this assessment, it is hardly surprising that, when in the mid-1960s Soviet leaders sanctioned the development and rapid growth of the country's third-generation strategic nuclear forces, those within the military vested with special responsibilities in this area, as well as their allies in the defense-industrial community, established precise and demanding performance criteria for these weapons. Principal among these were that the systems then under development prove highly resistant to preemption, once operational; such measures, ranging from the deployment of long-range, land-based systems in underground concrete and steel silos to the construction of ballistic missile submarines capable of launching their weapons while submerged, would serve to reduce significantly the military value of any surprise U.S. first strike.[8]

No less important, the new weapons, especially the intercontinental ballistic missiles (ICBMs) deployed on land, should have the combination of range, reliability, accuracy, and warhead yield to place as much of the U.S. strategic arsenal at risk as possible. Should the decision ever be made to attack the United States without waiting to be attacked first, the ability to employ such weapons effectively against military targets could mean the difference between victory and defeat by providing the leadership with at least some capacity to limit damage to the Soviet homeland. The ICBMs deployed by the Soviet Union from the late 1960s to the mid-1970s, including the very large (or "heavy") SS-9s and their successors, the SS-18s, as well as the SS-17s and SS-19s, were consistent with this military mission.[9] So too was the leadership's decision to invest hundreds of billions of rubles in the development and deployment of systems, such as surface-to-air and antiballistic missiles, to defend directly against nuclear attack.[10]

For the most part, Soviet arms control policies reflected these clear and demanding military priorities. For much of the SALT decade, Moscow's overarching goals were to negotiate significant constraints on U.S. strategic weapons programs—especially those most likely to contribute to the realization of U.S. wartime objectives and to frustrate those of the Soviet Union—while, at the same time, leaving Kremlin programs relatively unfettered. U.S. negotiators harbored similar goals, of course, only in reverse.

Even under the most favorable of circumstances, Soviet leaders would have found such ambitious goals difficult to achieve. Against an adversary as powerful, competitive, and technologically advanced as the United States, the difficult became all but impossible and it is doubtful that Soviet decision makers ever seriously expected to engineer such a blatantly one-sided outcome at any point during the SALT talks. When, in the course of the negotiations, the Soviets were faced with a choice between endangering the SALT dialogue by holding firm to their maximal position and salvaging the process by compromising, almost invariably they amended their proposals and scaled back their demands. Such behavior, while typical of the negotiating process, also suggested a keen sensitivity on Moscow's part to the broad political value of the negotiations, which at times took clear precedence over purely military considerations. As a reference point for the development of Soviet negotiating proposals, however, the ambition to utilize the SALT talks to buttress the Kremlin's military position and to weaken that of the United States never flagged during these years.

In the opening rounds of the SALT I negotiations, for example, the Soviets initially turned aside U.S. proposals for a freeze on the deployment of long-range land- and sea-based ballistic missile launchers (silos and submarine tubes), pressing instead for constraints on antiballistic missile systems.[11] With several hundred more deployed ICBMs and submarine-launched ballistic missiles (SLBMs) than the United States, and more under construction, Moscow had little real incentive to accede to a freeze. Moreover, Soviet leaders might have anticipated that further expansion of the country's strategic arsenal would yield tangible military benefits, assuming no sizable counterdeployments by the United States. Yet a treaty limiting antiballistic missiles (ABMs) would prevent the United States from deploying ballistic missile defense systems nationwide that, given the superior U.S. technological base, could eventually threaten the Soviet Union's "assured destruction" capability. Without a deterrent of unquestionable reliability and effectiveness, Soviet leaders could have found themselves in a most unpleasant, if not a desperate, military situation.

In the end, of course, the two sides were able to strike a deal. At the 1972 Moscow summit, Nixon and Brezhnev signed two arms control agreements: the ABM treaty, limiting the deployment of antiballistic missiles to two installations nationwide, and the Interim Agreement on Offensive Weapons, a kind of freeze in place on ICBM and SLBM launchers. Soviet negotiators sanctioned many similar trade-offs throughout the SALT decade, often agreeing to modest shifts in position in order to move the talks forward. At least during these years, however, none of the concessions required the leadership to renounce the commitment to the eventual development of a war-winning posture or to undertake a comprehensive reassessment of Soviet military strategy.

PHASE II: 1985 TO THE PRESENT

The second phase in Soviet arms control policy, coinciding with the coming to power of Mikhail Gorbachev, seems to be informed by a very different set of core beliefs. With varying degrees of conviction, Gorbachev's predecessors, from Krushchev to Chernenko, nurtured the image of a vigilant, well-armed, and well-defended Soviet state, ever ready to deal a "decisive rebuff" to any would-be aggressor poised to disturb the socialist community's "peaceful way of life." Rhetorically at least, the new Soviet leader rejects such imagery as atavistic, hopelessly grounded in the military logic of the past. A nuclear war, the Soviets now argue, can never be won and must never be fought.[12] In the place of unilateral military advantage, Gorbachev speaks of a mutuality of security interests and of a new and complex global interdependence, linking capitalist and socialist countries alike.[13] Such themes, while familiar to Western students of international relations and international political economy, are essentially without precedent in the Soviet context. That Gorbachev's new vocabulary denotes a fundamental break in Soviet thinking and not, as some have charged, a simple tactical shift designed to calm the external environment as the Soviet Union seeks to reform itself from within, has become increasingly clear over time. Not even those in the West who initially greeted the reforms with deep-seated skepticism now doubt the authenticity of the Gorbachev revolution. We know, for example, that the Soviet leader has advanced a series of strategic arms control proposals since 1985 that, if ever implemented, would interrupt, if not derail, any lingering ambitions on Moscow's part either to develop or to maintain a credible war-winning posture. Deep reductions in central strategic systems, when coupled with severe constraints on the development, testing, and deployment of strategic defenses, render all but impossible the essential task confronting any group of military decision makers determined to prevail in the event of war: significant damage limitation. The Soviets have endorsed both kinds of measures.[14]

Should the two sides come to terms in the START talks, and should the agreement concluded reflect key elements of the current Soviet negotiating position, the principal military effect would be to enshrine what Western analysts term an "offensively dominated strategic environment," in other words, a superpower military relationship in which peace is maintained through the capacity of each side not to defend itself against attack, but to deliver a crippling retaliatory blow in response to any first strike. Such a relationship, while stable, is hardly the ideal posture from the perspective of a military planner determined to acquire the means to fight and win a nuclear war.

Assuming, for purposes of analysis, that the shift in Soviet arms control policies reflects a prior shift in views regarding the nature of war in the nuclear age, one should be able to construct a hierarchy of beliefs for this second phase in Soviet policy that differs in important ways from the hierarchy characteristic of the first phase. For the most part, such is indeed possible, although it is interesting to note that for both periods in Soviet policy, the first-order objective—preventing the outbreak of general war with the West—remains the same. It is at the second and succeeding levels that change becomes manifest:

- If, during the first phase, a nuclear war can either be won or lost, then during the second phase, there can be no victors.

- If, during the first phase, the pursuit of military advantage has a positive heuristic (to the side enjoying the advantage could go victory), then during the second phase the heuristic is either neutral (no decisive advantage is possible) or negative (the pursuit of advantage simply forces the competition to a new and more expensive level, as the other side takes appropriate countermeasures to preserve the existing balance).

- If, during the first phase, the primary purpose of arms control agreements is to secure the most restrictive limitations possible on the adversary's military forces, while leaving one's own programs unrestrained, then during the second phase the overarching objective is the maintenance of a stable military relationship in which neither side has any incentive to attack and both are content with roughly equal forces.

- If, during the first phase, national security can be enhanced only by diminishing the security of others, then during the second phase security can be mutual (even if premised on the chilling pledge to incinerate the other side in response to military aggression).

Several cautionary notes are in order at this point. The first and most obvious is that Soviet rhetoric has outpaced Soviet action. As of this writing, the character and capabilities of Soviet strategic forces, offensive and defensive, have changed hardly at all. The same forces that provoked the "window of vulnerability" controversy in the late 1970s and early 1980s and that led conservative U.S. military analysts to pronounce Soviet nuclear forces superior to those of the United States are still deployed; several new and more advanced missile systems, in fact, have been introduced within the last several years.[15] Only slightly less disturbing are the occasional dissident voices from within various Soviet bureaucracies, including the professional military, that until quite recently articulated views more closely associated with the "victory is possible" than with the "security is mutual" school. The persistence of such disconfirming evidence is troubling, to say the least, seeming to suggest that Moscow's conversion on security-related issues may be less than complete. It also points up the very real difficulty in arriving at firm conclusions regarding political and military intentions during a time of change, when the process being investigated is still under way.

And yet, in several key policy areas the Soviets have manifested a willingness to move beyond the rhetoric and to undertake actions consistent with the new logic. The changing content of the Soviet Union's START proposals has already been noted and its significance should not be minimized. The conclusion of the treaty on intermediate-range nuclear forces (INF) in December 1987 is also important in this context.[16] Although the military significance of the agreement may be judged marginal—the vast majority of the Western European targets that would have been destroyed by the Soviet Union's arsenal of intermediate- and medium-range systems in the event of war can just as effectively be destroyed by a fraction of the Kremlin's central strategic forces—the agreement marks the first time that the Soviets have been willing to negotiate the elimination of several classes of nuclear delivery systems and to do so asymmetrically (unequal reductions to an equal outcome).

The most dramatic development, however, came with Gorbachev's December 1988 announcement of a 500,000-man unilateral reduction in Soviet military personnel over two years, of which some 50,000 would be drawn from the groups of Soviet forces in East Germany, Czechoslovakia, and Hungary.[17] In the same speech, the Soviet leader promised to withdraw considerable military equipment from the territory of the Warsaw Pact states, including some 5,000 Soviet tanks. In all Gorbachev pledged to eliminate 8,500 artillery systems, 800 tactical aircraft, and 10,000 tanks from Soviet military stocks in the European U.S.S.R. and Eastern Europe.[18] In response to charges that only outdated equipment was likely to be dismantled or repositioned, Gorbachev stated in January 1989 that

5,300 of the 10,000 Soviet tanks slated for elimination would be newer, "more advanced" models.[19]

Precisely why Gorbachev has been willing to sanction these and other military initiatives is unclear. Both Western analysts and their increasingly outspoken Soviet counterparts have advanced two kinds of explanations. The first looks principally to economics as the motivating factor. The Soviet economy is in such dismal and desperate shape, according to those making this case, that reductions in military spending, which accounts for between 15 and 25 percent of the country's gross national product, are absolutely essential if the leadership's plans to "restructure" the Soviet system are to have any realistic prospect of success.[20] Monies saved by cutting allocations to the military may be redirected to the civilian sectors of the economy, including the consumption and the investment accounts. Improving Soviet living standards is a key objective of the Gorbachev reform program; only through such material incentives, the new leadership appears to believe, can the economic system be made more productive and efficient, thereby ultimately generating greater wealth. The second explanation looks more toward a general attitudinal shift among Soviet leaders with respect to a wide range of issues as the primary engine of change.[21] From "democratization" and "glasnost" on the domestic front to "interdependence" and "reasonable sufficiency" in foreign and defense policy, Gorbachev's "new thinking" constitutes an abrupt break with the past and an explicit rejection of much of the Soviet experience; it also serves as a blueprint for the country's future development.

The two explanations are not, of course, mutually exclusive. In defense of his many policy initiatives, Gorbachev has repeatedly expressed his conviction that only through a process of fundamental and comprehensive change, attitudinal as well as structural, can the Soviet system be made to work. In this sense, the two kinds of change go hand in hand; efforts to reform the system by focusing narrowly on a single dimension of the problem are likely to prove ineffective, even counterproductive.

Due largely, then, to this broad mandate for change, Soviet foreign and defense policies have been extensively revised within the last half-decade. Among the particular forces dictating a change in Soviet arms control policy, however, has been a shift in core beliefs regarding the wagability and winability of nuclear war. At one level, the leadership's decision to reformulate its arms control policies consistent with the logic that "a nuclear war can never be won and must never be fought" can be attributed to the economic argument in favor of systemic change: given the stupendous scale of the resources required to implement Gorbachev's ambitious program for economic reform, the funds necessary to develop and maintain a war-winning military posture are simply unavailable, at least for the time being and perhaps for decades to come. Moscow's new look in arms control can also be said to reflect the more broadly based imperatives regarding the need for change associated with the Gorbachev revolution. Either explanation is probably sufficient to account for a shift in core beliefs of the kind being proposed here.

ACCOUNTING FOR THE SHIFT

There are, however, other ways to conceive of the forces working to transform Soviet thinking about the nature of war in the modern age and thus the Kremlin's arms control diplomacy. Such a reconception does not diminish the importance of either the economic or the broadly systemic explanation; rather, it supplements the former and refines the latter. More instrumentally, it is through such a reconception that one can most usefully speak of a learning process in Soviet arms control policy. It is also by reference to this analytical method that the unevenness of the learning process—the persistence within Soviet policy of contradictory elements, images, and themes, especially during the years of transition—is best seen.

The learning evident in the Soviet Union's arms control diplomacy has come about as a consequence of the interplay of three main factors: technology, experience, and regime change. Each is analyzed below. The learning itself, which far exceeds any reward-punishment conception, has been of three types, for the most part corresponding to the definitions elaborated earlier in this volume, namely changes in cognitive content, changes in cognitive structure, and greater efficiency. The *scope* of learning and the *rate* at which it has proceeded through different segments of the Soviet policy-making community are central but distinct issues; both are considered in a later section of this chapter.

LEARNING INDUCED BY TECHNOLOGY

The role of technology in contemporary strategic military affairs is complex. The innovations in weaponry and the means of delivery that we associate with the nuclear revolution place at the disposal of policymakers in Washington and Moscow (and, to a lesser extent, in London, Paris, and Beijing) military capabilities of unprecedented destructiveness. The coupling, in particular, of thermonuclear warheads (with yields ranging from hundreds of kilotons to several megatons) with long-range ballistic missiles makes it possible for one superpower to eviscerate the other in a matter of minutes. At the same time, the very technologies that have multiplied by a factor of several thousand the offensive striking power of the United States and the Soviet Union have rendered the task of effective nationwide defense problematic. Though present in latent form since the late 1950s, this peculiar and deeply disturbing feature of the bilateral strategic relationship has become a central preoccupation of U.S. and Soviet decision makers only over the course of the last 20 years.

For U.S. leaders, the understandable urge to undo deterrence—to return to traditional, prenuclear military logic in which a state's security is measured by its ability to defend as well as to destroy—has been counterbalanced for the most part by the recognition that human whims must yield to the laws of physics.[22] Since Robert McNamara's tenure as secretary of defense in the 1960s, successive U.S. administrations have been content in their public pronouncements to base the country's security on the pledge to retaliate in kind, should the Soviet Union ever unleash a nuclear attack against the United States or its principal allies.[23] Active defense against such an attack is currently beyond the capacity of the United States to effect, in any event.[24]

For the first 30 years after Hiroshima, Soviet authorities resisted the conclusion that nuclear weapons had changed fundamentally the laws of war, rejecting such Western claims as unscientific. While sensitive to the predictable consequences of any war fought with nuclear weapons, those responsible for maintaining the military security of the Soviet Union denounced as "defeatist" the proposition that the most effective way to deter the outbreak of hostilities with the United States was by sanctioning what amounted to a mutual suicide pact.[25] Well into the 1970s high-level spokesmen for the Soviet ministry of defense routinely described a military strategy that had as one of its central features the capacity to limit damage to the territory and population of the U.S.S.R.[26]

To implement such a strategy, the Soviets invested widely in a range of active defensive measures, most notably strategic air defenses (interceptor aircraft and surface-to-air missiles) and antiballistic missile systems, including the Galosh ABM deployments begun around Moscow in the early 1960s.[27] Doubtless, Soviet authorities also looked to the development during the late 1960s and early 1970s of the quick-reacting, reliable, and relatively accurate fourth-generation ICBMs—which could be employed in a preemptive first strike against U.S. military installations—as a vital step in the effort to construct a viable damage-limiting military posture. Western military analysts have long noted the Kremlin's interest in various "passive" defensive measures, including civil defense and industrial dispersion and hardening, although the utility of such measures has been and continues to be open to question.[28]

Given this defensive emphasis in both Soviet military writings and the country's strategic weapons programs, why the Kremlin's willingness in 1972 to conclude the ABM treaty, which, as written, limited active ABM sites to two, neither of which could be expected to afford much protection against a "dedicated" U.S. missile strike? Soviet leaders appear to have made their decision in response to two developments, both of a largely technical nature. The first concerned the relative state of U.S. and Soviet ballistic missile defense technologies. In the late 1960s the U.S. scientific and technical communities, in sworn testimony before Congress, characterized the U.S. ABM program as significantly more advanced than its Soviet counterpart, particularly with respect to important sensor and tracking technologies.[29] In the short run at least, U.S. systems, once deployed, were likely to perform their designated military mission more effectively. Were this in fact to be the case, the Kremlin could confront a military situation in which the bedrock of Soviet security, its assured retaliatory capabilities, might be threatened. At a minimum, a large-scale U.S. ABM program would compel the Soviet leadership to assume the worst militarily, necessitating additional efforts to safeguard the deterrent value of its offensive forces, even as it redoubled efforts to keep pace defensively.

The second development that appeared to induce caution on the part of Soviet leaders was the advent of multiple-warhead technology. MIRVs— multiple independently targetable reentry vehicles—served to multiply the military utility of long-range ballistic missiles by increasing from 1 to several the number of nuclear warheads that could be delivered by a single rocket booster. The United States began the deployment of the 3-warhead Minuteman III ICBM in 1970; the first Poseidon SLBM, equipped with from 10 to 14 warheads, entered service the following year.[30] Whereas Soviet military planners had confronted approximately 1,700 U.S. ballistic missile warheads as late as 1969, within 5 years the number was certain to grow to at least 7,000. The task of defending against a missile-borne attack, never a simple matter, would increase in difficulty proportionately. If, as appeared likely, the cost of constructing and upgrading antiballistic missile systems were to exceed the cost of deploying additional ballistic missile warheads, the economic advantage would lie with the attacker. In short, in any race between offensive and defensive strategic systems, the former was sure to prevail.

The best evidence in support of the proposition that the Soviets ran through precisely such calculations is their signing of the ABM treaty; had they reached a different set of conclusions regarding the relationship between strategic offensive and defensive systems, in other words, they would have held out for a less restrictive accord or rejected the treaty altogether.

It is also worth noting, however, that the conclusion of the agreement did not induce the leadership to reject as unworkable the *concept* of effective strategic defense, at least not initially. On the contrary, in those areas not limited by the ABM treaty, such as conventional air defense and ballistic missile defense research and development, Soviet efforts continued unabated, arousing deep suspicions on the part of U.S. officials that the Kremlin's commitment to nuclear deterrence keyed to the pre-eminence of the offensive was at best conditional.[31] Through the late 1970s Soviet military writings, which spoke of the continuing obligation of the country's armed forces to "seize the initiative" in the event of hostilities and to "defend" the socialist way of life through the application of appropriate military methods, tended to confirm this interpretation.[32]

An interesting situation had developed by the mid-1970s with respect to the issue of strategic military policy as well-placed Soviet analysts, many with links to the senior political leadership, began to advance ideas in connection with the U.S.–Soviet strategic relationship that departed in important ways from the views of the uniformed military. While for the most part shying away from the language used by students of strategic affairs in the United States, such Soviet commentators as Georgi Arbatov (and others associated with the Institute of the USA and Canada in Moscow) unequivocally endorsed the emerging arms control regime with Washington, taking special note of the importance of the various agreements in heading off a new and "destabilizing" round of the military competition.[33] The restraints contained in the several agreements concluded between the superpowers during these years, including though not limited to the ABM treaty, severely limited the ability of senior Soviet commanders to plan with confidence for "victory" in the context of strategic military operations. The ostensible gap between the views of civilian and military authorities widened in the late 1970s and early 1980s, as the civilians, led by Brezhnev himself, edged closer to an explicit endorsement of American-style deterrence. The gap did not begin to narrow again until late in Brezhnev's tenure, when many of those directly responsible for the maintenance of Soviet security took up a number of the themes associated with the critics of the "victory is possible" school. (The issue of differential learning curves among Soviet elites is treated in greater depth later in the chapter).

The views of Marshal Nikolai Ogarkov, the chief of the Soviet General Staff from 1977 to 1984, take on particular significance in this regard. Western analysts have frequently portrayed Ogarkov as an unreconstructed "hawk" on defense and military questions, a proponent of the view that more is always better in the struggle to provide for Soviet security.[34] In reality, during his years as chief Ogarkov sharply distinguished between *strategic* military requirements and the needs of Soviet armed forces at the *theater level*.[35] Informed, we may assume, by a particular understanding of the existing strategic military relationship between the superpowers, Ogarkov wrote in 1983, for example, of the inability of either side to overcome the paralytic effects of nuclear deterrence by military means. Under any and all conditions, he argued, the side struck first will retain sufficient retaliatory forces to inflict unacceptable damage on the aggressor. In what must have been a first for a chief of the General Staff, he paraphrased McNamara on the point approvingly.[36] The true threat to Soviet security, according to Ogarkov, was the rapidly changing character of the conventional battlefield, particularly in Europe, where Western innovations in weaponry—from advances in microchip circuitry to satellite imagery—threatened to neutralize Warsaw Pact advantages in deployed manpower and in most kinds of military equipment.[37] Ogarkov ran afoul of his civilian superiors (which culminated in his resignation as chief of the General Staff in September 1984) not for his views on strategic military policy and strategic arms control, but for his obvious displeasure with the state of Soviet theater military capabilities and for his implied criticism of those within the system who failed to recognize the problem. His calls for the devotion of new resources to the theater mission could not have won him many friends in the mid-1980s, as the political leadership had already served notice that the Soviet Union was entering a period of budgetary austerity in which military spending was likely to be held constant if not decreased.

The Soviet response to the Reagan administration's Strategic Defense Initiative (SDI) offers additional evidence in support of the argument that technological factors have served to influence the content of Soviet arms control policies in important ways. As a consequence of SDI, the post-Brezhnev leadership has moved from a kind of reluctant or grudging endorsement of the ABM treaty to enthusiastic support for the agreement in its narrowest construction. Through the mid-1980s the Soviets, in practice, adhered to a rather loose interpretation of the accord, undertaking a number of ABM-related activities that many in the United States construed as violating the intent if not the letter of the agreement. Principal among these has been the construction of a large-phased array radar near Krasnoyarsk, in east central Siberia.[38] While nothing in the treaty prohibits the building of such a radar, the installation must be located on the periphery of Soviet (or U.S.) territory and "oriented outward."[39] As the Soviets now admit, the Krasnoyarsk radar is neither. While the radar itself is of only marginal military value, as an indication of the Soviet Union's somewhat laissez-faire attitude toward the restraints contained in the ABM treaty, the episode was deeply troubling to U.S. policy makers.

Since the unveiling of SDI in 1983, the Soviet leaders have done an about-face concerning the ABM treaty. They now call for a "reaffirmation" of the accord, as well as a superpower agreement to abide by its provisions for an agreed number of years (the initial Soviet proposal was for a 20-year "no-cut" pledge, later reduced to 10). The particular interpretation of the agreement that the Soviets have put forward since 1985 in both their public and private diplomacy has been more restrictive than even the narrowest reading offered by U.S. analysts, including several who participated in the agreement's drafting.[40]

The Soviet Union's ardent embrace of the ABM treaty appears to be driven in large measure by the conviction that, in any renewed superpower competition involving strategic defensive systems, the predictable consequence will be a new and potentially ruinous arms race that, although unlikely to eventuate in decisive military advantage for either side, would place extraordinary demands on an already ailing Soviet economy. The need to earmark additional resources for the development of effective SDI countermeasures would inevitably compromise Gorbachev's plans to revitalize the country's domestic economy—plans that are keyed to the greater availability of funds for the consumption and nonmilitary investment accounts.

If Soviet leaders believed that the broad application of new military technologies would be likely to result in the overthrow of mutual assured destruction and its replacement with what Ronald Reagan once termed *mutual assured survival*, their response to the Strategic Defense Initiative might have been more positive. They may even have looked more favorably on SDI if they believed that the development and deployment of technologically advanced defensive systems could significantly reduce the damage certain to attend any widespread use of nuclear weapons against Soviet territory. They have been persuaded by neither argument, strongly suggesting that they reject as unrealizable any technologically driven solutions to the security dilemmas posed by nuclear deterrence.

The change in Soviet perspective on this particular issue—from an explicit endorsement of a "mixed" or balanced strategic military posture to a characterization of strategic defensive programs as "destabilizing" and a first-strike threat—is prima facie evidence of complex "learning" in Soviet arms control policy in response principally to certain perceived technological realities. The learning that appears to have taken place can perhaps best be characterized as the acquisition by policy makers of a progressively more differentiated understanding of the world in which they must operate (cognitive structural), which precipitates a change in strategic beliefs and preferences (a second order change in cognitive content).

The argument that such a learning process has occurred is difficult to substantiate, however, because of the obvious disconnect between what Soviet leaders say and the military forces at their command. Gorbachev's rhetoric notwithstanding, through 1987 the Kremlin spent at least as much on the procurement and deployment of strategic defensive systems as it did on long-range offensive forces.[41] Until the Soviets significantly reduce the level of spending in this area, allow their air defense and antiballistic missile capabilities to atrophy, and follow through on their commitment to abide by the "strict" interpretation of the ABM treaty, their newfound willingness to sanction a strategic military relationship with the United States based on the logic of assured destruction will be greeted skeptically by responsible U.S. and Western officials. The U.S. decision to reopen the strategic debate through SDI further complicates the situation. On one hand, it legitimizes any renewed Soviet effort to acquire a significant damage-limiting posture because the U.S. government has now endorsed the pursuit of the defensive option; on the other hand, should the Kremlin take up the U.S. challenge in earnest, those who detect in Soviet policy the military ambition to prevail in any strategic exchange with the United States are certain to sound the alarm bells. In a very real sense, the Soviet leaders are damned if they do and damned if they don't.

LEARNING THROUGH EXPERIENCE

The previous section focused on the ways in which technology appears to have contributed to a revision in Soviet arms control policies, culminating in an identifiable shift in the leadership's strategic beliefs and preferences. One attraction to discussing the role of technology is that it can be broken out, at least to a degree, from other factors that may induce learning because of its distinctive quality. We understand that, as an agent of learning or change, technology functions differently from and perhaps more predictably than other agents, although we may have difficulty explaining exactly why this is the case. Whatever analytical neatness attends consideration of the role of technology disappears, however, when the focus shifts to "experience" as a factor in learning.

That people learn as a consequence of experience is a truism. The problem with this particular conception of learning is its vagueness. What does it mean to say that the Soviet Union's arms control diplomacy has been influenced by the experience of negotiating with the Americans?

As the term is applied here, it is meant to suggest the changes in Soviet arms control policies that have come about largely as a result of the sustained interaction on security-related issues between U.S. and Soviet policy makers either directly, through personal dealings with their counterparts, or indirectly, through the experiences of those to whom they entrust responsibility. It is the type of learning that we associate with complex political processes. Although still disturbingly imprecise, such a definition serves to bring the analysis into sharper focus and to contain the distorting effect of having to consider all possible variants and conceptions of experience simultaneously.

For Soviet leaders, negotiating with the United States on the limitation of strategic offensive and defensive forces was part of a much larger process that they labeled the relaxation of tensions, better known in the

West as détente. From the first round of the SALT talks in November 1969 through the mid-1970s, Soviet analysts tended to divide the pursuit of better relations with Washington, and with the West more generally, into two distinct parts: the relaxation of political tensions (or political détente) and measures to reduce or alleviate the military confrontation (or military détente).[42] During these early years in particular the Soviets even developed a rather precise formula for the implementation of détente in which they linked the conclusion of arms control agreements to the normalization of superpower political relations; in the Soviet conception, steps to curtail the military competition should follow rather than precede an upturn in political ties.[43] The sequencing is important to understand in reconstructing the history of the period, because it serves to highlight how profoundly Soviet policy changed—from a rather rigid set of preferences and priorities to a much more flexible and adaptive approach—in response to the actual development of U.S.–Soviet relations during the first half of the 1970s.

The SALT I negotiations constituted the first important challenge to the Kremlin's strategy. U.S. pressure to conclude agreements limiting both ABM systems and offensive forces was unremitting; while favorably disposed toward the former, the Soviets were equivocal about the latter. By contrast, they attached singular importance to the generation of a joint declaration on political relations, intended, along with whatever arms limitation agreements might emerge, to symbolize Moscow's emergence as Washington's equal.[44]

U.S. policy makers, only recently reconciled to the notion of Soviet military equality, were distinctly unenthusiastic and manifested little interest in a document detailing, by Moscow's reckoning, the shared rights and obligations of the world's two leading nuclear weapons states.[45] The Nixon administration pressed for the conclusion of the arms control accords and sought to defer for as long as possible consideration of the political testament. The Brezhnev leadership induced various pauses in the SALT talks in order to focus U.S. attention on the declaration of principles. The compromise that emerged enabled both sides to claim victory: Washington secured Soviet assent to the ABM treaty and the Interim Agreement on Offensive Weapons, and Moscow obtained its cherished Basic Principles of Relations agreement.

During the first part of the second round of SALT, from November 1972 to the negotiations leading up to the conclusion of the Vladivostok accords two years later, the Kremlin's determination to remain faithful to its conception of the proper sequencing of détente reemerged. U.S. officials who participated in the negotiations were struck by the leadership's keen interest in the further development of U.S.–Soviet political and economic relations and by its manifest disinterest in arms control. William Hyland, a high-ranking member of the National Security Council staff during the Nixon and Ford administrations, has remarked that Brezhnev, in particular, was preoccupied with the conclusion of a possible U.S.–Soviet nonaggression pact and with trade issues, and that the Soviet leader seemed content throughout 1973 to leave SALT-related discussions to Foreign Minister Andrei Gromyko.[46] In his memoirs, Kissinger too describes the snaillike pace of the SALT II negotiations during their first year, which he attributes both to the administration's mounting preoccupation with the Watergate crisis and to the lack of Soviet initiative and responsiveness.[47] When the Soviets finally saw fit to bestir themselves in SALT, it was to propose that the interim agreement be converted, without significant revision, to a long-term treaty.[48] Their willingness to urge such a step strongly suggests, beyond their basic satisfaction with the military status quo, a decision to downgrade the role of arms control in détente and a determination to refocus Washington's attention on the nonmilitary dimensions of the relationship.

If such was in fact the Soviet purpose, the leadership must have watched with surprise and consternation as their preferred strategy fell victim to the vagaries of superpower relations, compounded in this instance by the slow unraveling of Richard Nixon's presidency. It is also, however, during these difficult months, from the introduction in January 1973 of the Jackson-Vanik amendment to Nixon's resignation some 20 months later, that it is possible to detect evidence of complex learning on the part of Soviet leaders as they sought to adapt their policies to the rapidly changing political environment.

Initially Moscow seemed content with the laggard pace of the early SALT II negotiations; by intentionally slowing the discussions on arms control, the Soviets sought to signal Washington that the detailed consideration of political and economic matters could no longer be deferred. By the spring of 1974, however, with the Nixon administration entering its final agonies, the Kremlin's perspective changed abruptly, as Soviet leaders came to realize that the president's fate and that of détente were intertwined.

As Nixon struggled to remain in office, the domestic critique of his foreign policies reached a crescendo, with the U.S.–Soviet détente a favorite target. To salvage the policy, if not the Nixon presidency, the Soviets permitted the pace of the SALT talks to quicken in the months leading up to the third Nixon-Brezhnev summit in June 1974. As the meetings drew to a close, the two sides announced two relatively minor arms control accords and recommitted themselves to conclusion in the nearest future of a 10-year treaty to replace the 1972 interim agreement.[49]

When Nixon was forced from office in August, Gromyko sought and obtained an early meeting with the new president, Gerald Ford, both to communicate the Kremlin's unflagging devotion to détente and to satisfy himself that Nixon's successor would stay the course. Most important, Gromyko brought word that the Soviet leadership was prepared to move ahead without delay on the signing of at least a framework agreement in SALT.[50] By so doing, Gromyko confirmed that the Soviet leadership would not hold progress in arms control hostage to the further development of political relations. It was a nearly complete reversal of the Soviet position during 1973 and the first part of 1974.

In November Ford and Brezhnev, meeting in Vladivostok, signed the memorandum of understanding that would guide the negotiations for the remainder of the president's term in office.[51] Significantly, the Vladivostok agreement contained several provisions that only months before the Soviets had dismissed in the negotiations as prejudicial to their interests. Prior to the November summit, the leadership had lobbied for the perpetuation of the unequal force levels contained in the interim agreement, asserting that the Soviet Union was entitled to such an advantage because of the combined threat posed to the country's security by the nuclear forces of the United States, Great Britain, France, and China. At Vladivostok Brezhnev abandoned this position and assented to strict numerical equality in the number of U.S. and Soviet deployed strategic systems.[52]

The trauma associated with the collapse of the Nixon presidency taught the Soviets several valuable lessons. First, they were reminded that both the content and conduct of U.S. foreign policy are context-dependent—that any administration's foreign policy initiatives are shaped to a greater or lesser degree by powerful domestic political currents that can change with dizzying speed and over which a president and his advisers exercise only modest influence. Second, they learned that their own actions can have an impact on the way in which the American public and their elected representatives perceive a particular policy course. In reinvigorating the moribund SALT negotiations in the fall of 1974, the Soviets not only energized a process to which they attached considerable importance but they also gave détente a new, if temporary, lease on life in the United States.

Much to their later chagrin, Soviet leaders learned the first lesson better than the second. While they never again lost sight of the intimate connection in the United States between domestic politics and foreign policy, they did not always act in a manner consistent with that critically important insight. In their own conduct of foreign policy, they regularly undertook actions that almost seemed designed to undermine the delicate domestic U.S. consensus in favor of arms control and détente more generally. Over time, Moscow's insistence that the relaxation of tensions with the United States could continue to develop despite the intensification of the "international class struggle"—best symbolized by the Soviet-assisted upturn in revolutionary activity in Africa during the mid- to late-1970s—destroyed U.S. confidence in the Kremlin's commitment to a new and more stable international political order.[53]

The Soviet tendency to "unlearn" the lessons of the Watergate crisis was also apparent in the way the leadership chose to pursue the modernization of its strategic nuclear arsenal. The history of the Soviet military buildup during the seven years between the SALT I agreements and the SALT II treaty has been told elsewhere and need not be rehearsed. Suffice it to say that its rate and intensity caught most U.S. policy makers off guard and contributed to the growing perception in this country that the Soviets were manipulating the SALT process to advance their military fortunes at the expense of their negotiating partner. It was as if Soviet leaders believed that their actions in this area were somehow external to the conduct of their relations with the United States.

In the end, of course, it was precisely the growth in Soviet military capabilities during these years that most exercised détente's critics in the United States, constituting perhaps the most effective charge in the bill of indictment leveled against the policy by its opponents. Various Soviet efforts to contain the damage and to signal an important departure in policy—from Brezhnev's renunciation of military superiority as a Soviet goal in January 1977 to his rather tortured statement four years later that the side that begins a nuclear war in hopes of emerging victorious "has decided to commit suicide"—were too little, too late.[54]

By the end of the 1970s the Brezhnev leadership had repeatedly manifested an ability to undertake significant and constructive tactical adjustments in its policies toward the United States, largely as a consequence of the sustained interaction between the two superpowers and its newfound sensitivity to the salience of domestic factors in U.S. foreign policy. Such adjustments, especially in arms control, probably served to prolong détente, even as other forces, some within the Kremlin's control and others beyond, contributed to its demise. That Soviet leaders had acquired through experience a progressively more refined understanding of the policy environment within which they were forced to function can scarcely be questioned. At the same time, the relatively minor modifications to policy sanctioned by the leadership, as well as the persistence of certain kinds of behavior to which Washington took strong exception, conspired to reduce the effectiveness of the attempt at reform.

In the absence of a shift in core Soviet beliefs and values regarding the utility of nuclear arms control (necessitating a prior shift in attitudes toward the wagability and winability of nuclear war), all efforts to restore the fabric of relations with the United States and to negotiate a new strategic arms reduction agreement to replace the discredited SALT II treaty were likely to be stillborn. As late as 1982, the realization that only a change of this magnitude could set U.S.–Soviet relations on a new, more productive, and less confrontational course had yet to work its way through key elements of the Soviet decision-making system.

LEARNING AND REGIME CHANGE

Most Western students of Soviet affairs characterize the last five years of the Brezhnev regime as a period of unrelieved torpidity, a time of profound social alienation, political regression, and accelerating economic decline. The Soviets, of course, now term the entire 18-year reign of Brezhnev "the period of stagnation." While doubtless true with respect to many, if not most, areas of Soviet life, the characterization does not hold for Soviet thinking on security-related issues, which, between the late 1970s and early 1980s, changed—or more correctly began to change— in important ways. It was during these years in the development of Soviet military thought that the belief systems associated with the first period yielded to those of the second.

As noted earlier, dating the transition is no simple matter. Depending on the point of departure, it spanned some 15 years (starting from the late 1960s), about a decade (from 1972), or five years (from the very late 1970s); some would argue that it is only now under way, coinciding with Gorbachev's accession to power. The present effort dates the initial change in Soviet thinking to the mid-to-late 1970s, at which time senior Soviet leaders, led by Brezhnev, began to advance a view of the U.S.–Soviet strategic military relationship significantly different from and more textured than analyses offered earlier. The reassessment continued in the years following Brezhnev's death late in 1982, although without much energy, and then rapidly intensified, culminating with the series of pronouncements on military strategy and arms control policies that have emanated from the Soviet policy-making community since 1985.

It is highly unlikely that Brezhnev sought to provoke a wide-ranging review of Soviet security policies in January 1977 when, in the course of his remarks in the city of Tula, long a center of Russian arms production, he rejected as a Soviet goal the attainment of strategic military superior- ity. Timed to coincide with the inauguration of Jimmy Carter, the Soviet leader's remarks were no doubt intended to help set a positive tone for the next phase in superpower relations and to answer charges, then widespread in the United States, that the modernization of Soviet strategic nuclear capabilities posed a grave and increasing threat to the U.S. and Western security.

At the same time, the central thrust of Brezhnev's speech—that in rejecting superiority as a goal, the Soviet Union had the right to expect corresponding forbearance on the part of the United States—seemed to presage an important branch point in Soviet policy. For the first time, the ranking Soviet leader had implicitly acknowledged the reciprocal, interactive character of the military competition between the superpowers and explicitly expressed his country's willingness to settle for a position of rough military equality with its principal adversary.[55] The general secretary's remarks were greeted with considerable skepticism in the West, as well they should have been, coming in the midst of the Kremlin's strategic military buildup, then in full swing. The disjunction between words and deeds notwithstanding, Brezhnev's contribution to the strategic dialogue represented a qualitatively new input.

More pronouncements and policy initiatives regarding military policy and arms control followed during the remaining years of Brezhnev's stewardship and throughout the abbreviated terms of Yuri Andropov and Konstantin Chernenko. Brezhnev's version of the suicidal character of nuclear war, offered in October 1981, has already been noted. In 1982 then Minister of Defense Dmitri Ustinov announced the Soviet Union's decision to undertake a commitment not to be the first to use nuclear weapons in the event of a conflict with the United States and its allies.[56] In March 1983, following Ronald Reagan's call to the U.S. scientific and technological communities to devise the means to render nuclear weapons "impotent and obsolete," Andropov lectured his U.S. counterpart from the pages of *Pravda* on the pernicious consequences of a renewed superpower competition in the development and deployment of strategic defensive systems.[57]

These and similar statements suggested a fairly wide-ranging, if less than completely coherent, reconsideration of many of the major tenets of Soviet military doctrine, including the possible utility of nuclear weapons in times of war. By so doing, Kremlin authorities also forced, willy nilly, a fresh look at Soviet arms control policies and the potential value of agreements to limit, in particular, certain kinds of nuclear weapons deployments.

The process begun by Brezhnev in 1977, and advanced with varying degrees of conviction by his successors from 1982 to 1985, did not, however, result in either a formal or an unequivocal renunciation of existing Soviet military and arms control policies. On the contrary, the leadership took considerable pains to emphasize the essential continuity of policy. Arguably the best indicators of the state of Soviet thinking, the country's START proposals, offered between the summer of 1982 when the negotiations began and November 1983 when they were suspended, were notable largely for their predictability and lack of imagination, constituting little more than amended versions of plans offered earlier. U.S. negotiators derisively termed the Soviet proposals SALT II 1/2.

Given their own roles in the development of Soviet policy over the course of the preceding 10 or in some cases 20 years, as well as their identification with and commitment to the goals these policies had been designed to serve, it would have taken an extraordinary set of circumstances to induce these Brezhnev-era policy makers to abandon their handiwork. In their own view, no such set of circumstances had arisen, despite the admittedly troubled state of the Soviet economic, political, and social systems. By their own reckoning, a change in Soviet foreign and military policy was indeed necessary in order to adjust to manifest shifts in the international environment. But such change as might be required was to be undertaken cautiously, in increments, and with due regard for Soviet prestige; and it certainly should not come at the cost of what had been achieved—diplomatically and politically—with such effort and over such time.

Between 1977 and 1985, Soviet leaders "learned" that many of the conceptions that had informed their understanding of the superpower relationship and guided their arms control diplomacy were of decreasing utility. In response, they encouraged, within strict limits, a reassessment of existing policy, incorporated those elements of change that could be accommodated within the extant system of beliefs and preferences, and, by reference to this revised cognitive framework, sanctioned a number of new departures in policy. Had Andropov, for example, been 10 years younger when he succeeded Brezhnev, this gradual and controlled evolution of Soviet policy might well have continued to the present time.

Andropov's tenure proved to be brief, however, and within 13 months of his passing the Soviet leadership had elected 53-year old Mikhail Gorbachev to succeed him. The anointing of Gorbachev signaled the long-awaited and much-anticipated generational shift in Soviet politics. With his selection the halting, confused, defensive, and profoundly conservative tenor of Soviet diplomacy ceased abruptly, and there ensued a veritable cascade of new initiatives and proposals, many of them in the areas of U.S.–Soviet security relations and nuclear and conventional arms control.

Partially in response to what several Western analysts termed Ronald Reagan's nuclear "allergy," best symbolized by his determined advocacy of SDI, Gorbachev in January 1986 went the U.S. president one better, offering a rhetorically elegant plan for the phased elimination of all nuclear weapons by the year 2000.[58] Ten months later, in a hastily prepared presummit meeting in Reykjavik, Iceland, Gorbachev returned to the offensive, endorsing deep cuts in U.S. and Soviet strategic nuclear forces in exchange for a U.S. commitment to abide by a new and more restrictive interpretation of the ABM treaty. Before the bidding came to an end on the third day, undone by Reagan's refusal to cut a deal on SDI, the Soviet leader had maneuvered the president into agreeing, in principle, to the former's plan for the gradual elimination of U.S. and Soviet nuclear weapons arsenals.[59] The U.S. side, criticized both at home and abroad for moving too far, too fast, quickly disavowed the commitment, arguing that the

United States had been prepared to consider reducing to zero only nuclear-armed ballistic missiles.[60] The "clarification" notwithstanding, the impression lingered that Gorbachev and his associates had dominated the Reykjavik meetings from start to finish.

Within several months, Gorbachev was at it again, this time proposing that the two sides conclude the negotiations on intermediate-range nuclear forces without further delay; to advance the talks, he embraced a slightly amended version of the so-called zero option, first proposed by the Reagan administration in November 1981—and denounced as unworkable by Gorbachev's three immediate predecessors—by which the United States and the Soviet Union would agree to dismantle and destroy all intermediate-range missiles.[61] When, during the final months of the negotiations, the administration attached a number of additional conditions to the U.S. proposal, the Kremlin balked momentarily but then conceded on all important points.[62] By the terms of the agreement, signed in Washington in December 1987, the Soviet Union agreed to eliminate 2 1/2 missiles for every U.S. Pershing-2 and ground-launched cruise missile either withdrawn from service with U.S. forces in Europe or scheduled for deployment.[63] Fearing a precedent, never before had the Soviet leadership consented to an arms control agreement requiring that the U.S.S.R. undertake sharply asymmetrical reductions. With the INF treaty, Gorbachev accepted the U.S. position of "unequal reductions to an equal outcome," seemingly without hesitation. In addition to the reductions, the Soviets also agreed in INF to a highly intrusive regime for monitoring compliance with the accord that included extensive provisions for on-site inspection.[64]

Accompanying Gorbachev's dramatic departures in arms control, only the most important of which have been noted here, have been similarly provocative and far-reaching statements on national and international security and on Soviet military doctrine. The Soviet leader's heavy emphasis on the need for new thinking in international relations—most especially his assertions that the world is now "interdependent" and "interconnected" and that the search for mutual security must displace the pursuit of national security through unilateral means—are by now familiar themes in Soviet foreign policy, tending to obscure just how radical the Gorbachev line has been.[65] His proposed revisions to Soviet military doctrine, particularly the introduction of the concept of "reasonable sufficiency" as a guide to the development of Soviet military capabilities and to the sizing of the country's armed forces, have surprised and perplexed Western observers, who struggle to decipher the substance of the reforms and to assess their possible implications for the role of military power in Soviet strategy.[66]

The rapid-fire promotions, demotions, and forced retirements that have characterized Soviet personnel policy in the last five years, especially within those bureaucracies associated with the formulation and implementation of the country's military and arms control policies, offer strong circumstantial evidence in support of the argument that Gorbachev's new line on Soviet security policy constitutes a decisive break with the past. Given the tendency, moreover, of those who have exercised power to resist, consciously and unconsciously, the dismantling of the policies with which they are closely identified and by reference to which they have secured their positions within the system, it is only through their replacement that a shift in core beliefs of the type suggested in this analysis can be successfully implemented.

Certainly the scale of the personnel changes under Gorbachev is consistent with a strategy to remake the Soviet decision-making apparatus in the area of security policy. Since March 1985 Gorbachev and his allies have engineered several key appointments, including, most importantly, the replacement of Andrei Gromyko by Eduard Shevardnadze as foreign minister and of Sergey Sokolov by Dmitri Yazov as defense minister. In December 1988 Ogarkov's replacement as chief of the General Staff, Marshal Sergey Akhromeyev, suddenly resigned (in part, it appears, because of Gorbachev's plan to reduce Soviet armed forces by some 500,000 troops within two years); Akhromeyev's replacement was General Mikhail Moiseyev, a man allegedly more sympathetic to the goals of the new regime.[67] Two months later, in February 1989, General Petr Lushev, first deputy minister of defense, was abruptly named to succeed Marshal Viktor Kulikov as commander-in-chief of Warsaw Pact forces; like Moiseyev, Lushev is seen to be a supporter of the Gorbachev-sponsored reforms in military policy.[68] At the same time, Gorbachev has revitalized and seemingly enhanced the policy-making role of the Central Committee's international department, long a conservative redoubt within the Soviet system, and placed it under the direct control of one of his closest associates, Aleksandr Yakovlev.[69] Turnover at the second and third levels of the party, state, and military bureaucracies has been extensive as well, with more changes to come.

Regime change of the kind outlined here would appear to facilitate two types of learning. The first, and more fundamental, may be thought of as a first-order shift in cognitive content. In other words, the advent of the new Soviet leadership has made possible a change in general policy objectives and values because those making decisions in 1990 bring to that task a different set of core beliefs and preferences from their predecessors. The second kind of learning would seem to accord with the concept of greater efficiency, in particular, the willingness to redefine one's goals more realistically. The relationship between these two types of learning is less than clear, although it would appear that while the second may proceed in the absence of the first, a first-order shift in cognitive content will always result in a revised set of objectives, in that a conscious effort is being made to match more effectively means and ends.

THE SYSTEM DISAGGREGATED: LEARNING DIFFERENT THINGS AT DIFFERENT TIMES

To this point in the analysis, the central thrust has been that three main factors—technology, experience, and regime change—account for much of the change in both the conduct and the content of the Soviet Union's strategic nuclear arms control policies since the late 1960s. It is also by reference to these three factors that a more refined argument can be advanced in support of the proposition that such change as we have witnessed in Soviet policy is due in large part to a complex learning process. While useful, such an approach is also misleading. Any explanation that fastens narrowly on policy, defined in this context as the *output* of the decision-making community, fails to provide much of a sense for the dynamics of the process. To restore some of the richness that might otherwise be lost, this section of the chapter shifts levels of analysis—from the Soviet decision-making *system* for national security to several of the *institutions* that comprise its key components.

Such an investigation reveals, among other insights, that not only do institutions learn at different rates, but they also, when presented with essentially the same evidence, learn different things. With respect to Soviet arms control policy, for example, it is apparent that the foreign and defense ministries have often seen developments of interest to both in ways not easily reconciled. While especially pronounced during the early days of SALT, the tendency persists (a point developed in a slightly different way later in the analysis).

In the months following the conclusion of the SALT I accords in May 1972 a spate of articles and analyses appeared in the Soviet press that explained in great detail why and how the ABM treaty and the interim agreement served Soviet national interests. The longer and more carefully argued pieces appeared under the signature of Georgi Arbatov, director of the Academy of Sciences' Institute of the USA and Canada.[70] Arbatov was thought to enjoy the patronage of key actors in both the Ministry of Foreign Affairs and the Central Committee apparatus. As such, the institute's line, so to speak, could be considered to reflect the views of at least some members of the senior political leadership.

The Soviet military offered a rather less enthusiastic assessment of the SALT agreements. Without criticizing the agreements directly, military spokesmen and analysts writing in the Soviet military press tended to downplay their military significance and to emphasize the undiminished relevance of the canons and precepts that had guided the development of Soviet military thinking since the late 1950s.[71] Most provocative were the subtle affirmations of the continuing role of *defensive* military forces—strategic as well as tactical—in Soviet military strategy at precisely the time that the country's senior political leaders had concluded an agreement that rendered illegal any large-scale effort to deploy antiballistic missile systems.[72] Many of these analyses also called for a redoubling of efforts to guard against complacency in the face of the imperialist military threat and for the devotion of additional resources to the defense mission.[73] For the most part, the nonmilitary types writing on U.S.–Soviet security issues paid lip service to the first injunction and ignored the second.

Although part of this difference in perspective might be explained by the perceived need to accent different things to different audiences, the contrast is striking nonetheless. Typically it fell to the senior-most Soviet leaders, most especially Brezhnev, but also on occasion to Alexei Kosygin and Nikolai Podgorny, to impose a degree of order and logical consistency by tying together in a single statement a number of disparate themes. The most skillfully crafted of these were reserved for the Communist Party congresses, held at five-year intervals after 1966. They made for interesting reading but were not always judged either convincing or intellectually satisfying to those in the West seeking to interpret them. It is likely, as well, that many Soviet readers found these explanations wanting. One of the most convoluted statements came some two weeks before Brezhnev's death in November 1982 as the aging Soviet leader, in what was billed as an important statement to an extraordinary gathering of the country's military leadership, commended the armed forces for their unflagging devotion to duty, urged them on to still greater exploits, and then informed their representatives that henceforth they would have to make do with the same, if not a reduced, level of resources.[74] Compounding the confusion of his audience was Brezhnev's failure to specify how and under what conditions Soviet military commanders should be prepared to employ their forces beyond such hollow bromides as "the constant readiness to defend their socialist homeland."[75]

Even within the same institution, different voices could be heard. When, in July 1982, Defense Minister Ustinov announced the Soviet decision not to be the first to use nuclear weapons should a war erupt involving the U.S.S.R., the reception accorded the initiative from within the ministry, as recorded on the pages of *Krasnaia zvezda*, was not altogether positive. As was to be expected, the opposition was muted, coming in the form of warnings, for example, that the danger of war with the West was lately on the rise and that the essential nature of U.S. military policy remained unchanged.[76] Ustinov took the unprecedented step of acknowledging such misgivings among the "Soviet people and our friends" in his statement containing the no-first-use pledge.[77]

Whether within or between institutions, the willingness to depart from officially sanctioned positions, while seldom done in an open fashion, is hardly unique to this era in Soviet politics. Neither were the debates concerning arms control and military policy somehow atypical in this regard. What is rather more unusual in the Soviet experience is the persistence over time of a coherent, internally consistent policy perspective sharply or identifiably at odds with the prevailing political line. At the risk of overstating reality, this appears to have been the case in Soviet arms control policy, as the professional military maintained a discreet but pointed critique of the enterprise from before the start of the SALT negotiations in 1969 through the early 1980s.

Since at least the reformulation of military doctrine in the late 1950s, the leadership of the Soviet armed forces had lent its unequivocal endorsement to the first of the two belief systems identified in this analysis—that despite the development of nuclear weapons and the advent of nuclear deterrence, a new world war could be either won or lost. In contrast to the political leadership's slow erosion of confidence in this judgment, however, the professional military seemed to hold firm to these beliefs until well into the 1980s. Whether they remain loyal to the "fight and win" school now, almost a decade later, is difficult to say, although the literal outpouring of military writings on such Gorbachev-favored concepts as "reasonable sufficiency" and "defensive defense" within the last several years would appear to indicate that the gap between civilian and military perspectives on security-related issues is once again beginning to close.[78]

Assuming, for purposes of argument, that the Soviet military's affection for the doctrinal revisions begun under Brezhnev and accelerated by Gorbachev was lukewarm, especially during the early years of the debate, the existence of such dissent raises interesting questions about learning in foreign policy and international relations. While in the aggregate Soviet arms control policies can be said to have evolved as a result of a complex learning process in the specific directions suggested in this analysis, it may also be true that learning of a different sort took place *within* particular institutions, in this case, the Soviet military establishment.

In other words, as Kremlin political leaders began to amend their views concerning such issues as the nature of war in the contemporary period and the character of U.S.–Soviet security relations in reaction to external and internal stimuli, those responsible for the development of Soviet military thought and for the posturing of the country's armed forces "learned" as well, only in ways that served, on balance, to reinforce rather than undermine their existing beliefs and convictions. This may account for the clear differences in emphasis that have been discussed. It may also help to explain why, from the late 1970s to the mid-1980s, very senior political and military authorities saw fit occasionally to intervene forcefully in the debates over military and arms control policy; by so doing, they may have been attempting to communicate the permissible parameters of debate and to quell dissent. This is one way, for example, to interpret Brezhnev's 1981 statement on the suicidal character of nuclear war and his October 1982 address to Soviet military commanders, as well as Ustinov's defense of the no-first-use pledge and Ogarkov's 1983 observations on the durability and robustness of nuclear deterrence.

The military's distinctive "cut" on security policy during the roughly 15-year period from the start of the SALT process in 1969 to Gorbachev's election as general secretary in March 1985 strongly suggests an institution-wide effort to ward off unwelcome change and to register its discomfort with politically driven revisions to doctrine. In and of itself, this is an interesting and relevant finding. Moreover, given the shift from one set of core beliefs to another at the political level, the military's resistance to change can only be seen as an attempt to reaffirm the continuing validity of existing doctrine. The "black box" of Soviet military planning makes it impossible, of course, to arrive at firm conclusions regarding this issue. Absent the opportunity to peruse actual Soviet war plans, no analyst can determine the extent to which an assured-destruction model of nuclear deterrence has come to replace within recent years various war-fighting strategies in Kremlin military planning. Admittedly, the argument that an important dichotomy existed—and may continue to obtain—between Soviet political and military leaders on sensitive national security issues rests largely on circumstantial evidence; nonetheless, the evidence is not inconsequential and the case seems compelling.

The tension between civilian and military perspectives would appear to be unique within the Soviet decision-making system. No such institutionally based conflicts seem to have arisen, for example, between ranking party officials and senior economic managers, or between the foreign ministry and prominent members of the Academy of Sciences' Institute of the USA and Canada or the Institute of World Economics and International Relations. To the extent that individuals representing different institutions have attached greater or lesser weight to this or that theme in connection with Soviet security policy, it would seem that they have done so not so much to dissent from the political line, but to amplify or to tailor it to a specific audience. Kosygin, when chairman of the Council of Ministers during the 1960s and 1970s, more than once justified the pursuit of strategic arms control agreements by reference to the debilitating costs of the arms race—a position not inconsistent with his role as the Soviet Union's preeminent economic manager.[79]

When, on rare occasions, senior officials did depart from the agreed text in ways difficult to explain by reference to their position, they were usually quick to find an appropriate opportunity to correct their mistake. Gromyko, addressing the Supreme Soviet in July 1969, went beyond the official Soviet position in seeming to subscribe to a kind of "action-reaction" model for understanding the strategic military competition, which could have been—and apparently was—interpreted as suggesting a degree of Soviet culpability for the arms race.[80] When he next addressed the subject in detail, in April 1971, the interactive character of the military competition between Washington and Moscow found no place in his remarks.[81] In examining the scores of major speeches made by or statements issued under the names of key Soviet officials from the late 1960s to the present, such deviations surface relatively frequently, although for the reasons indicated it is probably a mistake to accord them extraordinary significance without, at least, careful consideration as to context and follow-up.

"Disaggregating" the Soviet decision-making system reveals interesting if, for the most part, predictable schisms between and among institutions involved in the formulation and implementation of Soviet security policy. For the most part, these schisms have been neither deep nor enduring. The military's critique of the so-called Tula line is the exception. With the passage of time even this dissent has begun to fade, as the political leadership retires those in uniform opposed to change and promotes to positions of responsibility military officials more sympathetic to the new thinking. Barring the overthrow of Gorbachev, which could bring to power a group of leaders more to the liking of traditionalists within the Soviet defense community, the military has precious few resources either to obstruct the redefinition of Soviet security interests, now far advanced, or to prevent the restructuring of the country's armed forces.

CONCLUSION

Two particularly interesting conclusions are suggested by this review of the role of learning in the development of Soviet strategic arms control policies. The first concerns the tight coupling between shifts in core beliefs and regime change. While it is true that Brezhnev and his immediate successors demonstrated in their conduct of policy an impressive capacity to learn in a cognitive structural sense—that is, an ability to respond creatively to an increasingly complex negotiating environment—they did so by reference to a remarkably stable set of beliefs and images. Brezhnev, in particular, articulated a number of themes late in his tenure that could be interpreted as signaling an important departure in policy. But the pronouncements were often confused, incomplete, and lacking in logical coherence, suggesting a less than thoroughgoing willingness on the part of the senior leadership first to confront and then to accommodate the powerful forces militating for change. It would be difficult to demonstrate, in other words, that as a collective Soviet decision makers during the Brezhnev era ever underwent anything approximating a cognitive conversion in reference to the issues of national security and arms control. It would fall to a new and younger group of leaders, led by Gorbachev, for whom the words and deeds of their predecessors exercised no special magic, to break decisively with the failed policies of the past.

The second conclusion has to do less with the nature or the timing of learning than with its sources. On one hand, Soviet arms control policies, especially between the late 1960s and the early 1980s, can be said to have changed in response to what is described in the body of the analysis as *experience*, or the combination of environmental factors that prompted the leadership to revise its objectives and to amend its methods as it acquired a progressively more refined understanding of the enterprise on which it was embarked. The same can be said more narrowly with respect to the influence of *military technology*, which prompted those in charge of policy eventually to revisit their assumptions about the nature of war in the nuclear age.

What is remarkable about both kinds of learning, but especially the latter, is that it lacks an evidential base: no one knows that a nuclear war can be fought and won; no one knows that it cannot. Soviet decision makers, and their U.S. counterparts, have had to design their military and arms control policies by reference to the considered judgments of the various experts to whom they turn for advice and counsel. The manifest inability to predict with utter certainty the consequences of a strategic nuclear exchange between the superpowers has prolonged and intensified, in both capitals, the debates over military strategy and national security policy.

Largely for this reason, the notion of a learning process in U.S.–Soviet security relations remains problematic, particularly when it is meant to suggest a gradual convergence of perspectives around a given set of norms, such as the Reagan-Gorbachev formula on the nonwinability of nuclear war. At this time, and for reasons having to do with the existing state of military technology, both countries seem prepared to subscribe to such a dictum. Should, however, political leaders in Washington or Moscow, in response to advice provided by their respective technical, scientific, and military communities, ever have reason to doubt that assessment, the temptation to "unlearn" the lessons of the past 20 years— to "defect" from the cooperative game—could be irresistible, resulting in a spirited race for military advantage and strategic superiority. This, it would appear, is the single most important, if also the most disturbing, lesson to be learned from an examination of the Soviet Union's strategic arms control policies from the late 1960s to the late 1980s.

NOTES

1. I am grateful to W. Philip Ellis, Robert Macray, and Brian Davenport, all of whom provided valuable assistance in the preparation of this analysis.

2. The best English-language source on the development of Soviet military thinking during the 1950s remains Herbert S. Dinerstein, *War and the Soviet Union: Nuclear Weapons and the Revolution in Soviet Military and Political Thinking*, rev. ed. (Westport, Conn.: Greenwood Press, 1976), esp. 65–90, 167–262; see also David Holloway, *The Soviet Union and the Arms Race*, 2d. ed. (New Haven: Yale University Press, 1984), 29–64. For the 1960s, see V.D. Sokolovsky, ed., *Military Strategy: Soviet Doctrine and Concepts* (New York: Frederick A. Praeger, 1963); Raymond L. Garthoff, *Soviet Military Policy* (New York: Frederick A. Praeger, 1966); and Thomas W. Wolfe, *Soviet Strategy at the Crossroads* (Cambridge, Mass.: Harvard University Press, 1966). Writings on the development of Soviet military doctrine from the late 1960s to the late 1970s are voluminous; for a sense of the richness of the Western debate, see Richard Pipes, "Why the Soviet Union Thinks It Can Fight and Win a Nuclear War," *Commentary*, (July 1977): 21–32; and Raymond L. Garthoff, "Mutual Deterrence, Parity, and Strategic Arms Limitation in Soviet Policy," in *Soviet Military Thinking*, ed. Derek Leebaert (London: George Allen & Unwin, 1981), 92–124. See also Coit D. Blacker, "The Military Forces," in *After Brezhnev: Soviet Conduct in the 1980s*, ed. Robert F. Byrnes (Bloomington: Indiana University Press, 1983), 125–85; and Edward L. Warner III, "The Defense Policy of the Soviet Union," in *American Defense Policy*, 5th ed., eds. John F. Reichart and Steven R. Sturm (Baltimore: Johns Hopkins University Press, 1982), 48–61.

3. "The Speech of Comrade G.M. Malenkov at a Meeting of the Electors of the Leningrad District of the City of Moscow, 12 March 1954," *Pravda* (13 March 1954). Quoted in Herbert S. Dinerstein, *War and the Soviet Union*, 71.

4. Herbert S. Dinerstein, *War and the Soviet Union*, 96–128.

5. In a speech delivered on March 14, 1958, Krushchev noted that, in addition to the immediate destruction, "the employment of nuclear weapons will poison the atmosphere with radioactive fall-out and this could lead to the annihilation of almost all life, especially in the countries of small territory and high population density. They all will be literally wiped off the face of the earth" (quoted in Herbert S. Dinerstein, *War and the Soviet Union*, 79). In an interview with a *New York Times* correspondent 10 months earlier, the Soviet leader had said, ". . . it is not to be excluded that a [nuclear] war can be unleashed as a result of some kind of fatal error, which will lead to untold tragedy for the peoples not only of our two countries, but for the peoples of the whole world" (quoted in Herbert S. Dinerstein, *War and the Soviet Union*, 85). Krushchev's most famous warning about the terrors of a nuclear war, however, was conveyed in his message to President Kennedy on October 26, 1962, at the height of the Cuban missile crisis, when he cautioned against a further tightening of "the knot of war," which could well result in the "catastrophe of thermonuclear war"; see Graham T. Allison, *Essence of Decision: Explaining the Cuban Missile Crisis* (Boston: Little, Brown, 1971), 222.

6. Although analysts may dispute the extent to which Soviet decision makers ever *believed* in the proposition that a nuclear war could be fought and won, the evidence is compelling that, from the mid-1950s to the mid-1970s, the country's senior military authorities sought, through both the development of strategy and

the acquisition of forces, a military posture sufficiently robust to enable the Soviet Union to prevail in the event of a general nuclear war. Despite the passage of some 25 years since its initial publication, the best single Soviet source on the implications of the nuclear revolution for the development of doctrine and force capabilities remains V.D. Sokolovsky, *Military Strategy*, esp. Chs. 4 and 7 ("The Nature of Modern War" and "Preparing a Country to Repel Aggression").

7. The reference is to Marshal Nikolai Ogarkov, chief of the Soviet General Staff from 1977 to 1984. In a piece entitled, "Provide a Reliable Defense for Peace," published in *Izvestiia*, 23 September 1983, Ogarkov wrote:

> The U.S. is vigorously building up its strategic nuclear forces with the aim of giving them the capability to inflict a "disabling" nuclear strike against the U.S.S.R. This is a reckless step. Some 20 years ago the U.S., to some extent, could still count on the possibility of achieving such a result. Today this is pure illusion. . . . In today's conditions, putting one's stakes on a first nuclear strike can only be suicide.

Six months earlier, Ogarkov had advanced much the same argument, although on that occasion he was prepared to say only that "what was possible to achieve with nuclear weapons 20 or 30 years ago is now becoming impossible for an aggressor" without naming the potential aggressor. See Marshal N. Ogarkov, "Victory and the Present Day," *Izvestiia* (9 May 1983).

8. For an analysis of Soviet strategic force development during the 1960s, see Thomas W. Wolfe, *Soviet Power and Europe* (Baltimore: Johns Hopkins University Press, 1971), 178–84, 427–31; and Robert P. Berman and John C. Baker, *Soviet Strategic Forces: Requirements and Responses* (Washington, D.C.: Brookings Institution, 1982), 50–61.

9. Robert P. Berman and John C. Baker, *Soviet Strategic Forces*, 65–67.

10. For an informed discussion of the development of Soviet air defense capabilities during the 1960s and 1970s, see Robert P. Berman, *Soviet Airpower in Transition* (Washington, D.C.: Brookings Institution, 1978).

11. Raymond L. Garthoff, *Détente and Confrontation: American-Soviet Relations from Nixon to Reagan* (Washington, D.C.: Brookings Institution, 1984), 135–42.

12. See, for example, "Joint U.S.–Soviet Statement at Geneva, 21 November 1985," reprinted in *Survival* 28 (March/April 1986): 155.

13. Gorbachev dealt in some detail with these and related themes in both his February 1986 report to the 27th Congress of the Communist Party of the Soviet Union, reprinted in "The Political Report of the CPSU Central Committee to the 27th Congress of the Communist Party of the Soviet Union," *Pravda* (26 February 1986), and in his December 7, 1988, address to the United Nations General Assembly, reprinted in "Speech by M.S. Gorbachev at the United Nations," *Pravda* (8 December 1988).

14. For a concise discussion of the evolution of Soviet strategic arms control proposals since 1985, see *Strategic Survey 1987–88* (London: International Institute for Strategic Studies, 1987), 39–47.

15. *The Military Balance 1987–88* (London: International Institute for Strategic Studies, 1987), 205.

16. The text of the INF treaty is reprinted in *Survival* 30 (March/April 1988): 163–80.

17. Gorbachev could not have known, of course, that the decision to withdraw some 50,000 Soviet troops from Eastern Europe would constitute but the first installment of a process that is ongoing. In February and March 1990, the Soviets concluded agreements with the reform governments of Czechoslovakia and Hungary mandating the departure of all Soviet forces by mid-1991. As of this writing, the disposition of Soviet troops in the German Democratic Republic is highly uncertain, although it is extremely unlikely that Moscow will be able to station more than a fraction of the 380,000 troops it currently maintains on German soil much beyond the early 1990s.

18. "Speech by M.S. Gorbachev" (see note 13).

19. Bill Keller, "Gorbachev Promises Big Cuts in Military Spending," *New York Times* (19 January 1989).

20. The connection between Soviet defense spending and growth prospects for the Soviet economy is usefully explored in Abraham S. Becker, "Sitting on Bayonets: The Soviet Defense Burden and the Slowdown of Soviet Defense Spending," in *The Soviet Calculus of Nuclear War*, eds. Roman Kolkowicz and Ellen Popper Mickiewicz (Lexington, Mass.: Lexington Books, 1986), esp. 186–95. See also Timothy Colton, *The Dilemma of Reform in the Soviet Union*, rev. ed. (New York: Council on Foreign Relations, 1986), 198–203.

21. See, for example, Bruce Parrott, "Soviet National Security Under Gorbachev," *Problems of Communism* 37 (November/December 1988): 1–36; Raymond L. Garthoff, "New Thinking in Soviet Military Doctrine," *The Washington Quarterly* 11 (Summer 1988): 131–58; Stephen M. Meyer, "The Sources and Prospects of Gorbachev's New Political Thinking on Security," *International Security* 13 (Fall 1988): 124–63; and Edward L. Warner, III, "New Thinking and Old Realities in Soviet Defense Policy," *Survival* 31 (January/February 1989): 13–33.

22. Of the many treatments of postwar U.S. strategic nuclear policy, the most balanced assessment is Lawrence Freedman, *The Evolution of Nuclear Strategy* (New York: St. Martin's Press, 1983); see also Lawrence Freedman, "The First Two Generations of Nuclear Strategists," in *The Makers of Modern Strategy: From Machiavelli to the Nuclear Age*, ed. Peter Paret (Princeton, N.J.: Princeton University Press, 1986), 735–78.

23. Considerable confusion surrounds the role of "assured destruction" in U.S. strategic nuclear policy. McNamara and his successors (with the notable exception of Caspar Weinberger) were careful to describe the ability of the United States to inflict an unacceptable level of damage against key military and nonmilitary targets in the Soviet Union in response to any Soviet first strike as the essential *bedrock* of U.S. strategic nuclear policy; in other words, U.S. assured-destruction capabilities have never been designed to constitute more than one element of the U.S. strategic nuclear posture. U.S. defense officials have always understood that U.S. nuclear forces must be robust enough—with respect to both numbers and capabilities—to perform a wide range of military missions, including those associated with nuclear war fighting and extended deterrence.

24. During the early years of the Reagan administration, an explicit emphasis on defense through damage limitation made a brief reappearance as a central

element of U.S. strategic nuclear policy. In his fiscal 1984 annual report to Congress, Secretary of Defense Weinberger stated that, in the event of war with the Soviet Union, it would be U.S. policy to seek to terminate hostilities at the earliest possible time, with as little damage as possible and "on terms favorable to the United States." This particular formulation, which suggested that a nuclear conflict involving the two superpowers could be waged to a successful conclusion by the United States, was deleted from later reports. See Caspar Weinberger, *FY 1984 Annual Report of the Secretary of Defense to Congress* (Washington, D.C.: U.S. Government Printing Office, 1983), 32–36.

25. Soviet denunciations of the logic of mutual nuclear deterrence were routine during the 1960s and 1970s. Henry Trofimenko, a senior analyst with the Institute of the USA and Canada in Moscow, offered perhaps the best-developed critique of Western-style deterrence theory, as well as its practical implementation, in a 1980 monograph published in the United States. See Henry Trofimenko, *Changing Attitudes Toward Deterrence*, ACIS Working Paper #25 (Los Angeles: Center for International and Strategic Affairs, 1980).

26. See, for example, Marshal A. Grechko, "In Battle Born," *Pravda* (23 February 1970); and Col. I. Sidelnikov, "Peaceful Coexistence and the Security of the Peoples," *Krasnaia zvezda* (14 August 1973). Although the defensive emphasis in Soviet military writings persisted far into the SALT decade, the references to damage limitation grew progressively more oblique as the U.S.–Soviet strategic arms control negotiations became an ongoing feature of the bilateral relationship. The least guarded references to the importance of the strategic defensive mission are to be found during the early to mid-1960s in both the writings of military analysts and the occasional pronouncements of senior Defense Ministry officials. See Marshal R. Malinovskii, "Reliable Guard of the Homeland," *Pravda* (23 February 1965), in which the minister of defense declared that Soviet air defense forces "have mastered new methods of destroying flying targets when they are still far from the objectives being protected. *The Soviet Union has solved the complex and extremely important problem of destroying enemy rockets in flight*" [emphasis added]. The same themes are developed at considerably greater length in Col. Ye. Rybkin, "The Essence of a Nuclear Rocket War," *Kommunist vooruzhennikh sil* (September 1965): 51–57; and Col. S. Maliachikov, "The Nature and Characteristics of Nuclear Missile Warfare," *Kommunist vooruzhennikh sil* (November 1965): 69–74.

27. The U.S. Department of Defense, in fact, maintains that the Soviets have invested as much in the development, acquisition, and deployment of strategic defensive forces as they have in support of strategic offensive capabilities. See *Soviet Military Power 1987* (Washington, D.C.: U.S. Department of Defense, 1987), 45. For more historical (and refined) treatments, see Lawrence Freedman, *U.S. Intelligence and the Soviet Strategic Threat* (Princeton, N.J.: Princeton University Press, 1986), 81–96; and John Prados, *The Soviet Estimate: U.S. Intelligence Analysis and Soviet Strategic Forces* (Princeton, N.J.: Princeton University Press, 1986), 151–71.

28. *Soviet Military Power 1987*, 52. Several analyses, including a 1978 study prepared by the U.S. Central Intelligence Agency, have found the Soviet industrial base and technological infrastructure no more able to withstand the effects of a nuclear war than its U.S. counterpart, despite numerous claims—Western as well

as Soviet—to the contrary. See Director of Central Intelligence, *Soviet Civil Defense*, N178-10003, July 1978.

29. See, in particular, U.S. Congress, Joint Committee on Atomic Energy, 90th Cong., 2d sess., 6 and 7 November 1967, *Scope, Magnitude and Implications of the United States Antiballistic Missile Program* (Washington, D.C.: U.S. Government Printing Office, 1967).

30. *The Military Balance 1987–88*, 202.

31. *Soviet Military Power 1987*, 46–61.

32. See, in particular, Marshal N. Ogarkov, "Soviet Military Science," *Pravda* (19 February 1978); and Marshal S. Sokolov, "Mighty Guard of the Socialist Gains," *Krasnaia zvezda* (22 February 1978). For an unusually frank discussion of Soviet civil defense efforts, see "Campaign of Provocation: On Western Statements About Civil Defense in the USSR," *Literaturnaia gazeta* (19 January 1977). References in the Soviet military press to such concepts as "seizing the [military] initiative" and dealing a "decisive rebuff" to imperialist aggression decrease markedly following Brezhnev's Tula address in January 1977, suggesting a recognition of the need on the part of the senior leadership to bring into closer alignment pronouncements on Soviet military doctrine delivered by ranking political and military officials. A notable exception to this trend toward greater uniformity in expression is Marshal N. Ogarkov, "In the Name of Peace and Progress," *Izvestiia*, 9 May 1982, in which Ogarkov writes that the military-technical aspect of Soviet military doctrine directs that "in the event of aggression our Armed Forces would not simply engage in passive defense, conducting strictly defensive actions, but would decisively rout an aggressor that dared to attack our country, up to and including the complete destruction of the aggressor. . . ."

33. See G. Arbatov, "Soviet-American Relations at a New Stage," *Pravda* (22 July 1973); M.A. Mil'stein and L.S. Semeiko, "SALT: Problems and Prospects," *SShA: ekonomika, politika, ideologiia* (December 1973): 3–12; G. Arbatov, "New Frontiers of Soviet-American Relations," *Izvestiia* (13 July 1974); G. Arbatov, "On Soviet-American Relations," *Pravda* (2 April 1976); and, most interestingly, G. Arbatov, "Big Lie of Détente's Opponents," *Pravda* (5 February 1977).

34. See, for example, George Weickhardt, "Ustinov versus Ogarkov," *Problems of Communism* 34 (January/February 1985): 77–82.

35. Marshal N. Ogarkov, "For Our Soviet Motherland: Guarding Peaceful Labor," *Kommunist* (July 1981): 80–91. Also see Edward L. Warner, III, "New Thinking and Old Realities," 16–18.

36. Marshal N. Ogarkov, "Provide a Reliable Defense for Peace," *Izvestiia* (23 September 1983).

37. Marshal N. Ogarkov, "The Defense of Socialism: History's Experience and the Present Day," *Krasnaia zvezda* (9 May 1984).

38. The Krasnoiarsk radar controversy is considered in some detail in Gloria Duffy, project director, *Compliance and the Future of Arms Control* (Cambridge, Mass.: Ballinger Publishing Company, 1988), 105–112.

39. Article VI (b) of the ABM treaty stipulates that the parties undertake "not to deploy in the future radars for early warning of strategic ballistic missile attack except at locations along the periphery of its national territory and oriented outward." The treaty text is reproduced in Coit D. Blacker and Gloria Duffy, eds.,

International Arms Control: Issues and Agreements, 2d ed. (Stanford, Calif.: Stanford University Press, 1984), 413–17.

40. The evolution of Soviet attitudes toward the ABM treaty (and the Strategic Defense Initiative) since 1983 are cogently analyzed in Karen Puschel, "Can Moscow Live with SDI?" *Survival* 31 (January/February 1989): 34–51.

41. *Soviet Military Power 1987*, 45.

42. The Soviet tendency to distinguish conceptually between political and military détente is discussed at length in Coit D. Blacker, "The Soviet Union and Mutual Force Reductions: The Role of Military Détente in the European Security Policy of the USSR," (Ph.D. diss., Fletcher School of Law and Diplomacy, Tufts University, 1978), 43–59.

43. See Coit D. Blacker, "The Soviets and Arms Control: The SALT II Negotiations, November 1972–March 1976," in *The Other Side of the Table: The Soviet Approach to Arms Control*, ed. Michael Mandelbaum (New York: Council on Foreign Relations, 1990), 56–61.

44. The history of the negotiation of the Basic Principles of Relations agreement is recounted in Raymond L. Garthoff, *Détente and Confrontation*, 290–98. See also Coit D. Blacker, "The Kremlin and Détente: Soviet Conceptions, Hopes, Expectations," in *Managing U.S.–Soviet Rivalry: Problems of Crisis Prevention*, ed. Alexander L. George et al. (Boulder, Colo.: Westview Press, 1983), 119–37. The text of the agreement is reproduced in Coit D. Blacker and Gloria Duffy, *International Arms Control*, 429–30.

45. See, in particular, Henry A. Kissinger, *White House Years* (Boston: Little, Brown, 1979), 1131–32, 1150–51, 1250.

46. William Hyland's comments were made in the context of a November 1987 working group discussion, convened under the auspices of the Council on Foreign Relations (New York), to review the development of Soviet arms control policies from the early 1960s to the mid-1980s. For more on this period, see Coit D. Blacker," The Soviets and Arms Control," 43–55.

47. Henry A. Kissinger, *Years of Upheaval* (Boston: Little, Brown, 1982), 228–301.

48. Coit D. Blacker, "The Soviets and Arms Control," 44–46.

49. The two accords in question were the Threshold Test Ban Treaty and the protocol to the 1972 ABM treaty. The texts of the agreements are reproduced in Coit D. Blacker and Gloria Duffy, *International Arms Control*, 434–35 and 438–39. Also see Coit D. Blacker, "The Soviets and Arms Control," 51; and "Texts of Nuclear Accords and Joint Statement," *New York Times* (4 July 1974).

50. Raymond L. Garthoff, *Détente and Confrontation*, 443–44.

51. The "Joint Statement on Strategic Offensive Arms," issued at the conclusion of the Vladivostok summit (24 November 1974), is reproduced in Coit D. Blacker and Gloria Duffy, *International Arms Control*, 440. For additional discussion, see Coit D. Blacker,"The Soviets and Arms Control," 51–54.

52. Raymond L. Garthoff, *Détente and Confrontation*, 444–46; Henry A. Kissinger, *Years of Upheaval*, 1018.

53. See Larry C. Napper, "The African Terrain and U.S.–Soviet Conflict in Angola and Rhodesia: Some Implications for Crisis Prevention"; Larry C. Napper, "The Ogaden War: Some Implications for Crisis Prevention"; and George W. Breslauer,

"Why Détente Failed: An Interpretation," in *Managing U.S.–Soviet Rivalry*, 155–85, 255–53, 319–40.

54. Speech, Comrade L.I. Brezhnev, "Outstanding Exploit of the Defenders of Tula: Ceremonial Meeting Dedicated to the Presentation of the Gold Star Medal to the City," *Pravda* (19 January 1977); and "L.I. Brezhnev Answers a Question From a Pravda Correspondent," *Pravda* (21 October 1981). On the latter occasion, Brezhnev's exact words were ". . . that only he who had decided to commit suicide can start a nuclear war in the hope of emerging from it as a victor."

55. Although Brezhnev's remarks in Tula constituted an important branch point in the development of his own rhetoric, less exalted members of Soviet officialdom had anticipated key elements of the so-called Tula line by a number of years. In his book *Doubletalk*, Gerard Smith, the chief U.S. negotiator in SALT I, recounts the opening remarks of Soviet ambassador Vladimir Semenov in November 1969, in which Semenov, in an effort to explain the Kremlin's interest in the negotiations, describes the dangerously destabilizing effects of a nuclear arms race featuring modern strategic offensive and defensive weapons systems and notes the suicidal character of nuclear war. See Gerard Smith, *Doubletalk: The Story of the First Strategic Arms Limitation Talks* (Garden City, N.Y.: Doubleday, 1980), 83–84.

56. Marshal D. Ustinov, "To Avert the Threat of Nuclear War," *Pravda* (12 July 1982).

57. "Yu. V. Andropov Answers Questions from a Pravda Correspondent," *Pravda* (27 March 1983).

58. "Statement by M.S. Gorbachev, General Secretary of the CPSU Central Committee," *Pravda* (16 January 1986).

59. For coverage of the Reykjavik summit, see Bernard Weinraub, "Reagan-Gorbachev Meeting Opens With Plans to Pursue Arms Pact and Rights Issues," *New York Times* (12 October 1986); and Bernard Gwertzman, "Reagan-Gorbachev Talks End in Stalemate as U.S. Rejects Demand to Curb 'Star Wars,'" *New York Times* (13 October 1986).

60. See, in particular, Secretary of State George Schultz's press conference of October 17, 1986, as reported in Bernard Gwertzman, "Schultz Details Reagan's Arms Bid at Iceland to Clarify U.S. Position," *New York Times* (18 October 1986).

61. "General Secretary Gorbachev's Statement on INF, 28 February 1987," *Survival* 29 (July-August 1988): 361–63; and Bill Keller, "Moscow, In Reversal, Urges Agreement 'Without Delay,' to Limit Missiles in Europe," *New York Times* (1 March 1987).

62. Lewis A. Dunn, "NATO After Global 'Double Zero,'" *Survival* 30 (May–June 1988), 195–209.

63. "The INF Treaty," *Survival* 30 (March/April 1988): 163–80.

64. Ibid.

65. See M.S. Gorbachev, "The Political Report of the CPSU Central Committee to the 27th Congress of the Communist Party of the Soviet Union," *Pravda* (26 February 1987).

66. Ibid. See also "Speech by M.S. Gorbachev" (see note 13).

67. See Bill Keller, "Gorbachev Pledges Major Troop Cutback, Then Ends Trip, Citing Vast Soviet Quake," *New York Times* (8 December 1988); and R. Jeffrey Smith,

"Young, Obscure Officer Is Named Leader of Soviet Armed Forces," *Washington Post* (14 December 1988).

68. "Top Leadership of the Soviet Armed Forces," *Air Force* (March 1989): 77.

69. Harriet Fast Scott, "The New Soviet Elite," *Air Force* (March 1989): 47.

70. See, in particular, G. Arbatov, "The Strength of a Policy of Realism: On the Results of the Soviet-American Summit Talks," *Izvestiia* (22 June 1972). For an equally well-argued treatment written somewhat later in the process, see M. Mil'stein and L. Semeiko, "The Problem of the Inadmissability of Nuclear Conflict," *SShA: ekonomika, politika, ideologiia* (November 1974): 3–12.

71. See the comments of General Victor Kulikov in "In the Interests of Strengthening Peace," *Izvestiia* (24 August 1972); the comments of Marshal Andrei Grechko in "Meeting of the Presidium of the U.S.S.R. Supreme Soviet," *Izvestiia* (30 September 1972); and Gen. S. Sokolov, "Standing Guard Over Peace and Socialism," *Izvestiia* (23 February 1973).

72. The most interesting of these include Col. I. Sidelnikov, *Pravda* (14 August 1972); and Col. Ye. Rybkin, "The Leninist Concept of War and the Present," *Kommunist vooruzhennikh sil* (October 1973): 21–28; also see Marshal A. Grechko, "Guarding Peace and Socialism," *Pravda* (23 February 1974); and Gen. V. Kulikov, "Great Exploit," *Izvestiia* (8 May 1976).

73. Marshal A. Grechko, "On the Leninist Course of Creation and Peace," *Pravda* (8 November 1973); Gen. N. Ogarkov, "Great, Patriotic," *Sovietskaia Rossiia* (8 May 1975); and Gen. V. Tolubko, "The Grandeur of Our Victory," *Sel'skaia zhizn'* (8 May 1975).

74. "Conference of Military Leaders in the Kremlin," *Pravda* (28 October 1982).

75. Ibid.

76. See especially Maj. Gen. V. Larionov, "Scenarios of Unlimited Insanity," *Krasnaia zvezda* (16 July 1982). See also Col. V. Vasil'ev, "Notes From a Military Commander: What Is Behind the 'Target Selection' Concept?", *Krasnaia zvezda* (21 July 1982); and Lt. Col. Yu. Gavrilov, "Militarist Marathon," *Krasnaia zvezda* (8 August 1982).

77. Marshal D. Ustinov, *Pravda* (12 July 1982).

78. For a representative sample of the military's "spin" on "reasonable sufficiency" and "defensive defense," see S. Akhromeev, "The Doctrine of Preventing War and Defending Peace and Socialism," *Problemy mira i sotsializma* (December 1987), esp. 25–27; V. Kulikov, *Doktrina zashchity mira i sotsializma* (Moscow: Voenizdat, 1988); and D. Yazov, *Na strazhe sotsializma i mira* (Moscow: Voenizdat, 1987).

79. Kosygin was particularly drawn to this logic during the mid-1960s. See, for example, A.N. Kosygin, "The Directives of the 23rd C.P.S.U. Congress for the Five-Year Plan for the Development of the U.S.S.R. National Economy in 1966–70," *Pravda* (6 April 1966); and A.N. Kosygin, "Statement of the U.S.S.R. Government on Basic Questions of Domestic and Foreign Policy," *Pravda* (4 August 1966).

80. A.A. Gromyko, "Questions of the International Situation and the Foreign Policy of the Soviet Union," *Pravda* (11 July 1969).

81. "Speech by Comrade A. A. Gromyko, U.S.S.R. Minister of Foreign Affairs," *Pravda* (4 April 1971).

13

Soviet Policy Toward Western Europe Since World War II

Jonathan Haslam

The subject of this chapter is the problem of learning in the development of Soviet policy toward Western Europe since 1945. And to make the topic more manageable the focus chosen is the German question. Highlighting other dimensions might have yielded rich return, but no issue has been more critical to the Soviet Union or of greater importance to Europe. Its very importance suggests that an extensive analysis of Soviet policy toward Germany might most readily show the extent to which Soviet understanding of postwar Europe has been adequate to the needs of Soviet Realpolitik.

A caveat must be made before proceeding further. What do we mean by *learning*? In the author's view, learning in politics cannot be defined in anything other than subjective terms. It is therefore worth stating what learning would mean for the purposes of Soviet security policy. It is assumed throughout that a security policy is unsuccessful if it is so maladapted to prevailing conditions that, instead of reducing threats from the international system, the net result of behavior is an increase in enemies. It is also assumed that if a policy results in the net accumulation of foreign hostility, then the premises underlying the policy need reviewing and changing; and that an effective security policy is one that advances state interests with minimal friction to foreign relations. In these terms successful learning is equated with the adjustment of policy to achieve maximum security at minimal cost to good relations with other Powers.

It may, of course, be that a state willfully pursues interests of a universalist nature, as Iran has done since its Islamic revolution or as Soviet

Russia did during its formative years, whereby the costs are met by the state but the benefits accrue to a greater cause (Islam or communism). Yet I would argue that this has certainly not been the order of priorities in postwar Russia, at least toward Western Europe. On the contrary, it is the factor of Realpolitik rather than the factor of revolution that has overshadowed policy toward Western Europe. And it was the security policy that Stalin adopted in 1942–1945 to end all likely threats to the homeland that contributed so decisively to the resulting tension.

But how was it that so provocative a policy was adopted? What lessons had Stalin, in particular, learned from the experience of international relations since 1917? To what extent have Stalin's successors become aware that their own postwar security policies have disrupted relations with Western Europe? How far can changes in policy be attributed to an awareness that others were reacting adversely to Soviet policy? Have such changes been merely tactical? To what degree has Moscow learned from its mistakes? Can we identify the mechanisms by which learning has occurred? And, finally, what are the prospects for further improvement, and thereby an end to the cold war in Europe?

First a few words must be said about the development of Soviet attitudes towards Western Europe since the revolution.

HARMFUL LESSONS FROM EXPERIENCE

Western Europe was for long the focus of both the hopes and fears of Soviet foreign policy makers. These hopes and fears were closely connected. The hopes traditionally rested on the prospect of fraternal socialist revolutions relieving Soviet Russia of its isolation in a capitalist world. These hopes were reduced to ashes in the 1920s. Some bright embers could still be seen among the ashes: particularly in France and Italy after World War II. But more striking and more critical to policy toward Western Europe was the fear, or rather the expectation, of war than any residual hopes of revolution.

These expectations were not entirely without foundation in that the existence of an international revolutionary organization (Comintern) run from Moscow, which threatened the stability of the capitalist order in the West through local Communist parties funded by Soviet Russia, inevitably exacerbated Western European hostility toward the Soviet regime.[1] Direct and persistent interference in the internal affairs of other states is after all one of the most provocative and least advisable ways of conducting international relations. As a result, Soviet relations with the Western powers were plagued by mistrust, tension, the threat of retribution, and recurrent war scares. In 1918–1919 a British-led war of intervention failed to overthrow the Bolshevik regime. Thereafter war scares were not infrequent.

A genuine war scare arose in 1926–1927 as relations with Britain broke under the strain of Soviet support for the Chinese revolution.[2] A war scare arose in 1930, when relations with France threatened to collapse following Soviet support for the nationalist revolt in Indochina.[3] And from 1933 on, Hitler found the easiest rallying cry under which he could expand was that of anticommunism.[4] Ironically, by the time the Soviet regime was least committed to the expansion of the revolution abroad, it had to pay the highest price for having been too zealous in the past. And, as argued elsewhere, a significant reason for the failure of the Soviet policy of collective security in Europe from 1933 to 1939 was the ideological abyss that separated East from West.

HOW THE ORIGINAL MISTAKE WAS MADE

Stalin was not alone in assuming war was inevitable in a capitalist international system. It was taken for granted that sooner or later the capitalist world would unite and intervene to overthrow the Soviet regime because it represented the antithesis of the capitalist order. The Munich settlement in 1938 and the collapse of Litvinov's attempts to build a collective security system in Europe early in 1939 only underlined to the fundamentalist in Moscow that the antagonisms between capitalism and socialism far exceeded the supposed antagonisms between democratic and fascist regimes in the capitalist West.

It might be thought that the experience of close collaboration with Britain and the United States in World War II would disabuse the Russians of such a fatalistic and conflict-oriented vision. Certainly from his post as *polpred* (ambassadorial equivalent) in Washington, Litvinov very much hoped that this would be so. But he was almost alone in such expectations. The larger part of the Soviet diplomatic corps that had a lifetime's close contact with the realities of the West had been wiped out between 1937 and 1939. Their replacements could barely cope with the languages they were supposed to learn, let alone understand the frame of mind of those they had been brought up to see as the enemy.

In contrast to others, Stalin never supposed that the contradictions between capitalism and socialism would always prevail over contradictions between capitalist states. His support for Litvinov until 1939 testified to that, as did his statements in *The Economic Problems of Socialism*, published in 1952. But he was a man congenitally given to extreme suspicion. Fantastic as it may seem, it was this, though not this alone, that led by the end of 1942 to Stalin's deep suspicion that allied Britain was not only failing to come to Soviet Russia's aid but was also contemplating a separate peace, even an alliance, with Hitler's Germany.[5]

Thereafter, as the Soviet regime anticipated victory, the greater part of

Soviet planning was predicated on a unilateral—rather than a multilateral—solution to the postwar security dilemma. The unilateral solution had been prefigured in the expansion of Soviet power into Eastern Poland, Eastern Romania, and the Baltic states in 1939–1940; the extent and limits of this expansion fit so closely with the boundaries of the former czarist empire that it could be explained as much in terms of a sense of continuity with the past as the dictates of geopolitics.

A "friendly" Poland was essential, as even Litvinov agreed,[6] and it was no secret that only a Communist-dominated Poland would willingly befriend the Soviet Union. In some sense, therefore, Moscow held the broadest consensus that Poland should become a Soviet protectorate. Beyond that, however, the likes of Litvinov would not go. But he had no significant influence whatever. Recalled to Moscow in the spring of 1943 and put in charge of postwar foreign policy planning as deputy commissar for foreign affairs, he had no access to Stalin at all. He and Molotov, who had supplanted him as foreign commissar, hated one another.[7] And the postwar world was to be framed by Stalin and Molotov rather than Stalin and Litvinov. Within this framework, more than Poland was required.

In order to prevent Germany's speedy recovery as a menacing capitalist power bent on revenge, a Soviet occupation was deemed vital, as was the eradication of the old order and its substitution by a socialist order. Stalin had enormous respect for Germany. He insisted to the Yugoslav Communist Milovan Djilas that Germany would eventually recover. "Give them twelve to fifteen years and they'll be on their feet again. And this is why the unity of the Slavs is important," he said.[8] In this apocalyptic vision, Soviet hegemony over Eastern Europe was inevitable, regardless of how the Western powers behaved.

Once the Red Army had defeated the bulk of German forces and had occupied Eastern Europe, Soviet fears and suspicions gave rise to a highly provocative policy of seeking security unilaterally through territorial expansion and the brutal extension of the revolution wherever the Red Army triumphed. This potent combination of revolution with the bayonet and dogged refusal to withdraw from "liberated" territory had a dramatic and destructive impact on Soviet relations with Western Europe in the postwar era. And when the war in Europe ended in May 1945, Western objections to Soviet domination of Eastern Europe merely reinforced fundamentalist convictions in Moscow as to the implacability of capitalism.

The creation of a Soviet *cordon sanitaire* and the closing of an iron curtain dividing Europe at its center required a massive army of occupation that inevitably aroused fears in the West as to Soviet intentions. These fears were enhanced by Western Europe's chronic economic difficulties and compounded by the massive growth of influence of Communist parties in France and Italy.[9] The fact that the rank and file of these parties expected the Red Army to help them to power as it had done their comrades in Eastern Europe did not go unnoticed in London, Paris, and Rome. To shore up the economic recovery of Western Europe and to counter the military capability of the Soviets, the West Europeans called in the Americans, alarming them with dire interpretations of Soviet intentions. In the summer of 1948, when the Soviets were trying to squeeze the Western powers out of Berlin, the United States began flying into Europe the bombers that had rained death on the Japanese at Hiroshima and Nagasaki.[10] In 1950, with a U.S. presence established in Western Europe, the United States began to move toward the rearmament of West Germany.[11] Thus it was that, in the circumstances of the defeat of the Axis in Europe, Stalin's chosen course of security through the unilateral extension of Soviet military power set in motion a series of events that eventually brought both East and West to the brink of war.

TACTICAL MOVES TO FORESTALL RETRIBUTION

Did Stalin not realize that his strategy had been counterproductive? There is no evidence that he—or for that matter Molotov—concluded that a fundamental mistake had been made in taking too much in 1945. It seems that the reason why only tactical adjustments were made to mollify the West was because the lesson learned by Stalin was the wrong one: that, by relying on his own military power and by exploiting the antagonisms within the Western camp, he could further Soviet interests without having to concede anything of substance. This is certainly how the situation was seen in retrospect by those who had the problem of responding to Soviet moves. In 1955 the Soviets were once more threatening France with severe consequences should West German rearmament proceed. The French chargé d'affaires in Moscow noted: "This method had been used before, at the end of 1950, and appeared to bear fruit. The USSR had then proclaimed that it would not tolerate the rearmament of Germany; at the same time China was sending its volunteers into Korea. The anxiety thus provoked in Western public opinion had contributed, or at least, had appeared to the Kremlin to contribute to delay for several years the decision to rearm Germany which had been taken in principle as early as the autumn of 1950."[12]

Yet Stalin did not just use threats; blandishments were also tried, though not with much conviction. On March 10, 1952, Moscow came forward with a draft treaty of peace with Germany that provided for the evacuation of all foreign forces, reunification, neutralization, and minimal rearmament.[13] There were legitimate doubts whether the Soviets were sincere. An editorial on the subject did not appear in *Izvestiia* until March 14.

The leader-writer drew a conclusion which underlined the propaganda purpose of the note: "The Note . . . and the Soviet draft . . . will once again convince people of good will across the entire globe that in the person of the Soviet Union they have a true defender of peace, a resolute fighter for the friendship and the security of nations [narodov]."[14]

Other signs emerged that gave cause for skepticism. For instance, the note said that Germany should be "democratic," yet the Soviet zone broadcasting service on March 26 stated that the German Democratic Republic (GDR) would serve as the "core of a future democratic Germany."[15] Suspicious of Stalin's intentions—since the offer was so obviously timed to upset progress toward the European Defense Community (EDC)—the Western powers responded by objecting that the proposals did not provide for free elections. On April 9 the Soviets responded by accepting this provision, although they rejected the idea that these elections should be supervised through the United Nations, on the grounds that the United Nations had no right to interfere in German affairs.[16] Instead the Soviets talked of the four-power command, which inevitably meant allowing a Soviet veto—and, even then, Foreign Minister Andrei Vyshinsky "was very evasive" when asked whether the Russians contemplated the establishment of a four-power commission.[17]

The conclusion drawn was that the Soviet government "still has not committed itself to [the] holding of elections before the conclusion of a peace treaty and may still be aiming at [the] formation of [a] provisional non-elected all Ger[man] Govt."[18] The U.S.-drafted reply of May 13 needlessly objected to neutralization instead of just driving home the issue of free elections.[19] But in subsequent exchanges the Western powers succeeded in calling the Soviet bluff. The Soviet response of May 24[20] was not, as Ambassador George Kennan noted from Moscow, "the authentic, terse, collected, menacing voice of Stalin's Kremlin when functioning in high gear and pursuing an important Sov[iet] initiative. On the contrary," he concluded, "[the] document seems to me to show signs of having been prepared by hacks supplied only with grudging, cryptic and guarded instr[uction]s and told to make [the] best of it."[21] Indeed, the note of May 24 effectively retreated to the position of March 10: emphasizing the peace treaty rather than the issue of elections. The West therefore pursued with a vengeance the issue of free elections, and no reply was ever received from Moscow to the last allied note of September 23, 1952.[22] The note of March 10 had none the less served a useful tactical purpose. In France it attracted considerable attention and ultimately contributed to the collapse of the EDC.

Clearly some new thinking had momentarily broken through in Moscow, but as soon as the Western powers seized the initiative on the awkward issue of elections and the unforeseen implications of the proposal became clear to Stalin, the idea quickly lost its appeal and was thereafter retained merely for propaganda.

WHAT PRICE DÉTENTE?

Stalin thus died on March 5, 1953, leaving Soviet foreign policy only fleetingly touched by any innovation. The Soviets still held a third of Germany, but in other respects Stalin left unpropitious conditions for dealing with the capitalist camp: not just an array of hostile power organized into an alliance with an integrated military structure, but a foreign policy establishment that had been reconstructed de novo from 1939 out of novices with little, if any, knowledge of the outside world (this was seen as an advantage given the spy mania of the time); that had been disciplined by the authoritarian Molotov, who had not encouraged subordinates to act on their own initiative; that had seen the capitalist world only from the confines of the embassy compound; that had been intimidated by fundamentalist and xenophobic revivalism in 1946–1948; that was actively discouraged from acquiring any empathy for the adversary's perspective; and that had been deprived of the only related institution that could provide an alternative voice on foreign affairs—Varga's Institute of World Economy and World Politics—in 1948. It would take another generation, reeducated to simulate the experience of the Bolsheviks in (foreign) exile, both linguistically and culturally, as well as substantial institutional reform—the creation of specialist institutes at Mikoyan's instigation—to create a pluralist system of thought in international relations to compensate for the deficit left by the Stalin years. If a former lathe operator such as Valentin Falin could eventually become a leading Germanist and, through an instinctive feel for foreign affairs, ultimately rise to head the party's International Department, it was despite rather than because of the Stalinist freeze.[23] To Soviet detriment, the bulk of the intake in those years and, indeed, many later was (and some still is) totally unsuited to the conduct of diplomacy in any form.

Yet the proposal of March 10, 1952, had originated somewhere—we still have no precise idea where—within the monolith. The source might well have been Vladimir Semenov, political adviser to the chairman of the Soviet Control Commission in Germany.[24] The U.S. High Commission in Germany learned by the summer of 1952 that Semenov had been "the advocate of a more compromising policy"; he was "supposed to have favored the softer approach and to have been willing to sacrifice the SED [East German Communist coalition] initially, in order to get a unified Germany which could eventually be captured from within."[25] Certainly publications under his ultimate control in the Soviet zone in the month preceding the Soviet note of March 10, denying the proto-

socialist character of the GDR, anticipated the proposal that might ultimately have dispensed with the Grotewohl-Ulbricht regime.[26] And it is
significant that until April (before the third and defensive Soviet note
went to the allies), Semenov was seen as a critical influence on Soviet
German policy, but his rival, Pushkin, Soviet ambassador to the GDR,
who had consistently pressed for the reinforcement of the regime, gained
the upper hand and by June had been recalled to Moscow and promoted
to the post of deputy foreign minister.[27]

Moreover, a year later the degree and speed of change in Soviet policy
after the death of Stalin took the U.S. Central Intelligence Agency (CIA),
for instance, completely by surprise, as Gorbachev did over three decades later. The CIA had originally expected the Malenkov regime to be
cautious until power was concentrated into the hands of a new leader; it
thought the new regime would remain loyal to Stalin's policies for some
time. Yet by early April 1953 CIA chief Allen Dulles reported to the
National Security Council that they were now witnessing "quite shattering departures": the most significant changes in Russian domestic and
foreign policy since 1939.[28] What the CIA had underestimated was the
degree to which there was dissatisfaction within the new leadership as
to the progress of the economy (a steady deterioration in rates of growth
since 1950); the significance of the maldistribution of resources between
consumption and investment within the economy to the disadvantage of
the consumer; the degree of rivalry within the ruling group, which would
prompt some to court consumer popularity; and the intensity of concern
at the high degree of tension in relations with the West.[29]

In this extremely hierarchical system formed under Stalin, everything
depended on the calibre of the leadership, and several leading figures—
not least (initially) Beria, Malenkov, Khrushchev—Bulganin and Mikoyan
were only two conscious of the need for change, in foreign as well as
domestic policy. Khrushchev later recalled: "we had doubts of our own
about Stalin's foreign policy."[30] But how far did these doubts extend
across the field of foreign policy? And to what extent were doubts shared
by the entire leadership? Molotov, who took over the foreign ministry,
certainly did not share such doubts. This was critical, because he was
unquestionably the most inflexible figure of them all: committed to the
framework of security determined in 1943–1945. He was, indeed, prepared
to work within the leadership consensus, but he fought hard to shift the
consensus back onto the more traditional lines Stalin and he had originally
constructed. And the fact that the diplomatic apparatus responsible for
implementing policy and suggesting ideas for change was largely the
same as that under Stalin meant that, without persistent intervention
from above, foreign policy had a tendency to drift back into the doldrums.

World politics could not wait, however: the West was pressing ahead with the EDC. The specter of West German rearmament still haunted the Kremlin; action was urgently required. And on June 16–17 a new problem arose: an uprising in East Berlin that had to be crushed by Soviet troops to sustain the crumbling edifice of the Communist regime. It was apparently after the Berlin uprising, and most probably to consider the new Western proposal of July 15 for a four-power conference on the German question, that the Politburo met under Chairman of the Council of Ministers Malenkov to discuss the fate of Germany.

Deputy Foreign Minister Gromyko was present, though not a member. The discussion opened with expressions of support for East Germany (the GDR) and comments on its importance. Finally, Gromyko records, "suddenly Beria spoke up. 'The GDR? What does it amount to, this GDR? It's not even a real State. It's only kept in being by Soviet troops, even if we do call it the German Democratic Republic.'" Such open and brutal cynicism had obvious policy implications: the GDR was dispensable in the search for a German settlement. But Gromyko emphasizes that everyone was shocked and in outrage spoke up in defense of the GDR. Molotov was typically vehement in pressing the argument that the GDR "has the right to exist as an independent State."[31] But Beria was not alone. According to Khrushchev it was both Malenkov and Beria who proposed to countermand Stalin's decision to build socialism in the GDR. They had brought to the Presidium (Politburo) the text of a document laying out the proposal. But it had not been distributed to the rest of the leadership, all of whom backed Molotov in his resolute opposition to the Beria-Malenkov position.[32] What this underlines is the element of continuity between Beria and Malenkov's position in 1953 and the real implications of the exchange of notes in 1952. It also indicates why the proposals had such a short shelf life: most probably before, but certainly after, Stalin's death, the idea of sacrificing the GDR on the altar of free elections, reunification, and neutralization was not an easy one for the Politburo to contemplate. Far less were they capable of a fundamental reassessment of the bases of Stalin's European security policy.

DÉTENTE ON THE CHEAP?

However explosive, the German problem could not be wished away. At the very least, tactical adjustments were still needed; indeed, they appeared more urgently needed than ever. There is every sign that some Soviet leaders tacitly accepted that Stalin had been in error; that instead of deterring likely adversaries, Stalin had in fact multiplied their number and steeled their resolve; that, with the Soviet economy faltering, the need to satisfy domestic consumer demand rising, and the consequent pressure to end the nuclear arms race, some kind of détente with the

West was required. But, as in 1952, the hope was still that such a détente could be obtained at low cost, without sacrificing the basic security policy that Stalin had—perhaps mistakenly—undertaken. As West German rearmament looked increasingly likely, the Soviet leadership under Malenkov embarked on a train of concessions with no sure sense of the ultimate destination. Force of circumstance drove home the need for change, though the degree to which change was needed was still uncertain and a matter of intense debate within the leadership.

The dilemma faced by Soviet leaders lay in the fact that, although eager for some kind of détente, they were equally determined not to surrender what they had won at enormous cost in World War II. This was apparent when the foreign ministers of the four powers met in Berlin from January 25 to February 18, 1954. On January 29, the British raised the stakes by proposing the reunification of Germany through free elections.[33] This, particularly after the uprising of the previous summer in Berlin, threw the Soviets onto the defensive. The only novelty in Molotov's tired rejoinder appeared on February 4 when he expressed his fears of the consequences of such elections.[34] Recalling the years 1932–1933, when Hitler maneuvered his way to power along the constitutional road, Molotov—who had then made the grave error of underestimating the significance of German fascism for the future of Soviet security—was dogmatic: "We cannot permit Fascist degenerates again to occupy the dominating position in the central organs of power in Germany by some means or other—including the help of parliamentary procedure." Instead he suggested a provisional German government be formed "supported by all the democratic elements of Eastern and Western Germany." And this government was to ban "fascist, militarist and other organizations hostile to democracy and the preservation of peace."[35] Given that the Soviets defined the existing regime in the GDR as "democratic," the bottom line of Molotov's position was clearly to secure recognition of the GDR regime, and reunification only on the basis of a coalition including East German Communists and excluding those the Soviets disliked. To all appearances the Russians were retreating to their stance of March 10, 1952.

This much was evident on February 10 when Molotov put forward a plan for German reunification together with a draft all-European collective security treaty.[36] Bearing no mention of elections, free or otherwise, this plan provided for evacuation of German soil by all but a limited contingent of allied forces. It provided for reunification "on a democratic and peace-loving basis" (the kind of language that already defined the GDR); ominously, it also included this provision: "In the event that a threat to security in either part of Germany should arise, the Powers at present performing occupation functions in Germany shall have the right to call in their troops: the U.S.S.R. into Eastern Germany. . . ." To add insult to injury, the Soviet proposals on collective security not only provided for the liquidation of the North Atlantic Treaty Organization (NATO)—which inevitably caused the British and French to close ranks with the Americans—but also contained the inept provision in article 9 that the United States be involved only on a par with China, in the role of an "observer."[37] At that point in Molotov's statement, records special assistant to President Eisenhower, C.D. Jackson, "we all laughed out loud and the Russians were taken completely by surprise at our reaction . . . the Russian momentum was gone."[38]

The responses of Dulles, Bidault, and Eden then brought the Soviet house of cards tumbling down. Jackson continues: "Molotov was drawn, gray and angry and they were all scribbling furiously and avoiding looking up in our direction, which they always do when they think they are doing well. . . . Molotov's rebuttal . . . practically ruined him because he had practically to admit that his plan called for the liquidation of NATO which is the one thing France and England *know* is their salvation. He also admitted that his scheme would probably perpetuate the division of Germany for 50 years which certainly will endear him to his German audiences and he also admitted that this business of troop withdrawal was a phoney because the Russians could come back any time they wanted, literally without any pretext other than the unilateral announcement that they felt like coming back." And when Dulles "said that classifying the Americans as 'observers' may be considered by some a poor joke but by the Americans as an affront after the blood and treasure the U.S. had expended in Europe, Molotov actually went white and then red."[39]

Molotov had evidently learned nothing since 1945. The devastation of the Soviet Union at German hands in World War II inevitably made any far-reaching reconsideration of the German question an emotive matter, impossible to carry through without arousing strong objections to any solution that left Germany free to determine its future. But the Soviet solution was still excessively indifferent to the interests of others. It was only too apparent that the policy of security through unilateral means—the extension of Soviet hegemony over the greater part of Europe—was still the agreed policy of the Soviet government, and that the continuation of this policy still had the inadvertent effect of inciting Western suspicions and solidifying Western resistance. As Eden remarked in response to Molotov's recommendations: "It seems to me that these suggestions are in essential a kind of Monroe doctrine for Europe and that their purpose is to break up the North Atlantic Treaty Alliance and to keep the United States and her forces out of Europe."[40]

From a tactical point of view, the collapse of Soviet proposals for a collective security structure mattered little if the Soviets succeeded in forestalling West German rearmament, although this left the fundamental causes of the problem unresolved. Early in 1954 the signs looked promising in Moscow that French opinion might ultimately reject the projected EDC that was designed to make West German rearmament palatable. This surely goes some way to explain why Molotov's preferences were not overridden by the Politburo and why the Soviet proposals went no further than those of March 1952. Indeed, at Berlin Molotov tactlessly commented to French Premier Bidault: "It is understandable that in France the number of opponents of the European army [the EDC] is growing."[41] Molotov seemed vindicated on August 30, 1954, when the French Assembly voted down ratification of the EDC treaty. But it was a Pyrrhic victory. The Western powers then moved instead to integrate West German rearmament within the framework of NATO, arguably a worse outcome—if the Soviets could not also forestall this process—than the EDC option. As a result of the conferences of London (September 28 – October 3) and Paris (October 20–22), it was agreed that West Germany should enter NATO as a sovereign power, with armed forces of some 500,000 strong.

These accords had yet to receive ratification; the Soviets therefore still had time. But Malenkov's leading role was in doubt. His policy of favoring consumer goods over capital goods was under sustained assault from, among others, Khrushchev. In these circumstances the London and Paris accords pulled the rug from under his feet. For the capital goods sector of the economy was closely identified with the defense industries, and the argument for cutting defense spending was predicated on more détente; certainly not West German rearmament. Hence Malenkov's warning to the French ambassador early in December: "When the Soviet Government claims that ratification of the Paris agreements will inevitably lead us to increase our armaments, it is not making propaganda. The groundwork has all been laid [C'est un dessein bien arrêté], you should know that."[42]

Malenkov was clearly on probation and under some strain. But the approaching victory of the heavy industry lobby did not bring the search for détente to an end. Some evidently believed the peace movement might forestall ratification of the Paris accords. But others were also prepared to go one step further toward the West in sacrificing the reserved option for military intervention against a reunified Germany. On January 15, 1955, the Soviet government announced that "At present there still exist unused possibilities for the attainment of an agreement on the question of the unification of Germany, necessarily taking into account the legitimate interests of the German people, and to this end carrying out free all-German elections in 1955" provided, of course, that the Paris accords were not ratified.[43] This was the closest the Soviets had ever come to the offer made by Eden a year before and, as the Quai d'Orsay noted, "The publication of this declaration must have given rise to some lively discussions within the Soviet Government and Party."[44] Furthermore, the elections would be open to international inspection, provided East and West Germany agree. But there was an important caveat in the statement. The elections were to be based on the election laws of East and West Germany, yet only "democratic" parties and organizations were to be allowed to participate; reference to the future Germany as "peaceloving and democratic" looks very much as though the Russians were still not seeking genuinely free elections, but elections in which only organizations acceptable to Moscow were to be permitted to participate. In this respect the offer of January 15 appears to have been a compromise between innovators and diehards. It showed that, when faced with the real prospect of German rearmament, major concessions could be squeezed from the Soviets for a more democratic Germany. But it also revealed the limits of the consensus beaten out in Moscow: the composition of the new German government would be subject to a Soviet veto; for if certain organizations could not get elected, how could they govern? Clearly Molotov's bitter reflections on the experience of 1932–1933 had been accommodated, albeit in a more restricted fashion than he would have preferred.

Had the West accepted (which it did not), could the offer ever have been implemented? It is still not clear to what degree the majority within the Soviet leadership accepted that Stalin's security structure was fatally flawed. The level of disagreement within the leadership on foreign as well as domestic policy—which became apparent with Malenkov's removal on February 8 and with Molotov's self-criticism on September 15[45] and eventual resignation in June 1956—was considerable. In July 1955 Molotov was condemned for obstructing the improvement in relations with Yugoslavia, and at a Central Committee plenum on June 22–29, 1957, he was also condemned for having "put the brake on [the] conclusion of the Austrian State Treaty"; for having opposed the normalization of relations with Japan; for having opposed the agreed party position on the possibility of preventing war in current conditions; and, inter alia, for having "denied the value of establishing personal contacts between leading figures in the U.S.S.R. and statesmen of other countries."[46]

It does not appear that the Russians thought Western acceptance at all likely, anyway. The offer of January 15 was only partly conceived in terms of possible Western acceptance. More important, it also allowed for the prospect that the division of Germany would continue; in which case it benefited Moscow not to leave Adenauer entirely in the Western camp. The offer of January 15 was made in anticipation of the Bundestag decision on the ratification of the Paris accords. The innovative element in Soviet foreign policy making—still impossible to identify with any precision—evidently calculated that, whatever happened, the Soviet Union would sooner or later have to come to terms with Adenauer. The declaration of January 15 thus included a statement of the Soviet Union's determination to normalize relations with Bonn, and on January 25, 1955, the Supreme Soviet formally ended the state of war with Germany. In London a Soviet diplomat warned his French counterpart: "We will turn towards Germany, and you know, we are powerful. We have great resources to hand. We will not hesitate to make use of them. I wonder what you will say in two or three years."[47] But, once again, these were merely tactical adjustments. The Soviets were still skirting the real problem. The main hope for a basic change now rested with Khrushchev, who was less considered in his judgments, less inclined to defer to the consensus, and more inclined to take risks in all aspects of policy.

With Malenkov's resignation and replacement by Bulganin on February 8, Khrushchev emerged indisputably as the leading figure in the regime. He now adopted policies barely distinguishable from those of Malenkov; in this respect the promotion of Mikoyan as a first deputy chairman of the Council of Ministers on February 28 was a positive sign to those eager for détente with the West; this, in turn, was to ensure a collision with Molotov. Khrushchev ensured that the doors were not entirely closed to an accommodation with the West even after the Paris accords were ratified by France on March 27. A gesture of defiance was offered with the creation of the Warsaw Pact on May 14—as threatened.[48] But this alliance merely formalized preexisting arrangements between Moscow and its satellites. And the text of the resolution explicitly relegated East German participation in the military structure to some future date. Clearly Khrushchev did not consider the German question entirely settled, even then. In June the Russians renewed the peace offensive and dropped hints that the neutralization of Austria, secured on May 15, could serve as a model for Germany: genuinely free elections, reunification, and neutralization.[49] From then on, however, the Soviets began a retreat back to safer positions. Tensions were only too apparent in relations between Moscow and East Berlin (Ulbricht in particular).[50] Less and less talk was heard of free elections. And by November 6 Kaganovich—one of the known hard liners in Moscow—delivered a no-nonsense speech insisting that unity could be obtained only on the basis of a "democratic and peaceful" Germany (the old formula of 1954).[51]

Despite the proposals that were whispered in the corridors of power, and the zigzags only too evident in Moscow's policy on the German question, all designed to forestall German rearmament, the Soviet leadership as a whole could not steel itself to risk abandoning the GDR for a form of reunification that promised an uncertain future. Even those aware of the mistakes made in the past were at this stage still in no position to undo them. Perhaps the bottom line of Soviet policy was best summed up by

Zhukov who, as Bulganin's replacement at the head of the Defense Ministry, bluntly stated what others were only thinking: "We will not give back what we have conquered. Who would do so in our position?"[52] This, said in November 1955, was to be confirmed in the bloodiest manner one year later.

PROPPING UP THE BLOC

The impotence of the East German regime in the face of a workers' revolt in June 1953 had convinced Beria that the Soviets were best rid of Ulbricht and his followers. This suggests that for some, at least, in the Soviet leadership the growth of unrest within the Eastern bloc might drive home the lesson that hegemony over the region was no solution to Soviet security. Unfortunately, the events of 1956 had a rather different effect. As a direct consequence of the "thaw" that culminated in February 1956 with Khrushchev's denunciation of Stalin, expectations of liberation from Stalinism prompted unrest in Poland and Hungary in the summer and autumn of 1956. In Poland the unrest ensured the emergence of a new Communist leadership under Gomulka that, despite misgivings, the Soviet government ultimately found acceptable; at least it could control popular unrest. But in Hungary the leadership that emerged under Nagy was visibly incapable of stemming the anticommunist tide; and in November Soviet tanks rolled into Budapest to restore the kind of order Moscow preferred.[53] The NATO powers did nothing; though inflammatory broadcasts from radio stations in the West undoubtedly incited unrealistic popular expectations of liberation from Soviet rule. What this episode demonstrated all too clearly was Soviet determination to hold onto what had been conquered. Reluctance to reconsider the premises of this security policy was doubtless reinforced by fears that an ordered retreat might turn into a rout and that the NATO bloc, above all West Germany, would advance into any area deserted by Soviet forces. In this sense the Soviets were prisoners of the situation they had themselves done so much to create in the 1940s.

Once again, the only area of innovation was tactical. Holding what it had, the Soviet government then moved to forestall the worst consequences of West German rearmament: the location of tactical nuclear weapons on West German soil and, likely as not, their acquisition by the Federal Republic of Germany (FRG), which openly declared reunification as its goal. As early as March 27, 1956, Moscow had proposed establishing a nuclear-free zone in Central Europe.[54] This proposal was reiterated by Poland's Foreign Minister Rapacki at the United Nations in October 1957.[55] Neither offer had any appeal for the NATO powers. Having failed to forestall the arrival of nuclear weapons in West Germany; having failed in further attempts to gain Western recognition of the East German regime in 1957–1958; and faced with the prospect of growing West German economic and military power and the defection of skilled men from East Berlin into West Berlin, on November 27, 1958, Khrushchev forced the issue by delivering an ultimatum to the allies that demanded their evacuation of West Berlin and threatened to conclude a separate peace treaty with East Germany.[56]

On January 8, 1960, Khrushchev emphasized to President Gronchi from Italy the importance of "concluding a treaty of peace with Germany which would stabilize the situation in such a way that it would fix the state of affairs that had in fact come into being after the Second World War. We must reinforce this state of affairs with a de jure agreement and thereby also secure de jure approval for the change of frontiers that came into being after the Second World War. Should we not resolve these problems, forces that wish to change the situation . . . will arise and organize themselves.[57] But this attempt failed. And on August 13, 1961, the Soviets accepted the division of Berlin and blocked further emigration from East Germany by constructing a wall that bisected the city, handing over control of East Berlin to the East German regime.[58]

KHRUSHCHEV'S INITIATIVE FORESTALLED

By the early 1960s the Soviet occupation of East Germany was locked into a framework originally created by Stalin as a tactical device, but which had apparently become the only workable alternative to complete retreat—bringing the prospect of a rearmed, reunited, and anti-Soviet Germany—or war. The Soviets had inadvertently acquired an uncertain investment in the unpopular Ulbricht regime in East Berlin; as a consequence Ulbricht began to exert a constant negative influence on any progress toward an innovative solution to the German problem. Whenever Khrushchev tried to alleviate the consequences of this impasse by an attempted rapprochement with Bonn, a cry would go out from East Berlin that found echoes among hard liners in Moscow opposed to Khrushchev on other grounds. The threatened acquisition by West Germany of nuclear weapons— a specter that appeared over the horizon with the appointment of Strauss as defense minister in October 1956, that materialized in the generals' memorandum of 1959, and that was not exorcised until West German signature of the nonproliferation treaty 10 years later—polarized opinion within Moscow.[59]

For some it was merely confirmation of the need to rearm and confront the West from a position of strength—a lesson also drawn from the Cuban missile crisis in October 1962, wherein a Soviet retreat had resulted from both local naval inferiority and overall strategic nuclear inferiority.

For others—including Khrushchev—it prompted a renewed search for détente. This resulted in the signing of the partial test ban treaty in August 1963.[60] It also led to a new approach to West Germany, made on behalf of Khrushchev by his son-in-law Adzhubei on a visit to Bonn in the second half of July 1964. Although it is not clear to what extent Khrushchev was rethinking the German problem, his attempt to circumvent the diplomatic apparatus by using Adzhubei and the reports that reached Khrushchev's rivals of Adzhubei's meetings in Bonn played a not insignificant role in his overthrow that October. Soviet intelligence obtained tape recordings of Adzhubei's meetings. Khrushchev's son Sergei recalls: "In one of the reports it said that in reply to cautious enquiry whether an improvement in relations between Russia and West Germany would affect the existence of the Berlin wall, Adzhubei evidently replied that when Khrushchev came and saw for himself what good guys [*khoroshie rebyata*] the Germans were, not a stone of the wall would be left standing."[61] If Adzhubei's indiscretion reflected his father-in-law's own musings in private, then it would appear that Khrushchev had not entirely forsaken the option of a deal with West Germany at East German expense.

But Khrushchev's overthrow in October 1964 forestalled his trip to Bonn; indeed, it may well have been timed to that end. The new coalition led by First Secretary (later General Secretary) Brezhnev and Chairman of the Council of Ministers Kosygin ruled out any visit, let alone bilateral détente, with West Germany. Soviet goals reverted to form: maintenance of hegemony over Eastern and part of Central Europe and a campaign to forestall West German acquisition of nuclear weapons; all of this buttressed by the attainment of strategic nuclear parity with, if not superiority over, the United States; and substantial modernization of Soviet conventional armaments in Europe. The Soviet Union would negotiate with the West in Europe but negotiate from strength to secure Western recognition of the postwar status quo.

Thus Brezhnev announced that the Soviet Union "would welcome the normalization of relations with the Federal Republic of Germany." But he made equally clear that "normalization of this kind cannot be obtained on the basis of satisfying Bonn's revanchist claims. There can be no normalization at the expense of the interests of the German Democratic Republic, the Czechoslovakian Socialist Republic, the Polish People's Republic, or at the expense of any other socialist country."[62] This certainly indicated the possibility of such an option in the recent past; otherwise, why the need for such reassurance? These conditions rendered any innovative and constructive solution to the German problem impossible.

Instead, in a memorandum published on December 8, 1964, the Soviet government revived the suggestion originally made 10 years before, for "an effective and all-encompassing system of collective security in Europe" that would include the United States.[63] The Soviets sought a conservative solution that would, they hoped, neutralize the adverse consequences of the policy they had pursued since 1945, rather than remove the bases of the East-West confrontation in Europe by withdrawing to national frontiers.

SEEKING RECOGNITION OF THE STATUS QUO

The Soviet security proposal was echoed by Polish Foreign Minister Rapacki a week later in a speech to the United Nations General Assembly. But when the Warsaw Pact Political Consultative Committee met on January 19–20, 1965, the communiqué made no mention of U.S. participation in the new scheme, which inevitably gave the impression that this had turned into yet another transparent attempt to push the Americans out of Europe.[64] The belligerency with which Ulbricht pressed his case for tougher measures "to bring their [West German] aggressive plans to a halt"[65] reinforced the innate conservatism of the Brezhnev leadership with respect to the German question. And the "sharpening of contradictions in NATO"— evident in France's withdrawal from NATO's military structure—which Moscow attributed to "American imperialism's Vietnam adventure"[66] can only have encouraged the Soviets to believe that the correlation of forces might be shifting to their advantage in Europe.

But what would be the purpose of the European Security Conference (ESC)? The bottom line was drawn by the eminence grise of the Brezhnev regime, ideologist Suslov: "The borders that came into being in Europe as a result of the defeat of Hitler's Germany are fixed and final. . . ."[67] While dropping indelicate hints at the possibility of reviving the Franco-Russian alliance to counterbalance the U.S.–West German axis,[68] the Soviets pressed ahead with plans for the ESC that would in effect set the postwar European order in concrete. At a meeting of the Warsaw Pact Political Consultative Committee in Bucharest on July 4–5, 1966, a declaration was issued echoing Suslov's words: "One of the main preconditions for the guarantee of European security is the immutability [*nezyblemost'*] of existing frontiers between European states, including the borders of the sovereign German Democratic Republic, Poland, Czechoslovakia."[69] Thus by 1966 the Soviets had resigned themselves to the permanence of the division of Germany and the permanence of Stalin's unilateral solution to the problem of Soviet security in Europe. There was no sense in which the Soviet regime had collectively learned anything from experience about the dynamic that set the cold war in motion and that had sustained it over two decades. And if a policy looks as if it is succeeding, there is absolutely no incentive to reconsider its fundamental premises.

The only likely reason for reconsideration would be a clear sign that the maintenance of Soviet hegemony over Eastern Europe was unsustainable. Such a sign appeared in 1968, as it had in East Germany in 1953 and in Hungary in 1956. While Bonn was able to exploit the growth of centrifugal forces within Eastern Europe by the exertion of its considerable economic power in trade—and Romania was only the first country to take the bait—Soviet demands for Western recognition of the unalterability of the postwar status quo carried less credibility. And with the collapse of the Stalinist order in Czechoslovakia in December 1967, the West German coalition government naturally hoped the coming thaw would further weaken Soviet hegemony over Eastern Europe. But the policies pursued by the reformist Dubček regime in Prague in the following spring unfortunately coincided with unprecedented student unrest in neighboring Poland and East Germany. This underlined the fact that, if the dynamics of social and political change continued to operate freely, the net result would be fragmentation of the bloc and the loss of Stalin's *cordon sanitaire*. Only by demonstrating once and for all that these countries were permanent Soviet protectorates could the Brezhnev regime ever hope to undermine the grand coalition's Ostpolitik, forestall West German encirclement and isolation of East Germany, and force the West to accept the postwar status quo in Europe as immutable. Soviet and allied troops invaded Czechoslovakia on the night of August 20, 1968. Brezhnev told Dubček: "For us the results of the Second World War are inviolable, and we will defend them even at the cost of risking a new war."[70]

THE MIRAGE OF DÉTENTE

The West German Social Democratic Party (SPD) now accepted that the policy of divide and rule projected into the Soviet sphere of influence would never work; that it was, in fact, counterproductive; and that nothing remained but to come to terms with "the results of the Second World War." Breaking with the grand coalition and winning a victory over the Christian Democrats in September 1969, Willy Brandt led the SPD to power in coalition with the Free Democrats.[71] Inaugurating a new Ostpolitik, framed by Herbert Wehner,[72] Brandt immediately signed the nuclear nonproliferation treaty—finally relieving the East of a long-standing nightmare—and opened negotiations that led to Bonn's recognition of the postwar status quo in Eastern and Central Europe. This included the basic treaty with the Ulbricht regime (December 21, 1971) that paved the way for NATO recognition of the GDR.[73] The European Security Conference at Helsinki that followed in 1973–1975 put the finishing touches to NATO acceptance of the postwar order in Europe as "inviolable."[74] The Soviets had been angling for "immutable," but ultimately accepted that they had gained as much as could reasonably be expected. The goal that Khrushchev had sought in 1958 had finally been attained. The fact that this achievement was reached only after the forceful suppression of centrifugal tendencies within the Soviet bloc, and that it was accompanied by the steady reinforcement of Soviet military power in the region, inevitably strengthened the dominance of the least innovative elements in Soviet policy toward Europe. Although not everything attained at Helsinki in 1975 was to Soviet taste (notably Basket Three on human rights), the Soviets could be forgiven for believing that the correlation of forces, at least in Europe, had shifted and was continuing to shift to their advantage. In these conditions, any fundamental reconsideration of Stalin's framework for Soviet security was unthinkable.

A further, and critical, factor in growing Soviet complacency about the interests of the Western Europeans was the process of strategic arms negotiations with the United States. At SALT I (1969–1972) the Americans—against tough Soviet objection—worked hard to prevent and succeeded in preventing the inclusion of any U.S. forces in Europe in the agreements on arms limitation.[75] But during SALT II (1972–1979) U.S. eagerness for another agreement with the Soviet Union that would cap the strategic competition led the U.S. government to sacrifice systems that promised to maintain NATO superiority in theatre nuclear weapons over the Warsaw Pact. In pressing for these measures the Soviets showed themselves indifferent to their likely impact on Western Europe. What seemed to count most to a Soviet leadership that saw itself attaining equality with the other superpower was a deal with the United States. Now that the German question had been resolved essentially to Soviet satisfaction, the Western Europeans had essentially diminished to little more than objects of policy. The way onward and upward in the Soviet foreign policy hierarchy was as an Americanist, not a Europeanist. It was all too easy for Brezhnev and Foreign Minister Gromyko to assume that, once arms control was settled with the United States, everything else—except in the Third World, where the Soviets were rapidly undercutting U.S. influence through energetic support for wars of "national liberation"—would neatly fall into place. It was also a fallacy to believe that the cold war was a problem to be resolved merely through arms control or disarmament, whether in Europe or on the strategic level. The arms themselves were—as they are still—the symptoms of a deeper malaise. Despite the Soviet achievement in securing recognition for postwar frontiers, it was the continued division of Germany and the maintenance of Soviet hegemony over the eastern half of the divide that kept the arms race in Europe in being. While Soviet policy appeared to be exclusively concerned to preserve the status quo in Central Europe, a minimal form of détente was possible; however, once the Soviets were seen to be holding what they had but then also attempting to undermine the U.S. military presence that underwrote Western European security and the balance of power in Europe, no short-term stability, let alone long-term détente, was possible with Western Europe.

Thus when the Soviets not only focused almost exclusively on arms control in East-West negotiations but also, within that, focused almost exclusively on the U.S.–Soviet strategic balance, thereby ignoring particular European interests, they inadvertently compounded Stalin's original error and ended up raising rather than lowering tension in Europe and destroying détente in the process. How they did this was by deploying the SS-20.

DEPLOYMENT OF THE SS-20

At SALT I and SALT II the Soviets had tried to include U.S. theatre nuclear systems in the count, but to no avail. The deployment of the new intermediate-range SS-20 missile would, they hoped, not only offset NATO's advantage in theatre nuclear forces, but it might also serve as an essential bargaining chip to set against the U.S. forward-based nuclear-capable aircraft that so preoccupied the Soviet air defense forces. In Moscow no consideration was given to the impact deployment would have on Western European views of Soviet intentions. The significance of Europe was eclipsed by the larger mass of the United States. The Soviets were, indeed, right to see that Washington counted far more than Bonn, London, or Paris. But they were wrong to assume that the United States ran NATO in the way the Soviet Union ran the Warsaw Pact. As in the critical years 1945–1948, the Western Europeans collectively still possessed a critical power as catalyst to U.S. policy toward the Soviet Union; as a catalyst not merely toward détente but also, in these circumstances, as a lobby for the rectification of the balance of power in Europe to NATO advantage.[76] There were alternatives to détente. The correlation of forces was reversible, as the Soviets soon found to their cost.

The West Germans stood on the front line. Chancellor Helmut Schmidt was the first to raise the alarm publicly in Europe, in September 1977. But this proved insufficient, and, faced with apparent U.S. unconcern and complete Soviet indifference, Western European alarm increased rather than diminished. By November 1979, when Gromyko visited Bonn, the Western Europeans had set in motion a dynamic in U.S. foreign policy that would not merely rectify the expected imbalance of power in Europe but would also raise NATO's threat to Soviet security to new heights. Yet Gromyko, though concerned, appeared uncomprehending. After the meeting Schmidt came away with the sure impression that "the Soviet leadership still failed to see the situation in which they had placed Western Europe and Germany."[77] In December NATO resolved to deploy U.S.

cruise and Pershing-2 missiles in Western Europe should the Soviets fail to withdraw deployment of the SS-20.

The opening of the talks in 1981 did not stall SS-20 deployments. The Soviets still clung to their original position that the SS-20 was essentially a trade-off for U.S. forward-based aircraft and allied nuclear systems. And through their front organization, the World Peace Council, they attempted to mobilize the peace movement to outflank NATO.[78] Schmidt warned Brezhnev: "In the West the impression is widespread that the Soviet leadership is counting on the peace movements rather than on the negotiations."[79] But this had no effective impact on Soviet policy; with the deadline reached and SS-20 deployments continuing apace, U.S. deployment of cruise and Pershing-2 missiles began.

The Brezhnev leadership and its successors, under Andropov and Chernenko, had learned next to nothing from this unfortunate episode. To the extent that anything had been learned with respect to European policy, they had learned the wrong lessons. Their formative experience in power had been that of the 1960s: that by standing firm on long-held aims they could achieve substantially what they sought without major concessions. And it is extremely difficult for anyone, let alone aged leaders, to reconsider positions that have proved successful in the past. There were dissentient voices within the lower ranks, however. From the Institute for the Economics of the World Socialist System, headed by Oleg Bogomolov and long protected by Andropov, alternative voices could be heard, at least in private. Head of the international relations department Vyacheslav Dashichev had recommended accepting the Western negotiating position in 1981–1982.[80] But the Politburo was deaf to such voices. Only when the alarming decline of the Soviet economy coincided with the astonishing revival of U.S. economic and military power—highlighted by U.S. plans to accelerate the arms race into outer space with the Strategic Defense Initiative (SDI)—did doubts begin to find an echo in the Kremlin. Economic performance since the mid-1970s had been noticeably worse than before, even to the extent of prompting a stagnation in military procurement from 1976 to 1982. And it was this combination of growing domestic malaise and the emergence of an alarming new threat to Soviet security from the United States under Ronald Reagan that in March 1985 prompted the aging Politburo to elevate Mikhail Gorbachev to power on a platform of major reform.[81]

THE ADVENT OF NEW THINKING

Gorbachev's accession proved a critical turning point. Previous heresies soon found a willing ear. Pragmatic in the face of the country's domestic and international crises, Gorbachev introduced a new flexibility and realism into Soviet policy. Gromyko, judging by his actions as well as his memoirs, had learned nothing from the setbacks of the previous decade. Thus it took his ejection from the Foreign Ministry, his replacement by the reformist Eduard Shevardnadze in July 1985, and the appointment of former ambassador to Washington Anatoly Dobrynin to head the party's International Department to translate this spirit of pragmatism into the conduct of international relations. Bent on destroying the SDI, which symbolized the threat from ever-advancing U.S. technology and innovation, but unable to make headway toward the United States, Gorbachev accepted the need to appease the Europeans as an interim measure. In January 1985, while Chernenko was fatally ill and with Gorbachev in the ascendant as heir apparent, the Soviets had agreed to renegotiate theatre nuclear weapons only on condition that this would put the SDI on the bargaining table. But after Gorbachev assumed power, Soviet policy moved decisively toward the appeasement of Western Europe. His spokesmen even began talking positively about Western Europe as an independent entity in the international system. And at the 27th party congress in February 1986 he marked out a fundamental break with the past in declaring that the maintenance of Soviet security was "a political task" to be resolved "only through political means." Security had to be "mutual." And he announced that he favored "keeping military capability within the limits of reasonable sufficiency."[82]

Thus, by the end of his first year in office, Gorbachev had demonstrated that with respect to Europe he, at least, had learned a significant lesson from the events of the previous decade: the Americocentric focus of Soviet foreign policy, which treated the Western Europeans as mere objects, had distorted Soviet perceptions of reality and had driven the Soviet Union into a political cul-de-sac. While courting the Western Europeans through concessions on human rights and offering new openings for trade, Gorbachev now conceded position after position to the United States (and its allies) at the Geneva talks. This process culminated in the treaty of December 1987 providing for the destruction of all Soviet intermediate and medium-range missiles, together with the removal of all cruise and Pershing-2 missiles from Europe, leaving U.S. forward-based aircraft and allied nuclear forces intact.[83] Gorbachev then also moved to cut Soviet conventional forces through joint negotiation at the conference on conventional forces in Europe (CFE) that opened in 1989.

What we have witnessed in Soviet foreign policy since 1985 is the outcome of a great deal of new thinking. It is not that these ideas never existed in Moscow; but that, like Dashichev's proposals in 1981–1982, they never found a welcome at the highest levels. The learning that occurred within restricted circles of Moscow's think tanks since their creation in the 1950s and 1960s has now been disseminated in an increasingly public manner. Yet, for all progress clearly made, thus far those elements of the new thinking so far adopted as policy represented changes that rolled back only the surface of Soviet power. The substrata, consisting of Soviet domination of Eastern and part of Central Europe, remained. But, with domestic decline more rapid than ever and the gap in trust between East and West in Europe apparently as wide as ever, Moscow now moved beyond disarmament to build bridges with the West. The empty rhetoric about "Europe" the "common home" now needed putting into practice, and this inevitably entailed a change in policy on the German question.

THE GERMAN QUESTION REEMERGES

The importance of Germany was underlined in the autumn of 1988 with the appointment of the leading Germanist and former ambassador to Bonn, Valentin Falin, to the post of head of the Central Committee international department. Initially Falin's activities since that time appeared to have less in common with the new thinking than with Soviet tactics in the early 1950s, the formative period of his development as a diplomat. As the Soviets pressed for negotiations to remove all tactical nuclear weapons from Europe, in 1988–1989 they met stiff resistance from the United States (with Britain and France standing firm behind it). But West German public opinion and, as a consequence, the governing Christian Democrat–Free Democrat coalition were badly split on the issue. Eager to secure another zero option in this sphere, the Soviets could not resist the temptation to play on the divisions of opinion in Bonn and between Bonn and the other leading NATO powers.

Such behavior inevitably called into question the much-expressed denial in Moscow that the Soviet intention had always been to split NATO. Indeed, Soviet treatment of this issue began to look suspiciously like the measures taken to forestall deployment of the neutron bomb in 1977–1978 and to forestall cruise and Pershing-2 deployments in the early 1980s. In his address to a foreign policy congress held by the West German Christian Democratic Party on April 14, 1988, Soviet ambassador to Bonn (and former Falin protégé) Yuli Kvitsinsky struck a strongly anti-American and pro-European note. He carefully ruled out any changes in the existing "territorial political structure of Europe" (meaning its division between East and West), because that had "brought all of us 40 years of peace." Without a trace of irony, he went on to claim Soviet credit for the fact that "[a]fter the end of the Second World War we were the only European Power that, together with its allies, did not submit to the American demand for the role of world leader." And he highlighted the role West Germany might play in the new Europe envisioned by the

Soviet Union, insisting that "Europe must recover its specific weight in the world."[84] To cap it all, in Vienna on May 12, 1989, with NATO in disarray over tactical nuclear weapons and in response to the fears expressed by the U.S. secretary of defense of a reunified Germany, Falin chose this delicate moment not only to blame the United States for the division of Germany in the first place, but also to imply that the Soviet Union viewed the prospect of a reunified and neutralized Germany with equanimity.[85]

Falin's statement represented something much more substantial than a blatant attempt to draw tactical advantage in the struggle for influence over Bonn. The value of sustaining the Warsaw Pact had been called into question. With the Soviet economy in a state of secular decline since the mid-1970s,[86] unable to contemplate indefinite competition with the United States in the arms race and unable even to feed the people, attention turned to the socioeconomic stagnation of allies in Eastern Europe. Political order had been bought at the price of economic effort. In their condition as vassals, the countries of the pact were burdens rather than supports to the expansion of Soviet power. From 1985 to 1988 this area of Soviet foreign policy had been left untouched. But by the time Falin spoke out, something fundamental had begun to change. Proposals had gone to the Soviet leadership from Dashichev at the Institute for the Economics of the World Socialist System suggesting reunification and neutralization as a solution to the confrontation in Europe. And some time in the summer of 1988 Gorbachev received the results of a national security review that argued the case for complete withdrawal from Central and Eastern Europe. Forging a consensus within the leadership on such a contentious issue was not easy. Gorbachev hesitated. The sense of uncertainty was caught by remarks given by Falin in May 1989 and by a subsequent comment by the deputy head of the international department, Vladimir Zagladin, who in June pointed out that "[r]eunification is not on the agenda at present" but added, for emphasis: "At present."[87]

Yet by the time Zagladin had spoken, Gorbachev had already begun to put into effect the proposals presented to him a year before and to do so, as events later revealed, without a complete consensus within the Politburo behind him. Beginning with Poland, where free elections were won by Solidarity on June 4, the process spread to Hungary, which on September 10 opened its border with Austria, which resulted in a mad rush of East Germans into Budapest and through Hungary to Austria in the West; this crisis then spread to the GDR with the overthrow of Hönecker on October 18 and the opening of a breach in the Berlin Wall on November 9; once it hit the GDR, Prague could not hold out alone, and the creation of a non-Communist government in Czechoslovakia took place on December 10; free elections were called for in June 1990 in Bulgaria; and, last but not least, in Romania the fall of Ceaucescu occurred on December 22.

All of these events, with the exception of Romania, required a positive decision from Moscow to release control over the normal political development of each country.

The initial decision to let go of Poland had obvious long-term consequences for the maintenance of forward-based Soviet forces in East Germany. It is however clear that the speed—though not the direction—of developments ran far beyond what had been anticipated. But it is also true that here, as at home, having finally resolved to act, Gorbachev was characteristically quite prepared to risk unleashing forces that could not entirely be controlled in order to make the process of change irreversible.

As the process of change unfolded, Western governments were somewhat stunned to see Moscow unperturbed—unperturbed but silent. Gorbachev waited before openly embracing the changes as they affected the fate of the GDR, but embrace them he finally did on February 10 when Chancellor Kohl of West Germany visited Moscow. The communiqué read: "M.S. Gorbachev stated—and the Chancellor agreed with him— that now between the U.S.S.R., the FRG and GDR there are no disagreements about the fact that the question of the unity of the German nation must be decided by the Germans themselves and they must themselves make their choice as to what state forms, within what time, at what pace, and on what conditions this unity will be realized."[88] Evidently, to reassure the more nervous sectors of the Soviet population, the communiqué also spoke of the overall context of developments in Europe and the need to take into account "the security and interests of neighbors"— though Poland and Czechoslovakia were not specifically named. Yet, typically pragmatic, in his actions Gorbachev had shown himself rather indifferent to such consideration. "I long ago said that history will take care of the resolution of the German question," he said disarmingly. "And here we are, it has been worked out at an unexpected pace."[89] The problem that soon arose was, of course, the West German ambition to swallow East Germany whole while remaining within NATO and the European Economic Community (EEC), thus threatening an enlarged adversarial alliance while the Soviet alliance system had fallen apart. The other problem was that of German irredentism. The latter prompted an interview with *Pravda* on February 21 to reassure those alarmed at West German reluctance to commit themselves to the immutability of frontiers in Europe—something they had refused to do in 1970–1971 and had been backed by NATO in so refusing at Helsinki in 1974–1975. Here he indicated that the Soviet Union still had some leverage: he did so by restating the fact that the rights of the four powers were still in effect and that a peace treaty with Germany had yet to be signed.[90] Similarly, on the danger of East Germany ultimately entering NATO, Shevardnadze reminded readers that "[w]e have options of one kind or another in reserve."[91]

Clearly Gorbachev and Shevardnadze had been persuaded of the counterproductive results obtained from enforced membership of the communist camp in Eastern and Central Europe. They had learned the lessons of past mistakes and, what is more, dared put these lessons into practice that former Soviet leaders had been either unwilling or unable to do. But, as one might have guessed, not all in the leadership and indeed the foreign policy establishment agreed. The issue of what should be done about Germany had "repeatedly been raised in the Politburo"[92] and the policy pursued by Gorbachev and Shevardnadze came under attack at the Central Committee plenum early in February 1990 from Ligachev, Shevardnadze's most significant critic. It appears that Ligachev's remarks were not fully reported in the Soviet press. What they did report were the following remarks concerning "the approaching danger" consequent upon "the acceleration of German reunification, and effectively, the absorption of the GDR." He warned of the need to "prevent a pre-war Munich."[93] Whether it was Ligachev or the Soviet ambassador to Poland—a diehard opponent of all that perestroika has stood for—it is not entirely clear but, as Shevardnadze noted: "One comrade, speaking at the Plenum, said: not long ago the U.S.S.R. was a big state that exercised authority, the whole world admired it. And there was Eastern Europe— the guarantee of our security. . . . He implies that we have destroyed all this—both the grandeur and the guarantee. . . . We know in what way we were admired. . . . We introduced forces into Czechoslovakia, we eradicated the buds of progress. They believe that the world admired this? To Hungary we 'brought order' in 1956. Was Europe also de-lighted? We went into Afghanistan. How was this then called—an international duty? But it would be more correct to call it an invasion. And was the world once again admiring?. . . . And among us some even now pose puzzling questions: how is it possible that a massive Power with an army of five million was unable to deal with small Afghanistan?!"[94]

Clearly the Soviet leadership—now backed by many in the Central Committee—had learned some hard lessons from the counterproductive behavior of the past and had completely transformed Soviet foreign policy in the process. The "new thinking"—once a minority view shared by Moscow intellectuals epitomized by the late Andrei Sakharov—was now the triumphant new orthodoxy. Those preaching class war abroad had been forced to lower their voices within the Institute of Marxism-Leninism and the Central Committee apparatus; within the leadership itself they could talk as much as they like but could affect nothing of substance.

None of these changes—particularly with regard to German policy— was successfully predicted; nor are the long-term consequences easy to foresee. Under Gorbachev the Soviet government has not only success-fully reversed the disastrous policy of rearmament that his predecessors had initiated and stubbornly maintained, but has also learned that West

European interests must be correctly understood and allowed for in the search for understandings with the United States. In addition, the Soviet Union made the critical decision—perhaps the most important made since 1945—to pull back all its forward-based forces to the Soviet frontier in a fundamental revision of Stalin's postwar security policy.

CONCLUSIONS

What general conclusions can be drawn from this study of Soviet policy toward Western Europe since the war? In schematic form the pattern emerges somewhat like this: for a major change in existing policy, the premises underlying it have to be called into question. To do so will require certain objective and subjective preconditions: in this case an overwhelming crisis in both foreign and domestic policy. The costs of the policy have to be seen to outweigh the benefits: failure has to become apparent not necessarily to all, but certainly to the most dynamic element in the power structure.

The objective factors at work in both periods included external pressure, most notably from the United States, and the internal pressures arising from economic imbalance and declining rates of growth. In the case of the period 1953–1955 under Malenkov, the adjustments made to European policy (and other aspects of foreign policy) were prompted by the combination of a massive threat to Soviet security that, if Soviet security policy had not exactly precipitated, it had surely not removed, as well as severe economic problems at home, accompanied by strong doubts about the previous direction taken in domestic political life and internal disagreements as to the course to be taken. It is striking that these elements reappear—albeit in far greater form—when Gorbachev came to power. In 1953–1955 the economy had its problems; by 1985 it was visibly in crisis. In 1953–1955 the balance of military power between the United States and the Soviet Union was obviously to Soviet disadvantage; from the early 1980s it was less the actual balance than Soviet projections of the future balance—with the development of U.S. space weaponry, a conventional arms race in Europe at a higher level of technology, and the massive growth of British and French nuclear systems—that unnerved the Soviet leadership. Yet, however obvious such facts might seem to one observer, they may appear rather differently from another vantage point. One cannot afford to underrate the importance of the subjective preconditions for change, as the critical role of Gorbachev's powerful personality certainly underlines.

Clearly the direction of change has to come from the top in a society with a totalitarian structure of power. Certainly under Stalin nothing could be done without (at the very least) his patient acquiescence. The note of March 1952 very soon outlived its usefulness, and once the old dictator lost interest one of the very few innovations that appeared in his twilight years disappeared into the gloom from which it had, almost miraculously, emerged. The fact that his leading successor, Malenkov, was not only intelligent but also apparently indifferent to doctrine and totally unprincipled (as revelations about the notorious Leningrad affair now indicate) and determined to court popularity by redirecting the course of the Soviet economy from heavy industry to the production of consumer goods made all the difference to the emergence of new tactical flexibility in Soviet foreign policy from 1953 to 1955. Had Molotov emerged at the top, a resurgence of fundamentalism would have been the order of the day.

Much, then, depends on the leader. Malenkov's successor, Khrushchev, was no less innovative in spirit, though less so in practice: to have gone further would have required massive structural readjustments to Soviet security policy that could not have been produced without the establishment of a personal dictatorship over the party and state on the model of Stalin. In this respect the events of 1956 in Poland and Hungary, in undermining Khrushchev's authority—Molotov, Malenkov, and Kaganovich could blame it all on de-Stalinization when they were not blaming the CIA—forestalled any fundamental reassessment of policy. This underlines the fact that the existence of an innovative mind at the top of the leadership is to no avail if the prevailing objective conditions obstruct structural change.

But even in the realm of subjective factors, not everything depends exclusively on the nature of the leading figure in the Kremlin. The destruction of the old Soviet diplomatic corps and the creative intelligentsia with knowledge of the outside world, and the subsequent subjugation of their remnants and replacements in vicious campaigns against "cosmopolitanism," left a ruling elite substantially bereft of the human resources vital to objective assessments of the international situation, no less—indeed perhaps even more—than the domestic scene.

Whereas Malenkov was visibly working against the grain—certainly against Molotov, his allies, and his protégés—in changing Soviet foreign policy, Gorbachev has at his disposal a wealth of creative and supportive talent. The think tanks created at Mikoyan's suggestion since 1956, the widespread expansion of foreign language teaching, the enormous growth of Soviet foreign correspondents and diplomats (with the appearance of embassies in all the new Third World states), plus the not insignificant impact of the growth in foreign trade and cultural exchanges with foreign countries have all had the cumulative effect over the past three decades of restoring to the Soviet Union the mass of knowledge and insight with respect to the outside world that Stalin had feared and largely destroyed.

Many of these improvements themselves grew out of the attempted changes of the mid-1950s: in this sense without Malenkov (or, indeed, without Khrushchev), no Gorbachev.

Thus, when a leader of Gorbachev's calibre has doubts about the wisdom of past policy with respect to some issue or area of the world, he can find a variety of analyses and conclusions from which to draw; more important perhaps, those actually executing policy are more likely to follow the spirit of the changes and not sabotage them in implementation. It may also mean that, in contrast to the Malenkov phase, the changes made may be far more difficult to reverse should a less enlightened leadership emerge into power. The fact that Molotov's men were still in place when Brezhnev took power made it that much easier to revert to patterns of behavior more reminiscent of an earlier era. Institutional responsiveness to innovation through the recruitment of more knowledgeable *mezhdunarodniki* would thus seem to be an indispensable precondition to a foreign policy appropriately matched to Soviet interests. Learning that occurs only at the very top is therefore unlikely to have a long-term impact without learning from below. In this respect, greater availability of information on foreign affairs, anticipated under Brezhnev with more detailed and more open discussions of foreign affairs on radio and television from the mid-1970s, a process furthered by the creation of the international information department of the Central Committee in 1978, has also played a critical role.

But for all the progress made in the propagation of international information, we are still largely talking of an educated elite rather than an educated populace. Shevardnadze's expressed wish to see foreign policy debated in public forums such as the Supreme Soviet certainly suggests that the extension of general knowledge of international affairs is an important element in the development and implementation of the new thinking. How much of this will be achieved, and whether Soviet foreign policy will depart from the general European model of court politics rather than public policy, remains a matter of conjecture. But the degree and pace of learning in Soviet foreign policy cannot remain unaffected by the outcome of this uncertain process. Will this retard or hasten the learning process? To answer that, we will have to await future events.

NOTES

1. The best history of the Comintern in these years can be found in E.H. Carr's series of works on the history of Soviet Russia (London: Macmillan): *The Bolshevik Revolution, 1917–23*, Vol. 3 (1953); *The Interregnum, 1923–24* (1954); *Socialism in One Country, 1924–26*, Vol. 3 (1964); *Foundations of a Planned Economy, 1926–29*, Vol. 3 (1976); *Twilight of Comintern, 1930–35* (1982); *The Comintern and the Spanish Civil War, 1936–39* (1984).

2. Fairly conclusive evidence can be found in Foreign Office archives. In February 1927 the Commissariat for Military and Naval Affairs was, at a feverish pace, constructing a strategic railroad to facilitate the transfer of troops along the Polish frontier, with April as the deadline for completion. In Leningrad doctors and nurses were being registered for war service. Munitions plants were forced to raise output by six times the norm, and special military commissars were put in charge of them. Suspected counterrevolutionaries were moved from the frontier zones. See Hodgson (Moscow) to Chamberlain (London), 9 February 1927: *FO 371/12588* (Public Record Office, London).

3. J. Haslam, *Soviet Foreign Policy 1930–33: The Impact of the Depression* (London: Macmillan/New York: St. Martin's Press, 1983).

4. J. Haslam, *The Soviet Union and the Struggle for Collective Security in Europe 1933–39* (London: Macmillan/New York: St. Martin's Press, 1984).

5. "All of us in Moscow are getting the impression that Churchill is maintaining a course directed towards the defeat of the USSR in order then to come to terms with the Germany of Hitler or Bruning at the expense of our country." Stalin (Moscow) to Maisky (London), 19 October 1942: *Sovetsko-angliiskie otnosheniya vo vremya velikoi otechestvennoi voiny 1941–1945: Dokumenty i Materialy*, Vol. 1, 1941–1943 (Moscow 1983) doc. 147.

6. Discussion at the British embassy, 28 October 1943, with Eden and Harriman: W. Averell Harriman and E. Abel, *Special Envoy to Churchill and Stalin 1941–1946* (London: Hutchinson, 1976), 242–243.

7. There is considerable evidence for this, not least the testimony that Litvinov could be heard shouting *"durak"* (fool) at Molotov on the telephone: interview with Litvinov's daughter Tanya.

8. M. Djilas, *Conversations With Stalin* (New York/London: Harcourt Brace, 1962), 114.

9. P. Spriano, *I communisti europei e Stalin* (Turin: Einaudi, 1983); for a sense of the spirit of the time, turn to the reports from the various U.S. embassies in Europe from 1946 to 1948 in the series *Foreign Relations of the United States*.

10. See A. Bullock, *Ernest Bevin: Foreign Secretary 1945–1951* (London: Heinemann, 1983), 576; R. Futrell, *Ideas, Concepts, Doctrine: A History of Basic Thinking in the United States Air Force 1907–1964* (Maxwell Air Force Base, Alabama, 1971), 121.

11. For this process, see *Foreign Relations of the United States, 1950*, Vol. IV (Washington, D.C., 1980).

12. Le Roy (Moscow) to Pinay (Paris), 19 August 1955: *Documents Diplomatiques Français, 1955* (Paris, 1988), Vol. 2, doc. 125.

13. *Izvestiia*, 11 March 1952. A translation can be found in: *Cmnd. 1552: Selected Documents on Germany and the Question of Berlin 1944–1961* (London, 1961), doc. 54a.

14. "O mirnom dogovore s Germaniei," *Izvestiia*, 14 March 1952.

15. Secretary of state to the Office of the U.S. High Commissioner for Germany, at Bonn, 12 April 1952: *Foreign Relations of the United States 1952–1954*, Vol. VII, Part 1 (Washington, D.C., 1986) doc. 84.

16. *Izvestiia*, 11 April 1952.

17. Gifford (London) to Department of State, 17 April 1952: *Foreign Relations of the United States*, Vol. VII, doc. 86.

18. Ibid.

19. Ibid, doc. 101.

20. *Izvestiia*, 25 May 1952; a translation can be found in *Foreign Relations of the United States*, Vol. VII, doc. 102.

21. Kennan (Moscow) to Department of State (Washington), 25 May 1952: *Foreign Relations of the United States*, Vol. VII, doc. 103.

22. For the last note sent to Moscow: *Foreign Relations of the United States*, Vol. VII, doc. 138.

23. On Falin: A. Shevchenko, *Breaking with Moscow* (New York: Knopf, 1985), 168–69.

24. A brief biography of Semenov appears in the memoirs of U.S. negotiator at SALT I, Gerard Smith. He describes him thus: having once worked on a collective farm, Semenov "joined the Foreign Service in 1939 [the Molotov intake], after graduating from the Moscow Institute of History, Philosophy, and Literature. He was counselor in Berlin during the Soviet-German Non-Aggression pact years 1940–1941. He returned to Berlin in May 1945 as a political adviser, then served as high commissioner and finally as Soviet ambassador. . . . He became chief of the Foreign Ministry's Central European Division in 1954 and Deputy Foreign Minister in March 1955." G. Smith, *Doubletalk* (London: Doubleday, 1985), 45-46.

25. Director of the Berlin Element, *United States High Command for Germany* (Lyon) to Department of State, 5 June 1952: *Foreign Relations of the United States*, Vol. VII, Part 2, doc. 699.

26. For example, a full-page article in *Tägliche Rundschau* of 6 February 1952 on new economic policy, the Soviet Union, and the People's Democracies: analyzed in Chief of the Eastern Affairs Division, Berlin Element, *HICOG* (Barnes) to Department of State, 26 July 1952—*Foreign Relations of the United States*, Vol. VII, doc. 704.

27. Ibid, doc. 699.

28. 139th Meeting of the National Security Council, 8 April 1953: *Eisenhower Papers, Ann Whitman File, NSC, 4, 3* (Eisenhower Library, Abilene, Kansas).

29. For the state of the economy: A. Bergson, *The Real National Income of Soviet Russia Since 1928* (Cambridge, Mass.: Harvard University Press, 1961), 221. For the politics: R. Conquest, *Power and Politics in the USSR* (London: Macmillan, 1961), Chapter 10.

30. *Khrushchev Remembers* (London: Sphere Books, 1971), 356.

31. A. Gromyko, *Memories* (London: Hutchinson, 1989), 316. These comments do not appear in the original Russian edition.

32. N. Khrushchev, "Vospominaniya," *Ogonek*, No. 6 (February 1990):28.

33. *Cmd. 9080: Documents Relating to the Meeting of Foreign Ministers of France, the United Kingdom, the Soviet Union and the United States of America. Berlin, January 25–February 18, 1954* (London 1954), annex A.

34. Ibid., doc. 14.

35. Ibid., annex D.

36. Ibid., annex F.

37. Ibid., annex G.

38. Jackson (Berlin) to McCrum (White House), 10 February 1954: *Foreign Relations of the United States*, Vol. VII, Part 1, doc. 456.

39. Ibid.

40. 10 February 1954: *Cmd 9080*, doc. 24.

41. G. Bidault, *D'une résistance à l'autre* (Paris: Les Presses du Siècle, 1965), 192.

42. Joxe (Moscow) to Mendès France (Paris), 11 December 1954: *DDF, 1954* (Paris, 1987), doc. 437.

43. "Zayavlenie Sovetskogo Pravitel'stva po germanskomu voprosu," *Izvestiia*, 16 January 1955.

44. "Note de la sous-direction d'Europe orientale: Politique allemande de l'URSS," *DDF*, Vol. 2, doc. 127.

45. Molotov's letter of self-criticism, dated 16 September 1955, was published in *Kommunist* No. 14 (20 September 1955): 127–28. It referred directly only to his assessment of the level of development of socialism in the U.S.S.R. and in the People's Democracies. But it was taken to signify much more than that: see note 42. Also, by November CIA chief Allen Dulles offered the opinion "that the Russians now regarded Molotov as expendable." 265th Meeting, National Security Council, 10 November 1955: *Eisenhower Papers, Ann Whitman File, NSC, 7*.

46. "Plenum TsK KPSS 22-29 iyunya 1957g.: informatsionnoe soobshchenie," *Kommunisticheskaya Partiya Sovetskogo Soyuza v Rezolyutsiyakh i Resheniyakh S'ezdov, Konferentsii i Plenumov TsK*, Part IV, 1954–1960 (Moscow, 1960), 274–75.

47. Edgar Fauré (Paris) to François-Poncet (Germany), 11 February 1955: *DDF, 1955*, Vol. 1 (Paris, 1988), doc. 68.

48. *Organizatsiya varshavskogo dogovora 1955–1975: Dokumenty i Materialy* (Moscow, 1975), doc. 2.

49. See note 44.

50. Ibid.

51. *Pravda*, 7 November 1955.

52. Words spoken at a reception on 7 November 1955—Laloy (Moscow) to Pinay (Paris), 8 November 1955: *DDF*, doc. 351.

53. An interesting assessment of events by the CIA can be found in the minutes of the 305th Meeting of the National Security Council, 30 November 1956; *Eisenhower Papers, Ann Whitman File, NSC, 8*. All references to inflammatory broadcasts have been deleted from the documents in the archive.

54. *Istoriya vneshnei politiki SSSR*, Vol. 2, 1945–1980, ed. A. Gromyko et al. (Moscow, 1981), 244.

55. Ibid., 247.

56. *Izvestiia*, 28 November 1958. For the first full-length treatment of the resulting crisis: R. Slusser, *The Berlin Crisis of 1961* (Baltimore: Johns Hopkins University Press, 1973).

57. The text is quoted verbatim in G. Andreotti, *L'Urss vista da vicino* (Milan: Rizzoli, 1988), 37.

58. For a recent and vivid account by a former Berlin correspondent: N. Gelb, *The Berlin Wall: Kennedy, Khrushchev, and a Showdown in the Heart of Europe* (New York: Simon & Schuster, 1986).

59. For the German background: C. Kelleher, *Germany and the Politics of Nuclear Weapons* (New York: Columbia University Press, 1975).

60. For the background: G. Seaborg, *Kennedy, Khrushchev, and the Test Ban* (Berkeley: University of California Press, 1981).

61. S. Khrushchev, "Pensioner soyuznogo znacheniya," *Ogonek*, No. 42 (October 1988): 28.

62. Speech given on 14 September 1965: *Pravda*, 15 September 1965. This best illustrates adoption of a policy evident since October 1964.

63. *Pravda*, 8 December 1964.

64. Ibid., 22 January 1965. The initiative for the collective security proposals was attributed to the Poles: editorial, "Vo imya mira i bezopasnosti narodov," ibid.

65. Speech on the day of arrival in Moscow for talks. Ulbricht led a massive German delegation: *Pravda*, 18 September 1965.

66. Ibid., 13 March 1966.

67. Speech at an electoral meeting in Leningrad, 7 June 1966: *Pravda*, 8 June 1966.

68. See, for example, an article by the historian of the Franco-Russian alliance, Professor A. Manfred, "Traditsionnye uzy sotrudnichestva," *Pravda*, 18 June 1966. Also see the interview with Moscow-based French journalist and writer, Jean Cathala: J. Lacouture and R. Mehl, *De Gaulle ou l'éternel défi* (Paris: Seuil, 1988), 222.

69. The declaration was signed on 5 July but not published in *Pravda* until 9 July 1966.

70. Z. Mlynař, *Night Frost in Prague* (London: Hurst, 1980), 241. Mlynař was present at the encounter.

71. As soon as the new coalition made its intentions known, the Soviets publicly welcomed the change of heart: V. Nekrasov, "Sily sotsializma v nastuplenii," *Pravda*, 12 October 1969; then came Brezhnev's speech: *Pravda*, 28 October 1969.

72. Wehner's role is emphasized by Helmut Schmidt: H. Schmidt, *Menschen und Mächte* (Berlin: Siedler, 1987), 29.

73. *Cmnd. 6201*, doc. 154.

74. For the text of the final act: *Miscellaneous No. 17 (1977): Selected Documents Relating to Problems of Security and Cooperation in Europe, 1954–1977. Cmnd. 6932* (London, 1977) doc. 81.

75. For the background: R. Garthoff, *Détente and Confrontation* (Washington, D.C.: Brookings Institution, 1985).

76. See J. Haslam, *The Soviet Union and the Politics of Nuclear Weapons in Europe, 1969–1987* (Ithaca: Cornell University Press, 1990), chapters 4–5.

77. Schmidt, *Menschen*, 105.

78. Haslam, *The Soviet Union and the Politics of Nuclear Weapons*, chapters 5–6.

79. Schmidt, *Menschen*, 126.

80. Interview with Dashichev: *Der Spiegel*, 4 July 1988.

81. Haslam, *The Soviet Union and the Politics of Nuclear Weapons*, Chapter 7.

82. Speech, 25 February 1986: M. Gorbachev, *Izbrannye rechi i stat'i*, Vol. 3 (Moscow, 1987): 245 and 246.

83. Haslam, *The Soviet Union and the Politics of Nuclear Weapons*, Chapter 7.

84. *Vestnik Ministerstva Inostrannykh Del SSSR*, No. 16, 1 (September 1988):37–40.

85. *The Independent*, 13 May 1989.

86. See E. Hewett, *Reforming the Soviet Economy: Equality Versus Efficiency* (Washington, D.C.: Brookings Institution, 1988), 57.

87. Ibid., 7 June 1989.
88. "Vstrecha M.S. Gorbacheva i g. Kolya," *Izvestiia*, 11 February 1990.
89. Ibid.
90. *Pravda*, 21 February 1990.
91. Interview: *Izvestiia*, 19 February 1990.
92. *Pravda*, 8 February 1990.
93. Ibid., 7 February 1990.
94. *Izvestiia*, 19 February 1990.

14

Soviet Policy Toward China, 1969–1988

Allen S. Whiting

INTRODUCTION: PROBLEMS AND PROSPECTS

Lest one suspect the author of hubris in assuming a ready ability to determine the degree of "learning" in Soviet policy toward China during the period 1969–1988, several formidable obstacles and limitations must be acknowledged at the outset. These do not vitiate the effort, but they impose severe constraints on drawing firm conclusions.

The first problem is basically epistemological. How can we determine what has been learned from policy if we do not know what the Soviet goals or expectations of policy were beforehand? Illustrative of the difficulty in this effort is the frank admission by Charles E. Bohlen, "The development of [postwar] Soviet policy toward Germany is still shrouded in mystery. Although I attended most of the Council of Foreign Ministers meetings after the war, it was never clear to me what Soviet objectives were."[1] Bohlen started studying Russian in 1929, served in the Soviet Union in 1934–1935 and 1937–1940, acted as interpreter and note-taker for the Roosevelt-Stalin meetings at Teheran and Yalta, and interpreted for 10 days of Hopkins-Stalin exchanges in May 1945. He had access to all the available U.S. intelligence as well as close interaction with other Soviet specialists such as Loy Henderson and George Kennan. Writing his memoir in the early 1970s, Bohlen referred to subsequent scholarly monographs and acknowledged his own errors in the light of their research. Yet he still confessed an inability to determine Moscow's policy goals vis-à-vis Germany 25 years later.

Critics may make personal judgments about the poor perceptiveness of policy makers and State Department officers. But Bohlen's uncertainty about a question on which he witnessed so much interaction at the highest level cautions against academic inferences at long distance over the more elusive question of Soviet policy toward China. To anticipate briefly the starting point of our inquiry, 1969, at least two different policy goals have been attributed to Soviet behavior in that year of military buildup, border clashes, and threatened nuclear attack: (1) to deter Chinese bellicosity and risk-taking, (2) to force Beijing to negotiate border differences.[2] For some observers a "surgical strike" against Chinese nuclear weapons facilities was a serious option; for others, this was merely bluff to pressure Beijing. These goals are not necessarily exclusive; they could have constituted a minimum to maximum range of targeting. But depending on the analyst's choice of goal(s), Soviet military pressure succeeded, or so the Kremlin "learned"; alternatively it did not succeed, and a different lesson resulted.

This leads us to the problem of evidence in support of analysis. Nothing comparable to Khrushchev's memoirs has yet emerged for this period, *glasnost* to the contrary notwithstanding, apart from the question of such memoirs as source material. In the absence of direct evidence one is forced to inference from public statements and writings. This raises a third set of problems of which the most perplexing is one of linkage between publicists and policy makers. The term "publicist" refers to experts in various research institutes with varying status and proximity to policy. Whether such analysis reflects decisions or influences them has been seriously debated for the pre-Gorbachev period. On this point three different conclusions have been reached in highly specialized studies: (1) Soviet China scholars basically follow policy leads except when debate occurs at high levels, (2) the scholars are an important input to policy by providing explanatory concepts as well as information, and (3) Soviet writings address China as a surrogate for analysis of the Soviet Union.[3] Each of these interpretations has been argued at length on the available materials with obviously different implications for our inquiry.

This problem is not entirely insolvable. Interviews with Soviet specialists on China and a close reading of their work can provide clues as to their relative ranking in the policy elite. For many years M.S. Kapitsa enjoyed a unique role in government and academia as Moscow's top "China watcher."[4] He had served in the Soviet embassy in 1943–1946 and 1950–1952. In 1956 he became head of the Far East department in the Foreign Ministry and in that capacity accompanied Foreign Minister Andrei Gromyko to China for a critical meeting with Mao Zedong during the 1958 Quemoy bombardment. In 1982 he rose to deputy foreign minister. According to other China specialists, he cleared their writings before publication throughout the 1970s with full authority to delete or suppress entirely. Yet even his writings, some of which appear under alternate pseudonyms and others over his own name, must be mined meticulously with "Kremlinological" caution. Deliberate omission as well as commission can camouflage the true view of an author, an important clue in Kapitsa's case as we shall see. Thus a superbly insightful Soviet writer complained privately in the mid-1970s of being prevented from saying anything about the People's Liberation Army (PLA) in his analysis of Chinese politics, despite the PLA's salient role.

Another evidential problem concerns the decision-making process. Interviews and revealing press conferences were unknown before Mikhail Gorbachev's ascendancy. Informants, usually foreign, purported to provide "insider" knowledge of isolated policy discussions, but none of these bore on China policy. This leaves one at liberty to conceptualize alternative decision-making models, whether idiosyncratic, factional, bureaucratic, or rational actor. Each of these models has its scholarly support in extant monographs and essays, but none can be proven superior on the basis of firsthand evidence.

Finally there is the contextual problem. By assignment this essay has tunnel vision in focusing on a bilateral relationship in a multilateral environment. The limitations of time and space as well as the availability of other studies in this project preclude a detailed tracing of how Soviet perceptions of and policy toward the United States interacted with and impacted on China policy. But while reference to this factor will be made at the appropriate junctures, a more realistic approach would be comprehensive, embracing whatever contextual considerations must logically have arisen at the time, whether American, Japanese, Vietnamese, Indian, Middle Eastern, or European.

Having identified some of the negative aspects of our inquiry, we can proceed to the positive prospects for analysis. An invaluable resource is a doctoral dissertation by Chi Su, Soviet Image of and Policy Toward China: 1969–1979 (Columbia University, 1984). Dr. Su combines image as an organizational concept, cognitive psychology as a contributing discipline, content analysis as a nonquantitative tool, and political acumen for an insightful examination of Soviet publications and statements on China during the decade cited. My own intellectual orientation, reinforced by governmental experience, has been toward image and perception as shaping definition of the foreign policy problem, modified by organizational and bureaucratic behavior.[5] This differs from the more standard rational actor model, whether in a dyadic setting or subsumed in the larger systemic context. Thus both in terms of his conceptual approach and his careful research, Su's study provides the basis of much that follows without, however, my subscribing to all of his inferences and conclusions.

For some time now, scholars have wrestled with the problem of how empirically to determine images in inaccessible leadership groups. In addition there is the problem of demonstrating linkage between image and foreign policy decision. Images of China vary widely in the Soviet Union as elsewhere, whether by location, knowledge, age, or experience.[6] Thus, Kapitsa's implicit identification of Zhou Enlai as separate from "the Maoist clique" differed from authoritative analysts writing in *Kommunist* during the 1969 border crisis.[7] Presumably, however, his role in the foreign ministry had greater weight in shaping policy. Images are also subject to change over time as a function of the official line in addition to the objective reality of Chinese postures and actions. Again, Kapitsa's depiction of Zhou turned negative in a 1979 publication following the normalization of Sino-American relations.[8]

Apart from China specialists, a considerable degree of consensus, mainly negative, was evident during my visits and conversations in the 1970s. Many "inside" intellectuals shared a "yellow peril" image remarkably devoid of fact and logic. Thus in 1972 a nonspecialist in the Academy of Sciences privately admitted his fear of "China taking over our empty Siberia." This is the least likely avenue of Chinese expansionism given the forbidding environmental obstacles to mass settlement there. By contrast, that same week a historian of China who had taught in Beijing during the 1950s remarked enthusiastically, "Aren't the Chinese wonderful people?" Significantly, the latter remark was offered in a park, discussion in his office having been deliberately avoided because of likely surveillance.

These conversations illustrate the value of personal contact with Soviet Sinologists. Beginning in 1972 I was able to visit them every two or three years and many sought me out in Ann Arbor. The purpose of such contact varied on their part, depending on professional interest and personality, but as a rule they were trying to tap the views of American Sinologists with access to Washington. This provided possible insights to U.S. policy. Inevitably, however, these interactions reciprocally provided insights on their own views and the ambience of Sinology in the Soviet Union. This tacit quid pro quo furnished information not otherwise available although not necessarily verifiable or conclusive in itself.

Granted the lack of systematic empirical data, a brief review of Sino-Soviet developments prior to 1969, as perceived from Moscow, provides a general sense of the image or frame of reference within which the subsequent period was viewed as it unfolded. Following this prologue, chronological benchmarks in Soviet behavior will be focused on as reactions to external events or as new Soviet initiatives. These benchmarks will be examined according to what preceded them, what immediately triggered their actual occurrence, and what followed as consequences. This will structure our speculative scenario of what was learned, when, and with what results.

We can identify minimal or reward-punishment learning without much difficulty. When experience demonstrates failure and a change of verbal or behavioral policy follows, the consequence is visible and can be diagnosed as a simple cause-effect phenomenon, all other factors being constant. When these factors vary, however, as with a change in Soviet leadership, the analysis becomes highly inferential. Was it the individual leader's cognitive map, his choice of advisers, his political need to differ from his predecessor, or a collective change in the assessment of Beijing that occasioned a new policy in Moscow? Finally, did Soviet goals change altogether? Any, some, or all of the possibilities may be present to varying degree. Yet the evidence is inadequate to confirm or disconfirm alternative explanations.

In the absence of such evidence, the choice of reward-punishment learning, learning at the level of cognitive content, cognitive structure, or the basic change of goals as an explanation of change in verbal and behavioral policy will be made on the logic of the situation as intuited from public statements and private interaction with Soviet specialists on China. This highly subjective exercise invites disagreement, but space precludes the examination of alternative explanations and a rank-ordering of their plausibility.

The degree of detail offered to cover the two decades, 1969–1989, varies according to the importance of the development and the assumed knowledge on the part of the reader. A schematic approach could cover the period in much less space; a thorough study would require a book. Reordering the data according to theoretical and conceptual approaches would sacrifice necessary narrative for analysis. These compromises are identified here as an apologia for what follows.

PROLOGUE: PRE-1969

Sino-Soviet relations experienced wide swings from cooperation to confrontation during 1949–1969. Domination by Moscow and dependency by Beijing characterized the initial period, 1949–1953, personalized in the Stalin-Mao "elder brother–younger brother" interaction and Chinese conduct of the Korean War. Khrushchev's ascendancy shifted the respective political weight of the two leaderships. From 1954 through 1957 Moscow in effect bought Beijing's cooperation with far more generous terms of economic and military aid than previously, culminating in a critical nuclear-sharing agreement.

While it is impossible to determine Stalin's personal image of Mao, his general approach to the Chinese Communist movement resembled his handling of communist parties elsewhere. Control was a constant objective and internationalism was defined as total and unquestioning subordination to Soviet policy in addition to personal acknowledgment of Stalin's genius. However Mao's victory over Comintern appointees and the Chinese party's victory over the Kuomintang compelled Stalin to compromise somewhat his compulsive manipulation of the Chinese Communist Party (CCP) in order to secure its alliance against the United States.

Khrushchev's memoirs give a post hoc image of Mao that undoubtedly varies somewhat from that which he held during the two summits of 1954 and 1957. In addition to his own views, those of his colleagues probably differed from Stalin's with regard to both ends and means in the Sino-Soviet relationship. Domination was not to be demonstrated overtly and dependency was not to be crudely exploited. At least symbolic acknowledgment of the CCP's success necessitated concessions to Beijing's sensitivity over joint stock companies, the residual Soviet presence in Port Arthur, and the role of Mao in ideological innovation. However a continuity in cognitive structure consisted of an asymmetrical relationship offering Moscow ascendancy in the alliance. Whether in the denunciation of Stalin or the handling of East European dissidence, Khrushchev tended to act without seeking Mao's views in advance.

1958 was a benchmark year and so identified by Kapitsa both publicly and privately. It was then that Mao launched the disastrous Great Leap Forward in total disregard of Soviet economic advice and started the abortive bombardment of Quemoy without prior Soviet consultation. The former resulted in Khrushchev's withdrawal of all advisers and assistance in 1960. The bombardment caused him to terminate the far-reaching nuclear weapons agreement in 1959.[9] This agreement had been arrived at only in November 1957 to win Mao's backing at a critical point in Khrushchev's management of the international movement. Its provisions included the transfer of equipment as well as design for a gaseous diffusion plant, the outer construction of which was subsequently detected by overhead photography.[10] Nevertheless, according to Kapitsa who claims to have drafted the 1959 letter of termination, only one year after the initial agreement Mao's triggering of crisis in the Taiwan Strait prompted Khrushchev to end it.

That these unilateral Chinese actions aroused such shock and anger in Moscow warrants attention to their prior context in contributing to the Soviet image of Mao as decision maker during the decade 1959–1969. Between 1950 and 1960 approximately 8,000–10,000 Soviet specialists went to China, with another 1,200 from Eastern Europe.[11] Reciprocally, more than 38,000 Chinese trainees and students went to Soviet industrial enterprises, research centers, and institutions of higher education. Taking the broader period of 1949 to 1966, more than 110,000 Chinese students, undergraduate and graduate, completed courses of study or training in the Soviet Union. In addition to facilitating the construction or renovation of 256 major industrial projects, Moscow provided blueprints of machinery and equipment, licenses, technical manuals, and hundreds of thousands of books of science and technology. Some 140 Chinese scientists were trained at the Atomic Energy Institute in Dubna. Beijing's first atomic reactor and cyclotron were completed with Soviet assistance. Last but not least, the modernization of China's ground, air, and naval forces was wholly dependent on Soviet human and material aid.

This period was not one of plenty in the U.S.S.R., given the total devastation of European Russia in World War II. China's meager means of payment was in natural resources and foodstuffs. Moreover, China had no alternate source of assistance. The United States not only imposed a total economic embargo on its citizens but also prohibited American licensed products from being made available by other countries. While most Soviet material assistance came through loans rather than grants, the fact remains that Moscow provided the essential wherewithal for putting "New China" on its feet after nearly two decades of foreign invasion and civil war.

Yet despite this dependency and, from Moscow's view, Soviet generosity, in early 1958 Mao secretly announced his decision "to put self-reliance first and foreign aid second."[12] This suddenly lowered a barrier between Soviet advisers and their Chinese counterparts without explanation.[13] In like fashion, Mao began the bombardment of Quemoy in late August without having informed Khrushchev who, together with his minister of defense, had visited Beijing at the beginning of that month on other matters.[14] The first move flaunted Soviet advice; the second one preempted it, despite the risk of U.S. intervention and its attendant implications for the alliance. The Chinese attack on Indian forces in the disputed Himalayan frontier in 1962 further challenged Moscow's presumption of China's subordinate role in the political-military relationship.

Khrushchev's memoirs amply illustrate the anger and frustration caused by Mao's behavior, with virtually all of his criticism targeting the chairman but not his colleagues.[15] The image of an ungrateful and irresponsible ally was put privately by Kapitsa many years later in addressing the prospect of an emergent Sino-American alignment, "You'll see. They will squeeze you like a lemon and then throw you away when they have gotten what they want!" Beginning in 1960 Mao's polemical attacks against Khrushchev added insult to injury.

Khrushchev's style was idiosyncratic in its impulsiveness, but his policy at this juncture probably reflected consensus. By withdrawing all aid, Mao could be taught a lesson. If he refused to learn the limits imposed by dependency, his more pragmatic colleagues would certainly act on their best interests and force a change in Chinese behavior. Liu Shaoqi's titular headship of the government and Zhou Enlai's foreign policy expertise would accept subordination to Moscow at some point. But despite some compromising signals from Liu during his 1962 tour of the Soviet Union, no substantive change occurred. Instead, war with India later that year patently signaled disregard for Soviet interests in the subcontinent.

Nor did Beijing's polemics cease with Khrushchev's political demise in 1964, another benchmark year with two key Chinese developments. In July Mao voiced support to a Japanese delegation for demanding the return of four Kurile islands. These were occupied by the Red Army after World War II despite their lying outside the chain ceded under the terms of the Yalta agreement. But worse, he also elaborated on China's own territorial grievances, asserting that the vast area from Lake Baikal to the Kamchatka Peninsula, specifically including Vladivostok, had been seized by czarist imperialism, noting, "We have not yet settled this account."[16] Moscow protested the remarks but won no retraction. Then in October China detonated its first atomic bomb two days after Khrushchev's ouster.

Zhou's Moscow visit in the aftermath of the leadership change came to naught. However the anticipated increase in U.S. involvement in Vietnam prompted one more Soviet effort and in February 1965 Premier Alexei Kosygin conferred with Mao after having visited Hanoi. During that visit U.S. bombers struck North Vietnam, ostensibly in retaliation for the attack on U.S. military personnel and equipment at Pleiku but clearly as the long-threatened start of hitting the North until it stopped supporting guerrillas in the South. According to a reliable report, Mao dismissed Kosygin's proposal for joint aid to Hanoi as unnecessary. When Kosygin protested that the United States would bomb the North, Mao retorted that the Vietnamese could take it and pointed to the devastation of North Korea compared with that country's condition only a dozen years later.[17] If Kosygin and his colleagues thought Khrushchev had mismanaged Mao, the tenor of this conversation challenged that belief. The image of Mao's irresponsibility and perhaps irrationality was strengthened, although hope remained with Liu and Zhou. Indeed, Zhou reportedly agreed with Japanese Communist Party leaders on the need for joint Sino-Soviet support of Hanoi in mid-1965, only to be directly contradicted by Mao in their subsequent interview with the chairman.[18]

Then in August 1966 Mao's Red Guards began the Great Proletarian Cultural Revolution with massive demonstrations, sporadic violence, and harassment of East European diplomats.[19] In January 1967 the People's Liberation Army came under attack as did increasing numbers of top officials, Liu being denounced as "China's Khrushchev." While Chinese students demonstrated in the streets of Moscow, Red Guards ringed the Soviet embassy in Beijing for day and night bombardment with loudspeakers. As Soviet diplomats and their families finally fled the capital, they were physically assaulted en route to the plane. By midsummer dozens of cities were plunged into virtual anarchy with armed battles between rival Red Guard gangs. Meanwhile the PLA divided in its support of the movement and at the key city of Wuhan verged on civil war.

This recapitulation of developments is necessary to reconstruct the pre-1969 framework within which Soviet perceptions of and policy toward China emerged. Whether one adopts a rational actor model or more realistically introduces psychological and emotional variables, it is safe to say that at a minimum, the cognition of Mao was as a potentially dangerous neighbor. The degree to which his seeming irrationality was shared by his colleagues may have been debated. But Mao's ascendancy in 1966 and thereafter literally removed all of his former colleagues from power with the singular exception of Zhou Enlai. In their place Mao's wife and colleagues, subsequently dubbed the "Gang of Four," ran rampant over the entire range of domestic and foreign policy through 1969 and to some extent until Mao's death in 1976.

To anticipate somewhat, by the summer of 1969 U.S. intelligence analysts calculated that, at a minimum, the number of Soviet divisions opposite China had doubled from their pre-1965 level of roughly a dozen and were on the way to triple that amount.[20] Moreover the readiness of forces in Siberia had been appreciably increased. Three airfields had been built in the Mongolian People's Republic accompanied by five divisions of armor and infantry. Northeast China was ringed by 500 nautical mile, nuclear-capable missiles.

The extent of this military buildup suggests that it was decided on well before 1969, although it accelerated that spring when deployments closed the Trans-Siberian Railroad to foreigners for two months. Formidable logistical obstacles confronted those charged with laying down the infrastructure for a permanent force of this magnitude and complexity given the climate, terrain, and absence of communications in much of the region. This necessitated a major effort committed over time.

As early as January 1967 Mao referred to Chinese awareness of an increase in Soviet forces. It seems most likely that the increase began as a result of the aforementioned events in 1964–1965 and accelerated with the Cultural Revolution chaos in 1966–1968. In particular, the type of Red Guard aggressiveness that occurred on the borders of Hong Kong and Vietnam in 1967 may have been paralleled by similar activity along the Sino-Soviet border. At its extremity this border lay eight time zones away from Moscow's European power base and separated a population of some 70 million in Manchuria from less than 10 percent that number in the entire Soviet Far East. In addition to this objective reality, military worst-case threat estimates would have been consistent with traditional Russian overinsurance against offensive contingencies as well as self-serving for budgetary increases.

Any one of the 1964–1968 events alone might not have occasioned serious concern in Moscow, but their concatenation, from Mao's grandiose definition of "lost territory" to the near-total breakdown of institutionalized civilian and military authority, would have justified strengthening Soviet defenses along the 4,500-mile border. But Kapitsa's 1969 volume, treated below, went beyond earlier analyses of Maoist policy to stress its nationalistic aspects, which, in conjunction with Chinese demands over allegedly disputed territory, raised specific questions of Beijing's intent.

To be sure, according to conventional military calculations, whatever the intent, Chinese capability would seem wholly inadequate against a Soviet superiority in all categories of weaponry, most notably nuclear. But however much prudence rather than paranoia explains Soviet military behavior down to 1969, events in that year triggered a much more alarmist response in Moscow. The cumulative incremental impact of developments in the previous three years combined with the shock of actual conflict on the border to basically alter the image of Mao as a serious threat for whom a serious counterthreat was required.

1969: TO THE BRINK?
SELECTIVE CHRONOLOGY I: SINO-SOVIET 1969–1970

January	Moscow warns Beijing it will use force against further local challenges to Soviet control of islands in Ussuri River
March 2	Firefight on Damansky Island (Zhenbao) with 31 Soviet dead, 14 wounded, apparently from Chinese ambush
15	Second Damansky clash with 12 Soviet officers and non-commissioned officers, including colonel, killed, apparently Soviet initiated
29	Moscow proposes "consultations" on border, begun in 1964 but suspended by Beijing, to be resumed soonest
April 11	Moscow repeats proposal, names April 15 to start
June 7	Brezhnev makes first reference to collective security pact for Asia; Gromyko amplifies to Supreme Soviet June 10
June 18–August 8	Sino-Soviet joint commission on river navigation meets on shipping, signs protocol, agrees to meet in 1970
1970	
June	Soviet bomber wing transfers to Central Asia from East Europe, conducts mock exercises against targets in northwest China
Summer	Clashes occur along northeast and western border sectors, most serious in Xinjiang, apparently at Soviet initiative

August   Soviet soundings on reaction to surgical strike against
                Chinese nuclear facilities reported by U.S., Eastern European,
                and Indian sources
September 3   Ho Chi Minh dies, will calls for "restoration of unity on
                Marxism-Leninism and proletarian internationalism"
        11   Kosygin diverts en route home from Ho funeral to meet
                Zhou at Beijing airport; Chinese allege verbal agreement,
                denied by Moscow; no further major clashes reported
                thereafter

Soviet analysts logically had various alternative hypotheses they could have advanced to explain the initial Damansky incident: (1) local obstreperousness without higher authorization, (2) regional radicalism countering central authority, (3) Lin Biao seeking to enhance his power as PLA leader in the forthcoming April CCP congress, (4) a Mao-Lin effort to exploit anti-Soviet sentiment for unity at the CCP congress, the first since 1956, (5) a demonstration of defiance to deter an alleged Soviet threat voiced by Zhou after the Czech invasion, and (6) an irrational adventuristic action intended to mobilize the population for testing Soviet resolve on territorial differences. The last hypothesis characterized Soviet official and mass media statements in the following months. Differences arose describing the degree of unity in Beijing, with Kapitsa notably attributing a more moderate position to Zhou, but the main actor was uniformly identified as Mao.

Likewise a repertoire of responses lay at hand, depending on the explanation of Chinese behavior: (1) minimum public attention with a maximum concentration of force at so-called disputed points along the border to deter any repetition, (2) private demarches in Beijing through Soviet and other channels to query Chinese intention, (3) a punitive counterblow at Damansky Island without publicity, (4) the same action with low-key publicity for "Red Guard provocations," (5) a combination of local military counterblow and high-level diplomatic demarche, and (6) in addition to (5) a nationwide alert to the threat posed by an irrational, adventuristic China. As reflected in the above chronology, the final alternative characterized Moscow's main response. Again, however, the implications of Kapitsa's position called for diplomatic probes of leadership unity and intent, a course that eventually surfaced in September.

Kapitsa's work was sent to be typeset July 1, 1969, and signed to the press on August 22. Its timing and the author's status as the highest China specialist advising the Kremlin warrants attention to his subtle presentation of Zhou as a better hope for Sino-Soviet relations than Mao. Thus during the first major policy crisis, the 1958 bombardment of Quemoy, Mao is reported as telling Gromyko (in Kapitsa's presence), "It is impossible in a certain sense to not love war, one must prepare for it and prepare the people."[21] These remarks came amid "the senseless acts of the PRC [which] created a threat of military confrontation." Zhou, however, used diplomacy in reopening Sino-American ambassadorial talks when the crisis peaked. On the more immediate and sensitive issue of the border dispute, Kapitsa recalled Zhou's 1960 press conference in Katmandu in which he said, "On the map there are insignificant differences. It will be very easy to settle them peacefully."[22] By contrast, the "nationalistic, adventuristic thrust of Mao Zedong and his circle" prevailed over "the healthy internationalist forces" in the Chinese party.

But Kapitsa did not determine Moscow's basic approach. The choice of a worst-case explanation and reaction created a state of war-mindedness in the Soviet Union that intensified through spring and summer as the postures struck by both capitals mutually reinforced perceptions of each other's belligerency. A few examples suffice to illustrate this phenomenon, without exhausting the evidence that is readily available elsewhere.

Soviet television coverage of the first Damansky clash featured grim shots of mutilated bodies together with graphic accounts of the alleged Chinese attack and attendant atrocities. Evgenii Yevtushenko penned a pseudo-epic poem that luridly evoked images of the historic Mongol invasion with reference to "hordes" whereby "a heavy hand creeps across our border, the Chinese God-khan."[23] Andrei Voznesenskii echoed the reference, speaking of "Genghis-hog."[24] At a more authoritative level, Brezhnev addressed an international communist conference in June, recalling Mao's celebrated 1957 speech wherein the chairman had disparaged concern over nuclear war by noting that even if half the world perished, half would survive.

This was Brezhnev's first and last reference to Mao's remark, but it appeared in numerous less authoritative statements as purported evidence of Mao's irrationality.[25] A *Kommunist* editorial signed to the press less than two weeks after the second Damansky clash declared, "This bloody provocation on the Soviet-Chinese border, which has brought casualties to both sides, is a vivid illustration of the Maoists' adventurist and militarist policy, for whose sake—as Mao Zedong has said more than once— he is prepared to sacrifice half the population of China and even the majority of the world's population." At the same time this alarming analysis was released, the more widely read magazine, *New Times*, underscored the deliberateness of Chinese aggressiveness by quoting foreign press reports to the effect that Lin Biao as minister of defense, "acting on orders from Mao Zedong," had arrived in the border area before the second clash to direct the fighting himself.

The leitmotif of Soviet statements throughout the spring focused on "nationalism" as a key ingredient in Chinese behavior, extending its manifestations back to Chiang Kai-shek and Feng Yuxiang in the 1920s and culminating as "the alpha and the omega" of Maoism. An authoritative analysis in *Kommunist* charged that the March fighting resulted from a "delayed action mine" that the Maoist leadership had long waited to detonate in pursuit of its nationalist ambitions. In late June, 10 days after the international communist conference had ended, the Communist Party of the Soviet Union (CPSU) Central Committee amended its resolution warning against "revisionism, dogmatism, and left sectarianist adventurism" to read "revisionism, dogmatism, and *nationalism*" (emphasis added).

In the context of Mao's earlier allusion to territory seized by czarist imperialism for which the "account" had not been settled, the Chinese insistence that Moscow acknowledge that these territorial transfers had resulted from "unequal treaties" sounded a threatening note. Beijing's specific demand that Soviet forces withdraw from "disputed areas" as a precondition for negotiations likewise opened a possible Pandora's box. Thus the new emphasis on Chinese "nationalism" raised worrisome implications, practical as well as emotional. An additional dimension of threat lay in the attribution of irrationality, signaled in the term *adventurism* used in the initial *Kommunist* editorial cited above.

These concerns won reinforcement with the ninth CCP congress, which met from April 1–24. Soviet analysis showed a clean sweep of the 1956 Central Committee of which only 18 percent survived, replaced largely by a mixture of military personnel and newly rising Maoists. The elevation of "Mao Zedong Thought" as state ideology and the enshrinement of "Marxism-Leninism-Maoism" committed the CCP to following the chairman's words, regardless of their rationality. Lin Biao's political report and the concluding communiqué identified struggle with Soviet revisionism as a main line of policy.

Soviet proposals for "consultations" on the eve of and during the congress almost certainly were made for the record and not with serious expectation of a positive response. A *Kommunist* editorial before the congress convened warned against any hope that "opponents within the country" could prevail against "the military-bureaucratic regime" of the "Mao Zedong group." The next issue declared flatly, "The practice of recent years shows that all efforts at a compromise agreement with Mao Zedong's group, even on specific questions, have proved fruitless." The week after the congress ended, a major *Pravda* article anathematized Maoist policy as "a dangerous force . . . which is prepared—if given the chance—to confer on mankind not tens nor hundreds but tens and hundreds of millions of graves." In response, "this force must be made to feel that not a single one of its actions will go unpunished. Right from the beginning, right from the very first step."

Beyond these and numerous other open indicators of war-mindedness were secret moves cited above, including the accelerated military buildup and the deployment of bombers for exercising against targets in northwest China, the location of key nuclear weapons production facilities.[26] These facilities were vulnerable to conventional bombing and lacked any protective screen of fighter bases or surface-to-air missiles. A credible strike mounted from Central Asia could terminate at bases in Mongolia with assurance of sufficient damage to thwart China's growing nuclear capability.

It remains a moot point whether this contingency was made feasible for final consideration as an option in Moscow or merely to pressure Beijing to enter negotiations on the border. The June activity was certain to be detected by Chinese as it was by U.S. intelligence. Soviet queries to foreign diplomats in the following months concerning their government's reaction to a possible Soviet strike could simply have added to a war of nerves as these queries became known to Beijing.[27] But perhaps military circles argued seriously for the need to exploit this opportunity to perform "nuclear castration" with a surgical strike before Beijing acquired an eventual second-strike capability.

This raises the basic question: What decisions were made with what objective at what point in time? In purely objective terms, the PLA posed no offensive threat to the Soviet Union. It was deplorably weak in Xinjiang, with no railroad extending beyond the capital of Urumchi, a weak road network vulnerable to washouts, and little infrastructure to sustain prolonged action. Mongolia was not a prize worth the effort, serving as a convenient buffer between Siberia and China. Northeast China admittedly pressed on the Soviet periphery of the Maritime Province region, essential to Soviet power in the Pacific. But a ring of nuclear weapons, tactical and strategic, surely deterred any attack in this region. Finally, the Vietnam War still raged, and Taiwan remained a potential threat. This latter combination tied down a major portion of China's air and ground forces even though Washington had begun deescalation and Beijing had withdrawn its forces from North Vietnam accordingly. The PLA's outmoded weaponry would require reliance on vastly superior numbers against more capable Soviet equipment, yet no such massive redeployment was under way before 1969.

But purely objective calculations do not necessarily determine threat estimates. Taking into consideration the long interaction of the Soviet leadership with its opposite number, weight must be given to the cumulative effect of the previous decade as undermining confidence in Chinese rationality in risk-taking. The cautionary military buildup prior to 1969 testifies to this concern. Moreover a qualitative as well as quantitative shift in Soviet statements and Soviet behavior subsequent to the first Damansky clash suggests that it prompted an urgent upgrading of the threat estimate, which required prompt responses at all levels. The result was a change in the Soviet cognitive structure of the Chinese leadership.

Dr. Su notes the "disarray" in Soviet Sinology from 1960–1966, evidenced by the sharp drop in articles and books dealing with contemporary China compared to the halcyon 1950s.[28] No center of Chinese studies existed, nor did any authoritative periodical. Establishment of the Institute of Far East Studies in 1966 relied on a new cohort group of China specialists who had served in Beijing during the stormy 1960s. A Soviet variant of McCarthyism beclouded those who had prevailed during the relatively harmonious years of economic assistance.[29] The effect immobilized the "soft" approach in favor of the "hard." The net result left analysis of China in a state of transition just when the most turbulent and perplexing period of the Cultural Revolution emerged.

At this juncture other problems on the Soviet foreign policy agenda took priority over contentious China. U.S.–Soviet relations contained critical contradictions. On one hand, the Vietnam War demanded Soviet support, risking indirect clashes with Washington.[30] On the other hand, the nascent arms control relationship, begun under Kennedy, remained potentially promising under Johnson. Czechoslovakia posed a further complication for the U.S.–Soviet relationship and was of major importance in itself. The "Prague spring" of 1968 culminated in the Warsaw Pact invasion later that year. In this general context, China was troublesome but not of the greatest immediate concern. The Damansky clash and Beijing's treatment of it moved China to the top priority, presented in stereotypical "yellow peril" imagery.

The resultant policy contained negative as well as positive constructs. War should be avoided but not at all costs. On the contrary, no symbolic or substantive concessions should be made lest they invite further Chinese demands and perhaps further adventurism. Instead, a political standfast should accompany military rebuffs and, if necessary, military punishment limited to border areas. At the same time Beijing should be reminded of more far-reaching destruction that lay at hand.

As a minimum objective, the total policy aimed at reducing Chinese risk-taking. At the intermediate level, hope lay in some form of intermittent communication, whether through the joint navigation committee or "consultations" on the border, to minimize miscalculation. Kapitsa's book implicitly placed this hope in Zhou Enlai. The maximum goal of forcing a Chinese backdown on border demands was articulated but with low expectation of achievement so long as Mao remained in charge.

Increasing mutual intransigence and continued border clashes marked the summer as the post-Damansky decisions were implemented. Chinese overt behavior struck a defiant note with a nationwide mobilization to "dig tunnels deep and store grain," manifest in a labyrinth of hand-dug shelter complexes emerging under the major cities. Covert Chinese purchases of large earth-moving equipment and blood plasma on a cash-down, urgent delivery basis bespoke of serious planning for possible war.[31] Airfield construction in northwest China and the redeployment of air and ground units from their Vietnam War locus in southern areas underscored Beijing's preparation for the worst.

Suddenly the death of Ho Chi Minh provided a deus ex machina in the drama of Sino-Soviet confrontation. The degree of tension between the two sides was demonstrated by Zhou Enlai's refusal to attend ceremonies in Hanoi with the Soviet delegation, resulting in his arrival and departure in advance of the final rites. This, together with the fact that Kosygin's plane headed home before it suddenly diverted to Beijing for the airport rendezvous with Zhou, suggests that, in the familiar phrase, the two sides were eyeball to eyeball when one side—the Chinese—blinked.[32]

Parenthetically it is worth noting that Hanoi's plea for unity was more than funereal rhetoric. Conflict between the Soviet Union and China would remove the only deterrent against a U.S. invasion of the North, namely the possibility of Chinese intervention as in Korea. Whether the Vietnamese pursued this plea by acting as intermediaries cannot be determined. However, the timing of Zhou's presence in Hanoi and the subsequent diversion of Kosygin's aircraft from its original goal of Moscow to Beijing suggests some role for Ho's colleagues.

The secrecy and ambiguity surrounding the Zhou-Kosygin exchange preclude any firm conclusions therefrom. But the striking absence of any further reports of border clashes suggests that at a minimum the two men agreed to stop at the brink with a mutual standdown at the border. By confining talks to the airport and by omitting even the exchange of a memorandum of conversation, much less a joint statement, the official nature of the meeting was finessed. Nevertheless its reported duration of three and a half hours provided ample opportunity for clarifying the situation so as to reduce the immediate level of confrontation.

The meeting provided a logical time for the Kremlin to have assessed its policy up to that point. From its perspective the results were decidedly mixed. First and foremost, none of the military pressures, including nuclear blackmail, had changed Beijing's basic posture. Had it not been for Ho's death, there is no indication the Chinese would have dropped any of their preconditions or demands and entered into "consultations" or "negotiations." But second, military pressure had prevailed over Mao's "adventurism." The aggressive posture at Damansky and admonitions to "dig tunnels deep" had faded into verbal attacks on the "new czars." Zhou's willingness to cool the border confrontation showed that force had won the minimal objective of reducing Chinese risk-taking and opened the possibility of further diplomatic probes for a genuine modus vivendi.

On September 5, Washington suddenly signaled its opposition to a Sino-Soviet conflict that, under the circumstances, could only be construed as opposition to a Soviet attack on China.[33] The crowded context of that signal, coming as it did at the crescendo of Soviet nuclear warnings and on the eve of Ho's death, made it unlikely to have received exhaustive analysis or alarmist interpretations. Nevertheless, it did resonate with expressed apprehension over a coincidence in Sino-American anti-Soviet interests that might draw Beijing and Washington together and hence deserves separate attention.

SELECTIVE CHRONOLOGY II: U.S.–SOVIET 1969

April 3	Ambassador Anatoly Dobrynin queries National Security Council adviser re press reports of China policy review
22	Ambassador Beam gives Nixon letter to Kosygin omitting China reference, pointedly adds oral disclaimer of exploiting Sino-Soviet differences
July 21	State Department eases China trade and travel limits
August 2	Nixon hints softer China policy to Ceaucescu; Romanian leader promises to act as go-between
8	Secretary of State Rogers in Canberra stresses "opening up China" policy through "liberalized" trade, travel, and seeking "to remove irritants in our relations and to help remind people on mainland China of our historic friendship"
18	Mid-level State Department officer queried at Soviet embassy at luncheon on U.S. reaction should Soviets hit Chinese nuclear facilities
27	Central Intelligence Agency head Richard Helms background-briefs diplomatic correspondents re Moscow sounding Eastern Europeans on reaction to Soviet strike at Chinese nuclear plants
September 5	Undersecretary of State Elliott Richardson addresses American Political Science Association convention in Washington, declares "long run improvement in [China] relations in our own national interest" and declares "United States could not fail to be deeply concerned with escalation of [Sino-Soviet] quarrel into massive breach of peace." It is impossible to determine how much and at what level these developments impacted on the Kremlin consciousness, much less to what extent it affected calculations

prior to Kosygin's meeting with Zhou. Kapitsa's reference to a 1963 statement by Zhou purported to show an inclination toward the West. His citing A. Doak Barnett's 1966 proposal that the United States seek a constructive engagement with China hinted at Beijing's option.[34] As a standard intelligence item, Soviet monitoring of Sino-American relations had been a regular requirement, manifest in bugging the ambassadorial talks in Warsaw during the 1960s and remarks to U.S. officials.[35] But however routine may have been the earlier effort, developments in 1969 should have raised this priority of attention. The Nixon-Ceaucescu exchange in Bucharest may well have been picked up by Soviet intelligence. Certainly the Richardson remarks, singled out for front-page coverage in *The New York Times*, deserved special analysis in Moscow, although Kosygin's departure for Hanoi may have missed their immediate transmission.

The American factor aside, it seems reasonable to infer that by September 11 the Soviet leadership concluded it had no alternative but to stop its escalation of threatening behavior lest the border confrontation get out of hand. The Chinese had refused to back down, regardless of the risks. Reward-punishment learning as a result of experience modified tactics but nothing more. At the same time there was less cause for alarm. The six months since Damansky had failed to show greater Chinese aggressiveness. Meanwhile the domestic turbulence had been checked for more than a year, with the PLA virtually running the country. Last but not least important, Zhou remained as the one presumably sober and sophisticated voice in a regime dominated by Cultural Revolution cohorts. His meeting with Kosygin therefore provided some assurance against a worst-case eventuality. Thus a policy of calculated pressure and confrontation appeared both necessary and sufficient as a basic strategy. Its effectiveness could be tested by diplomacy, but no concessions would be made lest the appetite of Chinese chauvinism be whetted.

1969–1971: DETERRENCE PLUS DIPLOMACY
SELECTIVE CHRONOLOGY III: SINO-SOVIET 1969–1971

1969

September	Soviets propose nonaggression pledge; rejected
October 7	Chinese reply to Soviet June 13 note; agree to border talks
October 20	Border talks begin
December 14	Border talks end without agreement

1970

January 4	Border talks resume
April 14	Border talks end without agreement
July 8	Soviets propose nonaggression pact; no reply
October 10	New Soviet ambassador arrives, first since 1967
November 24	New Chinese ambassador arrives, first since 1967; Sino-Soviet trade agreement, first since 1967

1971

January 15	Soviets propose nonuse of force treaty; rejected after negotiation
March 21	Zhou-Ilychev meeting
April	Soviets propose reaffirmation of 1950 treaty; rejected

These developments make the period from late 1969 to the end of 1971 a time of transition in Soviet policy marked by renewed diplomatic efforts in the wake of unprecedented tensions and before the virtual freeze that followed. The Zhou-Kosygin exchange was the first summit meeting since the abortive Mao-Kosygin talk in 1965. As such it doubtless occasioned another Kremlin review of ends as well as means to be pursued. One possible token of this review came on October 27 when Brezhnev, for the first time in three years, referred to "Comrade" Zhou Enlai in a public address.[36]

Although neither side reversed its position, some modification occurred during this time. Each continued to accuse the other of threatening war and each strengthened its military confrontation. However, the tone of shrill urgency that had attended the border clashes lessened, and no publicity attended whatever incidents may have actually occurred. Meanwhile Soviet proposals and channels of communication opened up the possibility of secret diplomacy avoiding miscalculation.

As we have already noted, the Zhou-Kosygin meeting produced no communiqué, and both capitals subsequently differed sharply on what had actually happened.[37] They concurred, however, on the absence of any document for reference. Disagreement on the outcome may have resulted from the nature of the conversation. No member of Kosygin's party was an expert on the border dispute in particular or even on Sino-Soviet relations in general. Given the pressures attending this unanticipated summit, worsened by possible fatigue and jet lag, it is likely that the Soviet premier misspoke in response to Zhou's deft assertions. Then, when Kosygin returned to Moscow, his colleagues "corrected" whatever "oral understanding" may have been reached.

Nevertheless it cannot be a coincidence that border clashes stopped, at least in public reference, and that border "talks" began. Each side compromised to make the latter possible. Moscow dropped its insistence on "negotiations," settling for the lesser term while unilaterally describing subsequent meetings by its original preferred nomenclature. Reciprocally, Beijing dropped its demand that the czarist "unequal treaties" be so acknowledged as a precondition for border discussions. Most important, perhaps, was the simple fact of summitry itself, providing the most authoritative and direct communication at the most critical juncture in the relationship.

Given the agenda of issues confronting the two leaders, three and a half hours of discussion could hardly be expected to produce accord after a decade of acrimony and six months of recurrent firefights. Not only was this time reduced to half by the needs of interpreting, but no known staff talks or exchanges of proposals preceded the encounter. Afterward Beijing summarized its position with written proposals on September 18 and October 6, the gist of which being revealed in its statement of October 7. Notably, that statement was the first official response to Moscow's note of June 13.

According to a much later *Pravda* account, the two sides agreed to restore ambassadorial relations, to expand trade, to seek a border settlement in the process of normalizing relations, to avoid border clashes, and to settle disputes through negotiations. The first two points could be easily accomplished as the above chronology shows, although these nonsubstantive steps took another year. The remaining two points, however, constituted the essence of Chinese demands as spelled out in Beijing's statement: (1) both sides "first of all" should agree on provisional measures for maintaining the status quo along the border, for avoiding conflict, and for disengagement of forces and (2) both sides must withdraw from, or refrain from entering, all the areas where disagreement existed on maps exchanged during the 1964 negotiations.

Neither side published definitive versions of the 1964 maps. General references, however, identified three portions of territory alleged by the Chinese as "disputed": (1) islands in the Ussuri River lying to the west of the *thalweg* or main channel, (2) Bear Island, adjacent to Khabarovsk at the junction of the Ussuri and Amur rivers, and (3) the so-called Pamir knot adjoining the U.S.S.R., Afghanistan, and China. These points together with lesser parts of the border in Central Asia are estimated to total only some 33,000 square kilometers.[38] However, except for the Ussuri islands, their importance was a function of location, not of size. Later conversations with Kapitsa and other officials made clear that, while the Ussuri *thalweg* was easily conceded together with Damansky and the associated islands, neither Bear Island nor the Pamir area could be turned over to China because of military sensitivity. Under these circumstances, no Soviet agreement to withdraw from "disputed" areas prior to negotiations was possible, nor could any subsequent compromise be countenanced, at least at that time.

Soviet diplomacy perforce sought to finesse the territorial question in proposals to China, hence the recourse to "nonaggression" treaties. Conversely the Chinese adamantly refused to accept abstract accords that did not specifically address the border. Although the Soviet nonuse of force proposal evoked a semblance of negotiations, Beijing's standard position was either refusal to respond or outright rejection of Moscow's initiatives.

Nevertheless once the 1969 confrontation eased, both sides maintained strict secrecy on key aspects of the relationship. Moscow did not reveal its proposals until years later and then only piecemeal. Border talks remained closely held. No authoritative account of the unique Zhou-Ilychev meeting "leaked" from either capital. Ilychev's role as deputy foreign minister and head of the Soviet border delegation made this a potentially important meeting. Its late-night occurrence after a banquet for a Nepalese delegation together with its reported four-hour duration suggested a substantive exchange, yet its content could only be surmised.

In sum, Soviet diplomacy maintained a proper public posture, however unable it was in private to moderate the Chinese position. This suggests a serious effort beyond establishing a record of self-justification. Seriousness is also suggested by comparison with the publicity, timing, and content of subsequent initiatives. In short, the proposals of 1969–1971 emptied the coffers of compromise, Moscow's later offers basically repeating these earlier items.

Curiously Moscow's hopes seem to have peaked in the first half of 1971 only to disappear altogether thereafter. Two factors may account for this admittedly modest variation in the overall posture of pressure against Beijing: domestic developments in China and developments in Sino-American relations. These, in combination with negative reaction to its proposals, apparently caused the Kremlin to conclude that containment without compromise was the only recourse, thereby completing the cognitive restructuring that had begun in March 1969.

Soviet uncertainty over Chinese politics in 1970 was reflected by journal articles on the subject, which fell from 24 in 1969 to 2 in 1970, rising to 11 in 1971 and 49 in 1972.[39] The complicating factor probably was renewed struggle between moderates and radicals after the ninth congress in 1969. However the trend was viewed optimistically in 1971, according to a *Kommunist* article of July. It tempered the aforementioned 1969 analysis when "Mao Zedong's group" had "succeeded in overcoming resistance" by opponents. Now the writer declared, "The opposition that the Maoists encounter in the implementation of their plans testifies to the unceasing resistance offered by the healthy forces of the CCP. The genuine Chinese

Communists find themselves in a grave situation now, but they do exist, and evidently there are a good many of them."[40]

Understandably, whoever comprised the "healthy forces" remained unnamed. Any such identification could only have hurt the prospects of "the genuine Chinese Communists," given the overt anti-Soviet posture of "the Maoists." But high on the list, which could not have been long in any case, would have been Zhou Enlai. Kapitsa, the most authoritative and influential China specialist, implicitly favored Zhou in his writings. His major work, put to press in July 1969, had repeatedly attacked "the Maoists" by their words and actions while citing Zhou, almost without exception, in implicitly positive terms. This contrasted with *Kommunist* articles of the time. Given Kapitsa's role, he probably argued for diplomatic probes such as the Zhou-Ilychev meeting.

Yet just when Chinese domestic politics appeared promising for Soviet diplomacy, the American factor intervened, with Zhou playing a prominent role. The complications for Soviet analysis of linkages between Chinese domestic and foreign policy increased with the death of Lin Biao in September 1971, after his alleged plot to assassinate Mao aborted. Whatever else was involved, this removed a likely opponent to détente with Washington, thereby strengthening Zhou as well as Mao in the effort. Thus a long-standing concern suddenly became prominent with the announcement of Henry Kissinger's secret trip to Beijing in July 1971 and the simultaneous public scheduling of President Richard Nixon's visit in February 1972.

SELECTIVE CHRONOLOGY IV: U.S.–SOVIET 1969–1971

1969

October 20	Dobrynin warns Nixon not to exploit Sino-Soviet tension; Nixon agrees but says China not permanent enemy
December 11	Ambassador Stoessel invited to Chinese embassy in Warsaw, for first time; State Department terms talk "cordial"
18	Kissinger press briefing calls Chinese "great people . . . 25 percent of human race . . . cannot be ignored . . . we are prepared to engage in a dialogue with them"
22	United States ends destroyer patrol in Taiwan Strait

1970

January 21	Dobrynin queries Kissinger on Sino-American meeting at U.S. embassy in Warsaw, hopes United States not "using" China as military threat
October 26	Nixon toasts "People's Republic of China" first time at Ceausescu dinner

1971
February 25	President's foreign policy report uses PRC title
March 13	Nixon lifts all passport restrictions for PRC travel
April 6	Beijing invites U.S. ping-pong team
13	Kissinger tells Soviet chargé United States relaxing trade embargo for PRC though still stronger than for Soviet Union
14	Zhou calls ping-pong team visit "new page in relations of American and Chinese people"
July 18	Kissinger secret trip revealed, Nixon 1972 visit to Beijing announced

This chronology shows a careful monitoring of and cautionary response to U.S. moves toward China but no undue alarm in 1969–1970. The resumption of Sino-American ambassadorial talks in Warsaw after long suspension warranted attention, especially since the talks moved from Polish facilities susceptible to eavesdropping to secure quarters in the two embassies. But the talks were again suspended with the U.S.–South Vietnamese invasion of Cambodia in May 1970. Meanwhile Washington's relations with Moscow steadily improved.

Dobrynin's demarches reflected awareness of a possible U.S. effort to exploit Sino-Soviet problems, but it is not likely that the Kremlin envisaged a reciprocal tendency in Beijing, given the vociferous anti-imperialist rhetoric of the Cultural Revolution. In addition, the substantive issue of Taiwan could be presumed to block any such option for the PRC. As a further consideration, Beijing's willingness to treat Moscow's January 1971 proposal more seriously than its predecessors, together with the March Zhou-Ilychev conversation, may have reassured the Kremlin. A comparison of Brezhnev's description of the relationship in 1970 and 1971 reveals cautious optimism in the Chinese response to Soviet diplomatic moves.[41] In April 1970 he addressed the centennial celebration of Lenin's birth, to which representatives of all communist countries other than China and Albania were invited. There Brezhnev blamed "cooperation between socialist countries being disrupted in a most serious manner" on "the nationalistic policy of the Chinese leadership and its break with the principles laid down by Lenin." He claimed that "the virulent anti-Soviet campaign that has been conducted in China during the past few years . . . under the screen of an alleged threat from the Soviet Union" revealed its initiators "as apostates from the revolutionary cause of Lenin."

In marked contrast, Brezhnev's report to the 24th CPSU congress on March 30, 1971, noted: "In the past 18 months . . . there have been signs of some normalization in the relations between the USSR and the People's Republic of China." Beginning with the Zhou-Kosygin meeting in 1969, he recapitulated developments cited in the selective chronology above, terming them "useful steps." Again, whereas his 1970 address had merely made a general assertion "in favor of socialist internationalism and the restoration of good relations between socialist countries wherever they have been broken," the 1971 report declared, "Our party and the Soviet Government are profoundly convinced that an improvement in relations between the Soviet Union and the People's Republic of China would be in keeping with the fundamental long-term interests of both countries. . . . We are prepared to help in every way not only to normalize relations but also to restore neighborliness and friendship."

Brezhnev did not omit criticism of the Chinese "ideological-political platform which is incompatible with Leninism" and he specifically cited "an intensive and hostile propaganda campaign against our party and country, territorial claims on the Soviet Union," and "armed incidents along the frontier." He also attacked "nationalistic tendencies, especially those which assume the form of anti-Sovietism" in linking Beijing with "setting up splinter groupings in a number of countries."

Nevertheless, this indictment of Chinese sins was offset to some extent by the explicit listing of "normalization" developments in 1970–1971. Moreover, they were attributed to "the initiative displayed by us," crediting Soviet diplomacy with "useful steps." The border discussions won attention as "negotiations" that were "going forward slowly." Trade had "somewhat increased." In short, a more favorable image of the relationship emerged in Brezhnev's retrospective assessment of the previous year and a half than had been true in 1970.

Yet only two weeks later Zhou hailed a U.S. ping-pong team's visit to Beijing as a "new page" in Sino-American relations. Three months later, Kissinger's secret trip made world headlines, capped by the announcement of Nixon's forthcoming visit to Beijing in 1972. Early indicators may have been cited by Soviet intelligence along the way, including Edgar Snow's appearance next to Mao on Tiananmen Square during the national day celebrations of October 1, 1970, a photograph of which made the front page of *People's Daily* in December. Snow's interview with Mao wherein the chairman said he was willing to receive Nixon personally as either president or tourist belatedly appeared in *Life* magazine following the ping-pong team visit. But it is doubtful that these clues received their full weight at the highest level in Moscow. After all, the Kremlin was enjoying close contact with top officials in both Beijing and Washington with especially promising developments in the White House. Thus the Kissinger revelations probably came with shock and dismay.

The full implications of a Sino-American détente may not have been foreseen immediately, but some hint of the future came in November when East Pakistani turmoil led to rising tension between India and

Pakistan.[42] As each side jockeyed for support from its near-ally, respectively the Soviet Union and China, the United States became increasingly involved. Fierce polemical Sino-Soviet jousting at the United Nations paralleled military posturing in South Asia, which included the dispatch of a U.S. aircraft carrier task force.

Many of the accusations exchanged in the Soviet and Chinese press echoed those of the Sino-Indian war in 1962. However, a new line struck by Moscow accused Beijing of colluding with Washington. In the United Nations Security Council, Yakov Malik declared, "The Chinese representative, with his vicious pathological slander against the Soviet Union is aspiring to the role of the imperialists' court jester."[43] More seriously, *Pravda* asserted that China had encouraged the United States' naval mission, inter alia accusing Zhou of being the prime activator of anti-Soviet policies. This was the first time Zhou had been attacked in the Soviet press, and as such it signaled a subtle but significant change in posture.

Thus 1971 ended such diplomacy as Moscow was willing to attempt, with China policy further confounded by the new U.S. relationship. Viewed from the Kremlin, Mao had stolen a march on Moscow. His adroit diplomat, Zhou Enlai, had managed simultaneously to play both superpowers to China's interest. If anything was learned from the 18-month period covered by Brezhnev's report, it was further proof of Chinese perfidy in the willingness of Beijing to put anti-Soviet policy before anti-imperialism. This did not as yet endanger the substantive situation. Sino-American relations still confronted the Taiwan problem while U.S.–Soviet relations were moving toward anticipated summitry. But the new context opened up opportunities for China that called for one of two Soviet responses: competitive compromise or confrontational containment. Given the image of China derived from the decade 1959–1969, it is no surprise that the latter course continued with increased emphasis.

1972–1981: POLICY FREEZE

Compared with the military clashes and threats of 1969 and the diplomatic initiatives of 1970–1971, the period 1972–1981 was one of rigidity in Soviet policy toward China. Military strengthening in Siberia took qualitative as well as quantitative steps as part of a global arms race in addition to regional confrontation. Public posturing revealed Moscow's earlier diplomatic proposals in an effort to appear sensible and statesmanlike compared with continued perturbations by Mao's Cultural Revolution radicals, but basically no new proposals were offered. Polemical exchanges ebbed and flowed without much change in content or effect. Trade rose unevenly but remained a minuscule proportion of each country's total foreign trade. Meanwhile Moscow stepped up its effort at containment, focusing in particular on an Asian collective security pact and on a possible U.S.–Soviet condominium with implicit anti-Chinese overtones.

Important developments occurred: first and foremost, Mao's death in 1976. Moscow suspended polemics for the following months, but no change occurred in the Chinese posture. The CPSU sent a condolence message to the CCP, the first known contact between the two parties in many years. Beijing rejected it on the grounds that no such relations existed. Brezhnev's October 26 congratulatory message to Hua Guofeng as CCP chairman was similarly rejected, and Chinese press attacks against Moscow continued. Second, Sino-American relations took a more threatening turn in 1978 with National Security Adviser Zbigniew Brzezinski's trip to China, where he openly hinted at a common strategic interest in countering Soviet power. En route he also encouraged Tokyo to accept an antihegemony clause in the deadlocked Sino-Japanese Treaty of Peace and Friendship. Moscow had objected to the term as anti-Soviet, but Tokyo agreed to Beijing's language nevertheless. The year ended with President Carter's announcement transferring diplomatic recognition from Taipei to Beijing and terminating the U.S. treaty with Taiwan one year later.

Third, Sino-Vietnamese tensions suddenly escalated in 1978, placing new demands on Soviet policy as well as offering new opportunities. In June Beijing abruptly withdrew all economic aid in retaliation for Hanoi's exploitation and expulsion of more than 200,000 Chinese residents in Vietnam. This forced Moscow to increase its already heavy involvement in postwar reconstruction there. Then in November a new Soviet-Vietnamese treaty opened the door to Soviet air and naval facilities in Vietnam on the eve of anticipated Sino-Vietnamese hostilities. This realized the traditional goal of a warm-water site for West Pacific and Indian Ocean power projection. However it also challenged Soviet crisis management in a Sino-Vietnamese conflict.

None of these developments changed policy toward China. Moscow did propose less dramatic and far-reaching agreements in these years. In 1972 long-term trade contracts and resumption of border trade were suggested; in 1973, cooperation in health services; in 1974, participation by the Sino-Soviet Friendship Society in an all-U.S.S.R. conference on friendship with foreign countries; and, in 1977, the reestablishment of scientific and technological contacts. At a still lesser level, contact between the two academies of science and friendship societies, the exchange of newspaper correspondents, and similar people-to-people relations were suggested, all to no avail. The obvious political manipulation of broader proposals made these less credible, particularly given their paralleling similar developments already under way in Sino-American relations.

The only discernible move of substance concerned the disputed Bear Island (Heixiazi) opposite Khabarovsk.[44] Moscow claimed the channel on the southwestern side constituted the boundary as an arm of the Amur, the northeastern side being a second Amur arm and hence an inland waterway. Beijing countered that the two sides were arms of the Ussuri, hence the channel was a Chinese inland waterway and the boundary lay to the northeast of the island. In 1966 Soviet gunboats enforced Moscow's position by blocking the eastern route. This restricted Chinese ships to the southwestern channel, which became too shallow in summer for navigation.

However, during the joint commission meeting of July 27–October 6, 1977, the first in three years and the second longest on record, Moscow modified its stance and lifted the blockade subject to several conditions: (1) China will give advance notice for use of the eastern route, which the Soviet Union will agree to; (2) Soviet internal law will apply; (3) Chinese passage will be by day; (4) the agreement does not prejudice the positions of either side on the border. As the first navigation agreement in 8 years and as a reversal of a position enforced for more than 10 years, it is worth noting as a modest concession. Perhaps in conjunction with Moscow's reported willingness to accept the *thalweg* principle and cede most of the Ussuri islands, including Damansky, tacticians in the foreign ministry sought to elicit practical piecemeal concessions on the Chinese side. Chinese acceptance of Soviet internal law and the attendant provisions for passage may have strengthened such hope. If so, it was never realized in the separate ongoing border talks.

Discussions with Soviet Sinologists during the period 1972–1978 revealed a disregard of expertise that countered Kremlin imagery. China specialists who did not conform with the definition of Beijing as a dangerous threat suffered in silence. One analyst revealed a prohibition against writing "anything but brief book reviews on the Sino-Indian war—it is too sensitive for us on both sides." Another privately attacked the authorized version of Sino-Soviet relations by two highly placed authors, "It's just propaganda." Despite having acquired many documents during his years of teaching in Beijing, this scholar had been forced to abandon a history of PRC foreign policy. Instead he was writing about the earlier czarist period "to show that it was China, not Russia, that expanded in the Far East, contradicting the [Marc] Mancall version."

Nor were academic analysts the only frustrated experts. A young foreign service officer who had cut his teeth on Sino-Soviet relations in the 1950s later alluded to the futility of trying to propose policy changes during the 1970s. Even Kapitsa privately communicated a sense of imposed constraint in trying to keep the relationship alive for future opportunity. In sum, Kremlin learning would have to come through experience, not expertise.

Meanwhile the policy of containment proceeded apace. Brezhnev's call for a collective security pact in Asia, first surfaced in 1969, was actively promoted throughout the decade as an implicit anti-China move but won no adherents. India, the one Asian country that had been attacked by the PLA, refused to support the proposal, despite New Delhi's dependence on Moscow for economic and military assistance.

Moscow continued to signal security concerns in various ways. An indirect indicator of the rising influence of the Red Army came from Kapitsa's change in privately explaining why the southern Kurile Islands could not be returned to Japan as was demanded by Tokyo and justified by their history. In 1972 he had claimed that a range of "territorial demands" would become more active if this one were granted, including by implication demands of China. But in 1978 he dramatically covered the Sea of Okhotsk with his hand on a map, declaring that during World War II numerous Soviet ships had been sunk there by Japanese submarines despite the Soviet-Japanese neutrality pact. Therefore military necessity required "locking the door" to any potential enemy by controlling the entire Kurile chain.

More overtly, in March 1978 Brezhnev, accompanied by his defense minister, spent two weeks in the Soviet Far East viewing military exercises and publicly praising their performance. Sometime that year a new theater command coordinated the Far Eastern, Transbaikal, and Siberian military districts with the Pacific Ocean Fleet, the first such regional consolidation in the Far East since the Korean War.[45] Meanwhile the total force complement was triple that of a decade previous, with comparable qualitative improvements in air, sea, ground, and missile forces confronting China.

As a corollary development, a second railroad paralleling the Trans-Siberian but much further removed from the Chinese border began to take shape.[46] This massive project had been considered intermittently since the Japanese threat in the late 1930s, but its final construction was only begun in the mid-1970s. Its justification was mixed, economists having long heralded the potential exploitation of Siberia's vast mineral resources. But the assignment of military engineering units in addition to civilian ones properly signaled the logistical importance of the Baikal-Amur Mainline, or BAM as it came to be known. The inordinate cost occasioned by extremely formidable obstacles of permafrost, earthquakes, and extreme temperatures did not deter Brezhnev and his associates at a time when the Soviet economy was stagnating and was starved for efficient use of capital. Under the circumstances, military justification presumably met the need.

Krasnaia zvezda (Red Star) hammered away at the Chinese "threat" during 1977–1978, going well beyond the image projected by *Pravda* in timing and content.[47] In March 1978 it depicted a dangerous "fifth column" posed by overseas Chinese in Southeast Asia, a theme taken up by *Pravda* only in June. This anticipated Vietnam's expulsion of Chinese and the consequent Soviet access to military facilities there. The military newspaper ended the year by suggesting that President Carter's December 15 announcement on diplomatic relations with Beijing showed that "the American imperialists, the Japanese revanchists, and the Chinese great-power chauvinists" looked toward a military bloc. It further accused Beijing of plotting a U.S.–Soviet war that would clear the way for its "world hegemony." *Pravda* expressed no such concern at this point, probably sensitive to its overseas readership, especially in Washington.

Containment was not wholly passive, as shown by Soviet subversive broadcasts to Xinjiang, where anti-Han uprisings over the previous century had offered opportunity for Russian expansionism. In 1962 some 60–80,000 Turkic-speaking locals, mainly Uighur, had fled across the border to escape the catastrophic consequences of the Great Leap Forward and to join ethnically akin people who were much better off. Beijing closed the border and accused Moscow of seeking to "separate" Xinjiang. Then beginning in 1969 a noticeable increase in broadcasts beamed to Xinjiang, attention to local language publications on the Soviet side of the border, and exploitation of refugee reports juxtaposed suffering under Beijing with prosperity under Moscow.[48] Tibet, adjacent to Xinjiang, with its own history of anti-Han attitudes, was claimed by *Literaturnaya Gazeta* in November 1973 to have suffered more than 12,000 deaths in a revolt the previous year.[49] No such revolt was ever established by other sources. Beijing's policy was "close to genocide."

When challenged privately on the story, reputable Soviet specialists dismissed it: "Everybody knows that is only propaganda and not serious." Nevertheless, given the previous history of Russo-Chinese relations in Central Asia, it is possible that the KGB or its adherents in the Kremlin took this approach seriously. It is worth noting that the provocative broadcasts from Tashkent became noticeably restrained during the polemical standdown after Mao's death, only to resume their previous tone when the standdown ended in 1977.

In general the Soviet policy freeze of 1972–1981 did not change basic Chinese policy. However an important shift occurred in 1979 that Moscow failed to follow up, understandably in view of the crowded developments of that year. In January, Deng Xiaoping exploited a triumphal tour of the United States to attack U.S.–Soviet arms control negotiations and to call for "a united front of China and the United States, and Japan and Western Europe, against the Soviet Union."[50] Brezhnev warned through a *Time* interview that the United States was "playing with fire" in its China policy.[51] In February, Deng, with implied approval in Washington, made good his threat to "teach Vietnam a lesson" by launching the PLA on a limited ground invasion. Soviet military posturing on the Xinjiang border did not deter Beijing, although it may have contributed to Deng's terminating the attack at Longju after three weeks of an embarrassingly poor performance by Chinese forces.

1981–1982: MOSCOW CHANGES COURSE

In retrospect 1981 stands as a benchmark year for the Soviet reassessment and revision of China policy. Although the following years evidenced varying degrees of détente, a definite turning point occurred at this time in Moscow's approach to Beijing. The objective situation clearly called for a policy review. Not only had the frozen posture adopted in 1971 failed to win Chinese concessions on the border; it had proven counterproductive by inviting a Sino-American alignment that might possibly incorporate Japan, at best leaving Moscow odd man out in a strategic triangle and at worst isolating it in a quadrilateral setting. Brezhnev's 1980 subjective assessment added urgency to the situation. In addition to the previous goal of normalization by negotiation of bilateral differences, the Kremlin now faced the need to weaken and possibly break the emerging Sino-American alignment before it achieved a solid military foundation.

Just when necessity called for change in ends as well as means, so too did opportunity arise to invite it. Ronald Reagan's presidential campaign rhetoric included a "Taiwan tilt" that continued at his inauguration, protested by Beijing in private and in public. Six weeks later the first indicator of Soviet change came with Brezhnev's report to the CPSU congress on February 23, 1981.[52] He still saw "no grounds yet to speak of any change for the better in Beijing's foreign policy," which he characterized as "aimed at aggravating the international situation and aligned with the policy of the imperialist powers." However he reversed the image of his Alma Ata speech the previous August of China allegedly plotting to use the United States against the Soviet Union for Beijing's own interest. Now it was "the United States, Japan, and a number of NATO countries" who want to "use [China's] hostility to the Soviet Union . . . in their own imperialist interests." Whereas before Brezhnev was warning Washington to watch out for Beijing's designs, now the warning was implicitly aimed at Beijing to guard against Washington's manipulation.

This subtle but significant thrust was not repeated elsewhere at the time. Being buried in a lengthy report dominated by domestic subjects, it may have been inserted after some debate as a low-key test of Beijing's response. In any event, its reemergence later that year and its formal enunciation by Kapitsa in 1982 confirmed the shift in line as a substantive change of direction.

The visit to Beijing by Secretary of State Alexander Haig, June 14–17, 1981, dramatically demonstrated the threats and opportunities it reflected in Sino-American relations.[53] Prior to Haig's arrival, President Reagan approved moving the PRC to the category of "friendly but not allied" countries for U.S. export controls. This facilitated selling technology of higher caliber and dual-use items of military as well as civilian interest. It also allowed China to buy defensive weapons through commercial channels. In Beijing, Haig publicly announced Washington's willingness to sell defensive arms to China. In this connection he said that the PLA deputy chief of staff would visit Washington in the near future. The threat anticipated by Brezhnev's Alma Ata speech seemed about to materialize.

However, on the final day of Haig's visit, President Reagan reiterated his commitment to the Taiwan Relations Act (TRA) at a press conference, thereby reaffirming the sale of arms to the Chinese Nationalists as well as to the Chinese Communists. This touched a sensitive issue on which Deng was vulnerable, having already compromised on arms to Taiwan in 1978 to win diplomatic relations. The TRA had clearly not been antici- pated in Beijing, particularly its explicitly defining Taiwan's self-defense capability as a U.S. responsibility. News leaks before the Haig visit had alluded to the prospect of Beijing acquiescing in arms to Taiwan when Beijing could also receive them, but this evoked a public rejection by the foreign ministry spokesman.

Beijing's commentaries after Haig left addressed the weapons issue directly in negative terms. Moreover, when the PLA official's trip was confirmed, no reference to arms purchases appeared. Finally on August 25, a sympathetic Hong Kong journal published an interview with Deng wherein he bluntly warned, "The United States thinks that China is seek- ing its favor. In fact, China is not seeking any country's favor. . . . If worst comes to worst and the relations retrogress to those prior to 1972, China will not collapse. . . . When US Secretary of State Alexander Haig came to China, I told him the same thing."[54]

Meanwhile Soviet comment took an interesting turn. As might be expected, *Pravda* carried a long, authoritative article on June 27 that pointed to "a new stage in the development of the Chinese-American partnership . . . expressed primarily in a substantial expansion of the military aspects."[55] It claimed Washington had "expressed a readiness to provide Beijing with the means of waging a modern war, up to and including offensive weapons." Whereas the Carter decisions had led to "about 500 licenses for the sale of dual-purpose goods and technology (helicopters, transport aircraft, trucks and radar) . . . henceforth, China will have access not only to such classified high-technology products as strategic-missile guidance systems and military communications devices but also to various types of combat equipment—from antitank missiles to fighter-bombers."

However this was not an alliance cast in concrete. "No, the US and Chinese policy makers, having found common ground in bellicose anticommunism and anti-Sovietism, are by no means united in their global pretensions." Taiwan was the sticking point at which "the CPR leadership . . . agreed to a 'two Chinas' situation that is insulting to the prestige and sovereignty of a great power. Thus China is playing a shameful role *as junior partner* and accomplice of the US imperialists" (italics added).

This could be dismissed as patent cynicism, hypocritically lamenting the denigration of China's national interest as well as the betrayal of its ideological foundation. Alternatively it could be seen as more than the proverbial crocodile tears, thrusting into the sensitive area of Chinese nationalism so as to exacerbate Deng's vulnerability on the Taiwan question, inter alia worsening Sino-American relations. The second hypothesis was strengthened by the main Soviet commentary on a CCP Central Committee plenum that met immediately after the Haig visit and adopted a "decision on some questions of CCP history from the time the PRC was founded."[56] Moscow's analysis claimed its "clearly contradictory" provisions were forced on "the rival groupings in the Beijing leadership." The plenum "reflected a specific stage in the fierce power struggle in Beijing" wherein "Deng Xiaoping has not been able to completely realize his plans and has been forced to maneuver."

This was not the first time a power struggle had been alluded to, nor did it necessarily spill over into Chinese foreign policy. *Kommunist* carried an authoritative analysis in mid-1981 specifically addressing this latter question.[57] Because it was directly contradicted by Kapitsa in 1982, the two statements deserve quotation at length as evidence of divided views in Moscow, with Kapitsa winning out in the new policy. *Kommunist* warned:

> An acute power struggle continues within the ruling group itself. . . . However, the strife at the Beijing upper level does not affect the strategic goals proclaimed by Mao Zedong. All the Chinese leaders are united by the desire to turn the PRC into a strong military-industrial power. They all support the platform of the 'sinicization of Marxism' and positions of great-power chauvinism, hegemonism, and anti-Sovietism. The differences between them concern mainly the methods and pace of the accomplishment of the set tasks.

Kapitsa did not attack this analysis head on.[58] Instead he focused on the last point, arguing that it was precisely the difference in means, not ends, that was important in Chinese foreign policy choices. In doing so, he reiterated the theme of "junior partner" first hinted at by Brezhnev and alluded to in *Pravda*:

Quite a few Maoist leaders who imposed ethnocentrism on China are buried . . . but many of them are still alive, hold high posts, and continue to poison the atmosphere with national chauvinism. However an increasing number of people realize that the present-day world is not the "Celestial Empire" of time of the Tang or Qing Dynasties, that China is lagging behind some "barbarian" nations by dozens and even hundreds of years, that China must work hard for 50–70 years to carry out the necessary modernizations and pursue a correct policy instead of brainwashing their own people, and that finally, the imperialists will not help China modernize. As China acquires experience in international discourse, the following conviction is becoming widespread: the role of *junior partner* to imperialism runs counter to the interest and dignity of the Chinese people (italics added).

Kapitsa's projection of the time during which China must labor to "catch up" with advanced societies countered the image of threat implied by the attention given to incipient U.S. military assistance, manifest in the aforementioned *Pravda* article. It probably corresponded to Soviet military analyses of the PLA, which undoubtedly benefited from Hanoi's salutary experience in the 1979 fighting as well as from familiarity with PLA weaponry that was almost wholly derived from obsolete Soviet designs of the 1950s.

This did not negate the political implications for Moscow of the trend in Sino-American military relations evidenced by the Brown and Haig visits. Coincidentally, however, this trend had run afoul of the Taiwan question on which the Reagan administration appeared internally divided but externally committed so as to infuriate Beijing. Thus necessity and opportunity combined to call for a new Soviet line that could exploit the long-lamented Chinese nationalism to Moscow's advantage by focusing on the "junior partner" role and the issue of Taiwan. For dialecticians, the situation was excellent.

The culmination of this new line came on March 24, 1982, in a major address by Brezhnev at Tashkent.[59] As one of four points cited as basic Soviet policy, he declared, "We have never supported, and do not support now in any form, the so-called 'concept of two Chinas,' but have fully recognized and continue to recognize the PRC's sovereignty over Taiwan island." At that very time Washington and Beijing were wrestling to resolve the rising controversy over arms sales to Taiwan.

Another point stated, "We have never tried to interfere in the internal life of the PRC. We have not denied and do not deny now the existence of a socialist system in China." In addition to burying past polemical attacks, Brezhnev was obliquely alluding to growing Sino-American friction over such matters as human rights and birth control. His third point amplified normalization themes present in previous statements, noting, "We remember well the time when the Soviet Union and People's

China were united by bonds of friendship and comradely co-operation." Brezhnev specified "economic, scientific, and cultural as well as political relations" as areas of potential improvement. This responded belatedly to Huang Hua's proposal of 1979. Finally he reiterated the standard disavowal of "threat to the PRC from the Soviet Union." However he went beyond the usual proposal for border talks, adding, "We are also ready to discuss the matter of possible measures to strengthen mutual trust in the Soviet-Chinese border area." This hinted at some response to Beijing's demand that Moscow reduce its forces opposite China, one of the three "obstacles to normalization," the other two being the Soviet invasion of Afghanistan and Soviet support for Vietnam's invasion of Cambodia.

The Tashkent speech represented the fullest formulation of the new Soviet policy to date. However, it was anticipated by less dramatic indicators of decisions in Moscow and Beijing that must have preceded the previous year. A brief review of new Sino-Soviet interactions in the first half of 1982 illustrates the degree to which incremental steps finessed the larger questions as a token of incipient détente:

SELECTIVE CHRONOLOGY V: SINO-SOVIET 1982

January 12–19	PRC delegation to U.S.S.R. signs book trade agreement
February 6	Agree on PRC exports to Europe, Iran via U.S.S.R.
March 19	PRC economists arrive U.S.S.R. to study structure and management
March–April	Chinese gymnast team tours Moscow, Riga
June 16	U.S.S.R. participates Beijing track & field events, first since 1965
29	Friendship societies of U.S.S.R., PRC jointly celebrate 55th anniversary of Canton Commune

Equally noteworthy visits of Sergei Tikhvinsky, deputy leader of the Soviet delegation in the Moscow talks, and of Kapitsa occurred January 24 and May 14, respectively. While the former was shrouded in secrecy and the latter was publicly described merely as "a private visit," both individuals met with Chinese foreign ministry officials and presumably addressed the agenda of expanding relations.

This panoply of interaction argues for Soviet and Chinese decisions, followed by secret exchanges, to have occurred in 1981. Given the notoriously slow process of the bureaucracy in both countries, it is virtually inconceivable that these events could have taken place on short notice. This is particularly true for those interactions that resulted in signed agreements, such as book trade and Chinese exports transiting Soviet rail systems. The timing justifies our attention to Brezhnev's report of February 23 and *Pravda*'s commentary of June 27, 1981, as indicators of a new policy.

Thus developments in 1981–1982 indicate that the Kremlin learned from the past and the present in several ways reflective of cognitive structural changes.[60] First, it learned to listen to the Sino-American dialogue in a more subtle manner than previously, thereby enabling it to balance worst-case projections of threat against best-case projections of opportunity. Neither precipitate alarm nor passive optimism should dictate the Soviet response, but change was clearly called for under the circumstances. Second, it learned to listen to differing Sinologists whose past political fortunes had been simplistically tied to imputations of "hard" or "soft" positions on the question of China. Again, neither extreme was to be purged or put in policy positions, but alternative analyses could be argued with new insights emergent.

Third, Soviet policy learned to live with the stalemated border negotiations and redundant Chinese demands on Afghanistan, Vietnam, and troop concentrations while slowly but steadily expanding the range and level of interaction short of summitry and party-to-party ties. Tactically this offset the prior U.S. monopoly of relations with China. Strategically it lessened the prospect of a China threat, alone or in alliance with others, in this century. By reducing tension, Moscow thereby allowed Beijing to give priority to economic modernization, leaving military modernization for later.

Not all of these lessons may have been learned simultaneously or necessarily in these formulations. But the consistency of Kapitsa's implied favoring of Zhou Enlai in 1969 as against "the Maoists" and his depiction of divided Beijing counsels in 1982 is impressive, given the dominance of the "Maoist ascendancy" advanced by Soviet statements in the interim and their implementation in Soviet rigidity. The latter approach proved to be self-fulfilling as Deng joined Brzezinski against "the polar bear." If Moscow came to realize its own contribution to the Sino-American entente, no public acknowledgment occurred. In any event, the 1980s witnessed the unfreezing of Soviet policy with initial incremental steps that ultimately climaxed with full normalization of relations represented by the visit of General Secretary Mikhail Gorbachev to Beijing in May 1989.

1982–1985: LEADERSHIP CHANGES AND POLICY CHANGE

Brezhnev's lengthy rule was subsequently anathematized as "stagnation" by Mikhail Gorbachev and his associates. This term fit most of China policy during these years as we have seen. Nevertheless, a significant shift toward a new policy did begin in Brezhnev's final period. This deserves attention lest subsequent leadership changes be exaggerated as determining variables across time. True, the pace of policy movement varied under the brief regimes of Yuri Andropov (1982–1984) and Nikolai Chernenko (1984–1985). But whether this variation was a function of the particular individual or the brevity and obvious uncertainty to insiders of his tenure is not known. Suffice to say that the promise of 1982 was not realized as rapidly as might have occurred had Brezhnev lived or had a solid succession been established on his death.

The importance of continuous leadership lay in the degree to which the "three obstacles to normalization" posed by Beijing hit high-priority items on the agenda of domestic as well as foreign politics. All three issues involved major civilian and military interests. The reduction of forces opposite China could undercut appropriations for completing the Baikal-Amur Mainline, whose initial target date of 1985 was already unfeasible, in addition to threatening military allocations. Pressure on Hanoi to withdraw from Cambodia might jeopardize access to Cam Ranh Bay, Danang, and other facilities essential to the projection of Soviet military power in an arc extending from the South China Sea across the Indian Ocean. These facilities were not formally leased as bases for a fixed period so could be terminated at Hanoi's discretion. Finally, withdrawal from Afghanistan would publicly acknowledge disastrous decision making at the outset and military impotence in the implementation. The potential implications could be global as well as regional, rivaling those of the U.S. withdrawal from Vietnam.

In addition, these "gut-issue" demands from Beijing had no compensatory Chinese concessions as incentives. The PRC might abandon its claim of "disputed territories" and resolve the long-standing border problem. But then again, it might not, since no clear quid pro quo had been advanced beyond "normalization." Moreover, the threat of war from border incidents no longer existed. As for trade, it was already on the increase and in any event would not be of major importance because China could not meet Soviet needs for increased productivity through technology and know-how. Nor were the Chinese likely to back off from confronting Vietnam, now a Soviet ally by treaty, or competing for influence elsewhere, especially in North Korea.

On balance, then, the question of how fast and how far to pursue the changed policy turned less on a calculus of bilateral relations than of domestic and third country considerations. The third country question, in this case the United States, presented a dialectical conundrum of both inhibition and stimulus for change. An accelerated trend of Sino-American military cooperation argued for action to reverse it but also for caution lest either Washington or Beijing exploit the blackmail potential of such a trend. Acrimony in Sino-American relations offered the opportunity to intrude a favorable Soviet posture but also lessened the imperative to do so. In short, bureaucratic arguments framed solely in terms of the strategic triangle could fall on both sides of the choice between passivity and activity.

The larger frame of reference, namely Soviet global goals, could not be challenged by an aged transient leadership. To anticipate the next period under Gorbachev, a wholesale reassessment of Soviet economic and political priorities, domestic and foreign, engendered perestroika and glasnost. Professed strategic doctrine acknowledged security to be a mutual need, mutually determined. Bilaterally negotiated and unilaterally announced force reductions lowered confrontation in Asia as well as Europe. In this wider context, Afghanistan was expendable for the sake of reallocating human and material resources. A similar calculation would cancel support for Vietnam's decade-long occupancy of Cambodia, supplied and financed by the Soviet Union. Whatever gains these would bring in Sino-Soviet relations were a plus, but the basic determinants far transcended that concern.

So fundamental and far-reaching a set of decisions required a more vigorous leader with a stronger political base in the Politburo and the Central Committee than was possible in the virtual interregnum of 1982–1985. The inevitable resistance to reversals of this magnitude with rewards of such remote and uncertain payoff required more risk-taking and resilience than could be expected of two figures in declining health, wholly apart from the question of how committed they were personally to a more rapid improvement in Sino-Soviet relations.

Nevertheless, visible improvement did occur as a result of the change begun under Brezhnev. In addition to the developments already noted in the first half of 1982, the following summary shows the successive moves that ascended the ladder of relations thereafter.

SELECTIVE CHRONOLOGY VI: SINO-SOVIET 1982–1985[61]

1982

October 3–29	First round of consultations on normalization (repeated 11 times on semiannual basis to 1989)
November 16	Foreign ministers Huang Hua and Andrei Gromyko meet after Brezhnev funeral, first such contact in nearly 20 years

1984

February 15	PRC vice premier meets with first deputy chairman of Presidium of U.S.S.R. Council of Ministers, first such contact since 1969

June 30–	PRC vice foreign minister meets with Gromyko
July 4	during invited visit to U.S.S.R.
September 21–22	Foreign ministers meet twice at United Nations, first official meeting in many years
December 21–29	First deputy chairman of Presidium of U.S.S.R. Council of Ministers in PRC for agreements on economic and technical cooperation and to form Sino-Soviet Economic, Trade, Scientific, and Technological Cooperative Committee

1985

| March 14 | Vice Premier Li Peng meets with General Secretary Mikhail Gorbachev after Chernenko funeral |

At least three channels of communication opened during this period, apart from the funeral. Consultations on normalizing relations allowed ample time to cover a difficult agenda and associated counterproposals, totaling more than five months through a dozen semiannual sessions. Foreign minister exchanges at the annual United Nations sessions could focus on selected items to update or ratify previous exchanges. Separate visits facilitated high-level discussion on both sides. In addition, of course, there were always indirect means, privately through third parties and publicly by means of interviews, speeches, and other media signals. This last channel, for example, found Beijing censoring its transmission of anti-Soviet remarks made by President Reagan during his visit in April 1984. This facilitated the rescheduling of Arkhipov's visit in December after Moscow cancelled its original date in May because of the Reagan visit.

At the secondary level of relations, normalization was clearly under way, manifest in the slow rising status of official contacts. Negotiated trade grew by 2.7 times in 1983 and 1.6 times in 1984, albeit remaining well below 1950s figures.[62] Delegation exchanges increased in size, frequency, and constituency as noted in the expanded comment describing successive normalization consultations. Press polemics against domestic practices gave way to balanced presentations of developments in each country. Arkhipov's visit in particular explicitly evoked images on both sides of the halcyon days when Soviet economic assistance, which he had directed, had laid the basis of China's revived civilian and military industries in the 1950s.

However, Beijing kept up its attack on Soviet foreign policy in selected areas and its demand on the "three obstacles"—troop withdrawal opposite China, Afghanistan, and Vietnam-Cambodia. It required still a third change of leader and attendant changes in Moscow for Soviet policy to meet these demands.

SELECTIVE CHRONOLOGY VII: SINO-SOVIET
1985–1988 (TO THE SUMMIT)[63]

1985

May 30– June 14	U.S.S.R. director of consular affairs to PRC, agrees on new consulates in Leningrad, Shanghai
July 9–16	PRC vice premier on invited visit signs agreements on "goods exchanges and payment" and "construction and reform of industrial projects in China"
September 26	Foreign ministers exchange visit invitations at United Nations October 9; Deng asks Ceausescu to tell Gorbachev he can have summit if Moscow urges Hanoi to withdraw from Cambodia
October 10–18	Chairman of U.S.S.R. heads Supreme Soviet delegation to PRC, reciprocates March National People's Congress visit
December 5–13	Vice Foreign Minister Kapitsa on invited visit

1986

March 15–21	Agree on "exchange of engineering and technical personnel"
July 28	Gorbachev Vladivostok speech: agrees on *thalweg* for river boundary, withdrawal from Afghanistan in stages with six regiments out by the end of 1986, major troop withdrawal from Mongolia under discussion there
August 6	PRC spokesman claims speech had "new ideas that have never been mentioned before"
August 13	PRC foreign minister claims "cannot satisfy us since has sidestepped . . . withdrawal of Vietnamese troops from Cambodia"
October 6–14	Vice Foreign Minister Rogachev (replacing Kapitsa) in Beijing for ninth consultation; agrees to reopen boundary talks at vice foreign minister level in February and revive joint Amur Basin Commission

1987

January 15	Moscow announces withdrawal of division from Mongolia
February 9–23	Boundary talks agree to discuss eastern section
April 14–20	Tenth consultation discusses "regional conflicts"
August 7–21	Second boundary talks agree to resolve eastern boundary
October 5–16	Eleventh consultation to exchange Cambodian views
December 4	Deng claims "Gorbachev turned down my wish" for summit after Moscow presses Hanoi on Cambodia

1988
April 14   U.S.S.R. in Geneva agreement withdraws from Afghanistan
June 13-20   Twelfth consultation focuses on Cambodia, U.S.S.R. pro-
                poses special Sino-Soviet negotiation on it
July 2   Beijing agrees to special Cambodia negotiations
September 29   At U.N. foreign minister agrees to Moscow to press Hanoi
                on Cambodia, mutual visits discussed as step to summit
October 20–30   Third boundary talks agree on "most of eastern section"
                and begin on western section

> Substantial progress on Beijing's "three obstacles to nor-
> malization" reflected fundamental decisions in Moscow
> under Gorbachev's aegis. These decisions developed from
> wider considerations than the Sino-Soviet relationship,
> as we have noted, but they also brought a qualitative
> change of policy to the Moscow-Beijing discourse as shown
> by the chronology. Thus border talks, suspended in 1978,
> rapidly moved from two two-week sessions in 1987 to
> "work groups" meeting twice in 1988, with an agreement
> that October. Similarly, normalization consultations moved
> from the Soviet refusal to discuss "third country" interests
> to "regional conflict" as an agenda item with Cambodia
> eventually subject to "special negotiations." Finally, Moscow
> agreed to press Hanoi after exchanges with Beijing.

It would be wrong to credit Gorbachev exclusively for this record just
as it would be wrong to ignore Hanoi's internal decision making. Consensus in the Kremlin on the debit accounts from Afghanistan and Cambodia
presumably prevailed over whatever opposition remained in the aftermath of Gorbachev's political reshuffling of key party and government
personnel. Moscow's move was made easier by Vietnam's desperate
economic situation coupled with the stalemate in fighting the Khmer
Rouge. But Beijing's refusal to back down on the Cambodian "obstacle,"
singled out by Deng as a precondition for summitry and repeatedly hammered
home by official statements, necessarily weighed in the scales of Kremlin
argument.

On balance, the explanation for developments in 1985–1989 that culminated in a Sino-Soviet summit appears to lie more with a change of
goals in the broadest sense, combined with leadership change that enunciated
these goals, than with a change in the cognitive structure of Sino-Soviet
relations or a change of goals in China policy. The bilateral relationship
had progressed sufficiently not to justify substantive concessions to Beijing's
three demands. Negotiated trade increased 1.7 times in 1985. Ironically,

it peaked slightly in 1986, declined by nearly 30 percent in 1987, and increased by a similar amount in 1988 but remained well below the 1985–1986 level precisely when political relations improved the most.[64] Border agreements were welcome but not necessary given the overall military posture of both sides, especially after the INF agreement. In short, the improvements that flowed from Brezhnev's final years had accumulated by the time of Chernenko's death not only to meet a reasonable definition of normalized relations but also to sharply reduce the possibility of either Washington's or Beijing's exploiting Sino-Soviet relations in the triangular game.

SUMMARY AND RETROSPECT

In 1954–1957 Khrushchev handled Mao as a deserving but dependent junior partner in a socialist alliance. From 1958 to 1960, Mao's disregard for dependency and disrespect for Khrushchev prompted the latter to teach Mao a lesson on the calculation that his sensible socialist colleagues would recement the shaken alliance structure. The polemical dispute escalated until Khrushchev's fall in 1964, but Kosygin did no better meeting with Mao in 1965. The near-total elimination of the Long March veterans from power in 1966–1968 during the Cultural Revolution challenged the image of a rational ally dominated by a petty-bourgeois nationalist. The prospect of an overthrow of Mao or a post-Mao succession restoring the alliance faded. The shock of border clashes in 1969 produced a worst-case threat of an irrational Mao amid an expansionist elite that had to be both deterred and contained by the threat of force. A fundamental change resulted in the cognitive content and cognitive structure of Soviet China policy.

Except for a brief period in 1970–1971, deterrence and containment omitted serious diplomatic efforts to ameliorate tensions. Once Sino-American détente erupted in 1971–1972, Moscow proved unrelenting toward Beijing's effort to exploit the strategic triangle with a Sino-American-Japanese anti-Soviet entente. Mao's death introduced a brief testing period wherein Moscow's polemics ceased, to no avail. The eight-month duration and the absence of any serious initiatives showed that no basic cognitive change had occurred.

The years 1978–1981 strengthened the worst-case image with a steadily growing military component in Sino-American relations. Deterrence had reduced Chinese risk-taking to a minimum, but containment had failed to block the Beijing-Washington rapprochement. That alignment demanded fresh and urgent attention. Meanwhile Reagan's campaign rhetoric and initial presidential posture tilted toward Taiwan sufficiently to antagonize Deng Xiaoping. Thus necessity and opportunity combined with the ascendancy of Soviet Sinologists who argued for reintroducing diplomacy, pointedly put by Kapitsa, promoted to deputy foreign minister in 1982. A cognitive content change of policy responded belatedly to the 1979 Chinese invitation for improved relations without preconditions. Brezhnev's start in this direction was followed by Andropov and Chernenko, but the brevity of their tenures precluded any fundamental approach to China's three preconditions for full normalization.

This approach became possible with Gorbachev. Kapitsa was replaced as deputy foreign minister in 1986 by Rogachev. The latter began his China experience as interpreter for the joint Sino-Soviet Amur Basin Commission in 1955–1957 and brought a much younger and more sophisticated mind to this key post.[65] The "McCarthy" syndrome of the 1960s and 1970s ended as a more diverse and complex analysis of China's domestic reforms accompanied a more relaxed and optimistic depiction of its foreign policy, particularly with respect to Washington and Moscow.

However, the critical components responsible for the successful culmination of Soviet policy in the May 1989 summit lay in a much broader context than Sino-Soviet relations. By acknowledging that security was a mutual interactive phenomenon, Moscow conceded that its own posture affected how others perceived it. This in turn justified reducing forces opposite China as a means of détente in keeping with reductions in East Europe. In addition to a revised global posture, domestic economic needs dictated and permitted reassessment and reversal of policy on a wide front from Africa to Asia. Within this wider framework, withdrawal from Afghanistan and pressure on Hanoi to withdraw from Cambodia met China's demands but also met demands in Moscow.

This does not undervalue a second change in the cognitive structure of China policy in the 1980s, which proved as fundamental and far-reaching as that in the late 1960s. But while we have concentrated on Moscow's image of Beijing during this twenty-year span, it must ultimately be considered in the totality of Soviet policy, wherein learning also occurred as a function of experience, leadership change, and the cognitive restructing of ends and means.

BIBLIOGRAPHIC NOTE

This chapter draws on several major sources that are best described in advance of their citation at appropriate points. Such citation is often in summary reference to a section rather than offered at every possible instance, thereby lessening the reader's need to interrupt the analysis for hunting down an endnote.

First and foremost, as noted in the introduction, I have drawn on Chi Su, "Soviet Image of and Policy Toward China: 1969–1979," Ph.D. dissertation, Columbia University, May 1984. This is a comprehensive and close reading of Soviet statements and publications, cast within a conceptual scheme of cognitive analysis that concurs with my own intellectual approach and that embodied in this collection of essays on learning in foreign policy. The dissertation has extensive quotations that I have excerpted in the author's translation as noted.

Second, I am deeply indebted to my former graduate student, Dr. Eric Jones, for his research and analysis of articles by M.S. Kapitsa in comparison with contemporary writing by other Soviet Sinologists. In 1976, we began this collaborative effort on the annual collection, *Opasnyi kurs* [Dangerous Course], a selection of the most authoritative articles that had appeared each year on China in leading Soviet journals. A hypothesis we tested at that time concerning Kapitsa's view of Zhou Enlai as a potential moderate for negotiating Sino-Soviet problems was developed further by Dr. Jones for the present study, supplemented by Kapitsa's two major studies, *KNR: dva desiatiletiia—dve politiki* [PRC: Two Decades—Two Policies](Moscow: Izdatel'stvo Politicheskoi Literatury, 1969), and its successor, *KNR: tri desiatiletiia—tri politiki* [PRC: Three Decades—Three Policies] (Moscow: Izdatel'stvo Politicheskoi Literatury, 1979).

Third, much of the chronology and summary of major developments comes from Peter Jones and Sian Kevill, eds., *China and the Soviet Union: 1949–1984* (New York: Facts on File, 1985). For the broader focus on third country relations, especially with the United States, a detailed account of developments and secret negotiations culled from participant memoirs and interviews was provided by Raymond L. Garthoff, *Détente and Confrontation: American-Soviet Relations From Nixon To Reagan* (Washington: The Brookings Institution, 1985).

Fourth, my intermittent interaction with Soviet specialists on China, beginning in 1969, encompassed the Institute of the Far East, the Institute of Oriental Studies, and the Institute of the USA and Canada (all in the Academy of Sciences) and the Ministry of Foreign Affairs. My interviews took place in Ann Arbor, Michigan, until 1982 when these individuals visited the Center for Chinese Studies at the University of Michigan, and in Moscow until 1987. These conversations were professional but private and, with the exception of M.S. Kapitsa, must remain anonymous. There was no glasnost during most of this period, and I respect the tacit understanding that prevailed at the time, particularly in view of the fact that some of the specialists have since moved into sensitive official positions. But I wish to express my indebtedness to them for the frank exchanges and insights that they provided.

An excellent survey and analysis of these specialists, together with a good description of the constraints on access to their works, is provided by Gilbert Rozman, "Moscow's China-watchers in the Post-Mao Era: The

Response to a Changing China," *The China Quarterly*, 94 (June 1983): 215–41. While I differ with Rozman's categorization of "hard liners," taking exception to the inclusion of Kapitsa in this group, his prodigious research has been pathbreaking in the analysis of both Chinese and Soviet specialists in their reciprocal images of the opposite side.

I profited from the critical guidance provided by the editors of this volume, Professors George W. Breslauer and Philip Tetlock, together with the comments by colleagues at the Berkeley conference in December 1988. Dr. Jones also provided comment on a first draft. They are not responsible, however, for the final version.

NOTES

1. Charles E. Bohlen, *Witness to History, 1929–1969* (London: Weidenfeld and Nicolson, 1973), 274.

2. Among the many writings on this crisis, for thoughtful retrospection based on careful research see Richard Wich, *Sino-Soviet Crisis Politics* (Cambridge, Mass.: Harvard University Press, 1980); Tsien-hua Tsui, *The Sino-Soviet Border Dispute in the 1970s* (Oakville, Ontario: Mosaic Press, 1983); and Thomas G. Hart, "Sino-Soviet Relations 1969–1982: An Attempt at Clarification," *Cooperation and Conflict*, 18 (June 1983):79–99.

3. For each of these views see, respectively, Gretchen Ann Sandles, "Soviet Images of the People's Republic of China, 1949–1979," Ph.D. dissertation, University of Michigan, 1981; Chi Su, "Soviet Image of and Policy Toward China: 1969–1979," Ph.D. dissertation, Columbia University, 1984; Gilbert Rozman, *A Mirror for Socialism, Soviet Criticisms of China* (Princeton, N.J.: Princeton University Press, 1985).

4. For high praise from the long-time foreign minister, see A.A. Gromyko, *Pamiatnoe*, vol. 2 [Memoir](Moscow, Politizdat, 1988), 136–137, referring to Kapitsa's "high level knowledge of Chinese language, history, and culture."

5. See Allen S. Whiting, *Soviet Policies Toward China, 1917–1924* (New York: Columbia University Press, 1954).

6. During my travels I have found an inverse relationship between distance from China and hostile imagery. Interviews in Irkutsk and Khabarovsk and with persons from Vladivostok elicited little or no threat imagery in contrast with that advanced by intellectuals in Moscow.

7. Mikhail Stepanovich Kapitsa, *KNR: dva desiatiletiia—dve politiki* [The PRC: Two Decades—Two Policies] (Moscow: Izdatel'stvo Politicheskoi Literatury, 1969); compare with anonymous article, "Obstanovka v Kitae i Polozhenie v KPK na Sovremennom Etape" [The Situation in China and the Condition of the CCP at the Current Stage], *Kommunist* (1969): 86–103 in *Opasny kurs: Po povodu sobytii v Kitae*, vol. 1 [The Dangerous Course: Concerning Events in China] (Moscow: Politizdat, 1969), 89–115.

8. M.S. Kapitsa, *KNR: tri desiatiletiia—tri politiki* [The PRC: Three Decades—Three Policies](Moscow: Izdatel'stvo Politicheskoi Literatury, 1979).

9. Interview with M.S. Kapitsa.

10. Information available to author as special assistant to the director, Bureau of Intelligence and Research, Department of State, November 1961.

11. Data in this section is from Leo A. Orleans, "China's Science and Technology and Its American Connection: The View From Moscow," mimeo., June 1984. Orleans draws on L.V. Filatov, *Ekonomicheskaia Otsenka Nauchno-Tekhnicheskoi Pomoshchi Sovetskogo Soiuza Kitaiu 1949–1966* [Economic Estimate of Scientific-Technical Assistance by the Soviet Union to China, 1949–1966] (Moscow: Nauka Press, 1980).

12. Mao Zedong, "Talk at an Enlarged Central Work Conference," January 30, 1962, quoted in Stuart Schram, ed., *Chairman Mao Talks to the People* (New York: Pantheon, 1975), 176–78.

13. Interviews with Soviet specialists in China at that time.

14. Interview with M.S. Kapitsa.

15. Nikita Khrushchev, *Khrushchev Remembers* (Boston: Little Brown, 1970), translated and edited by Strobe Talbot, Ch. 18; also *Khrushchev Remembers: The Last Testament* (Boston: Little Brown, 1974), Ch. 11.

16. Mao Zedong, interview of July 10, 1964, in *Sekai Shuho*, August 11, 1964, quoted in Dennis J. Doolin, *Territorial Claims in the Sino-Soviet Conflict* (Stanford, Calif.: Hoover Institution, 1965), 43–44.

17. Information available to author as director, Office of Research and Analysis, Far East, in the Bureau of Intelligence and Research, Department of State, 1962–1966.

18. Kikuzo Ito and Minoru Shibata, "The Dilemma of Mao Tse-tung," *The China Quarterly*, 35 (July-September 1968): 58–77, fn. 9.

19. This paragraph draws on the author's knowledge as deputy principal officer, American Consulate General, Hong Kong, 1966–1968.

20. Information in this paragraph available to author from U.S. intelligence sources while consultant to the Rand Corporation, July 1969.

21. M.S. Kapitsa, *Dva desiatiletiia*, 210–11.

22. Ibid., 237–38.

23. Evgenii Yevtushenko, "On The Red Ussuri Snow," *Literaturnaia gazeta* 12 (March 19, 1969), quoted in Chi Su, "Soviet Image," 222.

24. Andrei Voznesenskii, "Prologue to a Poem," quoted in Chi Su, "Soviet Image," 222.

25. The following paragraphs draw on Su, 482 ff., unless otherwise noted.

26. Information from reliable U.S. sources.

27. Raymond L. Garthoff, *Détente and Confrontation: American-Soviet Relations from Nixon to Reagan* (Washington: The Brookings Institution, 1985), 208.

28. Chi Su, "Soviet Image," 431 ff.

29. Interviews with Soviet specialists in 1972.

30. Military memoirs published in 1989 revealed Soviet troops had manned surface-to-air batteries in Vietnam 20 years previously and claimed considerable success in shooting down U.S. planes, *The New York Times* (April 14, 1989): A4.

31. Information from reliable U.S. sources.

32. On Kosygin's flight, see Raymond L. Garthoff, *Détente*, 210.

33. Undersecretary Elliott L. Richardson, "The Foreign Policy of the Nixon Administration: Its Aims and Strategy," address to the American Political Science Association conference, quoted in Raymond L. Garthoff, *Détente*, 220.

34. For the 1963 reference see M.S. Kapitsa, *Dva desiatiletiia*, 286; for the A. Doak Barnett reference see p. 288.

35. Knowledge of the Sino-American ambassadorial talks being bugged emerged during the mid-1960s; information available to the author at the time.

36. Raymond L. Garthoff, *Détente*, 211.

37. Summaries and quotations for this period are in Raymond L. Garthoff, *Détente*, 211–12, and Peter Jones and Sian Kevill, eds., *China and the Soviet Union, 1949–84* (New York: Facts on File, 1985), 142–43.

38. This figure is offered by both sides; for the Chinese reference see Chi Su, "Soviet Image," 72; for the Soviet one, see Peter Jones and Sian Kevill, *China*, 148.

39. Chi Su, "Soviet Image," 444.

40. O. Vladimirov and V. Riazanov, "The 50th Anniversary of the CCP," *Kommunist*, 10 (1971): 88, quoted in Chi Su, "Soviet Image," 39.

41. For relevant excerpts of Brezhnev's speeches, see Peter Jones and Sian Kevill, *China*, 97–101.

42. Ibid., 157–60.

43. Ibid., 159.

44. Neville Maxwell, "Why the Russians Lifted the Blockade at Bear Island," *Foreign Affairs*, 57 (Fall 1978): 138–45.

45. Raymond L. Garthoff, *Détente*, 715.

46. Allen S. Whiting, *Siberian Development and East Asia: Threat or Promise?* (Stanford, Calif.: Stanford University Press, 1981).

47. William deB. Mills, "Comparing Soviet Civilian and Military Views of China," *The Korean Journal of International Studies*, 15 (Summer 1984): 285–305.

48. Chi Su, "Soviet Image," 156–65.

49. Peter Jones and Sian Kevill, *China*, 105.

50. "An Interview with Teng Hsiao-p'ing," *Time*, February 5, 1979, quoted in Raymond L. Garthoff, *Détente*, 718.

51. "An Interview with Brezhnev," *Time*, January 22, 1979, quoted in Raymond L. Garthoff, *Détente*, 717.

52. Peter Jones and Sian Kevill, *China*, 141.

53. For further details see Raymond L. Garthoff, *Détente*, 1038–41.

54. Interview with Deng Xiaoping, *Ming Bao*, August 25, 1981, quoted in Raymond L. Garthoff, *Détente*, 1040–41.

55. I. Aleksandrov, "Escalation of Folly—Regarding A. Haig's Visit to Peking," *Pravda* (June 27) in *Current Digest of the Soviet Press*, 33 (25): 2–4.

56. "On the Sixth Plenary Session of the CCP Central Committee," *Pravda* (July 5, 1981), *Izvestiia* (July 5, 1981), in *Current Digest*, 33 (27): 5 ff.

57. O. Borisov, "Certain Aspects of Chinese Policy," *Kommunist*, 6 (1981): 120–21, quoted in Chi Su, "Soviet Image," 551.

58. M.S. Kapitsa, "Soviet-Chinese Relations: Problems and Perspectives," *Problemy dalnego vostoka*, 2 (1982), quoted in Chi Su, "Soviet Image," 555.

59. Peter Jones and Sian Kevill, *China*, 175–76.

60. Chi Su, "Soviet Image," in his "Conclusion," 559–71, specifically addresses the question of "learning" in Soviet policy toward China but comes to very different findings.

61. This chronology is based in part on Wen Fu, "The Process of Heading

Toward Normalization—a Chronology of Major Events in Sino-Soviet Relations (1982-88)," *Shijie Zhishi* 3, (February 1, 1989): 10–14, quoted in *Foreign Broadcast Information Service*, China (February 17, 1989): 8–14.

62. Ibid., 10.

63. Ibid., 9–14.

64. Ibid., 10.

65. The author first met Rogachev in the early 1960s when he was assigned to the Soviet embassy in Washington after having served in Beijing.

15

Learning in Soviet Policy
Toward the Arab-Israeli Conflict

George W. Breslauer

Soviet policy in the Middle East has varied considerably over the past 43 years, as has Soviet policy in the Third World more generally. Indeed, in some respects, Soviet policy toward the Middle East has been a function of the general Soviet posture in, or thinking about, the Third World as an arena of East-West competition. For this reason, I have found it useful to conceptualize the evolution of Soviet Middle East policy in categories similar to those I have elsewhere found useful for conceptualizing dominant tendencies in Soviet Third World policy.[1] Although later in this chapter I will narrow the focus to concentrate on Soviet policy toward the Arab-Israeli conflict, I begin the analysis by focusing on Soviet policy in the region more generally.

There have been four dominant, though at times conflicting, orientations in Soviet policy toward Third World regions, including the Middle East. The orientations are defined by the dominant direction of policy within them; they may be thought of as "policy clusters." The first is *Russia-first*, which entails a concentration of attention on the home front, on relations with countries that directly border on the Soviet Union, or on the conventional East-West struggle in Europe and the Far East. The Russia-first orientation might be called a form of isolationism or avoidance, though it is not averse to (and may even seek) confrontation on matters of border security. It is then continental, rather than global, in its focus.[2]

The three other orientations are all globalist in their focus. One of these may be called *sectarian activism*. This entails heavy assistance to anti-imperialist forces in the Third World, preferably but not necessarily

551

radical forces that seek to emulate the Soviet developmental model. Sectarian activism may be marked by support of the revolutionary efforts of local communist forces or, as in the Middle East, by extensive military assistance to pro-Soviet regimes that are actively engaged in the "anti-imperialist struggle." This policy orientation pursues *exclusive* relations with the chosen Third World forces, at the expense of imperialist influence.

Another tendency may be called *ecumenical activism*. Like sectarian activism, this is a policy of competition for influence with imperialism. Unlike sectarian activism, however, it is willing to collaborate with a wide spectrum of political forces (both social and governmental), does not necessarily insist on exclusive relationships with those forces, and emphasizes means of competition that do not contain a high potential for escalation (political, cultural, and economic levers, but also low-grade military assistance).[3]

The final tendency, which is also globalist, is *crisis prevention*. By this I do not mean simply the caution that the Soviets have often displayed in crisis situations (which can be conceptualized as circumstantial confrontation avoidance). Rather, crisis prevention seeks superpower coordination of effort to reduce the escalatory potential of given Third World conflicts. Although the policy may emphasize bilateral (e.g., U.S.–Soviet) or multilateral (e.g., United Nations Security Council) means, it is decidedly inclusionary with respect to Soviet participation and status in the process of coordinating positions, defining interests, and guaranteeing outcomes. Thus, whereas Russia-first, sectarian activism, and ecumenical activism are all policies of either confrontation, competition, or avoidance, crisis prevention is a policy of cooperation.

Competitive policies may be oriented toward the *acquisition* or toward the *defense* of Soviet influence, allies, or assets. Cooperative policies may also be crafted in ways that will advance either acquisitive or defensive goals. However, to qualify as a cooperative policy of crisis prevention, they must be willing to sacrifice a measure of short-term self-interest for the sake of coordinating with the adversary in order to head off escalations that they both dread. They need not be generous, much less capitulationist, but they must not be entirely selfish either.[4]

Since World War II, Soviet policy in the Third World and the Middle East has never been marked by an exclusive reliance on only one of these four tendencies. Yet over time, it has been marked by shifting mixes of them. During Stalin's last years, for example, the Russia-first policy predominated. Under Khrushchev, global activism predominated, decisively subordinating the Russia-first orientation. That activism constituted a distinctive mix of sectarian and ecumenical approaches and was largely acquisitive in thrust. However, the crisis-prevention orientation remained weak and unelaborated. Khrushchev's mistake lay in overestimating the potential for achieving reliable and exclusive relationships with his allies in the Middle East and in his failure to anticipate the need for an elaborate strategy of crisis prevention. Under Brezhnev, sectarian activism, both defensive and acquisitive, came to predominate over ecumenical activism but came also to coexist with a much-strengthened and increasingly developed crisis-prevention orientation. The blind spot under Brezhnev lay in the belief that crisis prevention could be effective when acquisitive sectarian activism was also strong. Under Gorbachev, acquisitive sectarian activism has been decisively subordinated (though not eliminated) to a strategy that combines defensive sectarian activism, ecumenical activism, and a still stronger crisis-prevention orientation. It remains to be seen whether this distinctive mix of activism and crisis prevention succeeds in attaining major Soviet objectives in the Middle East.

An inquiry into the sources of change in Soviet policy toward the Arab-Israeli conflict and the role of elite learning as one explanation for change requires an examination of the turning points just noted (after Stalin, after Khrushchev, and after Brezhnev), along with an analysis of turning points within those administrations. The framework outlined above provides us with a dependent variable (i.e., changes in broad policy orientations) that is sufficiently encompassing to avoid having to explain myriad changes in tactics. We now must ask whether change in that variable has been triggered or accompanied by changes in the objectives of policy or the assumptions, perceptions, and beliefs that may inform the formulation of policy. If we find this to be the case, we must then ask whether those changes qualify as learning, or as a particular type of learning, according to the alternative definitions proposed by Philip Tetlock (Chapter 2) and Ernst Haas (Chapter 3) in this volume. Finally, we must attempt to explain the pattern of learning or nonlearning uncovered in the inquiry. This final exercise will seek to push the causal arrows one step further back: If learning of some sort contributes in varying degrees to explaining the pattern of policy change, what explains the types, degrees, and timing of the learning? To cope with these multiple tasks, this chapter will therefore combine an interpretive narrative of the evolution of Soviet policies in the Middle East with discussions of the character and causes of the turning points.

STALIN'S LAST YEARS

Between the end of World War II and Stalin's death in 1953, Soviet policy toward noncontiguous areas of the Third World and toward the Middle East was driven largely by a Russia-first orientation. To be sure, *some* elements of competitive activism existed. Stalin supplied low-grade military assistance to the Jews of Palestine in their struggle against British colonial rule. And, in political arenas, he backed "Arab nationalist demands for the withdrawal of French troops from Lebanon and Syria and of British forces from Egypt."[5] Then too, he tried to intensify conflict between the United States and Great Britain over the Palestine issue. Yet, despite these features of anti-imperialist activism, the dominant Soviet policy orientation was one of avoidance of involvement or engagement. Nowhere was this more manifest than in the Soviet denunciation of nationalist Third World leaders (Nasser included, after he came to power in 1952) as stooges of the imperialists.

The Russia-first orientation was based on a particular set of policy objectives, perceptions of opportunity and threat, and beliefs about the nature of the adversary. With respect to objectives, it placed highest priority on the mobilization of national resources to meet proximate threats to national security on the rim of the socialist world. It therefore placed a relatively low value on the anti-imperialist struggle in distant regions. This preference ordering derived in part from a perception that the Third World was dominated by the unalterably antagonistic imperialists, and that few opportunities existed for successful Soviet competitive activity in distant regions, or for indigenous radical forces to overcome the stranglehold of the imperialists and their henchmen. These policies and objectives were informed by a black-and-white, conspiratorial, and zero-sum view of the world, according to which one trusted nothing one could not directly control, and by a perception that imminent threats to national security required an overwhelming focus on border security. Doctrinally, Stalin justified these perspectives by arguing that a third world war was inevitable in this era of the "final crisis of capitalism" and that such a war could be won by socialism if the Soviet Union remained perpetually prepared for it. That war, in turn, would usher in a period of revolutionary transformation in the Third World. In the meantime, a policy of continental siege, not global competition, was deemed consistent with the perceptions of threat and opportunity and with the image of the adversary.

There were many individuals within the Soviet political establishment who were uncomfortable with either the implausibility of these perceptions or the level of tension and war preparation they required. Some of them tried to challenge prevailing policy, however circumspectly, in 1951–1952, during preparations for the 19th Party Congress (the first such Congress to be held in 13 years). But Stalin rebuffed them. Their voices would only be heard clearly, loudly, and publicly after Stalin's death in March 1953.

POST-STALIN REAPPRAISAL

During 1954–1955, a controversial reorientation of Soviet Third World and Middle East policy took place. That shift called for decisive subordination of the Russia-first orientation, in favor of intensified global competition. In the Middle East, this found expression in the huge Czech-Egyptian (read: Soviet-Egyptian) arms deal, in doctrinal acknowledgment that Nasser, like Nehru and Sukarno elsewhere, was not a stooge of imperialism but rather a nationalist leader performing a historically positive function, in large-scale technical and economic aid programs for Egypt, expanded cultural and economic ties with Yemen, Syria, and Lebanon, and a declaration that the Soviet Union would assist any country requesting Soviet aid.

This new competitive strategy was a mixture of sectarian and ecumenical activism. It was ecumenical in accepting as historically progressive allies so-called bourgeois-nationalist leaders in the Third World, in endorsing the nonaligned movement's emphasis on "positive neutralism," and in the heavy dose of competition by nonescalatory means (economic assistance, cultural exchange). It was sectarian in its commitment to substantially arming Third World governments for the struggle against imperialism and in its expectation of the development of exclusive relationships with states that would eventually, it was assumed, become left-wing regimes and ideologically close, reliable allies of the Soviet Union (i.e., the supplanting of imperialism by Soviet-allied and Soviet-type regimes).

The new policy cluster was based on a very different set of priorities, perspectives, and perceptions from those that marked Russia-first. It was based on a more differentiated (less black-and-white, conspiratorial, and zero-sum) perception of trends within the Third World and on an eagerness to compete for influence among the weak links in the imperialist global system of domination. It rejected the Stalinist belief that one could not trust any social forces one did not control directly. It was also based on a perception that the historical course of events (in particular, decolonization) was rapidly creating new opportunities for the advance of socialism: opportunities for the Soviet Union to aggravate contradictions among the imperialists, to undermine the containment barriers that imperialism was setting up to encircle the Soviet Union (the Southeast Asia Treaty Organization was formed in 1954, the Baghdad Pact in 1955), and to secure exclusive allies in this new arena of competition. Khrushchev also projected confidence that he could do all this without getting unwittingly embroiled in confrontations that might escalate to a war with the West— a war that he did not want in any case, and that he certainly was not willing even to contemplate in defense of newly declared Soviet interests in the Third World or the Middle East.

Indeed, Khrushchev revised Stalinist doctrine about war to justify the new policies and perspectives. To Khrushchev, the atomic era made World War III unaffordable. A continuing state of siege was therefore dangerous and threatened inadvertent nuclear war. Hence, he sought to negotiate limits to the arms race and to stabilize a situation of mutual deterrence. But with respect to the Third World, such mutual deterrence would allow the Soviet Union also to deter Western export of counter-revolution, which would in turn allow the forces of nationalism to throw off the bonds of colonialism. Thereafter, indigenous forces of socialism would eventually replace bourgeois-nationalist regimes with Soviet-type regimes.

This revised perspective on war was accompanied as well by a revised image of the adversary. Increasingly under Khrushchev, imperialism was defined as being a more differentiated entity, with a more complex goal structure, and with an antagonism that was mitigable or deterrable.

The new Soviet policy in the Middle East was based on the perception that opportunities had arisen that provided easy entry into the Middle East power game. Such entry was not defined by Moscow as primarily an anti-Israeli act or as incompatible with continued normal relations with Israel (which had gone quickly downhill under Stalin after 1949 but which improved immediately after Stalin's death). The Baghdad Pact was both the object of Soviet competitive counters and the source of opportunity for them to embrace an important prospective ally, Egypt. Since Nasser opposed the pact (for many reasons) and since the United States and Great Britain had engineered its creation as an anti-Soviet alliance, it followed logically that mutual aversion might lead the Soviet Union and Egypt into each other's arms. However, that would happen only if a new mentality prevailed in the Soviet leadership, one that was optimistic about the general Soviet capacity to compete and interested in doing so. In other words, a Russia-first mentality had to be overcome. What's more, there were also those within the Soviet political establishment (for example, V. Molotov) who were uncomfortable with the ecumenical dimension of this new policy: its willingness to create alliances with bourgeois-nationalist governments at the expense of local communist parties. Once these forces were outflanked, the main Soviet goals in the Middle East under Khrushchev became to erode or eliminate Western influence in the region, to expand Soviet influence there, and to do all this without causing a nuclear confrontation between East and West.

What kind of a change in thinking and policy did this constitute, and what were its causes? In one respect, the change can be viewed as an example of relatively simple learning: either trial and error or a revision of tactics based on the simple perception of a new opportunity. In Tetlock's terms, this would correspond to a change in cognitive content at the tactical level. In Haas's terms, it would be a form, not of learning, but of adaptation. Perceiving that Nasser's opposition to the Baghdad Pact made him available as a potential ally ("the enemy of my enemy is my friend") hardly required a major cognitive reorientation.

But this is an exceedingly narrow view of what was happening in

Soviet policy at the time. The Czech-Egyptian arms deal was but one manifestation of a much broader shift in policy clusters across several Third World regions. That shift toward acquisitive activism was accompanied by cognitive changes that were more far-reaching. Some of the most fundamental perceptions and beliefs associated with the late-Stalinist world view were rejected. Moreover, this change also entailed a change in short-term policy objectives. Khrushchev and his political allies valued more highly than did Stalin the urge to compete actively for influence and allies in noncontiguous regions. They also valued more highly the self-image of the Soviet Union as a global, not just a continental, power. Whether the new perceptions of opportunity and threat caused, accompanied, or were caused by the change in values may be impossible to determine. But the changes in both perceptions and objectives are undeniable.

In this light, the changes of the 1950s would constitute higher-order learning of two sorts presented by Tetlock: cognitive content and cognitive structure. The content of both objectives and strategies changed, as did the supporting beliefs and perceptions that had justified the previous objectives and strategies. And cognitive structure became more integratively complex: foreign policy makers acknowledged more complex trade-offs among values and beliefs, sought to reconcile these through more complex strategies, and sought to justify them through more complex doctrinal formulations. Even by Haas's more restricted definition of learning, the changes of the 1950s might qualify as learning. New goals and strategies were adopted, based on a redefinition of cause-and-effect relationships in the international environment.[6]

Yet one could also argue that the *limits* of the reevaluation of the 1950s are as salient as the scope. With respect to goals, the commitment to anti-imperialism is a point of continuity between the Russia-first and the global activism tendencies. Each tendency was also based on the optimistic assumption that time was on the side of progressive historical forces, and that socialism would eventually emerge victorious over capitalism. While global activism was based on a more differentiated image of imperialism, it still shared with the Stalinist mentality an image of the adversary as a malign force seeking to maintain or extend its spheres of domination. And while the image of the international order in the 1950s became more differentiated, it still essentially divided the world into antagonistic blocs between which the uncommitted states would eventually choose. Whether a break with these points of continuity is necessary to qualify the change as learning rather than adaptation may be a matter of definitional taste. These aspects of continuity become more important, however, as we seek to *explain* the scope and limits of change, which is the matter to which we now turn.

A contributory, but not sufficient, cause of the shift was Soviet ideology. The ideological tradition was decidedly universalist and globalist. Lenin's theory of imperialism posited that the colonial world would prove to be the weak link in the imperialist global chain. Once the colonies began to break away from the metropoles, the final crisis of capitalism would set in. Much discussion had taken place in the years following the Bolshevik revolution about Soviet obligations to support national liberation and the desirable or feasible Soviet role in the "anti-imperialist struggle." Thus, the changes that took place after Stalin constituted doctrinal reversion, not revelation or inspiration. Stalin had postponed the globalist mission, being more comfortable with a continental state of siege. Some of his lieutenants, however, interpreted the decolonization that followed World War II as a sign that a strategy of global activism could now be pursued with profit. Thus, the ideological heritage provided ideas that had lain dormant for many years (but visible, for they had been turned into ritual incantations) and that suddenly proved useful, first for identifying new opportunities and later for legitimizing the urge to pursue them.[7]

Ideology could only do so much in the face of Stalin's opposition, though. Clearly, a necessary condition for the change was the death of Stalin. This did not predetermine the outcome, however. There were at least three positions in the leadership following Stalin's death. Molotov argued for maintaining the Russia-first posture toward the outside world. He was willing to go along with selective measures to reduce the inordinate level of tension in East-West relations at the time (the Korean War was still going on, and Eisenhower-Dulles had just taken office, with talk of using atomic weapons in Korea and of "rolling back" communism in Eastern Europe). But beyond these measures, Molotov saw no reason to break with Stalin's view of the world. Malenkov, in contrast, argued for a sustained effort to engage the West in a negotiating process that would result in agreements to defuse the German and Central European situations. Malenkov was interested primarily in cooperation geared toward crisis prevention, but was Eurocentric, not Third World oriented. He saw the Third World as little more than an arena in which Soviet foreign trade might reach deals that would improve the consumer situation in the Soviet Union; he did not advocate military and economic assistance programs to those countries.[8]

Khrushchev struck a posture that sought to discredit both of these positions, though he dealt with them sequentially, not simultaneously, in the process dominating the center of the political spectrum. Malenkov was accused of being too easily intimidated and of giving away too much to the West. Molotov was accused of failing to recognize the danger of continuing in the old way. Khrushchev argued instead for a policy of negotiating *from strength*, both by building up Soviet nuclear capability and by competing for influence in the Third World. He defined global competition as a Soviet *right*, bestowed on her by her status as a superpower. At the same time, Khrushchev sought to demonstrate, through conciliatory gestures in 1955–1956, that he could strike deals with the West that would keep tensions from getting out of hand and that would extricate the Soviet Union from highly escalatory situations. His was a promise of both global competition and tough East-West negotiation on European and arms control issues. At that time, he did not envisage that such collaboration would extend to Third World conflicts. Rather, the Third World was one of several arenas in which Soviet advances would demonstrate to the imperialists that they had no choice but to do business with the Soviet Union on what Moscow defined as reasonable terms.

One can imagine how the ideological heritage facilitated the victory of Khrushchev's Third World strategy. Substantively, the heritage justified both the desirability and the feasibility of a reversion to global activism. In addition, the ideology's missionary optimism was perfectly suited to the strategy Khrushchev was articulating. I am not arguing that Khrushchev won the power struggle because of his Third World policy and its relationship to the ideological heritage. Rather, this policy was part of the package of domestic and foreign policies he put forth to bolster his appeal, and this part resonated with establishment audiences attracted to the idea of getting the country moving again on the global stage. But none of this would have been possible at the time it took place without the death of Stalin and the subsequent power struggle, which encouraged the leading competitors for leadership to propose alternative programs of domestic and foreign policies.[9] Thus, political competition and programmatic differentiation during a succession struggle, in the ideological context of Soviet elite political culture, at a time when previous policies had been substantially discredited, propelled the redefinition of Soviet goals, perceptions, self-image, and policies that took place during 1953–1955.

Although Third World and Middle Eastern issues may have proven useful to Khrushchev in formulating a distinctive program during the power struggle, they proved to be somewhat more confounding in the subsequent period of political ascendancy, when consensual problem solving became the greater imperative. Khrushchev did not anticipate how complex an arena of struggle the Middle East would prove to be: how difficult it would be to achieve exclusivity in relations with clients and how unreliable "progressive" allies would be in their treatment of indigenous communist parties, in their willingness to heed Moscow's urgings, and in their paths of development. Nor did Khrushchev anticipate the magnitude of the challenge involved in deterring Western military intervention in the region and in avoiding superpower confrontation should he seek to assist clients against Western military pressure. In sum, Khrushchev's optimistic assumptions about the course of history and his optimistic perceptions of opportunity and threat were quickly put to the test.

Although Khrushchev treated Europe and the arms race as appropriate arenas for superpower collaboration in the 1950s, he had not developed a strategy of East-West crisis prevention to complement his more assertive policies in the Third World. Moscow did call for joint U.S.– Soviet action against Britain, France, and Israel after their invasions of Suez, but this was hardly a "cooperative" offer, given that only U.S. allies would be the objects of the superpowers' collusive coercion. Moscow did periodically call for summit meetings to resolve conflicts peacefully and called for mutual pledges not to intervene in the Middle East. But these declaratory statements reflected Moscow's lack of substantial influence over events and her unwillingness to sign on as a military protector of the Egyptians against Israeli or Western actions. The primary means by which the Soviets sought to prevent East-West confrontation in the Middle East was by simply avoiding Soviet engagement in escalating trains of events.

Khrushchev had not counted on the contradictions and dilemmas his entry into the Middle East competition would spawn for Soviet foreign policy. The invasion of Suez by England, France, and Israel took place in November 1956. Turkey and Syria confronted each other in 1957. The United States sent troops to Lebanon, and England sent troops to Jordan, in 1958. A coup brought anti-Western forces to power in Iraq in July 1958, but the Iraqi regime remained a bitter rival of Egypt's Nasser. Nasser reached agreement with Syria in 1959 on establishment of the United Arab Republic, a move that the Soviet Union opposed.

More than anything, these instabilities highlighted the basic Soviet dilemma. On one hand, they wanted to be recognized as a legitimate (or at least undeniable) power in the region and sought to rally anti-imperialist forces in a bid to undermine Western hegemony. On the other hand, they wanted to avoid a military confrontation with the United States. This put them in the position of seeking to maintain their credibility as a *patron* of the Arabs against the imperialists without having to sign on as the *military protector* of the Arabs against Western counterthrusts. The maintenance of credibility was an especially taxing challenge, for the Soviets lacked the will to play chicken with the West in the Middle East, were substantially inferior to the West in power projection capability, and were attempting to hide the extent of their inferiority in the nuclear arms race. Hence, Moscow was put in the position of being forced to bluff to maintain or augment its prestige—a situation that constantly threatened exposure of its weakness or the limits of its commitment to that turbulent region.

The Suez crisis made salient to Soviet leaders at least part of the dilemma they were facing and the limits of their optimistic assumptions about their ability to combine competitive assertiveness with confrontation avoidance. Subsequent events only reinforced those lessons. Accordingly, "after the events of the summer and fall of 1956, the Soviet Union for two years pursued a policy of extreme caution in the Arab East. Its efforts were directed primarily at spreading Soviet influence economically, not politically."[10] As Smolansky further states: "Since there was no doubt in Khrushchev's mind that he would not commit his armed forces to the defense of Nasir or Qasim [the anti-Western Iraqi leader who came to power in the coup of July 1958], the crushing of one or both would reveal to all the world the basic Soviet weakness vis-à-vis the West, which the Kremlin had been trying so hard to avoid."[11]

The optimism that Khrushchev had propounded about the Soviet ability to compete in the Middle East, while dented by the Western interventions, nonetheless remained strong. For Soviet optimism was predicated not only on Soviet capabilities but more fundamentally on an ideologically conditioned belief that the course of history would reinforce anti-imperialism in the Third World, that progressive forces would come to power, or that nationalist forces would engage in progressive behavior. These premises were apparently reinforced by many other events of 1957–1959. Thus, in Jordan and Lebanon, after the Western military interventions, conservative governments collapsed. In Iraq, the coup brought to power a regime that renounced the Baghdad Pact, Western military assistance, and Western bases while also proving willing to bring Communists into the ruling coalition. In light of this, it is not surprising that Moscow in 1959 declared unprecedented doctrinal optimism about the probability that indigenous forces in the Arab world would soon undertake a determined struggle to expel Western economic, political, and military sources of influence or control.[12]

But Khrushchev remained apprehensive about the reliability or strength of these indigenous forces. His interactions with Nasser during 1959–1960 apparently led him to the conclusion that the Egyptian leader was pursuing a conscious policy of playing the superpowers against each other. This forced Khrushchev to face his own intolerance of ambiguity and his sectarian activist urge for exclusive patron-client relations with Third World governments. At the same time, Khrushchev felt the need to play the game out of fear that, should the Soviet Union fail to compete vigorously, the West would be accorded a clear field to reestablish its hegemony through economic penetration and dependence.[13] Implicit in these fears was the assumption that Soviet optimism about the indigenous course of events was fragile at best. Also implicit was an assumption that local regimes were controllable (that nationalism was not a sufficient obstacle to reconstitution of imperialist domination) and that the superpower rivalry in this arena was therefore a zero-sum game.

Instability continued to plague Syria and Iraq during 1961–1964, and intra-Arab feuds marked relations among Cairo, Baghdad, and Damascus. Soviet economic, technical, and military assistance was not purchasing stable or reliable allies, as Syria and Iraq experienced changes of government and renewed persecution of their communist parties. This persistent unpredictability reinforced the conclusion drawn in the Soviet leadership in 1961 that Moscow would have to value these allies primarily for their foreign policy contributions to the struggle against imperialism, rather than for any transition they might make to socialism or for their toleration of local communists. Thus, Khrushchev's optimism of 1959 that indigenous forces in the Third World, the Middle East included, would make an imminent transition to radical, pro-Soviet regimes was largely abandoned at the doctrinal level by 1961.

How should we conceptualize and explain the changes in Soviet thinking about the Middle East that took place during 1956–1961? For the most part, the cognitive changes would correspond to a change in cognitive content at the level of beliefs supportive of the use of certain tactics or strategies. Soviet leaders came to appreciate that reconciling sectarian activism with confrontation avoidance would be a major challenge. They also gained a heightened awareness of some of the complexities of the region and of its nonconformity to the most optimistic theories of historical development that Soviet officials were touting. One could argue that the doctrinal revision of 1961 constituted a higher level of integrative complexity, and thus a form of learning that was more than just a greater appreciation of the degree of complexity of the environment. However, subsequent events would suggest that the change did not run quite that deep: that Soviet perspectives were marked by greater *complexity*, but not by greater *integrative complexity*, since an alternative conception of the basic cause-and-effect relationships within the regional order, and a redefinition of value trade-offs, were not adopted. This limitation on reevaluation may reflect a universal tendency not to leap to drastic conclusions at the first signs of frustration. Or alternatively, it may have been a product of a political need to avoid admitting that previous perspectives were inadequate, given the highly optimistic promises Khrushchev had been making in the late 1950s. Or it may have derived from the fact that Soviet optimism about the direction of historical development is ideologically conditioned, and that ideology provides reassurance that the road to socialism will be one with many temporary detours ("two steps forward, one step back"). Whatever the cause, one thing that did *not* take place was change of a more fundamental sort: in goals, in the preference ordering among goals on the part of those making policy, or in the basic theory of how the international order is configured and develops—beyond those that had taken place in 1953–1954. In light of these limitations, what took place during 1956–1961 was, in Haas's terms, adaptation, not learning.

The modest changes that did take place, then, can be viewed as products of crises and shocks that violated optimistic Soviet expectations, that highlighted contradictions among Soviet goals, and, perhaps most important, that raised the salience to Soviet leaders of the risks and dangers associated with involvement as a patron of Arab governments. A decline in the perception of opportunity accompanied a rise in the perception of threat.

The Arab-Israeli conflict was not central to Soviet policy at the time; rather, the East-West competition for the allegiance of Arab governments was paramount. As Klinghoffer puts it, regarding Soviet-Israeli relations, "the period from 1956 to 1963 was mainly one of benign neglect from the standpoint of the Soviets. They curried favor with the Arabs, generally disregarded Israel, but did not act decisively against its interests."[14]

This policy of caution and avoidance did not last for long. An environmental change intervened in the early 1960s that deepened Soviet commitment to military competition in the region: naval decisions made after the Cuban missile crisis, reinforced by U.S. deployment of the Polaris nuclear submarine in the eastern Mediterranean, which posed a strategic threat to the Soviet heartland. "The Kremlin had no choice but to attempt to counter this new threat to its security. Attempted permanent deployment of the Soviet fleet in the Mediterranean in 1964 makes sense only in the light of this strategic necessity."[15] This perception led Moscow to push for closer tactical military cooperation with Egypt, still apparently the most reliable, stable, and strategically situated Arab client in the region. Indeed, according to Ro'i, the Soviets opted in 1964 for "joint Arab action against Israel within the framework of Arab summitry . . . as a manifestation of true Arab unity."[16] Thus, a higher priority for military competition in the Middle East entered Soviet policy toward the region in 1963–1964, primarily as a result of a perceived strategic challenge.[17] This did not entail a change in goals, goal structure, assumptions about historical development, beliefs about the dynamics of international politics, or even a redefinition of the image of the adversary. It only entailed an increased perception of threat, which triggered a tactical shift. Whether that shift was inevitable, given the nature of the challenge, or whether it was driven by the political need to compensate for a retrenchment in other aspects of Soviet Third World policy, is worth further investigation. But the tactical change does not appear to bear heavily on theories of learning. It is clearly a case of adaptation, in Haas's terms, or of Tetlock's reward-punishment conception of learning.

THE KHRUSHCHEV SUCCESSION

In Soviet policy toward the Middle East, then, the Khrushchev era ended (in October 1964) on a relatively militant note. His successors, while continuing to try to neutralize U.S. strategic assets in the Eastern Mediterranean (indeed, they received logistical rights at Egyptian airfields and ports in March 1966), sought to reduce the posture of militancy that Khrushchev had struck toward Israel. As Klinghoffer reports: "Soviet-Israeli relations hit their highest point in 1965 and early 1966, the apogée having been achieved briefly in 1948. The campaign against Jews as economic criminals was muted. . . . Synagogues were no longer closed down by the authorities. . . . Soviet behavior during the winter of 1965–1966 was related to the possibility that the Soviets would sponsor Arab-Israeli peace negotiations by convening another 'Tashkent' [a Soviet-sponsored mediation of the Indo-Pakistani dispute]."[18]

This posture did not last long, however. The Syrian revolution of February 1966 brought to power a self-proclaimed radical Ba'athist regime, which sought close ties with the Soviet Union. Moscow was more than willing to oblige. Soviet relations with Israel worsened very shortly thereafter, at Soviet initiative. And Soviet doctrinal pronouncements of 1966 came to stress the need for unity of all *progressive* forces in the Arab world against both Arab "reaction" and "imperialism," a sectarian emphasis. Arms flows to Syria and Egypt increased, as did Soviet rhetorical support for the Arab position in the conflict with Israel. Moscow was moving closer, it seems, to the role of military protector, not just supplier, of her clients in the region. We will later ask why this happened.

Soviet leaders again were quickly faced with the dilemma of reconciling competitive activism, in this case of an increasingly sectarian character, with confrontation avoidance. Heikal reports that Soviet leaders at this time were quite nervous about the prospects for uncontrolled escalation. They embraced the Arab cause and Arab demands, but were fearful that U.S. escalation in Vietnam, the U.S. invasion of the Dominican Republic, and Israeli efforts to destabilize the Syrian regime would force Moscow to protect her clients against military defeat by the "imperialists."[19] During the escalating tensions of early 1967 (which would eventually get out of control and result in the Six Day War in June), the Soviets toyed with the idea of playing the role of peacemaker, but Nasser vetoed the idea. In November 1966, Kosygin raised with the Egyptian commander-in-chief the question of whether the arms race in the region could be diminished.[20] A month or two later, "Deputy Foreign Minister Semenov met in Baghdad with Soviet ambassadors to Middle Eastern states and the main topic of conversation was how to curb Syria."[21]

While these initiatives were geared toward conflict management and confrontation avoidance, they hardly constituted a strategy of crisis prevention through superpower cooperation. Rather, they were part of an effort to solidify ties with radical or militant clients while simultaneously seeking ad hoc means of avoiding confrontation and escalation. Since

Soviet clients were generally more militant about regional issues than was Moscow, this proved to be a difficult set of objectives to reconcile. Moscow allowed its clients (Syria and Egypt) to veto its cooperative initiatives, while variously encouraging or tolerating those clients' competitive initiatives. Moscow would caution Cairo and Damascus about going too far and losing control of situations. But it would not threaten or pressure them materially to prevent an escalatory situation from getting out of hand. In the end, Soviet leaders had miscalculated. Lacking much control over the local actors, they sought to demonstrate their solidarity while avoiding responsibility for those actors' actions. They armed Egypt and trumpeted her case, but sought to prevent a war from breaking out. They encouraged Egypt to mobilize troops in the hope of deterring Israel from attacking Syria. But, lacking a cooperative relationship with either the United States or Israel, the Soviets were unable to judge the line between deterrence and provocation. They apparently rationalized either that Israel was too weak and weak-willed to do what it would do in June 1967, or that the United States would prevent Israeli preemption. In sum, the Soviet leadership was pursuing during 1966–1967 a strategy of sectarian activism and confrontation avoidance in the Middle East without a well-developed strategy of crisis prevention.

One could state this sequence in terms of a unitary actor pursuing mixed, and partially conflicting, goals and argue that the ambivalent actor miscalculated. That may well be what transpired. However, we cannot ignore evidence that politics may have lain at the root of Soviet behavior. The initial conciliation of Israel can be seen as the consensual policy of a collective leadership that seeks a benign international environment within which to sort out the messy domestic situation it inherited, as well as a reflection of the uncertain political relationships within the Politburo. That would be consistent with Soviet policy toward the United States, China, Germany, and the Third World generally during the first nine months or so of the Brezhnev-Kosygin regime. However, the international environment then heated up (the Vietnam War and the Cultural Revolution), fueling an ongoing political competition between Kosygin, who was in charge of many foreign policy realms, and Brezhnev, among several others.

Content analyses of the speeches of these two leaders reveal Kosygin to have been a conciliator, whereas Brezhnev emphasized support for national liberation movements in the Third World.[22] Kosygin was apparently attempting to build his authority by demonstrating competence as a peacemaker. He personally mediated the India-Pakistan peace talks in Tashkent and must have been behind the idea of applying the same model to the Arab-Israeli conflict. It was he who wondered aloud to Middle Eastern dignitaries whether there might be some way of deescalating the conflict. He was probably behind the efforts to prevent Syria from becoming adventuristic. In contrast, Brezhnev was probably seeking to undermine Kosygin's foreign policy authority and touted the Syrian revolution of 1966 as a sign that radical transformation in the region was a real prospect. The deepening of Soviet commitment to "progressive" governments in the Middle East, while simultaneously trying to avoid inadvertent escalation, was probably the result of these two forces shaping the definition of Soviet policy.

This interpretation gains force by comparison with the political succession following Stalin's death. In both successions, an initial period of conciliation was followed by political competition over the relative balance of activism versus caution, with the relative hard liner winning out, only to be followed by a situation (the Suez crisis of 1956 and the June war of 1967) that escalated out of Soviet control. In both cases, deepening Soviet commitment took place in a context of growing regional tensions (the Baghdad Pact in 1955 and the Israeli-Syrian tensions of 1966). In both periods, a perceived opportunity to counter Western influence (Nasser's opposition to the Baghdad Pact and the Syrian revolution of February 1966) led to a deepening of Soviet involvement and commitment, amidst a temporary resurgence of optimism about indigenous trends in the region. Finally, in both cases, the general secretary adopted a relatively hard-line position, in contrast to the premier, who either sought conciliation (Kosygin) or had a lesser stake in seizing the opportunities (Malenkov). The general secretary's position was justified in terms of the ideological commitment to struggle against imperialism. As in 1955, so in 1966, a perception of opportunity fed into the political competition during a power struggle, in an ideological context that favored both the desirability and the perceived feasibility (though not urgency) of seizing the opportunities. In 1955, this resulted in the Soviets' adopting the role of patron to Egypt; in 1966–1967, it resulted in the Soviets' deepening this commitment still further and edging toward the role of protector of Syria.

Surely neither Kosygin *nor* Brezhnev wanted or anticipated the devastating defeat inflicted on the Arab states in June 1967. That war, in fact, constituted a watershed in Soviet approaches to dealing with the Arab-Israeli conflict. Debates broke out in Moscow over whether to reinvest billions in Egypt and Syria, or whether to take the low-cost, lower-risk approach of financing guerrilla warfare against Israeli occupation. (Those who advocated the latter approach represented a variant of the Russia-first policy orientation.) Brezhnev won that battle, and the post-Stalin policy of placing bets more on states than on social movements prevailed. Egypt and Syria were resupplied to the tune of $5 billion worth of military assistance. The ambivalent protector role that Moscow had adopted in 1966 was now put to the test. And while Moscow did not physically intervene during the Six Day War, her postwar behavior indicated a deepening of commitment that affirmed her role as protector.

What changed most fundamentally, however, was the Soviet approach to crisis prevention. U.S.–Soviet collaboration in July 1967 to secure Israeli withdrawal from occupied lands in exchange for Arab recognition of Israel's right to exist and an end to the state of war in the region (embodied in United Nations Resolution 242) began a process of interaction that entailed persistent, ongoing U.S.–Soviet discussions and negotiations over the terms of a Middle East settlement. For the first time, a sustained process of mutual adjustment was in place, with superpower or great power cooperation geared, at most, toward conflict resolution and, at least, toward removing the escalatory potential from the Arab-Israeli conflict. Soviet policy in the region for the next 15 years would be predicated on a mix of sectarian activism and crisis-prevention orientations that coexisted very uneasily.

Before turning to the post-1967 period, however, let us reflect on the implications of events of 1964–1966 for our conceptualization of the character and causes of learning in Soviet Middle East policy during those years. Before the war of 1967, cognitive changes informing Soviet policy were an apparent response to the Syrian revolution and its aftermath. An increased perception of both opportunity and risk is in evidence, which deepened the Soviet interest in both sectarian activism and circumstantial confrontation avoidance. That Soviet leaders never reconciled the two reflects either the consequences of political competition for foreign policy or the cognitive failure to achieve a higher level of integrative complexity in regime thinking about the regional environment and the value trade-offs involved. Be that as it may, the cognitive evolution of 1964–1966 did not entail either a change of goals or of goal structure. Soviet objectives remained focused on the acquisition and defense of clients, anti-imperialism, and confrontation avoidance. Nor did the cognitive evolution entail a redefinition of cause-effect relationships in the regional or international orders. Thus, the changes do not qualify as learning by Haas's definition, and they qualify only as learning of new cognitive content at the level of beliefs about tactics by Tetlock's definitions.

The shock of the 1967 war, however, ushered in a shift in the policy clusters dominant in Soviet policy toward the region. By combining sectarian activism with a developing strategy of cooperation for purposes of crisis prevention, Soviet leaders embraced a set of conflicting objectives that would require for their integration a new level of integrative complexity in thinking about the region. They would be forced to acknowledge the irreconcilability of sectarian activism and confrontation avoidance in the absence of a cooperative relationship with Israel's patron. Hence, their appreciation of value trade-offs among goals would increase. This constituted, not an abandonment of previous goals, but rather a reordering of the relative priority among goals and a redefinition of cause-effect relationships in the region. This may not qualify as learning by Haas's definition, however, for it was not informed by consensual knowledge, may have represented a trade-off among bargainers, and did not result in an elaborate and integrated strategy for reconciling conflicts among goals. Indeed, the change may constitute that type of adaptation that Haas refers to as the grafting of new goals onto a preexisting goal structure, without new cause-effect schemata to deepen the understanding of value trade-offs.

By Tetlock's definitions, the change qualifies as cognitive structural learning, for it is based on a realization that trade-offs among old and new goals must be made, even if understanding as to the precise content of those trade-offs remains highly limited. If the new goal structure was a product of bargaining between political actors with conflicting preferences, the deal may have been reached without any individual's having achieved a higher level of integrative complexity in his thinking. But that is doubtful, given the magnitude of the shock inflicted by the June war. Moreover, failure to think through the nature of the conflicts among the goals would have been a transitory condition. The continuous bargaining that ensued between the United States and the Soviet Union during 1967–1972, in a context of military escalation in the region, would have forced Soviet leaders very quickly to think about ways of reconciling the conflicts within the new goal structure. As we shall see, the Brezhnev regime never found a satisfying policy to reconcile those conflicts, but that was in part due to lack of U.S. receptivity and is an issue distinct from the question of integrative complexity being addressed in this paragraph.

SECTARIAN ACTIVISM AND CRISIS PREVENTION 1967–1985

The sectarian activist strand in Soviet regional policy found plenty of opportunities for expression during 1967–1982. Indeed, the structure of the situation made that predictable. In contrast to the preceding 10 years, the Arab-Israeli conflict had now become the most salient, and imminently escalatory, conflict in the region. In addition, with the massive Soviet resupply of Egypt and Syria after the June 1967 war and the U.S. decision to sign on as Israel's military supplier (to compensate for France's decision to withdraw from that role), the Arab-Israeli conflict now became a direct U.S.–Soviet confrontation. Then too, the main local actors (Egypt and Syria on the Arab side, Israel on the other) happened to share the beliefs that: (1) it was in their respective interests to deepen their patrons' level of military and political commitment and (2) efforts at U.S.–Soviet collusion should be impeded by the actions of local states, in order to head off an imposed settlement. Since the local actors had the power to escalate violence in the region, thereby "forcing" their patron or protector to engage in acts expressive of its military commitment to defend its client, the local actors had leverage that allowed them to spoil delicate superpower efforts to coordinate policy and cooperate with each other.

Under these conditions, only a deep mutual commitment to conflict mitigation through superpower cooperation, informed by a commonly held theory about how to reshape regional dynamics through superpower collusion, could have broken through these constraints. Yet such a commitment did not exist in sufficient strength on either side, and such a theory was not held in common between the superpowers. The Soviets were apparently sincere in their efforts to strike a deal that would deescalate the conflict, by teaming with the United States to induce or coerce Israel to trade land for an armed peace and regional normalization of relations that would be guaranteed by the superpowers. However, whenever the Arabs or Israel escalated the situation on the ground, whenever the U.S. increased visibly its military support for Israel, or whenever the Soviets perceived themselves as being excluded from a budding peace process, their reaction was to up the competitive ante and demonstrate their anti-imperialist credentials and their reliability as a patron or protector.

In the United States the commitment to superpower collaboration was much weaker than it was in Moscow. The United States maintained a fairly constant commitment to protect Israel, to supply her sufficiently to ensure her continued military superiority, and to attempt to drive a wedge between the Soviet Union and her allies in the region in order to facilitate unilateral U.S. mediation of the peace process. U.S. exclusionary diplomacy, which began in earnest in 1970 and continued through the Reagan administration, represented a competitive challenge to the Soviet Union that usually resulted in Soviet efforts to deepen ties to other, typically more militant, allies (both social and governmental) in the region and to find ways of obstructing the exclusionary process. If the United States was going to try to deal with the Arab-Israeli conflict unilaterally and presumably at the expense of Soviet interests, then the challenge to Moscow was to find means of demonstrating that, whatever its weaknesses in the region, the Soviet Union could effectively spoil the American game. Yet defiant Soviet behavior in response to exclusion helped to validate politically the conclusion drawn in Washington that the Soviet commitment to peace through collaboration was disingenuous.

Throughout these years, dominant Soviet leaders were interested in conflict mitigation in the Middle East, or even in a settlement of the Arab-Israeli conflict. But the terms they proposed were geared toward both settling the conflict *and* maintaining or consolidating Soviet influence in the region. Conflict resolution, then, was not ranked as high in Soviet preference orderings as influence consolidation. Moscow's assumption was that unilateral U.S. mediation of the conflict would aim at settlement terms that would undermine Soviet influence with her allies in the region.

In order to prevent such an eventuality, Moscow defined fortification of exclusive, military ties with allies in the region as a vital component of the negotiation process. Since the Arab states had emerged from the 1967 war in a situation of obvious military inferiority and vulnerability, the purpose of building them up militarily was to ensure that they would not be forced to negotiate from a position of abject weakness. The immediate objectives of Soviet activism in the region during these 15 years, then, were manifold: (1) to fortify the negotiating position of her clients; (2) to heighten the potential military cost to Israel of another preemptive attack; (3) to demonstrate Soviet reliability as a patron in the face of tactical setbacks to her clients; (4) to demonstrate to the United States that Soviet claims to being a power in the region could not be simply ignored, and that exclusion of the Soviet Union from the negotiating process would be likely to undermine that process; and (5) to compensate for losses (such as Egyptian defection to the U.S. side or the Israeli invasion of Lebanon) by strengthening or expanding ties to more militant forces in the region (the Palestine Liberation Organization [PLO], Libya, Algeria).

The Soviet urge to cooperate with the United States in order to defuse the Arab-Israeli conflict had the objective of removing the escalatory potential from the Arab-Israeli conflict so as to place firmer ground under the dual policies of confrontation avoidance and influence consolidation, while simultaneously forging a collaborative relationship with the United States that would yield benefits in other realms of policy. The factors that caused this shift in the preference ordering among Soviet goals may be broken down into those reflecting an *increased* perception of *threat* and those reflecting a *reduced* perception of *opportunity*. The increased perception of threat included: (1) shock at the magnitude of the setback in the June 1967 war and (2) growing awareness of the unprecedented escalatory potential inherent in that conflict, as demonstrated in 1967, again in 1969–1970 during the war of attrition (when the Soviet Union assumed responsibility for the air defense of Egypt), again during the 1973 war, again during the mid-1970s when Israeli acquisition of nuclear capability became known, and again in the war in Lebanon in 1982. The perception of reduced opportunity for unilateral competitive gain grew from: (1) recognition that the Soviet Union had relatively little direct, nonmilitary leverage over Israel: that such leverage could only be exercised through Washington; (2) recognition that the Arab states were operating from a position of objective military weakness that was not likely to change in the foreseeable future; and (3) belief that a settlement (not peace and harmony, but an "armed peace" [23] based on superpower guarantees) might have a better chance of stabilizing Soviet presence and influence in the region, in contrast to a situation in which Soviet clients pursued their own interests and then dared the Soviet Union not to support them (Nasser in the war of attrition, Sadat in 1972–1973, Syria in Lebanon during 1975–1976 and again in the 1980s, the PLO in its use of terrorism and in its refusal to recognize Israel).

Thus, we find during the years in question a dualistic tendency in Soviet behavior, consistent with a simultaneous commitment to both sectarian activism and crisis prevention. But, while new perceptions and objectives informed this new goal structure, Soviet leaders had not interrelated the beliefs that informed their policies along each track. Or, alternatively, they had interrelated them but based on the most optimistic assumptions. The consequence of all this, however, was that the Soviets painted themselves into a militant corner. The United States was disinterested in Soviet collaborative initiatives, preferring instead to go it alone (with some exceptions, such as 1969 and 1977 [Secretaries of State Rogers and Vance], which never lasted long) and apparently confident that Moscow could be successfully excluded. The Soviet Union had almost no influence over Israeli policy, given the lack of diplomatic relations between the countries, and therefore could not compete with the United States for the role of mediator. Soviet arms did not purchase Soviet control over the behavior of clients, which limited Soviet ability to convince Washington that its collaborative initiatives were not disingenuous. The Soviets lacked the economic resources to purchase leverage through development assistance (a factor that the United States used continually to encourage Egyptian defection from Soviet patronage and, later, from the militant Arab bloc). Finally, the Soviet tendency to *deepen* ties with militant, "rejectionist" forces in the face of frustration, rather than to extend a hand to more moderate forces, constricted Soviet options, both in dealing with the United States and in the region.

The kinds of learning that took place during 1967–1985 were not profound. There surely took place some cognitive evolution at the level of beliefs supportive of discrete tactics. In particular, Soviet leaders surely learned more about the controllability of individual allies than they had anticipated in, say, 1966, when they embraced the radical Syrian regime. Soviet expectations were violated by Nasser, when he initiated the war of attrition; by Sadat, when he expelled the Soviets in 1972 and when he proved determined to go to war in 1973; by Syria, when it intervened militarily in Lebanon in 1975–1976 and attacked the PLO; by Libya's Qaddafi throughout much of this period; by factional leaders within the PLO, who persistently refused to heed Soviet advice to emphasize political over military struggle. Some cognitive evolution also took place regarding the volatility and danger of the general situation in the region, about the dangers of fundamentalism in the region (post-1979), about ways in which "Arab unity" could often work *against* Soviet interests, and about the deep sources of U.S. and Israeli opposition to Soviet participation in the peace process.

But none of these acknowledgments led to a more integratively complex appreciation of the nature of the regional political order, either in the speeches of top leaders or in the authoritative interpretations of *Pravda* analyses. A content analysis of the articles published by *Pravda's* main Middle East analyst, Pavel Demchenko, reveals that he continued, despite the frustrations, to tout both crisis prevention and sectarian activism, the former in order to cope with an increasingly dangerous and volatile environment, and the latter in order to compensate defiantly for Soviet exclusion and frustration. However, the same analyst never concluded that the nature of regional or international politics, or the nature of the adversary, precluded the success of efforts to reconcile sectarian activism and crisis prevention. Rather, he continued to tout the need for "anti-imperialist Arab unity" to frustrate the efforts of Washington and Jerusalem to prevent Palestinian self-determination or Soviet inclusion.[24] The assumption remained strong that ideological affinity and common "anti-imperialism" would eventually make possible the creation of exclusive and reliable ties between the Soviet Union and her clients in the Middle East. At the same time, the assumption also remained that imperialism would eventually see the light and recognize its inability to make permanent U.S. and Israeli hegemony in the region.

Indeed, the limits of Soviet learning during these years are also symptomatic of the limits of the cognitive change that took place after the June 1967 war. The shock of that war led the leadership to graft new goals onto the preexisting goal structure, without a consensual understanding of the contradictions and trade-offs among goals. One finds in the writings of Pavel Demchenko, and of others who sought to combine collaboration with competition, a puzzlement and dismay at the unwillingness of the United States and Israel to bend to the Soviet view of things and an occasional lack of confidence in Soviet assumptions about regional dynamics, although without articulation of an alternative set of relevant assumptions. I take this to be the mark of that form of adaptation that Haas expects when the goal structure is made more complex but the underlying theory about cause-effect relationships has not changed fundamentally.

This also means that Soviet learning from 1968 or so to the death of Brezhnev did not entail a further redefinition of goals. The main Soviet goals remained those that had emerged from the lengthy policy reevaluation that followed the shock of the 1967 war: to secure political influence and strategic assets in the region, to limit U.S. ability to acquire these things, to avoid a superpower military confrontation in the region, to prevent events in the region from undermining higher-priority goals in other spheres of the relationship with the United States, and to advance the cause of a peace settlement that would reduce or remove the escalatory potential from the Arab-Israeli conflict. The first three of these goals represented continuity with the goals ascendant since 1955; the last two were newly defined as operational priorities only in the aftermath of the 1967 war. But they all remained on the agenda, in roughly the same order of priority, in 1985.

As in many areas of foreign policy, Gorbachev's coming to power resulted in a comprehensive reevaluation of the assumptions underlying Soviet Middle East policy. Some experts and policy influentials who had never bought fully into the Brezhnevite strategy were now offered the opportunity to advocate alternative assumptions and perspectives. What we find during the Gorbachev years is the beginnings of a reevaluation that suggest a greater emphasis on ecumenical activism, at the expense of the sectarian variant, and a search for a new strategy for combining activism with crisis prevention. In short, we are witnessing an attempt to acknowledge and come to terms with the probable incompatibility of sectarian activism and crisis prevention.

SEARCH FOR A NEW MIX UNDER GORBACHEV

Gorbachev's reevaluation continues to this day and therefore cannot be evaluated as a finished product. But we can characterize the direction and, thus far, the extent of change, inquiring into the causes of each and the implications for our thinking about learning.

The reevaluation has not led to a renunciation of sectarian activism in the region.[25] Indeed, the Soviet Union continues to supply Syria with large quantities of advanced weaponry and continues to support a unified PLO as an instrument for waging the struggle against Israeli and U.S. policy. What's more, Soviet settlement terms have not changed substantially. They continue to back the demand for a Palestinian state, for a PLO role in the process and outcome of negotiations, for Israeli evacuation of occupied territories, and for a central Soviet role in both the negotiations and the guarantees of a settlement. What's more, the primary Soviet goals in the region remain as before: to maintain Soviet influence, to avoid confrontation with the United States, to seek a settlement of the conflict that would exorcise its escalatory potential, to frustrate U.S. efforts to exclude the Soviet Union from the region, and to limit the further expansion of U.S. military presence in the region.

There *has* been a tempering of the sectarian activist impulse, though. Gorbachev has resisted Syrian requests for weaponry that might allow that country to achieve military parity with Israel. Indeed, Gorbachev has publicly lectured Syrian President Assad to abandon his goal of military parity and of seeking a military solution to the conflict with Israel. And yet it is difficult to view these facts as a diminution of militancy relative to the Brezhnev era. For Brezhnev too had denied Egypt and Syria the most advanced offensive weaponry. And he too had lectured the leaders of those countries on the need for a political, not a military, solution to the Arab-Israeli conflict. Nor is it surprising that Gorbachev is maintaining the commitments to Syria and the PLO. The militant box into which the Soviets had painted themselves under Brezhnev, in seeking to create a radical bloc to obstruct U.S. exclusionary diplomacy, left the Soviets with only two palatable allies that were central to the Arab-Israeli conflict. Egypt had defected, Jordan and Saudi Arabia were treated as ideological incompatibles with the Soviet Union, and Libya was never treated as a trustworthy client. Gorbachev could hardly afford to jettison his only bases of access to the region, given his regime's continuing commitment to playing an important great power role in the region. What is distinctive about the sectarian activism under Gorbachev, though, has been its more selective and defensive character. In contrast to Brezhnev, who sought to expand and deepen ties with more militant forces in response to frustration, Gorbachev has pushed for the creation of a broad coalition of states and of factions within the PLO supportive of decisive movement toward a political settlement of the conflict.

Moreover, acquisitive sectarian activism has not only been subordinated to defensive sectarian activism (shoring up the capacity of Syria and the PLO to defend themselves); but it has also been decisively subordinated to two other orientations that have been strengthened in both an absolute and a relative sense. Ecumenical activism has been strengthened in a determined Soviet effort to expand political and economic ties with as many regimes as possible in the region. Relations have been opened or increased with the Gulf states: Kuwait, the United Arab Emirates, and Oman. Diplomatic feelers have been extended to Bahrain and Saudi Arabia, resulting ultimately in the announcement in September 1990 that the Soviet Union and these two countries will restore diplomatic relations. Relations with Jordan have been rocky but have resulted in an arms deal, in a Jordanian agreement to push for an international conference that would include the Soviet Union, and in the abrogation in April 1987 of an accord between Hussein and Arafat that had appeared to facilitate further U.S. exclusionary diplomacy. And, perhaps most important, the Soviet Union has restored diplomatic relations with Egypt, rescheduled Egyptian debts to the Soviet Union, and struck a series of bilateral economic deals with that country. The ecumenism behind this sustained effort to expand Soviet ties in the region was even given ideological sanction in the new party program approved under Gorbachev, in which expanded ties with states following the path of capitalist development were declared to be the main direction of contemporary Soviet Third World policy. This is the essence of ecumenical activism. The ties do not typically entail methods that contain escalatory potential, and they are nonexclusionary—that is, they accept the reality that Moscow is competing for influence within an arena that is likely to remain for long considerably open to U.S. influence.

The most dramatically ecumenical manifestation of policy change under Gorbachev has been the opening to Israel. The Soviets have been negotiating with Israel about the terms for restoring diplomatic ties at some level. They have resisted Israeli calls for full restoration of diplomatic relations, but have restored consular relations, reduced their anti-Zionist propaganda, increased Jewish emigration to record levels, released all Soviet Jews who had been imprisoned for Jewish activism, and softened their terms regarding the procedures to be followed within an international conference and the form that Palestinian participation would take. They have indicated that diplomatic relations between the Soviet Union and Israel could be fully restored once Israel accepted the convening of such a conference; previously, Moscow had conditioned such restoration on progress toward an acceptable settlement within the context of such a conference. They have been negotiating with Israel behind the scenes for an omnibus agreement that would expand Israeli-Soviet trade and garnered Israeli support for abrogation of U.S. restrictions on U.S.–Soviet trade and credits, among other things. In 1988–1989, they pressured the PLO to recognize Israel, to renounce terror, and to accept U.N. Resolutions 242 and 338. Moscow played a very active role behind the scenes to induce Yasir Arafat to change his language regarding acceptance of a two-state solution and rejection of the PLO Charter.

In a similar vein, in December 1988, Soviet Foreign Minister Eduard Shevardnadze made a highly publicized tour of the region, during which he met in Cairo with Israeli Foreign Minister Moshe Arens, as well as with Yasir Arafat. Throughout his journey, he played down the traditional Soviet settlement terms. Instead, he emphasized procedural innovations for getting negotiations started, as well as new military and political proposals for guaranteeing Israeli security in the context of a settlement (intrusive on-site inspections of military installations and the banning of chemical weapons and ballistic missiles from the region, for example).

In sum, the policy changes under Gorbachev (as of October 1990) constitute an upgrading of the importance placed on crisis prevention and ecumenical activism relative to sectarian activism. They have expressed themselves in greater flexibility about negotiating terms and competitive behavior that is less sectarian. While the Brezhnev regime was also interested in deescalating or settling the Arab-Israeli conflict, one gets the impression that the Gorbachev regime is even more interested in doing so—that it is willing to pay a higher price toward that end.

Neil Malcolm has written that to current Soviet leaders "the Middle East now represents more a problem to be solved than an opportunity to be exploited."[26] This interesting and accurate observation requires further specification. Under Khrushchev, the Middle East was viewed largely as an opportunity to be exploited, with a number of risks to be averted. After the shocks of the 1967 war and the suspense of the war of attrition (1969–1970), Soviet leaders viewed the area as *both* an opportunity to be exploited *and* a problem to be solved, for the cause-effect schemata they brought to deliberation of the problem still assumed that time was on the side of the Arabs. This assumption eroded but did not disappear during the 1970s and is sustained to this day by the belief that Palestinian rights cannot forever be denied. However, the Middle East competition has proven to be so risky, unpredictable, costly, and injurious to Soviet pursuit of high-priority goals, that one gets the impression that, under Gorbachev, Malcolm is correct in claiming that the situation is now viewed by the dominant coalition in Moscow as *more* a problem to be solved than an opportunity to be exploited.

What might explain this shift? One possibility is that Soviet authorities are reacting to the perceived ineffectiveness of Brezhnev's strategy for attaining goals common to both the Brezhnev and Gorbachev regimes (regional stabilization and Soviet influence consolidation, at acceptable cost and risk). Having boxed themselves into a corner, they are seeking to expand their options in pursuit of both competitive and collaborative goals. They have been less sectarian about the competitive game and less inflexible about negotiating terms, because the previous approach had discredited its ability to compete for influence and allies, its ability to gain inclusion in an international peace process, and its ability to reduce the risk of regional war and superpower confrontation. At a time when the deteriorating Soviet domestic situation dictated priority attention to the home front, Soviet leaders could rationalize both the desirability and the urgency of reevaluating previous policies and assumptions regarding the Middle East. The death of Brezhnev created the political space required to allow this subterranean learning to surface and become policy. The speed of Gorbachev's consolidation of power, which was made possible by the unprecedented interregna of Andropov and Chernenko, allowed the new Soviet leader to suppress much of the political competition that marked previous succession periods and to impose a policy consistent with the subterranean learning—a policy that ran counter to the optimistic, more hard-line biases of the ideology. To the extent that this divergence needs to be justified to political audiences that continue to buy into traditional thinking, Gorbachev can depict the changes in Middle East and Third World policy as a necessary breathing spell before the next historical period of opportunities for expansion. The implication of this interpretation is that, with respect to the Middle East, the kind of learning that has informed these changes has been merely a change in the content of the beliefs that inform tactics or strategies. In Haas's terms, this constitutes adaptation of tactics within the old goal structure. Until we have the opportunity to witness further evolution in Soviet policy toward the region, this pessimistic interpretation is at least plausible and cannot be ruled out.

However, a more optimistic interpretation can be posited. A broader epistemological revolution, which has been dubbed *new thinking*, has been taking place in Soviet foreign policy making. Since the content of new thinking has been analyzed by Robert Legvold in this volume (Chapter 18), I will not outline its components at any great length. But some elements are worth mentioning, if we are seeking the cognitive sources of a shift away from sectarian activism, and if we posit that an important change in values or goal structure has been under way.

The new thinking posits that: (1) the international order is marked by tight coupling (interdependence); (2) regional competition is often a negative-sum game, in which both sides lose; (3) security among adversaries must be mutual; political instruments and accommodation through reassurance must replace military instruments and deterrence through intimidation as the bases for security; (4) linkage is a reality in U.S. politics; and (5) local actors cannot be controlled and are not likely ever to be controllable. Acceptance of these premises makes it difficult to legitimize (either to oneself or to one's domestic audiences) the feasibility of an optimistic policy of sectarian activism, with its stress on struggle, exclusive relationships, reliable allies, military competition, and the supplanting of imperialist positions at acceptable risk. Acceptance of these new perspectives on the nature of the international order constitutes not just a new level of *complexity* in Soviet thinking, but also a new level of *integrative complexity*. It is a level of integrative complexity that throws into question certain philosophical assumptions basic to Leninist ideology, and thus can undermine belief in the feasibility of ever achieving the traditional normative ends (such as worldwide construction of socialism),[27] or even of ever achieving more immediate and modest objectives (such as the creation of Arab unity on an anti-imperialist basis). Moreover, to the extent that the new package dovetails with rhetorical and behavioral changes in Soviet Middle East policy, it constitutes a genuine upgrading of the relative value placed on the crisis-prevention tendency in Soviet policy.

Were the new thinking to define Soviet Middle East policy in a direct, deductive path of causation, we would expect to find cognitive changes that qualify as learning even by Haas's definition. For the new thinking is decidedly pessimistic about the attainment of traditional ideological goals and about the relevance of Marxist-Leninist theory to understanding the direction of global change in the twenty-first century. It does not conceptualize the present era as a breathing spell. We would therefore expect to witness a subordination of the competitive to the collaborative urge in Soviet foreign policy and a fundamental redefinition of the nature of competition. This would constitute both a redefinition of goals and a rearrangement of the preference ordering among goals. It would have been driven by a growing distaste for military competition in a region in which decades of such sectarian activism have proven so unrewarding. And it would have been informed by a new theory of the dynamics of international relations, as well as by the political ascendancy of a coalition that perceived the adoption of such a theory and of major policy reevaluations to be both desirable and necessary.

As noted, this is the optimistic interpretation of the new thinking, and especially of the applicability of that thinking to Soviet Middle East policy. The package of new thinking has been endorsed and trumpeted at the doctrinal level and has apparently been a factor driving (or rationalizing?) the markedly concessionary Soviet behavior in a number of policy realms, but Soviet officials are more reticent when asked to explain how these new principles have been applied in Middle East policy. Indeed, many of them say quite unabashedly that higher-priority issues have taken precedence (arms control, Europe, Afghanistan, China, Kampuchea), and that the new thinking will be applied to the Arab-Israeli conflict when that issue reaches the top of the foreign policy agenda. Yet when pressed to reveal the hypothetical content of new approaches to this region, Soviet officials do not have much that is new to offer; they appear to be searching for new ideas [personal communications]. But if this is indeed the case, we are left to wonder about the meaning of the changes that *have* taken place. For the time being, therefore, the pessimistic interpretation of changes in Soviet Middle East policy can compete with the optimistic interpretation.

Soviet responses to the Iraqi invasion of Kuwait in August 1990, however, may have provided a test of these alternative hypotheses. In response to the same action, Leonid Brezhnev would have condemned the invasion, urged Saddam Hussein to withdraw his troops from Kuwait, and *perhaps* withheld arms shipments for a period of time. But Brezhnev would probably not have joined the United States in coordinated military, economic, and political pressure on Iraq (a Soviet ally, albeit a fiercely independent one). He certainly would not have sanctioned a large U.S. military build-up in the Persian Gulf and on land, much less offered to cooperate with a United Nations-led military operation against Iraq.

It is true that this issue is not central to the Arab-Israeli conflict. Hence, the lessons of this test of new thinking cannot automatically be generalized to other realms of Soviet policy in the Middle East. Nonetheless, the strikingly conciliatory posture struck by Moscow in this crisis speaks well for the new thinking's grounding in philosophical and normative changes and could therefore portend far-reaching reevaluations of Soviet policy on related issues.

But how far-reaching could we expect the change to be? That is, even if the Gorbachev regime applies the new thinking more fully to the Arab-Israeli conflict, how much further change in Soviet policy can we expect? This question forces us to confront some basic questions about Soviet policy. First, thus far the leadership's felt need to create an international environment supportive of concentration on the home front does not constitute an extreme Russia-first orientation. This is not yet a throwback to Stalin's abdication of interest in global competition in favor of a continental focus, much less a posture of confrontation along the borders. Hence, unless Gorbachev is ready to abandon the Soviet role as a great power in the Middle East, we should not expect abandonment of the Soviet competitive track in the region. Second, ecumenical activists and crisis preventers should not be thought of as nonideological. A content analysis of their publications reveals that they share with sectarian activists a belief that Palestinian nationalism is an irresistible force, destined to achieve national liberation by some means, and that Israeli efforts to deny some form of self-determination to the Palestinians will ultimately prove futile or too costly.[28] Thus, while the level of normative dedication to the Palestinian cause may indeed vary among Soviet policy influentials, they are likely to find consensus among themselves at the level of philosophical beliefs about the intrinsic infeasibility of hard-line U.S. and Israeli policies. The Palestinian uprising of December 1987 to the present could only reinforce these beliefs, as well as the confidence that, if a war can be avoided, time is not on the side of the Israeli hard-line position. Given these points of consensus, abandonment of the basic Soviet commitment to Palestinian self-determination of some sort, or abandonment of the Soviet alliance with Arab states, is very unlikely.

A third reason to question the amount of change likely in Soviet policy stems from the structure of the situation in the Middle East. Quite simply, movement toward a negotiated settlement will depend largely on decisions made in Jerusalem and Washington, or in the capitals of key Arab states, not in Moscow. The Soviet Union has relatively few points of leverage through which to compel a negotiating process. The prevailing belief (or hope) under Brezhnev was that Soviet control of the war option would intimidate the U.S. and Israel into including the Soviet Union and negotiating a settlement. But that belief proved to be erroneous. Some Soviet leaders may still entertain the thought that their only lever could someday have that effect (say, after another Syrian-Israeli war), but their current fears of what such a war could do to world peace or U.S.–Soviet relations may take priority in their planning. And current Soviet policy in the region, while expanding influence among moderate allies, is not likely to develop levers that could compel or induce a change in Israeli positions. What's more, if the Soviets retain their determination to remain a power in the region and their commitment to the Arab cause, they will continue to be constrained in the depth and the timing of the flexibility they feel at liberty to display. I have elsewhere characterized Soviet-Arab relations as a game of "approach-avoidance" that reflects the ambivalence that each party feels about the commitments implicit in the relationship and the degree of overlap of interests between the two parties.[29] I do not see that ambivalence disappearing—though I do see a partial easing of the ambivalence as Soviet leaders have become more relaxed about the competitive process in the region and less fearful that U.S. patronage implies Soviet exclusion.

If the observer requires abandonment of the basic Soviet negotiating position as the criterion for declaring that fundamental learning has taken place, then we get at the heart of a problem involved in some discussions of the learning construct. For the philosophical assumptions that underpin the Soviet position may, after all, be correct, and the assumptions that underlie the positions advocated by Ariel Sharon and Itzhak Shamir may, after all, be wrong. The Soviet claim that a mobilized, aggrieved nation, with regional sources of support, cannot for long be denied independence at a price the occupiers are willing to pay may prove to be correct. If it is, then Soviet unwillingness to abandon the assumption constitutes wisdom, not a lack of learning.[30]

This problem is intrinsic to application of the efficiency definition of learning. As Tetlock explains it, the efficiency definition posits that an actor has learned when he has achieved a more efficient match of ends and means. This definition requires the observer to make a judgment as to the efficacy of different policies in achieving specified ends. Learning, in this sense, is learning to do something better or learning to adjust one's aspirations to one's capacities. In many instances, we can make such a judgment. We can claim with high confidence that Soviet leaders during the past 30 years have gained a much more accurate appreciation of the limits of their capacity to control clients and allies in the Middle East and have scaled down their aspirations accordingly. We can also point to the greater Soviet diplomatic skill displayed in seeking to woo a diverse coalition of moderate and militant states to press for an international conference on the Middle East. But, with respect to the grand issues, we cannot make the judgment required for application of an efficiency definition of learning without imposing our own theories of historical development on the analysis. Are current Soviet policies increasing the probability of crisis prevention and confrontation avoidance? Would a Palestinian state be a stabilizing force in the Middle East, compared with the present situation? Will the current Soviet effort to combine ecumenical activism with crisis prevention prove to be any more productive than was the previous effort to combine sectarian activism with crisis prevention?

It may be too soon to tell. We will probably not have to wait until the twenty-third century (as Haas playfully suggests in his chapter) to decide the grand issues, but it does seem reasonable to suggest that time will tell, and that there will inevitably be controversy over just how long we must wait before declaring that enough time has elapsed to draw conclusions.

CONCLUSIONS: SORTING THE CORRELATES OF CHANGE

We have identified a number of types and degrees of change in Soviet leaders' evaluation of the situation in the Middle East during the past 40 years. Some of these changes were more far-reaching than others and reflected a higher order of cognitive evolution. Specifically, during 1954–1955 we identified a change in goals, assumptions, self-image, and policies that substituted competitive activism for a Russia-first orientation. During 1967–1968 we identified a shift toward combining sectarian activism with crisis prevention that constituted a reshuffling of the goal structure informing Soviet Middle East policy. And under Gorbachev, we have witnessed a further reshuffling of the goal structure: subordination of sectarian activism to ecumenical activism, a relative strengthening of the crisis-prevention orientation, and a decisive subordination of competition to cooperation.

However we choose to characterize the changes in these time periods (1954–1955; 1967–1968; 1985–present)—as learning or adaptation—we must still inquire into their causes. In the cases of the first and the third, it is immediately evident that they took place during periods of political succession. But this is at best a partial explanation, for the outcomes were quite different. In the first case, political succession made possible the reevaluation of previous policy, while political competition encouraged programmatic differentiation: competing proposals for new directions in Soviet foreign policy. As it turned out, the optimistic global competitors were able to build their authority by plugging into the missionary optimism of the ideological heritage. The 1980s were quite different. It is true that political succession was again a necessary condition for the leadership to break with previous policy. But the optimism of the 1950s was no longer accepted by many political audiences in the Soviet establishment. And Gorbachev's speedy consolidation of power, after the deaths of two transitional leaders who differed among themselves over Middle East policy, may have preempted the kind of programmatic differentiation and political competition we saw earlier. In the case of the changes of 1967–1968, these were obviously a product of the shock of the June 1967 war. They were not a direct product of the political succession and its attendant political competition. They share with the new thinking a heightened valuation of crisis prevention in response to a perception of failure and danger. But they share with Khrushchev's policies a high valuation of sectarian activism.

Richard Anderson's contribution to this volume (Chapter 4) emphasizes the structuring impact of political competition on Soviet foreign policy choices. His argument captures an important measure of the truth, especially during periods of political succession.[31] We have seen the impact of programmatic differentiation on Soviet Middle East policy in the mid-1950s. We have also seen that such political competition was probably relevant to the Soviet embracing of the Syrian revolution in 1966 and the subsequent Soviet drift toward a protector role toward her clients in the region. Indeed, the authority-building process appears in both cases to have favored the general secretary's appeal to optimism and activism, as conditioned by the ideological heritage. But if this is so, the decisive cause of the choice was not political competition per se, but rather the substantive biases built into the ideological heritage, which disadvantaged competitors who did not play to those biases.

The Soviet ideological heritage has importantly conditioned the process of individual and regime learning. Leninism as a theory was relatively flexible, allowing for some reality testing and reevaluation. Stalinism, however, eventually purged that flexibility, and turned the ideology into a dogma that allowed no reevaluation of premises or interests in response to disappointment. After Stalin, the effort to "return to Leninism" was accompanied by limited de-dogmatization of the ideology, legitimation of the growth of scholarly communities charged with developing new understandings of Third World developments, and a somewhat greater capacity for reality testing. Nonetheless, the substantive biases of the Marxist-Leninist heritage and the regime's legitimation of its rule with reference to that heritage continued to delimit severely the space for reality testing and possible legitimation of alternative theories. Specifically, the optimistic and missionary biases, at the philosophical and normative levels of the ideological structure, lent weight to political actors propounding the inevitability of the desirable. Other elements of the ideology encouraged stereotypical images of the adversary and wishful thinking about the loyalties of local regimes. After 30 years of costly competition, which was heavily influenced by these cognitive predispositions, the combination of subterranean learning by specialists, and backstage learning by would-be party leaders in the wings, has perhaps led to the discrediting of certain philosophical tenets of Leninism as a guide to policy in the Middle East.

Other philosophical tenets, such as those that predict the undeniability of Palestinian nationalism, have not been discredited. If anything, the ongoing process of reality testing during the past 30 years has reinforced them. Hence, it is inappropriate to speak of the end of ideology in Soviet foreign policy. Rather, important (in some cases, core) features of the ideological structure are being redefined or discarded, while other core beliefs remain intact.

The link among ideology, authority building, and learning, it would seem, is *credibility*. By the 1980s, the optimism of the ideological heritage that had justified emphases on sectarian activism had lost its credibility in the face of 30 years of experience in the Middle East and the Third World more generally. This loss of credibility did not take place in a linear fashion. Several false starts and several surges of optimistic denial of earlier lessons intervened. This reflected either a universal tendency not to abandon deep-seated beliefs easily; or the distinctive potency of Soviet ideology's optimistic strand; or the potency of that strand in the thinking of party officials within the Khrushchev-Brezhnev generation that remained in power for 30 years (Boris Ponomarev, for example, remained in charge of the International Department of the Central Committee under both Khrushchev and Brezhnev); or the intervening impact of political succession in the 1960s, which encouraged political competitors to deny earlier lessons. Whatever the mix of these causes, the more fundamental lesson that reliable, exclusive allies are not on the horizon for the foreseeable future, and that the costs or dangers of sectarian competition may outweigh the gains, would not be learned until several false starts had taken place and a generational turnover had brought to power new personnel with very different backgrounds.

Thus, while ambivalence remains about the tension between long-standing normative commitments and some new-found beliefs informing Soviet Middle East policy, the requirements of credibility in the authority-building process today are different from what they were, because of a secular process of "regime learning" that provides the political base for individual learning at the top. While that individual learning may be subject to reversal as a result of shifting politics, personalities, and international pressures, the deeper regime learning, supported by epistemic communities unleashed by glasnost, may have generated more enduring consensual knowledge about the unpredictability and uncontrollability of events in the Middle East. This is not a theory of development; rather, it is a broadly shared belief (held now even by many conservative Soviet academics) in the untenability of previous assumptions that had underpinned the more optimistic and ambitious variants of sectarian activism.

NOTES

1. George W. Breslauer, "All Gorbachev's Men," *The National Interest* 12 (Summer 1988):91–100.

2. Galia Golan [*The Soviet Union and National Liberation Movements in the Third World* (London and Boston: Unwin Hyman, 1988)] suggests the term, *Soviet Union-first*, but she uses it to refer to any policy orientation that seeks to place a higher

priority on domestic development including, for example, the position espoused by Andropov. Her usage, then, is compatible with a conciliatory and nonisolationist foreign policy. In contrast, I use *Russia-first* to refer to a policy orientation analogous to that followed in Stalin's last years, connoting a confrontational posture of "fortress Russia."

3. In "All Gorbachev's Men," I characterized these tendencies as *radical activism* and *pragmatic activism*. I have since been persuaded by Kenneth Jowitt ["Developmental Stages and Conflict within the Leninist Regime World," *Social Science and Policy Research* 10 (1988)2:1–14] that *sectarian activism* and *ecumenical activism* better capture the distinction.

4. On defining cooperation, see Steven Weber, "Cooperation and Discord in Security Relationships: Toward a Theory of US–Soviet Arms Control," Ph.D. dissertation, Department of Political Science, Stanford University, 1988.

5. Oles Smolansky, *The Soviet Union and the Arab East Under Khrushchev* (Lewisburg, Penn.: Bucknell University Press, 1974).

6. This was not driven by "consensual knowledge" generated by "epistemic communities," but that part of Haas's definition (and theory of causation) appears to be a product of the issue areas and institutions on which Haas focuses his studies of governmental learning. In most modern states, there are well-defined epistemic communities for health, environmental, nuclear and, to a degree, economic issues, but not for the regional and geopolitical issues of the sort discussed in this and other chapters. This point is all the more relevant to the Soviet Union of the 1950s, in which Stalinist dogma had crippled almost all the social sciences.

7. George W. Breslauer, "Ideology and Learning in Soviet Third World Policy," *World Politics* 39 (1987) 3:429–48.

8. C. Grant Pendill, Jr. "'Bipartisanship' in Soviet Foreign Policy-Making," in *The Conduct of Soviet Foreign Policy*, eds. Erik P. Hoffman and Frederic J. Fleron, Jr. (New York: Aldine, 1971); James Richter, "Action and Reaction in Soviet Foreign Policy Under Khrushchev," Ph.D. dissertation, Department of Political Science, University of California at Berkeley, 1989; see also Chapter 2 of this volume.

9. Richard D. Anderson, "Competitive Politics and Soviet Foreign Policy: Authority Building and Bargaining in the Brezhnev Politburo," Ph.D. dissertation, Department of Political Science, University of California at Berkeley, 1989.

10. Smolansky, *Arab East*, 59.

11. Ibid., 94.

12. Ibid., 119.

13. See Smolansky, *Arab East*, 136–38.

14. Arthur Jay Klinghoffer with Judith Apter, *Israel and the Soviet Union* (Boulder, Colo.: Westview, 1985), 25.

15. Smolansky, *Arab East*, 301.

16. Yaacov Ro'i, *From Encroachment to Involvement: A Documentary Study of Soviet Policy in the Middle East, 1945–1973* (New York: John Wiley & Sons, 1974), 425.

17. The reactive shift that began in 1963–1964, which entailed an upgrading of the military dimension of competitive activism, was at variance with the drift of changes in Soviet Third World policy and thinking more generally. At this time, Khrushchev was seeking to deepen a détente relationship with the United States and was willing to subordinate the competitive impulse to the collaborative to further that cause. He indicated his intention to wash his hands of the commit-

ment to North Vietnam and leftist forces in Laos. He was ready to polemicize with Castro. He reduced the level of commitment to North Korea. In sum, Soviet policy toward the Middle East was no longer consonant with general Soviet Third World policy. I have speculated on possible reasons for this in *Soviet Strategy in the Middle East* (London and Boston: Unwin Hyman, 1989), and in Chapter 1 of this volume.

18. Klinghoffer, *Israel and the Soviet Union*, 30.

19. Mohamed Heikal, *The Sphinx and the Commissar* (New York: Harper and Row, 1978).

20. Klinghoffer, *Israel and the Soviet Union*, 38–39.

21. Ibid., 40.

22. Richard Anderson, "Authority Building and Bargaining in the Brezhnev Politburo"; and James Richter, "Action and Reaction Under Khrushchev." Note, while Anderson's content analysis [Chs. III, VII–IX] reveals Kosygin to have been a sponsor of collaborative strategies worldwide, and Brezhnev to have been a sponsor of national liberation worldwide, Anderson's interpretation of Kosygin's and Brezhnev's behaviors toward Syria in 1966 is different from my own, as presented in this and subsequent paragraphs. Anderson sees perverse circumstances at the time causing their roles in the Mideast during 1966 to diverge from their ordinary global postures.

23. Oded Eran, "Soviet Policy Between the 1967 and 1973 Wars" in *From June to October: The Middle East Between 1967 and 1973*, eds. Itamar Rabinovich and Haim Shaked (New Brunswick, N.J.: Transaction, 1978).

24. George Breslauer, *Soviet Strategy*.

25. The summary of policy changes in this section is based on Breslauer, *Soviet Strategy*, Chs. 6, 10, and Afterword.

26. Neil Malcolm, "Soviet Decision-Making and the Middle East" in *The Superpowers, Central America and the Middle East*, eds. Peter Shearman and Phil Williams (London: Brassey's, 1988).

27. George Breslauer, "Ideology and Learning," 429–48.

28. George Breslauer, *Soviet Strategy*.

29. Ibid.

30. At the same time, if the perspectives articulated by Shimon Peres emerge ascendant in Israeli politics, they would be based on a convergence with Soviet perspectives about the undeniability of Palestinian nationalism. Under those circumstances, Washington would presumably go along with a shift in Israeli policy. Learning in the East-West and Arab-Israeli positions would then be based on consensual knowledge about cause-effect relationships in the local environment, which is defined by Haas as a prerequisite for learning, rather than adaptation.

31. I am less persuaded that a political competition framework allows one to understand the evolution of Soviet Middle East policy during nonsuccession periods [see Breslauer, *Soviet Strategy*, Ch. 10]. Rather, after the Soviet leader has attained a position of relative ascendancy within the collective leadership, I would argue that the policy-making process conforms to the specifications of Achen's "focal actor" model [Christopher H. Achen, "When Is a State With Bureaucratic Politics Representable as a Unitary Rational Actor?" Paper prepared for the annual meeting of the International Studies Association, London, England, March 29–April 1, 1989].

16

Peripheral Visions:
Brezhnev and Gorbachev
Meet the "Reagan Doctrine"

Ted Hopf

Upon assuming the White House, the Reagan administration set out to challenge Soviet positions in the Third World. In doing so, it was behaving according to a long-established tradition in postwar U.S. foreign policy. Covert and not so covert actions in Korea, Iran, Guatemala, Vietnam, the Dominican Republic, Angola, Afghanistan, El Salvador, and Nicaragua all have elements of the same underlying rationale. The object of these policies was to teach the Soviet leadership a set of lessons about its external environment, lessons that would deter it, it was hoped, from future foreign policy behavior the U.S. leadership finds objectionable.

These lessons come in three varieties. First, the Soviets should learn that the United States is both willing and able to counter future Soviet efforts at expansionism in the Third World, and indeed in areas of greater strategic importance, such as Europe or the Persian Gulf. A U.S. failure to respond, conversely, leads to a loss of credibility and encourages the Soviet Union to adopt adventuristic policies that threaten U.S. interests around the globe.

Second, the Soviets should learn that the United States' strategic allies—Western Europe, Japan, and conservative Middle Eastern states—are reassured of Washington's commitment to their security. Hence, Soviet leaders are convinced that, if they embark on any future expansionism, they will be met by a united front of resistance to such efforts.

Third, the Soviets should learn that the neighbors of the state under contention are also both willing and able to resist any encroachments on their security. So, as a consequence of the Sandinistas being compelled to fight against the Contras, the Soviets discover that El Salvador, Honduras, Costa Rica, and Guatemala will not fall like dominoes in the face of the emergent Nicaraguan threat, but rather will ally with each other and the United States to resist. Hence, the Soviet leadership learns that the regional dynamics set off by a victory for progressive forces inevitably check the scope of the influence of that victory in the best case and are able to roll that influence back in the worst case.[1]

In fact, however, neither Brezhnev nor Gorbachev learned these kinds of lessons from U.S. efforts aimed at countering Soviet adventurism in the Third World. Instead, Brezhnev's peculiar belief system led him to be convinced of a highly credible America even in the face of apparent U.S. defeats in Mozambique, Angola, Nicaragua, and Afghanistan. His rigid and narrow views of how U.S. foreign policy is made by a small group of the ruling elite, axiomatically hostile to Soviet foreign policy activities in the Third World, made him overestimate U.S. resolve and capabilities following these U.S. losses. By focusing only on the executive branch of the U.S. government and not recognizing congressional and public opposition to U.S. adventurism in the Third World, Brezhnev exaggerated the probability of U.S. resistance to Soviet adventures.

But this did not deter Brezhnev from such adventures, since two other elements in his belief system and policy strategy pushed him toward continued involvement in the periphery regardless of levels of U.S. resistance. The first element is his orthodox Leninist view of the "world revolutionary alliance." Brezhnev believed there are three motive forces operating in the international arena—the socialist community, the international working class, and the global national liberation movement. Any Soviet retreats in the face of U.S. support for the Contras in Nicaragua or the Mujaheddin in Afghanistan would threaten the integrity of Brezhnev's world view. If Brezhnev were to reduce his commitment to national liberation movements around the world or the progressive "countries of socialist orientation" that such movements bring to power, he would have been faced with the psychological need to reorder his view of how the world revolutionary alliance operates. This extremely high psychological cost prevented Brezhnev from responding to the increased costs created by U.S. actions in Nicaragua and Afghanistan. Instead of being deterred by the costs imposed by U.S. behavior, Brezhnev was prevented from being deterred by the costs imposed by his own system of beliefs.

The second element of Brezhnev's belief system that prevented him from learning the deterrent lessons being taught by U.S. foreign policy was his policy commitment to "offensive détente."[2] Brezhnev believed that it was possible to reap the benefits of cooperation with the United States at the strategic level of détente on arms control and economic relations, while simultaneously continuing to support revolutionary change in the Third World. This policy commitment fit nicely into his view of how U.S. foreign policy was made by a narrow elite in the White House, impervious to any pressure from Congress, the media, or the American public. This commitment made Brezhnev ignore the evidence, accumulating quickly after the Popular Movement for the Liberation of Angola's (MPLA) victory in Angola, that public and elite support for strategic détente was threatened in the United States by Soviet activities in the Third World. Like his belief in and commitment to the world revolutionary process, Brezhnev's strategy of offensive détente led him to disregard the costs the United States was imposing on the Soviet Union for its actions in Nicaragua and Afghanistan.

In sum, due to Brezhnev's peculiar set of beliefs, he paradoxically both exaggerated U.S. credibility after the Soviet victory in Angola and could not be deterred by subsequent U.S. efforts to raise the price of such victories.

Gorbachev also did not learn the kinds of lessons that U.S. policy makers were trying to teach him by raising the costs of Soviet involvement in Angola, Nicaragua, and Afghanistan. But, unlike Brezhnev, Gorbachev has a set of beliefs and a policy strategy that leads him to recognize the need for disengagement from Third World adventures. Gorbachev also sees a narrow elite responsible for the formulation of U.S. foreign policy, though with one critical addition—the American public. Gorbachev, unlike Brezhnev, does not believe that U.S. policy is axiomatically hostile toward the Soviet Union, as the American people themselves do not hold the same hidebound beliefs of U.S. political leadership. If the Soviet Union can influence this public, it can change U.S. foreign policy for the better. This less rigid view of the U.S. polity allows Gorbachev to imagine making concessions in the periphery as an instrument with which to influence U.S. policy toward the Soviet Union.

The second critical difference with Brezhnev is the fact that Gorbachev does not have a world view that subscribes to a world revolutionary alliance. Reduced support for national liberation movements and progressive allies does not threaten Gorbachev's view of how the world works. On the contrary, Soviet circumspection in this regard opens up the prospects of realizing Gorbachev's primary objective of strategic détente. Indeed, Gorbachev's view of the Third World is not the Leninist-Brezhnevite perception of the periphery as the soft underbelly of imperialism, but rather as a constituent part of a world antinuclear alliance that will help further the cause of disarmament and the peaceful resolution of conflicts.

The third and perhaps most important difference with Brezhnev is Gorbachev's slow, but increasing, recognition that Soviet behavior in the Third World is partly responsible for the death of strategic détente. Brezhnev could not recognize such a causal nexus, given his commitment to offensive détente and the world revolutionary alliance and his view of U.S. foreign policy making. Gorbachev can, as he recognizes that such retreats influence the American public to press its government for détente with the Soviet Union. He also can because such Soviet adventurism threatens Gorbachev's central values of strategic détente and disarmament.

In sum, Gorbachev is not deterred by the costs imposed by U.S. support for the National Union for the Total Independence of Angola (UNITA), the Contras, and the Mujaheddin, but rather by the risk Soviet support to these embattled governments poses for his central objective—détente with the United States. In a sense, the Nixon-Kissinger assumptions about linking détente to Soviet behavior in the periphery were correct, but premature, given Brezhnev's beliefs and foreign policy strategy.

However, there is one possible problem with the view that Gorbachev has a dominant strategy of retreat from the periphery deriving from the beliefs noted above. U.S. policy makers assume that they must stand firm in the periphery; otherwise, Soviet leaders will learn the wrong lessons. But U.S. decision makers fail to recognize that Soviet leaders may be driven by the same assumptions. Gorbachev is apparently also concerned about Soviet credibility in the periphery and responds by continuing to arm those governments that are under attack by U.S.-backed insurgencies. In this sense, a U.S. policy aimed at deterring Gorbachev from future adventures may lead to precisely the opposite outcome— continued Soviet support for these embattled regimes.

Brezhnev and Gorbachev also share two characteristics that reduce the importance of U.S. behavior in the Third World as a relevant instrument of policy. First, events in the Third World have very low salience to both general secretaries. In making judgments about the international arena, they pay overwhelming attention to U.S. military programs and U.S. behavior in strategic areas of the globe, such as Western Europe, Northeast Asia, and the Persian Gulf. As a consequence, U.S. efforts to raise the costs of Soviet adventurism in the periphery are largely lost on Brezhnev and Gorbachev, whose attention is focused on more important arenas of competition with the United States.

Second, neither Brezhnev nor Gorbachev infer from Soviet successes in the Third World that the United States cannot credibly defend its interests in strategic areas of the globe. For example, Brezhnev did not interpret the victory of the MPLA in Angola as a sign of U.S. inability or unwillingness to protect its strategic interests in Western Europe or elsewhere.

THE CASES AND THE METHODOLOGY

I have chosen five quite different cases of U.S.–Soviet conflict in the Third World since 1975. Three of these—Afghanistan, Angola, and Nicaragua—are cases of U.S. efforts to overthrow Soviet allied governments. South African opposition to the Mozambican government is an example of a U.S. ally trying to overthrow a Soviet ally, without U.S. involvement. The successful U.S. and British diplomatic efforts bringing Zimbabwe independence are an example of the United States' thwarting of Soviet efforts to bring a national liberation movement to power by force, but with diplomatic and economic, not military, instruments.

I include the Mozambican and Zimbabwean cases in order to test whether Brezhnev and Gorbachev infer more powerful deterrent lessons when they are not faced with a military defeat at the hands of U.S.–armed insurgencies. I hypothesize that they will learn more, as their own need to maintain Soviet credibility will not be invoked.

Angola is an example of a U.S. loss at the hands of a Soviet-supplied, Cuban-supported national liberation movement that, from the withdrawal of South African forces in March 1976 to late 1988, was engaged in a counterinsurgency war against the South African–backed forces of UNITA. In 1985, the Reagan administration convinced Congress to repeal the Clark amendment, which had prohibited U.S. aid to UNITA. This case provides a fruitful test of whether the Soviet leadership shares the same anxiety about its credibility as U.S. policy makers. If so, then the Soviet commitment to Angola should increase, rather than decrease, after the repeal of the Clark amendment.

Mozambique is an example of a liberation movement coming to power, but largely with Chinese, not Soviet, support. Since the independence of Zimbabwe in 1980, the Mozambican Liberation Front (FRELIMO) government has been fighting a counterinsurgency war against the National Resistance Movement of Mozambique (RENAMO), a group first created by the white Rhodesian special services and then taken over by the South Africans. In the 1984 Nkomati accords with the Republic of South Africa (RSA), the Mozambican government essentially capitulated to South African demands with respect to denying safe haven to African National Congress (ANC) fighters. The fact that the Reagan administration refused to support RENAMO, despite calls from the Republican right, provides an interesting case for whether Soviet leaders are able to recognize the autonomy of regional actors, the RSA in this case, and so learn stronger lessons about the difficulty of protecting its revolutionary allies, than would be the case if the United States were directly backing their overthrow.

The Sandinista National Liberation Front (FSLN or Sandinistas) of Nicaragua overthrew the Somoza regime in July 1979 without any Soviet support, though with the significant backing of Cuba. From November 1981 until June 1985 and then from June 1986 until February 1988, it fought an insurgency financed, armed, and trained by the United States. This case is an opportunity to see whether Gorbachev responds to the period of congressionally mandated suspensions of U.S. military aid by reducing Soviet support for the Sandinistas.

The Mugabe government came to power in Zimbabwe as a consequence of the mediation efforts of the British and U.S. governments in 1980. Since that time, though sporadically raided by South African commandos, it has enjoyed a relatively secure environment. It is included as an example of a nonmilitary defeat for the Soviets in the Third World in order to compare the lessons Soviets learn from resisting insurgencies backed by the United States or its allies with those defeats it suffers as a consequence of the diplomatic and economic power of the West.

Finally, since 1979, the Afghani government has been fighting an insurgency armed and trained by the United States. The Soviet withdrawal in February 1989 has not led the United States to suspend military aid to the Mujaheddin. This continued military support provides an opportunity to test whether in fact Gorbachev feels the need to maintain Soviet credibility in the face of continued U.S. resistance by sustaining Soviet arms supplies to the Kabul government, providing more direct military support, and/or increasing military support to other Soviet allies in the Third World.

As a sample for Soviet perceptions I have used all the public speeches made by Brezhnev and Gorbachev since 1975 appearing in the party daily, *Pravda*.[3] I examine each speech for evidence of inferences made from any of the five cases. I use the inferences made by the two general secretaries as the data against which to test the three general assumptions held by U.S. decision makers about credibility, alliance behavior, and regional dynamics.

THE BREZHNEV YEARS

SALIENCE

Brezhnev devoted the bulk of his speeches to discussions of U.S. military preparations, the Chinese threat, the intermediate-range nuclear forces (INF) treaty, and Poland. However, he did comment somewhat frequently on at least some of the conflicts.[4] There is also a definite distribution of attention among the five events. Angola, and to a lesser extent, Zimbabwe, were the most salient cases from 1976 to 1979. In 1980–1981, he shifted his attention to Angola and Afghanistan. In the last year of his rule, he focused on Nicaragua and Angola. Mozambique received only sporadic and limited attention.

These are very crude measures of salience that must be conditioned by considerations of context and content. An analysis of both the audience before which a speech is delivered and the actual content of the remarks further demonstrates the low salience of the periphery for Brezhnev. A more detailed analysis of both is made in the section devoted to the lessons learned by the general secretary from the five cases, but let me raise two short points. First, concerning context, the vast bulk of attention to the five cases comes in situations in which Brezhnev addressed a Third World audience, hardly a time when he is going to ignore events there. Moreover, even when addressing this audience, a good part of the speech was still devoted to areas of strategic conflict, in this case U.S. armaments, the INF, the People's Republic of China (PRC), and others. Finally, Brezhnev only extremely rarely raised any of the cases here before a European, Middle Eastern, or Japanese audience.

In terms of content, most of the remarks cited are at most a line or two of text, while paragraphs are devoted to problems with the United States on such things as the INF and the Strategic Arms Limitation Talks (SALT). This is true even before Third World audiences, though not as often the case when addressing leaders of the affected countries.

LESSONS LEARNED

U.S. Credibility

Brezhnev's perception of U.S. capabilities and the will to use them did not weaken as a consequence of the victory of the MPLA in Angola, FRELIMO in Mozambique, or the FSLN in Nicaragua. Brezhnev did see U.S. behavior in Nicaragua and Afghanistan as evidence of aggressive U.S. intentions, but he did not make such attributions from South African support for RENAMO's campaign of subversion in Mozambique or from British and U.S. efforts to bring Zimbabwe independence peacefully. He did, however, perceive South African support for UNITA in Angola as proof of a continuing U.S. threat to progressive regimes in the Third World, despite the fact that the Clark amendment was still in force.[5] U.S.–sponsored resistance in Nicaragua and Afghanistan did contribute to Brezhnev's perceptions of U.S. credibility. But the influence of these events was insignificant compared with perceived U.S. behavior in the area of arms control, military expenditures, relations with China, and policy toward events in Poland. Brezhnev made 32 speeches in the period in which he made a judgment about U.S. capabilities and resolve. In fully 29 of them, he based these judgments on strategic U.S. behavior.[6]

Immediately after the Angolan victory, Brezhnev recognized that Soviet actions there had led the Ford administration to start accusing the Soviet Union of violating the rules of détente. In his final report to the twenty-fifth congress of the Communist Party of the Soviet Union (CPSU), Brezhnev argued that détente "does not in the slightest abolish the laws of class struggle." Furthermore, "when we are criticized for this [aid to national liberation movements, which in his formulation is synonymous with détente], we can hardly help thinking that those who rebuke us are not sure that capitalism can survive without resorting to aggression and threats of force, and without infringing on the independence and interests of other peoples."[7]

Several months later, at a gathering of European communists in East Berlin, he argued that those people in the West who want to destroy détente no matter what, "those who make fortunes on weapons production and who cannot think of any other political career other than heating up a holy crusade against socialist countries and communists" inflate the myth of the Soviet threat, in part by blaming the U.S.S.R. for "civil and national liberation wars."[8]

As evidence of U.S. resolve to prevent any future Angolas, Brezhnev argued that "now that Africa has shown that it itself can deal with the remnants of colonialism and racism, some, under the banner of helping this process, have begun to try to replace the true liberation of southern Africa with fictitious liberation; essentially to preserve the positions of imperialism in the region and to support the stronghold of racism—the RSA."[9]

Brezhnev was referring to the diplomatic efforts undertaken by Kissinger in the summer of 1976 to work out a peaceful solution for Rhodesian and Namibian independence. Clearly, Brezhnev feared that the Soviet Union's only possible entrée into the region—providing arms to the last remaining liberation fighters—was about to be closed. He reiterated this fear after the Carter administration embarked on its diplomatic efforts in the region.[10]

Brezhnev saw a U.S. willingness to resist backed up by growing military capabilities and he perceived the latter, at least in part, as a U.S. response to its Angolan debacle:

> The fact is that to these defeats in social battles, to the loss of colonial possessions, to the departure of an ever growing number of countries from capitalism, to the success of world socialism and the growth of influence of communist parties in bourgeois states—to all this the aggressive circles of the capitalist world react by feverishly unleashing military preparations. They inflate their defense budgets, create new types of weapons, build bases and undertake military demonstrations. Relying on this "position of strength," imperialism hopes to hold on to the possibility of commanding other countries and peoples which is slipping through its fingers.[11]

Already by late September 1977, Brezhnev saw an Angola under siege by imperialism, as it sees "the very existence of the PRA [People's Republic of Angola] as a threat to the bulwark of racism and neocolonialism."[12] Imperialism simply cannot reconcile itself to the existence of progressive "countries of socialist orientation" in general.[13] Brezhnev even dredged up the old Stalinist thinking, saying in paraphrase that "the stronger the states which have gained independence become, the more insistent become the efforts of imperialists to prevent their development, to turn them back and re-establish their lost influence there."[14]

By the end of 1978, according to Brezhnev, the U.S. elite had gone beyond simply accusing the Soviet Union of expansionism in the Third World as a pretext for undermining détente; now the United States itself was "aspiring to maintain the hotbeds of tension in the Middle East, southern Africa and Indochina."[15]

Brezhnev showed a peculiar understanding of the role of U.S. public opinion on the question of Third World conflicts and détente in his speech in Vienna at the summit with President Carter:

> Attempts continue to depict the social processes in one country or another and the struggle of peoples for independence as the "intrigues and machinations of Moscow." Soviet people are of course in solidarity with the liberation struggle of peoples. But the USSR is against interference in the internal affairs of other countries. So why lay responsibility on the USSR for the objective course of history and even more use it as a pretext for the exacerbation of our relations? All the same, I think that even now realism, a far-sighted approach and statesman-like wisdom will ultimately prevail. The more so as the advocates of the improvement and development of our relations have many allies—millions of citizens of both countries and all the peoples of the earth.[16]

In his February 1980 Supreme Soviet election speech, Brezhnev revealed both where he ranked the influence of events in Angola on subsequent U.S. decision making and also his perceptions of genuine U.S. intentions and their roots:

> The consolidation of peace and the success of the liberation struggle is not to the liking of the militaristic circles of imperialism—first of all U.S. imperialism. Let's see how they respond to the development of mutually-rewarding contacts with many capitalist countries, to the success of the Helsinki Conference and to the victory of the revolutionary peoples of Angola and Ethiopia over the intervenors and mercenaries of imperialism. They began to delay the SALT II negotiations and then the treaty's ratification. They encouraged the treachery of Sadat. They imposed a multi-year armaments program on the NATO countries and finally they decided to deploy INF. Against détente are big forces directly or indirectly working on war preparations: militarists, monopolies connected with them, their henchmen in the state bureaucracy and in the mass media. And the more the opportunities for imperialism to dominate other peoples and countries are reduced, the more fiercely its most aggressive and short-sighted representatives react to this.

But then, in at least an indirect recognition that American public opinion was pushing the administration to take a harder line against the U.S.S.R., he noted that "anti-Soviet hysteria [over Afghanistan] is not needed only so that someone can win the presidential elections . . . on the crest of this wave. The main thing is that the United States has plans to create a network of military bases in the Indian Ocean, in the Near and Middle East and in Africa. The United States would like to subordinate these countries to its hegemony and remove their natural resources freely and at the same time use their territories against the socialist world and popular-liberation forces."[17]

So, by this point, Brezhnev assessed the U.S. reaction to its defeat in Angola as more than a pretext for those who wanted to destroy détente. He now believed that the United States had economic and strategic interests in undermining and dominating Third World regimes, some of which were Soviet allies. This line of argument became the credo of Brezhnev for the rest of his term in office.[18]

Brezhnev expressed his very limited view of the efficacy of public opinion as a constraint on Western policy makers, asserting that "the efforts of people will ultimately disperse the threatening clouds of war," implying that, while they could not prevent the destruction of détente, the U.S. miliary buildup, or resistance in the periphery, at least they would be able to prevent the final conflagration.[19]

Brezhnev only belatedly came to the issue of Nicaragua as a sign of U.S. credibility. In May 1982, he obliquely accused the United States of "trying to preserve or re-establish positions of dominance and impose foreign oppression on peoples."[20] It should be noted here that the "loss" of Nicaragua to the Sandinistas was never mentioned by Brezhnev as being a blow to U.S. credibility.

In sum, Brezhnev did not reduce his estimation of U.S. credibility after its losses in Angola, Mozambique, and Nicaragua. Instead, he remarked on a renewed U.S. commitment to not allow repetitions of these events. To back up this evident intention, the United States diplomatically outmaneuvered the Soviets in southern Africa on Zimbabwe, increased its military potential, continued to economically and militarily harass Soviet allies in the Third World, and deployed U.S. military forces around the globe in new or expanded foreign bases. U.S. support for the Mujaheddin and the Contras contributed to this picture, as did South African support for UNITA, though by far the most powerful influence on Brezhnev's perceptions of U.S. credibility was its behavior at the strategic level.

Allied Behavior

Brezhnev's perceptions of U.S. allied reactions to U.S. foreign policy in the periphery were precisely the opposite of those predicted by U.S.

assumptions. First, after the MPLA victory, when U.S. allies were supposed to be considering accommodating themselves to the emergent Soviet threat, Brezhnev was instead declaiming Chinese cooperation with the United States in suppressing Third World revolutions and opposing socialism.[21] The two Western efforts to save Mobutu's government in Zaire from Katangese insurgents in Shaba province gave Brezhnev further evidence of allied cooperation with the United States, not estrangement:

> As if in a bad memory of colonial times, meetings in Western capitals at which African problems are discussed follow one after another. The only thing that is not clear is who empowered them to include Africa in the sphere of action of NATO. And who asked them, by means of arms, to interfere in Zairean events and knock together the so-called "inter-African forces," the goal of which is to kill Africans by the hands of Africans? Here I say briefly: the African plans of the imperialists are dangerous. Dangerous to Africans. Dangerous for the cause of peace and détente.[22]

And equally contrary to U.S. beliefs, after the insurgencies were in full swing against Angola, Mozambique, Afghanistan, and Nicaragua, Brezhnev argued that "this policy is provoking growing indignation in many countries, including among U.S. allies."[23]

Regional Dynamics

Of the three assumptions of U.S. policy makers, this is the one that receives the most empirical support, though even this evidence is mixed and limited. In the grossest terms, the Angolan victory and, to a much lesser extent, that of Mozambique, led Brezhnev to see brighter prospects for the liberation of Zimbabwe and Namibia and the elimination of the apartheid regime in the RSA. The independence of Zimbabwe, to an extent even less than Mozambique, was also seen as promoting progressive change in the RSA and Namibia. Yet Brezhnev did not credit the Sandinista victory with facilitating anyone's struggle in the region, not even the Faribundo Marti in El Salvador.

There are two factors that dampened Brezhnev's expectations about southern Africa. First, he recognized that the Pretoria regime was fiercely defending both itself and its Namibian colony and was engaged in a destabilization campaign against all front-line states (FLSs), but against Angola and Mozambique in particular. This caused the earlier optimistic lessons about Angola's positive influence in the region to disappear by 1980.[24]

Perhaps the turning point in Brezhnev's perceptions can be marked by the content of his speech before the visiting Angolan president in September 1977. For the first, but not the last time, he declared that, despite the attacks of South Africa and its accomplices, the gains in Angola and Mozambique were irreversible. He glaringly omitted any mention of these two countries' role in promoting any further progressive change in the region.[25]

In sum, Brezhnev learned from the Angolan case that strong regional actors, such as the RSA, were quite capable of resisting any encroachments on their interests threatened by new Soviet allies. Indeed, Brezhnev's assessment of the threat to Angola and Mozambique developed long before the United States resumed aid to UNITA in 1986. In the case of Mozambique, there never was such aid. Also of interest is that in cases of no U.S. resistance to the establishment of a regime to Soviet liking— Mozambique, Zimbabwe, and Nicaragua—Brezhnev failed to see much, if any, regional effect. If this is in fact a pattern of Soviet learning, then it implies that less U.S. involvement helps dampen Soviet perceptions of regional dominoes.

A last point is that Brezhnev never saw the dynamics being set off in the southern African and Central American regions as influencing events in strategic areas of the world. This relates both to cascading progressive dominoes around the globe and also to the possibility of other Soviet allies questioning Soviet security guarantees if the Soviet Union does not respond in any of these four cases.

Brezhnev's Rigid Belief System

Brezhnev's analysis of U.S. credibility is consistent with a tightly structured belief system, severely limited in its capacity to respond to new information. His ability to learn from Soviet behavior in the periphery was even further constrained by his policy commitment to his own peculiar version of détente, which, when challenged by reality, resulted not in his adjusting his policy to the new environment, but rather his reordering of reality so as to be consonant with the underlying postulates of his policy.

At the core of Brezhnev's belief system was his view of how U.S. foreign policy is made within a narrow elite circle. In his view, these ruling circles are rarely, if ever, subject to pressures from the legislative branch of government, let alone the popular masses. As was noted above, Brezhnev noted the role of domestic public opinion in the United States only once in the context of U.S. policy in the Third World,[26] and interpreted it as pushing the president to abandon concern over Soviet behavior in the Third World for the sake of détente. This is quite interesting, apart from the fact that Brezhnev was so far off the mark. What is striking and what demonstrates how strongly Brezhnev held to an elitist view of U.S. politics is his failure to note that it was Congress and public opinion that thwarted the Ford administration in Angola. This is very strong evidence, because, if he had recognized that the elite was constrained, he could have assumed the coast was clear for further Soviet adventures in the periphery, perhaps in Namibia or Zimbabwe. Given Soviet claims in the period about how détente made the world safe for national liberation movements, it is interesting to see that Brezhnev's beliefs about U.S. politics overrode his commitment to progressive change. In fact, his focus on the elite led to a condition of self-deterrence, an overestimation of U.S. resolve.

One perhaps can see the same dynamic working in the case of Nicaragua, where most observers of the U.S. political scene believe that U.S. public opinion restrained the Reagan administration from behaving more aggressively there. But Brezhnev, narrowly focusing on the actions and words of the Reagan team, probably overestimated the credibility of a U.S. response in Central America.

Brezhnev's view of détente as allowing for Soviet promotion of revolutionary change in the Third World creates a case of cognitive dissonance when he discovers that the United States is moving away from détente as a seeming consequence of these Soviet actions. How does Brezhnev bring his beliefs back into cognitive balance? First, he argued that certain members of the elite, most usually identified as broadly connected with the military-industrial complex or inveterate cold warriors, are simply seizing on events they do not like in Angola to weave myths about a growing Soviet threat to deceive public opinion in the United States so as to undermine its support for détente. Even though Brezhnev considered these actions to be illegitimate and insidious, it still seems that the logical and rational response to such actions, since Brezhnev placed military-economic détente with the United States at the center of his foreign policy program, would be to somehow manage the fallout from Angola in a way that would reassure the wavering U.S. elite.[27]

One can imagine a Soviet effort to explain to the U.S. side that Angola was simply an aberration, that the collapse of the Portuguese colonial empire was fortuitous, that if the South Africans had not intervened, the Soviets would not have provided such strong support to the MPLA, that the Soviet Union was willing to forswear all kinds of military activities in Angola, that they were willing to work with the administration on Zimbabwean and Namibian independence, and so on. Instead, Brezhnev attacked the United States for unjustifiably undermining détente and placed Angola in the context of an inexorable course of history leading to future revolutions. Hardly a strategy calculated to cool the hot-headed militarists in Washington. It is Brezhnev's view of détente and his orthodox understanding of the "world revolutionary process" submerged in that vision that prevented a response sensitive to U.S. domestic politics.[28]

Brezhnev also engaged in "bolstering" his beliefs about U.S. politics as détente came under increasing attack in the United States. By 1980, that is, after further revolutionary changes with varied degrees of Soviet participation in Ethiopia, Nicaragua, and Afghanistan, Brezhnev felt compelled to add additional motives for the U.S. elite to undermine détente. Still unable to make the connection between Soviet behavior and U.S. attitude change, he cited the orthodox Marxist argument about the imperialist need for raw materials in the Third World. In addition, the United States needs military bases around the globe to protect current clients and overthrow progressive governments. Once again, Brezhnev's vision of détente is protected by devising arguments to explain U.S. behavior that contradicts this vision.

This centralized view of decision making also extends to Brezhnev's analysis of allied behavior and regional dynamics, though in the former, shortly before his death, some hints of change are visible. Though he recognized that the RSA was militarily powerful and aggressive, Brezhnev never hinted that he understood that perhaps the leaders of Pretoria subvert their neighbors without waiting to receive orders from Washington. In fact, this focus on the U.S. elite undermines one of my initial hypotheses that Soviet leaders are more likely to learn from cases of resistance without U.S. involvement. At least in Brezhnev's case, this hypothesis is moot, as he was unable to discern any cases of U.S. noninvolvement.

Shortly after Angola, Brezhnev focused on Washington's direction of North Atlantic Treaty Organization (NATO) forces in Zaire in 1977 and 1978. In this context, he spoke of Washington convincing its NATO partners to extend the alliance's sphere of action to Africa, to prevent any future progressive change. However, in one of the last speeches before his death, Brezhnev remarked that even U.S. NATO allies object to excessively aggressive U.S. behavior in the Third World. Since Brezhnev presented no evidence for this observation, one can only surmise about its basis. One explanation may be that it is simply spillover from the European debates on the INF and Reagan and Haig's unfortunate comments on limited nuclear war in the period. This may not necessarily be the case, given rather open French and Spanish opposition to U.S. policy in Nicaragua.

SOVIET POLICY UNDER BREZHNEV

According to U.S. assumptions, the insurgencies in Angola, Mozambique, Afghanistan, and Nicaragua should have taught Brezhnev that the costs of maintaining these relationships are too high and hence Soviet commitments to them should diminish. In fact, both verbally and materially, this was not at all the case for Brezhnev. Moreover, it seems that Brezhnev was more committed to providing military aid against subversion than in providing the economic wherewithal to build socialism. There is, however, a hint that Brezhnev was willing to explore negotiated solutions to some conflicts, a position that did not appear immediately after events in Angola.

Brezhnev was consistent throughout the period in enunciating continued Soviet support for national liberation movements.[29] But in October 1977, for the first time, he raised the possibility of settling these conflicts by peaceful means. "We clearly see the dangers which increasingly lie in wait for détente. In one, then in another region of the world conflicts emerge, hotbeds of heightened regional tensions. They must be extinguished as rapidly as possible and problems must be moved to the plane of resolution by peaceful means at the negotiating table.[30] But this change of heart was no doubt related to the war then raging between Somalia and Ethiopia, whose resolution in late October the Soviets still hoped could be reached without losing their positions in either state.[31]

Perhaps a legitimate change in position was Brezhnev's attitude toward the war for Zimbabwean liberation. In May 1978 he called for the transfer of "all power to the people of Zimbabwe represented by the Patriotic Front."[32] But then just a month later he explained to the president of Madagascar that: "The USSR is on the side of national liberation movements in Africa. But this of course does not mean that it is the enemy of efforts, including diplomatic, aimed at the peaceful resolution of emerging problems, if such a solution addresses the legitimate interests of peoples."[33] In this case, of course, the Patriotic Front was already negotiating with the Smith government, so essentially Brezhnev was just ratifying a decision already taken, though warning against an illegitimate solution.

The one case in which he came out for negotiations from the start was Nicaragua. In an unusual place for a lengthy discussion of Nicaragua, Brezhnev suggested to President Koivisto of Finland that "if the good foundations which are the basis of our relations with you were more widely adopted in the world, then there would probably be significantly fewer hotbeds of tension and conflicts."[34] He then went on to support the views of Mexico, Cuba, and Nicaragua on lessening tensions in Central America. One can only speculate as to whether Brezhnev was suggesting the "Finlandization" of Nicaragua, as Westerners understand the notion. That is, Nicaragua's foreign and security policies would be subordinated to U.S. interests in exchange for virtual autonomy in its domestic affairs. In any case, throughout the rest of his term in office, Brezhnev continued to support a negotiated settlement in the region.[35]

Brezhnev continually hedged on providing economic support to Third World countries in general, and Soviet allies in particular. Even in his address before the party congress in 1976, he made no commitment to their economic needs, saying only that "it is quite clear now that, with the present correlation of world class forces, liberated countries are able to resist imperialist *diktat* and achieve equitable economic relations."[36] After describing to President Neto how hard it would be for Angola to overcome its colonial economy and the destruction wrought by the civil war, Brezhnev weakly offered: "I suggest that Soviet-Angolan cooperation will help resolve a number of questions."[37]

In a meeting with Fidel Castro, Brezhnev assured him that "socialist countries help peoples as far as we can with their economic growth."[38] Perhaps most striking was this peculiar passage in a speech at a dinner for Mengistu: "We fully share the thought expressed by Comrade Mengistu that Ethiopia won't arrive at socialism 'by oxen and plow.' And we are sincerely happy about the success of the Ethiopian revolution and wish Ethiopians new accomplishments in the construction of a peaceful, happy and secure life."[39] Clearly, Comrade Mengistu was fishing for more than best wishes from Brezhnev.

The levels of military aid given to Afghanistan and Nicaragua by the Brezhnev government also reflect a lack of responsiveness to the increased costs imposed by U.S. support for the Mujaheddin and the Contras. From the time that U.S. covert aid began to the Mujaheddin in 1979 until Brezhnev's death in November 1982, the Soviet Union substantially increased its supply of materiel to the Afghan government.[40] A similar aid pattern is seen in the case of Nicaragua, though on a much smaller scale. From the advent of covert U.S. aid to the Contras in 1981 until Brezhnev's death, the Soviet Union supplied the Sandinista government with 25 T-54/5 main battle tanks, 12 armored personnel carriers, a dozen large-caliber howitzers, two dozen 120mm mortars, 138 antiaircraft guns, and an undetermined quantity of SAM-7 antiaircraft missiles.[41]

These arms supplies are not consistent with U.S. assumptions that Brezhnev would be deterred from supporting Soviet allies in the face of increased costs of such support imposed by U.S. efforts. Instead, given Brezhnev's peculiar set of beliefs and policy commitments, such U.S. efforts were seemingly irrelevant to his calculations of support levels for progressive allies in the periphery.

THE GORBACHEV REVOLUTION

SALIENCE

In comparison to Brezhnev, Gorbachev pays substantially less attention to events in Afghanistan, Angola, Mozambique, Nicaragua, and Zimbabwe. In a total of 205 speeches in which he touches on foreign policy issues, Gorbachev remarks on one of these cases 80 times, or somewhat less than 40 percent.[42] Angola, Afghanistan, and Nicaragua were far more salient to Gorbachev than either Mozambique or Zimbabwe.[43] As political settlements became imminent in both Afghanistan and Angola, Gorbachev paid increasing amounts of attention to them at the expense of Nicaragua.[44]

Overall, however, consistent with Brezhnev, Gorbachev is overwhelmingly concerned about U.S. military activities, especially nuclear weapons and the Strategic Defense Initiative (SDI).[45] This priority further manifests itself by the fact that he evaluates the nuclear threat arising from the United States before Third World audiences, which normally would demand his treatment of issues such as international debt, the new international economic order, etc.[46] In fact, as is brought out in the discussion below, his treatment of the Third World in general is largely derivative of his concerns about the arms race. This is an enormous departure from the attitude of Brezhnev.

LESSONS LEARNED

U.S. Credibility

Gorbachev is remarkably consistent in seeing a U.S. political elite both disposed and able to resist revolutionary change in the Third World. This conviction preceded his selection as general secretary by some five years and continues to this day. He sees a vast and ever-growing array of motives driving the U.S. government to overthrow progressive governments, oppose national liberation movements, and dominate the rest of the Third World. He very often cites U.S. actions against Nicaragua, Angola, and Afghanistan as evidence of U.S. aggressiveness. As he does not see many divisions over policy in the U.S. leadership or take any note of the role of Congress in the U.S. political process to speak of, he focuses his attention on the U.S. executive and the American public. The latter he sees as an important factor in the ultimate curbing of the executive's aggressive tendencies.

I begin first with Gorbachev's analysis of U.S. motives for aggression, then the evidence he uses from the cases here to document that behavior, and finally his evaluation of U.S. domestic public opinion.

First, Gorbachev advances a variant of a theory of "social imperialism."[47] Speaking in Hanoi in March 1982, Gorbachev argued:

> The main cause of the significantly aggravated international situation is obvious to all Marxist-Leninists. It is the new aggravation of the general crisis of the capitalist system. The beginning of the 1980s was marked in a majority of developed capitalist countries by stagnation and production declines, the growth of inflation and unemployment and increased battles among monopolies for export markets and spheres of capital investment. As has happened more than once in history, clashing with domestic difficulties, imperialism searches for a way out by heating up international tensions, increasing the arms race and threatening socialist countries and liberation movements.[48]

But at the twenty-seventh party congress, Gorbachev reversed himself on this position and has not used it since. "True, the present stage of the general crisis of capitalism does not bear within it the absolute stagnation of capitalism, does not exclude possibilities of economic growth and mastery of new scientific-technological waves. It allows for the retention of concrete economic, military and other positions and in some sectors even the possibility of social revenge and the retrieval of positions lost earlier."[49]

A more durable line of analysis is that the narrow ruling elite that directs U.S. foreign policy has a direct economic interest in aggression in the Third World. This line of argument assumes several different forms, but it is used in some fashion throughout the period:

> For centuries imperialist states have exploited the labor and plundered the natural resources of colonies and kept people in poverty. And now they try to bind them to the capitalist system by any means—economic, military, threats and intimidation, bribery and sops. They try to prescribe to young states what kind of policies to adopt at home. They overthrow or kill those who are disobedient or whom they don't like. This is the common practice of the so-called "states of the free world." Precisely the unwillingness of the aggressive forces of capitalism to recognize the right of all states to sovereignty and independence and the free determination of their development paths and the desire to remake the world in their image no matter what— precisely this is also today the biggest source of danger for peoples.[50]

Gorbachev clearly saw U.S. imperial dependence on the exploitation of the Third World as something that had to change if the United States was ever to refrain from adventurism in the periphery. He asked the question:

> Can the capitalist system get along without neocolonialism which is one of the sources of its present life-support? How realistic is the hope that an understanding of the catastrophic danger in which the world is—and it, we know, penetrates even the elite echelons of the ruling elite of the Western world—will be turned into practical policy? After all, no matter how strong the arguments of reason, no matter how developed the feeling of responsibility and no matter how great the instinct for self-preservation, one cannot at all underestimate just how much is determined by economic, and consequently, class interests. Life will give the answers.[51]

In other words, U.S. adventurism will not abate unless and until the U.S. elite recognizes that it can maintain its country's standard of living without economically exploiting Third World countries.

A simpler answer given by Gorbachev was that U.S. aggression in the Third World is simply a necessary by-product of a more ambitious quest for global domination. As Gorbachev put it in a speech before the Portuguese Communist Party congress: "What are the causes of the present tension? Apparently, the answer to this question one should seek in a complex of factors—economic and political—which determines the present line of imperialism of confrontation, by means of threats, blackmail, interventions and wars, resolving the historical argument of the two world systems in its favor. The essence of the present militaristic course . . . is to guarantee itself dominant positions in the world."[52]

That the military-industrial complex and the ruling elite connected to it are interested in the arms race is a concept shared by Brezhnev. But Gorbachev is the first one to emphasize that both these groups are bent on increasing tensions in the Third World to serve as justification for increasing the arms race. This is a very common theme in Gorbachev's analyses of what drives U.S. decision makers to aggressive policies.[53]

Starting with his address at the party congress, Gorbachev adduces yet another explanation for U.S. interests in resisting revolutionary change— the U.S. government and military-industrial complex exploit Third World economies to pay for their military programs.[54] Yet another motive for U.S. adventurism is, by increasing tensions in the Third World and hence providing a justification for bloated military budgets, the U.S. leadership can force the Soviet Union into the arms race and economically exhaust it. Though rejecting the strategy as futile, Gorbachev said:

> [He] and his comrades try to understand for what this Administration aspires. What do all these efforts to preserve confrontation mean? Where are going to lead and what interests are served by U.S. actions in Nicaragua, against Libya and Afghanistan, the violation of our territorial waters by the U.S. Navy, support for the troglodyte apartheid regime in the RSA and much else which characterizes the international behavior of the United States today? We are familiar with the calculations to exhaust the USSR in the arms race. But they are ancient and frankly stupid.[55]

He further links this U.S. drive to bankrupt the Soviet economy with U.S. interests in the continued exploitation of the Third World, arguing that the United States wants "to limit the possibilities of the Soviet Union in its economic ties with developing countries and they, given such a situation, would be forced to all go begging to the United States."[56]

The most recent cause of U.S. adventurism that Gorbachev advanced is that it is a by-product of the U.S. strategy of deterrence:

> Let's look at deterrence from another angle. Essentially it is a policy of threats. The threat is an instrument of policy and naturally there is a desire that these threats be taken seriously by everyone. But for this it is necessary to periodically reinforce threats with action. In any given instance—the

use of force. So, there can only be one conclusion: the policy of deterrence not only does not reduce, but even increases, the possibility of military conflicts. How would we regard such a man if we met him on the street? Why are such standards, which were long ago recognized as savagery when speaking of relations between individuals still considered, by seemingly extremely enlightened people, as almost a natural norm in international relations?! These are stereotypes of past thinking, when it was considered "legitimate" to exploit other peoples and dispose of their resources. To what does the maintenance of such views lead? To the growth of regional conflicts.[57]

Gorbachev relatively frequently cited U.S. behavior toward Nicaragua, Angola, and Afghanistan as evidence of its aggressive foreign policy in the Third World.[58] He does not, however, differentiate among the causes for U.S. aggressiveness in any of the cases. So U.S. behavior in each of the three cases is driven by its need to exploit lesser-developed economies, to finance its military budgets, to exhaust the Soviet economy, and to pursue its deterrent strategy.

The only element that Gorbachev sees as restraining the aggressiveness of U.S. foreign policy in the United States itself is domestic public opinion. And on this score, Gorbachev is very deliberate in distinguishing between an American public that is against nuclear war and one that is against adventurism in the Third World. In the 82 speeches in which he speaks of U.S. military programs, Gorbachev mentions the potentially critical role U.S. public opinion has to play in their restraint in 51 of these speeches, or 62 percent. Only twice in 51 speeches that concern U.S. adventurism in the Third World does Gorbachev suggest that the American public can restrain its government.[59] He sees a struggle being conducted between a reactionary, militaristic elite who does everything to deceive its own people to get them to support an ever-expanding military budget. They are resisted by millions of people who want to put an end to the arms race once and for all.[60] He remained hopeful, however, that eventually the American people will resist the "doctrine of neoglobalism" as well.[61]

In sum, Gorbachev sees an America driven to resist progressive change in the Third World by a combination of factors. It needs to exploit the Third World economically, finance its military programs through such exploitation, create instability as a cover for pursuing the arms race, bankrupt the Soviet economy, and demonstrate its resolve through aggression in order to implement its strategy of deterrence. Gorbachev further does not expect any abatement in such aggressiveness until the U.S. elite, through the action of public opinion, comes to accept the "new realities" of the age.

Allied Behavior

U.S. foreign policy makers have assumed that efforts by the United States to confront Soviet adventurism in peripheral areas of the globe would reassure strategic allies in Western Europe, Japan, and elsewhere of the durability of U.S. security guarantees. As noted above, Brezhnev learned lessons about U.S. allies precisely contrary to those predicted. Gorbachev simply makes no connection whatever between U.S. behavior in the five cases here and the consequent attitudes of U.S. allies.[62] In fact, his analysis of U.S. allies is very similar to his evaluation of U.S. domestic public opinion. He asserts their security interests dictate their opposition to U.S. military programs and neoglobalism. But he recognizes that it is only very rarely that these countries heed his warnings on nuclear issues, and virtually never on Third World issues. Gorbachev, as in the case with the issue of U.S. credibility, pays the closest attention to U.S. allied attitudes toward U.S. military programs, not their attitudes toward U.S. actions in the Third World.[63]

The only time Gorbachev even hinted that a U.S. ally could restrain U.S. adventurism was in a speech before President Mitterand in Paris, when he suggested that French and Soviet cooperation on the Middle East, Central America, and southern Africa might be possible.[64] Moreover, Gorbachev treats public opinion in Europe and Japan similarly to public opinion in the United States, i.e., he differentiates between a very powerful antiwar/nuclear movement and a virtually nonexistent movement against U.S. adventurism.

Gorbachev has most commonly argued that the U.S. policy of the arms race evokes the resistance of broad public forces.[65] But, unfortunately for Gorbachev, these governments simply do not listen to their own people.[66] And even when there is some tangible allied opposition to a U.S. policy, such as the bombing raid on Libya, Gorbachev found that "in undertaking this action, the United States did not consider either world public opinion or a majority of its own NATO allies."[67]

Gorbachev gave his most sustained analysis of U.S.–allied relations at the twenty-sixth party congress, and his reviews were mixed:

To the degree that agreement in the positions of the three centers (of imperialism in the United States, Western Europe, and Japan), it most often is the consequence of U.S. pressure or open *diktat* which pursues the interests and aims of primarily the United States. This leads in turn to an aggravation of contradictions. It seems that they are increasingly beginning to ponder this causal nexus. For the first time, in the governments of a number of West European countries, in Social-Democratic and Liberal Parties and among the broad public, a rumor is circulating: aren't U.S. pretensions to leadership going too far? U.S. partners could be convinced, and not for the first time, that others' glasses do not replace one's own eyes.

But then Gorbachev concluded that "it is hard to expect that the complex of economic, military-political and other common interests of the three centers, in the real conditions of the modern world, can be broken. But, within the bounds of this complex, Washington should not expect the submissive obedience of its ally-competitors to U.S. *diktat*, especially when it harms their own interests."[68]

Despite the overall tone of frustration in the vast majority of Gorbachev's comments in this period, he does cite evidence that Soviet hopes are well placed on U.S. allies to turn the Reagan administration away from its nuclear madness. In his address before the Supreme Soviet after his return from the Geneva summit with Reagan, he noted that "even among its allies, confusion has emerged in the face of the clear scorn for their security interests and the readiness in Washington to stake everything in a race for the chimera of military superiority. [That SDI is the main obstacle to arms control] is not only our opinion. The governments of France, Denmark, Norway, Greece, the Netherlands, Canada and Australia have all refused to participate in SDI."[69] In sum, Gorbachev asserted, "we will count on the reason of the working people of all countries, on the good sense of simple people, on the growing feeling of self-preservation and on the recognition by political figures and parties, including NATO countries, of the new realities."[70]

Regional Dynamics

According to U.S. assumptions, Gorbachev should learn from U.S. support for UNITA, the Mujaheddin, and the Contras that, at a minimum, the prospects for further progressive change in southern Africa, South Asia, and Central America are very bleak. But Gorbachev simply makes no causal connection between events happening in Afghanistan and Nicaragua and the probability of future progressive revolutions in the respective regions. In the case of Angola, Gorbachev explicitly noted when direct U.S. support was resumed for UNITA in Angola, but he merely termed it an escalation of U.S. involvement, regrettable, but not any change from a policy of subversion that had been undertaken through its South African allies all along.[71] He recognizes that the RSA is bent on continuing "its aggressive actions against the Frontline States," but asserts that ultimately "apartheid is doomed." But in this he implies that Angola, Mozambique, and Zimbabwe will not be secure on their progressive paths until apartheid is eliminated in South Africa.[72]

Gorbachev hailed the political settlements in Angola and Afghanistan for their positive regional and global influence. In the case of the U.S.–

brokered Cuban troop withdrawal from Angola linked to Namibian independence and South African pledges to end their support for UNITA, Gorbachev argued that the agreement was "a very important step toward peace and security in southern Africa, opening the prospects for the peaceful development of Namibia and greater political and economic independence for the states in southern Africa."[73]

Gorbachev argued, prior to the Geneva accords on Afghanistan, that "when the Afghani knot is untied, it will exert the deepest influence on other regional conflicts. A political settlement (there) will be an important breach in the chain of regional conflicts. After the political settlement in Afghanistan, the question already looms: which conflict will be overcome next? And there definitely will be a next one. All regional conflicts could be done away with in several years."[74]

He went further in suggesting that "by participating as mediators and guarantors in the settlement, the Soviet Union and United States are creating a precedent of constructive interaction."[75] During his press conference at the conclusion of the June 1988 Washington summit, Gorbachev combined his hopes with a warning:

> I told the President directly that the signing of the agreements creates a precedent which goes far beyond the bounds of that problem in significance. Because this is the first time that the Soviet Union and the United States have signed an agreement which opens the way to a political solution. I think that if all parties do not adhere to the agreement, then this will not be a positive precedent; it will have far-reaching consequences and influence the approaches to those kinds of problems in other regions. And there is reason for concern. This was said to the President and the entire U.S. delegation with all frankness.[76]

In both of these cases, it should be noted that the Soviets, as yet, have only experienced half-defeats. While the Cubans have been compelled to agree to ultimately leave Angola, UNITA remains a military and political force with which the Angolan government must reckon. If UNITA ever becomes part of the government in Luanda, then it will be possible to gauge Gorbachev's reactions to a more total defeat of Soviet policy in that country.

Similarly in the case of Afghanistan, Soviet soldiers have been forced to withdraw, but the government in Kabul remains in place. If the Mujaheddin do take power, then it will be possible to see whether Gorbachev still perceives the outcome in Afghanistan as a model for conflict resolution in the Third World. Given his not-so-veiled warning at the Washington summit, it seems that his degree of willingness to make similar retreats in policy toward Nicaragua or the Middle East depends, at least in part, on the ultimate outcome in Afghanistan and U.S. policy toward that conflict.

GORBACHEV AS A BOUNDED RATIONAL ATTRIBUTION THEORIST

Gorbachev's pattern of perceptions of U.S. behavior in the periphery is consistent with a "naive scientist" using a crude model of Mills's method of difference.[77] Gorbachev identifies a number of causes for U.S. behavior in the Third World based both on his prior beliefs about the nature of imperialism and his observations of U.S. conduct abroad and domestic politics in the United States itself. He then develops various antidotes or responses to these causes, remedies that are designed to reduce future U.S. propensities for adventurism in the periphery. In this respect, his handling of information from the external environment accords quite closely to a model of a bounded rational attribution theorist. He identifies causes based on various sources of evidence and then develops a strategy to influence these causes. His only departure from this model of rationality is in his continued adherence to some elements of an orthodox Leninist approach to understanding the nature of imperialism. I examine both of these aspects of Gorbachev's beliefs below.

Gorbachev's beliefs about the inner workings of U.S. foreign policy are intimately bound up in his foreign policy strategy. As was noted above, he sees a number of factors driving U.S. aggressiveness in the Third World. Gorbachev advances several antidotes to U.S. aggressiveness. All of them turn on his recognition that U.S. domestic public opinion is the only avenue by which to influence the U.S. ruling circles. His prescriptions are a combination of Soviet domestic and foreign policies and verbal commitments to new ways of thinking about the nature of the international system. He believes that glasnost, democratization and perestroika at home will help erode the enemy images that grip the American public and elite and cause them to maintain hostile attitudes toward the Soviet Union. Bold arms control concessions and proposals coupled with cooperative behavior in the resolution of regional conflicts are expected to influence both public and elite opinion about the Soviet Union in the United States. Moreover, they provide substance for the verbal commitments to "new thinking" in foreign affairs.

Gorbachev continually argues that the military-industrial complex is an economic anachronism, asserting that economic growth is better served by civilian production. This is an effort to teach Americans that their own interests are being denigrated by the pursuit of the narrow anti-Soviet agenda of this militaristic grouping. Finally, Gorbachev's view of the Third World is a critical component of both his beliefs and his foreign policy strategy.

Unlike Brezhnev, who saw the global national liberation movement in the Third World as an integral part of the "world revolutionary alliance" aimed against imperialism, Gorbachev never mentions the existence of any kind of revolutionary alliance. Instead, he speaks of countries in the Third World as important participants in the struggle for nuclear arms control. This reformulation of the role of the periphery both reassures the U.S. public about Soviet intentions there and allows Gorbachev to sacrifice revolutionary allies on the altar of strategic détente with the United States.

In sum, Gorbachev's recognition of the role of public opinion in the formulation of U.S. foreign policy permits him to have confidence that Soviet behavior can have an eventual effect on the elite that makes that policy. His view of the Third World allows him to design a foreign policy that can credibly influence the American public in the desired direction. Below I provide evidence for this description of Gorbachev's set of beliefs and the policy strategy that is linked to it.

Gorbachev's commitment to changing and reinforcing the pressure of public opinion on Western governments, especially the United States, is reflected in his ever-broadening conception of the participants in antiwar/nuclear movements.

In order to make his reliance on public opinion more realistic, Gorbachev had to expand his conception of the same, going beyond the usual formulas of communist parties as being in the vanguard of the peace movement. This he does, and before audiences that lend power to the argument. For example, when addressing the Portuguese Communist Party congress, he did not even mention communists as part of the "tens of millions of honorable people who are coming out against the arms race." In his meeting with the Italian Communist Party general secretary, he told him that "left democratic forces, of which Communists are a part, could act in the struggle against the military threat more harmoniously."[78] Throughout this period, Gorbachev takes a very inclusive view of relevant domestic opinion in the West.

The fact that Gorbachev sees Western governments directing a good deal of their energies to deceiving public opinion is more proof that he believes that U.S. citizens are the weak link in U.S. foreign policy. For example, in his TV address to the Soviet people after the Reykjavik summit, he explained to his listeners that:

> the forces resisting disarmament with all their might aspire to lead people astray. They are trying to take under their control the feelings of wide circles of the world public, to extinguish their impulse toward peace and prevent governments from taking a clear position at this decisive historical moment. At the disposal of these circles are political power, economic levers and powerful media outlets. I said in Reykjavik that we hope that the President will consult with Congress and the American people. Something completely different occurred. [They] distorted the whole picture of

the talks in Reykjavik. They concealed the facts of Reykjavik from the American people. It looks like the United States is becoming an increasingly closed society; they are cleverly and effectively isolating their own people from objective information. This is a dangerous process. *The American people must know the truth about what is happening in the Soviet Union and the true content of Soviet foreign policy.* I would say that this is acquiring extraordinary significance (emphasis in original).[79]

Given his view of the critical role of U.S. domestic public opinion, Gorbachev has laid out a strategy that is designed to take advantage of this avenue for influence. Gorbachev argues that Soviet foreign policy initiatives and ideas, combined with reforms at home, can change U.S. policy toward the Soviet Union and regional conflicts, although changing the latter is far harder than influencing U.S. thinking on its strategic relationship with the Soviet Union.

Gorbachev only slowly and haltingly, though in recent times increasingly, has come to realize explicitly that concrete Soviet foreign policy actions have a significant effect on Western, including U.S., publics. Soviet foreign policy can empower the American people to resist its government's predisposition of hostility toward the Soviet Union. He more often and earlier has argued that Soviet domestic reforms have this desirable consequence. Before a meeting of Soviet trade union officials, Gorbachev admitted that "today we well know and understand that the massive attack—economic, political, psychological and militaristic—begun by reactionary forces at the end of the '70s and beginning of the '80s, was, along with other reasons, dictated by the state of our internal affairs."[80] Gorbachev later argued that "anti-Soviet forces are clearly worried about the interest of people and political circles in the West in what is happening now in the Soviet Union," worried that it will "erase the artificially created enemy image, an image which they have exploited for decades."[81]

Gorbachev first obliquely acknowledged the link between Soviet external behavior and U.S. foreign policy in July 1987. "Conservative forces do not apprehend and reject new thinking. All kinds of dogmatists and skeptics have ended up in alliance with them. Words alone are not destined to overcome this view of foreign policy. The problems and barriers there are colossal.[82] Gorbachev elaborated on this linkage in a speech in Murmansk in October of the same year. "If one judges the situation only by the speeches of certain highly-placed Western figures, then it would look as if everything is as it was before: the same anti-Soviet attacks, the same demands for us to prove our adherence to peace. However, with the passage of several days, no one remembers these speeches. It means something is changing. And one of the elements of the changes is that now it is hard to suggest to people that our foreign policy is only propaganda. New thinking's power is that it corresponds to popular common sense. That is why, despite all the efforts to belittle and slander our foreign initiatives, they are making their way."[83]

After returning from the summit in Washington, Gorbachev told the Soviet people he was encouraged by the fact that "the wave of goodwill on the part of average Americans has grown, to the degree that they, through television and the press, have found out what our real views are, what we want."[84]

In his speech on the seventieth anniversary of the Bolshevik revolution, Gorbachev admitted that postwar Soviet foreign policy made mistakes. It did not "take advantage of opportunities," or "reinforce the peace loving, democratic forces and stop the organizers of the Cold War." But new thinking has "begun to destroy the stereotypes of anti-Sovietism and the suspicion of [Soviet] initiatives and actions."[85] In the same vein, Gorbachev suggested at the nineteenth party conference that only a foreign policy characterized by realism could expect a "realistic attitude by those to whom it is directed," implying a previous lack of such realism in Soviet foreign policy. He admitted that the Soviet Union "inadequately responded to international events and the policies of other states and so erroneous decisions were made." In addition, alternative actions were not evaluated in terms "of how they would turn out or how much they would cost." Gorbachev also dwelt on the overemphasis of the military aspect of Soviet foreign policy:

> Having concentrated enormous resources and attention on the military side of the competition with imperialism, we did not always use the political opportunities which opened up in the world for reducing tensions and increasing mutual understanding among peoples. Meanwhile, the arms race approached a critical point. On this background, our political and public activity in favor of peace and disarmament began to lose its persuasiveness. And if one speaks more frankly—a failure to break the logic of such a development could have really ended up on the brink of military confrontation. That is why not merely a perfection, but rather the decisive renewal, of foreign policy is demanded. For this, new political thinking is needed.

He went on to argue that "precisely new thinking allows us to find new opportunities to resist a policy of force on a political basis," one that is far wider than before.[86]

In his speech before the Polish parliament, Gorbachev explained why détente failed in the 1970s and how a new Soviet approach to foreign policy is designed to avert an early death to détente now:

> Far from all opportunities were used either in the West or the East to slow and stop the dangerous process of the arms race. The concept of new

political thinking has allowed us to see things in their true measure. All members of the world community . . ., including of course also us, need to learn the high political art of a balance of interests. Western society knows the realities of the socialist world poorly. From the cradle, they drum into the people that communists are miscreants who have enslaved their own peoples and are sharpening their knives against the free nations of the West. Our foreign policy ideas and especially the processes of perestroika in the Soviet Union and other socialist countries, glasnost, openness and democratization—all this undoubtedly will destroy the primitive myths about socialism. This is extraordinarily important. After all, false stereotypes prevent the realistic conduct of affairs. I will observe that we also must rid ourselves of the simplistic approaches we have taken to depicting Western realities.[87]

In his official statement on Afghanistan, Gorbachev admitted for the first time, even if obliquely, that Soviet conduct in Afghanistan had made neighboring states anxious about their security. "Any armed conflict, including an internal one, is able to poison the atmosphere in the entire region, create a situation of unease and alarm for its neighbors. Regional conflicts are bleeding wounds able to cause patches of gangrene on the body of mankind. The earth is literally ulcerated with such dangerous hotbeds."[88] He went on to identify the situation in southern Africa and Central America as other examples of such "bleeding wounds."

Gorbachev also redefined the causes of conflicts in the Third World. By shifting the blame from imperialism to indigenous forces, two consequences follow. First, by removing the blame from imperialism, he hopes to convince the American public and elite that the Soviet Union is a credible negotiating partner. Second, by shifting the blame from Soviet shoulders, he hopes to convince the U.S. elite that their adherence to a deterrent strategy is misplaced. If changes in the status quo occur continually, almost randomly, but certainly inevitably, then no attributions will be made about U.S. credibility based on these completely arbitrary and autonomous events.

Until October 1985, Gorbachev argued that imperialism is the root cause of conflicts in the Third World.[89] But some six weeks later, at his press conference in Geneva after the conclusion of the summit, he reversed course:

Tension, conflict and even wars between different states have their roots either in the past or present socioeconomic conditions of these countries and regions. To depict things as if all these knots of contradictions are caused by the competition between East and West is not only wrong, but extremely dangerous. I said all this to the President. If today, for example, Mexico, Brazil and a number of other states cannot pay not only their debts, but even interest on them, then one can imagine what kind of processes are occurring in these countries. This can heat up the situation and lead to an explosion. And what then, they will speak of the "hand of Moscow" again? These banalities still occur everywhere, but they are impermissible at meetings such as this.[90]

In sum, Gorbachev expects that a combination of Soviet domestic reforms and foreign policy initiatives will succeed in changing the attitude of the American people toward the Soviet Union. It, in turn, will influence its government to adopt a more cooperative foreign policy. These Soviet actions operate on two elements that Gorbachev sees driving U.S. foreign policy—the cold war stereotypes held by the American public and the hostility toward the Soviet Union inherent to the U.S. ruling elite. Gorbachev's recognition that "unrealistic" Soviet foreign policy actions cause unnecessary hostility in the relationship operates on U.S. elite adherence to deterrent strategies. A search for a balance of interests is calculated to obviate the U.S. need to establish its "reputation for resolve" in peripheral conflicts.[91]

But this still leaves Gorbachev with two causal nuts yet to crack. First, the military-industrial complex still maintains an interest in pursuing the arms race and increasing tensions in the periphery. Second, interests in the exploitation of Third World economies still drive U.S. foreign policy toward adventurism in the Third World. Gorbachev's strategy deals with the military-industrial complex in several ways, but he never comes to grips with how to reduce U.S. interests in economic plunder.

Gorbachev identifies several factors he believes will ultimately cause a diminution in the pernicious influence exercised by the military-industrial complex on the formulation of U.S. foreign policy. First, he believes that this complex is an enormous drag on U.S. economic growth and that the U.S. people and elite are coming to share this concern. For example, before a group of visiting U.S. business leaders, he suggested that "business circles in the United States cannot help but be troubled by the economic and financial consequences of excessive military spending and the consequences caused by militarization of the economy, its lopsided development."[92]

In the same vein, Gorbachev has tried to demonstrate to the American people and government that the complex is indeed an obstacle to economic growth. Before an audience of U.S. teachers of the Russian language, he said that one of the biggest obstacles to reduced military budgets is the fact that people are concerned about the loss of jobs. He counterargued that "one can create three jobs in the civilian sector for the price of one job in the military-industrial complex. Second, there is surplus capacity in the military economy which can be used for peaceful aims. Third, we together can come up with big joint programs, combining our resources and scientific and intellectual potentials."[93] He buttressed his case by citing the experiences of Japan, West Germany, and Italy.[94] Gorbachev also differentiated between those U.S. business interests who are connected to the production of armaments and those "who really look at things as they are, who are not sick with the paranoia of anti-communism and who do not bind themselves to the profits from the arms race."[95] Gorbachev expects these latter interests to pose an obstacle to the continued dominance of U.S. foreign policy by the complex.

Gorbachev's constant refrain is that "the interests and goals of the military-industrial complex are not one and the same thing as the interests and goals of the U.S. people."[96] He expects that eventually the American people will realize this and oppose its influence.

While Gorbachev sees an array of factors that may ultimately ameliorate the negative influence exerted by the military-industrial complex in the United States, he does not offer any antidotes for U.S. economic dependence on the exploitation of the Third World. This is one of two areas in which Gorbachev displays signs of an orthodox and rigid set of beliefs. In continuing to adhere to the Leninist dogma of the need for imperialist states to exploit lesser-developed economies, Gorbachev logically threatens the success of his own policy strategy. On one hand, the ability to tolerate inconsistency is a sign of rationality. On the other hand, the fact that this particular belief has its origins in a far wider set of beliefs, namely, Leninist ideology, implies that Gorbachev is simply unable to shed one element of his own Leninist upbringing.

This interpretation is further supported by the fact that U.S. dependence on exploitation is a variable very easily subjected to empirical testing.[97] It is obvious to even the most casual observer that U.S. economic interests in the Third World in general are far less than its interests in Western Europe, East Asia, and the oil-producing areas of the Middle East. Moreover, the share of the Third World in total U.S. imports/exports, foreign investment, and repatriated profits has been in secular decline since the late 1960s. Gorbachev most certainly has been exposed to these facts.[98]

In addition, in the cases of U.S. adventurism in the 1980s—in Angola, Afghanistan, and Nicaragua—its economic interests in any one of these particular cases is less than meager. The case of Gulf Oil's interests in Angola further disconfirm Gorbachev's beliefs. There is no need for the United States to overthrow a government that allows itself to be exploited by U.S. monopoly capital.

Perhaps Gorbachev finds himself facing a very difficult value trade-off in his own mind. He needs to see economic motives at work in places like Afghanistan, Angola, and Nicaragua, as otherwise he would have to explicitly admit that it is Soviet involvement in these arenas that drives U.S. behavior. As noted above, Gorbachev did mention that the

United States is driven by elite adherence to deterrence theory and the need to demonstrate credibility in peripheral areas of the globe, implying an acknowledgment of partial Soviet responsibility for the U.S. responses. A good test of Gorbachev's further evolution away from ideological rigidity will be whether he comes to drop his economic explanation for U.S. behavior and begins to more consistently focus on the role of Soviet actions in influencing U.S. conduct.

The second area in which Gorbachev displays some form of motivated bias is in his evaluation of U.S. public opinion. Having committed himself to a policy based on the centrality of public opinion in the United States, he appears to use several mechanisms to protect these beliefs from disconfirming evidence. Of course, the biggest challenge to Gorbachev's beliefs is the fact that U.S. behavior has not changed during the period. Gorbachev gets around this with two devices that render his own beliefs unfalsifiable. First, he is rather careful in always describing enormous resistance to new thinking in Western ruling circles who are burdened with ancient stereotypes and habits. So he always hedges the success of his strategy with words like "eventually, ultimately, in the final account," etc., which can always provide him with a convenient counter to any challenges. Second, he is able to refer to the enormous and sustained disinformation campaign that reactionary circles and the military-industrial complex, through the media outlets they control, use to distort Soviet foreign policy initiatives and delude their publics.

He further protects his beliefs in this regard by asserting very frequently that the United States controls its allies, so that, even if public opinion in Western Europe or Japan were to break through elite prejudices and propaganda and actually influence policy, these governments would still be brought to heel by the United States.

Gorbachev also engages in a form of bolstering his beliefs. As my discussion of his assessments of motives makes clear, he continually adds new elements to the equation. I would suggest that this is done in order to continue to explain why the U.S. government feels it necessary to continue to resist Soviet proposals and the demands of the American public. Moreover, when one of his elements, his social imperialism hypothesis, contradicts his view of a public opinion for peace, he drops it. This is a critical piece of evidence for the view that public opinion is central to his belief system.

A last device used by Gorbachev to maintain his beliefs is selective attention and avoidance. As I noted above, Gorbachev did remark on the Reagan administration's resumption of aid to UNITA in Angola. However, what he did not choose to comment on was that Congress repealed the Clark amendment, with no effective resistance from the American public. If Gorbachev had recognized this fact, his belief system would have been threatened, and so he ignored this piece of disconfirming evidence. Moreover, Gorbachev seizes on clearly unrepresentative parts of the American public to make his case that U.S. public opinion is changing about Soviet foreign policy.[99]

It should be noted that Gorbachev's protection of his beliefs about the American public is not such that one could argue that it completely distorts his view of the U.S. domestic scene. As noted above, Gorbachev consciously distinguishes between an extant American public concerned about the nuclear threat and desirous of arms control and a nascent, if not absent, public opposed to Third World adventurism. If he were totally engaged in preserving his beliefs, he would argue that the American people are against such policies and the ruling elite is simply ignoring its wishes. This is a telling sign that Gorbachev is a rational attribution theorist. Another sign is the fact that he ignores evidence that would help him maintain confidence in his beliefs. Despite the enormous struggle between Congress and the Reagan administration over military aid to the Contras, and its suspension from June 1985 to June 1986 and from February 1988 until now, Gorbachev does not seize on U.S. domestic opposition to funding the Contras to buttress his beliefs about the sentiments of the American people.

So far, I have described Gorbachev's beliefs about what drives a U.S. foreign policy of adventurism and the factors he identifies that can alter it. The second half of Gorbachev's foreign policy strategy concerns his view of the Third World. Gorbachev's commitment to changing and reinforcing the pressure of public opinion on Western governments, especially the United States, is reflected in a new approach to the Third World. Before Third World audiences, Gorbachev tries to convince them that anti-imperialist concerns must be subordinated to the struggle against the nuclear threat. A most striking piece of evidence for this interpretation is how Gorbachev redefines the "world revolutionary alliance" at the party congress. Unlike Brezhnev, and indeed his other predecessors as general secretary, who all defined its constituent parts as the socialist community, the international working class, and the national liberation movement, Gorbachev couches it in terms of the antinuclear movement and in fact placed it in his report to the twenty-sixth party congress in that section of his address.[100]

Later in this speech, Gorbachev lumped the commitment of the CPSU to solidarity with "the forces of national and social liberation" together with a readiness to "develop close ties with noncommunist tendencies and organizations, including religious ones, who come out against war." This is indeed very strange company for Third World revolutionaries to find themselves among. And the next paragraph contained an appeal to cooperate with social democratic parties on the basis of antinuclear sentiments. Gorbachev believes "that in liberated states, they increasingly better understand that in order to achieve full independence, to increase economic growth and secure the democratic restructuring of international economic relations, they must be in close coordination with the struggle against the arms race and threat of war."[101]

Gorbachev explicitly tells his audiences that Third World objectives in the area of economic development and other problems must be subordinated to the issue of arms control. In India, for example, he told that country's parliament that only the "elimination of nuclear weapons will yield the resources necessary for an improvement in the lives of peoples. Ending the arms race will facilitate the realization of the idea of a new international economic order."[102] Later, in another forum, he said that all global problems—Third World conflicts, economic development, food shortages, and nuclear arms control—are interdependent. But then he declared that their "dependence on each other is not equal: without curtailing the arms race, one cannot really solve any of the other problems."[103] Gorbachev's ideas about how the United States finances the arms race through the exploitation of Third World economies provides a substantive basis for his appeals to his Third World allies to help resist U.S. military programs before turning to their agenda on the new international economic order.

In sum, Gorbachev's set of beliefs about the role of domestic opinion in the formulation of U.S. foreign policy and the role of the Third World in international affairs allow him to develop a strategy for détente with the United States far different from any that Brezhnev could have devised. Like an adept attribution theorist, Gorbachev discovered one of the causes of the downfall of détente was in U.S. reactions to progressive change in the Third World. Consistent with bounded rationality, he generated a menu of independent variables that can account for this kind of reaction. It includes economic motivations, the role of the military-industrial complex in U.S. politics, the cold war stereotypes that grip both the American people and the ruling elite, the latter's adherence to deterrence theory, and also Soviet behavior in various regional conflicts.

Gorbachev develops a policy that is consistent with his beliefs about both the U.S. political scene and the place of the Third World in the international arena. Through a combination of Soviet domestic and foreign policy initiatives, he expects to erode the enemy images held by the American people and the elite. Through a process of education, he expects to teach the American people that the military-industrial complex is inimical to U.S. national interests and can be profitably reconverted to civilian production tasks. Finally, through constructive Soviet behavior in regional conflicts, Gorbachev expects to be able to remove one of the conditions that motivates U.S. deterrent strategy. He hopes to convince U.S. leaders that they no longer have to worry about demonstrating their resolve in regional conflicts, because the Soviet Union is more than willing to accept a mutually arrived at conception of a "balance of interests" in any given case. Moreover, Gorbachev's conception of Third World actors as contributors to the process of arms control, rather than as revolutionary forces designed to shift the correlation of forces against imperialism, allows him to abandon long-time Soviet commitments to the victories of national liberation movements around the globe.

SOVIET POLICY UNDER GORBACHEV

The assumptions of U.S. foreign policy would predict that, as a consequence of rising costs associated with U.S. military support for UNITA, the Contras, and the Mujaheddin, Gorbachev would reduce the level of Soviet support for the respective embattled regimes. The evidence from Gorbachev's public speeches and amounts of Soviet military aid remains quite ambiguous. Consistent with U.S. assumptions, Gorbachev does not frequently state Soviet support for national liberation movements[104] and calls continually for negotiated solutions to the conflicts in Angola, Afghanistan, and Nicaragua.[105] But the lack of verbal support for national liberation movements is also consistent with the set of beliefs Gorbachev holds about the Third World and its role in Soviet strategy. Similarly, the expressed preference for negotiated settlements to these conflicts is congruent with his beliefs about how to best influence U.S. public and elite opinion. Contrary to U.S. assumptions, the Gorbachev government continues to increase the supply of arms to these embattled regimes.[106]

It would appear that these increased arms supplies contradict Gorbachev's verbal commitment to negotiations and lack of explicit commitments to national liberation movements. There are at least several alternative explanations for this apparent inconsistency. It is possible that Gorbachev is simply trying to enhance the bargaining positions of Soviet allies in these conflicts. It could be the case that this is a side payment being made by Gorbachev to his more conservative rivals in exchange for a free hand in other areas of diplomacy. For example, he is able to negotiate his way out of these alliances, but must continue to provide military support to these allies in order to appease his conservative critics.

An alternative explanation is that Gorbachev is trying to protect Soviet credibility. Driven by the same fears that motivate U.S. policy makers to demonstrate their resolve in peripheral areas of the globe, Gorbachev may feel the need to show the U.S. government that his retreats have limits and to show his Third World allies that the Soviet Union has not completely abandoned them to imperialist aggression. Gorbachev is doubly susceptible to concerns for credibility, since his policy strategy rests on the belief that Soviet concessions in Third World conflicts will lead the U.S. public to press its government to end its own involvement.

There is some limited evidence from Gorbachev himself that a concern for credibility drives his continued military commitment to these regimes. Gorbachev, unlike Brezhnev, singles out precisely those countries under imperialist attack for Soviet aid in their defense.[107] Indeed, while always hedging on Soviet commitments of economic support for these regimes, Gorbachev emphatically affirms Soviet support for their defense capabilities.[108] Brezhnev, on the contrary, singled out countries on an ideological basis, arguing for the need to defend "countries of socialist orientation."[109] In this respect, Gorbachev links his policy of maintaining military support to continued U.S. arms supplies to insurgencies against Soviet allies.

The credibility hypothesis argues that it is continued U.S. military supplies to the Mujaheddin after the Soviet withdrawal and to UNITA after the accords on Angola and Namibia that cause Gorbachev's continued flow of arms. The test for each of these alternative hypotheses will come once the United States ends it arms supplies to the Mujaheddin in Afghanistan and UNITA in Angola. We have already seen an end to Soviet arms supplies to the Sandinistas after the United States cut off military aid to the Contras. In this case, at least, the credibility hypothesis finds support.[110]

AMERICAN ASSUMPTIONS AND SOVIET LEARNING

This study shows that the kinds of lessons Soviet decision makers are likely to learn from U.S. efforts to raise the costs of Soviet adventurism in the Third World are highly contingent on the kinds of beliefs held by those leaders. Neither Brezhnev nor Gorbachev learned the kinds of deterrent lessons U.S. policy makers tried to impart.

Brezhnev had a very rigid and narrow set of beliefs. He saw a very small group within the U.S. ruling elite as responsible for the formulation of U.S. foreign policy, impervious to any influence exerted by Congress or the American public. He saw the national liberation movement as an integral part of a "world revolutionary alliance" along with the international working class and the socialist community. This alliance was aimed at continually shifting the global correlation of forces against imperialism. These two beliefs underlay Brezhnev's policy strategy of offensive détente.

The consequences of these beliefs and strategy for Brezhnev's perception of the costs imposed by U.S. efforts to resist Soviet adventurism were twofold. On one hand, Brezhnev did not learn from Soviet gains in Angola, Mozambique, and Nicaragua that the United States had lost its willingness or capacity to resist future progressive changes in the Third

World. By focusing his attention on a narrow U.S. elite axiomatically hostile to such changes, Brezhnev ignored the fact that the American people and Congress were exerting a constraining influence on the aggressive predispositions of the executive branch. In effect, Brezhnev overestimated U.S. credibility.

On the other hand, Brezhnev, through the operation of this same set of beliefs, could not be deterred from future support of revolutionary forces by U.S. efforts to increase the price of such support. His tightly constructed view of a world revolutionary alliance made the abandonment or even reduction of commitment to national liberation movements too psychologically costly. Such a revision of his beliefs would have compelled him to fundamentally alter his entire structure of beliefs about how the world operated. Moreover, since he saw no role for the American people and Congress in the foreign policy process, he could see no reason why any moderation in Soviet behavior in the periphery would have any affect on U.S. aggressiveness. As a consequence, Brezhnev was unable to make any effective adjustments in his strategy of offensive détente, even as the presumed centerpiece of that strategy—arms control and economic cooperation with the West—was lost through Soviet actions in the Third World.

Gorbachev also did not learn the kinds of deterrent lessons U.S. policy makers assumed he would from events in the periphery. Gorbachev approached his analysis of U.S. adventurism in the Third World as if he were a bounded rational attribution theorist. He identified the causes of this elite propensity for aggression and then set about designing a Soviet foreign policy strategy that could influence U.S. policy. Herein lies the first critical difference with Brezhnev's belief system. Unlike Brezhnev, Gorbachev singled out U.S. public opinion as a critical variable with the potential to ultimately alter the U.S. governing elite's predilection for interventionism in the periphery. The recognition of this causal connection made changes in Soviet foreign policy relevant to the endeavor of influencing U.S. policy. Brezhnev had no such understanding of U.S. foreign policy formulation and so did not see any role for Soviet foreign policy in altering the behavior of the United States.

The second critical difference with Brezhnev was Gorbachev's lack of adherence to a view of the international system whose conceptual centerpiece was the world revolutionary alliance. Unlike Brezhnev, Gorbachev did not see continual victories of progressive forces in the Third World as necessary to maintain his core set of beliefs about how the world operates. Hence, Gorbachev can reduce Soviet commitments to revolutionary change in order to cultivate U.S. public opinion, without having to abandon some critical component of his world view. Consequently, Gorbachev, when faced with the obvious failure of Brezhnev's strategy of offensive détente, was able to develop an alternative foreign policy strategy that takes into account both U.S. public opinion and the effect of Soviet foreign policy behavior on that opinion.

In sum, Brezhnev could not be deterred because of the costs Soviet foreign policy moderation would impose on his tightly structured belief system. Gorbachev was deterred, but not by the costs imposed by U.S. efforts to overthrow Soviet allies in the periphery. Instead, Gorbachev responded to the costs Soviet actions in the Third World had levied on Soviet efforts to continue strategic détente with the United States. And only Gorbachev's beliefs about U.S. public opinion and the role of the Third World in the international arena allowed him to make such a calculation.

NOTES

1. Several of the assumptions held by decision makers were developed by traditional deterrence theorists almost 30 years ago. These include the fear of falling dominoes, bandwagoning allies, and reduced credibility in subsequent conflicts in the Third World as a consequence of a loss in the periphery. Where U.S. decision makers go farther than their theorist counterparts is in worrying that Soviet leaders will make the inferential leap from the periphery to strategic areas of the globe. Except for this latter distinction, I could just as well be testing the postulates of deterrence theory, rather than the assumptions held by U.S. policy makers. I am grateful to Charles Glaser for bringing this difference to my attention. For the assumptions of traditional deterrence theory, see Thomas C. Schelling, *Arms and Influence* (New Haven: Yale University Press, 1966) and Glenn Snyder, *Deterrence and Defense* (Princeton, N.J.: Princeton University Press, 1961).

2. This typification of Brezhnev's foreign policy strategy was coined by Jack Snyder in "The Gorbachev Revolution: A Waning of Soviet Expansionism?" *International Security* 12 (Winter 1987/8): 103–9.

3. As a consequence of this reliance on a single source, my citations include only date and page number(s), unless I use another source.

4. From 1976 until his death in November 1982, Brezhnev made 104 speeches in which he touched on foreign policy issues. In 57 of these, or 55 percent of the total, he mentioned one of the five cases considered here.

5. The importance of each of these cases to the formation of Brezhnev's view of U.S. credibility varied widely. In the period 1976–1982, Brezhnev mentioned Mozambique eight times in speeches, but never drew any inferences about U.S. credibility in these addresses. For Zimbabwe, he did so only once in 14 instances. This compares to 3 out of 4 times for Afghanistan, 4 of 9 for Nicaragua, and 9 of 22 for Angola.

6. In 15 of these cases, Brezhnev was addressing a Third World audience, which is not a context that demands a discussion of INF deployments or U.S. relations with China. This stands in stark contrast to the fact that Brezhnev inferred lessons about U.S. credibility from the latter's actions in the Third World

only four times before non–Third World audiences, compared with 13 times before Third World audiences.

7. February 26, 1976, 5. He continued on this theme throughout the rest of his reign. See, for example, his speech at the eighteenth Komsomol congress, April 20, 1978, 2.

8. June 30, 1976, 1.

9. October 8, 1976, 2.

10. Speech at dinner for Ethiopian leader Mengistu, November 18, 1978, 2.

11. Address before Central Committee plenum, October 26, 1976, 2.

12. Speech at dinner for Angolan President Neto, September 29, 1977, 1–2. This is a theme maintained throughout by Brezhnev, namely, that the very existence of progressive regimes is sufficient to evoke U.S. resistance. See, for example, his speech at a dinner for Qaddafi, April 28, 1981, 2.

13. Speech on the sixtieth anniversary of the October revolution, November 3, 1977, 3.

14. Speech at dinner for Syria's President Hafez Assad, February 22, 1978, 2. It is most likely in this instance that Brezhnev was fulminating at the recent loss of Egypt.

15. Greetings to a Tashkent meeting of writers of Afro-Asian countries, October 11, 1978, 1.

16. June 17, 1979, 1.

17. February 23, 1980, 1–2.

18. See, for example, his speech to Qaddafi, April 28, 1981, 2.

19. Even this conclusion may be exaggerating Brezhnev's optimism, as this speech was given while awarding Romesh Chandra, president of the World Peace Council, an Order of Lenin. Since Chandra was in charge of mobilizing public opinion against war, one could expect Brezhnev to at least give him some encouragement about his prospects for success. June 19, 1981, 1.

20. Speech at dinner for Nicaragua's President Daniel Ortega, May 5, 1982, 2. Given the occasion, one could easily argue that even this instance of attention to Nicaragua's plight was an obligatory performance. However, Brezhnev did return to Central America in subsequent speeches before his death. For example, in a speech before a group of Soviet army and navy personnel, October 28, 1982, 1.

21. At twenty-sixth party congress, February 23, 1981, 2.

22. Speech at dinner for the president of Madagascar, Didier Ratsiraka, June 30, 1978, 2. Brezhnev noted these and other NATO activities in Africa in support of U.S. aims in, for example, his address to the sixteenth trade union congress, March 22, 1977, 2.

23. In speech before military officers, October 28, 1982, 1.

24. For Angola's revolutionizing effect on the region, see, for example, his report at twenty-fifth party congress, February 25, 1976, 2. For the South African threat to progressive regimes in southern Africa, see, for example, his speech before Ethiopian President Mengistu, November 18, 1978, 2. For the absence of effects for Nicaragua, see the same congress report, 2.

25. September 29, 1977, 2. Similar such omissions can be found, for example in his message to Angolan President Dos Santos on the fifth anniversary of the PRA, November 11, 1980, 1.

26. To be more accurate, Brezhnev often recognized the role of public opinion in pushing the U.S. ruling classes to conclude arms control agreements—the core of détente in Brezhnev's view—and prevent war, but these views are beyond the scope of this paper.

27. In fact, Brezhnev described the Carter administration in precisely these terms, as an elite caught between the forces of the cold war and détente.

28. There is a substantial body of experimental psychology literature that supports the idea that people with tightly organized belief systems will resort to all sorts of inconsistency-reducing mechanisms before they will submit to reordering their central beliefs. See, for example, William J. McGuire, "The Current Status of Cognitive Consistency Theories," in *Cognitive Consistency,* ed. Shel Feldman (New York: Academic, 1966), 15; Elliot Aronson, "Dissonance Theory: Progress and Problems," in *Theories of Cognitive Consistency,* ed. Robert P. Abelson (Chicago: Rand McNally, 1968), 5–26; Robert P. Abelson, "Psychological Implications," in Abelson, *Theories of Cognitive Consistency,* 116; and Paul D. Sweeney and Kathy L. Gruber, "Selective Exposure: Voter Information Preferences and the Watergate Affair," *Journal of Personality and Social Psychology* 46 (June 1984): 1208–20.

29. From his address before the twenty-fifth party congress, February 25, 1976, 3, to his message to the international conference on sanctions against the RSA, May 20, 1981, 1.

30. Speech at dinner for Indian prime minister, Morarji Desai, October 22, 1977, 2.

31. Similarly, beginning in the middle of 1980, Brezhnev called for the peaceful settlement of disputes, a line clearly linked to Afghanistan. See, for example, his speech awarding Yemen's prime minister, Ali Nasser Muhammed, an Order of the Friendship of Peoples, May 28, 1980, 1.

32. May 25, 1978, 1.

33. June 30, 1978, 2.

34. March 10, 1982, 2.

35. For example, in speech to Ortega himself, May 5, 1982, 2.

36. February 25, 1976, 3.

37. October 8, 1976, 2.

38. April 6, 1977, 1.

39. October 13, 1982, 2.

40. In this period, the Soviet Union sent more than 400 T-54/5 main battle tanks, more than 400 armored personnel carriers, close to 200 SAM-2/3 antiaircraft missiles, a dozen Su-17 fighter planes, 32 attack helicopters, and a dozen transport aircraft. All these levels of aid are taken from *The Military Balance* (London: International Institute of Strategic Studies), for 1979–1980, 1980–1981, 1981–1982 and 1982–1983.

41. The Brezhnev government also gave Mozambique and Angola substantial amounts of military aid in this period. This occurred, however, prior to the resumption of U.S. military aid to UNITA in Angola, so does not constitute fair evidence of a Soviet response to U.S.-imposed costs.

42. This compares with 55 percent for Brezhnev (57 cases in 104 speeches).

43. The figures are Angola–27, Afghanistan–24, Nicaragua–22, Mozambique–8, and Zimbabwe–1.

44. In 1986 Afghanistan and Angola accounted for 47 percent of Gorbachev's total comments on the five cases; in 1987, this increased to 63 percent and in 1988 to 79 percent.

45. In 108 of his 205 (53 percent) speeches that touch on foreign policy issues, Gorbachev explicitly notes the threat to peace that derives from U.S. military programs of various types.

46. Some representative examples are: speech before Ethiopia's Mengistu, November 2, 1985, 3; message to Zimbabwe's Robert Mugabe as chairman of nonaligned movement, September 1, 1986, 1; speech at dinner for Syria's Assad, April 25, 1987, 2; and speech at dinner given for him by Indian president, R. Venkataraman, November 19, 1988, 2.

47. This school of thought, at least in Western scholarship, was first formulated to describe Wilhelmine Germany's imperial policy prior to World War I. See, for example, Volker Berghahn, "Naval Armaments and Social Crisis: Germany Before 1914," in *War, Economics and the Military Mind*, eds. Geoffrey Best and Andrew Wheatcroft (London: Croon Helms, 1976), 61–84.

48. At the Vietnamese Communist Party's fifth party congress, March 29, 1982, 4.

49. February 26, 1986, 2–3.

50. Speech in Dnepropetrovsk metallurgical factory, June 27, 1985, 1–2. For a representative example from among many, see his speech at dinner for Mozambique's President Chissano, August 4, 1987, 2. Gorbachev's logic here is wanting. Since he admits that the United States is able to keep all Third World countries, even countries of socialist orientation, in the world capitalist economic system by a vast combination of devices, it makes no sense for the United States, if driven by purely economic motives, to try to subvert the progressive countries it is already exploiting.

51. Speech on the seventieth anniversary of Great October, November 3, 1987, 4–5. See also his conversation with the Australian prime minister, Robert Hawke, December 2, 1987, 2.

52. December 17, 1983, 4. See also his speech at a Central Committee plenum, October 16, 1985, 1–2.

53. See, from among many examples, his speech at dinner for Italian Communist Party general secretary Natta, January 29, 1986, 2.

54. See, for example, his answers to the questions of an Algerian journalist, April 3, 1986, 1–2.

55. Interview with Algerian journalist, April 3, 1986.

56. TV address after Reykjavik summit, October 15, 1986, 1–2.

57. Address before a meeting in Moscow "for a nuclear-free world and humanism in international relations," February 17, 1987, 1–2. He repeated a similar critique of deterrence policies in a dinner for England's Prime Minister Thatcher, March 31, 1987, 2.

58. He inferred lessons about U.S. credibility from its actions in Nicaragua 16 times, in Angola 11, and Afghanistan 10.

59. Speech awarding Vladivostok an Order of Lenin, July 29, 1986, 1–3, and in an NBC television interview with Tom Brokaw, December 2, 1987, 1–2.

60. This is perhaps the single most frequent theme in Gorbachev's speeches. From among many examples, see his remarks at a joint press conference with

President Mitterand in Paris, October 5, 1985, 1–2; text of his TV address to the American people on New Year's Day, January 2, 1986, 1; and his speech at eleventh party congress, German Socialist Unity Party, April 19, 1986, 1–2.

61. In a speech at a meeting of international scholars on ending nuclear tests in Moscow, July 15, 1986, 1–2.

62. Gorbachev comments on the relationship between the United States and its Japanese, Western European, and Chinese allies in 33 speeches. He does not once speak of their attitudes toward U.S. adventurism in the Third World or the effect of such adventurism on U.S. security guarantees for these allies.

63. In fully 24 of the 33 speeches in which U.S. allies are discussed, it is their position on U.S. military programs that Gorbachev singles out for attention. For a representative example, see his speech in Sofia on the fortieth anniversary of the Bulgarian revolution, September 9, 1984, 4.

64. October 4, 1985, 4.

65. For example, in his speech at the tenth party congress, Portuguese Communist Party, December 17, 1983, 4.

66. For example, his speech in Sofia, September 9, 1984, 4. One may somewhat discount this speech, as it is given in the context of defending the Soviet suspension of participation in the INF negotiations. For stinging criticisms of Japanese support for U.S. policy, see his speech before general secretary of the Vietnamese Communist Party, Le Zuan, June 29, 1985, 2, and his answers to a TASS correspondent, August 14, 1985, 1.

67. Speech in East Berlin, April 22, 1986, 1–2.

68. February 26, 1986, 2–3.

69. November 28, 1985, 1–2.

70. Speech in Togliatti, April 9, 1986, 1–3.

71. See his speech to Dos Santos, May 7, 1986, 2.

72. Speech at dinner for Mozambique's President Chissano, August 4, 1987, 1.

73. Congratulatory message to Fidel Castro, December 23, 1988, 1.

74. Statement on Afghanistan, February 9, 1988, 1. He repeated these expectations before other audiences as well. For example, see his message to the Chataqua conference meeting in Tbilisi, September 19, 1988, 1.

75. Speech at meeting with U.S.–Soviet commercial-economic council, April 14, 1988, 1.

76. June 2, 1988, 2–4.

77. For a clear statement of attribution theory, see Harold H. Kelley, "Processes of Causal Attribution," *American Psychologist* 28 (February 1973): 107–28.

78. January 29, 1986, 2. For an example from among many, see his speech at the nineteenth party conference, June 29, 1988, 3–4. The only exception to this expansive view of the relevant public is in a speech before the East German leader Honecker at the dedication of a monument to the German Communist, Ernst Thalmann, in which Gorbachev asserts that "the working class, even to this day, occupies a special place" in the antiwar movement. One can probably explain this exception by the context—a speech before one of the more orthodox ideologues of Eastern Europe about a man who oversaw the destruction of the German Communist Party after the rise of Hitler due to his slavish devotion to the Stalinist line of nonalignment with "social fascists."

79. October 23, 1986, 1–2. For another example of Gorbachev arguing that the U.S. ruling elite prevents its people from learning the truth about Soviet foreign policy, see his speech in the Polish parliament, July 12, 1988, 2.

80. February 26, 1987, 1–2. The high level of ideological orthodoxy of this audience gives added power to this admission by Gorbachev.

81. Speech in Murmansk, October 2, 1987, 2–3. In a speech to the Australian prime minister, Robert Hawke, Gorbachev argues that the erosion of the enemy image held by the American people made the INF treaty possible, December 2, 1987, 2. I am not at all implying in this argument that Gorbachev is adopting any domestic reforms in order to influence Western opinions. Instead, Gorbachev simply came to realize that one valuable by-product of such reforms has been its salutary affect on images of the Soviet Union abroad.

82. Speech at breakfast for Gandhi, July 4, 1987, 2.

83. October 2, 1987, 2–3. See also his speech at a Central Committe plenum, February 19, 1988, 3.

84. December 15, 1987, 1.

85. November 3, 1987, 4–5.

86. June 29, 1988, 3–4.

87. July 12, 1988, 2. It is noteworthy here that in the text of this speech, the word *free* in the phrase "free nations of the West" was not in quotation marks. This is the first time I have ever seen a speech by a Soviet leader in which this qualification is not added.

88. February 9, 1988, 1.

89. In a speech at a dinner with Mitterand in Paris, October 4, 1985, 4. This in itself is a sign of emphasis, as Soviet leaders generally go out of their way to avoid anti-imperialist statements before Western European audiences.

90. November 22, 1985, 1–3. Among many other examples, see his speech at dinner given for him by Reagan in Moscow, June 1, 1988, 2. This is not to say that Gorbachev completely absolves imperialism of responsibility for conflicts in the Third World. He continues to blame the United States for instability in Afghanistan: at a joint press conference with Gandhi in India, November 29, 1986, 1–2, and in his interview with Tom Brokaw, December 2, 1987, 1–2; the latter, however, is the last time he made such an attribution.

91. It is almost as if Gorbachev had read Snyder and Diesing's work that shows that a state's behavior in conflicts is driven by its perceived need to protect its credibility, as much as, if not more than, by its material interests in any given conflict. Glenn Snyder and Paul Diesing, *Conflict Among Nations* (Princeton, N.J.: Princeton University Press, 1977), 183–89.

92. December 11, 1985, 2.

93. August 8, 1987, 2. See also his speech on the seventieth anniversary of the revolution in which he proposed that the United States and Soviet Union jointly prepare programs to convert their military industries to civilian uses, November 3, 1987, 4–5. He repeated this offer in his speech before the United Nations, December 8, 1988, 1–2.

94. November 3, 1987, 4–5.

95. Speech awarding Vladivostok an Order of Lenin, July 29, 1986, 1–3.

96. Report to the twenty-seventh party congress, February 26, 1986, 7–9. For

one among many examples, see his answers to the questions of correspondents from *Newsweek* and the *Washington Post*, May 23, 1988, 1–2.

97. Experimental psychologists have found that people tend to handle quantitative data, such as would be available in any assessment of U.S. economic dependence on Third World countries, in a far more rational and rigorous manner than qualitative information. See, for example, Paul Slovic and Douglas MacPhillamy, "Dimensional Commensurability and Cue Utilization in Comparative Judgment," *Organizational Behavior and Human Performance* 11 (February 1974): 172–94.

98. Indeed, many Soviet scholars have written precisely about this phenomenon for well over a decade, including advisers who are very close to Gorbachev, such as Evgenii Primakov.

99. This is most obvious in his frequent citations of the February 16, 1987, meeting in Moscow with thousands of celebrities (e.g., John Denver) from around the world, as if this meeting were representative of the average American voter.

100. February 26, 1986, 7–9.

101. April 23, 1983, 1–3. Gorbachev argues for the primacy of antinuclear activities over revolutionary aims before audiences that usually demand precisely the opposite emphasis. For example, in a speech to Ethiopia's Mengistu, November 2, 1985, 3; speech before Indian parliament, November 28, 1986, 2; message to meeting of the OAU, May 25, 1988; and at a dinner for the Brazilian president, Jose Sarney, October 19, 1988.

102. November 28, 1986.

103. February 17, 1987.

104. Out of 205 speeches, Gorbachev advances such support only 12 times. More important, in only three of these cases did the context or audience not call for such expressions of support. In dozens of speeches before Third World audiences, Gorbachev does not express such support.

105. In 27 speeches over the last three and a half years, Gorbachev has called for political settlements for these three conflicts.

106. From 1986 to 1988, the Afghani regime has received more than 100 artillery pieces, more than 400 mortars, 250 antiaircraft guns, 35 Su-22 ground attack fighter planes, 20 Mig-19 fighter interceptors, 30 Mi-25 helicopter gunships, and 25 additional transport planes. In the same period, the Angolan government received 100 T-54/5 main battle tanks, 50 artillery pieces, an indefinite number of multiple rocket launchers and SAM-2/13 missile batteries, 75 antiaircraft guns, 14 Mig-21, 7 Su-22, and 30 Mig-23 ground attack fighters, 19 transport planes, 21 Mi-25 helicopter gunships, and 23 Mi-8/17 transport helicopters. Nicaragua obtained 30 T-54/5 tanks, 22 armored cars, 50 artillery pieces, 12 122mm multiple rocket launchers, over 350 antitank guns, over 400 antiaircraft guns, over 150 SAM-7/14/16s, 5 coastal patrol boats, 35 Mi-8/17 transport helicopters, six Mi-24/5 helicopter gunships, and 6 transport planes. I have omitted Soviet weapons deliveries for 1985, assuming that these were largely ordered prior to that year. This most probably understates the level of arms shipments for which Gorbachev is responsible, as he could have cancelled their delivery. *The Military Balance* (London: International Institute for Strategic Studies), 1986–1987, 1987–1988, 1988–1989.

107. For explicit commitments to regimes under attack, see, for example, his

speech at the Central Committee plenum, April 24, 1985, 1–2, and his interview with Tom Brokaw, December 2, 1987, 1–2.

108. For an example of expressions of the limitations on Soviet ability to provide economic aid and on the need to more efficiently utilize aid that has already been granted, see his speech at the fifth party congress of the Vietnamese Communist Party, March 29, 1982, 4, and his message to the OAU, May 25, 1988, 1.

109. Gorbachev, in 205 speeches, only twice even mentions countries of socialist orientation, let alone identifies them as meriting a special place in Soviet aid commitments.

110. One additional alternative explanation is not so easily tested. It is possible that Soviet military aid is the product of some standard operating procedure in a section of the Defense Ministry. A set package of military hardware and support may be preprogrammed for a five-year period, and the execution of this program may be relatively impervious to any alterations once it is under way. If this is the case, then the levels of Soviet military aid to any given country may not correlate at all with the Soviet leadership's actual level of commitment to that country. For example, the Soviet government contends that its military advisers in Iraq can come home only after the terms of their contracts expire. I am grateful to Mike Desch for bringing this alternative explanation to my attention.

17

Attempted Learning: Soviet Policy Toward the United States in the Brezhnev Era

Franklyn Griffiths

This chapter considers learning in Soviet behavior toward the United States in the decade surrounding Leonid Brezhnev's rise to primacy as leader in 1971. Détente became the major business of the day. The question for the Soviet Union was how to incorporate sustained cooperation into a conflictual relationship in which the U.S.S.R. was destined to prevail. Decision makers and other participants in the Soviet policy process had plenty of opportunity to learn about cooperation from the very lengthy preliminaries to the summit and agreements of May 1972, from the onset of détente in the following months, and from the ensuing experience of renewed discord. As might be expected, not everyone drew the same inferences from the same situation.

"New" thinking about the United States, international relations, and Soviet policy requirements was certainly to be observed in these years. New conservative thinking, which viewed cooperation essentially as a form of protracted conflict with the United States, was assimilated by the regime and incorporated into its outward behavior. It proved misguided in concept and unworkable in practice. Reformist new thinking, which in essence sought protracted cooperation as a means of demilitarizing the continuing conflict with the United States, was promoted at lower echelons of the regime and with some support from on high. But it failed to obtain equivalent expression at the leadership level and in external Soviet conduct. Although the regime remained wedded to détente with the United States and proceeded to tinker with its American policy as U.S.–Soviet relations began their slide into acrimony and then confronta-

630

tion, new strategic thinking about cooperation was put on hold by the mid-1970s. The Soviet performance in the decade to 1976 was thus one of attempted but arrested learning.

If the Soviet Union in the Brezhnev era proved unequal to the task of learning to cooperate effectively with the United States, why take the trouble to penetrate the shroud of secrecy and ideological controls that so obscured Soviet thinking in these years? In large part the answer is that learning to collaborate with the principal adversary has been a historical process where the U.S.S.R. is concerned. Little in the way of learning may be observed over a short period of time, even in the span of a decade. And yet all manner of insights, policy adjustments, and, to be sure, reversals do occur continuously on and below the surface of Soviet behavior. The cumulative effect has indeed been substantial. Consider the evolution of the Soviet stance toward the United States between February 1953 (to say nothing of February 1918) and February 1976. Consider also the decade of concern to us here: although the regime was unable to make a going concern of cooperation, as of February 1976 it was committed to a negotiating agenda that went far closer to the heart of Soviet security and well-being than anything contemplated 10 years before. Nor would the lessons of failed cooperation in the 1970s be lost on the generation of reformists that came to power under Mikhail Gorbachev after March 1985. While grievously flawed, the performance of the Brezhnev regime in pursuing a détente relationship with the United States warrants close consideration not only for what it may reveal about foreign policy learning in a given context, but also for an appreciation of learning as an evolutionary process.

The origins of the détente of the 1970s reach back to the early years of the Brezhnev-Kosygin regime and its dealings with the Johnson administration on matters of strategic arms control. The substance of détente became increasingly complex as the Brezhnev-Kosygin and then the Brezhnev leadership endeavored to come to terms with the Nixon administration, and subsequently contributed to the undoing of cooperation with Nixon's successor. Lest we lose ourselves in the welter of detail that bore on the Soviet Union's American policy in the decade ending with the twenty-fifth congress of the Communist Party in the Soviet Union (CPSU) in 1976, I will assume knowledge of U.S.–Soviet relations and focus this inquiry on indications of learning as revealed in internal Soviet discourse.[1]

As to learning per se, more will be said later but for now it is to be understood as a process in which consensual knowledge is altered to provide an improved basis for collective action. Access to the operative consensual knowledge of the regime, for example in its handling of the Jewish emigration issue or the Soviet-American-Chinese triangular relationship, is effectively denied us by the secrecy that surrounded Soviet foreign policy making in the Brezhnev years. As a result, we are unable to conduct a direct investigation of consensual learning as it figured in the strategic thinking of decision makers or in their processing of specific issues relating to the United States. The available data do, however, allow us to consider changes in the regime's overt consensual knowledge, and therefore any overt consensual learning that may have occurred in connection with U.S.–Soviet détente.

Though highly abstract and seemingly far removed from the operative consensus, overt consensual knowledge as it concerned the principal adversary served serious purposes. It legitimized the regime and its policies. It biased the making of policy in favor of certain options and at the expense of others. It also served to constrain the behavior of political participants, some of whom had an interest in altering the published consensus to favor preconceived policy needs. The particular set of participants to be considered here consists of representative leaders and specialists who were all occupied one way or another with U.S.–Soviet relations and with the maintenance and manipulation of consensus as such.[2]

Evidence of consensual learning will accordingly be sought in indications of attempted and achieved change in the overt consensus of the regime on (a) the situation it faced and (b) policy toward the United States. The reader is forewarned that what follows may at first appear to be an inquiry into priestly mutterings that had little to do with Soviet practice in cooperating with the United States. But as we begin to penetrate the fog that surrounded Soviet foreign policy discourse, we find that overt consensual knowledge may not have been entirely divorced from operative situational assessment and operative policy analysis. By the same token, overt consensual learning, and the lack thereof, provides a basis for judgment on the underlying ability of the Brezhnev regime to engage in situational and policy learning.

CRISIS AND STABILIZATION

Consensual knowledge has been defined as "the sum of technical information and of theories about that information which commands sufficient consensus at a given time among interested actors to serve as a guide to public policy designed to achieve some social goal."[3] In the Soviet case, overt consensual knowledge did not so much "guide" policy directly, as reflect unstated requirements of the regime for legitimacy and internal control, including control over policy debate. During the decade to 1976, as before, overt Soviet knowledge of the international situation was governed by a theory of imperialism. Two subsets of this theory will concern us here. The first of these, the general crisis of capitalism (GCC), drew attention on balance to internal and external U.S. decline, to conflict of opposed social systems, and to Soviet revolutionary goals. The second, state-monopoly capitalism (SMC), pointed broadly to stabilizing modifications of the capitalist order, to commonalities among advanced social systems, and to opportunities to further Soviet security and well-being through cooperation. Indeed, inherent in stated Soviet thinking on SMC was a redefinition of imperialism and a stabilized view of the international environment in which states from different social systems acted not only as class adversaries but also on the basis of what they had in common.

To the extent that a crisis perspective prevailed in the regime's overt consensus on the situation, Soviet policy debate would be inclined to the prosecution of conflict even as it cooperated with the United States, and to the maintenance of an internal order keyed to the marshaling of capabilities for struggle against imperialism. Conversely, to the degree that overt Soviet consensual knowledge was informed by concepts of capitalist stabilization, revolutionary objectives would be devalued relative to possible gains from collaborative action, and conservative preferences for internal policy would yield ground to reformism. As it happened, once a significant change in the overt consensus was authorized in 1967, the leadership's stated assessment of the situation remained constant in its essentials throughout the period under review. At the specialist level, however, reformist attempts to alter the consensus were made after 1969. Initial indications of situational learning are evident here.

The notion of the GCC crystallized at the sixteenth and seventeenth party congresses in the early 1930s, as Stalin rose to preeminence and the West was beset by the Great Depression.[4] Manifestations of the GCC included the division of the world into two counterposed social systems; the crisis of colonialism; aggravation of the problem of capitalist markets; chronic capitalist underutilization of industrial capacity; and continual mass unemployment in the capitalist countries. By the 1960s, the GCC was seen to have passed through three phases: the first marked by the October revolution; a second by the enlargement of the socialist camp as a consequence of World War II; and a third by further losses to imperialism due to decolonization. In principle, the GCC was a theory of a changing global correlation of forces in which ever more countries quit an imperialist camp in decay and moved with varying velocity into the ever stronger world socialist system, until the day when the capitalist order finally collapsed under the weight of its internal contradictions. But in practice there was plenty of technical information and no "theory" of the GCC. Quite simply, the inordinate complexity of the concept defied systematic inquiry.

As to state-monopoly capitalism, the term was coined by Lenin after he had completed *Imperialism, the Highest Stage of Capitalism* in 1916. Where *Imperialism* had designated monopoly capitalism as the highest and last stage of a reactionary and war-breeding social system prior to socialist revolution, wartime developments in the economic role of the imperialist state impelled Lenin to announce in September 1917 that monopoly capitalism had been replaced by SMC, which represented absolutely the highest "step" [*stupen'*] before, or the very antechamber to, socialism.[5] *Imperialism* lay at the heart of Leninist orthodoxy and could be read as assigning virtually omnipotent power to the most reactionary and belligerent elements of the ruling class. As such, it stood as a formidable obstacle to any attempt to reform or come to lasting terms with the opposing social system. In fact, it was constructed with this purpose in mind. The concept of SMC, by contrast, represented Leninist unorthodoxy. It lent itself to the thought that political considerations could acquire predominance over economic determinants in the behavior of imperialism; that capitalism had a capacity for self-stabilization and evolutionary growth toward socialism as contrasted with economic crisis and socialist revolution; and that the relative self-sufficiency of the state could be utilized in an effort to reform and otherwise modify the domestic and foreign policy of imperialist countries. Latent in the concept of SMC was a two-phase theory of the imperialist stage in which monopoly capitalism gave way to a stabilized, economically very potent, and reformist SMC that had no little in common with socialism.

The regime's consensus on these matters was established principally by the general secretary in speeches on the occasion of party congresses, historic anniversaries, and events such as international meetings of communist parties. These presentations for the most part addressed the overall condition of imperialism and did not make specific reference to the United States except on current matters of policy. We may nevertheless proceed on the assumption that the United States, as the leading imperialist country, was being referred to unless the context suggested otherwise. As of Brezhnev's address on the Lenin centenary in April 1970, the overt consensus of the Brezhnev-Kosygin leadership on imperialism and what to expect from it was essentially as follows.

The general crisis of capitalism continued to deepen and was becoming more severe.[6] It was manifested in a changing correlation of forces that increasingly favored socialism in the struggle of opposed social systems.[7] Elements of the altered correlation included growth of the economic and military might of the world socialist system, in indirect reference to Soviet attainment of strategic nuclear parity with the United States; liquidation of the colonial empires; upsurge of the workers' and national liberation movements; mounting signs of economic and social instability within the capitalist countries and heightened contradictions between them; and, in the case of the United States, militarization, deficits, unemployment, exploitation, racial conflict, collapse of the "Great Society," and the array of instabilities arising from the war in Vietnam—in brief, an unworkable social order governed by "reaction on all lines." Imperialism nevertheless remained a "serious and dangerous opponent."[8] Aside from its innate aggressiveness, it endeavored to "adapt to new conditions, to conditions of the struggle of the two systems."[9]

The concept of imperialist "adaptation" was first advanced in the Soviet Union in 1963 by one of Khrushchev's speech writers, the reformist F.M. Burlatskii.[10] Subsequently it was endorsed in passing by Suslov in 1965, and authorized by the general secretary in November 1967.[11] In legitimizing the thought of imperialist adaptation, the leadership had for the first time acknowledged change in the opposing social system. Indeed, the rudiments of a Soviet theory of American learning were to be found in the notion of adaptation. As Brezhnev had put it on the fiftieth anniversary of the October Revolution, the opponent "has learned much, it tries to draw lessons from its defeats, to adapt to the new situation."[12] Had the regime proceeded to articulate a theory of American adaptive learning, it would have been stated in the language of political economy and might well have located the sources of American learning in structural change at the international (GCC) and national (SMC) levels simultaneously. Assuming that the Soviets viewed the U.S. system in the light of their own experience and needs, we have here a hint about possible sources of Soviet learning behavior that should be filed away. Be that as it may, the general secretary's account of adaptive change in the United States and other advanced industrial societies remained grudging and constrained as of the Lenin centenary.

Responding principally to adverse change in the correlation of forces, imperialism had adapted by developing a "powerful, highly organized mechanism of production" to support the wealth and power of the largest monopolies, whose "omnipotence" was now greater than ever before.[13] As monopoly gave way to state-monopoly capitalism, the magnates made use of the state to achieve "some limitation of market anarchy," to maintain economic growth and weaken crisis phenomena, to exploit the scientific and technological revolution so as to increase production and trade, to make "partial concessions" to the working class, and to employ "more clever and exact" methods in exploiting other countries.[14] Furthermore, although "extreme aggressive circles" were active in the making of imperialist foreign policy, "more moderate" and "realistically-minded" elements were to be observed and taken into account.[15] Although these and other signs of imperialist adaptation added up essentially to tactical "maneuvers" and were doomed to fail as the contradictions of capitalism continued to aggravate, they did signify a "certain shift in the center of gravity of imperialist strategy" that could not be ignored.[16]

Stripped to its essentials, the leadership's declared view of what to expect from the United States early in 1970 was biased to the GCC and to a conservative view of things. A debilitated but aggressive U.S. imperialism that could "maneuver" but not alter its reactionary essence was steadily losing ground in the historic struggle with socialism. Nevertheless, favorable change in the global correlation of forces was also producing perverse effects in terms of an enhanced U.S. economic ability to stay the course. As well, there was the emergence of U.S. "realism" on foreign affairs. The consensus was not without ambiguity.

In my judgment, the collective leadership had privately decided, not long before April 1970, to act on a less ambiguous situational assessment. Opting in December 1969 to pursue the strategic arms limitation talks (SALT) beyond a preliminary first round, Soviet decision makers evidently resolved to seek a stabilization of relations with the principal adversary as well as its European allies.[17] Domestic politics aside, a wide range of international security and foreign political considerations would seem to have entered the decision to pursue a détente with the United States. Concern over Soviet economic backwardness relative to an increasingly adaptive capitalist system was also a critical factor. Referring in April 1970 to "difficulties, inadequacies, unresolved problems" discussed at the December 1969 Central Committee plenum, Brezhnev said it all in noting that, whereas success had been registered in economic competition with capitalism, the question was "at what cost, with what expenditure of labor."[18] And yet a regime that in December 1969 had come close to rehabilitating Stalin was in no position to countenance structural reforms, especially political reform.[19] In this tortured situation, the leadership chose to attach new significance not only to international security and political cooperation, but also to trade, credits, and transfers of technology from the United States as well as Western Europe.

But could a stabilization of U.S.–Soviet relations be effectively pursued when the leadership's outward thinking about the principal opponent was grounded in a crisis perspective that allowed little in the way of collaboration between opposed social systems? The answer to this question was itself ambiguous. Brezhnev's rendition of the leadership's assessment would harden somewhat when he addressed the twenty-fourth CPSU congress in March 1971, shortly before he assumed the position of prime leader. The GCC was deepening, he asserted, and the "adaptation" of imperialism did not signify its "stabilization."[20] Nevertheless, as of late 1969 the scene was set for reformist specialists to contest ambiguities in the regime's consensus on what to expect from the Nixon administration, and on what could be accomplished in a stabilization of U.S.–Soviet relations. Nor, given the controversial nature of the decision to seek a détente with the United States, would conservative analysts remain silent on the enduring elements of conflict in the relationship.

Specialist controversy intensified in 1969–1970 as representative voices were heard from all points on the political spectrum. M.F. Kovaleva of the Central Committee's Academy of Social Sciences delivered what was to be the last undisguised Stalinist presentation in the professional literature on the capitalist system.[21] M.S. Dragilev of the economics faculty of Moscow State University advanced an only somewhat less conservative case for the primacy of a crisis perspective on the West.[22] G.A. Arbatov, director of the U.S.S.R. Academy of Sciences' Institute of the USA, and N.N. Inozemtsev, director of the Academy's Institute of the World Economy and International Relations (IMEMO), put forward reformist views.[23] And S.I. Tiul'panov of the economics faculty of Leningrad State University began to move radical reformist thinking ahead by deploying a two-phase theory of the imperialist stage.[24]

In subsequent months through to the autumn of 1974, a wide-ranging discussion unfolded in a series of volumes and on the pages of the IMEMO and other journals.[25] Although Inozemtsev withdrew to a centrist standpoint as of 1972, Arbatov persisted in reformist argumentation.[26] Arbatov's principal backer, it should be noted, was Iurii Andropov, the KGB chairman and, as of April 1973, Politburo member.[27] Arbatov, moreover, obtained personal access to Brezhnev in this period. As to Tiul'panov, he proceeded to make a fundamental attack on conventional Soviet thought about imperialism in a volume sent to press in March 1973.[28] In October 1973, however, Tiul'panov was obliged to retire to a less radical position on the nature of change in the capitalist system.[29] This, it should be noted, was after the events in Chile and before the October war in the Middle East. Meanwhile, Brezhnev had become heavily and publicly committed to a restructuring (perestroika) of U.S.–Soviet relations after May 1972.[30] And yet the leader abstained from new thinking about imperialism, and repeatedly affirmed the competitive and transformational goals of the Soviet regime.[31]

But then Soviet attention was drawn to the severity and implications of the Western economic crisis. As of October 1974, Brezhnev had announced that "profound, in many ways unprecedented crisis phenomena" were evident in the West.[32] The following year, as U.S.–Soviet détente ran into mounting difficulty, Dragilev produced a conservative treatment of SMC, IMEMO began to prepare a triumphalist volume on the GCC under Inozemtsev's guidance, Arbatov continued to argue the case for U.S.–Soviet cooperation, and Tiul'panov had fallen silent (though he remained a member of the IMEMO journal's editorial board).[33] As of late 1975, reformist tendencies in Soviet thinking about Western "adaptation" and

U.S.–Soviet stabilization had suffered a multiple assault. Not only was détente being derailed in Angola and elsewhere, but the Western economic crisis of 1974–1975 had breathed new life into conservative hopes that a competitive U.S.S.R. might prevail more rapidly over a world capitalist system in decline.[34] To boot, Watergate and signs of the demise of the Keynesian state in the West presented a challenge to reformist argumentation that state-monopoly capitalism and the heightened political role of the American state offered new opportunities for U.S.–Soviet cooperation. Finally, the CPSU was now embroiled in an increasingly acrimonious dispute with reformist European communist or Eurocommunist parties, some of whose analysis had much in common with that of radical Soviet reformism. Accordingly, at the twenty-fifth congress in February 1976, Brezhnev added a conservative edge to the leadership's overt consensus of 1970. Although imperialism retained "powerful reserves" for use in competition with socialism, the Western crisis had "exploded the myth of reformists" that capitalism could stabilize itself.[35] Crisis and an improved outlook for revolutionary transformations had prevailed over adaptation and stability in the Soviet perspective on the West.

Far more was raised in the specialist discussion of 1969–1976 than need be considered here. To simplify, we may focus on the GCC and SMC as they figured in contrasting assessments of change in the nature and behavior of imperialism in 1969–1974, the high point of new thinking. Let us consider the differences first between Dragilev and Tiul'panov, and then between Inozemtsev and Arbatov.[36]

For Dragilev, a man with Stalinist proclivities, what had changed was not imperialism but the global conditions of its existence. Summed up by the GCC, these conditions had altered qualitatively and exerted "vast influence" on processes occurring within the capitalist system.[37] Internally, qualitative changes had occurred around the turn of the century, when monopoly capitalism or imperialism arose. Since then, not much had really altered: "In its internal nature, in its root features and characteristics, in its reactionary and anti-popular essence, capitalism remains unchanged over the whole imperialist stage."[38] State-monopoly processes in particular had set in before the October revolution and the GCC and were thus an inherent attribute of monopoly capitalism and nothing very new.

What was new, however, was the changing correlation of forces and the ensuing attempt of finance capital to adapt to it though the use of state-monopoly measures: "The broadening of state-monopoly relations is increasingly the reply of the monopoly bourgeoisie to the development of the general crisis of capitalism."[39] Although a "state-monopoly strategy of adaptation" yielded some improvement in the exploitation of scientific and technological advances, in higher growth rates, and in some evening out of the business cycle as compared with the interwar years, state intervention could only sharpen the contradictions of imperialism.[40] Moreover, though forced to rely on the state, the monopolists sought whenever they could to reduce and otherwise avoid it. As to the influence of the world socialist system in prompting the monopoly bourgeoisie to utilize the state, it evidently served not to strengthen but to waste the opposing system and hasten its demise.[41]

In the view of Tiul'panov, however, a qualitative change in the nature of imperialism had occurred in the late 1950s and early 1960s, when the transition from monopoly capitalism to SMC was completed.[42] Transformation and not adaptation was the proposition here. Productive forces, relations of production, social structure, and the institutions of advanced capitalist society had all been sufficiently altered to warrant the identification of SMC as a "new phase in the history of imperialism."[43] Moreover, while external factors had affected the form and rate of development of SMC, the sources of change were primarily *internal* to the capitalist system.[44] Technology, economics, and politics had impelled the state to assume a formidable array of national and international functions that could not be handled by monopoly capital alone. Although the monopoly bourgeoisie had coalesced with the state, the state had also acquired greater self-sufficiency. State-monopoly institutions undermined the regulatory role of the market and the corresponding role of party politics and the press and had led, in effect, to a corporatist capacity for the "conscious administration of social processes," including some degree of economic planning.[45]

The development of the "state principle" had also been accompanied by a "regrouping" within the ruling class. The affairs of the latter were managed not by the monopolists, but by a state-monopoly elite whose concerns were considerably broader than those of the "subsystem of private enterprise."[46] Notable here was the recognition by the ruling class and "more accurately its most far-sighted and influential representatives," of a general class interest in maintaining demand, growth, competitiveness, and social stability.[47] Nor was militarization a necessary feature of the capitalist system. In fact, pressure from the military-industrial complex—a "secondary phenomenon"—was offset by forces in the American ruling class interested in a limitation, if not the cessation, of the arms race.[48] More broadly, the socialization of production achieved through systemic participation of the state in the reproduction of social capital marked a qualitative leap in the creation of economic and social preconditions for a peaceful and lengthy but still revolutionary transition to socialism.

For Dragilev, substantial change in imperialism short of socialist revolution was out of the question. Accordingly he inveighed against the "two-phase" theory and was regarded by Tiul'panov as representative of its critics.[49] In Dragilev's view, such adaptation as the U.S. system was capable of would be highly strategic, forced on the United States by adverse change in the correlation of forces, and designed to enhance the existing order without changing it. For Tiul'panov, by contrast, U.S. imperialism had already experienced a transformation that eased the way for international cooperation. Further evolutionary change in the United States and its behavior would include substantial opportunities for internal reform and for collaboration between social systems that had increasingly more in common.

Moving toward the center of the spectrum, we find in Inozemtsev a more nuanced but still conservative assessment of the sources and potential for change in U.S. behavior. Inozemtsev's position was also subject to change. By 1976, it was in many respects not that different from Dragilev's where the GCC was concerned. In 1972, however, his assessment was more venturesome.

Not only had there been qualitative change in the conditions in which imperialism existed, that is in the GCC, but imperialism itself had also changed very substantially since the turn of the century.[50] Although its basic features remained unaltered, the opponent had been forced to adapt to external pressure in ways that "frequently contradict its exploitative and aggressive strivings."[51] Utilizing the state to mobilize resources for the struggle with socialism, monopoly capital had presided over an intergrowth of monopoly into SMC in which the financial oligarchy used the apparatus of the state to strengthen its positions at home and abroad. At the same time, internal processes had shaped the development of modern capitalism.

Chief among inner factors was the scientific and technological revolution. It allowed imperialism reduced labor costs, greater labor productivity, more room for "social maneuver," including higher real wages, greatly improved management practices, and the opportunity in the United States for simultaneous growth in military expenditure *and* living standards.[52] In fact, U.S. economic strategy had been altered to give priority not to military production per se, but to long-term economic growth and technological development, which also made for more effective weaponry.[53] As a proportion of gross national product, U.S. defense spending had consequently declined. In effect, the Americans had found a way of producing guns and butter simultaneously and without undue stress. Since commonalities existed between opposed but advanced social systems,[54] there was evidently something to be learned from American practice.

As to U.S. foreign policy, in Inozemtsev's view the loss of military invulnerability and the changing world correlation of forces had compelled the United States to adopt a more flexible and differentiated strategy in the struggle with socialism. Though "realistic trends" had also surfaced in America, the behavior of the adversary remained hostile and reactionary in its reliance not only on military force but also on other instruments of policy adding up to a "wider use of economic, political, diplomatic, and ideological forms of struggle."[55] Nevertheless, for Inozemtsev as of 1972, not only had the strategy of U.S. imperialism altered, but the "center of gravity" of the struggle of opposed social systems was itself subject to change.[56] Possibly there was some learning to be done here as well by the Soviet Union.

As for Arbatov, he all but stated what Inozemtsev left between the lines: having adapted to new circumstances, America would succeed unless the Soviet Union in turn found a way to "'adapt'" its own policies.[57] External factors, including the deepening GCC and an altered correlation of forces together with the disappearance of strategic invulnerability and the positive influence of Soviet diplomatic efforts, had all assisted in an adaptation of American thinking and practice.[58] Nevertheless, as Tiul'panov also argued, internal processes had been decisive.[59] Utilizing the scientific and technological revolution and the opportunities presented by the development of SMC, the monopoly bourgeoisie had acquired more scope for "maneuver" at home and abroad.[60] The monopolists were, however, split on foreign affairs, there were differences between the monopoly and nonmonopoly strata of the ruling class, the intelligentsia had a role to play, and there was public opinion and even the silent majority to be considered.[61] The result was to make the adaptation of U.S. policy highly contingent on internal developments in the United States. Two basic tendencies, to reaction and to realism, were nevertheless to be observed in U.S. policy. They also figured in the program of individual politicians, which invariably reflected both lines in varying proportion.[62]

Each tendency, in Arbatov's view, constituted a tactical variant of the same strategic objective of preserving monopoly rule in conditions of an aggravated GCC.[63] The forms of struggle represented by each were, however, very different. Adaptation of U.S. policy was represented by the realist tendency to employ "tactics characterized by greater flexibility, circumspection and willingness to agree to certain compromises in foreign policy, by a more subtle use of economic, political and ideological levers."[64] Realism in the selection of forms of struggle by the United States could suffer internal defeat and in any event represented no change in the nature of imperialism.[65] But its influence might also be fortified to allow a "channeling" of U.S.–Soviet relations that could reduce the threat of thermonuclear war and permit cooperation.[66] Indeed, for the first time in the overt Soviet discourse of the Brezhnev regime, Arbatov acknowledged in 1973 the existence of "common interests" between the Soviet

Union and the United States.[67] Aside from according greater strength to reaction in U.S. policy, Arbatov's reading of U.S. affairs remained basically unaltered into the 1980s.

Differences between Inozemtsev and Arbatov in the early 1970s were subtle. Both depicted imperialism as fundamentally hostile. Both acknowledged substantial adaptive change in the U.S. system and the forms of struggle it employed against the Soviet Union. But for Inozemtsev, the U.S. system had on balance altered more than the quality of U.S. conduct. Arbatov, possibly because he preferred not to take on the additional burden of demonstrating system change as Tiul'panov had done, seemed to see more substantial change in U.S. thinking and practice than in the system as such. Inozemtsev envisaged U.S. behavior in terms of strategic design tightly controlled by the monopolists. Arbatov, however, attributed great significance to internal process variables, including the readiness of reactionaries to "use" external events, Soviet behavior presumably included, in making their case in internal U.S. policy debate.[68]

In defining the sources of imperialist adaptation, Inozemtsev attached greater significance to external pressure and to crisis phenomena, whereas Arbatov stressed the evolution of internal political conflict over U.S. responses to external change. For Inozemtsev, adaptation served on the whole to improve U.S. competitiveness. For Arbatov, the heightened U.S. potential to cooperate appeared to be more important. Where Inozemtsev's hidden agenda seemed to be one of improving the Soviet capacity to compete economically and militarily, Arbatov's pointed more to cooperation in international security affairs.

Given the decay of détente and new evidence of decay in the West as crisis phenomena gained prominence after 1973, there was diminished urgency to Inozemtsev's implied argument for the adaptation of Soviet policy. But for Arbatov, a deteriorating international security outlook presumably made adaptation still more urgent. As of October 1974, shortly before the prospect of U.S.–Soviet trade expansion evaporated, Brezhnev himself was willing to state that crisis in the West had served to aggravate the arms race and heighten international tension, that crisis was *not*, in effect, good news.[69] By February 1976, however, the Soviet leader was content to note that, "The instability of capitalism is becoming ever more apparent."[70] Hopes of stabilization had not succeeded in displacing expectations of crisis in the situational consensus of the regime.

What, then, might be said by way of preliminary comment on overt situational learning in the decade to 1976? First, having certified the notion of adaptation in 1967, the collective leadership appeared to learn little or nothing. Despite new developments in Soviet policy toward the United States after 1969 and in U.S.–Soviet relations after May 1972, the leadership's overt consensus on the situation remained stable, if ambiguous. In common with the Nixon administration, which preferred to present détente as a triumph of traditional policy from strength and not as an adaptation forced upon the United States by adversity, the Soviet leadership's stated view of the situation minimized the need for adaptation in Soviet behavior. On the contrary, in accounting for détente in terms of a favorably altered correlation of forces that obliged the adversary to engage in tactical adjustments of traditional policy, the leadership in effect stated that military and economic cooperation was to proceed without touching the essentials of the world revolutionary process and conflict between opposed social systems. From this perspective, détente was inherently a "maneuver" governed by the pursuit of strength.

Second, the data point to an awareness within the regime that situational change did indeed call for adaptations in Soviet thinking and practice. Brezhnev was willing to take note of change in the "center of gravity" of U.S. strategy, and Inozemtsev acknowledged an equivalent shift in the nature of the struggle between opposed social systems. The case for reassessment however, was, made most forcibly by reformist specialists as represented by Arbatov and Tiul'panov. Had new thinking on the part of reformist commentators been followed by open support from the leadership for a redefinition of the situation, as was to occur in the Gorbachev years, the regime might well have engaged in overt consensual learning. Furthermore, it might have made itself more capable of a sustained effort to follow the United States in generating the capacity to rely less heavily on military forms of struggle. But this was not to be. On balance, a setting of conflict and crisis served the regime better than one of cooperation and stability. Accordingly, where overt situational evaluation was concerned, it seems appropriate to speak at most of attempted consensual learning in the Brezhnev years.

Third, the dividing line between situational and policy analysis proves to have been indistinct. In identifying an array of situational assessments at the specialist level, we have hit on a larger set of tendencies in the articulation of ends, analyses, and preferred means by leaders and lesser participants in the policy process. Which brings us to consensual learning as it concerned policy toward the United States.

CONFLICT AND COOPERATION

Compared with situational assessment, overt Soviet discourse on policy matters was highly guarded. As such, it seemed closer to the operative consensus of the regime. Contrasting conservative and reformist orientations were nevertheless to be observed in published Soviet comment on ends and means in dealing with the United States. Moreover, whereas reformist situational assessments failed to find their way into the regime's overt consensus, reformist policy thinking did surface in the statements of the general secretary and in outward Soviet behavior after May 1972, this as the regime continued to maintain a conservative assessment of the situation and to seek unilateral advantage in an increasingly favorable correlation of forces. By December 1974, however, reformist policy prescriptions had been very largely excised from Brezhnev's speeches and were to recede but not disappear at the level of specialist commentary. Whatever consensual learning had been achieved in relating ends and means on behalf of sustained cooperation with the United States was in large measure but not wholly undone by the time of the twenty-fifth congress in 1976.

In policy toward the United States, as in so many other domains, the consensus of the regime was to have things both ways. On one hand, strategic arms control was valued for its contribution to a homeland-sparing military doctrine that sought, as of 1966, to avert the nuclear devastation of the U.S.S.R. in the event of war with the United States.[71] Similarly, trade and technology transfer were sought, as of 1969, to improve Soviet economic competitiveness without far-reaching internal reform. On the other hand, there was absolutely no questioning of the Soviet commitment to further a historical process that would remake the world in the image of Soviet-style socialism.[72] Hence Soviet maneuvering for advantage in the Middle East and Europe, military and political support for the United States' Vietnamese adversaries, probing for revolutionary opportunity in Portugal in 1974–1975, intervention in Angola, and continued military modernization, including preparations to deploy the SS-20 intermediate-range nuclear missile in Europe. The regime's overt consensus on these highly disparate matters was stated in terms of a "two-spheres" concept of coexistence with the United States.

Speaking in December 1972, Brezhnev asserted that in view of the irreconcilable world outlook and class aims of the two social systems, the international class struggle would continue unabated in the sphere of economics, politics, and ideology. At the same time, the Soviet Union stood ready to cooperate with all governments and peoples prepared to uphold the peace.[73] Implicit in this incantation was a split-level conception of coexistence. As later elaborated by Arbatov:

> What we are talking about is essentially different spheres of political life in our day (though they can influence one another in various ways). One of them is the sphere of social development, which steadily makes headway in any international conditions—whether détente, 'cold' war or even 'hot' war. . . . The other is the sphere of interstate relations, in which other extremely important questions are resolved—questions of war and peace, methods of resolving controversial foreign policy questions, and possibilities for mutually advantageous international cooperation.[74]

Here we have the central problem of Soviet policy in establishing a détente with the United States: to sustain a process of interstate cooperation in the midst of intersystem conflict or international class struggle that could only favor the Soviet Union. To solve this problem, not only in concept but in also practice, was to learn.

Two main orientations to the "two-spheres" or have-it-both-ways dilemma could be discerned in overt Soviet discourse. One sought to "combine" (*sochetat'*) the two spheres by supporting anti-imperialist forces in the struggle of opposed systems so as to compel U.S. cooperation that enhanced Soviet security and competitiveness. The other favored an effort to "channel" (*pereiti v ruslo*) the struggle of opposed social systems by employing interstate cooperation to demilitarize the struggle and thereby accelerate the global advance of socialism. These two orientations corresponded, at a high level of generality, to long-standing tendencies in outward Soviet behavior toward the United States. Incorporating key elements of the situational assessment discussed above, we may specify the dominant tendencies in the regime's overt policy consensus as follows.[75]

Expansionist internationalism was based on the recognition that a harsh two-camp foreign policy such as had prevailed in the Stalin years served not only to isolate the U.S.S.R. from potential sources of international support, but also to underwrite U.S. leadership over a cohesive and mobilized imperialist camp. Sharing the Stalinist impulse to build military and economic strength and to prevail over the United States and a world capitalist system in crisis, Soviet expansionism favored a global and détente-oriented effort to make use of intermediate forces that disappeared from view when a tense two-camp confrontation was under way: differences between the United States and its European allies, broad-front revolutionary movements in the developed countries, Third World nationalism, anti-Americanism, pacifist and mass antiwar sentiment, "realistic" or "far-sighted" tendencies among Western policy makers, and other forces whose growth would in the ensemble serve to constrain and eventually isolate the principal adversary.

At the same time, state-monopoly processes in the West were seen not only to inhibit the emergence of revolutionary situations there, but to strengthen the economic and military competitiveness of the United States and its allies relative to the Soviet Union. Atmospheric and substantive negotiation with the West could thus serve a variety of Soviet goals: reduced danger of general nuclear war and of Soviet annihilation in the event of escalation from limited war, diminished risk of U.S. and North Atlantic Treaty Organization (NATO) overreaction to military and Third World changes in the global correlation of forces favoring the U.S.S.R., lessened coherence of the opposing camp, direct economic and political benefit from collaboration with America's allies, and overall improvement in the Soviet geopolitical position. As well, economic cooperation with the United States itself could improve the Soviet capacity to prevail.

But among Khrushchev's successors there was also a determination to avoid "appeasement" of the United States such as was seen to have occurred when the Soviet leader refrained from threat-producing activity and otherwise endeavored in reformist fashion to stabilize U.S.–Soviet relations by reinforcing "sober-moderate" tendencies in U.S. behavior following the Cuban missile adventure.[76] The preference of the new regime to deal with the United States as it was and from a situation of strength was surely stiffened by the decision of a newly elected Democratic administration to wage war directly against a Soviet ally in Southeast Asia after February 1965. The United States, initially the demandeur for strategic arms limitation talks, was thus to be forced to cooperate with the Soviet Union. It was not to be induced to negotiate by means of Soviet good behavior in the sphere of "social development."

From an expansionist perspective, cooperation was another form of conflict between opposed social systems. Agreements with the United States that strengthened Soviet security and the ability to compete were certainly appropriate, but not at the cost of constraining Soviet support for national liberation movements and related sources of global strength. Coexistence, in this view, could only be highly competitive. As Suslov put it in 1966, "The policy of peaceful coexistence of states with different social systems neither in theory nor in practice contradicts but combines with the policy of support for the peoples fighting for their national independence and freedom, of giving a rebuff to the aggressive intrigues of imperialism."[77] Nor did the advent of détente alter this view. As Politburo member V.V. Grishin put it in 1973, Soviet foreign policy was "based on the combination of the principle of peaceful coexistence of states with different social systems with support for the just struggle of the peoples for their liberation, with a firm rebuff to imperialism, to its aggressive intrigues."[78] Insofar as Soviet conduct was guided by the expansionist preference for "combined" action on the interstate and intersystem planes, continued improvement in the Soviet geopolitical position would produce U.S. cooperation on terms that not only preserved but also enhanced the Soviet ability to prevail.

And yet the fact remains that, as of 1969, Soviet expansionism had incorporated a far greater measure of cooperation with the United States than had been contemplated under Khrushchev. There may be an indication of conservative policy learning here. By the end of the 1960s, expansion-minded decision makers evidently concluded that the advent of strategic nuclear parity was to be followed not by an uninhibited pursuit of superiority, but by strategic arms control and an adapted global strategy that would diversify the Soviet ability to prevail. SALT would rationalize and possibly reduce the opportunity costs of continued military modernization while also creating a context conducive to intensified economic development with U.S. as well as West European and Japanese assistance. As cautiously voiced by Inozemtsev in 1972, Soviet policy was to be adapted to the task of economic modernization and all that could be expected to flow from it. Again, the United States could be expected to contribute to Soviet strength on Soviet terms because the altered correlation of forces left it little choice.

As passage of the Jackson-Vanik and Stevenson amendments made abundantly clear, expansionist conceptions of cooperation as a form of conflict were misguided in design and execution alike. Aside from an unrealistic evaluation of change in the correlation of forces, the sense that equality with the United States was now at hand may have engendered a false belief that the opponent would accord a greater measure of legitimacy to Soviet military might and regional intervention. Coupled with the expansionist image of the United States as a strategic actor capable at most of limited "maneuvering," an overweening Soviet sense of strength and the long-standing injunction against "appeasement" also encouraged a propensity to slight the president's need to obtain support for his actions. The effect was to suppress an awareness in Moscow that Soviet actions at home and abroad could evoke greater competitiveness rather than restraint from the U.S. policy process. In these and other respects, expansionist thinking about cooperation proved to be fatally flawed.

Nor would the expansionist mentality have been likely to learn from the debacle of December 1974. It would have attributed the failure of economic cooperation to innate U.S. aggressiveness, denied any fault on the part of the Soviet Union, and favored a greater measure of self-help in the "sphere of social development," while expecting the Soviet military buildup to sustain U.S. interests in cooperation on nuclear arms control. Indeed, the fact that Soviet interventionism in the Third World increased markedly after December 1974 suggests that an alternative and constraining tendency was at work in the Soviet policy process prior to that date.

Had U.S.–Soviet relations followed an expansionist script after May 1972, a cold détente would have ensued. But this of course is not what happened. For a time, as Brezhnev and Nixon engaged in summitry and the attempt to cooperate on a broadening array of issues, the détente relationship took on a life of its own. In so doing, it elicited reformist Soviet responses that had been largely but not wholly contained since the fall of Khrushchev. We find Brezhnev speaking of U.S.–Soviet relations in terms of perestroika, a "turn-around for the better," greater "stability," "long-term stable cooperation," and so on.[79] Moreover, in view of changes in the U.S.–Soviet relationship, Brezhnev found it appropriate to aspire to a "radical improvement" in the international atmosphere as a whole, and committed the U.S.S.R. to a perestroika of international relations in which détente acquired a "global, all-embracing character."[80] Such views were of course not wholly inconsistent with an expansionist promotion of U.S.–Soviet cooperation as a form of intersystem conflict. Nor, if regarded primarily as propaganda, did they represent a departure from Brezhnev's statement of the consensus on the instability of imperialism in crisis. But embedded within them was a conception of sustained cooperation that challenged the expansionist commitment to a zero-sum course in world affairs.

Sustained cooperation with the principal adversary was a key objective of *reformative internationalism*, which represented a Soviet propensity to demilitarize U.S.–Soviet conflict and thereby accelerate favorable change in the correlation of forces between opposed social systems.[81] Whereas expansionist thinking defined U.S. imperialism and opportunities provided by the general crisis in a manner that oriented the Soviet Union to coercive cooperation with the United States, reformative views were keyed to conciliation of the main opponent. Internal developments of U.S. state-monopoly capitalism were seen to endow the state with a significant capacity for reformist responses in implementing policy on behalf of the ruling class and, above all, monopoly capital. Similar effects in U.S. behavior were encouraged by changes in the world correlation of forces that favored socialism. In these circumstances, U.S. "realism" had appreciated to an extent that a reformation of U.S.–Soviet relations became possible. If only because of the continued predominance of monopoly capital within the United States, conflict between the two social systems remained inevitable in this view. But forms of conflict were very much a matter of choice.[82] Emphasizing the risks and costs of continued geostrategic competition, reformative thinking implied that military and economic cooperation were ultimately of greater significance than self-help and strength in determining the outcome of struggle between opposed social systems. Risks for the Soviet Union included crises and thermonuclear war.[83] Among the costs were the economic burden of defense and international conditions unsuited to rapid Soviet economic and political development.[84]

Seen from this standpoint, conventional Soviet thought on the general crisis and correlation of forces was off the mark. Rather than aspire to supremacy at the head of a militarily powerful but economically backward world socialist system, the Soviet Union was better advised to maintain the military strength necessary to deter U.S. aggressiveness and otherwise to explore the potential of cooperation in channeling U.S.–Soviet conflict from military-strategic into economic and ideological forms of struggle. Mutual security and well-being would thereby be advanced, the Soviet capacity to prevail by force of example would be enhanced, conservative tendencies in the United States and other Western countries would be progressively constrained, and social change would unfold more readily in the Third World and elsewhere. Though major difficulties in U.S.–Soviet affairs were unavoidable, the situation was such that the Soviet Union could join with U.S. "realists" in directing the relationship toward incrementally greater cooperation and nonmilitary competition over an extended period of time.

Given the early aversion of the regime to "appeasement" of the United States, the evaluation of U.S. realism had become a sensitive matter in Moscow. Indeed, the very act of acknowledging U.S. "farsightedness" could be construed as a tacit affirmation of the need to key Soviet policy to its support. Expansionist argumentation dealt with the problem by defining U.S. realism as the maneuvering of an innately hostile social formation faced with an increasingly adverse correlation of forces. Accordingly, there was nothing especially noteworthy in Brezhnev's acknowledgment by 1969 that not only were there "hawks" in the United States but also "significant strata" opposed to the arms race as well as the Vietnam War.[85] It was another matter, however, to state that Moscow would take into account "realistically-minded circles," a "more moderate wing," "far-sighted representatives of U.S. business," and the like who were engaged in struggle with U.S. advocates of cold war.[86] In making such comments through October 1974, Brezhnev lent his authority to a threat-reducing policy of unilateral Soviet restraint.

Under Khrushchev, the prototype for Soviet efforts to underwrite moderation in U.S. behavior toward the Soviet Union had been Lenin's instructions on Soviet policy for the Genoa economic conference of 1922. The basic objective at that time had been to enhance the influence of the pacifist and liberal wing of the ruling class in shaping the conduct of the principal adversary on matters of trade and stabilized political relations with Soviet Russia.[87] When Brezhnev referred to the existence of a "moderate wing," or when Arbatov and others cited Lenin's actions in 1922,[88] they were alluding to the need for Soviet threat-reducing behavior and cooperative action aimed at sustaining U.S. realism. Brezhnev could thus assert that the main Soviet influence on the world revolutionary process was by force of example and economic achievement.[89] As elaborated by Arbatov, this meant competition as to which social system could provide "the highest standard of living, genuine freedom, a flourishing culture and the best conditions for the development of the individual."[90]

What was moot here was a mutual adaptation of Soviet and U.S. policy that went considerably further than the domestic and foreign policy modifications envisaged by Soviet expansionism. Both sides would engage in an arduous and lengthy process that would see them reduce reliance on military forms of struggle including intervention in regional conflicts, and give correspondingly greater weight to ideological-political and economic competition. For the Soviet Union, military strength was of course required to sustain the correlation of forces that made possible an adaptation of conflict in the first place. But otherwise Moscow was best advised to negotiate, to refrain from actions that unnecessarily supported the arguments of U.S. advocates of strength, to erode anticommunist "stereotypes,"[91] and generally to affirm and broaden the coalition for realism within the United States.

Reformative interests in the demilitarization of U.S.–Soviet conflict received clearest expression at the very onset of détente. The Basic Principles Agreement (BPA) of May 29, 1972, committed the two sides to "peaceful coexistence," further arms limitation, abstention from "efforts to obtain unilateral advantage at the expense of the other," to crisis prevention and confrontation avoidance, and to the development of cooperation on a "firm and long-term basis."[92] All the essentials of a reformative foreign policy were there. As such, the BPA was in violation of the overt Soviet consensus on imperialism and the general crisis: no one had ever ventured to suggest that the United States could refrain from the pursuit of unilateral advantage. More important, the thought of Soviet abstention from support of national liberation movements at U.S. expense remained eccentric. Nevertheless, reformative internationalism called for reciprocal nonintervention.

Brezhnev could thus be found condemning the export of revolution and condoning Soviet resistance to the export of counterrevolution.[93] Similarly, Arbatov demanded "complete parity," presumably reciprocity, in nonintervention and then dropped the other shoe: the Soviet Union could not "guarantee the 'status quo' [and] halt the process of class and national liberation struggle engendered by the objective laws of historical development."[94] Moscow and Washington were thus to reduce rivalry in regional conflicts, cooperate in their resolution, and otherwise let them take their course, which would of course favor the cause of socialism.

Translated into "two-spheres" terminology, reformative thinking gave precedence to the sphere of U.S.–Soviet interstate cooperation over Soviet activity in the "sphere of social development" or international class struggle of the two systems. Arguing an increasingly reformative line as of December 1972, Brezhnev began to speak of the "channeling" of intersystem conflict so as to reduce the threat of war, regional conflict, and an uncontrolled arms race.[95] To the best of my knowledge, the concept of "channeling" conflict was first put forward by Arbatov in August 1963, at the height of reformative internationalism under Khrushchev and at the time when Burlatskii floated the notion of imperialist "adaptation."[96] Resurrected in 1970 and reiterated on various occasions to 1973,[97] the "channeling" formula represented an alternative to the expansionist preference for "combining" Soviet action on the interstate and intersystem planes. Eschewing the attempt to pursue cooperation together with continued acquisition of military might and geopolitical situations of strength, it called for an agreed U.S.–Soviet transition to nonmilitary forms of struggle in interstate and intersystem relations alike.

A reformative perestroika of U.S.–Soviet and international relations therefore aimed at greater Soviet security and well-being together with progressive global change through collaborative demilitarization of the continuing conflict between states with different social systems. Core transformational goals of the regime would thus be preserved as the Soviet Union engaged in ever deeper cooperation with the principal adversary. Moreover, while détente had already taken hold in Europe before the Moscow summit of May 1972, the advent of intensified U.S.–Soviet cooperation made it possible to envisage a demilitarization of international relations that would pervade all regions of the world. As of July 1973, Brezhnev referred to détente as "the remarkable turnaround in all postwar history."[98]

But this was about as far as reformative commentary on U.S.–Soviet and international relations would go. By late 1973, as had been the case with situational assessment at the specialist level, the tide began to turn and an expansionist perspective returned to predominance in leadership and specialist discourse. In 1976, Inozemtsev and his colleagues would greet developments in Angola and Ethiopia as powerful blows against the world capitalist system. For them, the perestroika of international relations, which "channeled" the competition of opposed social systems toward peaceful coexistence, would play a growing role in resolving the general crisis of capitalism through the victory of socialism.[99] Expansionism had not only displaced but appropriated the language of reformative internationalism. Nevertheless, the fact remains that for a period of time from May 1972, if not December 1969, to the collapse of trade expansion in December 1974, Brezhnev had presided over a limited incorporation of reformative thinking into Soviet policy toward the United States.

To persist in the "channeling" process, Soviet decision makers had to face a period of unrequited restraint and concessions in which the United States could all too readily be seen as taking advantage of Soviet "appeasement." Unilateral Soviet restraint and threat-reducing concessions were exactly what the expansionist mentality was determined to avoid, and avoid it did with some help from the U.S. side. As a result, the message of reformative internationalism decayed in the midst of continued expansionist signaling to the United States. Furthermore, reformative thinking pointed to the internalization of conflict between opposed social systems, and thus to Soviet democratization as well as economic reform. Despite Brezhnev's qualified readiness to assimilate reformative views, evident lack of consensus within the regime on an opening to the left in

Soviet policy made reformative internationalism no more workable than expansionism in producing sustained cooperation with the principal adversary. Again, the evidence points at most to attempted learning.

CONSENSUAL LEARNING

Consensus implies a divergence of views. The force of the Brezhnev regime's overt consensus on situational and policy matters turns out to have been more indicative than directive. Imposing a conceptual framework for public discussion of policy issues, it also left political participants significant room for maneuver, including maneuver to alter the framework itself. Substantive consideration of the situation faced by the Soviet Union and of policy toward the United States was marked by an interplay of tendencies. The correlation of tendencies in what was said and written was not immobile. On the contrary, it showed signs of oscillation across a limited range of outcome streams. We may therefore think in terms of a rolling consensus that shifted leftward to the advantage of reformative views after December 1969, halted its leftward movement as of October 1973, and swung back to the right and a renewed expansionist emphasis as of December 1974. The overt consensus rolled primarily in response to change in the operative consensus of the collective leadership as it dealt with adjustments of power among oligarchs and processed a never-ending sequence of foreign and domestic policy issues.

Overt consensual learning, insofar as there was any in the decade to 1976, may accordingly be viewed in terms of substance and process. As a substantive exercise, consensual knowledge was altered to provide an improved basis for sustained cooperation with the United States. As a political process, overt consensual learning consisted essentially of change in the correlation of tendencies to the advantage of reformist thinking. Utilizing the analytical framework that governs this volume, we will first consider the evidence for substantive learning and then examine process variables.

REWARD-PUNISHMENT LEARNING

My understanding of the phenomenon here is one in which an actor, having been sufficiently burned or gratified by an experience, subsequently averts or repeats prior behavior in analogous circumstances. Minimalist Soviet learning was error-averse, far from minimal in its consequences, and possibly quite elaborate in its thought processes. Insofar as it was reflexive, reward-punishment learning would seem to have been based more on feeling than thought.

Khrushchev provided his successors with plenty of experience to avoid in future. U.S. behavior not long after October 1964 served to drive the lessons home. The new management came in already inclined to resist "appeasement" in Soviet relations with the United States. Nor was it well disposed to the Khrushchevian conception of coexistence, which authorized unilateral Soviet abstention from supporting the world revolutionary process so as to reinforce U.S. moderation and thus U.S.–Soviet interstate cooperation. The new regime, for its part, was predisposed to a "two-spheres" view of coexistence as a form of combined interstate and international class struggle. As Brezhnev put it early on, "The *kto-kogo* question will be resolved in struggle and only in struggle."[100] The initiation of U.S. air attacks on North Vietnam in February 1965, when Kosygin was in Hanoi, further weakened the proposition that Soviet decision makers might rely on U.S. moderation or realism, much less exercise restraint to encourage it. Further, as U.S. aggressiveness was seen to increase with the Dominican Republic intervention and other moves, Brezhnev began to cite the consequences of appeasement before World War II.[101] Strength, unity, and the readiness to "rebuff" the Americans all became increasingly indispensable. Similarly, Moscow was to bargain with Washington from real strength and without Khrushchevian bluff or "scheming." All of this took place shortly before the period of interest to us here. The effect was to rededicate the regime to an expansionist course in world affairs.

As to reward-punishment learning in the decade to 1976, it too would seem to have favored expansionist thinking. Great gratifications and bad burns at the hands of the United States were, however, not very numerous. Burns that directly or indirectly involved the United States included the surprise Sino-American rapprochement following the U.S.–Soviet "conceptual breakthrough" of May 1971, Nixon's bombing of Hanoi and mining of North Vietnamese harbors shortly before the summit of May 1972, the expulsion of Soviet forces from Egypt in July 1972, the overthrow of Allende in September 1973, and above all the December 1974 denial of credits and trade expansion by the United States. None of these events was of a magnitude equivalent to the Khrushchev experience in shaping subsequent Soviet choices. But taken together, these and similar insults could only have bred resentment, mistrust, and the conviction that cooperation would not alter the essentials of U.S.–Soviet relations. Given the centrality of technology transfer and trade expansion to the expansionist perspective on cooperation, the events of December 1974 no doubt had special force in moving Soviet decision makers to rely more heavily on self-help. Moreover, the fact that concessions made on the question of Jewish emigration proved to be of no avail could well have underscored the fallacy of relying on U.S. realism to do the work of Soviet power.

And yet, Soviet relations with the United States were not without gratification. It came with the attainment of strategic parody, if the phrase may be allowed. As well, there was the prospect of recognized international equality with the principal opponent as manifested in summitry and bilateral negotiation on matters affecting all. But again the essential prerequisite for gratification was strength.

On the whole, the effect of reward-punishment learning was to "unlearn" the situational assessment and reformative policy priorities of Khrushchev's last years and to reinforce the outlook of expansionism. When learning is defined in terms of a heightened capacity to achieve lasting cooperation with the United States, little learning was to be observed under the reward-punishment heading.

COGNITIVE CONTENT LEARNING

As understood here, cognitive content learning entails the altering of tactics, of strategy when tactical modification fails, and ultimately the reconsideration of goals, but all within a stable conceptual framework that allows decision makers, in effect, to change their minds. The overall Soviet commitment to détente might be considered in this light. Especially where expansionist thinking was concerned, Moscow could be seen as doing the same old things in a situation that had not really changed. And yet, if only because of imperialist "adaptation," expansionist thought betrayed an awareness that the situation called for an assessment and for action that to some extent departed from the old. As for the reformative outlook, it clearly suggested that prevailing ways of perceiving and acting on the situation could no longer suffice. Nor do our categories allow us to distinguish readily between cognitive content and *attempted* efficiency learning in the matching of ends and means. In the circumstances, we are better advised to move directly to evidence of cognitive structural learning.

COGNITIVE STRUCTURAL LEARNING

Here we are interested in the acquisition of new and more highly differentiated understandings of the international environment and the Soviet relationship to it. The central issue was forms of struggle in conditions of military-strategic equivalence with the United States. Again, expansionist and reformative perspectives yielded diverging assessments and implications for Soviet policy.

However qualified the notion of imperialist "adaptation," it became increasingly clear to the expansion-minded Soviet observer that the United States was exploiting a superior array of capabilities that went far beyond the military. These capabilities presumably gained in significance as the Soviet Union proceeded to offset U.S. military might. The superior U.S. ability to compete was seen to arise from a highly productive economic mechanism that made effective use of the scientific and technological revolution. It allowed the Americans to employ a wide range of means in influencing developments in the Third World. It made for internal social stability. It gave the United States technological advantages in weapons acquisition. It also enhanced the U.S. appeal in the "struggle for the minds of other peoples."[102] Meanwhile, an inefficient Soviet economy had entered a stage of development in which it was no longer possible to "work in the old style," in which past experience was "a poor counsel."[103] The message was clear: given change in the "center of gravity" of struggle between opposed social systems, the Soviet Union had now to acquire new economic capabilities if it was not to lose out in economic, political, and ideological as well as military competition.

At the same time, the attainment of strategic equivalence with the United States provided an essential precondition for a transition to diversified competition. It gave the Soviet Union security in making the transition, a means to compel the United States to negotiate a stabilization of continuing defense efforts by both sides, and a point of departure for technology transfer and trade expansion. Coupled with the military-strategic utility of nuclear arms control, the effect of these varied considerations was to further an adaptation of expansionist thinking to favor competitive co-operation with the United States. Accordingly, as Soviet military might and security increased, so also did the overt recognition of U.S. realism.

But if expansionist thinking acquired a more differentiated understanding of forms of struggle and thus of international relations, it proved unable to integrate conflict and cooperation into a viable policy. The "two-spheres" concept certainly admitted increased complexity and differentiation into the understanding of U.S.–Soviet relations. But the expansionist mentality could not admit restraint in prosecuting the international class struggle, any more than it could accept that U.S. hostility was driven not solely by the inherent nature of imperialism but also by Soviet behavior. Aside from a deeply entrenched competitiveness framed in *kto-kogo* terms, the inability to sustain a process of cooperation that was of undoubted interest to the Soviet Union seems ultimately to have arisen from an unwillingness to open the door to reformism in Soviet internal affairs. In no way, for instance, could it be admitted that Soviet maneuvering for unilateral advantage in regional conflicts, or human rights denials in the U.S.S.R., were in reality arms race initiatives that sustained the U.S. capacity to resist cooperation. In a word, there was no empathy.

The expansionist admission of complexity was thus truncated. It certainly allowed for cooperation, but not for means other than strength to make a success of it.

Incorporating a wider range of situational variables than expansionist thinking, reformative internationalism provided a more integrated appreciation of the policy problems of sustained cooperation. A superior understanding of the international environment came with the assimilation of data relating to the domestic politics of U.S. foreign and military policy. Tacit acceptance of linkage as a reality, if not as an U.S. bargaining strategy, made for a more complex and integrated view of Soviet policy requirements in seeking to cooperate with the Americans.

The advent of strategic equivalence provided the occasion for a resurgence of reformative argumentation, as it did for modifications of expansionist thought. But reformative "new" thinking was keyed not so much to the acquisition of improved material means of competition, as to the need for adaptation to new realities that were shaping the ends and means of Soviet and U.S. policy alike. Since Arbatov laid out the arguments in by far the greatest detail, we may revert to his account for evidence of cognitive structural learning associated with the strengthening of reformism in Soviet behavior after 1969. Though Arbatov's case was made in part by reference to U.S. acknowledgments of the inability to continue as before, the message applied equally to the U.S.S.R.

International relations were in transition primarily as a result of the appearance of thermonuclear weapons and ensuing change in the consequences of war.[104] A government that was seen to have initiated nuclear war could well be swept away by the survivors.[105] Opportunities for the effective use of military power had waned, as had the ability to translate military means into influence.[106] A situation of mutual deterrence had in effect been achieved. It was fraught with risks but also presented opportunities. On the down side, dangers of accidental nuclear war and escalation from regional conflicts had to be addressed through arms talks and regional conflict resolution.[107] Yet the Soviet Union and the United States had common interests in reducing reliance on military forms of struggle. It was also possible to employ strategic deterrence as a "shield" for more active exploitation of alternative sources of strength—economic, scientific and technological, political, and ideological.[108] In particular, the capacity to influence the thinking of the opponent, its public opinion included, had become increasingly important as a "new factor of power" in international relations.[109] An expansionist Soviet strategy that stressed the acquisition of geopolitical strength would therefore court avoidable risks and losses. It would also fail to exploit available openings in the competition of opposed social systems. It would be playing the old game when in reality the game was changing. In fact, there was an element of urgency here since the United States was well positioned to exploit nonmilitary forms of struggle and had already begun to adapt to the new realities.

Relying on new means and methods—ranging from "bridge-building" and efforts to "erode" socialism, to forms of military and political cooperation that were not incompatible with coexistence—the United States was already acting in less confrontational ways toward the Soviet Union.[110] The underlying conception of U.S. behavior here, it should be noted, was quite different from the expansionist notion of a unitary actor adjusting its strategy and tactics, as though led by a "general staff," to an altered correlation of forces.[111] On the contrary, the relationship between U.S. policy and objective reality was mediated by sometimes acute internal political conflict. There were clashing assessments of the situation and of policy requirements.[112] And reactionaries stood ready to make use of "any favorable turn of events."[113] New realities, the correlation included, had certainly shaped adaptations of U.S. policy to the detriment of confrontation. But adaptation was heavily dependent on the course of U.S. politics.

It followed that Moscow could not rely primarily on strength and an improved global correlation of forces to evoke a continued U.S. willingness to cooperate. Nor could Moscow ignore the effects of perceived Soviet actions on the making of U.S. policies toward the Soviet Union. Like it or not, issues as diverse as human right denials, naval deployments, regional conflict moves, and the like were linked in the politics of U.S. policy making on strategic arms control and economic cooperation with the U.S.S.R. This had been understood but by no means always taken to heart since 1922 and the regime's first attempt to reduce the perceived Soviet threat to the West. The reality of linkage meant that cooperation on strategic arms control, technology transfer, and trade was unlikely to persist if at the same time the Soviet Union could readily be depicted in America as unrelenting in its pursuit of unilateral advantage. Across-the-board threat reduction, possibly including democratization of the Soviet system itself, was ultimately required.

Needless to say, a reformative adaptation of Soviet behavior would not entail unmitigated restraint and self-denial. Military strength sufficient for "shielding" purposes would be required. Restraint in regional intervention would have to be reciprocal, or this would at least be the Soviet demand as it endeavored at the margin to bring clients to negotiate and itself declined to exploit every advantage. More important, in reducing the perceived Soviet threat and striving to demilitarize U.S.–Soviet competition, the Soviet Union would aim at "undermining the spiritual unity of the class adversary and ensuring to itself the broadest possible influence in his ranks."[114] A reformation of U.S.–Soviet relations would serve to weaken the appeal of U.S. reactionaries and eventually to isolate them within the United States.[115] It would thereby reduce the capacity of reaction to contain progressive social change around the world.[116] It would underwrite realism at the elite level and help to mobilize U.S. public opinion on behalf of improved U.S.–Soviet relations. Where expansionist thinking regarded economic cooperation primarily as a means of acquiring new competitive capabilities, the reformative view saw it as a means of building vested U.S. interests in stable cooperation.[117] In sum, a reformative Soviet Union would ally itself with the adaptive processes of imperialism by adapting its own behavior to the new realities. It would not so much force as help the United States to learn.

But if reformative thinking outdid expansionism in cognitive structural learning about cooperation, the fact remains that it was a weak force in Soviet behavior. Appreciating in overt situational assessment at the specialist level, in the policy pronouncements of the general secretary, and to a degree in the outward behavior of the regime, it remained vulnerable to criticism. It was based on differentiated and less threatening conceptions of imperialism and U.S. policy making that were at variance with the overt consensus of the regime. It required recognition of inherent linkages among issues in U.S. politics at a time when Republican administrations were endeavoring to make offensive use of linkage as a bargaining technique. It called for Soviet good behavior. It implied that Moscow could not have things both ways in dealing with the United States. Frustrated by U.S. and Soviet actions, it suffered as conservative views gained strength in the United States following the defeat in Vietnam and the Western economic crisis. As the U.S. consensus rolled to the right and away from cooperation with the principal adversary, so also did the Soviet.

We may therefore conclude that the Soviet Union did engage in cognitive structural learning. The effort was limited and ultimately ineffectual. Nevertheless, "new" thinking was to be observed. Reformists did not have a monopoly here. Expansionist thought came to embrace cooperation on the basis of a new view of the situation and of Soviet policy requirements. But it could not solve the problem of sustained cooperation. On balance, there was more wishful thinking than new thinking here. As to reformative thought, it evinced a superior appreciation of the analytical and policy implications of sustained cooperation, but was unable to displace the mentality of expansionism.

EFFICIENCY LEARNING

Here we are interested in the Soviet ability to match ends and means in more effective ways, either by acting on more efficient strategies for the pursuit of existing goals or through goal redefinition to meet altered opportunities and constraints. Attempts at efficiency learning were certainly made. Where expansionist internationalism was concerned, an adaptive strategy that employed cooperation as a form of conflict was intended to diversify the Soviet capacity to prevail in interstate and intersystem conflict alike. As to reformative internationalism, the correlation of state and revolution in Soviet goals was to be altered to stress interstate cooperation as a means of enhancing security and well-being, while also creating more favorable conditions for global social change and internal Soviet reform. But for various reasons that have been discussed and others to be considered below, neither strategic nor goal-changing efficiency learning proved successful, if success is measured in terms of sustained cooperation with the United States.

Hairs might be split on the matter of residual efficiency learning that fell short of intention or that allowed readier achievement of subsidiary goals even as détente failed. But it seems appropriate to conclude that in the period under review there was ultimately no efficiency learning in Soviet behavior toward the United States. Efficiency learning failed largely because cognitive structural learning was either misguided in the case of expansionism or insupportable where reformative internationalism was concerned.

PROVENANCE AND QUALITY IN LEARNING

Our concern here is with structural constraints on the Soviet ability to engage in learning. Ambiguity notwithstanding, the overt consensual knowledge of the Brezhnev regime was highly injurious to innovative thought bearing on the problem of sustained cooperation with the United States. To be sure, the leadership permitted and moreover encouraged specialist discussion within the bounds of the overt consensus. Constricted debate was thus a commonplace. But consider the underlying assumptions to which all were expected to conform: a conception of imperialism that allowed for adaptation but no change in the essentials since Lenin wrote in 1916; a "two-spheres" understanding of international relations as an arena for class struggle; such deep-seated conflict between opposed social systems that it was odd even to acknowledge the existence of common interests. To deviate significantly from these and other conventions required not merely imagination but courage, such as was displayed by Tiul'panov. Far more often, deviation was surreptitious. As would seem to have been the case with Arbatov, it entailed a readiness to corrupt one's thought by assimilating it to the prevailing outlook. In short, leading specialists acted for the most part like bureaucrats. Subordinated by the party-state in the Stalin era, professional communities that had come to be known as *mezhdunarodniki* and *amerikanisty* continued to be crippled in their ability to report during the Brezhnev years.

In these debilitating circumstances, the substance of attempts to learn took two forms, archaic and current. Where archaic learning was concerned, the process consisted of rectifying consensual knowledge that had been wrong or inaccurate for years. Current learning was centered on the effort to figure out what was happening, and how best to respond, more or less as it occurred. So much of Soviet thinking about the United

States and U.S.–Soviet relations being behind the times, specialist learning attempts were in large measure archaic. This applied in particular to the revision of technical information and prevailing generalizations about the nature of imperialism and the range of capabilities employed all along by the United States in world affairs. On these and other matters there was considerable evidence of archaic learning in the published work of specialists, if not in the overt consensus of the regime once the notion of adaptation had been authorized. More interesting was current learning, especially as it concerned change in the efficacy of military and nonmilitary or civil forms of struggle under conditions of strategic equivalence with the United States. Overt learning was apparent here at the leadership as well as specialist levels, the most obvious case being Arbatov's articulation and Brezhnev's outward acceptance of the notion of "channeling." Nevertheless, lack of leadership consensus on the utility of a more civil relationship with the United States subverted specialist efforts to alter prevailing knowledge in this regard. In archaic and current terms alike, the result was at most a stunted ability to learn despite the appearance of conservative and reformist "new" thinking.

But what was new about Soviet thinking as it pertained to cooperation with the United States in the Brezhnev era? The notions of "adaptation" and "channeling," among others, were derived from the Khrushchev years. Suslov's speeches in the 1970s were little different from those of the 1950s. Kovaleva's Stalinist presentation of late 1969 was indistinguishable from that offered by a predecessor in 1949. Some sought guidance or justification in Lenin on imperialism in 1916, others in Lenin on threat reduction in 1922. As to notions like "mutual dependence," "stereotypes," and indeed the two-phase theory of the imperialist stage, they originated with Western social science and Western communist parties. Although the contextual detail was of course "new," as were policy problems such as comparative economic advantage under conditions of strategic equivalence, in the materials reviewed here it is impossible to identify a single major concept or idea that originated in the Soviet Union in the Brezhnev era. The regime was feeding on its past and on contemporary foreign thought.

We are faced with evidence of the far more widespread Soviet inability to innovate. Although the causes were many, Ernst Haas's insight (Ch. 3) that epistemic communities are essential to the creation of consensual knowledge directs us to the underlying structural disability. Since there were no epistemic communities in the Soviet Union on the questions of interest to us, Haas's view of the provenance and hence the nature of consensual knowledge suggests that no such knowledge was available in the Brezhnev years. And yet our evidence indicates that a great deal of effort went into the maintenance and modification of consensus as determined by central authorities endowed with great but incomplete control over professional communities. Haas's conception of consensual knowledge must surely be amended to allow for impure forms in which bodies of policy-related technical information and associated theories are created, maintained, and assured of acceptance with active intervention from on high. Ultimately, however, Haas is surely right in drawing attention to the relationship between provenance and quality in consensual knowledge. The simple message is this: the less the intellectual freedom allowed to professional producers of knowledge, the lower the quality of knowledge embodied in the consensus.

To set things right in the Soviet Union would in no way have been a simple task. It would have begun with the ungagging of professional communities by a thoroughgoing commitment to glasnost. It would have seen professionals rise to the challenge by thinking independently and speaking their minds after decades of control. It would have led to a restructuring of the Soviet order that saw the creation of autonomous intermediate social and political structures of a kind that had begun to appear before 1917, were ravaged under Lenin, and then incorporated in their remains by the Stalinist state. None of this being remotely feasible in the Brezhnev years, the Soviet regime remained incapable of autonomous innovative thought. In the circumstances, it proved able to conduct at most a disabled attempt at learning to collaborate with the principal adversary.

MIRRORED LEARNING

Turning more directly to the process dimension of Soviet learning behavior, let us assume that Soviet decision makers and specialists actually understood very little about the United States, and that those who were knowledgeable recognized parallels between their country and the United States when they cited militarism, alienation and cynicism of youth, economic contradictions, and so on. I am suggesting here that U.S. behavior and U.S. approaches to U.S.–Soviet relations were understood essentially in the light of Soviet experience and perceived Soviet needs. The GCC accordingly becomes the general crisis of socialism (GCS). Corrected to read not monopoly but oligarchy, SMC becomes state-oligarchy socialism or (appropriately enough) SOS. What Arbatov had to say about prevailing thought in the West applied equally to the overt consensual knowledge of the Brezhnev regime: "Instead of helping to understand reality and giving expression to the urgent tasks of social development, the ideas and doctrines [of the ruling minority] are increasingly aimed at defending and justifying outworn social patterns and institutions which hinder progress."[118] Without overworking the parallel, let us see what reported Soviet understandings of U.S. learning behavior might tell us about equivalent Soviet processes.

For those with a conservative outlook, the Soviet process added up to strategic efficiency learning by command from on high. The aim was to strengthen the Soviet system without altering its essentials. The impetus to learn was primarily exogenous. It arose from changing "conditions of existence" of the Soviet system. Of special significance here were the scientific and technological revolution and an overall correlation of forces that threatened to deteriorate if adaptive action were not forthcoming. Adaptation saw the party oligarchy rely more heavily on the apparatus of state and state-oligarchy measures to master the scientific and technological revolution, and to create new capabilities for competition with imperialism. As well, the oligarchy was willing to allow cooperation and other maneuvering in foreign affairs, which in no way compromised Soviet hostility to the opposing social system. The whole adaptive process was properly conceived and controlled by the oligarchs.

From a reformist perspective, however, the learning process transcended questions of efficiency. A two-phase theory of the presocialist stage of development suggested that the Soviet system was undergoing transformation, not adaptation. Let us call this *innovative learning* or the acquisition of capacities to do new things in new ways centered on the anticipation of future effects of present practice.[119] Productive forces, relations of production, social structure, education, and other factors had all been sufficiently altered to produce forward movement of the Soviet system from oligarchy socialism to SOS as a new phase in the history of socialist development—in effect the "antechamber" to an anticipated democratic socialism. Though the forms and rate of advance of SOS were influenced by external forces, the sources of innovative learning were primarily endogenous. The Soviet state was being obliged to assume an everwidening array of functions that could not be handled by the party oligarchy alone. Despite coalescence of the party and state apparatuses, the state was acquiring increased self-sufficiency under the effects of technological and economic change. Further, a fused state-oligarchic elite was taking shape. Its perspective was less that of the party oligarchy and increasingly that of the general interest in social reform, including international reform. Contrasting tendencies to reaction and reform were nevertheless at work in the elite and affected the learning process. Both tendencies could be found in the program of individual Soviet politicians, which varied with the needs of the moment. Even when those of reformist persuasion achieved superior position, tendency conflict persisted. Losers could seek "revenge." Reformist winners might not see eye to eye and could find it necessary to make concessions to conservative losers.[120]

Innovative Soviet learning was thus an intensely political process that occurred in a domestic socioeconomic and international setting that militated for reform in Soviet institutions, thinking, and practices. Over time, a changing internal and also international environment would oblige the Soviet Union to complete the state-oligarchic phase. It would also prepare the preconditions for an authentically democratic socialism. When the latter arrived, the organs of public representation—the soviets—would finally displace the oligarchy and ensure democratic control over an increasingly self-sufficient state apparatus. By then, the outdated ideas and doctrines that justified oligarchic rule would have been replaced by new ways of thinking and expression consistent with an exemplary socialism. By then the Soviet Union would have become markedly more capable of sustained cooperation with the United States.

The implicit reformist image of the Soviet learning process was thus one in which the ability to cooperate successfully with the United States was a by-product of deep-seated social change that eroded patterns of thought and action acquired under command socialism. In my view, this is ultimately where the sources of Soviet learning behavior were to be found. But domestic political reality in the Brezhnev era was something else again. Despite its recognition of the utility of cooperation with the United States, the oligarchy remained wedded to a conservative situational assessment, to policies of international expansion, and to the denial of internal reform. In these circumstances, reformists could hardly press for innovative learning. They had to settle for less, and some such as Arbatov were temperamentally inclined to do so. Accordingly, the conclusion stands that the reformative tendency was oriented in practice to efficiency learning, and no more, in the Brezhnev years.

INSTITUTIONAL LEARNING

This heading directs us to the effects of Soviet domestic political development on the capacity of the regime to generate new understandings and to translate them into a practice of sustained cooperation. A small universe opens up before us here.[121] To simplify, let us focus on rearrangements in the oligarchy, on institutional change as it affected information processing, and on Brezhnev's contribution in particular.

The collective leadership that followed Khrushchev attached high value to consensus and to stability of expectations. As indicated, it was also predisposed to an expansionist view of things. Reformist thinking was not, however, banished by the oligarchy. Kosygin in particular seemed willing to act on internal economic reform and on cooperation with the United States despite the Vietnam War. Indeed, Moscow did cooperate, as was evinced in the Outer Space Treaty of 1967, in U.S.–Soviet coordination in ending the Middle East war of 1967, in the Nuclear Non-proliferation Treaty of 1968, and in the abortive prenegotiation for strategic arms limitation talks to begin late in 1968. As Brezhnev gradually displaced Kosygin and moved to a position of primacy within the leadership, he evidently found it expedient to appropriate elements of Kosygin's program including economic cooperation with the United States—something Kosygin had advocated on behalf of the leadership as early as 1962.[122] This Brezhnev did by committing himself to strategic arms control and to détente with the Americans as a means of addressing Soviet problems of economic modernization and competitiveness. The result, as of late 1969, was a degree of cognitive structural and efficiency learning on expansionist lines and an internal political context that encouraged the assertion of reformative views in overt discourse.

In April 1971, Brezhnev's predominance within the leadership was revealed in a meeting with Willy Brandt. This was just after the twenty-fourth congress announced a modest "peace program" that would soon be inflated into a major undertaking. Again, the issue with Brandt was international peace and security, which had already served Brezhnev well. Then, as U.S.–Soviet détente broke out in May 1972, Brezhnev leaned into it. Quite likely he did so to elevate his stature within the oligarchy. Certainly he sought to confirm the arrival of the Soviet Union as a global power equal to the United States. In any event, the new dynamic of amity in U.S.–Soviet relations lent further authority to reformative thinking within the regime. It also evoked reformative behavior on Brezhnev's part, as evinced in the BPA, SALT, the June 1973 Agreement on the Prevention of Nuclear War, acceptance of Basket III in the agenda of the Conference on Security and Cooperation in Europe, and possibly in a measure of Soviet "good behavior" in regional conflicts even as the oligarchy as a whole continued to affirm the continued validity of Soviet expansionary goals.

Throughout the decade to 1976, the international department of the Central Committee secretariat played a significant role in the processing of information for foreign policy decision making. Headed by B.N. Ponomarev, a candidate member of the Politburo with experience dating back to Comintern days, the international department's main responsibility had previously been the management of CPSU relations with nonruling communist parties. Dealing inter alia with national liberation movements, the corporate culture of this office would seem to have been decidedly anti-imperialist and not well disposed to reformism. In the 1960s its mandate was broadened to include foreign policy as it concerned relations with capitalist governments, initially those of Western Europe and then the United States. Although the department could hardly have been averse in principle to cooperation between states with different social systems, a two-spheres expansionist perspective is almost certain to have conditioned its staff work for the Politburo. But the international department ran into competition.

At some point in the early 1970s and no doubt with Andropov's assistance, Arbatov gained personal access to Brezhnev. A pipeline was thus established for transmission directly to the general secretary of reformative views that made for improved cognitive structural and efficiency learning. Moreover, given the analytical capacity of the Institute of the USA and Canada to report on and anticipate U.S. reactions to Soviet moves, Arbatov's access signified the institutionalization of a goal-changing feedback loop. Ultimately, the loop was of little avail. But for a while, as the concept of "channeling" informed Brezhnev's behavior toward the United States, it constituted an institutional modification that improved the Soviet capacity to learn in ways not congenial to the international department.

Then, in April 1973, important changes were made in the Politburo that also affected sources of advice. Among the changes was Gromyko's abrupt elevation to full membership and an ensuing increase in the foreign ministry's capacity to feed analysis and recommendations directly to the inner circle and through the international department. Whether the foreign ministry's contributions were conservative or reformist in thrust, they were almost certainly more pragmatic than those of the international department. Gromyko's promotion also affected Inozemtsev's access. As head of the Academy's institute with overall responsibility for international affairs, Inozemtsev's leadership patrons were reported to be Suslov and Kosygin. But given the foreign ministry's resistance to "academic" advice, which persists today, Inozemtsev may have been obliged to conform more closely to the international department's view of things if he was to be heard over the foreign ministry. Hence one reason for Inozemtsev's trajectory toward a more decidedly expansionist outlook after 1972.

The Politburo changes of April 1973 also saw the chiefs of the ministry of defense and the KGB promoted to full membership. Together with Gromyko's rise, these developments further solidified Brezhnev's personal position. Though Andropov may well have been predisposed to a reformist view of things, the net effect of the April 1973 institutional changes was to add to the force of conservative opinion in Soviet decision making.

Utilizing the prerogatives of his office, Brezhnev had meanwhile proceeded to assimilate elements of the reformative outlook into his own pronouncements and into Soviet policy. Given the greater emphasis on self-help in Soviet conduct after December 1974, he may have sponsored a degree of unilateral restraint and sought the same from regional client states, most notably North Vietnam. In any event, Brezhnev appears to have got out ahead of the oligarchy's consensus. All remaining members of the leadership showered praise on Brezhnev personally for the development of détente. They did so in sycophantic fashion, or because they approved of some or all of what he was doing, or in order to distance themselves from a line of policy that might unleash reformism in domestic and foreign affairs. A capable leader fully committed to long-term cooperation with the United States would have found ways to widen the opening to the left in the consensus of the oligarchy, and in overt Soviet discourse and action. He might have begun by altering the overt consensus on imperialism, forms of struggle, and on the consequences of thermonuclear war even as the going got rough with the United States. But Brezhnev's personal shortcomings as a leader entered the picture here.

Brezhnev's principal failing appears to have been an inability to cope with the complexities of policy. Regarding himself as a specialist in "organization and psychology" when he took the position of party leader, he was unable to deal effectively with the substance of issues.[123] Politburo discussions chaired by Brezhnev could therefore be something of a shambles, as was implied by Gromyko in 1989.[124] Unable and possibly unwilling to fashion a reformist consensus by force of intellect, the general secretary was the prisoner of a conservative consensus fashioned by guile. The promise of cooperation with the United States had helped him gain the leadership, but the leadership ability required to sustain the process of cooperation was beyond him.

When it came, the denial of U.S. credits and technology could only have meant a personal defeat for Brezhnev. Economic cooperation with the United States had been a significant factor in his rise to preeminence within the leadership, a prime objective of Soviet expansionism, and a major consideration in expansionist learning, such as it was. Though Kosygin regarded the turn of events in December 1974 as merely a "zigzag" in U.S.–Soviet relations,[125] the regime and above all Brezhnev had suffered a setback. The situation may have demanded a clearer choice between reformative internationalism and a more aggressive expansion keyed to rapid advances in the "sphere of social development." Already stung by events in Chile, encouraged by the Western economic crisis, resisting the pretensions of reformist communist parties in Western Europe, and channeling large sums into Portugal on behalf of the ultra-doctrinaire party leader there,[126] the oligarchy seems to have been in no mood to admit further reformism. In the circumstances, conservative pressure would seem to have mounted for a change of course in Soviet foreign policy, if not a change in leadership as well.

According to one account, Brezhnev was confronted with a challenge from Politburo member A.N. Shelepin in the wake of the Stevenson and Jackson-Vanik amendments.[127] Although long since sidetracked by Brezhnev, Shelepin remained a thorn in the side of the general secretary. Shelepin now argued that "Brezhnev's détente had failed and it was time for a new course." The new line of policy was to begin with the dispatch of Soviet "volunteers" to Portugal, along the lines of Soviet assistance to the Republican forces in the Spanish Civil War. The response of Brezhnev and his handlers was to propose the dispatch of Cuban "volunteers" to Angola. The general secretary won out, Shelepin was put out to pasture in April 1975, and the Angolan venture was set in motion. In September 1975, Brezhnev crudely signaled his born-again orthodoxy and indicated support for a more conservative overt consensus by publicly endorsing the outlook of K.I. Zarodov, a Stalinist ideologue and resolute foe of reformism.[128]

Brezhnev's personal position was thus solidified, but at the expense of change in the correlation of Soviet tendencies that would prove exceedingly inimical to cooperation with the United States. Declining to press on toward a more clearly defined reformative course after 1973, Brezhnev first acquiesced in unlearning by the regime, and then put himself behind a renewed emphasis on expansion even as the leadership continued to seek further agreement with the United States on strategic arms control.

Insofar as conclusions can be drawn about the internal affairs of a secretive order, politics within the regime were the dominant factor in shaping the Soviet capacity to learn. External and internal situational variables, while having significance in affecting Soviet performance, had to be incorporated into behavior if they were to have any force. Political leadership was the major means of assimilating or denying situational change. All things considered, the fundamental impulse of the Brezhnev-Kosygin and then the Brezhnev leadership was to misread change. Misreading sprang from the desire to maintain the power, privileges, and priorities of a ruling minority that was hostile to pressure for reform, whatever its origin—from within, from the United States, from the Italian Communist Party. But learning was not wholly excluded even in this unpromising context.

Change and threatened change *of* the top leadership provided occasions for learning and unlearning as manifested in published comment and outward behavior. On this account, the experience of the regime was one of unlearning. Thinking and practice alike were altered in ways that impeded cooperation with the United States when Khrushchev was ousted in 1964, and possibly when policy failure threatened change in the general secretaryship a decade later.

But Brezhnev's gradual rise to primacy *within* the collective leadership made for limited cognitive and policy changes conducive to sustained cooperation with the Americans. It did so by furthering a consensus on competitive cooperation and by opening the way to reformative thinking. Brezhnev's rise to ascendancy was also accompanied by the establishment of a goal-changing feedback network that, if properly employed, might have abetted the process of cooperation. And yet changes in the Politburo designed to bolster the leader's position could also lend strength to conservative institutions, to counterreformist information processing, and thus to unlearning, as seems to have occurred in April 1973. Consensus could roll either way in response to leadership and institutional developments.

In the midst of relentless political maneuvering, Brezhnev appears as an uncommitted thinker ready to act on a repertoire of conflicting tendencies as the situation required. Indeed, as discussed by Deborah Larson (Ch. 10), he may have been one of those who constructed an outlook to suit the needs of the moment, including the need to maintain his position within the oligarchy. Lacking conviction and the ability to communicate it, he was not the man to lead in learning.

Learning attempts thus occurred in midcourse of the Brezhnev-Kosygin and Brezhnev regimes, and not with renewal of the top leadership. These attempts were made incrementally, in stultifying conditions, and without benefit of outstanding leadership abilities on the part of the general secretary. They proved half-hearted and ineffectual in sustaining cooperation with the United States.

CONCLUSIONS

Consensual learning was defined at the outset as a process in which consensual knowledge is altered to provide an improved basis for collective action. A distinction was then made between overt and operative consensual knowledge in the Soviet case. Contrasting expansionist and reformative tendencies were subsequently identified in overt situational and policy discourse. On this basis, an attempt was made to consider shifts in the operative consensual knowledge of the regime as it broached and then failed to obtain a lasting collaboration with the United States.

To summarize the results, it was found that reward-punishment learning added up very largely to unlearning where cooperation was concerned. Cognitive structural learning occurred but was asymmetrical, limited, and ultimately ineffectual for expansionist and reformative purposes alike. Efficiency learning was also attempted but came to naught. Modifications of expansionist thought amounted at most to attempted adaptive learning, whereas innovative learning was inherent but suppressed in the reformative tendency. Throughout, the absence of epistemic communities compromised the Soviet ability to learn, as did the unwillingness of the regime to alter the overt consensus on key situational and policy issues. Personal leadership and politics within the Politburo proved to be all-important in shaping the Soviet ability to create and employ consensual knowledge on behalf of sustained cooperation. Finally, I would add that learning disability and error in the performance of the Brezhnev regime would seem to have been heavily motivated. They sprang from a determination to resist the opening to the left in internal Soviet affairs that would have flowed from the perceptions and practices required to sustain cooperation once it had been initiated.

This much allowed, it should be clear that there is considerably more to consensual learning than the elaboration of new and agreed knowledge conducive to the achievement of collective goals. In the Soviet case we are dealing with a process consisting of several interdependent phases. To begin with, increasingly complex and integrated causal understandings are generated to account for developments in the international and domestic environments and for the achievement of the collective purpose in both settings. Second, situational and policy understandings are legitimized through professional discourse and assimilation into the practice of policy makers. Finally, the outward behavior of the collectivity is altered to realize the policy makers' intention. A collectivity or its representatives may come to the fullest understanding of what needs to be done, but if they prove unable to translate an altered state of awareness into effective action, learning cannot finally be said to have occurred. It remains in some sense academic.

On all three counts—the generation, legitimation, and effective use of consensual knowledge—the performance of the Brezhnev regime would seem pure and simple to have been a failure. Such a judgment would, however, be overly severe. Something *was* happening in a time now derided as the era of stagnation. To get to the heart of the matter, let us consider two technical challenges to any admission of learning in Soviet conduct toward the United States under Brezhnev.

Ernst Haas argues in Chapter 3 that adaptation and learning are two quite different phenomena. Adaptation he sees as problem solving, possibly even with the invention of new means, but without a thorough reevaluation of ends and beliefs about causation. Learning is said to require, among other things, a redefinition of ultimate purpose and the acceptance of new cause-and-effect understandings as originally devised by epistemic communities. Since the Soviets under Brezhnev were engaged in, and saw themselves as embarked on, a course of adaptation to change in international relations—and to prior adaptation in the nature and behavior of the U.S. system—even the attempt to "learn" would have to be ruled out if we follow Haas. As well, Richard Anderson (Ch. 4) argues that while public policy change normally occurs through adaptation, the dynamics of political competition within the Brezhnev Politburo were such as to produce effects that mimicked learning. The proposition here is that bargaining among the oligarchs evoked integrative complexity in Soviet statements and conduct, when in actuality leaders were highly unlikely to learn about external affairs and could in any event switch with relative ease to alternative perceptions and routines when the demands of Politburo competition required.

Whether the net result in the Brezhnev years was attempted adaptation, mimicked learning, or attempted learning is not a semantic question. At issue here are the nature of the collectivity that learns and the temporal framework within which consensual learning ordinarily occurs on matters of great moment.

To begin with mimicry, my evidence suggests that whereas persistence in the overt situational consensus was consistent with no outward learning at the leadership level, the operative consensus was altered to embrace an expanded set of interconnected ends. The aim was to diversify Soviet competitiveness through cooperation in conditions of strategic equivalence, enhanced significance of nonmilitary forms of struggle, and continued two-spheres conflict. The redefinition of Soviet ends was accompanied by diverging cause-and-effect understandings of the preconditions for success in global competition. Whether or not these understandings originated with specialists, they were articulated most clearly by spokesmen for contending schools of specialist thought and were not readily to be found in leadership presentations.

Furthermore, as described by Brezhnev, the character of the process that committed the Soviet Union to a course of competitive cooperation was one of "evaluation," "study," "knowing how to determine basic tasks," and "concluding," all of which occurred at some point before March 1971.[129] If Brezhnev's account is to be accepted, Soviet decision making for détente did indeed include a studied assessment of what the international and domestic environments could allow, and is not well represented in terms of introverted political competition among Politburo members or, for that matter, cybernetic information processing. Irrespective of learning on the part of individual Politburo members, collective processes analogous to individual learning would seem to have occurred as Soviet strategy was adapted to the task of marshaling strength in diversified competition with the United States. If so, who or what did the learning?

The entity that learns is ultimately an analytic construct and not a physical collectivity. I take it to be the political system through which values are allocated for society. The system is not to be reduced to interaction among its decision makers and key institutions. Society and uniformities in system behavior are also potent forces. As suggested earlier, socioeconomic change associated with economic and technological innovation, education, urbanization, and international development contributed in incremental but fundamental ways to the evolution of a systemic propensity to collaborate with the United States. Indeed, a society may ultimately "learn" not so much by acquiring new capabilities to accomplish old or new tasks, but by becoming something different, by displacing old tendencies in favor of new.

In the Brezhnev era, the pattern of interaction that made up the political system exhibited long-established but mutable tendencies whose correlation varied to produce a rolling consensus that structured the behavior of actors within. Two tendencies, expansionist and reformative internationalism, have been stressed here as they shaped the capacity of the Soviet Union to collaborate with the United States. But in reality there were four tendencies in play. Coercive (Stalinist) and democratic (radical reformist or Eurocommunist) variants of isolationism constituted significant but unequal forces at either end of the political spectrum.[130]

In politics, Soviet politics included, four is a crowd. Three seems optimal when differences are initially aggregated and compromise is repeatedly required. The story of Soviet conduct toward the United States from Stalin to Gorbachev is one of incremental change in the "center of gravity" of the tendency set. Change occurred as a consequence of domestic and international social forces mediated by an arduous and reversible effort on the part of actors within to displace coercive by democratic isolationism. Stated succinctly, the secular process of consensual learning not merely to engage in, but to sustain, a collaborative relationship with the United States consisted of the accentuation of reformist tendencies in system behavior at the expense of deep-seated conservative routines.

The Politburo or, more precisely, interaction among Politburo members played a critical role in determining the correlation of tendencies in Soviet conduct. And yet competition and cooperation within the Politburo were constrained by the established tendencies of the system. Politburo members in the Brezhnev years were in no position to invent qualitatively new routines for the Soviet system. On the contrary, unless very gifted, they were obliged to work within the repertoire of tried and tested practices, adapting them at the margin. Policy makers also regulated the generation as well as the legitimation and overt use of consensual knowledge. But again they were in no position themselves to create new bodies of knowledge. Professionals drawn into the central decision process had something to contribute here, as did bureaucratic institutions. Policy makers appeared and disappeared, but Soviet tendencies persisted, as did the intellectual and institutional milieu in which policy was made.

How then might learning have occurred at the level, not of the Politburo or regime, but of the political system taken as a whole? Evidently it occurred as consensual knowledge was incrementally assembled by reformist specialists embedded in a society disabled by persistent Stalinist assumptions about domestic and international affairs. As well, it would seem to have occurred as Politburo members—even those who may have shared Brezhnev's inability to deal with the substance of issues—processed recombinant pieces of perception and policy. Brezhnev may have been driven by personal ambition in opting for détente with the United States, but the effect of his actions was to alter the framework of discussion to the advantage of reformism. Subsequently, in drawing openly but weakly on reformist thought, Brezhnev also altered the correlation of tendencies in outward Soviet behavior in a manner that for a time made sustained cooperation more likely. And then the events of December 1974 fed into the Politburo to produce unlearning in an enhancement of adversarial perception and routines throughout the system. Nevertheless, in embarking on a course of action that produced the unintended consequence of SALT without trade expansion, even the most self-regarding of leaders had participated in a process of adaptive learning. This was done by committing the collectivity to a momentous collaborative venture that could neither be repudiated, nor subverted by free-wheeling adversarial activity, without incurring undue costs and risks.

A denial of foreign policy learning in the Brezhnev era on the grounds that it was being mimicked might therefore hold under three conditions: (1) when the system of interaction we call the Soviet Union is reduced to its decision makers; (2) when individual learning by decision makers is assumed to be a precondition for significant learning elsewhere in the system, or on the part of the system taken as a whole; and (3) when political competition among decision makers is regarded not as a standard feature of allocative behavior for Soviet society, including allocations that might contribute to adaptive learning by the whole, but as a singular impediment to learning by leaders. Separately and together, these conditions seem unwarranted. Policy oscillations of the kind observed in this paper occurred as a function of international and domestic developments mediated by political competition among Politburo members, virtually all of whom preferred to deny or avoid citing the need for adaptive action even as some sought it. To carry the point still further, in the scope and magnitude of its implications, the strategic course correction ventured in 1969–1974 was not wholly dissimilar to that undertaken in the Gorbachev years. The failed learning of the Brezhnev era was a very, very dry run for what followed when the prefiguration of economic crisis in 1969 had become a reality.

If we are dealing here with a disabled but authentic attempt at adaptive learning, what of Haas's sharp distinction between adaptation and learning? As with his insistence on the role of epistemic communities in the provenance of consensual knowledge, the adaptation-learning difference is useful in conceiving what might be at stake for organizational behavior. But it is too exacting to take us far in examining the confused, impure, and reversible processes that bring an entire society to learn for itself— that is, consensually and without high levels of coercion. There is no denying that learning comes hard. But it comes through cumulative adaptation and not in a flash. Even when it takes place quickly, as with the onset of European integration in 1948–1952 or the revolution in Soviet affairs since 1985, it remains the culmination of decades of experience and inference. Haas in fact recognizes this when he notes that learning is "a slow historical movement in which *some* epistemic communities successfully shake up *some* aspects of habitual behavior." When learning occurs in the course of extended incremental adaptation, learning and adaptation are synonymous. Although the end state will differ qualitatively from the beginning, the traverse is adaptive and cumulative.

Just as Brezhnev-era thinking that appeared "new" at first sight turned out to be either received from the Khrushchev and earlier years or recently imported knowledge, the evidence assembled here suggests that a good deal of the "new political thinking" of the Gorbachev years was not invented or imported after March 1985.[131] Elements of today's new thinking and practice are evident, albeit in fragmentary and distorted form, in the reformist discourse and behavior of the decade to 1976. Consider merely the following: the assertion of "common interests," "mutual dependence," and "pan-human" values; the desirability of prevailing by force of example including democratization, as distinct from international might; the heightened significance of nonmilitary forms of struggle and global issues such as the environment; the need to separate the two spheres rather than combine them; the two-phase theory of the imperialist stage; Soviet entry into the BPA, SALT, and the CSCE; "stereotypes" as an impediment to international cooperation; recognition of the realities of linkage; and above all the need to reduce the Soviet threat. Though by no means all of it was there, no little of Gorbachev's foreign policy program is to be seen in the tortured reformism of the Brezhnev era.

We do not need to rehabilitate Brezhnev to acknowledge significant continuities between his and Gorbachev's time. In its failed attempt to adapt Soviet expansionism to altered conditions, the Brezhnev regime abetted reformist adaptations of Soviet behavior that were to figure in Soviet actions under Gorbachev. In so doing, the regime contributed to a secular process of adaptive learning that promised higher levels of accommodation with the United States. Adaptive learning was furthered by committing the U.S.S.R. to the SALT process, by incorporating certain reformist conceptions and policy preferences into official allocations, and by permitting the maintenance of a repertoire of reformist knowledge and options that could be drawn on when circumstance warranted. For circumstance to warrant, the Soviet situation had to get substantially worse and better at the same time. Impending economic crisis had to narrow the regime's choices so severely that it became possible to steer the system hard to the left, to the advantage of long-standing reformist tendencies. As well, a leader had to come forward who was prepared to disabuse the regime of its vision of geopolitical mastery and to lend new legitimacy to reformist knowledge. When the preconditions for acceler-

ated reformist learning were at long last met, Gorbachev and his associates proceeded not to invent qualitatively new routines but to act forcibly
on the weak tendencies of the Brezhnev and Khrushchev years.

Consensual learning on vital questions of foreign and military policy
has thus been a painfully slow historical process for the Soviet Union.
So it was under Brezhnev, when learning took the form of truncated,
incremental, and substantially reversible adaptations. Though foreign
affairs learning under Gorbachev could yet prove reversible, today's explosive search for international accommodation is at once an extraordinary
break with history and the expression of historic continuities in Soviet
behavior.

NOTES

1. For accounts, see George W. Breslauer, "Why Détente Failed: An Interpretation," in Alexander L. George, ed., *Managing U.S. Rivalry: Problems of Crisis Prevention* (Boulder, Colo.: Westview, 1983), 319–40; Lawrence T. Caldwell, *Soviet
Approaches to SALT*, Adelphi Papers 75 (London: International Institute for Strategic Studies, 1971); Raymond L. Garthoff, *Détente and Confrontation: American-Soviet Relations from Nixon to Reagan* (Washington: Brookings, 1985); Harry Gelman,
The Brezhnev Politburo and the Decline of Détente (Ithaca, N.Y.: Cornell University
Press, 1984); Henry A. Kissinger, *White House Years* (Boston: Little, Brown, 1982);
and Bruce Parrott, *Trade, Technology and Soviet-American Relations* (Bloomington: Indiana
University Press, 1981).

2. Where leaders are concerned, the data base for this chapter consists of the
selected speeches of L.I. Brezhnev, V.V. Grishin, A.N. Kosygin, and M.A. Suslov
as compiled in the following volumes: L.I. Brezhnev, *Leninskim kursom: Rechi i stat'i*,
vols. 1–5 (Moscow: Politizdat, 1970–1976), hereafter *Brezhnev* I–V; V.V. Grishin, *Izbrannye
rechi i stat'i* (Moscow: Politizdat, 1982), hereafter *Grishin*; A.N. Kosygin, *Izbrannye
rechi i stat'i* (Moscow: Politizdat, 1974), hereafter *Kosygin* I; A.N. Kosygin, *K velikoi
tseli*, vol. 2 (Moscow: Politizdat 1979) hereafter *Kosygin* II; M.A. Suslov, *Izbrannye
rechi i stat'i* (Moscow: Politizdat, 1972), hereafter *Suslov* I; and M.A. Suslov, *Na putiakh
stroitel'stva kommunizma* (Moscow: Politizdat, 1977), hereafter *Suslov* II. To provide a minimal sense of context, dates are given for each citation throughout the
chapter. As to the specialist literature, it has been examined in sufficient detail to
identify leading spokesmen for contending schools of thought. A prior analysis
of specialist discourse is available in Franklyn Griffiths, "The Sources of American
Conduct: Soviet Perspectives and Their Policy Implications," *International Security*,
9 (Fall 1984): 3–50, which is drawn on liberally here.

3. Ernst B. Haas, "Why Collaborate: Issue-linkage in International Regimes,"
World Politics, 32 (April 1980):367–68. As elaborated by Haas (Ch. 3), the concept
of consensual knowledge has particular meanings that deserve comment. Consisting
of socially constructed understandings about cause-and-effect relationships in
phenomena of significance to a collectivity, it may be virtually indistinguishable
from ideology. Nor must consensus be complete: consensual knowledge may
entail understandings that are becoming more, or less, consensual. Consensual

knowledge is, however, to be distinguished from ideology in that its claims to comprehension and counsel are subject to what Haas terms "truth tests" centered on adversary procedures and demonstrated ability to solve problems. The ultimate test of "truth," especially when rival schools of thought are present, is decision by those who make use of knowledge for the collectivity. In these respects there is no great problem in applying the notion of consensual knowledge in the analysis of Soviet behavior. I would add only that, when ideology embraced everything said and done by a line of leaders from Marx to Brezhnev, consensual knowledge is best viewed in the Soviet case as a connective body of understandings that relates currently salient aspects of ideology to current social reality. A problem does, however, arise with Haas's insistence that the originators of consensual knowledge are "epistemic communities." By this he means groups of professionals, usually drawn from a variety of disciplines, who are committed to a given view of causation, share a set of political values, stand by "extra-community reality tests," and whose substantive knowledge draws them to public policy making and decision makers in particular. The problem here is that, aside from the spectrum of dissident groups, during the decade to 1976 no epistemic communities were to be found in a society governed by a regime that sought to regulate all public discourse. Are we therefore to conclude that the Soviet Union in the Brezhnev era was bereft of consensual knowledge? That Haas's conception of consensual knowledge is something of an ideal type? That official intolerance of policy-relevant epistemic communities was a factor in the Soviet inability to learn? More on these matters below.

4. For discussions, see M. Dragilev, "Leninskaia kharakteristika krizisa mirovogo kapitalizma i sovremennost'," *Mirovaia ekonomika i mezhdunarodnye otnosheniia* (hereafter *MEiMO*), 3 (March 1973):5–16; A.G. Mileikovskii, "Novye iavleniia v razvitii sovremennogo gosudarstvenno-monopolisticheskogo kapitalizma," *Znanie*, Ser. ekonomika, 7 (1972):4–16; and Erik P. Hoffman and Robbin F. Laird, *"The Scientific-Technological Revolution" and Soviet Foreign Policy* (New York: Pergamon, 1982), Ch 2.

5. V.I. Lenin, "Groziashchaia katastrofa i kak s nei borot'sia" (September 1917), *Pol'noe sobranie sochineniia*, vol. 34 (Moscow: Gospolitizdat, 1962), 193. For background, see P. Boccara, "Aperçu sur la question du capitalisme monopoliste d'état," *Economie et politique*, 138 (1966): 6–17; the materials assembled in "Conférence internationale sur le capitalisme monopoliste d'état," ibid., 143–44 and 145–46 (1967); and N.N. Inozemtsev et al., eds., *Uchenie V.I. Lenina ob imperializme i sovremennost'* (Moscow: "Nauka," 1967).

6. This was a constant theme. See *Brezhnev* I, 266, 273 (March 29, 1966); *Brezhnev* II, 108 (November 4, 1967), 243 (July 3, 1968), 369 (June 7, 1969), and 593–94 (April 21, 1970). See also *Suslov* I, 513 (November 11, 1967); *Brezhnev* III, 208 (March 30, 1971); *Suslov* II, 302 (December 21, 1971); *Grishin* 119 (November 6, 1971); *Suslov* II, 396 (June 11, 1974); *Brezhnev* V, 180 (October 11, 1974); *Suslov* II, 419 (October 22, 1974), 432 and 436 (April 22, 1975); and *Brezhnev* V, 479 (February 24, 1976). Kosygin, however, proved unwilling, referring not at all to the GCC in the collections under review here.

7. To be precise, leaders made frequent reference to favorable change in the global correlation of forces but did not associate the phenomenon directly with

the GCC. For some specialists, however, change in the correlation to the advantage of socialism was the "essence" of the GCC. Dragilev, "Leninskaya kharakteristika," 14. Encouraging leadership assessments of the correlation are to be found in *Brezhnev* I, 109 (April 8, 1965), 168 (June 20, 1965), 224 (September 29, 1965), 266 (March 29, 1966); and *Brezhnev* II, 235 (July 4, 1968). See also *Suslov* I, 414–15 (June 2, 1965), 433–35 (January 26, 1966), 588 (autumn 1969), 603 (June 9, 1970); *Brezhnev* III, 390 (June 11, 1971); *Grishin* 156 (March 14, 1972); *Suslov* II, 360 (July 13, 1973), 394 (June 11, 1974); *Brezhnev* V, 76–77 (June 14, 1974); *Suslov* II, 451 (June 9, 1975); *Brezhnev* V, 317 (June 13, 1975), and 465 (February 24, 1976). Kosygin again proved leery.

8. *Brezhnev* II, 430 (August 1969). See also *Brezhnev* II, 108 (November 4, 1967), 236 (July 4, 1968); *Kosygin* I, 438 (April 23, 1969); *Brezhnev* II, 369 (June 7, 1969); *Suslov* I, 603 (June 9, 1970); and *Brezhnev* V, 480 (February 24, 1976).

9. *Brezhnev* II, 368 (June 7, 1969).

10. F. Burlatskii, *Pravda*, July 25, 1963.

11. *Suslov* I, 415 (June 2, 1965), and *Brezhnev* II, 108 (November 4, 1967). For subsequent leadership comment on imperialist adaptation, see *Brezhnev* II, 236 (July 4, 1968), 368–69 (June 7, 1969); *Brezhnev* III, 207–208 (March 30, 1971); *Suslov* I, 651 (autumn 1971); *Grishin* 119 (November 6, 1971); *Suslov* II, 302 (December 21, 1971), 372 (November 23, 1973); and *Brezhnev* V, 479 (February 24, 1976). As of 1967, the Academy of Sciences' leading institute on these matters, the Institute of the World Economy and International Relations, had opted for the "adaptation" formula as against a "two-phase" conception of the imperialist stage.

12. *Brezhnev* II, 108 (November 4, 1967).

13. Ibid., 368 (June 1969), and 594 (April 21, 1970).

14. *Brezhnev* I, 273 (March 29, 1966); *Brezhnev* II, 109 ("partial concessions," "more clever," November 4, 1967), 213 (March 29, 1968), 368 ("anarchy," June 7, 1969), and 593–94 (April 21, 1970). See also *Suslov* I, 541 (May 5, 1968); *Kosygin* I, 438 (April 23, 1969); *Suslov* I, 589 (autumn 1969); and *Suslov* II, 302 (December 21, 1971).

15. *Brezhnev* II, 412–13 (June 7, 1969), and 587 (April 21, 1970). See also *Brezhnev* I, 438 (June 10, 1966), 473 (November 1, 1966); *Brezhnev* II, 258 (June 8, 1968); *Brezhnev* III, 56 (June 12, 1970); *Brezhnev* IV, 249 (August 15, 1973); *Suslov* II, 372 (November 23, 1973); *Brezhnev* IV, 377 (November 29, 1973); and *Brezhnev* V, 84 (June 14, 1974).

16. *Brezhnev* II, 369 (June 7, 1969). On "maneuvering," see for example *Brezhnev* I, 261 (January 15, 1966); *Brezhnev* II, 108 (November 4, 1967); and *Suslov* I, 651 (autumn 1971).

17. Franklyn Griffiths, "The Soviet Experience of Arms Control," *International Journal*, 44 (Spring 1989):326–41. On variables that may have entered the Soviet decision, see also Richard Anderson's contribution to this volume at note 2 therein. Speaking in June, 1974, Brezhnev noted that "several years" earlier the correlation of forces had been evaluated to suggest the possibility of a radical turn in the international situation; the "peace programme" announced at the twenty-fourth party congress in 1971 had "generalized" this objective, which seemingly had been established earlier. *Brezhnev* V, 76–77 (June 14, 1974). As I see it, the decision in principle for détente with the United States was taken in late November or very early December 1969. A key indicator was Soviet readiness to accept the

United States as a participant in the European security process, which was communicated to Washington in the first days of December 1969. Griffiths, "Soviet Experience," 340.

18. *Brezhnev* II, 520 (April 13, 1970). See also the analysis of stated Soviet thinking on comparative economic performance in Bruce Parrott, *Politics and Technology in the Soviet Union* (Cambridge, Mass.: MIT Press, 1983), Ch. 6.

19. Archie Brown, "Political Developments: Some Conclusions and an Interpretation," in Archie Brown and Michael Kaser, eds., *The Soviet Union Since the Fall of Khrushchev*, 2nd ed. (London: Macmillan, 1978), 228. Suslov evidently opposed rehabilitation. Roy Medvedev in *Argumenty i fakty*, April 22–28, 1989.

20. *Brezhnev* III, 208 (March 30, 1971).

21. M.F. Kovaleva, *K voprosu metodologii politicheskoi ekonomii kapitalizma* (Moscow: "Mysl'," 1969). Though Kovaleva's statement was in all respects a replay of I.I. Kuzminov, *O gosudarstvenno-monopolisticheskom kapitalizme* (Moscow: Gospolitizdat, 1949), the perennial discussion of crisis and stabilization in the West reached back to the 1920s and earlier. See Richard B. Day, *The 'Crisis' and the 'Crash': Soviet Studies of the West, 1917–1939* (London: NLB, 1981). Related Soviet commentary in the 1960s is considered in Parrott, *Politics and Technology*, Ch. 5.

22. M.S. Dragilev and V.I. Mokhov, *Leninskii analiz monopolitsicheskogo kapitalizma* (Moscow "Vysshaia shkola," 1970).

23. G.A. Arbatov, *Ideologicheskaia borb'a v sovremennykh mezhdunarodnykh otnosheniiakh* (Moscow: Politizdat, 1970), and N.N. Inozemtsev et al., eds., *Politicheskaia ekonomiia sovremennogo monopolisticheskogo kapitalizma*, 2 vols. (Moscow: "Mysl'," 1970). Arbatov's study is relied on heavily here. Indeed, it may be regarded as a programmatic statement of Soviet foreign policy reformism in the Brezhnev era. For ease of access, it is cited in its English translation, *The War of Ideas in Contemporary International Relations* (Moscow: Progress Publishers, 1973).

24. S.I. Tiul'panov, ed., *V.I. Lenin i problemy sovremennogo kapitalizma* (Leningrad: Izd-vo LGU, 1969). Others had tentatively spoken in favor of a "two-phase" theory. Among them was E.A. Ambartsumov who, in the Gorbachev era, was among the first to float the notion of pan-human values taking precedence over those of any particular class. See "Mezhdunarodnaia konferenstiia marksistov," *MEiMO*, 6 (June 1967):82, and E. Ambartsumov, *Izvestiia*, September 6, 1986. For Brezhnev-era comment on "the unity of humanity" and "the general human interest," see F.M. Burlatskii and A.A. Galkin, *Sotsiologiia. Politika. Mezhdunarodnye Otnosheniia* (Moscow: "Mezhdunarodnye otnosheniia," 1974), 290, 296–98, 304.

25. Dragilev, "Leninskaia kharakteristika" (March 1970); Arbatov, *War of Ideas* (1970); F.M. Burlatskii, *Lenin. Gosudarstvo. Politika* (Moscow: "Nauka," 1970); Dragilev and Mokhov, *Leninskii analiz* (1970); Inozemtsev, *Politicheskaia ekonomiia* (1970); S.I. Tiul'panov and V.L. Sheinis, "Kapitalizm i problemy planirovaniia," *Vestnik Leningradskogo universiteta*, Seriia ekonomika (hereafter *VLU*), 5 (1971):19–35; M. Dragilev, "Obshchii krizis i gosudarstvenno-monopolisticheskii kapitalizm," *MEiMO*, 7 (July 1971):94–108; E. Bregel', "O metode leninskogo issledovaniia imperializma," *Voprosy ekonomiki*, 7 (July 1971):104–14; S.I. Tiul'panov and S.I. Iakovleva, "Krupnoe nauchnoe sobytie," *VLU*, 11 (1971):131–36; E. Bregel', "O nekotorykh spornykh voprosakh teorii obshchego krizisa kapitalizma," *MEiMO*, 12 (December 1971):86–97; S.A. Dalin, *SShA: poslevoennyi gosudarstvennyi kapitalizm* (Moscow: "Nauka," 1972);

N.N. Inozemtsev, *Sovremennyi kapitalizm: Novye iavleniia i protivorechiia* (Moscow: "Mysl'," 1972); V. Zhelezova, "Obshchii krizis kapitalizma i GMK," *MEiMO*, 6 (June 1972):103–107; Mileikovskii,"Novye iavleniia" (1972); M. Dragilev, "Gosudarstvenno-monopolisticheskii kapitalizm — organicheskoe svoistvo imperializma," *Voprosy ekonomiki*, 9 (September 1972):82–91; M. Perovich and I. Prokopenko, "Eshche raz ob obshchem krizise kapitalizma," *MEiMO*, 3 (March 1973):107–109; I. Rudakova, "Mesto gosudarstvenno-monopolitsicheskikh protsessov v sisteme kapitalisticheskikh otnoshenii," ibid., 104–107; V.E. Guliev, *Sovremennoe imperialisticheskoe gosudarstvo* (Moscow: "Mezhdunarodnye otnosheniia," 1973); S.I. Tiul'panov and V.L. Sheinis, *Aktual'nye problemy politicheskoi ekonomii sovremennogo kapitalizma* (Leningrad: Izd-vo LGU, 1973); Iu. Borko, "O metodologii analiza gosudarstvenno-monopolisticheskogo kapitalizma," *MEiMO*, 5 (May 1973):102–10; "Obsuzhdaiut'sia problemy sovremennogo kapitalizma," ibid., 8 (August 1973):140–42; S. Tiul'panov, "Istoricheskoe mesto gosudarstvenno-monopolisticheskogo kapitalizma," ibid., 10 (October 1973):103–109; S.I. Iakovleva and S.I. Tiul'panov, "Tsennoe issledovanie novykh yavlenii v ekonomike imperializma," *VLU*, II, 1973, 145–48; L. Leont'ev, "Rol' gosudarstva v ekonomike sovremennogo kapitalizma," *MEiMO*, 1 (January 1974):104–12; A.A. Gromyko and V.V. Zhurkin, eds., *SShA: Naucho-technologicheskaia revoliutsiia i tendentsii vneshnei politiki* (Moscow: "Mezhdunarodnye otnosheniia," 1974), hereafter Gromyko and Zhurkin, *SShA: NTR*; Burlatskii and Galkin, *Sotsiologiia. Politika. Mezhdunarodnye otnosheniia* (1974); B. Ponomarev, "The World Situation and the Revolutionary Process," *World Marxist Review*, 6 (June 1974); and "Ob uglublenii obshchego krizisa kapitalizma," *MEiMO*, 9 (September 1974):3–18, which effectively closed the discussion.

26. Inozemtsev, *Sovremennyi kapitalizm* (1972), and G.A. Arbatov, "Sobytie vazhnogo mezhdunarodnogo znacheniia," *SShA: ideologiia, politika, ekonomika* (hereafter *SShA*), 8 (August 1972):3–12; "O sovetsko-amerikanskikh otnosheniiakh," *Kommunist*, 3 (February 1973):101–13; and "Sovetsko-amerikanskie otnosheniia v 70-e gody," *SShA*, 5 (May 1974):26–40.

27. Interviews, Moscow, May 1989.

28. Tiul'panov and Sheinis, *Aktual'nye problemy* (1973).

29. Tiul'panov, "Istoricheskoe mesto" (October 1973), which depicted change as occurring within, and not beyond, the monopoly stage of capitalism. The details of Tiul'panov's argument remained intact, but now it was stated in terms of phases within the monopoly stage only. See also S.I. Tiul'panov and S.I. Iakovleva, "Osobennosti ekspluatatsii trudiashchikhsia v usloviiakh GMK," *Rabochii klass i sovremennyi mir* (hereafter *RKiSM*), 3 (March 1978):54–68.

30. See for example *Brezhnev* IV, 150 (June 18, 1973); also 26 (November 13, 1972), 79 (December 21, 1972), and 188 ("edifice of peace," July 10, 1973).

31. Ibid., 15–16 (June 27, 1972), 66 and 72 (December 21, 1972), 186–87 (July 10, 1973), 227 (July 26, 1973), 279 (September 19, 1973), and 336 (October 26, 1973). See also *Kosygin* II, 212 (December 11, 1972), 221 (July 13, 1972), 244–45 (November 14, 1973); *Suslov* I, 651 (July 3, 1972); and *Suslov* II, 360 (July 13, 1973).

32. *Brezhnev* V, 180 (October 11, 1974).

33. M.S. Dragilev et al., eds., *Gosudarstvenno-monopolisticheskii kapitalizm: Obshchie cherty i osobennosti* (Moscow: Politizdat, 1975), hereafter Dragilev, *GMK*; N.N.

Inozemtsev et al., eds., *Uglublenie obshchego krizisa kapitalizma* (Moscow: "Mysl'," 1976); and G. Arbatov, *Izvestiia* September 4, 1975, and *Pravda*, April 2, 1976.

34. Suslov put it succinctly: the deepening crisis in the West meant that capitalism would not have a "'second wind'." *Suslov* II, 419 (October 22, 1974). See also ibid., 436 (April 22, 1975), 451 (June 9, 1975), and T.T. Timofeyev, "Rabochee dvizhenie na sovremennom etape obshchego krizisa kapitalizma," *RKiSM*, 5 (May 1975):21–35.

35. *Brezhnev* V, 479–80 (February 24, 1976).

36. Brief biographical notes are in order here. Dragilev had been slow to reject Stalinist views of the capitalist system in the Khrushchev era, and had come out in favor of a Stalinist perspective once again when an attempt was made to rehabilitate Stalin prior to the twenty-third party congress in 1966. Conversations with specialists at IMEMO in the 1970s suggested that Dragilev was aligned with V.V. Grishin, Politburo member and head of the Moscow party organization. Tiul'panov had been a professional military officer and had risen to the rank of general by the time he was demobilized in 1956 at the age of 55. Decorated several times in World War II and mentioned in Zhukov's memoirs, he drew comment in the West as head of the information office of the Soviet military adminstration in Germany, 1945–1949. From 1956 to 1961 he was prorector of Leningrad University, where he furthered studies of the capitalist system. He is said to have been a personal friend of General A.A. Epishev, head of the main political administration of the Soviet armed forces. Inozemtsev and Arbatov both graduated from the Institute of International Relations in the class of 1947. Initially an Americanist, Inozemtsev rose through the ranks of IMEMO to become director in 1965 and candidate member of the Central Committee in March 1971. His patrons in the 1970s were said to be Suslov and Kosygin. Arbatov became the founding director of the Institute of the USA (later USA and Canada) in 1967 and entered the Central Committee in 1976. As noted above, his principal patron was Andropov.

37. Dragilev, "Leninskaia kharateristika" (March 1970), 7.

38. *Ibid.* See also Dragilev, "Obshchii krizis" (July 1971), 96–99 and "Gosudarstvenno-monopolisticheskii kapitalizm" (September 1972), 90–91.

39. Dragilev, "Obshchii krizis" (July 1971), 108.

40. Dragilev, "Leninskaia kharakteristika" (March 1970), 8–9; Dragilev and Mokhov, *Leninskii analiz* (1970), 192–248; and Dragilev, *GMK* (1975), 27 on "strategy."

41. Dragilev, "Leninskaia kharakteristika" (March 1970), 16, suggests that growing Soviet political and military power aggravated the condition of U.S. capitalism by furthering its militarization, military interventions, balance of payments deficits, devaluation, tax increases, reduced real wages, and so on.

42. Tiul'panov, *Lenin i problemy* (1969), 32, and Tiul'panov and Sheinis, *Aktual'nye problemy* (1973), 6–7, 11.

43. Tiul'panov and Sheinis, *Aktual'nye problemy* (1983), 6. See also Tiul'panov, *Lenin i problemy* (1969), 6, 22–23.

44. Tiul'panov and Sheinis, *Aktual'nye problemy* (1973), 64.

45. Ibid., 12–13, 89–90, and Ch. 3 on planning.

46. Ibid., 88 ("subsystem"), and 94 ("state-monopoly elite"). See also Tiul'panov, *Lenin i problemy* (1969), 20–21. On "regrouping," and the "state principle," see Tiul'panov and Sheinis, *Aktual'nye problemy* (1973), 12.

47. Tiul'panov and Sheinis, *Aktual'nye problemy* (1973), 88–89.

48. Ibid., 74–75. On preconditions for socialism, see 240.

49. Ibid., 9.

50. Inozemtsev, *Sovremennyi kapitalizm* (1972), 14, 22–23, 82, 95.

51. Ibid., 22–23. See also 36.

52. Ibid., 36–49 ("social maneuver," 37).

53. Ibid., 116.

54. On commonalities, see ibid., 54, 112–13, and Inozemtsev's remarks in "Obshchee sobranie Akademii Nauk SSSR, 3-6 fevralia 1970g," *Vestnik Akademii Nauk SSSR*, 4 (April 1970):101.

55. Inozemtsev, *Sovremennyi kapitalizm* (1972), 115. See also 125 ("differentiated means, methods, forms of struggle"), 109–10 ("realistic trends"), and 117–18 (all in the service of "reaction"). Economic forms of struggle were a special concern of Kosygin. See esp. *Kosygin* I, 438 (April 23, 1969).

56. Inozemtsev, *Sovremennyi kapitalizm* (1972), III. See also the acknowledgment of a sharp increase in the significance of economic forms of struggle centered on scientific-technical education and research. Ibid., 110. Similar points were made by Arbatov in Gromyko and Zhurkin, *SShA: NTR* (1974), 18–19 and 34.

57. Arbatov, *War of Ideas* (1970), 240. The words used were: the adversary would prevail "until the working-class and liberation movements in their turn 'adapt' themselves to these modifications in the policies of their class enemy. . . ."

58. Ibid., 54, 57–79, 115, 228, 230, 245. See also Arbatov in *Pravda*, May 4, 1971; *Izvestiia*, June 22, 1977; "O sovetsko-amerikanskikh otnosheniyakh" (February 1973):104–105; and in *Pravda*, July 22, 1973.

59. Arbatov, *War of Ideas* (1970), 36, 234. On politics of adaptation within the monopoly bourgeoisie, see ibid., 227, 232–34, and *Izvestiia*, June 22, 1972.

60. Arbatov, *War of Ideas* (1970), 121–22, 227, 230–31, and Arbatov in Gromyko and Zhurkin, *SShA:NTR* (1974), 9–11.

61. Arbatov, *War of Ideas* (1970), 49, 103, 121, 122, 130, 227, and on the silent majority, Arbatov "Administratsiia Niksona u serediny distantsii," *SShA*, 8 (August 1970):14.

62. Arbatov, *War of Ideas* (1970), 225–29. On dualism in the position of individual politicians, see ibid., 229.

63. Ibid., 225–26, 228–30, 247.

64. Ibid., 227. See also ibid., 225, 230, 232, 241, 254. Adaptation in U.S. foreign and military policies was thus tactical: aims remained as before, but means and methods had been altered.

65. Ibid., 227, 233–34, and G. Arbatov, " Amerikanskaia vneshyaia politika na poroge 70kh godov," *SShA*, 1 (January 1970):32.

66. Arbatov, *War of Ideas* (1970), 245, 275. See also *Pravda*, May 4, 1971 and July 22, 1972.

67. Arbatov, "O sovetsko-amerikanskikh otnosheniiakh" (February 1973):109–110; *Pravda*, July 22, 1973; and Arbatov in Gromyko and Zhurkin, *SShA:NTR* (1974), 35 and also 37 (Soviet Union and United States as "partners").

68. Arbatov, "Administratsiia Niksona" (August 1970):13, on those standing ready to make use of any favorable turn of events.

69. *Brezhnev* V, 180 (October 11, 1974). Kosygin also ventured to suggest that crisis phenomena, the GCC, and the like did not "ease humanity's task of developing international cooperation." *Kosygin* II, 319 (November 2, 1974).

70. *Brezhnev* V, 480 (February 24, 1976).

71. Michael MccGwire, *Military Objectives in Soviet Foreign Policy* (Washington: Brookings, 1987), Chs. 3 and 11. On the homeland-sparing strategy, see also John G. Hines et al., "Soviet Military Theory, 1945–2000," *Washington Quarterly*, 9 (Fall 1986):117–37 and Mary FitzGerald, "Marshal Ogarkov on the Modern Theatre Operation," *Naval War College Review*, 39 (Autumn 1986):6–25.

72. Even for the reformist, the struggle of opposed social systems would lead "to the victory of the most advanced social system, socialism, and to the subsequent reorganization of all international reality in accordance with the laws of life and the development of the new society." Arbatov, *War of Ideas* (1970), 35.

73. *Brezhnev* IV, 81 (December 21, 1972).

74. Arbatov, *Izvestiia*, September 4, 1975.

75. The following passages owe much to Griffiths, "Sources of American Conduct," which, however, depicts Soviet behavior in terms of a varying correlation among four tendencies. To simplify for the moment, I have reduced the set to two.

76. On appeasement, see A.N. Iakovlev, *Prizyv ubivat': Amerikanskie falsifikatory problemy voiny i mira* (Moscow: Politizdat, 1965), 41; V. Golikov, "Vazhnyi printsip leninskoi vneshnei politiki," *Kommunist*, 18 (December 1965):98–99; V.I. Popov, "Vneshniaia politika SSSR," *Voprosy istorii*, 10 (October 1966):244; and A. Gorokhov, "Leninist Diplomacy: Principles and Traditions," *International Affairs* (Moscow), 4 (April 1968):43–44.

77. *Suslov* I, 435 (January 26, 1966).

78. *Grishin* 210 (July 12, 1973). See also Inozemtsev, *Pravda*, June 9, 1972 and August 20, 1974.

79. *Brezhnev* IV, 26 (November 13, 1972), 150 (June 18, 1973), 157, 166 (June 21, 1973), 169, 172 (June 24, 1973), 380 (November 29, 1973); V, 80, 82 (June 14, 1974), 200 (November 24, 1974), and 291 (May 8, 1975).

80. *Brezhnev* IV, 26 (November 13, 1972), 168, 173 (June 24, 1973), 187–88 (July 10, 1973), 278 (July 26, 1973); V, 76 (June 14, 1974), 179 (October 11, 1974), 317 (June 13, 1975), 469 (February 24, 1976).

81. Reliance on Griffiths, "Sources of American Conduct," is again acknowledged.

82. Arbatov, *War of Ideas* (1970), 225; *Pravda*, May 4, 1971; "Sobytie" (August 1972):8; *Pravda*, July 24, 1973; and Arbatov in Gromyko and Zhurkin, *SShA: NTR* (1974), 18–19 and 34.

83. See for example *Brezhnev* IV, 81 (December 21, 1972).

84. *Brezhnev* III, 390 (March 30, 1971), and *Brezhnev* IV, 81 (December 21, 1972). See also Arbatov, *War of Ideas* (1970), 306–307; and "Sobytie" (August 1972), 7, on "aimless waste" in military spending.

85. *Brezhnev* II, 258 (July 8, 1968).

86. Ibid. 412 (June 7, 1969), 587 (April 12, 1970); *Brezhnev* IV, 377 (November 29, 1973); *Brezhnev* V, 84 (June 14, 1974), 94 (June 27, 1974), and 180 (October 11, 1974).

87. Griffiths, "Soviet Experience," 306–26.

88. Arbatov, *War of Ideas* (1970), 226 and *Pravda*, May 4, 1971. See also V.V. Zhurkin, *SShA i mezhdunarodno-politicheskie krizisy* (Moscow: "Nauka," 1975), 302–303.

89. *Brezhnev* II, 441 (June 7, 1969).

90. Arbatov, *War of Ideas* (1970), 275. On force of example, see 304, 313.

91. Arbatov, "O sovetsko-amerikanskikh otnosheniiakh" (February 1973):106.

92. U.S. Senate, Committee on Armed Services, Hearings June-July 1972 (Washington: U.S. Government Printing Office, 1972), 12–13. Reformative preferences were also evident in Moscow's readiness to accept Basket III or a human rights agenda in preparatory talks for a conference on security and cooperation in Europe, held late in 1972 and into 1973.

93. See for example, *Brezhnev* IV, 187 (July 10, 1973). At the same time, détente created most favorable conditions for the national liberation struggle. *Brezhnev*, II, 412 (June 7, 1969); *Brezhnev* V, 52 (April 24, 1974), and 78 (June 14, 1974).

94. Arbatov, *War of Ideas* (1970), 269 ("complete parity"), and *Izvestiia*, October 1, 1975 (no "guarantee").

95. *Brezhnev* IV, 81 (December 21, 1972) and, less directly, 227 (July 26, 1973).

96. Arbatov, *Pravda*, May 13, 1963.

97. Arbatov, *War of Ideas* (1970), 245, 275; *Pravda*, May 4, 1971 and July 22, 1973. Arbatov, it should be noted, made use of the formula of "combined" operation in the two spheres, but in a manner that gave prominence to interstate relations and was not wholly unlike "two-track" thinking in the West. *Izvestiia*, June 22, 1972, and "O sovetsko-amerikanskikh otnosheniyakh" (February 1973):112. As of September 1975, however, he urged the drawing of a "clear line" between the two spheres. *Izvestiia*, September 4, 1975.

98. *Brezhnev* IV, 197 (July 11, 1973).

99. Inozemtsev, *Uglublenie* (1976), 106–107.

100. *Brezhnev* I, 109 (April 8, 1965).

101. For example, "Tens of millions paid with their lives for the policy of 'appeasement'." *Brezhnev* I, 193 (September 14, 1965). See also ibid., 122 (April 8, 1965), 148 (May 8, 1965), 246 (October 23, 1965), 291 (March 29, 1966); and *Brezhnev* II, 247 (July 3, 1968).

102. *Brezhnev* II, 109 (November 3–4, 1967).

103. Ibid., 519 (April 13, 1970).

104. Arbatov, *War of Ideas* (1970), 57–58.

105. Ibid., 76.

106. Ibid., 46–47 citing U.S. authorities; and "O sovetsko-amerikanskikh otnosheniyakh" (February 1973):105.

107. Arbatov, *War of Ideas* (1970), 270–72; "Shag, otvechaiushchii interesam mira," *SShA*, 11 (November 1971):55–56; *Pravda*, June 22, 1972; "Sobytie" (August 1972):10; and "O sovetsko-amerikanskikh otnosheniiakh" (February 1973):109.

108. Arbatov, *War of Ideas* (1970), 59.

109. Ibid., 28, 45–46, 47–48, 104.

110. Ibid., 227, 241 on less confrontational; 224–48, 230, 235, 241 on new means and methods.

111. Ibid., 230, 232.

112. Ibid., 233.

113. Arbatov, "Administratsiia Niksona" (August 1970):13.

114. Arbatov, *War of Ideas* (1970), 41.

115. Ibid., 270, speaks of "complete isolation" of the hawks. See also *Brezhnev* II, 122 (November 4, 1967): to fight for peace was "to isolate the most militant, aggressive circles, to disrupt their anti-popular plans."

116. *Brezhnev* IV, 157 (June 21, 1973), 172 (June 24, 1973); V, 54 (April 23, 1974), and 78 (June 14, 1974).

117. Arbatov, in Gromyko and Zhurkin, *SShA: NTR* (1974), 37, cites the stabilizing effects of "mutual dependence" on a range of issues. See as well *Brezhnev* V, 186 (October 15, 1974), 200 (November 24, 1974). By 1974, Arbatov had also added environmental issues to the agenda of Soviet–U.S. cooperation. Gromyko and Zhurkin, *SShA: NTR* (1974), 39–40.

118. Arbatov, *War of Ideas* (1970), 109.

119. James W. Botkin et al., *No Limits to Learning: Bridging the Human Gap. A Report to the Club of Rome* (New York: Pergamon, 1979). This book was drawn to my attention by Academician D.M. Gvishiani in Moscow, May 1989.

120. Arbatov, *War of Ideas* (1970), 227.

121. For detail, see George W. Breslauer, *Khrushchev and Brezhnev as Leaders: Building Authority in Soviet Politics* (London: Allen and Unwin, 1982); Gelman, *Brezhnev Politburo*; Parrott, *Politics and Technology*; and also Peter Volten, *Brezhnev's Peace Program: A Study of the Soviet Domestic Political Process* (Boulder, Colo.: Westview, 1982). Needless to say, estimates provided by the KGB remain a critical unknown in all Western analyses, the present one included.

122. *Kosygin* I, 139 (November 6, 1962).

123. F.M. Burlatskii, *Literaturnaia gazeta*, September 14, 1988.

124. "A Walk in the Woods with Gromyko," *The Observer*, April 2, 1989.

125. *Kosygin* II, 370 (June 11, 1975).

126. Gelman, *Brezhnev Politburo*, 163.

127. Boris Rabbot, "Détente: The Struggle Within the Kremlin," *Washington Post Outlook*, July 10, 1977. Rabbot's account has yet to be corroborated.

128. Gelman, *Brezhnev Politburo*, 163–64.

129. *Brezhnev* V, 76–77 (June 14, 1974), 365 (June 13, 1975), and 465 (February 24, 1976).

130. Griffiths, "Sources of American Conduct." Inequality is exemplified by the relative ease with which Dragilev, as distinct from Tiul'panov, was able to make his case. The term *isolationism* signifies not so much a withdrawal from international affairs (though self-isolating behavior was inherent in the Stalinist variant), as a propensity to subordinate foreign to domestic priorities and to fashion an external setting conducive to the realization of domestic purposes above all.

131. Gorbachev reports that a review of Soviet policies had begun prior to the April 1985 Central Committee plenum. Mikhail Gorbachev, *Perestroika: New Thinking for Our Country and the World* (New York: Harper & Row, 1987), esp. 24–27. My argument is not that Gorbachev appeared with a developed plan of action, but that contemporary Soviet reformism is an outgrowth of tendencies present in the Brezhnev and Khrushchev eras.

18

Soviet Learning in the 1980s

Robert Legvold

Explaining foreign policy, any country's foreign policy, is hard going. So hard, in fact, that no one ever fully explores from whence it comes. No one does, because no general theory exists integrating the different domains in which analysts find their explanations. Instead most commentators, including the theorists among them, do the lion's share of their explaining by featuring one of two settings. Either they dwell on the imperatives and logic of behavior set by the basic structure of the prevailing international system, the actions of other states, and the absence of authority, often of hegemony, and sometimes even of hierarchy outside everyone's national borders; or they stress what flows from the nature of a particular country's political system, the tugging and hauling of politics within the country, and the special dynamic of making decisions in bureaucratic settings.[1]

Policy, however, is obviously not the creature of influences from only one of these spheres, but from both. Major thinkers in international studies have always said so, although each then ends by stressing one more than the other.[2] Choice, in this case, represents more than intellectual fancy. Implicitly, and sometimes explicitly, the analyst who concentrates on the international dimension is saying that the rolling constraints and imperatives of the external environment are primary causes of behavior, while the impact of domestic politics or bureaucratic dynamics are of secondary or derivative importance.[3] Similarly, the analyst who makes the domestic setting his or her point of departure is suggesting that the imperatives and constraints of the international setting are so twisted and transformed by the political process within states that they in fact turn out to be the indirect and secondary element in the story.

What most from both sides ignore, however, is a third force, the intrusive, even decisive effect of beliefs—the hierarchy of beliefs guiding individuals and, in a more incoherent fashion, governments. Beliefs or even belief systems are those things that all analysts know exist, yet that in most of the literature are left to stand as empty boxes marking a spot in the universe. Their dynamic, their connection with the behavior of states, remains a pious disregard. Theorists who deal with the imperatives of the international setting sometimes tip their hat to the presence of beliefs, but nearly always populate their theories with states that have none.[4] Theorists who concentrate on the internal sources of policy actually reserve a place for beliefs, usually as part of the makeup of national leaders and policy makers, their unit of analysis, but neither the nature, content, nor role of beliefs is then developed. Instead, some of the most seminal work of this genre substitutes for beliefs the related, but narrower notion of perceptions (and misperceptions), and then proceeds systematically to explore their impact on decision making.[5] Perforce, however, the happenings in people's minds become a subordinate feature of the decision-making process, something that touches policy and the behavior of states only through the overshadowing influence of the politics of deciding.

In truth, however, the imperatives and constraints of the international environment have no impact except that which the minds of people give them, and this is very much shaped by beliefs and the hierarchies they form. Similarly, while beliefs work their effect in political environments, including bureaucracies, which distort or muffle this effect, those who engage in political struggles over policy have beliefs and, for the most part, act on them.

These are stark propositions, and I am mindful of the injustice they do to the work of a number of scholars who have studied the practical results of the images in people's minds. But I venture them because they drive home the special concern of this chapter, which is not simply with the effect of psychological processes on political action, but rather, with the specific habit of people to collect and arrange explanations for broad and basic political phenomena, explanations infused with personal values (of what is good and bad, just and unjust, wise and unwise). For these broader, more enduring, generalized insights into reality I reserve the term *beliefs*. For the narrower explanations of specific events, specific actions, and specific twists of fate I apply the notion of *perceptions*. Most of the best work done on the influence of cognition on political behavior concentrates on this second category.[6]

Yet beliefs and the hierarchies they form are crucial, not merely to the interpretation of particular happenings, but to the comprehension of whole chains of phenomena, of trends, of epochs, of the health of a foreign policy, not merely of specific policies. Perceptions have to do with one's understanding of why a particular foreign leadership took a particular step, what reactions a particular measure is likely to produce in a particular opponent, how a particular crisis took its particular shape, and so on. Beliefs have to do with one's understanding of the vaguer and broader sources of a country's behavior, of the underlying dynamic of international politics within a region or in the world as a whole, or of the right strategy to follow toward another state or bloc of states month after month, year after year.

The two are obviously related, indeed, overlapping. This overlap can be handled several ways. Normally perceptions are treated as the building blocks of beliefs, the cognitive raw material from which connected attitudes and ideas are fashioned.[7] Others would blur the distinction I am drawing and fold what I have called perceptions into the low end of a belief system, treating them as, in fact, the narrowest and most concrete form of belief.[8] Whether one regards, say, Dean Acheson's assessment of the likelihood of China's entering the Korean War as a belief or the function of beliefs is not, however, crucial to the argument of this essay. I have introduced the distinction only to highlight my focus on the other end of the spectrum: on the integrated, value-laden constructs by which people (and governments) give meaning to the flow of history, weight and order threats to national security, identify the principal dynamics of international politics, and set a foreign policy agenda.

While conceivably international relations theory will continue to advance without bothering greatly with these matters, foreign policy theory will not. International relations theory cares most about the *interactions* of states and can accomplish a good deal by treating states as letters of the alphabet—nations X, Y, and Z. Foreign policy theory, in contrast, must address the behavior of states with names, and nations with names come with histories, political cultures, and belief systems.

When the whole edifice of a regime's beliefs collapses into something else, as has happened in the Soviet Union since Mikhail Gorbachev's coming to power, nearly everyone notices, and the topic becomes spectacularly interesting. But, in fact, belief systems, even when they are not changing, contribute substantially to the policies and actions of states. The advantage of the current Soviet drama is to show how much. By studying the character of the change and its direct consequences—and, no less important, the nature of the process by which the change occurs—one begins to get an idea of how powerful an intervening variable beliefs are. Thus, while the hand that the international environment deals a leadership constitutes an important primary source of behavior, in times like these, one sees just how crude and indirect its influence is. Indeed, except as filtered and shaped by beliefs and their transformation, the world outside has no particular or precise effect on a country's foreign policy. In fact, as this century enters its last decade and the international order is sent spinning by the Eastern European revolution of 1989, the question can be fairly posed: Which has the greater influence—the international setting on Soviet beliefs? Or the change in these beliefs on the international setting?

Similarly, while no doubt the heaving and hauling of domestic politics— indeed, in today's Soviet Union the sheer turmoil of politics—leaves its mark again, the story of the conceptual revolution under way in Gorbachev's Soviet Union demonstrates how empty politics is as an explanation for foreign policy behavior when left to stand alone.

THE ROLE OF BELIEFS AND THE CONCEPT OF LEARNING

This chapter is about beliefs and the systems they form, and only in a secondary and subordinate fashion about learning. Whereas the concept of learning forms the central action in most of the chapters in this book, here it is merely a tool. My stake in the concept stems from the insight that it promises into the issue of when, why, and how beliefs change—in particular why and how a whole belief system would crumble. Its use is essentially as a measuring device, a way of distinguishing quantitative from qualitative change, a means of tracking change where it matters, in the realm of beliefs.

Moreover, if this book is not merely about learning but learning *theory*, my part is still more modest. Learning theory is addressed here only in the context of the theory of when, why, and how learning occurs, not where theory has its real payoff, that is, as an explanation for behavior. The neglect is intentional and comes from a judgment I will explain later that learning causes nothing; rather it sheds light on phenomena that are the real sources of altered behavior.

Because my use of the concept of learning is limited and specialized, so is my definition of learning. It contains two elements: the movement from simple to more complex generalizations and the more effective or efficient alignment of ends and means.[9] This is closely connected with a crucial distinction introduced by Joseph Nye. There is a difference, says Nye, between simple learning—or a shift in behavior instigated by failure, in which neither basic aims nor values change—and complex learning— or an awakening to conflicts among norms and goals in complex causal situations, leading to new priorities and an adjustment of trade-offs.[10] Simple learning might also be thought of as tactical. At this level, when learning involves "the more effective or efficient alignment of ends and means," those doing the learning are presumably focused on manipulating means, that is, on redirecting resources to the same goal. Or, when thought of as the "movement from simple to more complex generalizations," simple or tactical learning implies very little movement.

Complex learning, in contrast, has more to do with the ends end of the means/ends relationship, that is, with the issue of whether a goal survives and where it survives among other goals or, at a minimum, with the task of reducing the discrepancy between goals and resources by adjusting one or the other or both—not merely with the improved use of existing resources in pursuit of unchanging ends. It also entails more progress along the path from simple to complex generalization.

In terms of the four definitions offered by Tetlock in his initial chapter, mine is a combination of the last two: on one hand, Etheredge's notion of cognitive differentiation, modified to include what Tetlock calls cognitive and evaluative complexity (explanations of reality that are complex enough to be in tension one with another). On the other hand, it also includes the notion of matching means and ends in more efficient or effective ways, normally by redefining one's goals. Because I believe the distinction between complex and tactical learning is more important than any other, the fusion is important. I find it hard to imagine and still harder to identify historical instances in which great shifts meeting Etheredge's criteria have not either been inspired by or influenced the relating of means to ends. Moreover, there seems to me to be a qualitative difference between learning as the squaring of ends and means when done by improving tactics or even strategy and when done by revising goals or values.

Mine is meant to be a neutral or nonnormative definition of learning in two senses: first, I have tried not to define learning as simply whatever I regard to be intelligent or effective shifts in behavior, and, second and more important, I do not imply by it that any and all movement toward analytical complexity is progressive, good, or desirable. Doubtless, on occasion, more involved interpretations of reality can obscure the essential and paralyze effective action. But I would mislead the reader if I did not confess to believing that most of the time increasingly sophisticated or complex understandings of reality do lead to a more effective integration of ends and means or, at least, to attempts in this direction. And for me the more effective integration of ends and means is good in the sense of being more rational. Good in the ultimate sense, of course, depends on the character of a country's goals.

Finally, to finish with this definitional prologue, my concern is not with random or independent beliefs, but with the systems they form. Nearly all students of beliefs, whether psychologists or political scientists, have noted the hierarchical character of beliefs and the different levels they inhabit, some being more elemental, others, more immediate.[11] Moreover, it is generally accepted that beliefs on different levels interact—top down and bottom up—and that out of this interaction comes change in the belief system.

Different people have conceived the levels of a belief system differently, but none quite as I do. Thus, as I see matters, a political belief system begins to make itself felt at the level of assumptions—fundamental, fairly integral, and rather closed givens, serving as the solid but unobtrusive backdrop to a whole series of less immutable arguments, beliefs, and concepts. In the case of the Soviet Union, fundamental assumptions have to do with the notion of revolution, the image of capitalism, and the understanding of imperialism. While the scribes of ideology may worry about and, on occasion, argue over their content, for most people most of the time, these are silent realities, taken for granted as they go about the business of conceiving and explaining closer and less primary facts of life. (When that changes and fundamental assumptions are called into question, something momentous is happening.)[12]

There are then the host of beliefs produced by the efforts of nearly everyone to account for more immediate, practical realities. At their most tenuous, these are no more than valuations parading as judgments. As Bertrand Russell once said, "Every man, wherever he goes, is encompassed by a cloud of comforting convictions [about himself, his family, his class, and his nation], which move with him like flies on a summer day."[13] These, for a typical Soviet, could be anything from a conviction that U.S. presidents are the captive agents of Wall Street moguls or a military-industrial complex, to the belief Stalin once expressed that "the weak get beaten." It is at this level that one of Milton Rokeach's insights has utility. A belief system, he proposes, consists not only of those things that a person believes to be true, but at the same time of "a series of subsystems" containing "all the disbeliefs, sets, expectancies, conscious and unconscious, that, to one degree or another, a person at a given time rejects as false."[14] He called this the disbelief system, and he saw it as the symbiotic partner of the other system (for example, Lutheranism-Catholicism and communism-capitalism).

Beliefs, however, become more substantial as one proceeds down through the next levels, where they begin to embody concepts. Here beliefs cease to be merely acts of faith and become intellectual constructs for fathoming things by establishing their characteristics and the relationship among these characteristics. They come in two kinds, in effect representing two different levels in a belief system: what I call, in the first and higher instance, basic concepts and, second, policy concepts. *Policy concepts* are what bear directly on policy choice, the hard, practical notions that guide action, the concepts by which arms are accumulated and used, arms controls negotiators instructed, intervention in Third World crises undertaken, and international institutions supported or undermined. *Basic concepts* are broader and deeper understandings, more abstract and more remote from action. But, by the same token, they are the level at which meaning is attached to events, trends, and circumstances. In the foreign policy realm, they are the formulas by which a confusion of parties and actions is turned into an intelligible set of challenges (to national security, to national standing and prestige, and to national welfare), by which some processes are picked out as more important than others and by which problems, countries, and parts of the world are assigned priority.

WHEN, WHY, AND HOW COMPLEX LEARNING OCCURS

States, governments, regimes consist of individuals, but they are something more (and something less) than individuals. Hence, a problem arises when intellectual constructs designed for one, like the psychologist's theory of learning, are applied to the other. Still, if governments can be said to learn, at some level the process begins with the learning done by those who make and influence policy. A first step toward understanding how governments learn is to understand how individuals learn.

Learning occurs, according to a prominent psychological theory, in one of two ways. Either the concepts or schemata by which a person constructs reality are sharpened by exposure to more and more testing instances, revealing those that fit and those that do not, thus becoming a richer and more accurate representation of reality.[15] Growth of this kind might be thought of as the movement from simple to more complex generalizations. It is what happens to the concept of a dog when one encounters more breeds than a cocker spaniel, perhaps including a cat.

Or a schema gives way under the onslaught of discordant or incongruent instances. On too many occasions the unexpected happens, the unlikely appears, the improbable triumphs. The trouble can come from either of two directions. Either the setting changes, undoing a once good schema (what twentieth-century aeronautical engineering inflicted on sixteenth-century theories of human mobility). Or the schema, being oversimplified, misconceived, or defective in some other fashion, is eventually defied by the evidence (as, for example, the notion that the earth is flat or at the center of the universe).

Governments, however, are not the sum of their parts, and processes at work within an individual's mind do not necessarily apply to them. More precisely, the dynamics of a political setting interrupt, twist, and redirect the effects of change within the individual mind. What happens to people's political belief systems matters—obviously more so the more power or influence these people have—but, for the most part, in altered and attenuated ways, as we shall see.

Not always, however, is the effect to dilute the impact of change within individual belief systems. And the exceptions represent critical dimensions of the relationship between change at the level of the individual and the way governments learn. In two respects, the intervening impact of politics produces a sharper version of what takes place in the other sphere. The rise and fall of leaders—or simply the changing of personnel—in the normal course of the political process, for one, can greatly accentuate the effect of changes in the beliefs of individuals. Replace Hoover with Roosevelt, let alone, Nicholas with Lenin or the Shah with the Ayatollah, and the consequences appear faster and more dramatically than those from any personal conversion. Moreover, it is the coming and going of people that makes it possible for governments to accomplish what no nonneurotic individual can—that is, to reverse the process and unlearn.

Politics also intensifies the unsystematic quality of the learning process. If within a single individual's belief system change proceeds chaotically, then, when shifts in some people's beliefs at one level echo—maybe causing, maybe simply paralleling—modifications of others' beliefs at a *different* level, the effect is sharper yet. But the fact is that people do have different intellectual agendas and this, combined with the fact that individual agendas evolve in only the loosest logical sequence, adds greatly to the disorderly pattern by which dominant beliefs change.

Does this last sentence and, more importantly, the concept of governmental learning mean that governments have belief systems? Provided one can live with a much vaguer version of the concept, my answer is yes. At a general level, dominant fundamental assumptions, basic concepts, and policy concepts do exist, and in a hierarchy maintaining some logical order among them. They are, in effect, mainstream thinking, and mainstream thinking is largely the creature of those who dominate the political order, leaders in the first instance. Thus, the broader political belief system is more than a vast intellectual potluck dinner, assembled from whatever the whole of the foreign policy elite bring. But it is also less intact, complete, and internally consistent than the belief system of an individual.

These last deficiencies are the product of politics. Politics complicates the issue of when and how learning occurs. Because not all people are like-minded, the change taking place in some people's minds—or the change not taking place—will sometimes diverge from or even contradict the change in others'. When this happens in a political setting, in which outlooks and preferences are in competition, on occasion intense competition, the process by which the broader belief system forms and reforms, goes forward coughing and sputtering. When whole segments of the elite, say, much of the military leadership, dissent from an evolution in beliefs or concepts, the process will be delayed and quite conceivably altered.

When key individuals in the national leadership are learning different and mutually exclusive things, the broader learning process cannot escape internal contradictions and impediments. Even the normal free-for-all among people at many different points in the system tends to blunt and slow the impact of shifting beliefs and concepts.

Several students of politics, however, have suggested that the problem is more profound—that politics shapes the learning process more drastically. One of these is John Steinbruner, who is interested in the way decisions get made in a political environment with uncertainties, that is, when the pursuit of one objective threatens another and when not merely the probability of an outcome but even the full range of possible outcomes is unknown.[16]

Often, he notes, decision makers do respond in a generally analytic way; that is, they do decide based on the likelihood of achieving an objective, which in turn is embraced with some sense of its worth (to the decision maker) when compared with the worth of another whose feasibility is affected by the pursuit of the first. In short, when making decisions, they recognize and react to trade-offs, at least to a degree. They also attempt to anticipate the likely consequences of their policies farther down the road—that is, what new circumstances or challenges may come from the pursuit of a particular objective.

When the environment changes or can be expected to change in a way affecting the outcome they seek, their calculations adjust to take account of the change. This Steinbruner calls learning by "lateral expansion," that is, by adding to the decision makers' working model previously excluded critical environmental elements. (Because it relates to the effective pursuit of an objective without tampering with the original assessment of trade-offs, this kind of learning approximates what I earlier called *tactical learning*.) But decision makers are also capable of reconfiguring their hierarchy of objectives when changes in the environment dictate, and hence of rethinking the uses to which tools have been previously put. He calls this process learning by "upward expansion" of the working model. I have called it *complex learning*.

More often, however, according to Steinbruner's theory, decision makers are not so analytical, not so driven by the desire to maximize value. Rather they are tyrannized by the desire to reduce uncertainty, and they therefore behave like servomechanisms (a thermostat is an example) or army ants, particularly when they are part of a bureaucracy. They respond mechanically to a few feedback variables (the fewer the better when variety is the enemy), producing outcomes that need no conceptualizing in advance. Outcomes are the result of applying recipes and, when an outcome deviates from an acceptable norm, the "repertory of operations" adjusts, like a cat moving closer or farther from a fire when too cold or too hot. The decision maker runs through the repertory of operations in an ordered sequence that has nothing to do with assessing likely outcomes, only with past experience.

Learning in this case "manifests itself in terms of changes in behavior rather than changes in outcome calculation."[17] It occurs when the repertory of operations fails to keep a key variable within a tolerable range and is modified until the variable is brought back within range—truly tactical learning. Standard operating procedures adjust after an air defense shoots down a wayward commercial airliner. Steinbruner calls it instrumental learning.[18]

But this cybernetic model, Steinbruner argues, works best in understanding rote behavior at the low end of bureaucracy, not at the top where policy makers cannot so easily tame complexity by following bureaucratic routine. They in fact must confront trade-offs, and do so in an environment with other powerful actors who share in the action and who have competing interests.

Enter cognitive psychology. The mind is a wondrously powerful instrument for coping with complexity, but it does so, say the psychologists, by simplifying the processing of information. Steinbruner uses their insights to argue that normal cognitive processes provide an alternative to analytic procedures and, along the way, strengthen the effects of cybernetic behavior. For like cybernetic mechanisms, the mind struggles mightily to reduce uncertainty—in its case, by imposing structure on complexity. This is, says Steinbruner, a more elaborate process that results from coping with more complicated environments.[19] For example, rather than recognize and then respond to value trade-offs, people simply obscure from themselves the need to choose, assuming that conflicting objectives are in fact separate and compatible. When the mind has done its job—employing its peculiar "inference mechanisms" to "impose structure on uncertain situations in systematic ways"—the "cybernetic decision process" takes over.

When learning occurs in a political or bureaucratic environment—because new and troublesome information arrives—it is, to use Steinbruner's adjective, constrained. "The new ideas, new inferences, new perceptions" are allowed to intrude only at "lower levels of generality," and in this way "the general structure of conceptualization remains both stable and partial even over very extended periods."[20] For real learning to take place, the rascals have to be thrown out and new people with fewer preconceived notions given a chance.

The learning in which I am most interested is the part of policy that is not autonomous of environmental events or trends. The part that transcends the learning of the cybernetic bureaucrat and the simplicity-seeking political figure. That part that represents the upsetting and resetting of beliefs, including those at the very core. Such is the essence of complex learning, for which our day's most important illustration is the foreign policy of Gorbachev's Soviet Union. The merit of Steinbruner and others, who have carried the argument still further, is to demonstrate why politics makes complex learning so difficult.[21]

COMPLEX LEARNING AND CONTEMPORARY SOVIET FOREIGN POLICY

Something remarkable is happening to Soviet foreign policy under Gorbachev. Hardly anyone in the West, including many on the political right, has failed to notice. But do thoughts about the way governments or regimes learn help us to pinpoint what is special about the change? And, even if they contain certain insights, do they get to the heart of the matter?

Whatever learning theory does for the Soviet example, the Soviet example more than repays learning theory. So rich and full are the changes under way—the sheer turmoil of the last several years—that the grist they provide the mills of creative thought has been heaped high. From it, if the workings of learning cannot be glimpsed, the concept does not have much productive use. The Soviet Union has become the easy case.

A way to begin is with Soviet perspectives on learning. Merely for the Soviet side to raise the issue constitutes something strikingly new. No one before ever allowed that Soviet policy had been anything but sophisticated, accurate, and sound. Lately, however, particularly since early 1988, Soviet speakers high and low have suggested that lessons are being learned. The range of their views creates a new angle for contemplating the kinds of learning taking place.

In performing this step in the analysis I will offer four individual profiles. The four do not exhaust the full sweep of emerging Soviet wisdom. Nor do they constitute a systematic survey of who within the society is doing the learning and with what effect in the political arena. But these four examples demonstrate vividly the kinds of lessons being featured, and they provide the basis for imagining what a comprehensive comparison might look like.

Georgi Arbatov, the most senior of the academic specialists on the United States with long-standing connections to those at the pinnacle of power, not so long ago offered an accounting of what the Soviet Union had contributed to the "second cold war," as he termed the collapse of U.S.–Soviet relations in the post-1979 period.[22] Our gravest error, he suggested was to allow the Soviet economy and society to fall into great disrepair, indeed, to "the brink of economic, social and spiritual crisis." Because the Soviet Union had failed itself, "enemies" had their hopes raised that "the slightest pressure would get rid of the very problem of co-existence."[23] Second, he wrote, we permitted the other side to "impose on us" its preferred notion of the contest, trapping us in a military competition inherently favorable to an economically stronger opponent. "We accepted too many challenges in the sphere of military rivalry and sometimes were too eager and too enthusiastic in that rivalry." And, third, the Soviet Union, by accumulating great stores of conventional arms at the center of Europe, made it easier for adversaries to persuade the Western Europeans "to think of Soviet military supremacy as the big bad wolf, the main obstacle on the road to security."[24]

Even more interesting than the content of the lessons Arbatov draws is their nature. There is a theory in psychology that people tend to locate causality in what captures their attention. Explaining their own behavior, they tend to focus on the context or situation in which they acted, rather than on their basic nature or inner impulses, for it is naturally difficult to see oneself from the outside; the mind's eye fastens more easily on surrounding effects, extenuating circumstances, and external imperatives. But when judging others, people do exactly the opposite: with their attention focused more squarely on the person, they attribute behavior to his or her character and inclinations, not to the pressures of his or her situation.[25]

There is also a theory in political science to the effect that people tend to share one of two competing notions of what makes the world go round; more precisely, what motivates another (unfriendly) power.[26] One part of the universe believes the key to understanding the actions of the (unfriendly) state resides in the way its leaders calculate another state's resolve and capability. To an unfriendly leadership looking for the slightest sign of irresolution, policies of moderation and conciliation are a provocation. Only by holding the line even when the stakes are trivial can the adversary be thwarted. The other part of the universe finds the problem, not in the nature of the adversary, but in the condition of international politics, which makes every state, in fending for itself, invariably do things threatening the security of others. The first school stresses the imperative of deterring the other side. The second worries more about the interaction produced by the preoccupation with deterring.

The political scientist's proposition bears an obvious resemblance to the psychologist's, and both converge in Arbatov's three lessons learned. If a manifestation of complex learning is a newfound ability to understand (a) what in the other side's situation, not merely its disposition, causes it to behave as it does and (b) how the interaction between states, not merely the incorrigibility of one state, adds to the effect, then Arbatov appears to be somewhere in the anterior of complex learning.[27] His disgruntled assessment of the Soviet Union's earlier priorities does reflect a measure of complex learning; he is talking about a more effective alignment of ends and means, and he does imply more complex generalizations (for example, that national security may not necessarily be best assured by piling up arms). Moreover, his acknowledgment that Soviet military policies may have played into the opponent's hands by frightening the Western Europeans reflects some movement away from deterrence thinking toward a greater sensitivity to the effects of interaction. But what unites his three lessons is the image of the enemy: an enemy—by and large the United States—whose disposition creates the problem, not the challenges to which it is responding (challenges partly of Soviet making).

Henry Trofimenko works for Arbatov. He is the former chief of the Department on U.S. Foreign Policy at the Institute for the USA and Canada. Recently he commented on the Soviet part not only in the second but also the original cold war. Measured against the criteria introduced a moment ago, he is further along than his senior colleague. At the outset of the cold war, he argues, for example, whatever the merit of the change brought to Eastern Europe ("not without U.S.S.R. military assistance"),[28] "the enormous broadening of the socialist system" frightened the United States and convinced it of Soviet expansionism.[29] The effect grew with the formation of the Sino-Soviet alliance after the October 1949 revolution, the Soviet browbeating of Iran and Turkey, the creation of the Cominform, and the purge trials in Eastern Europe. Trofimenko, in this instance, has joined those who believe in interactive or spiral theory, rather than deterrence theory.

The same can be said of his criticism of Khrushchev's ham-handed nuclear threats against the Europeans in the mid-1950s, which he says only "fanned passions and led to overreaction on both sides."[30] But to skip to a third and qualitatively different example: Trofimenko also faults Soviet leaders for assuming in the early 1970s that détente could only come about by "imposing" it on the imperialist adversary. Hence, they not only invited the consequences that spiral theory predicts, for how else could they impose their preferences other than by pursuing some kind of military leg up, whatever their avowed devotion to strategic parity. More important, they got themselves in this foolish position in the first place by assuming that the nature of the adversary allowed them no other choice. Here Trofimenko has done better than shake free of deterrence thinking; he has recognized the folly of explaining the other side's behavior as only a function of its inner character.

Arbatov phrases his analysis as if he speaks for a substantial part of the Soviet political establishment. Trofimenko, in contrast, makes no pretense of speaking for anyone but himself. Vyacheslav Dashichev, my third example, not only speaks for himself, he offers lessons that establish the outer bounds of acceptable learning.[31] Unlike Trofimenko, his analysis did provoke a rebuff from better connected figures.

He, too, deals with his country's role in the cold war and its revival in the 1980s, but he goes much further than Trofimenko. He begins with a classic statement of the way governments manage to rally others against them. Dashichev is a specialist on Eastern Europe, and, with Stalin's postwar policies in mind, he writes: every state exists within a system of states that are "in a condition of a certain political equilibrium relative to one another." When a major state or bloc of states threatens to disrupt this equilibrium by setting about to "sharply expand its sphere of influence," the others band together to restore it. Hence, he says, "any hegemonism contains the seeds of its own downfall."

Putting the blame on Soviet hegemonism, to say the least, carries the explanation to a qualitatively different level. (He speaks of hegemonism as a force proceeding under "the banner of messianism," imposing "certain ideological values, a certain way of life, and a certain social setup on other peoples and states," and he traces its source, in Stalin's case, to the "overcentralization" of his domestic political order.) The "hegemonist, great-power ambitions of Stalinism," he writes, "repeatedly jeopardized the political equilibrium" between East and West. "In the process the interests of the expansion of social revolution pushed into the background the task of preventing the threat of war."

Dashichev is not merely saying that the West saw certain things in Soviet behavior and reacted; he is saying that what they saw was correct and what they saw correctly was deeply misguided. Not the least was it misguided, because it handed the United States a means by which to advance its own hegemony within the West, and in the process stimulate a vast and dangerous arms race. Later, when détente created the possibility of escaping this cycle, he suggests, Stalin's successors perpetuated the errors of the past. Could détente's demise at the end of the 1970s have been avoided, he asks, and then answers, "unquestionably so," had it not been for the "miscalculations and incompetent approach of the Brezhnev leadership." Stupidly the Soviet Union continued to believe the "struggle for social progress" could and should be a matter of an international political and military competition with the West—rather than understanding that the Soviet Union "can and must influence world social progress exclusively via its economic, political, scientific, and cultural successes." Stupidly the Soviet Union embroiled itself politically, militarily, and diplomatically in regional conflicts, disregarding their impact on détente. Stupidly the Soviet Union wrongly assessed the "global situation" and the "correlation of forces," and, worse, then made "no serious efforts to settle fundamental political contradictions with the West."

Whatever are the limits to the learning occurring among Soviet influentials, Dashichev's lessons, without much question, are outside them. He has been attacked by conservative colleagues directly, and indirectly by the senior figure in the party's international affairs apparat.[32] Nor are the scale and shape of his argument consistent with the kinds of lessons being drawn by most commentators, including the most powerful among them. Trofimenko's analysis, in contrast, is.[33] The reason for including Dashichev among these profiles is not that his views may be influential, but that they exist at all—not that they may instruct leaders, but that they have entered the discourse.

Eduard Shevardnadze is an entirely different case. As foreign minister and the third most important Soviet foreign policy figure after Gorbachev and Alexander Yakovlev, the Politburo member in charge of foreign policy, the lessons he brings to the policy debate do matter. Shevardnadze, like the others, has also had something to say about the Soviet role in the cold war and in what followed. To the question of who bears more of the responsibility for the tensions of the last 40 years, he answers, the imperialists. Their conduct, their anti-Soviet strategies, their enmity and determination to jeopardize "Soviet power" drove the whole affair.[34] But the Soviet Union was scarcely blameless, and for him the fault is not minor.

Shevardnadze delivers two indictments. First, the Soviet Union has at times been clumsy and short-sighted in dealing with others. He speaks of the foolish habit of "slamming doors" so prevalent in the Soviet Union's diplomacy of the 1950s, a habit from which Soviet leaders had still not freed themselves as late as the struggle over the Euromissiles 1979–1983. When the Soviet Union walked out of the negotiations in November 1983, he says, it simply "accelerated and facilitated the creation of an antagonistic second strategic front."[35]

Second, and more serious, the distorted character of the Soviet system undermined the quality of Soviet foreign policy—not, as Dashichev argues, because it generated hegemonism. But because the tyranny, the cult of personality, and the dogmatism denied the Soviet Union others' trust, betrayed the country's ideals, and devalued Soviet initiative.[36] The system's deformation warped Soviet relations with other communist and workers' parties. It deceived policy makers, leading them to underestimate the "progressive world community" and to overestimate the military dimension of the struggle with imperialism. By fostering a crude, ideologically rigid image of the enemy, it doomed the Soviet Union to squander inadequate resources on a misconceived threat, damaging rather than protecting the real welfare of the society.[37]

This may not represent a total escape from stereotypical thinking about the other side, but it does reflect a vast expansion of the Soviet capacity for self-criticism and long strides across the spectrum from deterrence to spiral theory. Learning, in its more advanced forms, can be said to have penetrated the innermost circles of power. Nor are the scale and extent of this learning, in at least the case of the foreign minister, noticeably inferior to what is under way at less elevated points in the system.

If, however, the issue were to be confined to this sort of articulated learning, much of what is happening to alter the base of Soviet foreign policy would be missed. Articulated learning forms one layer of an altogether more complex and dense phenomenon. Indeed, the most substantial forms of learning are neither so readily displayed nor, one would guess, so self-conscious.

What makes the Gorbachev era such a good—indeed, almost a pure—illustration of *complex* learning is, first, the change taking place at all levels of the belief system and, second, the scale of the change taking place on any given level. Start with the transformation of *fundamental assumptions*: no matters are more at the core of the Soviet belief system than assumptions concerning capitalism, imperialism, and revolution. Although never immobile, Soviet beliefs at this level have lately veered in radically different directions.[38] In extreme cases, the revision represents a literal reversal of the original assumption.

For example, far from arguing the historic exhaustion of capitalism, Soviet commentary now stresses its basic dynamism. True, Soviet analysis long ago conceded capitalism's ability to side-step momentarily the consequences of its inherent defects, but always on the unchallenged assumption that the reckoning could not be forever avoided. Now, not only is this proposition largely ignored, but also some notable voices dare to suggest that ultimately capitalism and socialism are not all that different (unless the difference be that capitalism, at this stage, is the more successful system). After all, says Georgi Shakhnazarov, socialism was born inside capitalism, and, therefore, is of and not alien to it.[39] Moreover, capitalism has changed, has undergone "a rudimentary socialist process," has ceased to represent only the "interests and will of the economically dominant class" (but rather now addresses "the basic demands of the whole of society") and thus has "lost part of its bourgeois character."[40] Writes another commentator in praise of Shakhnazarov, "that is why the division of the world into ours and theirs is abstract philosophizing pure and simple."[41] "We are different," Shakhnazarov argues, "but not opposed"; indeed, the real contrast is only a matter of different levels of economic development and political regime.[42]

The recasting of assumptions concerning the prospects for revolution is no less spectacular. Soviet observers for years have harbored few illusions concerning the revolutionary potential of the Third World, let alone of the developed capitalist nations. But, until recently, they kept alive the abstract hope that a certain number of local power struggles would go their way—enough, in fact, to justify the ideological placard of "national liberation struggle." None would have thought to say aloud that pep talk about the advance of the "world revolutionary process" was a fraud. None would have acknowledged that contemporary history had "showed" that this "process" had crested and so, too, the advance of socialism in the Third World. But now Soviet commentators do; in fact, in precisely the words of the last sentence.[43] Why, this person asks, is the "highest wave over for both the world revolutionary process in general and the socialist orientation in particular?" Because capitalism has "rejuvenated itself" and socialism has faltered, is his answer. "Until we attain superiority over capitalism in the decisive sphere, material production," he concludes, "we cannot expect a new wave" of either. He obviously would not predict such a turnabout any time soon. Meanwhile, "we can forecast in the group of socialist-oriented countries and in the Third World as a whole growing trends toward a capitalist model of development."

And then there is the concept of imperialism—the international face of capitalism, the source (and bane) of revolution. Not that nothing had happened to update it before. Soviet writers have long acknowledged the flexibility and resourcefulness of modern imperialism. But their image was of a cunning and adaptability designed to save the same old exploitations inflicted on peoples too poor and weak to resist. The story these days is quite different. It is not the predatory nature of imperialism that gets featured, but its strength, and Soviet analysts find this strength no longer in the wiliness of imperialism's strategists, but rather in the sheer dynamism and creativity of capitalism itself. If imperialism attracts a steadily growing number of the developing countries to the capitalist system, one writes, it is because of the effective role of "government regulation in the economy, the growth in the level of material consumption for the masses of workers, the distinct expansion of their democratic rights, and the progressive social reforms over several postwar decades."[44] In addition, imperialism is aided in the "competition between the two systems," says he, by the "accumulation of troubles and contradictions in the development of socialism—by the phenomena of stagnation and crisis in its economic and political system, by the strengthening of bureaucratism and anti-democratic tendencies."

In fact, say a number of commentators, does the concept of imperialism any longer make sense, at least, as it has been understood historically?[45] Just how imperialistic is imperialism, they ask, when the developing countries' share of direct foreign investment has shrunk from 65 percent of the total on the eve of World War II, to 32 percent in 1960, to 25 percent in 1985? When the flow of resources out of the Third World to the West equals $43 billion annually and the flow into them equals $54 billion? When the place of the Third World in the West's trade has diminished from 1950 to 1987 by more than a third? When the original notions of "parasitic" and "decaying" capitalism and of "nonequivalent exchange" no longer have any basis in fact?

Lenin's ideas had a point on the eve of World War I, when nations vying for colonial spoils risked war and when a revolution required a rationalization, but now the very term was of "increasing inadequacy" in charting the phenomena to which it supposedly applied.[46] To the question Gorbachev posed in 1987, "Can the capitalist order manage without neo-colonialism?" their answer comes back a resounding yes (an answer Gorbachev probably had in mind even in posing the question).[47]

Then come the wholesale changes at the next level: the rethinking of *basic concepts*, the conscious intellectual formulations explaining the phenomena that give foreign policy its tasks. At this level, Soviet leaders and analysts are reconceiving national security and the role of military power in it (the role is to be less); the basic dynamic of international politics and the place of class struggle in it (the place is already smaller); the character of international relations among socialist countries and parties and the legitimacy of Soviet intervention (the legitimacy was going even before the Eastern European revolution of 1989); and the nature of the East-West contest and the significance of Third World revolution (the significance is discounted, maybe even dismissed).[48]

Every dimension of Soviet foreign policy is touched. These four basic concepts—on the nature of national security, the nature of international politics, the nature of socialist relations, and the nature of the East-West competition in the Third World—do not exhaust the list, but they do suggest the sweep of what is happening. In the case of each the transformation involves far more than modest tinkering. When Soviet leaders, beginning with Gorbachev himself, question previous concepts of national security, their alternative concept cuts to the core. They want to substitute for the notion that the nation is threatened most by the military power of others and the possibility of war with them the thought that economic incompetence, political deformation, and social deterioration carry a far greater danger, one, in fact, that has something to do with the distortions and preoccupations caused by the older concept. When they locate the essence of international politics in interdependence—that is, in the weave of problems and trends enmeshing all states, even the most powerful—they, in the same breath, banish to secondary importance the notion of class struggle, the virtually sacred starting point of Soviet analysis for 70-odd years. When they grope for something to take the place of "socialist internationalism," the tutelary and, at times, ruthless concept of relations among socialist states dominant since the mid-1950s, they begin to sketch a far freer, more normal, even more chaotic and conflicted alliance. When they raise the issue of the Third World in the context of East-West relations, they are not only now allowing their behavior in one sphere to be linked to the prospects of improvement in the other, but they are also questioning much of what they have thought about the chances of change within the developing countries.

If basic concepts are about phenomena setting the foreign policy agenda, *policy concepts* are the formulations guiding the way Soviet leaders go about this agenda.[49] Policy concepts are in no less flux than fundamental assumptions and basic concepts. In the defense field, Gorbachev, Shevardnadze, and a number of other spokesmen have capped off the incipient, fragmentary changes of the late-Brezhnev period by introducing whole new notions, some of which turn old concepts on their heads. Reasonable sufficiency is one such concept, which not only repudiates the legitimacy of seeking military superiority, but even the need to insist on a pristine parity. Defensive defense abjures the offensive posture and strategy hallowed by a half-century of Soviet military thinking.

Parallel to the radically different way Soviet leaders now formulate the central dynamic of international politics, they have also begun featuring the priority of multilateralism as never before, urging the strengthening of international institutions and the circumscribing of unilateral (superpower) initiative. In the world of socialism, they have introduced in place of the "general laws of socialism" essentially a laissez-faire approach, told both Yugoslav and Hungarian leaders the Brezhnev Doctrine is no more (and never should have been), and then proved it by not merely tolerating but helping to bring about the collapse of socialism in Eastern Europe. And, in the Third World where clients and friends are embroiled in local and civil wars, they now preach the primacy of "national reconciliation" over the triumph of "national liberation struggle" and of political settlements over military solutions.

If words are taken at face value, if the ideas they express are real, not ploys or deceptions, then all of this amounts to a remarkably good example of complex learning. Not only does it involve at almost every turn movement from simpler to more complex generalizations, a sharper and more accurate sense of value trade-offs, and an enhanced reconciliation of ends and means or, at least, more candor and sophistication in addressing the problem. But, in addition, it includes strong traces from the larger checklist: an evolution away from deterrence thinking toward a greater appreciation of the "security dilemma," a readiness and capacity to comprehend others, behavior less as a matter of depravity and more as a matter of circumstance. Finally, it also entails a kaleidoscopic reordering of the belief system.

But how is one to know whether words are to be taken at face value? How is one to know whether the ideas they express are real? Although this is obviously a critical determination, it is not one that I want to resolve in this essay. Because it cannot be entirely skirted, however, I offer three tests: first, whether foreign policy behavior bears out the change in ideas—that is, whether policy makers act on their seemingly altered notions. Second, whether participants in the political arena take them seriously—that is, whether they debate them or do political battle over them. And, third, whether the new beliefs or concepts emerge in a natural, spontaneous fashion or in a contrived, manipulated way—that is, whether the process of change itself is compelling or suspect.

Without arguing in the detail necessary to make the case, let me simply assert that the change under way in the Soviet Union today meets all three tests. With each passing month, it is more manifest in actual behavior. (I will come back to the evidence later, when discussing the more basic problem of the relationship between belief and behavior.) Second, at all levels of the foreign policy establishment there have been sporadic signs that some take the new ideas seriously enough to express their discontent. At times it is an old military academy type denouncing a young civilian specialist's sense of defense priorities.[50] Or at times a serving general indirectly protests the appeal of academics to recast the concept of national security in less slavishly militaristic terms. On occasion, national leaders have weighed in, as when Yegor Ligachev in summer 1988 sounded off against the abandonment of a "class approach" to international affairs.[51]

Finally, the way the change has come about also lends authenticity to it. Perhaps in a single individual a cataclysmic challenge might strike at the roots of a belief system, letting loose a cascading tumult in subordinate values and concepts. But not in a larger social setting. A national leadership's belief system—slowly formed, ramified, and cumbersome—does not change in an orderly fashion. Had the vast shift in fundamental assumptions, basic concepts, and policy concepts, described a moment ago, emerged systematically, had they been one by one reconsidered, honed, and articulated, had revised assumptions preceded basic concepts, and basic concepts, policy concepts, none of it would be believable.

Instead, chaos is convincing. And chaos has reigned in the Soviet case. Gorbachev did not, from all the evidence, begin to offer innovative approaches to national security only after thinking his way through the many other elements of a revised foreign policy. He did not introduce the theme of interdependence among nations, knowing full well that conceptual adjustments of this sort would eventually be accompanied by turbulence in fundamental assumptions concerning capitalism, imperialism, and revolution. He did not suggest new basic concepts in any area, having clearly in mind a matching set of policy concepts by which to give them life. Nowhere did any agency or force organize the review, attempt to relate change at one level or in one area to change in another, or even keep track of the remarkable surge of new ideas erupting nearly everywhere.

Gorbachev began in 1985 with a few notable but scattered notions: a new way of discussing the link between Soviet national security and the security of other states; language suggesting that the interdependence of societies counted for more than the conflict across the capitalist-socialist divide; talk of deep cuts in nuclear weapons; and reference to a "common European home." With each subsequent foreign policy speech, more ideas were added and earlier ideas elaborated, so that by the time of his address to the international forum in March 1987 they had begun to form a web.[52]

Gorbachev's intellectual odyssey is itself instructive and important to the larger process, but hardly the whole story. He and other influential figures in the leadership, like the foreign minister, Eduard Shevardnadze, and the chief of the Politburo's Foreign Affairs Commission, Alexander Yakovlev, have not so much authored a redesign of the belief system as they have started a chain reaction within the foreign policy establishment. Prominent journalists, academics, diplomats, party and foreign ministry officials, and even soldiers play off of their ideas, filling them in, pushing beyond, enlarging the terrain of discourse. Gorbachev, from early 1986, began identifying "reasonable sufficiency" as an adequate basis for defense, but without defining the term; within a year, important civilian specialists began to give it content. Not all of what they proposed appealed to parts of the Soviet military, for it implied minimum deterrence as the basis for a strategic nuclear posture and the tolerance of considerable military inferiorities in other spheres—but, to judge from the tone of later leadership speeches, their elaborations suited the likes of Shevardnadze and Gorbachev.[53] In other instances, ideas originated outside leadership circles, and then captured the attention of those at the top. Gorbachev's new theme of multilateralism and the need to strengthen international institutions, unveiled in fall 1987 and raised to prominence in his December 7, 1988, address to the United Nations, for example, seems to have come from second-tier figures in the Foreign Ministry. With a gathering momentum, ideas tumbled forth in all areas of policy and at all levels of the value system anchoring policy.

Igor Malashenko is a highly regarded young specialist on the United States, who until recently made his career in the Institute of the USA and Canada. In early 1989, he took a senior staff position in the international department of the Central Committee, the party's primary foreign policy apparat, under the direction of Valentin Falin. Malashenko, more impatient and bolder than many of his colleagues, nonetheless typifies the infusion into the policy-making hierarchy of bright, imaginative specialists eager to cast off the ideas of the past. His progression over the last three years illustrates well the nature of the process of change.

As the Brezhnev era was drawing to a close, Malashenko began to shift his interest from domestic politics in the United States to the strategic nuclear relationship between the United States and the Soviet Union. He was intrigued not so much by the technical aspects of the balance as by its psychological dimensions, and he set about to explore the roots of strategic thinking in the United States. He also had in mind the sources of his own country's approach to nuclear weapons, but in this twilight period such questions were not pursued openly. His first efforts in 1984–1985 were intelligent and responsible, but constrained, not by political censorship, but by habits of mind that made the study of nuclear issues its own justification—a self-contained topic, disembodied, separated from broader issues of foreign policy. Gradually, as he wrestled with the problem, he came to see strategic nuclear dogma as but a symptom of the way political leaders, including his own, featured the role of military power in international politics. In response, he first sought to expose the malign interaction of each side's nuclear thinking and to urge a psychological break with the "archaic stereotypes that admit of no quantitative 'lag' from the rival" for fear of the other side gaining the "illusion of superiority."[54]

But this was already the middle of 1987, and the stirrings of bolder thought had begun. Others were venturing beyond the past silences to challenge the wisdom of staking Soviet security so much on arms and, when planning for war, putting so much stress on the offensive.[55] Encouraged, Malashenko pressed on. His own concerns now extended much beyond the strategic nuclear competition. In fall 1987, he wrote a piece denouncing the whole Soviet approach to defense as wasteful, crude, and antiquated. Scheduled for publication in *New Times*, the article ran into trouble with Eastern European authorities who read some of his criticism as directed against their own earlier decisions. Eventually the article appeared in *Twentieth Century and Peace*, formerly a dull and predictable organ, but now a radical, avant garde journal of the Soviet Peace Committee and home to otherwise unprintable essays.[56]

Malashenko's thinking continued to evolve and, by early 1989, had taken on still starker and more adventurous shape. But then so, too, had his opportunities to publish. In 1988 *International Affairs*, long a hopelessly stodgy organ of the Foreign Ministry, came under the editorship of Boris Piadyshev, an aggressive, bright member of the Ministry, and immediately livelier and more provocative offerings began to appear. In January 1989, the journal carried Malashenko's essay entitled, "Non-Military Aspects of Security."[57] In it, he sets out to demonstrate that "state security," by which he means sovereignty and territorial integrity, is "not an end in itself," but a preliminary to the more important objective of "guaranteeing the security of society as a whole."[58] And to the second the first must be subordinate. Hence, for example, while a tyrannical, martial state can conceivably neutralize (external) threats to its security, such a society "can hardly be seen as living in security," because it is ruining its deeper internal sources of strength. Only a "healthy and dynamic" society, he contends, can in the end be a secure society, and that means the profoundest and most serious threats to national security are internal, not external.

If so, he says, how sad and unwise has been the Soviet failure to escape its authoritarian past, how debilitating the tendency to concentrate on enemies abroad, often imagined enemies, when everything was going to hell on the inside, how foolish to see the threat as that of aggression, when it was really that of war. In these circumstances, matters were only made worse by a poor grasp of what military power can do for you.

> While making an emphasis on the military means of building our national security, we have neglected for too long the fact that the utility of military strength is steadily waning while its actual use can turn out to be counterproductive. Moreover, our own experience has demonstrated that the buildup of the nuclear potential has not only ceased to bring political benefits but is fraught with grave repercussions and that the attempt to resort to military force to settle the problem of Afghanistan has inflicted more damage on our security than the establishment of any unfriendly regime in that country.[59]

Malashenko then goes on to make a series of dramatic arguments against the excessive militarization of Soviet society, the folly of attempting to achieve national security unilaterally, and the threat to national security created by the Soviet Union's "self-isolation" and self-invited "dehumanized" image of Soviet society. He speaks of the mistake of "pursuing a line of self-aggrandizement," of underestimating the "viability and internal unity of Western civilization," of leaving political solutions too often in the "dead zone," and of disregarding "freedom of choice" as an "inalienable right of countries and nations." "Freedom of choice" was a principle endorsed in an intriguing but formless way by Gorbachev in his December 1988 speech before the United Nations General Assembly. Malashenko is quite concrete. Had we recognized the importance of freedom of choice by others, he says, we would have realized that Afghan society after 1978 "did not accept socialist transformations." It "sought to make a choice marked by a substantial measure of historical and national identity," and, therein, the Soviet Union might have saved itself some trouble.

Again, I introduce the example of Igor Malashenko not to suggest that his ideas are the essence of the new thinking nor even that they constitute a crucial input. (They, however, are certainly in the spirit of the new thinking, and many within the foreign policy establishment would find them congenial. Nor is it utterly immaterial that he has been recruited into the party's single most important foreign policy agency.) Rather, I use him to illustrate the nature of the process: the natural growth of his ideas, the organic rather than contrived character of their development.[60] In this, he is truly representative of the overwhelming portion of the foreign policy community who might be associated with the apparent uprooting of more traditional Soviet foreign policy thinking.

WHY LEARNING IS OCCURRING IN SOVIET FOREIGN POLICY

The task of determining whether the words are real, whether the new phrasing is more than dust in our eyes is one of two important problems given short shrift here. The other is the crucial matter of why the change is occurring, assuming the change is real.[61]

At least five explanations are likely to figure in a serious answer to the question. My hypothesis is that all five form part of a larger whole, not alternative explanations—thus, ingredients in a cake, not one good and sufficient cause and four false connections. Take away any one, and almost certainly the result would be significantly different. Enough can be said about each to establish its role; enough to challenge theory's need for parsimony; enough to suggest the hazards of underdetermining phenomena of this kind. But not enough at this stage to rank-order the five factors.

The growing numbers of Western politicians and publicists who take seriously the change in foreign policy under Gorbachev almost always offer a twofold explanation: first comes the force of the Soviet Union's domestic predicament, a severe task master demanding of Soviet leaders a trimmed agenda abroad and reduced military expenditure at home. The other half of the explanation is the unique leadership of Gorbachev himself. Alas, this leaves out important parts of the explanation—in fact, the more important parts.

The first of the missing pieces is the impact of failure, not on the home front, but in past foreign policy. If beliefs about the external world and Soviet approaches to it are in flux, if learning is under way, theory tells us to look for signs that relevant schemata are either being improved or under siege. The improvement or maturing of schemata occurs when more and different illustrations invade them, and they expand to take account of the new information. This can happen to political schemata, for example, when notions of democracy are enriched by the discovery of unexpected starting and stopping points. Or it may turn out that national security is also menaced by economic and political dangers, not only by the malign intent of armed aggressors.

Failure as a cause, however, involves the other source of learning, schemata under siege. As noted earlier, there are two versions: either change in one's surroundings renders schemata outmoded, or defective schemata are finally undone by an unyielding reality. Failure ordinarily has most to do with the second version. When leaders and elites sense policy has been a failure, usually they place the blame on inept formulations. They, or more likely their predecessors or political competitors, got things wrong by misconceiving problems, priorities, or possibilities. This also means that failure counts as an impetus to learning only when the judgment is made by those capable of influencing policy. The assessment of others, including pundits abroad, does not much matter within our terms of reference.

What these people judge to be the nature of the failure is also crucial. Much rides on whether they regret a particular policy action or even a series of specific policies or whether the lament is over foreign policy in general. In the Soviet case, ever since Alexander Bovin, the prominent commentator for *Izvestiia*, first looked back unapprovingly at the decision to deploy the modern SS-20 missile, Soviet commentators and policy makers have catalogued a considerable list of past Soviet missteps. Invading Afghanistan in 1979 is one. But other candidates—Shevardnadze's, for example—also include the mishandling of the Sino-Soviet conflict, a clumsy approach to the original Mutual and Balanced Force Reduction (MBFR) negotiations, and the short-sighted, wasteful, and dangerous urge to develop chemical weapons.[62]

Were all of these criticisms narrow—confined, say, to poor technique or tactical error—the indictment would be of one kind. In the case of the SS-20, for example, had only the decision to walk out of the negotiations in fall 1983 been condemned, the unhappiness might have been thought to be limited to the ways Brezhnev's people went about their objectives, went about blocking the decision by the North Atlantic Treaty Organization (NATO) to modernize its own intermediate-range nuclear weapons. But the whole mentality behind the decision to modernize and deploy this weapon system without regard for the political consequences abroad and economic consequences at home is what has been rejected.

Had criticism of Soviet policy in Third World conflicts been confined to a poorly chosen instance or two, the issue might have remained the Brezhnev generation's inferior sense of timing. But the problem, critics argue, was with its "scholastic approach" to the Third World as a "solid 'zone of expansion for socialism'" and as "in all cases a natural ally in the struggle with imperialism," which drew the country into the quagmire of regional conflicts and "polarized" the position of the two superpowers, when the Soviet Union should have been seeking mutually acceptable ways out of these situations.[63] The problem was that the Soviet Union, as much as the United States, "considered it inevitable, tolerable, and even desirable to maintain a high level of rivalry in the Third World," treated political competition in the Third World as a "zero-sum game," and, as its economic resources dwindled and the attraction of its model grew tarnished, shifted its emphasis "to the military sphere."[64] And it did all this "without looking too closely" at the social and political character of [the] regimes" it was "wooing."

Had criticism of the prior leadership's approach to foreign economic relations been only of a muffed deal or two, again, the issue would have been a lesser level of incompetence. Instead, as two academic critics put it, "the years of stagnation seriously deformed our international economic relations" by failing to turn them into an "effective instrument for promoting the intensive development of the economy" through the exploitation of the international division of labor. They served only as a way of making up "current and chronic national economic deficits."[65] Trade policy was driven by the need of deficient bureaucracies for import bailouts, and exports became simply a means to obtain them. These, in turn, grew increasingly concentrated in oil and gas, as the share of machinery and equipment in Soviet exports declined from 23.6 percent in 1972 to 12.5 percent in 1984, placing the Soviet Union behind many developing countries in the structure of its trade.

Failure in the eyes of those now speaking up was not simply a misadventure or two, not simply defective tactics, not simply a problem here and there, but, in general, a large and important misunderstanding of the key dynamics in contemporary international politics, a miscasting of priorities, and a distorted notion of the challenges facing the Soviet Union in the outside world. To listen to the foreign minister, "serious harm" was done to Soviet policy and, therefore, "to the nation" by the excessive emphasis on the military as a means of dealing with the adversary, and, to make matters worse, by the obtuseness of Soviet leaders who did not understand that "imperialism" meant to drag the Soviet Union into an arms race threatening its "economic exhaustion."[66] Soviet behavior fed the fears of the outside world and made it easy for others to create an image of the enemy best serving their purposes. Faith in the Soviet Union's "creative peacefulness was undermined by [domestic] repressions, by statements such as 'we will bury you,' by incorrect steps against friends, and during the period of détente by preaching the erroneous and, I would say, anti-Leninist thesis of peaceful coexistence as a specific form of class struggle."

Schemata also come under siege when the world changes and they no longer ring true. Thus, changes in the international setting, when comprehended by foreign policy elites, are a second source of learning. Like the perceived failure of prior policy, they, too, frequently fall out of the stock explanation for the Gorbachev innovations. But they are substantial and difficult to miss in much of Soviet commentary.

Gorbachev, from the beginning, has insisted that Soviet policy is shifting because the pressures and imperatives of the external world have shifted. Never has he confined, indeed, never has he started his explanation with the problems at home, although he has always confessed their importance. On the contrary, more than any other contemporary national leader, Gorbachev dwells on the deep and powerful changes in the international setting. More than any other he stresses the need for a wholesale revision of traditional foreign policy approaches, because the world is different. This must take place, he makes plain, not merely in devising the tactics of policy, but in shaping its underlying concepts.

Reduced to their essentials, his ideas center on (1) the perils of nuclear weapons, but, even more basically, the inuring to the dangers of a nuclear tragedy fostered by entrenched thinking about deterrence, (2) the rise of other phenomena—such as the "internationalization of economic life," ecological dangers, and the growing gap between the world's rich and poor—to a point at which they rival long-standing preoccupations, and (3) the interweaving of societies in every domain, leaving them more than ever dependent on the actions and policies of others, yet, (4) the growing capacity and determination of even the smallest countries to resist the overt dictates of the mightiest.

His response features, first, an altered conception of "international security," a "system based on the principle that one's own security cannot be ensured at the expense of others," and one that "organically connects all the main areas of security—the military, political, economic, and humanitarian."[67] Second, he argues that power must be thought of in different terms: not as the ability to compel—the means for which are weakening—but as the ability to influence through the force of attractive example.[68] Third, he concludes that national leadership must reconceive the cost-benefit analysis of policy, incorporating extended costs, instead of deciding only on the basis of immediate need or gain and in only one dimension. (What, for example, Soviet leaders now ask, has the Sino-Soviet "confrontation" cost the "two great socialist powers" from "the economic viewpoint?") Fourth, Gorbachev has set aside the holiest of Soviet foreign policy concepts, the notion that the most elemental dynamic of international politics resides in the tension between two historic social orders—socialism and capitalism. Class struggle, he maintains, is a reality, but no longer to be seen as *the* transcendent reality. Class interests, he claims, can and should have common human interests as a common denominator. No greater conceptual leap can be imagined for a Soviet leader, at least in the realm of foreign policy, than to place interdependence ahead of class struggle among the decisive forces shaping international politics.

These broad and basic notions are the apparent culmination of a long process of intellectual adjustment occurring among Soviet foreign policy specialists. Since the early 1970s, a great many scholars, diplomats, and news analysts had been slowly introducing a series of new ideas more attuned to the world Gorbachev and his colleagues now describe. Since the early 1970s, they had been discussing the increased complexity of international politics, eroding a simple bipolar contest; the changing nature of power or, as one leading scholar wrote in 1972, "the complexity, the diversity, and the breadth of the very notion of strength"; and the shrinking role of force as well as the unwinability of war. They had commented on the "constantly growing number and diversity of actors" on the international scene, disrupting and complicating the traditional games nations play. They had begun to recognize the nonsense of thinking in terms of "a single balance of power, when several exist, and when they must be viewed in a mutual relationship." Nikolai Inozemstev, then the director of the Institute of World Economy and International Relations, had by 1978 even begun to note the emergence of a new dimension in international politics, connecting "class and social problems with problems common to all mankind," interlacing the "contradictions between the two systems with the contradictions between nature and society."[69] In short, the disintegration and reformation of schemata has been a slow, diffuse process, rooted in the efforts of Soviet foreign policy professionals to understand the changing requirements of a changing international order.

But the complex learning now taking place in Soviet foreign policy cannot be fully understood as only the retreat of Brezhnev's successors from the failures of the past and, more broadly, as the slow readjustment of Soviet thinking to obtrusive international realities. The mess within also plays a role. Here I do not have in mind the direct incentive to restraint provided by the turmoil of internal political change and the urgency of economic collapse, great as that may be. Rather, I am pointing to the subtle effect acute problems at home have on the intellectual framework applied to foreign policy—that is, to their impact on concepts, not simply on strategy and tactics. For, it is at this level that complex, as opposed to tactical, learning emerges.

Contemporary Soviet leaders, like anyone else whose economic and political problems are boring in on them, have a natural tendency to find rationalizations for why it is wise, prudent, and safe to relax the notion of threat facing them on the outside. Doubtlessly Gorbachev, Shevardnadze, and the others are influenced by the psychological need to bring their view of the world and its challenges into line with their sense of what circumstances at home allow. At a minimum, hard times induce national leaders to worry a great deal more about the efficiency of foreign policy and therefore to favor conceptual refinements pointing in this direction.

But the effects can also be more subtle and profound. Gorbachev and in particular Shevardnadze have argued the need to integrate domestic and foreign policy, to understand the intimate link between developments within the Soviet Union and in the world beyond, and to overcome the tendency of past Soviet leaders to divorce foreign policy aims from internal consequences. What the Soviet Union can hope to accomplish abroad and in turn what the world outside will permit it to accomplish at home, Gorbachev has said since 1986, cannot be separated.[70] Unless foreign policy is understood to be a function of the domestic order—its reflection, servant, and victim or beneficiary—it will risk serving false goals, fail to count its real weaknesses and strengths, and undercut its own purposes. Indeed, it is when foreign policy becomes the disembodied preserve of specialized bureaucracies that it ends up being "a source of many calamities for which the popular masses had to pay."[71]

Shevardnadze refines the point further. Soviet influence abroad, he maintains, flows not only, not even primarily, from its military might, but from its image in the eyes of others. And this is a function of "the values and ideals which the nation defends and carries out," of its "economic example," and of its "attitude toward its own citizens, respect for their rights and freedoms, and recognition of the individual's sovereignty."[72] Since "our self-respect, our well-being, and our status in the world depend largely on the attitude [of others] toward us," he has said, who the Soviet Union is matters, and who the Soviet Union is must bear some resemblance to "what is termed civilized conduct in the world community," if we "wish to be accepted in it."

These first three explanations for the learning currently under way have in common the reworking of the standards, concepts, and beliefs in the minds of those who make and influence policy. The fourth part of the explanation is of a different sort—being political rather than intellectual or psychological. The arrival of Gorbachev must also be considered a crucial aspect. Another leader would have been subject to the same internal and external pressures for change, would have had the same reasons to learn, but nothing guarantees that he would have responded quite as Gorbachev has. Other less bold, less far-reaching, less refined lessons are entirely imaginable. Although learning, indeed, complex learning was under way throughout much of the Brezhnev era in far greater measure than has generally been appreciated, it is hard to imagine someone like Brezhnev adjusting his outlook with the same speed or on the same scale.

Nor would the society, the state, the regime have reacted necessarily the same under different leadership. Gorbachev's importance to this process derives not only from the impact of his own intellectual makeup—an indisputably vital part of the story—but from the political changes he has introduced. Two in particular. First, the opening under glasnost has enormously invigorated the foreign policy dialogue in the country, and out of this has come a more searching reexamination of policy and its premises than otherwise would have occurred. Second and more important, Gorbachev's consolidation of power has been accompanied by a critical changing of the foreign policy guard. As a result, almost to a person, key positions within the foreign policy hierarchy—with the important exception of the Soviet General Staff—have gone to people open to fresh ideas, critical of the past, and capable of improving on the new directions sketched by the leadership. Had the cast of senior figures within the Foreign Ministry, the international department of the Central Committee, the advisory councils to Politburo members, the upper ranks of the media, and the most powerful institutes within the Academy of Sciences been different, the same level and pace of complex learning are unlikely.

Finally, a fifth part of the explanation arises from the process of learning itself. With individuals, it well may be that one thing leads to another, when learning is swift and intensive. That is certainly the case with the learning taking place in Gorbachev's Soviet Union. Ideas are inspired by ideas. People are sparked to thoughts they have never had by others, equally novel thoughts. The process, therefore, generates an effect. The process produces learning.

To illustrate, let me offer the discussion of Soviet national interest opened in 1988 and continued into 1989, although a dozen different examples might be supplied. The path to it was for leaders and analysts alike a twisted and unpredictable one. When Gorbachev began discussing a different approach to national security issues in 1985–1986, dropping allusions to new concepts such as "reasonable sufficiency," he sparked the immediate interest of a number of academics. These were themes familiar to them, and many had been waiting for the chance to put forward their own ideas. By fall 1987, they were busy helping to define Gorbachev's vaguely offered notions of reasonable sufficiency, strategic stability, and the like.[73]

For some, the act of elaborating more elegant, sophisticated, and re-strained defense concepts awakened a more profound and adventurous concern: What was Soviet defense all about in the first place? Vitaly Zhurkin and his young coauthors, thus, soon found themselves writing a piece reexamining the whole Soviet concept of threat, challenging the overly crude, military-based notion of threat dominating Soviet defense policy in the postwar era, and urging greater attention to the economic and social costs of misconceiving the threat in this fashion.[74] Others, like young Malashenko, who already were restlessly challenging Soviet notions of defense and, indeed, of the place of military power in Soviet foreign policy, grasped the discussion of threat and catapulted it to the more fundamental level of national interest itself. Not what is the nature of the threat facing the Soviet Union in the 1980s, but what, he asked, are at root Soviet national interests? Surely they are not, he now boldly asserted, to engage the country in mindless commitments in distant quarters, or in a reflexive jockeying for international position, or in the struggle for spheres of influence.[75] Having gone this far, he and a growing number of young intellectuals next began to sketch the outlines of an entirely different foreign policy—one, that in the name of national interest, cut expensive Third World allies adrift, embraced minimal deterrence (even without the United States), and rejected the excesses induced by pretensions to superpower status.[76]

These are ideas that Malashenko and the others were long capable of having, but almost certainly they are ideas that, in fact, were not in their minds even a year earlier. The larger process of learning triggered them.

Meanwhile, the Soviet foreign minister had also raised the issue of where Soviet national interests lay. He, too, did so fully intending to challenge old Soviet priorities. National interests, he said—and merely to introduce the concept was a striking innovation—"are a very mobile category, dynamic, and constantly changing."[77] They are, because the world in which they exist has become "integral and mutually dependent," because the interests of others cannot be disentangled from them, because "one's own security cannot be separated from universal security," because— and he went on with the dramatically different conceptualization of international politics taking shape by 1988. A year earlier, when he spoke to Foreign Ministry cadres and the extended foreign policy community, he gave no evidence of such advanced views.[78]

To be clear, I am not arguing that Shevardnadze's education was the direct work of Zhurkin, Malashenko, or any other academic. Nor am I arguing that the conceptual innovations of any particular individual cause shifts in the views of another. I have no way of knowing who influences whom in this process. But it is evident that the broader tumult of criticism, fresh thought, and conceptual invention serves as an independent source of change. Out of the accumulation come new individual insights, leaps, propositions never dared before. In this case, the process of change is a cause of further change.

BELIEFS AND BEHAVIOR

None of this matters very much, however, unless it is of some consequence—unless it transfers to behavior. Learning only counts if it makes a difference to policy. Thus, the question arises, what is the link between learning and behavior? When learning takes place in a regime or a leadership, what effect does it have on the conduct of foreign policy?

Learning, in my view, even the most elaborate forms of complex learning, causes nothing. Learning is an evaluative standard, not a theory of change. Shifts in belief lead to shifts in behavior, and learning provides a yardstick of shifting belief, not a causal explanation of this relationship. It explains neither the readiness of national leadership to do something differently nor the reasons they change their minds. Rather it measures the change taking place in their minds. Complex learning, therefore, cannot be expected to account for the striking foreign policy departures of the Gorbachev period. Nor does it constitute a theory by which to predict what Gorbachev or his successors will do in the future. Instead, it provides an essential standard for understanding the change under way, a means for distinguishing qualitative from quantitative change.

The question asked earlier, why do regimes learn, should be rephrased: When complex learning is meant, the question is, why do the beliefs of a regime change in ways that add up to learning? That, in fact, is the question provisionally answered in the preceding section. The correct parallel question, therefore, is, what kind of behavior *reflects* complex learning (not what kind of behavior is caused by complex learning)?

What kind of behavior, indeed, because the term, to have a payoff, must capture more than a modest adjustment here and there. Something whole, with a chain of consequences, ought to be involved. Let me suggest what that different "whole" might be. Behavior reflecting complex learning should have one or more of the following five qualities: first, evidence of a greater sensitivity to value trade-offs. Second, evidence that a new causal explanation has replaced an old one, and that the new explanation contains more of what Ernst Haas calls "nested problem sets," by which he means the interlinking of problems and solutions in a way capitalizing on a more comprehensive and higher order of knowledge.[79] Third, evidence that in the pursuit of a better match between ends and means, it is goals, rather than tactics, that are changing. Fourth, evidence that in setting goals the movement is from lower to higher orders of purpose, a notion introduced by Karl Deutsch, signifying the evolution from narrowly conceived ends, affecting limited domains and superficial values, to more substantial ends, affecting basic domains and fundamental values.[80] And, fifth, evidence of a greater degree of self-reflection, that is, to use Tetlock's phrase, a greater "capacity to view one's own mental processes with a degree of detachment."

By way of contrast, behavior that may reflect learning, but not complex learning, meets more modest tests. Any one of the following three would suffice: (a) a steadiness of purpose and conduct buttressed by more ramified and elaborate rationalizations; (b) a more effective or efficient integration of ends and means achieved through an adjustment of either strategy or tactics; and (c) the pursuit of new goals added without bothering to integrate or reconcile them with other goals. Ernst Haas calls this kind of behavior adaptation rather than learning. Others characterize some forms of this behavior as instrumental or tactical learning. In any event, it is qualitatively different from behavior reflecting complex learning.

Gorbachev's foreign policy surprises by its progress toward not one but nearly all five qualities contained in the harder test. Moreover, the illustrations come not in wispy, isolated, well-spaced fashion, but in increasing number, rich and to the point. For a while, the signs of change were in what I call symptomatic behavior, the kinds of actions that, when taken as a whole, suggested that something was up, that new criteria were being applied, but not on issues at the heart of policy or at the center of East-West relations. Releasing Andrei Sakharov from exile in Gorky in 1986 was one such. Paying back dues on United Nations peacekeeping operations was another. Cooperating with the International Atomic Energy Agency evaluating the Chernobyl disaster, still another. The list grew rapidly between 1985 and 1987.

Even at this level, however, from an analytical point of view the importance of these steps, at least some of them, was not in their salience to the core East-West contest or lack of it, but in the traces they offered of, say, a heightened sense of trade-offs or of a redefinition of goals, even goals reflecting the evolution from lower to higher orders of purpose. Take the release of Sakharov from Gorky. Alone the decision seemed only a tactical correction, a deft move designed to rid Soviet policy of an inconvenient irritant in relations with the West. But, when accompanied subsequently by a searching discussion of human rights and then a far more supple and responsive diplomacy on the issue, the decision took on a different light. By 1988, having elevated human rights to a legitimate place on the U.S.–Soviet agenda, met most of Washington's pre-1985 demands, and even accepted a role for the International Court of Justice in these matters exceeding anything the United States was prepared to grant, the Soviet leadership appeared to be confronting trade-offs and reordering values, not simply moving their hands and feet more dexterously. Prior Soviet leaderships had always refused to weigh the trade-off between control at home and legitimacy abroad, never mind choosing the latter. Moreover, because the Gorbachev leadership chose legitimacy abroad as part of an introspective argument over the nature of power and influence in the modern world, in which the Soviet image was now said to matter as much if not more than carefully tallied stores of arms, Soviet actions suggested new and far more refined causal explanations.

When Soviet authorities in summer 1988 permitted representatives of

Arctic ethnic groups to attend the Inuit Circumpolar Conference, a gathering of Arctic peoples from Canada, Greenland, and Alaska, it seemed a small thing. But the Inuit from the high Arctic had been meeting every three years since 1977, and never before had the Soviet Union allowed its own Inuit to join them. Thus, the concession gave greater credibility to a theme Gorbachev had been sounding since fall 1987, namely the need for stronger multilateral cooperation to protect the Arctic environment and its indigenous peoples as well as for steps to demilitarize this part of the globe.[81] Considered in the context of a broad and diverse set of proposals designed to enhance international institutions and expand their role in dealing with everything from ecological emergencies to peacekeeping in local conflicts, this small step flowed into a pattern of action bearing out the leadership's stress on the interdependence of nations and the primacy of humanity's common problems. If so, a once narrow-minded and aggressively defensive regime was making considerable strides from, in Deutsch's phrase, lower to higher orders of purpose.

Even the decision to withdraw from Afghanistan, taken in 1987 and implemented in 1988, a decision seen by many as simply a hard-headed, pragmatic step to escape a mistake and no harbinger of new departures in Soviet behavior, in fact, reflects an important element of complex learning. Leaving Afghanistan by cutting and running, even when the motive is to cauterize a "bleeding wound," represents a reshuffling of a once important order of priority.[82] More to the point, because cutting and running risked heavy short-term losses, beginning with the trauma of seeing a client regime next door hacked to death, a more than plausible prospect when the decision was taken, Gorbachev's choice signified a readiness to protect the future by sacrificing some of the present. This, too, is the mark of complex learning.

By far the most compelling reflection of complex learning in Soviet behavior, however, is occurring in the arena that has mattered most to U.S.–Soviet relations in the postwar period: the fashioning of a military posture and the concept of security that it glorifies. Having laid down a trail of new ideas in this area—ideas stressing the intertwining of one country's security with another's as well as the need not to be overly enamored of the benefits of military power—the new Soviet leadership has added to its words a remarkable set of initiatives. Starting with a reworking of the Soviet negotiating stance in the strategic nuclear arms talks in October 1985, which in one stroke conceded U.S. concerns over the vulnerability of fixed land-based missiles, the Soviet Union has crossed a number of thresholds, each more impressive than the one before. In 1986, Gorbachev's people swiftly cut through the thatch of old objections to complete a more elaborate regime of confidence building measures in Europe, with intrusive on-site verifications provisions. A year later, in rapid sequence, he and his colleagues sacrificed demand after demand, until all that was left was an intermediate-range nuclear forces (INF) agreement 90 percent on NATO's terms, an agreement taken by them and then enlarged to include short-range systems, when NATO members worried about leaving them out. The following year, in December 1988, Gorbachev announced unilateral cuts in Soviet forces over the next two years amounting to 12 percent of total manpower and 100,000 officers, together with the withdrawal of 40 percent of forward-deployed tank divisions in Eastern Europe and a larger percentage of tanks. In March 1989, the Warsaw Pact came to the new conventional forces in Europe (CFE) negotiations in Vienna with a proposal whose first phase would reduce troops and armor in the two alliances to a level 10 percent below NATO's holdings, representing a reduction in Soviet forces ranging between 6 and 10 times that of the West, and then proceeded in the first months of the negotiations to accept most of the NATO alliance's key counter-proposals.

Maybe these steps were taken with narrow, malevolent aims in mind: the INF agreement to promote the denuclearization of Europe in hopes that Western European security might be decoupled from American; the conventional arms control proposal as a way of reducing NATO strength, while the Red Army carried out internal reforms making it a "leaner and meaner" fighting force. Or maybe their inspiration was simply pragmatic, reflecting no change in Soviet goals; maybe they were driven by the sheer need to save money, and not by any reconsideration of underlying values.

The trouble for those who think in these terms, however, is that such explanations may account for one departure or two at the most, but none covers them all. And none explains the overall pattern. Moreover, even if accepted as true, they do not gainsay far-reaching changes in Soviet approach, so extensive, in fact, that values are implicitly at stake. For example, the proposed cuts in Soviet conventional forces will perforce undo the military's long-standing preferred strategy for fighting a war in Europe. More significantly, economic need may be the impulse to reductions, but the reductions carry in their train consequences for the Soviet Union's comparative military strength that earlier Soviet leaders, given their value structure, flatly rejected.

Moreover, these actions or promised actions have a consistency most easily explained by the changes Soviet leaders say they have adopted toward national security questions. If so, then these shifts reflect every one of the five qualities that I attributed to behavior symptomatic of complex learning. They manifest a sensitivity to the trade-off between economic and social stability at home and military strength abroad, a relationship that has been almost wholly suppressed in the past. They place the matter of national security in a much broader context, integrating many dimensions, including economic, political, and even psychological concerns—no longer only military concerns. This more complex nested problem set, to use Haas's term, is, indeed, serviced by a wider array of more advanced intellectual concepts, integrating knowledge from many spheres.

They deal with the problem of reconciling ends and means by altering goals rather than strategy, and strategy rather than tactics. At the level of war and its prevention, strategy, not simply tactics, is changing, as military leaders are obliged to conceive another, less advantaged, and offensive path to their objectives. At the level of threat, goals are changing, as Soviet leaders seek to address plausible dangers rather than to defeat all comers. And, at the still more fundamental level at which foreign and defense policy intersects, again, goals, not merely strategy, are changing, as the Soviet leadership substitutes a less self-sufficient notion of security, elevates universal over parochial concerns, and questions purposes whose most natural instrument remains armed force.

And, if a respect for the anxieties of others and an awareness of how one's own actions fuel them indicate greater self-reflection, then this manifestation of complex learning is also present. Gorbachev and the rest of the Soviet leadership are acting as though they mean it, when they relate national to mutual security and confess the role their country has had in stimulating the arms race.

Recognizing in contemporary Soviet behavior striking reflections of complex learning, however, still does not establish the relationship between beliefs and behavior. On that score I would offer two hypotheses: first, that the relationship is functional, rather than mechanical, meaning that each is capable of causing change in the other. Cause does not flow only from beliefs to behavior. The second hypothesis is that belief change on the scale of complex learning sets the parameters of behavioral change, but does not necessarily determine its precise content.

If a person believes John Smith to be a good and generous soul and then discovers he, in fact, is mean-spirited and self-serving, his or her behavior toward Smith is almost certain to change. But, if that person believes mankind to be good and generous, and then finds his or her assumption undone, the impact on behavior will radiate far further. Complex learning represents more of the second kind of belief change. If Soviet leaders are altering as many key assumptions, concepts, and beliefs as the evidence suggests, their behavior is bound to be influenced.

But not in a simple way. For, whatever impulse Gorbachev's inchoate notions of "reasonable sufficiency" may provide to his defense and arms control policies, steps once taken, say, the unilateral cuts announced in December 1988, feed back into Soviet thinking and push it along. Indeed, many of these initiatives have other, separate motivation. Some are presumably prompted in part by economic imperative and the need to shift resources from defense to perestroika. Others, in part, by political calculations at home. But, once set in motion, Soviet actions give ideas an immediacy and substance, vindicating them, agitating them, encouraging their further development. So, the influence flows in both directions: new ideas spark new behavior; specific innovations, perhaps rationalized on other grounds, shape and strengthen the new ideas; and the process, as conceptual and behavioral change accumulates, begins to develop a synergy, making it difficult to disentangle cause and effect.[83]

The second hypothesis concerning the relationship between beliefs and behavior, when complex learning is involved, argues that extensive changes in beliefs determine a range within which behavior is likely to adjust but not the precise ways behavior will change. The advent of nuclear weapons profoundly influenced people's thinking about war, its prevention, its conduct, and its consequences. But this conceptual upheaval has led some to argue for a nuclear-free world and others to defend nuclear deterrence, albeit in safer and more stable forms. So, too, is the complex learning occurring in Gorbachev's Soviet Union compatible with a diversity of behavior. A certain diversity, that is—because, while the recasting of a belief system may not predict particular actions, complex learning promises that behavior will conform to a unique and critical set of characteristics.

THE PERILS OF PARSIMONY

At the outset I mentioned how difficult was the task of explaining foreign policy, any country's foreign policy. The winds of change swirling through contemporary Soviet foreign policy dramatize the point. Our schemes of explanation, including our formal theories, fail conspicuously. Most are relatively silent about the wholesale uprooting of a superpower's foreign policy when neither war nor revolution has intervened.

Not that the field suffers from a poverty of theory. On the contrary, there are theories to explain the regularities in national behavior dictated by the underlying (power) structure of the international political system. Theories to explain when and why nations cooperate—even in those moments when no power is strong enough to instigate and underwrite their cooperation. When and why they go to war. And theories to explain why they find it difficult to resist offensive military postures and the consequences these bring. We have theories to explain the reasons nations form alliances. The ways they use the instruments of power, particularly economic and military. And the ways they prevent, manage, and bargain in crises. But none of these, impressive as they are, can make sense of the broad, complex passage of Soviet policy in the 1980s. Nor is any much good at tracking and then explaining the slow, cumbersome process by which national foreign policy evolves over time.

The reasons seem to me threefold: first, the most venerable and dominant theory, realism and its offshoots (wherein nearly all explanations of the outside world's impact on national behavior reside) does not much care about the whole of a nation's foreign policy. Its mission is to reveal the source of the most essential *interactions* between or among states: why, for example, they go to war—the theme of the first and most venerable realist, Thucydides. Why also they band together. And why they bargain with one another as they do, particularly in the midst of crises. Kenneth Waltz, who practices the severest version of realism, expressly distinguishes between a "theory of international politics" and "a theory about foreign policy," underscoring the first's ability to "explain only certain aspects" of the foreign policies of nations, indeed, leaving "the behavior of states and statesmen" as "indeterminate."[84]

Those who respect the austerity and discipline of Waltz's approach, with its unyielding emphasis on structure defined as the distribution of power, but who want to explain more than Waltz's theory permits, propose adding to his stark structuralism the effect of international institutions and rules as well as of the distinguishing characteristics of states in one age versus those in another.[85] They also propose subtracting from it the notion that the "search for power" always obsesses states and always in the same form. But, in the end, they, too, are searching for insight into the game of nations, not the composite of any particular state's engagement in international politics. They, too, shed light on "only certain aspects" of foreign policy, not foreign policy as an integral or comprehensive matter.

For a second reason, international relations theory fails to account for the evolution of a nation's foreign policy—and the more rigorous it is, the more it falls short. Namely, the best theory, by which is meant theory whose internal logic is least open to challenge, is also the narrowest in focus. As Waltz states the case made by many others before him, "Whatever the means of simplifying may be, the aim is to try to find the central tendency among a confusion of tendencies, to single out the propelling principle even though other principles operate, to seek the essential factors where innumerable factors are present."[86] There are, however, great hazards in doing so. Invariably something critical gets left out; invariably impossible subordinations are insisted on.

Take, for example, the impressive work of Jack Snyder, in which one finds a technically accomplished theoretical explanation for why Soviet policy in the postwar period has veered from moderation to expansionism three different times, each time provoking chastening responses from the

West and gaining the Soviet Union little.[87] As a by-product, he believes that he has discovered the essential difference under Gorbachev and why the cycle is not likely to be repeated if his reform goes forward.[88]

Snyder theorizes that the answer lies in the stages of Soviet political development: until Gorbachev, Soviet politics were marked by the lingering effects of high Stalinism—cartel-like politics among oligarchs who competed for the support of narrow constituencies, such as the military, the police, the party, and the state bureaucracy, producing four basic foreign policy orientations. Because these orientations were in conflict—some saw the West as profoundly and permanently hostile, yet favored a defensive strategy in response; others agreed but advocated an offensive strategy; still others disagreed but nonetheless believed an aggressive policy was both safe and profitable; and a fourth group disagreed and therefore was convinced aggressive Soviet actions would only be counterproductive—any leader who wanted to make it to the top of the heap had to engage in logrolling. In Khrushchev and Brezhnev's cases, Snyder contends, this was done best by defending a strategy of "offensive détente" toward the West, a posture offering a little something to all four groupings.

But the Soviet system has outgrown Stalinism, and this, to continue with Snyder's argument, allows Gorbachev to try a different strategy of power, one outflanking the cartels by pressing them from above and below, reconsolidating power in the hands of a "unitary leadership," while at the same time unleashing democratic forces from below. In the process, he frees himself from the danger of having once more to patch together support from the cartels by advocating offensive détente; indeed, the economic reform whose urgency has replaced every other imperative in Soviet politics requires that he free himself.

In the hunt for "the central tendency among a confusion of tendencies," a great deal of theory strains to enthrone a cause, rather than integrating causes and exploring the ramified nature of explanation. Indeed, the process of choosing *the* cause, while dismissing inferior competitors, is taken as a virtue.

Snyder, for example, starting from a theory of foreign policy as a function of political development, ascribes variations in external behavior essentially to the requirements of domestic politics, moreover, to the structure of the domestic political contest, not merely to the issues at stake or the people and institutions in competition. The international environment plays its role off stage, as a catalyst to the action center stage. What goes on in the minds of people, beliefs and the like, are givens, whose real effect occurs not from their direct impact on behavior, but only as a subordinate feature of the political contest.[89]

In fact, however, the best theory explains a realm by identifying all *critical* relationships and exploring all *decisive* interactions, not merely one.

This is what a general theory of foreign policy would do, if we had the intelligence to devise it. But we are not so blessed, and will not soon be. In the study of foreign policy, and for that matter of international politics, there is no Newtonian intellectual system, no theory of relativity. No Keynesian general theory. In its absence, it is a mistake to overburden lesser theories capable of shedding light on a single dynamic or on a single relationship with the claim to explain when, why, and how a country's overall foreign policy changes.

Which leads to the third reason international relations theory fails us, when the task is to account for the whole of a nation's foreign policy, not its essence, let alone, merely one or another of its parts. Lacking a general theory, analysts have at times sought to compensate for the constricted scope of particular theories by cobbling them together, on the assumption that what Robert Keohane calls a "multidimensional network of theories" will be more productive."[90] But, in fact, few such fusions are available; few have been actually constructed and tried.[91] Thus, rather than integrate the causal connections among the international environment, domestic politics, and the happenings in people's minds, most international relations theory continues to divorce them.

These, of course, are different levels of analysis. In the standard social science discussion on this score, my place is among those who believe levels of analysis can and should be linked to achieve more complete (and, if necessary, less relentlessly systematic) theories. Thus, my emphasis on the importance of understanding changing beliefs is not meant as an alternative to other explanations, but as a separate, productive dimension of a larger explanation. The nature of the international setting and the dynamic of domestic politics are also both self-evidently important parts of the picture. The trick is to bring all of them together.

If this is to be accomplished, it will be, first, by finding commensurate categories permitting influences from all three levels to be discussed simultaneously; second, by identifying complex, multicausal relationships and, among these, often interactive, rather than unidirectional, cause; and, third, by deriving conclusions from broad and intensive empirical study of foreign policy, always playing specific areas of policy in the broadest possible context.

One might imagine the following sequence or set of analytical tiers: start with the external environment. Every nation sooner or later must reckon with the constraints, possibilities, and challenges presented it by the shape of the world on the outside—the agglomerations of power facing it, the temper, agenda, and wherewithal of other key members of the international community, the sources, location, and magnitude of instability abroad, the vitality and legitimacy of prevailing international institutions and regimes, and so on. All of this heavily affects a nation's basic foreign policy orientation, the role it conceives for itself, the agenda that it sets as a result, and the way that it goes about its business.

By external environment, I do not mean the underlying structure of the international political system, thought of as a distribution of power. Instead I have in mind the infinitely complex array of players, relationships, and trends that create the reality confronting governments when they look beyond their borders. While these elements are in constant motion, only slowly do their effects accumulate to the point at which substantially new imperatives, prospects, and problems arise. Only when a sufficient number of elements in the international environment have rearranged themselves, like the turn of a kaleidoscope, must a foreign policy be reordered.

These turns of the kaleidoscope—slow or fast—determine a range of likely behavior; they do not dictate particular behavior.[92] The depreciated utility of military force as a recourse in a world whose dominant challenges are nonmilitary obliges the Soviet leadership to rethink the nature of influence and the place of military power in it. But it does not guarantee a particular reformulation. The loosening, even disintegration, of alliance systems impels the Soviet leadership to recast the East-West contest. But the recasting can be done in a variety of ways.

Beliefs might be thought of as the next level of influence, further narrowing the range of likely response. Like the external environment, beliefs also create a spectrum of possibilities, not specific effects. Because, however, they are not the creature of the external environment alone, but, as discussed earlier, are shaped by several sources, including domestic politics, they set the parameters of behavior differently—usually, by bringing them closer to actual choice or to particular outcomes.

Thus, changes in the international environment may incline the Soviet leadership to reduce the role of military power in their foreign policy, but nothing says this must be according to the norms of "reasonable sufficiency" or "defensive defense." These notions are the corollaries of rethinking the meaning and requirements of national security. But neither a new conception of national security nor a notion like reasonable sufficiency, in turn, ensures that Moscow will unilaterally muster out 500,000 troops from the Red Army, accept widely disproportionate cuts in Soviet conventional forces on the way to a NATO–Warsaw Pact agreement, or do anything else in particular. The growing interdependence among nations may well favor a less bare-fisted Soviet approach to the competition with the United States, but not necessarily a new devotion to multilateralism. This has more directly to do with the process of rethinking the centrality of "class struggle" (including the role of the "national liberation struggles"). Again, however, conceptual innovation at neither level determines which international institutions will be made candidates for strengthening or in what ways.

And then there is the third, potent, vexatious level of analysis, that of domestic politics. It, too, shapes generic rather than specific behavior. At least, it does at the high end of effect. The high end is where the various elements of the domestic setting come together—where the environment facing leaders inside national borders takes form. Everything is included, from the intensity and character of economic, social, and political problems to the state of the political institutions by which the job must be done. It can be a powerful force, indeed, as Gorbachev's deepening plight in the late 1980s reveals, an overwhelming force, short circuiting and shoving aside nearly every other influence.

In reality this internal environment and the one outside create what is really a single foreign policy environment. For analytical purposes, they can be separated and dissected, but in the real world they work their effect in tandem. Where one's influence begins and the other's ends cannot be easily established (a further reason to conceive the international setting in terms that preserve this unity).

Just as in the case of the international environment, however, the internal setting pushes and cajoles leaders in certain directions. It does not predetermine the precise direction they will go. For example, in the Gorbachev era, the frightful condition of the Soviet economy and the trauma of reform would drive any leadership toward retrenchment. But retreats come in many shapes and sizes. They can be large-spirited or mean-spirited, leading to a constructive engagement abroad or to sulking and self-preoccupation. Which version prevails depends on the broader concatenation of beliefs that comes to dominate, including beliefs about the world on the outside.

Jack Snyder and others, however, have argued that more than environmental constraints are at work. The dynamic of politics also plays a role. Foreign policy outcomes—again, understood as a range of possibilities—are affected by the nature of the political contest: by which participants, and how many of them, must be brought on board; by the autonomy and strength of the national leader's power; and by how open or closed the process of deciding is. And, to take the links among different levels of analysis a step further, James Richter has shown how in the Soviet Union the same international conditions produce different responses depending on the stage of the domestic struggle for power.[93]

Only the domestic politics level of analysis, however, can do a third thing; only it can explain the particular policies adopted by a state. Whether a country does or does not accept intrusive on-site inspection in the course of an arms control negotiation, whether it decides to pressure or drop a client in some local crisis, whether it seeks to strengthen United Nations peacekeeping agencies, or even whether it chooses a flexible and forgiving strategy toward allies over an imperious, demanding one are matters resolved by domestic politics, not by underlying changes in the international environment or in the belief system. These other influences are crucial in orienting choice, but not in defining its fine grain. The fine grain emerges from the pulling and tugging of domestic and bureaucratic politics, and doubtlessly as well from the cognitive devices, short-cuts, and protections at work within each policy maker.

Those who care about understanding the behavior of particular countries, who want this effort to be more systematic without neglecting deep-flowing cultural, historical, and ideological features, and who believe that theorists of international relations have something to teach them (and something to learn from them) are thus left with a stiff challenge. Since explanations at no single level of analysis—indeed, at no two levels of analysis—will suffice, ways must be found of doing justice to influences at all three levels.

The point of this essay has been to argue that there are, indeed, three levels of analysis. Beliefs and the systems they form are an important, independent part of the story. Leave them out and critical links in the explanation are broken, other levels of analysis become weakened abstractions, become car engines without crankshafts. Understanding where beliefs come from and when, how, and why they change, therefore, matters to theorists at whatever level they seek to explain. And understanding where beliefs come from and when, how, and why they change requires formidable tools, which is where the notion of learning has a contribution to make.

NOTES

1. Beyond the two excellent editors of this volume, I want to thank a gifted group of friends and critics for reading my essay and doing what they could to improve it: Alexander George, Stanley Hoffmann, Robert Jervis, Robert Keohane, Joseph Nye, and Jack Snyder.

2. The most notable exception is Glenn H. Snyder and Paul Diesing, *Conflict Among Nations* (Princeton, N.J.: Princeton University Press, 1977), a book in which the authors not only deal with both dimensions evenhandedly, but then attempt a synthesis. Their synthesis, however, explains a particular behavior (namely, crisis behavior) rather than the whole complex of behavior that is foreign policy.

3. This is true even of those who embrace a modified version of "neorealism" but stress the need to include domestic politics as an explanation for things unexplained by the dictates of the international political system. The most sophisticated recent example is Robert O. Keohane, *After Hegemony* (Princeton, N.J.: Princeton University Press, 1984).

4. Stanley Hoffmann, in books like *Gulliver's Troubles* (New York: McGraw-Hill, 1965) and *Primacy or World Order* (New York: McGraw-Hill, 1978), stands apart.

5. The most important example is Robert Jervis's work, *Perception and Misperception in International Relations* (Princeton, N.J.: Princeton University Press, 1976).

6. Not all, by any means, and I have profited from the pioneering work of Ole R. Holsti and James N. Rosenau—both their "Vietnam, Consensus, and the Belief Systems of American Leaders," *World Politics* (October 1979): 1–56 and "America's Foreign Policy Agenda: The Post-Vietnam Beliefs of American Leaders," in Charles W. Kegley and Patrick J. McGowan, eds., *Challenges to America: U.S. Foreign Policy in the 1980s* (Beverly Hills, Calif.: Sage International Yearbook of Foreign Policy Studies, IV, 1979), 231–68.

7. In the political realm, see the work of Walter Carlsnaes, in particular, *Ideology and Foreign Policy: Problems of Comparative Conceptualization* (New York: Blackwell, 1987). Also Philip E. Converse, "The Nature of Belief Systems in Mass Publics," in David Apter, ed., *Ideology and Discontent* (New York: Free Press of Glencoe, 1964).

8. Robert Jervis, *Perception and Misperception*, is a good illustration.

9. I have taken this definition from Lloyd Etheredge, *Can Governments Learn?* (New York: Pergamon Press, 1985), 143, where the first element is stressed, and from Ernst Haas, "Why Collaborate? Issue-Linkage and International Regimes," *World Politics* (April 1980); 390, where both elements appear. Etheredge's definition, as Tetlock indicates in Chapter 1, is, in fact, somewhat more elaborate. Learning, he says, is a matter of increased (a) cognitive differentiation, (b) integration of thought, and (c) capacity for self-reflection, terms that Tetlock explains.

10. Joseph S. Nye, Jr., "Nuclear Learning and U.S.–Soviet Security Regimes," *International Organization*, 41 (3:Summer 1987): 371–402. He invents the labels, but the idea itself he borrows from Chris Argyris and Donald Schon, *Organizational Learning: A Theory of Action Perspective* (Reading, Mass.: Addison-Wesley, 1978).

11. Among the psychologists, see Milton Rokeach, *The Open and Closed Mind* (New York: Basic Books, 1960), in particular, pp. 31–53. The most important illustration among political scientists is Alexander George's, "The 'Operational Code': A Neglected Approach to the Study of Political Leaders and Decision-Making," *International Studies Quarterly* (June 1969).

12. Robert Jervis notes that my discussion of this level of belief reminds him of James Joll's analysis of "hidden assumptions," operating in 1914. See Joll's "The 1914 Debate Continues," *Past and Present*, 34 (July 1966).

13. From his *Sceptical Essays*, (George Allen & Unwin, 1948).

14. Milton Rokeach, *Open and Closed Mind*, 33.

15. This and the rest draws on Jennifer Crocker, Susan T. Fiske, and Shelley E. Taylor, "Schematic Bases of Belief Change," in J. Richard Eiser, ed., *Attitudinal Judgment* (New York: Springer-Verlag, 1984), 203–205.

16. John D. Steinbruner, *The Cybernetic Theory of Decision: New Dimensions of Political Analysis* (Princeton, N.J.: Princeton University Press, 1974).

17. Ibid., 78.

18. This cybernetic form of learning also resembles what passes for learning in the theory of so-called (structural) realists, those like Kenneth Waltz, who see national leaderships adapting reflexively to the structure of power in the international system in order to survive. Tetlock calls it *stimulus-response covariation*.

19. Ibid., 112.

20. Ibid., 137.

21. The related, although more extreme argument, which I have spared the

reader, has it that political leaders act not primarily in response to beliefs or perceptions of reality, but in response to what the nature of political competition requires of them in order to prevail. See Ernest May, *Imperial Democracy* (New York: Harcourt, Brace, 1961) and, more recently, Richard Anderson, "Competitive Politics and Soviet Global Policy: Authority Building and Bargaining in the Politburo, 1964–1972," Ph.D. dissertation, University of California at Berkeley, 1989.

22. George A. Arbatov, "Such Different Meetings: Soviet-American Relations and the Four Summit Meetings," in Abel Agenbegyan, ed., *Perestroika* (New York: Charles Scribner's Sons, 1988), 217–33.

23. Ibid., 219.

24. Ibid., 231.

25. For a good summary of this school of thought, called attribution theory, see Deborah Welch Larson, *Origins of Containment* (Princeton, N.J.: Princeton University Press, 1985), 34–42. Larson, a political scientist, makes interesting use of this theory and several others to analyze the Truman administration's changing attitude toward the Soviet Union in the immediate postwar period.

26. Robert Jervis has analyzed it best in *Perception and Misperception*, 58–113.

27. While my readiness to associate learning with the evolution from "dispositional" to "situational" explanations of the other side's behavior may not be particularly contentious, the same cannot be said of my parallel proposition concerning the movement from deterrence to interactive or "spiral" theory. My point, however, is not that deterrence theory is always wrong (anymore than dispositional explanations are always inapt); rather that deterrence theory as a general way of thinking is likely to be less compatible with complex generalizations.

28. Genrikh Trofimenko, "Towards a New Quality of Soviet-American Relations," *International Affairs*, 12 (December 1988): 13–25.

29. Ibid., 14.

30. Ibid., 17.

31. Vyacheslav Dashichev, *Literaturnaya gazeta* (May 18, 1988):14.

32. See Lev Bezymensky and Valentin Falin, *Pravda* (August 29, 1988): 6. One should not, they wrote, yield to the "temptation to seek the truth 'somewhere in the middle' and to metaphysically divide in two the blame for all prewar and postwar complexities, tribulations and tragedies, let alone to load these sins on Stalin and Stalinism just for the sake of 'breaking' with the past." (Falin, in November 1988, became the new chief of the Central Committee's international department.)

33. This discussion begs the question whether Dashichev, Trofimenko, and Arbatov have in fact been learning. If these views have been theirs all along, and only now in the era of glasnost have they dared to express them, this would not represent learning. For what it is worth, knowing Arbatov and Trofimenko, I believe they are reaching what for them are new conclusions. Not knowing Dashichev, I cannot say. But the equally important point is that they all are introducing perspectives that represent learning for the foreign policy community at large.

34. This is in his address to a conference of scholars and practitioners in the Ministry of Foreign Affairs, July 25, 1988. It is the single most elaborate and substantial foreign policy speech given by the foreign minister. See "Nauchno-

prakticheskaya konferentsiya MID SSSR, 'XIX vsesoyuznaya konferentsiya KPSS: vneshnyaya politika i diplomatiya,'" *Vestnik Ministerstva inostrannykh del*, 12 (August 15, 1988):27–46.

35. Ibid., 33.

36. Ibid., 31, 32.

37. Ibid., 32.

38. To be absolutely accurate, *articulated* beliefs have changed. Whether, in fact, these beliefs had shifted earlier, but remained "unpublished," I do not yet know.

39. G. Shakhnazarov, "Vostok—Zapad: K voprosy o deideologizatsii mezhgosudarstvennykh otnoshenii," *Kommunist*, 3 (February 1989): 70. Shakhnazarov, an official of the CPSU Central Committee, happens to be an adviser within Gorbachev's personal entourage.

40. Ibid., 72–73.

41. Vladimir Kulistikov, "The Last Dispatch from the Ideological Front," *New Times*, 11 (March 4–20, 1989): 15.

42. Georgi Shakhnazarov, "Vostok—Zapad," 77.

43. See Kim Tsagolov's contribution to a symposium reported in *International Affairs*, 12 (December 1988): 146. The symposium was a gathering of journalists, academics, and senior officials from the foreign ministry. Tsagolov, a military officer, is a senior faculty member at the Voroshilov Military Academy. He was among the prominent Soviet voices in the last critical phases of the Afghanistan war, one of the few military people with expertise in the region.

44. G. Diligenskii, "Revolyutsionnaya teorii i sovremennost," *MEMO*, 3 (March 1988): 17–18. Diligenskii is the new and innovative editor of *MEMO*, the Soviet Union's most important academic international affairs journal.

45. See, P. Khvoinik, "Imperializm: termin i soderzhanie," *MEMO*, 1 (January 1990): 5–19; and the two-part discussion, "Sovremennyi kapitalizm i razvivayushchii mir: kharakter i perspektivy vzaimotnosheniya," *Narody Azii i Afriki*, 5 and 6 (May and June 1988): 123–41 and 68–89, in particular, the comments of V. Sheinis in Part 1., p. 126–29.

46. P. Khvoinik, "Imperializm," 16–17.

47. Ibid., 13. The question is asked in his November 2, 1987 speech on the anniversary of the revolution.

48. I will not here develop or illustrate the change under way in any detail, because I want to avoid repeating what I have written elsewhere: first, in "The Revolution in Soviet Foreign Policy," *Foreign Affairs* (America and the World 1988–89): 82–98; and, second, in a forthcoming book, *The Soviet Union and the Other Superpower*.

49. They are not the same as strategy, which in effect is a game plan, a notion of how one gets from A to B, the technical mobilization of means to achieve ends. Strategies may reflect beliefs, but they are not beliefs. Policy concepts are beliefs about the proper relationship of means to ends.

50. See, for example, Vladimir Serebryannikov's attack on Alexei Arbatov in "More on the Defense Doctrine Dilemma," *New Times*, 12 (March 21–27, 1989): 17. Lieutenant-General Serebryannikov is the deputy chief of the V.I. Lenin Military-Political Academy. Other illustrations include Yu. Lyubimov, "O dostatochnosti

oborony i nedostatki kompetentnosti," *Kommunist vooruzhennii sil*, 16 (August 1989): 21–26, and Y. Volkov, "Ne razyacnyaet, a zatumanivaet," *Krasnaia zvezda* (September 28, 1989): 3.

51. See his speech in Gorky, *Pravda* (August 6, 1988): 2.

52. A close textual analysis of the speeches of Gorbachev and other prominent foreign policy figures given between 1984 and 1988, done by a group of scholars at Berkeley, bears out this general point. Measured against a standard of "integrative complexity"—by which they mean the degree of nuanced or differentiated causal explanation and the perception of "conceptual connections among differentiated idea-elements"—Gorbachev's ideas, as those of the others, have moved steadily in the direction of increased integrative complexity. (See Philip E. Tetlock, Shari Cohen, and Russell Faeges, "Growing Integrative Complexity of Soviet Views of the International Environment: The Impact of 'New Thinking,'" paper presented to the annual meeting of the American Association for the Advancement of Slavic Studies, Honolulu, November 1988.)

53. For a more detailed account of their ideas and the politics surrounding them, see Raymond Garthoff, "New Thinking in Soviet Military Doctrine," *Washington Quarterly*, 3 (1988): 131–58; Stephen M. Meyer, "The Sources and Prospects of Gorbachev's New Political Thinking on Security," *International Security*, 2 (Fall 1988): 124–63; David Holloway, "Gorbachev's New Thinking," *Foreign Affairs* (America and the World 1988–89): 66–81, and Stephen Shenfield, "Minimum Nuclear Deterrence: The Debate Among Soviet Civilian Analysts," Center for Foreign Policy Development, Brown University, November 1989.

54. I. Malashenko, "Reasonable Sufficiency and Illusory Superiority," *New Times*, 24 (June 22, 1987): 20.

55. A.G. Arbatov, A.A. Vasilev, and A.A. Kokoshin, "Yadernoe oruzhie i strategicheskaya stabilnost," *SShA*, 9 (September 1987): 3–13 and 10 (October 1987): 17–24; V.V. Zhurkin, S.A. Karaganov, and A.V. Kortunov, "O razumnoi dostatochnosti," *SShA*, 12 (December 1987): 11–21; and A. Kokoshin and V. Larionov, "Kurskaya bitva v svete sovremennoi oboronitelnoi doktriny," *MEMO*, 8 (August 1987): 32–40.

56. See I. Malashenko, "Bezopasnost i zatratnyi podkhod," *Vek XX i Mir*, 5 (May 1988): 23–27.

57. Igor Malashenko, "Non-Military Aspects of Security," *International Affairs*, 1 (January 1989): 40–51.

58. Ibid., 41.

59. Ibid., 42.

60. Were his writings not convincing enough, the many American specialists who know him personally would, I think, agree with this assessment.

61. Neither, however, is as key to the question addressed in this chapter: the nature of learning and its relationship to behavior. One cannot get far with other issues, however—for example, the matter of the durability of the change—without facing them.

62. July 25, 1988, speech to Ministry of Foreign Affairs in *Vestnik* (August 12, 1988): 37–38.

63. L. Lyubimov, "Novoe myshlenie i sovetsko-amerikanskie otnosheniya," *MEMO*, 3 (March 1988): 9. Lyubimov is the head of the American studies department in the Institute of World Economy and International Relations.

64. Andrei Kozyrev and Andrei Shumikhin, "East and West in the Third World," *International Affairs*, 3 (March 1989): 68–69. Kozyrev is deputy chief of the international organization department in the Foreign Ministry; Shumikhin is head of the Middle East sector in the foreign policy department of the Institute of the USA and Canada.

65. V. Spandaryan and N. Shmelev, "Problemy povysheniya effektivnosti vneshneekonomicheskikh svyazei SSSR," *MEMO*, 8 (August 1988): 10. Spandaryan was, at the time, an acting deputy director of the Institute of the USA and Canada, and Shmelev, a well-known economist at the institute.

66. Speech to MFA, *Vestnik* (July 25, 1988): 32.

67. Speech to the International Forum for a "Nuclear-Free World, for the Survival of Humanity," *Pravda* (February 17, 1987): 1–2.

68. As his foreign minister put it: "Postwar experience has begun to correct substantially the notion of the capabilities of force. Even when superior, force most often does not yield the aggressor's planned result, and sometimes boomerangs against his own positions." (MFA speech July 25, 1988, *Vestnik*, 35.)

69. This and the other quotations are drawn from Chapter 4 of my *The Soviet Union and the Other Superpower: Soviet Policy Toward the United States, 1969–1989.*

70. This has been a theme of his since the twenty-seventh party congress in February 1986, but he first developed it at length in a speech within the Foreign Ministry May 23, 1986. (For a synopsis, see "Vremya Perestroiki," *Vestnik: Ministerstva inostrannykh del SSSR*, 1 [August 5, 1987]: 4.)

71. Gorbachev's speech in Yugoslavia, March 16, 1988, in *Pravda* (March 17, 1988): 1, 2.

72. Speech to MFA, *Vestnik*, (July 25, 1988): 39.

73. See footnote 55.

74. Vitaly Zhurkin, Sergei Karaganov, and Andrei Kortunov, "Vyzovy bezopasnosti—starye i novye," *Kommunist*, 1 (January 1988): 42–50.

75. Igor Malashenko, "Ideals and Interests," *New Times*, 45 (November, 1988): 26–28.

76. I. Malashenko, "Interesy strany: mnimye i realnye," *Kommunist*, 13 (September 1989): 114–23; Radomir Bogdanov and Andrei Kortunov, "'Minimum Deterrent': Utopia or a Real Prospect," *Moscow News*, 23 (June 11–18, 1989): 6.

77. MFA Speech, *Vestnik* (July 25, 1988): 34.

78. "Doklad E.A. Shevardnadze na soveshchanii v MID SSSR, 3 maya 1987 g.," *Vestnik Ministerstva inostrannykh del SSSR*, 1 (August 5, 1987): 17–22.

79. Ernst B. Haas, "Collective Learning," from his *When Knowledge Is Power* (Berkeley: University of California Press, 1990), 84.

80. Ibid.

81. See his speech in Murmansk, October 1, in *Pravda* (October 2, 1987): 1–3.

82. "Bleeding wound" is, of course, the phrase used by Gorbachev to describe the Afghan intervention at the twenty-seventh party congress in February 1986.

83. My guess is that this process occurs in every state's foreign policy, only in most instances more slowly than in the current Soviet case. In part, because most foreign policy studies focus on either a specific dimension of policy—say, toward a region of the world or a particular problem—or deal with a relatively limited period of time, they fail to detect the complex learning taking place over an era and across the whole of policy. What, in the narrower context, appears as ration-

alization after the fact or—to use the concepts of this book, increased cognitive, but not evaluative, complexity when judged from greater remove—is likely to be part of this functional relationship between changing belief and behavior. The fair test would be to compare, for example, U.S. foreign policy in the 1980s with U.S. policy in the late 1940s to early 1950s by measuring the degree to which the five qualities I have attributed to behavior reflecting complex learning are more present.

I would be surprised if, in most instances, the attributes of complex learning do not become increasingly prominent. This suspicion rests on the assumption that, over time, all nonpathological regimes gradually, progressively, come to understand the logic and imperatives of a given international order. In short, over time all governments, although not necessarily all leaderships, learn. The international order that we have had since the end of World War II has taken time to comprehend, not the least because, like other historic international orders, it does not stand still.

84. Kenneth Waltz, *Theory of International Politics* (Reading, Mass.: Addison-Wesley, 1979), 72 and 68.

85. See the essays by Robert Keohane and John Ruggie in Robert O. Keohane, ed., *Neorealism and Its Critics* (New York: Columbia University Press, 1986).

86. Kenneth Waltz, *Theory of International Politics*, 10.

87. The three instances are Stalin's aggressive policies in the late 1940s, Khrushchev's militancy over Berlin in the late 1950s, and Brezhnev's adventures in the Third World in the mid and late 1970s. (See Chapter 6 "The Soviet Union," in Snyder's book in preparation, *Myths of Empire*.)

88. This part of the argument is developed more fully in Jack Snyder, "The Gorbachev Revolution: A Waning of Soviet Expansionism?" *International Security*, (Winter 1987–1988): 93–131.

89. Another student who has taken Snyder's kind of theory to an extreme, Richard Anderson, refuses even a role for the external environment and beliefs. (See his dissertation, cited in note 21.)

90. He proposes modifying Kenneth Waltz's strict structural realism by adding the variations among issue areas, information levels, and international institutions, and then combining this enhanced systemic theory with the "rich interpretations. . . of the historically oriented students of domestic structure and foreign policy." (See Robert Keohane, *Neorealism and Its Critics*, 196–97.)

91. Exceptions, however, include the well-argued work of Kenneth Waltz's own students. Barry Posen, for example, in *The Sources of Military Doctrine* (Ithaca, N.Y.: Cornell University Press, 1984), combines two levels of analysis (systems theory and organizational theory) to explain the origins of offensive and defensive national military postures.

92. My notion of the international environment is broader than even the loosest categories used by systems theorists, but most of them, including the "structuralists," would conceive the effect of the international system in the same terms.

93. James Richter, "Action and Reaction in Soviet Foreign Policy: How Leadership Politics Affect Soviet Responses to the International Environment," Ph.D. dissertation, University of California at Berkeley, 1988.

PART IV

Conclusions

19

Learning and the Evolution of Cooperation in U.S. and Soviet Nuclear Nonproliferation Activities

Peter R. Lavoy

The United States and the Soviet Union have long feared the spread of nuclear weapons to other countries, but over time they have interpreted the problem differently and employed various means to curb nuclear proliferation. In all, each superpower has altered its basic nonproliferation strategy five times. With these changes has come a growing, mutual appreciation of the limits of superpower influence and thus of the need to cooperate for nuclear nonproliferation. Initially viewing the transfer of nuclear technology as a competitive matter, Washington and Moscow gradually turned what were once parallel but rival nonproliferation practices into efforts that now converge on enhancing the global nuclear nonproliferation regime. Even in an era that sees the superpowers cooperating to solve an expanding range of problems, they concur on ends and coordinate means in this area as in few others.

Driving this chapter is an assumption that the evolution of cooperation and specific strategic changes in nonproliferation ensue from the way in which Americans and Soviets draw on past experience in response to new conditions and events. The study thus focuses on how the superpowers *learn*. Learning is a concept rooted at once in the decision-making research tradition—which describes how choices are made, how efficient these choices are, and how they might be improved—and in social change research traditions—which examine the rise of new norms and behavior patterns among states and other social groups.

This volume's contributors generally regard learning as a concept that offers potentially rich insight into the processes by which states interpret their experiences, reconsider their policies, and adapt their behavior to a complex and ever-changing world. But consensus is lacking on precisely what learning means. In the volume's introductory chapter, Phil Tetlock discusses five useful conceptions of learning, three of which are examined here, but in a form more closely resembling the trio of choice patterns John Steinbruner identified years ago in *The Cybernetic Theory of Decision*.[1] In a historical survey of nonproliferation activity, I classify each U.S. and Soviet strategic shift as an outcome of *causal, instrumental,* or *constrained* learning, types that Steinbruner linked to analytic, cybernetic, and cognitive decision styles.

The four objectives of this chapter are (1) to elaborate and expand on Steinbruner's original learning types; (2) to assess the analytic utility of these three types concerning the complex problem of change in nonproliferation activity; (3) to explain the five respective shifts in superpower strategies to slow the spread of nuclear arms; and (4) to reveal the sources of U.S.–U.S.S.R. and global collaboration against nuclear proliferation. I suggest that, while superpower cooperation and strategic change in nonproliferation usually follow instrumental or constrained learning, states must learn causally in order to establish a universal nonproliferation consensus and the coordination that is needed to effectively inhibit the further diffusion of nuclear weapons.

LEARNING IN A COMPLEX AND UNCERTAIN WORLD

Organizations and the people in them learn from their experience. They act, observe the consequences of their action, make inferences about those consequences, and draw implications for future action. The process is adaptively rational. If the information is accurate, the goals clear and unchanging, the inferences correct, the behavior modification appropriate, and the environment stable, the process will result in improvement over time.[2]

If this scenario usually held in global politics, there would be no need for this chapter or this book. Learning would induce better policies and perhaps a better world. Real conditions, however, do not abet state learning. National leaders often are unsure about what events occur (*information paucity*), why they occur (*causal uncertainty*), and whether they are good or bad (*value complexity*). The environment of those who make foreign policy seldom yields clear or complete feedback from events. The information that officials obtain often does not permit them to grasp complex cause-and-effect linkages. And to compound their difficulties, policy makers must evaluate competing political assumptions and preferences and make unpleasant trade-offs among them.[3]

Nuclear proliferation is an area in which uncertainties and complexities abound. Soviets and Americans occasionally obtain ample evidence about some aspects of the problem, such as the technological requirements for "going nuclear,"[4] the weapons potential of near-nuclear states,[5] the likely delivery vehicles of first-generation nuclear devices, and the destructive capacity of the arms themselves. But these "learner-friendly" attributes contrast with more cases of incomplete or unclear information. The superpowers must contend with ambiguous evidence about the propensity of nonnuclear states to go nuclear, about their strategies to obtain weapon-grade fissile material, and about their capacity to use nuclear arms during political or military crises.

Like information paucity, causal uncertainty limits the ability of state leaders to draw clear and accurate lessons from the past. Three examples show this point. First, although superpower opposition to the spread of nuclear arms stems largely from the judgment that proliferation is dangerous and destabilizing, the evidence available also allows one to believe that the bomb's presence reduces the likelihood of war by inducing caution among regional rivals.[6] As Joseph Nye writes, the relationship between nuclear arms and war is uncertain:

> . . . much of what passes for nuclear knowledge rests upon elaborate counterfactual argument, abstractions based on assumptions about rational actors, assumptions about the other nation's unknown intentions, and simple intuitions. The ambiguous structure of nuclear knowledge makes it difficult for new information to alter prior beliefs.[7]

Because of unclear evidence about nuclear proliferation's strategic outcomes, beliefs in this area tend to be *theory-driven* rather than *data-driven*: leaders considering the matter must base choices and actions on preconceptions rather than on insights drawn from the "objective" evidence.[8] After all, only the occurrence of nuclear war between nuclear-armed states can "confirm" a theory about proliferation's deleterious strategic consequences.[9]

Second, the impact of the superpowers' own possession of nuclear weapons on the desire of other states to go nuclear is highly ambiguous. On one hand, U.S. strategic forces provide a nuclear umbrella over Washington's nonnuclear allies, reducing their insecurity and thus their incentive to acquire independent nuclear forces. On the other hand, states not protected by U.S. or Soviet nuclear arms may feel less secure because of the threat posed by those weapons; insecurity makes these states likely candidates to seek the bomb.

Third, uncertainty colors the connection between the conventional arms transfers of a superpower and the prospect that a recipient (or its rivals) will go nuclear. Like the process discussed above, military aid can make a state feel more secure by providing it with an ability to defend itself and by reinforcing its confidence in the supplier country's support. However, arms transfers abet the recipient's nuclear effort if they provide a new means to deliver nuclear arms, and security assistance to one country may heighten the insecurity of its neighbors, thus whetting their appetite for bombs. In sum, the forces that drive proliferation are complex, varied, and poorly understood.

Even when officials obtain enough evidence to calculate the outcome of possible courses of action, they must make difficult trade-offs when a decision involves multiple, competing values. The economic benefit and military threat inherent in nuclear science furnishes one case of value complexity. Since the use of uranium and plutonium for industrial purposes unavoidably produces the fissile material needed to build bombs, and because military and civilian applications share much of the same technology and infrastructure, Soviet and U.S. leaders continually have been forced to judge whether their promotion of nuclear energy at home and abroad justifies the ensuing military risk.

The superpowers must also choose between removing the threat posed by the military atom and relying on its protection. McGeorge Bundy identifies this trade-off in the original U.S. debate over the bomb's global control:

> That tension has appeared in every debate and in every judgment political leaders have made. In 1946 it was what finally divided a Baruch from an Oppenheimer. Much deeper than any difference over the details of the American proposal (the Baruch plan) or the tactics of debate was the difference over the nature of nuclear reality. To both men that reality had more than one face. Oppenheimer knew the value of getting there first from intense and direct experience, and Baruch had spoken of choosing between life and death. But in the end what Baruch saw first was the "winning weapon," and ever since Trinity what Oppenheimer had seen more clearly was "the destroyer of worlds."[10]

The tension that generates debate in Washington and Moscow over the relative merits of nuclear deterrence and disarmament figures largely in choices about nonproliferation. Almost without exception, U.S. and Soviet leaders have chosen the security provided by nuclear deterrence over the security that disarmament might provide by possibly solving the problem of proliferation and perhaps removing the nuclear threat altogether.

Finally, nonproliferation may compete with other foreign policy goals. When considering the sale of a nuclear facility, policy makers must determine if the economic and diplomatic benefits of the sale outweigh its proliferation risk. They must also decide whether to continue providing assistance or to withdraw support and impose sanctions on a country that covertly attempts to develop a nuclear bomb-making capability. Value conflict in this instance is intensified when the state in question is an important strategic ally, such as Israel and Pakistan are to the United States and India is to the Soviet Union.

When considering how best to limit nuclear proliferation, U.S. and Soviet leaders must contend with the related problems that information paucity, causal uncertainty, and value complexity create for efficient information processing. Even when their experience is ambiguous and misleading, decision makers try to learn from that experience. There is no alternative. The pressing demands of their jobs induce government officials to devise ways to acquire useful data, reduce uncertainty, simplify complexity, and fashion effective policy. Three types of such behavior are instrumental, constrained, and causal learning. The following section identifies the central features of each learning type.

THREE LEARNING TYPES

TYPE 1: STRUCTURAL REALISM, CYBERNETICS, AND INSTRUMENTAL LEARNING

One way that decision makers may cope with the complexity and uncertainty inherent in global politics is to monitor a limited range of information about international conditions and to rely on a small set of policy responses fixed by prior experience. In this *cybernetic* process of choice, national leaders implicitly recognize that their rationality is "bounded"; they have "neither the sense nor the wits to discover an optimal path" among competing values or to understand outcomes in a complex world.[11] A cybernetic actor is motivated by the need to obtain a set of core values, the content of which is shaped by the actor's environment. These core values drive whatever action the actor performs, although intermediary, or strategic, goals are pursued when a core value's achievement depends on them.[12] The resulting set of intermediary values, or "strategic interests," determines the issues the actor will find critical and about which the actor will seek information. Strategic interests also set the decision rules and responses which determine the course of action the actor will take when pertinent information is received on critical issues.

The learning process implied by cybernetics is simple, instrumental, and sporadic. This type of learning results in "adaptive" changes in the actor's behavior rather than changes in his understanding and beliefs about the world; thus it is simple.[13] The cybernetic organization, John Steinbruner writes, proceeds with one sequence of actions until feedback on critical variables forces one of these variables out of its tolerable range. There is then a change in the response patterns which, if it restores the critical variable to its desired range, then persists until another disruption occurs. Learning occurs in the sense that there is a systematic change in the pattern of activity in the organization.[14]

Routines or patterned responses persist if they hold critical variables within desired parameters; unsuccessful ones drop out. Since disappointment with old policies induces the implementation of a new approach, cybernetic learning is instrumental. Adjustments occur only when new events and conditions disrupt existing routines, thus this type of learning usually is slow and sporadic.

Instrumental learning is implicit to structural realist theory.[15] While neorealism does not specify a learning process as such, the learning process subsumed by the theory operates by cybernetic logic. Waltz contends that the international system's anarchic structure "limits and molds" state behavior in two related ways. *Competition* among countries determines what kinds of global behavior are punished and rewarded and, as the result of *socialization*, what types of foreign policy seem prudent to national leaders.[16] Conforming to the cybernetic pattern, realist actors pursue a set of core values: sovereignty, survival, and security. Each state seeks these values and tries to maintain its position in the international system by following a set of decision rules and patterned responses commonly known as realpolitik. When Waltz writes that "Structural constraints explain why (Realpolitik) methods are repeatedly used despite differences in the persons and states who use them,"[17] he endorses Steinbruner's point that "repertories of (cybernetic) behavior are ordered in terms of past reinforcement."[18] Similar logic operates whether instrumental learning is structured by the actor's past experience or by her environment.

Structural realism provides a framework for explaining three important outcomes of instrumental learning about nonproliferation: (1) the origin and persistence of U.S. and Soviet opposition to the spread of nuclear arms; (2) the occurrence of superpower cooperation on nonproliferation; and (3) the timing of this cooperation.[19] Neorealism explains Soviet and U.S. resistance to proliferation in two ways. First, a desire to protect their relatively advantaged global military positions leads Washington and Moscow to seek to preserve the nuclear club's exclusive status.[20] As a director of the U.S. Arms Control and Disarmament Agency remarked, "When we consider the cost to us of trying to stop the spread of nuclear weapons, we should not lose sight of the fact that widespread nuclear proliferation would mean a substantial erosion in the margin of power which our great wealth and industrial base have long given us relative to much of the rest of the world."[21]

The superpowers oppose proliferation also on the grounds that nuclear arms racing may heighten tension in conflict-prone areas such as South Asia and the Middle East, tension that may lead to regional nuclear conflict and catalytic war involving the nuclear giants. "More likely than an all-out war beginning between superpowers is a nuclear exchange between small countries," warned one U.S. legislator, "and a nuclear war anywhere has to be assumed to risk escalation to superpower involvement whether by deliberate intervention or by miscalculation, bluff or panic."[22] Even if it occurs far away, nuclear conflict threatens the U.S. and Soviet core value of security.

Structural conditions induce the superpowers to curb proliferation. They also elicit U.S.–U.S.S.R. cooperation for this end provided that Moscow and Washington cannot reap significant strategic gains relative to one another. Although individuals in both states may still hope to "win" the nuclear arms race, it appears that each side accepted the basic implications of mutually assured destruction soon after the Cuban missile crisis and with the advent of strategic nuclear parity in the mid-1960s. This is exactly when Moscow and Washington became partners in promoting the Nonproliferation Treaty (NPT).[23]

TYPE 2: BELIEF SYSTEMS AND CONSTRAINED LEARNING

If global politics does not possess the properties of a stable system, if past experience does not adequately structure strategic values, or if one simply embraces the human capacity for purposeful choice, it may make sense to view learning in terms of shifts in the goals, beliefs, and self-understandings of individual decision makers. Many contributors to the volume equate learning with change in the mode of thinking of U.S. and Soviet officials. This analytic approach emphasizes the causal importance of belief systems in foreign policy. Belief systems are organized hierarchically so that core values and beliefs exert more influence on strategic preferences and beliefs than vice versa; strategic cognition likewise governs tactical beliefs and preferences. Change usually occurs in peripheral zones of cognition. Officials avoid replacing strategies until they exhaust all tactical measures; and they reconsider basic aims generally only after repeated strategic failures. Since beliefs at the system's periphery are in near-constant flux, most writers associate learning only with change at the belief system's core, or perhaps at strategic levels. For example, Nye regards the revision of core goals and beliefs as *complex learning;* he sees shifts in strategic aims and beliefs as *simple learning.*[24]

Steinbruner terms the belief system approach *constrained learning,* owing to the rigidity and resistance to change inherent in cognitive structures:

In constrained learning, new information and new decision problems are fit into already established conceptual structures without causing any general adjustment of the structure. New ideas, new inferences, new perceptions are formed at lower levels of generality, and thus a belief system in a process of constrained learning is not static. However, the general structure of conceptualization remains both stable and partial even over very extended periods.[25]

Cognitive psychological research shows that information paucity, causal uncertainty, and value complexity lead individuals unconsciously to use several simple information-processing procedures that serve both to reinforce existing value and assumptive sets and to obstruct the learning of lessons incompatible with these sets. For example, humans underestimate the impact of situational causes of behavior and overestimate the force of dispositional causes (the "fundamental attribution error"); our analogical reasoning is simplistic and biased; we rely on "noncompensatory choice heuristics" to avoid making tough value trade-offs; and we tend to bolster our present commitments at the risk of ignoring alternative policies with higher expected payoffs.[26]

It is hard to specify the precise features of constrained learning since present cognitive research is highly fragmented. Cognitive variables are not yet coherently organized into a tight theoretical framework, and contradictory claims abound for most, if not all, theoretical statements about the role that cognitive factors play in foreign policy.[27] But three key assumptions of the cognitive research program warrant our consideration of constrained learning as a unique learning type. First, despite uncertainty, the mind establishes strong beliefs through categorical inferences and acts on them. As stated above, U.S. and Soviet nonproliferation policy stands at least partially on the belief that nuclear proliferation is dangerous and destabilizing, even though this inference cannot be verified by scientific means. The idea underpinning superpower policy is speculative but superstitiously held. Second, cognitive inference processes inhibit change in the core structure of beliefs. Although no state has used nuclear arms in war since August 1945, and although Israel, South Africa, India, and Pakistan have so far managed to control their nuclear capabilities, no top U.S or Soviet official has publicly changed her views about proliferation's likely strategic impact. Third, multiple values of a complex problem generally are not linked together, but separated and pursued independently. Washington and Moscow rely on nuclear deterrence to ensure national security even though one source of insecurity, nuclear proliferation, is an outcome largely of the superpowers' active development of nuclear arms.

As with the cybernetic processes that shape instrumental learning, the cognitive framework of constrained learning drives actors to follow habits. "Habits are derivatives of systems," James Rosenau writes, "and their repeated performance in a systemic context helps to sustain that system."[28] Political and psychological systems differ, but in one important respect similar effects ensue. Global political forces affecting the ability of states to stay secure and sovereign *externally* induce habitual conduct in instrumental learners, and cognitive processes helping humans make up their minds quickly and confidently *internally* make constrained learners habitual.[29] Old habits die hard; states seldom revise realpolitik routines, and people rarely reconsider basic aims and assessments. But change does occur. These two learning types do not presume that habits remain fixed, but simply that most individuals and groups require powerful stimuli to overcome them. Perhaps only *crises*, shocking intrusions upon habits, can stimulate instrumental and constrained learning.[30]

TYPE 3: EXPERT-GENERATED KNOWLEDGE AND CAUSAL LEARNING

If learning as viewed above involves the breakdown of old mental and bureaucratic habits through the force of critical events, causal learning occurs if the disappointment over actual or anticipated outcomes causes actors to alter habits with the aid of *analytic* evaluation, choice, and bargaining techniques. Causal learning rests on analytic information processing: after recognizing a problem, actors seek relevant information, identify alternative courses of action, analyze probable outcomes for each alternative, acknowledge the major values involved, order outcomes by an integrated value set, and then choose the most beneficial option.[31] If officials follow analytic procedures over many decision problems, they are likely to develop both a more specific and sophisticated causal conception of their environment and a more coherent ordering of their values and preferences. Causal learners typically become more knowledgeable about themselves and about the world in which they exist.

Causal learning is implicit in numerous theories of global politics; it is explicit in the model of organizational change developed by Ernst Haas.[32] According to Haas, policy makers are likely to follow analytic procedures if they urgently wish to solve the problems that prevent them from achieving key social goals, and if experts can provide them with the *knowledge* required to guide effective public policy.[33] Knowledge is created by experts in a social context, thus it is not necessarily true or complete; it often is political. Officials choose brands of knowledge to steer government policy according to personal and political tastes. Ideological concerns can bias even expertise. "In the area of national policy toward nuclear weapons," Robert Gilpin writes, "all the conditions exist that permit and even encourage the expert to supply his own non-technical assumptions concerning policy goals and thus to exert a strong influence on the formulation of policy."[34] But knowledge differs from ideology in that "it is constantly challenged from within and without and must justify itself by submitting its claims to truth tests considered generally acceptable."[35] Knowledge thus arises from existing information and ideas if it is verified by experts using internally derived scientific methods.

Causal learning differs from instrumental and constrained learning over the handling of collective choice. Whereas the latter pay scant attention to processes of bureaucratic bargaining and policy institutional-ization, the sequence linking shifts in individual beliefs to changes in organizational behavior is critical to causal learning.[36] Rival expert groups continually compete over whose knowledge should guide policy, the outcome often hinging more on one group's ability to gain access to key advisory posts than on the substantive merit of its scientific views. But even strategically positioned experts must persuade peers and appease politicians if their views are to sway opinion in the corridors of power. Knowledge becomes consensual when bargains obtain among relevant personal and political interests. A common recognition of causes then may prompt a shared understanding of solutions.[37] Therefore causal learning occurs when "the bargaining positions of the parties begin to converge on the basis of consensual knowledge tied to consensual goals (or interests), and when the concessions that are exchanged by the parties are perceived as instrumental toward the realization of the joint gains."[38]

States are not the sole consumers of knowledge. Causal learning can occur within and among coalitions of states, although politically and culturally diverse nations usually cannot define even a common problem in similar terms, much less agree on a single explanation or a shared solution for it. Cultural dissimilarity, like habits, resists learned behavior. Thus bargaining between opposing coalitions of states and cultural styles does not favor learning, but such bargaining may encourage shared meanings within coalitions. Capabilities to build nuclear arms still spread mainly because the nuclear giants have been unable to *institutionalize* nonproliferation lessons in an intercoalitional context nearly as effectively as they have in the more restrictive confines of intragovernmental and intracoalitional decision making.[39] The global nuclear nonproliferation regime exists but since its bargains emerged on the basis of incomplete consensual knowledge, they now muster only partial legitimacy and authority.[40] A stronger re-gime would seem to require a reconceptualization of the proliferation problem, a reevaluation of the chief causal linkages, and a redefinition of the regime's purposes. But a program of regime transformation offers no guarantee of success. When the Carter administration learned in the late 1970s to shift its basic nonproliferation strategy from global control to technology denial, it quickly discovered that tampering with the structure of the nonproliferation regime risks overturning the bargains that produced it.

Before turning to the historical survey, we should recognize that the concern of this chapter is not to prove that governments learn, but rather to show *how* they do, to identify the conditions under which each learning type operates. With respect to learning, then, the study's aim is evaluative; it is explanatory concerning strategic changes and the evolution of cooperation in nonproliferation. Table 1 summarizes the learning typology.[41]

HISTORICAL SURVEY OF SUPERPOWER NONPROLIFERATION ACTIVITIES

Although the United States and the Soviet Union have always opposed the global diffusion of military nuclear capabilities, their perceptions of the problem and their strategic responses to it have changed considerably over the years. Nonproliferation strategies vary with time, yet observation of any one point in the nuclear era is likely to find the superpowers thinking and acting along similar lines. Sometimes intentionally, sometimes not, U.S. and Soviet leaders generally have pursued parallel policies to keep other states from going nuclear. The following historical survey divides each superpower's nonproliferation activity into five distinct phases, four of which Moscow and Washington share. These phases are demarcated in terms of the chief strategy that nonproliferation policy makers follow rather than the basic goals they pursue (which hardly vary) or the tactics they devise (which frequently vary).

Strategy changes when policy makers, dissatisfied with the status quo, alter at least one of the following four strategic features. Nonproliferation policy first may *focus* on either the technological capability or the political motivation of states to go nuclear; or the focus may be mixed as it currently is in U.S. and Soviet policy. Strategic approaches also vary in their *coverage* of various technologies, with early policies designed to conceal all nuclear information and materials, later policies aimed at inhibiting obvious military uses of nuclear technology, and recent policies directed against the spread of plutonium reprocessing, uranium enrichment, and other sensitive technologies. Third, the strategy's *target* can vary. One policy may address all possible proliferators, while another may target a limited number of states. The final feature concerns the evolution of cooperation in nonproliferation: the *forum* of activity may be unilateral, bilateral, multilateral, or mixed. Table 2 shows these features in U.S. and Soviet nonproliferation strategies.[42]

AMERICAN SECRECY AND DENIAL: 1941–1953

Nuclear proliferation became a global fact in October 1941 when Franklin Roosevelt committed the United States to develop atomic arms for possible

TABLE 1 Typology of Learning

Learning type	Instrumental	Constrained	Causal
Decision paradigm in which embedded	Cybernetic	Cognitive	Analytic
Empirical theory in which embedded	Structural realism	Numerous cognitive psychological claims	Haas's model of managed interdependence
Chief units of analysis	States and foreign policy bureaucracies	Individual decision makers	Experts and foreign policy bureaucracies
Core goals of the decision maker	Security, sovereignty & relative advantage	Cognitive stability	Effectively solving social problems
How information paucity is handled	Information inputs severely restricted	Information inputs severely restricted	Sensitivity to all pertinent information
How causal uncertainty is handled	Set routines & single outcome calculations	Firm beliefs & single outcome calculations	Probabilistic analysis of alternative outcomes
How value complexity is handled	Preservation of core values	Value separation & single value focus	Limited value integration
How collective decision process is handled	Coordinated routines	Coordination without necessarily consensus	Integration: consensus formation
Chief impetus for learning	Failure to reach goals with existing routines	Failure to reach goals with existing strategies	Rise of new problems and knowledge about them
Learning mechanisms	Programmed operations and selective feedback	Belief reinforcement & inconsistency management	Scientific methods for evaluating knowledge
Chief learning outcome	Change in content of bureaucratic routines	Change in content of beliefs & preferences	Sophisticated knowledge of causes of problems

TABLE 2 Features of U.S. and Soviet Nonproliferation Strategies

U.S. Strategy	Focus	Coverage	Target	Forum
1941–53: Secrecy and denial	Capability	Comprehensive	Comprehensive	Unilateral
1954–64: Atoms for Peace	Motivation	Military uses	All except Britain	Bilateral
1965–74: Global control	Mixed	Military uses	Nonnuclear states (NNS)	Multilateral
1975–80: Technology denial	Capability	Sensitive uses	NNS except Europe/Israel	Mixed
1981–90: Management	Mixed	Sensitive uses	NNS except Europe/Israel	Mixed

Soviet Strategy	Focus	Coverage	Target	Forum
1945–54: Secrecy and denial	Capability	Comprehensive	Comprehensive	Unilateral
1954–58: Atoms for Peace	Motivation	Military uses	All except China	Bilateral
1958–62: Political control	Mixed	Military uses	Nonnuclear states (NNS)	Bilateral
1963–74: Global control	Mixed	Military uses	NNS (especially Germany)	Multilateral
1974–90: Management	Mixed	Sensitive uses	All NNS except India	Mixed

use in the allies' wartime effort.[43] In order to prevent Germany and others from discovering U.S. atomic secrets, Roosevelt allowed only a handful of his closest advisers to help make judgments about the project. As Richard Rhodes observes, "Scientists were summarily denied a voice in deciding the political and military uses of the weapons they were (commissioned) to build."[44] Since Roosevelt chose not to seek the advice of technical experts, the United States conducted no early analysis of the political impact of building atom bombs; U.S. officials did not anticipate difficulties regarding nuclear technology's future control.

No doubt justified by the demands of war, Roosevelt's stress on secrecy and the concentration of decision-making authority created a situation in which the United States paid scant attention to issues peripheral to building a bomb as quickly as possible.[45] Although it is hard to imagine a government's executing a war in different fashion, the point is that Roosevelt's administration did not search for all information pertinent to the atomic project; it did not calculate the likely outcomes of going nuclear; it did not balance additional values at the time of decision; and it did not open debate to obtain bureaucratic consensus. At the very outset of the atomic era, Washington made policy in a nonanalytic manner; it did not learn causally when it chose to build the bomb.

The high stakes of the nuclear race with Germany soon pushed the United States to collaborate in a limited manner on nuclear research and development with its closest military allies, Britain and Canada. Though Moscow shared the allies' wartime burden, Roosevelt did not inform Stalin of the ongoing atomic project, much less invite the Soviets to participate. In what is the world's first nuclear nonproliferation accord, the secret Quebec agreement of August 1943 committed the Anglo-American allies not to communicate any atomic information or share any sensitive material with third parties without mutual consent.[46]

The course of secrecy and denial met with some opposition, particularly among American atomic scientists. Upon learning of the Quebec pact, Robert Oppenheimer, Niels Bohr, and other Manhattan Project scientists campaigned to convince Anglo-American officials of the impending menace of a postwar arms race and of the novel opportunities the bomb could provide for international cooperation.[47] These experts argued that the wartime stress on secrecy should be discarded in favor of efforts to set up a supranational control authority. They viewed the U.S. atomic monopoly as a temporary advantage; since other states were bound to acquire bombs, the risks of global control would be less than those of an anticipated atomic arms race. Of the few U.S. scientists that actually knew about the atomic program, most felt that the United States would be served better by nuclear disarmament than by reliance on the bomb for deterrence.

The tragic revelation of the bomb's awesome destructive force in August 1945 finally moved U.S. leaders to accept responsibility for defining the world's nuclear future. Though President Truman asserted that Americans alone "would constitute (themselves) trustees of this new force," he ordered the State Department to analyze the problem and formulate a plan for international control.[48] The resulting Acheson-Lilienthal report of March 1946 stated that the "development of atomic energy for peaceful purposes and the development of atomic energy for bombs are in much of their course interchangeable and interdependent," and concluded that no state can be trusted to develop atomic power since a government conducting an ostensibly peaceful program might at any time convert its fissile materials to the building of bombs.[49]

In June 1946 Washington presented the Acheson-Lilienthal report to the United Nations Atomic Energy Commission (UNAEC), but in a form severely modified by the American UNAEC representative, Bernard Baruch. The original plan called for multinational management of nuclear activities by an International Atomic Development Authority (IADA), but Baruch insisted that the proposed IADA should also be allowed to impose sanctions for minor treaty breaches and that a veto-free UN Security Council should be assigned to deal with major violations. Baruch further argued that Washington had the right to preserve its atomic arsenal until an acceptable system of control and inspection could be established. None of these schemes was implemented, however, for Moscow refused to accept global control before the United States sacrificed its atomic monopoly and divulged its nuclear secrets, conditions that Baruch flatly rejected.[50]

As the UN representatives debated the issue of global control, Congress officially mandated secrecy on all aspects of the U.S. atomic weapons program by enacting the Atomic Energy Act (AEA) in August 1946.[51] The AEA (also known as the McMahon Act) was a legislative victory for those scientists responsible for building the bomb—now organized as the Federation of Atomic Scientists—who argued convincingly that civilians, not the military, should control nuclear arms. The AEA called for an independent, civilian Atomic Energy Commission to oversee all atomic research and development activities. But the legislation curbed AEC autonomy by banning releases of sensitive data on weapon design and industrial atomic uses and by outlawing exports of fissile material to foreign powers. By these measures and through steps taken to buy up existing uranium supplies, the United States tried to check the spread of atomic bomb-making capabilities.

Washington's first approach to the bomb fits the instrumental learning pattern. The government made its initial atomic choices fully in line with wartime routines, habits that resisted change long after the war's conclusion. Designed to prevent Germany's discovery of U.S. atomic activities, the Manhattan Project's security system evolved into a means to keep the U.S.S.R. from breaking the U.S. atomic monopoly. Underpinning nonproliferation strategy at this time was Washington's belief in its unique right to build and own atomic arms. Although many scientists warned that the global disparity in national nuclear status would not endure, officials maintained that others could not soon match U.S. atomic achievements.[52] This view prevailed until Moscow's explosion of an atomic device in August 1949 dramatically demonstrated that Washington had exaggerated the problems Soviet scientists would meet before gaining the bomb. When Britain tested an atomic device in October 1952, when France began in the same year to build plutonium-producing reactors, and when in 1953 Moscow tested a thermonuclear device of a type the United States had not yet tested, Washington had to acknowledge the shortcomings of its initial nonproliferation strategy.

U.S. nonproliferation policy in the first decade of the atomic era was not an outcome of causal learning. Although the administration eventually widened the scope of debate to include opinions and calculations of effects originally neglected, Washington did not use analytic procedures throughout the decision process. If the Acheson-Lilienthal report provided a framework for consensus for much of the foreign policy bureaucracy, Baruch neither fully accepted nor formally advanced the analysis and recommendations contained in the document.

SOVIET SECRECY AND DENIAL: 1945–1954

When Joseph Stalin learned in the autumn of 1942 of the ongoing German, British, and American work on the bomb, he decided at once to initiate a Soviet atomic project.[53] Washington's subsequent use of the bomb against Japan prompted the Soviet leader to instruct his advisers in August 1945 to "give us atomic weapons in the shortest possible time."[54] The urgency of this decision appears to have been motivated by Stalin's postwar conviction never again to be caught militarily unprepared. In light of the differences rapidly emerging with its erstwhile wartime allies, the Soviet Union braced itself for a major conflict with the capitalist powers. Stalin's swift cognizance of the atom's awesome destructive power and of Washington's prowess in this area did not lead to a fundamental revision of Soviet foreign policy. Soviet learning was constrained and instrumental; it was not causal. As David Holloway puts it:

> Stalin and Molotov met the challenge of atomic diplomacy by tactical countermoves rather than by a wholesale revision of policy. Their response to the bomb was to interpret its significance in terms of the existing premises of policy, not to use it to question their own understanding of Soviet security or of international relations.[55]

Holloway further observes that "Stalin's policy after Hiroshima rested on three assumptions: that war was not imminent; that world war was inevitable in the longer term; and that the immediate threat to the Soviet Union was the threat of atomic diplomacy, of a war of nerves, not of war."[56] Determined to resist nuclear coercion at all costs, Moscow rejected U.S. proposals for international atomic control, viewing them as disingenuous attempts to freeze and legitimize the global atomic disparity, thereby preserving the U.S. capacity for nuclear coercion. Moreover, the idea of intimate inspection, proposed by Baruch as an essential component of durable arms control, was viewed in Moscow as a menace to national sovereignty. As Soviet Ambassador Andrei Gromyko said before the United Nations: "The USSR government has no intention of permitting a situation whereby the national economy of the Soviet Union or particular branches of that economy would be placed under foreign control."[57] Instead, Gromyko called on Washington to abolish its nuclear arsenal prior to the establishment of a less intrusive international control body. This scheme was similarly unacceptable to the Americans, and negotiations rapidly deteriorated.

The U.S.S.R. opposed the imminent acquisition of nuclear arms by Britain and France, but during the first years of the atomic era the most pressing Soviet concern was to counter Washington's nuclear superiority; further proliferation was an incidental problem.[58] Moscow at once discounted the bomb's political and military significance and proposed a total ban on nuclear arms, an end to all nuclear testing, and other diplomatic initiatives designed to inhibit U.S. nuclear expansion without limiting its own nuclear development.[59] The Soviets showed scant interest in finding common negotiating ground with Washington or in establishing an organization even remotely resembling an IADA. As McGeorge Bundy notes: "Baruch made little effort to negotiate. Gromyko made none."[60]

During the initial era of the Soviet nuclear program, Soviet scientists did not seem to worry about the political implication of their work, about the menace of an arms race or the threat of nuclear war, except to the extent that they felt obliged to help deter Washington from starting one.[61] Whether due to the secret and authoritarian Soviet decision-making style at this time, or because scientists simply believed that their state's survival rested with the expeditious execution of the atomic bomb project and then of the hydrogen bomb program, Soviet leaders were not directly exposed, as U.S. officials were, to the analytic process that had led Bohr and Oppenheimer and then Acheson and Lilienthal to urge global nuclear control. Though consensus surely obtained over Soviet nuclear policy, stillborn debate cost the U.S.S.R. critical expertise that was not provided, estimates about the possible outcomes of going nuclear that were not made, and thus causal lessons that were not learned.

In a fashion typical of constrained learners, Stalin severely restricted the input of information concerning the political dimension of nuclear arms; he focused on the single strategic objective of matching U.S. nuclear power as quickly as possible; he calculated that going nuclear would cause a purely positive outcome; and he rejected views that contradicted his basic assessment of the problem. Soviet learning during this era is better characterized as instrumental, however, since the core values of national sovereignty and security guided policy in a manner entirely consistent with prior wartime routines. Even as cold war replaced world war, Moscow continued to see itself in a hostile and highly competitive world; thus it did not seek to revise the patterns of activity that emerged in the harsh period preceding Berlin's fall.

World War II left a very noticeable mark on the original nuclear era. Since the new superpowers saw each other much as they had viewed their common enemy, Germany, Moscow and Washington would not cooperate to check the bomb's spread, even though they just had joined ranks to defeat Hitler. Thus cooperation for nuclear proliferation was improbable at this time, especially as the superpowers did not agree that the bomb was as much a threat to their own survival as Germany had been. Technical experts pushed this view high up into the U.S. foreign policy bureaucracy, but it remained alien to Moscow.

AMERICAN ATOMS FOR PEACE: 1954–1964

Moscow's atomic and thermonuclear tests confronted Washington with two thorny problems, one political and commercial, the other military. First, U.S. scientists informed the administration in the early 1950s that the U.S.S.R. would soon be able to offer other countries the benefits of the peaceful application of its nuclear research. Neither Washington, hampered by its own legislation on nuclear technology exchange, nor even London, still bound to the secrecy pledge of the Quebec agreement, could compete with the Soviet Union in this area if contemporary conditions remained unaltered.[62]

Second, Soviet nuclear successes forced Washington to reassess Moscow's military threat and to devise a new strategic response. The NSC-68 study of 1950 provided the impetus for cognitive and doctrinal reorientation, urging "containing the Soviet system . . . by all means short of war to . . . so foster the seeds of destruction within the Soviet system that the Kremlin is brought at least to the point of modifying its behavior to conform to generally accepted international standards."[63] The document also advised shelving plans for global nuclear control so long as Moscow refused to permit inspection within its borders. Responding to the need to obtain "more" defense at less cost—mounting economic pressures simultaneously required military spending cuts—Washington upgraded the military role of nuclear arms owing to their perceived capacity to provide "more bang for the buck."[64]

Increased reliance on nuclear capabilities, which came to be known as the "New Look," provided Washington with a novel dilemma. As Secretary of State Dulles lamented, "somehow or other we must manage to remove the taboo from the use of these weapons."[65] The chairman of the Joint Chiefs of Staff, Admiral Arthur Radford, echoed Dulles's conviction that nuclear technology's popular image needed to be improved. In his view, "we have been spending vast sums on the manufacture of these weapons and at the same time we are holding back on their use because of our concern for public opinion."[66]

Concern quickly prompted action. Speaking to the UN General Assembly in December 1953, President Eisenhower heralded a new U.S. Atoms for Peace campaign designed to "hasten the day when fear of the atom will begin to disappear from the minds of people."[67] Eisenhower warned that rampant nuclear proliferation posed a serious threat, affirmed that nuclear know-how was sure to spread, and admitted that atomic aggression was not defensible. On the brighter side, he remarked that atomic power could immediately be channeled to serve humankind. In order to redirect this technology away from military pursuits and toward "peaceful . . . efficient and economic usage," Eisenhower invited "the governments principally involved" to "make joint contributions from their stockpiles of . . . fissionable materials to an international atomic energy agency . . . set up under the aegis of the United Nations." Mandated to collect, store, and distribute fissile materials, the proposed IAEA thus would not be entitled to the ownership and punishment powers planned for the IADA.[68]

In the same speech, Eisenhower proposed to modify the McMahon Act so as to facilitate the spread of civil nuclear technology. While economic factors loomed large in the 1954 AEA revision, the amendment's commercial appeal was as much ideal as material.[69] U.S. leaders justified spending vast public funds and devoting huge shares of the nation's scientific and industrial resources on atomic research on the grounds that a scientific discovery as revolutionary as that of atomic energy simply had to be brought into widespread application. The first Atomic Energy Commission (AEC) chairman, David Lilienthal, recalled that "this prodigious effort was predicated on the belief and hope that this great new source of energy for mankind could produce results as dramatically and decisively beneficial to man as the bomb was dramatically destructive."[70] This optimism in the ability of U.S. technology to deliver the country, and perhaps the world, to prosperity, if not necessarily to security, did not abate until the late 1970s.

Although Washington was less than fully attentive to the risk that the enthusiastic sharing of atomic information and the promotion of peaceful uses might stimulate a demand for bombs and increase bomb-making capabilities, the government still sought to prevent the "promiscuous spread" of atomic arms.[71] Nonproliferation remained a basic American objective even as new perceptions, political priorities, and technical realities pulled nonproliferation strategy away from secrecy and denial and toward "constructive engagement."[72] As Glenn Seaborg, a former commissioner of the AEC, reflected in a 1966 speech:

> Most of us knew that it was only a matter of time before other countries could achieve a nuclear weapons capability independently of the U.S., the USSR, and the U.K. . . . Many countries had their own supplies of natural uranium and, perhaps more importantly, their own scientists. We also considered that, if we failed to cooperate in sharing peaceful nuclear technology and nuclear materials, other countries might be willing to do so, without, however, insisting as we did on a firm assurance as to peaceful end use. Aside from this, we could not overlook the positive aspects of nuclear energy and its possible contributions to human betterment.[73]

Three developments during Eisenhower's presidency caused his successor to perceive nuclear proliferation with a greater sense of alarm and pessimism. Washington discovered in the late 1950s that China was moving to build atomic bombs; France's first fission test came in February 1960; and U.S. intelligence officials realized in the same year that Israel, with French assistance, was building a plutonium reprocessing unit at its Dimona nuclear complex that soon would enable Tel Aviv to fabricate nuclear arms. These threatening conditions led John Kennedy to predict in March 1963 that 15 to 25 states might obtain military nuclear capabilities by the 1970s, the likely result of which would be instability, insecurity, reduced opportunities for disarmament, a greater chance of accidental war, and a heightened prospect of the global powers becoming entangled in otherwise local conflicts.[74]

Despite the new American beliefs about proliferation, government policy changed only in two tactical areas: Kennedy moved to ban nuclear testing in the atmosphere, and he pushed for an Atlantic multilateral nuclear force (MLF). The first measure was designed to prohibit a near-nuclear nation from testing a first device,[75] and the other was adopted partially as a means to dull European appetites for independent nuclear forces.[76] Atoms for Peace remained the centerpiece of U.S. nonproliferation strategy.

Atoms for Peace was an outcome of constrained learning. Washington did not automatically respond to the new reality of nuclear proliferation with a policy shaped primarily by prior experience, as it earlier had done in adopting the strategy of secrecy and denial. But if U.S. learning was not instrumental, neither was it causal. Altering the focus, coverage, target, and forum of U.S. nonproliferation policy, Atoms for Peace was a highly innovative initiative. And it emerged after long consideration from a new recognition of the dangers of both the arms race and civilian nuclear power industries, but the knowledge that stimulated its origin failed to materialize in an institutional form.[77] The relative stability of U.S. preferences and beliefs about nuclear deterrence and arms control constrained U.S. learning during this period.

SOVIET ATOMS FOR PEACE: 1954–1958

Although Moscow first reacted skeptically to the Atoms for Peace concept, the program's global appeal quickly convinced the Kremlin of the political benefit that might be gained from promoting peaceful atomic uses. In July 1954 Moscow declared its readiness to share atomic technology for civilian ends inside the Communist bloc and beyond. And after the U.S. AEC decided in December 1954 to release certain atomic information, Moscow quickly followed suit, asserting a month later that it too would share the technical data it had collected during the operation of its first atomic power plant.[78] Nuclear technology thus became a key part of the cold war competition: "by gradual degree the nuclear giants lifted their skirts of secrecy, each challenging the other to reveal more evidence of dedication to the peaceful atom."[79]

Moscow began to export not only nuclear know-how but also research reactors and fissile material. Soviet officials arranged nuclear assistance agreements first with China, Czechoslovakia, East Germany, Poland, and Romania in 1955; they signed similar collaborative pacts with Bulgaria and Hungary the next year.[80] Confirmed in April, the commitment to China involved sending Beijing a cyclotron, a nuclear reactor, and fissile material for research; in exchange, China pledged to give the Soviets diplomatic support and "necessary raw materials."[81] Curiously, Moscow chose not to apply safeguards on any of its nuclear exports. William Potter notes that this decision may have derived from the great confidence Moscow placed in its ability to control its allies' nuclear activities.[82] Gloria Duffy adds that Khrushchev may have accepted a limited risk of proliferation in exchange for immediate political gains.[83] Or the Kremlin simply may not have understood the ease with which these exports could serve military ends. In any case, Moscow did not attach top priority to nonproliferation during the 1950s. But this situation changed suddenly. As Sino-Soviet nuclear relations grew more and more disturbing for Moscow, Soviet leaders reconsidered the likelihood and consequences of nuclear proliferation.

As John Lewis and Xue Litai write in their cogent study of the Chinese nuclear program, *China Builds the Bomb*, Soviet nuclear assistance to Beijing began very slowly. Moscow originally provided aid in order to obtain Chinese uranium ores. At the close of 1955 the Kremlin pledged generous assistance in return for these valuable ores, and after considerable haggling Moscow finally redeemed the pledge in August 1956. Initially Moscow did not directly help to build Chinese arms; it agreed only to train technical and scientific personnel in industrial atomic applications. But by October 1956 Beijing's bargaining power rose markedly as anticommunist uprisings spread in Hungary and Poland. In order to gain backing for its eroding status in the socialist bloc, Moscow finally conceded to help Beijing build nuclear weapons. Sino-Soviet nuclear relations reached an apex in October 1957 with the signing of the New Defense Technical Accord, a pact that committed Moscow to give its socialist ally a prototype atomic bomb, missiles, and related technical data.

Although Khrushchev claims in his memoirs that the bomb was crated and about to be shipped off to China, it was in fact never delivered. By early 1959 Khrushchev concluded that Beijing was an unreliable partner and that the Sino-Soviet friendship was one-sided and dangerous. According to Benjamin Lambeth, the Taiwan Strait crisis of 1958 provided the final straw that ended Khrushchev's patience with Mao.[84] As China strayed further and further from the Soviet policy line, and when it finally in May declared its intention to acquire a national nuclear arsenal, Moscow reversed its perception of China from friend to foe. A month later all Soviet-Chinese nuclear accords ended, as did this exceptionally lax phase in Moscow's nuclear proliferation policy.

The Soviet Atoms for Peace approach clearly did not result from causal learning. Rather than relying on analytic decision procedures to reconsider the recent changes affecting proliferation, Moscow emulated a strategy that it believed was providing positive results for Washington. Like its chief rival, the Soviet Union learned in a constrained fashion to drop the veil of secrecy surrounding its nuclear activities and to provide nuclear aid to its friends.

As both superpowers turned away from the generous sharing of nuclear technology, it became evident that Atoms for Peace had failed in two important respects. First, Eisenhower's original emphasis on multilateralism did not materialize. The IAEA, which Moscow helped to establish in 1957, never become a depository and disseminator of fissile material; it only monitored transactions among member states. Bilateralism prevailed: Moscow and Washington insisted on choosing the recipients of nuclear technology and the terms of all aid packages.[85] Second, similar superpower approaches meant that many states eager to acquire nuclear assistance were compelled to accept fettering safeguards that they otherwise might not have tolerated, but, on the whole, the superpowers did not dampen proliferation incentives and actually provided many states, starting with France and China, the means to go nuclear.

SOVIET POLITICAL CONTROL: 1958–1962

Moscow's unsettling experience with China fueled a major reappraisal of its nuclear export policy and pushed nonproliferation upward in the hierarchy of Soviet foreign policy aims.[86] As Gloria Duffy writes, "The ease with which the Chinese transformed Soviet nuclear aid into a weapons program seemingly was taken by the Soviets as an ill presentiment of the way Soviet nuclear exports might be manipulated in the future by other recipient countries."[87] Never again would Moscow assist in the development of unsafeguarded foreign nuclear power programs. Whereas the Soviet Union had previously relied on its ability to dominate the nuclear decisions of recipient states, after 1958 Moscow imposed strict political and technical controls on all nuclear exports.

Following a short period of policy revision and retrenchment—soon after the nuclear rift with China, the Kremlin reneged on pledges to supply a 100 mw reactor to Hungary and to help Czechoslovakia construct a plutonium producing power plant[88]—Moscow decided again to promote nuclear technology abroad, but limited reactor exports to the more proliferation-resistant light-water type. As a precondition to any nuclear deal, the Soviets now insisted on strict and innovative safeguards, including a commitment by recipients of Soviet reactors to obtain nuclear fuel from Moscow and return the spent fuel rods to the U.S.S.R. In addition, the Kremlin prevented its East European clients from developing independent uranium enrichment and plutonium reprocessing facilities.[89]

Although now apparently convinced of the utility of safeguards, Moscow remained vehemently opposed to plans for the newly established IAEA to set up a global safeguards system. A director of the Soviet Atomic Committee likened the "American inspired" IAEA safeguards idea to "a spider's web which would catch in its threads all the scientific research and all the scientists of the world."[90] Moscow's unwillingness to support an IAEA safeguard system at least partially derived from its unpopularity among the developing and nonaligned states of the world. India led the opposition to Washington's call for other states to abide by safeguards that it itself was unwilling to accept. As the IAEA statute was being negotiated, Moscow sided with New Delhi and was able to derail the U.S. plan requiring the organization's members to accept safeguards. Besides decoupling IAEA membership from safeguards, Khrushchev and Nehru also ensured that participation in the IAEA would not automatically compel states to accept safeguards on bilateral nuclear assistance pacts. Since Moscow only exported nuclear technology to nations in its orbit or to politically friendly states, it could afford to oppose IAEA safeguards. "The Soviet Union could, as a result, pride itself on practicing a policy of trust and could accuse the Western system of safeguards and inspection of implying a lack of confidence in the pledge of peaceful commitments given by the assisted countries."[91]

This four-year phase in Soviet nonproliferation activity again appears to be an outcome of constrained learning. The crisis with China induced the Kremlin to reexamine the possible political and military consequences of its nuclear assistance programs. Moscow did not completely reappraise its basic nonproliferation approach (as it would have if it had learned causally), but it did recognize and redress a perceived flaw in the Atoms for Peace strategy. The U.S.S.R. now would focus as much on the capability of states to go nuclear as on their motivation to do so; no longer would it export unsafeguarded nuclear technology or material. The learning behind this shift was not instrumental, even though Moscow partially returned to an old routine (the prior secrecy and denial strategy's focus on bomb-making *capabilities*) to bring a critical variable (the nature and number of nuclear weapon states) back to a tolerable range. Moscow's switch to national (not IAEA) safeguards as a means to stop proliferation resulted from lessons learned in a constrained manner.

SOVIET GLOBAL CONTROL: 1963–1974

Soviet beliefs about nuclear matters changed again in 1963. Signaling that the possibility of a nuclear conflict involving the superpowers was less remote than earlier had been imagined, the Cuban missile crisis caused Moscow to reconsider its basic approach to the bomb. The sobering experience of October 1962 prompted Khrushchev and Kennedy to sign three major arms control measures in less than a year: a direct communications hot line linking Moscow and Washington was set up in June; the Partial Test Ban Treaty was concluded in August; and in September the superpowers agreed to support a UN resolution outlawing the placement of mass destruction weapons in space.[92] The missile crisis also reinvigorated Soviet and U.S. interest in nonproliferation.

Growing fears that Germany and Japan might soon acquire nuclear options compounded Moscow's incentive to act decisively to limit the spread of nuclear weapon capabilities. The Kremlin first reversed its position on international safeguards, agreeing in 1963 to help finance the IAEA system. And in the same year Moscow began to criticize NATO's MLF idea. Post-missile crisis concerns stiffened Moscow's resolve to keep German and other European fingers away from nuclear triggers. While the Kremlin apparently felt that the best way to curb proliferation was for each superpower to "take care of its own," as a Soviet nuclear energy official stated in 1963,[93] Washington's backing of MLF created serious doubt about its ability to keep the bomb out of its friends' reach. In fact, Moscow may have viewed MLF as a deliberate U.S. scheme to promote proliferation.

With the hope for superpower collusion in bloc management frustrated, Moscow shifted from a bilateral to a multilateral strategic forum, submitting its first nonproliferation treaty draft in September 1965.[94] The NPT actually originated with an Irish proposal in 1961, but productive treaty negotiations began only after the superpowers, in their capacity as cochairs of the Geneva Disarmament Conference, chose in earnest to promote an accord. But the NPT's conclusion remained distant as Moscow vehemently objected to the Western MLF scheme, which it perceived as "quenching the nuclear thirst of German revenge-seekers."[95] Soviet NPT negotiators eventually convinced their U.S. counterparts that unless the MLF was discarded Moscow could not subscribe to any agreement to prevent the spread of nuclear weapons.[96] By 1966 Andrei Gromyko and Dean Rusk reached a mutually acceptable compromise; their governments submitted identical draft treaties the next year; and the NPT was signed in July 1968.

Especially during the final rounds of bargaining that led to the NPT, U.S. and Soviet officials displayed an unprecedented level of tacit understanding and open collaboration. As George Quester observes, "The handling of the NPT negotiations from 1967 to 1968, and the handling of proliferation matters since then, might substantively and procedurally be viewed as almost the ideal of how smoothly Soviet-American dealings could run."[97] In an important sense, the NPT institutionalized a common nonproliferation approach between the two superpowers by inducing the creation of bureaucratic groups in Washington and Moscow that had vested interests in continuing bilateral collaboration in this area.[98] But U.S.–Soviet cooperation was not yet based on completely consensual knowledge. Soon after the NPT's conclusion, Moscow made several attempts to persuade Washington to agree on joint action in the event of a third country's military use of nuclear explosives. Nixon administration officials rejected this idea partially because they suspected that China was its focus.[99]

Soviet nonproliferation activity during this phase seems to have been produced by instrumental as well as constrained learning. Moscow's choice to cooperate with Washington may be viewed as a cybernetic reaction induced by a profound change in the global military environment; the rise of nuclear parity between the superpowers during the 1960s created a condition in which nuclear arms control became less costly and thus tolerable for the U.S.S.R. Situated in this new setting, Moscow may have decided to join the Western nonproliferation coalition when the Cuban crisis and the threat of German nuclear armament under MLF auspices disrupted its prior nonproliferation routine. If such a Soviet *reaction* is stressed over a deliberate and thorough Soviet reassessment of proliferation's new causal context, then the rise of U.S.–Soviet cooperation to inhibit nuclear proliferation can be considered an outcome of instrumental learning.

Moscow's decision to support rather than obstruct the nascent nonproliferation regime resulted from constrained learning. Moscow's promotion of international organizational solutions to the proliferation issue cannot be depicted in terms of Soviet realpolitik response patterns. Here the emphasis should be placed on the rise of new strategic ideas, on cognitive change. Since we do not yet have access to information that would allow us to determine if Soviet policy makers conducted the analytic information-processing procedures required of causal learning, we must view Moscow's strategic shift to global control as an outcome of constrained learning.

AMERICAN GLOBAL CONTROL: 1965–1974

During the mid-1960s Washington also learned in a constrained manner to see the NPT as a vital new means to attain its old goals of preventing nuclear war and halting the spread of nuclear weapons. The scare created by the Cuban crisis, combined with the emergence of "nuclear upstarts" such as de Gaulle's France and Mao's China,[100] joined with a growing concern that bombs might soon come into the possession of more and more states, convinced U.S. officials that global nuclear activities should no longer remain uncontrolled and that a multilateral treaty promised the greatest barrier to proliferation for states that previously had been unwilling or unable to build or procure nuclear arms.

Before it could be enacted, however, the NPT had to survive a number of tests at various organizational levels, the first of which was within the U.S. foreign policy apparatus. The Arms Control and Disarmament Agency (ACDA) was the original bureaucracy to promote the pact; the Atomic Energy Commission and the Defense Department subsequently added their support. The chief opposition to the treaty came from the State Department's MLF supporters. Thus in 1965 when MLF died, much of the internal opposition to the NPT expired with it.[101]

As the government grew united in favor of the NPT, U.S. officials began to promote the pact globally. But while the two superpowers and their closest clients gradually found themselves in agreement about the treaty's preferred contents (after they solved the MLF dispute), many developing states sided with India's UN representatives, who refused to sign an arms control pact that limited the horizontal proliferation of military nuclear capabilities but was silent about their vertical growth among the states that already owned them. In a 1965 IAEA meeting, India demanded "tangible progress toward disarmament including a comprehensive test ban treaty, a complete freeze on the production of nuclear weapons and means of delivery, as well as a substantial reduction of existing stocks."[102] The developing states added that they could only sign a treaty binding nuclear exporters to provide technical aid on generous terms.

The superpowers finally reached a compromise in 1967 acceptable to most nonweapon states that required a commitment by the latter to stay nonnuclear in exchange for IAEA safeguards on existing nuclear programs and guarantees mandating the transfer of civilian nuclear technology.[103] But the bargain did not codify consensual knowledge. The NPT's conclusion hinged on an ability to link safeguards, technical assistance, and strategic arms control, but this linkage turned out to be *fragmented* rather than *substantive*. In other words, consensus was lacking on the substantive need to join the three issues; Moscow and Washington linked them so as to gain the largest number of signatories.[104]

Despite the considerable problems involved in concluding the NPT, from the mid-1960s onward the two superpowers have learned in a constrained fashion that the cost of independent action in nonproliferation far exceeds the benefit of unilateralism. Owing to this cognition, global bargaining has become a critical component in contemporary U.S. and Soviet activities to slow the spread of nuclear arms. But one should not infer from this observation that the superpowers have remained vigilant regarding proliferation. On the contrary. Following the U.S. Senate's ratification of the NPT in 1970, the White House devoted very little high-level attention to the problem of proliferation until 1974.

AMERICAN TECHNOLOGY DENIAL: 1975–1980

Just as Washington grew complacent about the capacity of the NPT-based regime to stop the further spread of nuclear capabilities, the simultaneous occurrence of several startling developments during the mid-1970s stimulated Washington to radically revise its nonproliferation strategy. By far the most significant of these events was India's detonation of a crude nuclear device in May 1974, an act that acquired special significance because India was the first state to use civilian facilities as a technological base and fuel source for an explosive device.[105] Because New Delhi was not a party to the NPT, and because it defiantly defined the event as a peaceful nuclear explosion rather than a military test, India legally managed to sidestep safeguards that were intended to prevent civilian nuclear activities from serving military ends.[106]

The concern caused by India's explosion grew as Washington's existing commitment to sell nuclear reactors to Israel and Egypt fueled fears that New Delhi's achievement might be duplicated in a still more volatile region of the world. The oil crisis stimulated by OPEC's embargo and price rise provided an additional shock as it reinforced the desire of many states to rely on nuclear power as a means to secure a stable energy supply. Significant shifts on the supply side of the nuclear market compounded concerns. Washington's monopoly over the export of nuclear fuel and power plants suddenly unraveled with the rise of new suppliers who seemed less discriminating regarding the transfer of sensitive technologies. France's proposed sale of plutonium reprocessing facilities to Pakistan and South Korea and Germany's sale of enrichment facilities to Brazil were especially ominous in this regard.

Despite the sudden confluence of these troubling events and trends, Washington revised its estimate of the proliferation problem very slowly. The ability of the government to learn was constrained by a pessimistic belief in the inevitability of proliferation shared by President Nixon and Secretary of State Kissinger. In their view, Michael Brenner explains, "The only question was which and how many states would take up the nuclear option. . . . Therefore, it simply did not make sense for the United States to incur political costs in trying to avoid an eventuality that in all likelihood was beyond Washington's power to control."[107] Moreover, governmental bureaucracies that were inclined to view proliferation as a problem requiring greater U.S. vigilance, such as the ACDA, were politically much less important than agencies like the AEC, which tended to endorse the thinking of Nixon and Kissinger.[108]

A new round of U.S. learning about nonproliferation required the departure of President Nixon from the White House; Gerald Ford displayed a much greater sensitivity both to the threats posed by proliferation and to his government's capacity to contain them. During his brief term in office Washington reversed its commitment to new, proliferation-prone technologies; urged that spent fuel not be recycled but rather stored indefinitely as part of a "once-through" fuel system; and sought stricter conditions on nuclear-power-related exports, including uranium fuel. Moreover, the government once again "learned . . . that the United States could not unilaterally prevent the spread of facilities and fuels contributing to a weapons capability."[109] During Ford's tenure, the United States resumed secret negotiations in London with fellow nuclear suppliers to develop procedures to tighten export guidelines and coordinate export practices.

Although President Ford presided over the origin of one of the most far-reaching shifts in Washington's approach to proliferation, his administration did not complete a causal learning process. When Ford's term ended, the most significant bureaucratic bargains remained to be struck and the new nuclear consensus was only partially institutionalized in the U.S. foreign policy establishment. While the ACDA, the State Department, and Congress increasingly proposed that stricter nonproliferation considerations should guide technology exports and domestic nuclear activities, the Energy Research and Development Administration (ERDA) and the Nuclear Regulatory Commission (NRC)—the two organizations created when the AEC was legislatively bifurcated at the end of 1974—

remained powerful enough to prevent new assumptions about proliferation from acquiring legitimacy and authority in the White House.

True causal learning occurred only after President Carter succeeded in placing his imprint on nonproliferation policy, a development that took little time as the president promptly put the issue at the top of his foreign policy agenda. Carter's appointment of avowed arms controllers to key bureaucratic posts paved the way for a new nonproliferation strategy to gain legitimacy and authority. Officials such as Joseph Nye, Lawrence Scheinman, and Gerald Smith at State and Paul Warnke, Spurgeon Keeny, and Charles Van Doren at ACDA "were chosen not to register the debate over what should be done, but rather to formulate the means for realizing ends that, as the president already had determined in his own mind, were essential to the U.S. national interest."[110]

Carter's understanding of what was wrong with the existing U.S. strategy and of what should be done to improve it followed from the analysis and advice of key technical experts. Albert Wholstetter's *Swords From Plowshares* and the Ford/Mitre study, *Nuclear Power Issues and Choices*, isolated and recombined strategic variables in a manner that produced a radical reconceptualization of the proliferation problem, thereby providing a framework capable of supporting a new consensus.[111] In a major nonproliferation address of April 7, 1977, the president stated that the new strategy would involve "a major change in U.S. domestic nuclear energy policies and programs."[112] While Carter also signaled that Washington would seek a global consensus on proliferation, the new policy measures unilaterally condemned: (1) the reprocessing and recycling of plutonium produced in U.S. facilities; (2) the domestic promotion of breeder reactors; and (3) the export of uranium enrichment and plutonium reprocessing technologies. The enactment of the Nuclear Nonproliferation Act (NNPA) the next year legislatively institutionalized the new consensual knowledge. The NNPA required Washington to renegotiate all nuclear cooperation agreements with foreign states and to make further trade contingent on their acceptance of full-scope safeguards.[113]

Once the new wisdom on nonproliferation gained legitimacy and authority within the government, Washington set out to impart its knowledge to important global actors. In one forum, the U.S. attempted to forge a new consensus among the leading nuclear technology exporters. The London Suppliers Group, which came to include 15 states, finally agreed in January 1978 to establish a set of guidelines requiring recipients of nuclear technology to: (1) promise that items on a trigger list would not be used to produce nuclear explosives; (2) protect all nuclear facilities and material from theft or sabotage; (3) pledge not to retransfer items to third parties without permission from the supplier; and (4) accept IAEA safeguards on all trigger-list items.

The developing states reacted very strongly to the new strings attached to nuclear technology transfers. They argued that Washington and the London Suppliers Group had transformed the nonproliferation regime through unilateral measures rather than consensus and negotiation. In response to charges that the NPT's spirit had been violated, Washington inaugurated the International Fuel Cycle Evaluation program (INFCE), in which 500 experts from 46 countries participated, in order to convince other countries that they could do without reprocessing and breeder reactors and that they would be better off relying on proliferation-resistant fuel cycles like that based on thorium. By providing "a commonly accepted foundation of facts, by offering a range of reasonable projection of nuclear futures over the long term, and by estimating the relevant costs and benefits of different fuel-cycle arrangements," INFCE made causal learning a distinct possibility at the global level.[114] By concluding that fuel cycles cannot be ranked in terms of their relative proliferation risk, however, the conference failed to produce from a common understanding of technical conditions a shared understanding of political solutions.

The Carter administration followed an analytic decision process for much of its tenure, and it succeeded in promoting analytic procedures in the London meetings and in the INFCE. But whereas these procedures eventually led to the institutionalization of consensual knowledge at the intragovernmental and the intracoalitional levels, causal learning did not occur at the intercoalitional level of decision making about nonproliferation. In fact some *unlearning* may have taken place at the global level, for many consumers of nuclear technology, irritated by the new U.S. tendency to unilaterally declare what types of civilian nuclear facilities and technologies would be permitted in the global marketplace, asserted at the 1980 NPT review conference that Washington had nullified a central NPT bargain by circumscribing the mandated flow of nuclear technology and material to developing states.

By the close of Carter's term, Washington also *unlearned* some of the key nonproliferation lessons as new strategic conditions lowered the issue in the hierarchy of national priorities. The examples of Pakistan and India are most revealing. Whereas in 1979 Washington cut off all assistance except food aid to Pakistan because Islamabad refused to place its enrichment plant under IAEA safeguards, Moscow's invasion of Afghanistan resulted in a new military aid offer to Islamabad the very next year. And even though the NRC had determined that a proposed sale of 17,000 pounds of enriched uranium for India's Tarapur power plant stood to violate the recently enacted Nuclear Nonproliferation Act, the president authorized the shipment anyway, now insisting that the denial of U.S. technology and materials may thwart rather than assist efforts to curb the spread of bomb-making capabilities.

SOVIET MANAGEMENT: 1974–1990

Soviet fears about proliferation abated after Bonn signed and ratified the NPT, but New Delhi's 1974 nuclear test, the global oil crisis, and the rise of new nuclear suppliers stimulated a significant if subtle shift in the way Moscow henceforth would pursue nonproliferation. An outcome of constrained learning, the new strategy emphasized increased commercial activity involving nonsensitive nuclear materials, stressed the application of strict safeguards on sensitive technology transfers, promoted greater coordination among nuclear suppliers, and implied acceptance of India's de facto nuclear power status.

After Washington spread confusion in the nuclear marketplace by halting all exports of enriched uranium in 1974, Moscow decided to promote its nuclear commodity transfers more aggressively. Reversing a long-held policy, the U.S.S.R. declared in 1975 its readiness to sell nuclear fuel and facilities outside the Communist bloc. Nuclear technology comprised one of very few technical areas in which the Kremlin could compete globally, so Moscow quickly filled the void created by its rival's unilateral embargo on enriched uranium sales. Compared with the situation prevailing prior to 1974 when the United States supplied all of the European Community's uranium enrichment services, by 1977 the Soviet Union was carrying over half of this load.[115]

Moscow quickly set out to exercise its newly acquired commercial muscle. In negotiations among members of the London Suppliers Group, the U.S.S.R. pressed hard for an agreement requiring the strictest possible controls on nuclear exports, more than once rejecting guidelines suggested by the United States as "minimal requirements."[116] Throughout the London talks Moscow insisted on the global adoption of full-scope safeguards, a rule requiring nuclear recipients to accept IAEA safeguards on all of their nuclear equipment no matter where it was acquired or when it was obtained. Spurred on by Moscow, Canada agreed to full-scope safeguards in 1976; Australia and the United States soon followed suit.

Soviet concerns over unrestricted global sales of sensitive technologies became apparent in 1975 when the Kremlin openly registered its opposition to the recently announced Germany-Brazil nuclear export deal. From this point onward Moscow became increasingly vocal in protesting international transfers of reprocessing and enrichment technology. "If such growth is not hindered," a *Pravda* journalist warned in April 1977, "there will be from 200 to 300 such enrichment plants in the world by the end of this century, and control over the nonproliferation of nuclear weapons will become virtually impossible."[117] Despite the publication of a Soviet article rebuking Washington's hostility to the proposed sale of a French reprocessing plant to Pakistan—"This problem cannot be solved by unilateral bans, with one prohibiting to another what one does oneself"[118]—Moscow shared Carter's concern over the deal. Secretary Brezhnev reportedly raised the issue with President Giscard d'Estaing at a 1977 summit meeting. As a member of the Soviet delegation later confirmed, Brezhnev gave "very serious attention" to this matter, insisting "with complete clarity that the Soviet Union and France must follow common practices so as not to permit the spread of nuclear weapons" through all types of loopholes.[119]

This comment belies the Soviet preference to work with suppliers rather than recipients of nuclear technology in order to head off proliferation. The Kremlin has gone to especially great lengths to coordinate nonproliferation strategies with the United States; formally the superpowers have discussed the subject twice a year since 1983. Today Soviet and U.S. officials confer whenever an important development arises that affects nuclear proliferation.

Despite its vigilant efforts to prevent the spread of sensitive nuclear technology, Moscow has become increasingly fatalistic regarding the threshold nuclear states. Public attacks against the nuclear activities of Pakistan, Israel, and South Africa have diminished in recent years, but most telling is Moscow's obvious acceptance of India's new nuclear weapons capacity. Although India is one proliferator with which the U.S.S.R. may have real influence owing to the two country's extensive military and economic relations, Moscow reacted very mildly to New Delhi's 1974 test, openly accepting India's depiction of it as a *peaceful* nuclear explosion; soon after the test, Moscow replaced Canada as New Delhi's main supplier of heavy water.[120] More recently, the U.S.S.R. broke a de facto embargo on major nuclear sales to threshold nuclear powers in April 1988 when it agreed to sell two new 1,000 mw reactors and their fuel to India. Though the reactors will be subject to IAEA safeguards and Moscow will recover the plutonium-bearing spent fuel they produce, this was the first nuclear sale to a nation possessing a *parallel* unsafeguarded nuclear program since 1979.[121] Apparently, Moscow only presses New Delhi, even in private, on India's ongoing mission to undermine the NPT. A Soviet official confided that, "we can easily accept India as a nuclear power but its behavior is worrisome globally; it could lead to a breakdown of the international nonproliferation regime."[122]

Changes in the coverage (stressing sensitive nuclear uses over strictly military uses), target (accepting India as a nuclear power), and forum (mixing coalitional with international activities) of Soviet nonproliferation strategy appear to result from constrained learning. Although the Kremlin responded to the same trends and events that led Washington to learn causally, we have no evidence indicating that Moscow also followed analytic information-processing procedures as it moved away from a global control strategy. If not an outcome of causal learning, the new

Soviet strategy is stable. Moscow's *management* of nuclear proliferation rests on preferences and beliefs that have persisted for sixteen years.[123] Even as the issue evolves, the assumptions and aims Moscow acquired in the mid-1970s constrain change in Soviet nonproliferation policy.

AMERICAN MANAGEMENT: 1981–1990

As the Carter administration's term drew to a close, adverse foreign and domestic reactions to recent arms control activities—especially to the NNPA—resulted in a major reassessment of U.S. nonproliferation priorities. The new administration's emphasis seemed clear even before it came to power: in response to a reporter's query about U.S. efforts to prevent new countries from acquiring the capacity to develop nuclear arms, presidential candidate Reagan said: "I just don't think it's any of our business."[124] After taking office, however, President Reagan was constrained from making radical revisions in the U.S. approach to nuclear proliferation. Although U.S. military and economic objectives now took precedence over nonproliferation considerations in shaping how the government would relate to the rest of the world, U.S. nonproliferation strategy changed only in a single dimension; it now focused on the political motivation as much as on the technical capability of new states to go nuclear.

The Reagan administration was determined not to permit nonproliferation to damage ties with close friends and strategic allies. Aid cutoffs and other sanctions were to be avoided at all costs. U.S. officials justified the return to "constructive engagement" in nonproliferation on the grounds that the most effective way to limit proliferation was not to deny states technology in the hope that this will prevent them from gaining the capability to build nuclear arms, but rather to provide potential (anticommunist) proliferators military support so as to heighten their sense of security, thus mitigating an important incentive to go nuclear. "In the final analysis," Reagan stated in his major nonproliferation address, "the success of our efforts depends on our ability to improve regional and global stability and reduce those motivations that can drive countries toward nuclear explosives."[125] The speech contained a related reason for stressing *management* over technology denial: "We must reestablish this nation as a predictable and reliable partner for peaceful nuclear cooperation under adequate safeguards. . . . If we are not such a partner, other countries will tend to go their own ways, and our influence will diminish."

Congressional legislation and a faith still held by much of the foreign policy bureaucracy in the continued utility of export controls constrained the president from altogether abandoning the focus on the nuclear capabilities of threshold states. Although Reagan *rhetorically* distanced his strategy from Carter's, Washington has consistently insisted on strict safeguards for all of its nuclear technology exports. Moreover, the Reagan and Bush administrations have paid considerably more attention than Carter did to the issue of delivery systems for weapons of mass destruction. Recognizing recently that missile technology comprised an important element in emergent nuclear weapon systems, Reagan ordered the government in November 1982 to find a way to curb missile proliferation. This resulted in a pact among seven industrial countries to establish consensual restraint guidelines for missile-related exports.[126] The agreement was formalized in April 1987 as the Missile Technology Control Regime (MTCR). As one State Department official put it, the new U.S. approach meant that "we will help countries like India with satellites but not with missiles." But the same individual later admitted that much of the sensitive technology is dual-use and that Washington has few means to verify that exports to foreign space programs do not go to bomb-builders and missile-makers.[127]

Like Moscow, Washington now seems to believe that some states are bound to join the nuclear club. U.S. policy toward Pakistan in particular seems to be shaped by fatalism. The White House energetically worked first in 1981 and then in 1987 to secure two massive aid packages involving the transfer of F-16 aircraft to Islamabad even though it was known that General Zia was assembling equipment and material to build nuclear arms. While Reagan failed to pressure Zia to pledge that Pakistan would curtail work on the bomb in return for U.S. aid, the administration did convince Congress that U.S. aid would cause nuclear restraint. As Secretary of State Haig wrote to a U.S. senator:

> By providing Pakistan with conventional military equipment in the frame-
> work of confidence and mutual understanding, the United States will be in
> a better position to influence the fate and direction of Pakistan's nuclear
> progress in the future.[128]

For a nonnuclear weapon state that imports sensitive nuclear technology without safeguards, the NNPA prohibits U.S. aid unless the president can certify to Congress each year that this state does not own an explosive device. While White House officials and congressional lawmakers now treat Pakistan as a de facto nuclear weapon state, the certification was made every year until 1990 chiefly because of the Soviet involvement in Afghanistan. Washington attempted to contain communism at the risk of tolerating proliferation.

The certification process offers an indication of how nonproliferation has changed over the years. Today lawyers rather than scientists provide the expertise that politicians seek most. As one U.S. official lamented, "Science clearly has become a political tool. Science under Carter was more pure, more meaningful. Under Reagan it has become an instrument to serve political ends; we need science to certify that Pakistan has no nuclear arms. The technical discussion now boils down to a legal question: 'What constitutes a nuclear weapon capability?'"[129] This comment implies that Washington in the past 10 years has not learned causally. The Reagan administration learned new lessons about nonproliferation, but not because it sought the input of technical specialists and not because it acted analytically in its attempt to deal with information paucity, causal uncertainty, and value complexity.

Recent U.S. learning about nonproliferation has been less constrained than instrumental. It has been instrumental owing to the restriction domestic laws and commitments to the coalition of nuclear technology suppliers have placed on Washington's ability to fundamentally modify its approach. In an important sense, the institutional framework that Carter's causal learning established has since *routinized* U.S. nonproliferation activity. Even though Reagan entered office with a very different set of beliefs and preferences from those of Carter, the new belief system resulted in a relatively small policy change. Its commitment to check the global advance of communism constrained the Reagan administration's learning about the focus but not about the target, coverage, or forum of U.S. nonproliferation strategy.

CONCLUSIONS

The preceding historical survey suggests that Washington and Moscow each revised their strategy for nonproliferation five times. Conceptualizing these strategic changes as outcomes of learning proves useful not so much as a means to explain the sources of change—a task that does not require the concept of learning—but rather as a way to compare and contrast the decision styles that resulted in change. By directing our attention to three different approaches that governments follow in order to process information and choose new foreign policies under complex and uncertain conditions, the learning typology that Steinbruner introduced in *The Cybernetic Theory of Decision* enables us to show what is different and what is similar in the ways that U.S. and Soviet officials formulate nonproliferation strategies. Table 3 summarizes each of the strategic shifts in terms of the type of learning that produced it.

Owing to the ambiguous nature of the boundary that separates constrained learning from instrumental learning, comparing actual foreign policy decisions according to this pair of abstractions may disclose more about the observer's analytic preference than about the substantive issue itself. In each of the five respective strategic changes in nonproliferation, the superpowers broke out of both cognitive and bureaucratic habits. Although three strategic shifts are identified as end results of instrumental

TABLE 3 Summary of Strategic Shifts as Learning Outcomes

U.S. Strategy	Instrumental	Constrained	Causal
1941–53: Secrecy and denial	X		
1954–64: Atoms for Peace		X	
1965–74: Global control		X	
1975–80: Technology denial			X
1981–90: Management	X		

Soviet Strategy	Instrumental	Constrained	Causal
1945–54: Secrecy and denial	X		
1954–58: Atoms for Peace		X	
1958–62: Political control		X	
1963–74: Global control		X	
1974–90: Management		X	

learning and six as outcomes of constrained learning, the grounds for demarcation are admittedly subjective; both fixed routines and firm beliefs constrained and conditioned change in all of the cases. Recall that the Reagan administration's learning about nuclear nonproliferation was shaped by legislatively mandated routines and by a shift in beliefs about the subject. Stressing the causal influence of routines over beliefs in this case owes more to judgment than to an impartial survey of the evidence; we simply have no clear criteria on which to base the comparison.

Distinguishing between causal learning and either of the habit-dominated learning types is a simpler and more logical task. If the instrumental and constrained learning types imply that policy makers employ similar techniques to deal with information paucity (narrowing the range of information inputs), causal uncertainty (calculating the effects only of a single outcome), and value complexity (isolating values and focusing only on the most salient), but for different reasons, the causal learning type implies a different decision process altogether: guided by technical specialists, government officials seek all pertinent information, analyze alternative outcomes, and integrate values in an analytic fashion. Since the indicators of causal learning are clear, it is easy to identify President Carter's revision of nonproliferation policy as the sole instance in which Washington employed this process. Searching the history of Soviet nonproliferation activity for evidence of causal learning is more difficult, however, since we can neither trace Soviet decision patterns or analyze the role experts play in shaping Soviet nonproliferation strategy.

Though causal learning is rare, its outcomes seem more likely to endure than do strategies motivated by instrumental or constrained learning. Recall that causal learning implies the institutionalization of consensual knowledge. Consensual knowledge is not necessarily true or complete, but experts develop it according to generally accepted scientific methods and standards. Once institutionalized, therefore, a brand of knowledge may enjoy a longer run of legitimacy and authority than nonscientific, ideological understandings. I state this point speculatively rather than firmly because the historical study of superpower nonproliferation activities suggests but does not confirm it.

U.S. nonproliferation strategies based on ideology rather than consensual knowledge, that is, produced by instrumental or constrained learning, endured for periods of between 9 (global control) and 12 (secrecy and denial) years. The Carter administration's technology denial strategy was replaced by the Reagan administration's management strategy after only five years, but the change that occurred in 1981 did more to preserve than abandon the earlier approach. Whereas the first four strategic shifts fundamentally transformed U.S. activities to inhibit the spread of nuclear arms by changing at least two of the four features of nonproliferation strategy, Reagan revised only one strategic feature (replacing a strict focus on technical capabilities with a mixed focus). Therefore, much of the consensual knowledge institutionalized by Carter continues to enjoy legitimacy and authority in Washington.

The establishment and continuing growth of cooperative nonproliferation arrangements between Washington and Moscow and among the broader coalition of nuclear technology suppliers represent two important outcomes of the causal learning that took place in the late 1970s. As Table 4 indicates, although Moscow and Washington began to cooperate for nonproliferation in 1966, coordinated activities were limited to establishing the NPT and were not fully based on a mutual understanding of the problem's causes and solutions. With the establishment in 1977 of a Joint Committee for U.S.–Soviet Cooperation in Atomic Energy, the superpowers institutionalized a procedure for sharing what was rapidly becoming consensual knowledge about nonproliferation. And although the practice of meet-

TABLE 4 Summary of Cooperative Arrangements as Learning Outcomes

General Development	Instrumental	Constrained	Causal
U.S.–U.S.S.R. nonproliferation cooperation	1966 ⟶		1977–83
Nuclear supplier cooperation		1975 ⟶	1978
Global nonproliferation cooperation	1968		

ing twice a year ended after the Soviet move into Afghanistan, it resumed in the summer of 1983. The U.S.–Soviet consensus on nonproliferation
is now thorough; the focus, coverage, target, and forum of present superpower nonproliferation strategies are identical.[130]

In 1975 the leading suppliers of nuclear technology convened their
first round of discussions in London on how to inhibit the spread of
nuclear weapons without curbing exports of equipment to meet the world's
energy needs.[131] Debate persisted on this issue until the group reached
the London Suppliers' Agreement in January 1978, thereby indicating
that consensual knowledge had been achieved and institutionalized.

Consensual knowledge has proved to be most elusive at the global
level. Finally reached in 1968, the NPT's major bargains involve a fragmented
rather than substantive linkage of issues. The treaty's formalization depended as much on the superpowers' ability to influence other parties to
accept the pact as on global knowledge. The nonproliferation norm was
not universally shared then, and it is not now. Over 30 states have
refused to sign or ratify the NPT, including two early nuclear powers,
France and China, as well as each country poised on the threshold of
possessing nuclear arms, namely Argentina, Brazil, India, Israel, Pakistan, and South Africa. The willingness of these threshold states and
other nuclear aspirants to refrain from building bombs seems to depend
on the ability of the established nuclear powers, especially the United
States and the U.S.S.R., to widen the consensus and coordinated action
that produced the NPT. That treaty entered force partially because the
superpowers proposed—and the other parties accepted—a redefinition
of the proliferation problem to be solved. Because challenges to the
credibility of the NPT-based regime have mounted, it may now again be
time to reconceptualize the problem, especially as the NPT's extension
comes up for final consideration in 1995.

NOTES

I wish to thank George Breslauer, George Bunn, James Fearon, Clay Moltz,
Benjamin Schiff, David Schleicher, Leonard Spector, Philip Tetlock, and Steven
Weber for their helpful comments on earlier drafts.

1. John Steinbruner, *The Cybernetic Theory of Decision* (Princeton, N.J.: Princeton
University Press, 1974).

2. James C. March and Johan P. Olsen, "Organizational Learning and the
Ambiguity of the Past," in March and Olsen, *Ambiguity and Choice in Organizations*
(Oslo, Norway: Universitetsforlaget, 1976), 67.

3. On the problems that paucity, uncertainty, and complexity pose for efficient foreign policy decision making, see John Steinbruner, *The Cybernetic Theory
of Decision*, 15–18; Alexander L. George, *Presidential Decision Making in Foreign
Policy: The Effective Use of Information and Advice* (Boulder, Colo.: Westview Press,

1980), 25–47; and Janice G. Stein and Raymond Tanter, *Rational Decisionmaking* (Columbus: Ohio State University Press, 1980), 23–26.

4. For a credible nuclear weapon status, a state must possess (1) fissile material for an explosive charge (plutonium or highly enriched uranium); (2) components to enclose and trigger a device (beryllium, timing instruments, detonators, etc.); and (3) a means to deliver the device to proposed targets. The greatest obstacle involved in going nuclear is obtaining fissile material.

5. For example, India's 1974 explosion of a nuclear device provided firm evidence that New Delhi can construct nuclear arms. Pakistan has not tested a device, but enough information has leaked out of Islamabad to inform Americans (and Soviets) of the present military potential of Pakistan's nuclear program. Informative studies of South Asian nuclear programs are Leonard S. Spector, *The Undeclared Bomb* (Cambridge, Mass.: Ballinger, 1988); and David Albright and Tom Zamora, "India, Pakistan's Nuclear Weapons: All the Pieces in Place," *Bulletin of the Atomic Scientists* 45 (June 1989).

6. The leading Western proponent of the view that a world of nuclear porcupines would be more peaceful is Kenneth N. Waltz, *The Spread of Nuclear Weapons: More May Be Better*, Adelphi Paper 171 (London: IISS, 1981). See also the Indian defense expert, K. Subrahmanyam's work, such as "Preventing Proliferation of Nuclear Weapons—Forestalling 1995," *Strategic Analysis* (New Delhi) (November 1988).

7. Joseph S. Nye, Jr., "Nuclear Learning and U.S.–Soviet Security Regimes," *International Organization* 41 (Summer 1987): 382. For recent discussions of the status of evidence and knowledge about nuclear deterrence, see the introductory and concluding chapters of Paul C. Stern et al., eds., *Perspectives on Deterrence* (New York: Oxford University Press, 1989); and Robert Jervis's chapter on "The Symbolic Nature of Nuclear Politics" in *The Meaning of the Nuclear Revolution* (Ithaca, N.Y.: Cornell University Press, 1989).

8. See P.E. Tetlock and C. McGuire, "Cognitive Perspectives on Foreign Policy," in S. Long, ed., *Political Behavior Annual*, vol. 1 (Boulder, Colo.: Westview, 1986); John Steinbruner, *The Cybernetic Theory of Decision*, 131–35.

9. The occurrence of war in a nuclear region, however, does not *disprove* the argument that nuclear proliferation reduces war's likelihood; a single contradictory event is generally regarded as insufficient to falsify a social scientific theory. See I. Lakatos, *The Methodology of Scientific Research Programmes*, vol. 1 (London: Cambridge University Press, 1978), 32; and Bruce Bueno De Mesquita, "Toward a Scientific Understanding of International Conflict: A Personal View," *International Studies Quarterly* 29 (1985): 22.

10. McGeorge Bundy, *Danger and Survival: Choices About the Bomb in the First Fifty Years* (New York: Random House, 1988), 173.

11. Herbert A. Simon, "Rational Choice and the Structure of the Environment," *Psychological Review* 63 (1956): 136. Cybernetic concepts are applied to decision theory in John Steinbruner, *The Cybernetic Theory of Decision*; W. Ross Ashby, *A Design for a Brain* (New York: John Wiley and Sons, Inc., 1952); and Herbert A. Simon, "The Architecture of Complexity," in *The Sciences of the Artificial* (Cambridge, Mass.: MIT Press, 1969).

12. The precise processes by which officials create strategic interests from core

values is not specified in cybernetic models. These models also black-box the way in which organizations join interests with inferences drawn from history to set the routines that guide behavior. These omissions inhibit the application of cybernetic concepts to complete policy processes, but other learning types are no more thorough in this respect. In fact, the recent interest in learning as a distinct analytic category derives from our scant knowledge about how leaders draw on experience to form their conceptions of national interests. It is much easier to show how experiential inductions push individuals and groups to *revise*, rather than *create*, existing interests.

13. Instrumental learning is identical both to the reward-punishment concept of learning Tetlock identifies in this volume's introductory chapter and to many behavioral perspectives on organizational change. For example, Levitt and March write that "behavior in an organization is based on routines. Action stems from a logic of appropriateness or legitimacy more than from a logic of consequentiality or intention. It involves matching procedures to situations more than it does calculating choices." Barbara Levitt and James G. March, "Organizational Learning," *Annual Review of Sociology* 14 (1988): 320.

14. John Steinbruner, *The Cybernetic Theory of Decision*, 78.

15. Political realism has been a dominant intellectual paradigm of global political studies in the postwar period. The tradition's most sophisticated and widely cited variant is Waltz's structural realism (*neorealism*). Kenneth N. Waltz, *Theory of International Politics* (New York: Random House, 1979).

16. As Barbara Levitt and James G. March put it: "Competitors are linked partly through the diffusion of experience, and understanding learning within competitive communities of organizations involves seeing how experience . . . [is shared]. Competitors are also linked through the effects of their actions on each other. One organization's action is another organization's outcome. As a result, even if learning by an individual organization were entirely internal and direct, it could be comprehended only by specifying the competitive structure." See "Organizational Learning," 332.

17. Kenneth N. Waltz, *Theory of International Politics*, 117.

18. John Steinbruner, *The Cybernetic Theory of Decision*, 63 n.22.

19. Cybernetic-structural theories about foreign policy generally are too abstract to permit useful explanations of state behavior. Though Waltz offers a theory of international politics, not of foreign policy, his substantive assumptions are strong enough to generate at least these three expectations about U.S. and Soviet nonproliferation activities.

20. For Kenneth Waltz, "The first concern of states is not to maximize power but to maintain their positions in the system." *Theory of International Politics*, 126. Joseph M. Grieco elaborates: "Driven by an interest in survival, states are acutely sensitive to any erosion of their relative capabilities, which are the ultimate basis for their security and independence in an anarchical, self-help international context. Thus, realists feel that the major goal of states in any relationship is not to attain the best possible individual gain or payoff. Instead *the fundamental goal of states in any relationship is to prevent others from achieving advances in their relative capabilities*." "Anarchy and the Limits of Cooperation: A Realist Critique of the Newest Liberal Institutionalism," *International Organization* 42 (Summer 1988): 498.

21. William C. Foster, "Arms Control and Disarmament," *Foreign Affairs* 43 (July 1965): 591; cited by Kenneth N. Waltz, *Theory of International Politics*, 203.

22. Clarence D. Long, "Nuclear Proliferation: Can Congress Act in Time?" *International Security* 1 (Spring 1977): 52.

23. This study does not try to explain nuclear proliferation's sources, but if it did, neorealism would provide a useful starting point. Because security and well-being are scarce in the present world order, the states that manage to obtain them set behavioral standards for others. Kenneth Waltz writes: "if some do relatively well, others will emulate them or fall by the wayside." Insofar as the United States and the U.S.S.R. are seen as two of the world's greatest powers, and to the extent that nuclear arms figure into images of their success, others are induced to acquire their own nuclear forces. "Contending states imitate the military innovations contrived by the country of greatest capability and ingenuity. And so the weapons of major contenders, and even their strategies, begin to look much the same all over the world." Two conditions restrict the sweep of this argument. Since superpowers can guarantee the defense of some friendly states, the latter do not need to emulate the military practices of their patron. And not all states *contend*: many countries are neither able nor inclined to acquire the latest military means to defend possessions and pursue gains. So bounded, structural realism provides a powerful account for a state's motivation to go nuclear. *Theory of International Politics*, 118, 127.

24. Complex learning, in Nye's words, "involves recognition of conflicts among means and goals in causally complicated situations and leads to new priorities and tradeoffs." "Simple learning uses new information merely to adapt the means, without altering any deeper goals in the ends-means chain." "Nuclear Learning and U.S.–Soviet Security Regimes," 380.

25. John Steinbruner, *The Cybernetic Theory of Decision*, 137.

26. Useful surveys of these and other cognitive heuristics are provided by P.E. Tetlock and C. McGuire, "Cognitive Perspectives on Foreign Policy"; and Robert Jervis, *Perception and Misperception in International Politics* (Princeton, N.J.: Princeton University Press, 1976). One example of a noncompensatory choice heuristic is the "elimination by aspects rule": people compare choice options according to their single most important value, eliminating the options that do not serve this value, and evaluating remaining options in terms of their second most important value, and so on. See Amos Tversky, "Elimination by Aspects: A Theory of Choice," *Psychological Review* 79 (1972).

27. P.E. Tetlock and C. McGuire, "Cognitive Perspectives on Foreign Policy," 272.

28. James N. Rosenau, "Before Cooperation: Hegemons, Regimes, and Habit-driven Actors in World Politics," *International Organization* 40 (Autumn 1986):863.

29. The boundary separating cybernetic and cognitive processes is highly ambiguous, partly because three diverse approaches demarcate it. First, one may consider the distinction in terms of the timeless debate between free will and determinism. Cybernetic arguments presume that situations structure human action. Cognitive claims stress the human capacity to challenge and reshape existing structures. For discrete reasons, both expect conservative behavior, although proponents of the cognitive tradition perhaps expect habits to be broken more

easily. Second, one may differentiate the pair by their level of analytic abstraction: one approach focuses on the cognition of individuals and the other on the routines of bureaucracies and other substate groups (as in Graham T. Allison's *Essence of Decision* [Boston, Little, Brown, 1971]) or nation-states (as in Kenneth Waltz's *Theory of International Politics*). Third, one may discuss both cybernetic and cognitive processes at the individual level, treating the former as a subcomponent of the latter (as John Steinbruner usually does in *The Cybernetic Theory of Decision*). The first two approaches demarcate the boundary in this chapter.

30. See Robert A. Nisbet, *Social Change and History* (New York: Oxford University Press, 1969), 275–83.

31. Graham T. Allison, *The Essence of Decision*, 28–32; John Steinbruner, *The Cybernetic Theory of Decision*; Janice G. Stein and Raymond Tanter, *Rational Decision-making*, 27–32.

32. See Ernst B. Haas's contribution to this volume, "Collective Learning: Some Speculations"; and his recent book, *When Knowledge Is Power: Three Models of Change in International Organizations* (Berkeley: University of California Press, 1990). An early formulation of Haas's approach is "Why Collaborate? Issue-Linkage and International Regimes," *World Politics* 32 (April 1980).

33. Ernst B. Haas, *When Knowledge Is Power*, 27–28.

34. Robert Gilpin, *American Scientists and Nuclear Weapons Policy* (Princeton, N.J.: Princeton University Press, 1962), 16.

35. Ernst B. Haas, *When Knowledge Is Power*, p. 21.

36. Though Haas admits that learning does not necessarily produce more elaborate or holistic causal theories, this type seems to join the cognitive structural and the institutional learning conceptions that Tetlock identifies.

37. Ernst B. Haas, *When Knowledge Is Power*, 24.

38. Ernst B. Haas, "Why Collaborate?" 392–93. John Steinbruner (*The Cybernetic Theory of Decision*, 147) emphasizes that only causal learners bargain for consensus: "If cognitive (and cybernetic) actors are engaged in politics, the natural presumption is that the role of bargaining as traditionally understood will be sharply diminished. Bargaining implies a willingness and capacity on the part of actors to adjust their conflicting objectives in a process of reaching an accommodation—a clear case of value integration. It is natural to suppose, by contrast, that cognitive (and cybernetic) actors will not display the same degree of deliberate accommodation, will act more independently, and will by-pass bargains which under analytic assumptions would appear to be obvious."

39. Linking bargaining to learning, institutionalization occurs with "the development of new organs, subunits, and administrative practices that are designed to improve the performance of the organization in the wake of some major disappointment with earlier performance." Institutionalization depends both on the legitimacy and authority of lessons learned (or bargains reached). Ernst B. Haas, *When Knowledge Is Power*, 85–88. The norms of nonproliferation are more fully institutionalized within and between the U.S. and Soviet governments than among the broader coalition of nuclear technology suppliers. Notwithstanding the IAEA and the NPT, these norms are least institutionalized internationally.

40. The nonproliferation regime consists of consensual understandings, voluntary commitments, bilateral agreements, and treaties prohibiting the acquisition of

nuclear explosives that are verified through international inspection conducted chiefly by the International Atomic Energy Agency. The regime rests on four substantive norms: (1) the spread of nuclear weapons is bad, (2) nuclear technology can contribute to national economic development, (3) access to nuclear energy is inevitable and can be facilitated without increasing the risk of proliferation, and (4) nuclear nonproliferation is closely linked to the reduction of nuclear arms by nuclear weapon states. See Lawrence Scheinman, *The Nonproliferation Role of the International Atomic Energy Agency* (Washington, D.C.: Resources for the Future, 1985); and Benjamin N. Schiff, *International Nuclear Technology Transfer* (Totowa, N.J.: Rowman and Allanheld, 1984).

41. This learning typology mainly draws on John Steinbruner, *The Cybernetic Theory of Decision*. See also Robert Cutler, "The Cybernetic Theory Reconsidered," *Michigan Journal of Political Science* 1 (Winter 1981):60.

42. This periodization of superpower nonproliferation activities draws on the work of William Potter and Joseph Nye. See William C. Potter, "Nuclear Proliferation: U.S.–Soviet Cooperation," *Washington Quarterly* 8 (Winter 1985); William C. Potter, "Nuclear Export Policy: A Soviet-American Comparison," in Charles Kegley and Patrick McGowan, eds., *Foreign Policy: USA/USSR* (Beverly Hills, Calif.: Sage Publications, 1982); and Joseph S. Nye, Jr., "U.S.–Soviet Cooperation in a Nonproliferation Regime," in Alexander L. George, Philip J. Farley, and Alexander Dallin, eds., *U.S.–Soviet Security Cooperation* (New York: Oxford University Press, 1988).

43. Early U.S. atomic activities are discussed by Richard G. Hewlett and Oscar E. Anderson, *The New World, 1939–1946: A History of the United States Atomic Energy Commission*, vol. 1 (University Park, Pa.: Pennsylvania State University Press, 1962); Richard Rhodes, *The Making of the Atomic Bomb* (New York: Simon and Schuster, 1986); and McGeorge Bundy, *Danger and Survival*.

44. Richard Rhodes, *The Making of the Atomic Bomb*, 378.

45. McGeorge Bundy, *Danger and Survival*, 47.

46. The text of the Quebec agreement appears in Margaret Gowing, *Britain and Atomic Energy 1939–1945* (New York: MacMillan, 1964), 439–40.

47. Two letters that Oppenheimer and his colleagues wrote to the U.S. secretary of war are reprinted in Robert C. Williams and Philip L. Cantelon eds., *The American Atom*, (Philadelphia: University of Pennsylvania Press, 1984), 39–40, 64–66. See also Robert J. Oppenheimer, "Niels Bohr and Atomic Weapons," *New York Review of Books* (December 17, 1964).

48. Truman's remarks at Potsdam on August 9, 1945, are cited by McGeorge Bundy in *Danger and Survival*, 133.

49. The famous document was a product of compromise between a committee of scientists led by Robert Oppenheimer and chaired by David Lilienthal and a group of political and military officials directed by Dean Acheson. Whereas the scientists advocated immediate delegation of full control over the whole field of atomic energy activities to an Atomic Development Authority, the more conservative politicians and soldiers prevailed in arguing that authority over atomic matters should be relinquished gradually, and only after the compliance of all parties was ensured. U.S. Department of State, *A Report on the International Control of Atomic Energy* (Washington, D.C.: U.S. Government Printing Office, 1946).

50. Baruch's concern with intimate inspection and enforceable punishment may have derived from a belief that the atomic issue could be used to open Soviet society and thus remove a projected source of atomic war. As Senator Arthur Vandenberg noted, "What had begun with the Acheson-Lilienthal study as an attempt to disarm the world of nuclear weapons became instead a nine-year struggle to design a partial system of world order among nation-states fundamentally in disagreement about the nature and future of the world." Robert L. Beckman, *Nuclear Non-Proliferation: Congress and the Control of Peaceful Nuclear Activities* (Boulder, Colo.: Westview Press, 1985), 33.

51. The 1946 AEA is reprinted in R.C. Williams and P.L. Cantelon, eds., *The American Atom*, 79–92.

52. This is a classic example of wishful thinking: Washington's *desire* to retain an atomic monopoly and its *fear* of facing novel atomic threats seems to have influenced its *expectation* that Moscow would not acquire the bomb soon. See Robert Jervis, *Perception and Misperception in International Politics*, 356–81. Although affect at least partly caused this cognition, thus implying constrained learning, early U.S. nuclear choices are better viewed as instrumental learning outcomes. This case shows that these two learning types are complementary.

53. David Holloway, "Stalin and Hiroshima," unpublished manuscript prepared for the Workshop on Soviet Nuclear History, Center for International Security and Arms Control, Stanford University, 7 and 8 April 1989, 2–3.

54. David Holloway, "Entering the Nuclear Arms Race: The Soviet Decision to Build the Atomic Bomb, 1939–45," *Social Studies of Science* 11 (1981):183.

55. David Holloway, "Stalin and Hiroshima," 27.

56. Ibid., 15.

57. See Joseph L. Nogee, *Soviet Policy Towards International Control of Atomic Energy* (Notre Dame, Ind.: University of Notre Dame Press, 1961), 136.

58. German access to the bomb, soon to become a major Soviet fear, was not then possible; the allies allowed neither Germany to arm even conventionally.

59. Joseph L. Nogee, "Soviet Nuclear Proliferation Policy: Dilemmas and Contradictions," *Orbis* 59 (Winter 1981):753.

60. McGeorge Bundy, *Danger and Survival*, 181.

61. Matthew Evangelista, *Innovation and the Arms Race* (Ithaca, N.Y.: Cornell University Press, 1980), 168. A Soviet physicist who worked on the original bomb program recently asserted that he and his colleagues were true believers: "We had a supreme task: in the shortest period of time to create weaponry that could defend our country! When the problem was successfully resolved, we felt relief, even happiness—indeed, possessing such weaponry, we were removing the possibility of having it used against the USSR with impunity." Iulii Khariton, in an interview with V. Gubarev, "Fizika—eto moia zhizn" (Physics is my life), *Pravda* (20 February 1984).

62. Bernard Goldschmidt, "A Historical Survey of Nonproliferation Policies," *International Security* 2 (1977):71.

63. U.S. Department of State, *Foreign Relations of the United States, 1950*, vol. 1 (Washington, D.C.: U.S. Government Printing Office, 1977), 271.

64. The new U.S. defense doctrine was codified in October 1953 in the highly classified "Basic National Security Policy" (NSC-162/2), the key sentence of which

reads: "In the event of hostilities, the United States will consider nuclear weapons to be as available for use as other munitions." *Foreign Relations of the United States, 1952–54* (2):593.

65. See Glenn Snyder, "The New Look of 1953," in Warner R. Schilling, Paul Y. Hammond, and Snyder, *Strategy, Politics, and Defense Budgets* (New York: Columbia University Press, 1962), 427–437; McGeorge Bundy, *Danger and Survival*, 249.

66. Quoted in McGeorge Bundy, *Danger and Survival*, 249.

67. President Eisenhower's "Atoms for Peace" address appears in the *Congressional Record*, 100 (January 7, 1954):61–63.

68. Finally established in 1957, the IAEA became the first real institutional expression of Washington's interest in channeling nuclear technology globally for peaceful ends. Eisenhower's sponsorship of the agency implied that the idea of a supranational control authority invested with a mandate to prohibit all independent nuclear arsenals was now viewed by Washington as unobtainable. Though a significant body of scientific opinion ran counter to Eisenhower's new emphasis, "with Atoms for Peace," Mitchell Reiss observes, "proposals for international control would henceforth emphasize partial nuclear disarmament." See *Without the Bomb: The Politics of Nuclear Nonproliferation* (New York: Columbia University Press, 1988), 12.

69. There was another important reason for the amendment. After Moscow tested its first thermonuclear weapon, Washington became extremely concerned about the West's ability to meet the growing Soviet threat. The 1954 revision addressed this concern by allowing both the training of NATO personnel in the employment of U.S. atomic weapons and the transfer to NATO states of information on nuclear defense plans and on the external characteristics of nuclear arms. U.S. fears returned in 1957 with the Soviet Sputnik success and with the release of the secret Gaither Report, which argued that a major missile gap had risen between the United States and the U.S.S.R. Consequently, the AEA was loosened again in 1958 to permit transfers to U.S. allies of fissile material, nuclear equipment, and highly sensitive information. Because the powerful U.S. Joint Committee on Atomic Energy doubted the reliability of France as a nuclear partner, this legislation actually allowed nuclear sharing only with Britain.

70. David E. Lilienthal, *Change, Hope and the Bomb* (Princeton, N.J: Princeton University Press), 96.

71. Secretary Dulles's remark is cited by William B. Bader, *The United States and the Spread of Nuclear Weapons* (New York: Pegasus, 1968), 29–35.

72. National Academy of Sciences, *Nuclear Arms Control: Background and Issues* (Washington, D.C.: National Academy Press, 1985), 233. See Glenn T. Seaborg, *Stemming the Tide: Arms Control in the Johnson Years* (Lexington, Mass.: D.C. Heath and Company, 1987), 73.

73. Glenn T. Seaborg, *Stemming the Tide*, 73.

74. *New York Times* (March 23, 1963).

75. Defense Secretary McNamara stated the plan's nonproliferation logic to Congress: "With testing limited to the underground environment, the potential cost of a nuclear weapons program would increase sharply for all signatory states. And since testing underground is not only more costly but also more difficult and time-consuming, the proposed treaty would retard progress in weapons de-

velopment in cases where the added cost and other factors were not sufficient to preclude it altogether. One of the great advantages of this treaty is that it will have the effect of retarding the spread of nuclear weapons." *Nuclear Test Ban Treaty,* Hearing, Committee on Foreign Relations, U.S. Senate, 88th Congress, 1st Session (Washington, D.C.: U.S. Government Printing Office, 1963), 108. See William B. Bader, *The United States and the Spread of Nuclear Weapons,* 55.

76. William B. Bader, *The United States and the Spread of Nuclear Weapons,* 46.

77. The Atoms for Peace idea began with a report in which a panel of experts chaired by Robert Oppenheimer recommended a U.S. policy of *candor* in explaining the gloomy new nuclear realities, thus raising the incentive for meaningful arms control. While Eisenhower told the world that there was no way to defend populations from the bomb's enormous destructiveness, he offered the illusory hope that peaceful nuclear uses could replace dangerous military stockpiles, thereby solving "the fearful atomic dilemma." But in the end, "building more weapons remained the top priority, and the stockpiles continued to grow unchecked." McGeorge Bundy, *Danger and Survival,* 287–95.

78. *Izvestia* (January 18, 1955); cited by William C. Potter in "Nuclear Export Policy: A Soviet-American Comparison," 296–297.

79. Harold L. Nieburg, *Nuclear Secrecy and Foreign Policy* (Washington, D.C.: Public Affairs Press, 1964), 92–93.

80. Gloria Duffy, "Soviet Nuclear Exports," *International Security* 3 (Summer 1978):85.

81. John Wilson Lewis and Xue Litai, *China Builds the Bomb* (Palo Alto, Calif.: Stanford University Press, 1988), 41. Much of the following information about Sino-Soviet nuclear relations is drawn from this book.

82. William C. Potter, "The Soviet Union and Nuclear Proliferation," *Slavic Review* 44 (Fall 1985): 469.

83. Gloria Duffy, "Soviet Nuclear Exports," 84–85.

84. Benjamin S. Lambeth, "Nuclear Proliferation and Soviet Arms Control Policy," *Orbis* (Summer 1970):311.

85. Christer Jonsson, *Superpower: Comparing American and Soviet Foreign Policy* (London: Frances Pinter, 1984), 206.

86. W.W. Rostow, *The Diffusion of Power* (New York: Macmillan, 1972), 31.

87. Gloria Duffy, "Soviet Nuclear Exports," 86.

88. William C. Potter, "The Soviet Union and Nuclear Proliferation," 470.

89. Ibid. The source William Potter cites on this point is Karel Docek, "Czechoslovak Uranium and the USSR," *Radio Liberty Dispatch* (July 9, 1974), 3.

90. Quoted by B. Goldschmidt, "A Historical Survey of Nonproliferation Policies," 75.

91. B. Goldschmidt, "A Historical Survey of Nonproliferation Policies," 75.

92. See Raymond L. Garthoff, *Reflections on the Cuban Missile Crisis* (Washington, D.C.: The Brookings Institution, 1987), 64–88; James Clay Moltz, "Managing International Rivalry on High Technology Frontiers: U.S.–Soviet Competition and Cooperation in Space," (Ph.D. dissertation, University of California, Berkeley, 1989).

93. V.S. Emelyanov made this remark to Bernard Goldschmidt, "A Historical Survey of Nonproliferation Policies," 84.

94. Gloria Duffy writes: "Consciousness of nonproliferation as a global problem demanding broader cooperation only seemed to strike the Soviets when their security interests were threatened by the incapacity of the US to uphold its side of the bargain." "The Soviet Union and Nuclear Drift," in W. Raymond Duncan, ed., *Soviet Policy in the Third World* (New York: Peragmon Press, 1980), 26.

95. Deputy Foreign Minister Valerin Zorin's July 1964 remark is quoted by Glenn T. Seaborg, *Stemming the Tide*, 107.

96. Glenn T. Seaborg, *Stemming the Tide*, 106.

97. George Quester, "Preventing Proliferation: The Impact on International Politics," *International Organization* 35 (Winter 1981), 227–28.

98. George Quester, *The Politics of Nuclear Proliferation* (Baltimore: Johns Hopkins University Press, 1973), 23.

99. David Holloway, *The Soviet Union and the Arms Race* (New Haven: Yale University Press, 1983), 47.

100. Dean Rusk said this to the U.S. Senate Committee on Foreign Relations. See Hearings, *Nonproliferation Treaty*, 90th Congress, 2nd Session, 1968, 4.

101. Duncan L. Clarke writes that ACDA's persistence was central to the eventual U.S. backing of the NPT, but that an equally important reason for the treaty's success was that it didn't threaten AEC or DOD budgets. *Politics of Arms Control* (New York: Free Press, 1979), 72–73.

102. Quoted by William Sweet in *The Nuclear Age* (Washington, D.C.: Congressional Quarterly Inc., 1988), 134.

103. The agreement that was finally presented to the United Nations and is now endorsed by 140 states commits nonnuclear-weapon-state signatories not to build nuclear explosives (Article II) and to accept *full-scope* IAEA safeguards on all of their peaceful nuclear activities (Article III). Each party agrees to accept IAEA safeguards on exports of nuclear equipment or material to nonnuclear weapon states (Article III). And nuclear-weapon states pledge not to help nonnuclear weapon states obtain nuclear arms (Article I). The two other substantive terms of the NPT call for the fullest possible global sharing of peaceful nuclear technology (Article IV) and for the nuclear weapon states to conduct nuclear disarmament negotiations in "good faith" (Article VI).

104. See Ernst B. Haas, "Why Collaborate?"; and Benjamin N. Schiff, *International Nuclear Technology Transfer*.

105. At Trombay, India ran an unsafeguarded, locally built reprocessing plant to separate plutonium for use as the fissile material in a Canadian-supplied research reactor, moderated with U.S.–supplied heavy water.

106. The implications of the Indian test are nicely summarized by Michael Brenner: "Most worrisome was that the key critical technology employed, spent-fuel reprocessing, and the key material, plutonium, were on the point of entering the commercial market. If the then-current practice of closing the nuclear fuel-cycle by the recycling of plutonium were to continue, a host of countries would move to the nuclear weapons threshold. Although the critical facilities would remain under safeguards so far as U.S.–supplied technology was concerned, other suppliers were less strict. Moreover, safeguards themselves had suffered a blow to their credibility with the explosion in India's Western Desert. In the future

their adequacy for meeting a renewed proliferation threat would be in question." Michael J. Brenner, *Nuclear Power and Non-Proliferation* (New York: Cambridge University Press, 1981), 6.

107. Ibid., 63.

108. ACDA in fact had been purged by Nixon and Kissinger in December 1972: they slashed the budget by a third and fired outspoken arms control advocates. Duncan L. Clarke, *Politics of Arms Control*, 52.

109. Michael J. Brenner, *Nuclear Power and Non-Proliferation*, 93.

110. Ibid., 123.

111. The Ford/Mitre study was considered Carter's "Bible" on nuclear matters. Ford Foundation Nuclear Energy Policy Study Group and Mitre Corporation Report, *Nuclear Power Issues and Choices* (Cambridge, Mass.: Ballinger, 1977). Wholstetter's report is described by a former ACDA director as the work that "revolutionized the thinking in the U.S. (and in other countries as well), leading the way to the radical new departure in U.S. nonproliferation policy." Fred Charles Ikle, "Foreword," in Albert Wholstetter, *Swords from Plowshares: The Military Potential of Civilian Nuclear Energy* (Chicago: University of Chicago Press, 1977).

112. *Papers of the President: Jimmy Carter*, Washington, D.C.: Library of Congress Series 13 (Vol. 15) (April 18, 1977).

113. The NNPA also contained an important escape clause that allowed the president, subject to congressional veto, to waive certain requirements.

114. Michael J. Brenner, *Nuclear Power and Non-proliferation*, 203.

115. Horst Mendershausen, *Europe's Changing Energy Relations* (Santa Monica, Calif.: Rand Corporation, 1976), 45; cited by Gloria Duffy in "The Soviet Union and Nuclear Drift," 27.

116. "Despite Faith in Nuclear Trade Controls, USSR Rejects U.S. Policy," *Energy Daily* (24 May 1977): 2; cited by Gloria Duffy in "The Soviet Union and Nuclear Drift," 35.

117. V. Mikhailov, "Battles Over Deal of the Century," *Pravda* (17 April 1977); cited by Gloria Duffy in "The Soviet Union and Nuclear Drift," 36.

118. *Socialisticheskaya Industria*; cited by Shirin Tahir-Kelly, "Pakistan's Nuclear Option and U.S. Policy," *Orbis* 22 (Summer 1978): 363–64.

119. *Tass* (17 June 1977); cited by Gloria Duffy in "The Soviet Union and Nuclear Drift," 36.

120. Gloria Duffy, "Soviet Nuclear Exports," 97.

121. Leonard S. Spector, *The Undeclared Bomb*, 317.

122. Interview material, New Delhi, December 1988.

123. Management as a nonproliferation approach is discussed by Jed Snyder, "Is Nuclear Proliferation in the U.S. Interest?" *World & I* 3 (January 1988).

124. *New York Times* (1 February 1980).

125. "Nuclear Nonproliferation Policy," President's Statement, July 19, 1981, Department of State *Bulletin* 81 (September 1981): 60–61.

126. Janne E. Nolan, "Ballistic Missiles in the Third World: The Limits of Nonproliferation," *Arms Control Today* 19 (November 1989): 12.

127. Interview material, New Delhi, November 1989.

128. Secretary of State Haig's letter to Senator Percy is cited in *Security and Development Assistance*, Senate Hearing 100-361, Part 2, 70.

129. Interview material, New Delhi, January 1990.

130. See William C. Potter, "Nuclear Proliferation: U.S.–Soviet Cooperation," for a more complete discussion of the convergence in superpower nonproliferation practices.

131. Michael J. Brenner, *Nuclear Power and Non-Proliferation*, 95–96.

20

Interactive Learning in U.S.–Soviet Arms Control

Steven Weber

INTRODUCTION

Arms control, Levine suggests, is like theology. It is different from other issues in U.S. and Soviet foreign policy, because there is no concrete evidence about the effects of nuclear weapons and measures to control them on deterrence. There has been no nuclear war between the United States and the Soviet Union, but the nonoccurrence of a unique event is a very poor source of feedback about the efficacy of arms control policies. It is impossible to argue decisively that nuclear arms control has added to or subtracted from the likelihood that war might some day occur.

Deterrence has been a constant. Despite this, the United States and the Soviet Union have changed both their basic approach to arms control and their specific policies, sometimes dramatically, over the last 40 years. This is because arms control is about much more than deterrence. There has been considerable change in both states' ideas and belief systems that define precisely what arms control is about, and how it meshes with their security and other interests. For example, both superpowers have struggled with the question of whether nuclear weapons can be used in military operations, and whether it is possible to "prevail" in nuclear war. Both sides have asked whether nuclear weapons increase the degree to which they are interdependent in security; or whether security in the nuclear age remains a self-help responsibility and the primary province of sovereign states.

In a general sense, these questions address the uncertain relationship between nuclear weapons and power in international politics. That relationship is forged by particular sets of ideas and beliefs about nuclear weapons. These ideas do more than simply give purpose to power; they define what power is and how it operates. Are nuclear weapons a source of influence, prestige, and control, making it possible for the possessor to advance its political and military interests in world politics? What does it mean to be a superpower, and to behave like one, in a nuclear world? This chapter examines the reasons why the United States and the Soviet Union have answered these questions in different ways over time. I will argue that the superpowers have undergone a form of *interactive learning* in arms control, whose sources and consequences are different from the kind of learning that is the subject of the other chapters in this book.

Arms control learning is important whether or not it has affected the basic phenomena of deterrence. God may be a constant; but the practice of religion has changed over time, and these changes have had a profound impact on human society. So too has the practice of arms control deeply affected the superpower relationship.

COGNITIVE STRUCTURE AND NUCLEAR ARMS CONTROL

Theories about learning identify the set of basic ideas that underlie state objectives and behavior in a given area as cognitive structure.[1] In arms control, there are actually two tiers of cognitive structure. The first tier is made up of a state's fundamental *strategic model*. Strategic models are built on the answers to the elemental questions about nuclear weapons and power posed earlier; they capture fundamental beliefs about how the world works in the context of nuclear weapons. Strategic models are made up of a set of simple rules that become a kind of "generative grammar" for thinking about arms control. Like a Kuhnian paradigm, they demarcate interesting and relevant data from chaff and delineate what relationships among the data are potentially meaningful.[2] The American strategic model of 1945, for example, pictured nuclear weapons as analogous to other military capabilities as a source of power in international politics. For this strategic model, the U.S. nuclear monopoly was clearly relevant "data" and should have had an important impact on U.S.–Soviet dealings in the postwar world.

Strategic models become institutionalized within governmental decision-making systems. New bureaucracies and decision-making procedures are set up to handle the problems that are defined by the strategic model as relevant and solvable. Once in place, highly institutionalized strategic models effectively exclude alternative models. They are extremely resistant to change.

The second tier of cognitive structure follows indirectly from the first. This second tier is made up of hypotheses that flesh out implications of the basic strategic model. It includes the tactical approaches to nuclear politics and arms control policies that are the familiar stuff of U.S.–Soviet relations. Any strategic model can accommodate a wide range of hypotheses at this second tier. If nuclear weapons in 1945 were seen as a traditional source of power in international relations, decision makers could still argue about how to "use" them or perhaps only threaten to use them in order to achieve political objectives. These alternative approaches to tactics and methods, all of which fall within the bounds of the basic strategic model, constitute the second tier of cognitive structure.

The hypotheses that make up the second tier generate expectations about the effects of policy. There is an important difference between these expectations in arms control and expectations about the effects of policy in other issue areas. When it comes to problems like intervention in Third World conflicts, the superpowers' belief systems generate expectations about the impact of their behaviors *upon events in the external environment.* These expectations can be contradicted by the feedback of policy failures. In arms control, there has been no feedback of this sort about deterrence because there has been no event to distinguish between policies that succeed and those that fail. The second tier of cognitive structure in arms control generates expectations *about how the other side will behave.* What results is interactive learning, based on a very different kind of feedback. It is different because the other side is also acting according to a strategic model of its own. If the two sides are acting on the basis of similar strategic models, it is possible that expectations will be fulfilled. If they hold different strategic models, it is very unlikely that feedback will fall out as predicted.

ANOMALIES AND CHANGE

When expectations are contradicted, standard operating procedures do not provide clear guidance for policy making. Decision makers are driven to change the state's behavior. Under most circumstances, change takes place only at the second tier of cognitive structure. This is *adaptation.* Rarely, contradicted expectations drive change at the first tier of cognitive structure and lead to the adoption of a new strategic model. This is *learning.* The history of U.S.–Soviet arms control, as I will show, has been checkered with contradicted expectations and frequent adaptation. Yet learning has been remarkably rare. In fact, I will propose that there have been only two episodes of learning in the history of U.S.–Soviet arms control; in the United States during the early 1960s and in the Soviet Union during the 1980s. Why has adaptation been so frequent, and learning so scarce?

To press the analogy with Kuhn, most contradicted expectations are comparable to the *surprising anomalies* or puzzles that continually confront normal science. Although such events can be understood within the reigning strategic model, they were not anticipated by the current hypotheses of the second tier. This drives adaptation, a search for alternative hypotheses at the second tier of cognitive structure. Decision makers recognize that these events raise new issues and require a fresh effort at problem solving, but do not necessitate any fundamental redefinition of self-interest. In July 1945, Truman and many of his top advisers believed that the atomic monopoly would help the United States gain most of its postwar objectives vis-à-vis the Soviet Union.[3] Moscow did not respond as predicted. When the first subtle efforts at "atomic diplomacy" failed, the Americans tried to adapt by developing new ways to use the atomic advantage in the service of traditional national goals. Truman and his advisers changed their beliefs about what the United States could actually accomplish through atomic diplomacy and how it should be practiced. They did not revise their basic conceptions about the relationship between atomic weapons, military force, political power, and security.

Expectations can also fail in a more serious way. Some events constitute *fundamental anomalies* that actually *violate* basic principles of the first tier of cognitive structure. *Crisis* occurs when such events threaten basic structures and values at all three levels of analysis—in the international environment, in the domestic political system, and in the belief systems of individual decision makers.[4] The issue with regard to nuclear weapons is no longer how best to "use" them in support of traditional security goals, but what security in a nuclear world is all about.

Crisis results in a "critical learning period" in which the first tier of cognitive structure, the basic strategic model, is opened to change. *Learning* occurs when decision makers respond with a fundamental restructuring of belief systems and a redefinition of self-interest—in short, a shift in the first tier of cognitive structure. A new strategic model gets selected from a menu of available choices. The critical learning period comes to an end when the new model is institutionalized in the state's decision-making system. These institutions then constrain further change: they permit and sometimes even foster adaptation, but tenaciously protect the first tier of cognitive structure. It will not change again until the state confronts another critical learning period, if it ever does.

The second tier of cognitive structure changes much more readily. Adaptation is inherently unstable, because a particular adaptive solution must continually compete with alternatives, all of which are consistent with the basic strategic model. Second tier hypotheses and the individuals who represent them shift in and out of policy making as surprising anomalies appear. These hypotheses are not fully discredited by feedback, because the causal relationship between a particular tactical approach to arms control and the other side's behavior is almost impossible to establish. Did NATO's deployment of medium-range missiles contribute to the 1987 Intermediate-range Nuclear Forces (INF) treaty, or might an agreement have been reached through a more conciliatory approach? When one approach informs policy, the advocates of others take up consulting offices outside Washington or brood about in dark corners of the Kremlin. They return to power in a cyclical fashion as new surprising anomalies bump up against the expectations of the current second tier.

VOLATILITY AND CONVERGING STRATEGIC MODELS

When the state is not in a critical learning period, the decision-making system adapts its arms control policies within the confines of its current strategic model. This can be a serious problem if the two sides are operating with very different strategic models, because expectations are bound to be continually falsified. The result will be a volatile cycle of adaptations on each side. So long as the strategic models remain different, there is no reason to believe that this volatility will decrease over time. At best, this makes for a highly unstable arms control relationship that complicates the tasks of military planning for both sides. It may do more harm than good to the long-term political and military interests of both superpowers.

I will argue in the following stylized history that the United States and the Soviet Union have *never* shared the same strategic model for arms control. Starting in the 1940s, the superpowers developed different sets of ideas that defined the problem in very different ways. As a result, each side's behavior frequently contradicted the other's expectations. Each superpower underwent one critical learning period that led to the adoption of a new strategic model, but U.S. and Soviet leaders did not select the same one. At all other times the anomalies drove adaptation; but because adaptation was directed and constrained by the first tier of cognitive structure, Moscow and Washington usually adapted in different and incompatible directions.

For a short period of time in the 1970s, there was a paradoxical convergence between adaptations. The result was the first Strategic Arms Limitation Talks treaty (SALT I), but the overlapping policies that produced a treaty in 1972 were not derived from similar strategic models. Predictably, each side's expectations about the other's behavior were contradicted soon thereafter. Both sides adapted, but they did so again in different directions, leading to a breakdown of arms control cooperation in a remarkably short period of time. If the return of arms control in the late 1980s reflects a similar coincidence of adaptations at the second tier, it will turn out to be equally short-lived.

The instability of arms control that this rather gloomy picture suggests has not diminished much over time. Although it has probably had little effect on deterrence per se, it has been detrimental to the superpower relationship. This might have been different. Instability would have been less if the superpowers had learned about nuclear weapons and arms control in a coordinated fashion. But the processes of learning in the United States and the Soviet Union started from very different places and have proceeded in different directions. Two critical learning periods have not led to a convergence of strategic models.

The reason this is so is because of the extremely low level of interdependence and interconnection between the learning processes of the two sides. Interaction increased over time, in part because of the institutions that grew up to facilitate cooperation under SALT in the 1970s, but it did not develop sufficiently during this decade to keep pace with changes in behavior and technology. The United States and the Soviet Union continued to absorb different lessons at different rates about arms control. The level of interaction has again increased substantially in the late 1980s, but convergence of strategic models remains a problem. The question of whether learning is now sufficiently coordinated to bring the two sides' strategic models into line remains open.

This is a critical question for understanding the future possibilities of arms control. Paradoxically, it is even more important if one accepts the possibility that ideas themselves don't matter much to deterrence. If large nuclear arsenals act as an "existential deterrent," then it may be that almost any set of ideas would have worked—that is, kept the nuclear peace. Levine argues that American thinking about arms control "has been right all along." I suggest that we may as well have been wrong. Because nuclear deterrence is so robust, right or wrong matters less than that the two sides are both right or both wrong *in the same way*.[5]

If almost any particular set of ideas had been shared to start with, or if the two superpowers had converged around a single strategic model, there still would have been no nuclear war. What would have been different is the quality and volatility of the superpowers' political-military relationships. If the central issue is really convergence of strategic models, then the most important challenge of this chapter is to understand the conditions under which superpower arms control learning might converge, and what the consequences might be.

AN INTERPRETIVE HISTORY

The United States was the first state to deal with the difficult question of how the atom bomb could be pressed into the service of national goals. The answer, during and in the immediate aftermath of World War II, was "just as any other new weapon would be." This followed from the same basic strategic model that had guided the United States in thinking about the use of military power in the prenuclear age. The Roosevelt and Truman administrations acted, predictably, as if a weapon of unprecedented destructive capability ought to be a source of unprecedented power in international relations. It was also natural to assume that the power of nuclear weapons would prove highly fungible: that is, American decision makers believed that their nuclear advantage could be brought to bear in support of a wide range of U.S. interests in security and elsewhere.

It did not turn out to be so, at least vis-à-vis the Soviet Union. Stalin and Molotov did not respond to nuclear diplomacy and particularly to attempts at compellence as U.S. decision makers predicted they would.[6] Washington also discovered rather quickly that the power of atomic weapons was poorly fungible across issue areas. Short of coercing the Red Army into a retreat from Europe, which it did not, the atomic advantage proved almost irrelevant to the postwar dilemmas on the Continent. The atom bomb did not matter to the Communist parties of Greece and Turkey, and it did not contribute toward rebuilding the economies of Western Europe. Most important, atomic weapons did not solve the problem of postwar Germany, or even give the United States a convincing advantage in its dealings with Stalin on this issue. Despite Washington's lead in atom bombs, Truman and his successors found that they were not able to get 80 percent or perhaps even 50 percent of their objectives in negotiations with a frustratingly recalcitrant Soviet Union.

The events of the 1950s and the behavior of the Soviets during the several crises in Berlin and elsewhere also contradicted U.S. decision makers' expectations about nuclear deterrence. "Massive retaliation," like atomic diplomacy, was an adaptive response at the second tier of cognitive structure. Atomic bombs, both powerful and cheap, would provide a cost-effective means of deterring Soviet aggression around the globe. But at best, deterrence did not work in precisely the way it was supposed to. In the face of a significant U.S. atomic advantage, the Communists were still challenging U.S. positions in Europe, the Middle East, Indochina, and elsewhere. This apparent contradiction did not seriously weaken beliefs at the first tier of cognitive structure: if deterrence was not working properly, it was *not* because nuclear weapons were not useful for this purpose. The problem was assumed to lie at the second tier; and the result was further adaptation, the development of new tactics to make better use of the nuclear advantage. In one instance, B-29 bombers (of a type configured to carry atom bombs) were deployed to Germany and to Britain; in another, veiled threats of nuclear use were dropped at press conferences and passed along discreetly through third party diplomatic channels.[7]

In response to contradicted expectations about how Moscow would respond, U.S. policy for "using" atomic and then nuclear weapons underwent adaptation but not learning during the late 1940s and early 1950s. New tactics were developed, but the strategic model endured. The question remained how best to make use of a nuclear advantage to support U.S. goals in the postwar world.

The U.S. strategic model of the 1950s had little room for arms control, aside from mostly propagandistic bids for comprehensive disarmament. If nuclear weapons were an important source of power and the United States held the advantage, it made no sense to cooperate with a distrusted adversary against whose interests this power was supposed to be used. The talks of the 1950s failed to reach substantive agreements, but this was fully expected. Of greater importance was the failure of the United States and the Soviet Union to absorb any substantial knowledge about each other's developing perspectives on strategic doctrine, deterrence, and the general relationship between nuclear weapons and security. Both U.S. and Soviet decision makers were adapting their beliefs to take account of events and behaviors that contradicted their expectations, but each side did so without a substantial understanding of the strategic model that was guiding the other side's behavior. The lack of interaction between these processes in Washington and Moscow virtually guaranteed that the superpowers' adaptive "solutions" to the problem of security in the nuclear age would be asymmetric; it also reduced the possibility that the strategic models developing on each side would converge over time.

The Soviets too were facing a new set of problems and possibilities as a result of the development of nuclear weapons. The Soviet response, like that of the United States, was at first adaptive and did not involve learning. What is striking about Soviet behavior during the first postwar decade, however, is how *little* adaptation actually took place. Stalin's strategic model for thinking about nuclear weapons was built on his belief in the primacy of military force as the most important currency of power in international relations. A weapon with unmatched destructive force would certainly be a most important source of power, just as the tank had been for a previous generation. The Soviets' main problem was that they were several years behind in atomic know-how. If a final decisive war between capitalism and socialism remained inevitable, the Soviet Union would need to have the advantage in the most powerful of modern weapons at that time. Stalin took the obvious adaptive response: he bought time. While dealing with the Americans as if the bomb were of marginal significance, Stalin directed his military establishment to close the gap as quickly as possible.[8]

Stalin's adaptive solution was in fact severely limited: it did not extend to a reevaluation of military doctrine or an analysis of how nuclear weapons might actually be used in the case of war. Stalin's effort to downplay the importance of nuclear weapons inhibited adaptation. And there was no institutional basis for developing new hypotheses outside the Kremlin: Stalin arrogated to himself all issues of military doctrine as the sole "prerogative of the leader of genius" and until just before his death stifled any attempts by others (including military officers) to intrude. It was not until Stalin's death in 1953 that the Soviet Union began a serious effort at more extensive adaptation.[9]

The principal factor driving this cycle of adaptation was the recognition by the Communist Party's new leaders that war between social systems was no longer inevitable. This was in part a response to American behavior of the previous decade, which had contradicted Soviet expectations by being less aggressive than Moscow had anticipated. If Washington had shrunk from war when it had a convincing atomic advantage, it seemed increasingly unlikely that a U.S. leader would ever choose war as Soviet military capabilities caught up with and eventually overtook those of the United States. Khrushchev's conclusion, as proclaimed to the 20th Party Congress in 1956, was that growing Soviet military power and specifically Soviet nuclear capabilities could prevent the imperialists from unleashing war, making it possible for continuing progress in the correlation of forces to carry socialism to triumph by peaceful means. Nuclear weapons did not mean that war was impossible, but simply that it was neither inevitable nor a prerequisite for a worldwide transition to socialism. The Soviets had become officially agnostic about war as the handmaiden of world revolution.

This revision of thought about the inevitability of war, however, did not represent any fundamental change in the first tier of cognitive structure. It did not produce a basic reassessment of the role played by nuclear capabilities in national power. Superpower war *might* be avoided; but *if* war were to come, the side with greater military power would still prevail. As with any other technological innovation, the Soviet Union had to be prepared to fight wars. This called for adaptation: developing new strategies and tactics for using nuclear weapons in support of traditional state interests.

The first cycle of Soviet adaptation ended with Khrushchev's 1960 announcement of a new strategic doctrine for Soviet nuclear forces.[10] This doctrine rested on an additional assumption: that a nuclear war (if it were to occur) could not be controlled or limited like other wars, but would instead escalate rapidly to all-out exchanges against the superpowers' homelands. The ramifications for Soviet force posture and for the prospects of arms control were clear. The primary responsibility for nuclear weapons would be entrusted to the newly organized Strategic Rocket Forces (SRF), whose principal mission would be to *deter* U.S. nuclear strikes by maintaining the ability to incinerate American cities under any conceivable conditions. Should deterrence fail, it was the mission of the SRF to ensure that the Soviet Union would prevail and emerge from the cataclysm damaged but victorious.

According to the Soviet strategic model, there was no logical contradiction between these two objectives. Nor were there convincing reasons to engage in arms control with the United States. Only to the extent that an agreement would reinforce deterrence without constraining Soviet abilities to prevail in war did it make sense to "cooperate" with the West. Measures to reduce political sources of instability (if the United States were interested) were more promising than strictly military or technical agreements, because the former could reduce the likelihood of war without requiring changes in unilateral Soviet force decisions.

These adaptations actually reinforced Moscow's first tier of cognitive structure. Adaptation preserved three essential elements of the Soviets' basic strategic model linking military power to security goals: nuclear weapons (like other weapons) were a source of power in international relations; nuclear war (like other wars) could be won; and self-dependence and autarky remained the most desirable and efficacious route to security. This formulation would play a central role in defining Moscow's approach to arms control over the next three decades.

The 1960 revision of doctrine was made up of a new set of ideas and hypotheses at the second tier of cognitive structure. These hypotheses followed logically from Khrushchev's 1956 argument about the noninevitability of war, but they were not the *only* ideas that might have done so. Why did this particular adaptation occur? It seems that the range of ideas available to Soviet decision makers at this time must have been influenced by interpretations of what the Americans were doing— and thinking—about nuclear weapons at the same time. Some of the evidence for interactive learning is self-evident and not unique to nuclear issues. Soviet military policy obviously had to respond as best it could to "objective" constraints: the reality of U.S. superiority in nuclear systems and Washington's 1952 decision to begin deploying a large arsenal of tactical nuclear weapons in Europe.[11] Precisely *how* Moscow should respond to U.S. nuclear policy, however, may have been influenced by Soviet interpretation of American ideas. It seems plausible that Soviet military thinkers, shut out of nuclear issues by Stalin, would now look to the West for ideas about what nuclear weapons could and could not do, and how.

Although the evidence that they did so is largely circumstantial, Soviet behavior does suggest some lessons taken from the Americans. In particular, Khrushchev's "missile rattling" during the Suez and Berlin crises suggest that he may have been following on Eisenhower and Dulles's notions about atomic diplomacy. In historical retrospect, it seems that leaders on both sides must have been less than fully impressed by the results.[12]   But even limited success might have been convincing for Khrushchev, playing the game as he was from a position of weakness. To whatever extent the Soviets may have believed that a small nuclear capability and their essentially empty nuclear threats could be a source of considerable power and compensate for other weaknesses in crisis bargaining, the logical adaptive response would have been to seek to amass substantially larger nuclear forces that would promise even greater success in the future.

The entrance of the Soviet Union onto the stage of atomic diplomacy was at the same time driving reassessments of strategic thought in the United States. If atomic diplomacy and deterrence did not work precisely as expected when the United States had a convincing nuclear advantage, then the 1957 Sputnik launch promised to make matters considerably worse.[13]   Massive retaliation, never a particularly credible doctrine, was becoming obsolete in an uncomfortably visible way. As Levine points out, by 1959 U.S. analysts were worried not about how to use nuclear weapons for compellence, but about whether the "delicate balance of terror" was sufficiently robust to deter direct attacks against the American homeland.

This new set of problems drove the Kennedy administration to develop new ideas about nuclear weapons, which were at first confined to adaptive hypotheses at the second tier of cognitive structure. Kennedy appointed Dean Acheson to lead a review of U.S. strategic policy; Acheson turned to Albert Wohlstetter, who at this time represented the mainstream of U.S. thought about nuclear weapons. Wohlstetter and those around him, in Levine's parlance "the Extenders," argued that the United States could and should act to regain some kind of functional nuclear superiority.[14] The rapid strategic buildup of the early 1960s and the "no-cities" doctrine were two sides of a coherent (if imperfect) adaptive solution to the problem of how U.S. nuclear weapons could continue to be a source of power and to deter Soviet aggression, when the survival of American cities was now clearly becoming dependent on the forbearance of Soviet leaders.

While these adaptive solutions were being put into practice in U.S. policy, intellectual ferment in U.S. strategic thought expanded beyond the bounds of adaptation. A group of academics and civilian analysts at Harvard, the Massachusetts Institute of Technology, and the RAND Corporation became intrigued by the possibilities of applying ideas from other disciplines, principally economics and game theory, to the puzzles of the U.S.–Soviet nuclear relationship.[15] Schelling's *The Strategy of Conflict*, Schelling and Halperin's *Strategy and Arms Control*, and other products of this line of thought used insights from new work in other fields to develop a new, alternative strategic model: a competitor for the first tier of cognitive structure.

This alternative strategic model was built on different answers to the elemental questions about nuclear weapons, security, and power. Some of its tenets directly conflicted with fundamental elements of the reigning first tier of cognitive structure that had guided U.S. thought about nuclear weapons since 1945. It is no exaggeration to say that security took on a different meaning in the nuclear world as defined by the Schelling model. This model pictured nuclear weapons as having transformed the superpower military relationship from a zero-sum rivalry into a mixed-motive game of interdependent decision. In a mixed-motive game, reducing the security of the other side does not necessarily lead to an increase in security for the state. Although such games are still essentially competitive, there is also substantial room for cooperation. This had implications for unilateral security policies and for arms control that were unprecedented and profound.

It was not at all novel to think of military power as a political asset, or to consider controlled use of weapons to deter, communicate, or signal intentions. Nor was it unheard of for adversaries to limit an arms race through international agreement. But the Schelling model suggested other hypotheses that violated the strategic model of the 1950s. First, both sides could profit by acting to reduce some kinds of uncertainty, which would in turn lessen reciprocal fear of surprise attack. Second, the model implied that stability and the prospects for peace would be maximized if both states were fully confident of their own and their adversary's capability to obliterate cities. This meant that unilateral and bilateral measures aimed at *enhancing* the efficacy of offensive forces were in the interests of both states. It also meant that neither should attempt to protect its civilian population against nuclear attack. The notion that security could rest on the abject vulnerability of populations, rather than on the efforts of the state to protect them, was a revolutionary one when the logic was first laid out by American strategic thinkers in the late 1950s and early 1960s.[16]

For the United States to have adopted this new strategic model as a replacement for the current first tier of cognitive structure would require *learning*, but when it was first proposed the United States was not in a critical learning period as I defined it. As a result, the alternative strategic model remained just that—an alternative—even as key individuals from the Harvard-MIT arms control seminar and the RAND Corporation settled into influential positions in the Kennedy administration. Defense Secretary Robert S. McNamara apparently paid serious attention to their arguments but did not at first accept that any revision of the first tier of cognitive structure was necessary.

Yet in the several years between 1962 and 1967, McNamara's approach to nuclear weapons policy did undergo fundamental change.[17] In none of the other issues discussed in this book can one find a comparable instance in which a set of abstract ideas had such powerful influence on a top policy maker's thought, while he was in office, and in the absence of a catastrophic failure of policy. McNamara's dramatic shift is the most visible indication of a parallel shift in U.S. strategic thought and arms control behavior. Between the Ann Arbor doctrine of 1962 and the 1967 Sentinel speech, the United States underwent a transformation of basic strategic models that constitutes learning. The most striking evidence of this lies in the shift in American views and policies toward strategic defense. Until 1964 the United States pursued research and development of anti-ballistic missile (ABM) systems subject only to technological constraints; after that year ABM became steeped in doctrinal controversies about stability and instability according to the grammar of the new strategic model.

Was learning somehow necessary at this juncture, or overdetermined by events in the external environment?[18] Clearly not: although changes in nuclear technology and the balance of capabilities between the superpowers surely necessitated some modification of U.S. behavior, adaptive responses that could have preserved the old strategic model were readily available. The United States did not have to accept the transition to offensive parity and mutual assured destruction. It could have built many more land-based missiles (as the Air Force had wanted). It could have gone forward with ABM and other defensive systems to protect American cities.[19] To claim that the United States gave up on ABM simply because strategic defense was expensive and technically difficult is an ex post facto rationalization and neither logically nor historically accurate. ABM technology was indeed imperfect and expensive, but so are all means of defense; a competition in expensive high technology weapons systems would have played to American strengths vis-à-vis the Soviet Union. Adaptation under the old strategic model would have led the United States to push the competition in defense and bring its considerable resources to bear on the problem. Why, instead, did learning occur at this particular juncture?

Changes in the first tier of cognitive structure take place only during critical learning periods. Critical learning periods begin when fundamental anomalies violate central principles of the strategic model and threaten basic structures and values at international, national, and cognitive levels. Learning was possible only because the U.S. decision-making system entered such a period during the mid-1960s.

Washington's critical learning period was evoked by the experience of the Cuban missile crisis, which in several ways went beyond the difficult crises of the 1950s. For the first time, the nuclear balance itself was a

source of international crisis.   Other motivations aside, Khrushchev's
dangerous demarche signaled the depth of Moscow's commitment to
achieving functional nuclear parity as quickly and as convincingly as
possible. At the same time, the Cuban experience underlined the developing perception among U.S. strategists that nuclear deterrence was *concentrated*: while deterrence of attack against the superpower's homelands
was probably robust, deterrence of challenges elsewhere, even in areas
clearly central to security interests, could be perilously weak. The combination of Khrushchev's willingness to challenge the United States despite its nuclear advantage, these troubling lessons about deterrence, and
the recognition that a nuclear imbalance could itself "cause" a war reinforced the growing belief among U.S. decision makers that their nuclear
advantage, even if it could be sustained, was not a potent or fungible
source of power in international politics.[20]

Cuba also presented fundamental anomalies for the United States that
threatened basic structures and values at the national level. The experience
called into serious doubt the utility of force (conventional as well as
nuclear) for settling *any* dispute between nuclear armed states. As the crisis
came to a head, Washington acted as if the perceived risks of escalation
were such that avoiding any direct U.S.–Soviet conflict would take priority over all but the most central state interests. Hard-line rhetoric covered
a deeper willingness to make the concessions necessary to avoid war. It
is not particularly surprising that U.S. decision makers resisted temptation
to "use" their substantial nuclear advantage for coercive purposes during
the crisis. What was more telling was Washington's reluctance to employ
its convincing *conventional* superiority in the Caribbean in a more forceful
way than it did, as it very well might have under a "protective blanket"
of nuclear deterrence. At each stage of the crisis, Kennedy chose the
most moderate of military options available to him.[21] We now know that
the president had also prepared a fallback position for resolving the
crisis peaceably, had Khrushchev not conceded on that fateful Saturday.

Earlier that day, Kennedy had laid the groundwork for accepting an
open trade of the missiles in Cuba for American intermediate-range ballistic missiles in Turkey with only the shallowest of multilateral diplomatic
trappings.[22] The president was ready to take the politically disastrous
move of sacrificing the interests of an important ally in response to Soviet
pressure, after he had publicly staked U.S. prestige and reputation on
the resolve not to do so. The lesson must have been clear. In future
superpower crises, governments could be expected to worry less about
manipulating credibility, perceptions of commitment, and resolve than
about using the resources that had been built up in these areas to extract
themselves from the crisis without provoking war.

Events in Cuba also forced on U.S. decision makers a cognitive crisis, with the painful recognition that the United States had become inescapably vulnerable to Soviet nuclear strikes. It is true that through much of the 1950s, decision makers in Washington were warned that a nuclear war would bring horrendous U.S. casualties.[23] But it was not until 1962 that the paralyzing effects of vulnerability were so dramatically brought home. This meant that the efficacy of a basic cognitive principle for state decision makers—security self-help—was at the very least severely compromised and possibly forever lost.

This combination of crisis events at the international, national, and individual cognitive levels elicited a critical learning period for the U.S. decision-making system, during which the first tier of cognitive structure was open to change. But the fact that the system was relatively plastic at this juncture does not explain why the particular ideas of Schelling and others were selected and put into place as the new first tier of cognitive structure. There were alternative strategic models vying to take hold of the same position—based on arguments about moving to a defense-dominated world or restoring American "superiority."[24] That the strategic model based on Schelling's arguments has since become so deeply institutionalized within the U.S. decision-making system that it defines the basic grammar in which Americans think about nuclear weapons issues should not obscure the fact that the selection of this particular model was in no sense an inevitable outcome.

Because critical learning periods have been so infrequent, I cannot offer a convincing comparative historical explanation of why particular strategic models are selected in arms control. It is clear, however, that the process of selection cannot depend on the evidence of experience and feedback from the environment. Like the competition between Kuhnian paradigms during a period of scientific crisis, a strategic model gets selected from a set of alternatives before it is fully articulated and its implications explored.[25] Decision makers cannot know how well one strategic model will succeed in serving their interests relative to the others. Without concrete feedback, the competition between models becomes a preeminently political one.

The Schelling model had several sources of political power in this contest. Part of its power flowed from the individuals who were champions of the model. Academics and think-tank analysts, held in high esteem by an administration committed to seeking out the best and the brightest to inform policy debates, moved into important positions in the Washington bureaucracy where they were able to bring their arguments directly to the top echelons of the decision-making elite. It is also true that the ideas they were espousing had specific policy implications that fit comfortably with McNamara's general desire to "rationalize" the application of resources to defense. The possibilities for arms control and weapons limitations that followed from this model were also compatible with trends in public opinion, particularly a growing popular discontent with military spending related to the Vietnam experience. But I believe that the most important source of power for the Schelling model was the fact that the ideas themselves were intellectually compelling.[26] The model was derived in transparent and logical steps from straightforward deductive arguments. This produced a set of ideas with an elegant parsimony, which could be presented and argued in a concise and accessible way. At the same time, the model was sufficiently abstract that it held up under a wide range of assumptions about what kind of state the Soviet Union was, giving it robust appeal across the political spectrum.

The other chapters in this book demonstrate how unusual it is that a set of ideas that started the 1960s as the ruminations of a few academics had by the end of that decade come to inform the basic strategic model of U.S. policy toward nuclear weapons and arms control. By 1969, a new first tier of cognitive structure had been institutionalized within the U.S. decision-making system. Did it matter for deterrence? It is hard to imagine how the adoption of an alternative strategic model would have led to a nuclear war. The impact of the new model on the prevention of war was less important than the consequences it had for the overall progress of U.S.–Soviet relations. Some of these consequences were mutually undesirable and might have been avoided. The worst of these followed not from any inadequacy of the model itself, but from its incompatibility with the Soviet model. Neither side fully understood the logic of the other's strategic model, or the degree to which the two were for most purposes of cooperative arms control incompatible.

The Soviet leadership did not immediately understand the shift in U.S. thought, but Moscow did recognize visible consequences in U.S. military policy to which it had to adapt. At the same time that the Kremlin was being invited to join the United States in talks aimed at limiting certain kinds of "destabilizing" strategic weapons, the Soviet military was also faced with a revised U.S. doctrine of flexible response, which placed greater emphasis on conventional forces for deterrence and defense in Europe. Strategic models aside, the combination of these changes "on the ground" raised new problems and possibilities for Soviet military planning. In the previous decade, Khrushchev had proclaimed that war was no longer inevitable, but the Soviets continued to plan for war under the assumption that if it did come, it would quickly and inevitably be nuclear. The military was thus instructed to focus on the problem of fighting and winning a nuclear war.[27] But by the second half of the 1960s, the Soviet military was forced to consider the possibility that changes in American policy (whatever the underlying rationale) had rendered its strategy obsolete. It now seemed plausible that a superpower war might not escalate in short order to nuclear strikes, and it might not do so at all.

The Soviets responded with a second cycle of adaptation. The military was called on to expand its thinking beyond the primary focus on nuclear war. Changes in Soviet force posture and doctrine after about 1967 reflect new and very serious planning for the eventuality of a war with the United States that might involve a protracted conventional phase or even be entirely conventional.[28] Fresh attention was also directed at the problems of local wars and interventions. These adaptive changes again served to reinforce the Soviets' basic strategic model. The proper mix of capabilities and favored methods for applying force were modified, but ever-expanding military power remained the primary means of ensuring the security of the Soviet state and continuing progressive change in the correlation of forces.

Changes in American behavior also had important consequences for Soviet nuclear policy. Sometime in the early 1960s, perhaps in the wake of the Cuban missile crisis, the Kremlin had embarked on a massive, long-term deployment program aimed at expanding its arsenal of modern land-based ballistic missiles. This was also adaptation: a response to what Soviet leaders probably saw as a painful lesson about the effects of nuclear inferiority, and to the rapid buildup of U.S. strategic forces begun at the close of the Eisenhower administration. Several years later, the United States had gone through a critical learning period, but the Soviets had not. American strategists were now talking about the destabilizing impact of defense and counterforce and were trying to convince Soviet leaders and defense scientists of their new strategic model. While the Soviets were listening, they were also moving ahead with the deployment of an ABM system around Moscow and making decisions about the next generation of intercontinental ballistic missile (ICBM) systems that reflected an unmitigated commitment to counterforce.

That the Soviets eventually began to repeat the arguments of the U.S. strategic model, and that they came to accept several agreements consistent with its logic, was taken by many U.S. decision makers as evidence that the Soviets had undergone learning in response to their American tutors.[29] In retrospect, it seems painfully clear to both Blacker and Levine in this volume that this was probably a misinterpretation, and that the Soviet leaders never accepted the U.S. strategic model as it was presented to them at Pugwash, Glassboro, and elsewhere.

How, then, can we explain the dramatic shift in Moscow's willingness to negotiate limitations on ABM systems, which occurred sometime around 1969 and resulted three years later in the first SALT treaty? Authoritative Soviet statements of the early 1970s and the negotiators' behavior at SALT suggest that Moscow came to accept at least some of the Americans' arguments about instabilities in a mixed offense-defense arms race. But Blacker shows evidence that the uniformed military, at least, held tenaciously to the traditional Soviet strategic model. The logic of this model defined a certain Soviet interest in limiting ABMs, but it was a very different interest than that of the Americans, with different implications for future behavior.

Blacker explains how the Soviets may have feared that developments in strategic defense would come to threaten their position of strategic parity, which they believed to be the foundation of détente. ABMs were a demanding technological problem and thus played directly to U.S. strengths. If U.S. technology were to provide a solution to this problem at some point in the future, the United States might once again be in a position of relative invulnerability. The primary source of Soviet power vis-à-vis Washington would then be lost. While this was clearly a worst-case scenario, the risks and the potential costs were too large to be ignored.[30]

The shift in Moscow's position on the ABM treaty was a product of adaptation, but it did not involve learning. The agreement required that Moscow relinquish or at least amend its long-standing commitment to defense of its territory against ballistic missiles—probably an onerous sacrifice. But if the ABM treaty and other technical measures related to SALT I further reduced the risk of nuclear war, the agreements could be seen as furthering essentially unchanged Soviet goals. Most important, ensuring the long-term vulnerability of American cities preserved the "power value" of the Soviet offensive nuclear arsenal. There was no change in Moscow's first tier of cognitive structure.

Adaptation made learning unnecessary. The SALT deal, as the Kremlin seems to have understood it, was simply that neither side would deploy ABM systems in the near future. This did not imply any accompanying restraint of counterforce-capable offensive systems, because these would in fact be useful in waging and winning nuclear war should it still occur. It was essential for the Soviet military to continue its drive for such forces. The ability to fight and win a nuclear war was the best guarantee of peace. At the same time, further growth in Soviet military power promised to generate more concessions from a U.S. leadership still reluctant to accord the Soviet Union full and equal superpower status around the globe.

Washington understood the SALT process and its relationship to détente in a different light—the light shed by its own first tier of cognitive structure. In the U.S. strategic model, the 1972 accords were the first step toward a cooperatively managed relationship of nuclear parity. Washington's hypotheses at the second tier of cognitive structure extended beyond arms control toward a broader conception of a revised political relationship, based on controlled competition and more constructive cooperation in areas of clear mutual interest.[31]

The statements of Soviet leaders and the behavior of the Soviet negotiating team at SALT provided sufficient evidence for many U.S. elites, who were willing if not anxious to believe that Moscow had adopted the U.S. strategic model and come to share U.S. perspectives on SALT. This is not to say that the level of confidence was uniformly high; there were good reasons to be suspicious and some Americans did raise serious questions about the nature of the Soviet commitment even before the treaty was signed.[32] But had these worries come to guide U.S. policy, it is doubtful that Nixon would have traveled to Moscow and signed SALT I until the ambiguities had been further resolved, domestic political pressures notwithstanding. On balance, the Americans expected that the Soviets would now show unilateral restraint in deployment of counterforce-capable ICBMs—because these missiles, not strictly limited by SALT, were understood within the U.S. strategic model to be the major remaining source of potential instability in the nuclear balance now that the ABM threat had been eliminated.[33] It did not take long for these expectations to be sharply contradicted.

SALT I did not represent a convergence of strategic models on the two sides. It was instead a coincidental overlapping of second tier hypotheses. But like matching hypotheses derived from different theories, these second tier hypotheses were derived from different strategic models and were similar only on the surface. The United States and the Soviet Union signed the treaty for different and nearly incompatible reasons. The fundamental flaw of SALT I was the fact that neither side fully understood the source of the other's interest in the treaty, because they did not understand each other's strategic model.

Each side could thus maintain very different expectations about the future behavior of the other. The Soviets expected continued competition in weapons systems not covered by the treaty, and particularly in counterforce-capable ICBMs. Brezhnev told Nixon as much in May 1972, but this message was lost on the Americans.[34] U.S. leaders discounted these statements and expected that the Soviets would act consistently with the logic of their own strategic model. Disappointed expectations in this case not only led to new cycles of nuclear policy adaptation on each side, but they also became a source of spiraling recriminations and contributed in important measure to the severe downturn in superpower relations in the latter half of the decade.

Again, these events had no concrete impact on nuclear deterrence, which remained a constant through SALT, détente and its unraveling, and even through the new cold war of the early 1980s. But the way in which deterrence was "practiced" had a profound impact on the character of superpower relations. That impact, on balance, was probably detrimental. The absolute minimum criterion for success at SALT would have been to further reduce the already minimal risk of nuclear war. Considering the resources and attention that both sides lavished on it, SALT should have done something more: it should have contributed to a moderation of the arms race, and to the development of a more constructive political relationship. Judged by these standards, SALT was certainly not much of a success and may have been a serious failure. If arms control were like other issues in U.S. and Soviet foreign policy, we would expect to see considerable learning on both sides in the wake of this experience.

Learning was blocked in this case by the fact that neither side was, in the early 1970s, engaged in a critical learning period. Responses to the "failure" of SALT (which I will consider shortly) were confined to adaptation. Even adaptation was complicated by both sides' difficulties in diagnosing why SALT had gone wrong. Because they continued to operate with divergent strategic models, it is not surprising that their diagnoses were different. It is also not surprising, then, that the two sides' adaptations in the aftermath of SALT carried their nuclear policies in divergent and still incompatible directions.

This might have been expected. Since 1945, there had been remarkably little direct interaction between the two sides' learning processes about nuclear weapons. Each side periodically changed its behavior in nuclear weapons and arms control issues, responding to the adaptations of the other side. But reciprocal understanding of each other's strategic models started at an extremely low level and did not improve much over time.

The United States and the Soviet Union began the SALT process in 1969 with different strategic models. The negotiations did very little to bring them toward convergence or even to elucidate the differences. There was little open discussion of strategic doctrine, and almost no military-to-military contact. And the international institutions that were set up and grew up around SALT, which might have served as forums for such interaction, were at first barely used for this purpose. The Standing Consultative Commission (SCC), for example, in its early years focused mostly on treaty compliance and other technical issues. But interactive learning did increase somewhat as a result of SALT. The SCC occasionally delved into basic questions of doctrine and other matters at the heart of the two sides' strategic models. SALT also spawned several quasi-official forums for exchange along the lines of Pugwash. Proliferating channels of communication between defense scientists, strategic analysts, and some policy makers may not have had an immediate impact on policy, but they did produce some interactive learning. There was some growth in mutual understanding of strategic models, as well as some joint research into the problems and possibilities that would be raised by emerging weapons technologies.[35]

As the 1970s progressed, the two sides came to understand each other's strategic models somewhat better than they had at the start of SALT. But this understanding was neither deep enough nor did it come quickly enough to rescue SALT. Expectations on each side about what SALT would bring were contradicted much too fast. Levine shows that the next cycle of U.S. adaptation was well under way two years after the Moscow summit. The Schlesinger Doctrine of 1974 was more than just a shift in declaratory policy; it signaled a revitalized commitment to counterforce in weapons programs and war planning.[36] Still, it was not a repudiation of the basic U.S. strategic model; at the same time, Washington was in the midst of negotiating a SALT II agreement with the Soviets. It was only a tactical change, another cycle of adaptation, driven this time by a growing belief that the Soviets were more apt to take advantage of U.S. restraint. The United States was now operating with a new hypothesis at the second tier: that the road to a better SALT II treaty lay not in conciliation but in bargaining from a position of strength.

The Soviets were adapting as well, but within the context of their own strategic model. Their expectations of American behavior following SALT I were also contradicted on a number of fronts. One of the most surprising elements for Moscow must have been the vehemence with which powerful groups of U.S. elites were criticizing SALT, claiming that the Soviets had dealt in bad faith and had broken both explicit and implicit bargains. One way Moscow responded to this challenge was to make use of its increasingly sophisticated understanding of U.S. domestic politics to try to influence arms control policy making in Washington. Blacker cites Brezhnev's concessions that led to the 1975 Vladivostok accords as an example of Soviet efforts to "reassure" suspicious Americans and to undermine brewing opposition to SALT in Washington. It was a fleetingly successful adaptive response: the accords gave SALT and détente a new but only a temporary lease on life.[37]

It was only a temporary lease because Washington's adaptation was gaining momentum and carrying U.S. policy in a perpendicular direction. To negotiate from a position of strength came to mean more than simply revising strategic doctrine and being stingy with concessions; it also evolved into an unprecedented peacetime buildup of American military forces. Interestingly, this cycle of adaptation paralleled the logic of the Soviets' adaptation in the previous decade. Washington's second tier hypotheses now implied that the best way to elicit concessions and cooperation from Moscow was to strengthen U.S. military power and to generally intensify America's competitive stance. Brezhnev did not respond as predicted. By the end of the decade, SALT for all intents and purposes lay in ruins.

Could it have been different? SALT might have been more successful if the two superpowers had either shared a single strategic model or had developed a substantial understanding of each other's models and how they differed. The first of these conditions did not hold in 1969, and because neither side experienced a critical learning period during the 1970s, their strategic models were not subject to change.[38] The second condition might have rescued SALT. Both states could have adapted to changing circumstances in ways derived from their own strategic models. The adaptations would not have necessarily been the same, but they might have been compatible. The important thing is that each side's adaptations would have conformed to the other side's expectations. This would have reinforced mutual understanding of strategic models and probably reduced the multiplying volatility at the second tier of cognitive structure.

Cooperation on this basis probably would not work in most issues of superpower relations. It can work in nuclear arms control, because the specifics of the strategic model barely matter to deterrence. Arms control did not have to be based on the U.S. strategic model. Cooperation could have developed equally well on the basis of the Soviet model. If *both* sides had expected and planned for a full-fledged competition in counterforce during the 1960s, there would have been no "window of vulnerability" during the 1970s. There would indeed have been a lot of counterforce-capable ICBMs on both sides, but they would have had few potential targets. A shared expectation that this was the way the arms race was going to go would have pushed both sides to move toward some mixture of mobile ICBMS, hard-site defense of silos, and robust command-and-control facilities more quickly and more completely than at least the United States moved. Deterrence would have been as robust in this world as it was in the world that did emerge. But without the burden of contradicted expectations, some alternative version of arms control might have endured and even prospered. U.S.–Soviet political relations would have been different and perhaps better; certainly, they would have been less volatile.

As it was, both sides held illusions about the nature of their arms control cooperation. On one hand, that these illusions were not dispelled or at least reduced by interactive learning earlier in the decade was a basic failure of SALT. Because SALT was the first substantive U.S.–Soviet venture in arms control, it was a failure that has proven difficult to correct. On the other hand, SALT did lead to a tangible increase in mutual understanding of strategic models. And the institutions that were set up under SALT, limited and delicate as they were, did survive and contribute to the further development of interactive learning.

SALT itself did not really survive the maelstrom of the late 1970s. The U.S. strategic model did survive, despite some fraying at the margins. Revisions of strategic thought during the Carter and Reagan administrations did not involve learning and did not produce change at the first tier of cognitive structure. Clearly, the level of disappointment with SALT was such that the reigning strategic model was seriously challenged, and alternatives were given serious attention in policy circles. The SALT treaties came under widespread criticism from all sides of the U.S. political spectrum. A powerful part of the U.S. elite tried to redefine U.S. nuclear security in purely self-help terms, arguing that the United States should now mount a full-fledged effort to reestablish uncompromised superiority in military forces. But while the Reagan administration effectively challenged the particular provisions of the treaties, it did not succeed in discrediting the strategic model that produced SALT. By the end of the first Reagan term, the controversy within the administration and without had been more or less resolved in favor of those who believed that negotiated nuclear arms control, with a new label (Strategic Arms Reduction Talks—START) but still based essentially on the SALT model, had an important role to play in American security policy.[39]

The strategic model survived this serious challenge because the United States was not in the midst of a critical learning period. The importance of Reagan's quixotic Strategic Defense Initiative (SDI) was symptomatic of the depth of the challenge, but the subsequent withering away of SDI confirmed the strength of the first tier of cognitive structure. In historical retrospect, SDI will appear as a remarkably brief flirtation with an alternative strategic model that was rather quickly disavowed. By the middle of the 1980s, adaptation had won out over learning in Washington.

The Soviet reaction to the failure of SALT was different. The Kremlin was at first remarkably slow to recognize the extent to which its behavior during the 1970s was provoking the Americans, because it did not make sense that it do so according to the logic of the Soviet strategic model.[40] The Vladivostok concessions were the first signs of adaptation; this was followed by the famous 1977 Tula speech and other official renunciations of military superiority as a goal. As time went on, these moves had less and less impact on U.S. behavior. During the late 1970s and early 1980s, the Soviet Union responded with several additional cycles of adaptation—ranging from the conciliatory approach of the late 1970s, to the hard-line approach of withdrawing from Intermediate-range Nuclear Forces (INF) and strategic arms negotiations in 1983, to the rather sullen resignation under the Chernenko regime that it would be difficult to deal with the United States at all. Each was notably unproductive.

This succession of failures did not by itself provoke any revision of the Soviets' first tier of cognitive structure. It was not until the beginning of a critical learning period for the Soviet decision-making system that learning and a shift to a new first tier of cognitive structure could supersede adaptation. While alternative ideas and strategic models had been under consideration in Moscow for some time, none really threatened to replace the old model until the accession of Gorbachev in 1985.

Soviet arms control behavior since that time reflects learning, a change in the first tier of cognitive structure. Moscow's new policies evidence a fundamental reconceptualization of the relationship between nuclear weapons, security, and power.[41] The specific details of the unprecedented arms control proposals and offers the Soviets have made over the last few years are less important than the fact that they cannot be explained solely as adaptation within the bounds of the old strategic model. The new Soviet arms control approach accepts three general principles—asymmetric and unilateral reductions, intrusive verification, and a deemphasis of military force as a source of power in international relations—all of which directly contradict basic tenets that made up the old first tier of cognitive structure.

The new Soviet strategic model recognizes the validity of U.S. theories about the technical determinants of strategic stability, but goes beyond them. It extends deeply into the political realm and includes a revised conception of Soviet security based on a new understanding of the sources of power in world politics. Some of the changes in Moscow's policy reflect both elements. For example, the Soviets have come to understand how offensive military doctrines and force postures can reduce stability in crises. But they also seem to have learned that proliferating counterforce weapons can exacerbate general hostility and insecurity between the superpowers, even if the weapons are justified by a supposedly defensive political stance. "Reasonable sufficiency" as a new guiding concept for nuclear forces does not necessarily imply a reduction to what some Americans call minimal deterrence. It does explicitly negate the twin goals of escalation dominance and the ability to prevail in nuclear war. It is aimed at reducing both technical sources of instability and political sources of tension and hostility. The concept of defensive or nonprovocative defense for conventional forces in Europe has similar goals. All together, these new organizing concepts make up something called *common security*, a notion that was suspiciously abstract when first introduced in 1985, but that has since been fleshed out with some convincing details. The Soviet leadership seems now to believe that by *decreasing* the size and the potency of their nuclear arsenal, they can reduce the risk of war, improve the context of superpower relations, and facilitate their relations both political and military with the rest of the world.

This is unprecedented. The old strategic model was built on the principle that military force remained the basic and most important currency of power in world politics. Gorbachev and his compatriots apparently no longer accept this. The INF agreement, in which the Soviets chose to make asymmetrical reductions for the sake of eliminating an entire class of nuclear weapons, proved to be only the beginning, only one of many startling hypotheses that would begin to spring forth from the new strategic model. The potential START bargain, involving 30 percent or greater reductions in strategic forces, would be further convincing evidence that learning has occurred. Should Moscow agree to substantial reductions in nuclear forces, it would be making a definitive statement to the United States and to the rest of the world that it no longer regards nuclear weapons as the most valuable source of international power. This is particularly curious coming from a state whose primary claim to superpower status has been precisely its military power, particularly nuclear. Recall that in the old strategic model, it was exactly these capabilities that made it possible for the Soviet Union to promote its interests in the world. By consciously devaluing this source of power, the Soviets would be taking a step uncharacteristic of the way we traditionally think that states tend to behave in an anarchic world—they do not voluntarily resign themselves to lesser status. The best explanation for this behavior is that the Soviets have in fact revised their understanding of the relationship between nuclear weapons, military force, and power. That is clear evidence of learning.

As was true of the United States in the 1960s, Soviet learning was not overdetermined by changes in the external environment—the cycle of adaptive responses could have been perpetuated. Learning occurred because the Soviet Union entered a critical learning period in the mid-1980s. Just as it had happened for the United States some 20 years before, fundamental anomalies violated central principles of the old strategic model and threatened basic structures and values at the international, national, and cognitive levels.

At the level of international politics, the Soviets in 1985 faced a world significantly more threatening than the world of a decade earlier, in considerable measure as a result of their own foreign policy initiatives. Washington had revitalized its military forces and shown new willingness to use them abroad. Defense cooperation between Western Europe, the United States, China, and Japan had grown closer, further isolating Moscow and increasing the possibility that if war came, the Soviet Union's enemies might join forces against it. SDI raised the spectre of a nuclear arms race redirected toward advanced technologies in which the United States and its allies held the potential trump cards. A basic principle of the old strategic model was that expanding Soviet military capabilities would lead to greater security, but all sorts of adaptive policies based on that model had not fostered either a safer or a more beneficial international environment for the Soviet Union in the 1980s.

This was accompanied by anomalies that threatened basic structures and values at the national level. During the 1970s, social and economic stagnation at home had been minimally acceptable to the leadership, for two reasons. First, the domestic system could maintain broad (if not deep) legitimacy among the populace so long as living conditions were improving at the margins or at least not deteriorating. Second, the Soviet system drew substantial and increasing international influence and prestige from Moscow's position as a military superpower. But neither condition lasted into the mid-1980s. Gorbachev and his cohort were faced with the fact that the legitimacy of the domestic political and economic system was weakening among the populace. They also recognized that the system was failing to provide the resources and capabilities necessary to maintain Moscow's power vis-à-vis a revitalized West. This went beyond the valid concern that the Soviet system could not match Western economic and technological achievements or compete effectively in a postindustrial world economy—it has never had to do so. The issue now was simply whether the state could provide enough to hold the society together and to retain superpower status through military competitiveness, something that Brezhnev had been relatively certain of. Whatever the currency of international power was likely to be in the twenty-first century, the Soviet system seemed poorly positioned to produce very much of it.

At the same time, a new generation of Soviet leaders was confronted with crucial anomalies that went beyond international and domestic concerns, to threaten fundamental values at the individual cognitive level. Gorbachev and his colleagues face an abject failure of the "correlation of forces" model, a crucial part of the Soviet *Weltanschauung* for dealing with the superpower relationship since at least 1945.[42] This model was supposed to provide an explanation of events and trends and a guide for action. It failed at both tasks. In contradiction to the correlation of forces argument, the Soviet leaders were challenged by the recognition that the advancement of socialism, the development of the Soviet state, and the maintenance of peace might *not* be mutually compatible goals. This suggested that the correlation of forces model was wrong. It could not serve as a guide for Soviet policy, and the manifest failures of past policies both foreign and domestic could not be blamed on faulty tactics. Nor could they be corrected through adaptation. The failures of the old thinking were the direct and incontrovertible results of a system of thought that showed itself ill-suited to guide a state's behavior in the modern world.

The new Soviet strategic model downplays military capabilities as a source of power in world politics. In fact, Moscow now seems to believe that an emphasis on military power is a definite hindrance to achieving Soviet goals. The Soviets are clearly trying to cultivate other sources of power in the international system, by posing as a leader in regional peacemaking efforts, global environmental issues, human rights, and the like. The change is made even more convincing by the fact that in each of these areas, Moscow is far less capable and has fewer potential resources than the United States.

Where did the new ideas that make up this strategic model come from? Although we have less information in this case than in the U.S. case of the 1960s, interactive learning has clearly been important in the development of a new first tier of cognitive structure. The new Soviet model shows evidence of diffusion of ideas from Western thought through expanded contacts with Soviet thinkers. It is an interesting hybrid that combines certain elements drawn from the U.S. strategic model with left-wing European thought and some traditional Soviet ideas. Soviet leaders seem to have taken from Washington the notion that meaningful political cooperation requires technically oriented arms control measures as a prerequisite. They have borrowed from the Europeans certain strands of thought about "defensive" and "nonprovocative" defense, as well as the importance of confidence-building measures and other forms of reassurance. Finally, the model includes traditional Soviet interests in political measures aimed at reducing general tensions and ameliorating possible sources of conflict.

How did this particular strategic model get selected as the new first tier of cognitive structure? This is an even more difficult question than it was in the American case, because we do not know much about possible alternative models that might have been contending for power in Moscow during the critical learning period.[43] The new strategic model does seem to share a characteristic that I suggested was a crucial factor in the American selection process two decades earlier. This is the quality of elegant parsimony or the scientific aesthetic. On its own terms, before the model produced any evaluable results in interaction with the United States, it offered a simplicity and elegance that was logically compelling. The selection process in the Soviet Union, like that in the United States, must be a preeminently political one. In that kind of environment, be it Washington or Moscow, a model based on simple, logically compelling arguments may have a crucial comparative advantage.

CONCLUSION

THE LEARNING EXPERIENCE

Learning in nuclear arms control is different from other issues in U.S.–Soviet relations because there has been no feedback to distinguish between policies that succeed or fail to maintain deterrence. But arms control is about much more than deterrence, and both superpowers have learned a substantial amount about how states behave in a nuclear world. They discovered that nuclear weapons breed prudence, even when one side is clearly superior.[44] They recognized that a security dilemma bound U.S. and Soviet nuclear weapons programs and operational doctrines in a tight grip. They realized that one result could be an aggravation of mistrust and insecurity that encouraged worst-case threat assessment and military planning. This could in turn produce mutually undesirable conflict spirals or "action-reaction" arms races. They found that it might be possible to limit the effects by engaging in some combination of unilateral policies targeted at reducing the security dilemma and cooperative arms control arrangements. This contributed to the growth of new ideas about arms control, its proper role in a state's security policy, and the means to sustain cooperative agreements in an anarchic international environment. Each superpower also learned something about the learning processes of the other side. Over time, they came to understand somewhat better how the adversary thought about each of these issues and, more generally, about nuclear weapons as a source of power in world politics.

There has been substantial change in the superpowers' arms control behaviors over time. If learning were just change, we would have to say there has been considerable learning in U.S.–Soviet arms control. But the point of this book is to go beyond the simplistic, minimalist conception of learning that sees learning whenever there is a change in the probability of a particular response.

Even accepting this definition, the patterns of change remain unexplained. The simple realist argument would start with the notion that the superpowers respond as rational actors to feedback from the environment. In a world in which feedback rests on the interdependent expectations and resulting behaviors of two large actors, realism expects that the superpowers would come to imitate each other's arms control behavior over time, for the same reasons that oligopolists tend to converge on a coordinated solution to their market problem.[45] But this argument does not stand up to either logical or historical scrutiny. It is impossible to distinguish between successful and failing "product lines" in arms control. And U.S. and Soviet arms control behavior have not become very much more like each other; this "market" has if anything tended to move further away from a coordinated solution or equilibrium over time.

This chapter proposes an alternative explanation. The basic argument is that U.S. and Soviet arms control behavior has been exceedingly volatile because each side's expectations of how the other would behave in response to its policies have been repeatedly contradicted. I began by distinguishing between two tiers of cognitive structure. The first tier comprises a basic strategic model, made up of fundamental beliefs about nuclear weapons and their relationship to power in world politics. The second tier includes instrumental or tactical hypotheses about how to pursue the goals and outcomes that the first tier identifies as relevant, desirable, and achievable. Changes in the first tier (*learning*) are rare, and can occur only during critical learning periods. Changes in the second tier (*adaptation*) are more frequent. Many different sets of hypotheses at the second tier can be consistent with a given first tier. When expectations about how the other side will behave are contradicted, adaptation and a recycling of alternative sets of hypotheses at the second tier are the primary responses.

Expectations have been repeatedly contradicted because the United States and the Soviet Union have never shared the same first tier; the superpowers have been operating on the basis of different strategic models that defined interests and expectations about the future in divergent and often incompatible ways. This produced repeated cycles of adaptation on each side. Any particular adaptation is unstable. There are always alternative adaptive responses available that are equally consistent with the reigning strategic model. Because the two sides were operating with different strategic models, their adaptations have tended to be asymmetrical and often incompatible. Because they were responding to each other's behavior, adaptation has also been dissynchronous. And because any particular adaptive response was thus destined to be volatile, achieving and maintaining substantial international cooperation in arms control have been exceedingly difficult.

Cycles of adaptation did not by themselves weaken basic strategic models. These change only during critical learning periods, when fundamental anomalies violate principal tenets of the first tier and threaten basic values and structures at the international, national, and individual cognitive levels. Each side experienced one such period, during which change at the first tier of cognitive structure took place. These episodes of learning did not happen at the same time. They did not result in any substantial convergence between the two sides' strategic models. Learning is path-dependent. Because the superpowers' original strategic models followed from very different historical traditions and ideologies, decision-making systems, and power positions in the international system, it is not surprising that these critical learning periods did not lead to convergence. Given the extremely low level of interaction between the two sides' learning processes over the last 45 years, these sources of asymmetry were not likely to be overcome.

The results are familiar to any historian of U.S.–Soviet arms control. For both Washington and Moscow, the experience has had an equivocal legacy. Neither side "trusts" the other, but trust in this type of relationship comes primarily from the ability to predict how the adversary is expected to behave. The superpowers' arms control experience has not made a notable contribution either to this ability or to trust. U.S. decision makers have not settled very basic questions about Soviet behavior in arms control. For example, we still do not know if moving toward strategic defense would elicit negotiated reductions in offensive forces or a proliferation of offensive systems and countermeasures.[46] That is because we do not understand why the Soviets behave in arms control as they do. This complicates the problem of coordination in an oligopolistic market. If oligopolists cannot understand *why* the other large firms are acting as they do, it is less likely that their behaviors will converge on each other over time.[47]

Looking at arms control from a larger perspective, as a manifestation of international cooperation, yields a similarly equivocal legacy.[48] Deterrence persists, but that would have been the case regardless. Beyond deterrence, superpower arms control has followed a paroxysmal course. Along the way, it has left behind a framework of partial agreements and weak institutions. Neither has been particularly successful in dealing with the challenges of new technology and other environmental shocks.[49] Cooperation has not made a convincing contribution to either strategic or political stability in the U.S.–Soviet relationship. It has done remarkably little to facilitate either learning or adaptation in ways that might have contributed to its own growth. Innovation in arms control has come almost exclusively from national sources and not from international institutions. The international institutions have not done much to coordinate these innovations. Nuclear security—and thinking about security in a nuclear era—remains principally a self-help domain.

STRATEGIC MODELS

Arms control policies follow from a first tier of cognitive structure—a basic strategic model—ensconced within decision-making systems in Washington and Moscow. Where do the ideas that make up any particular model come from? The answer to this question cannot rest on a stark realist argument that ideas are epiphenomenal to power and material interests.[50] Nor do the ideas that underlie nuclear arms control seem to follow from historical analogy: if that were true, we would expect to see a greater and more consistent commitment to defenses and stronger emphasis on the notion that more weapons are always better than fewer.[51]

In an issue without convincing empirical feedback, we might expect the *ideas themselves* and the intellectual entrepreneurship that accompanies them to play a uniquely important role. Innovation is certainly driven to some extent by technology and other material factors, but it is also driven by intellectual processes that are sometimes quite independent of both. The Cambridge Arms Control Seminar imported a set of ideas from other disciplines and developed them into an alternative strategic model for nuclear weapons, a model with its own internal and highly compelling logical strength. During the first two decades of U.S.–Soviet nuclear competition, this kind of innovation was almost entirely confined within national borders. But as a result of the increased level of direct interaction that began in the 1960s, there is now another, increasingly important source of innovation: ideas imported from the other side. The new Soviet strategic model clearly owes a debt to certain strands in American and European strategic thought. Interactive learning expands the range of ideas that either side can access and increases the probability that they might in fact choose the same or at least compatible ones.

The issue of choice is most important. During critical learning periods, one particular strategic model gets selected and enshrined in the first tier of cognitive structure, while contending models do not. Selection is not a passive process. Decision makers choose actively and consciously from a menu of alternative models that are available at the time.[52] How do they do so? The competition among alternative sets of ideas during critical learning periods is a preeminently political process, and the contending strategic models could derive political power from a number of sources. The positions that are held by individuals who champion one or another model are significant but not decisive. The ability of the ideas to mesh with other important beliefs and values that are widely held in the domestic political system is also a source of power, but again not a decisive one. It is worth noting that ideas can overcome what are thought to be inviolable political and domestic obstacles. That the United States should voluntarily renounce superiority and accept (in explicit terms) a mutual hostage relationship with a powerful and distrusted adversary was an idea that fell far outside the bounds of current political wisdom and legitimacy when McNamara and others first proposed this. Moscow's willingness to accede to intrusive inspection procedures in the 1987 INF accord, or to make substantial unilateral reductions in conventional forces across Europe in 1989, were actions equally at odds with at least what Americans thought to be politically legitimate inside the Kremlin.

Selection of a strategic model *cannot* depend on feedback, as theories about learning typically conceive of it. Decision makers cannot compare the results of a particular strategic model with the results of competitors or with the results of the old strategic model. That is because the new strategic model, when it is selected, has not yet produced any results. No one knew, in the mid-1960s, whether the Schelling model would lead to a better outcome than the alternatives. That depended in part on how the Soviets would respond. It also depended upon what criteria were used to define *better*. Alternative strategic models, like contending scientific paradigms, often define their own criteria for success and those criteria may be very different. Success for the Schelling model meant a stable deterrent relationship, jointly managed to reduce the risks of inadvertent war and the costs of the arms race. Success for an alternative model that sought to reassert U.S. superiority was something quite different. Contending strategic models are not like hypotheses that make differential predictions subject to testing with empirical data, or in this case with feedback from the other side's behavior. When they are selected during critical learning periods, strategic models are more like contending and usually incommensurable paradigms.[53] Selection is a decision made largely on faith, a faith that the new strategic model will in the long term do at least as well with the problems that the old strategic model solved and do better with others.

Where can this faith come from? Kuhn noticed that during periods of scientific crisis, scientists begin to act more like philosophers than investigators. They start to focus on the purely abstract characteristics of contending paradigms, to examine them *as paradigms* for logical deductive power and not for the hypotheses or results that they promise to produce. So it appears to be with contending strategic models. The most potent source of political power for selection lies in the nature of the ideas themselves. I discussed two cases of selection during critical learning periods: in both, the successful competitors had a compelling intellectual power, a logical coherence and elegant simplicity, that gave them a kind of scientific aesthetic. It was this scientific aesthetic that endowed a winning strategic model with decisive political power in Washington and Moscow.

The problem is that Washington and Moscow did not select the same strategic model. After starting from different places, they encountered critical learning periods at different times, and at those moments each was faced with a different menu of alternatives. The dissynchronous and asymmetrical cycles of adaptation that followed have made arms control cooperation difficult. Each side has been disappointed with the payoffs from cooperation; at worst, each has suspected the other of engaging in deception and taking advantage of attempts at conciliation and restraint. The efficiency definition of learning cannot be applied to arms control if the end is simply nuclear deterrence, but it can be applied if the end is broadened to include the impact of arms control on the larger context of superpower relations. The results are not encouraging. SALT, for example, led to disappointments and recriminations that were surely a major source of the sharp turn toward confrontation in U.S.–Soviet relations during the late 1970s. Learning has not had an obvious payoff in efficiency.

LEARNING AND U.S.–SOVIET ARMS CONTROL IN THE 1990s

Could it be different in the future? Deterrence will hold in the 1990s, but will U.S.–Soviet arms control make a more positive contribution to the superpower relationship? If the pattern of the past were to continue, the answer would have to be no. Washington may not respond constructively to new Soviet initiatives, because U.S. decision makers fail to understand how these initiatives follow from a new strategic model in Moscow. If Soviet behavior is interpreted according to the logic of the *old* strategic model, it makes sense for Americans to conclude that the expansion of U.S. military power and competitiveness during the 1980s made the Soviets more "tractable" and will continue to do so. The logical adaptation for Washington is to push even harder in search of greater concessions in arms control agreements.[54]

The Soviets would in turn be forced into their own adaptation, driven by failed expectations about American behavior. Their options would be limited. Economic constraints, albeit real, are not so severe as to dictate capitulation. And because Gorbachev's economic, political, and military reforms have forged closer entanglements between Moscow and the West, the option of a strategic "retreat," with maximum possible disengagement and autarky as goals, is probably ruled out as well. What is more likely is that the Soviets would adapt, much as the U.S. did in the late 1970s, and return to a new round of competition in nuclear weapons. The outlook for U.S.–Soviet relations following another failed attempt at détente and arms control would not be auspicious.

The argument of this chapter suggests two ways in which volatility in the arms control relationship might be reduced and these disagreeable consequences avoided. The first would be if the two sides were to converge on a similar strategic model, a shared first tier of cognitive structure. I believe this is unlikely for a number of reasons. Learning can occur only during critical learning periods, and there is no reason to suspect that the two sides are likely to undergo this experience at the same time. If they did, there is also no reason to assume that Moscow and Washington, in selecting a new strategic model, would in fact choose the same one. Because there has been some increase in the level of interactive learning, the menu of alternatives facing decision makers would look more alike than in the past. But learning is a path-dependent process. The current strategic models and their accompanying institutions remain quite different in Moscow and Washington. Because these beliefs and institutions constrain and direct both learning and adaptation, the United States and the Soviet Union will probably continue to absorb different lessons from even the most similar events.

There is another possible route to stability, through a series of *compatible adaptations* that could develop from different strategic models on the two sides. To be compatible, adaptations do not have to be identical. Nor do the superpowers have to share the same first tier of cognitive structure. If both states were working with a deeper understanding of each other's strategic model, it would be possible to predict better than they have how the other side will behave in the future. They might not behave in the same way, but they would not have to. The more important difference would be that expectations would not be so consistently contradicted. Adaptation to the other side's behavior and to changing technologies would be more gradual and less paroxysmal. This would diminish the principal sources of volatility in arms control policies. It would also provide greater time and opportunity for further interaction between the two sides, so that they could come to understand the logic behind each other's responses more fully. Under these conditions, it becomes possible to determine where two sides' conceptions of self-interest actually do coincide, and to construct agreements that serve mutual interests *and* remain stable over time.

The prospects for compatible adaptations are improved in the 1990s for a number of reasons. The weight of previous experience matters. Both sides have had 20 additional years since their first arms control experience to watch each other think about nuclear weapons. More important is the fact that the level of interaction between this thought on the two sides, interactive learning, has substantially increased. There has been a dramatic expansion of sources for information and ideas about arms control in both Washington and Moscow, ranging from government bureaucracies, to quasi-official organizations, to citizens and public interest groups. Many of the new actors on both sides are linked by transnational ties to additional sources of ideas outside their national borders, particularly in Europe. Many are also linked to the other superpower. On balance, there has been a small proliferation of channels for interactive learning. Even the two sides' military establishments, which had been carefully isolated from each other for most of the postwar era, have expanded their range of contacts and now engage in periodic discussions of military doctrine and related matters.[55] Political decision makers may not always pay attention to the ideas and information that are garnered through these contacts, but it is clear that each side can now know more about the other's strategic model as a result.

Interactive learning in arms control, which began at a remarkably low level, has increased over time. This is not likely to lead to convergence of strategic models in Washington and Moscow, at least in the foreseeable future. It should facilitate more compatible adaptations. But it is impossible to say definitively in 1990 whether interaction has increased sufficiently to dampen the volatility in arms control that has impeded progress and made cooperation a principal source of contention in superpower relations. There are many potential arms control "solutions" to the problem of deterrence and stability in a nuclear world. Precisely which of those solutions the superpowers choose is less important than understanding each other's choice and the reasons it was made.

NOTES

1. Philip Tetlock, "Learning in U.S. and Soviet Foreign Policy: In Search of an Elusive Concept," Chapter 2 in this volume.

2. Thomas Kuhn, *The Structure of Scientific Revolutions* (Chicago: University of Chicago Press, 1962), Chapter 1.

3. Even before the successful test at Alamogordo, Truman had been impressed by James Byrne's belief that "the bomb might well put us in a position to dictate our own terms at the end of the war." Harry Truman, *Year of Decisions* (Garden City, N.Y.: Doubleday, 1955), 87.

4. Theories about learning typically argue that major changes in belief systems can occur only during a crisis, but crisis is often defined as a period in which major change occurs. This is a tautology. Kuhn's work suffers from a similar problem. He argues that paradigm shifts occur only during crises of normal science, but he offers no consistent and independent definition of what constitutes a crisis. (Kuhn, *The Structure of Scientific Revolutions*, 82–86.) A major goal of this essay is to propose an independent definition of crisis. I argue that learning can occur only when its criteria are fulfilled.

5. Robert Levine, "The Evolution of U.S. Policy Toward Arms Control," Chapter 5 in this volume. "Existential deterrence," for McGeorge Bundy, follows from the vast destructive power of nuclear weapons and the resulting "nuclear danger" that is shared by all states. See McGeorge Bundy, *Danger and Survival: Choices About the Bomb in the First Fifty Years* (New York: Random House, 1988).

6. For a detailed account, including anecdotes that are both revealing and entertaining, see Gregg Herken, *The Winning Weapon: The Atomic Bomb in the Cold War, 1945–1950* (New York: Random House, 1981), Chapters 2 and 3.

7. For the Berlin case, see Avi Shlaim, *The United States and the Berlin Blockade, 1948–1949: A Study in Crisis Decisionmaking* (Berkeley: University of California Press, 1983), 237. For the Korea case, see Richard Betts, *Nuclear Blackmail and Nuclear Balance* (Washington, D.C.: Brookings, 1987), 32–37; Dwight Eisenhower, *Mandate for Change* (Garden City, N.Y.: Doubleday) 181.

8. See Herken, *The Winning Weapon*, 19–20; and David Holloway, "Entering the Nuclear Arms Race: The Soviet Decision to Build the Atomic Bomb, 1939–45," *Social Studies of Science* 11 (1981):183.

9. David Holloway, *The Soviet Union and the Arms Race* (New Haven: Yale University Press, 1983), 28 and 31. There was in fact some reconsideration of doctrine within the military before 1953, but this was effectively squelched by Stalin.

10. Holloway, *The Soviet Union and the Arms Race*, 35, 38.

11. For details, see Robert Osgood, *The Entangling Alliance* (Chicago: University of Chicago Press, 1966), 107.

12. For contending historical arguments about Korea, see Roger Dingman, "Atomic Diplomacy During the Korean War," and Rosemary Foot, "Nuclear Coercion and the Ending of the Korean Conflict," *International Security* 13:3 (Winter 1988–89). Dulles's bravado notwithstanding, the evidence that Eisenhower's implicit nuclear threat was instrumental in the Chinese and North Korean decision to stop stalling at the Panmunjom truce talks was and remains extremely weak. On the Soviet side, it is notable that Khrushchev's atomic diplomacy threats were typically made *after* the

climax of the Suez and Berlin crises, when the shape of the eventual resolution had already become clear. They may have thus been more for the consumption of domestic actors and Communist allies than serious attempts to coerce the West.

13. To repeat: the evidence of the previous decade suggested that while central deterrence might be comparatively robust, extended deterrence in Europe was potentially tenuous. When it came to compellence or coercive diplomacy, nuclear weapons appeared to be strikingly impotent.

14. See John P. Steinbrunner, *The Cybernetic Theory of Decision: New Dimensions of Political Analysis* (Princeton, N.J.: Princeton University Press, 1974), 200–202.

15. Thomas Schelling, whose name I will use as a label for the strategic model that this group constructed, was the exemplary member; others included Morton Kaplan, Glenn Snyder, Daniel Ellsberg, and Malcolm Hoag.

16. The first detailed studies of the potential destabilizing effects of a competition in ballistic missile defenses were carried out by the Department of Defense and by civilian analysts in 1963 and 1964. See Jerome Wiesner, *Where Science and Politics Meet* (New York: McGraw-Hill), 209–240; Ernest J. Yanarella, *The Missile Defense Controversy: Strategy, Technology, and Politics* (Lexington: University Press of Kentucky), 104.

17. As is now well known, U.S. nuclear *employment* policy (i.e., how weapons would actually be used in war) never changed as fully as did *declaratory* doctrine or policy. Nonetheless, the shift to a declaratory policy that emphasized assured destruction criteria did substantially affect targeting plans, as well as budget and procurement decisions for nuclear forces. For a recent review, see Scott Sagan, *Moving Targets: Nuclear Strategy and National Security* (Princeton, N.J.: Princeton University Press, 1989), 26–39.

18. Deborah Welch Larson, at the author's conference preceding this volume, made the important point that we must be careful to exclude an alternative explanation based on *rationalizing behavior*: when situationally induced changes in behavior *precede* and *cause* a change in belief systems. This argument would contend that U.S. decision makers, faced with an expanding Soviet arsenal and growing domestic constraints on their ability to expend the resources necessary to maintain a lead in nuclear weapons, created a new set of ideas to rationalize a fated reality, the development of parity. History does not support this alternative explanation. The ideas that made up the new strategic model go back in time to the early 1960s; by 1964 they were the subject of serious debate in circles of government. Parity, however, did not come until the end of the decade or the beginning of the next. While parity was anticipated much earlier than that, it was by no means a predetermined event over which the United States had no control.

19. Both measures would have been expensive and would have required at the very least a substantial redistribution of resources within the federal budget. This would have been politically difficult but hardly impossible. Economic and domestic political constraints on U.S. defense programs, real though they were, were not so inviolable that a determined administration could not have dismantled or bypassed them. Certainly the constraints were at least as great in the late 1970s, but they did not then prevent a concerted and at least partially successful effort by American elites to influence public perceptions of what was necessary and appropriate to do for America's nuclear security.

20. At least when it came to conflicts or issues involving other nuclear powers.

21. Historians of the crisis disagree on this point, but there is considerable evidence to suggest that Kennedy was apt to continue this course of moderate action even after the weekend of October 27, 1962, despite his warning to Khrushchev that the crisis *must* be resolved in short order. Even though he reports that members of the executive committee of the National Security Council seemed to fear that events were starting to slip out of their control, McGeorge Bundy agrees with Alexander George's argument that Kennedy would not have ordered an air strike or an invasion early in the next week so long as other options remained open to him. Bundy, *Danger and Survival*, 426–27; Alexander George, David Hall, and William Simons, *The Limits of Coercive Diplomacy: Laos, Cuba, Vietnam* (Boston: Little Brown, 1971), 128–29.

22. On Saturday evening, Kennedy took Dean Rusk's suggestion that they make use of Andrew Cordier (of Columbia University and a former deputy to U Thant) to propose to the United Nations secretary general that he appeal for an open trade, which the United States would then accept. See Rusk's letter quoted in James G. Blight, Joseph S. Nye, Jr., and David A. Welch, "The Cuban Missile Crisis Revisited," *Foreign Affairs* (Fall 1987): 179. The fact that Kennedy laid the foundation for an open trade does not necessarily mean he would have chosen this option had push come to shove, but it is at least as plausible as the other option he had instructed McNamara to prepare—an air strike. For a similar argument, see Bundy, *Danger and Survival*, 435.

23. For details, see Richard Betts, "A Nuclear Golden Age? The Balance Before Parity," *International Security* 11 (Winter 1986–87).

24. For representative arguments, see the testimony of Donald Wigner in *Strategic and Foreign Policy Implications of ABM Systems*, U.S. Senate, International Law and Disarmament Affairs Subcommittee of the Foreign Relations Committee, 91st Congress, 1st Session, 1969, Part II, 559; Paul Nitze, "Assuring Stability in an Era of Détente," *Foreign Affairs* 1976: 207–32.

25. See Kuhn, *The Structure of Scientific Revolutions*, Chapter 12. I will return to Kuhn and discuss further implications of this model in the Conclusion.

26. This is analogous to Kuhn's argument about the importance of what he calls the *scientific aesthetic* attached to contending paradigms. Kuhn, *The Structure of Scientific Revolutions*, 72–73 and 158.

27. Holloway, *The Soviet Union and the Arms Race*, 40.

28. For a detailed discussion, see Michael MccGwire, *Military Objectives in Soviet Foreign Policy* (Washington, D.C.: Brookings, 1987), 22–59.

29. But not, certainly, by all. For details (and implications) of the controversy in Washington, see Steve Weber, *Cooperation and Discord in US–Soviet Arms Control* (Princeton, N.J.: Princeton University Press, 1991), Chapter 4. For an account that stresses the interpretation that the Soviets had in fact accepted the logic of the American strategic model, see Gerard Smith, *Doubletalk: The Story of SALT I* (New York: Doubleday, 1980), 93–94.

30. Despite considerable and growing public sentiment against ABMs in the United States, the Soviets could hardly rely on U.S. domestic politics to stop the race.

31. See George Breslauer, "Why Détente Failed," in Alexander George, ed., *Managing US–Soviet Rivalry* (Boulder, Colo.: Westview, 1983), 319–40.

32. Paul Nitze, Dean Acheson, and Albert Wohlstetter, founders of the Committee to Maintain a Prudent Defense Policy, were particularly important proponents of the alternative view. There were many others, although this remained a minority viewpoint in Washington in 1972 and for at least several years thereafter. See Robert Newhouse, *Cold Dawn: The Story of SALT* (New York: Holt, Rinehart, and Winston, 1973), 201.

33. At the Moscow press conference following the treaty signing ceremony in May 1972, Chief U.S. negotiator Gerard Smith claimed "a commitment on [the Soviets'] part not to build any more of these ICBMs that have concerned us," reflecting what he and others believed to be a shared "recognition that the deterrent forces of both sides are not going to be challenged." White House Press Release, 26 May 1972, in *Documents on Disarmament 1972*, 210 and 212. Smith's optimism reflected a widespread sentiment among U.S. decision makers. See U.S. Senate, Armed Services Committee, *Military Implications of the Treaty on the Limitations of Anti-Ballistic Missiles and the Interim Agreement on the Limitation of Strategic Offensive Arms*, 92nd Congress, 2nd Session, 1972.

34. The first explicit indications actually came earlier, in April 1972, when Soviet negotiators told their U.S. counterparts in private conversation that Moscow was about to test a new large ICBM. This was later confirmed by reports by the Central Intelligence Agency (CIA). See *New York Times*, 23 April 1972, 1.

35. For details on the experience of the SCC, see Robert W. Buchheim and Philip J. Farley, "The US–Soviet Standing Consultative Commission," in Alexander George, Philip Farley, and Alexander Dallin, eds., *US–Soviet Security Cooperation: Achievements, Failures, Lessons* (New York: Oxford, 1988), 254–70; Sidney Graybeal and Michael Krepon, "Making Better Use of the Standing Consultative Commission," *International Security* (Fall 1985). One of the more important and influential channels for informal communication, the Committee for International Security and Arms Control (CISAC), was set up under the auspices of the two countries' Academies of Science. Many of the prominent scientists who took part in the meetings of this and other groups had good access to top decision makers in Washington. Under Gorbachev, Soviet defense scientists, some of whom have close ties to their Western counterparts, seem to be achieving similar access.

36. What became known in popular parlance as the Schlesinger Doctrine was formalized in National Security Decision Memorandum 242. Early public presentation of the new doctrine can be found in the testimony of James R. Schlesinger, secretary of defense, *U.S.–U.S.S.R. Strategic Policies*, Hearings before the Subcommittee on Arms Control, International Law, and Organization of the Committee on Foreign Relations, U.S. Senate, 93rd Congress, 2nd Session, March 4, 1974. For an assessment, see Lawrence Freedman, *The Evolution of US Nuclear Strategy* (New York: St. Martin's Press, 1983), 377–83.

37. Coit Blacker, "Learning in the Nuclear Age," Chapter 12 in this volume.

38. This is not to say that if strategic models had changed, they would have necessarily done so in a convergent rather than a divergent direction. In fact, given the continuing low level of interactive learning, divergence seems equally likely.

39. Alexander Dallin provides a concise analysis of the internal battles in the Reagan administration over this issue: Alexander Dallin, "Learning in U.S. Policy Toward the Soviet Union in the 1980s," Chapter 11 in this volume. For a more detailed account, see Strobe Talbott, *The Master of the Game: Paul Nitze and the Nuclear Peace* (New York: Knopf, 1988), Chapters 8–13.

40. Leonid Brezhnev in particular seems to have found it hard to understand why the Americans were surprised by his ICBM program. He seems to have believed for a time that the rumblings in Washington were the insidious work of incorrigible imperialist warmongers dedicated to overthrowing SALT and détente and intimidating the Soviets. Ted Hopf, "Soviet Decisions to Intervene," Chapter 16 in this volume.

41. Other sources of evidence include significant remodeling of the structure of Soviet decision making for defense. Blacker (Chapter 12 in this volume) points to concrete changes in personnel and in the institutions that make decisions for arms control and defense policy. He also describes the revamping of rhetoric and negotiating behavior that has emerged from the emended system.

42. This argument belongs to David Holloway, "Gorbachev's New Thinking," *Foreign Affairs* 68:1 (1989): 66–81.

43. I assume for the sake of argument here that the model has indeed been finally selected and is well along in the process of being institutionalized. Blacker (Chapter 12 in this volume) shows evidence of changes in personnel and decision-making structures that support this assumption. However, I am not fully convinced that the model has been fully institutionalized or that the Soviets' critical learning period of the 1980s has come to a close. A crucial test may come if the new strategic model is forced to accommodate adaptations that will have to be made if the United States does not respond as predicted. Washington has so far been recalcitrant in the face of unusual Soviet efforts. After the INF treaty, the two sides have made substantial progress toward a START accord, a bilateral chemical weapons treaty, and a broad agreement to limit conventional forces in Europe under the CFE arrangement. If these agreements do not come to fruition, and if the Soviets are still in the midst of a critical learning period, we might expect to see an alternative strategic model replace the current one in Moscow. If the critical learning period were over and the model fully institutionalized, then adaptation would be the predicted response. In that case, the Soviets would not jettison their general goals, but would instead develop new tactics to try to bring the Americans along.

44. This came as a surprise to Stalin, who seems to have feared that the United States might try to capitalize on its nuclear advantage far more aggressively than it did. Similarly, Herman Kahn and other influential Americans in the 1950s predicted that the Soviets would become far more aggressive as they moved toward and possibly beyond nuclear parity with the United States. A December 1960 review of American security policy prepared for the incoming Kennedy administration, NSC 6013, argued that "as the Soviet nuclear ballistic missile . . . capabilities grow, the element of pressure and threat will probably become more pronounced in communist dealings with the rest of the world. In their continual probing of the strength and determination of the West they will be more aggressive. . . ." Eisenhower Library, White House Office, Office of the Special Assis-

tant for National Security Affairs, Special Assistant Series, Presidential Subseries, Box 5.

45. That solution need not be the perfect solution of joint maximization of profits. In fact, except under special conditions that clearly do not hold in the U.S.–Soviet relationship, it will not be. U.S.–Soviet arms control, like most cases of oligopolistic competition, is not then expected to produce an optimal outcome. However, the outcome is expected to tend toward *some* equilibrium, which Fellner calls *qualified joint maximization*. See William Fellner, *Competition Among the Few: Oligopoly and Similar Market Structures* (New York: Knopf, 1949), 33–36.

46. For contending arguments, see Herbert F. York with Ashton B. Carter, *Does Strategic Defense Breed Offense?* (Lanham, Md.: University Press of America, 1987). For an illustration of how this controversy was played out in Washington under the Reagan administration, see Talbott, *Master of the Game*, 200–6 and 367.

47. Fellner, *Competition Among the Few*, 32–33 and 43.

48. I discuss this issue and why it has been so at length in *Cooperation and Discord in US–Soviet Arms Control.*

49. For those who think of U.S.–Soviet arms control as an international regime, this failure should be particularly troublesome. One of the most important functions of a regime, according to Keohane, is to facilitate states' efforts to develop compatible adaptations or adjustments to changes in the environment. Robert Keohane, *After Hegemony* (Princeton, N.J.: Princeton University Press, 1984), Chapter 6. Although developments in weapons technology have been an important and persistent source of challenges, technology poses new problems for any regime and the U.S.–Soviet arms control regime has been remarkably unsuccessful in this area. Environmental shocks from other aspects of the superpower relationship have also intruded on arms control (the Soviet invasion of Afghanistan, for example), but the putative regime has dealt poorly with these as well.

50. Unless one is willing to accept the tautology that what states do is, by definition, to seek power. This begs the question. How do decision makers define power at any given time? What resources are relevant? What is the contribution of nuclear weapons?

51. *Conventionalization,* as this is sometimes called, has in fact been a remarkably weak trend in thinking about nuclear weapons and arms control.

52. This is an observation based on only two historical cases. There is no logical reason that new ideas and new strategic models could not be built during a critical learning period, except that there may not be time to do so during the heat of crisis. Instead, top decision makers tend to draw on the menu of ideas that others have been working on and thinking through during the interim.

53. Again, I draw this argument from Kuhn, *Structure of Scientific Revolutions*, especially Chapters 7, 8, 12.

54. Talbott (*Master of the Game*, Chapters 11–14) provides a wealth of anecdotes that show that this line of adaptation was already well established in Washington during the second Reagan administration, and that it gained considerable strength from the INF "success." The Bush administration, at least in its early months, seems to have carried on with a similar approach. An example: after having secured agreement in principle on a 50 percent reduction in Soviet SS-18 deployments, the administration at the urging of national security adviser Brent Scowcroft

aimed to push the Soviet Union toward a total ban on these missiles. *New York Times,* 16 April 1989, 1).

55. This may be particularly important in the Soviet Union, where military institutions appear to have been the most persistent advocates of the old strategic model. Not surprisingly, military thinkers have also been the group involved in arms control most consistently isolated from contact with the West.

21

What Have We Learned About Learning?

George W. Breslauer

The purpose of this volume has been to introduce a category of analysis—learning—into discussions of U.S. and Soviet security policy, to explore the uses and utility of such a concept, to inquire into the conditions under which policy makers reevaluate their beliefs, and to understand when such reevaluations result in changes in policy and increases in policy effectiveness. The normative impulse for the project was to understand the conditions for ending the cold war and reducing the incidence of large-scale international conflict. As Philip Tetlock, in Chapter 2, has mined the case studies for examples and explanations of varied types and degrees of learning, I will emphasize in this chapter the implications of our findings for thinking about the relationship between varied types of learning and the duration and intensity of the cold war. I will also address explanations alternative to a learning framework for its duration, intensity, and prospective termination.

WHAT'S IN A DEFINITION?

The first, and most obvious, lesson to be drawn from this project is that the very definition of *learning* is a matter of dispute among those who apply the term to the study of foreign policy evolution. In part this derives from the inherent tension between the everyday use of the term *learning* as engendering "greater realism" (*learning that*) or "greater skill" (*learning how*), and the varied uses of the term in specialized psychological, organizational, and political science literatures. Beyond these distinctions, which are analyzed in Chapter 1, we find that learning remains a term in dispute even among those contributors to this volume who prefer to use it without reference to the greater realism or effectiveness of cognitive or behavioral changes involved in learning. Here the dispute revolves around the *magnitude* of change.

Thus, Philip Tetlock (Chapter 2), a social psychologist, treats learning as a generic concept. He defines it very broadly, and then seeks to differentiate among many types and degrees of learning, both individual and governmental. Not surprisingly in light of this definitional choice, he sees learning per se as a phenomenon that is to be observed fairly frequently in foreign policy making. However, some types of learning in his typology are much more commonly encountered in the real world than are others, with changes in tactical beliefs proving to be more frequent occurrences than changes in strategic beliefs or goals.

Ernst Haas (Chapter 3), in contrast, defines the concept very narrowly, treating many of Tetlock's forms of learning as manifestations of adaptation. Haas distinguishes among several types of adaptation and argues that these are common, whereas learning is rare. Given the fact that Haas's definition of learning is both highly restrictive and demanding of far-reaching change, it should come as no surprise that he finds relatively little evidence of genuine learning among Soviet or U.S. leaders. As he puts it, "We must conclude that nothing *irreversible* has occurred to *totally* alter the *cognitive universe* of Soviet and U.S. foreign policy makers" (emphasis added).

What is at stake here? When the issue is the relative magnitude of belief change along given dimensions, and not the observer's vouching for the greater realism or skill engendered by the change, does it matter whether we refer to learning and varying types of adaptation, or to tactical and fundamental learning (Legvold, Chapter 18), trial and error, cognitive content, and cognitive structural learning (Tetlock, Chapter 2), simple and complex learning?[1] Are these differences simply matters of taste? If they are, does it matter which definitions we employ, as long as we make clear the usage we are employing? In the abstract, it seems to me that the choice need not be consequential, as long as the reader is aware of the definitional choices at work. Learning is used by these authors as a subset of a broader phenomenon—belief change—and the choice of thresholds for distinguishing magnitudes of change—minor or major, insignificant or significant—is often (perhaps inherently?) a normative, or at least an arbitrary, exercise in all areas of the humanities and the social sciences.

When not treating the matter abstractly, but as a matter of the *utility* of alternative approaches, the choice may be more consequential. We may then ask: What does a given definition highlight? For example, if we are interested in specifying the conditions for improving the reliability of superpower crisis management, we may be primarily concerned with elite ability to read signals properly or to understand technical distinctions between, say, offensive and defensive deployments (i.e., realism). And we may be interested principally in the ability of leaders to learn cumulative lessons over time about the requisites of escalation control (i.e., skill).

Thinking of belief systems as a hierarchy ranging from instrumental to philosophical beliefs,[2] or from peripheral to core beliefs,[3] we would be concerned primarily with changes in instrumental or peripheral beliefs. Thinking of cognitive structure as informed by a means-ends (or a tactics-strategies-goals) chain, we would be interested primarily in changes in means or tactics. Thinking of learning as a continuum from simple to complex learning, we would be interested primarily in simple learning. However, this need not be equated with insignificant or minor change, since failure to improve one's understanding of the modalities of successful crisis management can have apocalyptic consequences. Thus, the larger question about the significance of change is ultimately: Significant for what?

In Chapter 1 we quoted Henry Kissinger's observation that policy makers do not gain in profundity with experience on the job; they must live off the intellectual capital they bring to office. This generalization is clearly not true with respect to the type of simple learning I have been discussing. Indeed, the case studies in this volume testify to the many types of lower-order learning that took place during the course of presidential administrations and Soviet leaders' terms in office (see Chapter 2).

Similarly with respect to other types of simple learning: much of the literature on analogical reasoning in foreign policy decision making is concerned with potentially momentous decisions (such as whether to Americanize the war in Vietnam) that are based on judgments about the extent to which a given situation closely resembles an analogous situation previously encountered. Ernest May and Richard Neustadt have written extensively on this subject[4] and prescribe guidelines for policy makers faced with such decisions. Essentially, their guidelines call for improving the information-processing capacity of decision makers by inducing them to examine more fully whether the analogies that underlie prevailing definitions of the situation constitute tight or loose analogical fits. In Chapter 9 of this volume Yuen Foong Khong explores the use of analogical reasoning by U.S. policy makers, although his concerns are analytic and explanatory, not prescriptive.

When our interest in significant change in beliefs is driven by a concern to improve crisis management, crisis prevention, other forms of limited cooperation, or the process of analogical reasoning, we are interested in learning as a process that improves skill (*learning how*) and realism (*learning that*). Thus, in the cases just noted, a low-magnitude change in beliefs (simple or tactical learning) is considered to be sufficient and vital to improving the realism and skill commensurate with the task in question. If the task is more ambitious—for example, to create a sustained collaborative relationship between rival powers across many issue areas— we may find that complex, strategic learning is required. This would force us to focus largely on changes in core beliefs, philosophical assumptions, strategies, and goals.

Such an approach flows naturally from the normative concern driving our interest in cold war history: to understand what it would take to effect sustained, broadly based superpower cooperation that goes beyond the avoidance of shared aversions.[5] There is a large and growing literature on great power security cooperation in an anarchic international system. Some of that literature employs comparative case study methodologies.[6] Other work on this problem employs game-theoretical and computer simulation techniques.[7] One of the most common findings of these studies is that cooperation in the real world of international politics is a *learned* technique. Preferences cannot be taken as given and immutable; they evolve over time, as does the perception of the realizability of given preferences. Hence, a focus on learning that highlights how leaders of rival powers *come to believe* that cooperation is necessary to advance their interests, or come to redefine their interests per se, is warranted given the state of our knowledge about international politics.

Hence, given the realities of cold war, it is reasonable to assume that complex learning, defined as changes in core beliefs and goals, is a necessary condition for broad and sustained superpower cooperation. We would especially like to know, therefore, what is required for such complex learning to occur. Accordingly, most of our contributors were asked to specify the major continuities and discontinuities in U.S. and Soviet elite thinking during the postwar era and the factors that determined those patterns. Do major discontinuities in prevailing assumptions and goals require a leadership change? With or without such leadership change, what circumstances must obtain for such major discontinuities in thought to take place, find their way into policy, and be sustained?

The chapter by Steven Weber (Chapter 20) is instructive in this regard. Weber accepts the utility of distinguishing between learning and adaptation. Adaptation, he finds, is a common phenomenon; learning is rare. This is because Weber defines learning narrowly. He demands a change of "strategic model" before a cognitive change qualifies as learning. And he posits that this occurs very infrequently—only once in U.S. arms control policy and once in Soviet arms control policy, in the past 40 years.

Weber's definitional choice in turn derives from his larger purposes.

He is interested, not only in the conditions under which learning occurs, but also in the circumstances under which rival powers come to cooperate in arms control. In this case, Weber posits that sustained cooperation is unlikely (but not impossible) in the absence of a parallelism between the strategic models embraced by the leading policy makers of the rival powers. *Given preexisting and incompatible strategic models*, the question is whether symmetrical changes occur in or within those models until they become sufficiently compatible as to facilitate cooperation. By acknowledging that plenty of adaptation had taken place *within* each country's preexisting strategic models, Weber is able to concede the frequency of change but still explain the frequent inadequacy of that change, relative to the requisites for achieving the goal of cooperation.

Weber allows that cooperation is possible if certain types of "compatible adaptations" take place within each strategic model, and if those adaptations are sufficiently symmetrical to build on complementary interests. He argues that if two states understand the basic components of each other's strategic model, and they limit cooperative endeavors to areas in which their conceptions of self-interest are actually compatible, then limited cooperation can be achieved and sustained even when their broader strategic models are not the same. But Weber is clearly skeptical of the *scope* of the possibilities for cooperation likely to emerge through that route. In sum, Weber's conceptual apparatus allows him to highlight the cognitive conditions that would have to obtain for the two sides to be sufficiently on the same wavelength to make possible the creation and maintenance of a cooperative relationship.

Weber's approach to cooperation circumvents the problem of vouching for the greater realism of cognitive change, which the everyday usage of the term *learning*, ordinarily requires (see Chapter 1). By defining learning as a change of strategic model, he makes learning synonymous with a certain magnitude of change of strategic beliefs. Had the Strategic Defense Initiative been widely accepted and institutionalized in U.S. politics, he allows, that would have qualified as learning, even though many observers would argue, based on their view of reality, that it was a case of madness. This highlights the difficulty of confining use of the term to instances in which the observer can persuasively vouch for the validity of new beliefs (*learning that*). For his purposes, Weber is more interested in parallel processes of cognitive evolution that increase the prospects of superpower cooperation. He is, in a sense, more interested in the issue of *learning how*, with learning that results in a parallelism of strategic models being a necessary condition for cooperation.

However, Weber is not an idealist; he does not view cognitive parallelism as a sufficient condition for cooperation. Like Ernst Haas,[8] he attempts to specify the environmental and political conditions under which policy makers will engage in fundamental reevaluations. Haas, for example, argues that learning occurs when a condition of perceived urgency, feasibility, and desirability of such change converges. Similarly, Weber argues that a "critical learning period" is required for a change in strategic model to take place. We will return later to this relationship between conditions and cognition.

Thus, in the cases of both Weber and Haas, a highly restrictive (and demanding) definition of learning proved useful in sorting the evidence brought forth to explain the limits of interstate cooperation. In this respect, their approach dovetails with premises of neorealist thought about international relations: (1) that in the contemporary state-system, conflict between rivals is the norm and broadly based, sustained cooperation very much the exception and (2) that states will ultimately adjust in response to repeated failure, but that far-reaching redefinition of the national interest is an extremely rare occurrence. Those concerned with explaining why the cold war has lasted as long as it has, and those concerned with determining what it would take to end the cold war (i.e., to effect multi-issue, far-reaching, and sustained superpower cooperation), will be drawn to restrictive definitions of learning and to a concern with the major turning points. That will be the approach of this chapter in seeking to synthesize and push beyond the material assembled in this book.

My approach parallels and builds on that adopted by Weber in the previous chapter, with one important exception. I will tackle the problem of learning as increased realism and skill in ways that do not allow the Strategic Defense Initiative to qualify as learning. Rather, I will begin with the incompatibility of the strategic models of each side, which I refer to as cold war paradigms. The cold war paradigms are much broader in their claims than are Weber's strategic models, which are more specific and suited to his focus on the arms control arena. The paradigms deal with fundamental assumptions about the course of history, the nature of the international system, and the nature of international conflict.

For the purposes of this essay, then, I treat learning as any reevaluation of the goals and philosophical assumptions built into the cold war paradigms, if the reevaluation undercuts unilateral approaches to ensuring national security, in favor of cooperative approaches. This may be an arbitrary or normative choice, but it is no more arbitrary than any approach that seeks to employ in the analysis of international relations the everyday usage of the learning construct. In my usage, then, *realism* is defined as any fundamental reevaluation of the cold war paradigm that argues for the principle of increased superpower cooperation. This is based on my belief that the assumptions built into the cold war paradigms on each side have been fundamentally at odds with reality. The worst-case U.S.

and Soviet assumptions about each other, and the best-case images on each side about the course of history, strike me as virtually indefensible.

COLD WAR PARADIGMS: U.S.–U.S.S.R.

When we turn to the case studies in this volume, we find that elites in Washington and Moscow clung for many decades to variants of a cold war paradigm that may only now be coming apart. By the *cold war paradigm*, I mean the basic structure of thought about the values to be pursued abroad, the nature of international politics and of history, the nature of the adversary, and the nature of the conflict relationship that prevailed in Washington and Moscow for most of the postwar era.

The cold war paradigm prevailing in Moscow reflected the Leninist ideological tradition on which the Soviet state was based. Normatively, Leninist ideology included a commitment to "make the world safe for socialism," both by maintaining Soviet power in the Soviet Union and by providing varied sorts and degrees of assistance to "anti-imperialist" forces abroad. Soviet strategies in pursuit of this goal were in turn conditioned by largely unfalsifiable philosophical assumptions: that, historically, time was on the side of socialism; that, ultimately, the victory of socialism was inevitable; and that, until then, history would proceed in ebbs and flows to which the Soviet Union must adjust. Soviet behavior in any given historical period was shaped by slightly more falsifiable beliefs about the anti-imperialist struggle: that the enemy was unalterably antagonistic and conspiratorial, and that the struggle with the enemy was usually zero-sum in character. The realities of the nuclear age later required that Moscow and Washington manage their relationship to prevent the struggle from eventuating in uncontrolled escalation. But under this managerial umbrella, the struggle would continue toward a predetermined, albeit increasingly distant, end. In light of these beliefs and justifications, it is quite appropriate to refer to the Soviet Union during the cold war as "an ambitious but cautious great power"[9] or to refer to Soviet strategy during much of 1953–1985 as "offensive détente."[10]

The varied dimensions of the U.S. cold war paradigm have been strikingly similar in form, though not in content, to the corresponding dimensions of the Soviet paradigm. Normatively, the United States was committed to "making the world safe for democracy," by resisting the spread of radicalism or the expansion of revisionist great powers. Prevailing U.S. thought was based on philosophical assumptions with deep roots in the American political heritage: that humankind ultimately yearns for political freedom and individualistic initiative; that the U.S. system of governance is broadly, if not universally, applicable; and that economic development will ultimately create political stability. U.S. tactics in the cold war were in turn shaped by empirical beliefs about the anticommunist struggle: that communism is diabolical and conspiratorial, and that the struggle is zero-sum in nature. Given such beliefs and justifications, it is not surprising that "for most of the cold war, U.S. grand strategy has leaned towards global containment, with occasional attempts to roll back Soviet clients."[11]

The parallels between the cold war paradigms in Moscow and Washington might be explained with reference to the bipolarity of the international system and the tendency on each side to mirror-image the other. Such an explanation, however, would be seriously incomplete, for it ignores the fact that long-standing ideological and political traditions in each country were parallel in form, but potentially antagonistic in content. That is to say, the cores of Soviet Leninism[12] and American liberalism[13] are both *optimistic* about what can be achieved through the mobilization of will, *missionary* in their commitment to seeing the world (actively or hopefully) transformed in their own image, *progressive* in their thinking about history, and based on philosophical assumptions that are largely *unfalsifiable*. Yet the danger for civilization resided in the fact that these formal parallels were filled with incompatible content, as each side directed its unfalsifiable optimism, viewed its mission, and defined its progress in opposite ways. Bipolarity might have created an analogous situation of hostility in any case, but the sharp ideological differences exacerbated their threat perceptions and the security dilemma, encouraged worst-case analysis, and intensified the geopolitical rivalry. All of which contributed to both the intensity and the duration of the cold war.

The chapters in this volume provide testimony to the tenacity of the cold war paradigm in shaping both thought and action in the U.S.–Soviet relationship from Stalin through Brezhnev, Truman through Reagan. Furthermore, the Sovietological chapters are nearly unanimous in their claim that a fundamental break with the cold war paradigm is taking place under Gorbachev. We have, then, clear examples of both nonlearning and learning to explain. Let me begin with the Soviet Union.

THE SOVIET COLD WAR PARADIGM IN ACTION

Jonathan Haslam, analyzing Soviet policy toward Europe since World War II (Chapter 13), argues that Soviet thinking under Stalin, Khrushchev, and Brezhnev was driven by a common set of assumptions. These assumptions were that national security hinged on Soviet domination of Eastern Europe, the partition of Europe and Germany, and an offensive strategy of military and/or political intimidation of the North Atlantic Treaty Organization (NATO) geared toward buttoning-down Western acceptance of the existing division of Europe. To be sure, the tactics employed by different Soviet leaders to effect this goal varied. Stalin pursued the goal through a state of military siege; Khrushchev through military threats, political pressure, and selective accommodation; Brezhnev through a combination of détente and military buildup. But their assumptions about the requisites of Soviet national security were similar.

In contrast, Gorbachev has ushered in a period of rethinking that challenges the inviolability of those assumptions. He has therefore been more willing to respond to the uncontrolled pace of change by abstaining from invasion and by entertaining (albeit ambivalently) alternative, post-partition visions that accept an end to Soviet domination of Eastern Europe, an end to communist rule in those countries, an end to offensive military-political intimidation of Western Europe, and an end to the partition of Germany. It is partially true but insufficient to say that he is merely adjusting to an unanticipated and uncontrolled situation, both because there is evidence that he helped to instigate the collapse of conservative regimes in Eastern Europe, and because his predecessors would have responded very differently to the current turmoil, especially regarding German reunification.

In Coit Blacker's study of Soviet arms control policy (Chapter 12), we find a similar pattern. As Weber has gone over this material in his concluding chapter, I will not rehearse the history here. But the significant point (for our purposes) is that, however important the changes in Soviet nuclear policy under Khrushchev and Brezhnev, those changes did not challenge optimistic assumptions about winnability, or the basically offensive posture assigned to military force-structuring that prevailed under Stalin. Nor did Khrushchev or Brezhnev abandon the perceived utility of nuclear weapons as a political weapon that emerged in the post-Stalin era. The large break comes with the current "new political thinking," with its stress on defense, minimum deterrence, global interdependence, mutual security, and "nonwinnability."

My own chapter on Soviet policy toward the Arab-Israeli conflict (Chapter 15) can be reinterpreted in analogous terms. Even though Khrushchev abandoned Stalin's continental isolationism for global competition, and even though Brezhnev added a collaborative track to Khrushchev's competitive track, all three leaders shared certain assumptions about the Third World and the Middle East as arenas of zero-sum conflict between imperialist and anti-imperialist forces, a component of the "world revolutionary process" in which progressive forces were destined ultimately to emerge supreme over imperialist forces. It is only Gorbachev's new political thinking that begins to challenge these most basic assumptions and to develop a new way of thinking about Third World competition (indeed, perhaps to redefine the very desirability of such competition).

The chapters by Franklyn Griffiths (Chapter 17) and Robert Legvold

(Chapter 18), though covering shorter time periods, reinforce the conclusions of the other chapters. Griffiths treats the Soviet détente policy under Brezhnev as a change of course but emphasizes its limitations. He points to Brezhnev's inability or unwillingness to reduce the preponderant strength of "expansionist internationalism" within Soviet policy-making circles, which placed restrictions on the trade-offs possible in U.S.–Soviet bargaining. Those restrictions, in turn, made it likely that superpower cooperation would fail, since the unbalanced mix of "expansionist" and "reformative" internationalism in Soviet policy making was incompatible with U.S. expectations about the terms of U.S.–Soviet cooperation. Thus, for the purposes of his analysis, and given his retrospective awareness of the collapse of détente, Griffiths too stresses the Soviet failure to embrace a more fundamental change in paradigm that might have made détente a more enduring success.

Robert Legvold's chapter on Gorbachev's new thinking has special importance in light of earlier chapters on continuity among the Stalin, Khrushchev, and Brezhnev eras. Legvold argues that changes in Soviet thinking under Gorbachev qualify as fundamental learning (or, in Haasian terms: learning, not just adaptation). He highlights, in Griffiths's terms, the victory of the reformative internationalist over the expansionist internationalist tendency in Soviet foreign policy, but in the process also demonstrates, I believe, that the reformative internationalism of today is much different from that of the early 1970s. It is based on a set of interconnected propositions that break more fully with the philosophical assumptions of the Leninist tradition than anything we have witnessed before. Legvold acknowledges that plenty of lower-order learning, or adaptation, marked Soviet foreign policy evolution before the Gorbachev era. But, in retrospect, we can see the limits of its break with traditional Soviet philosophical assumptions and normative commitments, and we can understand therefore, at least in part, the fragility of earlier conditions for cooperation between the superpowers.

THE U.S. COLD WAR PARADIGM IN ACTION

The chapters on U.S. policy toward Europe, China, and the Middle East (by Wallace Thies, Banning Garrett, and Steven Spiegel, respectively) nicely display the incompatibility of the U.S. cold war paradigm with that embraced by Soviet leaders. Thies, for example, shows the continuity in U.S. policy toward Western Europe from the late 1940s to the present (Chapter 6). The basic premise driving U.S. policy has been the perceived requirement that the United States lend its nuclear deterrent and ground forces to prevent Soviet domination of Western Europe. Similarly, Garrett (Chapter 7) demonstrates that U.S. policy toward China has consistently been driven by the belief that U.S. national security hinged on the ability to drive a wedge between the People's Republic of China and the Soviet Union, but almost never through an anti-Chinese alliance or a one-sided rapprochement with the Soviet Union.[14] And Spiegel (Chapter 8) demonstrates that a constant strategic goal of U.S. policy in the Middle East has been to prevent Soviet expansion in the region. In all three cases, administrations have differed regarding the strategies employed to realize these goals and the relative weight to place on competing goals—just as the Stalin, Khrushchev, and Brezhnev regimes differed on these scores, despite a continuity of basic perspectives. But the points of continuity are consistent with a cold war paradigm that treats as a given the desirability, necessity, and feasibility of containing Soviet expansionism, and that assumes a zero-sum perspective on the bipolar struggle.

Deborah Larson's study of Kissinger's and Nixon's strategy of détente nicely parallels the study of Brezhnev by Griffiths. Just as Griffiths showed how the Brezhnev regime incorporated conciliators into its coalition and pursued a cooperative track vis-à-vis the United States, so Larson shows how Nixon and Kissinger sought to develop cooperative relations with the Soviet Union on issues on which the Soviets proved flexible and U.S. public opinion demanded progress. At the same time, just as Griffiths showed how the Brezhnev regime rested on a fragile coalition of conciliators and determined competitors, so Larson shows how the Nixon administration was forced to allow Congress to link issues of trade, human rights, and Third World competition, while many other studies show how Nixon and Kissinger perceived the struggle against pro-Soviet regimes in Latin America (Cuba, Allende's Chile), the Middle East, and Southeast Asia to be essentially zero-sum in character.[15]

In each case, we observe a move away from the worst-case version of the cold war paradigm, through the addition of a collaborative track to the relationship. In Weber's terms, we observe some compatible adaptations within each side's strategic model. But in each case we find a tenuous balance between the competitive and the collaborative tracks, political factors that force more ambitious pursuit of unilateral advantages in many policy realms, a resultant perception of the adversary as pursuing zero-sum strategies in those realms, and the collapse of the fragile coalition in relatively short order.

Alexander Dallin, in examining the return to détente in the second Reagan term (Chapter 11), also downplays the notion that a fundamental break with the cold war paradigm had taken place. Rather, he sees pragmatic Republicans ascending within the hierarchy and exploiting the opportunities presented by Gorbachev's concessionary offerings. The change in U.S. policy looks highly significant compared with the rigidity and belligerence of the first Reagan term. But compared with Kennedy's or Kissinger's postures toward the East-West struggle, the new Reagan policy was not novel. What had changed fundamentally was Gorbachev's willingness to accept U.S. terms that previous Soviet leaderships had rejected.

In this light, it is not surprising that U.S.–Soviet cooperation proved to be so fragile throughout so much of the postwar era. The prevailing paradigms on *each* side were biased in the direction of a zero-sum view of the anti-imperialist and anticommunist missions, even as they also incorporated an awareness of the imperative of avoiding direct military clashes between the superpowers or an unrestrained arms race.[16] On each side, the competitive track of the relationship was less politically controversial than the cooperative, and the toughest bargaining terms were insisted upon in negotiations. Many of the agreements reached during the détente years were made possible by the *postponement* of the knottiest issues (multiple independently targetable reentry vehicles—MIRVs; conventional force reductions; compatible definitions of human rights). Only when Gorbachev came to power and led an assault on the basic premises of Soviet thinking, did the prospects for cooperation across a range of issue areas begin to soar.

This characterization and explanation is intuitively satisfying, but it may be based on too deterministic a conception of the causes of the cold war's lengthy duration. It implies that far-reaching and sustainable cooperation in the past was necessarily foreclosed or short-circuited by the prevailing incompatibility of cold war paradigms. The periodization, however, submerges too much historical contingency and may therefore be misleading. It smacks of what Fischhoff calls "creeping determinism" or "certainty-of-hindsight."[17] For one thing, the paradigms were not uniformly incompatible throughout the postwar era. For another, while it may be true that the paradigms still remained largely incompatible, and that the cold war could not end under those circumstances, it remains to be explored just why paradigmatic incompatibility remained. Or, to put it in counterfactual terms: What would it have taken to overcome the incompatibility of paradigms during periods of paradigmatic flexibility? By glancing at selected periods of reevaluation in Soviet and U.S. foreign policy, we may arrive at a more probabilistic explanation for the duration and intensity of the cold war, one that appreciates degrees of cognitive and political openness while noting the frequent asymmetry in the scope and timing of such openness in Moscow and Washington.

TURNING POINTS AND CONTINGENCIES

My depiction of the continuity described by Thies, Garrett, and Spiegel obscures the fact that each of these scholars also documents breaks and discontinuities that lend grist to the mill of those who vigorously deny the historical inevitability of the cold war's lasting as long, or becoming as intense, as it did. In U.S. policy toward Western Europe before 1950, U.S. policy makers operated with a more flexible conception of the means required to prevent West European domination by the Soviet Union or pro-Soviet internal forces. Specifically, according to Thies, the emphasis was on political-psychological reassurance, a balance between military and nonmilitary instrumentalities of deterrence, and self-help by the Europeans; the assumption was that a Soviet invasion was neither imminent nor likely, and the vision of alliance was of a loose coalition with a U.S. guarantee. In contrast, after the shock of the Korean War, the emphasis was on political-military measures of reassurance, heavy reliance on the United States for protection, and the creation of an integrated, unified command. All of which derived from a preoccupation with Soviet invasion scenarios. Only today are new approaches being considered, in light of the breakdown of Soviet power in Eastern Europe and Gorbachev's reevaluation of Soviet military doctrine.

The late 1940s also play an important role in the story told by Banning Garrett. Although U.S. leaders consistently looked for ways to drive a wedge between China and the Soviet Union, U.S. images of the adversary were quite different before 1949–1950 than after that time. Unitl then, it was still assumed that China need not become an unalterable antagonist of the United States, that Mao might become an Asian Tito. Although the climate of opinion in Washington political circles still made it unfeasible to offer positive assistance to China, policy makers were concerned not to threaten China either, for fear of driving her into the Soviets' arms. That set of beliefs was finally destroyed by the experience of the Korean War. Thereafter, China was perceived as an unalterable antagonist of the West. The new strategy then became to drive a wedge between the two communist giants by so pressuring China militarily that China would make excessive demands for protection and assistance on the Soviet Union.

Here again, the Korean War played an important role in shifting U.S. strategic thinking toward an exclusive preoccupation with military power as the means of ordering relations with adversaries, and toward a more uniformly diabolical image of the communist adversaries. Whatever openness existed in the thinking that drove U.S. policy in Europe and Asia before 1950 disappeared thereafter. This is not surprising from the standpoint of cognitive theory, which predicts that high-magnitude traumas, directly experienced, will have the greatest impact on cognitive reorganization.[18]

Indeed, that proposition is further reinforced by the compelling evidence presented in the chapter by Yuen Foong Khong (Chapter 9). Khong demonstrates that the Korea analogy was foremost in the minds of U.S. policy makers in 1963–1965, as they tried to make sense of the situation in Southeast Asia and to fashion an appropriate U.S. response. Analogical reasoning prevailed in policy deliberations, and the Korea analogy was more determinant of advocacy than were any of the competing analogies. Assuming that the Korean War was not a historical inevitability, one might assume that, in its absence, the U.S.–Soviet relationship in Europe, and the U.S.–Soviet–Chinese relationship in Asia might have been very different in the 1950s and 1960s. Possibly also, Americanization of the Vietnam War might have been averted. This does not necessarily mean that the cold war would have been averted entirely, only that its duration and intensity might have varied. For the Korean War's impact on U.S. thinking about Europe was primarily tactical. Still, in an atmosphere unpolluted by the Korean War, paradigmatic flexibility could potentially have been built on to avert the costly expenditures and dangerous confrontations that awaited us in the 1950s and 1960s.

It is true that, after the Benes coup in Czechoslovakia in 1948, it was very hard to find any prominent U.S. decision maker arguing for anything else but a bipolar competitive balance-of-power system. Alternative paradigms, such as Roosevelt's cooperative multipolar balance-of-power system, or Kennan's balance by denial, were premised on the notion that spheres of influence could be loosely constructed, and not be areas of exclusive superpower dominance. Those conceptions lost official legitimacy in 1948, while the tight bipolar conception informed U.S. decisions regarding the necessity of a European defense alliance, first in the Brussels Pact and then in NATO. However, the same hardening did not take place in the Congress or in the public in 1948. That happened with the Korean War.[19]   A further hardening of the official paradigm did take place in 1950, as Thies points out, leading to a preoccupation with invasion scenarios. Perhaps we can say that the cold war paradigm's application to the European theatre emerged ascendant within the administration in 1948, but that its further dogmatization and militarization was a consequence of Korea, as was its broader acceptance within Congress and the attentive public.[20]

Dogmatization and militarization of the cold war paradigm prevailing in Washington in turn affected the U.S. ability to perceive accurately periods of cognitive and political openness in Moscow, though it remains a mystery whether pre-Korea, post-1948 thinking (tight bipolar competitive) would have been sufficient to block such awareness. After the death of Joseph Stalin in 1953, a power struggle among Malenkov, Khrushchev, and Molotov revolved, at least in part, around foreign and defense policy issues. Molotov represented the militants, while Malenkov adopted a conciliatory position on East-West issues. Khrushchev occupied the center of the political spectrum, but emerged victorious in the power struggle in part by adopting a relatively hard-line position on defense issues. We cannot rerun history to determine whether Khrushchev would have adopted this position on the policy spectrum and won the power struggle, regardless of the condition of the international environment. However, considerable circumstantial evidence supports the hypothesis that Malenkov's conciliatory position was undermined politically by the militant rhetoric of John Foster Dulles and, especially, by the progress being made toward West German rearmament and a European Defense Community, which was itself a product of the post-1950 preoccupation with invasion scenarios. Had the West struck a more accommodative posture, the argument goes, Malenkov's arguments would have gained credibility and his position would have been bolstered.[21]

Khrushchev subsequently forged a détente policy of his own. It was considerably more hard-line than Malenkov's, but more accommodative than Khrushchev himself had been espousing during the power struggle. It corresponds to what Jack Snyder calls "offensive détente."[22] It proclaimed "peaceful coexistence" henceforth to be "the general line of the Party," and it purged the apocalyptic dimension (i.e., World War III) from Soviet conceptions of the process of transition from a capitalist-dominated to a socialist-dominated world. It retained the optimistic assumption that time was on the side of socialism, and expanded the Soviet commitment to assisting the "world revolutionary process." It sought to consolidate Soviet control over Eastern Europe, solve the Berlin problem on Soviet terms, and force the West to treat the Soviets as negotiating equals by exaggerating Soviet nuclear and missile capacity in public statements and threats. In light of these hard-line elements, and in light of the dogmatization and militarization of the U.S. cold war paradigm after the Korean War, it should come as no surprise that official Washington treated Khrushchev's conciliatory gestures during 1956–1959 as largely disingenuous, and Khrushchev's competitive initiatives as confirmation of Soviet determination to bury the West. But would Washington's reactions and perceptions have been the same had the Korean War never taken place?

A period of intense East-West confrontation followed during 1960–1962, reaching a crescendo in the Cuban missile crisis. One consequence of that crisis was a reevaluation of the cold war paradigm in both Moscow and Washington, but especially in Moscow. As Zimmerman has so well documented,[23] and as Griffiths mentions in his chapter, fundamental reappraisals of Soviet perspectives on international relations entered into Soviet elite discourse during Khrushchev's last two years in power. Many of the premises that comprise Gorbachev's "new political thinking" appeared suddenly in Soviet doctrinal statements in this period. Minimal deterrence, mutual security, global interdependence, and (in Griffiths's terms) subordination of the expansionist to the reformative tendency in aspects of

Soviet Third World policy characterized this interlude. A U.S.–Soviet détente emerged at this time. It even included (as Garrett notes) discussions at U.S. initiative about the possibility of joint action to destroy Chinese nuclear capacity. And it was not aborted until both the overthrow of Khrushchev and the Americanization of the war in Vietnam.

This consequence of Khrushchev's "new thinking" lends support to the argument that an end to the cold war required, as a minimal condition, Soviet subordination of the competitive to the cooperative tendency. But it also undermines support for the larger tendency to homogenize the Khrushchev and Brezhnev eras in general, in order to contrast them to the present era. Such homogenization desensitizes the observer, both to the historical contingency involved at various turning points in U.S.–Soviet relations and to the origins of Gorbachev's new thinking. That new thinking appears to have emerged ultimately as a product of a long-term, cumulative process of learning. Elements of the new thinking have existed in Soviet doctrine since Lenin, but had typically been treated as rationalizations for a breathing spell before the next global offensive. Khrushchev embraced and expanded on many of those premises, justifying them in nontemporary, noninstrumental terms, because of the crisis he was experiencing at home and abroad. Khrushchev's despair about the prospects for bringing China back into the fold, his intense fear that Chinese adventurism could result in accidental or catalytic nuclear war, and the personal authority crisis he was experiencing within the Soviet political establishment in 1963 combined to make this for Khrushchev (what Weber, in Chapter 20, calls) a "critical learning period." However, Khrushchev did not succeed in transforming the Soviet establishment, which was still biased toward expansionist internationalism.

Khrushchev's overthrow allowed the expansionist tendency to reassert itself, though the political battle to resubordinate reformative internationalism was not decided until after Americanization of the war in Vietnam. Just as Malenkov's conciliatory approach was undermined by militancy in Washington and in Western Europe, so continuation of Khrushchev's conciliatory posture of 1964 was undermined by the escalation of U.S. involvement in Vietnam.[24]   It is again intriguing to propose the counterfactual: had Khrushchev not been overthrown, had Kennedy not been assassinated, and/or had the United States not Americanized the Vietnam War, the history of the cold war might have taken a very different turn.

Brezhnev, then, built his authority within a political context biased toward the political reascendancy of hard-line tendencies. Like Khrushchev in 1954, he adopted a relatively hard-line position in the power struggle and discredited conciliators in part by pointing to the threatening international environment. Like Khrushchev in 1955 to 1959, he thereafter forged a comprehensive program that combined détente and expansionism. Unlike Khrushchev's initial efforts, Brezhnev created a synthesis of expansion and détente that succeeded for a time in forging a cooperative relationship with the United States, and for an even longer time in fostering "European détente." Unlike Khrushchev's relationship with Eisenhower in 1959–1960, Brezhnev's interlocutors in Washington, Nixon and Kissinger, both understood and shared his urge for expanded cooperation. For a brief period of time, the Soviet and U.S. leaderships appeared to be cooperating across a range of issue areas. Each side tempered its aspirations and adjusted its expectations sufficiently to make possible a new détente. Each side dedogmatized its cold war paradigm somewhat. Indeed, as Weber has argued elsewhere, there emerged at this time a tacit understanding in Moscow and Washington that the two superpowers shared responsibility for a "joint trusteeship" of sorts over the international order.[25]

The détente of 1969–1974, however, was based on only a very limited convergence of paradigms, for both sides continued to treat the Third World as an arena of zero-sum struggle, while the U.S. Congress would not accept Brezhnev's insistence that Soviet human rights and Third World policies be decoupled from existing areas of U.S.–Soviet cooperation (such as trade). The terms for cooperation therefore proved unacceptable to the U.S. Congress, which responded to Soviet foreign and domestic behavior with restrictions that helped to fuel a defiant Soviet response. This dynamic created a political escalation spiral that led to the collapse of U.S.–Soviet cooperation by the end of the decade.

Only when Gorbachev came to power did the political conditions emerge for the premises of 1963–1964, and other reformative premises incorporated since then, to become ascendant once again in Soviet politics. This followed several intervening periods of frustration with Soviet foreign policy fortunes under the weighted synthesis of tendencies favoring expansionist internationalism and was catalyzed by the multilevel crisis at home and abroad in the 1980s. Gorbachev has been able to legitimize the far-reaching changes in thought he advocates and the highly conciliatory postures he has struck on specific issues because he can persuasively argue that alternatives based on expansionism and tough negotiating terms have demonstrated both their unaffordability and their unworkability. In other words, multiple periods of frustration have led the new generation of officials to include a considerable number of cooptable individuals who have drawn fundamental lessons from experience. Gorbachev's challenge has been to coopt these individuals and transform the institutional context of policy making so as to institutionalize a new paradigm.

The shock of Gorbachev's conciliatory policies at home and abroad, reinforced in 1989 by the collapse of communism throughout Eastern Europe, has created a crisis for the reigning U.S. cold war paradigm. In the eyes of many of its adherents, that paradigm was appropriate for understanding and dealing with the Soviet Union in the past, but it now requires substantial revision in light of the systemic changes taking place within the camp of the adversary. Both during Ronald Reagan's second term and during the first years of the Bush administration, discussion and debate have revolved around the extent of revision of traditional assumptions to accept and to translate into policy. Since most of the impulse for reevaluation has come from Soviet and East European capitulations to long-standing Western hopes or demands, behavioral adjustment on the part of the West is currently running far ahead of cognitive reevaluation of paradigms. The traditional cold war paradigm, in both its dogmatized and less dogmatic forms, appears to many of its previous adherents to have served its historical purpose and now to be inappropriate for the new era, but an alternative paradigm has not yet been embraced.

Perhaps what we are witnessing on the Western side is a manifestation of what Deborah Larson claims to be a frequent occurrence in foreign policy: behavioral change that comes later to be rationalized in order to bring beliefs into line with behavior.[26] At present, a form of liberal internationalism prevails in Moscow's "new thinking," but with pressure from those who are ambivalent about the scope of Soviet concessions. In Washington, realpolitik continues to prevail, but with pressure from liberal internationalists in Congress and in the executive branch who would like the response to current events to return us to an era of East-West cooperation analogous to the ideas expounded by Franklin Roosevelt.

The Iraqi invasion of Kuwait on August 2, 1990, prompted a further deepening of U.S.–Soviet cooperation and a partial convergence of paradigms. Moscow joined Washington in imposing an arms embargo on Iraq; the Soviets also endorsed and participated in an economic embargo of that country. A summit meeting between George Bush and Mikhail Gorbachev, held in Helsinki, Finland, on September 9, 1990, symbolically reinforced this new level of superpower collusion and coordination. The two leaders pledged to continue the isolation and embargo of Iraq until Baghdad withdrew from Kuwait. Increasingly, each side refers to the nonadversarial partnership emerging between Moscow and Washington in this post-cold war era. The United Nations Security Council has maintained its unity against Iraq, prompting both sides to view this crisis as a possible impetus to the partial realization of Franklin Roosevelt's vision of a new concert of the great powers. The Bush administration has accordingly announced that it is formally dropping its opposition to a central Soviet role in negotiating a settlement of the Arab-Israeli conflict.[27] And mutual concern over the Iraqi possession of chemical weapons and pursuit of nuclear weapons may deepen U.S.–Soviet collusion on matters of nuclear proliferation (see Chapter 19 of this volume).

Whether the partial convergence of paradigms that has already taken place will be sufficient to forge a lasting cooperative relationship between the superpowers remains to be seen. Even the extraordinary degree of U.S.–Soviet coordination against Iraq has not been free of potentially serious strains. Some Soviet military and civilian leaders have expressed alarm about the prospect of a large and long-term U.S. military presence in Saudi Arabia. Gorbachev himself has expressed strong reservations about the prospect of a shooting war between the United States (and her allies) and Iraq, arguing instead for patience and a political solution to the crisis, preferably led by Arab states. Moscow has been wary of making a commitment of its own forces to the military blockade. Hence, should Western and Arab unity break down due to differences over the price to be paid for containing or eliminating the regime in Baghdad, U.S.–Soviet cooperation on this issue could dissolve, and expanding definitions of *partnership* could be reevaluated.

Thus, whether U.S. and Soviet interests will converge across a wider range of issues, and whether that will be sufficient to forge broad, sustained cooperation, remains to be seen. But the 40-year duration of the cold war cannot be understood without an appreciation of the frequency with which prevailing cold war paradigms in Washington and Moscow did not converge, and the frequency with which one-sided partial convergence took place precisely when the other side was not ready for it—or (in the cases in the 1950s) was not even aware of it.

ALTERNATIVE EXPLANATIONS

When we use *learning* as the main (or only) independent variable to explain policy changes, and when we focus on each side's cold war paradigm, there is always a danger of overintellectualizing foreign policy analysis. This danger takes two forms: (1) inadequate appreciation of the political bases of foreign policy making and (2) overestimation of the importance of learning in foreign policy, as opposed to explanations that seek the sources of foreign policy in deeper, objective conditions that force states in given directions. The latter objection is at the basis of neorealist analyses and of neorealist criticisms of a learning perspective.[28] Let me take these issues in reverse order.

Neorealists might argue that the cold war lasted as long as it did because conflict is the norm in international politics. Superpower cooperation in a bipolar system is likely to take the limited form of escalation control in order to avoid shared aversions. This accounts for the relative ease with which the superpowers have managed crises.[29] Beyond this, superpower cooperation geared toward conflict resolution, rapprochement, or entente is likely to fail. To the extent that it does not fail, the basic cause of success will be the underlying power equation between the two adversaries. From this perspective, the Gorbachev revolution in Soviet foreign policy reflects the relative weakness of the Soviet Union at home and abroad. It took some time, and many false starts, for Soviet elites to wake up to this reality, but ultimately they did. They came to appreciate that their domestic economic, social, and political base was inadequate to support the survival of a regime with pretensions to being a stable empire, an imperial controller of Eastern Europe, an ideological and organizational leader of the world communist movement, and a competitive global superpower. When they finally came to this realization, they contracted their ambitions and proceeded to reform their system, thereby doing what neorealist theory would predict: they imitated the successful strategies of competitors. The unwillingness of the United States to treat the Soviet Union as an equal, by this accounting, was a recognition of the fact that, when military, economic, political, diplomatic, and other forms of power are added up, the United States and the Soviet Union were never equals. The neorealist would conclude that learning is epiphenomenal; it reflects underlying power realities, which in turn are the deeper explanation for the cold war's apparently coming to an end in the 1990s. States adjust to reality or are punished for their obstinacy. The Soviet Union ultimately adjusted to avoid further punishment, which was taking its toll.

This is a powerful alternative explanation, and not one that can or should be refuted. But we can cast doubt on some of its premises and demand qualifications. First, while it may partially account for what is happening today, it alone cannot account for the intensity and duration of the cold war (that is, the length of time it took for reality to sink in and the extent of conflict that marked those years). Ideological differences and domestic politics much exacerbated the structurally derived U.S.–Soviet conflict. What's more, had certain major events (the Korean War, Kennedy's assassination) not transpired, it is entirely conceivable that the intensity and duration of the cold war would have been even less than they were. Nor can a neorealist theory account for the periodic expansions and contractions of paradigmatic openness on each side during the previous 40 years. It would require a counterfactual assertion of a dubiously deterministic sort to argue, as neorealists would have to, that previous manifestations of openness were doomed to fail because of the objective balance of power at the time.

Second, the measurement of relative power is a controversial matter, both because nuclear weapons offset for certain purposes the other forms of power available, and because some other forms of power are often not easily measured, much less discerned by policy makers (for example, domestic morale, political stability, diplomatic-political skill and influence, and economic stability). The Soviet Union, for example, suddenly had much greater economic power in the 1970s after the oil shocks, just as the United States had correspondingly less. This changed again in the 1980s, when oil prices fell.

Third, individual learning and leadership has played an important role in the development and political legitimation of the new thinking. Had Chernenko or Andropov lived longer than they did (say, if either had lived for six or eight more years) or had one of Gorbachev's rivals won the power struggle, the lessons drawn by new thinkers might not have become doctrine and guides to policy. Indeed, to this day the new thinking remains controversial within the Soviet political-military establishment. In sum, much of the course of the cold war, and much of the contingency in the past and the present, cannot easily be explained by what is admittedly a powerful hypothetical explanation for the Gorbachev revolution.[30]

The other objection to my outline of contingency in the evolution of the cold war is that conceptualization of superpower conflict and cooperation in terms of incompatibilities between cold war paradigms is an intellectualization and reification that does violence to the *political* character of foreign policy decision making in both capitals. The point is well taken in principle, but misunderstands the purpose of the exercise, both in this chapter and in Weber's analysis of strategic models. The misunderstanding can be averted, I think, by invoking the familiar distinction between individual and governmental learning.

INDIVIDUAL AND GOVERNMENTAL LEARNING

Extensive and lasting cooperation between the superpowers results when both governments come to be controlled by a dominant coalition that considers the cost of noncooperation by far to exceed the cost or risk of cooperation. Usually, this condition will either be preceded or succeeded by a convergence (or growing compatibility) of the strategic models or paradigms informing or justifying policy in the two capitals. What's more, both the extent and the duration of the cooperation will be a function of the extent to which the new perspectives sink deep political roots in the two countries. One could refer to this as the level of institutionalization of "new thinking" on each side, as measured by: (1) the extent to which institutions with a stake in the old order are restaffed, reorganized, and given redefined missions; (2) the size and strength of the dominant coalition's hold on governance; and (3) the extent of broader public and broader elite acceptance of the desirability or necessity of superpower cooperation.

Using the analytic categories of this book, this means that lasting cooperation is not a product of only individual learning on one or both sides. It can result only from governmental learning or a cognitive reorientation that is broadly institutionalized. To be sure, governmental learning is impossible without individual learning, for governments are composed of individuals, and leading individuals within the government must surely be on board for new thinking to be accepted politically. But the distinction is valuable for understanding the duration of the cold war.

Malenkov's posture of 1953–1954 reflected individual learning that had very little political support (and that found it difficult to pick up support given events abroad). Soviet changes of 1963–1964 reflected individual learning by Khrushchev and other individuals within the political and scientific establishments, but it was not very broadly based within the political establishment. Brezhnev's strategy of détente was a partial break with traditionalist Soviet thinking but, at the political level, reflected a shaky coalition of moderates and militants. I will call it *partial governmental learning*. Gorbachev's base of support for new thinking appears to be much broader and deeper, due to the discrediting of much of traditionalist advocacy by events of the past 15 years. Given the controversial nature of the new thinking, however, it might appropriately be referred to as *substantial but incomplete governmental learning*.

On the U.S. side, we can also point to instances of individual breaks with key premises of the cold war paradigm that lacked a sufficiently broad political base to inform policy. In some cases, such as Eisenhower's endorsement of minimal deterrence or Jimmy Carter's flirtation with an interdependence framework for thinking about international relations, the learner was in power. In other cases, such as Eugene McCarthy or George McGovern, the learner was an American Malenkov. The Nixon-Kissinger strategy of détente was an example of partial governmental learning, in that a shaky coalition of new thinkers and traditionalists was in power—a coalition that, as in the Soviet case, fell apart within a few years. During Ronald Reagan's first term in office, the traditional thinkers controlled government, reverting back to the dogmatized version of the cold war paradigm. But this gave way during Reagan's second term to a return to the dedogmatized version of the paradigm, which has also been embraced by the Bush administration. The events of 1989 in the Soviet Union and Eastern Europe, however, put even that version under considerable pressure, largely because the Soviet Union has violated a primary expectation of the cold war paradigm: it has permitted, even encouraged, the reversibility of communist rule in Eastern Europe, thus undermining diabolical images of the enemy. This leaves the administration searching for a new way of thinking about East-West relations and about the nature of international politics in the post–cold war era. In contrast to the idealist new thinking, the Bush administration currently is searching for a conception of détente that combines realpolitik with a U.S.–Soviet partnership. In other words, we are faced with a situation today in which substantial governmental learning in Moscow is paired with compatible adaptations, but as yet no new paradigm, in Washington. Whether this will result in lasting cooperation remains to be seen, but it is worthy of note that this may be as close as the two sides have come in the postwar era to a significant convergence of ways of thinking.

Most competing political-institutional explanations for the duration of the cold war tend toward more pessimistic conclusions. One such explanation focuses on the interests of the military-industrial complex in each country and its preponderant influence on politics, economics, and ideology. There is much to be said for this focus, despite the fact that many cold war ideologues and crusaders have no personal material stake in military expenditures or status. (A variant of this "entrenched interests" explanation might avoid this criticism by factoring in the strength of the China lobby or the Israeli lobby, but it would still have difficulty accounting for U.S. policy toward the Soviet Union.) The basic point of this theory is that officials of institutions charged with safeguarding national security have developed entrenched interests that largely determine their perceptions of national interest and their policy advocacy. They are unusually resistant to learning or reevaluation precisely because the missions, status, and economic base of their institutions provide them a motivated bias against reevaluation. And they are powerful precisely because of the resources, prestige, and media access they developed during the cold war.

A second type of political explanation focuses less on political institutions and more on the political culture in which they are embedded. Here the reference, in the case of the Soviet Union, is to the synergistic impact of Leninist-Stalinist ideology and popular xenophobia and, in the case of the United States, to the synergistic impact of capitalist anticommunism and the liberal tradition in America. The political strength of military-industrial complexes on each side is not denied, but that strength is derived from, and reinforced by, the deeper political cultural receptivity—at the level of both elites and masses—to Manichean views of the relationship with the adversary. The material interests and the ideal interests come to reinforce each other in a powerful mix.

Each of these political explanations identifies an important ingredient in the recipe for an extended cold war and minimal cooperation between the superpowers. However, the problem with each is that it predicts only *continuity*; the theory contains no component that would allow us to anticipate, or even explain, change. Neither the individual learning nor the partial governmental learning that we have witnessed on each side is explicable in these terms. When something changes, the theorists of political continuity either deny the actuality or significance of the change or revert to highly idiosyncratic or circumstantial explanations that lose force with each additional manifestation of change.

We need to supplement these theories, which have explanatory value as far as they go, with approaches that both avoid overintellectualizing the study of foreign policy and appreciate the possibility of interest redefinition. The concept of governmental learning, it seems to me, fits this bill. While employing a metaphor that anthropomorphizes governments (by applying a concept from individual cognitive psychology), it nonetheless incorporates the political dimension by requiring a collective and institutional redefinition of interests and assumptions. Given our intellectual concern to understand what it would take to effect lasting superpower cooperation, an understanding of the conditions for governmental learning is more important for our purposes than a focus simply on individual learning. Moreover, anthropomorphizing per se need not be an obstacle either to understanding or to conceptual clarity. Some of the best work on leadership, for example, has used to good effect such concepts as organizational character, organizational mission, and organizational identity.[31]

VOLUNTARISM, DETERMINISM, AND GOVERNMENTAL LEARNING

Throughout this essay, there is a tension between deterministic and voluntaristic thinking about the course of the cold war. Theories that point to incompatible cold war paradigms, and their political-cultural and political-institutional grounding in each system, tend toward the deterministic conclusion that the cold war could not have ended earlier and is not necessarily coming to an end at this time. Neorealist explanations focus more on international factors than internal ones but reach a similar conclusion, that the cold war was not likely to end until a major change in the balance of power forced a redefinition of national interest onto the weaker side.

Voluntaristic thought about the possible earlier termination of the cold war focuses on historical turning points and contingencies, raising counterfactual questions about how the course of the cold war might have been altered by *virtú* and *fortuna*. Here the focus was largely on individual learning and partial governmental learning that was ultimately undermined by internal and external events.

The methodology of counterfactual analysis is underdeveloped and deserves fuller treatment than I could or should supply in this context. The credibility of a counterfactual claim initially depends on in-depth historical research into the *availability* of alternative pathways, both in terms of elite awareness and elite support at the time. However, having demonstrated such availability, one is still forced to assess the relative *weight* of the manifest and latent support for such alternatives. Otherwise, it is difficult to make credible the claim that altered circumstances would have *decisively* affected the political feasibility of the alternative's being enacted and sustained. Given the intrinsic limits on our ability to establish historical causality, much less counterfactual causality, we are then forced to bridge the gaps in our knowledge more or less deductively, through the application of an implicit or explicit theory of how things work in analogous types of systems and circumstances.

In this connection, the explanatory power one ultimately attributes to a learning framework may hinge on the relative importance one assigns to voluntarist-idealist versus determinist-materialist approaches to understanding history. Those who subscribe to the strong form of the "actor dispensability thesis" will find my counterfactuals unpersuasive, for they can readily imagine history unfolding pretty much the same way regardless of *virtú* and *fortuna*. Those who think that people and the ideas they embrace do matter decisively in history may find such counterfactuals quite compelling, for they reveal the contingent nature of events.[32]

I have sought to push beyond such dichotomization in my discussions of governmental learning, which led us back from voluntarism toward a more, but not fully, deterministic line of thought. Governmental learning highlighted the difficulty of building broad, stable coalitions on behalf of a redefinition of basic assumptions, goals, or identity. We saw that earlier efforts to change the cold war paradigm in directions that might have led to a convergence often foundered due to insufficient political support at home. Even the Gorbachev revolution in Soviet foreign policy remains controversial—a case of substantial but incomplete governmental learning.

While it is tempting to allow this political-institutional perspective to bias our conclusions toward determinism (if only because we know that the cold war in fact did *not* end earlier and still may not be brought to a conclusion), there is intellectual danger in doing so. Political configurations can change. Definitions of institutional interests can evolve. Leadership can make a difference. Political histories are not based on static definitions of interests, be they institutional or national; nor do such redefinitions always require for their realization a fundamental shift in the balance of power. The alternative, of course, is not to embrace pure voluntarism or idealism. It is rather to ask, in the case of the cold war: What would it have taken, at given points of partial convergence, for conciliatory leaders to have built a coalition on behalf of ending the cold war?

A focus on leadership, politics, learning, and persuasion as capable in principle of stretching constraints differs from a political-cultural and political-institutional explanation in that it does not beg the question of change. At the same time, an empirical, as opposed to a normative, theory of political change must incorporate as well the powerful political-cultural and political-institutional obstacles to change. Finally, such a theory must incorporate the ways in which international factors influence the internal political struggle.

Richard Anderson's chapter in this volume (Chapter 4), which builds on (and improves) my earlier work on authority-building in Soviet politics,[33] provides a start toward building such a mixed materialist-idealist, determinist-voluntarist statement, even though Anderson would surely protest my conclusions.

Politics is in good measure a process of justification of one's power and policies to audiences whose support is required to stay in power or to sustain given policies. In Soviet politics, I have conceptualized this as a process of authority-building and authority-maintenance, whereby leaders attempt to build and sustain dominant coalitions by convincing key audiences that they are uniquely capable of solving problems and building consensus. In U.S. politics, Alexander George has conceptualized this as a process of building "policy legitimacy."[34] We mean essentially the same thing, though my formulation would additionally highlight the building of "personal legitimacy." This does not mean that real or anticipated coercion, and material and status side-payments, are not also important components of the ways in which leaders build coalitions. It simply means that legitimizing appeals are a link between the material interests and the ideals of both the authorities and their publics, and are often crucial to one's ability to sell a strategy of cooperation with adversaries.[35]

Both the cognitive appeal of policies (i.e., their perceived feasibility) and the normative appeal of policies and personalities (i.e., the desirability of policy based on the values they invoke or elicit) are crucial to building the *credibility* that leaders of dominant coalitions require. When they lose that credibility, we say that they suffer a crisis of confidence.[36]

Credibility, both cognitive and normative, is a concept that allows us to factor change into a political model of superpower policy. The cold war paradigm can lose credibility over time as it comes to be perceived as increasingly unnecessary, senseless, costly, or risky as a guide to policy. As Keynes once argued: "the power of vested interests is vastly exaggerated compared with the gradual encroachment of ideas."[37] Garrett, for example, demonstrates the gradual loss of credibility of the pro-Taiwan rejectionist lobby during the 1960s.

If we ignore the counterfactual analyses outlined above, we would of course be inclined toward more deterministic interpretations of political evolution. We could argue on the basis of what has transpired, for example, that the process of discrediting may take a long time. If that statement is true, the duration of the cold war may be capable of being explained by applying to governments a principle of cognitive theory: that a single setback may be insufficient to induce the subject to undertake an inconvenient reevaluation of fundamentals. Only several periods of frustration, with cumulative lessons to be drawn, makes such a complete reappraisal politically feasible.

The process of discrediting may also be a long one because of cognitive dissonance-reduction mechanisms, because some ideas are more falsifiable than others, or because some are more central to the coherence of the prevailing paradigm than others. Many peripheral beliefs may be discredited without undermining confidence in the basic approach to policy.

Then too, on the basis of the record, one could argue that politicians and statesmen rarely abandon their philosophical assumptions (i.e., fundamentally learn) on the job. As the case studies in this volume suggest, changes in the politically dominant paradigm *in the direction of cooperation* have not typically taken place without a political succession. (Changes in the direction of intensified competition, which runs with, not against, the grain of the cold war paradigms, are more frequent and may not require a political succession.) Thus, Henry Kissinger's generalization is partially validated: while tactical or peripheral beliefs are often reevaluated on the job, deeper assumptions about the nature of the adversary and the nature of international politics typically are not.

If new elites come to power having embraced a new paradigm, does this qualify as governmental learning? If our concern were individual learning, we would have to ask whether those newly elected elites believed all along what they are currently advocating. But if our concern is governmental learning, we can combine an authority-building approach with a theory of political succession and instead ask: What made it possible for those new elites to legitimize and politically institutionalize a new paradigm? For these purposes, the concept of credibility, and Keynes's notion about the gradual encroachment of ideas, become relevant to our understanding of change.[38]

On the basis of the cold war record, the determinist might argue that an institutionalized cold war paradigm cannot be dislodged without a chain of causality that would include: (1) an extended period of dysfunction, during which doubts about the utility of the paradigm for advancing national security build up, and considerable backstage or subterranean learning takes place on the part of the "outs" (both politicians and specialists); (2) a critical learning period (as defined by Weber, Chapter 20), during which cumulative crises create a sense of urgency about the search for an alternative paradigm; and (3) a political succession period, which creates both the *opportunity* for dislodging the forces defending (and advantaged by) the prevailing paradigm and the incentive for competing political actors to offer alternative programs, as well as a new paradigm, as the basis for differentiating themselves from elites in power. When the political succession takes place, the new paradigm will still require a period of institutionalization, which may or may not be successful.

The cold war record, then, could be used to support varied types of deterministic argumentation, including neorealist theory, that view learning (i.e., fundamental learning that rejects philosophical assumptions, as opposed to tactical learning that may improve crisis-management or crisis-prevention capabilities) as epiphenomenal: unlikely to occur until forced by a major shift in the balance of power or an accumulation of costs that becomes undeniable. Indeed, when the issue becomes one of *economic costs*, security policy becomes somewhat more learner-friendly, for it becomes possible to develop scientifically grounded "consensual knowledge" (see Haas, Chapter 3) that specifies the price being paid for pursuing policies based on traditional assumptions. Otherwise, security policy, in contrast to environmental, economic, and other technical aspects of foreign policy, is typically more impervious to the creation of consensual knowledge. Orthodoxies, in fact, become so tenacious in part because persuasive reality tests in the security realm are so difficult to construct.

However, a commitment to counterfactual analysis and attention to competing propositions and evidence about the cold war record lead us back toward a voluntarist corrective to the determinist bias. Cumulative setbacks is one route to governmental learning, but it is also possible that single, high-magnitude traumas can have an equivalent, more immediate impact. For example, Khrushchev's fundamental reappraisal of 1963–1964 did not require a political succession to take place (he learned on the job) and was justified at the time by a highly salient traumatic event: the Sino-Soviet schism and the prospect of Chinese nuclearization. Had Khrushchev avoided overthrow (which was due primarily to failed domestic policies) and had Kennedy not been assassinated, there might have been more time and opportunity to institutionalize Khrushchev's new thinking and to strike deals with the United States that could have undermined the power of the cold war paradigm in Washington. Had Washington been receptive, and had the United States avoided Americanization of the Vietnam War, Khrushchev, in turn, might have been able to broaden the base of political support for the new thinking he was advocating. Of course, it would not have been easy to meet all these counterfactual contingencies, and counterfactual analysis is not well suited to establishing just how difficult it would have been. But the point remains that only "creeping determinism" would lead us to reject the exercise as misguided.

Use of the learning construct for understanding the conditions for superpower cooperation alerts us to the contingent and subjective dimensions of the origins of programmatic change. Use of the governmental learning construct alerts us to the political and justificatory dimensions of processes of adjustment. Nothing in this volume would contradict neo-realist pessimism about the difficulties and improbabilities of bringing about far-reaching, multi-issue, and sustained superpower cooperation in a bipolar world. However, we should be thinking more about possibilities than probabilities and should be constructing conditional generalizations rather than probability statements. By the same token, nothing in my argument would counsel optimism about what would have been involved in trying to effect an early end to the cold war (in the 1950s or the 1960s). Yet no theory can persuasively rule out the emergence of such cooperation, early or late, especially when counterfactuals control for traumatic events, such as the Korean War, that may have shaped later policy changes. If current trends continue, and if sufficient superpower convergence of assumptions takes place, leading to sustained cooperation on many fronts, that eventuality will not be capable of being explained without models of both individual and governmental learning.

What is at issue is the matter of leadership. Authority-building and authority-maintenance are not simply products of adjustment to prevailing biases within constituencies. They are also matters of mobilizing new constituencies into politics and of transforming or stretching the biases of mobilized constituencies and audiences. The outcome of efforts to legitimize extensive cooperation with rival great powers will depend not just on objective domestic political and international conditions or on a static subjective "field" within the polity, but also on the imaginative powers of the leadership and on the willingness to take risks and to push the limits of the latitude of acceptance.

Combining a theory of leadership with counterfactual examination of possible missed opportunities to end the cold war earlier will alert us to how much would have been enough in this respect. Without a theory of leadership, however, we are left only with implausible theories to the effect that *total* change (in personnel and in cognitive orientation) is required for complete governmental learning, and that complete governmental learning is a necessary condition for broad-based and sustainable superpower cooperation. Building on Jack Snyder's most recent work,[39] we can perhaps posit that "strongly institutionalized liberal coalitions" must be in power in Moscow and Washington for such cooperation to be achieved.

But that still leaves us searching for a statement of the requisites of strong institutionalization. Since almost all governmental learning in which we are interested is bound to be incomplete, we want to know how varied leadership strategies and capacities may determine whether instances of incomplete governmental learning are *sufficient* to sustain and expand support for a strategy of cooperation.

NOTES

1. Joseph Nye, "Nuclear Learning and U.S.-Soviet Security Regimes," *International Organization*, 41(1987)3: 371–402. Note that any of these levels of adaptation or learning could be defined, in everyday usage, as engendering greater realism or skill.

2. Alexander George, "The 'Operational Code': A Neglected Approach to the Study of Political Leaders and Decision-Making," *International Studies Quarterly* (June 1969).

3. Milton Rokeach, *The Open and Closed Mind* (New York: Basic Books, 1960).

4. Ernest May and Richard Neustadt, *Thinking in Time: The Uses of History for Decision Makers* (New York: The Free Press, 1986).

5. The distinction between "positive cooperation" that goes beyond "negative cooperation based on shared aversions" is Steven Weber's.

6. Alexander L. George, Philip J. Farley, and Alexander Dallin, eds., *U.S.-Soviet Security Cooperation* (New York: Oxford University Press, 1988); Kenneth Oye, ed., "Cooperation Under Anarchy" a special issue of *World Politics*, 38(October 1985)1; Steven Weber, "Cooperation and Discord in Security Relationships: Toward a Theory of U.S.-Soviet Arms Control," Ph.D. dissertation, Department of Political Science, Stanford University, 1988.

7. Robert Axelrod, *The Evolution of Cooperation* (New York: Basic Books, 1984).

8. See his chapter in this volume (Chapter 3) and "Why Collaborate? Issue-Linkage and International Regimes," *World Politics*, 32(1980)3:357–405; *When Knowledge Is Power* (Berkeley: University of California Press, 1989).

9. Stephen Walt, "The Case for Finite Containment: Analyzing U.S. Grand Strategy," *International Security* (Summer 1989):32.

10. Jack Snyder, "The Gorbachev Revolution: The Waning of Soviet Expansionism?" *International Security* (Winter 1987/88).

11. Walt, "Finite Containment," 9–10.

12. See Alfred G. Meyer, *Leninism* (New York: Praeger, 1962); Tony Smith, *Thinking Like a Communist* (New York: Norton, 1987).

13. See Louis Hartz, *The Liberal Tradition in America* (New York: Harcourt, Brace & World, Inc., 1955).

14. One exception noted by Garrett was the U.S.-Soviet discussions of 1963–1964 regarding possible joint action against Chinese nuclear facilities, which were clearly based on limited but intense shared aversions.

15. Seyom Brown, *The Faces of Power* (New York: Columbia University Press, 1983); Seymour Hersch, *The Price of Power* (New York, 1980); Raymond Garthoff, *Détente and Confrontation* (Washington: Brookings, 1985).

16. On the latter points, see John Lewis Gaddis, *The Long Peace* (New York: Oxford University Press, 1987).

17. Baruch Fischhoff, "For Those Condemned to Study the Past: Reflections on Historical Judgment," in *New Directions for Methodology of Behavioral Science: Fallible Judgment in Behavioral Research*, eds. R.A. Shweder and D.W. Fiske (San Francisco: Jossey-Bass, 1980).

18. Robert Jervis, *Perception and Misperception in International Politics* (Princeton, N.J.: Princeton University Press, 1976), Chapter 6.

19. To this point, this paragraph is based on a personal communication from my colleague, Steven Weber.

20. Similar qualifications are not required regarding the Asian theatre, where a looser conception of spheres of influence and balancing requirements prevailed within the administration until the Korean War.

21. See Herbert S. Dinerstein, *War and the Soviet Union* (New York: Praeger, 1959); and, most recently, James Richter, "Action and Reaction in Khrushchev's Foreign Policy," Ph.D. dissertation, Department of Political Science, University of California at Berkeley, 1989, Chs. 2–3.

22. Snyder, "The Gorbachev Revolution."

23. William Zimmerman, *Soviet Perspectives on International Relations, 1956–1967* (Princeton, N.J.: Princeton University Press, 1969).

24. See Richter, *Action and Reaction*, Ch. 7; also Richard D.Anderson, "Competitive Politics and Soviet Foreign Policy: Authority-Building and Bargaining in the Brezhnev Politburo," Ph.D. dissertation, Department of Political Science, University of California at Berkeley, 1989.

25. Steven Weber, "Realism, Détente, and Nuclear Weapons," *International Organization*, 44 (Winter 1990)1:55–82.

26. In addition to her chapter in this volume, see her *Origins of Containment: A Psychological Explanation* (Princeton, N.J.: Princeton University Press, 1985). Larson is applying to foreign policy an approach developed in psychology by Bem.

27. *The New York Times*, 11 September, 1990, p. 1.

28. For the fullest and best statement of neorealism, see Kenneth Waltz, *Theory of International Politics* (New York: Addison-Wesley, 1979); Robert O. Keohane, ed., *Neorealism and Its Critics* (New York: Columbia University Press, 1986); Nye, "Nuclear Learning."

29. See, for example, Benjamin Miller, "Perspectives on Superpower Crisis Management and Conflict Resolution in the Arab-Israeli Conflict," in *Soviet Strategy in the Middle East*, ed. George W. Breslauer (Boston: Unwin Hyman, 1990).

30. Another way to state this point is to argue the possibility for multiple equilibria—a range of possible solutions to the problem of biopoly, many of which could be stable (personal communication from Steven Weber).

31. Philip Selznick, *Leadership in Administration* (New York: Harper & Row, 1957).

32. My thanks to Philip Tetlock (personal communication) for the observations in this paragraph.

33. George W. Breslauer, *Khrushchev and Brezhnev as Leaders: Building Authority in Soviet Politics* (Boston: Allen & Unwin, 1982).

34. Alexander L. George, "Domestic Constraints on Regime Change in U.S. Foreign Policy: The Need for Policy Legitimacy," in *Change in the International System*,

eds. Ole R. Holsti, Randolph Siverson, and Alexander George (Boulder, Colo.: Westview, 1980).

35. Recall that Richard Neustadt [*Presidential Power: The Politics of Leadership* (New York: John Wiley & Sons, 1960), 10] argued that "Presidential *power* is the power to persuade"; also, that John Kennedy, after learning of Soviet missiles in Cuba, exclaimed, "How could he do that to me!"

36. The distinction between cognitive and normative dimensions of legitimation is from George, "Domestic Constraints on Regime Change."

37. Quoted in John S. Odell, *U.S. International Monetary Policy: Markets, Power, and Ideas as Sources of Change* (Princeton, N.J.: Princeton University Press, 1982): 12–13, as noted in Matthew Evangelista, "Sources of Moderation in Soviet Security Policy" (typescript, 1989).

38. In an unstable authoritarian regime, in which military coups regularly bring to power people with differing perspectives from those they overthrew, it would violate common sense to refer to this as governmental learning. However, the authority-building framework I propose is relevant to U.S. and Soviet politics since Stalin, when in both states a nonautocratic political process has been sufficiently institutionalized that a continuing debate over ideas and principles has taken place. Discrediting of the assumptions underlying the cold war paradigm has therefore required a continuing struggle, not just over interests but also over ideas. Political successions in both countries have provided contexts in which these debates have intensified. And while it is not possible to conclude that debates over foreign policy have decided political successions, they have certainly contributed to deciding the foreign policy agendas of successful insurgent elites.

39. "International Leverage on Soviet Domestic Change," *World Politics* (October 1989). Snyder argues that the impact of U.S. pressure or conciliation will depend on whether a liberal or an imperial coalition is in power in Moscow. Snyder describes all such coalitions in the post-Stalin era as "weakly institutionalized."

Index